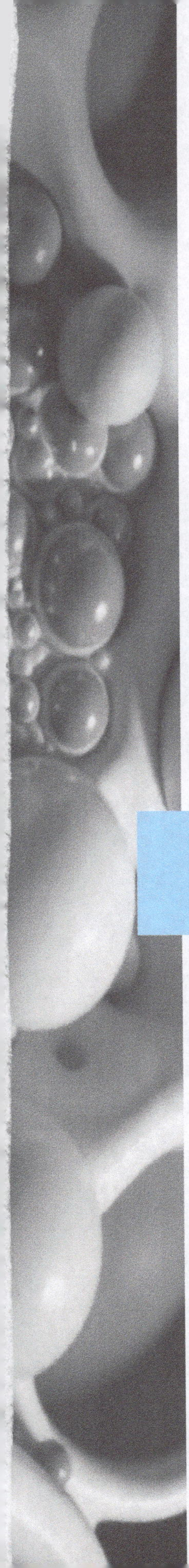

Master the NCERT

Line by Line MCQs from Latest NCERT Books

for NEET/JEE

CHEMISTRY XII

Master the NCERT

Line by Line MCQs from Latest NCERT Books

for NEET/JEE

CHEMISTRY XII

DR. NARENDRA JHA

Co-Authored by

SWATI CHAUHAN

PRERANA NIRMAL

arihant

SUCCESS AND NOTHING LESS

arihant
SUCCESS AND NOTHING LESS

Arihant Prakashan (Series), Meerut

卐 **Administrative & Production Offices**

Regd. Office
'Ramchhaya' 4577/15, Agarwal Road, Darya Ganj, New Delhi -110002
Tele: 011- 47630600, 43518550

Head Office
Kalindi, TP Nagar, Meerut (UP) - 250002
Tel: 0121-7156203, 7156204

卐 **Sales & Support Offices**
Agra, Ahmedabad, Bengaluru, Bareilly, Chennai, Delhi, Guwahati, Hyderabad, Jaipur, Jhansi, Kolkata, Lucknow, Nagpur & Pune.

卐 **PRICE** ₹475.00

卐 **PO No :** TXT-XX-XXXXXXX-X-XX

Published by Arihant Publications (India) Ltd.

For further information about the books published by Arihant, log on to www.arihantbooks.com or e-mail at info@arihantbooks.com

Follow us on

Preface...

For any aspirant of competitions, a proper grip over NCERT books is the necessity now. After rationalisation of syllabus in competitions like NEET, JEE Main and their syncing with different State Boards, it is very much expected that their test papers will contain most of the questions from NCERT. To cater this situation the need of dual synchronous preparation, i.e. study of NCERT for school and competitive exams simultaneously is increasing day by day.

Arihant's Master the NCERT Series is framed, developed and now revised with the same philosophy of such synchronous preparation. These books serve as the complete resource for gripping NCERT with learning, practice and assessment tools. The specialised features of this revised edition are-

- **3 level Chapter Analysis** is incorporated in the beginning of each Chapter.
- **Key Notes** are more elaborative and enriched with NEET/JEE exclusive features like **NEET PYQ markings, Marks Maximiser, Mnemonics, Caution Points & PYQ Notes.**
- **Concept Master** is present at places as concept explanatory videos of key notes.
- Major key points of the chapter are further mapped as multicoloured **Chapter at a Glance** for better visualisation and quick revision.
- Exercise portion is scientifically designed for step-by-step mastering through **Concept Builders,** followed by **Topical MCQs, Assertion – Reason, Statement Based, Matching, Numericals, NCERT Exemplar's, Past Exams'** and **Skill Boosters.**
- Questions of Exercises are tagged with NCERT page numbers.
- For Assessment of self-preparation levels **MCQs Based Online Chapter Tests** and **3 Online Mock Tests** (2 NEET & 1 JEE Main pattern) are incorporated with this revised edition.

The variety in types of questions framed will also be helpful in analysis of self – performances and exposure to face tough problems of competitive exams.

Huge efforts have been made from our side to keep this book error free, but inspite of that if any error or whatsoever is skipped, then that will be purely incidental. Please write to us your feedbacks for further improvement of the book.

Authors

Key Features

3 Level Chapter Analysis

On the first page of each chapter NEET Analysis of 5 years is given on following 3 basis -
(i) Topics
(ii) Special format Questions
(iii) Chapter weightage

Topicwise No. of Ques asked in 5 Years (NEET)

Topics	No. of Questions				
	2024	2023	2022	2021	2020
Topic-1: Werner's Theory of Coordination Compounds	–	–	–	–	–
Topic-2: Definition of Some Important Terms Used in Coordination Compounds	1	2	–	1	–
Topic-3: Nomenclature of Coordination Compounds	–	–	1	–	–
Topic-4: Isomerism in Coordination Compounds	1	–	–	–	–
Topic-5: Bonding in Coordination Compounds	1	–	1	1	2
Topic-6: Bonding in Metal Carbonyls	–	–	–	–	–
Topic-7: Importance and Applications of Coordination Compounds	–	–	–	–	–

Special Type of Ques asked in 5 Years (NEET)

Types	Years				
	2024	2023	2022	2021	2020
A-R	–	–	–	–	–
Statement Based	2	–	–	–	–
Matching	1	–	–	1	1

Last 5 Year Weightage (NEET)

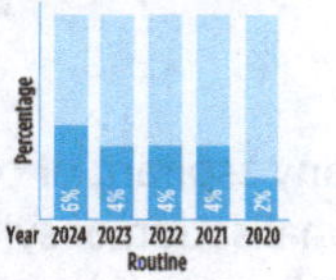

Marks Maximiser

Specialised box matter with NEET/JEE exclusive important Information which may or may not be present in NCERT.

Marks Maximizer

Effective atomic number (EAN) **rule** is also known as the "18-electron rule". This rule may be used to predict the number of ligands in compounds as well as the products of their reactions.

EAN = Atomic number of metal (Z) – oxidation number + 2 × coordination number

Mnemonics

Specialised learning tricks as easy to memorise sentences for retaining concepts and avoiding confusions.

Mnemonics Recall Spectrochemical Series

You can remember the spectrochemical series just by rembering one sentence.

I Bought Some Copies to Study Fundamental of Chemistry

$I^{\ominus} < Br^{\ominus} < SCN^{\ominus} < Cl^{\ominus} < S^{2-} < F^{-} < OH^{\ominus} < C_2O_4^{2-}$

He Nurtured Excellence in Necessary Coordination Compounds

$H_2O < NCS^{-} < edta^{4-} < NH_3 < en < CN^{-} < CO$

Crystal Field Theory (CFT)

- It is an electrostatic model which considers the metal-ligand bond to be ionic arising purely from electrostatic interactions between the metal ion and the ligand. The ligands are treated as point charges in case of anions or point dipoles in case of neutral molecules.
- According to CFT, under the influence of ligand field, degeneracy of the d-orbital is destroyed and it splits into two or more energy levels.

Chemistry Through Concept Master

Unique video support to explain difficult Topics/Concept of NCERT in simple and easy to understand language.

Key Features

PYQ Notes

1. Cobalt chloride when dissolved in water forms pink coloured complex $[Co(H_2O)_6]^{2+}$ which has octahedral geometry. This solution on treating with conc. HCl forms deep blue complex $[CoCl_4]^{4-}$ which has tetrahedral geometry. **JEE Main 2023**
2. For the complexes, having same oxidation state the order of CFSE will be **JEE Main 2022**
   $3d$-series < $4d$-series < $5d$-series.
3. Identification of Ni^{2+} carried out by dimethyl glyoxime (a bidentate neutral ligand) in the presence of NH_4OH. **JEE Main 2021**
4. Wavelength (λ) of absorption is inversely proportional to CFSE (Δ_o value) of the central metal ion. **NEET 2017**
5. The formula, which is used for the calculation of CFSE of an octahedral coordination compound.

$$CFSE = -0.4\ \Delta_o \times \text{number of electrons in } t_{2g} \text{ orbital} + 0.6\ \Delta_o \times \text{number of electrons in } e_g \text{ orbital}$$

NEET 2014

PYQ Notes

NEET/JEE specific important points, which were asked in past years but not incorporated in present Rationalised NCERT .

Solutions (Chapter at a Glance)

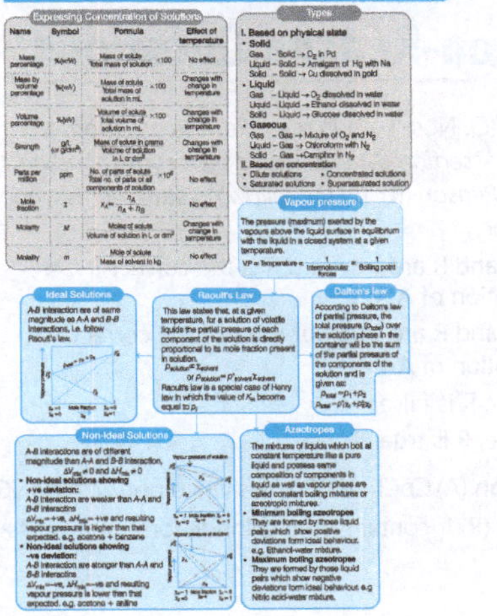

Chapter at a Glance

Fully Coloured Glorified Infographics to map all the key points of a chapter for quick review. These are present at the end of chapters.

Step by Step

Mastering NCERT

- Concept Builders
- Topical Questions
- Assertion-Reason
- Statement Based
- Matching Type
- Numerical Value
- NCERT Exemplar
- Past Exams
- Skill Boosters

Concept Builders

1 The primary valences are .... and are satisfied by .... ions.

2 The .... valency is equal to the coordination number and is fixed for a metal.

3 Write the number of ions given on complete ionisation of one mole of $[Co(NH_3)_3Cl_3]$.

4 The ions or groups bound by the secondary linkages to metal have characteristic spatial arrangement with respect to different coordination number. [T/F]

5 Double salt and complexes are formed by combination of two or more stable compounds in stoichiometric ratio. [T/F]

15 Name the isomerism exists between $[Cr(H_2O)_6]Cl_3$ and $[Cr(H_2O)_5Cl]Cl_2 \cdot H_2O$ complexes.

16 Valence bond theory does not give quantitative interpretation of kinetic stability of coordination compounds. [T/F]

17 Small splitting of d-orbitals occurs only in case of strong field ligands. [T/F]

18 $[Co(NH_3)_6]^{3+}$ is called low spin complex, while $[CoF_6]^{3-}$ is called high spin complex. [T/F]

19 $[Mn(CN)_6]^{3-}$ has magnetic moment of two unpaired electrons, while $[MnCl_6]^{3-}$ has magnetic moment of three unpaired electrons. [T/F]

Step by Step Mastering NCERT

The scientifically designed practice exercise with all possible type of questions to be asked in competition like NEET/JEE.

Concept Builders

1 The primary valences are .... and are satisfied by .... ions.

2 The .... valency is equal to the coordination number and is fixed for a metal.

3 Write the number of ions given on complete ionisation of one mole of $[Co(NH_3)_3Cl_3]$.

4 The ions or groups bound by the secondary linkages to metal have characteristic spatial arrangement with respect to different coordination number. [T/F]

Concept Builders

These are present as simple teasers like T/F, Fill ups and one word question. Thus, structured to build foundation stone of NCERT concepts.

Key Features

Topical Question

NEET/JEE like MCQs form line by line text of NCERT with complete tagging of pages. All these MCQs are arranged as per the Topic headings of NCERT.

Topical Questions

Werner's Theory of Coordination Compounds

1 Given, the molecular formula of some hexa coordinated complex. NCERT Pg 119

A. $CoCl_3 \cdot 6NH_3$ B. $CoCl_3 \cdot 5NH_3$
C. $CoCl_3 \cdot 4NH_3$

If the number of coordinated NH_3 molecules in *A*, *B* and *C* respectively are 6, 5 and 4, the primary valency, in (*A*), (*B*) and (*C*) respectively.

(a) 6, 5 and 4 (b) 3, 2 and 1
(c) 0, 1 and 2 (d) 3, 3 and 3

Assertion-Reason Questions

Directions (Q. Nos. 1-10) *In the following questions, a statement of Assertion (A) is followed by a corresponding statement of Reason (R). Of the following statements, choose the correct one.*

(a) Both A and R are true and R is the correct explanation of A.
(b) Both A and R are true but R is not the correct explanation of A.
(c) A is true, R is false.
(d) A is false, R is true.

1 **Assertion** (A) $CoCl_3 \cdot 4H_2O$ gives white ppt. with $AgNO_3$.
Reason (R) It contains free chloride ion. NCERT Pg 120

A-R Questions

Most Important special format MCQs category. All of these are also tagged with NCERT page numbers as well .

Statement type Question

In NEET Chemistry paper 3 types of statement based questions are asked
(i) Statement I & II
(ii) 4 statements with codes
(iii) 5 statements with codes
All these 3 categories are overed in step by step practice with NCERT page tagging.

Statement Type Questions

Direction (Q. Nos. 1-6) *In the following questions, two statements (I & II) are given. In the light of the given statements, choose the correct option given below.*

(a) Both Statement I and Statement II are false.
(b) Statement I is true but Statement II is false.
(c) Statement I is false but Statement II is true.
(d) Both Statement I and Statement II are true.

1 **Statement I** NO_2^- and SCN^- ion are ambidentate ligand.
Statement II SCN^- and NO_2^- ion can coordinate only through N to a central atom or ion. NCERT Pg 121

Matching Type Questions

1 Match the Column I with Column II. NCERT Pg 133

	Column I (Complex)		Column II (Colour)
A.	$[Co(NH_3)_6]^{3+}$	1.	Violet
B.	$[Ni(H_2O)_6]^{3+}$	2.	Pale blue
C	$[Ti(H_2O)_6]^{3+}$	3.	Yellowish orange
D.	$[Ni(H_2O)_4(en)]^{2+}$	4.	Green

Matching Type Questions

Step by step practice includes both the matching type MCQs (i.e. with and without codes. These are placed just after statement based MCQs and all are tagged with NCERT page numbers.

Key Features

NCERT Exemplar Questions

1 When 0.1 mole of $CoCl_3(NH_3)_5$ is treated with excess of $AgNO_3$, 0.2 mole of AgCl is obtained. The conductivity of solution will correspond to

(a) 1 : 3 electrolyte (b) 1 : 2 electrolyte
(c) 1 : 1 electrolyte (d) 3 : 1 electrolyte

2 When 1 mole of $CrCl_3 \cdot 6H_2O$ is treated with excess of $AgNO_3$, 3 moles of AgCl are obtained. The formula of the complex is

(a) $[CrCl_3(H_2O)_3] \cdot 3H_2O$ (b) $[CrCl_2(H_2O)_4]Cl \cdot 2H_2O$
(c) $[CrCl(H_2O)_5]Cl_2 \cdot H_2O$ (d) $[Cr(H_2O)_6]Cl_3$

NCERT Exemplar's Questions

NCERT Exemplar books are considered as one of the best problem books for competitive exams. Each chapter has selected exemplar problems to provide consolidation for preparations.

Past Exams' Questions

NEET Archive

1. Given below are two statements : NCERT Pg 130, NEET 2024

Statement I Both $[Co(NH_3)_6]^{3+}$ and $[CoF_6]^{3-}$ complexes are octahedral but differ in their magnetic behaviour.

Statement II $[Co(NH_3)_6]^{3+}$ is diamagnetic whereas $[CoF_6]^{3-}$ is paramagnetic.

In the light of the above statements, choose the correct answer from the options given below:

(a) Both Statement I and Statement II are true.
(b) Both Statement I and Statement II are false.
(c) Statement I is true but Statement II is false.
(d) Statement I is false but Statement II is true.

Past Exams' Question

Selected PYQs with NCERT page tagging are present as the final check of preparation.

Skill Boosters

1. The complex $[Fe(H_2O)_5NO]^{2+}$ is formed in the brown ring test for nitrates when freshly prepared $FeSO_4$ solution is added to aqueous solution of $NO_3^{\ominus}$ followed by addition of conc. H_2SO_4. Select the incorrect statement about this complex.

(a) Colour change is due to charge transfer.
(b) It has iron in + 1 oxidation state and nitrosyl as $NO^{\oplus}$.
(c) It has magnetic moment of 3.87 BM confirming three unpaired electrons in Fe.
(d) In complex Fe has d^2sp^3-hybridisation.

2. Magnetic moment of a complex, compound can be determined experimentally and theoretically by using spin only formula. The value of spin only magnetic moment for octahedral complex of the following configuration is 2.84 BM. The electronic configuration which shows given magnetic moment is

Skill Boosters

Brain Teasers present at the end of step by step practice to provide extra edge for preparation.

Step by Step

Decoding the Questions

Concept Builders

1 ionisable, negative
2 secondary 3 One
4 True 5 True
6 Lewis acids 7 False
8 False 9 True
10 Trigonal bipyramidal
11 Geometrical isomerism
12 $K_3[Cu(CN)_4]$
13 Three
14 hydrate
15 Solvate isomerism
16 True 17 False

2 (*c*) $[Cr(H_2O)_6]Cl_3$ contains maximum number of ionisable anion ($3Cl^-$). Hence, it will consume more equivalents of aqueous solution of $AgNO_3$ and forms three moles of AgCl (white ppt.).

3 (*d*)

4 (*c*) Since, conductivity corresponds to two ions. Thus, it shows that $2Br^-$ ions are ionisable.

$\therefore [Co(NH_3)_5Br]Br_2 \xrightarrow{H_2O} [Co(NH_3)_5Br]^{2+} + 2Br^-$

$2Br^- + 2AgNO_3 \longrightarrow 2AgCl + 2NO_3^-$

So, the complex is $[Co(NH_3)_5Br]Br_2$.

So, the formula of complex will be $[Pd(NH_3)_4]Cl_2$. Similarly, complex III does not precipitate any AgCl. So, the formula wil be $[Pt(NH_3)_4Cl_2]$.

So, the secondary valencies of I and III are 4 and 6 respectively.

8 (*b*) Only $[CoCl_3(NH_3)_3]$ complex does not ionised in solution, as no ion is present outside the coordination sphere. Rest all can be ionised.

9 (*c*)

10 (*b*)

Decoding the Questions

Answers and explanatory solutions of selected questions for better gripping of NCERT concepts.

Contents

01

Scan for **Chemistry Through Concept Master** *Videos*

Solutions

In our daily life, we rarely come across the pure substances. Most of these are mixtures containing two or more pure substances. Solution is one of the most important class of mixture that contains more than one components. The importance of solution in life depends on their composition. Almost all process in living body occur in some kind of liquid solutions.

Topicwise No. of Ques asked in 5 Years (NEET)

Topics	No of Questions				
	2024	2023	2022	2021	2020
Types of Solutions	–	–	–	–	–
Expressing Concentration of Solutions	–	–	2	–	–
Solubility	1	1	–	1	–
Vapour Pressure of Liquid Solutions	–	–	–	–	1
Ideal and Non-Ideal Solutions	–	–	–	–	1
Colligative Properties and Determination of Molar Mass	1	–	–	1	2
Abnormal Molar Masses	–	–	–	–	–

Special Type of Ques Asked In 5 Years (NEET)

Types	Years				
	2024	2023	2022	2021	2020
A-R	–	1	–	–	–
Statement Based	–	–	–	–	–
Matching	–	–	–	–	–

Last 5 Years Weightage (NEET)

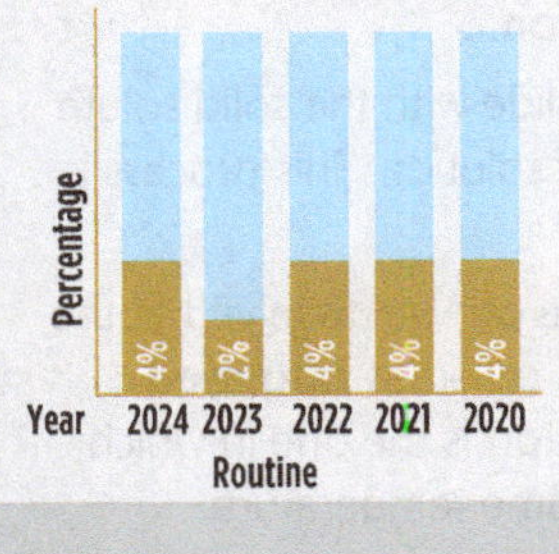

Types of Solutions

A homogeneous mixture of two or more substances is called a **solution**. **Homogeneous mixture** means its composition and properties are uniform throughout the mixture.

- The component of solution which is present in excess amount is called **solvent**, while the other which is present in relatively smaller quantity is called **solute**.
- Solvent determines the physical state in which solution exists.

Depending upon the number of components, solutions can be of the following types : Binary, ternary, quaternary etc.

Binary solution consist of two components while **ternary** and **quaternary** composed of three or four components respectively. In case of binary solutions, each component may be solid, liquid or in gaseous state.

On this basis, different types of solutions are possible as summarised in the following table.

Type of solutions	Solute	Solvent	Examples
Solid solutions	Solid	Solid	Alloys (copper dissolved in gold).
	Liquid	Solid	Hydrated salts, amalgam of Hg with Na.
	Gas	Solid	Solution of hydrogen in palladium.
Liquid solutions	Solid	Liquid	Salt/sugar solution in water.
	Liquid	Liquid	Alcohol in water.
	Gas	Liquid	Aerated drinks, O_2 in water.
Gaseous solutions	Solid	Gas	Iodine vapours in air, camphor in N_2 gas.
	Liquid	Gas	Water vapours in air, $CHCl_3$ mixed with N_2 gas.
	Gas	Gas	Air ($O_2 + N_2$).

Expressing Concentration of Solutions

The amount of solute present in the given quantity of the solution is called concentration of solution. It can be expressed either qualitatively (concentrated or dilute) or quantitatively.

The methods to express the concentration of the solution quantitatively are as follows

(a) **Mass percentage** (w/W) NEET 2022

The mass percentage of a component (solute) in a given solution is the mass of component per 100 g of the solution.

$$\text{Mass\%} = \frac{\text{Mass of component in solution}}{\text{Total mass of solution}} \times 100$$

(b) **Volume percentage** (V/V)

It is defined as the volume of component (solute) in mL dissolved in 100 mL of the solution.

$$\text{Volume\%} = \frac{\text{Volume of the component}}{\text{Total volume of solution}} \times 100$$

(c) **Mass by volume percentage** (w/V)

It is defined as the mass of component (solute) in grams dissolved in 100 mL of solution.

$$\text{Mass by volume\%} = \frac{\text{Mass of solute}}{\text{Total volume of solution}} \times 100$$

(d) **Strength** (g/L)

It is defined as the mass of component (solute in grams) dissolved in 1000 mL of solution.

$$\text{Strength} = \frac{\text{Mass of solute (g)}}{\text{Volume of solution (L or dm}^3\text{)}}$$

(e) **Parts per million** (ppm)

When a component (solute) is present in trace quantities, the concentration is expressed in parts per million.

Parts per million

$$= \frac{\text{Number of parts of the component}}{\text{Total number of parts of all components of the solution}} \times 10^6$$

(f) **Mole fraction** (χ)

It is the ratio of number of moles of one component to the total number of moles of all the components present in the solution.

Mole fraction

$$= \frac{\text{Number of moles of the component}}{\text{Total number of moles of all the components}}$$

For i number of components

$$\chi_i = \frac{n_i}{n_1 + n_2 + n_3 + \ldots\ldots n_i} = \frac{n_i}{\Sigma n_i}$$

and $\chi_1 + \chi_2 + \ldots\ldots\ldots\ldots\ldots\ldots + \chi_i = 1$

(g) **Molarity** (M)

It is defined as the number of moles of solute dissolved in one litre (or one cubic decimetre) of the solution.

$$\text{Molarity} = \frac{\text{Number of moles of solute}}{\text{Volume of solution (in L)}}$$

$$= \frac{w_B}{M_B \times V} \text{ mol L}^{-1}$$

(h) **Molality** (m)

It is defined as the number of moles of solute per kilogram of the solvent.

$$\text{Molality} = \frac{\text{Number of moles of solute}}{\text{Mass of solvent (in kg)}}$$

$$= \frac{w_B}{M_B \times W_A} \text{ mol kg}^{-1}$$

Marks Maximizer

Mass %, ppm, mole fraction and molality are temperature independent, whereas mass by volume %, strength and molarity depends on temperature. This is because volume depends on temperature but mass does not.

Solubility

The maximum amount of a substance that can be dissolved in a given amount of solvent at a given temperature is termed as solubility at that temperature.

Solubility of a Solid in a Liquid

Every solid does not dissolve in a given liquid, e.g. naphthalene and anthracene dissolve readily in benzene but NaCl and sugar do not. The various factors affecting solubility of a solid in a liquid are as follows

- **Nature of Solute and Solvent** Polar solutes dissolve in polar solvents and non-polar solutes are soluble in non-polar solvents. In general, a solute dissolves in a solvent if the intermolecular interactions are similar in the two, i.e. **like dissolves like.**
- When a solid solute is added to the solvent, some solute dissolves and its concentration increases in the solution. This process is known as **dissolution.**
- The solute particles in solution collide with the solid solute particles and get separated out of solution. This process is known as **crystallisation.**
- A solution in which no more solute can be dissolved at the same temperature and pressure is called as **saturated solution**, while **unsaturated solution** is the one in which more solute can be dissolved at same temperature.

- **Effect of Temperature** The solubility of a solid in a liquid is significantly affected by temperature changes. These changes occur in accordance with Le-Chatelier's principle.
  – In general, if in a nearly saturated solution, the dissolution process is **endothermic** (i.e. $\Delta_{sol}H > 0$), the solubility should increase with increase in temperature.
  – If it is **exothermic** (i.e. $\Delta_{sol}H < 0$), the solubility should decrease with increase in temperature.
- **Effect of pressure** Pressure does not have any significant effect on solubility of solids in liquids as these are highly incompressible.

Solubility of a Gas in a Liquid

Many gases dissolve in water while some dissolves only to a small extent. Solubility of gases in liquids is considerably affected by pressure and temperature.

- **Effect of Pressure** The solubility of gases increases with increase of pressure.
  – Henry gave a quantitative relation between pressure and solubility of a gas in solvent which is known as **Henry's law.** NEET 2023

  This law states that, *"the solubility of a gas in a liquid is directly proportional to the partial pressure of the gas present above the surface of liquid or solution".*

  If we use the mole fraction of a gas in the solution as a measure of its solubility, then it can be written as the mole fraction of gas in the solution is proportional to the partial pressure of the gas over the solution.

  The most commonly used form of Henry's law states that *"the partial pressure of the gas in vapour phase (p) is proportional to the mole fraction of the gas (χ) in the solution"* and is expressed as

  $$p = K_H \chi$$

  K_H depends on the nature of the gas. Generally, **higher** the value of K_H at a particular pressure, **lower** is the solubility of gas in the liquid. NEET 2024

  – A graph between the partial pressure of gas against the mole fraction of the gas in the solution gives a straight line passing through the origin. Slope of the line will give Henry's law constant (K_H).

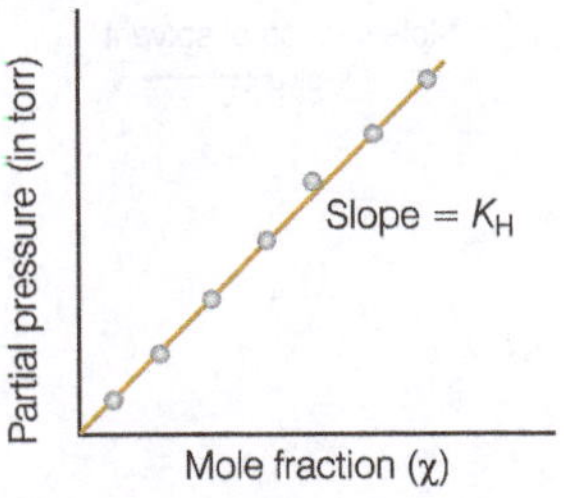

Applications of Henry's Law

– Soft drinks and soda water bottle are sealed under high pressure to increase the solubility of CO_2.

– Scuba divers must cope with high concentrations of dissolved gases while breathing air at high pressure underwater. Higher the pressure, more the solubility of atmospheric gases in blood.

When the divers come towards surface, the pressure gradually decreases resulting in the release of dissolved gases. This leads to the formation of bubbles of nitrogen in the blood which blocks capillaries and give rise to a disease called **bends.**

To avoid bends, the tanks used by scuba divers are field with air diluted with helium (11.7% He, 56.2% N_2 and 32.1% O_2).

– At high altitudes, the partial pressure of oxygen is less than that at ground level. This leads to low concentrations of oxygen in the blood and tissues of people living at high altitudes or climbers. Low concentration of oxygen in blood causes **anoxia** (weak and unable to think).

- **Effect of Temperature** Dissolution is an exothermic process, then according to Le-Chatelier's principle, the solubility should **decrease with increase of temperature.**

Vapour Pressure of Liquid Solutions

Vapour pressure is defined as the pressure exerted by the vapours of solvent, when they are in dynamic equilibrium with its liquid at a particular temperature. Liquid solutions are formed when solvent is a liquid. The solutions containing two components are (i) Liquids in liquids and (ii) Solids in liquids.

Vapour Pressure of Liquid-Liquid Solutions

- **Raoult's law** states that for a solution of volatile liquids, the partial vapour pressure of each volatile component in the solution is directly proportional to its mole fraction present in solution.

  For component 1, $p_1 \propto \chi_1$ or $p_1 = p_1^\circ \chi_1$

  Similarly, for component 2, $p_2 = p_2^\circ \chi_2$

  where, p_1° = vapour pressure of pure component 1

  p_2° = vapour pressure of pure component 2

  χ_1 and χ_2 are mole fractions of components 1 and 2 respectively.

For Concept Master Video

- **According to Dalton's law of partial pressures,** the total pressure (p_{Total}) over the solution phase in the container will be the sum of the partial pressures of the components of the solution and is given as,

$$p_{total} = p_1 + p_2$$
$$= p_1^\circ \chi_1 + p_2^\circ \chi_2$$
$$= (1 - \chi_2) p_1^\circ + \chi_2 p_2^\circ$$
$$= p_1^\circ + (p_2^\circ - p_1^\circ)\chi_2$$ NEET 2021

where, p_1 = partial vapour pressure of component 1
p_2 = partial vapour pressure of component 2
p_{Total} = total vapour pressure of solution

A graph of p_1 or p_2 *versus* the mole fractions χ_1 and χ_2 for a solution gives a linear plot.

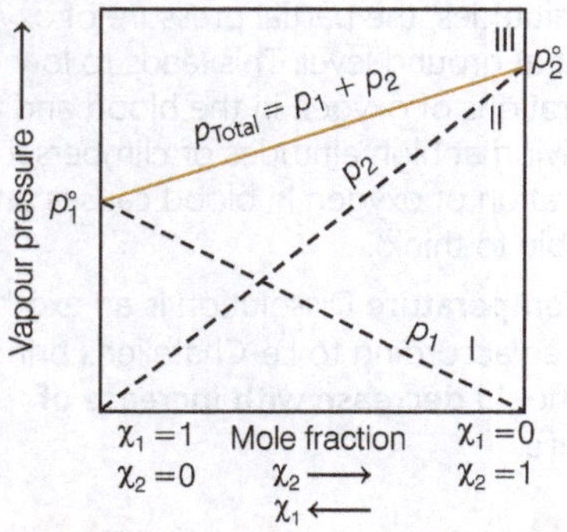

- The **mole fractions** of 1 and 2 in the vapour phase y_1 and y_2 can be determined as,

$$y_1 = \frac{p_1}{p_{Total}} = \frac{\chi_1 p_1^\circ}{\chi_1 p_1^\circ + \chi_2 p_2^\circ}$$ NEET 2019

Similarly, $$y_2 = \frac{p_2}{p_{Total}} = \frac{\chi_2 p_2^\circ}{\chi_1 p_1^\circ + \chi_2 p_2^\circ}$$

- **Raoult's law as a special case of Henry's law** According to Raoult's law, the vapour pressure of a volatile component in a given solution is given by

$$p_1 = \chi_1 p_1^\circ \quad \text{...(i)}$$

According to Henry's law, the partial pressure of the volatile component (gas) is proportional to its mole fraction in the solution.

$$p_1 = K_H \chi_1 \quad \text{...(ii)}$$

From Eqs. (i) and (ii) Raoult's law becomes a special case of Henry's law in which K_H becomes equal to p_1°.

Vapour Pressure of Solutions of Solids in Liquids

- Vapour pressure of a solution of non-volatile solute is lower than that of pure liquid.

  Reason When a non-volatile solute is added to a solvent, the surface has molecules of solute and solvent both.

  Thus, the number of molecules of solvent present in upper surface is less. The number of solvent molecules escaping from the surface is reduced. Thus, vapour pressure decreases.

- The decrease in the vapour pressure of solvent depends only on the quantity of non-volatile solute present in the solution irrespective of its nature, e.g. decrease in vapour pressure of 1 mole solution of sucrose and urea in water are same at same temperature.
- **Raoult's law for liquid solution of non-volatile solute** In a binary solution of non-volatile solute, the total vapour pressure of solution is only due to the vapour pressure of solvent.

  So, according to Raoult's law,

$$p_1 \propto \chi_1 \text{ and } p_1 = \chi_1 p_1^\circ$$

p_1 = vapour pressure of solvent
χ_1 = mole fraction of solvent
p_1° = vapour pressure of pure solvent.

- A graph between the vapour pressure of solution and mole fraction of solvent is a straight line passing through origin.

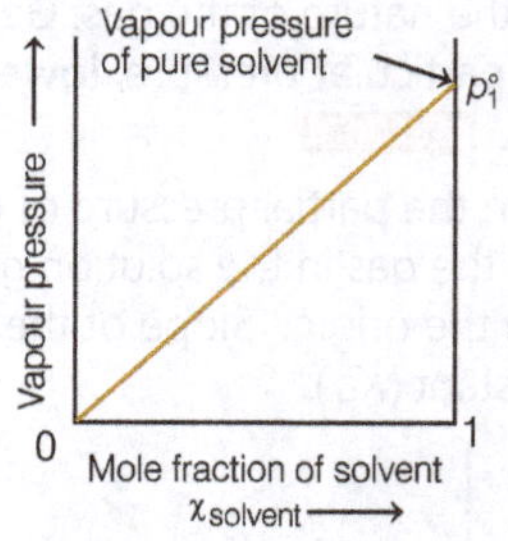

Ideal and Non-Ideal Solutions

On the basis of Raoult's law, liquid-liquid solutions can be divided into two types of solutions, i.e. ideal and non-ideal solutions as discussed below.

Comparison between Ideal and Non-Ideal Solutions

Ideal solutions NEET 2019	Non-ideal solutions NEET 2020, 2019	
	Positive deviation from Raoult's law	**Negative deviation from Raoult's law**
Each component obeys Raoult's law over the entire range of concentration. i.e. $p_1 = p_1^\circ \chi_1$ and $p_2 = p_2^\circ \chi_2$	Their components do not obey Raoult's law, over the entire range of concentration. i.e. $p_1 > p_1^\circ \chi_1$ and $p_2 > p_2^\circ \chi_2$	Their components do not obey Raoult's law, over the entire range of concentration. i.e. $p_1 < p_1^\circ \chi_1$ and $p_2 < p_2^\circ \chi_2$
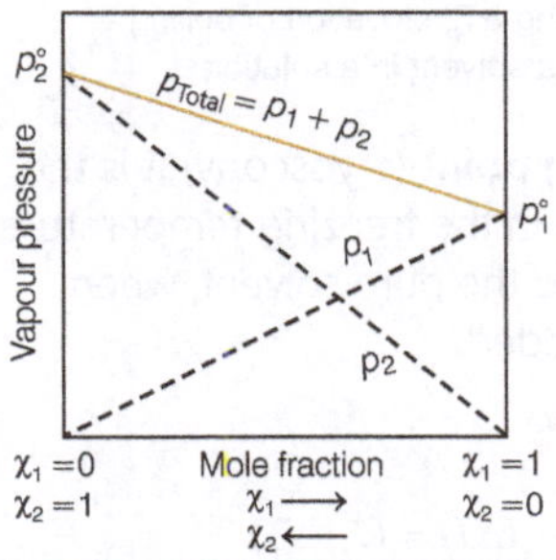	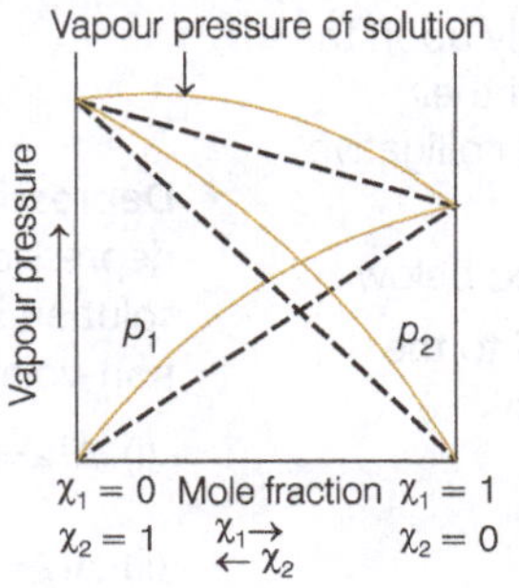	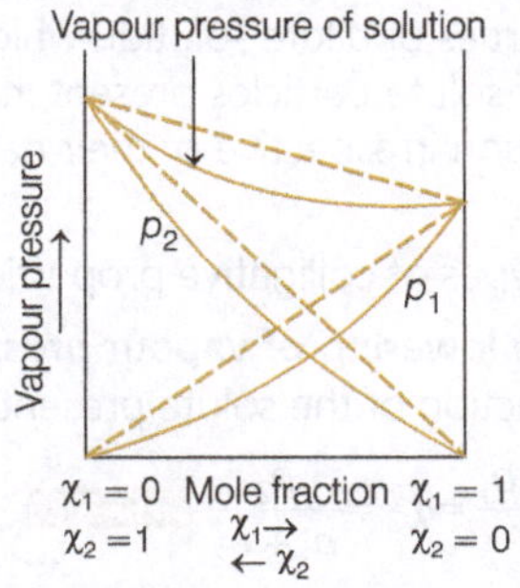
$\Delta_{mix}V = 0$, $\Delta_{mix}H = 0$	$\Delta_{mix}V > 0$, $\Delta_{mix}H > 0$ (endothermic)	$\Delta_{mix}V < 0$, $\Delta_{mix}H < 0$ (exothermic)
Intermolecular interactions, i.e. *A*—*B* interactions are same as present in pure components, i.e. *A*—*A* or *B*—*B*.	Intermolecular interactions, i.e. *A*—*B* interactions are weaker than in pure components, i.e. between *A*—*A* or *B*—*B*.	Intermolecular interactions, i.e. *A*—*B* interactions are stronger than in pure components, i.e. between *A*—*A* or *B*—*B*.
Do not form azeotropes.	Form minimum boiling azeotropes	Form maximum boiling azeotropes.
Examples Benzene and toluene, *n*-hexane and *n*-heptane; chlorobenzene and bromobenzene; ethyl bromide and ethyl iodide; *n*-butyl chloride and *n*-butyl bromide.	**Examples** Ethanol and water, ethanol and acetone, acetone and benzene, carbon disulphide and acetone, carbon tetrachloride and methanol, cyclohexane and ethanol, water and methanol, carbon tetrachloride and benzene.	**Examples** Acetic acid and methanol, acetic acid and pyridine, acetone and aniline, acetone and chloroform, benzene and chloroform, water and hydrochloric acid, water and nitric acid.

Trick to remember examples of ideal and non-Ideal solutions

- **Ideal solution**

  These are usually formed by compounds of nearly similar nature.
  e.g. Ethyl bromide and ethyl iodide, chlorobenzene and bromobenzene.

- **Non-ideal solution**

  +ve deviation Mostly formed with alcohols, CS_2, CCl_4, e.g. CH_3OH and H_2O, C_2H_5OH and H_2O, acetone and CS_2
  –ve deviation Mostly formed with acids, e.g. HCl and H_2O, HNO_3 and H_2O.

Azeotropes

The binary mixture (liquid) having the same composition in liquid and vapour phase and boil at constant temperature are called azeotropes or **azeotropic mixtures**. These have sharp boiling point like a pure liquid, components of these mixture cannot be separated by fractional distillation. These are formed by non-ideal solutions.

There are two types of azeotropes

- **Minimum boiling azeotropes** The solutions which show a large positive deviation from Raoult's law form minimum boiling **azeotrope** at a specific composition.

  e.g. 95% ethanol by volume in water forms azeotropic mixture which has constant boiling point 351.15 K. At this point, they have same composition in liquid and vapour phase which cannot be separated by fractional distillation. Due to this, pure ethanol cannot be obtained from ethanol-water mixture by fermentation of sugar.

- **Maximum boiling azeotropes** The solutions which show large negative deviation from Raoult's law form maximum boiling azeotrope at a specific composition.

  e.g. Nitric acid (68%) and water (32%) by mass with a boiling point of 393.5 K. NEET 2019

Marks Maximizer

Zeotropes are mixtures of liquid that have different boiling points. The components of the zeotrope can be separated by fractional distillation.

Colligative Properties and Determination of Molar Mass

The properties of dilute solution which depends only upon the number of solute particles present in a solution and their concentration irrespective of their nature are called colligative properties.

The four types of colligative properties are discussed below.

- **Relative lowering of vapour pressure** It is equal to the mole fraction of the solute present in the solution.

  (i) $\frac{p_1^\circ - p_1}{p_1^\circ} = \chi_2 = \frac{n_2}{n_1 + n_2}$ NEET 2020

  where, p_1° = vapour pressure of pure solvent
  p_1 = vapour pressure of solvent in solution
  χ_2 = mole fraction of solute

  (ii) For dilute solution, $n_2 << n_1$

  $$\frac{p_1^\circ - p_1}{p_1^\circ} = \frac{n_2}{n_1}$$

  or $$\frac{p_1^\circ - p_1}{p_1^\circ} = \frac{w_2 \times M_1}{M_2 \times w_1}$$

  where, M_2 = molecular weight of solute,
  w_2 = weight of solute
  M_1 = molecular weight of solvent
  w_1 = weight of solvent

- **Elevation of boiling point** (Ebullioscopy) It is an elevation or increase in the boiling temperature of the solution as compared to the pure solvent, when non-volatile solute is added. $\Delta T_b = T_b - T_b^\circ$

  (i) $\Delta T_b = K_b m$

  (ii) $\Delta T_b = \frac{K_b \times w_2 \times 1000}{M_2 \times w_1}$

  where, ΔT_b = elevation in boiling point.
  K_b = molal elevation constant or ebullioscopic constant $(RM_1 T_b^2 / 1000 \Delta_{vap} H)$
  m = molality
  $\Delta_{vap} H$ = enthalpy of vapourisation of pure solvent
  T_b° = boiling point of pure solvent

  (iii) Unit of K_b = K kg mol^{-1}

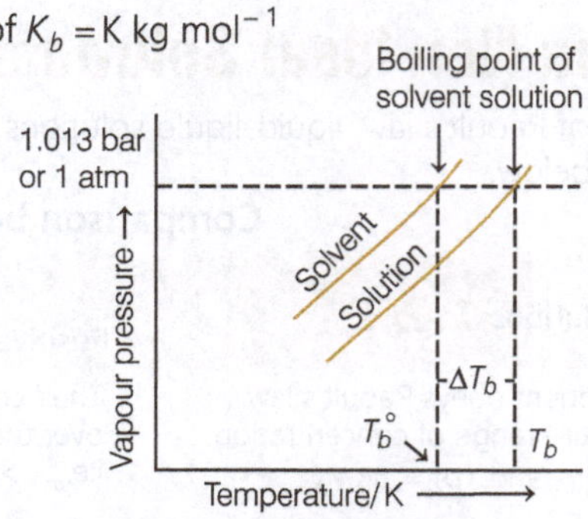

Graph showing ΔT_b elevation of boiling point of a solvent in a solution

- **Depression of freezing point** (cryoscopy) It is the depression or decrease in the freezing temperature of the solution as compared to the pure solvent, when non-volatile solute is added.

  (i) $\Delta T_f = K_f \times m$ NEET 2020

  (ii) $\Delta T_f = \frac{K_f \times w_2 \times 1000}{M_2 \times w_1}$ $(\Delta T_f = T_f^\circ - T_f)$

  ΔT_f = depression in freezing point
  whereas, K_f = molal depression constant or cryoscopic constant $(RM_1 T_f^2 / 1000 \Delta_{fus} H)$
  T_f° = freezing point of pure solvent
  $\Delta_{fus} H$ = enthalpy of fusion of pure solvent

  (iii) Unit of K_f = K kg mol^{-1}

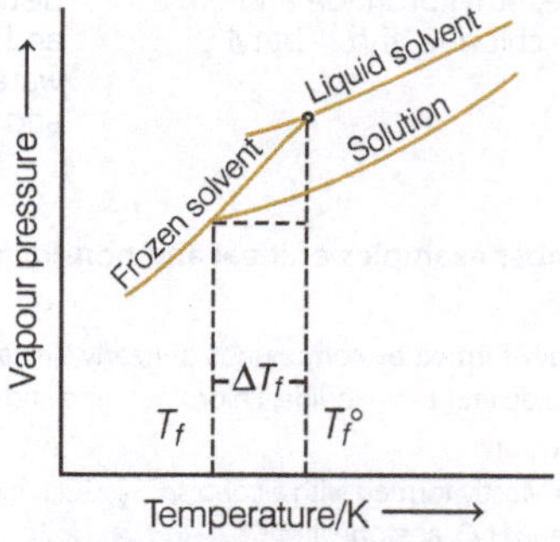

Graph showing ΔT_f, depression in freezing point of a solvent in a solution

Osmosis and Osmotic Pressure

- Spontaneous flow of solvent from dilute solution into the concentrated solution through a semipermeable membrane is called **osmosis**.

  e.g. People taking a lot of salt or salty food experience water retention in tissue cells and intercellular spaces because of osmosis. This resulting puffiness or swelling is called **edema**.

- The **osmotic pressure** of a solution is the excess pressure that must be applied to a solution to prevent osmosis, i.e. to stop the passage of solvent molecules through a semipermeable membrane into the solution.
- For dilute solution, osmotic pressure is proportional to the molarity (C) of the solution of given temperature (T).

  (i) $\pi = CRT = hdg$ **NEET 2021, 2024**

  where, h = height of liquid raised on capillary attached to solution chamber

  d = density of solution

  g = acceleration due to gravity

  $$C = \frac{\text{number of moles of solute}}{\text{volume of solution (in L)}}$$

  (ii) $\pi = \dfrac{w_2 RT}{M_2 \times V}$

- Two or more solutions having equal osmotic pressure under given conditions are called **isotonic solutions**.
- A solution having lower or higher osmotic pressure than the other is said to be **hypotonic** or **hypertonic** respectively.

  It is used for determination of molar mass of solutes, particularly for biomolecules as they are generally not stable at higher temperature and have poor solubility.

- The phenomena in which the direction of osmosis can be reversed, if a pressure larger than the osmotic pressure is applied to solution side so that the pure solvent flows out of the solution through the semipermeable membrane is known as **reverse osmosis**. It is used in desalination of sea water.

Marks Maximizer

For dilute solutions, the relation between osmotic pressure and relative lowering of vapour pressure, $\dfrac{p_1^\circ - p_1}{p_1^\circ} = \dfrac{\pi M_1}{dRT}$

where, d = density, M_1 = molecular mass of solvent

Abnormal Molar Masses

- For the association or dissociation of compounds in solution, molar masses determined by the study of colligative properties is different from the theoretical value and the compound is said to show abnormal molar mass.
- **van't Hoff factor** (i) gives the extent of association or dissociation of the solute particles in the solution.

  For Concept Master Video

  $$i = \frac{\text{Normal molecular mass}}{\text{Abnormal molecular mass}}$$

  $$\text{or } i = \frac{\text{Observed colligative property}}{\text{Calculated colligative property}}$$

  $$\text{or } i = \frac{\text{Total number of moles of particles after dissociation / association}}{\text{Number of moles of particles before dissociation / association}}$$

  For dissociation, $i > 1$, while for association, $i < 1$.

- **Colligative properties and van't Hoff factor,**

  Inclusion of van't Hoff factor modifies the equations for colligative properties as follows

  (i) $\dfrac{p_1^\circ - p_1}{p_1^\circ} = i\chi_2$ (ii) $\Delta T_b = iK_b\, m$

  (iii) $\Delta T_f = iK_f m$ (iv) $\pi = iCRT$

Caution Points

- If observed colligative property is less than the normal colligative property, then the solute undergoes association.
- If observed colligative property is more than the normal colligative property, then the solute undergoes dissociation.
- For an electrolyte A_xB_y undergoing dissociation,

  $$A_xB_y \rightleftharpoons xA^{y+} + yB^{x-}$$

  $$i = \alpha(x + y - 1) + 1 \quad \text{or} \quad \alpha = \frac{i-1}{x+y-1}$$

  where, i = van't Hoff factor and α = degree of dissociation
- The experimentally determined molar mass is always lower than the true value.

PYQ Notes

1. Relation between van't Hoff factor i and degree of association, $\alpha = \dfrac{1-i}{1-1/n}$. **JEE Main 2022**
2. The molal depression constant (K_f) is unchanged, when molality of the dilute solution is doubled. **NEET 2017**
3. For an ideal solution, change in Gibbs free energy of mixing is not equal to zero, i.e. $\Delta G_{mix} \neq 0$. **NEET 2016, Phase II**
4. The van't Hoff factor for a dilute aqueous solution of the strong electrolyte barium hydroxide is 3. **NEET 2016**
5. For an ideal solution, change in entropy of mixing is not equal to zero, i.e. $\Delta S_{mix} \neq 0$. **NEET 2015**

Step by Step

Mastering NCERT

- Concept Builders
- Topical Questions
- Assertion-Reason
- Statement Type
- Matching Type
- Numerical Value
- NCERT Exemplar's
- Past Exams'
- Skill Boosters

Concept Builders

1 State one example of liquid in solid solution.

2 If 22 g of benzene is dissolved in 122 g of carbon tetrachloride, mass percentage of benzene and carbon tetrachloride is .... and .... respectively.

3 Commercial bleaching solution contains 3.62 mass percentage of sodium hypochlorite in water. [T/F]

4 Mole fraction of ethylene glycol ($C_2H_6O_2$) in a solution containing 20% of $C_2H_6O_2$ by mass is ....

5 1m KCl solution means 74.5 kg of KCl dissolved in 1 kg of water. [T/F]

6 What is the molality of solution containing 40 g NaOH in 1000 mL of water?

7 100 g of A is dissolved in water to form a solution B on further addition of small amount of A, it remains as a solid on the bottom of solution B. Thus, solution B is ....

8 If dissolution process is exothermic, then solubility .... with rise in temperature.

9 What will be the value of Henry's law constant of H_2S, if the solubility of H_2S in water at STP is 0.195 m?

10 If gas A is more soluble in water than gas B at the same temperature then which gas has higher value of K_H?

11 The low concentration of oxygen in the blood and tissue of people living at high altitude is due to .... atmospheric pressure.

12 Scuba divers may experience a condition called .... To avoid this, the tanks used by them are filled with air diluted with ....

13 Name the law which represents the given graph.

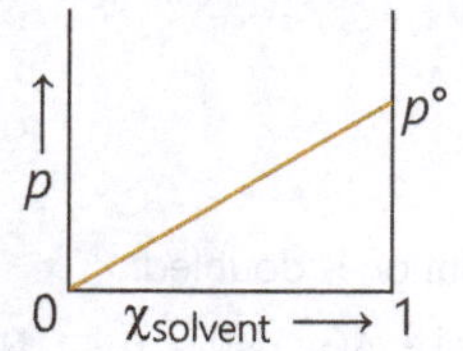

14 Nitric acid and water is an example of .... azeotrope, which has 68% nitric acid and 32% water by mass with a boiling point of 393.5 K.

15 In non-ideal solutions, what type of deviation shows the formation of maximum boiling azeotropes?

16 Name the type of deviation shown by the mixture of ethanol and acetone?

17 The unit of ebullioscopic constant is ....

18 Give the other name of boiling point elevation constant (K_b).

19 The boiling point of a liquid .... with decrease in atmospheric pressure.

20 Two different solutions of glucose of same molality prepared in different solvents will have the same depression is freezing point. [T/F]

21 If the molality of the dilute solution is doubled the value of molal depression constant becomes halved. [T/F]

22 State the formula showing relationship between depression in freezing point of a solution and molecular mass of the solute.

23 Colligative properties depend only on identity of solute and concentration of solute and independent of solvent identity. [T/F]

24 Solutions having less than 0.9% (mass/volume) concentration with respect to water is ....

25 The blood cells will shrink when placed in water containing more than 0.9% (mass/volume) NaCl solution. [T/F]

26 Name the phenomenon which is helpful in desalination of sea water?

27 Higher intake of salt results in puffiness or swelling called edema. [T/F]

28 A bacterium on salted meat loses water, shrivels and dies through osmosis process. [T/F]

29 The values of van't Hoff factors for KCl and K_2SO_4 are .... and .... respectively.

30 Dimerisation of ethanoic acid is due to .... bonding which results in the .... of calculated molar mass.

Topical Questions

Types and Expressing Concentration of Solutions

1 Which of the following statements is not correct about homogeneous mixtures? **NCERT Pg 1**
(a) These have uniform composition throughout the mixture.
(b) These show same physical properties throughout the mixture.
(c) These have same chemical properties throughout the mixture.
(d) These always contain only one solute and only one solvent.

2 Which of the following pair represents the liquid in liquid solution? **NCERT Pg 2**
(a) CO_2 in water, Brass
(b) Amalgam of Hg with Na, Alcohol in water
(c) Aerated drink, I_2 in CCl_4
(d) Hydrogen peroxide in water, Benzene in toluene

3 A solution is obtained by mixing 300 g of 30% and 200 g of 20% solution by weight. The percentage of solute in the resulting solution will be **NCERT Pg 2**
(a) 50% (b) 26% (c) 62% (d) 32%

4 The amount of water required to make 10% ethanol in water solution using 10 mL of pure ethanol is **NCERT Pg 2**
(a) 90 mL (b) 50 mL (c) 30 mL (d) 60 mL

5 184 g ethyl alcohol is mixed with 72 g of water. The ratio of mole fraction of alcohol to water is **NCERT Pg 3**
(a) 3 : 4 (b) 1 : 2
(c) 1 : 4 (d) 1 : 1

6 If molarity of Cu^{+2} ions is 3×10^{-4} M, then express this in ppm **NCERT Pg 3, 4**
(a) 0.3 (b) 0.2 (c) 0.1 (d) 0.6

7 The molarity of K^+ in aqueous solution that contains 17.4 ppm of K_2SO_4 is
(Molar mass $= 174$ g mol^{-1}) **NCERT Pg 3, 4**
(a) 2×10^{-2} M (b) 2×10^{-3} M
(c) 4×10^{-4}M (d) 2×10^{-4}M

8 Molarity of one litre solution of 22.2 g $CaCl_2$ is **NCERT Pg 4**
(a) 0.4 M (b) 0.2 M
(c) 0.8 M (d) 0.6 M

9 The molarity of H_2SO_4 solution, which has a density 1.84 g/cc at 35°C and contains 98% by weight is **NCERT Pg 4**
(a) 1.84 M (b) 18.4 M
(c) 20.6 M (d) 24.5 M

10 The molarity of a solution obtained by mixing 750 mL of 0.5 M HCl with 250 mL of 2M HCl will be **NCERT Pg 4**
(a) 0.875 M (b) 1.00 M
(c) 1.75 M (d) 0.0975 M

11 29.2% (w/W) HCl stock solution has density of 1.25 g mL^{-1}. The molecular weight of HCl is 36.5 g mol^{-1}. The volume (mL) of stock solution required to prepare a 200 mL solution of 0.4 M HCl is **NCERT Pg 4**
(a) 5.0 mL (b) 6.0 mL
(c) 8.0 mL (d) 15.0 mL

12 25.3 g of sodium carbonate, Na_2CO_3 is dissolved in enough water to make 250 mL of solution. If sodium carbonate dissociates completely, molar concentration of sodium ion, Na^+ and carbonate ions, CO_3^{2-} respectively are (Molar mass of $Na_2CO_3 = 106$ g mol^{-1}) **NCERT Pg 4**
(a) 0.477 M and 0.477 M (b) 0.955 M and 1.910 M
(c) 1.910 M and 0.955 M (d) 1.90 M and 1.910 M

13 Mole fraction is temperature independent. However, strength is a function of temperature because **NCERT Pg 5**
(a) volume depends on temperature and mole fraction involves volume
(b) mole fraction involves non-volatile solute
(c) mass of solute dissolved in 1 L solution do not change with temperature
(d) volume depends on temperature and strength involves volume

14 A 5.2 molal aqueous solution of methyl alcohol, is supplied. What is the mole fraction of methyl alcohol in the solution? **NCERT Pg 5**
(a) 1.10 (b) 0.090 (c) 0.086 (d) 0.050

15 The molality of 20% (mass/mass) aqueous solution of KI will be? (Molar mass of KI $= 166$ g mol^{-1}) **NCERT Pg 5**
(a) 1.48 (b) 1.51 (c) 1.35 (d) 1.08

16 If two bottles A and B contain 1 M and 1 m aqueous solution ($d = 1$ g/mL) of sulphuric acid respectively. **NCERT Pg 4, 5**
(a) A is more concentrated than B.
(b) B is more concentrated than A.
(c) Concentration of A is equal to concentration of B.
(d) It is not possible to compare the concentration.

17 The density of 2M aqueous solution of NaOH is 1.28g/cm^3. The molality of the solution is
[Given : Molecular mass of NaOH= 40 g mol^{-1}] **NCERT Pg 5**
(a) 1.20 m (b) 1.56 m (c) 1.67 m (d) 1.32 m

18 The approximate mole fraction of the solute in 1 molal aqueous solution is **NCERT Pg 5**

(a) 0.036 (b) 1.80
(c) 0.18 (d) 0.018

19 The molality of 1 L solution of 80% H_2SO_4 (w/V), (given that the density of the solution is $1.80\ g\ mL^{-1}$) is **NCERT Pg 5**

(a) 8.16 (b) 8.6
(c) 1.02 (d) 10.8

Solubility

20 15 g of sucrose is dissolved in 50 mL of water and some pressure is applied on the surface of solution formed. It will result in **NCERT Pg 6**

(a) increased solubility
(b) decreased solubility
(c) slight increase in solubility
(d) no effect on solubility

21 In the graph given below, what does the slope of the line represent? **NCERT Pg 7**

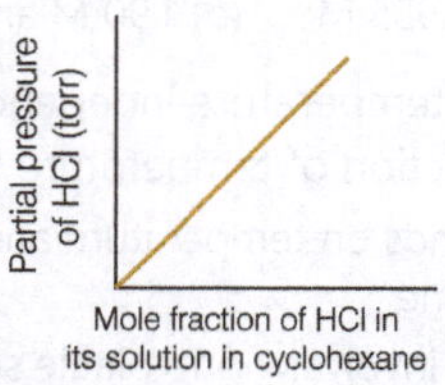

(a) Partial pressure of the gas in vapour phase (p)
(b) Mole fraction of gas in the solution (χ)
(c) Henry's law constant (K_H)
(d) Total pressure of gas

22 The value of Henry's law constant for helium (He), hydrogen (H_2) and oxygen (O_2) are respectively 144.97 kbar, 69.16 kbar and 34.86 kbar at 293 K. The correct order of their solubility is **NCERT Pg 7**

(a) $O_2 < He < H_2$ (b) $He < O_2 < H_2$
(c) $He < H_2 < O_2$ (d) $H_2 < He < O_2$

23 Ratio of O_2 and N_2 in the air is 1 : 4. Find out the ratio of their solubilities in terms of mole fractions of O_2 and N_2 dissolved in water at atmospheric pressure and room temperature.

$$\begin{bmatrix} K_H(O_2) = 3.30\times 10^7 \text{ torr} \\ K_H(N_2) = 6.60\times 10^7 \text{ torr} \end{bmatrix}$$ **NCERT Pg 7**

(a) 1 : 2 (b) 2 : 1 (c) 1 : 1 (d) 2 : 3

24 Henry's constant for Ar is 40 kbar in water. Then, molal concentration of Ar in water kept at 10 bar pressure will be **NCERT Pg 8**

(a) 0.09 (b) 0.05
(c) 1.25 (d) 0.014

25 Which of the following is correct? **NCERT Pg 7**

(a) The solubility of a gas in water increases with increase of temperature.
(b) The solubility of a gas in water increases with increase of pressure.
(c) Higher the value of K_H at a particular pressure, higher is the solubility of the gas in the liquid.
(d) Henry's law is valid if the gas reacts chemically with the solvent and dissociates or associates in the solvent.

26 K_H for $H_2(g)$/water system is 5.34×10^7 torr. If the partial pressure of H_2 over a solution at 25°C is 760 torr, then determine the solubility of hydrogen. Assume density of H_2O and solutions are same. **NCERT Pg 7**

(a) 6.4×10^{-3} mol L^{-1} (b) 7.89×10^{-4} mol L^{-1}
(c) 5.9×10^{-3} mol L^{-1} (d) 8.9×10^{-4} mol L^{-1}

27 The solubility of N_2 in water at 300 K and 500 torr partial pressure is $0.01 g\ L^{-1}$. The solubility in ($g\ L^{-1}$) at 750 torr partial pressure is **NCERT Pg 7**

(a) 0.02 (b) 0.015 (c) 0.0075 (d) 0.005

28 Henry's law constant for the solubility of methane in benzene at 298 K is 4.27×10^5 mm Hg. The solubility of methane in benzene at 298K under 760 mmHg will be. **NCERT Pg 7**

(a) 1.78×10^{-3} (b) 1.78×10^{-2}
(c) 1.78×10^{-1} (d) 1.78

29 The air is a mixture of a number of gases. The major components of air are oxygen and nitrogen with approximate proportion of 20% to 79% by volume at 298 K. The water is in equilibrium with air at a pressure of 10 atm. At 298 K, if the Henry's law constants for oxygen and nitrogen are 3.30×10^7 mm Hg and 6.51×10^7 mm Hg respectively, calculate the composition of these gases in water. **NCERT Pg 7, 8**

(a) $N_2 = 4.6\times 10^{-5}$; $O_2 = 9.22\times 10^{-5}$
(b) $N_2 = 2.3\times 10^{-5}$; $O_2 = 4.8\times 10^{-5}$
(c) $N_2 = 9.22\times 10^{-5}$; $O_2 = 4.6\times 10^{-5}$
(d) $N_2 = 4.8\times 10^{-5}$; $O_2 = 2.3\times 10^{-5}$

30 Which of the following gases have the least Henry's law constant at 298 K when dissolved in water? **NCERT Pg 8**

(a) He, Ar (b) N_2, He
(c) O_2, H_2 (d) CO_2, HCHO

31 Which of the following statement is not true? **NCERT Pg 8, 9**

(a) Pressure is higher under water than at the surface of a sea.
(b) Low surface pressure is responsible for the formation of bends in the body of scuba divers.
(c) Bends are actually the bubbles of nitrogen in the blood.
(d) Due to high pressure, solubility of atmospheric gases in the blood decreases.

32 Anoxia is a condition, generally seen in climbers because of **NCERT Pg 9**

(a) high concentration of oxygen at high altitudes
(b) high concentration of air at high altitudes
(c) high partial pressure of oxygen at high altitudes
(d) low partial pressure of oxygen at high altitudes

33 What is the composition of gases in the tanks used by the scuba divers? **NCERT Pg 9**

(a) 11.7% helium, 32.1% nitrogen, 56.2% oxygen
(b) 11.7% helium, 56.2% nitrogen, 32.1% oxygen
(c) 56.2% helium, 11.7% nitrogen, 32.1% oxygen
(d) 56.2% helium, 32.1% nitrogen, 11.7% oxygen

Vapour Pressure of Liquid Solutions

34 When a binary solution of two volatile liquids is taken in a closed vessel, then **NCERT Pg 9**

(a) both the components would evaporate and an equilibrium would be established between vapour phase and liquid phase
(b) both the components would evaporate but equilibrium would not be established between vapour phase and liquid phase
(c) none of components would evaporate and no equilibrium would be established between vapour phase and liquid phase
(d) none of the components would evaporate and an equilibrium would be established between vapour and liquid phase

35 p_A and p_B are the vapour pressure of pure liquid components A and B respectively of an ideal binary solution. If χ_A represents the mole fraction of component A, the total pressure of the solution will be **NCERT Pg 10**

(a) $p_A + \chi_A (p_B - p_A)$
(b) $p_A + \chi_A (p_A - p_B)$
(c) $p_B + \chi_A (p_B - p_A)$
(d) $p_B + \chi_A (p_A - p_B)$

36 At 300 K two pure liquids A and B have 150 mm Hg and 100 mm Hg vapour pressures, respectively. In an equimolar liquid mixture of A and B, the mole fraction of B in the vapour mixture at this temperature is **NCERT Pg 10**

(a) 0.6
(b) 0.5
(c) 0.8
(d) 0.4

37 Vapour pressure of chloroform ($CHCl_3$) and dichloromethane (CH_2Cl_2) at 25°C are 200 mm of Hg and 41.5 mm of Hg respectively. Vapour pressure of the solution obtained by mixing 25.5 g of $CHCl_3$ and 40 g of CH_2Cl_2 at the same temperature will be (Molecular mass of $CHCl_3$ = 119.5 u and molecular mass of CH_2Cl_2 = 85 u) **NCERT Pg 10**

(a) 173.9 mm Hg
(b) 615.0 mm Hg
(c) 347.9 mm Hg
(d) 90.63 mm Hg

38 The vapour pressure of pure $CHCl_3$ and CH_2Cl_2 are 200 and 41.5 atm respectively. The weight of $CHCl_3$ and CH_2Cl_2 are respectively 11.9 g and 17 g. The vapour pressure of solution will be **NCERT Pg 10**

(a) 80.5 atm
(b) 79.5 atm
(c) 93.4 atm
(d) 105.5 atm

39 Two volatile liquids A and B form a binary solution. At 350 K, the vapour pressures of pure A and pure B are 7×10^3 Pa and 12×10^3 Pa, respectively. The composition of the vapour in equilibrium with a solution containing 40 mole percent of A at this temperature is **NCERT Pg 10**

(a) $y_A = 0.76$; $y_B = 0.24$
(b) $y_A = 0.28$; $y_B = 0.72$
(c) $y_A = 0.4$; $y_B = 0.6$
(d) $y_A = 0.37$; $y_B = 0.63$

40 In three beakers labelled as P, Q, R, 100 mL of water, 100 mL of 1 M solution of glucose in water and 100 mL of 0.5 M solution of glucose in water are taken respectively and kept at same temperature. **NCERT Pg 12**

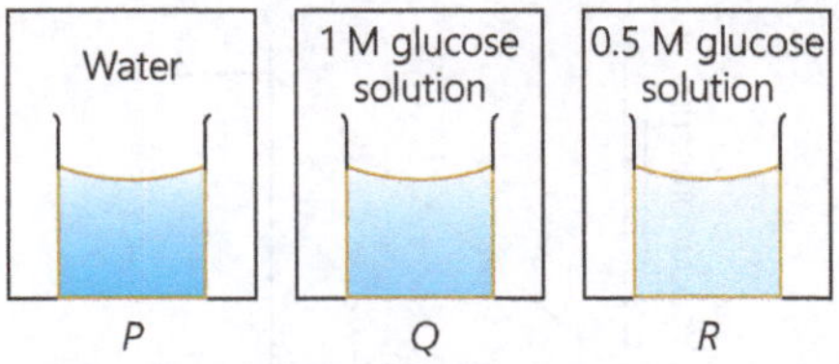

Which of the following statements is correct?

(a) Vapour pressure in all the three beakers is same.
(b) Vapour pressure of beaker R is lowest.
(c) Vapour pressure of beaker Q is highest.
(d) Vapour pressure of beaker Q is lower than that of R and vapour pressure of beaker R is lower than that of P.

41 In the three beakers labelled as X, Y and Z, following solutions are taken and kept at same temperature respectively. **NCERT Pg 12**

(i) Beaker $X \rightarrow$ 250 mL of water.
(ii) Beaker $Y \rightarrow$ 250 mL of 0.8 M solution of sucrose in water.
(iii) Beaker $Z \rightarrow$ 250 mL of 3 M solution of sucrose in water.

Which among the given beaker will have the highest vapour pressure?

(a) Beaker X
(b) Beaker Y
(c) Beaker Z
(d) Vapour pressure in all the beakers are same.

42 Vapour pressure of pure benzene is 119 torr and that of toluene is 37.0 torr at the same temperature. Mole fraction of toluene in vapour phase which is in equilibrium with solution of benzene and toluene having a mole fraction of toluene 0.50, will be **NCERT Pg 12**

(a) 0.137 (b) 0.237 (c) 0.435 (d) 0.205

43 Interpret the correct statement for the following figure. **NCERT Pg 12**

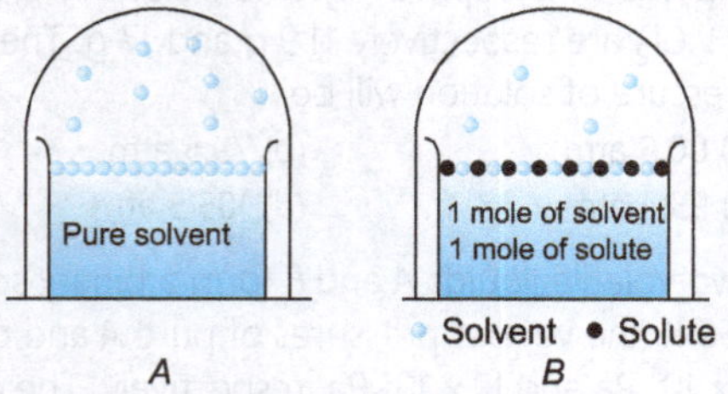

(a) Vapour pressure of pure solvent in beaker *A* is more than in the beaker *B*.
(b) Vapour pressure of the pure solvent in beaker *A* is less than in the beaker *B*.
(c) Vapour pressure of pure solvent in both the beakers is same.
(d) Vapour pressure of the solution *B* is very high as compared to *A*.

44 What does *A* point signifies in the figure given below? **NCERT Pg 13**

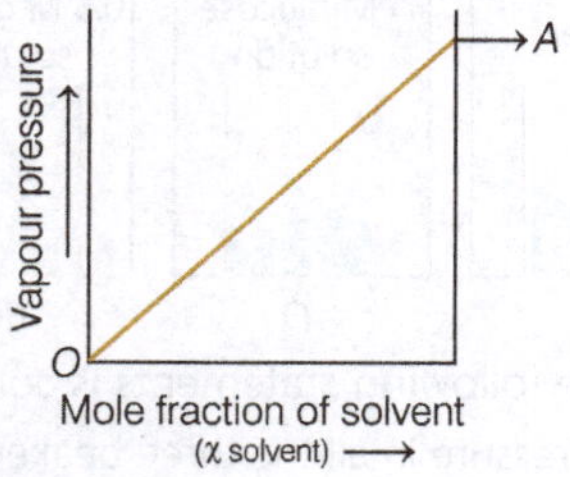

(a) Vapour pressure of solute
(b) Vapour pressure of pure solvent
(c) Vapour pressure of solution
(d) Mole fraction of solute

Ideal and Non-ideal Solutions

45 Solution of bromoethane and chloroethane **NCERT Pg 13**
(a) obeys Raoult's law over the entire range of concentration
(b) is a non-ideal solution
(c) has $\Delta_{mix}V \neq 0$
(d) has $\Delta_{mix}H \neq 0$

46 The solution which shows large positive deviation from Raoult's law form **NCERT Pg 14**
(a) maximum boiling azeotrope at a specific composition.
(b) maximum freezing azeotrope at a specific composition.
(c) minimum boiling azeotrope at a specific composition.
(d) minimum freezing azeotrope at a specific composition.

47 Which of the following azeotropic solutions has the boiling point less than the boiling point of its constituents molecules? **NCERT Pg 14**
(a) $CHCl_3$ and CH_3COCH_3 (b) CS_2 and CH_3COCH_3
(c) CH_3CH_2OH and CH_3COCH_3 (d) CH_3CHO and CS_2

48 Azeotropic mixture of water and C_2H_5OH boils at 351 K. By distilling the mixture, it is possible to obtain **NCERT Pg 14**
(a) pure C_2H_5OH only
(b) pure water only
(c) Both water and C_2H_5OH in pure state
(d) Neither C_2H_5OH nor water

49 Which of the following statement is correct regarding a mixture of benzene and chloroform? **NCERT Pg 14**
(a) $\Delta_{mix}H = 0$ at constant *T* and *P*.
(b) $\Delta_{mix}V = 0$ at constant *T* and *P*.
(c) Shows negative deviation since there is decrease in vapour pressure.
(d) Form minimum boiling azeotrope.

50 Which of the following statement is true for the diagram? **NCERT Pg 14**

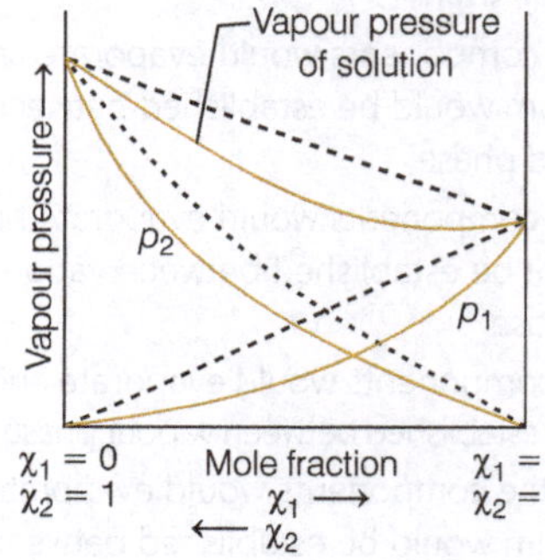

(a) The escaping tendency of molecule decreases for each component.
(b) Vapour pressure of the solution increases.
(c) Solution shows positive deviation from Raoult's law.
(d) It is true for ethanol and acetone.

51 Select the incorrect statement. **NCERT Pg 13, 14**
(a) Solution of chloroform and acetone shows negative deviation from Raoult's law.
(b) Solution of ethanol and acetone shows positive deviation from Raoult's law.
(c) In case of solution of phenol (*A*) and aniline (*B*), *A*—*A* and *B*—*B* interactions are stronger than *A*—*B* (i.e. phenol and aniline) interactions.
(d) Azeotropes are constant boiling mixtures, which are separated by azeotropic distillation.

52 The solution that forms maximum boiling azeotrope is **NCERT Pg 14, 15**
(a) carbon disulphide – acetone
(b) benzene – toluene
(c) acetone – chloroform
(d) *n*-hexane – *n*-heptane

Colligative Properties and Determination of Molar Mass

53 Colligative properties are observed when **NCERT Pg 15**

(a) a non-volatile solid is dissolved in a volatile liquid
(b) a gas is dissolved in non-volatile liquid
(c) a volatile liquid is dissolved in another volatile liquid
(d) a liquid is dissolved in non-volatile liquid

54 Relative lowering of vapour pressure is a colligative property because **NCERT Pg 15**

(a) it depends on the concentration of a non-electrolyte solute in solution and does not depend on the nature of the solute molecules
(b) it depends on number of particles of electrolytic solute in solution as well as on the nature of the solute particles
(c) it depends on the concentration of a non-electrolyte solute in solution and does not depend on the number of the solute molecules
(d) it depends on the concentration of an electrolyte or non-electrolyte solute in solution as well as on the nature of solute molecules

55 At room temperature, a dilute solution of urea is prepared by dissolving 0.60 g of urea in 360 g of water. If the vapour pressure of pure water at this temperature is 35 mm Hg, lowering of vapour pressure will be (Molar mass of urea = 60 g mol^{-1}) **NCERT Pg 15**

(a) 0.027 mm Hg (b) 0.031 mm Hg
(c) 0.017 mm Hg (d) 0.028 mm Hg

56 Lowering of vapour pressure of an aqueous solution of a non-volatile, non-electrolyte 1M aqueous solution at 100°C is **NCERT Pg 15**

(a) 14.12 torr (b) 312 torr (c) 13.45 torr (d) 352 torr

57 For a solution containing a non-volatile, non-electrolytic solute the relative lowering in vapour pressure is 0.2. If total number of moles present in the solution is 5, then which of the following is correct? **NCERT Pg 15**

(a) Mole fraction of solvent, $X_{solvent} = 0.8$
(b) Mole fraction of solute, $X_{solute} = 0.8$
(c) Number of moles of solute = 4
(d) Number of moles of solvent = 2

58 What does points *A* and *B* represent in the following diagram? **NCERT Pg 17**

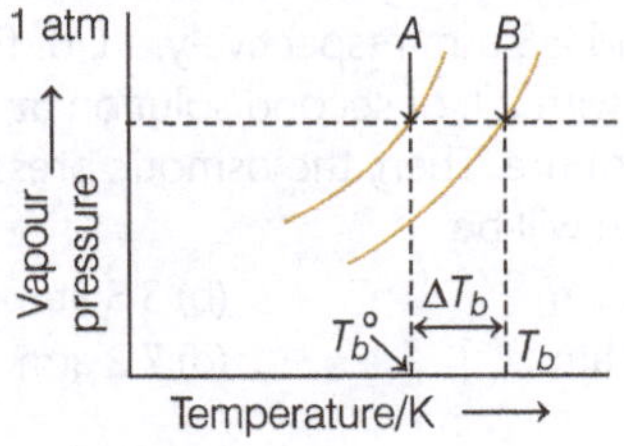

	Point *A*	Point *B*
(a)	Boiling point of solvent	Boiling point of solution
(b)	Boiling point of solution	Boiling point of solvent
(c)	Boiling point of solute	Boiling point of solvent
(d)	Boiling point of solvent	Boiling point of solute

59 For a dilute solution containing 2.5 g of a non-volatile, non-electrolyte solute in 100 g of water, the elevation in boiling point at 1 atm pressure is 2°C. Assuming concentration of solute is much lower than the concentration of solvent, the vapour pressure (mm of Hg) of the solution is (Take, $K_b = 0.76$ K kg mol^{-1}) **NCERT Pg 17**

(a) 724 (b) 740
(c) 750 (d) 720

60 Identify (i), (ii) and (iii) in the following diagram. **NCERT Pg 18**

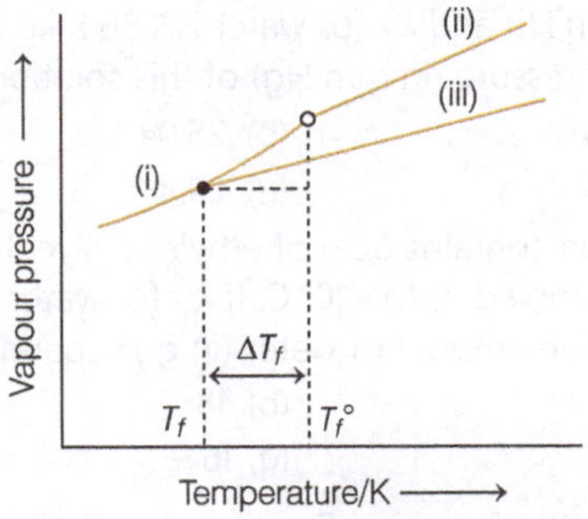

(a) (i) Solution (ii) Frozen solvent (iii) Liquid solvent
(b) (i) Frozen solvent (ii) Solution (iii) Liquid solvent
(c) (i) Frozen solvent (ii) Liquid solvent (iii) Solution
(d) (i) Solution (ii) Liquid solvent (iii) Frozen solvent

61 The freezing point of a 4% aqueous solution of '*A*' is equal to the freezing point of 10% aqueous solution of '*B*'. The molecular weight of *A* is 60, find out the molecular weight of *B*. Assume both *A* and *B* are non-electrolyte. **NCERT Pg 18**

(a) 160 (b) 90 (c) 45 (d) 180

62 An element '*X*' exists as a polymer X_n. When 3.26 g of *X* is dissolved in 200 g of a solvent ($K_f = 5$ K $molal^{-1}$), the freezing point is lowered by 0.125°C. The molecular formula of X_n is (Atomic wt. of $X = 80$) **NCERT Pg 18**

(a) X_2 (b) X_4 (c) X_8 (d) X_6

63 Ethylene glycol is used as an antifreeze in a cold climate. Mass of ethylene glycol which should be added to 4 kg of water to prevent it from freezing at −6°C will be (K_f for water = 1.86 K kg mol^{-1} and molar mass of ethylene glycol = 62 g mol^{-1}) **NCERT Pg 19**

(a) 800.00 g (b) 204.30 g
(c) 400.00 g (d) 304.60 g

64 How many grams of methyl alcohol should be added to 10 L tank of water to prevent its freezing at 268 K? [K_f for $H_2O = 1.86$ K kg mol^{-1}] **NCERT Pg 19**
(a) 880.07 g
(b) 899.04 g
(c) 886.02 g
(d) 868.06 g

65 K_f for water is 1.86 K kg mol^{-1}. If your automobile radiator holds 1.0 kg of water, how many grams of ethylene glycol ($C_2H_6O_2$) must you add to get the freezing point of the solution lowered to −2.8°C? **NCERT Pg 19**
(a) 72 g (b) 93 g
(c) 39 g (d) 27 g

66 A solution of a non-volatile solute in water freezes at −0.30°C. The vapour pressure of pure water at 298 K is 23.51 mm Hg and K_f for water is 1.86 K kg mol^{-1}. The vapour pressure (in mm Hg) of this solution at 298 K is
(a) 23.44 (b) 25.04 **NCERT Pg 16, 19**
(c) 28.34 (d) 29.44

67 A solution contains 62 g of ethylene glycol in 250 g of water is cooled upto −10° C. If K_f for water is 1.86 K kg mol^{-1}, then amount of water (in g) separated as ice is
(a) 32 (b) 48 **NCERT Pg 19**
(c) 64 (d) 16

68 Consider the following figure, **NCERT Pg 20**

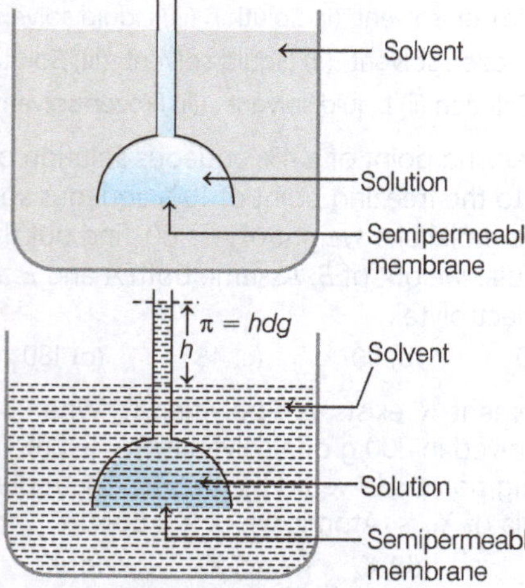

After 10 min

Mark the incorrect information derived from the figure.
(a) Solute molecule passes through the semipermeable membrane from pure solvent to the solution.
(b) The level of solution increases due to osmosis.
(c) Solvent molecules flow from pure solvent to solution.
(d) Osmotic pressure is needed to prevent this process.

69 0.1 M $CaCl_2$ and 0.005 M $BaCl_2$ solutions are separated by a semipermeable membrane in a container. For this system, choose the correct statement. **NCERT Pg 21**
(a) There is no movement of any solution across the membrane.
(b) Water flows from $BaCl_2$ solution to $CaCl_2$ solution.
(c) Water flows from $CaCl_2$ solution to $BaCl_2$ solution.
(d) Osmotic pressure of 0.1 M $CaCl_2$ is lower than that of $BaCl_2$ (assume complete dissociation).

70 If osmotic pressure of 4% (*w*/*V*) solution of sucrose is same as 2% (*w*/*V*) solution of '*X*', then the molecular mass of *X* (g/mol) is **NCERT Pg 21**
(a) 171 (b) 205.2 (c) 570 (d) 150

71 Which of the following material is used for making semipermeable membrane for carrying reverse osmosis in desalination of water? **NCERT Pg 23**
(a) Potassium nitrate (b) Cellulose acetate
(c) Cell membrane (d) Parchment membrane

72 A 6% solution of urea is isotonic with **NCERT Pg 22**
(a) 0.05 M solution of glucose
(b) 6% solution of glucose
(c) 25% solution of glucose
(d) 1 M solution of glucose

73 Osmotic pressure method is used to determine molar mass of protein, macromolecules like polymers, biomolecules etc., because **NCERT Pg 22**
(a) osmotic pressure is measured at body temperature
(b) osmotic pressure depends upon molality
(c) these are not stable at higher temperature and have poor solubility
(d) they have high molecular weight

74 If 0.5 M solution of sucrose and 0.5 M solution of glucose are placed on two sides of semipermeable membrane to equal heights, then the correct statement is **NCERT Pg 21**
(a) there will be no net movement across the membrane
(b) glucose will flow towards sucrose solution
(c) sucrose will flow towards glucose solution
(d) water will flow from glucose solution to sucrose solution

75 Two solutions of glucose have osmotic pressure 1.5 atm and 2.5 atm respectively. 1 L of first solution is mixed with 2 L of second solution at the same temperature. Then, the osmotic pressure of resultant solution will be **NCERT Pg 21**
(a) 2.16 atm (b) 3.5 atm
(c) 5.12 atm (d) 7.2 atm

76 Osmotic pressure present in the fluid inside the blood cell is equivalent to NCERT Pg 22
(a) 0.9% (*m/V*) NaCl solution
(b) less than 0.9 % (*m/V*) NaCl solution
(c) more than 0.9 % (*m/V*) NaCl solution
(d) 0.9% (*m/V*) Na_2SO_4 solution

Abnormal Molar Masses

77 58.5 g of NaCl and 180 g of glucose were separately dissolved in 1000 g of water. Identify the correct statement regarding the elevation of boiling point (b.p.) of the resulting solution. NCERT Pg 24
(a) NaCl solution will show higher elevation of boiling point.
(b) Glucose solution will show higher elevation of boiling point.
(c) Both the solutions will show equal elevation of boiling point.
(d) The boiling point elevation will be shown by none of the solutions.

78 The degree of dissociation (α) of a weak electrolyte, A_xB_y is related to van't Hoff factor (*i*) is given by the expression NCERT Pg 24
(a) $\alpha = \dfrac{i-1}{(x+y-1)}$ (b) $\alpha = \dfrac{i-1}{x+y+1}$
(c) $\alpha = \dfrac{x+y-1}{i-1}$ (d) $\alpha = \dfrac{x+y+1}{i-1}$

79 The van't Hoff factor for 0.1 M $Ba(NO_3)_2$ solution is 2.74. The degree of dissociation is NCERT Pg 24
(a) 91.3% (b) 87% (c) 100% (d) 74%

80 Compound *A* undergoes tetramerisation in a given solvent. The van't Hoff factor is NCERT Pg 24
(a) 2.0 (b) 0.5 (c) 0.25 (d) 0.125

81 Which one of the following electrolytes has the same value of van't Hoff factor (*i*) as that of $K_4[Fe(CN)_6]$? NCERT Pg 24
(a) $Al_2(SO_4)_3$ (b) K_2SO_4
(c) $K_3[Fe(CN)_6]$ (d) $Al(NO_3)_3$

82 The van't Hoff factor of $BaCl_2$ at 0.01 M concentration is 1.98. The percentage of dissociation of $BaCl_2$ at this concentration is NCERT Pg 24
(a) 49 (b) 69 (c) 89 (d) 98

83 A molecule *M* associates in a given solvent according to the equation $M \rightleftharpoons (M)_n$. For a certain concentration of *M*, the van't Hoff factor was found to be 0.9 and the fraction of associated molecules was 0.2. The value of *n* is
(a) 3 (b) 5 (c) 2 (d) 4 NCERT Pg 24

84 Solutions *A*, *B*, *C* and *D* are respectively 0.1 M glucose, 0.05 M NaCl, 0.05 M $BaCl_2$ and 0.1 M $AlCl_3$. Which one of the following pairs is isotonic? NCERT Pg 24
(a) *A* and *B* (b) *B* and *C* (c) *A* and *D* (d) *A* and *C*

85 Molal depression constant for a solvent is 4.0 K kg mol^{-1}. The depression in the freezing point of the solvent for 0.03 mol kg^{-1} solution of K_2SO_4 is (Assume complete dissociation of the electrolyte) NCERT Pg 24
(a) 0.18 K (b) 0.36 K
(c) 0.12 K (d) 0.24 K

86 Relative lowering in vapour pressure of a solution containing 1 mole K_2SO_4 in 54 g H_2O is (K_2SO_4 is 100% ionised). NCERT Pg 24
(a) $\frac{1}{55}$ (b) $\frac{3}{55}$ (c) $\frac{3}{4}$ (d) $\frac{1}{2}$

87 The elevation in boiling point of a solution containing 13.44 g of $CuCl_2$ in 1 kg of water using the following information will be (Molecular weight of $CuCl_2$= 134.4 g mol^{-1} and K_b = 0.52 K kg mol^{-1}) NCERT Pg 24
(a) 0.16°C (b) 0.05°C (c) 0.1°C (d) 0.2°C

88 Which of the following has least freezing point?
(a) 1% Sucrose (b) 1% NaCl NCERT Pg 24
(c) 1% $CaCl_2$ (d) 1% Glucose

89 KBr is 80% dissociated in aqueous solution of 0.5 m concentration. (Given, K_f for water = 1.86 K kg mol^{-1}). The solution freezes at NCERT Pg 24
(a) 271.326 K (b) 272 K
(c) 270.5 K (d) 268.5 K

90 The freezing point depression constant for water is 1.86°C $molal^{-1}$. If 5.00 g Na_2SO_4 is dissolved in 45.0 g of H_2O, the freezing point is changed to −3.82°C. Calculate the van't Hoff factor for Na_2SO_4. NCERT Pg 24
(a) 0.381 (b) 2.05 (c) 2.63 (d) 3.11

91 A solution of 1.25 g of *P* in 50 g of water lowers the freezing point of water by 0.3°C. Molar mass of *P* is 94 g mol^{-1}, $K_{f(\text{water})}$ = 1.86 K kg mol^{-1}. The degree of association of *P* in water is NCERT Pg 24
(a) 79% (b) 60% (c) 65% (d) 75%

92 Consider 0.1 m solution of two solutes *X* and *Y*. Solute *X* dissociates in two ions whereas *Y* dimerises in the solution. Which of the following is false? (*X* and *Y* represents solution containing *X* and *Y* respectively).
(a) $(\Delta T_b)_X > (\Delta T_b)_Y$ (b) $(B.P)_X > (B.P)_Y$ NCERT Pg 24
(c) $(F.P)_X > (F.P)_Y$ (d) $(\Delta T_f)_X > (\Delta T_f)_Y$

93 A complex is represented as $CoCl_3 \cdot xNH_3$. Its 0.1 molal solution in water shows melting point = 0.558 K. (K_f of H_2O = 1.86 K $molality^{-1}$). Assuming 100% ionisation of complex and coordination number of Co is 6, formula of complex is NCERT Pg 24
(a) $[Co(NH_3)_5Cl]Cl_2$ (b) $[Co(NH_3)_6]Cl_3$
(c) $[Co(NH_3)_4Cl_2]Cl$ (d) $[Co(NH_3)_3Cl_3]$

94 0.01 m solution of KCl and $BaCl_2$ are prepared in water. The freezing point of KCl is found to be −2°C. What is the freezing point of $BaCl_2$ to be completely ionised? **NCERT Pg 24**
(a) −3°C (b) +3°C
(c) −2°C (d) −4°C

95 The depression in freezing point of 0.01 m aqueous CH_3COOH solution is 0.02046°C. 1m urea solution freezes at −1.86°C. Assuming molality equal to molarity, pH of CH_3COOH solution is **NCERT Pg 24**
(a) 2 (b) 3 (c) 3.2 (d) 4.2

96 Which of the following would exert maximum osmotic pressure? **NCERT Pg 24**
(a) Aluminium sulphate (b) Barium chloride
(c) Sodium chloride
(d) A solution obtained by mixing equal volumes of (b) and (c).

97 The osmotic pressure of 0.1M monobasic acid, if pH = 2.0 at 25°C is **NCERT Pg 24**
(a) 2.69 atm (b) 26.9 atm
(c) 0.269 atm (d) 269 atm

98 1.2% (*w/V*) NaCl solution is isotonic with 7.2% (*w/V*) glucose solution. What will be the van't Hoff factor '*i*' for NaCl? **NCERT Pg 24**
(a) 0.5 (b) 1 (c) 2 (d) 6

99 The osmotic pressure of a dilute solution of an ionic compound *XY* in water is four times than that of a solution of 0.01 M $BaCl_2$ in water.
Assuming complete dissociation of the given ionic compounds in water, the concentration of *XY* (in mol L^{-1}) in solution is **NCERT Pg 24**
(a) 4×10^{-2} (b) 16×10^{-4}
(c) 4×10^{-4} (d) 6×10^{-2}

100 Osmotic pressure of a sucrose solution is 4.926 atm at 27°C. Which of the following is not isotonic with the given solution? **NCERT Pg 24**
(a) 3.6% glucose solution (b) 1.2% urea solution
(c) 0.585% NaCl solution (d) 1.7% $NaNO_3$ solution

101 The osmotic pressure of the solution prepared by dissolving 25 mg of K_2SO_4 in 2 L of water at 25°C will be (Assuming it is to be completely dissociated)
(a) 5.27×10^{-4} atm (b) 5.27×10^{-3} atm **NCERT Pg 24**
(c) 5.27×10^{-2} atm (d) 5.27×10^{-1} atm

102 Arrange the following aqueous solutions in the order of their increasing boiling points. **NCERT Pg 25**
I. 10^{-2} M NaCl II. 10^{-3} M $MgCl_2$
III. 10^{-4} M Urea IV. 10^{-4} M NaCl
(a) I < II < IV < III (b) III < IV < II < I
(c) II < I < III < IV (d) IV < III < I = II

Assertion-Reason Questions

Direction (Q. Nos. 1-10) *In the following question Assertion (A) followed by Reason (R) is given below. Choose the correct option out of the choices given below.*
(a) Both A and R are true and R is the correct explanation of A.
(b) Both A and R are true and R is not the correct explanation of A.
(c) A is false but R is true.
(d) A is true but R is false.

1 **Assertion** (A) Molarity of a solution in liquid state changes with temperature.
Reason (R) The volume of a solution changes with change in temperature. **NCERT Pg 5**

2 **Assertion** (A) When scuba divers come towards surface, their capillaries get blocked which is painful and dangerous to life.
Reason (R) This occur due to release of dissolved gases, as the pressure decreases and leads to the formation of bubbles of nitrogen in the blood. **NCERT Pg 8**

3 **Assertion** (A) The water pouch of instant cold pack for treating athletic injuries breaks when squeezed and NH_4NO_3 dissolves in water to lower the temperature.
Reason (R) Addition of non-volatile solute into solvent results into depression of freezing point of the solvent. **NCERT Pg 9**

4 **Assertion** (A) When NaCl is added to water, a depression in freezing point is observed.
Reason (R) The lowering of vapour pressure of a solution causes depression in the freezing point. **NCERT Pg 18**

5 **Assertion** (A) When a solution is separated from the pure solvent by a semipermeable membrane, the solvent molecules pass through it from pure solvent side to the solution side.
Reason (R) Diffusion of solvent occurs from a region of high concentration solution to a region of low concentration solution. **NCERT Pg 21**

6 **Assertion** (A) When methyl alcohol is added to water, boiling point of water increases.

Reason (R) When a volatile solute is added to a volatile solvent, elevation in boiling point is observed. NCERT Pg 17

7 **Assertion** (A) If blood cells are placed in pure water, they swell and burst.

Reason (R) Due to osmosis, the movement of water molecules into the cell dilute the salt content. NCERT Pg 22

8 **Assertion** (A) High blood pressure patients are advised to take the minimum quantity of salt.

Reason (R) From salt Na^+ and Cl^- ion concentration increases in the body fluid which may rupture the blood cells. NCERT Pg 23, 24

9 **Assertion** (A) Experimentally determined molar mass of an ionic compound is lower than the true value.

Reason (R) Lower molar mass is due to dissociation of solute into ions. NCERT Pg 24

10 **Assertion** (A) The molecular mass of the polymers cannot be calculated using the boiling point or freezing point method.

Reason (R) The freezing point or boiling point method is used for determining the molecular mass of small molecules. NCERT Pg 21, 22

Statement Type Questions

Direction (Q. Nos. 1-6) *In the following questions, two statements (I & II) are given. In the light of the given statements, choose the correct option given below.*

(a) Both Statement I and Statement II are false.
(b) Statement I is true but Statement II is false.
(c) Statement I is false but Statement II is true.
(d) Both Statement I and Statement II are true.

1 **Statement I** Azeotropes are binary mixtures having the same composition in liquid and vapour phase and boil at a constant temperature.

Statement II Benzene and toluene form maximum boiling azeotropes. NCERT Pg 13, 14

2 **Statement I** Colligative properties depend on the number of solute particles and not on their nature.

Statement II The molality of a solution changes with temperature as mass remains unaffected with temperature. NCERT Pg 5, 15

3 **Statement I** Depression in the freezing point depends on the nature of the solvent.

Statement II Adding a non-volatile solute to a solvent decreases the freezing point. NCERT Pg 15, 18

4 **Statement I** Lowering of vapour pressure takes place in both ideal and non-ideal solution.

Statement II Cryoscopic constant depends on the nature of solvent. NCERT Pg 15, 18

5 **Statement I** Osmotic pressure is an extra pressure applied on solution, so that solvent cannot move through semipermeable membrane.

Statement II For isotonic solutions, osmotic pressure of solutions are equal. NCERT Pg 21, 22

6 **Statement I** KCl in water and ethanoic acid in benzene show abnormal molecular mass.

Statement II The value of i for aqueous KCl solution and ethanoic acid is close to 2. NCERT Pg 24

7 Select the incorrect statements from the following. NCERT Pg 3, 7, 12, 14, 15

A. Azeotropic mixture are binary mixture having same composition in solid and liquid phase.
B. 35% $\left(\frac{W}{V}\right)$ solution of ethylene glycol is used for cooling the car engines.
C. The solubility of HCl gas increases with increase in pressure.
D. Chloroform and diethyl ether shows negative deviation from Raoult's law.
E. Raoult's law becomes a special case of Henry law when K_H equals to p_i°.

Choose the correct answer from the options given below.

(a) B, C and E (b) A and B
(c) D and E (d) C and D

8 Which of the following statements are true? NCERT Pg 3, 14, 22

I. In a binary mixture, mole fraction of A is,
$$\chi_A = \frac{n_A}{n_A + n_B}$$
II. For solution containing (i) number of components,
$$\chi_i = \frac{n_i}{\Sigma n_i}$$
III. Sum of mole fractions of all the components of a solution is one.
IV. The concentration of different solution are always equal for isotonic solution.
V. Ethanol and acetone shows negative deviation from Raoult's law.

Select the correct option with true statements.
(a) I and IV (b) II and V
(c) III and I (d) I, II, III and IV

9 Which of the following statements are correct? NCERT Pg 15, 16, 18, 24

A. The value of K_b depends upon the nature of solvent.
B. The value of van't Hoff factor is more than unity in case of dissociation.
C. Addition of non-volatile solute in a solvent decreases the vapour pressure of the solvent.
D. Solvents with higher boiling points have higher vapour pressure at a given temperature.
E. For dilute solutions, Raoult's law may be written as $\frac{p^\circ - p_s}{p_s} = \frac{n}{N}$.

Choose the correct answer from the options given below.
(a) C and E (b) A, B, C and E
(c) B, C and D (d) D and E

10 Select the correct statements from the following. NCERT 19, 20, 24, 25

A. The depression in freezing point of 1 M urea and 1 M NaCl are in the ratio 1 : 2.
B. Cryoscopic constant (K_f) decreases with increase in enthalpy of fusion.
C. Semipermeable membrane appears to be continuous sheets or films.
D. Osmotic pressure method uses molarity instead to molality.
E. Witted flower revive when placed in fresh water due to osmosis.

Choose the correct answer from the options given below.
(a) A, B and E
(b) C and E
(c) C, D and E
(d) A, B, C, D and E

Matching Type Questions

1 Match the Column I with Column II. NCERT Pg 2

Column I (Solution example)	Column II (Type of solution)
A. Chloroform mixed with nitrogen gas	1. Gaseous solution
B. Ethanol dissolved in water	2. Solid solution
C. Amalgam of mercury with sodium	3. Liquid solution

Codes

	A	B	C		A	B	C
(a)	1	2	3	(b)	1	3	2
(c)	2	1	3	(d)	2	3	1

2 Match the Column I with Column II. NCERT Pg 2

Column I (Example of solution)	Column II (Type of solution)
A. Sucrose solution	1. Either solute or solvent is liquid
B. Soda water	2. Solid solution
C. Brass	3. Solution of gas in solid.
D. Hydrogen gas in palladium	4. A solution of gas in liquid.

Codes

	A	B	C	D		A	B	C	D
(a)	1	4	2	3	(b)	2	1	3	4
(c)	2	4	3	1	(d)	3	2	1	4

3 Match the terms given in Column I with expression given in Column II. NCERT Pg 22

Column I	Column II
A. Isotonic solution	1. Salt concentration is less than 0.9% (m/V), water will flow into cell and it will swell.
B. Hypertonic solution	2. Salt concentration is more than 0.9% (m/V) NaCl, water will flow out of cell and it will shrink.
C. Hypotonic solution	3. No osmosis occurs, if solution is separated by semipermeable membrane.
D Saturated solution	4. A solution which contains maximum amount of solute that can be dissolved in a given amount of solvent at a given temperature.

Codes

	A	B	C	D		A	B	C	D
(a)	4	3	2	1	(b)	3	2	1	4
(c)	1	2	3	4	(d)	2	1	3	4

4 Match the following terms given in Column I with the Column II (van't Hoff factor approx). NCERT Pg 24, 25

Column I	Column II
A. KCl in water	1. 0.5
B. Ethanoic acid in benzene	2. 2
C. K_2SO_4 in water	3. 3
D. $C_{12}H_{22}O_{11}$ in water	4. 1

Codes

	A	B	C	D		A	B	C	D
(a)	2	3	1	4	(b)	1	3	2	4
(c)	2	1	3	4	(d)	1	2	3	4

5 Match the Column I with Column II. NCERT Pg 24

Column I	Column II
A. $i > 1$	1. Dissociation
B. $i < 1$	2. Neither association nor dissociation
C. $i = 1$	3. Association
D. $i < 0$	4. Not possible

Codes

	A	B	C	D
(a)	3	2	1	4
(b)	2	4	3	1
(c)	1	3	2	4
(d)	3	1	2	4

Numerical Value Questions

1 A solute X dimerises in water. The boiling point of a 2 molal solution of X is 100.52°C. The percentage association of X is .... (Nearest integer)
[Use : K_b for water $= 0.52$ K kg mol^{-1}, Boiling point of water = 100°C]. NCERT Pg 17, 24

2 2.92 g of a biopolymer dissolved in a 100 mL water at 300 K exerted an osmotic pressure of 4.84×10^{-6} bar. The molar mass of the biopolymer is .... $\times 10^7$ g mol^{-1}
[Use : $R = 0.083$ L bar mol^{-1}K^{-1}] (Nearest integer) NCERT Pg 21

3 The mass of non-volatile, non-electrolyte solute (molar mass = 50 g mol^{-1}) needed to be dissolved in 114 g octane to reduce its vapour pressure to 75% is .... NCERT Pg 15, 16

4 150 g of acetic acid was contaminated with 10.2 g ascorbic acid ($C_6H_8O_6$) to lower down its freezing point by $(X \times 10^{-1})$°C. The value of X is .... (Nearest integer)
[Given, $K_f = 3.9$ K kg mol^{-1}, Molar mass of ascorbic acid = 176 g mol^{-1}]. NCERT Pg 18, 19

NCERT Exemplar's Questions

1 4 L of 0.02 M aqueous solution of NaCl was diluted by adding 1 L of water. The molality of the resultant solution is ....
(a) 0.004 (b) 0.008 (c) 0.012 (d) 0.016

2 Which of the following units is useful in relating concentration of solution with its vapour pressure?
(a) Mole fraction (b) Parts per million
(c) Mass percentage (d) Molality

3 Match the items given in Column I with the type of solutions given in Column II.

Column I	Column II
A. Soda water	1. A solution of gas in solid
B. Sugar solution	2. A solution of gas in gas
C. German silver	3. A solution of solid in liquid
D. Air	4. A solution of solid in solid
E. Hydrogen gas in palladium	5. A solution of gas in liquid

4 On the basis of information given below, mark the correct option.

Information On adding acetone to methanol some of the hydrogen bonds between methanol molecules break.

(a) At specific composition, methanol-acetone mixture will form minimum boiling azeotrope and will show positive deviation from Raoult's law.
(b) At specific composition, methanol-acetone mixture will form maximum boiling azeotrope and will show positive deviation from Raoult's law.
(c) At specific composition, methanol-acetone mixture will form minimum boiling azeotrope and will show negative deviation from Raoult's law.
(d) At specific composition, methanol-acetone mixture will form maximum boiling azeotrope and will show negative deviation from Raoult's law.

5 K_H value for Ar(*g*), CO_2 (*g*), HCHO (*g*) and CH_4(*g*) are 40.39, 1.67, 1.83×10^{-5} and 0.413 respectively.

Arrange these gases in the order of their increasing solubility.

(a) HCHO < CH_4 < CO_2 < Ar
(b) HCHO < CO_2 < CH_4 < Ar
(c) Ar < CO_2 < CH_4 < HCHO
(d) Ar < CH_4 < CO_2 < HCHO

6 Two beakers of capacity 500 mL were taken. One of these beakers, labelled as '*A*', was filled with 400 mL water, whereas the other beaker is labelled as "*B*" was filled with 400 mL of 2 M solution of NaCl. At the same temperature, both the beakers were placed in closed containers of same material and same capacity as shown in figure.

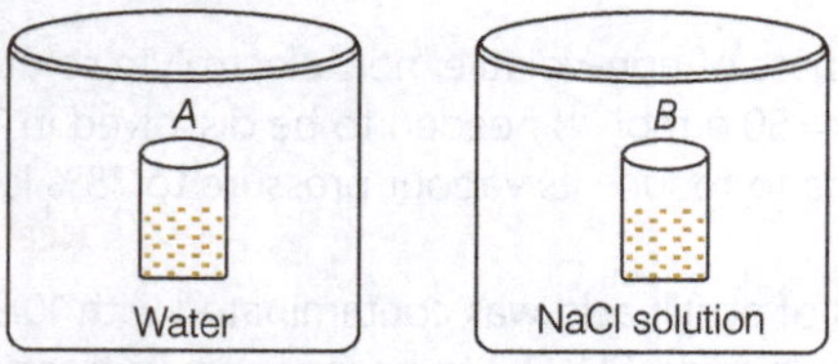

At a given temperature, which of the following statement is correct about the vapour pressure of pure water and that of NaCl solution?

(a) Vapour pressure in container *A* is more than that in container *B*.
(b) Vapour pressure in container *A* is less than that in container *B*.
(c) Vapour pressure is equal in both the containers.
(d) Vapour pressure in container *B* is twice the vapour pressure in container *A*.

7 Which of the following aqueous solutions should have the highest boiling point?

(a) 1.0 M NaOH
(b) 1.0 M Na_2SO_4
(c) 1.0 M NH_4NO_3
(d) 1.0 M KNO_3

8 In comparison to a 0.01 M solution of glucose, the depression in freezing point of a 0.01 M $MgCl_2$ solution is

(a) the same (b) about twice
(c) about three times (d) about six times

9 An unripe mango placed in a concentrated salt solution to prepare pickle shrivels because

(a) it gains water due to osmosis
(b) it loses water due to reverse osmosis
(c) it gains water due to reverse osmosis
(d) it loses water due to osmosis

10 Consider the figure and mark the correct option.

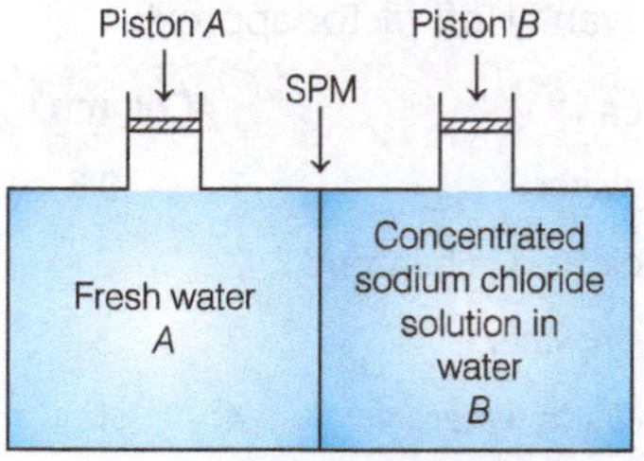

(a) Water will move from side *B* to side *A*, if a pressure lower than osmotic pressure is applied on piston *B*.
(b) Water will move from side *B* to side *A*, if a pressure greater than osmotic pressure is applied on piston *B*.
(c) Water will move from side *B* to side *A*, if a pressure equal to osmotic pressure is applied on piston *B*.
(d) Water will move from side *A* to side *B*, if pressure equal to osmotic pressure is applied on piston *A*.

11 At a given temperature, osmotic pressure of the concentrated solution of a substance

(a) is higher than that of the dilute solution
(b) is lower than that of the dilute solution
(c) is same as that of the dilute solution
(d) cannot be compared with osmotic pressure of dilute solutions

12 Which of the following statements is incorrect?

(a) Units of atmospheric pressure and osmotic pressure are the same.
(b) In reverse osmosis, solvent molecules move through a semipermeable membrane from a region of lower concentration of solute to higher concentration of solute.
(c) The value of molal depression constant depends on nature of solvent.
(d) Relative lowering of vapour pressure is a dimensionless quantity.

13 The value of van't Hoff factors for KCl, NaCl and K_2SO_4 respectively are

(a) 2, 2 and 2 (b) 2, 2 and 3 (c) 1, 1 and 2 (d) 1, 1 and 1

14 Which of the following statements is incorrect?

(a) Two different solutions of sucrose of same molality prepared in different solvents will have the same depression in freezing points.
(b) The osmotic pressure of a solution is given by the equation $\pi = CRT$ (where, *C* is the molarity of the solution).
(c) Decreasing order of osmotic pressure for 0.01 M aqueous solutions of barium chloride, potassium chloride, acetic acid and sucrose is $BaCl_2$ > KCl > CH_3COOH > sucrose.
(d) According to Raoult's law, the vapour pressure exerted by a volatile component of a solution is directly proportional to its mole fraction in the solution

15 We have three aqueous solutions of NaCl labelled as *A*, *B* and *C* with concentrations 0.1 M, 0.01 M and 0.001 M, respectively.

The value of van't Hoff factor for these solutions will be in the order:

(a) $i_A < i_B < i_C$
(b) $i_A > i_B > i_C$
(c) $i_A = i_B = i_C$
(d) $i_A < i_B > i_C$

16 On the basis of information given below mark the correct option.

I. In bromoethane and chloroethane mixture, intermolecular interactions of *A*—*A* and *B*—*B* type are nearly same as *A*—*B* type interactions.

II. In ethanol and acetone mixture, *A*—*A* or *B*—*B* type intermolecular interactions are stronger than *A*—*B* type interactions.

III. In chloroform and acetone mixture, *A*—*A* or *B*—*B* type intermolecular interactions are weaker than *A*—*B* type interactions.

(a) Solution II and III will follow Raoult's law.
(b) Solution I will follow Raoult's law.
(c) Solution II will show negative deviation from Raoult's law.
(d) Solution III will show positive deviation from Raoult's law.

17 Match the laws given in Column I with expressions given in Column II.

Column I	Column II
A. Raoult's law	1. $\Delta T_f = K_f m$
B. Henry's law	2. $\pi = CRT$
C. Elevation in boiling point	3. $p = \chi_1 p_1^\circ + \chi_2 p_2^\circ$
D. Depression in freezing point	4. $\Delta T_b = K_b m$
E. Osmotic pressure	5. $p = K_H \cdot \chi$

18. At equilibrium the rate of dissolution of a solid solute in a volatile liquid solvent is ....

(a) less than the rate of crystallisation
(b) greater than the rate of crystallisation
(c) equal to the rate of crystallisation
(d) zero

19. Maximum amount of a solid solute that can be dissolved in a specified amount of a given liquid solvent does not depend upon ....

(a) temperature (b) nature of solute
(c) pressure (d) nature of solvent

20. The unit of ebullioscopic constant is

(a) K kg mol^{-1} or K (molality)$^{-1}$
(b) mol kg K^{-1} or K^{-1}(molality)
(c) Kg mol^{-1}K^{-1} or K^{-1} (molality)$^{-1}$
(d) K mol kg^{-1} or K (molality)

Past Exams' Questions

NEET Archive

1. The Henry's law constant (K_H) values of three gases (*A, B, C*) in water are 145, 2×10^{-5} and 35 kbar, respectively. The solubility of these gases in water follow the order:

(a) *B* > *A* > *C* (b) *B* > *C* > *A* **NCERT Pg 7, NEET 2024**
(c) *A* > *C* > *B* (d) *A* > *B* > *C*

2. The plot of osmotic pressure (π) *vs* concentration (mol L^{-1}) for a solution gives a straight line with slope 25.73 L bar mol^{-1}. The temperature at which the osmotic pressure measurement is done is
(Use, $R = 0.083$ L bar mol^{-1}K^{-1}) **NCERT Pg 21, NEET 2024**

(a) 37°C (b) 310°C
(c) 25.73°C (d) 12.05°C

3. Given below are two statements, one is labelled as Assertion (A) and the other is labelled as Reason (R).

Assertion (A) Helium is used to dilute oxygen in diving apparatus. **NCERT Pg 9, NEET 2023**

Reason (R) Helium has high solubility in O_2.

In the light of the above statements, choose the most appropriate answer from the options given below.

(a) Both (A) and (R) are true but (R) is not the correct explanation of (A).
(b) (A) is true but (R) is false.
(c) (A) is not false but (R) is true.
(d) Both (A) and (R) are correct but (R) is not the correct explanation of (A).

4. In one molal solution that contains 0.5 mole of a solute, there is **NCERT Pg 5, NEET 2022**

(a) 500 g of solvent (b) 100 mL of solvent
(c) 1000 g of solvent (d) 500 mL of solvent

5. The correct option for the value of vapour pressure of a solution at 45°C with benzene to octane in molar ratio 3 : 2 is [At 45°C vapour pressure of benzene is 280 mm Hg and that of octane is 420 mm Hg. Assume ideal gas]. **NCERT Pg 11, NEET 2021**

(a) 160 mm of Hg (b) 168 mm of Hg
(c) 336 mm of Hg (d) 350 mm of Hg

6. Isotonic solutions have same **NCERT Pg 22, NEET 2020**
(a) vapour pressure (b) freezing temperature
(c) osmotic pressure (d) boiling temperature

7. The mixture which shows positive deviation from Raoult's law is **NCERT Pg 14, NEET 2020**
(a) benzene + toluene (b) acetone + chloroform
(c) chlorethane + bromoethane (d) ethanol + acetone

8. The freezing point depression constant (K_f) of benzene is 5.12 K kg mol^{-1}. The freezing point depression for the solution of molality 0.078 m containing a non-electrolyte solute in benzene is (rounded off upto two decimal places) **NCERT Pg 24, NEET 2020**
(a) 0.80 K (b) 0.40 K (c) 0.60 K (d) 0.20 K

9. For an ideal solution, the correct option is
(a) $\Delta_{mix}V \neq 0$ at constant T and p **NCERT Pg 13, NEET 2019**
(b) $\Delta_{mix}H = 0$ at constant T and p
(c) $\Delta_{mix}G = 0$ at constant T and p
(d) $\Delta_{mix}S = 0$ at constant T and p

10. The mixture that forms maximum boiling azeotrope is
(a) ethanol + water **NCERT Pg 14, NEET 2019**
(b) acetone + carbon disulphide
(c) heptane + octane
(d) water + nitric acid

11. Which of the following statements is correct regarding a solution of two compounds A and B exhibiting positive deviation from ideal behaviour?
NCERT Pg 13, NEET Odisha 2019
(a) Intermolecular attractive forces between A—A and B—B are stronger than those between A—B.
(b) $\Delta_{mix}H = 0$ at constant T and p.
(c) $\Delta_{mix}V = 0$ at constant T and p.
(d) Intermolecular attractive forces between A—A and B—B are equal to those between A—B.

12. In water saturated air, the mole fraction of water vapour is 0.02. If the total pressure of the saturated air is 1.2 atm, the partial pressure of dry air is
NCERT Pg 11, NEET Odisha 2019
(a) 1.18 atm (b) 1.76 atm (c) 1.176 atm (d) 0.98 atm

13. At 100°C the vapour pressure of a solution of 6.5 g of a solute in 100 g water is 732 mm. If $K_b = 0.52$, the boiling point of this solution will be **NCERT Pg 17, NEET 2016**
(a) 100°C (b) 102°C (c) 103°C (d) 101°C

14. Which of the following statements about the composition of the vapour over an ideal 1:1 molar mixture of benzene and toluene is correct? Assume that the temperature is constant at 25°C. (Given, vapour pressure data at 25°C, benzene = 12.8 kPa, toluene = 3.85 kPa) **NCERT Pg 9, 10, NEET 2016**
(a) The vapour will contain a higher percentage of toluene.
(b) The vapour will contain equal amounts of benzene and toluene.
(c) Not enough information is given to make a prediction.
(d) The vapour will contain a higher percentage of benzene.

15. Out of the following 0.10 m aqueous solutions, which one will exhibit the largest freezing point depression?
NCERT Pg 24, CBSE-AIPMT 2014
(a) KCl (b) $C_6H_{12}O_6$ (c) $Al_2(SO_4)_3$ (d) K_2SO_4

16. 6.02×10^{20} molecules of urea are present in 100 mL of its solution. The concentration of solution is
NCERT Pg 4, CBSE-AIPMT 2013
(a) 0.02 M (b) 0.01 M (c) 0.001 M (d) 0.1 M

JEE Main Archive

17. 2.5 g of a non-volatile, non-electrolyte is dissolved in 100g of water at 25°C. The solution showed a boiling point elevation by 2°C. Assuming the solute concentration is negligible with respect to the solvent concentration, the vapour pressure of the resulting aqueous solution is...... mm of Hg. (Nearest integer)
[Given: Molal boiling point elevation constant of water (K_b) = 0.52 K kg mol^{-1}, 1 atm pressure = 760 mm of Hg, molar mass of water = 18 g mol^{-1}] **NCERT Pg 17, JEE Main 2024**

18. A solution containing 10 g of an electrolyte AB_2 in 100 g of water boils at 100.52°C. The degree of ionisation of the electrolyte (α) is .... $\times 10^{-1}$. (Nearest integer)
[Given : Molar mass of AB_2 = 200 g mol^{-1}, K_b (Molal boiling point elevation const. of water) = 0.52 K kg mol^{-1}, boiling point of water = 100°C, AB_2 ionises as $AB_2 \longrightarrow A^{2+} + 2B^{-}$] **NCERT Pg 13, JEE Main 2024**

19. Identify the mixture that shows positive deviations from Raoult's law. **NCERT Pg 13, JEE Main 2024**
(a) $(CH_3)_2CO + CS_2$ (b) $CHCl_3 + C_6H_6$
(c) $(CH_3)_2CO + C_6H_5NH_2$ (d) $CHCl_3 + (CH_3)_2CO$

20. Match List-I with List-II.

List-I	List-II
A. van't Hoff factor, i	1. Cryoscopic constant
B. K_f	2. Isotonic solutions
C. Solutions with same osmotic pressure	3. $\frac{\text{Normal molar mass}}{\text{Abnormal molar mass}}$
D. Azeotropes	4. Solutions with same composition of vapour above it

NCERT Pg 14, 18, JEE Main 2023

Choose the correct answer from the options given below:
(a) A-3, B-1, C-4, D-2 (b) A-1, B-3, C-2, D-4
(c) A-3, B-1, C-2, D-4 (d) A-3, B-2, C-1, D-4

21. What weight of glucose must be dissolved in 100 g of water to lower the vapour pressure by 0.20 mm Hg ? (Assume, dilute solution is being formed.)
(Given : Vapour pressure of pure water is 54.2 mm Hg at room temperature. Molar mass of glucose is 180 g mol^{-1}.) **NCERT Pg 15, 16, JEE Main 2023**
(a) 3.69 g (b) 3.59 g (c) 2.59 g (d) 4.69 g

22. A solution is prepared by adding 2 g of "X" to 1 mole of water. Mass percent of "X" in the solution is **NCERT Pg 2, JEE Main 2023**
(a) 20% (b) 10% (c) 5% (d) 2%

23. Boiling point of a 2% aqueous solution of a non-volatile solute *A* is equal to the boiling point of 8% aqueous solution of a non-volatile solute *B*. The relation between molecular weights of *A* and *B* is **NCERT Pg 17, JEE Main 2022**
(a) $M_A = 4M_B$ (b) $M_B = 4M_A$ (c) $M_A = 8M_B$ (d) $M_B = 8M_A$

24. Given below are two statements, one is labelled as Assertion (A) and the other is labelled as Reason (R).
Assertion (A) At 10°C, the density of a 5M solution of KCl [atomic masses of K and Cl are 39 and 35.5 g mol^{-1} respectively], is 'x' g mL^{-1}. The solution is cooled to −21°C. The molality of the solution will remain unchanged.
Reason (R) The molality of the solution does not change with temperature as mass remain unaffected with temperature. **NCERT Pg 5, JEE Main 2022**
In the light of the above statements, choose the most appropriate answer from the options given below.
(a) Both (A) and (R) are correct and (R) is the correct explanation of (A).
(b) Both (A) and (R) are correct but (R) is not the correct explanation of (A).
(c) (A) is correct but (R) is not correct.
(d) (A) is not correct but (R) is correct.

25. The depression in freezing point observed for a formic acid solution of concentration 0.5 mL L^{-1} is 0.0405°C. Density of formic acid is 1.05 g mL^{-1}. The van't Hoff factor of the formic acid solution is nearly (Given, for water K_f = 1.86 K kg mol^{-1}) **NCERT Pg 24, JEE Main 2022**
(a) 0.8 (b) 1.1
(c) 1.9 (d) 2.4

Skill Boosters

1 The freezing point of an aqueous solution of a compound (*PQ*) is −0.45° C. At this temperature, *PQ* acts as a non-electrolyte. The same solution boils at 100.25°C at a pressure of 1 atm (for water, $\frac{K_f}{K_b} = \frac{7}{2}$)
The correct conclusion about the compound *PQ* at the boiling point of solution is,
(a) dimerises completely in solution
(b) degree of association is 50%
(c) acts as a non-electrolyte
(d) dissociates in solution

2 A motor vehicle radiator was filled with 16 L of water to which 2 L of methyl alcohol (density 0.8 g/mL) were added. The lowest temperature at which the vehicle can be parked out doors without a danger that water in the radiator will freeze ? (K_f of water = 1.86 K m^{-1})
(a) 5.81 (b) −5.81 (c) 0.17 (d) −0.17

3 A student experimented to measure the vapour pressure of liquids *A, B, C* and *D* to know the nature of liquid. He obtained a vapour pressure-temperature curve as shown below.

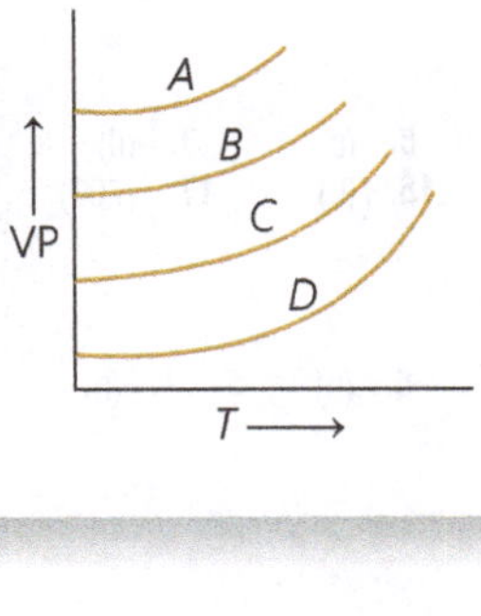

Liquids *A, B, C* and *D* respectively are
(a) diethyl ether, acetone, ethyl alcohol, water
(b) acetone, ethyl alcohol, diethyl ether, water
(c) water, ethyl alcohol, acetone, diethyl ether
(d) ethyl alcohol, acetone, diethyl ether, water

4 A complex is represented as $PtBr_4 \cdot 6H_2O$. 2 molal aqueous solution of the complex has value of ΔT_f of 7.45° C. Assuming 100% ionisation of the complex and K_f for H_2O = 1.86° C mol^{-1} kg. The correct formula of the complex is
(a) $[Pt(H_2O)_6]Br_4$ (b) $[Pt(H_2O)_3Br_3]Br \cdot 3H_2O$
(c) $[Pt(H_2O)_4Br_2] \cdot Br_2 \cdot 2H_2O$ (d) $[Pt(H_2O)_2Br_4] \cdot 4H_2O$

5 A solution is prepared by mixing 50 mL each of ethanol (d = 0.998 g/mL) and methanol (d = 0.791 g/mL). If M_1 is molarity of solution described as EtOH solute in MeOH solvent and M_2 is molarity of solution described as MeOH solute in EtOH solvent. The correct interpretation is
(a) $M_2 < M_1$ (b) $M_2 + M_1 < 50$
(c) $M_1 = M_2$ (d) $M_1 \times M_2 < 120$

6 A certain mass of a substance when dissolved in 100 g of benzene lowers the freezing point by 1.05°C. The same mass of solute dissolved in 100 g water lowers the freezing point by 1.14°C If the substance has normal molecular weight in benzene and is completely

dissociated in water? The number of ions in which the solute is completely dissociate is
[Given : K_f (C_6H_6, l) = 5.12 Km^{-1}, K_f (H_2O, l) = 1.86 Km^{-1}]
(a) 1 (b) 3
(c) 2 (d) 4

7 Prerana took three beakers *A*, *B* and *C* containing different types of solution and then she put raisin into each beaker. The following changes were observed.

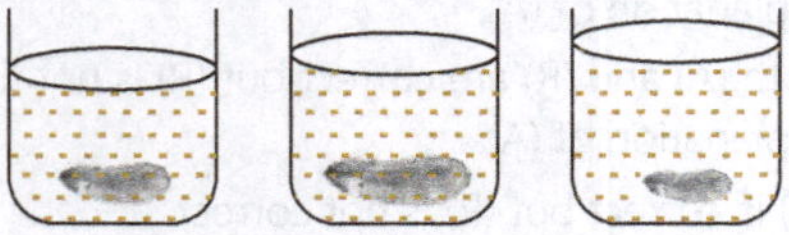

A *B* *C*

If beaker *A* contains water, *B* and *C* contains

	B	*C*
(a)	hypotonic solution	hypertonic solution
(b)	hypertonic solution	hypotonic solution
(c)	isotonic solution	isotonic solution
(d)	hypotonic solution	isotonic solution

8 Two 5 molal solutions are prepared by dissolving a non-electrolyte, non-volatile solute separately in the solvents *A* and *B*. The molecular weight of the solvents are M_A and M_B, respectively where $M_A = \frac{5}{4} M_B$. The relative lowering of vapour pressure of the solution in *A* is '*x*' times that of the solution in *B*. Given number of moles of solute is very small. The value of '*x*' is
(a) $\frac{3}{4}$ (b) $\frac{1}{4}$ (c) $\frac{5}{4}$ (d) $\frac{3}{4}$

Correct Codes

Topical Questions

1. (d) 2. (d) 3. (b) 4. (a) 5. (d) 6. (a) 7. (d) 8. (b) 9. (b) 10. (a)
11. (c) 12. (c) 13. (d) 14. (c) 15. (b) 16. (a) 17. (c) 18. (d) 19. (a) 20. (d)
21. (c) 22. (c) 23. (a) 24. (d) 25. (b) 26. (b) 27. (b) 28. (a) 29. (c) 30. (d)
31. (d) 32. (d) 33. (b) 34. (a) 35. (d) 36. (d) 37. (d) 38. (c) 39. (b) 40. (d)
41. (a) 42. (b) 43. (a) 44. (b) 45. (a) 46. (c) 47. (c) 48. (d) 49. (c) 50. (a)
51. (c) 52. (c) 53. (a) 54. (a) 55. (c) 56. (c) 57. (a) 58. (a) 59. (a) 60. (c)
61. (a) 62. (c) 63. (a) 64. (c) 65. (b) 66. (a) 67. (c) 68. (a) 69. (b) 70. (a)
71. (b) 72. (d) 73. (c) 74. (a) 75. (a) 76. (a) 77. (a) 78. (a) 79. (b) 80. (c)
81. (a) 82. (a) 83. (c) 84. (a) 85. (b) 86. (c) 87. (a) 88. (c) 89. (a) 90. (c)
91. (a) 92. (c) 93. (a) 94. (a) 95. (b) 96. (a) 97. (a) 98. (c) 99. (d) 100. (d)
101. (b) 102. (b)

Assertion-Reason

1. (a) 2. (a) 3. (a) 4. (a) 5. (b) 6. (d) 7. (a) 8. (a) 9. (a) 10. (a)

Statement Type

1. (b) 2. (b) 3. (c) 4. (d) 5. (d) 6. (b) 7. (b) 8. (d) 9. (b) 10. (d)

Matching Type

1. (b) 2. (a) 3. (b) 4. (c) 5. (c)

Numerical Value

1. (100) 2. (15) 3. (150) 4. (15)

NCERT Exemplar's

1. (d) 2. (a) 3. A-5, B-3, C-4, D-2, E-1 4. (a) 5. (c) 6. (a) 7. (b) 8. (c) 9. (d)
10. (b) 11. (a) 12. (b) 13. (b) 14. (a) 15. (c) 16. (b) 17. A-3, B-5, C-4, D-1, E-2 18. (c)
19. (c) 20. (a)

Past Exams'

1. (b) 2. (a) 3. (b) 4. (a) 5. (c) 6. (c) 7. (d) 8. (b) 9. (b) 10. (d)
11. (a) 12. (c) 13. (d) 14. (d) 15. (c) 16. (b) 17. (707) 18. (5) 19. (a) 20. (c)
21. (a) 22. (b) 23. (b) 24. (a) 25. (c)

Skill Boosters

1. (d) 2. (b) 3. (a) 4. (b) 5. (b) 6. (b) 7. (a) 8. (c)

Step by Step

Decoding the Questions

Concept Builders

1 Amalgam of mercury with sodium.

2 15.28, 84.72

[**Hint** mass % of component

$$= \frac{\text{Mass of the component in the solution} \times 100}{\text{Total mass of the solution}}]$$

3 True

4 0.068

$$\left[\textbf{Hint } \chi_{\text{glycol}} = \frac{\text{Moles of } C_2H_6O_2}{\text{Moles of } C_2H_6O_2 + \text{Moles of } H_2O}\right]$$

Molar mass of $C_2H_6O_2 = 62 \text{ g mol}^{-1}$

5 True

6 1 molal

7 saturated

8 decreases

9 282 bar

10 Gas *B*

11 low

12 bends, helium

13 Raoult's law

14 maximum boiling

15 Negative deviation

16 Positive deviation

17 K kg mol^{-1}

18 Molal elevation constant or ebullioscopic constant.

19 decreases

20 False

21 False

22 $M_B = \dfrac{K_f \times w_B \times 1000}{\Delta T_f \times W_A}$

23 False

24 hypotonic

25 True

26 Reverse osmosis

27 True

28 True

29 2 and 3

30 hydrogen, decrease

Topical Solutions

1 (*d*) Statement (*d*) is incorrect. It's correct form is as follows

A homogeneous mixture may have two or more than two components, so it may contain more than one solute.

2 (*d*)

3 (*b*) Solute in 300 g of 30% solution

$= 90$ g

Solute in 200 g of 20% solution

$= 40$ g

Mass of solute $= 130$ g

Mass of solution $= 300 + 200 = 500$ g

% of solute in the final solution

$$= \frac{130}{500} \times 100 = 26\%$$

4 (*a*) Volume % of ethanol

$$= \frac{\text{Volume of ethanol}}{\text{Total volume of solution}} \times 100$$

$$\text{or } 10 = \frac{10}{\text{Total volume of solution}} \times 100$$

$\Rightarrow$ Total volume of solution $= 100$ mL

Thus, the amount of water used

= Total volume of solution − amount of ethanol $= 100 - 10 = 90$ mL

5 (*d*) Number of moles of C_2H_5OH

$$= \frac{184}{46} = 4 \quad (M_{C_2H_5OH} = 46 \text{ g/mol})$$

$$\text{Number of moles of } H_2O = \frac{72}{18} = 4;$$

$$(M_{H_2O} = 18 \text{ g/mol})$$

$$\text{Mole fraction, } \chi_{C_2H_5OH} = \frac{4}{4+4} = \frac{4}{8}$$

$$\chi_{H_2O} = \frac{4}{4+4} = \frac{4}{8}$$

$$\Rightarrow \frac{\chi_{C_2H_5OH}}{\chi_{H_2O}} = \frac{4/8}{4/8} = \frac{1}{1} = 1:1$$

6 (*a*) 1000 mL of solution contains

$= 3 \times 10^{-4}$ mole of Cu^{2+} ions

($\because$ 1 M means 1 mole of solute dissolved in 1000 mL of solution)

$$10^6 \text{ mL of solution} = \frac{3 \times 10^{-4}}{1000} \times 10^6$$

$= 0.3$ ppm

7 (*d*) K_2SO_4 is 17.4 ppm, i.e. 10^6 mL has 17.4 g K_2SO_4.

$$1 \text{ L } (10^3 \text{ mL}) \text{ has } K_2SO_4 = \frac{17.4 \times 10^3}{10^6}$$

$$= 0.0174 \text{g/L} = \frac{0.0174}{174} \text{ mol/L}$$

$\therefore \quad [K_2SO_4] = 1 \times 10^{-4}$ M

$$K_2SO_4 \rightleftharpoons 2K^+ + SO_4^{2-}$$

$\therefore \quad [K^+] = 2 \times 10^{-4}$ M

8 (*b*) $\text{Molarity} = \dfrac{22.2 \text{ g}}{111 \text{ g mol}^{-1} \times 1 \text{ L}}$

[$\because$ Molecular weight of $CaCl_2$ $= 111 \text{ g mol}^{-1}$]

$\Rightarrow \quad 0.2 \text{ mol L}^{-1} = 0.2$ M

9 (*b*) $V = \dfrac{\text{Mass}}{\text{Density}} = \dfrac{100}{1.84}$

$$\text{Molarity} = \frac{98 \times 1000 \times 1.84}{98 \times 100}$$

$= 18.4$ M

10 (*a*) Given, $M_1 = 0.5\text{M}, M_2 = 2\text{M}$

$V_1 = 750 \text{ mL}, V_2 = 250 \text{ mL}$

$$\because \quad M_f = \frac{M_1V_1 + M_2V_2}{V_1 + V_2}$$

$$\therefore \quad M_f = \frac{750 \times 0.5 + 250 \times 2}{750 + 250}$$

$$= \frac{875}{1000} = 0.875 \text{ M}$$

11 (*c*) Mass of HCl in 1.0 mL stock solution $= 1.25 \times \dfrac{29.2}{100} = 0.365$ g

Also, Molarity

$$= \frac{\text{Mass of solute (in g)}}{\text{Molecular weight of solute} \times V \text{ (in L)}}$$

Mass of HCl required for 200 mL solution of 0.4 M HCl

$$= \frac{200}{1000} \times 0.4 \times 36.5$$

$= 0.08 \times 36.5$ g

$\because$ 0.365 g of HCl is present in 1.0 mL stock solution.

$\therefore$ 0.08×36.5 g HCl will be present in $\dfrac{0.08 \times 36.5}{0.365} = 8.0$ mL

12 (c) ∴ Molarity of Na_2CO_3 solution

$$=\frac{25.3\times1000}{106\times250}=0.955\text{ M}$$

$$Na_2CO_3 \longrightarrow 2Na^+ + CO_3^{2-}$$

	Na_2CO_3	$2Na^+$	CO_3^{2-}
Initial conc.	0.955	0	0
After dissociation		2×0.955	0.955

∴ $[Na^+]=2\times0.955\text{ M}=1.910\text{ M}$

$[CO_3^{2-}]=0.955\text{ M}$

13 (d) Strength is mass of solute dissolved in 1 litre solution. It has volume term which changes with temperature.

14 (c) ∴Molality

$$=\frac{\text{Number of moles of solute}}{\text{Mass of solvent (in kg)}}$$

∴Number of moles of methyl alcohol $=5.2\text{ m}\times1\text{ kg}$ [∵ 1kg = 1000 g]

$n_1(CH_3OH)=5.2,$

$$n_2(H_2O)=\frac{1000}{18}=55.56$$

∴ $n_1+n_2=5.20+55.56$

$=60.76$ mol

$$\therefore \chi_{CH_3OH}=\frac{n_1}{n_1+n_2}$$

$$=\frac{5.2}{60.76}=0.086$$

15 (b) 20% aqueous solution of KI means 20 g of KI is present in 80 g solvent.

$$m=\frac{20}{166}\times\frac{1000}{80}=1.506\approx1.51\text{ mol/kg}$$

16 (a) Molecular mass of H_2SO_4=98 g/moL

As density is 1g/mL, we can assume that the volume of solution is equals to the mass of solution in grams.

1 molar solution means,

1 mole H_2SO_4 in 1000 mL solution

1 mole H_2SO_4 in 1000 grams solution

Mass of water = 1000 − 98 = 902

Therefore, the molality of sulphuric acid in bottle *A*.

$$=\frac{1\times1000}{902}=1.108\text{ molal}$$

And the concentration (molality) of sulphuric acid in bottle *B* = 1 molal. Hence, concentration of *A* is more than *B*.

17 (c) We know that,

∴ Mass of solution $=d\times V$

$1.28\text{ g cm}^{-3}\times1000\text{ mL}=1280\text{ g}$

$$\text{Molarity}=\frac{\text{Number of moles of solute}}{\text{Volume of solution (in L)}}$$

$$\therefore\ 2=\frac{\text{Mass of solute}}{40}=80\text{ g}$$

∴Mass of solvent = 1280 − 80

= 1200g = 1.2 kg

$$\text{Now, }=\frac{\text{Number of moles of solute}}{\text{Mass of solvent (in kg)}}$$

$$=\frac{2}{1.2}=\frac{5}{3}=1.67\text{ m}$$

18 (d) 1 molal aqueous solution means that 1 mole of a solute is dissolved in 1000 g of solvent.

In case of water (density = 1 g /mL)

$$\text{Moles of solvent}=\frac{1000}{18}=55.5$$

Mole fraction of solute

$$=\frac{1}{1+55.5}=0.018$$

19 (a) The sample of H_2SO_4 is 80% by volume.

Therefore, weight of H_2SO_4 = 800 g in 1000 mL.

$$\text{Moles of }H_2SO_4=\frac{800}{98}=8.16$$

Weight of solution = 1000 × 1.80

= 1800 g

Weight of solvent = 1800 − 800

= 1000 g

$$\text{Molality}=\frac{8.16\times1000}{1000}=8.16\text{ M}$$

20 (d) Pressure does not have any significant effect on solubility of solids in liquids.

21 (c)

22 (c) Higher the value of Henry's law constant, lower is the solubility of gas in water (or in liquid solvent).

The order of K_H value is:

He > H_2 > O_2

144.97 kbar 69.16 kbar 34.86 kbar

Thus, the order of solubility is

$$He<H_2<O_2$$

23 (a)

$$p_{O_2}=\frac{1}{5}\times1=0.2\text{ bar}$$

$$p_{N_2}=\frac{4}{5}\times1=0.8\text{ bar}$$

∵ $p=K_H\,\chi$ (from Henry's law)

$$\therefore\ \frac{\chi_{O_2}}{\chi_{N_2}}=\frac{p_{O_2}}{K_H(O_2)}\times\frac{K_H(N_2)}{p_{N_2}}$$

$$=\frac{0.2\times6.60\times10^7}{0.8\times3.30\times10^7}=\frac{1}{2}$$

$$\chi_{O_2}:\chi_{N_2}=1:2$$

24 (d) According to Henry's law,

$$\chi_{Ar}=\frac{p}{K_H}=\frac{10}{40\times10^3}=2.5\times10^{-4}$$

Also, we know that

$$\chi_{Ar}=\frac{n_{Ar}}{n_{Ar}+n_{H_2O}}\left[n=\frac{1000}{18}=55.5\right]$$

$$2.5\times10^{-4}=\frac{n_{Ar}}{n_{Ar}+n_{H_2O}}\quad(n_g<<<55.5)$$

$$2.5\times10^{-4}=\frac{n_{Ar}}{55.5}\quad n_{Ar}=0.0139\text{ mol}$$

$$m=\frac{1.39\times10^{-2}}{1\text{kg}}$$

$=0.0139$

≈0.014 m

25 (b) The correct statement is (b)

26 (b) $\chi_{H_2}=\dfrac{p}{K_H}$

$$=\frac{760}{5.34\times10^7}=142.3\times10^{-7}$$

If n_{H_2} moles of H_2, then moles of water

$$=\frac{1000}{18}=55.5$$

$$\chi_{H_2}=\frac{n_{H_2}}{n_{H_2}+55.5}\quad(n_{H_2}<<55.5)$$

$$142.3\times10^{-7}=\frac{n_{H_2}}{55.5}$$

$$n_{H_2}=7.89\times10^{-4}\text{ mol L}^{-1}$$

27 (b) According to Henry's law,

$$\frac{p_1}{p_2}=\frac{S_1}{S_2}$$

[p_1 and p_2 are partial pressures and S_1 and S_2 are solubilities]

$$\Rightarrow\ \frac{500}{750}=\frac{0.01}{S_2}$$

$$\Rightarrow\ S_2=0.015\text{g L}^{-1}$$

28 (*a*) From Henry's law,

$$p = K_H \times \chi$$

$$\chi = \frac{(760 \text{ mm of Hg})}{4.27 \times 10^5 \text{ mm of Hg}} = 178 \times 10^{-5} = 1.78 \times 10^{-3}$$

29 (*c*) $p = \chi\, p_{\text{total}}$;

$$p_{O_2} = 10 \times \frac{20}{100} = 2 \text{ atm} = 2 \times 760 \text{ mm Hg}$$

$$p_{N_2} = 10 \times \frac{79}{100} = 7.9 \text{ atm} = 7.9 \times 760 \text{ mm Hg}$$

$$\chi_{O_2} = \frac{p_{O_2}}{K_H} = \frac{2 \times 760 \text{ mm Hg}}{3.3 \times 10^7 \text{ mm Hg}} = 4.6 \times 10^{-5}$$

$$\chi_{N_2} = \frac{p_{N_2}}{K_H} = \frac{7.9 \times 760 \text{ mm Hg}}{6.51 \times 10^7 \text{ mm Hg}} = 9.22 \times 10^{-5}$$

30 (*d*) As the solubility increases, value of Henry law constant decreases. Since CO_2, HCHO are most soluble in water among the given set of gases.
Therefore, they have the lowest value of Henry law constant.

31 (*d*) Statement (d) is incorrect.
It's correct form is as follows
Due to high pressure, solubility of atmospheric gases in the blood increases which is responsible for the formation of bends in the body of scuba divers.

32 (*d*) At high altitudes, the partial pressure of oxygen is less than that at the ground level. This leads to low concentration of oxygen in the blood and tissues of climbers which results in a medical condition known as anoxia.

33 (*b*) **34** (*a*)

35 (*d*) Total pressure,

$$p_T = p'_A + p'_B \quad \text{...(i)}$$

$$p_T = p_A\chi_A + p_B\chi_B \quad \text{..(ii)}$$

$$[\chi_B = 1 - \chi_A]$$

From Eq. (ii), we get

$$p_T = p_B + \chi_A(p_A - p_B)$$

36 (*d*) In equimolar liquid mixture,

$$\chi_A = 0.5, \quad \chi_B = 0.5$$

$$\because \quad p_T = p_A^\circ \chi_A + p_B^\circ \chi_B$$

So, $\quad p_T = 0.5 \times 150 + 0.5 \times 100 = 125$

Now, let Y_B be the mole fraction of vapour *B* then

$$Y_B = \frac{\chi_B p_B^\circ}{p_T} = \frac{0.5 \times 100}{125} = 0.4$$

37 (*d*) Number of moles of $CHCl_3$,

$$n_A = \frac{w}{M} = \frac{25.5}{119.5} = 0.213 \text{ mol}$$

Number of moles of CH_2Cl_2,

$$n_B = \frac{40}{85} = 0.47 \text{ mol}$$

Mole fraction of $CHCl_3$,

$$\chi_A = \frac{n_A}{n_A + n_B} = \frac{0.213}{0.683} = 0.31$$

Mole fraction of CH_2Cl_2

$$\chi_B = 1 - \chi_A = 0.69$$

$$p_{\text{total}} = p_A\chi_A + p_B\chi_B = 200 \times 0.31 + 41.5 \times 0.69 = 90.63 \text{ mm Hg}$$

38 (*c*) Number of moles (n_1) of

$$CHCl_3 = \frac{11.9}{119} = 0.1 \text{ mol}$$

Number of moles (n_2) of

$$CH_2Cl_2 = \frac{17}{85} = 0.2 \text{ mol}$$

$$\chi_1 = \frac{n_1}{n_T} = \frac{0.1}{0.3} = 0.33$$

$$\chi_2 = \frac{n_2}{n_T} = \frac{0.2}{0.3} = 0.66$$

$$\therefore \quad p_{\text{total}} = p^\circ\chi_1 + p^\circ\chi_2$$

$$p_{\text{Total}} = 200 \times 0.33 + 41.5 \times 0.66 = 93.39 \text{ atm}$$

39 (*b*) We know that,

$$p_{\text{total}} = x_A p_A^\circ + x_B p_B^\circ \quad \text{...(i)}$$

On substituting the given values in Eq. (i), we get

$$p_{\text{total}} = 0.4 \times 7 \times 10^3 + 0.6 \times 12 \times 10^3 = 10 \times 10^3 \text{ Pa} = 1 \times 10^4 \text{ Pa}$$

In vapour phase,

$$y_A = \frac{x_A p_A^\circ}{p_{\text{total}}} = \frac{0.4 \times 7 \times 10^3}{1 \times 10^4} = 0.28$$

$$\therefore y_B = 1 - 0.28 = 0.72 \quad [\because y_A + y_B = 1]$$

40 (*d*) Vapour pressure of a solution containing non-volatile solute is less than that of the pure solvent.
If the concentration of solute is higher, the number of solvent molecules escaping from the surface correspondingly reduced, thus the vapour pressure also reduced.
Hence, vapour pressure of $P > R > Q$.

41 (*a*) Beaker *X* will have the highest vapour pressure. This is because, the decrease in vapour pressure depends upon the quantity of a non-volatile solute present in it.

42 (*b*) From Raoult's law, for ideal solution

$$p_{\text{total}} = p^\circ{}_B\, \chi_B + p^\circ{}_T\, \chi_T$$

$$[B = \text{benzene}, T = \text{toluene}]$$

$$= 119 \times 0.5 + 37 \times 0.5 = 78 \text{ torr}$$

$\therefore$ Mole fraction of toluene in vapour phase $(y_T)_V = \dfrac{p^\circ{}_T\, \chi_T}{p_{\text{total}}} = \dfrac{18.5}{78} = 0.237$

43 (*a*) Vapour pressure of pure solvent is higher than the vapour pressure of solution, because solute particles occupy some surface sites and, hence less surface is available for evaporation.

44 (*b*) **45** (*a*)

46 (*c*) The solution which shows large positive deviation from Raoult's law forms minimum boiling azeotrope at a specific composition, e.g. ethanol-acetone, ethanol-water etc.

47 (*c*) Among the given solutions, mixture of CH_3CH_2OH and CH_3COCH_3 is non-ideal and shows positive deviation.

Hence, it has lesser boiling point or higher vapour pressure, than its constituent molecules.

48 (*d*) Azeotropic mixture is constant boiling mixture. it is not possible to separate the component of azeotropic mixture by distillation.

49 (*c*)

50 (*a*) The given diagram represents the solution showing negative deviation from Raoult's law. It is due to the strong intermolecular forces of the resultant solution which leads to decrease in vapour pressure, e.g. mixture of phenol and aniline.

51 (c) Statement (c) is incorrect.

It's correct form is as follows

In the mixture of phenol and aniline, the intermolecular hydrogen bonding between phenolic proton and lone pair on nitrogen atom of aniline is stronger than the respective intramolecular hydrogen bonding between similar molecules.

52 (c) Solution which shows negative deviation from Raoult's law is called maximum boiling azeotrope. Hence, acetone and chloroform forms maximum boiling azeotrope.

53 (*a*) When any one of the components of binary mixture either solvent or solute is non-volatile, it causes deviation in vapour pressure of solution which causes change in its colligative properties.

Hence, colligative properties is observed when a non-volatile solid is dissolved in a volatile liquid.

Thus, statement (a) is correct.

54 (*a*) Relative lowering of vapour pressure is a colligative property because

(i) it does not depend upon nature of solute.

(ii) it depends upon number of solute particles.

(iii) it depends upon concentration of non-electrolyte solution.

55 (*c*) χ_B = mole fraction of solute (urea)

$$= \frac{n_B}{n_A + n_B} = \frac{\frac{0.60}{60}}{\frac{360}{18} + \frac{0.60}{60}} \simeq 0.0005$$

Now, lowering of vapour pressure is

$$\Delta p = \chi_B \times p^\circ$$

$$\Delta p = 0.0005 \times 35$$

$$= 0.0175 \text{ mm Hg}$$

56 (*c*) 1 M aqueous solution contains 1 mole of solute in 1000 mL of water.

$$\chi_B = \frac{1}{1 + 55.5} = \frac{1}{56.5}$$

$\because$ $p^\circ = 760$ torr at 100°C

$$\frac{\Delta p}{p^\circ} = \chi_B, \Delta p = p^\circ \chi_B$$

$$= \frac{760 \times 1}{56.5} = 13.45 \text{ torr}$$

57 (*a*) Relative lowering of vapour pressure,

$$\frac{\Delta p}{p^\circ} = 0.2. \ \frac{\Delta p}{p^\circ} = \chi_{\text{solute}}$$

$$\chi_{\text{solute}} = 0.2$$

$$\frac{n_{\text{solute}} \text{ (number of moles of solute)}}{n_{\text{total}} \text{ (total number of moles)}} = 0.2$$

$$\frac{n_{\text{solute}}}{5} = 0.2$$

$$n_{\text{solute}} = 1 \text{ mol}$$

$$n_{\text{solvent}} = 5 - 1 = 4$$

$$\text{Mole fraction of solvent} = \frac{n_{\text{solvent}}}{n_{\text{total}}} = \frac{4}{5} = 0.8$$

58 (*a*) Since, boiling point of a solution is always higher than that of pure solvent and from figure $B > A$. So, B is the boiling point of solution and A is of pure solvent.

59 (*a*) From elevation in boiling point,

$$\Delta T_b = K_b \times m$$

$$m = \frac{2}{0.76} = \frac{2.5 \times 1000}{M_2 \times 100} \quad \text{...(i)}$$

M_2 = molar mass of the solute

When the concentration of solute is much lower than the concentration of solvent,

$$\frac{p^\circ - p}{p^\circ} = \frac{\text{No. of moles of solute}}{\text{No. of moles of solvent}}$$

$$\frac{760 - p}{760} = \frac{2.5/M_2}{100/18} \quad \text{...(ii)}$$

From Eqs (i) and (ii), $p = 724$ mm.

60 (*c*)

61 (*a*) 4% solution means 4g of A is present in 100 g of solution.

10% means 10 g of B is present in 100 g of solution.

$$\Delta T_f = K_f m$$

$$(\Delta T_f)_1 = (\Delta T_f)_2 \quad \text{(Given)}$$

$$\frac{K_f \times \frac{4}{60}}{\frac{96}{1000}} = \frac{K_f \times \frac{10}{M_2}}{\frac{90}{1000}}$$

$$M_2 = \frac{10 \times 60 \times 96}{4 \times 90} = 160$$

62 (*c*) Molar mass of $X = M_x$

$$= \frac{K_f \times w_x \times 1000}{\Delta T_f \times w_1}$$

$$= \frac{5 \times 3.26 \times 1000}{0.125 \times 200}$$

$$= 652 \text{ g mol}^{-1}$$

For $X_n = 652$

$$n = \frac{652}{80} = 8.15 = 8$$

So, the formula of $X_n = X_8$.

63 (*a*) As we know that,

$$\Delta T_f = \frac{1000 \times K_f \times w_2}{M_2 \times w_1}$$

$$w_2 = \frac{6 \times 62 \times 4000}{1000 \times 1.86} = 800 \text{ g}$$

64 (*c*) Normal freezing point of water = 273.15K. In order to prevent freezing at 268 K, let the amount of methanol added be x g.

$$\therefore \text{Molality, } m = \frac{x}{32 \times 10} = \frac{x}{320}$$

[$\because$ Molar mass of CH_3OH = 32g mol^{-1}]

Now, $\Delta T_f = K_f \cdot m$

$$(273.15 - 268) = 1.86 \times \frac{x}{320}$$

$$x = \frac{5.15 \times 320}{1.86} = 886.02 \text{ g}$$

65 (*b*) $\Delta T_f = 0 - (-2.8) = 2.8$°C or 2.8 K

$$\because \quad \Delta T_f = \frac{1000 \times K_f \times w_2}{M_2 \times w_1}$$

$$\Rightarrow \quad 2.8 = \frac{1000 \times 1.86 \times w_2}{62 \times 1000}$$

$$\therefore \quad w_2 = 93.33 \text{ g} \approx 93 \text{ g}$$

66 (*a*) Depression in freezing point,

$\Delta T_f = 0 - (-0.30) = 0.30$ K

Now we know that, $\Delta T_f = K_f m$

$\therefore \quad m = \frac{\Delta T_f}{K_f} = \frac{0.30}{1.86} = 0.161 \text{ mol kg}^{-1}$

According to Raoult's law

For dilute solution,

$$\frac{p^\circ - p}{p^\circ} = \frac{\text{No. of moles of solute}}{\text{No. of moles of solvent}}$$

$$\frac{23.51 - p}{23.51} = \frac{0.161}{1000/18} = \frac{0.161 \times 18}{1000}$$

$$\Rightarrow \frac{23.51 - p}{23.51} = 0.002898$$

$p = 23.44$ mm Hg.

67 (*c*) $\Delta T_f = K_f \times m$

$$T_f^\circ - T_f = K_f \times \frac{w_2 \times 1000}{M_2 \times W_1 (\text{in g})} \quad ...(i)$$

Here, $T_f^\circ = 0^\circ$ C, $T_f = -10^\circ$ C

$$0 - (-10) = 1.86 \times \frac{62 \times 1000}{62 \times w_1}$$

$$\Rightarrow \quad w_1 = \frac{1.86 \times 62 \times 1000}{10 \times 62} = 186 \text{ g}$$

So, amount of water separated as ice (solid solvent)

$= 250 - w_1 = (250 - 186)$ g $= 64$ g

68 (*a*) Statement (a) is incorrect.

It's correct form is as follows

Solute molecules can never pass through the semipermeable membrane, only solvent molecules can do that. They move from the lower concentration or from pure solvent to solution of higher concentration.

69 (*b*) The concentration of $BaCl_2$ solution is lower, thus solvent (water) moves from the $BaCl_2$ solution to $CaCl_2$ solution, when 0.1 M $CaCl_2$ and 0.005 M $BaCl_2$ solutions are separated by a semipermeable membrane.

70 (*a*) 4% solution of sucrose (*w/V*) means 4g of sucrose is dissolved in 100 mL of solution. Similarly, 2% (*w/V*) solution of '*X*' means 2g of *X* present in 100 mL of solution.

Since, π_1 (for sucrose solution) $= \pi_2$ (for *X* solution)

$$\therefore \quad \frac{n_1}{V_1} RT = \frac{n_2}{V_2} RT \quad (V_1 = V_2)$$

$$\frac{4}{342} = \frac{2}{\text{Molecular weight of } X}$$

$$\left[\because n = \frac{\text{Mass of solute}}{\text{Molecular weight of solute}}\right]$$

$$\text{Molecular weight} = \frac{2}{4} \times 342 = 171$$

71 (*b*)

72 (*d*) When a solution of urea (6%) is isotonic with a solution of glucose, then

$\pi_{\text{glucose}} = \pi_{\text{urea}}, C_{\text{glucose}} = C_{\text{urea}}$

$$\therefore \quad \left(\frac{w_g \times 1000}{M_g \times 100}\right) = \left(\frac{w_u \times 1000}{M_u \times 100}\right)$$

$$\therefore \frac{x \times 1000}{180 \times 100} = \frac{6 \times 1000}{60 \times 100} \Rightarrow x = 18 \text{ g}$$

Thus, 18 g of glucose is present in 100 mL of solution.

In other words, 1 M solution of glucose (18 g in 100 mL) is isotonic with 6% solution of urea.

73 (*c*)

74 (*a*) As both the solutions are isotonic hence, there is no net movement of the solvent occurs through the semipermeable membrane between two solutions.

75 (*a*) Osmotic pressure of solution 1 is

$$\pi_1 = \frac{n_1}{V_1} RT \Rightarrow n_1 = \frac{1.5}{RT}$$

Osmotic pressure of solution 2 is

$$\pi_2 = \frac{n_2}{V_2} RT \Rightarrow n_2 = \frac{5}{RT}$$

Osmotic pressure of resultant solution, $\pi = \frac{(n_1 + n_2)}{V_1 + V_2} RT$

$$= \frac{\left(\frac{1.5}{RT} + \frac{5}{RT}\right) RT}{3} = 2.16 \text{ atm}$$

76 (*a*)

77 (*a*) Elevation in boiling point,

$$\Delta T_b = i \times K_b \times m \quad ...(i)$$

Using Eq. (i) we get same molality for both solution.

So, it depends on but values of *i*, i.e. van't Hoff factor for NaCl and glucose are 2 and 1 respectively.

Hence, NaCl will show higher elevation in boiling point.

78 (*a*) $A_xB_y \rightleftharpoons xA^{y+} + yB^{x-}$

$(1-\alpha) \qquad x\alpha \qquad y\alpha$

After dissociation,

$$i = (A_xB_y) + (A^{y+}) + (B^{x-})$$

$$= 1 - \alpha + x\alpha + y\alpha$$

$$\therefore \quad \alpha = \frac{i-1}{(x+y-1)}$$

79 (*b*) $Ba(NO_3)_2 \rightleftharpoons Ba^{2+} + 2NO_3^-$

	$Ba(NO_3)_2$	Ba^{2+}	$2NO_3^-$
Initial	1 mol	0	0
After dissociation	$1-\alpha$	α	2α

Total number of moles

$= 1 - \alpha + \alpha + 2\alpha$

$= 1 + 2\alpha$

Then, van't Hoff factor, $i = 1 + 2\alpha$

or $\quad \alpha = \frac{i-1}{2}$

or $\quad \alpha = \frac{2.74 - 1}{2} = 0.87$ %

Degree of dissociation $= 87\%$

80 (*c*) $4A \rightleftharpoons A_4$

$\therefore \quad 1-\alpha \qquad \alpha/4$

$$i = \frac{1 - \alpha + \frac{\alpha}{4}}{1} = 1 - \frac{3}{4}\alpha \ (\alpha = 1)$$

$$i = 1 - \frac{3}{4} = 0.25$$

81 (*a*) $Al_2(SO_4)_3$ has the same value of van't Hoff factor as that of $K_4[Fe(CN)_6]$, i.e. $i = 5$

82 (*a*) $BaCl_2 \rightleftharpoons Ba^{2+} + 2Cl^-$

	$BaCl_2$	Ba^{2+}	$2Cl^-$
Initial	0.01 M	0	0
At equil.	(0.01 – *x*) M	*x* M	2*x* M

$$i = \frac{(0.01 - x) + x + 2x}{0.01}$$

$$= \frac{0.01 + 2x}{0.01} = 1.98$$

$\Rightarrow \quad x = 0.0049$

Percentage of dissociation of

$$BaCl_2 = \frac{x}{0.01} \times 100 = 49\%$$

83 (c) Let the degree of association be α.

$$M \rightleftharpoons (M)_n$$

Initially 1 0

After time t $1-\alpha$ $\frac{\alpha}{n}$

Total moles after association

$$=1-\alpha+\frac{\alpha}{n}=1+\left(\frac{1}{n}-1\right)\alpha$$

$$i=\frac{\text{Total moles after association}}{\text{Initial moles}}$$

$$=\frac{1+\left(\frac{1}{n}-1\right)\alpha}{1} \quad \text{...(i)}$$

We have, $i=0.9$ and $\alpha=0.2$

On putting values of i and α in Eq. (i) we get $n=2$

84 (a) Isotonic solutions have same molar concentration of solute particles in solution, i.e. $i \times C$.

Molar concentration of solute particles in solution are 0.1 M in glucose,
2×0.05 M (=0.1 M) in NaCl, 3×0.05 (0.15 M) in $BaCl_2$ and 4×0.1 (0.4 M) in $AlCl_3$.

Therefore, 0.1 M glucose and 0.05 M NaCl solutions are isotonic.

85 (b) For K_2SO_4, $i=3$

Using formula,

$$\Delta T_f = iK_f \times m$$

$$\Delta T_f = 3 \times 4 \times 0.03 = 0.36 \text{ K}$$

86 (c) $K_2SO_4 \longrightarrow 2K^+ + SO_4^{2-}; i=3$

Using relation,

$$\frac{\Delta p_1}{p_1^\circ}=\frac{p_1^\circ-p_1}{p_1^\circ}=i x_2$$

$$\frac{\Delta p_1}{p_1^\circ}=3\times\frac{1}{1+\frac{54}{18}}=\frac{3}{4}$$

87 (a) $CuCl_2$ is an electrolyte, which ionises in solution as follows

$$CuCl_2 \rightleftharpoons Cu^{2+} + 2Cl^-$$

At $t=0$ 1 mol 0 0

After ionisation $(1-\alpha)$ mol α mol 2α mol

$$(i)=\frac{1+2\alpha}{1} \text{ (on 100\% ionisation, } \alpha=1)$$

$$=\frac{1+2\times 1}{1}=3$$

Molality of $CuCl_2$ solution (m)

$$=\frac{\dfrac{\text{Weight of } CuCl_2 \text{ (in g)}}{\text{Molecular weight of } CuCl_2}}{\text{Weight of water (solvent) (in kg)}}$$

$$=\frac{\dfrac{13.44}{134.4}}{1}=0.1 \text{ m}$$

$$\Delta T_b = i \times K_b \times m$$

$$\Delta T_b = 3 \times 0.52 \times 0.1 = 0.16°\text{C}$$

88 (c) 1% $CaCl_2$ will have the least freezing point because it produces maximum number of ions.

89 (a) $\Delta T_f = i \times K_f \times$ molality

Here, degree of dissociation = 80%

$$KBr \rightleftharpoons K^+ + Br^-$$

Initial 1 0 0

At equilibrium $1-\alpha$ α α

$$i=1-\alpha+\alpha+\alpha=1.8$$

$$\therefore \Delta T_f = 1.8 \times 1.86 \times 0.5$$

$$\Rightarrow \Delta T_f = 1.674 \text{ K}$$

$$\Delta T_f = T_f^\circ - T_f$$

$$\Rightarrow 1.674 = 273 - T_f$$

$$\Rightarrow T_f = 271.326 \text{ K}$$

90 (c) Using, $\Delta T_f = i \times K_f \times m$

$$i=\frac{3.82\times 45}{1.86\times\left(\frac{5}{142}\right)\times 1000}=2.63$$

91 (a) $\Delta T_f = i \times K_f \times m$

$$0.3 = i \times 1.86 \times \frac{1.25\times 1000}{50\times 94}$$

$$\Rightarrow i = 0.6064$$

Degree of association, α

$$=\frac{i-1}{\frac{1}{n}-1}=\frac{0.6064-1}{\frac{1}{2}-1}$$

$$=\frac{-0.3936}{-0.5}\approx 79\%$$

92 (c) X is an electrolyte, which dissociates into 2 ions, i.e. $i=2$

Y dimerises in solution, $2Y \rightleftharpoons Y_2$ so its van't Hoff factor is $\frac{1}{2}$.

Since, the concentration of both X and Y are same, colligative properties depends on the value of van't Hoff factor (i), i.e. $i \propto \Delta T_f$ or ΔT_b.

As i is greater for X, $(\Delta T_b)_X$ and $(\Delta T_f)_X$ is higher than $(\Delta T_b)_Y$ and $(\Delta T_f)_Y$.

So, (a) and (d) are true.

Also, $\Delta T_b = T_b - T_b^\circ$

As ΔT_b is higher for X, T_b will also be higher. So, (b) is also true.

$$\Delta T_f = T_f^\circ - T_f$$

As ΔT_f increases, T_f decreases, i.e.

$$(F.P.)_Y > (F.P)_X$$

So, (c) is false.

93 (a) $\Delta T_f = iK_f m$

$$0.558 = i \times 1.86 \times 0.1 \Rightarrow i=3$$

So, the compound gives 3 ions in solution.

$$[Co(NH_3)_5Cl]Cl_2 \longrightarrow [Co(NH_3)_5Cl]^{2+} + 2Cl^-$$

Therefore, the formula of complex is $[Co(NH_3)_5Cl]Cl_2$.

94 (a) i for KCl = 2, i for $BaCl_2$ = 3

$$\because \Delta T_f \propto i; \frac{\Delta T_f(KCl)}{\Delta T_f(BaCl_2)}=\frac{2}{3}$$

$$\therefore \Delta T_f(BaCl_2)=\frac{3}{2}\times 2=3°\text{C}$$

$\therefore$ Freezing point of KCl = $-3°$C

95 (b) $\Delta T_f = iK_f m$

For CH_3COOH

$$0.02046 = i \times K_f \times 0.01 \quad \text{...(i)}$$

For urea

$$1.86 = K_f \times 1 \quad \text{...(ii)}$$

From (i) and (ii)

$$i=\frac{0.02046}{1.86\times 0.01}=1.1=1+\alpha$$

$$\alpha = i-1 = 1.1-1 = 0.1.$$

$$[H^+] = C\alpha = 0.01 \times 0.1$$

$$[H^+] = 10^{-3}$$

$$pH = 3$$

96 (a) Aluminium sulphate $Al_2(SO_4)_3$ produces maximum number of ions, so it will have highest osmotic pressure.

97 (a)

$$HA \rightleftharpoons H^+ + A^-$$

C 0 0

$C(1-\alpha)$ $C\alpha$ $C\alpha$

$$[H^+] = C\alpha$$

$$[H^+] = 10^{-pH} = 10^{-2} \text{ M} \quad [\because pH = 2]$$

$$C\alpha = 10^{-2}$$

$$\alpha = \frac{10^{-2}}{0.1} = 0.1 \quad [\because C = 0.1\,M]$$

van't Hoff factor (i)

$$= \frac{C(1+\alpha)}{C} = 1 + \alpha = 1 + 0.1 = 1.1$$

$$\pi = iCRT = 1.1 \times 0.1 \times 0.0821 \times 298$$
$$= 2.69 \text{ atm}$$

98 (*c*) For NaCl, $\pi_1 V_1 = i \times n_1 RT$

$$\pi_1 \times \frac{100}{1000} = \frac{1.2}{58.5} \times 0.0821 \times T \times i \quad \text{...(i)}$$

For glucose, $\pi_2 V = n_2 RT$

$$\pi_2 \times \frac{100}{1000} = \frac{7.2}{180} \times 0.0821 \times T \quad \text{...(ii)}$$

($\because$ For glucose $i = 1$)

$\because$ NaCl and glucose solutions are isotonic.

$$\therefore \quad \pi_1 = \pi_2$$

$$\Rightarrow \quad i = \frac{7.2}{180} \times \frac{58.5}{1.2} = 1.95 \approx 2$$

99 (*d*) $\pi_{XY} = 4\pi_{BaCl_2}$ (Given)

$$i \times CRT = 4 \times i \times CRT \quad \text{...(i)}$$
$$2 \times [XY] = 4 \times 3 \times [BaCl_2]$$
$$[XY] = \frac{12 \times 0.01}{2}$$
$$= 6 \times 10^{-2} \text{ mol L}^{-1}$$

100 (*d*) Condition for isotonic solution.

$$\pi_1 = \pi_2 \text{ or } i_1C_1 = i_2C_2$$

For sucrose,

$$iC = \frac{\pi}{RT} = \frac{4.926}{0.0821 \times 300} = 0.2$$

(a) For glucose, $i = 1$,

$$i \times C = \frac{3.6}{180 \times 100} \times 1000 = 0.2$$

(b) For urea, $i = 1$

$$i \times C = \frac{1.2}{60 \times 100} \times 1000 = 0.2$$

(c) For NaCl, $i = 2$

$$i \times C = \frac{2 \times 0.585}{58.5 \times 100} \times 1000 = 0.2$$

(d) For $NaNO_3$, $i = 2$

$$i \times C = \frac{2 \times 1.7}{100 \times 85} \times 1000 = 0.4$$

Hence, (d) is not isotonic with sucrose solution.

101 (*b*) K_2SO_4 dissociates into 2 K^+ and SO_4^{2-} ions, so $i = 3$

$$\pi = iCRT$$
$$\Rightarrow \quad \pi = i \times \frac{w}{M} \times \frac{RT}{V}$$
$$= 3 \times \frac{0.025}{174} \times \frac{1}{2} \times 0.0821 \times 298$$
$$= 5.27 \times 10^{-3} \text{ atm}$$

102 (*b*) More the value of $i \times C$, more will be the boiling point. Hence, increasing order of boiling points is

$$\underset{(i=1)\ [III]}{10^{-4}\,M\,\text{Urea}} < \underset{(i=2)\ [IV]}{10^{-4}\,M\,\text{NaCl}}$$
$$\underset{(i=3)\ [II]}{10^{-3}\,M\,MgCl_2} < \underset{(i=2)\ [I]}{10^{-2}\,M\,\text{NaCl}}$$

Assertion-Reason

1 (*a*) Both A and R are true and R is the correct explanation of A.

2 (*a*) Both A and R are true and R is the correct explanation of A.

3 (*a*) Both A and R are true and R is the correct explanationof A.

4 (*a*) Both A and R are true and R is the correct explanation of A.

5 (*b*) Both A and R are true but R is not the correct explanation of A.

6 (*d*) A is false but R is true. When methyl alcohol is added to water, boiling point of water decreases due to hydrogen bonding.

7 (*a*) Both A and R are true and R is the correct explanation of A.

8 (*a*) Both A and R are true and R is the correct explanation of A.

9 (*a*) Both A and R are true and R is the correct explanation of the A.

10 (*a*) Both A and R are true and R is the correct explanation of A.

Statement Type

1 (*b*) Statement I is true but statement II is false. The correct form of statement II is :

Benzene and toluene does not form an azeotrope.

2 (*b*) Statement I is true but Statement II is false.

The corrected form is : Molality of solution does not depend on the temperature as it depends on the moles of solute and mass of solvent. It does not depend on volume.

3 (*c*) Statement I is false but Statement II is true.

The correct form of Statement I is Depression in the freezing point depends on the number of solute particles.

4 (*d*) Both Statements I and II are true.

5 (*d*) Both Statements I and II are true.

6 (*b*) Statement I is true and Statement II is false.

The value of i for aqueous KCl is 2 while for ethanoic acid is nearly 0.5.

7 (*b*) A and B are incorrect. Their correct forms are

A. Azeotropic mixture are binary mixture having same composition in liquid and vapour phase.

B. $35\%\left(\frac{V}{V}\right)$ solution of ethylene glycol is used for cooling the car engine.

8 (*d*) Statements I, II, III and IV correct. The correct form of V is : Ethanol and acetone show positive deviation.

9 (*b*) Solvents with higher boiling points tends to have lower vapour pressure at a given temperature.

10 (*d*) All the given statements are correct.

Matching Type

1 (*b*) The correct match is A-1, B-3, C-2.

2 (*a*) The correct match is A-1, B-4, C-2 D-3.

3 (*b*) The correct match is A-3, B-2, C-1, D-4.

4 (c) The correct match is A-2, B-1, C-3, D-4.

5 (c) The correct match is A-1, B-3, C-2, D-4.

Numerical Value

1 (100) $2X \longrightarrow X_2$

Initial 1 0

Final $1-\alpha$ $\frac{\alpha}{2}$

$$i = 1-\alpha+\frac{\alpha}{2}$$

Also, $\Delta T_b = iK_b m$

$$\Delta T_b = T_b - T_b^\circ = 100.52 - 100 = 0.52$$

$$\Rightarrow 0.52 = i \times 0.52 \times 2,\ i = \frac{1}{2}$$

$$\Rightarrow \quad i = \frac{1}{2} = 1-\alpha+\frac{\alpha}{2}$$

$$\Rightarrow 1-\frac{\alpha}{2} = \frac{1}{2} \quad \Rightarrow \alpha = 1$$

So, percentage of association of X is 100%.

2 (15) As we know,

$$\pi = CRT \text{(Osmotic pressure)}$$

$$\pi = \frac{w_B \times R \times T}{M_B \times V \text{ (in L)}}$$

$$4.84 \times 10^{-6} = \frac{2.92 \times 0.083 \times 300}{M_B \times 0.1}$$

$$M_B = 15.02 \times 10^7 \approx 15 \times 10^7 \text{ g/mol}$$

3 (150) $\frac{\Delta p}{p^\circ} = \frac{\frac{w_2}{M_2}}{\frac{w_2}{M_2}+\frac{w_1}{M_1}}$

$$\frac{75}{100} = \frac{\frac{w_2}{50}}{\frac{w_2}{50}+\frac{114}{114}} \Rightarrow w_2 = 150 \text{ g}$$

4 (15) Moles of ascorbic acid

$$= \frac{10.2 \text{ g}}{176 \text{ g mol}^{-1}} \approx 0.058 \text{ mol}$$

$$\Delta T_f = K_f \times m$$

$$= 3.9 \times \frac{0.058}{150} \times 1000$$

$$= 1.5\ ^\circ\text{C} = 15 \times 10^{-1}\ ^\circ\text{C}$$

Thus, the value of X is 15.

NCERT Exemplar's

1 (d) As we know, $M_1V_1 = M_2V_2$

$$0.02 \times 4 \text{ L} = M_2 \times 5 \text{ L}$$

$$M_2 = \frac{0.08}{5} = 0.016 \text{ M}$$

For NaCl, molality = molality

∴ Molecular weight = equivalent weight

2 (a)

3 A-(5), B-(3), C-(4), D-(2), E-(1).

4 (a) At specific composition, methanol-acetone mixture will form minimum boiling azeotrope and will show positive deviation. This is due to weaker A—B interaction than A—A or B—B interaction. i.e. A—B < A—A and B—B.

5 (c) Higher the value of K_H at a given pressure, the lower is the solubility of the gas in the liquid.
Hence, correct order is

$$Ar < CO_2 < CH_4 < HCHO.$$

6 (a) When NaCl (non-volatile) is dissolved in a liquid, its vapour pressure decreases.
Thus, vapour pressure in container A is more than that in container B.

7 (b) As we know, greater the value of van't Hoff factor (for equimolar solutions), higher will be the elevation in boiling point and, hence higher will be the boiling point of solution.

For 1.0 M Na_2SO_4 $i = 3$ hence, it has highest value of boiling point.

8 (c) As we know that, depression in freezing point is directly related to van't Hoff factor (i) and greater the value of i, greater will be the depression in freezing point (for equimolar so motions).

0.01 M glucose,	$i = 1$
0.01 M $MgCl_2$,	$i = 3$

Hence, depression in freezing point of $MgCl_2$ is about 3 times of glucose.

9 (d) When an unripe mango is placed in a concentrated salt solution to prepare pickle, then it loses water due to osmosis.

10 (b) We know that, if a pressure higher than the osmotic pressure is applied on the solution (on piston B), the solvent will flow from the solution into the pure solvent through the semipermeable membrane. This process is called reverse osmosis.

11 (a)

12 (b) Statement (b) is incorrect.
It's correct form is as follows
In reverse osmosis, solvent molecules move through a semipermeable membrane from a region of higher concentration of solute to lower concentration of solute.

13 (b)

Substances	van't Hoff factor (i)
KCl	2
NaCl	2
K_2SO_4	3

14 (a) Statement (a) is incorrect.
It's correct form is as follows
Two different solutions of sucrose of same molality prepared in different solvents will have different depression in freezing point.

15 (c) Being strong electrolyte, in all cases will be independent of the concentration of ions.
Thus, $i_A = i_B = i_C$ [i.e. $i = 2$ (equal)]

16 (b) Chloroform and acetone mixture is an example of non-ideal solution showing negative deviation.
While ethanol-acetone mixture shows positive deviation.

17 A-(3), B-(5), C-(4), D-(1), E-(2)

18 (c) 19 (c) 20 (a)

Past Exams'

1 (b) The relation between solubility and Henry's law constant is

$$\text{Solubility} \propto \frac{1}{K_H}$$

if K_H decreases then solubility increases.
K_H for gas B is lowest (2×10^{-5} kbar) and A has highest (145 k bar).
Hence, the order of solubility is given by $B > C > A$.

2 (*a*) Osmotic pressure is given by,

$$\pi = CRT$$

Plot is of between osmotic pressure and concentration, i.e. π *vs* C.

On comparing with $y = mx + C$

Slope $m = RT$

$$25.73 = 0.083 \times T$$

$$T = 310\text{ K} = 37°\text{C}$$

3 (*b*) (A) is true while (R) is false. This is because at normal temperature and pressure helium is practically insoluble in oxygen. However, under extreme conditions very small amount of helium dissolve in oxygen.

4 (*a*) We know that,

$$\text{Molality} = \frac{\text{Number of moles of solute}}{\text{Weight of the solvent (g)}} \times 1000$$

$$1 = \frac{0.5\,\text{mole}}{\text{Weight of the solvent (g)}} \times 1000$$

Weight of the solvent (g) = 500 g

5 (*c*) Molar ratio of benzene to octane,

$$\frac{n_B}{n_O} = \frac{3}{2}$$

Let $n_B = 3x$ mol, $n_O = 2x$ mol

Total number of moles $= n_B + n_O$

$$= 3x + 2x = 5x \text{ mol}$$

Mole fraction of benzene,

$$\chi_B = \frac{n_B}{n_B + n_O} = \frac{3x}{5x} = \frac{3}{5}.$$

Mole fraction of octane,

$$\chi_O = \frac{n_O}{n_B + n_O} = \frac{2x}{5x} = \frac{2}{5}$$

Total vapour pressure of solution,

$$p_S = \chi_B p_B^\circ + \chi_O p_O^\circ$$

$$= \frac{3}{5} \times 280 + \frac{2}{5} \times 420$$

$$= 336 \text{ mm of Hg}$$

6 (*c*)

7 (*d*) In positive deviation the resulting solution has more vapour pressure than the ideal solution of the constituent liquids. This is because the A—B interactions are weaker than A—A and B—B.

e.g. Ethanol-acetone.

8 (*b*) $\Delta T_f = K_f \times m \times i$

$$= 5.12 \times 0.078 \times 1$$

$$= 0.39936 \approx 0.40 \text{ K}$$

9 (*b*) For an ideal solution,

$\Delta V_{mix} = 0$, $\Delta H_{mix} = 0$,

$\Delta G_{mix} < 0$, $\Delta S_{mix} > 0$.

Hence, option (b) is correct.

10 (*d*) The solutions that show large negative deviation from Raoult's law forms maximum boiling azeotrope, e.g. nitric acid and water.

11 (*a*) Solution exhibits positive deviation from ideal behaviour if the intermolecular interactions, i.e. A—B interactions are more stronger than in pure components, i.e. between A—A and B—B.

The remaining options are valid only for ideal solutions.

12 (*c*) Partial pressure of dry air = total pressure × mole fraction of dry air

$$\Rightarrow p_{\text{dry air}} = p_{\text{total}} \times \chi_{\text{dry air}}$$

$$\chi_{\text{dry air}} = 1 - 0.02 = 0.98$$

$$\therefore p_{\text{dry air}} = 1.2 \text{ atm} \times 0.98 = 1.176 \text{ atm}$$

13 (*d*) From Raoult's law of partial pressure,

$$\frac{p_1^\circ - p_0}{p_1^\circ} = \frac{n_2}{n_1}$$

$$\Rightarrow \frac{760 - 732}{760} = \frac{w_2 \times M_1}{M_2 \times w_1}$$

$$\Rightarrow \frac{28}{760} = \frac{6.5 \times 18}{M_2 \times 100}$$

$$\Rightarrow M_2 = 31.75$$

$$\therefore \Delta T_b = 0.52 \times \frac{6.5 \times 1000}{31.75 \times 100} = 1.06$$

$\therefore$ Boiling point = 100 + 1.06

$$= 101.06 \approx 101°\text{C}$$

14 (*d*) Since, component having higher vapour pressure will have higher percentage in vapour phase. Benzene has vapour pressure 12.8 kPa which is greater than toluene 3.85 kPa.

Therefore, the vapour will contain a higher percentage of benzene.

15 (*c*) $Al_2(SO_4)_3$ will exhibit largest freezing point depression due to the highest value of *i*.

$$Al_2(SO_4)_3\,(aq) \Rightarrow 2Al^{3+} + 3SO_4^{2-}\ (i = 5)$$

16 (*b*) Given, number of molecules of urea $= 6.02 \times 10^{20}$

$$\therefore \text{Number of moles} = \frac{6.02 \times 10^{20}}{N_A} = \frac{6.02 \times 10^{20}}{6.02 \times 10^{23}} = 1 \times 10^{-3} \text{ mol}$$

Volume of the solution

$$= 100 \text{ mL} = \frac{100}{1000} \text{ L} = 0.1 \text{ L}$$

Concentration of urea solution (in mol L^{-1})

$$= \frac{1 \times 10^{-3}}{0.1} = 0.01 \text{ mol L}^{-1}$$

17 (*707*)

> **Key Idea** To solve this question, use the formula $\Delta T_b = k_b m$ to calculate the value of molality (m). After that use this value of molality in the equation $\frac{\Delta p}{p^\circ} = \frac{m}{100} \times M_{\text{solvent}}$, as the solution is diluted, to calculate Δp. Then using this Δp calculate the required value of p_s.

Given that, $\Delta T_b = 2$

$$K_b = 0.52$$

$$p^\circ = 760 \text{ mm Hg}$$

$$M_{\text{solvent}} = 18$$

Now using $\Delta T_b = K_b m$

$$2 = 0.52 \times m$$

$$m = \frac{2}{0.52}$$

Now, according to question, since the solution is diluted much. Hence,

$$\frac{\Delta p}{p^\circ} = \frac{n_{\text{solute}}}{n_{\text{solvent}}} \Rightarrow \frac{\Delta p}{p^\circ} = \frac{m}{1000} \times M_{\text{solvent}}$$

$$\Rightarrow \Delta p = 760 \times \frac{\left(\frac{2}{0.52}\right)}{1000} \times 18$$

$$\Delta p = 52.615$$

So, $p_s = 760 - 52.615$

$$p_s = 707.385 \text{ mm Hg}$$

Hence, nearest integer is 707.

18 (5) $\Delta T_b = 0.52°C$

$$\Delta T_b = i \times K_b \times m$$

$$0.52 = i \times 0.52 \times \frac{10}{200 \times 0.1}$$

$$i = 2 \quad ...(i)$$

$$\alpha = \frac{i-1}{n-1}$$

$$AB_2 \longrightarrow A^{2+} + 2B^-$$

$$n = 3$$

$$\alpha = \frac{2-1}{3-1} = \frac{1}{2} = 0.5 = 5 \times 10^{-1}$$

Hence, degree of ionisation is 5×10^{-1}.

19 (a) Among the given options $(CH_3)_2CO + CS_2$, i.e. shows positive deviation from Raoult's law. Since acetone-CS_2 attractions are and weaker than acetone-acetone attractions and $CS_2 - CS_2$ attractions.

Concept Enhancer

The liquid solutions which shows positive deviation from the Raoult's law form minimum boiling azeotropes.

20 (c) The correct match is

A-3, B-1, C-2, D-4.

21 (a) According to Raoult's law, for dilute solution, $\frac{p° - p}{p°} = \frac{n}{N}$

[where, n = number of moles of glucose, N = number of moles of H_2O]

On substituting the given values, we get

$$\frac{0.2 \text{ mmHg}}{54.2 \text{ mmHg}} = \frac{w \times 18 \text{ g/mol}}{180 \times 100 \text{ g}}$$

$$w = \frac{100}{271 \times 18} \times 180 = 3.69 \text{ g}$$

22 (b) Mass of solution $= 18 + 2 = 20$ g

$$\text{Mass \% of } X = \frac{\text{Mass of solute}}{\text{Mass of solution}} \times 100$$

$$= \frac{2}{20} \times 100 = 10\%$$

23 (b) $\Delta T_b = K_b \times m$

$(\Delta T_b)_A = (\Delta T_b)_B$ (given)

$\therefore \quad m_A = m_B$

Molality

$$= \frac{\text{Mass of solute} \times 1000}{\text{Molecular mass of solute} \times \text{Weight of solvent (in g)}}$$

$$\frac{2 \times 1000}{M_A \times 98} = \frac{8 \times 1000}{M_B \times 92}$$

$$\therefore \quad M_B \simeq 4M_A$$

24 (a) Both (A) and (R) are correct and (R) is the correct explanation of (A).

25 (c) Now, $p = \frac{M}{V} \Rightarrow M = p \cdot V$

$$= 1.05 \times 0.5 = 0.525 \text{ g}$$

According to formula,

$$\Delta T_f = iK_f m \quad (m = \text{molality})$$

Let us take, mass of solution = 1 kg = 1000 g

Mass of solvent $= 1000 - 0.525$
$= 999.475$ g (formic acid)

$$\text{So, } m = \frac{0.525 \times 1000}{46 \times 999.475} = 0.0114$$

$$\Delta T_f = iK_f (0.0114)$$

$$\Rightarrow \quad i = \frac{0.0405}{1.86 \times 0.0114} \approx 1.9$$

Skill Boosters

1 (d) $\Delta T_f = K_f m$

$$0.45 = K_f \times m \quad ... (i)$$

$$\Delta T_b = iK_b m$$

$$0.25 = iK_b m \quad ... (ii)$$

On dividing Eqs. (i) and (ii) we get,

$$i = 1.944$$

Since, van't Hoff factor, $i > 1$, its a case of dissociation.

2 (b) $\Delta T_f = \frac{K_f \times 1000 \times w_B}{w_A \times M_B}$

$$(w_B = 2000 \times 0.8 = 1600 \text{ g})$$

$$= \frac{1.86 \times 1000 \times 1600}{16000 \times 32} = 5.81$$

Freezing point $= 0 - 5.81 = -5.81°C$

3 (a) The vapour pressure increases with decrease in intermolecular forces.

When the forces are weak, the liquid has high volatility and maximum vapour pressure. Diethyl ether has highest vapour pressure while water has lowest vapour pressure.

4 (b) $\Delta T_f = iK_f m$

$$7.45 = i \times 1.86 \times 2.0 \Rightarrow i = 2.0$$

So, the formula is $[Pt(H_2O)_3Br_3]Br \cdot 3H_2O$ which ionise in solution as $[Pt(H_2O)_3Br_3]^+$ and Br^- ions.

5 (b) Mass of MeOH

$$= 50 \times 0.791 = 39.55 \text{ g}$$

Mass of EtOH $= 50 \times 0.998 = 49.9$ g

$$M_1 = \frac{49.9 \times 1000}{46 \times 100} = 10.84$$

$$M_2 = \frac{39.55 \times 1000}{32 \times 100} = 12.36$$

Thus, $M_2 > M_1$

and $M_1 + M_2 = 12.36 + 10.84$
$= 23.2 < 50$

6 (b) In benzene, $m = \frac{\Delta T_f}{K_f} = 0.205$

In H_2O, ionisation occurs ($\alpha = 1$),

$$i = \frac{\Delta T_f}{K_f m} = 3$$

7 (a) In hypotonic solution, the water is drawn in and the raisin swells while in hypertonic solution the water is drawn out and the raisin shrink.

8 (c) The relationship between molar masses of two solvents is

$$M_A = \frac{5}{4} M_B \quad ...(i)$$

The relative lowering of vapour pressure α mole fraction of solute.

Given 5 molal solution means 5 moles of solute.

The number of moles of solvent

$$= \frac{1000 \text{ g}}{M}$$

The mole fraction of solute

$$= \frac{5 \times M}{1000}$$

$$\text{Hence, } M_A \times \frac{5}{1000} = x \times M_B \times \frac{5}{1000} \quad ... (ii)$$

Substitute Eq. (i) in Eq. (ii)

$$\frac{5}{4} \times M_B \times \frac{5}{1000} = x \times M_B \times \frac{5}{1000}$$

$$x = \frac{5}{4}$$

02

Scan for **Chemistry Through Concept Master** Videos

Electrochemistry

Electrochemistry is the study of production of electricity from energy released during spontaneous chemical reactions and the use of electrical energy to bring about non-spontaneous chemical transformations.

Electrochemical Cells

- An electrochemical cell is a device in which chemical energy of the redox reaction is converted into electrical energy. e.g. Daniell cell.
- The cell which has an electrical potential equal to 1.1 volt and concentration of Zn^{2+} and Cu^{2+} ions is unity (1 mol dm^{-3}), known as Daniell cell. Such a device is also called a **galvanic cell** or a **voltaic cell**,

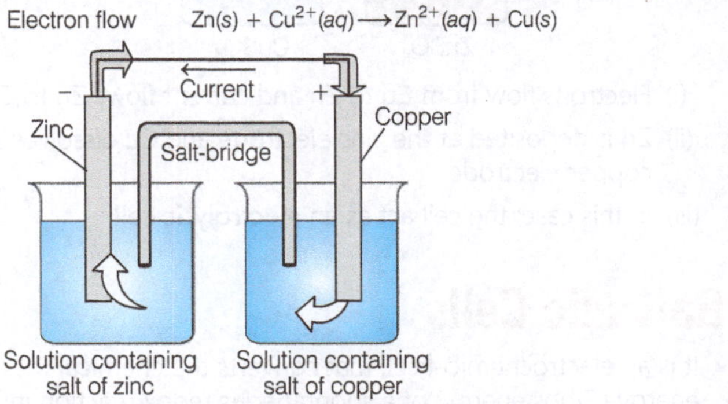

Daniell cell having electrodes of zinc and copper dipped in the solutions of their respective salts.

- If an external opposite potential is applied in the galvanic cell, three cases are seen.
  – **Case I** When $E_{ext} < 1.1\,V$

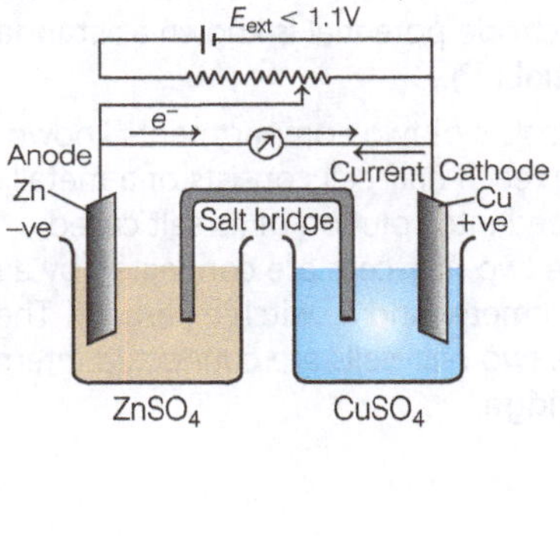

Topicwise No. of Ques asked in 5 Years (NEET)

Topics	No. of Questions				
	2024	2023	2022	2021	2020
Electrochemical and Galvanic Cells	–	–	2	–	1
Nernst Equation	–	–	1	–	–
Conductance of Electrolytic Solutions	–	1	–	2	–
Electrolytic Cells and Electrolysis	2	–	–	–	2
Batteries, Fuel Cells and Corrosion	–	–	–	–	1

Special Type of Ques Asked In 5 Years (NEET)

Types	Years				
	2024	2023	2022	2021	2020
A-R	–	–	–	–	–
Statement Based	–	–	–	–	–
Matching	1	–	–	–	–

Last 5 Years Weightage (NEET)

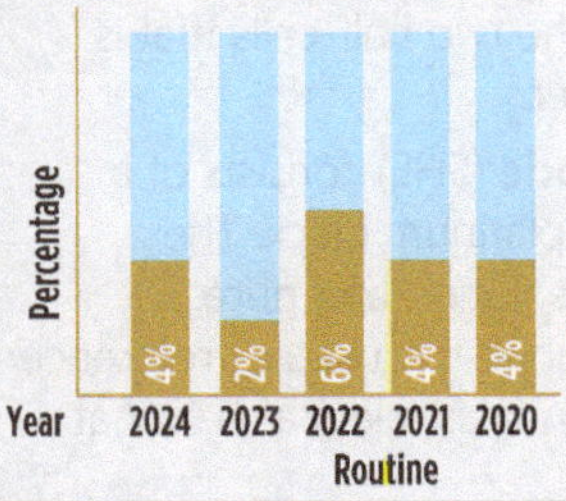

(i) Electrons flow from Zn rod to Cu rod, hence current flows from Cu to Zn.

(ii) Zn dissolves at anode and copper deposited at cathode.

– **Case II** When $E_{ext} = 1.1\,V$

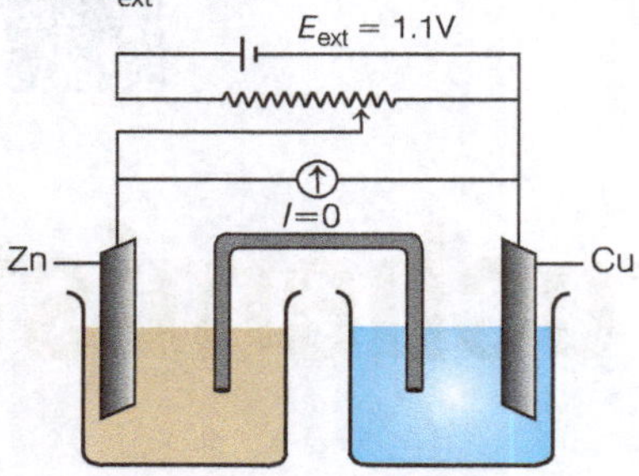

(i) No flow of current or electrons.

(ii) No chemical reaction.

– **Case III** When $E_{ext} > 1.1\,V$

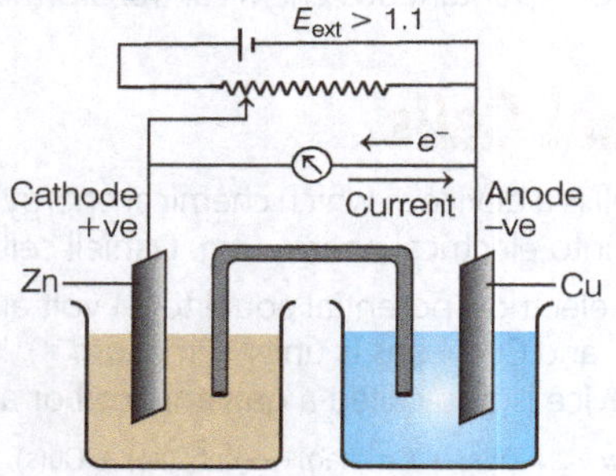

(i) Electrons flow from Cu to Zn and current flows Zn to Cu.

(ii) Zn is deposited at the zinc electrode and Cu dissolves at copper electrode.

(iii) In this case, the cell act as an **electrolytic cell**.

Galvanic Cells

- It is an electrochemical cell that converts the chemical energy (Gibbs energy) of a spontaneous redox reaction into electrical energy, which may be used for running a motor or other electrical gadgets like heater, fan, geyser, etc.
- A potential difference develops between the metal and the metal ion of solution in which electrode is dipped is called **electrode potential**. At 1 atm pressure and 1M concentration of electrolyte, electrode potential is known as **standard electrode potential** ($E°$).
- A galvanic cell consists of two compartments known as **half-cells**. Further, each half-cell consists of a metallic rod, i.e. electrode dipped into solution of its salt called **electrolyte**. These two half-cells are connected by a metallic wire through a voltmeter and a switch externally. The electrolytes of the two half-cells are connected internally through a **salt-bridge**.
- Salt-bridge plays an important role in working of an electrochemical cell as it completes the circuit and maintains the electrical neutrality of solutions in each of the respective half-cells.
- The electrode on which oxidation takes place is called **anode**. It has a negative potential with respect to the solution. Hence, denoted by (–ve) sign. It is written in the left side in the cell representation.
- The electrode on which reduction takes place is called **cathode**. It has a positive potential with respect to the solution. Hence, denoted by (+ve) sign. It is written in the right side in the cell representation.

General representation of an electrochemical cell is given as

$$\underset{\text{Anode}}{M_1(s)} \mid \underset{\text{Oxidation half-cell}}{M_1^{n+}(aq)} \parallel \underset{\text{Reduction half-cell}}{M_2^{n+}(aq)} \mid \underset{\text{Cathode}}{M_2(s)}$$

$$\xrightarrow{\text{Flow of electrons}}$$

In place of M_1 and M_2 there may be different metals.

- According to the IUPAC convention, standard reduction potential of cell is now called **standard electrode potential**.
- The difference in electrode potentials (reduction potential) of the two half-cells of a cell is known as **cell potential**.
- **Electromotive force** (emf) of a cell is the potential difference, when no current is drawn through the cell. It is measured in volts (V).

$$E_{cell} = E_{right} - E_{left}$$

or

$$E_{cell} = E_{cathode} - E_{anode}$$

For a cell reaction to be spontaneous E_{cell} must be positive.

Marks Maximizer

Salt-bridge prevents or minimises liquid-liquid junction potential which arises because of the difference in the rate of diffusion of cations and anions from more concentrated solution to less concentrated solution.

Measurement of Electrode Potential

The potential of individual half-cell cannot be measured. It is the potential difference between the two half-cells that is measured in a circuit by a voltmeter.

- The **standard hydrogen electrode** (SHE) consists of a platinum electrode coated with platinum black. The electrode is dipped in an acidic solution and pure hydrogen gas is bubbled through it. It is used as reference electrode whose electrode potential is taken as 0.00V at 298 K.

For the cell,

$$H^+(aq) + e^- \longrightarrow \frac{1}{2}H_2(g); E° = 0.00\text{ V}$$

- At 298K, the emf is measured by taking the SHE as anode (reference half-cell) and another half-cell as cathode, gives the reduction potential of the other half-cell.

$$\text{Emf of the cell} = E^\circ_{cell} = E^\circ_R - E^\circ_L$$ NEET 2022

As E°_L for SHE is zero, $E^\circ = E^\circ_R - 0 = E^\circ_R$

e.g. The measured emf of the cell

(a) $Pt(s) \mid H_2(g, 1\text{ bar}) \mid H^+(aq, 1M) \parallel Cu^{2+}(aq, 1\text{ M}) \mid Cu$ (=0.34 V)

(b) $Pt(s) \mid H_2(g, 1\text{ bar}) \mid H^+(aq, 1M) \parallel Zn^{2+}(aq, 1\text{ M}) \mid Zn$ (=−0.76 V)

- The positive value of the standard electrode potential in the first case indicates that Cu^{2+} ions get reduced more easily than H^+ ions. While the negative value of the standard electrode potential in the second case indicates that hydrogen ions can oxidise zinc.

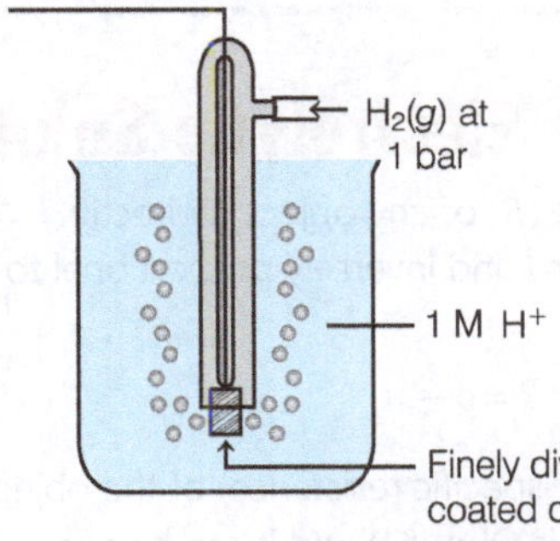

Standard Hydrogen Electrode (SHE)

- Sometimes metals like platinum or gold are used as inert electrodes. They do not participate in the reaction but provide their surface for oxidation or reduction and for the conduction of electrons.
- Electrochemical cells are used for determining the pH of solutions, solubility product, equilibrium constant and other thermodynamic properties and for potentiometric titrations.

Marks Maximizer

Calomel electrode is now used as a secondary reference electrode. It is a type of half-cell in which the electrode is mercury coated with calomel (Hg_2Cl_2) and the electrolyte is a solution of KCl and saturated calomel.

The overall reaction is

$$Hg_2Cl_2(s) + 2e^- \longrightarrow 2Hg(l) + 2Cl^-$$

Electrochemical Series

The arrangement of various standard half-cells in the order of their decreasing value of standard reduction potential is called electrochemical series. NEET 2020

Standard Reduction Potentials at 298 K (Electrochemical Series)

(Left side, upward arrow: Increasing strength of oxidising agent; right side, downward arrow: Increasing strength of reducing agent)

Reaction (oxidised form + ne^-	$\longrightarrow$ reduced form)	$E^\ominus$/V
$F_2(g) + 2e^-$	$\longrightarrow 2F^-$	2.87
$Co^{3+} + e^-$	$\longrightarrow Co^{2+}$	1.81
$H_2O_2 + 2H^+ + 2e^-$	$\longrightarrow 2H_2O$	1.78
$MnO_4^- + 8H^+ + 5e^-$	$\longrightarrow Mn^{2+} + 4H_2O$	1.51
$Au^{3+} + 3e^-$	$\longrightarrow Au(s)$	1.40
$Cl_2(g) + 2e^-$	$\longrightarrow 2Cl^-$	1.36
$Cr_2O_7^{2-} + 14H^+ + 6e^-$	$\longrightarrow 2Cr^{3+} + 7H_2O$	1.33
$O_2(g) + 4H^+ + 4e^-$	$\longrightarrow 2H_2O$	1.23
$MnO_2(s) + 4H^+ + 2e^-$	$\longrightarrow Mn^{2+} + 2H_2O$	1.23
$Br_2 + 2e^-$	$\longrightarrow 2Br^-$	1.09
$NO_3^- + 4H^+ + 3e^-$	$\longrightarrow NO(g) + 2H_2O$	0.97
$2Hg^{2+} + 2e^-$	$\longrightarrow Hg_2^{2+}$	0.92
$Ag^+ + e^-$	$\longrightarrow Ag(s)$	0.80
$Fe^{3+} + e^-$	$\longrightarrow Fe^{2+}$	0.77
$O_2(g) + 2H^+ + 2e^-$	$\longrightarrow H_2O_2$	0.68
$I_2 + 2e^-$	$\longrightarrow 2I^-$	0.54
$Cu^+ + e^-$	$\longrightarrow Cu(s)$	0.52
$Cu^{2+} + 2e^-$	$\longrightarrow Cu(s)$	0.34
$AgCl(s) + e^-$	$\longrightarrow Ag(s) + Cl^-$	0.22
$AgBr(s) + e^-$	$\longrightarrow Ag(s) + Br^-$	0.10
$2H^+ + 2e^-$	$\longrightarrow H_2(g)$	0.00
$Pb^{2+} + 2e^-$	$\longrightarrow Pb(s)$	−0.13
$Sn^{2+} + 2e^-$	$\longrightarrow Sn(s)$	−0.14
$Ni^{2+} + 2e^-$	$\longrightarrow Ni(s)$	−0.25
$Fe^{2+} + 2e^-$	$\longrightarrow Fe(s)$	−0.44
$Cr^{3+} + 3e^-$	$\longrightarrow Cr(s)$	−0.74
$Zn^{2+} + 2e^-$	$\longrightarrow Zn(s)$	−0.76
$2H_2O + 2e^-$	$\longrightarrow H_2(g) + 2OH^-(aq)$	−0.83
$Al^{3+} + 3e^-$	$\longrightarrow Al(s)$	−1.66
$Mg^{2+} + 2e^-$	$\longrightarrow Mg(s)$	−2.36
$Na^+ + e^-$	$\longrightarrow Na(s)$	−2.71
$Ca^{2+} + 2e^-$	$\longrightarrow Ca(s)$	−2.87
$K^+ + e^-$	$\longrightarrow K(s)$	−2.93
$Li^+ + e^-$	$\longrightarrow Li(s)$	−3.05

- Reducing power $\propto \dfrac{1}{\text{Standard reduction potential}}$ NEET 2019

i.e. more negative the value of standard reduction potential, higher is the reduction power.

- If the standard electrode potential of an electrode is greater than zero, then its reduced form is more stable as compared to hydrogen gas and *vice-versa*.

Nernst Equation

- The relationship between electrode potential and concentration of solution is given by Nernst equation.

For Concept Master Video

For a general electrochemical reaction,

$$aA + bB \xrightarrow{ne^-} cC + dD$$

$$E_{cell} \text{ or EMF} = E^\circ_{cell} - \frac{2.303\,RT}{nF}\log Q$$ NEET 2022, 2019

where, n = total number of electrons gained or lost

$1F = 96500\text{ C}$

T = temperature

R = gas constant ($8.314\text{ JK}^{-1}\text{mol}^{-1}$)

Q = reaction quotient of overall reaction $\left(\frac{[C]^c[D]^d}{[A]^a[B]^b}\right)$

- Concentration of pure solids are taken as unity

At 298 K, $E_{cell} = E^\circ_{cell} - \frac{0.0591}{n}\log Q$

Equilibrium Constant from Nernst Equation

At equilibrium, $E_{cell} = 0$

(i) $E^\circ_{cell} = \frac{2.303\,RT}{nF}\log K_C$

where, K_C = equilibrium constant.

(ii) At, $T = 298$ K, $E^\circ_{cell} = \frac{0.0591}{n}\log K_C$

Electrochemical Cell and Gibbs Energy of Reaction

$$\Delta_r G = -nFE_{cell}$$

If the concentration of all the reacting species is unity then $E_{cell} = E^\circ_{cell}$.

$$\Delta_r G^\circ = -nFE^\circ_{cell}$$

or $$\Delta_r G^\circ = -RT\ln K$$ NEET 2019

Note E_{cell} is an intensive property, while $\Delta_r G$ is an extensive property.

Marks Maximizer

- Nernst equation for hydrogen electrode can be written as

$$E_{H^+/H} = E^\circ_{H^+/H_2} - \frac{0.0591}{n}\log\frac{1}{[H^+]} = -0.0591\text{ pH } [\because \text{pH} = -\log[H^+]]$$

- For concentration cell, EMF is given by

$$E_{cell} = \frac{RT}{nF}\ln\frac{C_2}{C_1} \quad [\text{where, } C_2 > C_1]$$

- When different number of electrons are involved in two different reactions. The overall standard electrode potential can be calculated by using the given formula,

$$\Delta G^\circ_3 = \Delta G^\circ_1 + \Delta G^\circ_2 \text{ and } -n_3FE^\circ_3 = -n_1FE^\circ_1 + n_2FE^\circ_2$$

$$E^\circ_3 = \frac{n_1E^\circ_1 + n_2E^\circ_2}{n_3}$$

- Relation between free energy and cell potential for different cell.

Type of cell	ΔG	E	Type of reaction
Galvanic	−ve	+ve	Spontaneous
Electrolytic	+ve	−ve	Non-spontaneous
Dead battery	0	0	Equilibrium

Conductance of Electrolytic Solutions

- The **electrical resistance** (R) of any object is directly proportional to its length l and inversely proportional to its area of cross-section (A).

Thus, $$R \propto \frac{l}{A} \text{ or } R = \rho\frac{l}{A}.$$

where, ρ is **resistivity** (or specific resistance) of the object. The SI unit of resistance is Ohm (Ω) and it can be measured with the help of a **Wheatstone bridge**.

- **Resistivity** (specific resistance) is defined as the resistance offered by a substance of 1 m length with area of cross-section to 1 m^2. Its SI unit is ohm metre (Ωm).
- The quantity $\frac{l}{A}$ is called the **cell constant**.

It is denoted by the symbol G^*. It will be given by,

$$G^* = \frac{l}{A} = R \times \kappa$$

The unit of cell constant (G^*) is m^{-1}.

- **Conductance** (G) is the reciprocal of resistance and may be defined as the ease with which the electric current flows through the conductor, $G = \frac{1}{R} = \frac{A}{\rho l}$

Here, R = Resistance [SI unit = Siemens (S) or ohm^{-1} (mho)]

- **Conductivity or specific conductance** (κ) of an electrolytic solution may be defined as the conductance of a solution of 1 m length with its area of cross-section equal to 1 m^2.

$$\kappa = \frac{1}{R} \times \text{cell constant}$$ NEET 2023

Its unit is Sm^{-1} or $ohm^{-1}\ m^{-1}$.

Types of Substances on the Basis of Conductivity

Materials are classified into conductors, insulators and semiconductors depending on the magnitude of their conductivity.

- Substances like glass, ceramics, coal etc., which have very low conductivity are called **insulators**.
- Substances like silicon, doped silicon and gallium arsenide which have moderate conductivity are called **semiconductors**.
- Substances which have very large conductivity are known as **conductors**, e.g. metals and their alloys, certain non-metals like carbon black, graphite and some organic polymers.
- Materials which have zero resistivity and infinite conductivity are called **superconductors**, e.g. metals and their alloys at very low temperature (0 to 15 K).

Types of Conductance

Electrical conductance through metals is called **metallic** or **electronic conductance** and is due to the movement of electrons. It depends on

- nature and structure of the metal
- the number of valence electrons per atom
- temperature (it decreases with increase of temperature)

The conductance of electricity by ions present in the solutions is called **electrolytic** or **ionic conductance**. It depends on

- the nature of the electrolyte added.
- size of the ions produced and their solvation.
- the nature of the solvent and its viscosity.
- concentration of the electrolyte.
- temperature (it increase with the increase of temperature).

Measurement of the Conductivity of Ionic Solutions

- Conductance of an ionic solution is measured accurately by measuring its resistance with the help of Wheatstone bridge.
- The cell constant is usually determined by measuring the resistance of the cell containing a solution (generally KCl) whose conductivity is already known, by using the formula

$$G^* = \frac{l}{A} = \kappa \cdot R$$

The set up for the measurement of the resistance is shown in figure.

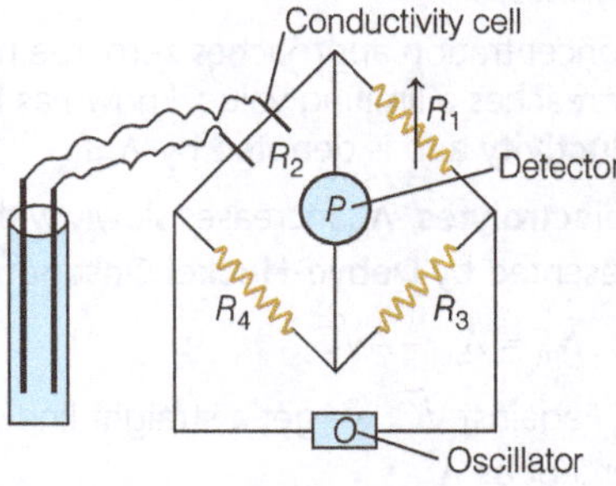

Arrangement for measurement of resistance of a solution of an electrolyte

(i) It consists of two resistances R_3 and R_4, a variable resistance R_1 and the conductivity cell having the unknown resistance R_2.

(ii) The bridge is balanced when no current passes through the detector. At equilibrium,

$$\frac{R_1}{R_2} = \frac{R_3}{R_4} \text{ or } R_2 = \frac{R_1 \cdot R_4}{R_3}$$

- Once, the cell constant and the resistance of the solution in the cell is determined, then the conductivity of the solution is measured by the formula.

$$\kappa = \frac{\text{Cell constant}}{\text{Resistance}} = \frac{G^*}{R}$$

Molar conductivity (Λ_m) is defined as the conducting power of all the ions produced by dissolving one gram mole of an electrolyte placed between two electrodes with area of cross-section '*A*' and at a distance of 1 cm.

It is given by $$\Lambda_m = \frac{\kappa}{C}$$

Here, κ is expressed in $S\ m^{-1}$ and the concentration C is $mol\ m^{-3}$ thus, unit of Λ_m is $S m^2\ mol^{-1}$ or $ohm^{-1}\ m^2\ mol^{-1}$.

$$1 S\ m^2\ mol^{-1} = 10^4\ S\ cm^2\ mol^{-1}$$

Variation of Conductivity and Molar Conductivity with Concentration

- Conductivity always decreases with decrease in concentration both for weak and strong electrolyte. This is due to the fact that the number of ions that carry current in a unit volume of solution always decreases with decrease in concentration.
- The molar conductivity can also be written as,

$$\Lambda_m = \frac{\kappa A}{l} = \kappa$$

Since, $l = 1$ and $A = V$ (volume containing 1 mole of electrolyte)

$$\therefore \quad \Lambda_m = \kappa V$$

- Molar conductivity increases with decrease in concentration because the total volume V of solution containing 1 mole of electrolyte increases.
- When the concentration approaches zero, the molar conductivity reaches a limiting value, known as **limiting molar conductivity** and is denoted by Λ_m°.
- For **strong electrolytes**, Λ_m increases slowly with dilution. This can be represented by **Debye-Huckel Onsager equation**,

$$\Lambda_m = \Lambda_m^\circ - A\sqrt{C}$$

If we plot Λ_m against $\sqrt{C}$, we get a straight line with slope as $-A$ and intercept as Λ_m°.
- The value of constant 'A' depends upon the type of electrolyte, i.e. the charges on the cation and anion produced on the dissociation of the electrolyte in the solution.
- For **weak electrolytes**, like acetic acid, have a lower degree of dissociation at higher concentration and hence, there is a rapid increase in the value of Λ_m with dilution.
- In low concentration region, the graph of weak electrolytes in a plot of Λ_m against $\sqrt{C}$ becomes parallel to the Y-axis. So, the limiting molar conductivity (Λ_m°) cannot be determined by the extrapolation of the plot. It can be determined by using **Kohlrausch law of independent migration of ions**.
- The variation of Λ_m with the concentration for strong and weak electrolytes is shown by the following graph :

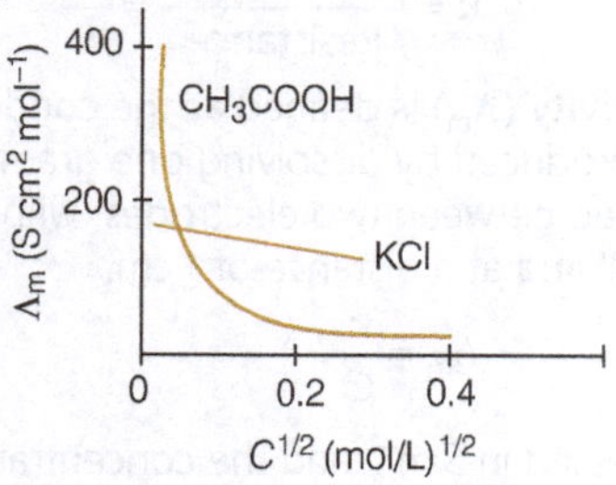

Marks Maximizer

Equivalent conductivity (λ_{eq}) is the conductance of a volume of solution containing one equivalent of an electrolyte.

$$\lambda_{eq} = \frac{\kappa \times 1000}{\text{Normality}}$$

Its units are ohm^{-1} cm^2 eq^{-1} or S cm^2 eq^{-1} or mho cm^2 eq^{-1}. It increases with dilution.

Kohlrausch's Law

For Concept Master Video

It states that "Limiting molar conductivity of an electrolyte is the sum of individual contributions of conductivity of cation and anion of the electrolyte".

$$\Lambda_m^\circ = x\lambda_m^\circ + y\lambda_m^\circ$$ NEET 2019

(x and y = number of cations and anions)

e.g. Limiting molar conductivity for sodium chloride is given as $\Lambda_{m(NaCl)}^\circ = \lambda_{Na^+}^\circ + \lambda_{Cl^-}^\circ$

Some important applications of Kohlrausch law are as follows

(i) **Degree of dissociation** of weak electrolyte can be determined as $\alpha = \dfrac{\Lambda_m}{\Lambda_m^\circ}$ NEET 2022

[Λ_m = molar conductivity at a given concentration, Λ_m° = limiting molar conductivity].

(ii) **Dissociation constant** (for weak electrolyte) can be determined as

$$K_a = \frac{C\alpha^2}{(1-\alpha)} = \frac{C\Lambda_m^2}{\Lambda_m^\circ(\Lambda_m^\circ - \Lambda_m)}$$

[C = concentration, α = degree of dissociation]

Electrolytic Cells and Electrolysis

- In an **electrolytic cell** external source of voltage is used to bring about a chemical reaction.
- **Electrolysis** is the process of decomposition of an electrolyte by passing electricity through its aqueous solution or molten state.
- The **quantitative aspect of electrolysis** was studied extensively by Michael Faraday and his law of electrolysis are known as **Faraday's law of electrolysis.**

  (i) **Faraday's first law of electrolysis** states that, "The amount of chemical reaction occurring at any electrode during electrolysis by passing a current is directly proportional to the quantity of electricity passed through the electrolyte (in solution or in molten electrolysis state)" i.e. NEET 2020, 2024

$$W \propto Q$$
$$W = ZQ$$
$$W = Zit \qquad (\because Q = i \times t)$$

where, Q = quantity of electricity
i = current (in A)
t = time (in s)
Z = constant of proportionality called electrochemical equivalent.

Charge on one electron is equal to 1.6021×10^{-19} C. Therefore, the charge on one mole of electron is equal to

$$N_A \times 1.6021 \times 10^{-19}\,C = 6.02 \times 10^{23}\,mol^{-1} \times 1.6021 \times 10^{-19} = 96487\,C\,mol^{-1}$$

This quantity of electricity is called **Faraday** and is represented by the symbol 'F'.

For approximate calculations we use $1\,F \approx 96500\,C\,mol^{-1}$.

(ii) **Faraday's second law of electrolysis** states that, "When the same quantity of electricity is passed through different electrolytes, the amount of different substances liberated/deposited are directly proportional to their equivalent weights. i.e. $\frac{w_1}{w_2} = \frac{E_1}{E_2}$

where, w is the mass of the substance and E is its equivalent weight.

$$E = \frac{\text{Atomic mass of element}}{\text{No. of electrons gained or lost by one atom /ion of the element}}$$

Products of Electrolysis

It depends upon the nature of material being electrolysed and the type of electrodes being used. It depends on the different oxidising and reducing species present in the electrolytic cell and their standard electrode potentials and over potential. Some important examples of electrolysis are as follows :

- Molten sodium chloride is electrolysed to produce sodium metal at cathode and chlorine gas at the anode.
- Electrolysis of aqueous NaCl solutions give hydrogen gas at cathode and chlorine gas at anode.

Note At cathode, H_2 is produced due to higher value of $E°$ and at anode due to over potential (extra potential) of oxygen liberation of chlorine gas is preferred.

- Dilute sulphuric acid is electrolysed using platinum electrodes, oxygen gas is liberated at anode and hydrogen gas is liberated at the cathode. NEET 2020
- Electrolysis of concentrated sulphuric acid leads to the oxidation of sulphuric acid to $S_2O_8^{2-}$ ion at anode and hydrogen gas liberated at cathode

Marks Maximizer

Discharge potential The minimum potential that must be applied across the electrodes to bring about the electrolysis and thus, discharge of the ions on the electrode is known as discharge potential. In case of negative ions, lower standard reduction potential value indicates lower discharge potential and incase of positive ions, higher standard reduction potential value indicate lower discharge potential.

Differences between Electrolytic Cell and Electrochemical Cell

Electrolytic cell	Electrochemical cell (Galvanic or Voltaic cell)
Non-spontaneous redox reaction is made to occur. Only when electrical energy is supplied. i.e. $\Delta G = +ve$	Gibbs energy of the spontaneous redox reaction is converted into electrical work. e.g. Daniell cell. i.e. $\Delta G = -ve$
No salt-bridge is required.	Salt-bridge is essential to maintain electroneutrality.
Cathode is negative and anode is positive electrode.	Cathode is positive and anode is negative electrode.
The electrodes materials may be same or different and suspended in electrolyte in the same beaker.	The electrodes involved are of different materials and usually set up in two separate beakers.

Batteries

A **cell** or a battery (arrangement of 1 or more than 1 cells connected in series) is basically a galvanic cell where the chemical energy of the redox reaction is converted into electrical energy.

Some commercial batteries are

- The **primary batteries** are those in which the cell reaction occurs only once and the battery becomes dead after use over a period of time and cannot be used again. e.g. Dry cell
- A **secondary cell** or **battery** can be recharged by passing current through it in the opposite direction so that it can be used again. e.g. Ni-Cd cell.

Difference between Primary and Secondary Cell

	Primary Cell		Secondary Cell	
Cell	Dry cell or Leclanche cell	Mercury cell	Lead storage cell	Nickel-cadmium cell
Anode	$Zn(s) \longrightarrow Zn^{2+}(aq) + 2e^-$	$Zn(Hg) + 2OH^-(aq) \longrightarrow ZnO(s) + H_2O(l) + 2e^-$	$Pb(s) + SO_4^{2-}(aq) \longrightarrow PbSO_4(s) + 2e^-$	$Cd(s) + 2OH^-(aq) \longrightarrow Cd(OH)_2(s) + 2e^-(aq)$
Cathode	$MnO_2(s) + NH_4^+(aq) + e^- \longrightarrow MnO(OH)(s) + NH_3(g)$	$HgO(s) + H_2O(l) + 2e^- \longrightarrow Hg(l) + 2OH^-(aq)$	$PbO_2(s) + SO_4^{2-}(aq) + 4H^+(aq) + 2e^- \longrightarrow PbSO_4(s) + 2H_2O(l)$	$NiO_2(s) + 2H_2O(l) + 2e^- \longrightarrow Ni(OH)_2(s) + 2OH^-(aq)$
The overall reaction :	$Zn(s) + 2MnO_2(s) + 2NH_4^+(aq) \longrightarrow Zn^{2+}(aq) + 2MnO(OH)(s) + 2NH_3(g)$	$Zn(Hg) + HgO(s) \longrightarrow ZnO(s) + Hg(l)$	$Pb(s) + PbO_2(s) + 2H_2SO_4(aq) \longrightarrow 2PbSO_4(s) + 2H_2O(l)$	$Cd(s) + 2Ni(OH)_3(s) \longrightarrow CdO(s) + 2Ni(OH)_2(s) + H_2O(l)$

Fuel Cells

- It is a galvanic cell in which chemical energy from combustion of fuels like hydrogen, methane, methanol, etc., is converted into electrical energy, e.g. H_2-O_2 fuel cell. NEET 2020
- H_2-O_2 fuel cell is used for proceeding electrical power in Apollo space programme. The water-vapours are condensed and added to the drinking water supply for the astronauts.
- In fuel cell, following electrode reactions takes place.

  At cathode, $O_2(g) + 2H_2O\,(l) + 4e^- \longrightarrow 4OH^-(aq)$

  At anode, $2H_2(g) + 4OH^-(aq) \longrightarrow 4H_2O\,(l) + 4e^-$

  Overall reaction, $2H_2(g) + O_2(g) \longrightarrow 2H_2O\,(l)$

  Fuel cells producing electricity with an efficiency (70%) as compared to the efficiency of thermal power plant (40%). Fuel cells are pollution free.

*Corrosion

- It is an electrochemical process in which a metal is oxidised to metal oxide or other salt of the metal by losing electrons to oxygen or other electronegative element and forms a coating on the metal surface.
- The rusting of iron, tarnishing of silver surface, surface of copper and bronze turning green are some of the examples of corrosion.
- **Rusting or corrosion of iron** occurs in the presence of water and air. Following anodic and cathodic reactions takes place

  At anode, $2Fe\,(s) \longrightarrow 2Fe^{2+}(aq) + 4e^-, E^\circ_{(Fe^{2+}/Fe)} = -0.44\text{ V}$

  At cathode, $O_2(g) + 4H^+(aq) + 4e^- \longrightarrow 2H_2O\,(l);$

  $$E^\circ_{(H^+/O_2/H_2O)} = 1.23\text{ V}$$

  Overall reaction,

  $$2Fe\,(s) + O_2(g) + 4H^+\,(aq) \longrightarrow 2Fe^{2+}(aq) + 2H_2O\,(l);$$

  $$E^\circ_{cell} = 1.67\text{ V}$$

  The ferrous ions are further oxidised by atmospheric oxygen to ferric ions and form rust, i.e. hydrated ferric oxide ($Fe_2O_3 \cdot xH_2O$).
- The corrosion can be prevented by coating the surface with paint or some chemicals (e.g. *bis*-phenol); by covering the surface with other metals (e.g. Sn, Zn, etc.) and by an electrochemical method, i.e. providing a sacrificial electrode of another metal (like Mg, Zn, etc.) which corrodes itself but saves the object.

* *This topics not include in latest NEET syllabus, but it is given in latest rationalised NCERT.*

The Hydrogen Economy

- At present the main source of energy that is driving our economy is fossil fuels such as coal, oil and gas.
- Hydrogen can be used as renewable and non-polluting alternative source of energy. Water will split into hydrogen and oxygen using solar energy.

  $$H_2O(l) \xrightarrow{h\nu} H_2(g) + \frac{1}{2}O_2(g)$$

  Combustion of hydrogen in a fuel cell will produce water.

  $$H_2(g) + \frac{1}{2}O_2(g) \longrightarrow H_2O(l)$$
- Both the production of hydrogen by electrolysis of water and hydrogen combustion in a fuel cell will be important in the future.

Caution Points

- A cell reaction is spontaneous only when E_{cell} is positive and Gibbs free energy is negative.
- While applying the Nernst equation, electrode potential is always taken as reduction potential.
- While balancing the half-cell reaction, one must be remembered that the electrode potential value does not change.

PYQ Notes

1. For hydrogen electrode, Nernst equation is

$$E = \frac{0.0591}{2}\log\frac{p_{H_2}}{[H^+]^2}$$

NEET 2016

2. The graph between molar conductivity (Λ_m) *versus* $\sqrt{C}$ for KCl and NaCl is

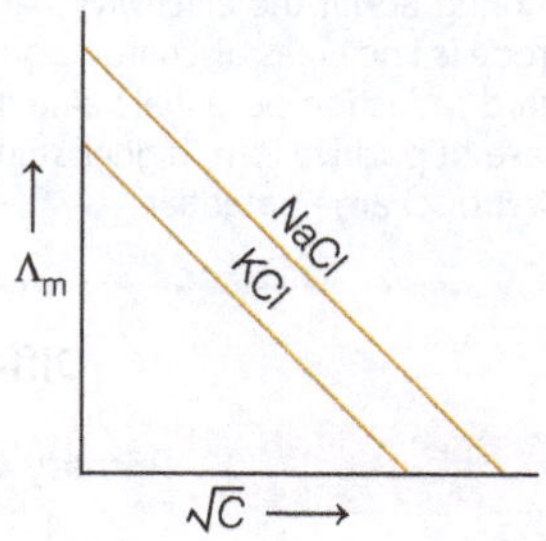

JEE Main 2019

3. Cell reaction is spontaneous, when ΔG° is negative.

NEET 2014

4. The decreasing order of reducing power of the metal is

K ($E^\circ_{K^+/K} = -2.93$ V) > Al ($E^\circ_{Al^{3+}/Al} = -1.66$ V) > Cr ($E^\circ_{Cr^{3+}/Cr} = -0.74$ V) > Ag ($E^\circ_{Ag^+/Ag} = 0.80$ V)

NEET 2019

Step by Step

Mastering NCERT

- Concept Builders
- Topical Questions
- Assertion-Reason
- Statement Type
- Matching Type
- Numerical Value
- NCERT Exemplar's
- Past Exams'
- Skill Boosters

Concept Builders

1. All chemical reaction produce electrical energy. [T/F].
2. In Daniell cell, current flows from .... to .... electrode.
3. In Galvanic cell, Gibbs energy of non-spontaneous redox reaction is converted into useful electrical work. [T/F]
4. In Galvanic cell, anode and cathode are negative and positive electrodes respectively. [T/F]
5. Name the term used for the cell potential when no current is drawn in a cell.
6. The potential of an individual half-cell cannot be measured. [T/F]
7. Element which will be easily reduced than H^+ ions is ...... (Cu^{2+}/Zn^{2+}).
8. .... (Positive/Negative) value of standard potential indicate that hydrogen ion cannot oxidise Cu.
9. A negative $E°$ means that the redox couple is a weaker reducing agent than the H^+/H_2 couple. [T/F]
10. What will be standard cell potential for the following Galvanic cell?

$$Cr\,|\,Cr^{3+}||Cd^{2+}|Cd$$

[Given : $E^\circ_{Cr^{3+}/Cr} = -0.74V$, $E^\circ_{Cd^{2+}/Cd} = -0.40V$]

11. Greater reduction potential represents greater reducing power of the substance. [T/F]
12. In Daniell cell, the E_{cell} increases with increase in the concentration of Cu^{2+} and decrease with increase in concentration of Zn^{2+} ions. [T/F]
13. At equilibrium, in Daniell cell concentration of Zn^{2+} and Cu^{2+} .... (remains same/changes proportionally) and voltmeter gives .... (zero/unity) reading.
14. In standard hydrogen electrode, the pressure of H_2 gas is 100 bar and the concentration of hydrogen ion is 2 molar. [T/F]
15. The potential of hydrogen electrode in a solution of pH = 10 will be ....
16. On increasing length of wire to double, resistance of wire will be halved. [T/F]
17. Metallic conductance decreases with increases in temperature. [T/F]
18. Out of 0.01 M KCl and 0.01 M HAc, which one will shows more conductivity?
19. The cell constant of a conductivity cell do not depend on the distance between the electrodes and their area of cross-section. [T/F]
20. λ°_m for NaCl, HCl and NaAc are 126.4, 425.9 and 91.0 S $cm^2\ mol^{-1}$ respectively. The value of λ°_m for HAc is ....
21. Conductivity of a solution .... with dilution because number of ions .... in a unit volume.
22. The mass of the substance deposited when one coulomb of electricity is passed through its solution is called .... of the substance.
23. According to Faraday's law, the amount of chemical reaction which occurs at any electrode is directly proportional to quantity of electricity passed through solution. [T/F]
24. What amount of Al is produced by passing 96500 C of electricity through aqueous Al_2O_3?
25. Name the electrolyte used in mercury cell.
26. In lead storage battery, the cathode consists of ....
27. Write the value of cell potential of mercury cell.
28. Ni-Cd cell has longer life as well as cheaper than lead storage cell. [T/F]
29. Name the cell which is used as a primary source of electrical energy on the Apollo space program.
30. Presence of electrolytes in water do not show an significant effect on rusting of iron. [T/F]

Topical Questions

Electrochemical Cells and Galvanic Cells

1 In a electrochemical cells, **NCERT Pg 32**

(a) the potential energy of the cell is converted into electrical energy.

(b) the energy of the cell is utilised in conduction of the reduction and oxidation reaction.

(c) the chemical energy liberated during the redox reaction is converted to electrical energy.

(d) the electrical energy of the cell is converted to chemical energy.

2 What happens when applied external opposite potential in a Daniell cell reaches to 1.1 V? **NCERT Pg 32**

(a) Chemical reaction stops and no current flows.

(b) Current starts flowing in a direction opposite to that of the electrons.

(c) Current starts flowing in the same direction as of electrons.

(d) The cell behaves like an electrolytic cell.

3 Consider the following given figure, **NCERT Pg 32**

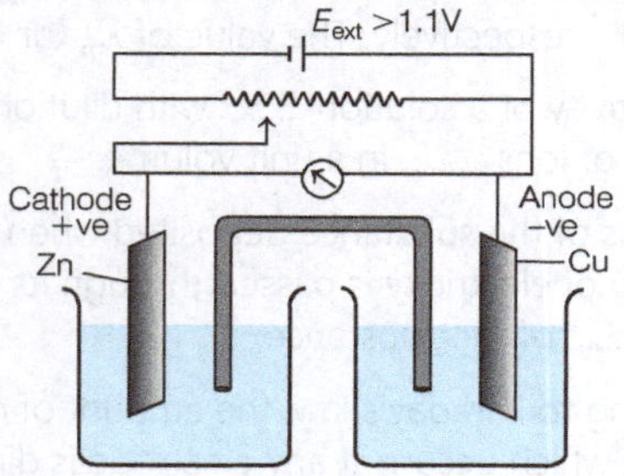

Choose the correct statement regarding the above figure.

(a) Zn dissolves at anode and copper deposits at cathode.

(b) Zn dissolves at cathode and copper deposits at anode.

(c) Zn deposits at cathode and copper dissolves at anode.

(d) Zn deposits at anode and copper dissolves at cathode.

4 Look at the Daniell cell, **NCERT Pg 32**

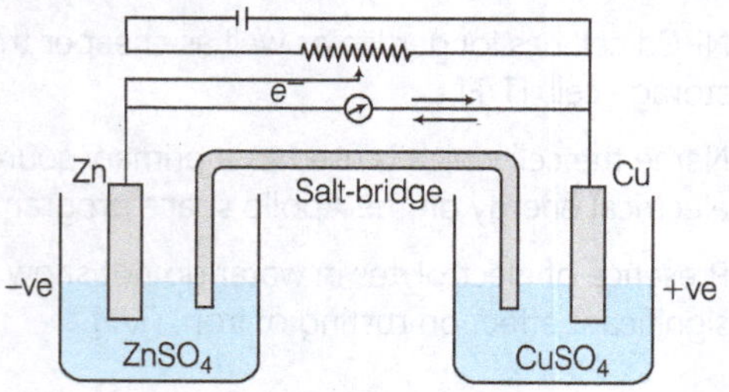

The incorrect statement related to this cell is

(a) electron flow from zinc to copper electrode, when applied external potential is 0.9 V.

(b) current flow from zinc to copper electrode, when applied external potential is 1.5 V.

(c) current flow from zinc to copper electrode when applied external potential is 0.9 V.

(d) zinc electrode acts as cathode and copper as anode when applied external potential is 1.5 V.

5 The electrode potential is known as standard electrode potential **NCERT Pg 33**

(a) when it is reduction potential and concentration of all the species involved in half-cell is unity.

(b) when it is reduction potential and concentration of species involved in half-cell is greater than unity.

(c) when it is oxidation potential and concentration of species involved in half-cell is greater than unity.

(d) when it is oxidation potential and concentration of all the species involved in half-cell is unity.

6 Select the incorrect statement. **NCERT Pg 34**

(a) Cell potential is the difference between electrode potentials of cathode and anode.

(b) Cell potential is unitless quantity.

(c) It is also called cell electromotive force (emf) when no current is drawn through cell.

(d) In a cell anode is kept on left and cathode on right.

7 The correct cell representation of the following cell is

$$Zn + 2Ag^+ \longrightarrow Zn^{2+} + 2Ag$$ **NCERT Pg 34**

(a) $Zn(s)|\,Zn^{2+}(aq)||\,Ag^+(aq)|\,Ag(s)$

(b) $Zn^{2+}\,|\,Zn\,||\,Ag\,|\,Ag^+$

(c) $Zn(aq)\,|\,Zn^{2+}(s)||\,Ag^+(s)|\,Ag(aq)$

(d) $Zn(s)|\,Ag^+(aq)||\,Zn^{2+}(aq) + Ag(s)$

8 For the electrochemical cell, $Ag\,|\,AgCl|\,KCl\,||\,AgNO_3|\,Ag$, the overall cell reaction is **NCERT Pg 34**

(a) $Ag^+ + KCl \longrightarrow AgCl(s) + K^+$

(b) $Ag + AgCl \longrightarrow 2Ag + \frac{1}{2}Cl_2$

(c) $AgCl(s) \longrightarrow Ag^+ + Cl^-$

(d) $Ag^+ + Cl^- \longrightarrow AgCl(s)$

9 The standard reduction potential for the half-cell reaction, $Cl_2 + 2e^- \longrightarrow 2Cl^-$ will be

(Given, $Pt^{2+} + 2Cl^- \longrightarrow Pt + Cl_2, E^\circ_{cell} = -0.15$ V;

$Pt^{2+} + 2e^- \longrightarrow Pt, E^\circ = 1.20$ V) **NCERT Pg 35**

(a) – 1.35 V (b) + 1.35 V (c) – 1.05 V (d) + 1.05 V

10 For the cell, $Cu\,|Cu^{2+}||\,Ag^{+}|\,Ag$, $E^{\circ}_{cell} = +0.46$ V
If concentration of Cu^{2+} ions is doubled, then E°_{cell} will be **NCERT Pg 35**
(a) halved (b) doubled
(c) four times (d) remains the same

11 Standard electrode potential for Sn^{4+} / Sn^{2+} couple is + 0.15V and that for the Cr^{3+} /Cr couple is – 0.74V. These two couples in their standard state are connected to make a cell. The cell potential will be **NCERT Pg 35**
(a) + 1.83 V (b) +1.19 V
(c) + 0.89 V (d) + 0.18 V

12 E°_{cell} of the reaction is **NCERT Pg 35**
$Zn\,(s) + Cu^{2+}(aq) \longrightarrow Zn^{2+}(aq) + Cu\,(s)$;
[If $E^{\circ}_{Zn^{2+}/Zn} = -0.76, E^{\circ}_{Cu^{2+}/Cu} = 0.34$ V]
(a) 0.34V (b) – 0.76 V (c) + 1.10 V (d) – 1.10 V

13 Given, $E^{\circ}_{Ni^{2+}/Ni} = 0.25$ V, $E^{\circ}_{Cu^{2+}/Cu} = 0.34$ V
$E^{\circ}_{Ag^{+}/Ag} = 0.80$V and $E^{\circ}_{Zn^{2+}/Zn} = -0.76$V
Which of the following reactions under standard condition will not take place in the specified direction? **NCERT Pg 35**
(a) $Ni^{2+}(aq) + Cu\,(s) \longrightarrow Ni(s) + Cu^{2+}(aq)$
(b) $Cu\,(s) + 2Ag^{+}(aq) \longrightarrow Cu^{2+}(aq) + 2Ag(s)$
(c) $Zn\,(s) + 2H^{+}(aq) \longrightarrow Zn^{2+}(aq) + 3\,H_2(g)$
(d) $Zn\,(s) + Cu^{2+}(aq) \longrightarrow Zn^{2+}(aq) + Cu(s)$

14 For the cell, $Zn(s)|\,Zn^{2+}(aq)\,||\,M^{x+}(aq)\,|\,M(s)$, different half-cells and their standard electrode potentials are given below. **NCERT Pg 35**

$M^{x+}(aq)/M(s)$	$Au^{3+}(aq)$/ Au(s)	$Ag^{+}(aq)$/ Ag(s)	$Fe^{3+}(aq)$/ $Fe^{2+}(aq)$	$Fe^{2+}(aq)$/ Fe(s)
$E^{\circ}_{M^{x+}/M}$/V	1.40	0.80	0.77	– 0.44

If $E^{\circ}_{Zn^{2+}/Zn} = -0.76$ V, which cathode will give a maximum value of E°_{cell} per electron transferred?
(a) Ag^{+}/Ag (b) Fe^{2+}/Fe
(c) Au^{3+}/Au (d) Fe^{3+}/ Fe^{2+}

15 Given below are the half-cell reactions,
$Mn^{2+} + 2e^{-} \longrightarrow Mn; E^{\circ} = -1.18$ V
$2Mn^{3+} + 2e^{-} \longrightarrow 2Mn^{2+}; E^{\circ} = +1.51$ V
The E° for $3Mn^{2+} \longrightarrow Mn + 2Mn^{3+}$ will be **NCERT Pg 35**
(a) –2.69 V, the reaction will not occur
(b) –2.69 V, the reaction will occur
(c) –0.33 V, the reaction will not occur
(d) –0.33 V, the reaction will occur

16 Given the standard electrode potentials.
$E^{\circ}_{Fe^{2+}/Fe} = -0.44$ V
and $E^{\circ}_{H^{+}/O_2/H_2O} = 1.23$ V
Calculate the E°_{cell} of the corrosion. **NCERT Pg 35**
(a) – 0.79 V (b) – 1.67 V
(c) 1.67 V (d) + 0.79 V

17 Which of the following statement is correct with respect to $Cu(s)|Cu^{2+}(aq)||Ag^{+}(aq)|\,Ag\,(s)$ cell? **NCERT Pg 34**
(a) $E_{cell} = E_{Cu^{2+}/Cu} - E_{Ag^{+}/Ag}$
(b) $Cu(s)/Cu^{2+}(aq)$ represent cathode and $Ag^{+}(aq)/Ag(s)$ is anode electrodes respectively.
(c) Reaction at cathode $Cu(s) \longrightarrow Cu^{2+}(aq) + 2e^{-}$
(d) Cu electrode loses mass and Ag electrodes gains mass.

18 Choose the incorrect statement regarding standard hydrogen electrode. **NCERT Pg 34, 35**
(a) It has zero potential at all temperatures.
(b) It is represented as $Pt(s)\,|\,H_2(g)\,||\,H^{+}(aq)\,|$.
(c) It consist of a platinum electrode coated with platinum black.
(d) The electrode is dipped in basic solution.

19 A cell is set up as shown in the figure. It is observed that EMF of the cell comes out to be 2.87 V. Which of the given statement is not correct about the cell? **NCERT Pg 34, 35**

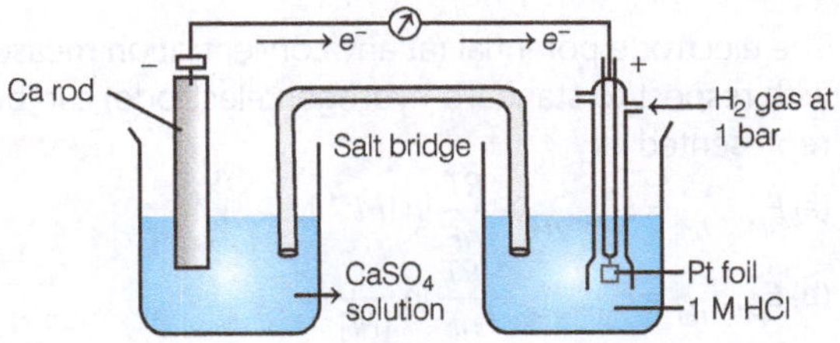

(a) Reduction takes place at calcium electrode and oxidation at SHE.
(b) Oxidation takes place at calcium electrode and reduction at SHE.
(c) Standard electrode potential of Ca^{2+}/Ca will be – 2.87 V.
(d) Electrons flow from calcium electrode to hydrogen electrode.

20 Zn gives hydrogen with H_2SO_4 and HCl but not with HNO_3 because **NCERT Pg 35**
(a) Zn acts as oxidising agent when reacts with HNO_3.
(b) HNO_3 is weaker acid than H_2SO_4 and HCl.
(c) Zn is above the hydrogen in electrochemical series.
(d) NO_3^{-} is reduced in preference to H^{+} ion.

21 Electrochemical cells are not used for determining the
(a) pH of solutions NCERT Pg 36
(b) solubility product
(c) equilibrium constant
(d) dissociation constant

22 Standard electrode potential of three metals *X*, *Y* and *Z* are –1.2V, +0.5V and –3.0V respectively. The reducing power of these metals will be NCERT Pg 36
(a) $X > Y > Z$ (b) $Y > Z > X$
(c) $Y > X > Z$ (d) $Z > X > Y$

23 The standard electrode potential ($E°$) values of Al^{3+}/Al, Ag^+/Ag, K^+/K and Cr^{3+}/Cr are – 1.66 V, 0.80V, – 2.93 V and – 0.74 V, respectively. The correct decreasing order of reducing power of the metal is NCERT Pg 36
(a) Ag > Cr > Al > K (b) K > Al > Cr > Ag
(c) K > Al > Ag > Cr (d) Al > K > Ag > Cr

24 The standard reduction potential for $Zn^{2+}/Zn, Ni^{2+}/Ni$ and Fe^{2+}/Fe are –0.76,–0.23 and –0.44 V respectively. The reaction $X + Y^{2+} \longrightarrow X^{2+} + Y$ will be spontaneous, if NCERT Pg 36
(a) $X = Ni, Y = Fe$ (b) $X = Ni, Y = Zn$
(c) $X = Fe, Y = Zn$ (d) $X = Zn, Y = Ni$

Nernst Equation

25 For the hypothetical half-cell reaction,

$$M^{n+}(aq) + ne^- \longrightarrow M(s)$$

The electrode potential (at any concentration measured with respect to standard hydrogen electrode) can be represented as NCERT Pg 36

(a) $E_{M^{n+}/M} = E°_{M^{n+}/M} - \frac{RT}{nF}\ln[M^{n+}]$

(b) $E_{M^{n+}/M} = E°_{M^{n+}/M} - \frac{RT}{nF}\ln\frac{1}{[M]}$

(c) $E_{M/M^{n+}} = E°_{M/M^{n+}} - \frac{RT}{nF}\ln\left[\frac{M^{n+}}{M}\right]$

(d) $E_{M^{n+}/M} = E°_{M^{n+}/M} - \frac{RT}{nF}\ln\frac{1}{[M^{n+}]}$

26 Select the correct statement for Daniell cell containing Cu^{2+} and Zn^{2+} ions. NCERT Pg 38
(a) E_{cell} does not depend on the concentration of Cu^{2+} and Zn^{2+} ions.
(b) E_{cell} decreases with increase in the concentration of Cu^{2+} ions.
(c) E_{cell} increases with decrease in the concentration of Zn^{2+} ions.
(d) E_{cell} increases with increase in concentration of Cu^{2+}, Zn^{2+} ions.

27 Mark the correct Nernst equation for the given cell.

$Ni(s)|Ni^{2+}(aq)||Ag^+(aq)|Ag(s)$ NCERT Pg 38

(a) $E_{cell} = E°_{cell} + \frac{RT}{2F}\ln\frac{[Ni^{2+}]}{[Ag^+]^2}$

(b) $E_{cell} = E°_{cell} - \frac{RT}{2F}\ln\frac{[Ni^{2+}]}{[Ag^+]^2}$

(c) $E_{cell} = E°_{cell} - \frac{RT}{2F}\ln\frac{[Ni^{2+}]^2}{[Ag^+]}$

(d) $E_{cell} = E°_{cell} + \frac{RT}{2F}\ln\frac{[Ni^{2+}]^2}{[Ag^+]}$

28 Select the option which is the incorrect match of the expression with their respective reaction. NCERT Pg 38

(a) For, $M^{n+}(aq) + ne^- \longrightarrow M(s)$; $E = E° - \frac{0.0591}{n}\log\left[\frac{1}{M^{n+}}\right]$

(b) For, $aA + bB \overset{ne^-}{\rightleftharpoons} cC + dD$ at equilibrium;

$$E°_{cell} = \frac{0.0591}{n}\log\frac{[C]^c[D]^d}{[A]^a[B]^b}$$

(c) For, $2Ag^+ + H_2(1\text{ atm}) \longrightarrow 2Ag + 2H^+(1\text{ M})$;

$$E_{cell} = E°_{cell} - \frac{0.0591}{2}\log\frac{[Ag^+]^2}{[H^+]^2}$$

(d) For, $Ag|Ag^+(C_1)||Ag^+(C_2)|Ag$; $E_{cell} = -\frac{0.0591}{1}\log\frac{C_1}{C_2}$

29 What is the potential of the cell containing two hydrogen electrodes as represented below?

$Pt, \frac{1}{2}H_2(g)|H^+(10^{-8}M)||H^+(0.001\text{ M})|\frac{1}{2}H_2(g), Pt$ NCERT Pg 38

(a) –0.2955 V (b) – 0.0591 V
(c) 0.2955 V (d) 0.0951 V

30 In which of the following cells, $E_{cell} = E°_{cell}$? NCERT Pg 38
(a) $Cu(s)|Cu^{2+}(0.01\text{ M})||Ag^+(0.1\text{ M})|Ag(s)$
(b) $Pt(H_2)|pH = 1||Zn^{2+}(0.1\text{ M})|Zn(s)$
(c) $Pt(H_2)|pH = 1||Zn^{2+}(1\text{ M})|Zn(s)$
(d) $Pt(H_2)|H^+(0.01\text{ M})||Zn^{2+}(0.01\text{ M})|Zn(s)$

31 If $E°_{(Zn^{2+}/Zn)} = -0.763$ V and $E°_{(Fe^{2+}/Fe)} = -0.44$ V, then the emf of the cell

$Zn|Zn^{2+}(a = 0.001)||Fe^{2+}(a = 0.005)|Fe$ is

(Given, log 0.2 = –0.699) NCERT Pg 38

(a) equal to 0.323 V (b) less than 0.323 V
(c) greater than 0.323 V (d) equal to 1.103 V

32 For the given cell notation, $M|\underset{0.01}{M^{2+}}||\underset{0.0001}{M^{2+}}|M$, if the value of $E°_{cell}$ is 4 volt
(Given : ln 10 = 0.06) then, the emf of the cell is NCERT Pg 38
(a) 3.94 V (b) 4.0591 V
(c) 2.03 V (d) 8.18 V

33 Given, $E^{\circ}_{(Cr^{3+}/Cr)} = -0.72$ V, $E^{\circ}_{(Fe^{2+}/Fe)} = -0.42$ V. The potential for the cell $Cr|Cr^{3+}(0.1\text{ M})||Fe^{2+}(0.01\text{ M})|Fe$ is

(a) – 0.339 V (b) – 0.26 V (c) 0.26 V (d) 0.3 V **NCERT Pg 38**

34 The reduction potential of hydrogen half-cell will be negative if **NCERT Pg 38**

(a) $p(H_2) = 1$ atm and $[H^+] = 2.0$ M
(b) $p(H_2) = 1$ atm and $[H^+] = 1.0$ M
(c) $p(H_2) = 2$ atm and $[H^+] = 1.0$ M
(d) $p(H_2) = 2$ atm and $[H^+] = 2.0$ M

35 In the cell, $Pt(s)|H_2(g, 1\text{ bar})|HCl(aq)||AgCl(s)|Ag(s)|Pt(s)$ the cell potential is 0.92 V when a 10^{-6} molal HCl solution is used. The standard electrode potential of $(AgCl/Ag, Cl^-)$ electrode is

$$\left\{\text{Given}, \frac{2.303RT}{F} = 0.06 \text{ V at } 298 \text{ K}\right\}$$ **NCERT Pg 38**

(a) 0.40 V (b) 0.20 V
(c) 0.94 V (d) 0.76 V

36 If the standard electrode potential for a cell is 2V at 300 K, the equilibrium constant (*K*) for the reaction,

$$Zn(s) + Cu^{2+}(aq) \rightleftharpoons Zn^{2+}(aq) + Cu(s)$$

at 300 K is approximately

$(R = 8\text{ JK}^{-1}\text{mol}^{-1}, F = 96000\text{ C mol}^{-1})$ **NCERT Pg 39**

(a) e^{-160} (b) e^{160} (c) e^{-80} (d) e^{320}

37 Given the equilibrium constant (K_C) of the reaction :

$$Cu(s) + 2Ag^+(aq) \longrightarrow Cu^{2+}(aq) + 2Ag(s)$$

is 10×10^{15}, calculate the E°_{cell} of this reaction at 298 K. $\left[2.303\frac{RT}{F} \text{ at } 298\text{ K} = 0.059 \text{ V}\right]$ **NCERT Pg 39**

(a) 0.472 V (b) 0.0472 mV
(c) 0.472 mV (d) 0.0472 V

38 Calculate the standard cell potential (in V) of the cell in which following reaction takes place

$$Fe^{2+}(aq) + Ag^+(aq) \longrightarrow Fe^{3+}(aq) + Ag(s)$$

Given that, $E^{\circ}_{Ag^+/Ag} = x$ V, $E^{\circ}_{Fe^{2+}/Fe} = y$ V

$E^{\circ}_{Fe^{3+}/Fe} = z$ V **NCERT Pg 40**

(a) $x + 2y - 3z$ (b) $x - y$
(c) $x + y - z$ (d) $x - z$

39 The Gibb's energy for the decomposition of Al_2O_3 at 500°C is as follows **NCERT Pg 40**

$$\frac{2}{3}Al_2O_3 \longrightarrow \frac{4}{3}Al + O_2;\ \Delta_rG = -960 \text{ kJ mol}^{-1}$$

The potential difference needed for the electrolytic reduction of aluminium oxide (Al_2O_3) at 500°C is atleast.

(a) 4.5V (b) 3.0V (c) 2.5V (d) 5.0V

40 The electrode potentials for

$Cu^{2+}(aq) + e^- \longrightarrow Cu^+(aq)$ and

$Cu^+(aq) + e^- \longrightarrow Cu(s)$ are +0.15V and + 0.50V respectively. The value of $E^{\circ}_{Cu^{2+}/Cu}$ will be **NCERT Pg 40**

(a) 0.150 V (b) 0.500 (c) 0.325 V (d) 0. 650 V

41 $M | M^{2+}$ (saturated solution of a sparingly soluble salt, MX_2) $|| M^{2+}$ (0.00001 mol dm^{-3}) | M.

The emf of the given electrochemical cell at 298 K is 0.0591 V.

The value of ΔG (kJ mol^{-1}) for the given cell is (take 1F = 96500 C mol^{-1}) **NCERT Pg 40**

(a) –5.7 (b) 5.7 (c) 11.4 (d) –11.4

42 In the given reaction, **NCERT Pg 40**

$$2Cu^+(aq) \longrightarrow 3Cu^{2+}(aq) + Cu(s)$$

$E^{\circ}_{Cu^+/Cu} = 0.6$ V and $E^{\circ}_{Cu^{2+}/Cu^+} = 0.41$ V

The equilibrium constant for this reaction will be

(a) $10^{6.44}$ (b) $10^{8.44}$
(c) $10^{7.44}$ (d) $10^{5.44}$

43 $E^{\circ}_{cell} = 1.1$ V for Daniell cell. Which of the following expressions is correct description of state of equilibrium in this cell? **NCERT Pg 40**

(a) $1.1 = K_C$ (b) $\log K_C = \frac{2.2}{0.059}$
(c) $\log K_C = \frac{3.4}{0.059}$ (d) $\log K_C = 1.1$

44 For a Ag-Zn button cell, net reaction is

$Zn(s) + Ag_2O(s) \longrightarrow ZnO(s) + 2Ag(s)$

$\Delta_fG^{\circ}(Ag_2O) = -11.21$ kJ mol^{-1}

$\Delta_fG^{\circ}(ZnO) = -318.3$ kJ mol^{-1}

Then, E°_{cell} of the button cell is **NCERT Pg 40**

(a) 3.182 V (b) –1.621 V
(c) 1.591 V (d) –1.591 V

45 ΔG° for the reaction, $Cu^{2+} + Fe \longrightarrow Fe^{2+} + Cu$ is

[Given : $E^{\circ}_{Cu^{2+}/Cu} = +0.34$, $E^{\circ}_{Fe^{2+}/Fe} = -0.44$ V]

(a) –151540 J (b) –150540 J
(c) –180545 J (d) –302150 J

Conductance of Electrolytic Solutions

46 Select the incorrect statement. **NCERT Pg 41**

(a) SI units of resistance is kg m^2/S^{3}A^2.
(b) Wheatstone bridge is used to measure unknown resistance.
(c) Conductivity meter can directly read the conductance or resistance of solution.
(d) Inverse of resistance is called specific conductance.

47 Electrical conductance through metals is called metallic or electronic conductance and is due to the movement of electrons. The electronic conductance does not depends on **NCERT Pg 42**
(a) the nature and structure of the metal
(b) the number of valence electrons per atom
(c) change in temperature
(d) change in composition

48 Which of the following statements is correct? **NCERT Pg 42, 43**
(a) Electrolytic conductance decreases but electrical conductance increases with increase in temperature.
(b) Electrolytic conductance increases but electrical conductance decreases with increase in temperature.
(c) Electrolytic as well as electrical conductance decrease with rise in temperature.
(d) Electrolytic as well as electrical conductance increase with rise in temperature.

49 What happen to the composition of metallic conductor when electron enters at one end and go out through other end? **NCERT Pg 43**
(a) There will be change in metallic conductor.
(b) Metallic conductor remains unchanged.
(c) There will be change on metallic conductor only in the presence of applied pressure.
(d) Metallic conductor will behave as insulator.

50 Select the correct statement about ionic conductance.
I. It is the conductance of electricity by ions present in the solutions.
II. It depends on nature of solvent, its viscosity and concentration of electrolyte.
III. It depends upon the size of ions produced and solvation.
IV. It depends on the viscosity of solvent.
V. It increases with increase in the temperature.

Choose the correct option. **NCERT Pg 43**
(a) I, III and V (b) I, II, III, IV and V
(c) III, IV and V (d) I, II, III and IV

51 Alternating current (AC) is used instead of direct current (DC) for the measurement of conductivity of ionic solutions. This is because **NCERT Pg 43**
(a) alternating current changes the composition of the solution
(b) direct current changes the composition of the solution
(c) direct current is more powerful
(d) direct current changes the charges on the ions in the solution

52 Conductivity of an electrolytic solution depends on **NCERT Pg 43**
(a) surface area of electrode
(b) concentration of electrolyte
(c) power of AC source
(d) distance between the electrodes

53 Which of the following statement is correct regarding the cell constant? **NCERT Pg 44**
(a) It is the ratio of distance between the electrodes and their area of cross-section.
(b) Its SI unit is cm^{-1}.
(c) It is the measured directly from l and A.
(d) It is denoted by the symbol G.

54 KCl solution is generally used to determine the cell constant because **NCERT Pg 44**
(a) it is highly ionic in nature
(b) its conductivity is known accurately at various concentration and different temperatures
(c) size of cations and anions are comparable
(d) charge on both the ions are same

55 The resistance of the cell containing KCl solution at 23°C was found to be 55 Ω. Its cell constant is 0.616 cm^{-1}. The conductivity of KCl solution ($\Omega^{-1}\ cm^{-1}$) is **NCERT Pg 44**
(a) 1.21×10^{-3} (b) 1.12×10^{-2}
(c) 1.12×10^{-3} (d) 1.21×10^{-2}

56 Resistance of 0.2 M solution of an electrolyte is 50 Ω. The specific conductance of the solution is 1.3 Sm^{-1}. If resistance of the 0.4 M solution of the same electrolyte is 260 Ω, its molar conductivity is **NCERT Pg 44, 45**
(a) 6250 S m^2 mol^{-1}
(b) 6.25×10^{-4} S m^2 mol^{-1}
(c) 625×10^{-4} S m^2 mol^{-1}
(d) 62.5 S m^2 mol^{-1}

57 If resistance of a conductivity cell filled with 0.1 mol L^{-1} KCl solution is 100 Ω. The resistance of the same cell when filled with 0.02 mol L^{-1} KCl solution is 520 Ω. Then the conductivity of 0.02 mol L^{-1} KCl solution will be

(Given the conductivity of 0.1 mol L^{-1} KCl solution is 1.29 S/m.) **NCERT Pg 45**
(a) 0.248 S cm^{-1} (b) 0.248 S m^{-1}
(c) 2.48 S cm^{-1} (d) 2.48 S m^{-1}

58 The specific conductivity of $N/10$ KCl solution is 0.0212 ohm^{-1} cm^{-1} and the resistance of cell containing this solution is 55 ohm. The cell constant is **NCERT Pg 44**
(a) 3.324 cm^{-1} (b) 2.173 cm^{-1}
(c) 1.166 cm^{-1} (d) 4.616 cm^{-1}

59 The molar conductivity is minimum for the solution of concentration. NCERT Pg 45

(a) 0.004 M (b) 0.002 M (c) 0.005 M (d) 0.001 M

60 Specific conductance of 0.2 M NaCl solution is 1.01×10^{-2} ohm^{-1} cm^{-1}. Its molar conductance in ohm^{-1} cm^2 mol^{-1}. NCERT Pg 45

(a) 1.01×10^2 (b) 1.01×10^3

(c) 1.01×10^4 (d) 50.5

61 Which of the following statements is not true for molar conductivity? NCERT Pg 45, 47

(a) When concentration approaches to infinity, the molar conductivity is known as limiting molar conductivity.

(b) $\Lambda_m (S\,m^2\,mol^{-1}) = \dfrac{\kappa\ (S\ m^{-1})}{1000\ L\ m^{-3} \times \text{Molarity}\ (mol\ L^{-1})}$

(c) $\Lambda_m\ (S\,cm^2\,mol^{-1}) = \dfrac{\kappa (S\,cm^{-1}) \times 1000\ (cm^3/L)}{\text{Molarity}\ (mol\ L^{-1})}$

(d) $\Lambda_m = \dfrac{\kappa A}{l}$

62 Select the correct statement. NCERT Pg 46, 47

(a) Conductivity decreases but molar conductivity increases with increase in dilution.

(b) Conductivity increases but molar conductivity decreases with increase in dilution.

(c) Conductivity decreases but molar conductivity increases with increase in concentration .

(d) Conductivity as well as molar conductivity decrease with decrease in concentration.

63 The graph of molar conductivity *versus* $C^{1/2}$ is plotted. Which type of electrolyte are used in *A* and *B* ? NCERT Pg 47

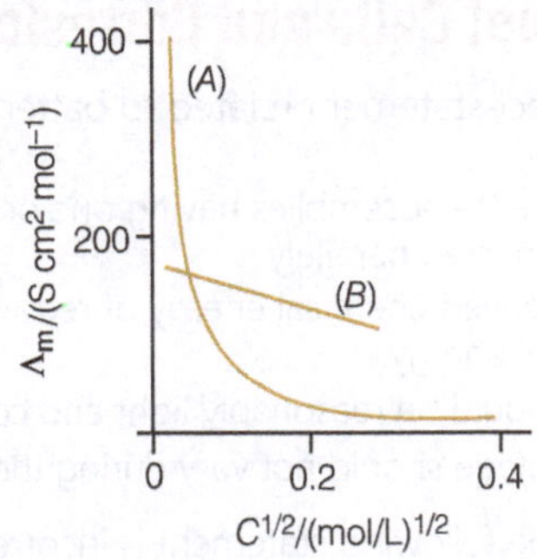

	A	*B*
(a)	Weak electrolyte	Strong electrolyte
(b)	Strong electrolyte	Weak electrolyte
(c)	Weak electrolyte	Weak electrolyte
(d)	Strong electrolyte	Strong electrolyte

64 Limiting molar conductivity of which ion in water is least at 298 K? NCERT Pg 49

(a) Na^+ (b) K^+ (c) Ca^{2+} (d) Mg^{2+}

65 If molar conductivity of Ca^{2+} and Cl^- ions are 119 S cm^2 mol^{-1} and 71 S $cm^2 mol^{-1}$ respectively, then the molar conductivity of $CaCl_2$ at infinite dilution is

(a) 215 S cm^2 mol^{-1} (b) 340 S cm^2 mol^{-1} NCERT Pg 49

(c) 126 S cm^2 mol^{-1} (d) 261 S cm^2 mol^{-1}

66 At 25°C, the molar conductance at infinite dilution for the strong electrolytes NaOH, NaCl and $BaCl_2$ are 248×10^{-4}, 126×10^{-4} and 280×10^{-4} Sm^2mol^{-1} respectively. $\lambda^\circ_m Ba(OH)_2$ in S m^2mol^{-1} is NCERT Pg 49

(a) 362×10^{-4} (b) 402×10^{-4} (c) 524×10^{-4} (d) 568×10^{-4}

67 Molar conductivity of 0.025 mol L^{-1} methanoic acid is 46.1 S cm^2mol^{-1}, the dissociation constant will be (Given : $\lambda^\circ_{H^+}$ =349.6 S cm^2mol^{-1}, and $\lambda^\circ_{HCOO^-}$=54.6 S cm^2mol^{-1}) NCERT Pg 50

(a) 3.67×10^{-4} mol L^{-1} (b) 1.83×10^{-4} mol L^{-1}

(c) 4.25×10^{-4} mol L^{-1} (d) 3.67×10^{-6} mol L^{-1}

68 Which of the following statement incorrect about the application of Kohlrausch law? NCERT Pg 50

(a) The molar conductivity of weak electrolytes at infinite dilution can be calculated.

(b) It is helpful in calculating of degree of dissociation of weak electrolyte.

(c) Solubility of the sparingly soluble salt can be calculated.

(d) λ°_m for any electrolyte can be calculated from the $\lambda°$ of individual ion.

Electrolytic Cell and Electrolysis

69 Which of the following statements is incorrect for electrolytic cell? NCERT Pg 51

(a) External source of voltage is applied to carry the chemical reaction.

(b) These cells are mainly used in laboratory and chemical industry.

(c) Simplest electrolytic cell consists of two copper strips dipped in an aqueous solution of $CuSO_4$.

(d) Galvanic or voltaic cell is a common example of this type of cell.

70 In order to obtain pure copper from impure copper by electrolysis. NCERT Pg 51

I. Anode is made from impure copper.

II. Copper is oxidised at anode and deposited at cathode.

III. A solution of copper sulphate is used as electrolyte.

IV. Cathode is made from impure copper.

V. Copper is oxidised at cathode and deposited at anode.

Choose the correct option.

(a) I and II (b) III, IV and V

(b) IV and V (d) I, II and III

71 An electrolytic cell contains alumina. If we have to obtain 50 g Al by using 105 A of current, the time required is **NCERT Pg 51**
(a) 1.54 hr (b) 2.15 hr (c) 1.42 hr (d) 1.32 hr

72 1.5 A current is flowing through a metallic wire. If it flows for 3 hrs, the number of electrons would flow through the wire is **NCERT Pg 52**
(a) 2.05×10^{22} electrons (b) 1.0×10^{23} electrons
(c) 10^{24} electrons (d) 4.5×10^{23} electrons

73 How many Coulombs are required in order to reduce 12.3 g of nitrobenzene to aniline? **NCERT Pg 52**
(a) 579 C (b) 5790 C
(c) 57900 C (d) 579000 C

74 The time required to deposit 2×10^{-3} cm thick layer of silver (density 1.05 g cm^{-3}) on the surface of area 100 cm^2 by passing a current of 10 A through silver nitrate solution will be **NCERT Pg 52**
(a) 125 s (b) 115 s (c) 18.8 s (d) 27.25 s

75 A 4.0 M aqueous solution of NaCl is prepared and 500 mL of this solution is electrolysed. This leads to evolution of chlorine gas at one of the electrodes. The total charge required for the complete electrolysis will be
(a) 96500 C (b) 24125 C **NCERT Pg 52**
(c) 48250 C (d) 193000 C

76 2F of electricity is passed through a solution of $CuSO_4$. The mass of copper deposited at the cathode is (atomic mass of Cu = 63.5 u) **NCERT Pg 52**
(a) 0 g (b) 63.5 g (c) 2 g (d) 127 g

77 6 A current with 75% efficiency is passed through a cell for 6 h? ($Z = 4 \times 10^{-4}$). The amount of metal deposited will be **NCERT Pg 51, 52**
(a) 22.4 g (b) 36.0 g (c) 32.4 g (d) 38.9 g

78 What will be the weight of silver deposited, if 96.5 A of current is passed into aqueous solution of $AgNO_3$ for 100 s? **NCERT Pg 52**
(a) 1.08 g (b) 10.8 g (c) 108 g (d) 1080 g

79 10 F of electricity is passed through the solutions of silver nitrate, copper sulphate and ferric chloride. The amount of metal deposited at cathode in each case respectively are **NCERT Pg 51, 52**
(a) Ag = 1080 g Cu = 3175 g Fe = 186.7 g
(b) Ag = 108 g Cu = 31.75 g Fe = 18.67 g
(c) Ag = 1080 g Cu = 317. 5 g Fe = 186.7 g
(d) Ag = 10.8 g Cu = 317.5 g Fe = 186.7 g

80 The incorrect statement among the following is **NCERT Pg 52**
(a) Charge required for the oxidation or reduction of a substance depends upon the stoichiometry of the electrode reaction.
(b) 2 moles of electrons are required for the reduction of 1mole of calcium ion.
(c) 50,000 A current is equal to 0.518 F per second.
(d) Charge required for reducing 1 mole of MnO_4^- into Mn^{2+} is 2F.

81 When aqueous sodium chloride solution is electrolysed
(a) H^+ is reduced at cathode instead of Na^+. **NCERT Pg 53**
(b) Na^+ is reduced to Na at cathode and H^+ is reduced to H_2.
(c) Cl^- is oxidised into Cl_2 at cathode.
(d) Na^+ is reduced to Na at cathode and Cl^- is oxidised into Cl_2.

82 What will happen during the electrolysis of aqueous solution of $CuSO_4$ by using platinum electrodes?
(a) Copper will deposit at cathode **NCERT Pg 53**
(b) Copper will deposit at anode
(c) SO_2 will be released at anode
(d) Copper will dissolve at anode

83 For the given cell, $Mg|Mg^{2+}||Cu^{2+}|Cu$, which of the following is correct? **NCERT Pg 53**
(a) Mg is cathode.
(b) Cu is anode.
(c) The cell reaction is $Mg + Cu^{2+} \longrightarrow Mg^{2+} + Cu$
(d) Cu is not the oxidising agent.

Batteries, Fuel Cells and Corrosion

84 The incorrect statement related to batteries is **NCERT Pg 54**
(a) these are the assemblies having one or more than one cell connected parallely.
(b) these convert chemical energy of redox reaction into electrical energy.
(c) these should be reasonably light and compact.
(d) their voltage should not vary during the use.

85 Which of the following statement is incorrect for dry cell?
(a) Reaction at cathode **NCERT Pg 54**
$$MnO_2 + NH_4^+ + e^- \longrightarrow MnO(OH) + NH_3$$
(b) Manganese is reduced from +5 to +4 oxidation state.
(c) Cell potential is 1.5 V.
(d) Ammonia form complex with Zn^{2+} to give $[Zn(NH_3)_4]^{2+}$.

86 The correct statement about mercury cell is

(a) It is used in high current devices. **NCERT Pg 54, 55**

(b) Zn-Hg amalgam acts as cathode and a paste of C + HgO as anode.

(c) The cell potential remains constant.

(d) The cell potential is approximately 1.5 V.

87 What is the anode and cathode in the cell given in the figure? **NCERT Pg 54**

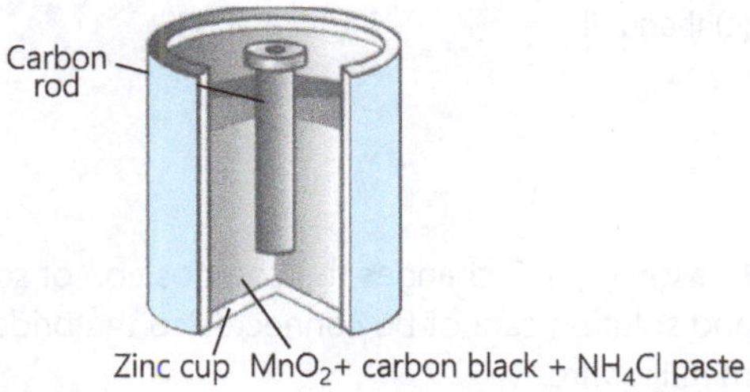

	Anode	Cathode
(a)	Zinc cup	Carbon rod
(b)	Carbon rod	Zinc cup
(c)	Carbon black	Carbon cup
(d)	Zinc cup	MnO_2

88 In the given mercury cell, **NCERT Pg 54**

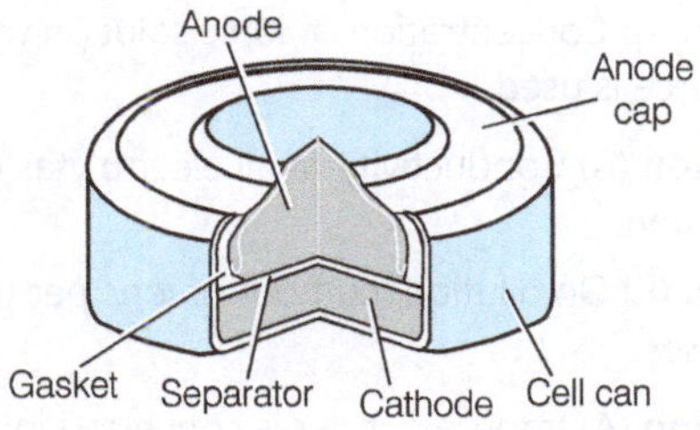

the reaction occurring at cathode will be

(a) $Zn(Hg) + 2OH^- \longrightarrow ZnO(s) + H_2O + 2e^-$

(b) $HgO + H_2O + 2e^- \longrightarrow Hg(l) + 2OH^-$

(c) $Zn + 2OH^- \longrightarrow ZnO(s) + H_2O + 2e^-$

(d) $Zn(Hg) + HgO(s) \longrightarrow ZnO(s) + Hg(l)$

89 The incorrect statement about lead storage battery is **NCERT Pg 55**

(a) it is used in high current devices like invertors

(b) here lead acts as anode and lead packed with lead dioxide acts as cathode

(c) during discharging, Pb and PbO_2, both form $PbSO_4$

(d) during charging PbO_2 is formed at anode

90 Which of the following statements/ reactions is correct regarding the lead storage battery? **NCERT Pg 55**

(a) Cathode reaction

$$Pb(s) + SO_4^{2-}(aq) \longrightarrow PbSO_4(s) + 2e^-$$

(b) Anode reaction

$$PbO_2(s) + SO_4^{2-}(aq) + 4H^+(aq) + 2e^- \longrightarrow PbSO_4(s) + 2H_2O(l)$$

(c) On charging the battery $PbSO_4$ give Pb at anode and PbO_2 at cathode.

(d) A 48% solution of sulphuric acid is used as an electrolyte.

91 In the following figure of lead-storage battery, I; II and the electrolyte represents. **NCERT Pg 55**

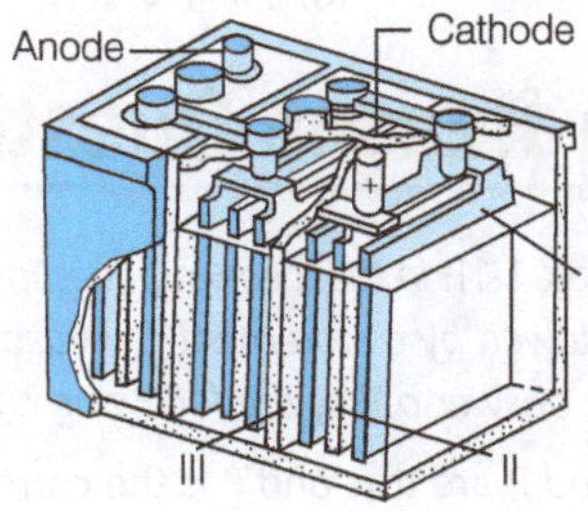

	I	II	Electrolyte
(a)	Positive plates; Spongy lead	PbO_2; Negative plates	50% H_2SO_4 solution
(b)	Negative plates; Spongy lead	PbO_2; Positive plates	38% H_2SO_4 solution
(c)	PbO_2; Positive plates	Spongy lead; Negative plates	50% H_2SO_4 solution
(d)	PbO_2; Negative plates	Spongy lead; Positive plates	38% H_2SO_4 solution

92 The anodic half-cell of lead-acid battery is recharged using electricity of 0.05 Faraday. The amount of $PbSO_4$ electrolysed in g during the process is (Molar mass of $PbSO_4 = 303 g mol^{-1}$) **NCERT Pg 52, 55**

(a) 11.4 (b) 7.6

(c) 15.2 (d) 22.8

93 Mark the incorrect statement for fuel cells. **NCERT Pg 56**

(a) It is used in Apollo space programme and for drinking water supply for astronauts.

(b) Hydrogen and oxygen are bubbled through porous carbon electrodes.

(c) Catalyst like finely divided Pt or Pd are incorporated into electrodes.

(d) Anode reaction is $O_2 + 2H_2O(l) + 4e^- \longrightarrow 4OH^-(aq)$

94 Galvanisation is **NCERT Pg 57**

(a) zinc plating on aluminium sheet

(b) zinc plating on iron sheet

(c) iron plating on zinc sheet

(d) aluminium plating on zinc sheet

95 Which of the following reactions regarding rusting of iron is correct? **NCERT Pg 57**

I. $Fe(s) \longrightarrow Fe^{2+}(aq) + 2e^-$ (at anode)

II. $O_2(g) + 4H^+(aq) + 4e^- \longrightarrow 2H_2O(l)$ (at cathode)

III. $2Fe + O_2 + 4H^+ \longrightarrow 2Fe^{2+} + 2H_2O$

IV. $Fe_2O_3(s) + xH_2O\,(l) \longrightarrow Fe_2O_3 \cdot xH_2O$

Choose the correct answer from the options given below.

(a) Only I (b) I and II
(c) I, II and III (d) I, II, III and IV

96 Which of the following statement are correct? **NCERT Pg 57**

I. Rusting of iron and tarnishing of silver surface are the examples of corrosion.

II. Covering the surface of iron by *bis*-phenol protect iron from rusting.

III. Sn and Zn are used to protect iron from rusting.

Choose the correct answer from the options given below.

(a) I and II (b) I and III
(c) II and III (d) I, II and III

Assertion-Reason Questions

Directions (Q.Nos. 1-11) *In the following questions a statement of Assertion (A) followed by a statement of Reason (R) is given. Choose the correct answer out of the following choices.*

(a) Both A and R are true and R is the correct explanation of A.
(b) Both A and R are true but R is not the correct explanation of A.
(c) A is true but R is false.
(d) A is false but R is true.

1 Assertion (A) For a Daniell cell $Zn|Zn^{2+}||Cu^{2+}|Cu$ with $E_{cell} = 1.1$ V, the application of opposite potential greater than 1.1 V results into the flow of electrons from anode to cathode.

Reason (R) Zn is deposited at zinc electrode and Cu is dissolved at copper electrode. **NCERT Pg 32**

2 Assertion (A) Cu does not dissolve in HCl but dissolves in HNO_3.

Reason (R) In nitric acid Cu is oxidised by nitrate ion not by hydrogen ion. **NCERT Pg 35**

3 Assertion (A) Copper sulphate solution cannot be stored in zinc pot. **NCERT Pg 36**

Reason (R) Zinc is more reactive than copper so it displaces copper from copper sulphate solution.

4 Assertion (A) Conductivity of pure water is very low, i.e. 3.5×10^{-5} Sm^{-1}.

Reason (R) High amounts of hydrogen and hydroxyl ions are present in pure water. **NCERT Pg 43**

5 Assertion (A) DC cannot be used during measurement of resistance of an ionic solution.

Reason (R) DC changes the composition of solution and solution cannot be connected to the bridge like metallic wire. **NCERT Pg 43**

6 Assertion (A) $E_{Ag^+/Ag}$ increases with increase in concentration of Ag^+ ions.

Reason (R) $E_{Ag^+/Ag}$ has a positive value. **NCERT Pg 38**

7 Assertion (A) For measuring resistance of an ionic solution, an AC source is used.

Reason (R) Concentration of ionic solution will change if DC source is used. **NCERT Pg 43**

8 Assertion (A) Conductivity of all electrolytes decreases on dilution.

Reason (R) On dilution, number of ions per unit volume decreases. **NCERT Pg 47**

9 Assertion (A) Impure copper is converted into pure copper by electrolysis.

Reason (R) Copper is dissolved at cathode and deposited at anode. **NCERT Pg 51**

10 Assertion (A) A solution of $Ni(NO_3)_2$ is electrolysed between platinum electrodes using current of 5 A for 20 minute. The weight of Ni deposited is 1.825 g. **NCERT Pg 51**

Reason (R) The mass of substance deposited during the electrolysis of an electrolyte is inversely proportional to the quantity of electricity passed through the electrolyte.

11 Assertion (A) Now-a-days H_2-O_2 fuel cell is used over the ordinary cell.

Reason (R) They do not cause any pollution and its efficiency is 60-70%. **NCERT Pg 56**

Statement Type Questions

Direction (Q. Nos. 1-6) *In the following questions, two statements (I & II) are given. In the light of the given statements, choose the correct option given below.*

(a) Both Statement I and Statement II are false.
(b) Statement I is true but Statement II is false.
(c) Statement I is false but Statement II is true.
(d) Both Statement I and Statement II are true.

1 Statement I In standard hydrogen electrode, the pressure of H_2 gas is 10 bar and the concentration of hydrogen ion is 1 M.

Statement II In standard hydrogen electrode, the concentration of both the reduced and oxidised forms of hydrogen is maintained at unity. **NCERT Pg 35**

2 Statement I Copper liberates hydrogen from a dilute solution of hydrochloric acid.

Statement II Hydrogen is present above copper in the electrochemical series. **NCERT Pg 35, 37**

3 Statement I For the following given reactions, $\Delta G°$ and equilibrium constant (K) are quite different.

(i) $CrO_4^{2-} + 4H_2O + 3e^- \longrightarrow Cr(OH)_3 + 5OH^-$; $E_1 = -0.11$ V

(ii) $[Cu(NH_3)_2]^+ + e^- \longrightarrow Cu^+ + 2NH_3; E_2 = -0.10$ V

Statement II $\Delta G°$ and k are independent of standard, electrode potential. **NCERT Pg 40**

4 Statement I Conductivity always increases with decrease in the concentration of electrolyte.

Statement II Molar conductivity always increases with decrease in the concentration of electrolyte. **NCERT Pg 46, 47**

5 Statement I Na and Mg metals are produced by the electrolysis of their fused chlorides.

Statement II Aluminium is produced by electrolysis of aluminium oxide in presence of cryolite. **NCERT Pg 51**

6 Statement I The cell potential of mercury cell is 1.35 V which remains constant during its life.

Statement II In mercury cell, the electrolyte is a paste of KOH and ZnO. **NCERT Pg 54, 55**

7 Which of the following statement is/are incorrect?

I. For strong electrolytes, λ_m increases slowly with dilution. **NCERT Pg 35, 36, 47, 55**
II. In lead storage battery, during discharging phase, sulphuric acid is formed as byproduct in overall cell reaction.
III. As the electrode potential values decrease oxidising power decreases.
IV. Zn gives hydrogen with H_2SO_4 and HCl.
V. NaCl shows a straight line in the plot of Λ_m vs $\sqrt{C}$.

Choose the correct answer from the options given below.

(a) I, III and IV (b) I and II (c) II and V (d) Only II

8 Which of the following statements are correct?

I. In dry cell, a moist paste of NH_4Cl and $ZnCl_2$ is present in between the electrodes. **NCERT Pg 41, 47, 54**
II. Ammonia gas is produced in Leclanche cell.
III. A paste of KOH and ZnO is used as electrolyte in mercury cell.
IV. NaCl, $CaCl_2$, $MgSO_4$ are known as 1-1, 1-2, and 2-2 type electrolytes respectively.
V. Conductance is directly proportional to resistance.

Choose the correct answer from the options given below.

(a) I and V (b) I and III
(c) II and IV (d) I, II, III and IV

9 Select the incorrect statements from the following.

I. E_{cell} is temperature independent.
II. If the system is at equilibrium no net reaction occurs.
III. A reaction occurs from right to left if $E_{cell} < 0$.
IV. A reaction is spontaneous from left to right if $E_{cell} > 0$.
V. The half-cell of standard hydrogen electrode is represented by $Pt(s) | H_2(g) | H^+(g)$.

Choose the correct answer from the options given below. **NCERT Pg 33, 35, 38**

(a) I and V (b) II, III and V
(c) I, II and V (d) III and IV

10 Select the correct statements from the following.

I. The molar conductivity at infinite dilution of an electrolyte can be represented as the sum of individual ions (cations and anions) of the electrolyte.
II. The change in Λ_m with dilution is due to increase in the degree of dissociation
III. Degree of dissociation can be obtained by the ratio of molar conductivity Λ_m to the limiting molar conductivity at any concentration C.
IV. Λ_m° can be obtained by extrapolation of Λ_m to zero concentration for weak electrolyte.
V. Kohlrausch law is only applicable for calculation of limiting molar conductivity of weak electrolyte.

Choose the correct answer from the options given below. **NCERT Pg 46, 47, 49**

(a) I, II and III (b) II, III and V
(c) II and V (d) I, II, III and IV

Matching Type Questions

1 Match the following Column I (expressions) with Column II (terms) and choose the correct option from the codes given below. **NCERT Pg 41**

Column I (Expressions)	Column II (Terms)
A. $\rho l / A$	1. Conductivity
B. $1/R$	2. Conductance
C. RA/l	3. Resistance
D. $1/\rho$	4. Resistivity

Codes

	A	B	C	D		A	B	C	D
(a)	3	4	2	1	(b)	3	2	4	1
(c)	4	3	1	2	(d)	4	1	3	2

2 Match the physical quantities given in Column I with their units given in Column II and choose the correct options from the codes given below. **NCERT Pg 41**

Column I (Physical quantities)	Column II (Unit)
A. Resistance	1. Ω
B. Resistivity	2. $S\ m^2\ mol^{-1}$
C. Molar conductivity	3. Ωm
D. Specific conductance	4. $\Omega^{-1} m^{-1}$

Codes

	A	B	C	D		A	B	C	D
(a)	4	2	1	3	(b)	2	3	1	4
(c)	1	3	2	4	(d)	3	2	1	4

3 Match the items of Column I and Column II on the basis of data given below.

$$E^\circ_{F_2/F^-} = 2.87\ V, E^\circ_{Li^+/Li} = -3.05\ V,$$
$$E^\circ_{Au^{3+}/Au} = 1.4\ V, E^\circ_{Br_2/Br^-} = 1.09\ V$$

Column I	Column II
A. F_2	1. Metal is the strongest reducing agent.
B. Li	2. Metal ion which is the weakest oxidising agent.
C. Au^{3+}	3. Non-metal which is the best oxidising agent.
D. Br^-	4. Unreactive metal.
E. Au	5. Anion that can be oxidised by Au^{3+}.
F. Li^+	6. Anion which is the weakest reducing agent.
G. F^-	7. Metal ion which is an oxidising agent.

Codes

	A	B	C	D	E	F	G
(a)	3	1	5	7	2	4	6
(b)	3	1	7	5	4	2	6
(c)	3	1	5	7	4	6	2
(d)	1	3	5	7	4	2	6

4 Match the terms given in Column I with the items given in Column II.

Column I	Column II
A. Λ_m	1. Intensive property
B. E°_{cell}	2. Depends on number of ions/volume
C. κ	3. Extensive property
D. $\Delta_r G_{cell}$	4. Increases with dilution

Codes

	A	B	C	D
(a)	1	4	3	2
(b)	1	4	2	3
(c)	4	1	3	2
(d)	4	1	2	3

5 Match the items of Column I and Column II.

Column I	Column II
A. κ	1. $I \times t$
B. Λ_m	2. $\Lambda_m / \Lambda^\circ_m$
C. α	3. κ / C
D. Q	4. G^* / R

Codes

	A	B	C	D		A	B	C	D
(a)	4	3	2	1	(b)	1	3	2	4
(c)	3	2	1	4	(d)	2	4	3	1

6 Match the items of Column I and Column II.

Column I	Column II
A. Lead storage battery	1. Maximum efficiency
B. Mercury cell	2. Prevented by galvanisation
C. Fuel cell	3. Gives steady potential
D. Rusting	4. Pb is anode, PbO_2 is cathode

Codes

	A	B	C	D		A	B	C	D
(a)	2	4	3	1	(b)	4	3	1	2
(c)	3	1	2	4	(d)	1	2	3	4

Numerical Value Questions

1 Consider the following cell reaction.

$2Fe(s) + O_2(g) + 4H^+(aq) \longrightarrow 2Fe^{2+}(aq) + 2H_2O(l)$; $E° = 1.67$ V

At $[Fe^{2+}] = 10^{-3}$M, $p(O_2) = 0.1$ atm and pH = 3, the cell potential at 25°C is .... $\times 10^{-3}$ V. NCERT Pg 38

2 Consider the cell

$Pt(s)|H_2(g, 1 \text{ atm})|H^+(aq, 1\text{ M})||Fe^{3+}(aq)|Fe^{2+}(aq)|Pt(s)$

When the potential of the cell is 0.712 V at 298 K, the ratio $[Fe^{2+}]/[Fe^{3+}]$ is .... (Nearest integer)

[Given : $Fe^{3+} + e^- \rightleftharpoons Fe^{2+}$, $E^\circ_{Fe^{3+}|Fe^{2+}/Pt} = 0.771$ V, $\frac{2.303\,RT}{F} = 0.059$ V] NCERT Pg 38

3 For the given reactions, $Sn^{2+} + 2e^- \longrightarrow Sn$

$Sn^{4+} + 4e^- \longrightarrow Sn$

The electrode potentials are $E^\circ_{Sn^{2+}/Sn} = -0.140$ V and $E^\circ_{Sn^{4+}/Sn} = 0.010$ V. The magnitude of standard electrode potential for Sn^{4+}/Sn^{2+}, i.e. $E^\circ_{Sn^{4+}/Sn^{2+}}$ is ...... $\times 10^{-2}$ V. (Nearest integer) NCERT Pg 40

4 The limiting molar conductivities of NaI, $NaNO_3$ and $AgNO_3$ are 12.7, 12.0 and 13.3 mS m^2mol^{-1}, respectively (all at 25°C).

The limiting molar conductivity of AgI at this temperature is ...... mS m^2 mol^{-1}. NCERT Pg 49

5 The specific conductance of 0.0025 M acetic acid is 5×10^{-5} S cm^{-1} at a certain temperature. The dissociation constant of acetic acid is .... $\times 10^{-7}$. (Nearest integer)

[Consider limiting molar conductivity of CH_3COOH as 400 S cm^2 mol^{-1}]. NCERT Pg 50

6 For a cell, $Cu(s)|Cu^{2+}(0.001\text{ M})||Ag^+(0.01\text{ M})|Ag(s)$ the cell potential is found to be 0.43 V at 298 K. The magnitude of standard potential for Cu^{2+}/Cu is .... $\times 10^{-2}$ V NCERT Pg 38

[Given: $E^\circ_{Ag^+/Ag} = 0.80$ V and $\frac{2.303\,RT}{F} = 0.06$ V]

NCERT Exemplar's Questions

1 Which cell will measure standard electrode potential of copper electrode?

(a) Pt (s) | H_2 (g, 0.1 bar) | H^+(aq., 1 M) || Cu^{2+}(aq, 1 M) | Cu

(b) Pt (s) | H_2 (g, 1 bar) | H^+(aq, 1 M) || Cu^{2+}(aq, 2 M) | Cu

(c) Pt (s) | H_2 (g, 1 bar) | H^+(aq, 1 M) || Cu^{2+}(aq, 1 M) | Cu

(d) Pt (s) | H_2 (g,0.1bar) | H^+(aq,0.1M) || Cu^{2+}(aq,1M) | Cu

2 Which of the following statements is not correct about an inert electrode in a cell?

(a) It does not participate in the cell reaction.

(b) It provides surface either for oxidation or for reduction reaction.

(c) It provides surface for conduction of electrons

(d) It provides surface for redox reaction.

3 Electrode potential for Mg electrode varies according to the equation,

$$E_{Mg^{2+}/Mg} = E^\ominus_{Mg^{2+}/Mg} - \frac{0.059}{2}\log\frac{1}{[Mg^{2+}]}.$$

The graph of $E_{Mg^{2+}/Mg}$ vs log $[Mg^{2+}]$ is

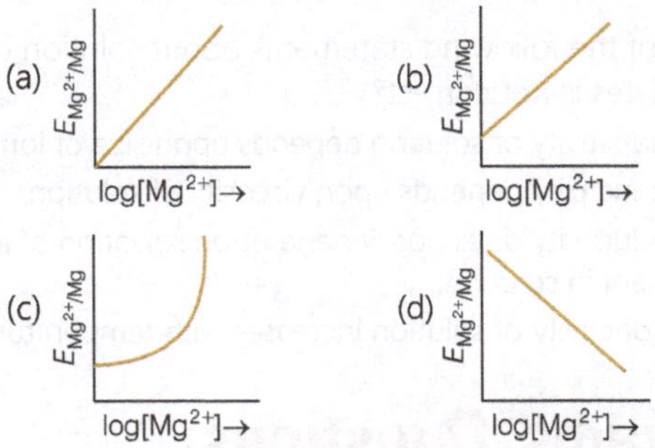

4 Which of the following statement is correct?

(a) E_{cell} and Δ_rG of cell reaction both are extensive properties.

(b) E_{cell} and Δ_rG of cell reaction both are intensive properties

(c) E_{cell} is an intensive property while Δ_rG of cell reaction is an extensive property.

(d) E_{cell} is an extensive property while Δ_rG of cell reaction is an intensive property.

5 Using the data given below, find out the strongest reducing agent.

$E^{\circ}_{Cr_2O_7^{2-}/Cr^{3+}} = 1.33\ V$; $E^{\circ}_{Cl_2/Cl^-} = 1.36V$

$E^{\circ}_{MnO_4^-/Mn^{2+}} = 1.51V$; $E^{\circ}_{Cr^{3+}/Cr} = -0.74V$

(a) Cl^- (b) Cr (c) Cr^{3+} (d) Mn^{2+}

6 Using the data given in Q.5 find out in which option the order of reducing power is correct ?

(a) $Cr^{3+} < Cl^- < Mn^{2+} < Cr$

(b) $Mn^{2+} < Cl^- < Cr^{3+} < Cr$

(c) $Cr^{3+} < Cl^- < Cr_2O_7^{2-} < MnO_4^-$

(d) $Mn^{2+} < Cr^{3+} < Cl^- < Cr$

7 Use the data of Q. 5 and find out the most stable oxidised species.

(a) Cr^{3+} (b) MnO_4^- (c) $Cr_2O_7^{2-}$ (d) Mn^{2+}

8 Use the data given in Q. 5 and find out the most stable ion in its reduced form.

(a) Cl^- (b) Cr^{3+} (c) Cr (d) Mn^{2+}

9 Use the data given in Q. 5 and find out which of the following is the strongest oxidising agent?

(a) Cl^- (b) Mn^{2+} (c) MnO_4^- (d) Cr^{3+}

10 The cell constant of a conductivity cell ....

(a) changes with change of electrolyte.

(b) changes with change of concentration of electrolyte.

(c) changes with temperature of electrolyte.

(d) remains constant for a cell.

11 Which of the following statements about solution of electrolytes is not correct?

(a) Conductivity of solution depends upon size of ions.

(b) Conductivity depends upon viscosity of solution.

(c) Conductivity does not depend upon solvation of ions present in solution.

(d) Conductivity of solution increases with temperature.

12 $\Lambda^{\circ}_{m\,(NH_4OH)}$ is equal to ....

(a) $\Lambda^{\circ}_{m\,(NH_4OH)} + \Lambda^{\circ}_{m\,(NH_4Cl)} - \Lambda^{\circ}_{m\,(HCl)}$

(b) $\Lambda^{\circ}_{m\,(NH_4Cl)} + \Lambda^{\circ}_{m\,(NaOH)} - \Lambda^{\circ}_{m\,(NaCl)}$

(c) $\Lambda^{\circ}_{m\,(NH_4Cl)} + \Lambda^{\circ}_{m\,(NaCl)} - \Lambda^{\circ}_{m\,(NaOH)}$

(d) $\Lambda^{\circ}_{m\,(NaOH)} + \Lambda^{\circ}_{m\,(NaCl)} - \Lambda^{\circ}_{m\,(NH_4Cl)}$

13 The quantity of charge required to obtain one mole of aluminium from Al_2O_3 is

(a) 1 F (b) 6 F

(c) 3 F (d) 2 F

14 While charging the lead storage battery

(a) $PbSO_4$ anode is reduced to Pb.

(b) $PbSO_4$ cathode is reduced to Pb.

(c) $PbSO_4$ cathode is oxidised to Pb.

(d) $PbSO_4$ anode is oxidised to PbO_2.

15 The difference between the electrode potentials of two electrodes when no current is drawn through the cell is called........

(a) cell potential

(b) cell emf

(c) potential difference

(d) cell voltage

16 An electrochemical cell can behave like an electrolytic cell when ....

(a) $E_{cell} = 0$ (b) $E_{cell} > E_{ext}$

(c) $E_{ext} > E_{cell}$ (d) $E_{cell} = E_{ext}$

17 In the electrolysis of aqueous sodium chloride solution which of the half cell reaction will occur at anode?

(a) $Na^+(aq) + e^- \longrightarrow Na(s); E^{\ominus}_{cell} = -2.71\ V$

(b) $2H_2O(l) \longrightarrow O_2(g) + 4H^+(aq) + 4e^-; E^{\ominus}_{cell} - 1.23\ V$

(c) $H^+(aq) + e^- \longrightarrow \frac{1}{2}H_2(g); E_{cell} = 0.00\ V$

(d) $Cl^-(aq) \longrightarrow \frac{1}{2}Cl_2(g) + e^-; E^{\ominus}_{cell} = 1.36\ V$

Past Exams' Questions

NEET Archive

1. Mass in grams of copper deposited by passing 9.6487 A current through a voltmeter containing copper sulphate solution for 100 seconds is (Given : Molar mass of Cu : 63 mol^{-1}, 1 F = 96487 C) **NCERT Pg 52, NEET 2024**

(a) 3.15 g

(b) 0.315 g

(c) 31.5 g

(d) 0.0315

2. Match List I with List II. **NCERT Pg 52, NEET 2024**

	List I (Conversion)		List II (Number of Faraday required)
A.	1 mole of H_2O to O_2	I.	3F
B.	1 mole of MnO_4^- to Mn^{2+}	II.	2F
C.	1.5 mole of Ca from molten $CaCl_2$	III.	1F
D.	1 mole of FeO to Fe_2O_3	IV.	5F

Choose the correct answer from the options given below:
(a) A-II, B-IV, C-I, D-III (b) A-III, B-IV, C-I, D-II
(c) A-II, B-III, C-I, D-IV (d) A-III, B-IV, C-II, D-I

3. The conductivity of centimolar solution of KCl at 25°C is 0.0210 ohm^{-1} cm^{-1} and the resistance of the cell containing the solution at 25°C is 60 ohm. The value of cell constant is **NCERT Pg 44, NEET 2023**
(a) 3.28 cm^{-1} (b) 1.26 cm^{-1} (c) 3.34 cm^{-1} (d) 1.34 cm^{-1}

4. Given below are half-cell reactions
$MnO_4^- + 8H^+ + 5e^- \rightarrow Mn^{2+} + 4H_2O$, $E^\circ_{Mn^{2+}/MnO_4^-} = -1.510$ V
$\frac{1}{2}O_2 + 2H^+ + 2e^- \rightarrow H_2O$, $E^\circ_{O_2/H_2O} = +1.223$ V
Will the permanganate ion, MnO_4^- liberate O_2 from water in the presence of an acid?
(a) No, because $E^\circ_{cell} = -0.287$ V **NCERT Pg 34, 37, NEET 2022**
(b) Yes, because $E^\circ_{cell} = +2.733$ V
(c) No, because $E^\circ_{cell} = -2.733$ V
(d) Yes, because $E^\circ_{cell} = +0.287$ V

5. At 298 K, the standard electrode potentials of Cu^{2+}/Cu, Zn^{2+}/Zn, Fe^{2+}/Fe and Ag^+/Ag are 0.34 V, – 0.76 V, – 0.44 V and 0.80 V, respectively. On the basis of standard electrode potential, predict which of the following reaction can not occur? **NCERT Pg 36, NEET 2022**
(a) $CuSO_4(aq) + Fe(s) \longrightarrow FeSO_4(aq) + Cu(s)$
(b) $FeSO_4(aq) + Zn(s) \longrightarrow ZnSO_4(aq) + Fe(s)$
(c) $2CuSO_4(aq) + 2Ag(s) \longrightarrow 2Cu(s) + Ag_2SO_4(aq)$
(d) $CuSO_4(aq) + Zn(s) \longrightarrow ZnSO_4(aq) + Cu(s)$

6. Find the emf of the cell in which the following reaction takes place at 298 K
$Ni(s) + 2Ag^+(0.001\ M) \longrightarrow Ni^{2+}(0.001\ M) + 2Ag(s)$
(Given that, $E^\circ_{cell} = 1.05$ V, $\frac{2.303\,RT}{F} = 0.059$ at 298 K) **NCERT Pg 39, NEET 2022**
(a) 1.385 V (b) 0.9615 V (c) 1.05 V (d) 10.4115 V

7 The molar conductivity of 0.007 M acetic acid is 20 S cm^2 mol^{-1}. What is the dissociation constant of acetic acid? Choose the correct option.
[$\lambda^\circ_{H^+} = 350$ S cm^2 mol^{-1}, $\lambda^\circ_{CH_3COO^-} = 50$ S cm^2 mol^{-1}]
NCERT Pg 50, NEET 2021
(a) 1.75×10^{-4} mol^{-1} L^{-1} (b) 2.50×10^{-4} mol^{-1} L^{-1}
(c) 1.75×10^{-5} mol^{-1} L^{-1} (d) 2.50×10^{-5} mol^{-1} L^{-1}

8 Identify the reaction from following having top position in EMF series (Standard reduction potential) according to their electrode potential at 298 K. **NCERT Pg 37, NEET (Oct.) 2020**
(a) $Mg^{2+} + 2e^- \longrightarrow Mg(s)$
(b) $Fe^{2+} + 2e^- \longrightarrow Fe(s)$
(c) $Au^{3+} + 3e^- \longrightarrow Au(s)$
(d) $K^+ + 1e^- \longrightarrow K(s)$

9 The number of Faraday's (F) required to produce 20 g of calcium from molten $CaCl_2$ (Atomic mass of Ca = 40 g mol^{-1}) is **NCERT Pg 51, NEET 2020**
(a) 2 (b) 3 (c) 4 (d) 1

10 For the cell reaction,
$2Fe^{3+}(aq) + 2I^-(aq) \longrightarrow 2Fe^{2+}(aq) + I_2(aq)$
$E^\ominus_{cell} = 0.24$ V at 298 K. The standard Gibb's energy ($\Delta_r G^\circ$) of the cell reaction is [Given that, Faraday constant F = 96500 C mol^{-1}] **NCERT Pg 40, NEET 2019**
(a) –23.16 kJ mol^{-1} (b) 46.32 kJ mol^{-1}
(c) 23.16 kJ mol^{-1} (d) – 46.32 kJ mol^{-1}

11 For a cell involving one electron $E^\circ_{cell} = 0.59$ V at 298 K, the equilibrium constant for the cell reaction is **NCERT Pg 39, NEET 2019**
[Given that $\frac{2.303RT}{F} = 0.059$ V at T = 298 K]
(a) 1.0×10^5 (b) 1.0×10^{10} (c) 1.0×10^{30} (d) 1.0×10^2

12 Following limiting molar conductivities are given as
$\lambda^\circ_{m\,(H_2SO_4)} = x$ S cm^2mol^{-1}
$\lambda^\circ_{m\,(K_2SO_4)} = y$ S cm^2mol^{-1}
$\lambda^\circ_{m\,(CH_3COOK)} = z$ S cm^2mol^{-1}
λ°_m (in S cm^2mol^{-1}) for CH_3COOH will be
NCERT Pg 49, NEET (Odisha) 2019
(a) $x - y + 2z$ (b) $x + y - z$
(c) $x - y + z$ (d) $\frac{(x-y)}{2} + z$

13 The number of electrons delivered at the cathode during electrolysis by a current of 1 ampere in 60 seconds is (charge on electron = 1.60×10^{-19} C) **NCERT Pg 51, NEET 2016, Phase II**
(a) 6×10^{23} (b) 6×10^{20} (c) 3.74×10^{20} (d) 7.48×10^{23}

14 The molar conductivity of a 0.5 mol/dm^3 solution of $AgNO_3$ with electrolytic conductivity of 5.76×10^{-3} S cm^{-1} at 298 K is **NCERT Pg 45, NEET 2016, Phase II**
(a) 2.88 S cm^2/mol (b) 11.52 S cm^2/mol
(c) 0.086 S cm^2/mol (d) 28.8 S cm^2/mol

15 Zinc can be coated on iron to produce galvanised iron but the reverse is not possible. It is because
(a) zinc is lighter than iron. **NCERT Pg 37, NEET 2016, Phase II**
(b) zinc has lower melting point than iron.
(c) zinc has lower negative electrode potential than iron.
(d) zinc has higher negative electrode potential than iron.

16 If the E°_{cell} for a given reaction has a negative value, which of the following gives correct relationships for the values of ΔG° and K_{eq}? **NCERT Pg 40, NEET 2016**
(a) $\Delta G^\circ > 0$; $K_{eq} < 1$ (b) $\Delta G^\circ > 0$; $K_{eq} > 1$
(c) $\Delta G^\circ < 0$; $K_{eq} > 1$ (d) $\Delta G^\circ < 0$; $K_{eq} < 1$

17 When 0.1 mole of MnO_4^{2-} is oxidised, the quantity of electricity required to completely oxidise MnO_4^{2-} to MnO_4^- is **NCERT Pg 52, CBSE-AIPMT 2014**
(a) 96500 C (b) 2 ×96500 C (c) 9650 C (d) 96.50 C

JEE Main Archive

18 Which of the following statements is not correct about rusting of iron? **NCERT Pg 57, JEE Main 2024**
(a) Dissolved acidic oxides SO_2, NO_2 in water act as catalyst in the process of rusting.
(b) Rusting of iron is envisaged as setting up of electrochemical cell on the surface of iron object.
(c) When pH lies above 9 or 10, rusting of iron does not take place.
(d) Coating of iron surface by tin prevents rusting, even if the tin coating is peeling off.

19 How can an electrochemical cell be converted into an electrolytic cell? **NCERT Pg 51, JEE Main 2024**
(a) Reversing the flow of ions in salt bridge.
(b) Exchanging the electrodes at anode and cathode.
(c) Applying an external opposite potential greater than E°_{cell}
(d) Applying an external opposite potential lower than E°_{cell}

20 Identify the factor from the following that does not affect electrolytic conductance of a solution. **NCERT Pg 42, JEE Main 2024**
(a) The nature of the electrode used.
(b) Concentration of the electrolyte.
(c) The nature of the electrolyte added.
(d) The natural of solvent used.

21 Which one of the following statements is correct for electrolysis of brine solution? **NCERT Pg 53, JEE Main 2023**
(a) Cl_2 is formed at cathode. (b) OH^- is formed at cathode.
(c) O_2 is formed at cathode. (d) H_2 is formed at anode.

22 The reaction

$$\frac{1}{2}H_2(g) + AgCl(s) \rightleftharpoons H^+(aq) + Cl^-(aq) + Ag(s)$$

occurs in which of the given galvanic cell. **NCERT Pg 35, JEE Main 2023**
(a) $Pt| H_2(g)| HCl(aq) || AgCl(s)\ Ag(s)$
(b) $Pt| H_2(g)| KCl(aq)|| AgCl(s) Ag(s)$
(c) $Ag| AgCl(s)| KCl(aq)|| AgNO_3(aq) Ag(s)$
(d) $Pt| H_2(g)| HCl(aq)|| AgNO_3(aq)Ag(s)$

23 For lead storage battery pick the correct statements.
A. During charging of battery, $PbSO_4$ on anode is converted into PbO_2.
B. During charging of battery, $PbSO_4$ on cathode is converted into PbO_2.
C. Lead storage battery consists of grid of lead packed with PbO_2 as anode.
D. Lead storage battery ~ 38% solution of sulphuric acid is used as an electrolyte.

Choose the correct answer from the options given below. **NCERT Pg 55, JEE Main 2023**
(a) B and D (b) B and C
(c) B, C and D (d) A, B and D

24 The molar conductivity of a conductivity cell filled with 10 moles of 20 mL NaCl solution is Λ_{M_1} and that of 20 moles another identical cell having 80 mL NaCl solution is Λ_{M_2}. The conductivities exhibited by these two cells are same. The relationship between Λ_{M_2} and Λ_{M_1} is **NCERT Pg 45, JEE Main 2022**
(a) $\Lambda_{M_2} = 2\Lambda_{M_1}$ (b) $\Lambda_{M_2} = \Lambda_{M_1}/2$
(c) $\Lambda_{M_2} = \Lambda_{M_1}$ (d) $\Lambda_{M_2} = 4\Lambda_{M_1}$

25 Match List-I with List-II.

List-I	List-II
(A) $Cd(s) + 2Ni(OH)_3(s) \longrightarrow CdO(s) + 2Ni(OH)_2(s) + H_2O\ l$	(I) Primary battery
(B) $Zn(Hg) + HgO(s) \longrightarrow ZnO(s) + Hg(l)$	(II) Discharging of secondary battery
(C) $2PbSO_4(s) + 2H_2O(l) \longrightarrow Pb(s) + PbO_2(s) + 2H_2SO_4(aq)$	(III) Fuel cell
(D) $2H_2(g) + O_2(g) \longrightarrow 2H_2O(l)$	(IV) Charging of secondary battery

Choose the correct answer from the options given below. **NCERT Pg 55, 56, JEE Main 2022**
(a) A-I, B-II, C-III, D-IV (b) A-IV, B-I, C-II, D-III
(c) A-II, B-I, C-IV, D-III (d) A-II, B-I, C-III, D-IV

26 Compound *A* used as a strong oxidising agent is amphoteric in nature. It is the part of lead storage batteries. Compound *A* is **NCERT Pg 55, JEE Main 2021**
(a) PbO_2 (b) PbO (c) $PbSO_4$ (d) Pb_3O_4

27 Match List-I with List-II.

List-I (Parameter)	List-II (Unit)
A. Cell constant	1. $S\ cm^2\ mol^{-1}$
B. Molar conductivity	2. Dimensionless
C. Conductivity	3. m^{-1}
D. Degree of dissociation of electrolyte	4. $\Omega^{-1}m^{-1}$

Choose the most appropriate answer from the options given below. **NCERT Pg 41,44,45,50, JEE Main 2021**

	A	B	C	D
(a)	3	1	4	2
(b)	3	1	2	4
(c)	1	4	3	2
(d)	2	1	3	4

Skill Boosters

1. A student has following four electrodes

A. $Au^{3+}(0.0005\,M)|Au(s)$ *B.* $Au^{3+}(0.5\,M)|Au(s)$

C. $Au^{3+}(0.05\,M)|Au(s)$ *D.* $Au^{3+}(0.005\,M)|Au(s)$

If the standard reduction potential of $Au^{3+}|Au$ is 1.50 V. Then the decreasing order of reducing potential of the given electrode is

(a) $A > C > D > B$ (b) $B > C > D > A$

(c) $C > A > B > D$ (d) $A > D > C > B$

2. Consider the following laboratory observation?

$$Sn + 2AgBr \longrightarrow 2Ag + SnBr_2$$

$$2Ag + SnBr_2 \longrightarrow \text{No reaction}$$

Which of the following statements in not true on the basis of the above observations?

(a) Sn is stronger reducing agent than Ag.

(b) Ag^+ is a stronger oxidising agent than Sn^{2+}.

(c) The reduction potential for Ag^+ is more than the reduction potential for Sn^{2+}.

(d) Sn^{2+} is a stronger oxidising agent than Ag^+.

3. Standard electrode potential data is useful understanding the suitability of an oxidant in a redox titration. Some half-cell reactions and their standard potentials are given below .

$$MnO_4^-(aq) + 8H^+(aq) + 5e^- \longrightarrow Mn^{2+}(aq) + 4H_2O(l); \quad E° = 1.51\text{ V}$$

$$Cr_2O_7^{2-} + 14H^+(aq) + 6e^- \longrightarrow 2Cr^{3+}(aq) + 7H_2O(l); \quad E° = 1.33\text{ V}$$

$$Fe^{3+}(aq) + e^- \longrightarrow Fe^{2+}(aq); E° = 0.77\text{ V}$$

$$Cl_2(g) + 2e^- \longrightarrow 2Cl^-(aq); E° = 1.36\text{ V}$$

Identify the false statement regarding the quantitative estimation of aqueous $Fe(NO_3)_2$.

(a) MnO_4^- can be used in aqueous HCl.

(b) $Cr_2O_7^{2-}$ can be used in aqueous HCl.

(c) MnO_4^- can be used in aqueous H_2SO_4.

(d) $Cr_2O_7^{2-}$ can be used in aqueous H_2SO_4.

4. Vidit electrolysed a solution of 1 mole per litre each of $Cu(NO_3)_2$, $AgNO_3$, $Hg_2(NO_3)_2$ and $Mg(NO_3)_2$ using inert electrodes. The values of standard reduction electrode potential in volts are $Ag^+/Ag = 0.80$, $Cu^{2+}/Cu = 0.34$, $Mg^{2+}/Mg = -2.37$, $Hg_2^{2+}/2Hg = +0.79$.

If he increase the voltage, the sequence of deposition of these metals on the cathode will be

(a) Ag, Mg, Cu, Hg (b) Ag, Hg, Mg, Cu

(c) Ag, Hg, Cu, Mg (d) Mg, Cu, Hg, Ag

5. When a bright silver object is placed in the solution of gold. Chloride acquires a golden tinge but nothing happens when it is placed in a solution of copper chloride. The correct reason which explain this behaviour of silver is/are

I. The standard electrode potential of silver is higher than gold.

II. The standard electrode potential of silver is lower than gold.

III. The standard electrode potential of copper is lower than silver.

IV. The standard electrode potential of silver is lower than copper.

Choose the correct answer from the options given below.

(a) I and IV (b) II and III (c) I and III (d) II and IV

6. Two students use same stock solution of $ZnSO_4$ and a solution of $CuSO_4$. The emf of one cell is 0.03 V higher than the others. The concentration of $CuSO_4$ in the cells with higher emf value is 0.5 M. The concentration of $CuSO_4$ in the other cell is

(a) 0.5 M (b) 0.1 M (c) 0.05 M (d) 0.01 M

7. Ajeet brought some silver jewellery for his mother. Over a span of time, it get dull and a black layer of Ag_2S is formed on it. Now, he wants to remove the black tarnishing in order to make it shine again.

The suitable method he can adopt from the option given below is

[Given : $E^\circ_{(Ag_2S/2Ag,S^{2-})} = -0.71$ V, $E^\circ_{(Al^{3+}/Al)} = -1.66$, $E^\circ_{(Br_2/Br^-)} = 1.09$, $E^\circ_{(Au^{3+}/Au)} = 1.40$, $E^\circ_{(Cu^{2+}/Cu)} = 0.34$]

(a) Place jewellery in aluminium pan containing NaCl as electrolyte.

(b) Place jewellery in bromine solution.

(c) Place jewellery in gold pan containing an inert electrolyte.

(d) By placing the jewellery in copper pan containing NaCl as electrolyte.

8. A gas *P* at a 1 atm is bubbled through a solution containing a mixture of 1 MQ^- and 1MR^- at 25°C. If the reduction potential of *P*, *Q*, *R* is in the order of $R > Q > P$, then

(a) *Q* will oxidise *P* and not *R*.

(b) *Q* will oxidise *R* and not *P*.

(c) *P* will oxidise both *P* and *Q*.

(d) *Q* will reduce both *P* and *R*.

Correct Codes

Topical Questions

1. (c)	2. (a)	3. (c)	4. (c)	5. (a)	6. (b)	7. (a)	8. (d)	9. (b)	10. (d)
11. (c)	12. (c)	13. (a)	14. (a)	15. (a)	16. (c)	17. (d)	18. (d)	19. (a)	20. (d)
21. (d)	22. (d)	23. (b)	24. (d)	25. (d)	26. (c)	27. (b)	28. (c)	29. (c)	30. (a)
31. (c)	32. (b)	33. (c)	34. (c)	35. (b)	36. (b)	37. (a)	38. (a)	39. (c)	40. (c)
41. (d)	42. (a)	43. (b)	44. (c)	45. (b)	46. (d)	47. (d)	48. (b)	49. (b)	50. (b)
51. (b)	52. (b)	53. (a)	54. (b)	55. (b)	56. (b)	57. (b)	58. (c)	59. (c)	60. (d)
61. (a)	62. (a)	63. (a)	64. (a)	65. (d)	66. (c)	67. (a)	68. (c)	69. (d)	70. (d)
71. (c)	72. (b)	73. (c)	74. (c)	75. (d)	76. (b)	77. (d)	78. (b)	79. (c)	80. (d)
81. (a)	82. (a)	83. (c)	84. (a)	85. (b)	86. (c)	87. (a)	88. (b)	89. (d)	90. (c)
91. (b)	92. (b)	93. (d)	94. (b)	95. (d)	96. (d)				

Assertion-Reason

1. (a)	2. (a)	3. (a)	4. (c)	5. (a)	6. (b)	7. (a)	8. (a)	9. (c)	10. (c)
11. (a)									

Statement Type

1. (c)	2. (a)	3. (b)	4. (c)	5. (d)	6. (d)	7. (d)	8. (d)	9. (a)	10. (a)

Matching Type

1. (b)	2. (c)	3. (b)	4. (d)	5. (a)	6. (b)

Numerical Value

1. (1567)	2. (10)	3. (16)	4. (14)	5. (66)	6. (34)

NCERT Exemplar's

1. (c)	2. (d)	3. (b)	4. (c)	5. (b)	6. (b)	7. (a)	8. (d)	9. (c)	10. (d)
11. (c)	12. (b)	13. (c)	14. (a)	15. (b)	16. (c)	17. (d)			

Past Exams'

1. (b)	2. (a)	3. (b)	4. (d)	5. (c)	6. (b)	7. (c)	8. (c)	9. (d)	10. (d)
11. (b)	12. (d)	13. (c)	14. (b)	15. (d)	16. (a)	17. (c)	18. (d)	19. (c)	20. (a)
21. (b)	22. (a)	23. (a)	24. (a)	25. (c)	26. (a)	27. (a)			

Skill Boosters

1. (b)	2. (a)	3. (a)	4. (c)	5. (b)	6. (c)	7. (a)	8. (b)

Step by Step

Decoding the Questions

Concept Builders

1 False
2 copper, zinc
3 False
4 True
5 Electromotive force (EMF)
6 True
7 Cu^{2+}
8 Positive
9 False
10 +0.34 V [**Hint**: $E^\circ_{cell} = E^\circ_{right} - E^\circ_{left}$]
11 False
12 True
13 remain same, zero.
14 False
15 –0.591 V

[**Hint**: $E_{cell} = E^\circ - \frac{0.0591}{n}\log\frac{[p_{H_2}]}{[H^+]}$]

16 False
17 True
18 0.01 M KCl
19 False
20 390.5 S cm² mol⁻¹

[**Hint**: $\lambda^\circ_m(HAc) = \lambda^\circ_m(HCl) + \lambda^\circ_m(NaAc) - \lambda^\circ_m(NaCl)$]

21 decreases, decreases
22 gram equivalent mass
23 True
24 9 g. $\left[\textbf{Hint}: W = \frac{E \times Q}{96500}\right]$
25 Paste of KOH and ZnO.
26 grid of lead packed with PbO_2.
27 ≈1.35 V
28 False
29 Fuel cell
30 False

Topical Solutions

1 (c) In a electrochemical cells, the chemical energy liberated during the redox reaction is converted to electrical energy.

2 (a) When applied external opposite potential (E_{ext}) reaches to 1.1 V in a Daniell cell, chemical reactions stops and no electron or current flows through the cell.

3 (c) The given figure represents Daniell cell, in which $E_{ext} > 1.1$ V. In this case, electron flows from Cu to Zn and current flows from Zn to Cu. Therefore, Zn is deposited at the zinc electrode (cathode) and Cu dissolves at copper electrode (anode).

Thus, statement (c) is correct.

4 (c) Statement (c) is incorrect.
It's correct form is as follows :
In Daniell cell, cell potential is 1.1 V.
Since, $E_{ext}(0.9) < 1.1$, so in this case, current flows from copper to zinc electrode.
Rest other statements are correct.

5 (a) The electrode potential under the conditions of unit concentration at 1 atm pressure and 25°C of all species in the half-cell is called standard reduction potential.

6 (b) Statement (b) is incorrect.
It's correct form is as follows :
Unit of cell potential is volt.
Rest other statements are correct.

7 (a) For the reaction,

$$Zn + 2Ag^+ \longrightarrow Zn^{2+} + 2Ag$$

The correct representation of the cell is,

$$Zn(s) \mid Zn^{2+}(aq) \,||\, Ag^+(aq) \mid Ag(s)$$

8 (d)

9 (b) At anode,

$$2Cl^- \longrightarrow Cl_2 + 2e^-; E^\circ_{anode} = ?$$

At cathode, $Pt^{2+} + 2e^- \longrightarrow Pt; \quad E^\circ_{cathode} = 1.20$ V

$$Pt^{2+} + 2Cl^- \longrightarrow Pt + Cl_2 \quad E^\circ = -0.15 \text{ V}$$

$$E^\circ_{cell} = E^\circ_{cathode} - E^\circ_{anode}$$
$$-0.15 = 1.20 - E^\circ_{anode}$$
$$E^\circ_{anode} = 1.20 + 0.15$$
$$= 1.35 \text{ V}$$

10 (d) $E^\circ_{cell} = E^\circ_{cathode} - E^\circ_{anode}$

i.e. E°_{cell} does not depend upon the concentration of ions, so, remains the same. Hence, if the concentration of Cu^{2+} ions is doubled, then E°_{cell} will remains the same.

11 (c) The cell potential is given as,

$$E^\circ_{cell} = E^\circ_{cathode(RP)} - E^\circ_{anode(RP)}$$
$$\therefore E^\circ_{cell} = 0.15 - (-0.74) = +0.89 \text{ V}$$

12 (c) For the given reaction,

$$E^\circ_{cell} = E^\circ_{Cu^{2+}/Cu} - E^\circ_{Zn^{2+}/Zn}$$
$$= 0.34 - (-0.76) = +1.10 \text{ V}$$

13 (a) E°_{cell} is not positive only for the reaction (a), i.e.

$$Ni^{2+}(aq) + Cu(s) \longrightarrow Ni(s) + Cu^{2+}(aq)$$
$$E^\circ_{cell} = E^\circ_{Ni^{2+}/Ni} - E^\circ_{Cu^{2+}/Cu}$$
$$= 0.25 - 0.34 = -0.09 \text{ V}$$

Therefore, it will not take place in the specified direction.

14 (a) $E^\circ_{cell} = E^\circ_{cathode} - E^\circ_{anode}$

$$= 0.80 - (-0.76) = 1.56 \text{ V for } 1e^-$$

$\therefore E^\circ_{cell}$ for $1e^- = 1.56$ V

$\therefore Ag^+/Ag$ will give a maximum value of E°_{cell} for electron.

15 (a) If E°_{cell} is positive, reaction is spontaneous, otherwise if it is negative than non-spontaneous.

At cathode,

$$Mn^{2+} + 2e^- \longrightarrow Mn; E^\circ = -1.18 \text{ V}$$

At anode,

$$2Mn^{2+} \longrightarrow 2Mn^{3+} + 2e^-; E^\circ = -1.51 \text{ V}$$

$$3Mn^{2+} \longrightarrow Mn + 2Mn^{3+};$$

$$E^\circ_{cell} = E^\circ_{red} + E^\circ_{ox}$$
$$= -1.18 + (-1.51)$$
$$= -2.69 \text{ V}$$

Negative E°_{cell} of the reaction indicates that reaction is non-spontaneous.

16 (c) $E^\circ_{cell} = E^\circ_{H^+/O_2/H_2O} - E^\circ_{Fe^{2+}/Fe}$

$= 1.23 - (-0.44) = 1.67$ V

17 (d) Among the given statements only (d) is correct.

(a) $E_{cell} = E_{Ag^+/Ag} - E_{Cu^{2+}/Cu}$

(b) $Cu(s) \mid Cu^{2+}(aq)$ is anode and $Ag^+(aq)/Ag(s)$ is cathode electrodes respectively.

(c) Reaction at anode :
$Cu(s) \longrightarrow Cu^{2+}(aq) + 2e^-$

18 (d) Among the given statement (d) is incorrect. The electrode is actually dipped in acidic solution.

19 (a) The correct form of (a) is Oxidation takes place at calcium electrode and reduction at hydrogen electrode.

20 (d) Due to reduction of NO_3^- in preference to H^+ ion. H^+ ion is not reduced to give H_2 gas.

21 (d) Electrochemical cells are not used for determining the dissociation constant.

22 (d) Higher the reduction potential, lesser the reducing power. The order of standard electrode potential of given metals X, Y and Z is $Y(+0.5\text{ V}) > X(-1.2\text{ V}) > Z(-3.0\text{ V})$.

Thus, the correct order of reducing power of these metals will be $Z > X > Y$.

23 (b) More negative is the value of standard reducting potential, higher is the reduction power.

Thus, the correct decreasing order of reducing power of the metal is K > Al > Cr > Ag.

24 (d) A cell reaction is spontaneous, if $\Delta G^\circ < 0$

Since, $\Delta G^\circ = -nFE^\circ_{cell}$

Thus, $E^\circ_{cell} > 0$

$X = Zn,\ Y = Ni,$

$Zn + Ni^{2+} \longrightarrow Zn^{2+} + Ni$

$E^\circ_{cell} = E^\circ_{Zn/Zn^{2+}} + E^\circ_{Ni^{2+}/Ni} = 0.53$ V

This reaction is spontaneous.

While, for other options E°_{cell} is –ve, so reaction will be non-spontaneous.

Thus, the option (d) is correct.

25 (d)

26. (c) E_{cell} depends on the concentration of both Cu^{2+} and Zn^{2+} ions. It increases with increase in the concentration of Cu^{2+} ions and decrease in the concentration of Zn^{2+} ions.

Thus, statement (c) is correct.

27 (b) For the given cell the reaction is

$Ni(s) + 2Ag^+(aq) \longrightarrow Ni^{2+}(aq) + 2Ag(s)$

The Nernst equation can be written as

$$E_{cell} = E^\circ_{cell} - \frac{RT}{2F} \ln \frac{[Ni^{2+}]}{[Ag^+]^2}$$

28 (c) Among the given relations, (c) is incorrect.

For, $2Ag^+ + H_2\,(1\text{ atm}) \longrightarrow 2Ag + 2H^+\,(1\text{M});$

$$E_{cell} = E^\circ_{cell} - \frac{0.0591}{2} \log \frac{[H^+]^2}{[Ag^+]^2}$$

29 (c) Cell reaction,

$H^+_{(cathode)} \longrightarrow H^+_{(anode)};\ E^\circ_{cell} = 0$ V

$$\therefore \quad E_{cell} = 0 - 0.0591 \log \frac{[H^+]_{anode}}{[H^+]_{cathode}}$$

$$= -0.0591 \log \frac{[10^{-8}]}{0.001}$$

$$= -0.0591 \times (-5)$$

$$= +0.2955 \text{ V}$$

30 (a) From Nernst equation,

$$E_{cell} = E^\circ_{cell} - \frac{0.0591}{n} \log Q.$$

If $Q = 1$, $\log Q = 0$ so, $E_{cell} = E^\circ_{cell}$

This condition is found only in the cell :

$Cu(s) \mid Cu^{2+}(0.01\text{M}) \| Ag^+(0.1\text{M}) \mid Ag(s)$

$$E_{cell} = E^\circ_{cell} - \frac{0.0591}{n} \log \left[\frac{Cu^{2+}}{(Ag^+)^2}\right]$$

$$= E^\circ_{cell} - \frac{0.0591}{n} \log \left[\frac{0.01}{(0.1)^2}\right]$$

$\therefore\ E_{cell} = E^\circ_{cell}$

31 (c) The cell reaction is,

$Zn + Fe^{2+} \longrightarrow Zn^{2+} + Fe$

From Nernst equation,

$$E_{cell} = E^\circ_{cell} - \frac{0.0591}{n} \log \frac{a_{Zn^{2+}}}{a_{Fe^{2+}}}$$

$$= (0.763 - 0.44) - \frac{0.0591}{1} \log \frac{0.001}{0.005}$$

$$= 0.364 \text{ V}$$

32 (b) For Nernst equation,

$$E_{cell} = E^\circ_{cell} - \frac{0.0591}{n} \log \frac{[M_p]^{n+}}{[M_r]^{n+}}$$

$$\therefore \quad E_{cell} = 4 - \frac{0.0591}{2} \log \frac{10^{-4}}{10^{-2}}$$

$$E_{cell} = 4 + 0.0591 = 4.0591 \text{ V}$$

33 (c) $E^\circ_{cell} = E^\circ_{cathode} - E^\circ_{anode}$

$= -0.42 - (-0.72) = 0.3$

Net reaction,

$2Cr + 3Fe^{2+} \longrightarrow 2Cr^{3+} + 3Fe$

$$\therefore \quad E = E^\circ_{cell} - \frac{0.0591}{6} \log \frac{[Cr^{3+}]^2}{[Fe^{2+}]^3}$$

$= 0.26$ V

34 (c) $2H^+ + 2e^- \longrightarrow H_2(g)$

$$E_{H^+/H_2} = E^\circ_{H^+/H_2} - \frac{0.0591}{2} \log \frac{p(H_2)}{[H^+]^2},$$

$[E^\circ_{H^+/H_2} = 0]$

For the negative value of E_{H^+/H_2}

$\frac{p(H_2)}{[H^+]^2}$ should be +ve, i.e. $p(H_2) > [H^+]$.

35 (b) The overall cell reaction can be written as,

$\underset{(1\text{ bar})}{H_2(g)} + 2AgCl(s) \longrightarrow \underset{(10^{-6}\text{ M})}{2HCl(aq)} + 2Ag(s)$

According to Nernst equation,

$$E_{cell} = (E^\circ_{cathode} - E^\circ_{anode}) - \frac{2.303 \times RT}{n \times F} \log \frac{[HCl]^2 [Ag]^2}{p_{H_2} [AgCl]^2}$$

$\Rightarrow 0.92 = (E^\circ_{cathode} - 0) - 0.06 \times \log \frac{(10^{-6})^2 \times 1^2}{1 \times 1^2}$

$\Rightarrow E^\circ_{cathode} = 0.92 - 0.72 = 0.20$ V

Note 10^{-6} molal HCl is a very dilute solution.

So, 10^{-6} m $\approx 10^{-6}$ M

36 (*b*) The relationship between standard electrode potential ($E°$) and equilibrium constant (K) of the given cell reaction, can be expressed as,

$$E° = \frac{RT}{nF} \ln K$$

$$\Rightarrow \quad K = e^{nFE°/RT}$$

$$\therefore \quad K = e^{\frac{2 \times 96000 \times 2}{8 \times 300}} = e^{160}$$

37 (*a*) According to Nernst equation,

At equilibrium, $E_{cell} = 0$

$$E^\circ_{cell} = \frac{0.059}{n} \log K_C$$

$$\therefore \quad E^\circ_{cell} = \frac{0.059}{2} \log (10 \times 10^{15})$$

$$= 0.472 \text{ V}$$

38 (*a*) $Fe^{2+}(aq) + Ag^+(aq) \longrightarrow Fe^{3+}(aq) + Ag(s)$

$$\therefore \quad E^\circ_{cell} = E^\circ_{Ag^+/Ag} - E^\circ_{Fe^{3+}/Fe^{2+}}$$

$$= x - E^\circ_{Fe^{3+}/Fe^{2+}} \quad \text{... (i)}$$

Now, for two half-cells

(i) $Fe^{2+} + 2e^- \longrightarrow Fe;$

$E^\circ_{Fe^{2+}/Fe} = E^\circ_1 = y$V; $\Delta G^\circ_1 = -2FE^\circ_1$

(ii) $Fe^{3+} + 3e^- \longrightarrow Fe;$

$E^\circ_{Fe^{3+}/Fe} = E^\circ_2 = z$V; $\Delta G^\circ_2 = -3FE^\circ_2$

So, $Fe^{3+} + e^- \longrightarrow Fe^{2+};$

$E^\circ_{Fe^{3+}/Fe^{2+}} = E^\circ_3 = ?;$

$\Delta G^\circ_3 = -1 \times FE^\circ_3$

Again, $\Delta G^\circ_3 = \Delta G^\circ_2 - \Delta G^\circ_1$

$\Rightarrow \quad E^\circ_3 = 3E^\circ_2 - 2E^\circ_1$

$\Rightarrow \quad E^\circ_{Fe^{3+}/Fe^{2+}} = (3z - 2y)$ V

So, from equation (i)

$E^\circ_{cell} = (x - 3z + 2y)$ V

39 (*c*) The half-cell reactions are

$$4Al^{3+} + 12e^- \longrightarrow 4Al$$

$$6O^{2-} \longrightarrow 3O_2 + 12e^-$$

or $\frac{4}{3} Al^{3+} + 4e^- \longrightarrow \frac{4}{3} Al$

$$2O^{2-} \longrightarrow O_2 + 4e^-$$

As we know that, $\Delta G° = -nFE°$

$\therefore -960 \times 1000 = -4 \times 96500 \times E°$

$$E° = \frac{960000}{4 \times 96500} = 2.487 \text{ V}$$

$$\approx 2.5 \text{ V}$$

40 (*c*) $\because \Delta G_{Cu^{2+}/Cu} = \Delta G_{Cu^{2+}/Cu^+} + \Delta G_{Cu^+/Cu}$

$\therefore -2FE° = -1F \times 0.15 + (-1F \times 0.50)$

$-2FE° = -0.15F - 0.50F$

$= -F(0.15 + 0.50)$

$$E° = \frac{0.65}{2} = 0.325 \text{ V}$$

41 (*d*) As we know that,

$\Delta G = -nFE_{cell}$

$$\therefore \Delta G = -\frac{2 \times 0.0591 \times 96500}{1000} \text{ kJ}$$

$$= -11.406 \text{ kJ} \approx -11.4 \text{ kJ}$$

42 (*a*) $\therefore$ Cell potential

$(E^\circ_{cell}) = E^\circ_{Cu^+/Cu} - E^\circ_{Cu^{2+}/Cu^+}$

$= 0.60 - 0.41 = 0.19$ V

As we know that,

$-nFE° = -RT \ln K_{eq}$

$$\Rightarrow \log K_{eq} = \frac{nE°}{(2.303RT/F)}$$

$$= \frac{2 \times 0.19 \text{ V}}{0.059 \text{ V}} = 6.44$$

$$K_{eq} = 10^{6.44}$$

43 (*b*) At the state of equilibrium,

$\Delta G = -RT \ln K_C$

$-nFE° = -RT \, 2.303 \log K_C$

$$E° = \frac{RT 2.303 \log K_C}{2F}$$

($n = 2$ for Daniell cell)

$\because$ At equilibrium, $E^\circ_{cell} = 1.1$

$$\therefore \quad \frac{2.303 \, RT}{2F} \log K_C = 1.1$$

$$\Rightarrow \log K_C = \frac{2.2}{0.0591} \quad \text{[on solving]}$$

44 (*c*) As we know that,

$\Delta G° = \Delta G^\circ_f(ZnO) - \Delta G^\circ_f(Ag_2O)$

$\therefore \Delta G° = (-318.30 + 11.21)$ kJ mol^{-1}

$= -307.09$ kJ

$= -307.09 \times 10^3$ J

$\because \Delta G° = -nFE^\circ_{cell}$

$\therefore -307.09 \times 10^3 = -2 \times 96500 \times E^\circ_{cell}$

or $E^\circ_{cell} = 1.591$ V

45 (*b*) $E^\circ_{cell} = E^\circ_{Cu^{2+}/Cu} - E^\circ_{Fe^{2+}/Fe}$

$= 0.34 \text{ V} - (-0.44) \text{ V} = 0.78$ V

$\Delta G° = -nFE^\circ_{cell}$

$= -2 \times 96500 \times 0.78$

$= -150540$ J

46 (*d*) Statement (d) is incorrect.

It's correct form is as follows

Reciprocal or inverse of resistance is called conductance, while specific conductance or conductivity is the reciprocal of resistivity.

Rest other statements are correct.

47 (*d*) **48** (*b*) **49** (*b*)

50 (*b*) All the given statements are correct.

51 (*b*)

52 (*b*) Conductivity of electrolytic solution is due to presence of mobile ions in the solution. This type of conductance is known as ionic conductance.

Conductivity of these type of solutions depend upon

(i) the nature of electrolyte added

(ii) size of the ion produced and their solvation

(iii) concentration of electrolyte

(iv) nature of solvent and its viscosity

(v) temperature

While power of source, surface area and distance between electrodes has no effect on conductivity of electrolyte solution.

Hence, options (b) is the correct.

53 (*a*) Statement (a) is correct, while other statements are incorrect.
Corrected form are as follows
Cell constant $= l/A$.
But rest of the given statements are incorrect.
Corrected form are as follows
(b) Its SI unit is m^{-1}.
(c) It is measured from resistance and conductivity.
(d) It is denoted by the symbol of G^*.

54 (*b*)

55 (*b*) Conductivity, $(\kappa) = \frac{\text{Cell constant}}{\text{Resistance}}$
$$= \frac{0.616 \text{ cm}^{-1}}{55 \Omega}$$
$$= 1.12 \times 10^{-2} \Omega^{-1} \text{cm}^{-1}$$

56 (*b*) As we know that,
Specific conductance = conductance × cell constant
$$\therefore \; 1.3 \text{Sm}^{-1} = \frac{1}{50} \text{S} \times \text{cell constant} \quad \left(C = \frac{1}{R}\right)$$
$$\Rightarrow \text{Cell constant} = 1.3 \times 50 \text{ m}^{-1}$$
$$= 65 \text{ m}^{-1} = \frac{65}{100} \text{cm}^{-1}$$
Molar conductivity
$$= \frac{1000 \times \text{conductance} \times \text{cell constant}}{\text{molarity}}$$
$$= \frac{1000}{0.4} \times \frac{1}{260} \times \frac{65}{100}$$
$$= 6.25 \times 10^{-4} \text{ S m}^2 \text{ mol}^{-1}$$

57 (*b*) Cell constant,
$$G^* = \text{conductivity} \times \text{resistance}$$
$$= 1.29 \text{ S/m} \times 100 \Omega = 129 \text{ m}^{-1}$$
Conductivity of 0.02 mol L^{-1} KCl solution
$$= \frac{G^*}{R} = \frac{129 \text{ m}^{-1}}{520 \Omega}$$
$$= 0.248 \text{ S m}^{-1}$$

58 (*c*) Cell constant $= \kappa \cdot R$
$$= 0.0212 \times 55 = 1.166 \text{cm}^{-1}$$

59 (*c*) The molar conductivity $\Lambda_m \propto \frac{1}{M}$
Hence, the solution having minimum molar conductivity has to be more concentrated. Hence, option (c) is the correct one.

60 (*d*) $\Lambda_m = \frac{\kappa \times 1000}{M}$
$$= \frac{1.01 \times 10^{-2} \times 1000}{0.2}$$
$$= 50.5 \text{ ohm}^{-1} \text{cm}^2 \text{mol}^{-1}$$

61 (*a*) When concentration approaches to zero, the molar conductivity is known as limiting molar conductivity.

62 (*a*) Conductivity always decreases with decrease in concentration because the number of ions (current carrying species) per unit volume decreases on dilution.

Molar conductivity, however, increases on dilution because total volume of solution containing one mole of electrolyte also increases.

Thus, statement (a) is correct.

63 (*a*)

64 (*a*) The size of the given ion increases as $Na^+ < K^+ < Mg^{2+} < Ca^{2+}$ but order of the size of the hydrated ion is $Na^+ > K^+ > Mg^{2+} > Ca^{2+}$ and limiting molar conductivity depends on the size of hydrated ion. Thus, the limiting molar conductivity of Na^+ is least as its size of hydrated ion is largest.

65 (*d*) As we know that,
$$\Lambda^\circ_{(CaCl_2)} = \Lambda^\circ_{Ca^{2+}} + 2 \times \lambda^\circ_{Cl^-}$$
$$\therefore \quad = 119 + 2 \times 71$$
$$= 261 \text{ S cm}^2 \text{ mol}^{-1}$$

66 (*c*) The reaction for the formation of $Ba(OH)_2$ can be written as
$$BaCl_2 + 2NaOH \longrightarrow Ba(OH)_2 + 2NaCl$$
$$\because \quad \lambda^\circ_{m\,[Ba(OH)_2]} = \lambda^\circ_{m(BaCl_2)} + 2\,\lambda^\circ_{m(NaOH)} - 2\,\lambda^\circ_{m(NaCl)}$$
$$\therefore \; \lambda^\circ_{m\,[Ba(OH)_2]} = 280 \times 10^{-4} + 2 \times 248 \times 10^{-4} - 2 \times 126 \times 10^{-4}$$
$$= (280 + 496 - 252) \times 10^{-4}$$
$$= 524 \times 10^{-4} \text{Sm}^2 \text{mol}^{-1}$$

67 (*a*) $\lambda^\circ_{HCOOH} = \lambda^\circ_{H^+} + \lambda^\circ_{HCOO^-}$
$$= 349.6 + 54.6 = 404.2 \text{ S cm}^2 \text{ mol}^{-1}$$
$$\alpha = \frac{\Lambda_m}{\Lambda^\circ_m} = \frac{46.1}{404.2} = 0.114$$
$$K_a = \frac{C\alpha^2}{1 - \alpha} = \frac{0.025 \times (0.114)^2}{1 - 0.114}$$
$$= \frac{0.025 \times 0.114 \times 0.114}{0.886}$$
$$= 3.67 \times 10^{-4} \text{mol L}^{-1}$$

68 (*c*) Solubility of the sparingly soluble salt cannot be calculated by Kohlrausch law.

69 (*d*) Galvanic or voltaic cell is an example of electrochemical cell.

70 (*d*) Among the given statement I, II and III are correct. To obtain pure copper from impure copper by electrolysis, anode is made from impure copper and copper is oxidised at anode and deposited at cathode. A solution of copper sulphate is used as an electrolyte.

71 (*c*) $Al^{3+} + 3e^- \longrightarrow Al$
Equivalent weight of Al $= \frac{27}{3} = 9$
From Faraday's first law,
$$w = Zit = \frac{E}{96500} it$$
$$\therefore \; t = \frac{w \times 96500}{E \times i} = \frac{50 \times 96500}{9 \times 105}$$
$$= 5105.82 \text{ s} = 1.418 \text{ hr} \approx 1.42 \text{ hr}$$

72 (*b*) We know that,
Charge, $Q = it = 1.5 \times 3 \times 60 \times 60$
$$= 16200 \text{C}$$
$\because$ Charge on one electron
$$= 1.6 \times 10^{-19} \text{C}$$
$$\therefore \; 16200 \text{ C charge is on } \frac{1 \times 16200}{1.6 \times 10^{-19}}$$
$$\approx 1.0 \times 10^{23} \text{ electrons}$$

73 (c) The conversion of nitrobenzene to aniline is as follows

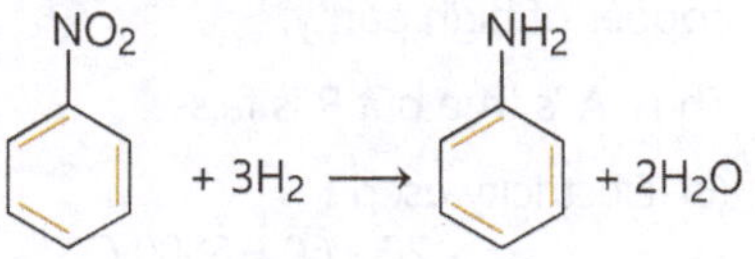

123 g (1 mol) 6 g (3 mol)

Nitrogen gains a total of 6 electrons during this reduction process.

Moles of nitrobenzene used in the reaction $= \frac{12.3}{123} = 0.1$ mol

H_2 required for reduction $= 0.1 \times 3 = 0.3$ mol

Amount of charge required to liberate 0.3 mole of hydrogen $= 2 \times 96500 \times 0.3 = 57900$ C.

74 (c) Mass of silver in coating $= V \times d$

$$= (A \times l) \times d$$

$$= 2 \times 10^{-3} \times 100 \times 1.05 = 2 \times 0.105 \text{ g}$$

$$\because w = \frac{i \times t \times E}{96500}$$

$$\text{or } t = \frac{w \times 96500}{i \times E} = \frac{0.105 \times 2 \times 96500}{10 \times 108}$$

$$= 18.76 \text{ s} \approx 18.8 \text{ s}$$

75 (d) $Na^+ + e^- \xrightarrow{Hg} Na(Hg)$

$$2Cl^- \longrightarrow Cl_2 + 2e^-$$

Moles of NaCl electrolysed

$$= 4 \times \frac{500}{1000} = 2.0$$

Two Faraday of electric charge is required for electrolysis of 2 moles of NaCl.

Total Coulombs $= 2 \times 96500$

$$= 193000 \text{ C}$$

76 (b)

77 (d) $\because \quad w = Zit$

$$= 4 \times 10^{-4} \times 6 \times \frac{75}{100} \times 6 \times 3600$$

$$= 38.88 \approx 38.9 \text{ g}$$

78 (b) $Q = it = 96.5 \times 100 = 9650$ C

96500 C charge deposits 108 g of Ag

9650 C will deposit $= \frac{108 \times 9650}{96500}$

$$= 10.8 \text{ g of Ag}$$

79 (c) $\underset{1\text{ mol}}{Ag^+ + e^-} \longrightarrow Ag;$ (1 mol, 1 F)

$$Cu^{2+} + \underset{\substack{2\text{ mol}\\2\text{ F}}}{2e^-} \longrightarrow Cu$$

$$Fe^{2+} + \underset{\substack{3\text{ mol}\\3\text{ F}}}{3e^-} \longrightarrow Fe$$

Gram of Ag liberated

$$= \frac{108 \times 10}{1} = 1080 \text{ g}$$

Gram of Cu liberated

$$= \frac{63.5 \times 10}{2} = 317.5 \text{ g}$$

Gram of Fe liberated

$$= \frac{56 \times 10}{3} = 186.7 \text{ g}$$

80 (d) Statement (d) is incorrect.

It's correct form is as follows

The charge required for reducing 1 mole of MnO_4^- into Mn^{2+} is,

$$\overset{+7}{Mn}O_4^- + 5e^- \longrightarrow Mn^{2+}$$

$$5e^- \equiv 5F = 5 \times 96500$$

or $\quad 4.82 \times 10^5$ C

Rest other statements are correct.

81 (a) When aqueous solution of NaCl is electrolysed, there is a competition between the following reduction reactions at cathode.

$$Na^+ + e^- \longrightarrow Na; E^\circ_{cell} = -2.71 \text{ V}$$

$$H^+ + e^- \longrightarrow \frac{1}{2}H_2 \,;\, E^\circ_{cell} = 0.00 \text{ V}$$

The reaction with higher value of E° is preferred and therefore, the second reaction occurs at cathode, i.e. H^+ is reduced instead of Na^+.

82 (a) For electrolysis of aqueous solution of $CuSO_4$.

$$CuSO_4\,(aq) \longrightarrow Cu^{2+} + SO_4^{2-}$$

$$H_2O \longrightarrow 2H^+ + O^{2-}$$

At anode, $2O^{2-} \longrightarrow O_2 + 2e^-$

At cathode, $Cu^{2+} + 2e^- \longrightarrow Cu(s)$

83 (c) Left side of cell reaction represents oxidation half cell, i.e. oxidation of Mg and right side of cell represents reduction half cell reactions, i.e. reduction of copper.

Cu is reduced and reduction occurs at cathode.

Mg is oxidised and oxidation occurs at anode.

Whole cell reaction can be written as

$$\overbrace{Mg + Cu^{2+} \longrightarrow Mg^{2+}}^{\text{Oxidation}} + Cu$$

(Oxidation: Mg → Mg^{2+}; Reduction: Cu^{2+} → Cu)

Hence, options (c) is correct.

84 (a) Statement (a) is incorrect.

It's correct form is as follows

In batteries, cells are connected in series, not parallely.

Rest other statements are correct.

85 (b) At cathode,

$$MnO_2 + NH_4^+ + e^- \longrightarrow MnO(OH) + NH_3$$

Here, manganese is reduced from +4 oxidation state to +3 oxidation state.

Thus, statement (b) is incorrect.

86 (c) Statement (c) is correct, while the other statements are incorrect.

Corrected form are as follows

(a) Mercury cell is a low current device.

(b) Zn-Hg amalgam acts as anode and a paste of C + HgO acts as a cathode.

(d) The cell potential is approximately 1.35 V.

87 (a) The cell consists of zinc container/cup that act as anode and cathode is a carbon (graphite) rod surrounded by powdered manganese dioxide and carbon.

The space between electrodes is filled by moist paste of NH_4Cl and $ZnCl_2$.

88 (b)

89 (d) Statement (d) is incorrect. It's correct form is as follows

On charging the battery, the reaction is reversed and $PbSO_4(s)$ at anode and cathode is converted into Pb and PbO_2 respectively.

Rest other statements are correct.

90 (*c*) Statement (c) is correct, while the other statements are incorrect. Corrected form are as follows :

At the time of charging, a reverse reaction takes place. In which $PbSO_4(s)$ at anode and cathode is converted into Pb and PbO_2 respectively. A 38% solution of sulphuric acid is used as an electrolyte.

91 (*b*)

92 (*b*) During charging:

$$PbSO_4 + 2e^- \longrightarrow Pb + SO_4^{2-}$$

$$\Rightarrow \quad 1\text{ F} \equiv 1\text{ g-equiv. of } PbSO_4$$

$$= \frac{1}{2}\text{ mol of } PbSO_4$$

$$\Rightarrow \quad \frac{303}{2}\text{ g } PbSO_4$$

$$\therefore \quad 0.05\text{ F} \equiv \frac{303}{2} \times 0.05\text{ g of } PbSO_4$$

$$= 7.575\text{ g of } PbSO_4$$

93 (*d*) Statement (d) is incorrect. It's correct form is as follows

In hydrogen-oxygen fuel cell, anode reaction is

$$2H_2(g) + 4OH^-(aq) \longrightarrow 4H_2O(l) + 4e^-$$

Rest other statements are correct.

94 (*b*) Galvanisation is the process of applying a protective zinc coating on iron or steel, to prevent rusting.

95 (*d*) All the given reactions take place during rusting of iron.

96 (*d*) All the given statements are correct.

Assertion-Reason

1 (*a*) On applying external voltage greater than 1.1V in a Daniell cell, the current flows in the reverse direction, i.e. from Zn to Cu (anode to cathode). The electrons flow from copper to zinc.
Zn is deposited at Zn electrode and Cu dissolves at Cu electrode. The reaction is

$$Zn^{2+} + Cu \longrightarrow Zn + Cu^{2+}$$

Thus, both A and R are true and R is the correct explanation of A.

2 (*a*) Both A and R are true and R is the correct explanation of A. Also, in electrochemical series Cu is placed above the H^+ ion. Thus, the electrode potential value of H^+/H_2 is less than Cu^{2+}/Cu whereas, the electrode potential of NO_3^-/NO (+0.97) is higher than that of copper electrode and it oxidise Cu to Cu^{2+}.

3 (*a*) Both A and R are true and R is the correct explanation of A.

4 (*c*) Pure water has small amount of hydrogen and hydroxyl ions ($\sim 10^{-7}$ M) due to which it has very low conductivity (3.5×10^{-5} S m^{-1}).

Thus, A is true but R is false.

5 (*a*)

6 (*b*) $\because E = E° - \frac{0.0591}{1}\log\frac{1}{[Ag^+]}$

$$= E° + 0.0591 \log [Ag^+]$$

Thus, $E_{Ag^+/Ag}$ increases with increase in concentration of Ag^+ ions .

Thus, both A and R are true but R is not the correct explanation of A.

7 (*a*) Both A and R are true and the R is the correct explanation of A.

8 (*a*) Since, conductivity depends upon the number of ions per unit volume. Therefore, the conductivity of all electrolytes decreases on dilution due to decrease in number of ions per unit volume.

Thus, both A and R are true and R is the correct explanation of A.

9 (*c*) Cu gets discharged at cathode, i.e. copper metal is deposited at cathode.

$$Cu^{2+}(aq) + 2e^- \longrightarrow Cu(s)$$

At anode, copper is converted into Cu^{2+} ion, i.e. copper is dissolved at anode.

$$Cu(s) \longrightarrow Cu^{2+}(aq) + 2e^-$$

It is the industrial process by which impure copper is converted into copper of high purity.

Thus, A is true but R is false.

10 (*c*) Electricity used

$$= 5 \times 20 \times 60 = 6000\text{ C.}$$

$$Ni(NO_3)_2 + 2H^+ + \underset{2\text{ F}}{2e^-} \longrightarrow \underset{58.7\text{ g}}{Ni} + 2HNO_3$$

Charge required to deposit 1 mole Ni $= 2$ F $= 2 \times 96500 = 1.93 \times 10^5$ C

1.93×10^5 C of charge produce Ni $= 58.7$ g

6000 C of charge will produce

$$Ni = \frac{58.7 \times 6000\text{ C}}{1.93 \times 10^5}$$

$$= 1.8248 \approx 1.825\text{ g}$$

As, mass of substance deposited is directly proportional to the quantity of electricity passed.

Thus, A is true but R is false.

11 (*a*) H_2-O_2 fuel cell is used over ordinary cell because they do not cause any pollution and have high efficiency of 60-70%.

Thus, both A and R are true and R is the correct explanation of A.

Statement Type

1 (c) Statement I is false but Statement II is true.

The correct form of Statement I is :

In standard hydrogen electrode, the pressure of hydrogen gas is 1 bar and the concentration of hydrogen ion in the solution is 1 molar.

2 (*a*) Both Statement I and Statement II are false.

- Copper does not liberate hydrogen from a dilute hydrochloric acid solution.
- Copper is present above hydrogen in the electrochemical series.

3 (*b*) Statement I is true but Statement II is false.

The correct form of statement II is $\Delta G°$ and K are dependent on standard electrode potential.

$$\Delta_r G° = -nFE°_{cell} = -RT \ln K.$$

4 (c) Statement I is false but Statement II is true.

Conductivity increases with an increase in concentration of electrolyte.

5 (d) Both Statement I and Statement II are true.

6 (d) Both Statement I and Statement II are true.

7 (d) Statement II is incorrect. It's correct form is :

In lead storage battery, during discharging phase H_2SO_4 is consumed (as electrolyte).

$$Pb(s) + PbO_2(g) + 2H_2SO_4(aq) \longrightarrow 2PbSO_4(s) + 2H_2O$$

8 (d) All the given statements are correct except V.

Conductance is inverse of resistance.

9 (a) Among the given statements I and V are incorrect. While II, III and IV are correct. The correct form of statement I and V are

- E_{cell} is temperature dependent as per Nernest equation.
- A half-cell is called standard hydrogen electrode represented by $Pt(s) | H_2(g) | H^+(aq)$

10 (a) Among the given statements I, II and III are correct whereas IV and V are incorrect. Their correct form is

- Λ_m° cannot be obtained by extrapolation of Λ_m to zero concentrations for weak electrolytes.
- Kohlrausch law is applicable for calculation the limiting molar conductivity of any (weak and strong) electrolyte.

Matching Type

1 (b) The correct match is

A - 3, B - 2, C - 4, D - 1.

2 (c) The correct match is

A - 1, B - 3, C - 2, D - 4.

3 (b) The correct match is

A - (3), B - (1), C - (7), D - (5), E - (4), F - (2), G - (6).

A. F_2 is a non-metal and best oxidising agent because SRP of F_2 is + 2.87 V.

B. Li is a metal and strongest reducing agent because SRP of Li is – 3.05 V.

C. Au^{3+} is a metal ion which is an oxidising agent as SRP of Au^{3+} is +1.40 V.

D. Br^- is an anion that can be oxidised by Au^{3+} as $E°$ for Au^{3+}/Au (i.e. 1.40 V) is greater than $E°$ for Br_2/Br^- (i.e. 1.09 V).

E. Au is an unreactive metal.

F. Li^+ is a metal ion having least value of SRP (– 3.05 V), hence it is the weakest oxidising agent.

G. F^- is an anion which is the weakest reducing agent as F^- / F_2 has low oxidation potential (–2.87 V).

4 (d) The correct match is

A-(4), B-(1), C-(2), D-(3).

5 (a) The correct match is

A-(4), B-(3), C-(2), D-(1).

6 (b) The correct match is

A-(4), B-(3), C-(1), D-(2).

Numerical Value

1 (1567) Here, $n = 4$ and

$[H^+] = 10^{-pH} = 10^{-3}$

Applying Nernst equation

$$E = E° - \frac{0.059}{n} \log \frac{[Fe^{2+}]^2}{[H^+]^4 p_{O_2}}$$

$$= 1.67 - \frac{0.059}{4} \log \frac{(10^{-3})^2}{(10^{-3})^4 \times 0.1}$$

$$= 1.67 - \frac{0.059}{4} \log 10^7$$

$$= 1.67 - 0.103$$

$$= 1.567 \text{ V} \approx 1567 \times 10^{-3} \text{ V}$$

2 (10) Reactions involved in the cell are

At anode, $\frac{1}{2}H_2 \longrightarrow 1H^+ + 1e^-$

At cathode, $Fe^{3+} + e^- \longrightarrow Fe^{2+}$

Overall equation,

$$\frac{1}{2}H_2 + Fe^{3+} \longrightarrow H^+ + Fe^{2+}$$

$$E_{cell} = E°_{cell} - \frac{0.059}{1} \log \left(\frac{[Fe^{2+}][H^+]}{[Fe^{3+}] p_{H_2}^{1/2}} \right)$$

$$0.712 = 0.771 - 0.059 \log \left(\frac{[Fe^{2+}][H^+]}{[Fe^{3+}] p_{H_2}^{1/2}} \right)$$

$$\log \left(\frac{Fe^{2+}}{Fe^{3+}} \right) = \frac{0.059}{0.059} = 1$$

$$\Rightarrow \quad \frac{Fe^{2+}}{Fe^{3+}} = 10$$

3 (16) Given, $Sn^{2+}(aq) + 2e^- \longrightarrow Sn(s)$; $E°_{Sn^{2+}/Sn} = -0.140$ V

$$\Delta G_1^\circ = -nFE°_{Sn^{2+}/Sn} = -2 \times (-0.14) \text{ F}$$

$$= 0.28 \text{ F} \quad \text{...(i)}$$

$Sn^{4+}(aq) + 4e^- \longrightarrow Sn(s)$; $E°_{Sn^{4+}/Sn} = 0.010$ V

$$\Delta G_2^\circ = -nFE°_{Sn^{4+}/Sn} = -4 \times 0.01$$

$$\Delta G_2^\circ = -0.04 \text{ F} \quad \text{...(ii)}$$

$Sn^{4+}(aq) + 2e^- \longrightarrow Sn^{2+}(aq)$; ΔG_3° ...(iii)

To get Eq. (iii), subtract Eqs. (i) from (ii)

$$-nFE°_{Sn^{4+}/Sn^{2+}} = -0.04\text{F} - 0.28 \text{ F}$$

$$-2FE°_{Sn^{4+}/Sn^{2+}} = -0.32 \text{ F}$$

$$E°_{Sn^{4+}/Sn^{2+}} = \frac{0.32 \text{ F}}{2 \text{ F}} = 0.16 \text{ V}$$

$$E°_{Sn^{4+}/Sn^{2+}} = 16 \times 10^{-2} \text{ V}$$

4 (14) $\Lambda^\infty_{AgI} = \Lambda^\infty_{AgNO_3} + \Lambda^\infty_{NaI} - \Lambda^\infty_{NaNO_3}$

$$= 13.3 + 12.7 - 12.0$$

$$= 14 \text{ mS m}^2 \text{ mol}^{-1}$$

5 (66) $\Lambda_m = \frac{\kappa}{C} \times 1000$

$$= \frac{5 \times 10^{-5} \times 10^3}{0.0025}$$

$$= \frac{5 \times 10^{-2}}{2.5 \times 10^{-3}} = 20 \text{ S cm}^2 \text{ mol}^{-1}$$

$$\alpha = \frac{20}{400} = \frac{1}{20}$$

$$K_a = \frac{C\alpha^2}{1-\alpha} = \frac{0.0025 \times \frac{1}{20} \times \frac{1}{20}}{\frac{19}{20}}$$

$$= \frac{0.0025}{19 \times 20} = 6.6 \times 10^{-6}$$

$$= 66 \times 10^{-7}$$

6 (*34*) The cell reaction is represented as

$$Cu + 2Ag^+ \longrightarrow Cu^{2+} + 2Ag$$

According to Nernst equation,

$$E_{cell} = E^\circ_{cell} - \frac{0.06}{2} \log \frac{[Cu^{2+}]}{[Ag^+]^2}$$

$$0.43 = E^\circ_{cell} - \frac{0.06}{2} \log \frac{(0.001)}{(0.01)^2}$$

$$= 0.46 \text{ V}$$

$$E^\circ_{cell} = E^\circ_{Ag^+/Ag} - E^\circ_{Cu^{2+}/Cu}$$

$$\Rightarrow 0.46 = 0.80 - E^\circ_{Cu^{2+}/Cu}$$

$$E^\circ_{Cu^{2+}/Cu} = 0.34 \text{ volt} \Rightarrow 34 \times 10^{-2}$$

NCERT Exemplar's

1 (*c*) Standard electrode potential of copper electrode can be calculated by constructing a electrochemical cell composed of two half-cell reactions in which standard hydrogen electrode as anode (reference half-cell) and the other half-cell as cathode.

$$\underbrace{Pt(s) \mid H_2(g, 1 \text{ bar}) \mid H^+(aq, 1 \text{ M})}_{\text{Oxidation half-cell reaction}} \Big| \underbrace{Cu^{2+}(aq, 1 \text{ M}) \mid Cu}_{\text{Reduction half-cell reaction}}$$

2 (*d*) It does not provide surface for redox reaction. Thus, statement (d) is not correct while other given statements are correct.

3 (*b*) Electrode potential for Mg electrode varies according to the equation,

$$E_{Mg^{2+}/Mg} = E^\circ_{Mg^{2+}/Mg} - \frac{0.059}{2} \log \frac{1}{[Mg^{2+}]}$$

or, $$E_{Mg^{2+}/Mg} = \frac{0.059}{2} \log [Mg^{2+}] + E^\circ_{Mg^{2+}/Mg}$$

This equation represents equation of straight line, i.e. $y = mx + c$.

So, intercept $(c) = E^\circ_{Mg^{2+}/Mg}$

This, equation can be graphically represented as

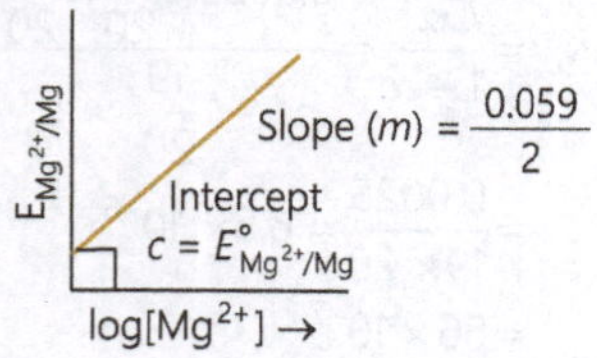

4 (*c*) E_{cell} is an intensive property as it does not depend upon mass of species (number of particles) but $\Delta_r G$ of the cell reaction is an extensive property because this depends upon mass of species (number of particles).

Thus, statement (c) is correct.

5 (*b*) Here, out of given four options standard reduction potential of chromium has highest negative value, hence most powerful reducing agent is chromium (Cr).

6 (*b*) On moving top to bottom SRP value decreases from positive to negative value which will increase the reducing capacity. So, the correct option is (b).

7 (*a*) $E^\circ_{Cr^{3+}/Cr}$ has most – ve value equal to – 0.74 among given four choices. So, Cr^{3+} is the most stable oxidised species.

8 (*d*) $E^\circ_{MnO_4^-/Mn^{2+}}$ has + ve value equal to 1.51 V which is highest among given four choices. So, Mn^{2+} is most stable ion in its reduced form.

9 (*c*) Higher the positive value of standard reduction potential of metal ion higher will be its oxidising capacity.

Since, $E^\circ_{MnO_4^-/Mn^{2+}}$ has value equal to 1.51 V hence it is the strongest oxidising agent.

10 (*d*)

11 (*c*) Statement (c) is incorrect. It's correct form is as follows

Conductivity depends on solvation of ions present in solution.

Greater the solvation of ions of an electrolyte, lesser will be the electrical conductivity of the solution.

12 (*b*)

13 (*c*) The quantity of charge required to obtain one mole of aluminium from Al_2O_3 is equal to number of electrons required to convert Al_2O_3 to Al.

$$Al^{3+}(aq) \xrightarrow{+3e} Al(s)$$

Hence, total charge 3F is required.

14 (*a*) While charging the lead storage battery, the reaction occurring in the cell is reversed and $PbSO_4$ (*s*) on anode and cathode is converted into Pb and PbO_2 respectively.

15 (*b*) **Cell emf** The difference between the electrode potential of two electrodes when no current is drawn through the cell is called cell emf.

16 (*c*) If an external opposite potential is applied on the galvanic cell and increased reaction continues to take place till the opposing voltage reaches the value 1.1 V.

At this stage no current flow through the cell and if there is any further increase in the external potential then reaction starts functioning in opposite direction.

Hence, this works as an electrolytic cell.

17 (*d*) In case of electrolysis of aqueous NaCl oxidation reaction occurs at anode as follows

$$Cl^-(aq) \longrightarrow \frac{1}{2} Cl_2(g) + e^-; \quad E^\circ = 1.36 \text{ V}$$

$$2H_2O(l) \longrightarrow O_2(g) + 4H^+(aq) + 4e^-; \quad E^\circ_{cell} = 1.23 \text{ V}$$

But due to lower E°_{cell} value water should get oxidised in preference of Cl^- (*aq*).

However, the actual reaction taking place in the concentrated solution of NaCl is (d) and not (b), i.e. Cl_2 is produced and not O_2.

This unexpected result is explained on the basis of the concept of 'overvoltage', i.e. water needs greater voltage for oxidation to O_2 (as it is kinetically slow process) than that needed for oxidation of Cl^- ions to Cl_2. Thus, the correct option is (d) not (b).

Past Exams'

1 (*b*) Given, current (i) $= 9.6487$ A

$1F = 96487$ C

$t = 100$ s

$$w = \frac{E(it)}{96487}$$

$$\Rightarrow w = \frac{\frac{63}{2} \times 9.6487 \times 100}{96487}$$

$w = 0.315$ g of Cu

2 (*a*) The correct match is

A-II, B-IV, C-I, D-III.

A. $2H_2O \longrightarrow O_2 + 4H^+ + 4e^-$

2 mol H_2O require 4F charge

1 mol H_2O will require 2F charge.

B. $8H^+ + MnO_4^- + 5e^- \longrightarrow Mn^{2+} + 4H_2O$

1 mole of MnO_4^- will require 5F charge.

C. $CaCl_2 + 2e^- \longrightarrow Ca + 2Cl^{-1}$

1 mole of Ca will require 2F charge.

1.5 moles of Ca will require 3F charge.

D. $FeO + H_2O \longrightarrow Fe_2O_3 + 2H^+ + 2e^-$

2 moles of FeO will require 2F charge.

1 mole of FeO will require 1 F charge.

3 (*b*) Given, conductivity (κ) $= 0.0210\, \Omega^{-1}\text{cm}^{-1}$

Resistance $= 60\, \Omega$ and

Cell constant = ?

We know that, $\kappa = \frac{1}{R} \times \frac{l}{a}$

Cell constant $= \frac{l}{a} = \kappa \times R$

$= 0.0210 \times 60 = 1.26\text{ cm}^{-1}$

4 (*d*) Reaction at cathode (reduction)

$2MnO_4^- + 16H^+ + 10e^- \longrightarrow 2Mn^{2+} + 8H_2O$; $E°_{RP} = 1.510$ V

Reaction at anode (oxidation)

$5H_2O \longrightarrow \frac{5}{2}O_2 + 10H^+ + 10e^-$;

$E°_{OP} = -1.223$ V

The overall reaction is

$2MnO_4^- + 6H^+ \longrightarrow 2Mn^{2+} + \frac{5}{2}O_2 + 3\,H_2O$

$$E° = E°_{MnO_4^-/Mn^{2+}} - E°_{O_2/H_2O}$$

$$= 1.510 - 1.223 = 0.287 \text{ V}$$

Here, since the value of $E°$ is positive, the reaction is spontaneous. Hence, MnO_4^- will liberate O_2.

5 (*c*) Standard reduction potential values is given to us which can be arranged as follows

$E°_{Zn^{2+}/Zn} < E°_{Fe^{2+}/Fe} < E°_{Cu^{2+}/Cu} < E°_{Ag^+/Ag}$

So, the reactivity order will be

Zn > Fe > Cu > Ag.

The reactions given in the options are displacement reaction. In case of displacement reaction, more reactive metals (i.e. low SRP) can displace less reactive metals (higher SRP) from their salt solution.

So, $CuSO_4(aq) + 2Ag(s) \longrightarrow Cu(s) + Ag_2SO_4\ aq)$ is not possible.

As, Ag is less reactive as compared to Cu. Hence, the correct option is (c).

6 (*b*) Given, $E°_{cell} = 1.05$ V

$$\frac{2.303\,RT}{F} = 0.059$$

Using Nernst equation,

$$E_{cell} = E°_{cell} - \frac{0.059}{n}\log\frac{[Ni^{+2}]^1}{[Ag^{+1}]^2}$$

$$= 1.05 - \frac{0.059}{2}\log\frac{(10^{-3})}{(10^{-3})^2}$$

$$= 1.05 - \frac{0.059}{2} \times 3$$

$= 1.05 - 0.0885$; $E_{cell} = 0.9615$

7 (*c*) According to Kohlrausch's law,

$$\lambda°_{CH_3COOH} = \lambda°_{H^+} + \lambda°_{CH_3COO^-}$$

$$= 400\text{ S cm}^2\text{ mol}^{-1}$$

Degree of dissociation,

$$\alpha = \frac{\lambda_{CH_3COOH}}{\lambda°_{CH_3COOH}}$$

$$\alpha = \frac{20}{400} = \frac{1}{20} = 0.05 = 5 \times 10^{-2}$$

	CH_3COOH	$\rightleftharpoons$	CH_3COO^-	$+ H^+$
$t = 0$	C		–	–
$t = t_{eq}$	$C - C\alpha$		$C\alpha$	$C\alpha$

Equilibrium constant,

$$K = \frac{C^2\alpha^2}{C(1-\alpha)} = \frac{C\alpha^2}{1-\alpha}$$

As $\alpha << 1; 1 - \alpha \approx 1$

$$K = C\alpha^2 = 0.007 \times (0.05)^2$$

$$= 0.007 \times 25 \times 10^{-4}$$

$$= 1.75 \times 10^{-5}\text{ mol}^{-1}\text{ L}^{-1}$$

8 (*c*) Let us consider the segment of EMF series (standard reduction potential) of the given reduction half-cell reactions

Reduction half reaction	$E°$/V at 298K
(a) $Mg^{2+} + 2e^- \longrightarrow Mg$	-2.36
(b) $Fe^{2+} + 2e^- \longrightarrow Fe$	-0.44
(c) $Au^{3+} + 3e^- \longrightarrow Au$	$+1.40$
(d) $K^+ + e^- \longrightarrow K$	-2.93

Hence, option (c) is correct.

9 (*d*) $\underset{\text{Molten}}{CaCl_2} \rightleftharpoons Ca^{2+} + 2Cl^-$

At cathode, $Ca^{2+} + 2e^- \longrightarrow Ca$
(Reduction)

According to Faraday's first law,

Charge passed in Faraday = Gram equivalent of product

$$= \frac{\text{Given mass}}{\text{Atomic mass}} \times \text{no. of } e^- \text{ released}$$

$$= \frac{20}{40} \times 2 = 1\text{ F}$$

So, one Faraday (F) is required for the process.

10 (*d*) The relation between $E°_{cell}$ and $\Delta_r G°$ is as follows

$$\Delta_r G° = -nFE°_{cell}$$

For the cell reaction,

$$2Fe^{3+}(aq) + 2I^-(aq) \longrightarrow 2Fe^{2+}(aq) + I_2(aq)$$

$n = 2$

Given, $F = 96500\text{ C mol}^{-1}$,

$E°_{cell} = 0.24$ V

Now, we know that $\Delta_r G° = -nFE°_{cell}$

On substituting the given values in above equation we get

$$\Delta_r G^\circ = -2\ \text{mol} \times 96500\ \text{C mol}^{-1} \times 0.24\ \text{J mol}^{-1}$$
$$= -46320\ \text{J mol}^{-1}$$
$$= -46.32\ \text{kJ mol}^{-1}$$

Hence, option (d) is correct.

11 (b) We know that,

$$E_{cell} = E^\circ_{cell} - \frac{2.303RT}{nF}\log Q$$

At equilibrium, $Q = K_{eq}$

and $E_{cell} = 0$

$$\therefore\ E^\circ_{cell} = \frac{2.303\ RT}{nF}\log K_{eq} \quad ...(i)$$

Given : $E^\circ_{cell} = 0.59$ V, $\frac{2.303RT}{F} = 0.059$ V,

$T = 298$ K, $n = 1$

On substituting the given values in Eq. (i), we get

$$0.59 = \frac{0.059}{1}\log K_{eq}$$

$$\therefore\ \log K_{eq} = \frac{0.59}{0.059} = 10$$

$$\Rightarrow\ K_{eq} = 10^{10} = 1 \times 10^{10}$$

12. (d) Given

$$\lambda^\circ_{m(H_2SO_4)} = 2\lambda^\circ_{H^+} + \lambda^\circ_{SO_4^{2-}} = x\ \text{S cm}^2\text{mol}^{-1} \quad ...(i)$$

$$\lambda^\circ_{m(K_2SO_4)} = 2\lambda^\circ_{K^+} + \lambda^\circ_{SO_4^{2-}} = y\ \text{S cm}^2\text{mol}^{-1} \quad ...(ii)$$

$$\lambda^\circ_{m(CH_3COOK)} = \lambda^\circ_{CH_3COO^-} + \lambda^\circ_{K^+} = z\ \text{S cm}^2\text{mol}^{-1} \quad ...(iii)$$

To find : $\lambda^\circ_{m(CH_3COOH)} = \lambda^\circ_{CH_3COO^-} + \lambda^\circ_{H^+}$

The above equation can be obtained by

$$\text{Eq. (iii)} + \frac{\text{Eq. (i)}}{2} - \frac{\text{Eq. (ii)}}{2}$$

$$\therefore\ \lambda^\circ_{m(CH_3COOH)} = \lambda^\circ_{m(CH_3COOK)} + \frac{\lambda^\circ_{m(H_2SO_4)}}{2} - \frac{\lambda^\circ_{m(K_2SO_4)}}{2}$$

$$= \left(z + \frac{x}{2} - \frac{y}{2}\right)\text{S cm}^2\ \text{mol}^{-1}$$

$$= \left(\frac{x-y}{2} + z\right)\text{S cm}^2\ \text{mol}^{-1}$$

13 (c) Using first law of electrolysis,

$Q = it = 1\text{A} \times 60s = 60\text{As}$ or 60 C

96500 C charge $= 6.022 \times 10^{23}$ electrons

$$60\ \text{C charge} = \frac{6.022 \times 10^{23}}{96500} \times 60 = 3.74 \times 10^{20}\ \text{electrons}$$

14. (b) Given, concentration of solution,

$M = 0.5$ mol / dm^3

Electrolytic conductivity,

$\kappa = 5.76 \times 10^{-3}$ S cm^{-1}

Temperature, $T = 298$ K

∴ Molar conductivity,

$$\lambda_m = \frac{\kappa \times 1000}{M} = \frac{5.76 \times 10^{-3} \times 1000}{0.5} = 11.52\ \text{S cm}^2/\text{mol}$$

15. (d) The metal with higher negative standard reduction potential, have higher tendency to get oxidised.

$$Zn^{2+} + 2e^- \longrightarrow Zn\ ;\ E^\circ = -0.76\ \text{V}$$
$$Fe^{2+} + 2e^- \longrightarrow Fe\ ;\ E^\circ = -0.44\ \text{V}$$

Thus, Zn works as anode and protects iron from rusting by making iron as cathode.

16. (a) Given, $E^\circ_{cell} = -ve$

Now, the relation between ΔG° and E°_{cell} is given as

$$\Delta G^\circ = -nFE^\circ_{cell} \quad ...(i)$$

as E°_{cell} is negative , so ΔG° comes out to be positive. Again, relation between ΔG° and K_{eq} is given as

$$\Delta G^\circ = -2.303nRT\log K_{eq} \quad ...(ii)$$

From Eq. (i) we get that ΔG° is positive. Now, if ΔG° is positive then K_{eq} comes out to be negative from eq (ii).

i.e. $\Delta G^\circ > 1$ and $K_{eq} < 1$

17. (c) $\underset{(+6)}{MnO_4^{2-}} \xrightleftharpoons{[1\ \text{mol}\ e^- = 1\ F]} \underset{(+7)}{MnO_4^-}$

As per the equation, for 1 mole of MnO_4^{2-}, 1 F of electricity is required. Thus, for 0.1 mole of MnO_4^{2-}, 0.1 F of electricity is required.

Since, 1 F = 96500 C

∴ 0.1 F = 0.1× 96500 C = 9650 C

Hence, 9650 C of electricity is required to completely oxidise MnO_4^{2-} to MnO_4^-.

18. (d) Option (d) is incorrect among the given options while remaining all other options are correct.

The correct form of option (d) is as follows

As tin coating is peeled off, then iron is exposed in atmosphere.

19. (c) An electrochemical cell can be converted into an electrolytic cell by applying an external potential greater than E°_{cell}.

The entire cell reaction will be reversed. The oxidised species will be reduced and the reduced species will be oxidised.

20. (a) Among the given options only nature of electrode does not affect electrolytic conductance of a solution.

21. (b) Reaction involved in electrolysis of brine solution is as follows

$$NaCl(aq) \xrightarrow{H_2O} Na^+(aq) + Cl^-(aq)$$

At anode, $2Cl^-(aq) \longrightarrow Cl_2(g) + 2e^-$

$2H_2O(l) \longrightarrow O_2(g) + 4H^+ + 4e^-$

At cathode,

$2H_2O\ (l) + 2e^- \longrightarrow H_2(g)\uparrow + 2OH^-(aq)$

$2Na^+ + 2OH^- \longrightarrow 2NaOH$

Thus, OH^- is formed at cathode.

22. (a) For the reaction,

$$\frac{1}{2}H_2(g) + AgCl(s) \rightleftharpoons H^+(aq) + Cl^-(aq) + Ag(s)$$

At anode, $\frac{1}{2}H_2(g) \longrightarrow H^+(aq) + e^-$

At cathode,

$AgCl(s) + e^- \longrightarrow Ag(s) + Cl^-(aq)$

∴ Cell representation is

$Pt|H_2(g)|HCl(aq)\ ||\ AgCl(s)|\ Ag\ (s)$

23. (a) Statements given in B and D are correct.
On charging the lead storage battery, the reaction is reversed and $PbSO_4(s)$ on anode is converted into Pb instead of PbO_2.
Lead storage battery consists of lead anode and a grid of lead packed with lead oxide as cathode, a 38% solution of H_2SO_4 is used as an electrolyte.

24. (a) Molar conductivity,
$$\Lambda_M = \frac{\kappa \times 1000}{M}$$
$$\Lambda_{M_1} = \frac{\kappa_1 \times 1000}{\frac{10}{20} \times 1000} = 2\kappa_1$$
and $$\Lambda_{M_2} = \frac{\kappa_2 \times 1000}{\frac{20}{80} \times 1000} = 4\kappa_2$$
Given, $\kappa_1 = \kappa_2 = \kappa$
$\therefore$ $\Lambda_{M_1} = 2\kappa;\ \Lambda_{M_2} = 4\kappa$
$$\frac{\Lambda_{M_2}}{\Lambda_{M_1}} = \frac{4\kappa}{2\kappa} = \frac{4}{2}$$
$\Rightarrow$ $\Lambda_{M_2} = 2\Lambda_{M_1}$

25. (c) The correct match is
A-II, B-I, C-IV, D-III.

26. (a) PbO_2 or Pb_3O_4 can be the compound A. But out of these two compounds only PbO_2 is used in lead storage batteries where a grid of lead packed with PbO_2 acts as cathode and also it is amphoteric in nature. It reacts with both acids and alkali.

27. (a) The correct match is
A-3, B-1, C-4, D-2.

Skill Boosters

1. (b) $E = E° - \frac{0.059}{n} \log \frac{1}{[M^{n+}]}$
Lower the concentration of M^{n+} lower is the reduction potential.
Hence, the correct order is
$B > C > D > A$

2. (a) The reaction $2Ag + SnBr_2 \longrightarrow$ No reaction because Sn^{2+} is a stronger reducing agent than Ag^+.

3. (a) MnO_4^- cannot be used in aqueous HCl because MnO_4^- will not only oxidise Fe^{+2} to Fe^{+3} instead of that it also oxidise Cl^- to Cl_2.

4. (c) Higher the reduction potential, higher is the tendency to deposition. Mg^{2+} will not be reduced as its reduction potential is much lower than water. Hence, the sequence of deposition of the metals will be Ag, Hg, Cu, Mg

5. (b) The standard electrode potential $E°$ for silver is 0.80 V and that of gold is 1.5 V, hence silver can displace gold from its solution.
The replaced gold is deposited on silver object due to which golden tinge is obtained. On the other hand, $E°$ for Cu is 0.34 V which is lower than that of silver, thus silver cannot replace copper from its solutions.

6. (c) The cell reaction is
$$Zn(s) + Cu^{2+}(aq) \rightleftharpoons Zn^{2+}(aq) + Cu(s)$$
$$E_{cell} = E°_{cell} - \frac{2.303RT}{2F} \log \frac{[Zn^{2+}]}{[Cu^{2+}]}$$
$$E_1 = E°_{cell} - \frac{0.06}{2} \log\left(\frac{Zn^{2+}}{Cu^{2+}}\right)$$
$$E_2 = E°_{cell} - \frac{0.06}{2} \log \frac{Zn^{2+}}{0.5}$$
$$E_2 - E_1 = \frac{0.06}{2}\left\{\log\left(\frac{Zn^{2+}}{Cu^{2+}}\right) - \log\left(\frac{Zn^{2+}}{0.5}\right)\right\}$$
$$0.03 = 0.03 \log \frac{0.5}{Cu^{2+}}$$
$$\log \frac{0.5}{Cu^{2+}} = 1$$
$$\frac{0.5}{Cu^{2+}} = 10$$
$$[Cu^{2+}] = 0.05\ M$$

7. (a) Tarnished silver contains Ag_2S. This can be removed by placing tarnished silver in an aluminium pan.
$$Ag_2S + Al \longrightarrow Al^{3+} + 2Ag + S^{2-}$$
$$E° = E°_{(Ag_2S/2Ag,S^{2-})} - E°_{(Al^{3+}/Al)}$$
$$= -0.71 - (-1.66) = +0.95\ V$$
$E°_{cell}$ is positive, the reaction is feasible and hence tarnish will be removed.
Other reactions will not occur as $E°_{cell} = -ve$ and hence cannot be used to remove the tarnishing.

8. (b) Higher reduction potential, means self reduction of species but oxidises others (means good oxidising agent).
Thus, Q will oxidise R and not P.

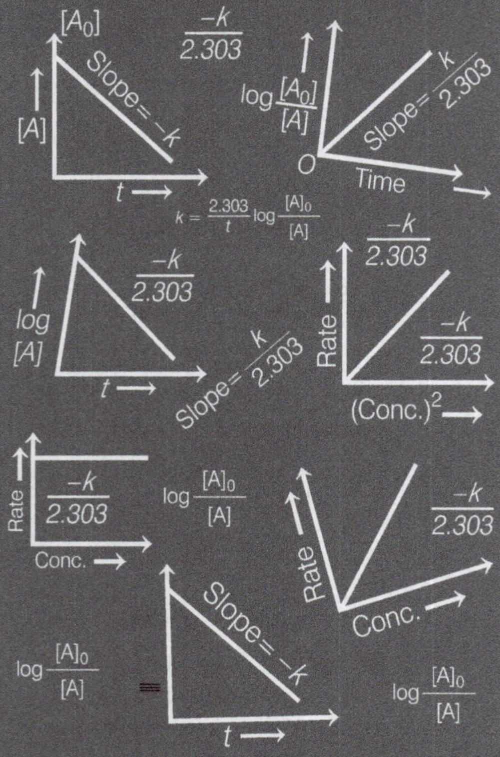

Scan for **Chemistry Through Concept Master** Videos

03 Chemical Kinetics

The branch of chemistry that deals with the study of reaction rates (speed) and their mechanisms is known as chemical kinetics. It also describes the conditions (like temperature, concentration etc.) by which rates can be altered.

Topicwise No. of Ques asked in 5 Years (NEET)

Topics	2024	2023	2022	2021	2020
Rate of a Chemical Reaction	–	–	–	–	–
Factors Influencing Rate of a Reaction	–	1	–	–	–
Integrated Rate Equations	–	–	2	–	2
Temperature Dependence of the Rate of a Reaction	2	1	–	2	–
Collision Theory of Chemical Reactions	–	–	–	–	2

Special Type of Ques Asked In 5 Years (NEET)

Types	2024	2023	2022	2021	2020
A-R	–	1	–	–	–
Statement Based	–	–	–	–	–
Matching	–	1	–	–	–

Last 5 Years Weightage (NEET)

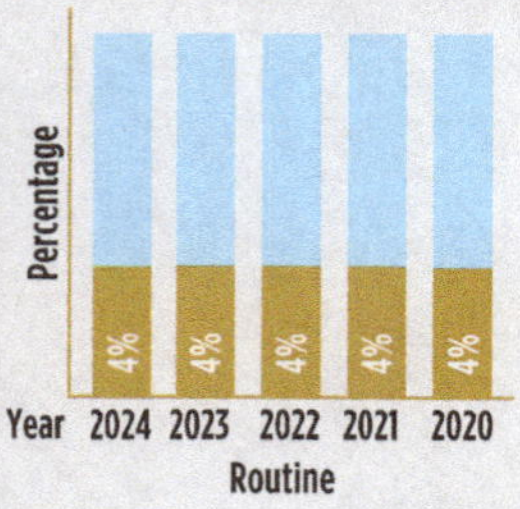

Rate of a Chemical Reaction

The rate of a chemical reaction is the change in molar concentration of the species taking part in the chemical reaction per unit time.

For the reaction, $A \longrightarrow B$

Rate of disappearance of reaction

$$= \frac{\text{Decrease in concentration of reactant}}{\text{Time taken}} = \frac{-\Delta[A]}{\Delta t}$$

Rate of appearance of reaction

$$= \frac{\text{Increase in concentration of product}}{\text{Time taken}} = \frac{\Delta[B]}{\Delta t}$$

- **Average rate of reaction** is the average value of reactant or product concentration during a specified interval of time.

$$r_{av} = \frac{-\Delta[A]}{\Delta t} = + \frac{\Delta[B]}{\Delta t}$$

- **Units of rate of reaction** is concentration time^{-1}, i.e. mol L^{-1} s^{-1} or atm s^{-1} (in gaseous reactions).
- **Instantaneous rate of reaction** is the rate of change of concentration of any one of the species involved in the reaction at a particular instant of time (i.e. when Δt approaches zero).

$$r_{inst} = \frac{-d[A]}{dt} = \frac{+d[B]}{dt}$$

Note For expressing the rate of such a reaction where stoichiometric coefficients of reactant or product are not equal to one, rate of disappearance of any of the reactants or the rate of appearance of products is divided by their respective stoichiometric coefficients.

Rate of reaction can be determined from the slope of the graph between the concentration of the reactants or products and time.

- Graph between the concentration of reactants and time comparing both the instantaneous and average rate of reaction is shown below.

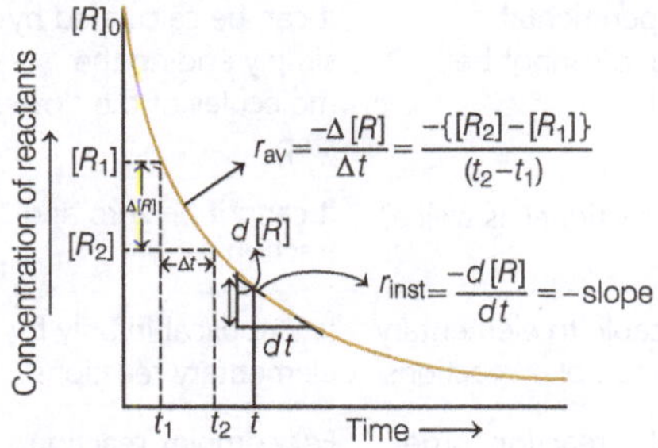

- Graph between the concentration of products and time comparing both the instantaneous and average rate of reaction is shown below.

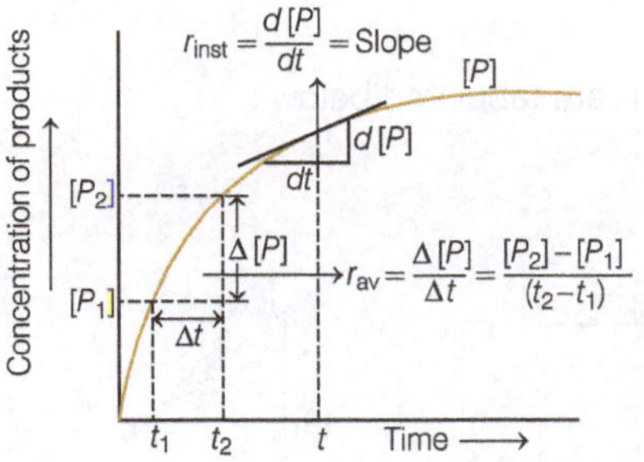

Here, Δ used for a larger change in defining the average rate of reaction while in instantaneous rate of reaction 'd' is used as a small change in concentration.

Factors Influencing Rate of a Reaction

- **Concentration** Greater the concentration of the reactants, or lesser the concentration of products, faster is the rate of reaction.
- **Physical state of reactants** Reactions involving gaseous reactants are faster than reactions containing solid and liquid reactants.
- **Surface area of reactants** For a reaction involving a solid reactant or catalyst, the greater the surface area, the faster is the reaction.
- **Temperature** The rate of reaction increases with increase in temperature. For most of the reactions, rate of reaction becomes almost double with 10° rise in temperature.
- **Presence of catalyst** A catalyst is a substance that accelerates a reaction by involved in it without being consumed.

Rate Expression and Rate Constant

Rate law is the expression in which reaction rate is given in terms of molar concentration of reactants with each terms raised to some power, which may or may not be same as the stoichiometric coefficient of the reacting species in a balanced chemical equation.

It is also called as **rate expression**.

For a general reaction,

$$aA + bB \longrightarrow cC + dD$$

Rate $= k[A]^x[B]^y$,

where, x and y may or may not be equal to the stoichiometric coefficients (a and b) of the reactants.

$$\text{Rate} = \frac{-d[R]}{dt} = k[A]^x[B]^y$$ **NEET 2023**

The above equation is known as **differential rate equation**, where k is a proportionality constant called **rate constant**.

Rate law for any reaction cannot be predicted by merely looking at the balanced chemical equation, i.e. theoretically, but must be determined experimentally.

Order of a Reaction

It is the sum of powers of the concentration of the reactants in the rate law expression.

If rate $= k[A]^x[B]^y$; order of a reaction $= x + y$

Order of a reaction can be 0, 1, 2, 3 and even a fraction.

Reactions occurring only in one step are called **elementary reactions** while that involving a sequence of elementary reactions, are called **complex reactions**. In case of complex reactions, the slowest step is called **rate determining step**.

Examples

- **Zero order** $2NH_3 \xrightarrow[1130\,K]{Pt} N_2 + 3H_2$; Rate $= k[NH_3]^0 = k$
- **1st order** $2N_2O_5 \longrightarrow 4NO_2 + O_2$; Rate $= k[N_2O_5]$
- **2nd order** $2NO_2 \longrightarrow 2NO + O_2$; Rate $= k[NO_2]^2$
- **3rd order** $2NO + O_2 \longrightarrow 2NO_2$; Rate $= k[NO]^2[O_2]$
- **Fractional order** $CH_3CHO \longrightarrow CH_4 + CO$; Rate $= k[CH_3CHO]^{3/2}$

Units of Rate Constant

The units of rate constants of different orders are different. Considering SI units of concentration, mol L^{-1} and time, s. The units of k for different orders of reaction are given below.

Reaction	Order	Unit of rate constant (k)
Zero order	$n = 0$	$= \frac{\text{mol L}^{-1}}{\text{s}} \times \frac{1}{(\text{mol L}^{-1})^0} = \text{mol L}^{-1}\,\text{s}^{-1}$
First order	$n = 1$	$= \frac{\text{mol L}^{-1}}{\text{s}} \times \frac{1}{(\text{mol L}^{-1})^1} = \text{s}^{-1}$
Second order	$n = 2$	$= \frac{\text{mol L}^{-1}}{\text{s}} \times \frac{1}{(\text{mol L}^{-1})^2} = \text{mol}^{-1}\text{Ls}^{-1}$
n^{th} order	n	$= \frac{\text{mol L}^{-1}}{\text{s}} \times \frac{1}{(\text{mol L}^{-1})^n} = (\text{mol L}^{-1})^{1-n}\text{s}^{-1}$

Molecularity of a Reaction

It is the number of the reacting species (atoms, ions or molecules) taking part in an elementary reaction, which must collide simultaneously in order to bring about a chemical reaction.

Depending on the collision between the number of species molecularity can be explained as

Unimolecular reaction $NH_4NO_2 \longrightarrow N_2 + 2H_2O$

Bimolecular reaction $2HI \longrightarrow H_2 + I_2$

Trimolecular reaction $2NO + O_2 \longrightarrow 2NO_2$

Note The probability that more than three molecules can collide and react simultaneously is very small. Thus, reactions with the molecularity three are very rare and slow to proceed.

Difference between Order and Molecularity of a Reaction

Order of reaction	Molecularity of reaction
It is an experimental quantity and cannot be calculated.	It can be calculated by simply adding the molecules of the slowest step.
It can be fractional as well as zero.	It cannot be zero and fractional
It is applicable to elementary as well as complex reactions.	It is applicable only for elementary reactions.
For complex reaction, order is given by the slowest step.	For complex reaction, molecularity has no significance.

For Concept Master *Video*

Integrated Rate Equations

The differential and integrated rate equations for zero and first order reactions are tabulated below :

Reaction	Order	Differential equation	Integral equation	$t_{1/2}$	Plot
(i) $A \longrightarrow$ Product $[A]_0$ = initial concentration of reactants	Zero order	$\frac{d[A]}{dt} = -k$	$k = \frac{\{[A]_0 - [A]\}}{t}$	$\frac{[A]_0}{2k}$ NEET 2022, 2020	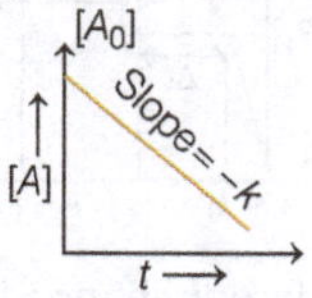
(ii) $A \longrightarrow$ Product	First order	$\frac{d[A]}{dt} = -k[A]$	$k = \frac{2.303}{t}\log\frac{[A]_0}{[A]}$ NEET 2020, 2019	$\frac{0.693}{k}$	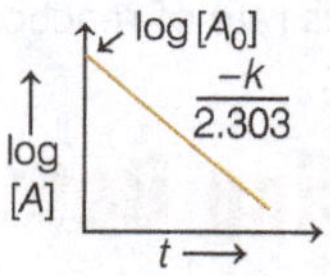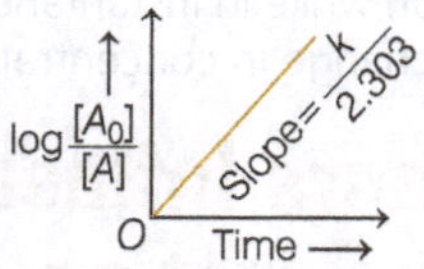

Marks Maximizer

- General expression for the time taken for n^{th} fraction of a reaction of 1st order to complete.

$$t_{1/n} = \frac{2.303}{k}\log\frac{n}{n-1}$$

- The time taken for any fraction of the first order reaction is independent of initial concentration.
- General expression for the time taken by reactant to reduce to n^{th} fraction.

$$t = \frac{2.303}{k}\log n$$

Pseudo First Order Reaction

The reactions which are not actually of first order but behave so due to altered conditions are called pseudo first order reaction.

In such a chemical reaction, between two substances, one reactant is present in large or excess amounts. e.g.

- **Acid hydrolysis of ethyl acetate**

$$CH_3COOC_2H_5 + \underset{(Excess)}{H_2O} \xrightarrow{H^+} CH_3COOH + C_2H_5OH;$$

$$Rate = k[CH_3COOC_2H_5]$$

- **Inversion of cane sugar**

$$C_{12}H_{22}O_{11} + \underset{(Excess)}{H_2O} \xrightarrow{H^+} C_6H_{12}O_6 + C_6H_{12}O_6;\ Rate = k[C_{12}H_{22}O_{11}]$$

Marks Maximizer

- Integrated rate equations for reactions of higher order

Reaction	Order	Rate law	Rate constant
$2R \rightarrow$ Products	2	Rate $= k[R]^2$	$k = \frac{1}{t}\left(\frac{1}{[R]} - \frac{1}{[R]_0}\right)$
$A + B \rightarrow$ Products	2	Rate $= k[A][B]$	$k = \frac{1}{t}\frac{2.303}{([A]_0 - [B]_0)}\log\frac{[B]_0[A]}{[A]_0[B]}$

- Some typical linear plots for reactions of different orders are given below.

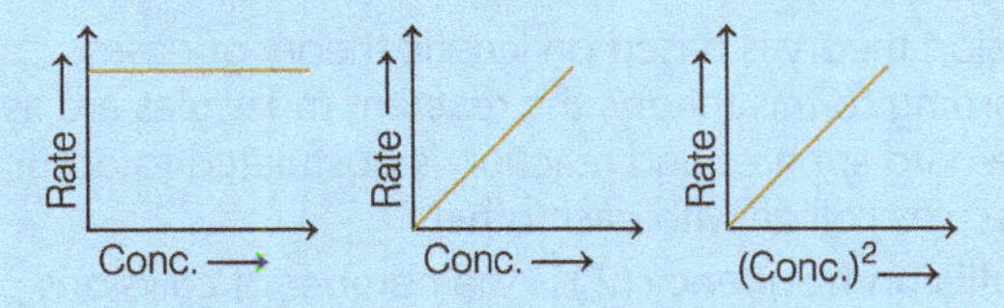

- Plots from integrated rate equations

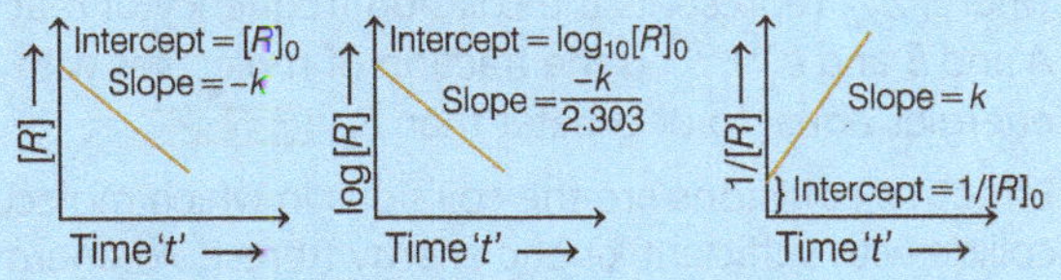

- Plots of half-lives vs concentration ($t_{1/2} \propto [R]_0^{1-n}$)

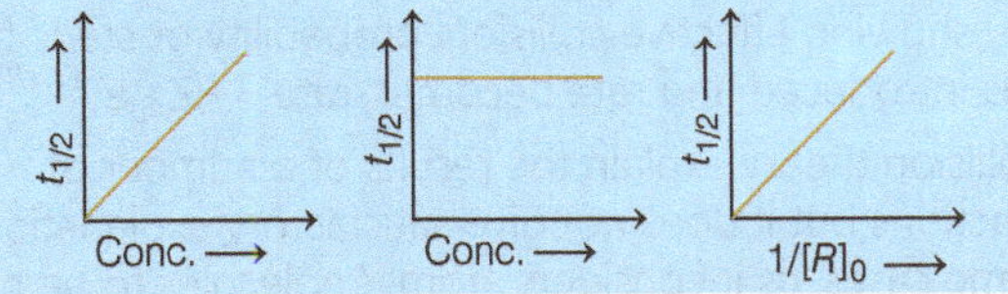

Temperature Dependence of the Rate of a Reaction

- Most of the chemical reactions are accelerated by increase in temperature.
- For a chemical reaction with rise in temperature by 10°C, the rate constant is nearly doubled.
- The temperature dependence of the rate of a chemical reaction can be exactly explained by Arrhenius equation.

Arrhenius Equation NEET 2024

The quantitative relationship between rate constant of a reaction and temperature was proposed by Arrhenius equation, $k = Ae^{-E_a/RT}$

For Concept Master Video

Here, A = Arrhenius factor or frequency factor or pre-exponential factor.

E_a = activation energy, (Joules/mole), R = gas constant T = temperature.

$e^{-E_a/RT}$ corresponds to the fraction of molecules having kinetic energy equal to or greater than E_a and is called **Boltzmann factor** in general terms.

- According to Arrhenius, a reaction can takes place only when reactant molecules collide with each other.
- Collision of reactant molecules forms an unstable intermediate which exists for a short time and then breaks up to form the product molecules.

  e.g. $H_2(g) + I_2(g) \longrightarrow 2HI(g)$
- **Activation energy** is the extra amount of energy which has to be supplied to the reacting species in their normal energy state to make their energy equal to threshold energy.
- Energy is released when activated complex decomposes to form products. Profile of energy when reactants go into products is represented by the following diagram. NEET 2021

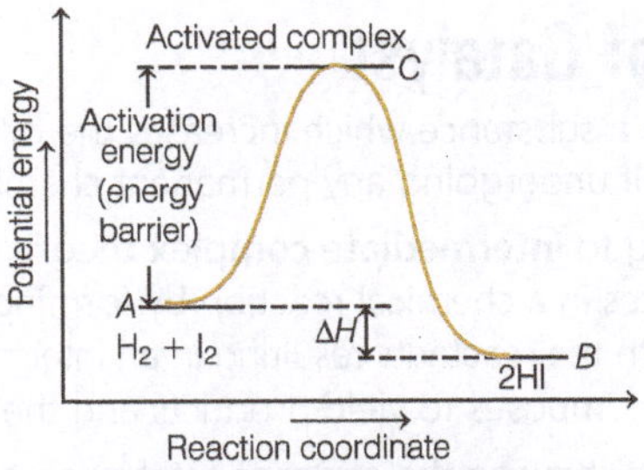

Diagram showing plot of potential energy *versus* reaction coordinate

- The distribution of kinetic energy may be described by plotting the fraction of molecules (N_E/N_T) with given kinetic energy (E) vs kinetic energy. This is called **Maxwell's distribution curve of energy**. Here, N_E is the number of molecules with energy (E) and (N_T) is the total number of molecules.

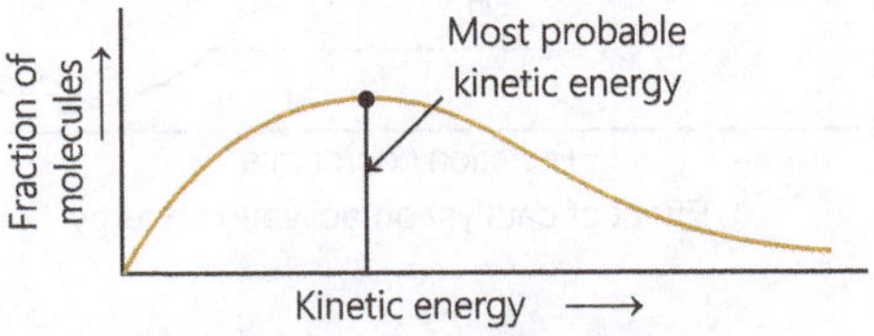

Distribution curve showing energies among gaseous molecules

- When the temperature is raised, the maximum of the curve moves to the higher energy value and the curve broadens out. Thus, proportion of molecules with higher energy increases, i.e. the fraction of reactant molecules which collide with energies greater the E_a increases with increasing temperature.

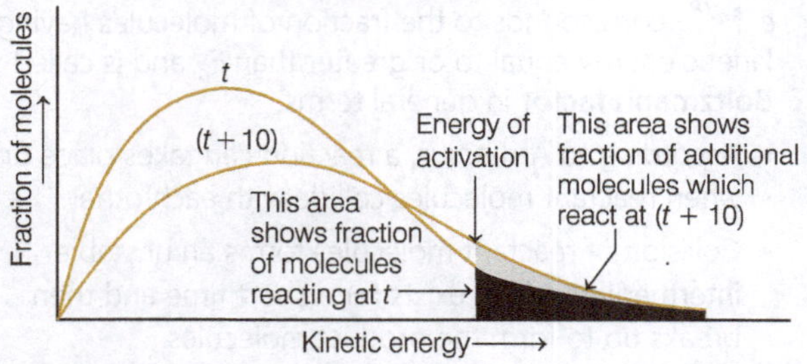

Distribution curve showing temperature dependence of rate of a reaction

- The logarithm expression for Arrhenius equation is, NEET 2024

$$\ln k = \frac{-E_a}{RT} + \ln A$$

$$\log k = \log A - \frac{E_a}{2.303RT} \quad \text{NEET 2021}$$

$$\log \frac{k_2}{k_1} = \frac{E_a}{2.303R}\left[\frac{1}{T_1} - \frac{1}{T_2}\right] \quad \text{NEET 2019}$$

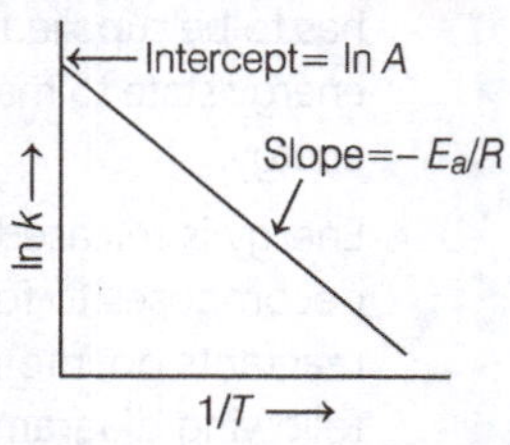

Graph between ln k vs $1/T$

Effect of Catalyst

A catalyst is a substance which increases the rate of reaction without itself undergoing any permanent chemical change.

- According to **intermediate complex theory**, a catalyst participates in a chemical reaction by forming temporary bonds with the reactants resulting in an intermediate complex, which decomposes to yield products and the catalyst.
- The graph showing the effect of catalyst on activation energy is shown below.

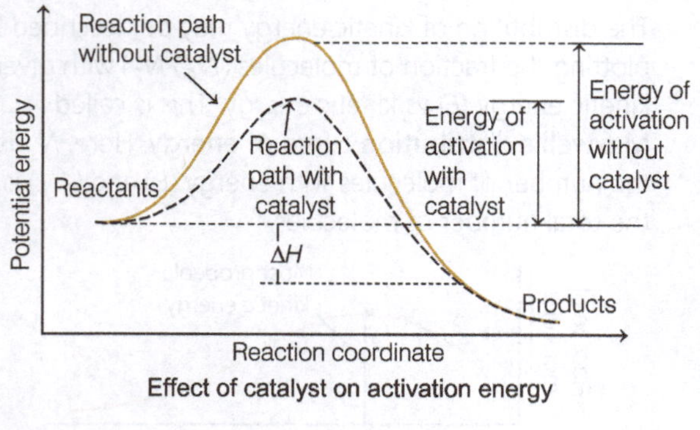

Effect of catalyst on activation energy

- From the above graph, it is clear that, the catalyst provides an alternate pathway or reaction mechanism by reducing the activation energy between reactants and products, hence lowering the potential energy barrier.
- A catalyst catalyses the spontaneous reactions but does not catalyses non-spontaneous reactions.
- A catalyst does not alter Gibbs energy of a reaction, also it does not change the equilibrium constant of a reaction.

Collision Theory of Chemical Reactions

Collision theory is based on kinetic theory of gases. According to this theory, the reactant molecules are assumed to be hard spheres and reaction is postulated to occur when molecules collide with each other.

- **Collision frequency** (Z) is the number of collisions per second per unit volume of the reaction mixture.
  It is related with rate as, rate $= Z_{AB}e^{-E_a/RT}$
  where, Z_{AB} represents the collision frequency of reactants A and B and $e^{-E_a/RT}$ is the fraction of molecules with energies equal to or greater than E_a. NEET 2020
- **Effective collisions** are the collisions in which molecules collide with sufficient kinetic energy (threshold energy which is equal to the sum of activation energy and energy possed by reacting species) and with proper orientation.
  For showing effective collision, probability or steric factor, P is introduced and rate becomes, rate $= PZ_{AB}e^{-E_a/RT}$
- Collision theory explain the results of a number of reactions but it does not give satisfactory explanation in some cases, as it considers atoms/molecules to be hard spheres and ignores their structural aspect.

Caution Points

- A reaction can not have zero activation energy. When a reaction have zero activation energy, the initial energy of the reactant will be equal to the activation energy of the reaction. That means every collision result into a chemical reaction which is not possible.
- Order of a reaction can change with change in conditions such as temperature, pressure etc. But molecularity of a reaction cannot be changed.

PYQ Notes

1. An increase in the concentration of the reactants of a reaction leads to change in collision frequency. **NEET 2020**
2. The half-life of a first-order reaction does not depend on initial concentration but the half-life of a second order reaction depends on intial concentration.
   i.e. $t_{1/2} = \frac{1}{k[A_0]}$ **NEET 2018**
3. Amount of the substance left after 'n' half-lives $= \frac{[R]_0}{2n}$
   where, $[R]_0$ is initial concentration. **JEE Main 2022**
4. Higher order reactions are rare due to low probability of simultaneous collision of all the reacting species. **JEE Main 2015**
5. The relationship between half-life and concentration (pressure) is as follows $t_{1/2} \propto (p_0)^{n-1}$ **JEE Main 2023**

Step by Step

Mastering NCERT

- Concept Builders
- Topical Questions
- Assertion-Reason
- Statement Type
- Matching Type
- Numerical Value
- NCERT Exemplar's
- Past Exams'
- Skill Boosters

Concept Builders

1 Chemical kinetics deals with the study of .... and their ....

2 The feasibility of a chemical reaction can be predicted by thermodynamics. [T/F]

3 The average and instantaneous rate of a reaction are equal when both of them have a time interval of zero. [T/F]

4 .... rate can be used to predict the rate of a reaction at a particular instant (Average/Instantaneous).

5 Unit of rate equation will be atm s^{-1}, if the concentration of gases is expressed in terms of their partial pressure. [T/F]

6 Average rate depends upon the change in concentration of reactants or products and the time taken for that change to occur. [T/F]

7 In a reaction, $2A \rightarrow P$, concentration of A decreases from 0.5 mol L^{-1} to 0.4 mol L^{-1} in 10 min. The average rate will be 5×10^{-3}M min^{-1}. [T/F]

8 ..... of a reaction can only be determined experimentally.

9 The unit of rate constant for n^{th} order gaseous reaction is ....

10 In a complex reaction, ... of slowest step is same as the ...... of overall reaction.

11 What is the molecularity of hydrolysis of cane sugar?

12 The molecularity of a reaction is always greater than order of a reaction. [T/F]

13 Write the order of reaction in which rate of reaction is equal to rate constant.

14 Thermal decomposition of HI on gold surface is an example of .... order reaction.

15 For a zero order reaction, plot, of $[A]$ *vs* t is a horizontal line. [T/F]

16 Radioactive decay of unstable nuclei takes place by zero order kinetics. [T/F]

17 What is the slope of $\log\left(\frac{[A]_0}{[A]}\right)$ *versus* time graph for a first order reaction?

18 $t_{1/2}$ for a zero order reaction is directly proportional to the .... and inversely proportional to ....

19 Half-life of first order reaction having $k = 5.5 \times 10^{-14} s^{-1}$ will be ....

20 The half-life of first order reaction does not depend on $[A]_0$ and the half-life of a second order reaction depends on $[A]_0$. [T/F]

21 Hydrolysis of ethyl acetate in an aqueous solution is of .... order.

22 Write the formula for half-life period for a second order reaction.

23 In a mixture of $KMnO_4$ and $H_2C_2O_4$, $KMnO_4$ gets decolourised slowly at a higher temperature. [T/F]

24 In general, energy is .... (released/absorbed) when activated complex decomposes to form products.

25 Name the minimum amount of extra energy required by a reacting molecule to get converted into product.

26 All the molecules in the reacting species do not have same kinetic energy. [T/F]

27 What is the value of slope for a graph plotted between $\ln k$ and $\frac{1}{T}$?

28 Name the substance which reduces the rate of a reaction.

29 Catalyst form permanent bonds with reactants which results in making an intermediate complex to yield product. [T/F]

30 Increase in rate of reaction with rise in temperature is mainly due to increase in .... (collision frequency/ effective collisions).

Topical Questions

Rate of a Chemical Reaction

1 Rate of which of the following reactions can be determined easily? **NCERT Pg 62**

(a) Rusting of iron in the presence of air and moisture.
(b) Hydrolysis of starch.
(c) Reaction of silver nitrate with sodium chloride.
(d) Weathering of rocks.

2 The value of r_{av} from the graph shown below is **NCERT Pg 63**

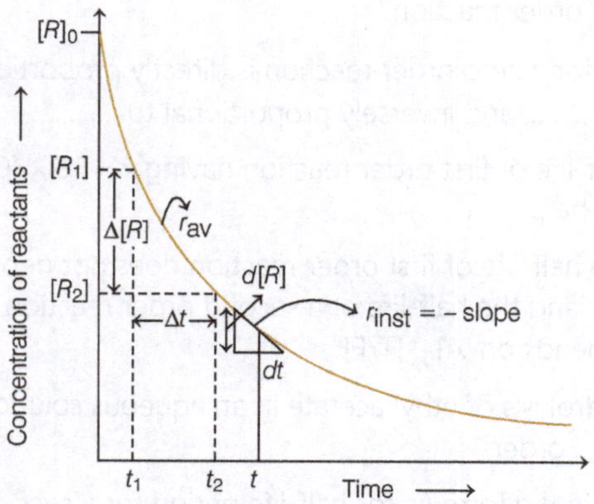

(a) $r_{av} = \dfrac{+\Delta[R]}{\Delta t}$

(b) $r_{av} = \dfrac{-[R_2]-[R_1]}{(t_1 - t_2)}$

(c) $r_{av} = \dfrac{-d[R]}{dt}$

(d) $r_{av} = \dfrac{-\{[R_2]-[R_1]\}}{(t_2 - t_1)}$

3 For a reaction,

$$A + B \longrightarrow C + D$$

The curve which depicts the variation of the concentration of products is **NCERT Pg 63**

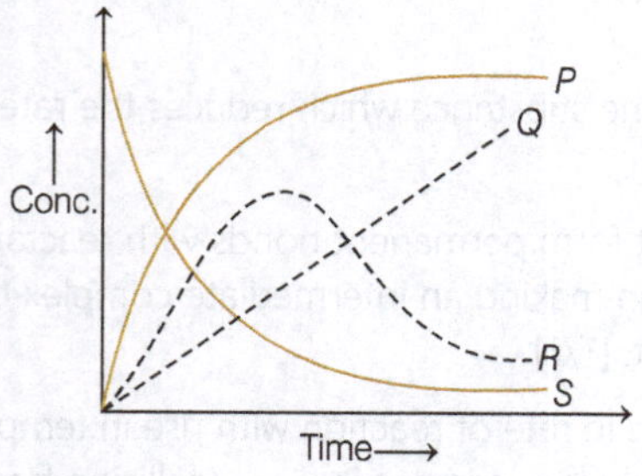

(a) P (b) Q
(c) R (d) S

4 A reaction follows the given concentration-time graph.

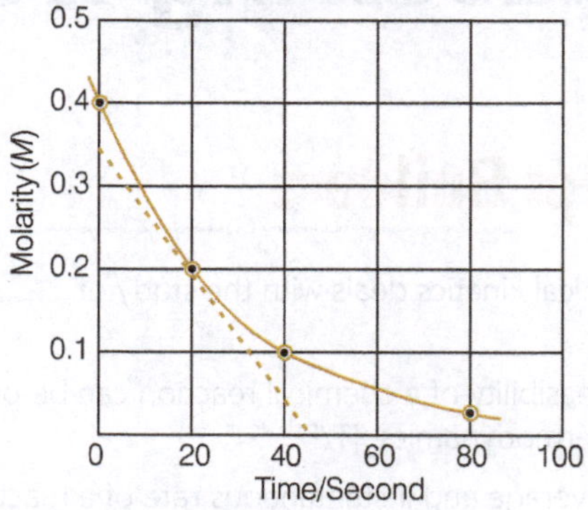

The rate for this reaction at 20s will be **NCERT Pg 64**

(a) $4\times10^{-3}\ Ms^{-1}$ (b) $8\times10^{-3}\ Ms^{-1}$
(c) $3\times10^{-3}\ Ms^{-1}$ (d) $7\times10^{-3}\ Ms^{-1}$

5 For the reaction,

$$2X + Y \longrightarrow X_2Y$$

The expression for instantaneous rate of the reaction is **NCERT Pg 65**

(a) $\dfrac{-d[X]}{2dt}$ (b) $+\dfrac{1}{2}\dfrac{d[Y]}{dt}$

(c) $-\dfrac{1}{2}\dfrac{d[X_2Y]}{dt}$ (d) $\dfrac{-d[X_2Y]}{dt}$

6 Choose the correct value of $\dfrac{d[NH_3]}{dt}$ for the reaction,

$$N_2 + 3H_2 \longrightarrow 2NH_3$$ **NCERT Pg 65**

(a) $-\dfrac{2}{3}\dfrac{d[H_2]}{dt}$ (b) $\dfrac{2}{3}\dfrac{d[H_2]}{dt}$ (c) $\dfrac{3}{2}\dfrac{d[N_2]}{dt}$ (d) $-\dfrac{3}{2}\dfrac{d[N_2]}{dt}$

7 Consider the following reaction. **NCERT Pg 65**

$$2NO_2 \longrightarrow 2NO + O_2$$

If rate of disappearance of $[NO_2]$ is 6.0×10^{-12} mol $L^{-1}s^{-1}$, then the rate of appearance of $[O_2]$ is

(a) 3×10^{-12} mol $L^{-1}s^{-1}$ (b) 6×10^{-12} mol $L^{-1}s^{-1}$
(c) 1×10^{-12} mol $L^{-1}s^{-1}$ (d) 1.5×10^{-12} mol $L^{-1}s^{-1}$

8 Contact process is used in the formation of sulphur trioxide, **NCERT Pg 65**

$$2SO_2(g) + O_2(g) \rightleftharpoons 2SO_3(g)$$

The rate of reaction can be expressed as

$$\frac{-\Delta[O_2]}{\Delta t} = 2.5\times10^{-4}\ \text{mol L}^{-1}\ \text{s}^{-1}.$$

Then rate of disappearance of $[SO_2]$ will be

(a) 50.0×10^{-5} mol L^{-1} s^{-1} (b) 3.75×10^{-4} mol L^{-1} s^{-1}
(c) 2.5×10^{-4} mol L^{-1} s^{-1} (d) 4.12×10^{-4} mol L^{-1} s^{-1}

9 For the reaction, NCERT Pg 65

$$5Br^- + BrO_3^- + 6H^+ \longrightarrow 3Br_2 + 3H_2O$$

if $-\frac{d[Br^-]}{dt} = k_1[Br^-]$, $-\frac{d[BrO_3^-]}{dt} = k_2[Br^-]$, $\frac{d[Br_2]}{dt} = k_3[Br^-]$ then k_1, k_2 and k_3 are related as

(a) $k_1 = 5k_2 = 1.66k_3$
(b) $3k_1 = k_2 = 5k_3$
(c) $5k_1 = 3k_2 = k_3$
(d) $k_1 = k_2 = k_3$

10 The progress of the reaction, $P \rightarrow nQ$ with time is represented in the graph shown below. NCERT Pg 65

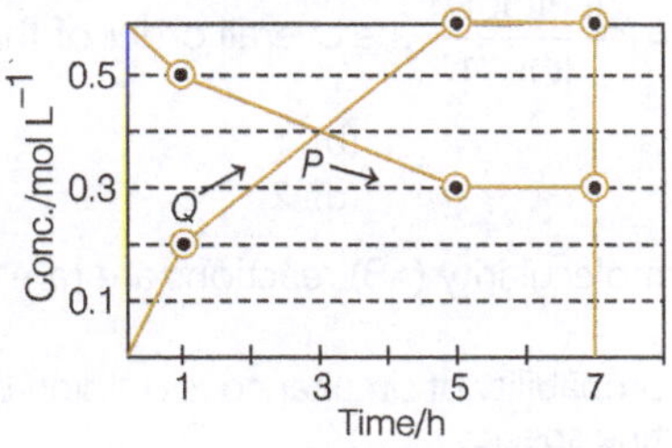

The initial rate of conversion of P will be

(a) $0.2 \text{ mol L}^{-1}\text{h}^{-1}$
(b) $0.4 \text{ mol L}^{-1}\text{h}^{-1}$
(c) $0.8 \text{ mol L}^{-1}\text{h}^{-1}$
(d) $0.1 \text{ mol L}^{-1}\text{h}^{-1}$

11 In a reaction, $2x \rightarrow y$, the concentration of x decreases from 3.0 M to 1.5 M in 4 min.
The rate of the reaction is NCERT Pg 65

(a) 0.187 M min^{-1} (b) 1.87 M min^{-1}
(c) $3.75 \times 10^{-1} \text{M min}^{-1}$ (d) 0.75 M min^{-1}

Factors Influencing Rate of Reaction

12 The rate law for a reaction, $P + Q \longrightarrow R + S$ is given by the expression $k[Q]$. The rate of reaction will be NCERT Pg 66

(a) increased on increasing the concentration of P
(b) decreased on increasing the temperature of the reaction
(c) unchanged by any change in concentration
(d) halved on decreasing the concentration of Q to half

13 In a reaction, $A + B \longrightarrow$ Product, rate is doubled when the concentration of B is doubled and rate increases by a factor of 8, when the concentrations of both the reactants (A and B) are doubled. Rate law for the reaction can be written as NCERT Pg 67

(a) rate $= k[A][B]^2$
(b) rate $= k[A]^2[B]^2$
(c) rate $= k[A][B]$
(d) rate $= k[A]^2[B]$

14 The rate law for a reaction between the substances P and Q is given by rate $= k[P]^a[Q]^b$. On doubling the concentration of P and reducing the concentration of Q to one-half, the ratio of the new rate to the earlier rate of the reaction will be NCERT Pg 67

(a) $\frac{1}{2^{(a+b)}}$ (b) $2^{(a-b)}$ (c) $(a-b)$ (d) $(a+b)$

15 For the non-stoichiometric reaction
$2A + B \longrightarrow C + D$, the following kinetic data were obtained in three separate experiments, all at 298 K. NCERT Pg 67

Initial concentration $[A]$	Initial concentration $[B]$	Initial rate of formation of C ($\text{mol L}^{-1}\text{s}^{-1}$)
0.1 M	0.1 M	1.2×10^{-3}
0.1 M	0.2 M	1.2×10^{-3}
0.2 M	0.1 M	2.4×10^{-3}

The rate law for the formation of C is

(a) $\frac{dC}{dt} = k[A][B]$ (b) $\frac{dC}{dt} = k[A]^2[B]$
(c) $\frac{dC}{dt} = k[A][B]^2$ (d) $\frac{dC}{dt} = k[A]$

16 Consider the following reaction,

$$CH_3Cl(g) + H_2O(g) \longrightarrow CH_3OH(g) + HCl(g)$$

following kinetic data were obtained for this reaction.

Initial concentration $[CH_3Cl]$	$[H_2O]$	Initial rate of disappearance of $[CH_3Cl \text{ M s}^{-1}]$
0.2	0.2	1
0.4	0.2	2
0.4	0.4	8

The rate law for the reaction is NCERT Pg 67

(a) $r = k[CH_3Cl]^2[H_2O]^1$
(b) $r = k[CH_3Cl]^2[H_2O]^2$
(c) $r = k[CH_3Cl][H_2O]^2$
(d) $r = k[CH_3Cl]^2[H_2O]^4$

17 Consider the following reactions,

$$O_3 \rightleftharpoons O_2 + O \text{ (fast)} \quad \text{...(i)}$$
$$O + O_3 \longrightarrow 2O_2 \text{ (slow)} \quad \text{...(ii)}$$

The rate law expression should be NCERT Pg 67

(a) $r = k'[O_3]^2[O_2]^{-1}$ (b) $r = k'[O_3][O_2]$
(c) $r = k'[O_3]^2$ (d) $r = k'[O_2]^{-1}$

18 In acidic medium, the rate of reaction between $[BrO_3]^-$ and Br^- ions is given as

$$-\frac{d[BrO_3]^-}{dt} = k[BrO_3^-][Br^-][H^+]^2$$

It means that, NCERT Pg 67

(a) the change in pH of the solution will not affect the rate of reaction
(b) rate constant of the reaction is $2s^{-1}$
(c) the reaction rate increases by 4 times on doubling the concentration of $[H^+]$ ions
(d) rate constant of the reaction is $4s^{-1}$

19 On mixing 1 dm^3 of 3M ethanol with 1 dm^3 of 2 M ethanoic acid, an ester is formed.

$$C_2H_5OH + CH_3COOH \longrightarrow CH_3COOC_2H_5 + H_2O$$

If each solution is diluted with an equal volume of water, the decrease in the initial rate would be NCERT Pg 68

(a) 0.5 times (b) 3 times
(c) 0.25 times (d) 2 times

20 When $CH_3COOC_2H_5$ was hydrolysed in presence of 0.1 M HCl, the rate constant obtained as $5.40\times 10^{-5}\ s^{-1}$. But when 0.1 M H_2SO_4 was fused for hydrolysis, the rate constant obtained as $6.20\times 10^{-5} s^{-1}$. NCERT Pg 68

From these, it can be said that

(a) H_2SO_4 is stronger than HCl
(b) H_2SO_4 is weaker than HCl
(c) Both HCl and H_2SO_4 are of same strength
(d) insufficient data to compare the strength of H_2SO_4 and HCl

21 For the elementary reaction $M \longrightarrow N$, the rate of disappearance of M increases by a factor of 8 upon doubling the concentration of M. NCERT Pg 68

The order of the reaction with respect to M is

(a) 4 (b) 3 (c) 2 (d) 1

22 Consider the data given below for a hypothetical reactions, $M \rightarrow N$ NCERT Pg 68

Time(s)	Rate of reaction (mol L^{-1} s^{-1})
0	4.20×10^{-4}
10	4.20×10^{-4}
20	4.20×10^{-4}
30	4.20×10^{-4}
40	4.18×10^{-4}

For the above data, the order of reaction is

(a) first (b) second (c) third (d) zero

23 For a reaction $X + Y \longrightarrow Z$, rate of reaction $\propto [X]$. What are the molecularity and order of reaction? NCERT Pg 69

(a) 2 and 1 (b) 2 and 2 (c) 1 and 1 (d) 1 and 2

24 Reaction of chloroform with chlorine is an example of fraction order reaction.

Its rate law expression is rate $= k[CHCl_3][Cl_2]^{1/2}$. If both are assumed in gaseous state and pressure is measured in bar, then units of rate and rate constant respectively are NCERT Pg 69

(a) bar min^{-1}, bar^2 min^{-1}
(b) bar min^{-1}, $bar^{-3/2}$, min^{-1}
(c) $bar^{-1/2}$ min^{-1}, bar^2 min^{-1}
(d) bar min^{-1}, $bar^{-1/2}$ min^{-1}

25 For the reaction, $I^- + OCl^- \longrightarrow IO^- + Cl^-$

in aqueous medium, the rate of a reaction is given by $\frac{d[IO^-]}{dt} = k\frac{[I^-][OCl^-]}{[OH^-]}$ the overall order of the reaction is NCERT Pg 68

(a) −1 (b) 1
(c) 0 (d) 2

26 Higher molecularity (>3) reactions are rare due to NCERT Pg 70

(a) low probability of simultaneous collision of all the reacting species
(b) increase in entropy and activation energy as more molecules are involved
(c) shifting of equilibrium towards reactants due to elastic collisions
(d) loss of active species on collision

27 The reaction, $2N_2O_5 \rightleftharpoons 2N_2O_4 + O_2$ is NCERT Pg 70

(a) bimolecular and first order
(b) unimolecular and second order
(c) bimolecular and second order
(d) unimolecular and first order

Integrated Rate Equations

28 Four reactions are given below. Which one of them is of zero order? NCERT Pg 72

(a) $PCl_5 \longrightarrow PCl_3 + Cl_2$
(b) $2FeCl_3 + SnCl_2 \longrightarrow 2FeCl_2 + SnCl_4$
(c) $2HI \xrightarrow[\text{Au catalyst}]{\Delta} H_2 + I_2$
(d) $N_2O_5 \longrightarrow 2NO_2 + \frac{1}{2}O_2$

29 The rate constant for a reaction of zero order is 0.0030 mol L^{-1} s^{-1}. The time taken for the initial concentration of reactant to fall from 0.10 M to 0.075 will be NCERT Pg 72

(a) 8.5 (b) 8.9
(c) 8.3 (d) 8.7

30 Which of the following graph is correct for a zero order reaction? **NCERT Pg 72**

(a) 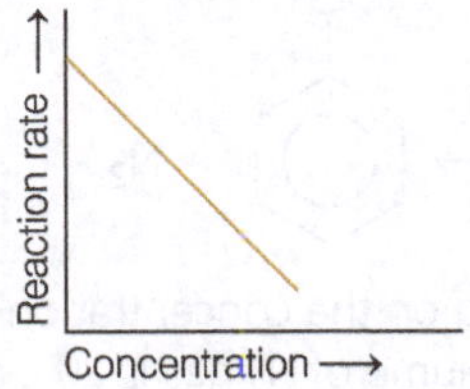

(b) 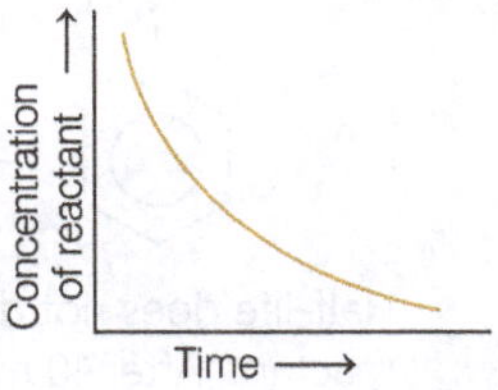

(c) 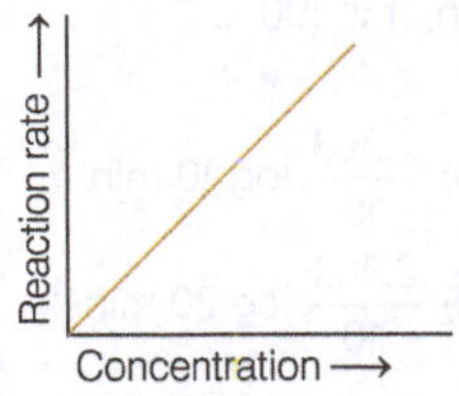

(d) 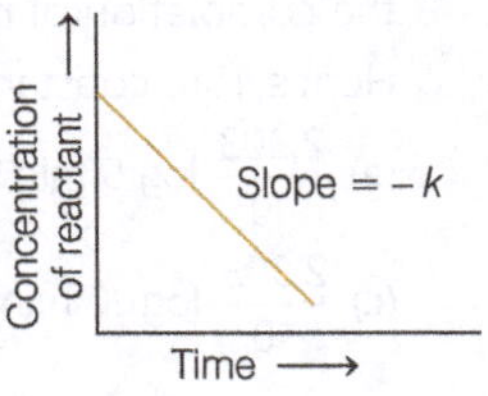

31 For a zero order reaction, a graph of concentration (along *y*-axis) and time (along *x*-axis) is linear with **NCERT Pg 72**

(a) a zero intercept and a +ve slope
(b) a zero intercept and a –ve slope
(c) a non-zero intercept and a –ve slope
(d) a non-zero intercept and a +ve slope

32 The rate constant of the reaction, $A \rightarrow B$ is 0.6×10^{-3} mole per litre per second. If the concentration of *A* is 5 M then, concentration of *B* after 20 min is **NCERT Pg 72**

(a) 1.08 M (b) 3.60 M
(c) 0.36 M (d) 0.72 M

33 Which of the following statements are incorrect?

I. For first order reactions, the rate of reaction is proportional to the first power of the concentration of the reactant *R*.

II. The zero order rate equation can be represented as,

$$k = \frac{2.303}{t} \log \frac{[R]_0}{[R]}$$

III. All natural and artificial radioactive decay of unstable nuclei take place by first order kinetics.

Choose the correct answer from the options given below. **NCERT Pg 72, 73**

(a) I and II (b) II and III
(c) Only III (d) Only II

34 In a first order reaction, reactant concentration '*C*' varies with time '*t*' as **NCERT Pg 73**

(a) *C* decreases with $\frac{1}{t}$

(b) log *C* decreases with $\frac{1}{t}$

(c) $\frac{1}{C}$ increases linearly with *t*

(d) log *C* decreases linearly with *t*

35 The example of first order reaction is **NCERT Pg 70, 73**

(a) $CH_3COOCH_3 + H_2O \xrightarrow{H^+} CH_3COOH + CH_3OH$

(b) $2H_2O_2 \xrightarrow{I^-,\text{ alkaline medium}} 2H_2O + O_2$

(c) $CH_3COOC_2H_5 + NaOH \longrightarrow CH_3CO\overset{-}{O}\overset{+}{Na} + C_2H_5OH$

(d) $C_{12}H_{22}O_{11} + H_2O \longrightarrow C_6H_{12}O_6 + C_6H_{12}O_6$

36 The given plots represent the variation of the concentration of a reactant *R* with time for two different reactions (i) and (ii). **NCERT Pg 74 & 72**

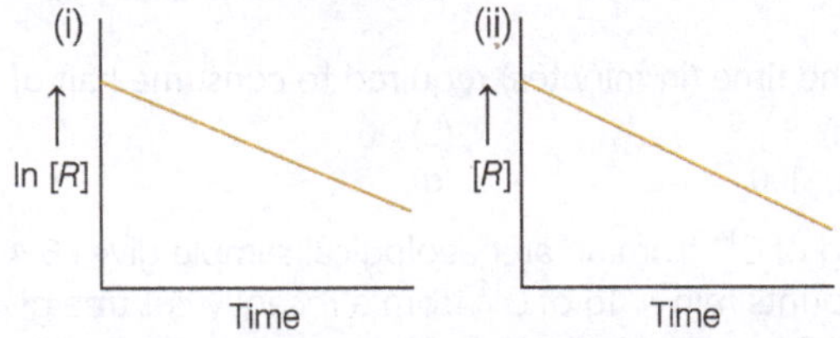

The respective orders of the reactions are

(a) 1, 1 (b) 0, 2 (c) 0, 1 (d) 1, 0

37 N_2 is obtained by the decomposition of benzene diazonium chloride at constant temperature. It is a first-order reaction the various volumes obtained at different time intervals are as, **NCERT Pg 74**

Time (min)	0	20	50	∞
N_2 (mL)	0	10	25	162

The rate constant of the reaction is

(a) 3.54×10^{-2} min^{-1} (b) 3.2×10^{-3} min^{-1}
(c) 3.89×10^{-3} min^{-1} (d) 3.1×10^{-5} min^{-1}

38 For a first order gas phase reaction, **NCERT Pg 75**

$$A(g) \longrightarrow B(g) + C(g)$$

(a) $k = \frac{2.303}{t} \log \frac{p_i}{p_i - p_t}$ (b) $k = \frac{2.303}{t} \log \frac{p_i}{2p_i - p_t}$

(c) $k = \frac{2.303}{t} \log \frac{2p_i}{p_i - p_t}$ (d) $k = \frac{2.303}{t} \log \frac{p_i}{p_i - 2p_t}$

39 For the decomposition of azoisopropane into hexane and nitrogen at 543 K, the following data is obtained. **NCERT Pg 75**

$$(CH_3)_2CHN{=}NCH(CH_3)_2 \longrightarrow N_2 + C_6H_{14}$$

Experiment	**Time** (s)	**Total pressure** (mm Hg)
I	0	35.0
II	360	54.0

The value of rate constant at 360s is

(a) 2.17×10^{-3}s^{-1} (b) 3.25×10^{-3}s^{-1}
(c) 3.25×10^{-3} min^{-1} (d) 1.98×10^{-3}s^{-1}

40 The following results were obtained during kinetic studies of the reaction; NCERT Pg 76

$2A + B \longrightarrow$ Product

Experiment	$[A]$ (in mol L^{-1})	$[B]$ (in mol L^{-1})	Initial rate of reaction (in mol L^{-1} min^{-1})
I.	0.10	0.20	6.93×10^{-3}
II.	0.10	0.25	6.93×10^{-3}
III.	0.20	0.30	1.386×10^{-2}

The time (in minutes) required to consume half of A is
(a) 5 (b) 10
(c) 100 (d) 1

41 2g of C^{14} from an archaeological sample gives 8.4 counts min^{-1}. 1g of C^{14} from a recently cut tree given 15.5 counts min^{-1}. Under the same conditions. How old is the archaeological sample ? ($t_{1/2}$ of C^{14} is 5750 years). NCERT Pg 76
(a) 5084 yrs (b) 7525 yrs
(c) 4548 yrs (d) 7255 yrs

42 Which of the following represent the expression for 5/6 life of a first order reaction? NCERT Pg 76
(a) $\frac{k}{2.303} \log \frac{6}{5}$ (b) $\frac{2.303}{k} \log \frac{5}{6}$
(c) $\frac{2.303}{k} \log 6$ (d) $\frac{2.303}{k} \log 5$

43 99% completion of a first order reaction takes place in 32 min. The time taken in 99.9% completion of the reaction will be NCERT Pg 76
(a) 48 min (b) 52 min (c) 56 min (d) 44 min

44 If the half-life period of a first order reaction is 20 min, then the percentage of the reaction is completed in 100 min. NCERT Pg 76
(a) 86.4% (b) 96.83%
(c) 40.2% (d) 99.9%

45 The half-life for radioactive decay of C-14 is 48750 years. An archaeological artifact containing wood had only 60% of the C-14 found in a living tree.
The age of the sample is NCERT Pg 76
(a) 63420 yrs (b) 64548 yrs
(c) 48540 yrs (d) 25320 yrs

46 Cyclopropane rearranges to form propene.
This follows first order kinetics. The rate constant is 2.714×10^{-3} s^{-1}. The initial concentration of cyclopropane is 0.29 M. What will be the concentration of cyclopropane after 200 s? NCERT Pg 76
(a) 0.169 M (b) 0.44 M (c) 1.153 M (d) 0.56 M

47 For the reaction,

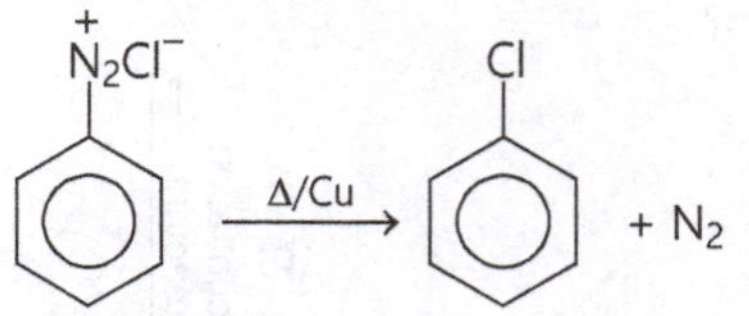

Half-life does not depend on the concentration of the reactant. After 10 min, volume of N_2 gas is 20 L and after the completion of reaction, it is 100 L. NCERT Pg 77
Hence, rate constant is
(a) $\frac{2.303}{10} \log 5$ min^{-1} (b) $\frac{2.303}{10} \log 10$ min^{-1}
(c) $\frac{2.303}{10} \log 10$ min^{-1} (d) $\frac{2.303}{10} \log 20$ min^{-1}

48 A bimolecular reaction may be of first order, if NCERT Pg 78
(a) the activation energy of reaction is less
(b) both reactants have same concentration
(c) one of the reacting species is in large excess
(d) the activation energy of reaction remains constant

49 The rate constant 'k' for pseudo first order reaction is NCERT Pg 78
(a) $\frac{2.303}{t} \log C_0 - C$ (b) $\frac{2.303}{t} \log \frac{C}{C_0}$
(c) $\frac{2.303}{t} \log C_0 + C$ (d) $\frac{2.303}{t} \log \frac{C_0}{C}$

Temperature Dependence of the Rate of a Reaction

50 The temperature coefficient of a reaction is NCERT Pg 78
(a) the ratio of rate constant at two temperatures
(b) the ratio of rate constant differing by 10° preferably 25°C and 35°C
(c) the rate constant at a fixed temperature
(d) the ratio of rate constant differing by 1°.

51 In a zero order reaction for every 10°C rise of temperature, the rate is doubled. If the temperature is increased from 10°C to 100°C, the rate of the reaction will become NCERT Pg 78
(a) 256 times (b) 512 times
(c) 64 times (d) 128 times

52 The correct increasing order of the time taken for half of the decomposition of N_2O_5 at the temperature 50°C, 0°C and 25°C will be NCERT Pg 78
(a) 50°C < 0°C < 25°C
(b) 50°C < 25°C < 0°C
(c) 0°C < 25°C < 50°C
(d) 0°C < 50°C < 25°C

53 Consider the following graph, NCERT Pg 79

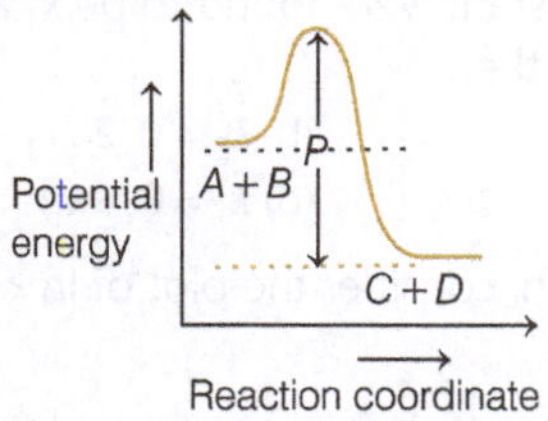

The above graph represents the change in energy for the reaction,

$$A+B \longrightarrow C+D.$$

Here, P is the

(a) energy change for the reaction, $C+D \longrightarrow A+B$
(b) energy change for the reaction, $A+B \longrightarrow C+D$
(c) activation energy for the reaction, $A+B \longrightarrow C+D$
(d) activation energy for the reaction, $C+D \longrightarrow A+B$

54 The rate constant of a reaction is shown as

$$k = 2.1 \times 10^{10}\, e^{-2700/RT}$$ NCERT Pg 79

It means that

I. $\log k$ vs $1/T$ will be a straight line with intercept $= \log 2.1 \times 10^{10}$.
II. The fraction of molecules having kinetic energy greater than E_a is 2.1×10^{10}.
III. Half-life of a reaction increases with increase in temperature.
IV. $\log k$ vs $1/T$ will be a straight line with slope $= -\dfrac{2700}{2.303R}$.

Choose the correct statement from the options given below.

(a) I and II (b) II and III
(c) III and IV (d) I and IV

55 Consider the given curve

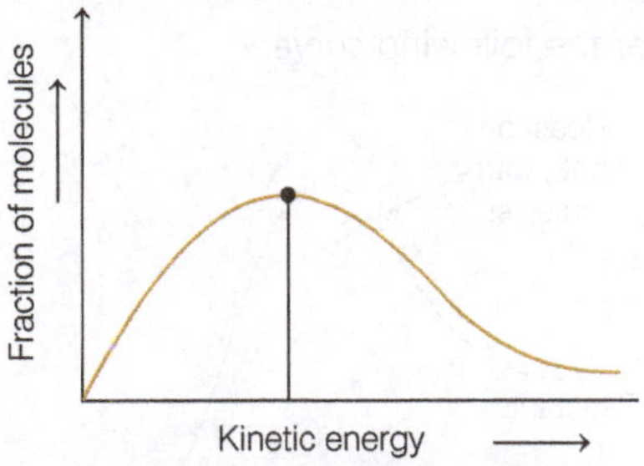

Distribution curve showing energies among gaseous molecules

The peak of the above shown curve corresponds to

(a) most probable kinetic energy NCERT Pg 79
(b) activation energy of forward reaction
(c) activation energy of backward reaction
(d) cannot be predicted

56 In the figure shown below, fraction of molecules represents. NCERT Pg 79

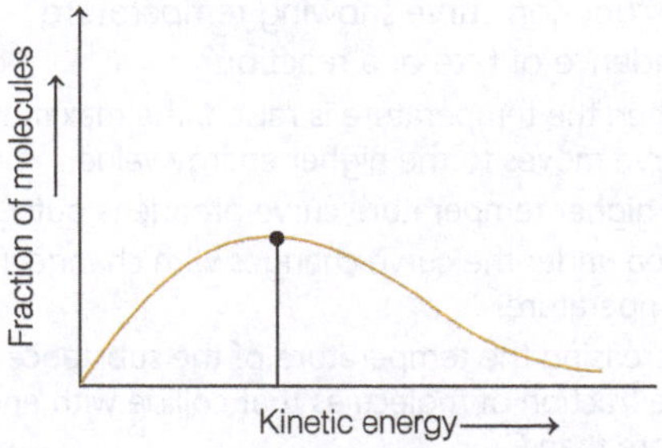

(a) $\dfrac{N_E}{N_T}$ (b) $\dfrac{N_T}{N_E}$ (c) $\dfrac{E}{N_E}$ (d) $\dfrac{E}{N_T}$

57 Consider the given plots for a reaction obeying Arrhenius equation (0°C < T < 300°C) : (k and E_a are rate constant and activation energy, respectively) NCERT Pg 79

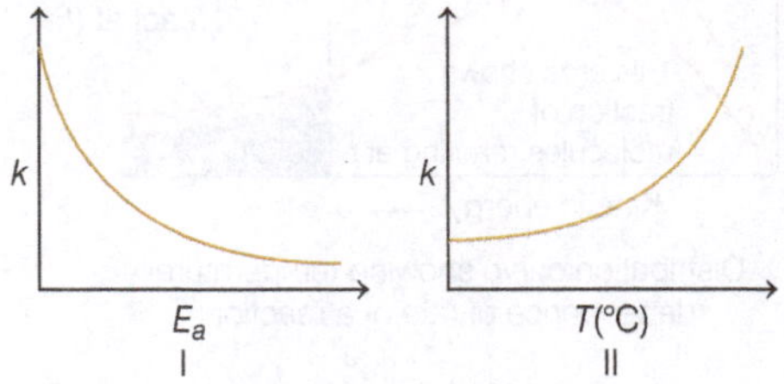

Choose the correct option.

(a) Both I and II are wrong. (b) Both I and II are correct.
(c) I is a wrong but II is right. (d) I is right but II is wrong.

58 For the following reactions, at a particular temperature, NCERT Pg 79

1. $2N_2O_5 \longrightarrow 4NO_2 + O_2;\, k_1$
2. $2NO_2 + \frac{1}{2}O_2 \longrightarrow N_2O_5,\, k_2$

If the value of $E_1 > E_2$, activation energies of reaction 1 and 2 respectively, then

(a) $k_1 > k_2$ (b) $k_1 < k_2$
(c) $k_1 = 2k_2$ (d) $\sqrt{k_1 > k_2^2} = 1$

59 If a reaction, $A + B \rightarrow C$ is exothermic to the extent of 30 kJ/mol and the activation energy of the forward reaction is 249 kJ/mol, then the activation energy of reverse reaction (in kJ/mol) is NCERT Pg 79

(a) 324 (b) 279
(c) 40 (d) 100

60 In the Arrhenius equation, $k = Ae^{-E_a/RT}$, the factor $e^{-E_a/RT}$ corresponds to the **NCERT Pg 80**

(a) fraction of molecules that have kinetic energy $= E_a$
(b) fraction of molecules that have kinetic energy $> E_a$
(c) fraction of molecules that have kinetic energy $< E_a$
(d) fraction of molecules that have kinetic energy $\leq E_a$

61 Which of the following statement is incorrect regarding the distribution curve showing temperature dependence of rate of a reaction? **NCERT Pg 80**

(a) When the temperature is raised, the maximum of the curve moves to the higher energy value.
(b) At higher temperature curve broadens out.
(c) Area under the curve changes with change in temperature.
(d) Increasing the temperature of the substance increases the fraction of molecules that collide with energies more than E_a.

62 Analyse the figure given below and answer the following questions. **NCERT Pg 80**

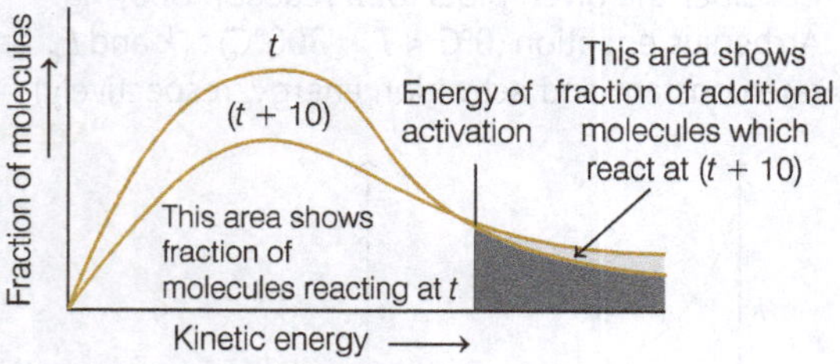

Distribution curve showing temperature dependence of rate of a reaction

The curve shown in the above figure is known as

(a) Ludwig-Clark curve
(b) Arrhenius-van't Hoff curve
(c) Maxwell-Boltzmann distribution
(d) None of the above

63 Consider the following plot between ln k and $1/T$, **NCERT Pg 80**

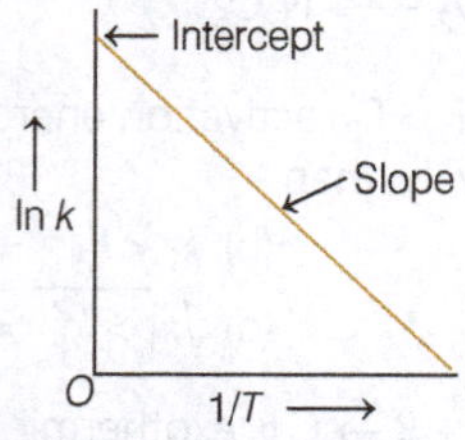

In this plot, the intercept and slope respectively are

(a) $-\frac{E_a}{R}$; ln A
(b) ln A; $-\frac{E_a}{R}$
(c) $\frac{E_a}{R}$; $-$ln A
(d) $\frac{E_a}{R}$; A

64 A chemical reaction was carried out at 300 K and 280 K. The rate constant were found to be k_1 and k_2 respectively, then **NCERT Pg 81**

(a) $k_2 = 4k_1$
(b) $k_2 = 0.25\,k_1$
(c) $k_2 = 2k_1$
(d) $k_1 = 0.5\,k_1$

65 For a reaction, consider the plot of ln k *versus* $1/T$ given in the figure. **NCERT Pg 81**

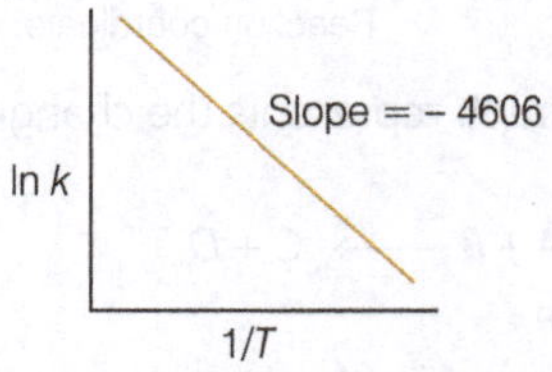

If the rate constant of this reaction at 400 K is $10^{-5}\ s^{-1}$, then the rate constant at 500 K is

(a) $4 \times 10^{-4}\ s^{-1}$
(b) $10^{-6}\ s^{-1}$
(c) $10^{-4} s^{-1}$
(d) $2 \times 10^{-4}\ s^{-1}$

66 The rate of a certain biochemical reaction at physiological temperature (T) occurs 10^6 times faster with enzyme than without. The change in the activation energy upon adding enzyme is **NCERT Pg 82**

(a) $+ 6\,RT$
(b) $-6\,(2.303)\,RT$
(c) $+ 6\,(2.303)\,RT$
(d) $- 6\,RT$

67 If a homogeneous catalytic reaction can take place through four alternative paths as shown below. **NCERT Pg 82**

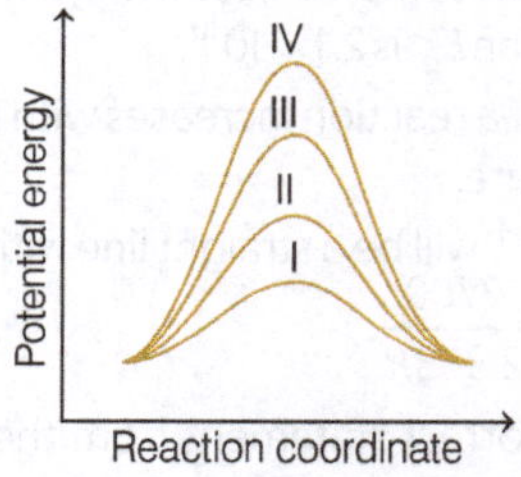

The catalytic efficiency of I, II, III, IV representing the relative case would be

(a) I > II > III > IV
(b) I < II < III < IV
(c) I = II = III = IV
(d) IV > II > III > I

68 Consider the following curve.

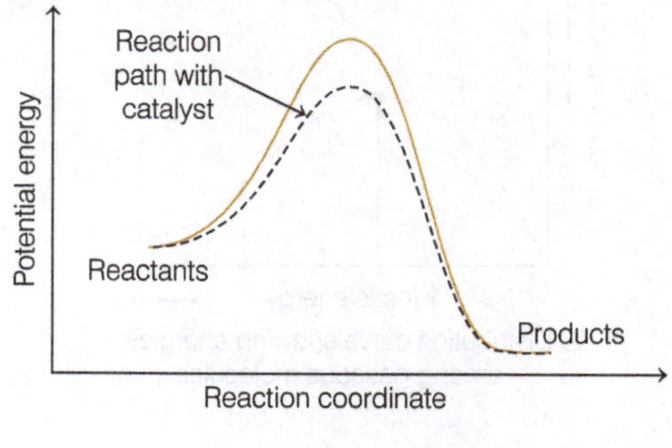

On the basis of the curve shown above, identify the incorrect statement. **NCERT Pg 82**

(a) Catalyst provides an alternate pathway or reaction mechanism.
(b) Catalyst increases the activation energy between reactants and products.
(c) Catalyst lowers the potential energy barrier.
(d) Catalyst reduces the activation energy between reactants and products.

Collision Theory of Chemical Reaction

69 Which of the following statements is not correct for the given expression?

$$\text{Rate} = Z_{AB}e^{-\frac{E_a}{RT}}$$

NCERT Pg 83

(a) Z_{AB} is collision frequency and is equal to number of collisions per second per unit volume of the reaction mixture.
(b) $e^{\frac{-E_a}{RT}}$ is the fraction of molecules with kinetic energy equal to or greater than E_a.
(c) E_a is activation energy of the reaction.
(d) All the molecules which collide with one other are effective collisions.

70 Relationship among threshold energy, activation energy and energy possessed by reacting species is **NCERT Pg 83**

(a) threshold energy = activation energy + energy possessed by reacting species
(b) thershold energy = activation energy − energy possessed by reacting species
(c) activation energy = threshold energy − energy possessed by reacting species
(d) activation energy = threshold energy + energy possessed by reacting species

71 In order to produce the effective collisions, the colliding molecules must have **NCERT Pg 83**

(a) a certain minimum amount of energy
(b) proper orientation
(c) Both threshold energy and proper orientation
(d) energy equal to or greater than threshold energy

72 The rate constant is given by the equation, $k = P \cdot Z_{AB}e^{-E_a/RT}$. To increase the rate of reaction, which of the factor should decrease? **NCERT Pg 83**

(a) Z (b) T
(c) P (d) E_a

73 Which of the following statement is correct about the collision theory of chemical reaction? **NCERT Pg 83**

(a) It considers reacting molecules or atoms to be hard spheres and explains their structural features.
(b) All collisions determines the rate of reaction.
(c) Collision of atoms or molecules possessing sufficient threshold energy results into the product formation.
(d) Molecules should collide with sufficient threshold energy and proper orientation for the collision to be effective.

74 Consider the following reaction

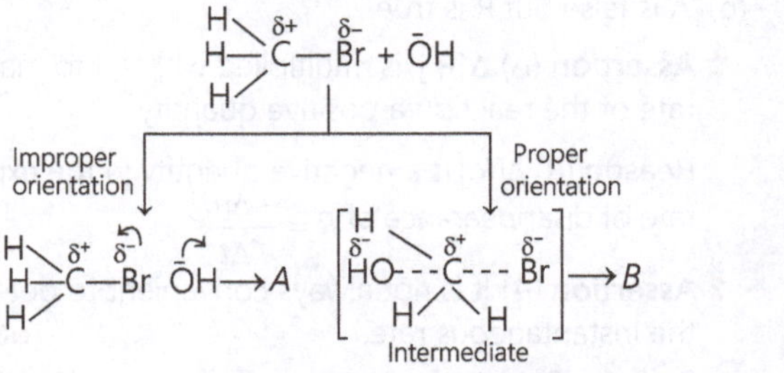

What will come in place of A and B in the above reaction ? **NCERT Pg 83**

(a) No products = A ; $HO—C(H)(H)—OH = B$
(b) No products = A ; $HO—C(H)(H)—H + Br^- = B$
(c) $HO—C(H)(H)—H = A$, No products = B
(d) $HO—C(H)(H)—H + Br^- = A$; No products = B

75 For a certain reaction, a large fraction of molecules has energy more than the threshold energy, still the rate of reaction is very slow. The possible reason for this could be that **NCERT Pg 83**

(a) the colliding molecules could be large in size
(b) the colliding molecules must not be properly oriented for effective collisions.
(c) the rate of reaction could be in dependent of energy
(d) one of the reactants could be in excess

Assertion-Reason Questions

Directions (Q. Nos. 1-20) *In the following question Assertion (A) followed by Reason (R) is given below. Choose the correct option out of the choices given below.*

(a) Both A and R are true and R is the correct explanation of A.
(b) Both A and R are true but R is not the correct explanation of A.
(c) A is true but R is false.
(d) A is false but R is true.

1 Assertion (A) $\Delta[R]$ is multiplied with -1 to make the rate of the reaction a positive quantity. **NCERT Pg 63**

Reason (R) $\Delta[R]$ is a negative quantity in the expression, rate of disappearance of $R = \frac{-\Delta[R]}{\Delta t}$.

2 Assertion (A) It is not always convenient to determine the instantaneous rate. **NCERT Pg 64**

Reason (R) Instantaneous rate is measured by the determination of slope of the tangent at point 't' in concentration *versus* time plot.

3 Assertion (A) The molecularity can never a fraction. **NCERT Pg 70**

Reason (R) The molecularity of a reaction is the number of molecules whether of the same or different species that must collide simultaneously in a single step in order to a reaction to occur.

4 Assertion (A) Order of the reaction can be zero or fractional. **NCERT Pg 68, 69**

Reason (R) We cannot determine order from balanced chemical equation.

5 Assertion (A) The multimolecular reactions are quite rare in comparison with bimolecular reactions. **NCERT Pg 70**

Reason (R) At normal pressure, triple collisions are much less frequent than double ones.

6 Assertion (A) Order and molecularity are same.

Reason (R) Order is determined experimentally and molecularity is the sum of the stoichiometric coefficient of rate determining elementary step. **NCERT Pg 69, 70**

7 Assertion (A) Rate of a zero order reactions depend on the concentration of reactants.

Reason (R) Order cannot be determined from balanced chemical equation. **NCERT Pg 68, 70**

8 Assertion (A) For a complex reaction, order is given by the slowest step of the reaction. **NCERT Pg 71**

Reason (R) Molecularity of the slowest step is same as the order of the overall reaction.

9 Assertion (A) Zero order reactions are relatively uncommon but these occur under special conditions. **NCERT Pg 72**

Reason (R) Thermal decomposition of HI on gold surface is a zero order reaction.

10 Assertion (A) Decomposition of gaseous ammonia on a hot platinum surface is a zero order reaction at high pressure. **NCERT Pg 72**

Reason (R) At high pressure, the metal surface gets saturated with gas molecules.

11 Assertion (A) The $t_{1/2}$ of zero order reaction depends on concentration of reactants. **NCERT Pg 76**

Reason (R) $t_{1/2}$ and rate constant of zero order reaction are related to each other as, $t_{1/2} = \frac{[R]_0}{2k}$.

12 Assertion (A) In a mixture of $H_2C_2O_4$ and $KMnO_4$, the later decolourises faster at a higher temperature than that at a lower temperature. **NCERT Pg 78**

Reason (R) No effect of temperature on decolourisation.

13 Assertion (A) A bimolecular reaction takes place when two properly oriented reactant molecules come together in a sufficiently energetic collision. **NCERT Pg 78, 83**

Reason (R) When the temperature is increased by 10°C, the reaction rate tends to be doubled.

14 Assertion (A) The enthalpy of reaction remains constant in the presence of a catalyst. **NCERT Pg 81**

Reason (R) A catalyst participating in the reaction forms different activated complex and lowers down the activation energy but the difference in energy of reactant and product remains the same.

15 Assertion (A) All collision of reactant molecules lead to product formation. **NCERT Pg 82**

Reason (R) Only those collisions in which molecules have correct orientation and sufficient kinetic energy lead to product formation.

16 Assertion (A) Rate constant determined from Arrhenius equation are fairly accurate for simple as well as complex molecules. **NCERT Pg 78, 82**

Reason (R) Reactant molecules undergo chemical change irrespective of their orientation during collision.

17 Assertion (A) A positive catalyst increases the rate of reaction. **NCERT Pg 82**

Reason (R) A positive catalyst decreases the energy of activation by providing a new and more efficient mechanism.

18 Assertion (A) Collision theory provides a greater insight into the energetic and mechanistic aspects of reactions in the expression obtained by collision theory. NCERT Pg 83

Reason (R) Collision theory has no link with kinetic theory of gases.

19 Assertion (A) To account for effective collisions another factor *P* is introduced in the expression obtained by collision theory. NCERT Pg 83

Reason (R) In a collision, molecules must be properly oriented.

20 Assertion (A) All collisions of reactant molecules does not lead to the formation of product. NCERT Pg 83

Reason (R) Only those collisions in which molecules have correct orientation and sufficient kinetic energy lead to formation of compound.

Statement Type Questions

Directions (Q. Nos. 1-5) *In the following questions, two statements (I & II) are given. In the light of the given statements, choose the correct option given below.*

(a) Both Statement I and Statement II are false.
(b) Statement I is true but Statement II is false.
(c) Statement I is false but Statement II is true.
(d) Both statement I and Statement II are true.

1 Statement I Molecularity greater than three is not observed. NCERT Pg 69

Statement II The overall molecularity of a complex reaction is equal to molecularity of the slowest step.

2 Statement I The rate of change of concentration per unit time for zero order reaction remains constant. NCERT Pg 71, 82

Statement II Lower the activation energy, faster is the reaction.

3 Statement I The rate of a chemical reaction increases rapidly for a small temperature increase.

Statement II Increase in temperature increases fraction of molecules with energies in excess of activation energy. NCERT Pg 80

4 Statement I Catalyst catalyse only spontaneous reactions.

Statement II The catalyst increases the activation energy which in turn increases the rate of the reaction. NCERT Pg 82

5 Statement I All molecular collisions lead to the formation of products.

Statement II Reactant molecules undergo chemical change irrespective of their collisions. NCERT Pg 80

6 Which of the following statements are correct? NCERT Pg 69, 70, 83

I. The molecularity of a reaction is always equal to the sum of the stoichiometric coefficient of reactants in the balanced chemical equation for a reaction.
II. A reaction involving two different reactants can never be unimolecular reaction.
III. Number of effective collisions determines the rate of reaction.
IV. Higher order reactions are rare due to low probability of simultaneous collision of all the reacting species.

Choose the correct answer from the options given below.

(a) I and III (b) II and IV
(c) I, II, III and IV (d) II, III and IV

7 Consider the following statements.

I. Average rate of a reaction is the instantaneous rate when time interval approaches zero.
II. Rate of a reaction depends on concentrations of reactants present at any time *t*.
III. Order and molecularity both are defined for complex reactions.
IV. Increase in temperature increases the fraction of molecules colliding.
V. A catalyst catalyses non-spontaneous as well as spontaneous reactions.

Choose the correct statements from the options given below. NCERT Pg 64, 66, 70, 80, 82

(a) I, II and V (b) III and V
(c) I, II and IV (d) III, and IV

8 Which of the following statements are correct?

I. Rate law is an experimental fact while law of mass action is a theoretical proposal.
II. Rate law is more informative than law of mass action for the development of mechanism.
III. Rate law is always different from the expression of law of mass action.
IV. Hydrogenation of ethene follows first order kinetics.
V. All the molecules which collide with one another are not effective collisions

Choose the correct answer from the options given below. NCERT Pg 66, 73, 83

(a) I, IV and III
(b) III, IV and II
(c) I and II
(d) I, II, IV and V

9 Which of the following statements are correct?

I. The energy required to form the intermediate called activated complex is known as activation energy.
II. All the molecules in the reacting species have same kinetic energy.
III. In Arrhenius equation, the factor $e^{-E_a/RT}$ corresponds to the fraction of molecules that have kinetic energy greater than E_a.
IV. Increasing the temperature or decreasing the activation energy will result in an increase in the rate of reaction and an exponential increase in rate constant.
V. Half-life for a zero order reaction is directly proportional to rate constant. NCERT Pg 76, 79, 78, 80

Choose the correct answer from the options given below.

(a) Both I and II (b) Both II and IV
(c) III and V (d) I, III and IV

10 Which of the following statements are correct?

I. Order of a reaction can be known from experimental result and not from the stoichiometry of reaction.
II. Overall molecularity of a reaction may be determined in a manner similar to overall order of reaction.
III. Overall order of reaction.

$A^m + B^n \longrightarrow AB_x$ is $(m+n)$ NCERT Pg 68, 69

Choose the correct answer from the options given below.

(a) I and III (b) I, II and III
(c) II and III (d) I and II

Matching Type Questions

1 Match the items of Column I and Column II. NCERT Pg 70

Column I (Type of reaction)	Column II (Example)
A. Unimolecular	1. $2HI \longrightarrow H_2 + I_2$
B. Bimolecular	2. $2NO + O_2 \longrightarrow 2NO_2$
C. Trimolecular	3. $NH_4NO_2 \longrightarrow N_2 + 2H_2O$

Codes

	A	B	C		A	B	C
(a)	2	1	3	(b)	2	3	1
(c)	3	1	2	(d)	3	2	1

2 Match the items of Column I and Column II. NCERT Pg 67, 69, 70, 71

Column I	Column II
A. Mathematical expression for rate of reaction	1. Rate constant
B. Rate of reaction for zero order reaction is equal to	2. Rate law
C. Units of rate constant for zero order reaction is same as that of	3. Order of slowest step
D. Order of a complex reaction is determined by	4. Rate of reaction

Codes

	A	B	C	D		A	B	C	D
(a)	1	2	3	4	(b)	2	1	4	3
(c)	4	3	2	1	(d)	3	4	1	2

3. Match the items of Column I with Column II. NCERT Pg 72, 78

Column I	Column II
A. Inversion of cane sugar.	1. Zero order reaction
B. Decomposition of N_2O.	2. First order reaction
C. Thermal decomposition of HI on gold surface.	3. Pseudo first order reaction

Codes

	A	B	C		A	B	C
(a)	1	2	3	(b)	2	3	1
(c)	3	2	1	(d)	2	1	3

4 Match the statements given in Column I and Column II. NCERT Pg 70, 76, 80, 82

Column I	Column II
A. Catalyst alters the rate of reaction.	1. Cannot be fraction or zero.
B. Molecularity	2. By lowering the activation energy.
C. Second half-life of first order reaction.	3. Is same as the first.
D. $e^{-E_a/RT}$	4. Refers to the fraction of molecules with energy equal to or greater than activation energy.

Codes

	A	B	C	D		A	B	C	D
(a)	2	1	3	4	(b)	1	2	3	4
(c)	4	3	2	1	(d)	4	2	3	1

5 Match the statements given in Column I and Column II. **NCERT Pg 69, 79, 70, 82**

Column I	Column II
A. Molecularity	1. Proper orientation is not there.
B. $e^{-E_a/RT}$	2. Can not be fraction or zero.
C. Energetically favourable reactions are sometimes slow.	3. Total probability is one.
D. Area under the Maxwell, Boltzmann curve is constant.	4. Refers to the fraction of molecules with energy equal to or greater than activation energy.

Codes

	A	B	C	D		A	B	C	D
(a)	2	4	1	3	(b)	4	2	1	3
(c)	2	4	3	1	(d)	3	2	4	1

Numerical Value Questions

1 The rate of the reaction, $P + Q + R \longrightarrow S$ is given by $r = \frac{-d[A]}{dt} = k[P]^{\frac{1}{2}}[Q]^{\frac{1}{2}}[R]^{\frac{1}{4}}$ the order of the reaction is $\frac{x}{4}$. The value of x is........ **NCERT Pg 68**

2 For a reaction $A \rightarrow B$, the rate of reaction becomes twenty seven times when the concentration of A is increased three times. The order of the reaction is .... **NCERT Pg 68**

3 The number of correct statements for order of reaction is/are .... **NCERT Pg 68, 70**

A. Order can be determined experimentally.

B. Order of reaction is equal to the sum of powers of concentration terms in rate law expression.

C. Order cannot be fractional.

D. Order is not affected by stoichiometric coefficient of the reactants.

4 Half-life period of a first order reaction is 10 min. The percentage of the reaction will be completed in 100 min .... (Nearest integer) **NCERT Pg 77**

5 The rate constant of the chemical reaction doubles for an increase of 10 K in absolute temperature from 295 K. The value of E_a will be .... kJ mol^{-1}. (Nearest integer) **NCERT Pg 81**

NCERT Exemplar's Questions

1 Consider the reaction, $A \longrightarrow B$. The concentration of both the reactants and the product varies exponentially with time. Which of the following figure correctly describes the change in concentration of reactant and product with time?

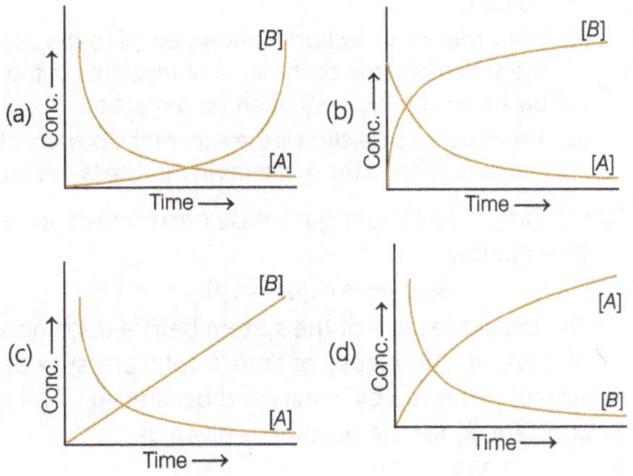

2 A graph of volume of hydrogen released *vs* time for the reaction between zinc and dil. HCl is given in figure. On the basis of this mark the correct option.

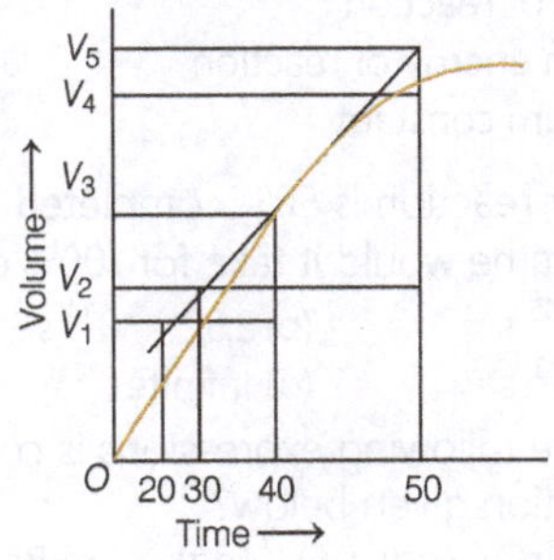

(a) Average rate upto 40 s is $\frac{V_3 - V_2}{40}$

(b) Average rate upto 40 s is $\frac{V_3 - V_2}{40 - 30}$

(c) Average rate upto 40 s is $\frac{V_3}{40}$

(d) Average rate upto 40 s is $\frac{V_3 - V_1}{40 - 20}$

3 Consider the graph given below. Which of the following option does not show instantaneous rate of reaction at 40s?

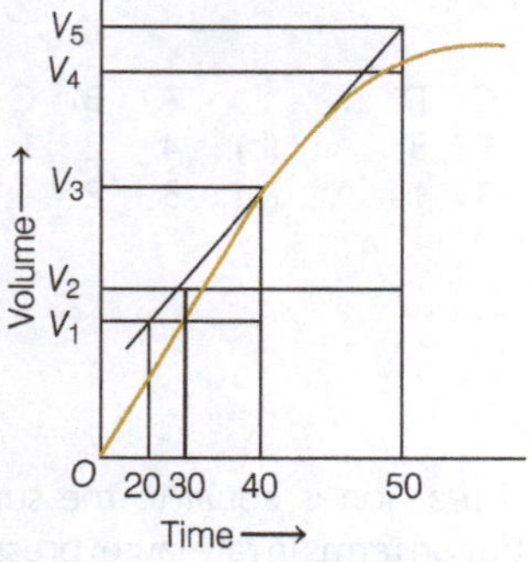

(a) $\frac{V_5 - V_2}{50 - 30}$ (b) $\frac{V_4 - V_2}{50 - 30}$

(c) $\frac{V_3 - V_2}{40 - 30}$ (d) $\frac{V_3 - V_1}{40 - 20}$

4 The value of rate constant of a pseudo first order reaction ....

(a) depends on the concentration of reactants present in small amount

(b) depends on the concentration of reactants present in excess

(c) is independent of the concentration of reactants

(d) depends only on temperature

5 The role of a catalyst is to change ....

(a) Gibbs energy of reaction

(b) enthalpy of reaction

(c) activation energy of reaction

(d) equilibrium constant

6 A first order reaction is 50% completed in 1.26×10^{14} s. How much time would it take for 100% completion?

(a) 1.26×10^{15} s (b) 2.52×10^{14} s

(c) 2.52×10^{28} s (d) Infinite

7 Which of the following expressions is correct for the rate of reaction given below?

$5Br^-(aq) + BrO_3^-(aq) + 6H^+(aq) \longrightarrow 3Br_2(aq) + 3H_2O(l)$

(a) $\frac{\Delta[Br^-]}{\Delta t} = 5\frac{\Delta[H^+]}{\Delta t}$ (b) $\frac{\Delta[Br^-]}{\Delta t} = \frac{6}{5}\frac{\Delta[H^+]}{\Delta t}$

(c) $\frac{\Delta[Br^-]}{\Delta t} = \frac{5}{6}\frac{\Delta[H^+]}{\Delta t}$ (d) $\frac{\Delta[Br^-]}{\Delta t} = 6\frac{\Delta[H^+]}{\Delta t}$

8 Rate law for the reaction, $A + 2B \longrightarrow C$ is found to be

$$\text{Rate} = k[A][B]$$

Concentration of reactant B is doubled, keeping the concentration of A constant, the value of rate constant will be.......... .

(a) the same (b) doubled

(c) quadrupled (d) halved

9 Compounds A and B react according to the following chemical equation,

$$A(g) + 2B(g) \longrightarrow 2C(g)$$

Concentration of either A or B were changed keeping the concentration of one of the reactant constant and rates were measured as a function of initial concentration. Following results were obtained. Choose the correct option for the rate equations of this reaction.

Exp.	Initial concentration of $[A]$/mol L^{-1}	Initial concentration of $[B]$/mol L^{-1}	Initial concentration of $[C]$/mol $L^{-1}s^{-1}$
1.	0.30	0.30	0.10
2.	0.30	0.60	0.40
3.	0.60	0.30	0.20

(a) Rate $= k[A]^2[B]$ (b) Rate $= k[A][B]^2$

(c) Rate $= k[A][B]$ (d) Rate $= k[A]^2[B]^0$

10 Which of the following statements is incorrect about the collision theory of chemical reaction?

(a) It considers reacting molecules or atoms to be hard spheres and ignores their structural features.

(b) Number of effective collisions determines the rate of reaction

(c) Collision of atoms or molecules possessing sufficient threshold energy results into the product formation.

(d) Molecules should collide with sufficient threshold energy and proper orientation for the collision to be effective.

11 Which of the following statements is incorrect about order of a reaction?

(a) The order of a reaction can be a fractional number.

(b) Order of a reaction is experimentally determined quantity.

(c) The order of a reaction is always equal to the sum of the stoichiometric coefficients of reactants in the balanced chemical equation for a reaction.

(d) The order of a reaction is the sum of the powers of molar concentration of the reactants in the rate law expression.

12 Consider a first order gas phase decomposition reaction given below.

$$A(g) \longrightarrow B(g) + C(g)$$

The initial pressure of the system before decomposition of A was p_i. After lapse of time 't' total pressure of the system increased by x units and became 'p_t'. The rate constant (k) for the reaction is given as ....

(a) $k = \frac{2.303}{t}\log\frac{p_i}{p_i - x}$ (b) $k = \frac{2.303}{t}\log\frac{p_i}{2p_i - p_t}$

(c) $k = \frac{2.303}{t}\log\frac{p_i}{2p_i + p_t}$ (d) $k = \frac{2.303}{t}\log\frac{p_i}{p_i + x}$

13 Consider the figure and mark the correct option.

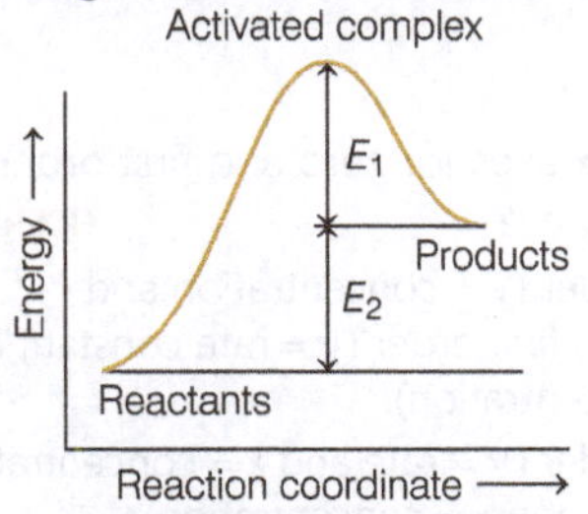

(a) Activation energy of forward reaction is $E_1 + E_2$ and product is less stable than reactant.
(b) Activation energy of forward reaction is $E_1 + E_2$ and product is more stable than reactant.
(c) Activation energy of both forward and backward reaction is $E_1 + E_2$ and reactant is more stable than product.
(d) Activation energy of backward reaction is E_1 and product is more stable than reactant.

14 Which of the following graphs represents exothermic reaction?

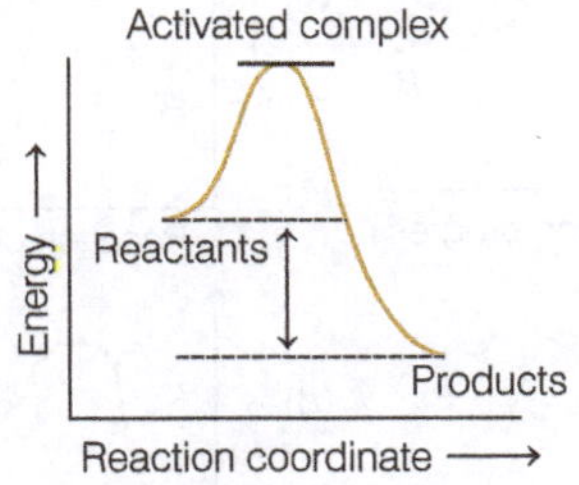

(I)

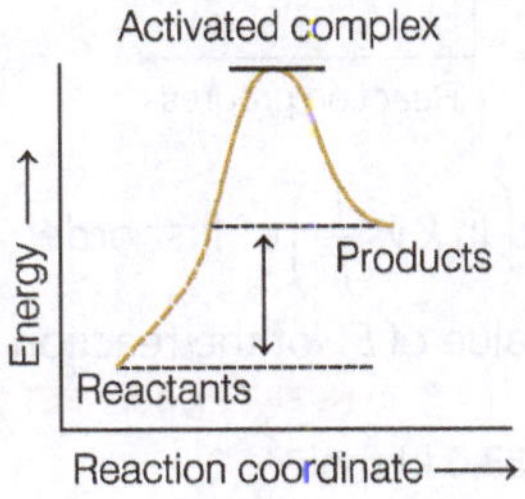

(II)

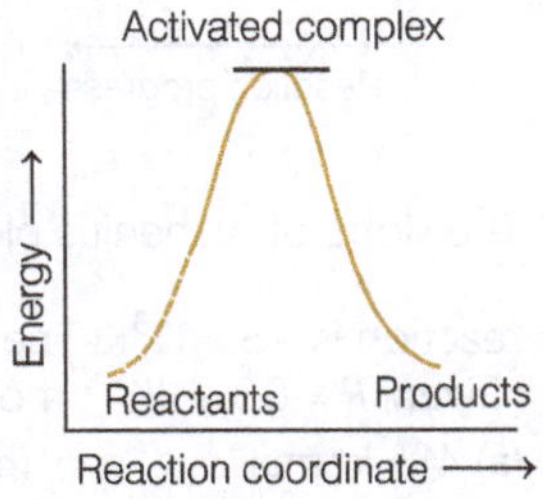

(III)

(a) Only I (b) II and III (c) Only III (d) I and II

15 Consider the Arrhenius equation given below and mark the correct option.

$$k = Ae^{-E_a/RT}$$

(a) Rate constant increases exponentially with increasing activation energy and decreasing temperature.
(b) Rate constant decreases exponentially with decreasing activation energy and decreasing temperature.
(c) Rate constant increases exponentially with decreasing activation energy and decreasing temperature.
(d) Rate constant increases exponentially with decreasing activation energy and increasing temperature.

16 According to Arrhenius equation rate constant (k) is equal to $Ae^{-E_a/RT}$. Which of the following options represent the graph of $\ln k$ vs $\frac{1}{T}$?

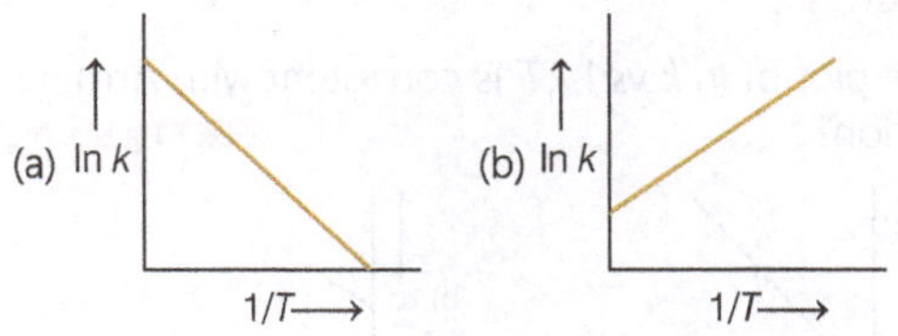

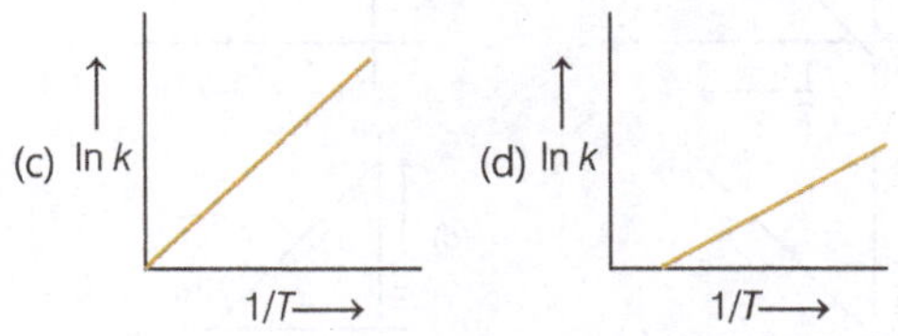

17 Activation energy of a chemical reaction can be determined by ....
(a) determining the rate constant at standard temperature
(b) determining the rate constant at two temperatures
(c) determining probability of collision
(d) using catalyst

18 In the presence of a catalyst, the heat evolved or absorbed during the reaction ....
(a) increases (b) decreases
(c) remains unchanged (d) may increase or decrease

19 Which of the following statement is correct?
(a) The rate of a reaction decreases with passage of time as the concentration of reactants decreases.
(b) The rate of a reaction is same at any time during the reaction.
(c) The rate of a reaction is independent of temperature change.
(d) The rate of a reaction decreases with increase in concentration of reactants.

20 Match the items of Column I and Column II.

Column I	Column II
A. Diamond	1. Short interval of time
B. Instantaneous rate	2. Ordinarily rate of conversion is imperceptible
C. Average rate	3. Long duration of time

21 Which of the following statement is not correct for the catalysts?
(a) It catalyses the forward and backward reactions to the same extent.
(b) It alters ΔG of the reaction.
(c) It is a substance that does not change the equilibrium constant of a reaction.
(d) It provides an alternate mechanism by reducing activation energy between reactants and products.

Past Exams' Questions

NEET Archive

1. Which plot of ln k vs $1/T$ is consistent with Arrhenius equation? **NCERT Pg 80, NEET 2024**

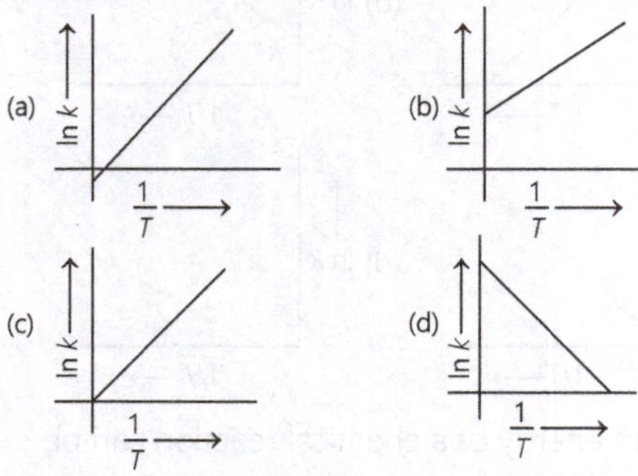

2. Activation energy of any chemical reaction can be calculated if one knows the value of **NCERT Pg 79, NEET 2024**

(a) rate constant at standard temperature
(b) probability of collision
(c) orientation of reactant molecules during collision
(d) rate constant at two different temperatures

3. For a certain reaction, the rate $= k[A]^2[B]$, when the initial concentration of A is tripled keeping concentration of B constant, the initial rate would **NCERT Pg 66, NEET 2023**

(a) increase by a factor of six
(b) increase by a factor of nine
(c) increase by a factor of three
(d) decrease by a factor of nine

4 Given below are two statements, one is labelled as Assertion (A) and the other is labelled as Reason (R).

Assertion (A) A reaction can have zero activation energy.

Reason (R) The minimum amount of energy absorbed by reactant molecules so that their energy becomes equal to threshold value, is called activation energy.

In the light of the above statements, choose the correct answer from the options given below. **NCERT Pg 79, NEET 2023**

(a) Both A and R are true and R is not the correct explanation of A.
(b) A is true but R is false.
(c) A is false but R is true.
(d) Both A and R are true and R is the correct explanation of A.

5. The given graph is a representation of kinetics of a reaction.

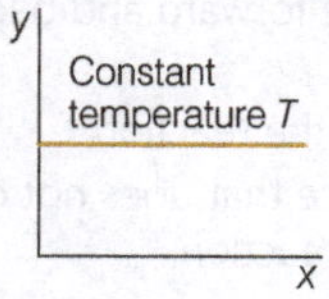

The y and x axes for zero and first order reactions, respectively are **NCERT Pg 77, NEET 2022**

(a) zero order (y = concentration and x = time), first order (y = rate constant and x = concentration).
(b) zero order (y = rate and x = concentration), first order ($y = t_{1/2}$ and x = concentration).
(c) zero order (y = rate and x = concentration), first order (y = rate and $x = t_{1/2}$).
(d) zero order (y = concentration and x = time), first order ($y = t_{1/2}$ and x = concentration).

6 For a reaction, $A \rightarrow B$, enthalpy of reaction is -4.2 kJ mol^{-1} and enthalpy of activation is 9.6 kJ mol^{-1}. The correct potential energy profile for the reaction is shown in option. **NCERT Pg 79, NEET 2021**

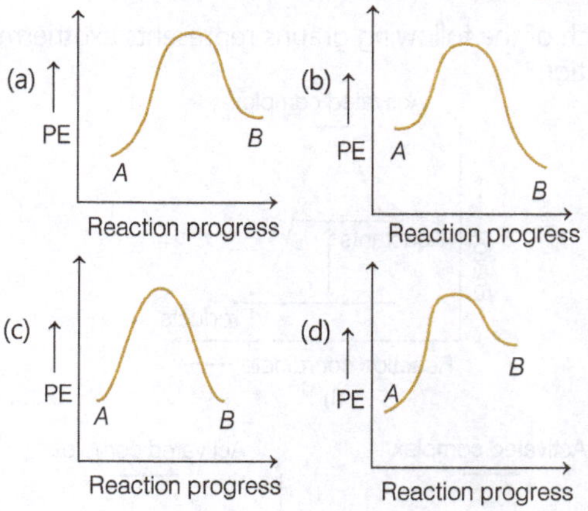

7 The slope of Arrhenius plot $\left(\ln k \text{ vs } \frac{1}{T}\right)$ of first order reaction is -5×10^3 K. The value of E_a of the reaction is [Given, $R = 8.314$ JK^{-1} mol^{-1}] **NCERT Pg 80, NEET 2021**

(a) 41.5 kJ mol^{-1} (b) 83.0 kJ mol^{-1}
(c) 166 kJ mol^{-1} (d) -83 kJ mol^{-1}

8 The half-life for a zero order reaction having 0.02 M initial concentration of reactant is 100 s. The rate constant (in mol L^{-1} s^{-1}) for the reaction is **NCERT Pg 76, NEET 2020**

(a) 1.0×10^{-4} (b) 2.0×10^{-4} (c) 2.0×10^{-3} (d) 1.0×10^{-2}

9 In collision theory of chemical reaction, Z_{AB} represents **NCERT Pg 83, NEET 2020**

(a) the fraction of molecules with energies greater than E_a
(b) the collision frequency of reactants, A and B
(c) steric factor
(d) the fraction of molecules with energies equal to E_a

10 The rate constant for a first order reaction is $4.606 \times 10^{-3}\ s^{-1}$. The time required to reduce 2.0 g of the reactant to 0.2 g is **NCERT Pg 73, NEET 2020**
(a) 200 s (b) 500 s (c) 1000 s (d) 100 s

11 If the rate constant for a first order reaction is k, the time (t) required for the completion of 99% of the reaction is given by **NCERT Pg 73, NEET (National) 2019, 2017**
(a) $t = 6.909/k$ (b) $t = 4.606/k$
(c) $t = 2.303/k$ (d) $t = 0.693/k$

12 A first order reaction has a specific reaction rate of $10^{-2} s^{-1}$. How much time will it take for 20 g of the reactant to reduce to 5 g? **NCERT Pg 73, NEET (Odisha) 2019, 2017**
(a) 238.6 s (b) 138.6 s (c) 346.5 s (d) 602 s

13 For a reaction, activation energy $E_a = 0$ and the rate constant at 200K is $1.6 \times 10^6\ s^{-1}$. The rate constant at 400 K will be [Given that gas constant $R = 8.314\ JK^{-1}\ mol^{-1}$] **NCERT Pg 81, NEET (Odisha) 2019**
(a) $3.2 \times 10^4\ s^{-1}$ (b) $1.6 \times 10^6\ s^{-1}$
(c) $1.6 \times 10^3\ s^{-1}$ (d) $3.2 \times 10^6\ s^{-1}$

14 When initial concentration of the reactant is doubled, the half-life period of a zero order reaction **NCERT Pg 76, NEET 2018**
(a) is tripled (b) is doubled
(c) is halved (d) remains unchanged

15 The rate of a first-order reaction is 0.04 mol $L^{-1} s^{-1}$ at 10 s and 0.03 mol $L^{-1} s^{-1}$ at 20 s after initiation of the reaction. The half-life period of the reaction is **NCERT Pg 73,76, NEET 2016**
(a) 34.1 s (b) 44.1 s (c) 54.1 s (d) 24.08 s

16 The activation energy of a reaction can be determined from the slope of which of the following graphs? **NCERT Pg 80, CBSE-AIPMT 2015**
(a) $\ln k$ vs T (b) $\frac{\ln k}{T}$ vs T (c) $\ln k$ vs $\frac{1}{T}$ (d) $\frac{T}{\ln k}$ vs $\frac{1}{T}$

17 When initial concentration of a reactant is doubled in a reaction, its half-life period is not affected. The order of the reaction is **NCERT Pg 77, CBSE-AIPMT 2015**
(a) zero (b) first
(c) second (d) more than zero but less than first

JEE Main Archive

18 Integrated rate law equation for a first order gas phase reaction is given by (where p_i is initial pressure and p_t is total pressure at time t) **NCERT Pg 72,73, JEE Main 2024**
(a) $k = \frac{2.303}{t} \times \frac{p_i}{(2p_i - p_t)}$ (b) $k = \frac{2.303}{t} \times \log \frac{p_i}{(2p_i - p_t)}$
(c) $k = \frac{2.303}{t} \times \log \frac{2p_i}{(2p_i - p_t)}$ (d) $k = \frac{2.303}{t} \times \log \frac{(2p_i - p_t)}{p_i}$

19 $r = k[A]$ for a reaction, 50% of A is decomposed in 120 minutes. The time taken for 90% decomposition of A is .... minutes. **NCERT Pg 76, JEE Main 2024**

20 During kinetic study of reaction, $2A + B \longrightarrow C + D$, the following results were obtained. **NCERT Pg 67, JEE Main 2024**

	A[M]	B[M]	Initial rate of formation of D
I.	0.1	0.1	6.0×10^{-3}
II.	0.3	0.2	7.2×10^{-2}
III.	0.3	0.4	2.88×10^{-1}
IV.	0.4	0.1	2.40×10^{-2}

Based on above data, overall order of the reaction is ....

21 For a chemical reaction, $A + B \longrightarrow$ Product, the order is 1 with respect to A and B.

Rate mol $L^{-1} s^{-1}$	[A] mol L^{-1}	[B] mol L^{-1}
0.10	20	0.5
0.40	x	0.5
0.80	40	y

What is the value of x and y? **NCERT Pg 67, JEE Main 2023**
(a) 80 and 4 (b) 80 and 2 (c) 40 and 4 (d) 160 and 4

22 The correct reaction profile diagram for a positive catalyst reaction. **NCERT Pg 82, JEE Main 2023**

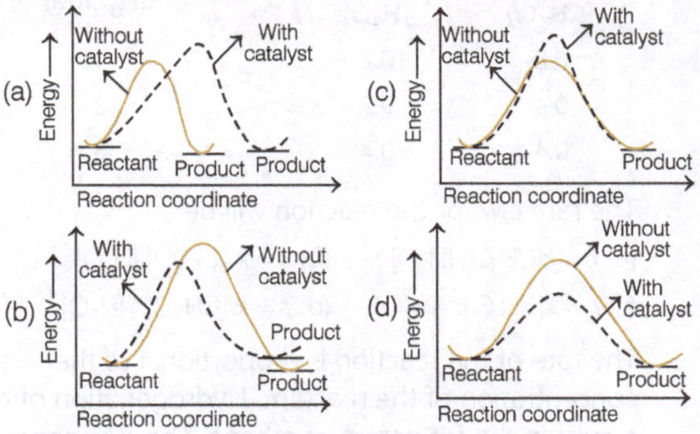

23 Consider the following reaction that goes from A to B in three steps as shown below. **NCERT Pg 79, JEE Main 2023**

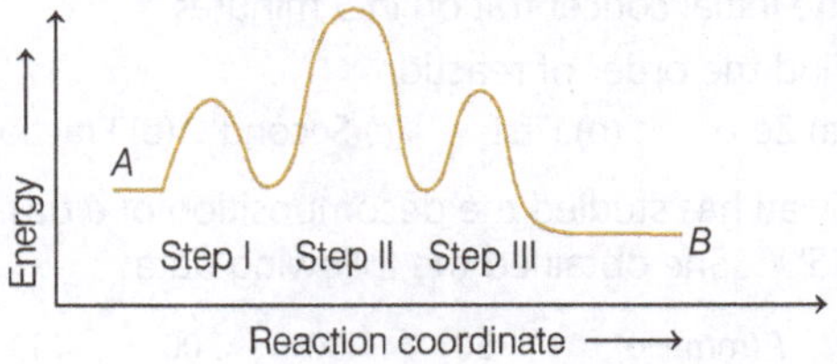

Choose the correct option.

	Number of intermediates	Number of activated complexes	Rate determining step
(a)	2	3	III
(b)	3	2	II
(c)	2	3	II
(d)	2	3	I

24 For a first order reaction, the time required for completion of 90% reaction is 'x' times the half-life of the reaction. The value of 'x' is (Given, ln10 = 2.303 and log 2 = 0.3010) **NCERT Pg 76, JEE Main 2022**

(a) 1.12 (b) 2.43
(c) 3.32 (d) 33.31

25 At 30°C, the half-life for the decomposition of AB_2 is 200 s and is independent of the initial concentration of AB_2. The time required for 80% of the AB_2 to decompose is (Given, log 2 = 0.30, log 3 = 0.48) **NCERT Pg 73, JEE Main 2022**

(a) 200 s (b) 323 s (c) 466 s (d) 532 s

Skill Boosters

1 A sample of milk turns sour at room temperature (27°C) in 48 hours. In a refrigerator at 2°C, milk can be stored three times longer before it sours. The activation energy of the souring of milk is (kJ mol^{-1}).

(a) 30.210 (b) 30.146 (c) 30.0 (d) 35.126

2 Consider the reaction represented by the equation.

$CH_3Cl(g) + H_2O(g) \longrightarrow CH_3OH(g) + HCl(g)$

These kinetic data were obtained for the given reaction concentrations.

Initial conc. (M)		Initial rate of disappearance of $CH_3Cl(Ms^{-1})$
$[CH_3Cl]$	$[H_2O]$	
0.2	0.2	1
0.4	0.2	2
0.4	0.4	8

The rate law for the reaction will be

(a) $r = k[CH_3Cl]\,[H_2O]$ (b) $r = k\,[CH_3Cl]\,[H_2O]^2$
(c) $r = k[CH_3Cl]^2\,[H_2O]$ (d) $r = k\,[CH_3Cl]^2\,[H_2O]^4$

3 The rate of the reaction is proportional to the concentration of the reactant. Hydrogenation of ethene results in the formation of ethane. The rate constant (k) for the reaction was found to be $2.5 \times 10^{-15} s^{-1}$. The concentration of the reactant reduces to one-third of the initial concentration in 5 minutes.

Find the order of reaction.

(a) Zero (b) First (c) Second (d) Fractional

4 Swati has studied the decomposition of a gas AB_3 at 25° C. She obtained the following data.

P(mm Hg)	50	100	200	400
Relative $t_{1/2}$(s)	4	2	1	0.5

The order of the reaction is

(a) 1 (b) 0 (c) 0.5 (d) 2

5 Consider the following reactions .

$A \rightarrow P1$; $B \rightarrow P2$; $C \rightarrow P3$; $D \rightarrow P4$,

The order of the above reactions are a, b, c and d respectively. The following graph is obtained what log[rate] vs log [conc.] are plotted.

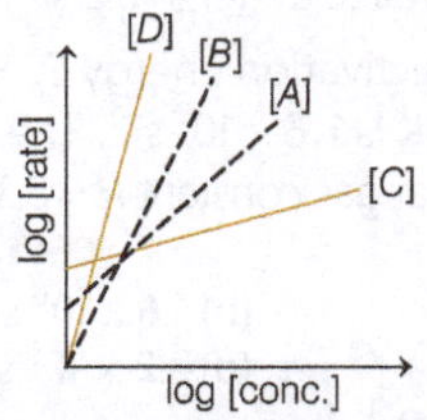

Among the following, the correct sequence for the order of the reactions is

(a) $d > a > b > c$ (b) $a > b > c > d$
(c) $c > a > b > d$ (d) $d > b > a > c$

6 Consider the given plot of enthalpy of the following reaction A and B

$A + B \longrightarrow C + D$

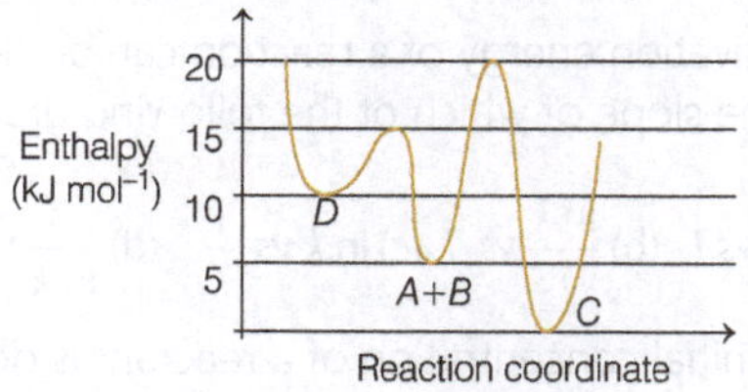

Identify the incorrect statement.

(a) D is kinetically stable product.

(b) Formation of A and B from C has highest enthalpy of activation.

(c) C is the thermodynamically stable product.

(d) Activation enthalpy to form C is 5 kJ mol^{-1} less than that to form D.

7 An exothermic chemical reaction proceeds by two stages

Reactants $\xrightarrow{\text{Stage 1}}$ Intermediate $\xrightarrow{\text{Stage 2}}$ Products.

The activation energy of state 1 is 50 J mol^{-1}. The overall enthalpy change for the reaction is –100 J mol^{-1}. Which graph could represent the energy level diagram for the reaction?

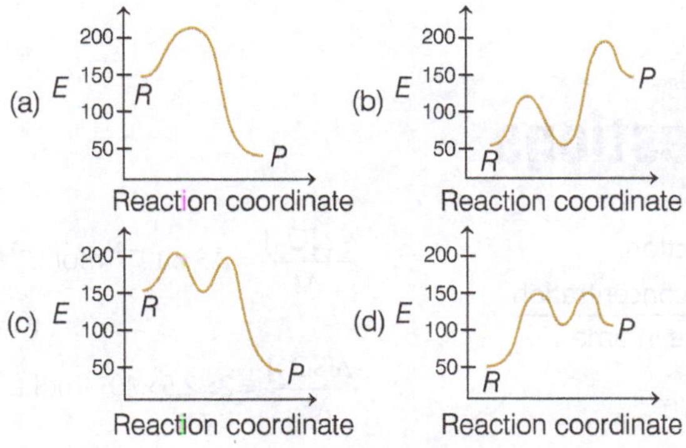

8 The rate constant for the decomposition of a certain reaction is described by the equation

$$\log k(s^{-1}) = 14 - \frac{1.25 \times 10^4 \text{ K}}{T}$$

At what temperature, rate constant is equal to pre-exponential factor?

(a) $T = \frac{1.25 \times 10^4}{14}$ (b) $T = \infty$

(c) $T = 0$ (d) $T = 14 - 1.25 \times 10^4$

9 The energy change accompanying the equilibrium reaction $A \rightleftharpoons B$ is $-33.0 \text{ kJ mol}^{-1}$. Assuming the pre-exponential factor is same for forward and backward reaction. The equilibrium constant K for the reaction at 300 K.

(a) 5.55×10^5 (b) 5.67×10^3 (c) 5.55×10^6 (d) 5.67×10^2

10 For an exothermic chemical process occurring in two steps as

I. $P + Q \longrightarrow R$ (slow) II. $R \longrightarrow PQ$ (fast)

The progress of the reaction can be best described by

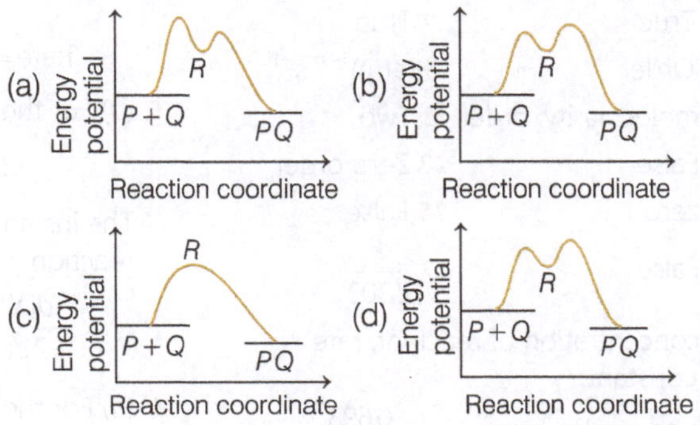

Correct Codes

Topical Questions

1. (b)	2. (d)	3. (a)	4. (d)	5. (a)	6. (a)	7. (a)	8. (a)	9. (a)	10. (d)
11. (a)	12. (d)	13. (d)	14. (b)	15. (d)	16. (c)	17. (a)	18. (c)	19. (c)	20. (d)
21. (b)	22. (d)	23. (a)	24. (d)	25. (b)	26. (a)	27. (a)	28. (c)	29. (c)	30. (d)
31. (c)	32. (d)	33. (d)	34. (d)	35. (b)	36. (d)	37. (b)	38. (b)	39. (a)	40. (b)
41. (a)	42. (c)	43. (a)	44. (b)	45. (b)	46. (a)	47. (a)	48. (c)	49. (d)	50. (b)
51. (b)	52. (b)	53. (d)	54. (d)	55. (a)	56. (a)	57. (b)	58. (b)	59. (b)	60. (b)
61. (c)	62. (c)	63. (b)	64. (b)	65. (c)	66. (b)	67. (a)	68. (b)	69. (d)	70. (a)
71. (c)	72. (d)	73. (d)	74. (b)	75. (b)					

Assertion-Reason

1. (a)	2. (a)	3. (a)	4. (b)	5. (a)	6. (d)	7. (d)	8. (b)	9. (b)	10. (a)
11. (a)	12. (c)	13. (b)	14. (a)	15. (d)	16. (c)	17. (a)	18. (c)	19. (b)	20. (a)

Statement Type

1. (b)	2. (d)	3. (d)	4. (b)	5. (a)	6. (c)	7. (c)	8. (d)	9. (d)	10. (d)

Matching Type

1. (c)	2. (b)	3. (c)	4. (a)	5. (a)

Numerical Value

1. (5)	2. (3)	3. (3)	4. (100)	5. (52)

NCERT Exemplar's

1. (b)	2. (c)	3. (b)	4. (a)	5. (c)	6. (d)	7. (c)	8. (b)	9. (b)	10. (c)
11. (c)	12. (b)	13. (a)	14. (a)	15. (d)	16. (a)	17. (b)	18. (c)	19. (a)	
20. A-2, B-1, C-3		21. (b)							

Past Exams'

1. (d)	2. (d)	3. (b)	4. (c)	5. (b)	6. (b)	7. (a)	8. (a)	9. (b)	10. (b)
11. (b)	12. (b)	13. (b)	14. (b)	15. (d)	16. (c)	17. (b)	18. (b)	19. (399)	20. (3)
21. (b)	22. (d)	23. (c)	24. (c)	25. (c)					

Skill Boosters

1. (b)	2. (b)	3. (b)	4. (d)	5. (d)	6. (d)	7. (c)	8. (b)	9. (a)	10. (a)

Step by Step

Decoding the Questions

Concept Builders

1 reaction rate, mechanism

2 True
3 True

4 instantaneous
5 True

6 True
7 True

8 Order
9 $(\text{atm})^{1-n}\ \text{s}^{-1}$

10 molecularity, order
11 Two

12 False
13 Zero order

14 zero
15 False

16 False
17 $\frac{k}{2.303}$

18 concentration of reactant, rate constant.

19 $1.26\times 10^{13}\text{s}\left[\textbf{Hint}: t_{1/2}=\frac{0.693}{k}\right]$

20 True
21 Pseudo first

22 $t_{1/2}=\frac{1}{k[A_0]}$
23 False

24 released

25. Activation energy
26 True

27 $\frac{-E_a}{R}$
28 Inhibitor

29 False

30 effective collisions

Topical Solutions

1 (*b*) Rate of only those chemical reactions can be determined easily which occurs at moderate speed, e.g. hydrolysis of starch, inversion of cane sugar etc.

2 (*d*) From the given graph, the average rate of reaction is given as,

$$r_{av}=\frac{-\{[R_2]-[R_1]\}}{(t_2-t_1)}$$

3 (*a*) In the given graph, the curve P depicts the variation of the concentration of products, as there is gradual increase in concentration of products with passage of time.

4 (*d*) The rate of the reaction

$$=\frac{\text{Change in concentration}}{\text{Change in time}}$$

$$\text{Rate}=\frac{0.35}{50}=7\times 10^{-3}$$

$$\text{Rate}=7\times 10^{-3}\ \text{Ms}^{-1}$$

5 (*a*) For the reaction,

$$2X+Y\longrightarrow X_2Y$$

The instantaneous rate of the reaction is given as,

$$-\frac{d[X]}{2dt}=\frac{-d[Y]}{dt}=+\frac{d[X_2Y]}{dt}$$

6 (*a*) For the reaction,

$$N_2+3H_2\longrightarrow 2NH_3$$

The instantaneous rate of reaction is given as

$$-\frac{d[N_2]}{dt}=-\frac{d[H_2]}{3dt}=+\frac{d[NH_3]}{2dt}$$

$$\therefore\quad \frac{d[NH_3]}{dt}=\frac{2}{3}\frac{d[H_2]}{dt}$$

7 (*a*) For the reaction,

$$2NO_2\longrightarrow 2NO+O_2$$

$$\text{Rate}=-\frac{1}{2}\frac{d[NO_2]}{dt}=\frac{d[NO]}{2dt}=\frac{d[O_2]}{dt}$$

$$\because\quad -\frac{d[NO_2]}{dt}=6\times 10^{-12}\text{mol L}^{-1}\ \text{s}^{-1}$$

$$\therefore\quad \frac{d[O_2]}{dt}=-\frac{1}{2}\frac{d[NO_2]}{dt}=\frac{1}{2}\times 6\times 10^{-12}=3\times 10^{-12}\ \text{mol L}^{-1}\text{s}^{-1}$$

8 (*a*) For the reaction,

$$2SO_2(g)+O_2(g)\rightleftharpoons 2SO_3(g)$$

the rate of reaction is given as

$$\frac{-\Delta[SO_2]}{\Delta t}=2\left(-\frac{\Delta[O_2]}{\Delta t}\right)$$

$$\because\quad \frac{-\Delta[O_2]}{\Delta t}=2.5\times 10^{-4}\ \text{mol L}^{-1}\ \text{s}^{-1}\quad\text{(Given)}$$

$$\therefore\quad \frac{-\Delta[SO_2]}{\Delta t}=2\times 2.5\times 10^{-4}\text{mol L}^{-1}\text{s}^{-1}=50.0\times 10^{-5}\ \text{mol L}^{-1}\ \text{s}^{-1}$$

9 (*a*) For the reaction,

$$5Br^-+BrO_3^-+6H^+\longrightarrow 3Br_2+3H_2O$$

$$\frac{-1}{5}\frac{d[Br^-]}{dt}=-\frac{d[BrO_3^-]}{dt}=\frac{1}{3}\frac{d[Br_2]}{dt}$$

$$\frac{1}{5}k_1\ [Br^-]=k_2\ [Br^-]=\frac{1}{3}k_3\ [Br^-]$$

$$3k_1=15k_2=5k_3 \text{ or } k_1=5k_2=1.66k_3$$

10 (*d*) In the given graph, from $t=0$ to $t=1$ h for P.

The change in concentration of P, i.e. $[\Delta P]=0.6-0.5=0.1\ \text{mol L}^{-1}$

$\therefore$ Initial rate of conversion of

$$P=\frac{\Delta[P]}{\Delta t}=\frac{0.1\ \text{mol L}^{-1}}{1\ \text{h}}=0.1\ \text{mol L}^{-1}\ \text{h}^{-1}$$

11 (*a*) Rate of reaction $=-\frac{1}{2}\frac{d[x]}{dt}$

$$=-\frac{1}{2}\frac{[1.5-3.0]}{4}=\frac{1.5}{8}=0.187\ \text{M min}^{-1}$$

12 (*d*) For the given reaction, rate depends upon concentration of Q only. So, on reducing the concentration of Q rate of reaction also reduces.

13 (*d*) For the reaction,

$$A+B\longrightarrow \text{Product}$$

Let the rate of reaction be

$$r_1=k[A]^\alpha[B]^\beta \quad\text{...(i)}$$

$$r_2=2r_1=k[A]^\alpha[2B]^\beta \quad\text{...(ii)}$$

$$r_3=8r_1=k[2A]^\alpha\ [2B]^\beta \quad\text{...(iii)}$$

On dividing Eq. (ii) by Eq. (i), we get

$$\frac{r_2}{r_1}=\frac{2r_1}{r_1}=\frac{k[A]^{\alpha}[2B]^{\beta}}{k[A]^{\alpha}[B]^{\beta}}$$

$\Rightarrow \quad \beta = 1$

Similarly, on dividing Eq. (iii) by Eq. (ii), we get

$$\frac{r_3}{r_2}=\frac{8r_1}{2r_1}=\frac{k[2A]^{\alpha}[2B]^{\beta}}{k[A]^{\alpha}[2B]^{\beta}} \Rightarrow \alpha = 2$$

$\therefore \quad$ Rate $(r_1) = k[A]^2[B]^1$

14 (*b*) $\because$ Initial rate $= k[P]^a[Q]^b$

$\therefore$ New rate $= k[2P]^a\left[\frac{Q}{2}\right]^b$

$= k\cdot 2^a[P]^a\cdot\frac{[Q]^b}{2^b}$

$= 2^{(a-b)}\cdot k[P]^a[Q]^b$

$= 2^{(a-b)}\cdot$ Initial rate

Thus, $\frac{\text{New rate}}{\text{Initial rate}} = 2^{(a-b)}$

15 (*d*) Rate law for the formation of C is

$$r=\frac{dC}{dt}=k[A]^x[B]^y$$

where, x = order of reaction w.r.t. A.

y = order of reaction w.r.t. B.

$1.2\times10^{-3}=k(0.1)^x(0.1)^y$

$1.2\times10^{-3}=k(0.1)^x(0.2)^y$

$2.4\times10^{-3}=k(0.2)^x(0.1)^y$

On solving the above equations, we get, $x=1$ and $y=0$

$\therefore r=\frac{dC}{dt}=k[A]^1[B]^0$

or $\quad r=\frac{dC}{dt}=k[A]$

16 (*c*) Let rate law,

Rate $= k[CH_3Cl]^x\,[H_2O]^y$

$1=k[0.2]^x\cdot[0.2]^y$ ...(i)

$2=k[0.4]^x\cdot[0.2]^y$ ...(ii)

$8=k[0.4]^x\cdot[0.4]^y$ ...(iii)

On dividing Eqs. (ii) by (i)

We get, $\frac{2}{1}=\left(\frac{0.4}{0.2}\right)^x$

$\Rightarrow \quad x=1$

On dividing Eq. (iii) by (ii)

We get, $\frac{8}{2}=\left(\frac{0.4}{0.2}\right)^y$

$\Rightarrow \quad y=2$

Hence, rate $= k[CH_3Cl]\,[H_2O]^2$.

17 (*a*) Given, $O_3 \rightleftharpoons O_2 + O$ (fast) ...(i)

$O + O_3 \longrightarrow 2O_2$ (Slow) ...(ii)

From Eq. (i) $K_{eq}=\frac{[O_2][O]}{[O_3]}$

or $\quad [O]=\frac{K_{eq}[O_3]}{[O_2]}$

From Eq. (ii)

rate law $= k[O_3][O]$

or $\quad r=\frac{k[O_3][O_3]}{[O_2]}K_{eq}$

or $\quad r=k'\,[O_3]^2\,[O_2]^{-1}\,[k'=k\times K_{eq}]$

18 (*c*) Since, the rate law given is

$$\frac{-d[BrO_3]^-}{dt}=k[BrO_3^-]\,[Br^-]\,[H^+]^2$$

Thus, the reaction rate increases by 4 times on doubling the concentration of $[H^+]$ ions. Moreover, since it contains $[H^+]$ term. This means that, rate changes with variation in the value of pH.

19 (*c*) For the given reaction,

$C_2H_5OH + CH_3COOH \longrightarrow CH_3COOC_2H_5 + H_2O$

$r = k[CH_3COOH][C_2H_5OH]$

or $r=k\left[\frac{n}{V}\right]\left[\frac{n}{V}\right]$

Increasing volume (V) by twice (due to dilution) will reduce the rate by 4 times.

i.e. $r = 0.25\,k\,[CH_3COOH][C_2H_5OH]$

20 (*d*) The strengths of two acids can be compared only by knowing their dissociation constants and not by value of rate constants.

Thus, the given data is insufficient to compare the strength of H_2SO_4 and HCl.

21 (*b*)

22 (*d*) As it is clear from the given data that, the rate of the reaction remains constant with time, therefore. reaction is of zero order.

23 (*a*)

24 (*d*) Given, rate $= k[CHCl_3]\,[Cl_2]^{1/2}$

$\because \quad$ Order $=1+\frac{1}{2}=\frac{3}{2}$

$\therefore$ Units of rate constant

$$=\frac{\text{Units of rate}}{[CHCl_3]\,[Cl_2]^{1/2}}$$

$$=\frac{\text{bar min}^{-1}}{\text{bar}^{3/2}}=\text{bar}^{-1/2}\text{min}^{-1}$$

and units of rate is bar min^{-1}.

25 (*b*) $\because$ The rate of reaction is given by,

$$\frac{d[IO^-]}{dt}=\frac{k\,[I^-]\,[OCl^-]}{[OH^-]}.$$

Therefore, overall order of reaction

$=1+1-1=1$

26 (*a*)

27 (*a*) The given reaction,

i.e. $\quad 2N_2O_5 \rightleftharpoons 2N_2O_4 + O_2$

occurs in two steps and, hence bimolecular reaction and the rate determining step is the slowest step which is of first order.

28 (*c*)

29 (*c*) $t=\frac{1}{k}[[A_0]-[A]]$

$=\frac{1}{0.0030}[0.10-0.075]$

$=\frac{1}{0.0030}\times 0.025=\frac{25}{3}=8.3$ s

30 (*d*) For a zero order reaction,

$[R]=(-k)\,t+[R]_0$ ...(i)

On comparing with equation of straight line; $y=mx+c$

$y=[R]$ concentration of reactant

$x=t$ (time)

Slope $(m)=-k$ (rate constant)

Intercept $(c)=[R]_0$ (initial concentration)

Thus, the graph between conc. of reactant and time is given in option (d).

31 (c)

32 (d) For a zero order reaction, unit of rate constant is $(\text{mol L}^{-1}\ \text{s}^{-1})$.
Hence, we can easily calculate the concentration of B after 20 min by the following formula,

$$X = kt = 0.6 \times 10^{-3} \times 20 \times 60$$
$$= 0.72\ \text{M}$$

33 (d) The correct form of statement II is the first order rate equation can be represented as $k = \frac{2.303}{t} \log \frac{[R_0]}{[R]}$.

34 (d) For first order reaction,

$$\frac{k \cdot t}{2.303} = \log [C_0] - \log [C]$$

or, $\log [C] = \log [C_0] - \frac{k \cdot t}{2.303}$

On comparing the above equation with equation of straight line, i.e. $y = mx + c$; plot of $\log [C]$ *vs* t is a straight line with negative slope.

Thus, $\log C$ decreases linearly with t.

35 (b) Among the given reaction,

$$2H_2O_2 \longrightarrow 2H_2O + O_2$$

is an example of first order reaction, while (c) is second order and the other given reactions are example of pseudo first order.

36 (d) For first order,

$$-\ln [R] = kt - \ln [R_0]$$

The graph for first order reaction is

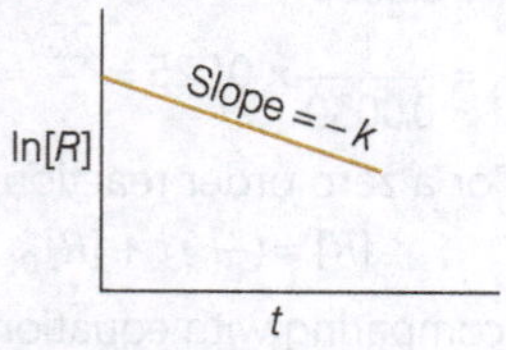

For zero order reaction,

$$[R]_t = [R]_0 - kt$$

The graph for zero order reaction is

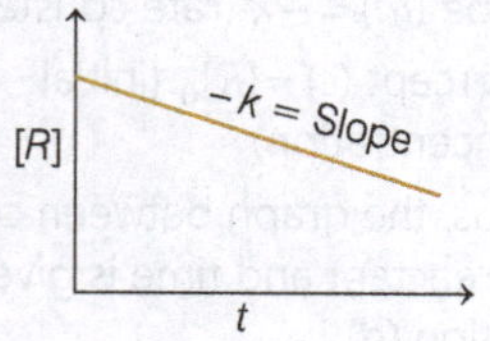

37 (b) Decomposition of benzene diazonium chloride occurs in the following manner.

$$C_6H_5\overset{+}{N}{\equiv}N\overset{-}{Cl} \longrightarrow C_6H_5Cl + N_2\uparrow$$

The volume of nitrogen obtained shows the extent of decomposition of benzene diazonium chloride, so

$$a \propto V_\infty = 162\ \text{mL}$$
$$(a - x) \propto (V_\infty - V_t)\ \text{mL}$$

For first order reaction,

$$k = \frac{2.303}{t} \log \frac{V_\infty - V_0}{V_\infty - V_t}$$

or $k = \frac{2.303}{t} \log \frac{V_\infty}{V_\infty - V_t} \quad (\because V_0 = 0)$

At 20 min,

$$k = \frac{2.303}{20} \log \frac{162}{162 - 10}$$
$$= \frac{2.303}{20} \log \frac{162}{152}$$
$$= 3.18 \times 10^{-3}\ \text{min}^{-1}$$
$$\approx 3.2 \times 10^{-3}\ \text{min}^{-1}$$

38 (b) For gas phase reaction,

	$A(g)$	$\longrightarrow$	$B(g)$	+	$C(g)$
At $t = 0$	p_i atm		0 atm		0 atm
At time = 't'	$(p_i - x)$ atm		x atm		x atm

$$k = \frac{2.303}{t} \log \frac{p_i}{(2p_i - p_t)}$$

39 (a) Let the initial pressure of azoisopropane is p_0 and after (t) time, its pressure reduces by x.

So, $(CH_3)_2CHN{=}NCH(CH_3)_2 \longrightarrow N_2 + C_6H_{14}$

		N_2	C_6H_{14}
At $t = 0$	p_0	0	0
After 360 s	$p_0 - x$	x	x

Total pressure after 360s

$$(p_t) = p_0 - x + x + x$$
$$\Rightarrow \quad = 35 + x = 54$$
$$x = 54 - 35 = 19\ \text{mm Hg}$$
$$p_0 - x = 35 - 19 = 16\ \text{mm Hg}$$

For first order reaction,

$$\text{Rate constant, } (k) = \frac{2.303}{t} \log \frac{p_0}{p_0 - x}$$
$$= \frac{2.303}{360} \log \frac{35}{16} = \frac{2.303}{360} \log 2.187$$
$$= \frac{2.303}{360} \times 0.34 = 2.17 \times 10^{-3}\ \text{s}^{-1}$$

40 (b) Let, the rate expression is

$$r \propto [A]^a\ [B]^b.$$

From experiments I and II

$$\frac{r_2}{r_1} = \left(\frac{0.1}{0.1}\right)^a \times \left(\frac{0.25}{0.20}\right)^b$$
$$\Rightarrow \frac{6.93 \times 10^{-3}}{6.93 \times 10^{-3}} = 1 \times \left(\frac{5}{4}\right)^b$$
$$\Rightarrow \quad 1 = \left(\frac{5}{4}\right)^b$$
$$\Rightarrow \quad b = 0$$

From experiments I and III

$$\frac{r_3}{r_1} = \left(\frac{0.2}{0.1}\right)^a \times \left(\frac{0.30}{0.20}\right)^b$$
$$\Rightarrow \frac{1.386 \times 10^{-2}}{0.693 \times 10^{-2}} = (2)^a \times (1.5)^0$$
$$\Rightarrow \quad a = 1$$

$\Rightarrow$ So, $r \propto [A]^1 [B]^0$

$\Rightarrow \quad r \propto [A]$

Order of the reaction $(n) = 1$

$\Rightarrow$ Now, let for the 1st experiment,

$$r_1 = k \cdot [A]$$
$$\Rightarrow \quad k = \frac{r_1}{[A]} = \frac{6.93 \times 10^{-3}}{0.1}$$
$$= 6.93 \times 10^{-2}\ \text{min}^{-1}$$
$$\Rightarrow t_{1/2}\% = \frac{0.693}{k} = \frac{0.693}{6.93 \times 10^{-2}} = 10\ \text{min}$$

41 (a) We know, $\lambda = \frac{0.693}{t_{1/2}}$

So, for first order reaction, the equation is $\lambda = \frac{2.303}{t} \log \frac{R_0}{R}$

Substituting the value for λ, we get

$$\frac{0.693}{5750} = \frac{2.303}{t} \log \frac{15.5}{8.4}$$

So, $t = 5084$ yrs

42 (c) For a first order reaction,

$$t = \frac{2.303}{k} \log \frac{[A]_0}{[A]}$$

$$\therefore \quad t_{5/6} = \frac{2.303}{k} \log \frac{[R_0]}{[R_0]/6}$$

$$\therefore \quad t_{5/6} = \frac{2.303}{k} \log 6$$

43 (a) For first order reaction,

$$k = \frac{2.303}{t} \log \frac{a}{a-x}$$

$$\therefore k = \frac{2.303}{32 \text{ min}} \log \frac{a}{a-0.99a}$$

$$= 0.1439 \text{ min}^{-1}$$

$$\Rightarrow t = \frac{2.303}{0.1439} \log \frac{a}{a-0.999a} = 48 \text{ min}$$

44 (b) For first order, the half-life period is given as

$$t_{1/2} = \frac{0.693}{k}$$

$$\Rightarrow \quad k = \frac{0.693}{20} \quad (\because t_{1/2} = 20 \text{ mins})$$

Now, $k = \frac{2.303}{t} \log \frac{[A]_0}{[A]_t}$

$$\Rightarrow \frac{0.693}{20} \times \frac{100}{2.303} = \log \frac{100}{100-x}$$

$$1.50 = \log \frac{100}{100-x}$$

$$\Rightarrow \quad x = 96.83\%$$

45 (b) Since, the radioactive decay follows first order kinetics;

$$\therefore k \text{ or decay constant } (\lambda) = \frac{0.693}{t_{1/2}}$$

$$\Rightarrow \frac{0.693}{48750} = \lambda$$

$$\Rightarrow \quad \lambda = 1.42 \times 10^{-5}$$

Given, $[A_0] = 100$

$$\therefore \quad [A] = 100 - 60 = 40$$

$$t = \frac{2.303}{\lambda} \log \frac{[A_0]}{[A]} = \frac{2.303}{1.42 \times 10^{-5}} \log \frac{100}{40}$$

$$\because t = \frac{2.303}{1.42 \times 10^{-5}} [\log (5) - \log(2)]$$

$$= 64548 \text{ yrs}$$

46 (a) $k = \frac{2.303}{t} \log \frac{a}{a-x}$

$(a-x)$ is the concentration left after 200 s.

$$2.714 \times 10^{-3} = \frac{2.303}{200} \log \frac{0.29}{(a-x)}$$

$$\frac{2.714 \times 10^{-3} \times 200}{2.303} = \log \frac{0.29}{a-x} = 0.235$$

$$\Rightarrow (a-x) = 0.169 \text{ M}$$

47 (a) Since, half-life does not depend on the concentration of the reactant.

$\therefore$ It is a first order reaction. As, the volume of N_2 gas (product) after completion of reaction is 100 L.

Thus, $\frac{[R]_0}{[R]} = \frac{100}{20} = 5$

Given, $t = 10$ min

As we know that,

$$k = \frac{2.303}{t} \log \frac{[R]_0}{[R]}$$

$$\therefore \quad k = \frac{2.303}{10} \log 5 \text{ min}^{-1}$$

48 (c) **49** (d)

50 (b) The temperature coefficient of a reaction is the ratio of rate constant differing by 10° preferably 25°C and 35°C.

51 (b) For 10° rise in temperature, $n = 1$

So, rate $= 2^n = 2^1 = 2$

when temperature is increased from 10°C to 100°C change in temperature $= 100 - 10 = 90°C$

$\therefore \quad n = 9$

So, $\quad$ rate $= 2^9$

$= 512$ times

52 (b) For a chemical reaction with rise in temperature by 10°, the rate constant is nearly doubled and, therefore the correct increasing order of the time taken for half of the decomposition of N_2O_5 at the temperatures 50°C, 0°C and 25°C will be 50°C < 25°C < 0°C.

53 (d)

54 (d) Statements I and IV are correct, while the statements II and III are incorrect. Corrected form are as follows

II. The fraction of molecules having kinetic energy greater than E_a can be determine by the factor $e^{-2700/RT}$

III. Rate of a reaction increases with increase in temperature.

55 (a) In Maxwell velocity distribution curve the peak point corresponds to most probable kinetic energy.

56 (a) In the given figure, fraction of molecules represents $\frac{N_E}{N_T}$, where N_E is the number of molecules with energy E and N_T is the total number of molecules.

57 (b) The Arrhenius equation is,

$$k = A \cdot e^{-E_a/RT}$$

where, k = rate constant,

A = Arrhenius constant,

E_a = activation energy,

and T = temperature in K.

From the equation, it is clear that k decreases exponentially with E_a. So, the plot-I is correct.

In the plot-II, k is plotted with temperature (in °C but not in K). So, at 0°C, $k \neq 0$ and k will increase exponentially with temperature upto 300°C. Therefore, the plot-II is also correct.

58 (b) Since $E_1 > E_2$; therefore $k_1 < k_2$. This is because, as the value of activation energy (E_a) increases, the value of rate constant (k) decreases.

59 (b) Activation energy diagram for the given exothermic reaction;

$A + B \longrightarrow C$ is given as

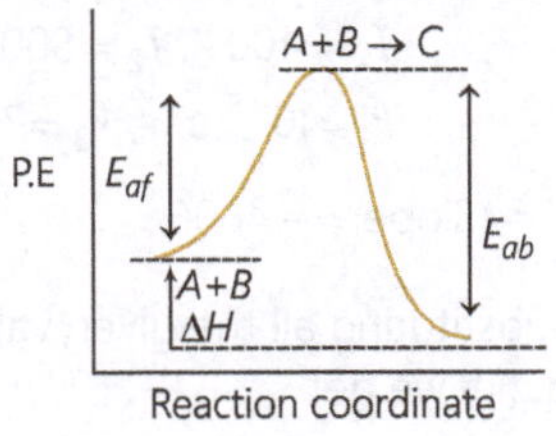

$\therefore E_{ab} = \Delta H + E_{af}$

$= (249 + 30)$ kJ/mol

$= 279$ kJ/mol

60 (*b*)

61 (*c*) Statement (c) is incorrect.

It's correct form is as follows

The total area under the curve must be constant, since total probability must be one at all times.

62 (*c*) The distribution of kinetic energy described by plotting the fraction of molecules with a given kinetic energy is called Maxwell's distribution of energies and the curve shown in the given figure is known as Maxwell-Boltzmann distribution curve.

63 (*b*) In the given plot of ln *k v/s* $1/T$; the intercept is ln *A* and slope is $\frac{-E_a}{R}$.

64 (*b*) For every 10°C rise, rate constant gets doubled.

Hence, for every 20° C rise, rate constant will be 4 times.

Therefore, according to the given statement,

Temperature	280K	300K
Rate constant	k_2	k_1 (or $4k_2$)

Thus, $k_1 = 4k_2$

$\Rightarrow k_2 = 0.25\, k_1$

65 (*c*) Arrhenius equation at two different temperatures for a reaction is

$$\ln \frac{k_2}{k_1} = \frac{E_a}{R}\left(\frac{1}{T_1} - \frac{1}{T_2}\right) \quad ...(ii)$$

$\Rightarrow$ In the given problem,

$T_1 = 400$ K, $T_2 = 500$ K,

$k_1 = 10^{-5}$ s^{-1}, $k_2 = ?$

$-\frac{E_a}{R}$ (Slope) $= -4606$

On substituting all the given values in Eq. (ii), we get

$$\ln \frac{k_2}{10^{-5}} = 4606\left(\frac{1}{400} - \frac{1}{500}\right)$$

$$\ln \frac{k_2}{10^{-5}} = 2.303$$

$\Rightarrow k_2 = 10^{-4} s^{-1}$

66 (*b*) Let the activation energy with and without enzyme be E_a^* and E_a.

Rate constant of reaction without catalyst is given by Arrhenius equation.

$$k = Ae^{-E_a/RT}$$

Taking log on both sides, we get

$$\log k = \log A - \frac{E_a}{RT(2.303)} \quad ...(i)$$

With catalyst, rate constant is 10^6 times more

$$\therefore \quad 10^6 k = Ae^{\frac{-E_a^*}{RT}}$$

$$\therefore \quad \log k = \log A - \frac{E_a^*}{RT(2.303)} - 6 \quad ...(ii)$$

Comparing Eqs. (i) and (ii)

$$\frac{E_a}{RT(2.303)} = \frac{E_a^*}{RT(2.303)} + 6$$

$$\therefore \quad E_a^* - E_a = -6(2.303)RT$$

67 (*a*) Since,

$$\text{Rate of reaction} \propto \frac{1}{\text{activation energy}}$$

Therefore, the catalytic efficiency of I, II, III and IV are representing the relative case would be, I > II > III > IV.

68 (*b*) Statement (b) is incorrect.

It's correct form is as follows

Catalyst reduces the activation energy between reactants and products.

Rest other statements are correct.

69 (*d*) Only those collisions in which molecules collide with sufficient energy, called threshold energy and proper orientation are effective collisions. Rest of the molecules collide and bounce back.

70 (*a*) **71** (*c*)

72 (*d*) Since $k \propto e^{-E_a}$; E_a should be decreased in order to increase the rate of reaction.

73 (*d*) Statement (d) is correct. Collision of atoms or molecules possessing sufficient threshold energy and proper orientation results into the product formation.

74 (*b*)

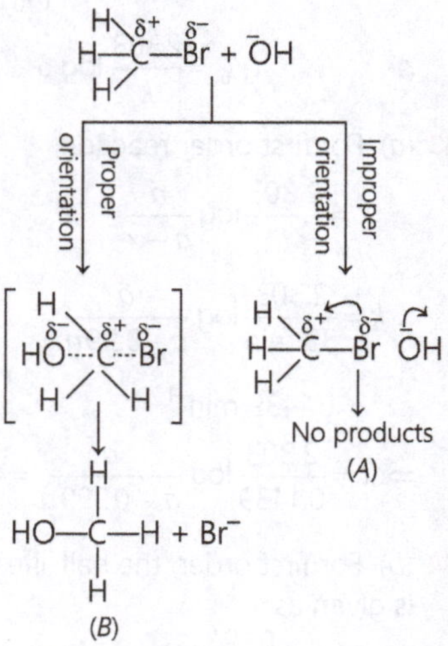

75 (*b*) For effective collisions to take place the colliding molecules should have proper orientation apart from energy considerations.

Assertion-Reason

1 (*a*) Both A and R are true and R is the correct explanation of A.

2 (*a*) Both A and R are true and R is the correct explanation of A.

3 (*a*) Both A and R are true and R is the correct explanation of A.

4 (*b*) Both A and R are true but R is not the correct explanation of A.

Order of reaction can be zero or fractional as order of reaction is directly related to sum of power of reactants.

5 (*a*) Both A and R are true and R is the correct explanation of A.

6 (*d*) A is false but R is true. The correct form of A is

Order and molecularity may or may not be same.

7 (*d*) A is false but R is true.

The correct form of A is :

Rate of a zero order reaction is given as, Rate $= k[R]^0$ or Rate $= k$
Therefore, for zero order reactions rate is independent of the concentration of reactants.

8 (*b*) For a complex reaction, order of reaction is given by slowest step of the reaction.
For the reaction,
$$CH_3CHO(g) \longrightarrow CH_4(g) + CO(g)$$
Rate $= k[CH_3CHO]^{3/2}$
Hence, the order of reaction is 3/2 or 1.5 and molecularity of reaction is 1, since only one reactant is involved.
Moreover, molecularity of slowest step is same as the order of overall reaction.
Thus, both A and R are true but R is not the correct explanation of A.

9 (*b*) Zero order reactions are not so common and they occur under special conditions, like some enzyme catalysed reactions and reactions which occur on metal surfaces are a few examples of zero order reactions.
Moreover, thermal decomposition of HI on gold surface is a zero order reaction.
Thus, both A and R are true but R is not the correct explanation of A.

10 (*a*) The reaction is given as,
$$2NH_3(g) \xrightarrow[\text{Pt catalyst}]{1130\text{ K}} N_2(g) + 3H_2(g);$$
Rate $= k[NH_3]^0 = k$
∴ In this reaction, Pt acts as a catalyst and the metal surface gets saturated with gas molecules at high pressure.
Thus, a further change in reaction conditions does not alter the amount of ammonia on the surface of the catalyst making rate of the reaction independent of its concentration.
Thus, both A and R are true and R is the correct explanation of A.

11 (*a*) Both A and R are true and R is the correct explanation of A.

12 (*c*) In a mixture of $KMnO_4$ and $H_2C_2O_4$, $KMnO_4$ gets decolourised faster at a higher temperature than that at a lower temperature.
Therefore, decolourisation also depends on temperature.
Thus, A is true but R is false.

13 (*b*) A bimolecular reaction takes place when two properly oriented reactant molecules come together in a sufficiently energetic collision which is explained by activated complex theory.
Also, when the temperature is increased by 10°C, the reaction rate tends to be doubled.
Thus, both A and R are true but R is not the correct explanation of A.

14. (*a*) A and R both are true and R is the correct explanation of A.

15. (*d*) A is false but R is true.
Correct A is "only effective collision lead to formation of product."

16. (*c*) A is true but R is false. The correct form of R is :
Only those molecules which have proper orientation during collision (i.e. effective collision) and sufficient kinetic energy lead the chemical change.

17 (*a*) Both A and R are true R is the correct explanation of A.

18 (*c*) Collision theory provides a greater insight into the energetic and mechanistic aspects of reactions as it is based on kinetic theory of gases.
Thus, A is true but R is false.

19 (*b*) According to assumption of collision theory for effective collisions another factor *P* is introduced.
Also, in a collision, molecules must be properly oriented to result into effective collisions.
Thus, both A and R are true but R is not the correct explanation of A.

20 (*a*) Both A and R are true and R is the correct explanation of A.

Statement Type

1 (*b*) Statement I is true but Statement II is false.
The correct form of statement II is for complex reactions, molecularity has no meaning.

2 (*d*) Both Statement I and Statement II are true.

3 (*d*) Both Statement I and Statement II are true.

4 (*b*) Statement I is true but Statement II is false.
The correct form of Statement II is Catalyst decreases the activation energy which in turn increase the rate of reaction.

5 (*a*) Both Statement I and statement II are false. Their correct form is
Only effective collisions result into product formation, i.e. collisions in which molecules collide with sufficient kinetic energy and proper orientation, so as to facilitate breaking of bonds between reacting species and formation of new bonds to form products.

6 (*c*) All the given statements are correct.

7 (*c*) Statements I, II and IV are correct, while III and V are incorrect. Their correct statements are
III. Molecularity is applicable only for elementary reaction.
V. A catalyst catalyses only spontaneous reaction.

8 (*d*) Statements I, II, IV and V are correct, while the statement III is incorrect. It's correct form is as follows
Rate law expression may come out to be similar to that predicted by law of mass action.

9 (*d*) Statements I, III and IV are correct, while the statement II and V are incorrect.

Their correct form are as follows

II. All the molecules in the reacting species do not have the same kinetic energy but the fraction of molecules having particular kinetic energy at a particular temperature remains constant.

V. Half-life of zero order reaction is inversely proportional to the rate constant.

10 (*d*) Among the given statements I and II are correct. While statement III is incorrect. The correct form of III is

$$A^m + B^n \longrightarrow AB_x$$

In this case, overall order of reaction may or may not be $= m + n$

Matching Type

1 (*c*) The correct match is A-3, B-1, C-2.

2 (*b*) The correct match is A-2, B-1, C-4, D-3.

3 (*c*) The correct match is A-3, B-2, C-1.

4 (*a*) The correct match is A-2, B-1, C-3, D-4.

5 (*a*) The correct match is A-2, B-4, C-1, D-3.

A. Molecularity can't be fraction or zero. If molecularity is zero, then reaction is not possible.

B. $e^{-E_a/RT}$ refers to the fraction of molecules with kinetic energy equal to or greater than activation energy.

C. Energetically favourable reactions are sometimes slow due to improper orientation of molecule cause some ineffective collision of molecules.

D. Area under the Maxwell, Boltzmann curve is constant because total probability of molecule taking part in a chemical reaction is equal to one.

Numerical Value

1 (5) For a reaction, $P + Q + R \longrightarrow S$

Here for the given reaction, order of reaction is

$$= \frac{1}{2} + \frac{1}{2} + \frac{1}{4} = \frac{5}{4} = \frac{x}{4}$$

The value of x is 5.

2 (3) Let rate of reaction $R = k[A]^n$ ...(i)

$$27R = k[3A]^n \quad ...(ii)$$

On dividing Eqs. (ii) by (i),

$$27 = 3^n$$

$$3^n = 3^3$$

$$n = 3$$

3 (3) Among the given statements A, B and D are correct.

The corrected statement of C is :

The order of a reaction can be a fractional number.

4 (100) For a first order reaction,

$$k = \frac{2.303}{t} \log\left(\frac{a}{a-x}\right) \quad ...(i)$$

$$k = \frac{0.693}{t_{1/2}} \quad ...(ii)$$

From Eqs. (i) and (ii)

$$\frac{0.693}{t_{1/2}} = \frac{2.303}{t} \log \frac{a}{(a-x)}$$

$$\frac{0.693}{10} = \frac{2.303}{100} \log\left(\frac{100}{100-x}\right)$$

$$x = 99.9\% \approx 100\%$$

5 (52) According to Arrhenius equation

$$\log \frac{k_2}{k_1} = \frac{E_a}{2.303R}\left[\frac{1}{T_1} - \frac{1}{T_2}\right]$$

$$\frac{k_2}{k_1} = 2$$

$$\log(2) = \frac{E_a}{2.303 \times 8.314} \times \left[\frac{1}{295} - \frac{1}{305}\right]$$

$$\Rightarrow E_a = 51.86 \text{ kJ mol}^{-1}$$

$$E_a \approx 52 \text{ kJ mol}^{-1}$$

NCERT Exemplar's

1 (*b*) For the reaction, $A \longrightarrow B$

Concentration of reactants and products which varies exponentially with respect to time are given as follows

(i) Concentration of reactant (here, *A*) decreases exponentially with respect to time.

(ii) Concentration of product (here, *B*) increases exponentially with respect to time.

2 (*c*) The given reaction is,

$$Zn + \text{Dil. HCl} \longrightarrow ZnCl_2 + H_2\uparrow$$

Average rate of reaction upto 40s

$$= \frac{\text{Change in concentration of } H_2}{\text{Change in time}}$$

$$= \frac{V_3 - 0}{40 - 0} = \frac{V_3}{40}$$

3 (*b*) Instantaneous rate of reaction at 40 s is rate of reaction during a small interval of time close to 40 s. Volume change during a small time interval is close to 40 s, i.e. 40 – 30 s, 50 – 40 s, 50 – 30 s , 40 – 20 s .

Instantaneous rate of reaction

$$= \frac{\text{Change in volume}}{\text{Time interval close to 40 s}}$$

(a) r_{inst} (20 s) $= \frac{V_5 - V_2}{50 - 30}$ correct.

(b) r_{inst} (10 s) $= \frac{V_4 V_2}{50 - 30}$ is incorrect,

correct is $\frac{V_5 - V_3}{50 - 40}$.

(c) r_{inst} (10 s) $= \frac{V_3 - V_2}{40 - 30}$ is correct.

(d) r_{inst} (20 s) $= \frac{V_3 - V_1}{40 - 20}$ is correct.

4 (*a*)

5 (*c*) The role of a catalyst is to change the activation energy of reaction. This is done by either increasing or decreasing activation energy of molecule by the use of catalyst.

6 (*d*) The time taken for half the reaction to complete, i.e. the time in which the concentration of a reactant is reduced to half of its original value is called half-life period of the reaction.

But it is impossible to perform 100% of the reaction. Whole of the substance never reacts because in every half-life , 50% of the substance reacts.

Hence, time taken for 100% completion of a reaction is infinite.

7 (c) Rate of reaction expression for the given equation can be written as

$$-\frac{1}{5}\frac{\Delta[Br^-]}{\Delta t} = -\frac{\Delta[BrO_3^-]}{\Delta t} = \frac{-1}{6}\frac{\Delta[H^+]}{\Delta t}$$
$$= \frac{+1}{3}\frac{\Delta[Br_2]}{\Delta t} = +\frac{1}{3}\frac{\Delta[H_2O]}{\Delta t}$$
$$\Rightarrow \quad \frac{1}{5}\frac{\Delta[Br^-]}{\Delta t} = \frac{1}{6}\frac{\Delta[H^+]}{\Delta t}$$
$$\Rightarrow \quad \frac{\Delta[Br^-]}{\Delta t} = \frac{5}{6}\frac{\Delta[H^+]}{\Delta t}$$

8 (b) Rate $= k[A][B]$

Rate of reaction with respect to B is of first order.

$$R_1 = k\,[A]\,[B]$$

When concentration of reactant 'B' is doubled then rate (R_2)

$$R_2 = k\,[A]\,[2B] = 2k\,[A]\,[B] = 2R_1$$

Therefore, as concentration of B is doubled keeping the concentration of A constant, rate of reaction gets doubled.

9 (b) Let x be the order w.r.t A and y be the order w.r.t B. Therefore, rate law for the given reaction can be written as,

$$r = k[A]^x[B]^y$$
$$\frac{\text{Rate of exp. 1}}{\text{Rate of exp. 2}} = \frac{[0.30]^x\,[0.30]^y}{[0.30]^x\,[0.60]^y}$$
$$\Rightarrow \quad \frac{0.10}{0.40} = \frac{[0.30]^y}{[0.60]^y}$$
$$\therefore \quad \frac{1}{4} = \left[\frac{1}{2}\right]^y \Rightarrow \left[\frac{1}{2}\right]^2 = \left[\frac{1}{2}\right]^y$$
$$\Rightarrow \quad y = 2$$
$$\frac{\text{Rate of exp. 1}}{\text{Rate of exp. 3}} = \frac{[0.30]^x\,[0.30]^y}{[0.60]^x\,[0.30]^y}$$
$$\therefore \quad \frac{0.10}{0.20} = \left[\frac{0.30}{0.60}\right]^x\left[\frac{0.30}{0.30}\right]^y$$
$$\text{or} \quad \frac{1}{2} = \left[\frac{1}{2}\right]^x$$
$$\Rightarrow \quad \frac{1}{2} = \left[\frac{1}{2}\right]^x, \text{ i.e. } x = 1$$

Thus, Rate $= k[A]^1\,[B]^2$

10 (c) According the postulates of collision theory there are following necessary conditions for any reaction to be occur.

(i) Molecule should collide with sufficient threshold energy.

(ii) Their orientation must be proper.

(iii) The collision must be effective.

11 (c) Order is not always equal to sum of the stoichiometric coefficients of reactants in the balanced chemical equation. For a reaction, it may or may not be equal to sum of stoichiometric coefficient of reactants.

Rest other statements are correct.

12 (b) The rate constant (k) for the given reaction is as follows

$$A(g) \longrightarrow B(g) + C(g)$$

	$A(g)$	$B(g)$	$C(g)$
Initially	p_i	0	0
At time, t	$p_i - x$	x	x

$$p_t = p_i - x + x + x = p_i + x$$
$$\therefore \quad x = p_t - p_i$$

For first order reaction,

$$k = \frac{2.303}{t}\log\frac{p_i}{p_i - x}$$
$$= \frac{2.303}{t}\log\frac{p_i}{p_i - (p_t - p_i)}$$
$$\therefore \quad k = \frac{2.303}{t}\log\frac{p_i}{2p_i - p_t}$$

13 (a) In the given question, the energy gap between reactants and activated complex is sum of E_1 and E_2.

$\therefore$ Activation energy of forward reaction $= E_1 + E_2$

Product is less stable than reactant as energy of product is greater than the reactant.

14 (a) The chemical reaction in which energy is evolved during the reaction is known as exothermic reaction, i.e. activation energy of product is greater than activation energy of reactants. In the given question, only (I) denotes correct picture of exothermic reaction.

15 (d) According to Arrhenius equation,

$$k = Ae^{-E_a/RT}$$
$$\therefore \quad k \propto e^{-E_a} \text{ and } k \propto e^{-1/T} \text{ or } \propto e^T$$

It indicates that as activation energy decreases, rate constant increases and as temperature increases, rate of reaction increases.

16 (a) According to Arrhenius equation,

$$k = Ae^{-E_a/RT}$$

Taking ln on both side

$$\ln k = \ln Ae^{-E_a/RT}$$
$$\Rightarrow \ln k = \ln A - \frac{E_a}{RT}$$
$$\Rightarrow \ln k = -\frac{E_a}{R} \times \frac{1}{T} + \ln A$$

This equation can be related to equation of straight line, i.e. $y = mx + c$.

From the graph, it is very clear that slope of the plot $= \frac{-E_a}{R}$ and intercept $= \ln A$.

Therefore, the graph given in option (a) correctly represents the graph of $\ln k$ vs $1/T$ as this is the only graph with negative slope.

17 (b) Activation energy of a chemical reaction is related to rate constant of a reaction at two different temperatures, i.e. k_1 and k_2 respectively, $\ln\left(\frac{k_2}{k_1}\right) = \frac{E_a}{R}\left[\frac{1}{T_1} - \frac{1}{T_2}\right]$

18 (c) In the presence of catalyst, the heat absorbed or evolved during the reaction remains unchanged as there is no change in stability of reactant and product.

19 (a) Statement (a) is correct, while the statements (b), (c) and (d) are incorrect. Corrected form of (b), (c) and (d) are as follows

(b) The rate of reaction changes with time.

(d) The rate of reaction increases with increase in concentration of reactants.

(c) The rate of reaction depends on the temperature change.

20 The correct match is A-2, B-1, C-3.

A. Diamond can't be converted into graphite under ordinary condition.

B. Instantaneous rate of reaction completes at very short span of time.

C. Average rate of reaction occurs to a long duration of time.

21 (b) *Characteristics of catalyst*

(a) It catalyses the forward and backward reaction to the same extent as it decreases energy of activation hence, increases the rate of both the reactions.

(b) Since, reaction quotient is the relation between concentration of reactants and products.

Hence, catalyst does not alter Gibbs free energy as it is related to reaction quotient. Thus, Gibbs free energy does not change during the reaction when catalyst is added to it.

$$\Delta G = -RT \ln Q$$

where, Q = reaction quotient

(c) It doesn't alter equilibrium of reaction as equilibrium constant is also concentration dependent term.

(d) It provides an alternate mechanism by reducing activation energy between reactants and products.

Past Exams'

1 (d) According to Arrhenius equation,

$$k = A.e^{-E_a/RT}$$

$$\ln k = \ln A - \frac{E_a}{RT}$$

$$\ln k = \frac{-E_a}{R}\left(\frac{1}{T}\right) + \ln A$$

Compare it with $y = mx + c$

$\ln k \rightarrow y$ and $1/T \rightarrow x$

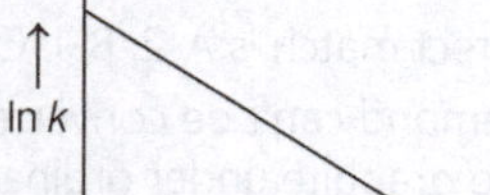

Hence, option (d) match the correct graph.

2 (d) Formula for calculating activation energy is given by

$$\log_{10}\left(\frac{k_2}{k_1}\right) = \frac{E_a}{2.303\,R}\left[\frac{1}{T_1} - \frac{1}{T_2}\right]$$

Here, k_1 is rate constant at T_1

k_2 is rate constant at T_2.

Hence, rate constant at two different temperatures should be known to calculate the activation energy of any chemical reaction.

3 (b) Given, rate $(r) = k[A]^2[B]$ ...(i)

$$r_1 = k[3A]^2[B] \quad ...(ii)$$

Dividing Eqs. (i) by (ii) we get

$$\frac{r}{r_1} = \frac{k\,[A]^2\,[B]}{k\,[3A]^2\,[B]}$$

$$\frac{r}{r_1} = \frac{1}{9} \Rightarrow r_1 = 9r$$

The initial rate would increase by a factor of nine.

4 (c) (A) is false but (R) is true. When a reaction have zero activation energy, the initial energy of the reactant will be equal to the activation energy of the reaction. That means every collision results into a chemical reaction which is not possible.

Mathematically, If $E_a = 0$, then according to Arrhenius equation.

$$k = Ae^{-E_a/RT} = Ae^0 = A$$

5 (b)

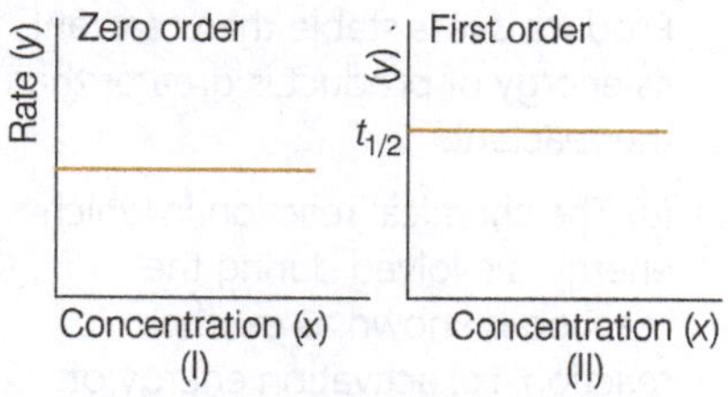

Here, graph I is of zero order if y-axis is representing rate and x represents concentration. For zero order, reaction rate is independent of concentration and remains constant. While II graph represents first order if y is half-life $(t_{1/2})$ and x is concentration.

Here, $t_{1/2}$ is independent of concentration.

Hence, option (b) is correct.

6 (b) The enthalpy of reaction is negative, -4.2 kJ mol^{-1}. The reaction is an exothermic reaction, i.e. the energy of product B, is less than the energy of reactant A. So, the potential energy profile for the reaction is

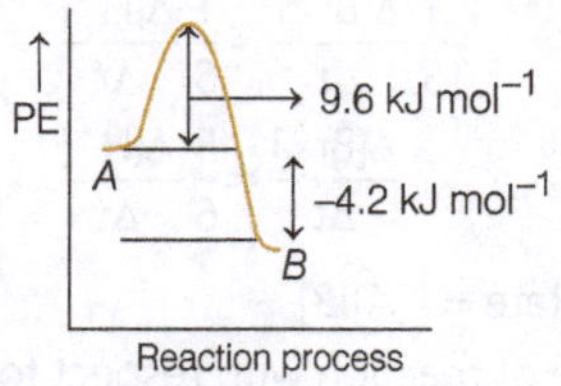

7 (a) As we know,

$$\ln k = \ln A - \frac{E_a}{R}\left(\frac{1}{T}\right)$$

$\frac{-E_a}{R}$ is the slope of Arrhenius plot and $\ln A$ is the intercept.

$$\text{Slope} = -5 \times 10^3 \text{ K}$$

$$R = 8.314 \text{ J K}^{-1} \text{ mol}^{-1}$$

So, $-\frac{E_a}{R} = -5 \times 10^3$ K

$$\Rightarrow E_a = 5 \times 10^3 \times R$$

$$= 5 \times 10^3 \times 8.314$$

$$= 41.57 \times 10^3 \text{ J mol}^{-1}$$

$$= 41.5 \text{ kJ mol}^{-1}$$

8 (a) For a zero order reaction,

$$t = \frac{1}{k}(a_0 - a)$$

$$\Rightarrow t_{50} = \frac{1}{k} \times \frac{a_0}{2}$$

$[\because \text{at } t_{50}, a = a_0/2]$

$$\Rightarrow k = \frac{a_0}{2 \times t_{50}} = \frac{0.02 \text{ M}}{2 \times 100 \text{ s}}$$

$$= 1 \times 10^{-4} \text{Ms}^{-1}$$

$$= 1 \times 10^{-4} \text{mol L}^{-1}\text{ s}^{-1}$$

9 (b)

10 (b) For a first order reaction,

Rate constant $(k) = 4.606 \times 10^{-3}$ s^{-1}

Initial amount $(a_0) = 2$g

Final amount $(a) = 0.2$g

So, time required,

$$t = \frac{2.303}{k} \log \frac{a_0}{a}$$

$$= \frac{2.303}{4.606 \times 10^{-3}} \times \log \frac{2}{0.2} = 500 \text{ s}$$

11 (*b*) Let the initial concentration $(a) = 100$. After time t, final concentration $(a - x) = 100 - 99 = 1$

We know that, $t = \frac{2.303}{k} \log \frac{a}{a-x}$

On substituting the given values in above Eq. we get

$$t = \frac{2.303}{k} \log \frac{100}{1} = \frac{2.303}{k} \log 10^2$$
$$= \frac{2.303}{k} \times 2 \log 10 = \frac{4.606}{k}$$

12. (*b*) For first order reaction,

$$t = \frac{2.303}{k} \log \frac{a}{a-x} \quad ...(i)$$

On substituting the given values in Eq. (i) we get

$$t = \frac{2.303}{10^{-2}} \log \frac{20}{5} = 138.6 \text{ s}$$

13. (*b*) Given,

$E_a = 0, T_1 = 200 \text{ K}, k_1 = 1.6 \times 10^6 \text{s}^{-1}$

$T_2 = 400 \text{ K}, R = 8.314 \text{ JK}^{-1} \text{mol}^{-1}$

According to Arrenius equation,

$$\log \frac{k_2}{k_1} = \frac{E_a}{2.303R}\left[\frac{1}{T_1} - \frac{1}{T_2}\right]$$

On substituting the given values in above equation, we get

$$\log \frac{k_2}{1.6 \times 10^6} = \frac{0}{2.303 \times 8.314}\left[\frac{1}{200} - \frac{1}{400}\right]$$
$$\log\left(\frac{k_2}{1.6 \times 10^6}\right) = 0$$
$$\frac{k_2}{1.6 \times 10^6} = 10^0 = 1$$
$$k_2 = 1.6 \times 10^6 \text{s}^{-1}$$

14. (*b*) For zero order reaction,

$$t_{1/2} = \frac{[R]_0}{2k}$$

Thus, $t_{1/2}$ for zero order reaction is directly proportional to the initial concentration of the reactant.

$$t_{1/2} \propto [R]_0$$

∴ For zero order reaction, when the concentration of reactant is doubled, the half-life $(t_{1/2})$ will also get doubled.

15. (*d*) Given, order of reaction $= 1$

Rate at $10 \text{ s} = 0.04 \text{ mol L}^{-1} \text{ s}^{-1}$

Rate at $20 \text{ s} = 0.03 \text{ mol L}^{-1} \text{ s}^{-1}$

∴ Half-life period $(t_{1/2}) = ?$

As we know,

$$k = \frac{2.303}{t} \log \frac{[A]_0}{[A]_t}$$
$$= \frac{2.303}{10} \log \frac{0.04}{0.03}$$
$$k = 0.028773 \text{ s}^{-1}$$
$$t_{1/2} = \frac{0.6931}{0.028773} = 24.08 \text{ s}$$

16 (*c*) By Arrhenius equation

$$k = Ae^{-E_a/RT}$$

Applying ln on both the side,

$$\ln k = \ln A - \frac{E_a}{RT} \quad ...(i)$$

Compare the above equation w.r.t. straight line equation of $y = mx + c$.

Thus, if a plot of $\ln k$ vs $\frac{1}{T}$ is a straight line, the validity of the equation is confirmed.

Slope of the line $= -\frac{E_a}{R}$

Thus, measuring the slope of the line, the value of E_a can be calculated.

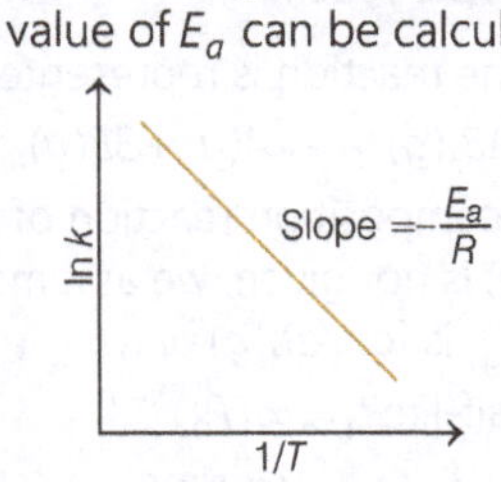

17 (*b*) Half-life period of first order is independent of initial concentration of a reactant.

$$t_{1/2} = \frac{0.693}{k}$$

18 (*b*)

	$A(g)$	$\longrightarrow$	$B(g)$	+	$C(g)$
At $t = 0$	p_i		0		0
At $t = t$	$p_i - x$		x		x

$$p_t = p_i - x + x + x$$
$$p_t = p_i + x$$
$$p_i - x = p_i - p_t + p_i$$
$$= 2p_i - p_t$$

So, $$k = \frac{2.303}{t} \log \frac{p_i}{(2p_i - p_t)}$$

19 (*399*) Rate of reaction $r = k[A]$

So, order of reaction $= 1$

$$t_{1/2} = 120 \text{ min}$$

For 90% completion of reaction

$$k = \frac{2.303}{t} \log\left(\frac{a}{a-x}\right)$$
$$\frac{0.693}{t_{1/2}} = \frac{2.303}{t} \log\left(\frac{100}{10}\right)$$
$$t = 398.7 \approx 399 = 399 \text{ min}$$

Hence, 399 min is required for 90% decomposition.

20 (*3*) Reaction rate, $r = k\,[A]^x\,[B]^y$

for I, $r = 6 \times 10^{-3}, A = 0.1, B = 0.1$

$6 \times 10^{-3} = k\,[0.1]^x\,[0.1]^y$

Similarly for IV,

$$2.4 \times 10^{-2} = [0.4]^x\,[0.1]^y$$

Now divide IV by I

$$4 = 4^x \Rightarrow x = 1$$

For III,

$$2.88 \times 10^{-1} = k\,[0.3]^x\,[0.4]^y$$

For II,

$$7.2 \times 10^{-2} = k\,[0.3]^x\,[0.2]^y$$

III/II, $4 = 2^y \Rightarrow y = 2$

Overall order $= x + y = 1 + 2 = 3$

21 (*b*) We know that,

$$r = k[A]^1[B]^1$$

From the given data

$$0.1 = k[20]^1[0.5]^1 \quad ...(i)$$
$$0.40 = k[x]^1[0.5]^1 \quad ...(ii)$$
$$0.80 = k[40]^1[y]^1 \quad ...(iii)$$

From Eqs. (i) and (ii) we will get $x = 80$ and from Eqs. (i) and (iii) we will get $y = 2$.

22 (*d*) A catalyst provides an alternate pathway or reaction mechanism by reducing the activation energy between reactants and products and hence lowering the potential energy barrier. Hence, the correct reaction profile diagram is in option (d).

23 (*c*)

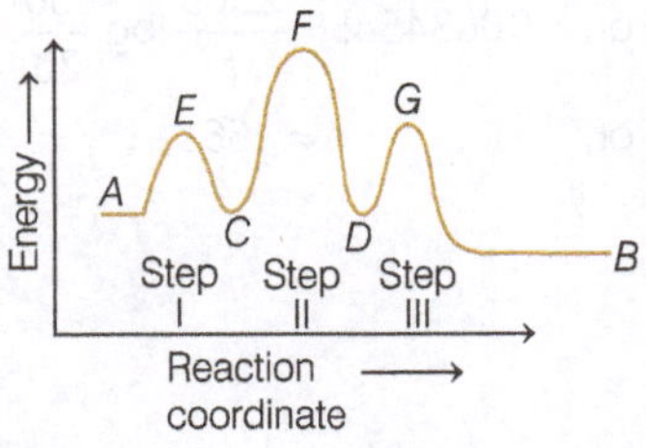

This is a 3-step reaction. Total number of intermediates are 2

(*C* and *D*) and transition states are 3 (*E*, *F* and *G*). The rate determining step is step II.

Since, it has highest activation energy and higher energy correspond to slowest step.

24 (c) Given, $t_{90\%} = x\, t_{50\%}$

$$t_{90\%} = \frac{2.303}{k}\log\left(\frac{100}{100-90}\right)$$

$$t_{50\%} = \frac{2.303}{k}\log(2) \quad ...(ii)$$

Eq. (i) divided by Eq. (ii)

$$\frac{t_{90\%}}{t_{50\%}} = \frac{\frac{2.303}{k}\log 10}{\frac{2.303}{k}\log 2} = \frac{1}{0.3010}$$

So, $\frac{t_{90\%}}{t_{50\%}} = 3.32$

$\Rightarrow \quad x = 3.32$

25 (c) It is a first order reaction because the half-life is independent of initial concentration of reactants.

For first order reaction,

$$k = \frac{2.303}{t}\log\frac{[A]_0}{[A]}$$

For 50% reaction,

$$k = \frac{2.303}{t}\log\frac{100}{(100-50)}$$

or, $k = \frac{2.303}{200}\log 2$

$= 0.0034545$

For 80% reaction,

$$k = \frac{2.303}{t}\log\frac{100}{100-80}$$

or, $0.0034545 = \frac{2.303}{t}\log\frac{100}{20}$

or, $t = 466\,s$

Skill Boosters

1 (b) At 2°C (275 K), the reaction is three times slower than at 27°C (300K). This implies that for souring of milk.

$$\frac{k_{300}}{k_{275}} = 3, T_1 = 275K, T_2 = 300\text{ K}$$

Applying Arrhenius equation,

$$\log\frac{k_{300}}{k_{275}} = \frac{E_a}{2.303R}\left[\frac{T_2 - T_1}{T_2T_1}\right]$$

$$\log 3 = \frac{E_a}{2.303 \times 8.314}\left[\frac{300-275}{275\times 300}\right]$$

$$E_a = 30.146\text{ kJ mol}^{-1}$$

2 (b) Comparing the rate law, the order w.r.t. CH_3Cl = 1 and w. r. t. $H_2O = 2$

$\therefore \quad r = k[CH_3Cl][H_2O]^2$

3 (b) The rate of reaction is proportional to the concentration for the reactant, i.e. ethene so, it is first order reaction.

4 (d) The reaction is represented as

$$AB_3(g) \longrightarrow A(g) + 3B(g)$$

as decomposition reaction of $AB_3(g)$ is not given, we assume that $P_{(\text{mm Hg})}$ is for $AB_3(g)$ only.

So, half-life $t_{1/2} \propto (P_0)^{1-n}$

$$\frac{(t_{1/2})_1}{(t_{1/2})_2} = \frac{(P_0)_1^{1-n}}{(P_0)_2^{1-n}}$$

$$\frac{4}{2} = \left(\frac{50}{100}\right)^{1-n}$$

$$2 = \left(\frac{1}{2}\right)^{1-n}$$

$$n = 1 + 1 = 2$$

5 (d) As we know, Rate = $k(\text{conc.})^n$

Taking log on both sides

log (Rate) = log k + $n$log [conc.]

Slope of graph is the order of reaction greater the slope, greater is the order of reaction.

∴Correct sequence for the order of reaction is

$d > b > a > c$.

6 (d) Only statement (d) is incorrect.

The correct form is

Activation enthalpy to form *C* is 15 kJ mol^{-1} which is more than 5 kJ mol^{-1} that is required to form *D*.

7 (c) Graph (c) represents exothermic reaction with

$E_a = 200 - 150 = 50$ J mol^{-1}

$\Delta H = 50 - 150 = -100$ J mol^{-1}

8 (b) $\log k = \log A - \frac{E_a}{2.303\,RT}$

$\therefore \quad \log A = 14$

$\Rightarrow \quad k = A$, when $T = \infty$

9 (a) $K_f = Ae^{-\frac{E_f}{RT}}, K_b = Ae^{-\frac{E_b}{RT}}$

$$\therefore \quad K = \frac{K_f}{K_b} = \frac{Ae^{-\frac{E_f}{RT}}}{Ae^{-\frac{E_b}{RT}}} = e^{\frac{E_b - E_f}{RT}}$$

or $\log K = \frac{E_b - E_f}{2.303RT}$

$$= \frac{33000\text{ J mol}^{-1}}{2.303 \times 8.314\text{ JK}^{-1}\text{ mol}^{-1} \times 300}$$

$= 5.745$

$\therefore K = \text{antilog}(5.745)$

$= 5.55 \times 10^5$

10 (a) As conversion of *P* + *Q* to *R* is slow which suggests that the process has a very high activation energy, while conversion of *R* to *PQ* is fast. It suggests that, the process has a very low activation energy.

Thus, graph (a) best represents the progress of reaction.

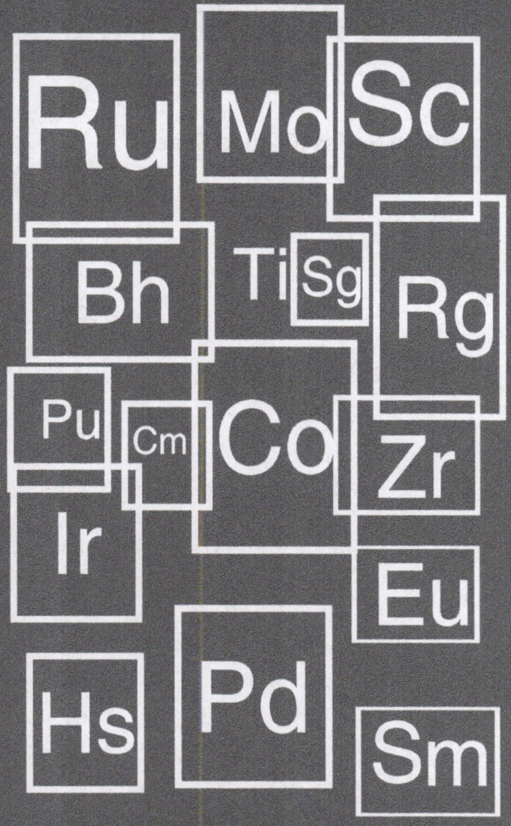

04

Scan for **Chemistry Through Concept Master** Videos

The *d*- and *f*-Block Elements

- The *d*-block of the periodic table contains the elements of the group 3-12. They are formed by progressive filling of *d*-orbitals. They are often called as **transition metals.**
- There are mainly four series of the transition metals 3*d*-series (Sc to Zn), 4*d*-series (Y to Cd), 5*d*-series (La and Hf to Hg) and 6*d*-series (Ac and Rf to Cn).
- The *f*-block element consists of elements in which 4*f* and 5*f*-orbitals are progressively filled. They are often called as **inner-transition elements.**
- The two series of the inner transition metals, i.e. 4*f* (Ce to Lu) and 5*f* (Th to Lr) are called as **lanthanoids** and **actinoids** respectively.

Now, let us study about transition and inner transition elements one by one.

Topicwise No. of Ques asked in 5 Years (NEET)

Topics	No. of Questions				
	2024	2023	2022	2021	2020
Introduction and Properties of *d*-Block Elements	2	1	–	–	2
Important Compounds of Transition Elements	–	1	1	1	1
The Lanthanoids	1	–	1	1	–
The Actinoids	–	–	–	1	–
Some Applications of *d*- and *f*-Block Elements	–	–	–	–	–

Special Type of Ques asked in 5 Years

Types	Years				
	2024	2023	2022	2021	2020
A-R	–	1	–	–	–
Statement Based	–	1	1	1	1
Matching	–	1	–	–	1

Last 5 Years Weightage (NEET)

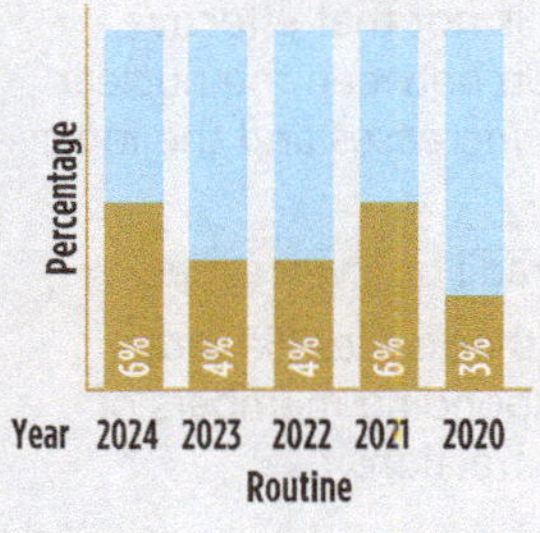

The Transition Elements (*d*-Block)

Position in the Periodic Table

The *d*-block lies in between *s* and *p*-block elements in long form of periodic table.

Electronic Configurations of the *d*-Block Elements

- The general electronic configuration of outer orbitals of these elements is given by $(n-1)d^{1-10}\ ns^{1-2}$, except palladium (Pd). Electronic configuration of Pd is $4d^{10}\ 5s^{0}$.
- The electronic configuration of outer orbitals of zinc (Zn), cadmium (Cd), mercury (Hg) and copernicium (Cn) are represented by $(n-1)d^{10}\ ns^{2}$.
- The orbitals of Zn, Cd, Hg and Cn are completely filled in the ground state as well as in their common oxidation states. So, they are not regarded as transition elements.

Electronic Configuration of Elements of 3*d*, 4*d*, 5*d* and 6*d* Transition Series (Ground State)

First (3*d*) Transition Series (Sc-Zn)

Elements (Symbol)	Sc	Ti	V	Cr	Mn	Fe	Co	Ni	Cu	Zn
Atomic number	21	22	23	24	25	26	27	28	29	30
Electronic configuration	$3d^1 4s^2$	$3d^2 4s^2$	$3d^3 4s^2$	$3d^5 4s^1$	$3d^5 4s^2$	$3d^6 4s^2$	$3d^7 4s^2$	$3d^8 4s^2$	$3d^{10} 4s^1$	$3d^{10} 4s^2$

Second (4*d*) Transition Series (Y-Cd)

Elements (Symbol)	Y	Zr	Nb	Mo	Tc	Ru	Rh	Pd	Ag	Cd
Atomic number	39	40	41	42	43	44	45	46	47	48
Electronic configuration	$4d^1 5s^2$	$4d^2 5s^2$	$4d^4 5s^1$	$4d^5 5s^1$	$4d^6 5s^1$	$4d^7 5s^1$	$4d^8 5s^1$	$4d^{10} 5s^0$	$4d^{10} 5s^1$	$4d^{10} 5s^2$

Third (5*d*) Transition Series (La-Hg)

Elements (Symbol)	La	Hf	Ta	W	Re	Os	Ir	Pt	Au	Hg
Atomic number	57	72	73	74	75	76	77	78	79	80
Electronic configuration	$5d^1 6s^2$	$5d^2 6s^2$	$5d^3 6s^2$	$5d^4 6s^2$	$5d^5 6s^2$	$5d^6 6s^2$	$5d^7 6s^2$	$5d^9 6s^1$	$5d^{10} 6s^1$	$5d^{10} 6s^2$

Fourth (6*d*) Transition Series (Ac-Cn)

Elements (Symbol)	Ac	Rf	Db	Sg	Bh	Hs	Mt	Ds	Rg	Cn
Atomic number	89	104	105	106	107	108	109	110	111	112
Electronic configuration	$6d^1 7s^2$	$6d^2 7s^2$	$6d^3 7s^2$	$6d^4 7s^2$	$6d^5 7s^2$	$6d^6 7s^2$	$6d^7 7s^2$	$6d^8 7s^2$	$6d^{10} 7s^1$	$6d^{10} 7s^2$

General Properties of the Transition Elements (*d*-Block)

Physical Properties

- Nearly, all the transition elements (except Zn, Cd, Hg and Mn) display typical metallic properties such as high tensile strength, ductility, malleability, high thermal and electrical conductivity and metallic lustre.
- The transition metals (except Zn, Cd and Hg) are very hard and have low volatility.

Melting and Boiling Points

- Their melting and boiling points are high due to involvement of greater number of electrons from $(n-1)d$ in addition to the *ns*-electrons in the interatomic metallic bonding.
- In any row, the melting points of these metals rise to a maximum at d^5 except for anomalous values of Mn and Tc and fall regularly as the atomic number increases.

Enthalpies of Atomisation ($\Delta_a H°$ kJ/mol)

- They have high enthalpies of atomisation.
- The metals of the second and third series have greater enthalpies of atomisation than the corresponding elements of the first series.
- The order of enthalpy of atomisation for 3*d*-series is V > Ti > Ni > Co > Fe > Cr > Cu > Sc > Mn > Zn.

Atomic and Ionic Sizes

- In general, ions of the same charge in a given series show progressive decrease in radius with increasing atomic number.
- The shielding effect of a *d*-electron is not that effective, hence the net electrostatic attraction between the nuclear charge and the outermost electron increases and the ionic radius decreases.
- Similar trend is observed in atomic radii of given series.
- It should be noted that, the radii of third series (5*d*) are virtually the same as those of corresponding members of second series due to lanthanoid contraction.

- The filling of 4*f*-orbitals before 5*d*-orbitals results in a regular decrease in atomic radii called **lanthanoid contraction** which essentially compensates for the expected increase in atomic size with increasing atomic number.
- The decrease in metallic radius coupled with increase in atomic mass results in a general increase in the density of these elements.

Ionisation Enthalpies

- There is an increase in ionisation enthalpy along each series of the transition elements from left to right due to an increase in nuclear charge which accompanies the filling of inner *d*-orbitals.
- The first ionisation enthalpy, in general, increases, but the magnitude of the increase in the second and third ionisation enthalpies for the successive elements is much higher along a series.
- Variation in ionisation enthalpy for an electronic configuration d^n depends on attraction of each electron towards nucleus, repulsion between the electrons and the exchange energy.
- Zn, Cd and Hg have highest ionisation energy. It is due to fully-filled configuration.
- The trend of steady increase in second and third ionisation enthalpy breaks for the formation of Mn^{2+} and Fe^{3+} respectively. In both cases, ions have d^5 configuration.
- Cr and Cu show unusually high values of second ionisation enthalpies due to disruption of d^5 and d^{10} configuration of M^+ ion respectively.

Oxidation States

- The transition elements show variety of oxidation states due to very small difference between $(n-1)d$ and *ns*-orbitals.

For Concept Master Video

- The highest oxidation state is equal to total number of *s*- and *d*-electrons.
- Maximum oxidation state increases from Sc to Mn and then decreases to Zn.
- The compounds in +2 and +3 oxidation states are mostly ionic. NEET 2023
- The elements which give the greatest number of oxidation states occur in or near the middle of the series, e.g. Mn show +2 to +7 oxidation state.
- Sc does not exhibit variable oxidation states.
- Low oxidation states are found, when a complex compound has ligands capable of π-acceptor character in addition to the σ-bonding. e.g. In $Ni(CO)_4$ and $Fe(CO)_5$, the oxidation state of nickel and iron is zero.
- The highest oxidation numbers are achieved in TiX_4, VF_5 and CrF_6. Beyond Mn no metal has a trihalide except FeX_3 and CoF_3.
- Mn does not form simple halide in +7 state but MnO_3F is known.
- The ability of fluorine to stabilise the highest oxidation state is due to either higher lattice enthalpy or higher bond enthalpy for higher covalent compounds, e.g. VF_5 and CrF_6.
- All Cu(II) halides are known except the iodide because Cu^{2+} oxidises I^- to I_2.

$$2Cu^{2+}(aq) + 4I^-(aq) \longrightarrow Cu_2I_2(s) + I_2(s)$$

- Cu^{2+} is more stable than Cu^+ due to highly negative hydration energy $\Delta_{hyd}H°$ of Cu^{2+} compounds. NEET 2023
- Many Cu(I) compounds are unstable in aqueous solution and undergo disproportionation.

$$2Cu^+ \longrightarrow Cu^{2+} + Cu$$

- The highest oxidation number in oxides coincide with the group number and is attained in Sc_2O_3 to Mn_2O_7. NEET 2023
- Beyond group 7, no higher oxides of Fe above Fe_2O_3 are known.
- Besides the oxides, oxocations stabilise V^V as VO_2^+, V^{IV} as VO^{2+} and Ti^{4+} as TiO^{2+}. The ability of oxygen to stabilise these high oxidation states exceeds that of fluorine. Thus, the highest Mn fluoride is MnF_4, whereas the highest oxide is Mn_2O_7 and it has Mn—O—Mn bridge in structure.
- The tetrahedral ions VO_4^{3-}, CrO_4^{2-}, MnO_4^{2-} and MnO_4^- ions are also known.

Trends in M^{2+}/M Standard Electrode Potentials

- There is a general trend towards less negative $E°$ values across the series. It is due to general increase in the sum of the I[st] and IInd ionisation enthalpies.
- Cu has positive $E°$ value due to its low hydration enthalpy.
- $E°$ values of Mn, Ni and Zn are more negative than expected from the trend.
- $Mn^{2+}(d^5)$ and $Zn^{2+}(d^{10})$ has more negative value due to stable configuration. While for Ni it is due to highest negative $\Delta_{hyd}H°$.

Trends in M^{3+}/M^{2+} Standard Electrode Potentials

NEET 2024

- There is a varying trend for M^{3+}/M^{2+} standard electrode potential.
- The highest $E°_{M^{3+}/M^{2+}}$ for Zn is due to the removal of an electron from the stable d^{10}-configuration of Zn^{2+}.
- Similarly, low value for Sc reflects the stability of $Sc^{3+}(d^0)$, which has a noble gas configuration.
- The comparatively high value for Mn shows that $Mn^{2+}(d^5)$ is stable, whereas low value of Fe shows the extra stability of $Fe^{3+}(d^5)$.
- The low value for V is related to the stability of V^{2+} (half-filled t_{2g} level).

Chemical Reactivity and $E°$ Values

- The metals of the first series with the exception of copper are relatively more reactive and are oxidised by 1M H^+ ion.
- The $E°$ values for M^{2+}/M indicates the decreasing tendency to form divalent cations across the series.
- The $E°$ values for M^{3+}/M^{2+} indicates that Mn^{3+} and Co^{3+} ions are the strongest oxidising agents in aqueous solutions.
- The ions Ti^{2+}, V^{2+} and Cr^{2+} are strong reducing agents and will liberate hydrogen from a dilute acid.

Magnetic Properties

For Concept Master Video

- Transition metal ions and their compounds that contains unpaired electrons in its $(n-1)d$-orbitals are paramagnetic in nature. While those transition elements that have no unpaired electrons are diamagnetic in nature.
- Magnetic moment is determined by the number of unpaired electrons. NEET 2024
  It is calculated by using the 'spin-only' formula $\mu = \sqrt{n(n+2)}$.
  where, n = number of unpaired electrons. NEET 2020
  μ = magnetic moment in Bohr Magneton (BM)
- Paramagnetism and magnetic moment increases as the number of unpaired electrons increases (from 1 to 5).

Marks Maximizer

Antiferromagnetic substances are expected to possess paramagnetism or ferromagnetism on the basis of unpaired electrons but actually have zero net magnetic moment. **Antiferromagnetism** occurs when the number of parallel magnetic momenta is equal to the number of anti-parallel magnetic momenta. This results in a net zero magnetic momentum.

Magnetic Moments of Some Ionic Species

Ion	Configuration	Number of unpaired electrons	Magnetic moment	
			Calculated	Observed
Sc^{3+}	$3d^0$	0	0	0
Ti^{3+}	$3d^1$	1	1.73	1.75
Ti^{2+}	$3d^2$	2	2.84	2.76
V^{2+}	$3d^3$	3	3.87	3.86
Cr^{2+}	$3d^4$	4	4.90	4.80
Mn^{2+}	$3d^5$	5	5.92	5.96
Fe^{2+}	$3d^6$	4	4.90	5.3–5.5
Co^{2+}	$3d^7$	3	3.87	4.4–5.2
Ni^{2+}	$3d^8$	2	2.84	2.9–3.4
Cu^{2+}	$3d^9$	1	1.73	1.8–2.2
Zn^{2+}	$3d^{10}$	0	0	0

Formation of Coloured Ions

- When an electron is excited from a lower energy d-orbtial to higher energy d-orbital, the energy of excitation corresponds to the frequency of light absorbed.
- The frequency generally lies in the visible region.
- The colour observed corresponds to the complementary colour of the light absorbed.
- The frequency of light depends on nature of ligands and in aqueous solution water molecules acts as ligand.

Formation of Complex Compounds

The transition metal forms a large number of complex compounds. It is due to

- small size of metal ions.
- high ionic charges.
- availability of empty d-orbitals for bond formation.

Catalytic Properties

- Transition metals show catalytic property due to their ability to adopt multiple oxidation states and to form complexes. NEET 2020
- Catalysts at a solid surface involve the formation of bonds between reactant molecules and atoms of the surface of the catalyst.
- Vanadium (V) oxide (in Contact process), finely divided iron (in Haber's process) and nickel (in catalytic hydrogenation) are some of the examples.

Formation of Interstitial Compounds

- These compounds are formed when small atoms like H, C or N are trapped inside the crystal lattices of metals. NEET 2020
- They are usually non-stoichiometric and are neither typically ionic nor covalent. e.g. TiC, Mn_4N, Fe_3H, $VH_{0.56}$ and $TiH_{1.7}$ etc.
- The interstitial compounds have high melting points, are very hard, retain metallic conductivity and are chemically inert.

Alloy Formation

- An alloy is a blend of metals, formed by mixing the components.
- They may be homogeneous solid solutions.
- Due to similar atomic radii, transition metals forms alloys easily.
- Examples of alloys in which transition metals and non-transition metals are the constituents such as brass (copper-zinc) and bronze (copper-tin).

Some Important Compounds of Transition Elements

Oxides and Oxoanions of Metals

- Reaction of transition metal with oxygen at high temperature gives metal oxides.
- In 3*d* series upto Mn all the metals, except Sc form MO oxides, which are ionic.
- Highest oxidation number of metal in its oxides is equal to its group number in periodic table.
- For example oxidation state of Sc, Ti, V, Cr, Mn in Sc_2O_3, TiO_2, V_2O_5, CrO_3, Mn_2O_7 are 3, 4, 5, 6 and 7 respectively.
- After Mn the only higher oxides known is Fe_2O_3.
- As the oxidation number of metal increases covalent character of oxides increases and ionic character decreases, e.g. V_2O_5, CrO_3 have low melting point and Mn_2O_7 is a covalent green oil.
- As the oxidation number increases, acidic character of oxides increases. For example, in the oxides vanadium V_2O_3 is basic, V_2O_4 is less basic and V_2O_5 is amphoteric.
- V_2O_5 reacts with alkalies and acids to give VO_4^{3-} and VO_4^{+} respectively. NEET 2023
- CrO is basic but Cr_2O_3 is amphoteric. NEET 2023
- CrO_3 and Mn_2O_7 are acidic as they give acid in water.

Potassium Dichromate ($K_2Cr_2O_7$)

Preparation

It is generally prepared by fusion of chromite ore ($FeCr_2O_4$) with sodium or potassium carbonate in free access of air. The complete sequence of reaction involved in formation of $K_2Cr_2O_7$ is as follows

$$\underset{\text{Chromite ore}}{4FeCr_2O_4} + \underset{\text{Sodium carbonate}}{8Na_2CO_3} + 7O_2 \longrightarrow \underset{\text{Sodium chromate}}{8Na_2CrO_4} + 2Fe_2O_3 + 8CO_2$$

$$\underset{\text{Sodium chromate}}{2Na_2CrO_4} + 2H^+ \longrightarrow \underset{\text{Sodium dichromate}}{Na_2Cr_2O_7} + 2Na^+ + H_2O$$

$$\underset{\text{Sodium dichromate (orange)}}{Na_2Cr_2O_7} + \underset{\text{Potassium chloride}}{2KCl} \longrightarrow \underset{\text{Potassium dichromate}}{K_2Cr_2O_7} + \underset{\text{Sodium chloride}}{2NaCl}$$

Structure

The structures of chromate ion (CrO_4^{2-}) and dichromate ion ($Cr_2O_7^{2-}$) are as follows

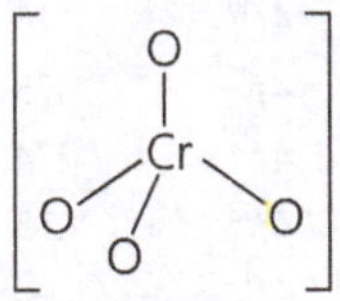

Chromate ion (Tetrahedral)

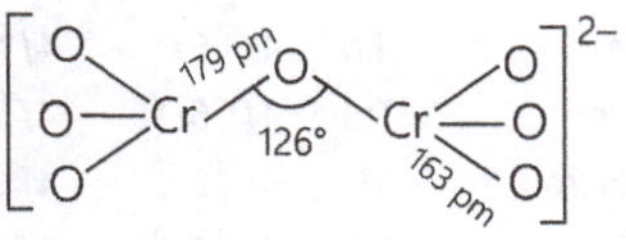

Dichromate ion

Properties

- Depending upon the pH of the solution, the chromates and dichromates are interconvertible in aqueous solution.

$$\underset{\text{(Orange)}}{Cr_2O_7^{2-}} + H_2O \rightleftharpoons \underset{\text{(Yellow)}}{2CrO_4^{2-}} + 2H^+$$

- In **acidic medium** backward reaction is favoured.

$$2CrO_4^{2-} + 2H^+ \longrightarrow \underset{\text{(Orange)}}{Cr_2O_7^{2-}} + H_2O$$

- In **alkaline medium** forward reaction is favoured.

$$Cr_2O_7^{2-} + 2OH^- \longrightarrow 2CrO_4^{2-} + H_2O$$

- The oxidation state of chromium in chromate and dichromate ion is same.
- Sodium and potassium dichromate are strong oxidising agents, the sodium salt has a greater solubility in water and is extensively used as an oxidising agent.
- Potassium dichromate is used as a primary standard in volumetric analysis. Its oxidising action in acidic solution can be represented as follows

$$Cr_2O_7^{2-} + 14H^+ + 6e^- \longrightarrow 2Cr^{3+} + 7H_2O$$

- It oxidises I^- to I_2, H_2S to S, Sn^{2+} to Sn^{4+} and Fe^{2+} salts to Fe^{3+}. The half-cell reactions for these oxidations are as follows

$$6I^- \longrightarrow 3I_2 + 6e^- \qquad 3Sn^{2+} \longrightarrow 3Sn^{4+} + 6e^-$$

$$3H_2S \longrightarrow 6H^+ + 3S + 6e^- \qquad 6Fe^{2+} \longrightarrow 6Fe^{3+} + 6e^-$$

- The complete ionic reaction is obtained by adding the half-cell reaction for potassium dichromate to the half reaction for the reducing agent.

e.g. $Cr_2O_7^{2-} + 14H^+ + 6Fe^{2+} \longrightarrow 2Cr^{3+} + 6Fe^{3+} + 7H_2O$

Marks Maximizer

- **Orange crystals** of dichromate ion are moderately soluble in cold water but readily soluble in hot water.
- In basic medium $K_2Cr_2O_7$ does not undergo redox reactions and it forms **chromate ion**.

Potassium Permanganate ($KMnO_4$)

Preparation

$KMnO_4$ can be prepared from pyrolusite ore (MnO_2) the reaction involved is as follows

$$2MnO_2 + 4KOH + O_2 \longrightarrow 2K_2MnO_4 + 2H_2O$$

$$3MnO_4^{2-} + 4H^+ \longrightarrow 2MnO_4^- + MnO_2 + 2H_2O$$

- Commercially, it can be prepared as follows

$$MnO_2 \xrightarrow{\text{Fused with KOH, oxidised with air or } KNO_3} \underset{\text{Manganate ion}}{MnO_4^{2-}}$$

$$\underset{\text{Manganate}}{MnO_4^{2-}} \xrightarrow{\text{Electrolytic oxidation in alkaline solution}} \underset{\text{Permanganate ion}}{MnO_4^-}$$

- In laboratory, it can be prepared as follows

$$2Mn^{2+} + 5S_2O_8^{2-} + 8H_2O \longrightarrow 2MnO_4^- + 10SO_4^{2-} + 16H^+$$

Structure

The structure of manganate and permanganate ions are as follows

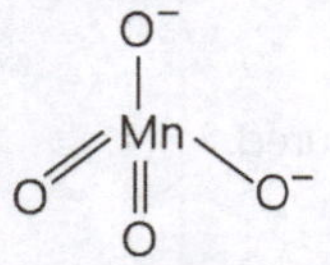

Tetrahedral manganate ion (green)[Paramagnetic] NEET 2019

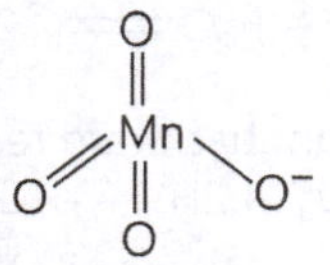

Tetrahedral permanganate ion (purple) [Diamagnetic] NEET 2019

Properties

- $KMnO_4$ has two physical properties of considerable interest. Its intense colour and its diamagnetism along with temperature dependent weak paramagnetism.
- MnO_4^{2-} is paramagnetic in nature and has $d\pi$-$p\pi$ bonding.
- Potassium permanganate forms dark purple (almost black) crystals which when heated it decomposes at 513 K.

$$2KMnO_4 \longrightarrow K_2MnO_4 + MnO_2 + O_2\uparrow$$

- Acidified permanganate solution undergoes the following reactions.

$$5\begin{vmatrix}COO^-\\COO^-\end{vmatrix} \longrightarrow 10CO_2 + 10e^-$$

$$5Fe^{2+} \longrightarrow 5Fe^{3+} + 5e^-$$

$$5NO_2^- + 5H_2O \longrightarrow 5NO_3^- + 10H^+ + 10e^-$$

$$10I^- \longrightarrow 5I_2 + 10e^-$$

- The concentration of hydrogen ion of the solution plays an important part in influencing the reaction as shown below.

$$MnO_4^- + e^- \longrightarrow MnO_4^{2-}$$

$$MnO_4^- + 4H^+ + 3e^- \longrightarrow MnO_2 + 2H_2O$$

$$MnO_4^- + 8H^+ + 5e^- \longrightarrow Mn^{2+} + 4H_2O$$

- Oxidising reactions of $KMnO_4$ are as follows
  - **In acid solutions**

$$10I^- + 2MnO_4^- + 16H^+ \longrightarrow 2Mn^{2+} + 8H_2O + 5I_2$$

$$5Fe^{2+} + MnO_4^- + 8H^+ \longrightarrow Mn^{2+} + 4H_2O + 5Fe^{3+}$$

$$5C_2O_4^{2-} + 2MnO_4^- + 16H^+ \longrightarrow 2Mn^{2+} + 8H_2O + 10CO_2$$

$$5S^{2-} + 2MnO_4^- + 16H^+ \longrightarrow 2Mn^{2+} + 8H_2O + 5S$$

$$5SO_3^{2-} + 2MnO_4^- + 6H^+ \longrightarrow 2Mn^{2+} + 3H_2O + 5SO_4^{2-}$$

$$5NO_2^- + 2MnO_4^- + 6H^+ \longrightarrow 2Mn^{2+} + 5NO_3^- + 3H_2O$$

  - **In neutral or faintly alkaline solutions**

$$2MnO_4^- + H_2O + I^- \longrightarrow 2MnO_2 + 2OH^- + IO_3^-$$

$$8MnO_4^- + 3S_2O_3^{2-} + H_2O \longrightarrow 8MnO_2 + 6SO_4^{2-} + 2OH^-$$

$$2MnO_4^- + 3Mn^{2+} + 2H_2O \longrightarrow 5MnO_2 + 4H^+$$

- Permanganate titrations in presence of hydrochloric acid are unsatisfactory, since hydrochloric acid is oxidised to chlorine.

Uses

- Besides, its use in analytical chemistry, potassium permanganate is used as a favourite oxidant in preparative organic chemistry.
- It is used for the bleaching of wool, cotton, silk and other textile fibres.
- It is used for the decolourisation of oils due to its strong oxidising power.

The Inner Transition Elements (*f*-Block)

- The elements in which the last electron enters into f-orbital are called f-block elements. These f-block elements are also called as inner transition elements.
- The f-block consists of two series each containing 14 elements, i.e. lanthanoids (following lanthanum from Ce to Lu) and actinoids (following actinium from Th to Lr).

Lanthanoids

Position in the Periodic Table

They are placed in a separate panel at the bottom of the periodic table.

Electronic Configurations

These elements have electronic configuration with $6s^2$ common but with variable occupancy of $4f$ level (Given in table below).

Electronic Configurations and Radii of Lanthanum and Lanthanoids

Atomic number	Name	Symbol	Electronic configurations*				Radii/pm	
			Ln	Ln^{2+}	Ln^{3+}	Ln^{4+}	Ln	Ln^{3+}
57	Lanthanum	La	$5d^1 6s^2$	$5d^1$	$4f^0$		187	106
58	Cerium	Ce	$4f^1 5d^1 6s^2$	$4f^2$	$4f^1$	$4f^0$	183	103
59	Praseodymium	Pr	$4f^3 6s^2$	$4f^3$	$4f^2$	$4f^1$	182	101
60	Neodymium	Nd	$4f^4 6s^2$	$4f^4$	$4f^3$	$4f^2$	181	99
61	Promethium	Pm	$4f^5 6s^2$	$4f^5$	$4f^4$		181	98
62	Samarium	Sm	$4f^6 6s^2$	$4f^6$	$4f^5$		180	96
63	Europium	Eu	$4f^7 6s^2$	$4f^7$	$4f^6$		199	95
64	Gadolinium	Gd	$4f^7 5d^1 6s^2$	$4f^7 5d^1$	$4f^7$		180	94
65	Terbium	Tb	$4f^9 6s^2$	$4f^9$	$4f^8$	$4f^7$	178	92
66	Dysprosium	Dy	$4f^{10} 6s^2$	$4f^{10}$	$4f^9$	$4f^8$	177	91
67	Holmium	Ho	$4f^{11} 6s^2$	$4f^{11}$	$4f^{10}$		176	89
68	Erbium	Er	$4f^{12} 6s^2$	$4f^{12}$	$4f^{11}$		175	88
69	Thulium	Tm	$4f^{13} 6s^2$	$4f^{13}$	$4f^{12}$		174	87
70	Ytterbium	Yb	$4f^{14} 6s^2$	$4f^{14}$	$4f^{13}$		173	86
71	Lutetium	Lu	$4f^{14} 5d^1 6s^2$	$4f^{14} 5d^1$	$4f^{14}$	–	–	–

Only electrons outside [Xe] core are indicated.

Note The electronic configuration of all the tripositive ions (most stable oxidation state of lanthanoids) are of form $4f^n$ ($n = 1$ to 14 with increasing atomic number).

Atomic and Ionic Sizes

The overall decrease in atomic and ionic radii from lanthanum to lutetium is a unique feature of the lanthanoids. This gradual and steady decrease across the period is called **lanthanoid contraction.**

Causes of Lanthanoid Contraction

For Concept Master Video

- As the atomic number increases from La(57) to Lu(71), the number of protons increases in the nucleus.
- Electrons are added to $4f$-orbitals which have very poor shielding power. Due to this imperfect shielding occurs.
- As a result, effective nuclear charge increases and radius decreases.
- The decrease in atomic radii is irregular due to irregular electronic configuration. But ionic radii decrease in regular manner.

Consequences of Lanthanoid Contraction

- It causes the atomic radii of the members of 2nd and 3rd transition series to be very similar. e.g. Atomic radii of Za (160 pm) and Hf (159 pm) are similar. NEET 2021
- Lanthanoid contraction accounts for their occurrence together in nature and difficulty faced in their separation.

Oxidation States

- All the lanthanoids and the lanthanum shows +3 oxidation state commonly.
- However, some lanthanoids also show +2 and +4 ions in solution or in solid compound.
- The irregularity is due to extra stability of empty, half-filled or fully-filled f-subshell. e.g. $Ce^{4+}(4f^0)$, $Eu^{2+}(4f^7)$, $Yb^{2+}(4f^{14})$.
- The formation of Ce^{4+} is favoured by its noble gas configuration, but it is a strong oxidant and $E°$ for Ce^{4+}/Ce^{3+} is 1.74 V.

  Thus, Ce^{4+} can oxidise water. However, the reaction rate is very slow and hence Ce(IV) is a good analytical reagent.
- Pr, Nd, Tb and Dy also exhibit +4 state, but only in oxides, MO_2.
- Eu^{2+} is formed by losing the two s-electrons and its f^7 configuration accounts for the formation of this ion.
- Eu^{2+} is a strong reducing agent changing to the common +3 state.
- Yb^{2+} has f^{14} configuration is a reductant.
- Tb^{IV} has half-filled f-orbitals and is an oxidant.
- Samarium exhibits both +2 and +3 oxidation states.

General Characteristic

- **Action of air** All the lanthanoids are silvery white soft metals and tarnish rapidly in moist air.
- **Hardness** It increases with increasing atomic number. Samarium is exceptionally steel hard.
- **Melting point** The range of melting point lies between 1000 to 1200 K, but samarium melts at 1623 K.
- **Conductivity** They have typical metallic structure and are good conductor of heat and electricity.
- **Density** and other properties change smoothly except for Eu and Yb and occasionally for Sm and Tm.
- **Colour** Many trivalent lanthanoid ions are coloured both in the solid state and in aqueous solution.

  La^{3+} and Lu^{3+} ion does not show any colour due to empty $(4f^0)$ or fully-filled $4f^{14}$-orbitals.

Magnetic Properties NEET 2024

The lanthanoids ions except f^0 type (La^{3+} and Ce^{4+}) and f^{14} type ($Yb^{2+}$and Lu^{3+}) are paramagnetic.

Ionisation Enthalpy

- The first ionisation enthalpies of the lanthanoids are around 600 kJ/mol.
- The second ionisation enthalpy is about 1200 kJ/mol.
- The abnormally low value of the third ionisation enthalpy is due to exchange enthalpy consideration which imparts a certain degree of stability to empty (f^0), half-filled (f^7) and completely filled (f^{14}) orbital, e.g. Lanthanum, gadolinium and lutetium.

Standard Electrode Potentials

The $E°$ values for the half-cell reaction is,

$Ln^{3+}(aq) + 3e^- \longrightarrow Ln(s)$ are in the range of -2.2 V to -2.4 V. Except for Eu for which its value is -2.0 V.

Chemical Behaviour

The earlier members of the series are quite reactive similar to calcium but with increasing atomic number, they behave more like aluminium. The chemical reactions of lanthanoids are as follows

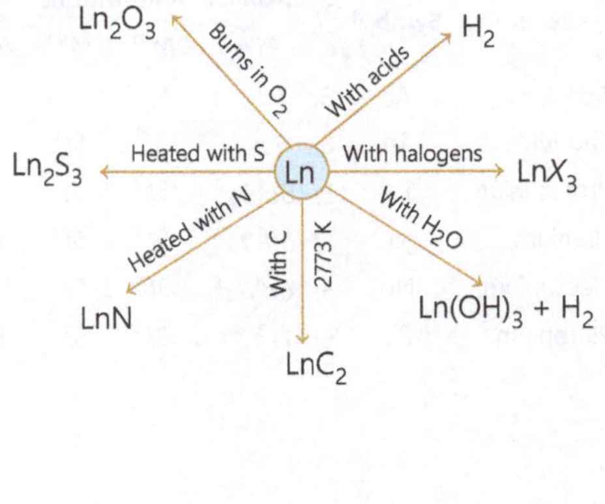

Note When metals are heated with carbon, then carbides like Ln_3C, Ln_2C_3 and LnC_2 are formed.

Uses

- Lanthanoids are used for the production of alloy steels for plates and pipes.
- A well known alloy is **misch-metal** which consists of lanthanoid metal (~ 95%) and iron (~ 5%) and traces of S, C, Ca and Al.
- Misch-metal is used in Mg based alloy to produce bullets, shell and lighter flint.
- Mixed oxides of lanthanoids are employed as catalysts in petroleum cracking.
- Some individual Ln oxides are used as phosphorus in television screens and similar fluorescing surfaces.

Actinoids

- They include the 14-elements from Th to Lr.
- They are radioactive elements and the earlier members have relatively long half-lives.
- The latter members have half-life values ranging from a day to 3 minutes for lawrencium ($Z = 103$).
- The latter members can be prepared in nanogram quantities only.

Electronic Configurations

- All the actinoids are believed to have the electronic configuration of $7s^2$ and variable occupancy of the $5f$ and $6d$-subshells.
- The general electronic configuration of actinoids are $5f^{1-14}6d^{0-1}7s^2$.
- The 14 electrons are added to $5f$-orbitals, except in thorium, but filling of $5f$ continues again after thorium till $5f$-orbitals are complete at lawrencium ($Z = 103$).
- The irregularities in the electronic configuration of actinoids are due to extra stability of f^0, f^7 and f^{14} orbitals.

Electronic Configuration and Radii of Actinium and Actinoids

Atomic number	Name	Symbol	Electronic configurations*			Radii/pm	
			M	M^{3+}	M^{4+}	M^{3+}	M^{4+}
89	Actinium	Ac	$6d^1 7s^2$	$5f^0$		111	
90	Thorium	Th	$6d^2 7s^2$	$5f^1$	$5f^0$		99
91	Protactinium	Pa	$5f^2 6d^1 7s^2$	$5f^2$	$5f^1$		96
92	Uranium	U	$5f^3 6d^1 7s^2$	$5f^3$	$5f^2$	103	93
93	Neptunium	Np	$5f^4 6d^1 7s^2$	$5f^4$	$5f^3$	101	92
94	Plutonium	Pu	$5f^6 7s^2$	$5f^5$	$5f^4$	100	90
95	Americium	Am	$5f^7 7s^2$	$5f^6$	$5f^5$	99	89
96	Curium	Cm	$5f^7 6d^1 7s^2$	$5f^7$	$5f^6$	99	88
97	Berkelium	Bk	$5f^9 7s^2$	$5f^8$	$5f^7$	98	87
98	Californium	Cf	$5f^{10} 7s^2$	$5f^9$	$5f^8$	98	86
99	Einstenium	Es	$5f^{11} 7s^2$	$5f^{10}$	$5f^9$	–	–
100	Fermium	Fm	$5f^{12} 7s^2$	$5f^{11}$	$5f^{10}$	–	–
101	Mendelevium	Md	$5f^{13} 7s^2$	$5f^{12}$	$5f^{11}$	–	–
102	Nobelium	No	$5f^{14} 7s^2$	$5f^{13}$	$5f^{12}$	–	–
103	Lawrencium	Lr	$5f^{14} 6d^1 7s^2$	$5f^{14}$	$5f^{13}$	–	–

Ionic Size

- There is a gradual decrease in the size of atoms or M^{3+} ions across the series. This may be referred to as the **actinoid contraction.**
- The contraction is greater from element to element due to poor shielding by $5f$-electrons. NEET 2021

Oxidation States

- There is a greater range of oxidation states, which is in part attributed to the fact that the $5f$, $6d$ and $7s$ levels are of comparable energies.
- The actinoids show in general +3 oxidation state. The elements in the first half of the series frequently exhibit higher oxidation states.
- The maximum oxidation state increases from +4 in Th to +5, + 6 and +7 respectively in Pa, U and Np but decreases in succeeding elements.

Oxidation States of Actinium and Actinoids

Ac	Th	Pa	U	Np	Pu	Am	Cm	Bk	Cf	Es	Fm	Md	No	Lr
+3		+3	+3	+3	+3	+3	+3	+3	+3	+3	+3	+3	+3	+3
	+4	+4	+4	+4	+4	+4	+4	+4						
		+5	+5	+5	+5	+5								
			+6	+6	+6	+6								
				+7	+7									

Note All the elements are present in positive oxidation state.

General Characteristics

- Actinoids are silvery in appearance. They are highly reactive metals, especially when finely divided. They tarnish rapidly in **air**.
- They are less reactive towards **acids**, due to formation of protective oxide layers.
- The have no action of **alkalies** on them.
- They are **strongly paramagnetic**.
- They have low **ionisation energy**.

Difference between Lanthanoids and Actinoids

Lanthanoids	Actinoids
They show +2 and +4 oxidation states in few cases besides +3.	They show higher oxidation states of +4, +5, +6 and +7 besides +3.
Except promethium, they are non-radioactive.	All actinoids are radioactive.
They do not form oxo-cations.	They form oxo-cations like UO_2^{2+}, PuO_2^{2+}, UO_2^{+}, etc.
The compounds of lanthanoids are less basic.	Actinoids compounds are more basic.
They have less tendency of complex formation.	They have greater tendency of complex formation.

Some Applications of *d*- and *f*-Block Elements

- Iron and steel are the most important construction materials.
- TiO is used in pigment industry.
- MnO_2, Zn, Ni/Cd are used in battery industry.
- Cu/Ni alloy are the 'silver' UK coins.
- V_2O_5 catalyses the oxidation of SO_2 in the manufacture of sulphuric acid.
- $TiCl_4$ with $Al(CH_3)_3$ is used in the manufacture of polyethylene. NEET 2019
- Iron catalyst is used in manufacturing of ammonia in Haber's process.
- Ni catalysts is used in hydrogenation of fats.
- $PdCl_2$ is used as a catalyst in the oxidation of ethyne to ethanal in Wacker process. NEET 2019
- Nickel complexes are useful in polymerisation of alkynes and other organic compound such as benzene. NEET 2019
- Light sensitive property of AgBr are used in photographic industries.

Caution Points

- Volumetric titrations involving $KMnO_4$ are carried out only in the presence of dil. H_2SO_4 but not in the presence of HCl or HNO_3.
- Cu^{2+} is more stable than Cu^{+} except for the cases of large anions, i.e. CuI is more stable than CuI_2.
- A metal chloride on heating with solid $K_2Cr_2O_7$ and conc. H_2SO_4 gives red vapours of chromyl chloride.

PYQ Notes

1. The reaction of aqueous $KMnO_4$ with H_2O_2 in acidic conditions given Mn^{2+} and O_2. **NEET 2014**
2. The number of *d*-electrons in $Fe^{2+}(Z = 26)$ is not equal to *p*-electrons in $Cl(Z = 17)$. **NEET 2015**
3. MnO_4^{2-} exhibits *d*-*d* transition and paramagnetism. **NEET 2018**
4. CrO_5 has a butterfly structure with 2 peroxide linkage. The oxidation state of Cr in CrO_5 is +6. **NEET 2019**

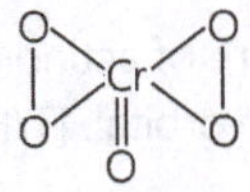

5. The size of Bk^{3+} ion is less than Np^{3+} ion due to actinoid contraction. **JEE Main 2021**

Step by Step

Mastering NCERT

- Concept Builders
- Topical Questions
- Assertion-Reason
- Statement Type
- Matching Type
- Numerical Value
- NCERT Exemplar's
- Past Exams'
- Skill Boosters

Concept Builders

1 In case of chromium, electron jumps from .... to .... to attain half-filled configuration.

2 Electronic configuration of transition element *X* in +3 oxidation state is [Ar] $3d^5$. What is its atomic number?

3 Which element has the least enthalpy of atomisation?

4 Zinc and mercury do not show variable valency like *d*-block elements. [T/F]

5 The radii of members of third transition series are similar to members of second series due to lanthanoid contraction. [T/F]

6 The third ionisation enthalpy of Fe is .... than that of Mn.

7 Name the element that has the highest first ionisation enthalpy in 3*d*-series.

8 Mo (VI) and W (VI) are more stable than Cr (VI). [T/F]

9 In *p*-block and *d*-block elements, the lower oxidation states are favoured by heavier members. [T/F]

10 Name an element from first series of transition elements which exhibit all oxidation states from +2 to +7.

11 Manganese and .... have more negative E°_{value} than expected from general trend.

12 Paramagnetic nature of actinoids is due to unpaired electrons in $(n-2)f$-orbital. [T/F]

13 ...... is approximately proportional to the total number of possible pairs of parallel spins in the degenerate orbitals.

14 The frequency of light absorbed by transition metal ion is determined by the nature of ligand. [T/F]

15 Cuprous ion is colourless but cupric ion is coloured. [T/F]

16 Name the alloy which contain copper and zinc as transition and non-transition metal.

17 Stainless steel contains manganese, ... and nickel alongwith 0.5 to` 1.5% of carbon.

18 Catalysts combine with reactant molecules to form .... and lower their .... energy.

19 .... compounds are formed when small atoms are trapped inside the crystal lattice of metals.

20 Name the ion formed when acidified $K_2Cr_2O_7$ solution is added to Sn^{2+}.

21 Cr(VI) in the form of dichromate in acidic medium is a strong oxidising agent, whereas Mo(VI) in MoO_3 and W(VI) in WO_3 are not. [T/F]

22 In the reaction between potassium permanganate and potassium iodide, permanganate ions acts as oxidising agent. [T/F]

23 Green manganate ion is paramagnetic, while purple permanganate ion is .... in nature.

24 Name the phenomenon which is responsible for almost similar size of Zr and Hf.

25 Name the product formed when lanthanoids heated with nitrogen.

26 Misch-metal is used in .... based alloy to produce bullets, shell and lighter flint.

27 Actinoids can utilise their 5*f*-orbitals along with 6*d*-orbitals in bonding but lanthanoids do not use their 4*f*- orbital for bonding. [T/F]

28 The actinoids are highly reactive metals, especially when finely divided. [T/F]

29 Name an actinoid that can show oxidation states upto+7.

30 Which catalyst can be used in the manufacturing of polyethylene?

Topical Questions

Introduction and Properties of *d*-Block Elements

1 Select the incorrect statement. NCERT Pg 90

(a) Cadmium is the end member of second transition series.
(b) Elements of 4*f* series are called lanthanoids.
(c) Elements of group-12 have complete shell configuration.
(d) The *d*-block occupies the large middle section flanked by *s* and *f*-blocks in the periodic table.

2 Ground state configuration of element having atomic number = 24 is $[Ar]3d^5 4s^1$. This is because, NCERT Pg 90

(a) the energy of 3*d* and 4*s*-orbitals is very low
(b) 3*d* and 4*s*-orbitals are of comparable energy
(c) energy of 3*d*-orbital is lower than the energy of 4*s*-orbital
(d) energy gap between third and fourth shell is very large

3 The configuration which exhibits highest oxidation state in transition metals is NCERT Pg 96

(a) $(n-1)d^8 ns^2$ (b) $(n-1)d^5 ns^1$
(c) $(n-1)d^3 ns^2$ (d) $(n-1)d^5 ns^2$

4 Classify the following elements into 1st, 2nd, 3rd and 4th series, Cr, Hs, Tc, Os, Mo. NCERT Pg 90, 91

(a) 1st series-Cr; 2nd series-Tc, Mo; 3rd series-Os; 4th series-Hs
(b) 1st series-Tc, Mo; 2nd series-Os; 3rd series-Hs; 4th series-Cr
(c) 1st series-Tc, Mo; 2nd series-Hs; 3rd series-Cr; 4th series-Os
(d) 1st series-Os; 2nd series-Tc; 3rd series-Hs, Mo; 4th series-Cr

5 Which one of the following transition metals have different lattice structure? NCERT Pg 92

(a) Rh (b) Pd
(c) V (d) Ag

6 Arrange the following elements in decreasing order of their melting point :

V, Cr, Mn and Fe NCERT Pg 92

(a) Cr > V > Fe > Mn (b) Cr > Fe > V > Mn
(c) V> Cr > Mn > Fe (d) V > Cr > Fe > Mn

7 Which one of the following does not correctly represent the correct order of the property indicated against it? NCERT Pg 92

(a) Ti < V < Cr < Mn, increasing number of oxidation states
(b) $Ti^{3+} < V^{3+} < Cr^{3+} < Mn^{3+}$, increasing magnetic moment
(c) Ti < V < Cr < Mn, increasing melting points
(d) Ti < V < Mn < Cr, increasing 2nd ionisation enthalpy

8 The filling of 4*f* before 5*d*-orbital results in a regular decrease in atomic radii called NCERT Pg 93

(a) lanthanoid contraction (b) shielding effect
(c) actinoid contraction (d) exchange energy

9 Which of the following statements is incorrect? NCERT Pg 93

(a) In general, ions of the same charge in a given series show progressive increase in radius with increasing atomic number.
(b) Shielding effect of a *d*-electron is not that effective hence the ionic radius decreases.
(c) As the nuclear charge increases along the series there is fairly regular decrease in the size of entire 4*f*-orbitals.
(d) There is an increase ionisation enthalpy along each series of the transition elements.

10 The transition element having least enthalpy of atomisation is NCERT Pg 94

(a) Zn (b) V
(c) Fe (d) Cu

11 The correct order of $E^\circ_{M^{2+}/M}$ values with negative sign for the four successive elements, Cr, Mn, Fe and Co is NCERT Pg 94

(a) Fe > Mn > Cr > Co
(b) Cr > Mn > Fe > Co
(c) Mn > Cr > Fe > Co
(d) Cr > Fe > Mn > Co

12 Which of the following arrangements does not represent the incorrect order of the property stated against it? NCERT Pg 94

(a) $Sc^{3+} < Cr^{3+} < Mn^{3+} < Ni^{3+}$; ionisation enthalpy
(b) $Ni^{3+} < Cr^{3+} < Mn^{3+} < Ti^{3+}$; ionic size
(c) $Ti^{2+} < V^{2+} < Mn^{2+} < Ti^{3+}$; standard electrode potential
(d) $V^{2+} < Cr^{2+} = Fe^{2+} < Mn^{2+}$; paramagnetic behaviour

13 The atomic radii decrease less rapidly in case of 3*d*-series because NCERT Pg 95

(a) 4*s*-electrons shield 3*d*-electrons more effectively than the other outershell electrons
(b) 3*d*-electrons shield 4*s*-electrons more effectively than the other outershell electrons
(c) 3*d*-electrons shield 4*s*-electrons less effectively than the other outershell electrons
(d) 4*s*-electrons shield 3*d*-electrons less effectively than the other outershell electrons

14 The correct order of the first ionisation enthalpies is NCERT Pg 94

(a) Mn < Ti < Zn < Ni (b) Ti < Mn < Zn < Ni
(c) Zn < Ni < Mn < Ti (d) Ti < Mn < Ni < Zn

15 Four successive members of the first row transition elements are listed below with their atomic numbers. Which one of them is expected to have the highest third ionisation enthalpy? **NCERT Pg 95**

(a) Vanadium (Z = 23) (b) Chromium (Z = 24)
(c) Iron (Z = 26) (d) Manganese (Z = 25)

16 The transition element which does not exhibit variable oxidation states is **NCERT Pg 97**

(a) titanium (b) scandium
(c) copper (d) zinc

17 In the form of dichromate, Cr(VI) is a strong oxidising agent in acidic medium but Mo(VI) in MoO_3 and W(VI) in WO_3 are not because

I. Cr(VI) is more stable than Mo(VI) and W(VI).
II. Mo(VI) and W(VI) are more stable than Cr(VI).
III. Higher oxidation states of heavier members of group 6 of transition series are more stable.
IV. Lower oxidation states of heavier members of group 6 of transition series are more stable.

The correct statement are **NCERT Pg 97**

(a) I and II (b) II and III
(c) I and III (d) II and IV

18 Four successive members of the first series of the transition metals are listed below. For which one of them, the standard potential ($E^\circ_{M^{2+}/M}$) value has a positive sign? **NCERT Pg 98**

(a) Co (Z = 27) (b) Ni (Z = 28)
(c) Cu (Z = 29) (d) Fe (Z = 26)

19 The value of $E^\circ_{M^{2+}/M}$ for which of the following transition elements are more negative than expected? **NCERT Pg 98**

(a) Cr, Mn and Zn (b) Mn, Ni and Zn
(c) V, Mn and Cu (d) Fe, Co and Ni

20 Consider the following statements. **NCERT Pg 99**

I. Highest oxidation numbers are achieved in TiX_4, VF_5 and CrF_6.
II. +7 state for Mn is not represented in simple halides but MnO_3F is known.
III. Fluorides of transition elements are unstable in the low oxidation states.
IV. The ability of fluorine to stabilise the highest oxidation state is due to either higher lattice energy or higher bond enthalpy.

Choose the correct statements and select the correct option.

(a) I and II (b) II and III
(c) III and IV (d) I, II, III and IV

21 Which of the following statements is incorrect? **NCERT Pg 100**

(a) Stability of Cu^{2+} is more rather than Cu^+ due to much more positive $\Delta_{hyd}H^\circ$ of Cu^{2+} than Cu^+.
(b) Highest oxidation number in the oxides coincides with the group number and is attained in Sc_2O_3 to Mn_2O_7.
(c) Besides the oxides, oxocations stabilise V^V as VO_2^+, V^{IV} as VO_2^+ and Ti^{IV} as TiO^{2+}.
(d) Highest Mn fluoride is MnF_4, whereas the highest oxide is Mn_2O_7.

22 Which of the following statement is incorrect regarding $E^\circ_{M^{3+}/M^{2+}}$? **NCERT Pg 99**

(a) Sc has low value due to stability of Sc^{3+}.
(b) Zn has highest value due to stable d^{10}-configuration of Zn^{2+}.
(c) Comparatively low value of V is due to stability of V^{2+}
(d) Mn^{3+} and Co^{3+} ions are weak oxidising agents in aqueous solution.

23 The incorrect statement about magnetic behaviour of transition elements is **NCERT Pg 101, 102**

(a) paramagnetic substances are attracted by an applied magnetic field
(b) magnetic moment, $\mu = \sqrt{n(n+2)}$ where, n = number of paired electrons
(c) diamagnetic substances are repelled by an applied magnetic field
(d) magnetic moment increases with increase in number of unpaired electrons

24 Which one of the following ions is the most stable in aqueous solution? [Atomic number of Ti = 22, V = 23, Cr = 24 and Mn = 25] **NCERT Pg 101**

(a) Cr^{3+} (b) V^{3+}
(c) Ti^{3+} (d) Mn^{3+}

25 Which of the following are strongest oxidising and reducing agents, respectively in aqueous solution. **NCERT Pg 101**

(a) Mn^{3+}, Co^{3+} and Ti^{2+}, V^{2+}, Cr^{2+}
(b) Ti^{2+}, V^{2+}, Cr^{2+} and Mn^{3+}, Co^{3+}
(c) Mn^{3+}, Cr^{3+} and Ti^{2+}, Co^{2+}, V^{2+}
(d) V^{3+}, Co^{3+} and Mn^{2+}, Ti^{2+}, Cr^{2+}

26 Consider the hydrated ions of Ti^{2+}, V^{2+}, Ti^{3+} and Sc^{3+}. The correct order of their spin-only magnetic moment is **NCERT Pg 102**

(a) $Sc^{3+} < Ti^{3+} < Ti^{2+} < V^{2+}$
(b) $Sc^{3+} < Ti^{3+} < V^{2+} < Ti^{2+}$
(c) $Ti^{3+} < Ti^{2+} < Sc^{3+} < V^{2+}$
(d) $V^{2+} < Ti^{2+} < Ti^{3+} < Sc^{3+}$

27 The highest value of the calculated spin only magnetic moment (in BM) among all the transition metal complexes is **NCERT Pg 102**

(a) 5.92 (b) 3.87 (c) 6.93 (d) 4.90

28 The paramagnetic species among the following are **NCERT Pg 102**

(a) Zn^{2+} (b) Ni^{2+} (c) Cu^{+} (d) Hg^{2+}

29 Magnetic moment of a transition metal ion is found to be 3.87 BM. The number of unpaired electrons present in it is **NCERT Pg 102**

(a) 2 (b) 3 (c) 4 (d) 5

30 Arrange the following in decreasing order of number of unpaired electrons.

I. Cu^{2+} II. Cr^{3+} III. Ni^{2+} IV. Fe^{3+} **NCERT Pg 102**

(a) I > III > II > IV (b) III > I > IV > II
(c) IV > II > III > I (d) II > IV > III > I

31 Which of the following statements about magnetic moment is incorrect? **NCERT Pg 102**

(a) It increases with increasing number of unpaired electrons
(b) It gives indication about the number of unpaired electrons present in the atom, molecule or ion
(c) Its unit is Bohr magneton (BM). A single unpaired electron has 1.73 BM magnetic moment
(d) The magnetic moment of Co^{2+} ion is 2.84 BM.

32 Arrange the following species in the decreasing order of their magnetic moment. **NCERT Pg 102**

I. V^{4+} II. Mn^{4+}
III. Fe^{3+} IV. Ni^{2+}

(a) II > III > I > IV (b) III > IV > II > I
(c) III > II > IV > I (d) I > IV > III > II

33 Which of the following aqueous solutions will be coloured? **NCERT Pg 103**

(a) $Zn(NO_3)_2$ (b) $LiNO_3$
(c) $CoNO_3$ (d) $HgCl_2$

34 When an electron from a lower energy *d*-orbital is excited to a higher energy *d*-orbital

I. The energy of excitation corresponds to the frequency of light absorbed.
II. This frequency generally lies in the visible region.
III. The colour observed corresponds to the complementary colour of the light absorbed.
IV. The frequency of the light absorbed is determined by the nature of the ligand.

Which of the above statements are correct? **NCERT Pg 103**

(a) I, II and IV (b) I, II and III
(c) I, II, III and IV (d) II and IV

35 Out of TiF_6^{2-}, CoF_6^{3-}, Cu_2Cl_2 and $NiCl_4^{2-}$ (at. no. of Ti = 22, Co = 27, Cu = 29 and Ni = 28), the colourless species are

(a) TiF_6^{2-} and CoF_6^{3-} (b) Cu_2Cl_2 and $NiCl_4^{2-}$ **NCERT Pg 103**
(c) TiF_6^{2-} and Cu_2Cl_2 (d) CoF_6^{3-} and $NiCl_4^{2-}$

36 Which of the following factors is not responsible for the formation of the complex compounds by transition elements? **NCERT Pg 104**

(a) Smaller size of metal ions
(b) High ionic charges on metal
(c) Availability of only *d*-orbitals
(d) Availability of both *d*-and *f*-orbitals

37 Which of the following will not form interstitial compounds? **NCERT Pg 104**

(a) Fe (b) Mn (c) Ti (d) Zn

38 What role do interstitial compounds play in improving the properties of alloys? **NCERT Pg 104**

(a) They decrease the hardness of alloys.
(b) They increase the brittleness of alloys.
(c) They increase the toughness and strength of alloys.
(d) They reduce the density of alloys.

39 Interstitial compounds are formed when small atoms are trapped inside the crystal lattice of metals. Which of the following are the characteristic properties of interstitial compounds? **NCERT Pg 104**

I. They have high melting points in comparison to pure metals.
II. They are very hard.
III. They retain metallic conductivity.
IV. They are chemically very inert.

Choose the correct option.

(a) I, II, III and IV (b) II, III and IV
(c) I, III and IV (d) I, II and IV

Some Important Compounds of Transition Elements

40 Consider the following statements. **NCERT Pg 105**

I. As the oxidation number of a metal increases, ionic character decreases.
II. In case of Mn, Mn_2O_7 is a covalent green oil which possess predominantly acidic character and it gives $KMnO_4$.
III. V_2O_5 is amphoteric, it gives VO_4^{3-} as well as VO_2^{+} salts.
IV. CrO is basic, while Cr_2O_3 is amphoteric.

The correct set of statements is/are (choose the appropriate option)

(a) I, II, III and IV (b) Only II
(c) Both II and III (d) Both II and IV

41 Which of the following transition metal show a gradual change in oxides from basic to less basic and to amphoteric? NCERT Pg 105
(a) Copper (b) Titanium
(c) Vanadium (d) Manganese

42 All the transition metals except one form molecular type of oxides which are ionic. That one metal is NCERT Pg 105
(a) vanadium (b) scandium
(c) iron (d) manganese

43 Which of the following compounds is used as the starting material for the preparation of potassium dichromate? NCERT Pg 105
(a) $K_2SO_4 \cdot Cr_2(SO_4)_3 \cdot 24H_2O$ (chrome alum)
(b) $PbCrO_4$ (chromite yellow)
(c) $FeCr_2O_4$ (chromite)
(d) $PbCrO_4 \cdot PbO$ (chrome red)

44 Acidified potassium dichromate does not oxidises NCERT Pg 106
(a) iodides to iodine (b) sulphides to sulphur
(c) tin (IV) to tin (II) (d) iron (II) to (III)

45 Which of the following can react with $K_2Cr_2O_7$? NCERT Pg 106
(a) SO_3^{2-} (b) CO_3^{2-} (c) SO_4^{-2} (d) NO_3^-

46 The structures of chromate and dichromate ions are ...*A*... and ...*B*... . Here, *A* and *B* respectively are NCERT Pg 106

	A	*B*
(a)	tetrahedral	octahedral
(b)	tetrahedral	two tetrahedrals
(c)	octahedral	two tetrahedrals
(d)	two octahedral	octahedral

47 In the following figure, the Cr—O—Cr bond angle is of *X*°. What is the exact value of *X*°? NCERT Pg 106

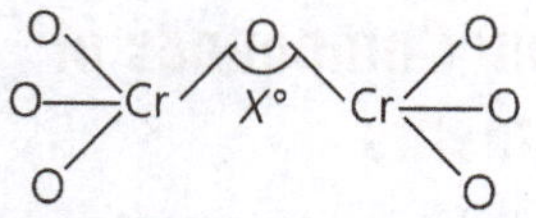

(a) 126° (b) 136° (c) 116° (d) 106°

48 The green manganate and purple permanganate are respectively. NCERT Pg 107
(a) Paramagnetic, diamagnetic
(b) Diamagnetic, paramagnetic
(c) Paramagnetic, paramagnetic
(d) Diamagnetic, diamagnetic

49 K_2MnO_4 is formed, when NCERT Pg 106
(a) Cl_2 is passed into $KMnO_4$
(b) MnO_2 is fused with KOH in air
(c) formaldehyde reacts with potassium permanganate in presence of a strong alkali
(d) Sodium dichromate reacts with potassium chloride

50 The true statement about the structure of dichromate anion is NCERT Pg 106
(a) all the Cr — O bonds are equivalent
(b) only 6 Cr — O bonds are equivalent
(c) only 3 Cr — O bonds are equivalent
(d) no bond is equivalent

51 Consider the following statements. NCERT Pg 106
I. Sodium dichromate is more soluble than potassium dichromate.
II. Crystals of potassium dichromate are of orange colour.
III. The chromates and dichromates are interconvertible in aqueous solution depending upon pH of the solution.
IV. The oxidation state of chromate and dichromate is different.

The correct statements are
(a) I, II, III and IV (b) Both II and IV
(c) I, II and III (d) Both I and II

52 Which of the following statements are correct? NCERT Pg 106
I. In acidic solution chromate ions are converted to dichromate ions.
II. An acidified solution of $K_2Cr_2O_7$ liberates iodine from iodides.
III. Potassium dichromate is used as a secondary standard in volumetric analysis.
IV. The dichromate ion consists of two tetrahedral showing one corner with Cr—O—Cr bond angle of 126°.

Choose the correct option.
(a) I, II and III
(b) II, III and IV
(c) I, II and IV
(d) Both II and III

53 A purple compound of manganese (*X*) decomposes on heating to give manganese compounds *Y*, *Z* and evolve oxygen gas.
Also, compound (*Z*) reacts with potassium hydroxide in the presence of potassium nitrate to give compound *Y*. From the given information, identify *X* to *Z*. NCERT Pg 107

	X	*Y*	*Z*
(a)	$KMnO_4$	K_2MnO_4	MnO_2
(b)	K_2MnO_4	$KMnO_4$	MnO_2
(c)	$KMnO_4$	MnO_2	K_2MnO_4
(d)	MnO_2	$KMnO_4$	K_2MnO_4

54 Which of the following is isostructural with $KMnO_4$?

(a) K_2SO_4 (b) K_2MnO_4 **NCERT Pg 107**

(c) $KClO_4$ (d) $K_2Cr_2O_7$

55 Permanganate ion (MnO_4^-) is dark purple coloured though Mn is in +7 oxidation state with d^0 configuration. This is due to **NCERT Pg 107**

(a) *d-d* transition

(b) charge transfer from metal to ligand

(c) charge transfer from ligand to metal

(d) unpaired electrons

56 The manganate and permanganate ions are tetrahedral, due to **NCERT Pg 107**

(a) there is no π-bonding

(b) the π-bonding involves overlap of *p*-orbitals of oxygen with *p*-orbitals of manganese

(c) the π-bonding involves overlap of *d*-orbitals of oxygen with *d*-orbitals of manganese

(d) the π-bonding involves overlap of *p*-orbitals of oxygen with *d*-orbitals of manganese

57 A purple coloured solution is made alkaline with KOH and is treated with KI forming potassium iodate. This solution is then acidified with H_2SO_4 and again it is treated with KI. But this time instead of potassium iodate, iodine gas is liberated.

This purple coloured solution is of **NCERT Pg 107, 108**

(a) $K_2Cr_2O_4$ (b) K_2MnO_4

(c) $KMnO_4$ (d) $K_2Cr_2O_7$

58 Permanganate at $[H^+] = 1$ should oxidise water in practice but the reaction is extremely slow. Which of the following factor increases the rate of reaction? **NCERT Pg 107**

(a) manganese (II) ions are present

(b) temperature is decreases

(c) temperature is constant

(d) manganese (III) ions are present

59 Consider the following reactions. **NCERT Pg 107**

I. $5\begin{array}{c}COO^- \\ | \\ COO^-\end{array} \longrightarrow 10CO_2 + 10e^-$

II. $5Fe^{2+} \longrightarrow 5Fe^{3+} + 5e^-$

III. $5NO_2^- + 5H_2O \longrightarrow 5NO_3^- + 10H^+ + 10e^-$

Which of the following reagent will oxidise above reactions?

(a) Acidified permanganate

(b) Acidified manganate

(c) Acidified chromate

(d) Acidified dichromate

60 Identify *A*, *B* and *C* in the following reactions and choose the correct option using code given below. **NCERT Pg 108**

I. $2MnO_4^- + H_2O + I^- \longrightarrow 2A + 2OH^- + IO_3^-$

II. $MnO_4^- + 5Fe^{2+} + 8H^+ \longrightarrow B + 5C + 4H_2O$

	A	*B*	*C*
(a)	MnO_2	Mn^{2+}	Fe^{3+}
(b)	Mn^{2+}	MnO_2	Fe^{3+}
(c)	MnO_2	MnO_4^{2-}	$Fe(OH)_3$
(d)	MnO_4^{2-}	Mn^{2+}	Fe_2O_3

61 When $KMnO_4$ reacts with oxalic acid in acidic medium its colour disappears. This is because **NCERT Pg 108**

(a) addition of oxalic acid change pH of solution

(b) $KMnO_4$ oxidises oxalic acid to CO_2 and itself changes to colourless Mn^{2+}

(c) $KMnO_4$ is oxidised to colourless K_2SO_4

(d) acidic solution of $KMnO_4$ is colourless in air

62 Which of the following compounds have no unpaired electrons but shows colour? **NCERT Pg 107, 108**

(a) $KMnO_4$ (b) K_2MnO_4 (c) $MnSO_4$ (d) $MnCl_2$

63 Choose the correct option. **NCERT Pg 108**

I. $MnO_4^- + 2H_2O + 3e^- \longrightarrow A + 4OH^-$

II. $5NO_2^- + 10OH^- \longrightarrow B + 5H_2O + 10e^-$

III. $5SO_3^{2-} + 2MnO_4^- + 6H^+ \longrightarrow 2Mn^{2+} + C + 3H_2O$

	A	*B*	*C*
(a)	MnO_2,	$5NO_3^-$,	$5SO_4^{2-}$
(b)	Mn^{2+},	$3N_2$,	$6SO_2$
(c)	MnO_4^{2-},	$2NO_3^{2-}$,	$3SO_4^-$
(d)	$2MnO_2$,	NO_3^-,	$2S^{2-}$

64 In the following reactions, which reaction do not occur in acid solution? **NCERT Pg 108**

(a) $10I^- + 2MnO_4^- + 16H^+ \longrightarrow 2Mn^{2+} + 8H_2O + 5I_2$

(b) $5Fe^{2+} + MnO_4^- + 8H^+ \longrightarrow Mn^{2+} + 4H_2O + 5Fe^{3+}$

(c) $5NO_2^- + 2MnO_4^- + 6H^+ \longrightarrow 2Mn^{2+} + 5NO_3^- + 3H_2O$

(d) $2MnO_4^- + 3Mn^{2+} + 2H_2O \longrightarrow 5MnO_2 + 4H^+$

The Lanthanoids

65 Lanthanoids are **NCERT Pg 108**

(a) 14 elements in the sixth period (atomic number = 90 to 103) that are filling 4*f*-sublevel

(b) 14 elements is the seventh period (atomic number = 90 to 103) that are filling 5*f*-sublevel

(c) 14 elements in the sixth period (atomic number = 58 to 71) that are filling the 4*f*-sublevel

(d) 14 elements in the seventh period (atomic number = 50 to 71) that are filling the 4*f*-sublevel

66 Consider the following statements. **NCERT Pg 109**

I. Eu^{2+} has f^7 configuration and it is a strong reducing agent.

II. Yb^{2+} has f^{14} configuration and it is a reductant.

III. Tb^{IV} has half-filled f-orbitals and is an oxidant.

The correct statement(s) is/are (choose the appropriate option)

(a) Only I (b) Both II and III
(c) Both I and II (d) I II and III

67 Identify the incorrect statement among the following. **NCERT Pg 109**

(a) There is a decrease in the radii of the atoms or ions as one proceeds from La to Lu.
(b) Lanthanoid contraction is the accumulation of successive shrinkages.
(c) As a result of lanthanoid contraction, the properties of 4d-series of the transition elements have no similarities with the 5d-series of elements.
(d) Lanthanoid contraction is due to effective shielding power of 4f-electrons.

68 Terbium belongs to 4f-series. It's atomic number is 65. Which of the following is the correct electronic configuration of terbium? **NCERT Pg 110**

(a) $[Xe]4f^9 6s^2$ (b) $[Xe]4f^9 5s^1$
(c) $[Xe]4f^7 5d^2 6s^2$ (d) $[Xe]4f^6 5d^3 6s^2$

69 Which of the following pairs has the same size? **NCERT Pg 109**

(a) Zn^{2+}, Hf^{4+} (b) Fe^{2+}, Ni^{2+}
(c) Zr^{4+}, Ti^{4+} (d) Zr^{4+}, Hf^{4+}

70 Although, +3 is the characteristic oxidation state for lanthanoids yet cerium also shows +4 oxidation state because **NCERT Pg 109**

(a) it has a tendency to attain noble gas configuration
(b) it has variable ionisation enthalpy
(c) it resembles Pb^{4+}
(d) it has a tendency to reduce from Ce^{4+} to Ce^{3+}.

71 The correct order of ionic radii of Ce, Pm, Gd and Dy in +3 oxidation state is **NCERT Pg 110**

(a) $Ce^{3+} < Gd^{3+} < Pm^{3+} < Dy^{3+}$
(b) $Ce^{3+} < Pm^{3+} < Gd^{3+} < Dy^{3+}$
(c) $Dy^{3+} < Gd^{3+} < Pm^{3+} < Ce^{3+}$
(d) $Pm^{3+} < Ce^{3+} < Dy^{3+} < Gd^{3+}$

72 Which of the following statements are incorrect regarding characteristics lanthanoids? **NCERT Pg 110, 111**

(a) These are silvery white soft metals.
(b) These tarnish rapidly in air.
(c) The hardness decreases with increasing atomic number.
(d) Their melting points range betwen 1000 to 1200 K but samarium melts at 1623 K.

73 Which of the following statement is incorrect? **NCERT Pg 111**

(a) $La(OH)_3$ is less basic than $Lu(OH)_3$.
(b) In lanthanide series ionic radius of Lu^{3+} ions decreases.
(c) La is actually an element of transition series rather lanthanoid series.
(d) Atomic radii of Zr and Hf are same because of lanthanoid contraction.

74 Choose the appropriate option about the misch-metal. **NCERT Pg 111**

(a) It is an alloy which consists of a lanthanoid metal (~95%) and iron (~5%) an traces of S, C, Ca and Al.
(b) Used in Na based alloy to produce bullets, shell and lighter flint.
(c) It finds application in making aeroplane body.
(d) It is a non-metal.

75 The correct order of basic lanthanoids of lanthanoid hydroxides given below is **NCERT Pg 111**

$$\underset{\text{I}}{La(OH)_3},\ \underset{\text{II}}{Lu(OH)_3},\ \underset{\text{III}}{Ce(OH)_3}$$

(a) I > III > II (b) I < III < II
(c) I > II > III (d) I < II < III

76 Chemical reactions of lanthanoids are as follows **NCERT Pg 111**

I. $Ln \xrightarrow{\text{with halogen}} A$

II. $Ln \xrightarrow{\text{with } H_2O} B$

III. $Ln \xrightarrow[\text{2773 K}]{\text{with C}} C$

A, B and C are

(a) $LnX_3, Ln(OH)_3 + H_2, LnC_2$ (b) LnX_3, Ln_2O_3, Ln_2C
(c) Ln_3X, LnO, Ln_2C (d) Ln_3X_2, Ln_2O_2, LnC

The Actinoids

77 The maximum number of possible oxidation states of actinoides are shown by **NCERT Pg 112**

(a) berkelium (Bk) and californium (Cf)
(b) nobelium (No) and lawrencium (Lr)
(c) actinium (Ac) and thorium (Th)
(d) neptunium (Np) and plutonium (Pu)

78 Which of the following elements shows maximum number of different oxidation states in its compounds? **NCERT Pg 112**

(a) Pa (b) Th
(c) Fm (d) Am

79 The actinoids resemble the lanthanoids in having more compounds in **NCERT Pg 112**

(a) +3 state (b) +4 state
(c) +5 state (d) +2 state

80 Actinoids in general show more oxidation states than the lanthanoids. The main reason for this is **NCERT Pg 113**

(a) higher energy difference between 5*f* and 6*d* orbitals than between 4*f* and 5*d* orbitals
(b) lower energy difference between 5*f* and 6*d* orbitals than between 4*f* and 5*d* orbitals
(c) higher reactivity of actinoids than lanthanoids
(d) lower tendency to form complex.

Some Applications of d- and f-Block Elements

81 Production of iron and steel is based on **NCERT Pg 113**

(a) the reduction of iron oxides
(b) the removal of impurities
(c) addition of carbon and alloying metals such as Cr, Mn and N
(d) All of the above

82 Compound(s) which is not used the battery industries is/are **NCERT Pg 113**

(a) MnO_2 (b) Zn
(c) Ni/Cd (d) TiO

83 Which of the following statement is incorrect regarding transition elements? **NCERT Pg 112, 114**

(a) Iron catalysts are used in Haber process.
(b) Nickel catalysts enable the hydrogenation of fats to proceed.
(c) In Wacker process the oxidation of ethyne to ethanal is catalysed by $PdCl_2$.
(d) Manganese complexes are useful in polymerisation of alkynes.

84 Contemporary 'copper' coins and 'silver' coins in UK respectively are **NCERT Pg 114**

(a) copper-coated steel; Cu/Ni alloy
(b) Cu/Ni alloy; Cu/Ni alloy
(c) Cu/Ni alloy; copper-coated steel
(d) copper-coated steel; copper-coated steel

85 Catalyst used in the oxidation of SO_2 in the manufacture of H_2SO_4 is **NCERT Pg 114**

(a) $CuCl_2$ (b) V_2O_5
(c) MnO_2 (d) None of these

86 Which of the following compounds form the basis, if Ziegler-Natta catalysts is used to manufacture of polythene? **NCERT Pg 114**

(a) $TiCl_4$ (b) $Al(CH_3)_3$
(c) $TiCl_4$ with $Al(CH_3)_3$ (d) V_2O_5

87 The photographic industry relies on the special light-sensitive properties of **NCERT Pg 114**

(a) AgCl (b) AgBr
(c) $PdCl_2$ (d) AgI

Assertion-Reason Questions

Directions (Q. Nos. 1 to 14) *In the following questions a statement of Assertion* (A) *followed by a statement of Reason* (R) *is given. Choose the correct answer out of the following choices.*

(a) Both A and R are true and R is the correct explanation of A.
(b) Both A and R are true but R is not the correct explanation of A.
(c) A is true but R is false.
(d) A is false but R is true.

1 Assertion (A) Cr and Cu are extra stable elements in the 3*d*-series.

Reason (R) Half and completely filled set of orbitals are relatively more stable. **NCERT Pg 90**

2 Assertion (A) Although, Zn is the member of 1st series, yet not a transition element.

Reason (R) The orbitals in Zn are completely filled in ground as well as in excited state. **NCERT Pg 91**

3 Assertion (A) Transition elements exhibit higher enthalpies of atomisation.

Reason (R) There are large number of unpaired electrons in the atoms of transition elements. They have stronger interatomic interactions. **NCERT Pg 92**

4 Assertion (A) The three series of the transition metals are 3*d*-series (Sc to Zn), 4*d* series (Y to Cd) and 5*d*-series.

Reason (R) The two series of the inner-transition metals (4*f* and 5*f*) are known as actinoids and lanthanoids respectively. **NCERT Pg 93**

5 Assertion (A) The second and third rows of transition elements resemble each other much more than they resemble the first row.

Reason (R) Due to lanthanoid contraction, the atomic radii of the second and the third row transition elements is similar. **NCERT Pg 93**

6 **Assertion** (A) First ionisation enthalpy of Cr is lower than that of Zn.

Reason (R) Chromium ion (Cr^+) has extra stability due to d^5 configuration. NCERT Pg 94

7 **Assertion** (A) Oxidising power increases in the order:

$$VO_2^+ < Cr_2O_7^{2-} < MnO_4^-$$

Reason (R) Oxidising power increases due to the increasing stability of lower species to which they are easily reduced. NCERT Pg 96

8 **Assertion** (A) Cu cannot liberate hydrogen from acids.

Reason (R) Cu has positive electrode potential. NCERT Pg 98

9 **Assertion** (A) Permanganate titrations in the presence of HCl are unsatisfactory.

Reason (R) HCl is oxidised to chlorine. NCERT Pg 108

10 **Assertion** (A) Separation of Zr and Hf is difficult.

Reason (R) Zr and Hf lie in the same group of the periodic table. NCERT Pg 109

11 **Assertion** (A) Many trivalent lanthanoid ions are coloured both in solid state and in aqueous solution.

Reason (R) Colour of these ions is due to the presence of unpaired electrons in f-orbitals. NCERT Pg 110

12 **Assertion** (A) Actinoid contraction is, greater than lanthanoids.

Reason (R) There is poor shielding by $5f$-electrons. NCERT Pg 112

13 **Assertion** (A) Actinoid metals display a variety of structures.

Reason (R) Structural variability of actinoids has no relationship with their metallic radii. NCERT Pg 112

14 **Assertion** (A) Actinoids form relatively less stable complexes as compared to lanthanoids.

Reason (R) Actinoids can utilise their $5f$-orbitals along with $6d$-orbitals in bonding but lanthanoids do not use their $4f$-orbitals for bonding. NCERT Pg 112, 113

Statement Type Questions

Direction (Q. Nos. 1-7) *In the following questions, two statements (I & II) are given. In the light of the given statements, choose the correct option given below.*

(a) Both Statement I and Statement II are false.
(b) Statement I is true but Statement II is false.
(c) Statement I is false but Statement II is true.
(d) Both statement I and Statement II are true.

1 **Statement I** For titanium ($Z = 22$) to copper ($Z = 29$) there's a significant decrease in density can be seen.

Statement II The increase in metallic radius coupled with increase in atomic mass occurs across the period. NCERT Pg 93

2 **Statement I** The $E°$ value of Ce^{4+}/Ce^{3+} is 1.74 V.

Statement II Ce is more stable in Ce^{4+} state than Ce^{3+} state. NCERT Pg 99

3 **Statement I** For Mn, Ni, Zn and Cu the value of $E°$ are more negative than expected from the trend.

Statement II All Cu(II) halides are known except the fluoride. NCERT Pg 98, 100

4 **Statement I** Cuprous ion is colourless whereas cupric ion is blue in the aqueous solution.

Statement II Cuprous ion has unpaired electrons while cupric ion does not. NCERT Pg 103

5 **Statement I** The transition metals and their compounds are known for their catalytic activity.

Statement II Transition metals have ability to adopt multiple oxidation states. NCERT Pg 104

6 **Statement I** Manganous salt is oxidised to MnO_2 in the presence of copper sulphate.

Statement II Acidified permanganate solution oxidises nitrites to nitrates. NCERT Pg 107, 108

7 **Statement I** The carbides Ln_3C, Ln_2C_3 and LnC_2 liberate CO_2 form dilute acids and burn in halogens to form halides. NCERT Pg 110, 111

Statement II The given carbides are formed when the metals are heated with carbon.

8 Select the incorrect statements from the following. NCERT Pg 93, 100, 109

I. Fe^{3+} compounds are more stable than Fe^{2+} because at stable half-filled d-orbitals.
II. The salts at Cu(I) are unstable because Cu(I) easily disproportionate to Cu(0) and Cu(II).
III. Ce^{4+} can act as an oxidising agent in nature.
IV. The correct order of ionic radii of Ce, La, Pm and Yb in +3 oxidation state is $La^{3+} < Ce^{3+} < Pm^{3+} < Yb^{3+}$.
V. 10 mL of 1M $KMnO_4$ solution oxidises 10 ml of 5M $FeSO_4$ solution.

Choose the correct answer from the options given below.

(a) I, II and IV (b) III and IV
(c) II, III and V (d) II and IV

9 Which of the following statements are correct? **NCERT Pg 95, 97**

I. Mo(VI) and W(VI) are more stable than Cr(VI).
II. The factors responsible for it are nuclear charge repulsion between the electrons and the exchange energy.
III. Ionisation enthalpy of Mn^{2+} is lower than that of Fe^{2+}.

Choose the correct answer from the options given below.

(a) I and II (b) II and III
(c) I and III (d) I, II and III

10 Select the incorrect statements from the following. **NCERT Pg 99, 100**

I. Beyond Mn, only Fe and Co form trihalides with fluorine.
II. MnO_3F is the compound in which oxidation state of Mn is +7.
III. The oxidation state of Cr is highest in $CrCl_4$.
IV. Fluorine stabilises the highest oxidation state due to its higher lattice energy.

Choose the correct answer from the options given below.

(a) III only (b) I and III
(c) II and IV (d) III and IV

11 Select the incorrect statements from the following. **NCERT Pg 99, 104**

I. The transition metal ions can change their oxidation states they become more effective as catalysts.
II. Vanadium (V) oxide, finely divided iron and nickel are some examples of transition metals as catalyst.
III. Iron catalyses the reaction between iodide and persulphate ions.
IV. Alloys are readily formed by transition metals because of different radii.

Choose the correct answer from the options given below.

(a) I and IV (b) III only
(c) I, II and III (d) IV only

12 Select the correct statements from the following. **NCERT Pg 96, 106, 107**

I. Exchange energy is approximately proportional to the total number of possible pairs of parallel spins in the degenerate orbitals.
II. 5*f* orbitals are not as buried as 4*f* orbitals and hence 5*f* electrons can't participate in bonding to a far greater extent.
III. Mn(VII) Compound is used in the decolourisation of oils.
IV. Mn_4N gives Mn^{2+} ions when reacting in acidic medium.
V. Potassium permanganate is used as an oxidising agent for the preparation of dimethyl amino azobenzene.

Choose the correct answer from the options given below.

(a) I and III
(b) II, III and V
(c) IV and V
(d) II and IV

13 Select the incorrect statements.

I. Lanthanoids have electronic configuration with $6s^2$ common but with variable occupancy of 4*f* level
II. Overall decrease in atomic and ionic radii from lanthanum to lutetium is called lanthanoid contraction
III. In lanthanoids, La (II) and Ln (III) compounds are predominant
IV. Eu^{2+} is a strong reducing agent, Yb^{2+} and Tb^{2+} are reductant **NCERT Pg 106, 109, 110**

Choose the correct answer from the options given below.

(a) I and IV (b) III only
(c) I, II and III (d) IV only

14 Select the correct statements from the following. **NCERT Pg 106, 111, 112, 114**

I. $PtCl_2$ catalysis the oxidation at ethyne to ethanal in the wacker process.
II. *M* is the element at actinoid series, the highest degree at complex formation is M^{4+}.
III. Misch-metal is composed at 95% of an actinoid metal. 5% of iron and traces at S, C, Ca and Al.
IV. Actinoids shows more oxidation states than the lanthanoids because at higher energy difference between 5*f* and 6*d* orbitals than between 4*f* and 5*d* orbitals.
V. In the dichromate ion all Cr—O bonds are not equal.

Choose the correct answer from the options given below.

(a) I and V (b) II and V
(c) I, IV and V (c) II, III and V

Matching Type Questions

1 Match the properties given in Column I with the metals given in Column II.

Column I (Property)	Column II (Metal)
A. An element which can show +8 oxidation state.	1. Mn
B. 3*d*-block element that can show upto +7 oxidation state.	2. Cr
C. 3*d*-block element with highest melting point.	3. Os

Codes NCERT Pg 90, 91

	A	B	C		A	B	C
(a)	1	2	3	(b)	3	2	1
(c)	3	1	2	(d)	2	3	1

2 Match the properties given in Column I with the metals given in Column II and choose the correct option from the codes given below.

Column I (Property)	Column II (Metal)
A. Element with highest second ionisation enthalpy	1. Co
B. Element with highest third ionisation enthalpy	2. Cr
C. *M* in $M(CO)_6$ is	3. Cu
D. Element with highest heat of atomisation	4. Zn

NCERT Pg 93, 95

Codes

	A	B	C	D		A	B	C	D
(a)	1	2	3	4	(b)	3	4	2	1
(c)	4	3	2	1	(d)	2	1	4	3

3 Match the symbols of actinoid with Column I with correct electronic configuration given in Column II and choose the correct option from the codes given below.

Column I (Actinoid)	Column II [Electronic configuration (*M*)]
A. Pa	1. $5f^{10}6d^1 7s^2$
B. Np	2. $5f^{11}7s^2$
C. Am	3. $5f^2 6d^1 7s^2$
D. Es	4. $5f^7 7s^2$

Codes NCERT Pg 111

	A	B	C	D		A	B	C	D
(a)	2	1	4	3	(b)	4	3	2	1
(c)	3	1	4	2	(d)	3	4	2	1

4 Match the following columns.

Column I (Compounds)	Column II (Uses)
A. V_2O_5	1. Oxidative fusion at MnO_2 followed by electrolytic oxidation.
B. Potassium permanganate	2. Chemical inertness
C. Interstitial compounds	3. Volumetric analysis
D. $K_2Cr_2O_7$	4. Contact process

Codes NCERT Pg 104, 106, 105,

	A	B	C	D		A	B	C	D
(a)	4	2	3	1	(b)	4	1	2	3
(c)	3	4	1	2	(d)	1	3	4	2

5 Match the property given in Column I with the element given in Column II.

Column I (Property)	Column II (Element)
A. Lanthanoid which shows + 4 oxidation state.	1. Pm
B. Lanthanoid which can show stable +2 oxidation state.	2. Ce
C. Radioactive lanthanoid	3. Lu
D. Lanthanoid which has $4f^7$ electronic configuration in +3 oxidation state.	4. Eu
E. Lanthanoid which has $4f^{14}$ electronic configuration in +3 oxidation state.	5. Gd

Codes NCERT Pg 110, 111

	A	B	C	D	E		A	B	C	D	E
(a)	2	4	1	5	3	(b)	1	2	5	3	4
(c)	2	3	4	5	1	(d)	3	4	2	1	5

6 Match the compounds/elements given in Column I with uses given in Column II.

Column I (Compound/element)	Column II (Use)
A. Lanthanoid oxide	1. Production of iron alloy
B. Lanthanoid	2. Television screen
C. Misch-metal	3. Petroleum cracking
D. Magnesium based alloy is constituent of	4. Lanthanoid metal + iron
E. Mixed oxides of lanthanoids are employed	5. Bullets

Codes NCERT Pg 113, 114

	A	B	C	D	E		A	B	C	D	E
(a)	2	1	5	4	3	(b)	5	4	3	2	1
(c)	2	1	4	5	3	(d)	1	2	3	4	5

Numerical Value Questions

1 The oxidation states of transition metal atoms in $K_2Cr_2O_7$, $KMnO_4$ and K_2FeO_4, respectively, are *x*, *y* and *z*. The sum of *x*, *y* and *z* is .... NCERT Pg 96, 97

2 The spin-only magnetic moment value of M^{3+} ion (in gaseous state) from the pairs Cr^{3+}/Cr^{2+}, Mn^{3+}/Mn^{2+}, Fe^{3+}/Fe^{2+} and Co^{3+}/Co^{2+} that has negative standard electrode potential, is .... BM. (Nearest integer) NCERT Pg 94

3 The spin-only magnetic moment value of the most basic oxide of vanadium among V_2O_3, V_2O_4 and V_2O_5 is .... BM. (Nearest integer) NCERT Pg 102

4 The disproportionation of MnO_4^{2-} in acidic medium resulted in the formation of two manganese compounds *A* and *B*. If the oxidation state of Mn in *B* is smaller than that of *A*, then the spin-only magnetic moment (μ) value of *B* in BM is .... (Nearest integer) NCERT Pg 106

5 The number of 4*f* electrons in the ground state electronic configuration of Gd^{2+} is .... [Atomic number of Gd is 64]. NCERT Pg 109

NCERT Exemplar's Questions

1 The electronic configuration of Cu(II) is $3d^9$, whereas that of Cu(I) is $3d^{10}$. Which of the following is correct?
(a) Cu(II) is more stable than Cu(I)
(b) Cu(II) is less stable than Cu(I)
(c) Cu(I) and Cu(II) are equally stable
(d) Stability of Cu(I) and Cu(II) depends on nature of copper salts

2 Generally, transition elements form coloured salts due to the presence of unpaired electrons. Which of the following compounds will be coloured in solid state?
(a) Ag_2SO_4 (b) CuF_2 (c) ZnF_2 (d) Cu_2Cl_2

3 The magnetic moment is associated with its spin angular momentum and orbital angular momentum. Spin only magnetic moment value of Cr^{3+} ion is
(a) 2.87 BM (b) 3.87 BM
(c) 3.47 BM (d) 3.57 BM

4 Match the catalysts given in Column I with the processes given in Column II.

Column I (Catalyst)	Column II (Process)
A. Ni in the presence of hydrogen	1. Ziegler-Natta catalyst
B. Cu_2Cl_2	2. Contact process
C. V_2O_5	3. Vegetable oil to ghee
D. Finely divided iron	4. Sandmeyer reaction
E. $TiCl_4 + Al(CH_3)_3$	5. Haber's process
	6. Decomposition of $KClO_3$

5 Highest oxidation state of manganese in fluoride is +4 (MnF_4) but highest oxidation state in oxides is +7(Mn_2O_7) because
(a) fluorine is more electronegative than oxygen
(b) fluorine does not possess *d*-orbitals
(c) fluorine stabilises lower oxidation state
(d) in covalent compounds, fluorine can form single bond only while oxygen forms double bond

6 Which of the following statements is not correct?
(a) Copper liberates hydrogen from acids.
(b) In its higher oxidation states, manganese forms stable compounds with oxygen and fluorine.
(c) Mn^{3+} and Co^{3+} are oxidising agents in aqueous solution.
(d) Ti^{2+} and Cr^{2+} are reducing agents in aqueous solution.

7 Which of the following are amphoteric oxide?
Mn_2O_7, CrO_3, Cr_2O_3, CrO, V_2O_5 and V_2O_4
(a) V_2O_5, Cr_2O_3 (b) Mn_2O_7, CrO_3
(c) CrO, V_2O_5 (d) V_2O_5, V_2O_4

8 The magnetic nature of elements depends on the presence of unpaired electrons. Identify the configuration of transition element which shows highest magnetic moment.
(a) $3d^7$ (b) $3d^5$ (c) $3d^8$ (d) $3d^2$

9 Interstitial compounds are formed when small atoms are trapped inside the crystal lattice of metals. Which of the following is not the characteristic property of interstitial compounds?
(a) They have high melting points in comparison to pure metals.
(b) They are very hard.
(c) They retain metallic conductivity.
(d) They are chemically very reactive

10 On addition of small amount of $KMnO_4$ to conc. H_2SO_4, a green oily compound is obtained which is highly explosive in nature. Identify the compound from the following.

(a) Mn_2O_7 (b) MnO_2 (c) $MnSO_4$ (d) Mn_2O_3

11 Match the solutions given in Column I and the colours given in Column II.

Column I (Aqueous solution of salt)	Column II (Colour)
A. $FeSO_4 \cdot 7H_2O$	1. Green
B. $NiCl_2 \cdot 4H_2O$	2. Light pink
C. $MnCl_2 \cdot 4H_2O$	3. Blue
D. $CoCl_2 \cdot 6H_2O$	4. Pale green
E. Cu_2Cl_2	5. Pink
	6. Colourless

12 When $KMnO_4$ solution is added to oxalic acid solution, the decolourisation is slow in the beginning but becomes instantaneous after sometime because

(a) CO_2 is formed as the product
(b) reaction is exothermic
(c) MnO_4^- catalyses the reaction
(d) Mn^{2+} acts as auto-catalyst

13 $KMnO_4$ acts as an oxidising agent in acidic medium. The number of moles of $KMnO_4$ that will be needed to react with one mole of sulphide ions in acidic solution is

(a) $\frac{2}{5}$ (b) $\frac{3}{5}$ (c) $\frac{4}{5}$ (d) $\frac{1}{5}$

14 $KMnO_4$ acts as an oxidising agent in alkaline medium. When alk. $KMnO_4$ is treated with KI, iodide ion is oxidised to

(a) I_2 (b) IO^-
(c) IO_3^- (d) IO_4^-

15 Why is HCl not used to make the medium acidic in oxidation reactions of $KMnO_4$ in acidic medium?

(a) Both HCl and $KMnO_4$ act as oxidising agents.
(b) $KMnO_4$ oxidises HCl into Cl_2 which is also an oxidising agent.
(c) $KMnO_4$ is a weaker oxidising agent than HCl.
(d) $KMnO_4$ acts as a reducing agent in the presence of HCl.

16 When acidified $K_2Cr_2O_7$ solution is added to Sn^{2+} salt then Sn^{2+} changes to

(a) Sn (b) Sn^{3+}
(c) Sn^{4+} (d) Sn^{+}

17 Electronic configuration of a transition element *X* in +3 oxidation state is $[Ar]3d^5$. What is its atomic number?

(a) 25 (b) 26
(c) 27 (d) 24

18 Although, zirconium belongs to 4*d*-transition series and hafnium to 5*d*-transition series even then they show similar physical and chemical properties because

(a) both belong to *d*-block
(b) both have same number of electrons
(c) both have similar atomic radius
(d) both belong to the same group of the periodic table

Past Exams' Questions

NEET Archive

1 'Spin only' magnetic moment is same for which of the following ions?

A. Ti^{3+} B. Cr^{2+}
C. Mn^{2+} D. Fe^{2+} E. Sc^{3+}

Choose the most appropriate answer from the options given below. **NCERT Pg 102, NEET 2024**

(a) B and D only (b) A and E only
(c) B and C only (d) A and D only

2 The $E°$ value for the Mn^{3+}/Mn^{2+} couple is more positive than that of Cr^{3+}/Cr^{2+} or Fe^{3+}/Fe^{2+} due to change of **NCERT Pg 99, NEET 2024**

(a) d^5 to d^4 configuration
(b) d^5 to d^2 configuration
(c) d^4 to d^5 configuration
(d) d^3 to d^5 configuration

3 The pair of lanthanoid ions which are diamagnetic is **NCERT Pg 102, NEET 2024**

(a) Ce^{4+} and Yb^{2+} (b) Ce^{3+} and Eu^{2+}
(c) Gd^{3+} and Eu^{3+} (d) Pm^{3+} and Sm^{3+}

4 Which of the following statements are incorrect?

I. All the transition metals except scandium form *MO* oxides which are ionic.
II. The highest oxidation number corresponding to the group number in transition metal oxides is attained in Sc_2O_3 to Mn_2O_7.
III. Basic character increases from V_2O_3 to V_2O_4 to V_2O_5.
IV. V_2O_4 dissolves in acids to give VO_4^{3-} salts.
V. CrO is basic but Cr_2O_3 is amphoteric.

Choose the correct answer from the options given below: NCERT Pg 105, NEET 2023

(a) II and IV (b) III and IV
(c) II and III (d) I and V

5 The stability of Cu^{2+} is more than Cu^{+} salts in aqueous solution due to NCERT Pg 100, NEET 2023

(a) enthalpy of atomisation
(b) hydration energy
(c) second ionisation enthalpy
(d) first ionisation enthalpy

6 In the neutral or faintly alkaline medium, $KMnO_4$ oxidises iodide into iodate. The change in oxidation state of manganese in this reaction is from NCERT Pg 108, NEET 2022

(a) + 6 to + 4 (b) + 7 to + 3
(c) + 6 to + 5 (d) + 7 to + 4

7 The incorrect statement among the following is NCERT Pg 110, 112, 113, NEET 2021

(a) Actinoid contraction is greater for element to element than lanthanoid contraction.
(b) Most of the trivalent lanthanoid ions are colourless in the solid state.
(c) Lanthanoids are good conductors of heat and electricity.
(d) Actinoids are highly reactive metals, especially when finely divided.

8 Zr ($Z = 40$) and Hf ($Z = 72$) have similar atomic and ionic radii because of NCERT Pg 108, NEET 2021

(a) belonging to same group
(b) diagonal relationship
(c) lanthanoid contraction
(d) having similar chemical properties

9 Match the followings aspects with the respective metal. NCERT Pg 89, 96, 97, 100, NEET 2020

Aspects		Metal
A.	The metal which reveals a maximum number of oxidation states.	1. Scandium
B.	The metal although placed in 3*d* block is considered not as a transition element.	2. Copper
C.	The metal which does not exhibit variable oxidation states.	3. Manganese
D.	The metal which in +1 oxidation state in aqueous solution undergoes disproportionation.	4. Zinc

Codes

	A	B	C	D		A	B	C	D
(a)	1	4	2	3	(b)	3	4	1	2
(c)	3	1	4	2	(d)	2	4	1	3

10 Identify the incorrect statement. NCERT Pg 106, NEET 2020

(a) The transition metals and their compounds are known for their catalytic activity due to their ability to adopt multiple oxidation states and to form complexes.
(b) Interstitial compounds are those that are formed when small atoms like H, C or N are trapped inside the crystal lattices of metals.
(c) The oxidation states of chromium in CrO_4^{2-} and $Cr_2O_7^{2-}$ are not the same.
(d) $Cr^{2+}(d^4)$ is a stronger reducing agent than $Fe^{2+}(d^6)$ in water.

11 When neutral or faintly alkaline $KMnO_4$ is treated with potassium iodide, iodide ion is converted into '*X*'. '*X*' is NCERT Pg 108, NEET 2019

(a) I_2 (b) IO_4^- (c) IO_3^- (d) IO^-

12 Identify the incorrect statement from the following. NCERT Pg 109, 108

(a) Zirconium and hafnium have identical radii of 160 pm and 159 pm, respectively as a consequence of lanthanoid contraction.
(b) Lanthanoids reveal only +3 oxidation state.
(c) The lanthanoid ions other than the f^0 type and the f^{14} type are all paramagnetic.
(d) The overall decrease in atomic and ionic radii from lanthanum to lutetium is called lanthanoid contraction.

13 Match the metal ions given in Column I with the spin magnetic moments of the ions given in Column II and assign the correct code : NCERT Pg 102, NEET 2018

	Column I		Column II
1.	Co^{3+}	1.	$\sqrt{8}$ BM
2.	Cr^{3+}	2.	$\sqrt{35}$ BM
3.	Fe^{3+}	3.	$\sqrt{3}$ BM
4.	Ni^{2+}	4.	$\sqrt{24}$ BM
		5.	$\sqrt{15}$ BM

Codes

	A	B	C	D		A	B	C	D
(a)	4	1	2	3	(b)	1	2	3	4
(c)	4	5	2	1	(d)	3	5	1	2

14 The reason for greater range of oxidation states in actinoids is attributed to NCERT Pg 112, NEET 2017

(a) the radioactive nature of actinoids
(b) actinoid contraction
(c) 5*f*, 6*d* and 7*s* levels having comparable energies
(d) 4*f* and 5*d* levels being close in energies

15 Which one of the following statements related to lanthanons is incorrect? NCERT Pg 110, NEET 2016

(a) Europium shows +2 oxidation state.

(b) The basicity decreases as the ionic radius decreases from Pr to Lu.
(c) All the lanthanons are much more reactive than aluminium.
(d) Ce (+4) solution are widely used as oxidising agent in volumetric analysis.

16 Magnetic moment 2.84 BM is given by
(At. no. Ni = 28, Ti = 22, Cr = 24, Co = 27)
NCERT Pg 102, CBSE-AIPMT 2015

(a) Ni^{2+} (b) Ti^{3+} (c) Cr^{3+} (d) Co^{2+}

17 Gadolinium belongs to 4*f* series. It's atomic number is 64. Which of the following is the correct electronic configuration of gadolinium? **NCERT Pg 110, CBSE-AIPMT 2015**

(a) $[Xe]4f^8 6d^2$ (b) $[Xe]4f^9 5s^1$
(c) $[Xe]4f^7 5d^1 6s^2$ (d) $[Xe]4f^6 5d^2 6s^2$

18 Reason of lanthanoid contraction is
NCERT Pg 109, CBSE-AIPMT 2014

(a) negligible screening effect of *f*-orbitals
(b) increasing nuclear charge
(c) decreasing nuclear charge
(d) decreasing screening effect

JEE Main Archive

19 Consider the following reaction.

$$MnO_2 + KOH + O_2 \longrightarrow A + H_2O$$

Product '*A*' in neutral or acidic medium disproportionate to give products '*B*' and '*C*' along with water. The sum of spin-only magnetic moment values of *B* and *C* is...... BM. (Nearest integer). (Given atomic number of Mn is 25) **NCERT Pg 102, JEE Main 2024**

20 A transition metal '*M*' among Sc, Ti, V, Cr, Mn and Fe has the highest second ionisation enthalpy. The spin-only magnetic moment value of M^+ ion is .... BM. (Nearest integer) **NCERT Pg 95, 102, JEE Main 2024**

(Given, atomic number Sc : 21, Ti : 22, V : 23, Cr : 24, Mn : 25, Fe : 26)

21 Which of the following compounds show colour due to *d-d* transition? **NCERT Pg 103, JEE Main 2024**

(a) K_2CrO_4 (b) K_2CrO_7
(c) $KMnO_4$ (d) $CuSO_4 \cdot 5H_2O$

22 During the reaction of permanganate with thiosulphate, the change in oxidation of manganese occurs by value of 3. Identify which of the below medium will favour the reaction. **NCERT Pg 108, JEE Main 2023**

(a) Both aqueous acidic and faintly alkaline
(b) Aqueous acidic
(c) Aqueous neutral
(d) Both aqueous acidic and neutral

23 Highest oxidation state of Mn is exhibited in Mn_2O_7. The correct statements about Mn_2O_7 are

A. Mn is tetrahedrally surrounded by oxygen atoms.
B. Mn is octahedrally surrounded by oxygen atoms.
C. contains Mn—O—Mn bridge.
D. contains Mn—Mn bond.

Choose the correct answer from the options given below.
NCERT Pg 100, JEE Main 2023

(a) B and D (b) B and C (c) A and C (d) A and D

24 Given below are two statements, one is labelled as Assertion (A) and the other is labelled as Reason (R).

Assertion (A) 5*f* electrons can participate in bonding to a far greater extent than 4*f* electrons.

Reason (R) 5*f* orbitals are not as buried as 4*f* orbitals.

In the light of the above statements, choose the correct answer from the options given below.

(a) A is true but R is false. **NCERT Pg 113, JEE Main 2023**
(b) Both A and R are true and R is the correct explanation of A.
(c) Both A and R are true but R is not the correct explanation of A.
(d) A is false but R is true.

25 Given below are two statements, one is labelled as Assertion (A) and the other is labelled as Reason (R).

Assertion (A) In the complex $Ni(CO)_4$ and $Fe(CO)_5$ the metals have zero oxidation state.

Reason (R) Low oxidation states are found when a complex has ligands capable of π-donor character in addition to the σ-bonding.

In the light of the above statements, choose the most appropriate answer from the options given below.
NCERT Pg 97, JEE Main 2023

(a) Both A and R are correct but R is not the correct explanation of A.
(b) Both A and R are correct and R is the correct explanation of A.
(c) A is correct but R is not correct.
(d) A is not correct but R is correct.

26 Given below are two statements.

Statement I Iron (III) catalyst, acidified $K_2Cr_2O_7$ and neutral $KMnO_4$ have the ability to oxidise I^- to I_2 independently.

Statement II Manganate ion is paramagnetic in nature and involves $p\pi$-$p\pi$ bonding.

In the light of the above statements, choose the correct answer from the options given below.
NCERT Pg 107, 108, JEE Main 2022

(a) Both Statement I and Statement II are true.
(b) Both Statement I and Statement II are false.
(c) Statement I is true but Statement II is false.
(d) Statement I is false but Statement II is true.

27 In neutral or alkaline solution, MnO_4^- oxidises thiosulphate to **NCERT Pg 108, JEE Main 2022**
(a) $S_2O_7^{2-}$ (b) $S_2O_8^{2-}$ (c) SO_3^{2-} (d) SO_4^{2-}

28 Cerium (IV) has a noble gas configuration. Which of the following is correct statement about it? **NCERT Pg 109, JEE Main 2022**
(a) It will not prefer to undergo redox reactions.
(b) It will prefer to gain electron and act as an oxidising agent.
(c) It will prefer to give away an electron and behaves as reducing agent.
(d) It acts as both, oxidising and reducing agent.

29 In neutral or faintly alkaline medium, $KMnO_4$ being a powerful oxidant can oxidise, thiosulphate almost quantitatively, to sulphate. In this reaction overall change in oxidation state of manganese will be **NCERT Pg 108, JEE Main 2022**
(a) 5 (b) 1 (c) 0 (d) 3

30 The electrode potential of M^{2+}/M of 3*d*-series elements shows positive value for **NCERT Pg 98, JEE Main 2021**
(a) Fe (b) Co (c) Zn (d) Cu

31 The nature of oxides V_2O_3 and CrO is indexed as '*X*' and '*Y*' type respectively. The correct set of *X* and *Y* is **NCERT Pg 105, JEE Main 2021**
(a) *X* = acidic *Y* = acidic
(b) *X* = basic *Y* = amphoteric
(c) *X* = basic *Y* = basic
(d) *X* = amphoteric *Y* = basic

Skill Boosters

1 Transition metal compounds are coloured either *d-d* or due to charge transfer transitions. Colour due to *d-d* transition is shown by transition metal compounds having d^1 to d^9 electrons whereas the compounds containing d^0 and d^{10} configurations are intensely coloured due to charge transfer transitions, which of the following compounds is not coloured?
(a) Na_2CuCl_4 (b) Na_2CdCl_4 (c) $K_4Fe(CN)_6$ (d) $K_3Fe(CN)_6$

2 A transition metal *A* has 'spin-only' magnetic moment value of 1.8 BM when it is reacted with dilute sulphuric acid in the presence of air, its compound *B* is formed. *B* reacts with compound *C* to give compound *D* with the liberation of iodine. Then, the metal *A* and compounds *B*, *C* and *D* are respectively.
(a) Ti, $TiSO_4$, KI and TiI_2 (b) Zn, $ZnSO_4$, KI and Zn_2I_2
(c) Cu, $CuSO_4$, KI and Cu_2I_2 (d) Cu, $CuSO_4$, Cu_2I_2 and CuI_2

3 When a white crystalline compound *X* is heated with $K_2Cr_2O_7$ and concentrated H_2SO_4, a reddish brown gas *P* is evolved. On passing *P* into caustic soda solution, a yellow coloured solution of *Q* is obtained. Neutralising the solution *Q* with acetic acid and on subsequent addition of lead acetate, a yellow precipitate *R* is obtained. When *X* is heated with NaOH solution, a colourless gas is evolved and on passing this gas into K_2HgI_4 solution, a reddish brown precipitate *S* is formed. Identify *P*,*Q*,*R*,*S* and *X*.
(a) $P = CrO_2Cl_2$, $Q = Na_2CrO_4$, $R = PbCrO_4$, $S = NH_2HgOHgI$, $X = NH_4Cl$
(b) $P = CrO_2Cl_2$, $Q = K_2Cr_2O_7$, $R = Pb_2O_3$, $S = NH_2HgOHgI$, $X = NaCl$
(c) $P = K_2Cr_2O_7$, $Q = Na_2CrO_4$, $R = Pb_2O_3$, $S = NH_2NH_2$, $X = NH_4Cl$
(d) $P = K_2Cr_2O_7$, $Q = NaOH$, $R = PbCrO_4$, $S = NH_2NH_2$, $X = NaCl$

4 A man made white silvery metal, radioactive in nature has a strong tendency to form oxocations and complexes. It is used as a nuclear fuel in atomic reactors. The metal is a
(a) lanthanide (b) actinide
(c) transition metal (d) representative element

5 When H_2S gas is passed through an orange red solution (*X*), the solution turns milky. When an alkali is added to this orange red solution it turns yellow and on acidifying this yellow solution again turns orange red *X* is
(a) K_2CrO_4 (b) $KMnO_4$ (c) $Na_2Cr_2O_7$ (d) $K_2Cr_2O_7$

6 Transition metals and many of their compounds show paramagnetic behaviour, where there are unpaired electron. The magnetic moment arises from the spin and orbital motions in ions or molecule. The magnetic moments of Cr ($Z = 24$), Mn^+($Z = 25$) and Fe^{2+}($Z = 26$) are *x*, *y* and *z* respectively. Which of the following order is correct ?
(a) $x < y < z$ (b) $x = y < z$ (c) $z < x = y$ (d) $x = y = z$

7 To measure the quantity of $MnCl_2$ dissolved in an aqueous solution, it was completely converted to $KMnO_4$ using the reaction.
$MnCl_2 + K_2S_2O_8 + H_2O \longrightarrow KMnO_4 + H_2SO_4 + HCl$
Few drops of concentrated HCl were added to this solution and gently warmed. Futher, oxalic acid (225g) was added in portions till the colour of the permanganate ion disappeared. What is the quantity of $MnCl_2$ (in mg) present in the initial solution)?
(Atomic weights in g mol^{-1}: Mn=55, Cl = 35.5)
(a) 130 mg (b) 148 mg (c) 126 mg (d) 120 mg

8 $KMnO_4$ acts as an oxidising agent in the neutral, alkaline as well as acidic medium. In acidic medium, it is used in volumetric analysis for estimation of Fe^{2+}, $Cr_2O_4^{2-}$ salts

etc. Before using it as a titrant, it is first standardised with standard oxalic acid solution or Mohr's salt solution. Mohr's salt $(FeSO_4 \cdot (NH_4)_2SO_4 \cdot 6H_2O)$ is preferred over $FeSO_4 \cdot 7H_2O$ for standardisation of $KMnO_4$ solution because

(a) Mohr's salt is a double salt while ferrous sulphate is a single salt
(b) Mohr's salt is not hygroscopic but $FeSO_4 \cdot 7H_2O$ is hygroscopic
(c) Mohr's salt contains only ferrous ions whereas ferrous sulphate contains some ferric ions
(d) Mohr's salt solution can be titrated even in the absence of H_2SO_4

9 A blackish brown coloured solid *P*, when fused with alkali metal hydroxides in presence of air, produces a dark green coloured compound *Q*, which on electrolytic oxidation in alkaline medium gives a dark purple coloured compound (*R*). Identify *P*, *Q* and *R* ?

(a) MnO_4^{2-}, $KMnO_4$, K_2MnO_4
(b) MnO_2, K_2MnO_4, $KMnO_4$
(c) MnO_2, Na_2CO_3, $NH_2HgOHgI$
(d) K_2MnO_4, $KMnO_4$, MnO_2

10 The dichromate ion is in equilibrium with chromate ion in aqueous solution as

$$\underset{\text{(Orange-red)}}{Cr_2O_7^{2-}(aq)} + H_2O \rightleftharpoons \underset{\text{(Yellow)}}{2CrO_4^{2-}(aq)} + 2H^+(aq)$$

the oxoanion has

The oxoanion has

(a) Similar oxidising property in alkaline or acidic solutions
(b) better oxidising power in acidic solution
(c) better oxidising power in alkaline solution
(d) no oxidising power in acidic or alkaline solution

Correct Codes

Topical Questions

1. (d)	2. (b)	3. (d)	4. (a)	5. (c)	6. (a)	7. (c)	8. (a)	9. (a)	10. (a)
11. (c)	12. (c)	13. (b)	14. (d)	15. (d)	16. (b)	17. (b)	18. (c)	19. (b)	20. (d)
21. (a)	22. (d)	23. (b)	24. (a)	25. (a)	26. (a)	27. (a)	28. (b)	29. (b)	30. (c)
31. (d)	32. (c)	33. (c)	34. (c)	35. (c)	36. (d)	37. (d)	38. (c)	39. (a)	40. (a)
41. (c)	42. (b)	43. (c)	44. (c)	45. (a)	46. (b)	47. (a)	48. (a)	49. (b)	50. (b)
51. (c)	52. (c)	53. (a)	54. (c)	55. (c)	56. (d)	57. (c)	58. (a)	59. (a)	60. (a)
61. (b)	62. (a)	63. (a)	64. (d)	65. (c)	66. (d)	67. (d)	68. (a)	69. (d)	70. (a)
71. (c)	72. (c)	73. (a)	74. (a)	75. (a)	76. (a)	77. (d)	78. (d)	79. (a)	80. (b)
81. (d)	82. (d)	83. (d)	84. (a)	85. (b)	86. (c)	87. (b)			

Assertion-Reason

1. (a)	2. (a)	3. (a)	4. (c)	5. (a)	6. (a)	7. (a)	8. (a)	9. (a)	10. (b)
11. (a)	12. (a)	13. (c)	14. (d)						

Statement Type

1. (a)	2. (b)	3. (a)	4. (b)	5. (d)	6. (c)	7. (c)	8. (d)	9. (a)	10. (a)
11. (d)	12. (a)	13. (d)	14. (b)						

Matching Type

1. (c)	2. (b)	3. (c)	4. (b)	5. (a)	6. (c)

Numerical Value

1. (19)	2. (4)	3. (3)	4. (4)	5. (7)

NCERT Exemplar's

1. (a) 2. (b) 3. (b) 4. A-3, B-4, C-2, D-5, E-1 5. (d) 6. (a) 7. (a) 8. (b) 9. (d)
10. (a) 11. A-4, B-1, C-2, D-5, E-6 12. (d) 13. (a) 14. (c) 15. (b) 16. (c) 17. (b)
18. (c)

Past Exams'

1. (a)	2. (c)	3. (a)	4. (b)	5. (b)	6. (d)	7. (b)	8. (c)	9. (b)	10. (c)
11. (c)	12. (b)	13. (c)	14. (c)	15. (c)	16. (a)	17. (c)	18. (a)	19. (4)	20. (6)
21. (d)	22. (c)	23. (c)	24. (b)	25. (c)	26. (b)	27. (d)	28. (b)	29. (d)	30. (d)
31. (c)									

Skill Boosters

1. (b)	2. (c)	3. (a)	4. (b)	5. (d)	6. (c)	7. (c)	8. (c)	9. (b)	10. (b)

Step by Step

Decoding the Questions

Concept Builders

1 4s, 3d
2 26
3 Zinc
4 False
5 True
6 less
7 Zinc
8 True
9 False
10 Manganese
11 zinc
12 True
13 Exchange energy
14 True
15 True
16 Brass
17 chromium
18 transition state, activation
19 Interstitial
20 Sn^{4+}
21 True
22 True
23 diamagnetic
24 Lanthanoid contraction
25 LnN
26 magnesium
27 True
28 True
29 Neptunium or Plutonium
30 $TiCl_4 + Al(CH_3)_3$

Topical Solutions

1 (*d*) Statement (d) is incorrect.
It's correct form is as follows
The *d*-block occupies the large middle section of the periodic table flanked between *s* and *p*-blocks in the periodic table.
Rest other statements are correct.

2 (*b*) One electron in case of atomic number 24, moves from 4*s* to 3*d*-orbital to achieve the state of more stability. This is because, energy of 3*d* and 4*s*-orbitals are of comparable energy.

3 (*d*) The configuration which exhibits highest oxidation state in transition metals is $(n-1)d^5 ns^2$. It show maximum oxidation state equal to +7.

4 (*a*)

5 (*c*) Among the given options, vanadium (V) has a bcc lattice structure whereas, Rh, Pd and Ag has a ccp lattice respectively.

6 (*a*) The correct decreasing order of melting point is

$$Cr > V > Fe > Mn$$

7 (*c*) The correct order of increasing melting point is $Mn < Ti < V < Cr$.

8 (*a*) The filling of 4*f*-orbital before 5 *d*-orbital results in a regular decrease in atomic radii called lanthanoid contraction.

9 (*a*) Statement (a) is incorrect.
It's correct form is as follows
In general, ions of the same charge in a given series shows progressive decrease in radius with increasing atomic number.
Rest other statements are correct.

10 (*a*) Among the given transition element, zinc will have least enthalpy of atomisation their correct order is

$$\underset{(515\ kJ/mol)}{V} > \underset{(416\ kJ/mol)}{Fe} > \underset{(339\ kJ/mol)}{Cu} > \underset{(126\ kJ/mol)}{Zn}$$

11 (*c*) $E°$ values of M^{2+}/M ions are

$Mn^{2+}/Mn = -1.18$ V,
$Cr^{2+}/Cr = -0.90$ V,
$Fe^{2+}/Fe = -0.44$ V,
$Co^{2+}/Co = -0.28$ V

So, the correct order is

$$Mn > Cr > Fe > Co.$$

12 (*c*) The correct order of standard electrode potential is

$$Ti^{2+} < V^{2+} = Mn^{2+} < Ti^{3+}.$$

13 (*b*) As we move along the period in a 3*d*-series, nuclear charge increases from Sc to Zn but electrons are added to the orbital of inner subshell, i.e. 3*d*-orbitals. These 3*d*-electrons shield the 4*s*-electrons from the increasing nuclear charge more effectively than the outershell electrons can shield one another.
Therefore, the atomic radii decreases less rapidly in case of 3*d*-series.

14 (*d*) IE order of the given elements will be, Ti < Mn < Ni < Zn.

15 (*d*) In all elements, shells and subshells are same. Required amount of energy (enthalpy) is based upon the stability of *d*-subshell.
The $3d^5$-subshell has the highest stability in an ion because it is half-filled subshell (while other are incomplete).
So, Mn shows highest third ionisation enthalpy.

16 (*b*) Among the given elements, Sc and Zn do not show variable oxidation state but Zn is not a transition element.

17 (*b*) Statements II and III are correct, while the Statement I and IV are incorrect.
Corrected form of Statements I and IV are as follows

I. Mo(VI) and W(VI) are more stable then Cr(VI).
IV. Higher oxidation states of heavier members of group 6 of transition series are more stable.

18 (*c*) In electrochemical series, metals with positive standard potential are placed below hydrogen. Out of given transition metals, only Cu is placed below hydrogen in electrochemical series.
Therefore, it must have positive sign for standard potential $[E°_{M^{2+}/M}]$.

19 (*b*) The value of $E°$ for Mn, Ni and Zn are more negative than expected from the trend.
The stability of the half-filled *d*-subshell in Mn^{2+} and the completely filled d^{10}-configuration in Zn^{2+} are related to their $E°$ values, whereas $E°$ for Ni is related to the highest negative $\Delta_{hyd}H°$.

20 (*d*) All the given statements are correct.

21 (*a*) Statement (a) is incorrect.
Its correct form is as follows
The stability of Cu^{2+} (*aq*) is more rather than Cu^{+} (*aq*) due to the much more negative $\Delta_{hyd}H°$ of Cu^{2+} (*aq*) than Cu^{+}.
Rest other statements are correct.

22 (*d*) Statement given in option (d) is incorrect. Its correct form is Mn^{3+} and Co^{3+} ions are the strongest oxidising agents in aqueous solutions.

Rest other statements are correct.

23 (b) Statement (b) is incorrect.

It's correct form is as follows

The magnetic moment of transition metal can be calculated as

$$\mu = \sqrt{n(n+2)}$$

where, n = number of unpaired electrons.

Rest other statements are correct.

24 (a) Among the given ions, Cr^{3+} is most stable in aqueous solution because of half-filled t_{2g} orbital.

25 (a) $E°$ values for the redox couple M^{3+}/M^{2+} shows that Mn^{3+} and Co^{3+} ions are the strongest oxidising agents in aqueous solutions.

The ions Ti^{2+}, V^{2+}, Cr^{2+} are strong reducing agents and will liberate hydrogen from a dilute acid.

26 (a) The spin only magnetic moment (μ) of each ion can be calculated as

$$\mu = \sqrt{n(n+2)} \text{ BM}$$

Thus, the correct order of spin only magnetic moments of given hydrated ions will be

$$Sc^{3+} < Ti^{3+} < Ti^{2+} < V^{2+}$$

27 (a) The spin only magnetic moment (μ) (in BM) is given by

$$\mu \text{ (in BM)} = \sqrt{n(n+2)}$$

The highest value of n in transition metal complex is 5 in its d^5-configuration.

$$\therefore \quad \mu = \sqrt{5(5+2)} \text{ BM} = 5.916 \text{ BM}$$

28 (b) On considering the given options. Only Ni^{2+} contains unpaired electrons, so it is paramagnetic.

29 (b) Magnetic moment of a transition metal ion (μ) = $\sqrt{n(n+2)}$

$$\therefore \quad 3.87 = \sqrt{n(n+2)} \text{ (Given, } \mu = 3.87)$$

On solving, $n = 3$

Thus, number of unpaired electrons are 3.

30 (c) The correct order of number of unpaired electrons is IV > II > III > I.

31 (d) Statements given in (a), (b) and (c) are correct about magnetic moment. But statement (d) is incorrect. It is because Co^{2+} has 3 unpaired electrons.

So, its magnetic moment will be 3.87 BM.

32 (c) The correct order of the magnetic moment is

$$Fe^{3+} > Mn^{4+} > Ni^{2+} > V^{4+}$$

i.e. III > II > IV > I

33 (c) Due to presence of unpaired electrons in d-orbitals of $CoNO_3$, it shows d-d transition and, hence it is coloured.

34 (c) All the given statements are correct.

35 (c) Among the given species, TiF_6^{2-} and Cu_2Cl_2 are colourless species as they do not have unpaired electrons while other (CoF_6^{3-} and $NiCl_4^{2-}$) have unpaired electrons.

36 (d) Transition metals form a large number of complex compounds due to the comparatively smaller sizes of metal ions, their high ionic charges and availability of d-orbitals for bond formation, availability of f-orbital has no role in complex formation.

Therefore, availability of both d and f-orbitals is not responsible for the formation of complex compounds by transition elements.

37 (d) Transition elements having unpaired electrons generally form interstitial compounds. Among the given elements, Zn has $3d^{10}$ configuration. That is, it does not have unpaired electrons. Thus, it will not form interstitial compounds.

38 (c) Interstitial compounds increase the toughness and strength of alloys.

39 (a) All the given statements are correct.

40. (a) All the given sets of statements are correct.

41 (c) Vanadium (V) show a gradual change in oxides from basic to less basic and to amphoteric.

42. (b) Scandium (Sc) is the transition metal which form molecular type of oxides in ionic form.

43. (c) Among the given compounds, chromite ($FeCr_2O_4$) is used as the starting material for the preparation of potassium dichromate.

44 (c) Acidified potassium dichromate oxidises iodides to iodine, sulphides to sulphur, tin(II) to tin(IV), iron(II) salts to iron (III). Thus, option (c) is the correct answer.

45 (a) $K_2Cr_2O_7$ is a strong oxidising agent it can oxidise the species, which is not in its most possible positive oxidising state.

Thus, among the given only SO_3^{2-} can react with $K_2Cr_2O_7$.

46 (b) The structure of chromate ion and dichromate ion is tetrahedral (A) and two tetrahedral (B) (sharing one corner with Cr—O—Cr bond angle of 126°) respectively.

47 (a) The bond angle of Cr—O—Cr is 126°.

48 (a) The green manganate is paramagnetic because of one unpaired electron but the purple permanganate is diamagnetic due to absence of unpaired electron.

49 (b) K_2MnO_4 is formed when MnO_2 is fused with KOH in air. The reaction is as follows

$$2MnO_2 + 4KOH + O_2 \longrightarrow 2K_2MnO_4 + 2H_2O$$

50. (b)

51 (c) Statements I, II and III are correct, while the statement IV is incorrect. It's correct form is as follows

The oxidation state of Cr in both chromate and dichromate is same, i.e. +6.

52 (c) Statements I, II and IV are correct, while statement III is incorrect. It's correct form is as follows

Potassium dichromate is used as a primary standard in volumetric analysis.

53 (a)

$$\underset{\text{Purple (X)}}{2KMnO_4} \xrightarrow{\Delta} \underset{(Y)}{K_2MnO_4} + \underset{(Z)}{MnO_2} + O_2 \uparrow$$

$$\underset{(Z)}{MnO_2} + 4KOH + O_2 \xrightarrow{KNO_3} \underset{(Y)}{2K_2MnO_4} + 2H_2O$$

Thus, $X = KMnO_4$, $Y = K_2MnO_4$, $Z = MnO_2$.

54 (c) Isostructural compounds are those compounds which have same structure. Potassium permanganate forms a dark purple crystals which are isostructural with $KClO_4$. They both have tetrahedral structure.

55 (*c*) In MnO_4^-, Mn is in +7 oxidation state with d^0 configuration hence, no unpaired electrons. Thus, it will not show *d*-*d* transition. It is dark purple coloured due to charge transfer from ligand to metal.

56 (*d*)

57 (*c*) The purple coloured solution is of $KMnO_4$.

The ionic reactions are as follows

$$2MnO_4^- + H_2O + I^- \longrightarrow 2MnO_2 + 2OH^- + IO_3^-$$

$$2MnO_4^- + 10I^- + 16H^+ \longrightarrow 2Mn^{2+} + 8H_2O + 5I_2$$

58 (*a*) Permanganate at $[H^+] = 1$ should oxidise water but in practice the reaction is extremely slow unless either manganese (II) ions are present or the temperature is raised.

59 (*a*) Acidified permanganate solution will oxidise the above reactions. It oxidises oxalates to carbon dioxide, iron (II) to iron (III) and nitrites to nitrates.

60 (*a*) I. $2MnO_4^- + H_2O + I^- \longrightarrow \underset{(A)}{2MnO_2} + 2OH^- + IO_3^-$

II. $MnO_4^- + 5Fe^{2+} + 8H^+ \longrightarrow \underset{(B)}{Mn^{2+}} + \underset{(C)}{5Fe^{3+}} + 4H_2O$

Thus, *A* is MnO_2, *E* is Mn^{2+} and *C* is Fe^{3+}.

61 (*b*) When $KMnO_4$ reacts with oxalic acid in acidic medium, it oxidises to CO_2 and itself changes to Mn^{2+} which is colourless. Thus, the colour of $KMnO_4$ disappears.

62 (*a*) Mn has 7 valence electrons and all are involved in bond formation. Hence, it has no unpaired electron.

The colour is not due to *d*-*d* transition but it is due to charge transfer from oxygen to manganese.

So, $KMnO_4$ have no unpaired electrons but shows colour.

63 (*a*) The complete reactions are as follows

I. $MnO_4^- + 2H_2O + 3e^- \longrightarrow \underset{(A)}{MnO_2} + 4OH^-$

II. $5NO_2^- + 10OH^- \longrightarrow \underset{(B)}{5NO_3^-} + 5H_2O + 10e^-$

III. $5SO_3^{2-} + 2MnO_4^- + 6H^+ \longrightarrow 2Mn^{2+} + \underset{(C)}{5SO_4^{2-}} + 3H_2O$

Hence, the compounds *A*, *B* and *C* are MnO_2, $5NO_3^-$ and $5SO_4^{2-}$.

64. (*d*) **65.** (*c*)

66 (*d*) All the given statements, i.e. I, II and III are correct.

67 (*d*) Statement (d) is incorrect.

It's correct form is as follows

Lanthanoid contraction is due to ineffective shielding produced by 4*f*-electrons than *d*-electrons.

Rest other statements are correct.

68 (*a*)

69 (*d*) Zr^{4+} and Hf^{4+} have same size due to lanthanoid contraction.

70 (*a*) **71** (*c*)

72 (*c*) Statement (c) is incorrect.

It's correct form is as follows

The hardness of lanthanoids increases with increasing atomic number. Rest other statements are correct.

73 (*a*) Statement given in option (a) is incorrect.

It's correct form is as follows

$La(OH)_3$ is more basic than $Lu(OH)_3$, because size of Lu^{3+} is smaller than La^{3+} and when *M*—OH bond length decrease then tendency to release electrons decreases.

Rest other statements are correct.

74 (*a*)

75 (*a*) Smaller cations form a more stable covalent compounds and hence form more basic lanthanoid hydroxide. Thus, the correct order of basic strength is

$$\underset{(I)}{La(OH)_3} > \underset{(III)}{Ce(OH)_3} > \underset{(II)}{Lu(OH)_3}.$$

76 (*a*) The lanthanoids reactions are

I. $Ln \xrightarrow{\text{with halogen}} \underset{(A)}{LnX_3}$

II. $Ln \xrightarrow{\text{with } H_2O} \underset{(B)}{Ln(OH)_3 + H_2}$

III. $Ln \xrightarrow[\text{2773 K}]{\text{with C}} \underset{(C)}{LnC_2}$

Hence, *A*, *B* and *C* are LnX_3, $Ln(OH)_3 + H_2$ and LnC_2 respectively.

77 (*d*) The maximum number of possible oxidation states of actinoids are shown by neptunium (Np) and plutonium (Pu). These actinoids exhibit oxidation states of +3, +4, +5, +6 and +7.

78 (*d*) Among the given options, Am (Americium) shows maximum number of different oxidation states in its compounds.

79 (*a*) The actinoids resemble the lanthanoids in having more compounds in +3 oxidation state.

80 (*b*)

81 (*d*) Production of iron and steel is based on the reduction of iron oxides, removal of impurities and addition of carbon and alloying metals such as Cr, Mn and N.

82 (*d*) MnO_2, Zn and Ni/Cd compounds are useful in the battery industries. While TiO is used in pigment industry.

83 (*d*) Statement (d) is incorrect.

It's correct form is as follows

Nickel complexes are useful in the polymerisation of alkynes and other organic compounds such as benzene.

Rest other statements are correct.

84 (*a*)

85 (*b*) V_2O_5 catalyst used in the oxidation of SO_2 in the manufacture of H_2SO_4.

86 (*c*)

87 (*b*) The photographic industry relies on the special light-sensitive properties of AgBr.

Assertion-Reason

1 (*a*) Both A and R are true and R is the correct explanation of A.

2 (*a*) Both A and R are true and R is correct explanation of A.

3 (*a*) Both A and R are true and R is the correct explanation of A.

4 (*c*) A is true but R is false.

The correct form of R is :

The two series of the inner-transition metals, (4*f* and 5*f*) are known as lanthanoids and actinoids respectively.

5 (*a*) Both A and R are true and R is the correct explanation of A.

6 (*a*) Both A and R are true and R is the correct explanation of A.

7 (a) Both A and R are true and R is the correct explanation of A.

8 (a) Both A and R are true and R is the correct explanation of A.

9 (a) Both A and R are true; R is the correct explanation of A.

10 (b) Both A and R are true; R is not the correct explanation of A. The correct explanation of A is:
Separation of Zr and Hf is difficult. This is due to lanthanoid contraction which causes almost similar radii for both of them.

11 (a) Both A and R are true and R is the correct explanation of A.

12 (a) Both A and R are true and R is the correct explanation of A.

13 (c) A is true but R is false.
The correct form of R is :
Structural variability of actinoids due to irregularities in their metallic radii.

14 (d) A is false but R is true. The correct form of A is : Actinoids form relatively more stable complexes as compared to lanthanoids.

Statement Type

1 (a) Both Statements I and II are false. Their correct form is titanium ($Z = 22$) to copper ($Z = 29$), atomic mass grows more rapidly than atomic volume does thus, significant increase in density is seen.
Decrease in metallic radius coupled with increase in atomic mass occurs across the period.

2 (b) Statement I is true but Statement II is false. The correct form of Statement II is :
Ce^{4+} can be reduced to Ce^{3+} and can oxidise water.

$$Ce^{4+} + e^- \longrightarrow Ce^{3+}$$

Ce^{4+} has noble gas configuration [Xe] $4f^0$ but it is strong oxidant and get converted to Ce^{3+}.

3 (a) Both Statements I and II are false.
Their correct form is :

- Among the given transition metal Mn, Ni and Zn has the more negative value of $E°$ than expected from the trend. Cu has positive value of $E°$.
- All Cu(II) halides are known except the iodide.

4 (b) Statement I is true but Statement II is false.
The correct form of Statement II is :
Cuprous ion has no unpaired electrons in $3d$-subshell while the cupric ion has one unpaired electron.

5 (d) Statements I and II are true.

6 (c) Statement I is false but Statement II is true.
The correct form of Statement I is : manganous salt is oxidised to MnO_2 in the presence of zinc sulphate.

7 (c) Statement I is false but Statement II is true.
The correct form of Statement I is :
The carbides Ln_3C, Ln_2C_3 and LnC_2 liberate hydrogen from dilute acids and burn with halogens to form halides.

8 (d) The statements II and IV are incorrect while statements I, III and V correct. The correct explanation of II and IV is :

I. Cu(I) salts are unstable in aqueous solution because stability of $Cu^{2+}(aq)$ rather than $Cu^{+}(aq)$ is due to the much more negative $\Delta_{hyd} H°$ of $Cu^{2+}(aq)$ than Cu^+. Hence, Cu^+ reduces to Cu^{2+}.

II. The correct order of ionic radii is
$$Yb^{3+} < Pm^{3+} < Ce^{3+} < La^{3+}$$

9 (a) Statements I and II are correct, while the Statement III is incorrect.
It's correct form is as follows
Ionisation enthalpy of Mn^{2+} is higher than that of Fe^{2+}.

10 (a) Statement III is incorrect.
It's correct form is as follows
The oxidation state of Cr is highest in its hexafluoride (CrF_6).
Rest other statements are correct.

11 (d) Among the given statements, IV is incorrect.
It's correct form is as follows
Alloys are readily formed by transition metals because of similar radii.
Rest other statements are correct.

12 (a) Statements I and III are correct and II, IV and V are incorrect statements. The correct form of these statements are

II. $5f$-orbitals are not as buried as $4f$-orbitals and hence $5f$-electrons can participate in bonding to a far greater extent.

IV. Mn_4N is an interstitial compound. They are chemically inert.

V. $K_2Cr_2O_7$ (potassium dichromate) is used as an oxidising agent for the preparation of many azo compounds (dimethylamino azo benzene).

13 (d) Among the given statements, (IV) is incorrect.
It's correct form is as follows
Eu^{2+} is a strong reducing agent changing to the common +3 state. Similarly, Yb^{2+} which has f^{14} configuration is a reductant Tb^{4+} has half-filled f-orbitals and is an oxidant.
Rest other statements are correct.

14 (b) Statements II and V are correct. But statements I, III and IV are incorrect. Their correct from is

I. $PdCl_2$ catalysis the oxidation of ethyne to ethanal in the Wacker process.

III. Misch-metal is composed of 95% of a lanthanoid metal, 5% of iron and traces of S, C, Ca and Al.

IV. Actinoids shows more oxidation states than the lanthanoids because of lower energy gap between $5f$ and $6d$ the outer e^- are easily excited hence show variable oxidation state.

Matching Type

1 (c) The correct match is A-3, B-1, C-2.

2 (b) The correct match is
A-3, B-4, C-2, D-1.

3 (c) The correct match is
A-3, B-1, C-4, D-2.

4 (b) The correct match is
A-4, B-1, C-2, D-3.

5 (a) The correct match is
A-2, B-4, C-1, D-5, E-3.

6 (c) The correct match is
A-2, B-1, C-4, D-5, E-3.

Numerical Value

1 (19) Oxidation of Cr in $K_2Cr_2O_7$ is
$$2 + 2x + 7(-2) = 0 \Rightarrow 2x = 12$$

Similarly, $x = +6$
and oxidation of Mn in $KMnO_4$ is +7.
Oxidation of Fe in K_2FeO_4 is +6
Thus, sum of the oxidation state in
$$= 6 + 7 + 6 = 19$$

2 (4) Cr^{3+} has lowest number of d-electrons. So, it has lowest, reduction potential and is actually negative as shown in electrochemical series. Cr^{3+} has 3 unpaired electrons.
So, spin-only magnetic moment is
$$\mu = \sqrt{n(n+2)} = \sqrt{3(3+2)}$$
$$= \sqrt{15} = 3.87 \approx 4 \text{ BM}$$

3 (3) Most basic oxide of vanadium is V_2O_3. Electronic configuration of $V^{3+} = [Ar]\,3d^2$
So, the magnetic moment is
$$\mu = \sqrt{n(n+2)}$$
(n = no. of unpaired electrons)
$$= \sqrt{2(2+2)} = \sqrt{8}$$
$$= 2.84 \approx 3 \text{ BM}$$

4 (4) The disproportionation reaction of MnO_4^{2-} in acidic medium is as follows
$$3MnO_4^{2-} + 4H^+ \longrightarrow \underset{(B)}{MnO_2} + 2\underset{(A)}{MnO_4^-}$$
Oxidation state of Mn in MnO_2 is + 4.
Oxidation state of Mn in MnO_4^- is + 7.
Hence, $A = MnO_4^-$, $B = MnO_2$
$$Mn = [Ar]\,3d^5 4s^2$$
$$Mn^{4+} = [Ar]\,3d^3$$
Total number of unpaired electrons (n) = 3
Magnetic moment (μ) spin only of B is
$$\mu = \sqrt{n(n+2)} = \sqrt{3(3+2)} = \sqrt{15}$$
$$= 3.87 \text{ BM} \approx 4 \text{ BM}$$

5 (7) The electronic configuration of Gd is as follows
$$Gd = [Xe]4f^7 5d^1 6s^2$$
So, electronic configuration of
$$Gd^{2+} = [Xe]4f^7 5d^1$$
∴The number of $4f$ electrons in ground state configuration of Gd^{2+} is 7.

NCERT Exemplar's

1 (a)

2 (b) Transition elements form coloured salt due to the presence of unpaired electrons. In CuF_2, Cu(II) [d^9 configuration] contain one unpaired electron.
Hence, CuF_2 is coloured in solid state.

3 (b) The electronic configuration of Cr^{3+} ion is $3d^3$.
Spin magnetic moment
$$(\mu) = \sqrt{n(n+2)} \text{ BM}$$
Here, $n = 3$
So, $\mu = \sqrt{3(3+2)}$
$$= \sqrt{15} = 3.87 \text{ BM}$$

4 The correct match is
A-3, B-4, C-2, D-5, E-1.

5 (d)

6 (a) Statement (a) is incorrect. It's correct form is as follows
Copper lies below hydrogen in the electrochemical series and, hence does not liberate H_2 from acids. Rest other statements are correct.

7 (a) V_2O_5 and Cr_2O_3 are amphoteric oxide because they both react with alkalies as well as acids.

8 (b) Greater the number of unpaired electron, higher will be its value of magnetic moment.
Since, $3d^5$ has 5 unpaired electrons hence highest magnetic moment.
$$\mu = \sqrt{5(5+2)}$$
$$= \sqrt{35} = 5.95 \text{ BM}$$

9 (d) Interstitial compounds acquire chemical inertness.

10 (a) On addition of $KMnO_4$ to conc. H_2SO_4, a green oily compound Mn_2O_7 is obtained which is highly explosive in nature.

11 The correct match is
A-4, B-1, C-2, D-5, E-6.

12 (d)

13 (a) The reaction of $KMnO_4$ in which it acts as an oxidising agent. In acidic medium is
$$2KMnO_4 + 3H_2SO_4 \longrightarrow K_2SO_4 + 2MnSO_4 + 3H_2O + 5[O]$$
$$H_2S + [O] \longrightarrow H_2O + S] \times 5$$
$$\overline{2KMnO_4 + 3H_2SO_4 + 5H_2S \longrightarrow K_2SO_4 + 2MnSO_4 + 8H_2O + 5S}$$
5 moles of S^{2-} ions react with 2 moles of $KMnO_4$.
So, 1 mole of S^{2-} ion will react with 2/5 moles of $KMnO_4$.

14 (c) $KMnO_4$ acts as an oxidising agent in alkaline medium. When alk. $KMnO_4$ is treated with KI, iodide ion is oxidised to IO_3^-.

15 (b) HCl is not used to make the medium acidic in oxidation reactions of $KMnO_4$ in acidic medium. The reason is that if HCl is used, the oxygen produced from $KMnO_4$ + HCl is partly utilised in oxidising HCl to Cl_2, which itself acts as an oxidising agent and partly oxidises the reducing agent.

16 (c) When acidified $K_2Cr_2O_7$ solution is added to Sn^{2+} salts then Sn^{2+} changes to Sn^{4+}.

17 (b) Electronic configuration of X^{3+} is $[Ar]3d^5$. It represents the total number of $e^{\ominus}$ and oxidation state. Therefore, atomic number of $X = 18 + 5 + 3 = 26$
Hence, option (b) is correct.

18 (c) Due to lanthanoid contraction, zirconium (Zr) and hafnium (Hf) possess nearly same atomic and ionic radii, i.e. Zr = 160 pm and Hf = 159 pm, $Zr^{4+} = 79$ pm and $Hf^{4+} = 78$ pm.
Therefore, these two elements show similar properties (physical and chemical properties).

Past Exams'

1 (a) Spin only magnetic moment is given by,
$$\mu_s = \sqrt{n(n+2)}$$
where, n = number of unpaired electrons

A. $Ti^{3+} \longrightarrow 3d^1, n = 1$
$$\mu_s = \sqrt{1(1+2)} = \sqrt{3}$$
B. $Cr^{2+} \longrightarrow 3d^4, n = 4$
$$\mu_s = \sqrt{4(4+1)} = \sqrt{20}$$
C. $Mn^{2+} \longrightarrow 3d^5, n = 5$
$$\mu_s = \sqrt{5(5+1)} = \sqrt{30}$$
D. $Fe^{2+} \longrightarrow 3d^6, n = 4$
$$\mu_s = \sqrt{4(4+1)} = \sqrt{20}$$
E. $Sc^{3+} \longrightarrow 3d^0, \mu_s = 0$

Hence, B and D have same value of magnetic moment.

2 (c) $E° = +ve$ for Mn^{3+} / Mn^{2+}

$Mn = 25 \longrightarrow 3d^5 4s^2$

$Mn^{2+} \longrightarrow 3d^5$

$Mn^{3+} \longrightarrow 3d^4$

Mn^{2+} has half-filled ($3d^5$) stable configuration.

Thus, Mn^{3+} has very high tendency to gain an electron due to this it has high +ve value of electrode potential ($E°$) while in other case, they does not gain electron easily.

Hence, the reason is change of d^4 to d^5-configuration.

3 (a) $Ce^{4+} = [Xe]\, 4f^0\, 5d^0$

$Yb^{2+} = [Xe] 4f^{14} 5d^0$

Both ions does not contain any unpaired electrons.

Hence, they are diamagnetic.

4 (b) Among the given statements III and IV statements are incorrect. Their correct forms are as follows

III. Basic character decreases from V_2O_3 to V_2O_4 to V_2O_5. In general, the oxides in lower oxidation states of metals are basic and in their higher oxidation states they are acidic.

IV. V_2O_4 dissolves in acids to give VO^{2+} salts.

5 (b) The highest stability of Cu^{2+} ion in aqueous solution is due to negative enthalpy of hydration.

6 (d) The reaction that takes place in the given condition is as follows

$$\underset{+7}{2KMnO_4} + I^- + H_2O \xrightarrow[\text{Weak alkaline medium}]{\text{Neutral}} \underset{+4}{2MnO_2} + IO_3^- + 2OH^-$$

So, the change in oxidation state of manganese in this reaction is from + 7 to + 4.

Hence, option (d) is correct option.

7 (b) Trivalent lanthanoid ions are coloured in the solid state and in aqueous state due to presence of f-electrons.

∴ Statement (b) is incorrect.

8 (c) Zr(Z = 40) and Hf(Z = 72) have similar atomic and ionic, radii because of lanthanoid contraction.

9 (b) The correct match is

A-3, B-4, C-1, D-2.

10 (c) Statements in options (a), (b) and (d) are correct.

Statement in option (c) is incorrect, because oxidation states of Cr in CrO_4^{2-} (chromate) and $Cr_2O_7^{2-}$ (dichromate) are same and it is +6.

11 (c) When neutral or faintly alkaline $KMnO_4$ is treated with potassium iodide, $KMnO_4$ is converted into MnO_2 while iodide (I^-) ion is converted into IO_3^- (iodate).

12 (b) + 3 oxidation state is common to lanthanoids in their compounds. However, + 4 and + 2 ions in solution or in solid are also known.

Hence, (b) is the incorrect statement.

13 (c) The correct match is

A-4, B-5, C-2, D-1.

14 (c) The reason for greater range of oxidation states in actinoid is attributed to the $5f$, $6d$ and $7s$ levels having comparable energies.

15 (c) Among the given statements only (c) is incorrect. The reactivity of lanthanons is similar to that of aluminium.

16 (a) Magnetic moment, $\mu = \sqrt{n(n+2)}$ BM

where,

n = number of unpaired electrons

$\mu = 2.84$ (given)

$$\therefore \quad 2.84 = \sqrt{n(n+2)} \text{ B.M}$$

$$(2.84)^2 = n(n+2)$$

$$8 = n^2 + 2n$$

$$n^2 + 2n - 8 = 0$$

$$n^2 + 4n - 2n - 8 = 0$$

$$n(n+4) - 2(n+4) = 0 \text{ and } n = 2$$

$Ni^{2+} = [Ar]\, 3d^8\, 4s^0$

(two unpaired electrons)

$Ti^{3+} = [Ar] 3d^1 4s^0$

(one unpaired electrons)

$Cr^{3+} = [Ar] 3d^3$,

(three unpaired electrons)

$Co^{2+} = [Ar] 3d^7, 4s^0$

(three unpaired electrons)

So, only Ni^{2+} has 2 unpaired electrons.

17 (c) The electronic configuration of gadolinium is $_{64}Gd = [Xe]\, 4f^7 5d^1 6s^2$.

18 (a) Lanthanoid contraction is the regular decrease in atomic and ionic radii of lanthanides. This is due to the imperfect shielding [or poor screening effect] of f-orbitals due to their diffused shape, which is unable to counterbalance the effect of the increased nuclear charge.

Hence, the net result is a contraction in size of lanthanoids.

19 (4) The given reaction proceeds as follows

$$MnO_2 + KOH + O_2 \longrightarrow \underset{(A)}{K_2MnO_4} + H_2O$$

$$K_2MnO_4 \xrightarrow[\text{medium}]{\text{Neutral/Acidic}} \underset{(B)}{KMnO_4} + \underset{(C)}{MnO_2}$$

Here Mn is in +4 oxidation state, in MnO_2

$Mn^{+4} = [Ar] 3d^3$

$\Rightarrow n = 3, \mu = \sqrt{3(3+2)} = 3.87$ BM

$\mu = 0$ for $KMnO_4$

sum of spin only magnetic moment of $B + C$ is 3.87.

So, the nearest integer is 4.

20 (6) Among the given metals, chromium has maximum second ionisation enthalpy because

2nd electron is removed from stable configuration $3d^5$.

$Cr^+ = [Ar] 3d^5 4s^0$

∴ Number of unpaired e^- in Cr^+ is 5 i.e.

$n = 5$

So, $\mu = \sqrt{n(n+2)}$ BM $= \sqrt{5(5+2)}$

$= 5.92$ BM ≈ 6 BM

21 (d) Among the given options, the colour of $CuSO_4 \cdot 5H_2O$ which acts as liquid cause crystal field splitting.

> **Concept Enhancer** The colour of $KMnO_4$, $K_2Cr_2O_7$ and $K_2Cr_2O_4$ is due to charge transfer transition caused by visible light adsorptiona nd which not by d-d transition which is commonly seen in d-block elements. Charge transfer transition involves the redistribution of charge density between the ligand and the metal ion orbitals.

22 (c) In aqueous neutral medium, thiosulphate is oxidised by $KMnO_4$ to SO_4^{2-}. In this manganese changes its oxidation state from +7 to +4.

23 (*c*) The correct statements regarding Mn_2O_7, are A and C only.

24 (*b*) Both (A) and (R) are true and (R) is the correct explanation of (A).

25 (*c*) A is correct but R is not correct. The correct form of R is :

Low oxidation state of metals can be stabilised by synergic bonding. So, ligand has to be π-acceptor.

26 (*b*) Both Statement I and Statement II are false. Their correct form are

- Neutral $KMnO_4$ oxidises I^- to IO_3^-. Acidified potassium dichromate reacts with potassium iodide and oxidises it to I_2.
- Manganate ion (MnO_4^{2-}) is paramagnetic with tetrahedral structural and has $d\pi$ - $p\pi$ bonding, i.e. *p*-orbital of oxygen and *d*-orbital of Mn.

27 (*d*) In alkaline medium, $\overset{+7}{Mn}O_4^-$ get reduced to $\overset{+4}{Mn}O_2$ and in this reaction, it oxidises,

$$\underset{\text{Thiosulphate ion}}{S_2O_3^{2-}} \longrightarrow \underset{\text{Sulphate ion}}{SO_4^{2-}}$$

28 (*b*) All the lanthanoids show +3 oxidation state as most stable oxidation state hence, Ce(IV) act as oxidising agent so that it can get converted to Ce(III).

29 (*d*) The reaction involved in neutral or faintly alkaline medium is

$$8\overset{+7}{Mn}O_4^- + 3S_2O_3^{2-} + H_2O \longrightarrow 8\overset{+4}{Mn}O_2 + 6SO_4^{2-} + 2OH^-$$

So, change in oxidation state of Mn is $7-4=3$.

30 (*d*) In the electrode potential series, only copper have positive value for electrode potential because copper has lower tendency than hydrogen to form ions.

$\therefore$ Electrode potential of Cu, $E^\circ_{Cu^{2+}/Cu}$ show positive value.

31 (*c*) V_2O_3 is a basic oxide as on dissolving in acids, give solution of vanadium (III) complexes.

In case of transition metal oxide, the metal with lower oxidation states are basic.

So, CrO is also basic as oxidation state of Cr is +2.

Skill Boosters

1 (*b*) Na_2CdCl_4 compound is not coloured because in this complex Cd is in +2 oxidation state and outer configuration is $4d^{10}$. All the orbitals are completely filled and there is no excitation of electrons, Thus, it is colourless.

2 (*c*) Cu(*A*) = Copper(27)= $3d^{10}4s^1$

'Spin only' magnetic moment

$$=1.8\,\text{M} = \sqrt{n(n+2)}$$

$$3.24 = n(n+2) \Rightarrow n=1$$

$$Cu^{2+} = [Ar]3d^9 4s^0$$

$$Cu^{2+} + H_2SO_4 \longrightarrow \underset{(B)}{CuSO_4} + H_2 \xrightarrow{KI\,(C)} \underset{(D)}{Cu_2I_2} + I_2 + K_2SO_4$$

Hence, $A = Cu$, $B = CuSO_4$, $C = KI$, $D = Cu_2I_2$

3 (*a*) The chemical reaction involved are as follows

$$\underset{(X)}{4NH_4Cl} + K_2Cr_2O_4 + \underset{(Conc.)}{6H_2SO_4} \longrightarrow \underset{\substack{(P)\\ \text{Reddish brown}}}{2CrO_2Cl_2} + 4NH_4HSO_4 + 2KHSO_4 + 3H_2O$$

$$\underset{(P)}{CrO_2Cl_2} + 2NaOH \longrightarrow \underset{\substack{(Q)\\ \text{Yellow ppt.}}}{Na_2CrO_4} + 2HCl$$

$$Na_2CrO_4 + Pb(CH_3COO)_2 \longrightarrow \underset{\substack{(R)\\ \text{Yellow ppt.}}}{PbCrO_4} + 2\,CH_3COONa$$

$$\underset{(X)}{NH_4Cl} + NaOH \longrightarrow NaCl + NH_3 + H_2O$$

$$2K_2HgI_4 + NH_3 + 3KOH \longrightarrow \underset{(S)}{NH_2HgOHgI} + 7KI + 2H_2O$$

4 (*b*) Actinides are man-made and radioactive in nature. They are used in nuclear fuels and have a strong tendency to form complexes.

5 (*d*) *X* can be either $Na_2Cr_2O_7$ or $K_2Cr_2O_7$. However, $K_2Cr_2O_7$, gives orange red solution.

$$K_2Cr_2O_7 + 2KOH \rightarrow \underset{\text{(Yellow solution)}}{2K_2CrO_4} + H_2O$$

$$\downarrow H_2SO_4$$

$$\underset{\text{(Orange red)}}{K_2Cr_2O_7} + K_2SO_4 + H_2O$$

6 (*c*) Electronic configuration of Cr (24) $=3d^5\ 4s^1$

3d						4s
1	1	1	1	1		1

The number of unpaired electrons (n) $=6$

Electronic configuration of

$$Mn^+(25) = 3d^5 4s^1$$

The number of unpaired electrons (n) $=6$

Electronic configuration of

$$Fe^{2+}(26) = 3d^6 4s^0$$

The number of unpaired electrons (n) $=4$

Magnetic moment (μ) $=\sqrt{n(n+2)}$ BM.

Greater the number of unpaired electrons, greater will be the magnetic moment. Thus, the correct order is $x = y > z$.

7 (*c*) The reaction is represented as

$$2MnCl_2 + 5K_2S_2O_8 + 8H_2O \longrightarrow 2KMnO_4 + 4K_2SO_4 + 6H_2SO_4 + 4HCl$$

$$2KMnO_4 + 5H_2C_2O_4 + 3H_2SO_4 \longrightarrow K_2SO_4 + 2MnSO_4 + 8H_2O + 10\,CO_2$$

Mass of oxalic acid added = 225 mg

Millimoles of oxalic acid added

$$= \frac{225}{90} = 2.5$$

Millimoles of $KMnO_4$ used to react with 2.5 millimoles of oxalic acid = 1

Millimoles of $MnCl_2$ required initially = 1

$\therefore$ Mass of $MnCl_2$ required initially

$$= 1 \times 126 = 126 \text{ mg}$$

8 (*c*) Mohr's salt contains only ferrous ions and volume of $KMnO_4$ reacting with Mohr's salt solution can be determined as it oxidises then to ferric ions. In order to reduce the oxidation of ferric ion, Mohr 's salt is preferred.

9 (*b*) The chemical reactions involved are as follows

$$\underset{\substack{\text{Pyrolusite blackish}\\ \text{brown } (P)}}{MnO_2} + 4KOH + O_2 \xrightarrow{\text{Fuse}} \underset{\substack{\text{Potassium manganate}\\ (Q)\text{-green coloured}}}{2K_2MnO_4} + 2H_2O$$

$$2K_2MnO_4 + H_2O + [O] \xrightarrow[\text{medium}]{\text{Alkaline}} \underset{\substack{\text{Potassium permanganate}\\ (R) \text{ purple coloured}}}{2\,KMnO_4} + 2KOH$$

10 (*b*) If H^+ ion concentration increases reaction shifts towards left and concentration of $Cr_2O_7^{2-}$ increases and orange red coloured appear.

Scan for **Chemistry Through Concept Master** Videos

05 Coordination Compounds

Topicwise No. of Ques asked in 5 Years (NEET)

Topics	No. of Questions				
	2024	2023	2022	2021	2020
Topic-1: Werner's Theory of Coordination Compounds	–	–	–	–	–
Topic-2: Definition of Some Important Terms Used in Coordination Compounds	1	2	–	1	–
Topic-3: Nomenclature of Coordination Compounds	–	–	1	–	–
Topic-4: Isomerism in Coordination Compounds	1	–	–	–	–
Topic-5: Bonding in Coordination Compounds	1	–	1	1	2
Topic-6: Bonding in Metal Carbonyls	–	–	–	–	–
Topic-7: Importance and Applications of Coordination Compounds	–	–	–	–	–

Special Type of Ques asked in 5 Years (NEET)

Types	Years				
	2024	2023	2022	2021	2020
A-R	–	–	–	–	–
Statement Based	2	–	–	–	–
Matching	1	–	–	1	1

Last 5 Year Weightage (NEET)

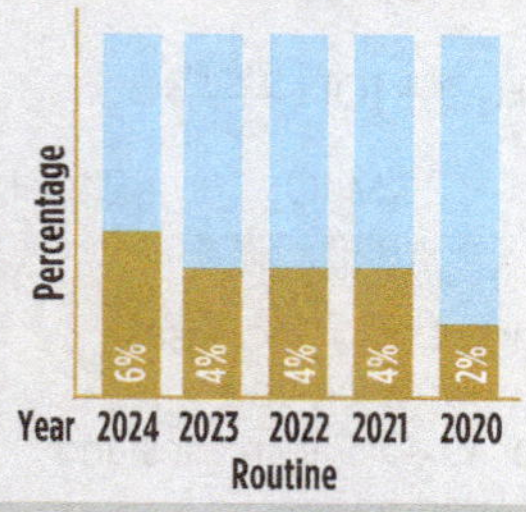

Certain elements, that include mostly transition metals, form a large number of **complex compounds** in which the metal atoms are bound to a number of anions or neutral molecules by sharing of electrons. Today, such compounds are named as coordination compounds.

e.g. Chlorophyll, haemoglobin and vitamin B_{12} are coordination compounds of magnesium, iron and cobalt metals respectively.

Werner's Theory of Coordination Compounds

- **Alfred Werner** (in 1866-1919) a Swiss chemist was the first to formulate his ideas, about the structures of coordination compounds. He proposed the concept of **primary valence** and **secondary valence** for a metal ion.
- Werner's theory of complex compounds is based upon his experimental work with complex compounds of cobalt (III) chloride and ammonia.

The observations, together with the results of conductivity measurements in solution is shown below.

Formulation of Cobalt(III) Chloride-Ammonia Complex

Complex compounds	Colour	No. of Cl^- ion precipitated per molecule of the complex by Ag^+	Formula	Solution conductivity corresponds to
$CoCl_3 \cdot 6NH_3$	Yellow	3	$[Co(NH_3)_6]^{3+}\ 3Cl^-$	1 : 3 electrolyte
$CoCl_3 \cdot 5NH_3$	Purple	2	$[Co(NH_3)_5Cl]^{2+}\ 2Cl^-$	1 : 2 electrolyte
$CoCl_3 \cdot 4NH_3$	Green	1	*trans*-$[Co(NH_3)_4Cl_2]^+ Cl^-$	1 : 1 electrolyte
$CoCl_3 \cdot 4NH_3$	Violet	1	*cis*-$[Co(NH_3)_4 Cl_2]^+ Cl^-$	1 : 1 electrolyte

- The last two compounds have identical empirical formula but distinct properties. These are called **isomers**.

Postulates of Werner's Theory

The Werner in 1898, propounded his theory of coordination compounds and the main postulates are as follows

- In coordination compounds, metal has two types of linkages or valences, i.e. primary and secondary valences.
- Primary valences is equal to the oxidation number of central ion. It is non-directional and ionisable. It is satisfied by negative ions. e.g. In $CrCl_3$, the primary valence is three.
- Secondary valences is equal to the coordination number of central atom/ion. It is directional and non-ionisable. It is commonly satisfied by neutral molecules or negative ions and is always fixed for a metal. Each metal ion has a fixed number of secondary valences.

  e.g. In $[Co(NH_3)_6]Cl_3$, six NH_3 groups are held by secondary valences.

  They are directed in space and account for shape or structure of a complex ion, e.g. $[Co(NH_3)_6]^{3+}$ has octahedral shape.

  e.g. Structure of $[CoCl_2(NH_3)_4]^+ Cl^-$ is as follows

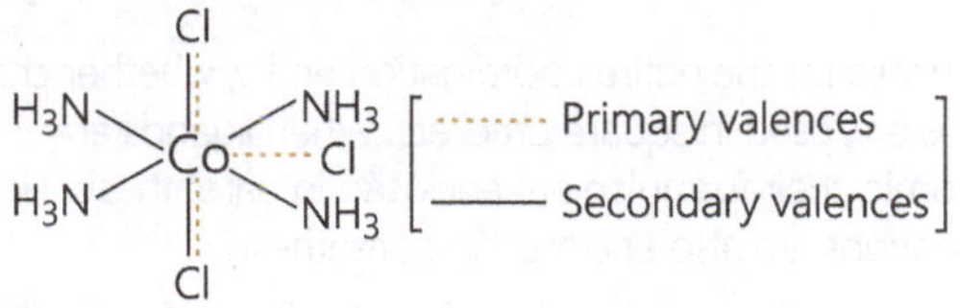

  The solid and dotted lines together indicate Cl-atom satisfying both primary and secondary valences.
- The ions or groups bounded by the secondary valences to the metal have characteristic spatial arrangements (called **coordination polyhedra**) corresponding to different coordination number.
- The species within the square bracket are coordination **entities** or **complexes.**
- The ions present outside the square bracket are called **counter ions.**
- Werner further postulated that octahedral, tetrahedral and square planar geometrical shapes are more common in coordination compounds of transition metals, thus $[Co(NH_3)_6]^{3+}$, $[CoCl(NH_3)_5]^{2+}$ and $[CoCl_2(NH_3)_4]^+$are octahedral entities, while $[Ni(CO)_4]$ and $[PtCl_4]^{2-}$ are tetrahedral and square planar, respectively.

Difference Between a Double Salt and a Complex (Coordination Compound)

Both double salts as well as complexes are formed by the combination of two or more stable compounds in stoichiometric ratio.

- **Double salts** when dissolved in water dissociate completely into ions, e.g. Mohr's salt $[FeSO_4(NH_4)_2SO_4 \cdot 6H_2O]$, potash alum $KAl(SO_4)_2 \cdot 12H_2O$, Carnallite $KCl \cdot MgCl_2 \cdot 6H_2O$.
- **Complex** do not dissociate completely into simple ions and do not completely lose their identity in solution, e.g. $K_4[Fe(CN)_6]$ or $[Fe(CN)_6]^{4-}$ do not dissociate into Fe^{2+} and CN^- ions.

Definitions of Some Important Terms Used in Coordination Compounds

Definitions of these terms are as follows

Coordination Entity

It constitutes a central metal atom or ion bonded to a fixed number of ions or molecules.

e.g. $[CoCl_3(NH_3)_3]$ is a coordination entity in which the cobalt ion is surrounded by three ammonia and three chloride ions.

Central Metal Atom/Ion

In a coordination entity, the atom/ion to which a fixed number of ions/groups are bound in a definite geometrical arrangement around it, is called the central atom or ion.

e.g. In $[NiCl_2(H_2O)_4]$, $[CoCl(NH_3)_5]^{2+}$ and $[Fe(CN)_6]^{3-}$ the central metal atom/ion are Ni^{2+}, Co^{3+} and Fe^{3+} respectively.

The central metal atom or ion can act as **Lewis acid.**

Ligands

Ions or molecules which can donate a lone pair of electron to the central atom or ion are called ligands.

- When a ligand is bound to a metal ion through a single donor atoms (e.g. Cl^-, H_2O), the ligand is said to be **unidentate.**
- When a ligand can bind through two donor atoms as in oxalate, the ligand is said to be **didentate.**
  e.g. $H_2NCH_2CH_2NH_2$ (ethane-1,2 diamine), $C_2O_4^{2-}$ (oxalate) and DMG (dimethyl glyoxime).
- When several donor atoms are present in a single ligand as in $N(CH_2CH_2NH_2)_3$, the ligand is said to be **polydentate.**
  e.g. EDTA (Ethylene diamine tetraacetate). NEET 2021
- When a di-or polydentate ligand uses its two or more donor atoms simultaneously to bind a single metal ion, it is said to be a **chelate** ligand. These chelate complexes are more stable than similar complexes containing unidentate ligand. NEET 2023
- The number of such ligating groups is called the **denticity** of the ligand. e.g. EDTA is a hexadentate with four oxygen atom and two nitrogen atoms.
- Ligand which has two different donor atoms and either of the two ligetes in the complex is called **ambidentate ligands.** e.g. NO_2^- and SCN^- ion.

Coordination Number

It can be defined as the number of ligand donor atoms to which the metal is directly bonded.

e.g. In the complex ion $[PtCl_6]^{2-}$ and $[Ni(NH_3)_4]^{2+}$ the coordination number of Pt and Ni are 6 and 4 respectively.

Similarly, for complex $[Co(en)_3]^{3+}$, the coordination number of Co is 6 as (ethane-1,2-diamine) is a didentate ligand.

Note Coordination number of the central atom/ion is determined only by the number of sigma bonds formed by the ligands with the central atom/ion.

Coordination Sphere

The central atom/ion and the ligands attached to it are enclosed in the square brackets are collectively known as coordination sphere. The ionisable groups are written outside the bracket and are called **counter ion**.

e.g. In the complex $K_4[Fe(CN)_6]$, the coordination sphere is $[Fe(CN)_6]^{4-}$ and the counter ion is K^+.

Coordination Polyhedron

The spatial arrangement of the ligand atoms which are directly attached to the central atom/ion defines a coordination polyhedron about the central atom. e.g. $[PtCl_4]^{2-}$ is square planar, $[Ni(CO)_4]$ is tetrahedral and $[Co(NH_3)_6]^{3+}$ is octahedral.

Oxidation Number

The charge present on central metal atom or ion, if all the ligands are removed along with the electron pairs that are shared with it is called **oxidation number of central atom.** The oxidation number is represented by a Roman numeral in parenthesis following the name of the coordination entity. e.g. Oxidation number of copper in $[Cu(CN)_4]^{3-}$ is +1 and is written as Cu(I).

Marks Maximizer

Effective atomic number (EAN) **rule** is also known as the "18-electron rule". This rule may be used to predict the number of ligands in compounds as well as the products of their reactions.

EAN = Atomic number of metal (Z) − oxidation number + 2 × coordination number

Homoleptic Complexes

Complexes in which metal is bound to only one kind of donor groups are known as homoleptic complexes. e.g. $[Co(NH_3)_6]^{3+}$.

NEET 2023 NEET 2024

Heteroleptic Complexes

Complexes in which a metal is bound to more than one kind of donor groups are known as heteroleptic complexes. e.g. $[Co(NH_3)_4Cl_2]^+$.

Nomenclature of Coordination Compounds

The formulas and names adopted for coordination entities are based on the recommendation of IUPAC.

Formulae of Mononuclear Coordination Compounds

Mononuclear coordination entities contain a single central metal atom. The following rules are applied while writing the formulas

- The central atom is listed first.
- The ligands are then listed in alphabetical order. The placement of a ligand in the list does not depend on its charge.
- **Polydentate ligands** are also listed alphabetically. In case of abbreviated ligand, the first letter of the abbreviation is used to determine the position of the ligand in the alphabetical order.
- The formula for the entire coordination entity, whether charged or not is enclosed in square brackets. When ligands are polyatomic, their formulae are enclosed in parenthesis. Ligand abbreviations are also enclosed in parenthesis.
- There should be no space between the ligands and the metal within a **coordination sphere.**
- When the formula of a charged coordination entity is to be written without counter ion, the charge is indicated outside the square brackets as a right superscript with the number before the sign (+ or –). e.g. $[Co(CN)_6]^{3-}$, $[Cr(H_2O)_6]^{3+}$, etc.
- The charge of the cation(s) is balanced by the charge of the anion(s) as the complex is consider as electrically neutral.

Naming of Mononuclear Coordination Compounds

The following rules are used while naming the coordination compounds

- The cation is named first in both positively and negatively charged coordination entities.
- The ligands are named in an alphabetical order before the name of the central atom/ion.
- Name of the anionic ligands end in -'o', those of neutral and cationic ligands are the same except aqua for H_2O, ammine for NH_3, carbonyl for CO and nitrosyl for NO. These are placed within enclosing brackets ( ).

  If ambidentate ligand is present, then it is named by placing the symbol of donor atom or by using different names. e.g. ONO (nitrito-O), —NO_2 (nitrito-N).

- Prefixes mono, di, tri, etc., are used to indicate the number of the individual ligands in the coordination entity.

  When the names of the ligands include a numerical prefix, then the terms, *bis, tris, tetrakis* are used, the ligand to which they refer is placed in parenthesis. e.g. $[NiCl_2(PPh_3)_2]$ is named as dichlorido*bis*(triphenylphosphine)nickel(II).
- Oxidation state of the metal in cation, anion or neutral coordination entity is indicated by Roman numeral in parenthesis.
- If the complex ion is a cation, the metal is named same as the element, e.g. Co in a complex cation is called cobalt and Pt is called platinum.
- If the complex ion is an anion, the name of the metal ends with the suffix—'ate', e.g. Co in a complex anion, $[Co(SCN)_4]^{2-}$ is called cobaltate. For some metals, the Latin names are used in the complex anions, e.g. ferrate for Fe.
- The neutral complex molecule is named similar to that of the complex cation.

  Few examples, to illustrate the nomenclature for coordination compounds are

  1. $[Cr(NH_3)_3(H_2O)_3]Cl_3$-Triamminetriaquachromium(III)-chloride
  2. $K_3[Fe(C_2O_4)_3]$-Potassium trioxalatoferrate(III)
  3. $[CoCl(ONO)(en)_2]^+$-Chlorido*bis* (ethane-1,2-diamine)-nitrito-O-cobalt(III)ion.
  4. $[Ag(NH_3)_2][Ag(CN)_2]$-diamminesilver(I) dicyanidoargentate(I) NEET 2022

Isomerism in Coordination Compounds

NEET 2024

Two or more compounds having the same chemical formula but a different arrangement of atoms are called isomers and the phenomenon is known as isomerism.

The isomerism in coordination compounds is discussed as follows

Types of Isomerism	Examples
1. **Structural isomerism** Isomers having same chemical formula but different chemical bonds.	
(a) **Linkage isomerism** It arises in a coordination compound containing ambidentate ligand.	Thiocyanate (NCS^-) ligand that can bind through nitrogen gives *M*—NCS or through sulphur to give *M*—SCN $[Co(NH_3)_5SCN]^{2+}$ (Violet) and $[Co(NH_3)_5NCS]^{2+}$ (Orange)
(b) **Coordination isomerism** It arises from the interchange of ligands between cationic and anionic entities of different metal ions present in a complex.	$[Co(NH_3)_6][Cr(CN)_6]$ and $[Cr(NH_3)_6][Co(CN)_6]$
(c) **Ionisation isomerism** It arises when the counter ion in a complex salt is itself a potential ligand and can displace a ligand which can then become the counter ion.	$[Co(NH_3)_5SO_4]Br$ and $[Co(NH_3)_5Br]SO_4$
(d) **Solvate isomerism** (Hydrate isomerism) These complexes differ in number of water molecules present as ligands (inside the coordination sphere) and as free molecules (outside the coordination sphere)	$[Cr(H_2O)_6]Cl_3$ (Violet) and $[Cr(H_2O)_5Cl]Cl_2 \cdot H_2O$ (Grey-green)
2. **Stereoisomerism** Isomers haveing same chemical formula and chemical bonds but different spatial arrangements.	

(a) **Geometrical isomerism**

- This type of isomerism arises in heteroleptic complexes.
- It arises due to different possible geometric arrangements of ligands.
- It is found in complexes with coordination number 4 and 6.
- In MX_2L_2 two ligands *X* are arranged as *cis* and *trans*.
- *MABXL* shows three isomers, two *cis* and one *trans*.
- Octahedral complexes of type $[Ma_3b_3]$, $[Ma_4b_2]$ and $[M(aa)_2b_2]$ shows geometrical isomerism.
- Ma_3b_3 shows *facial* (*fac*) and *meridional* (*mer*) isomer.

- MX_2L_2 (square planar complex)

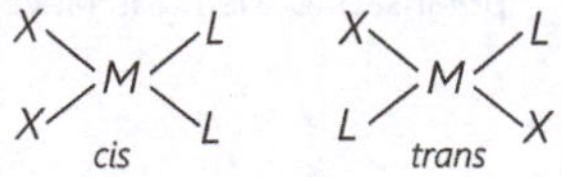

cis *trans*

- *MABXL* (square planar complex)

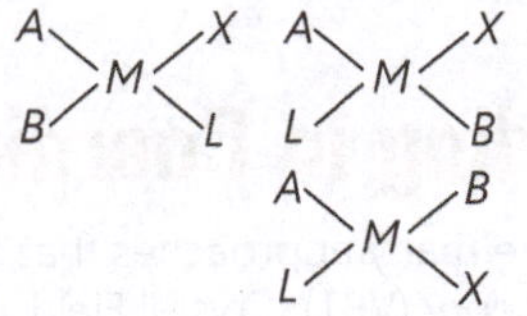

- Ma_4b_2 (octahedral complexes)

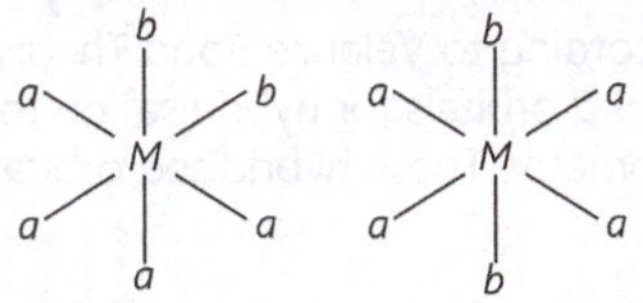

cis *trans*

- $M(aa)_2b_2$ (octahedral complexes) e.g. $[CoCl_2(en)_2]$

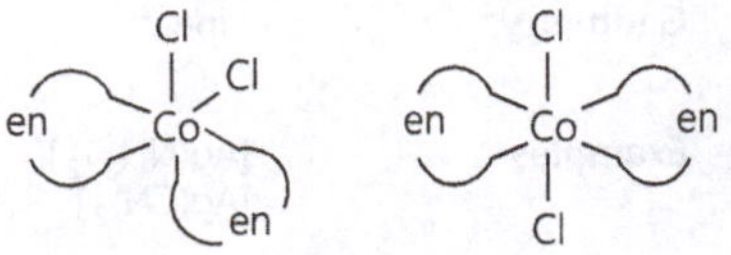

cis *trans*

- Ma_3b_3 (octahedral complexes)

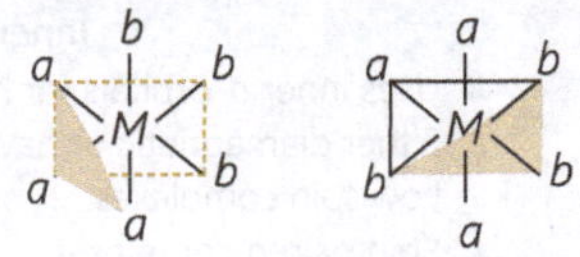

fac– *mer*–

Types of Isomerism	Examples
(b) **Optical isomerism**	
• It occurs in compounds having mirror images that are non-superimposable on each other. These are called **enantiomers**.	• $[M(aa)_3]$, e.g. $[Co(en)_3]^{3+}$ 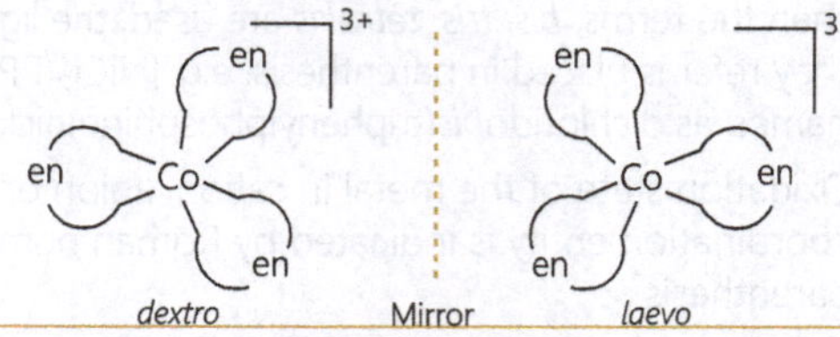
• These are common in octahedral complexes involving didentate ligands of type $[M(aa)_3]$ and $[M(aa)_2b_2]$.	• $[M(aa)_2b_2]$, e.g. $[Pt(en)_2Cl_2]^{2+}$ 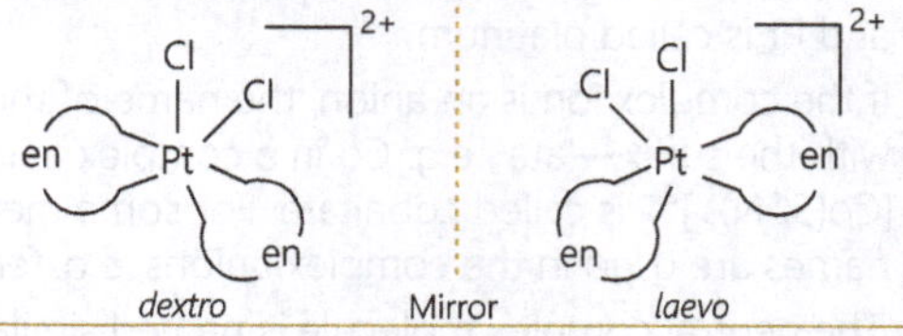
• These generally occur in two forms, i.e. *dextro* and *laevo*. (Dextro rotates plane polarised to the right, laevo rotates plane polarised to the left).	• $[M(aa)b_2c_2]$, e.g. $[Co(en)(NH_3)_2Cl_2]^{2+}$ 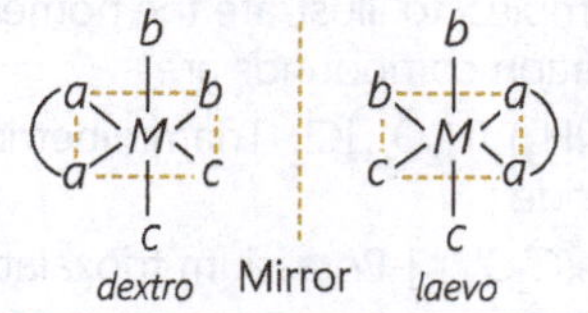

Bonding in Coordination Compounds

There are many approaches that are put forward to explain the nature of bonding in coordination compounds. *viz.* Valence Bond Theory (VBT), Crystal Field Theory (CFT), Ligand Field Theory (LFT) and Molecular Orbital Theory (MOT). In this chapter, we shall discuss VBT and CFT only.

Valence Bond Theory

For Concept Master Video

According to Valence Bond Theory (VBT), the metal atom or ion under the influence of ligands can use $(n-1)d$, ns np, nd orbitals for hybridisation to yield a set of hybridised orbitals such as square planar, tetrahedral and octahedral geometry. These hybridised orbitals overlap with ligand orbitals which can donate an electron pair for bonding.

Hybridisation and Geometry of Complexes

Type of hybridisation	sp	sp^2	sp^3	dsp^2	dsp^3	sp^3d	d^2sp^3	sp^3d^2
Coordination number	2	3	4	4	5	5	6	6
Geometry	Linear	Trigonal planar	Tetrahedral	Square planar	Square pyramidal	Trigonal bipyramidal	Octahedral (inner orbital)	Octahedral (outer orbital)
Examples	$[Ag(NH_3)_2]^+$ $[Ag(CN)_2]^-$	$[HgI_3]^-$	$Ni(CO)_4$ $[ZnCl_4]^{2-}$	$[Ni(CN)_4]^{2-}$ $[Cu(NH_3)_4]^{2+}$ $[Ni(NH_3)_4]^{2+}$	$Fe(CO)_5$,	$[SbF_5]^{2-}$ $[CuCl_5]^{3-}$	$[Cr(NH_3)_6]^{3+}$ $[Fe(CN)_6]^{3-}$	$[FeF_6]^{3-}$ $[Fe(H_2O)_6]^{2+}$ $[Ni(NH_3)_6]^{2+}$ NEET 2020

Difference Between Inner and Outer Orbital Complex

Inner orbital Complexes	Outer orbital Complexes
• Uses inner *d*-orbitals for hybridisation, i.e. $(n-1)$ *d*-orbitals.	• Uses outer *d*-orbitals for hybridisation, i.e. *nd*-orbitals.
• Either diamagnetic or have lesser number of unpaired electrons.	• Have larger number of unpaired electrons.
• Low spin complexes.	• High spin complexes.
• Spin paired complexes.	• Spin free complexes.
• e.g. $[Fe(CN)_6]^{3-}$ and $[Co(NH_3)_6]^{3+}$	• e.g. $[Fe(H_2O)_6]^{3+}$ and $[CoF_6]^{3-}$

Magnetic Properties of Coordination Compounds

- The magnetic behaviour of coordination compounds can be explained on the number of unpaired electrons. If no unpaired electron is present, the complex is diamagnetic. If unpaired electron(s) is/are present, complex is paramagnetic.
- The magnetic moment of $[Fe(CN)_6]^{3-}$ is 1.73 BM, $[Fe(H_2O)_6]^{3+}$ is 5.92 BM, $[Fe(CN)_6]^{4-}$ is 0 and $[Fe(H_2O)_6]^{4-}$ is 4.90. NEET 2021
- Generally, low spin complexes are diamagnetic and high spin complexes are paramagnetic. Some examples are shown in table.

S.N.	Atom/Ion complex	Configuration	Oxidation state of metal	Type of hybridisation	Geometry (Shape)	No. of unpaired electrons	Magnetic nature
1.	$Cu^{2+}(d^9)$	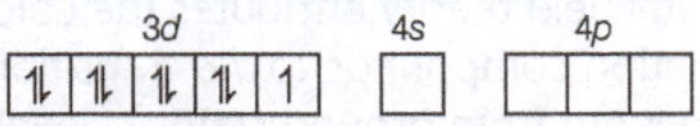	+2			1	Paramagnetic
	$[CuCl_4]^{2-}$	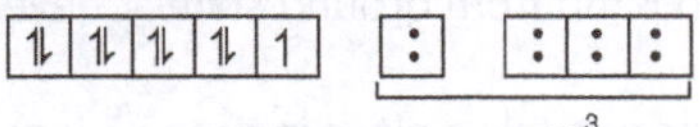	+2	sp^3	Tetrahedral	1	Paramagnetic
	$[Cu(NH_3)_4]^{2+}$	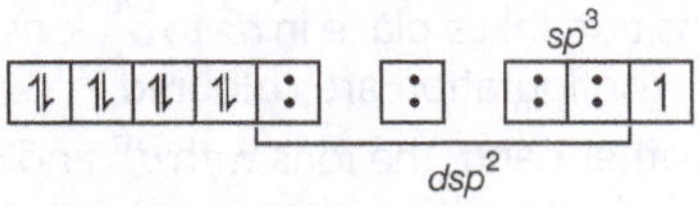 One electron is shifted from 3*d* to 4*p*-orbital.	+2	dsp^2	Square planar	1	Paramagnetic
2. NEET 2024	$Co^{3+}(d^6)$	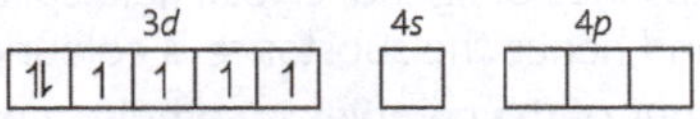	+3			4	Paramagnetic
	$[Co(NH_3)_6]^{3+}$	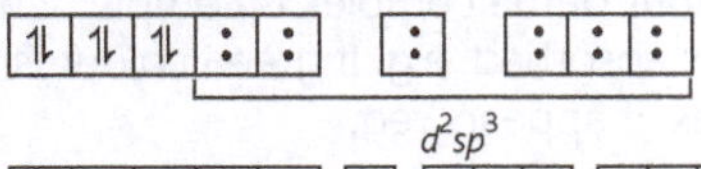	+3	d^2sp^3 (Inner)	Octahedral	0	Diamagnetic
	$[CoF_6]^{3-}$	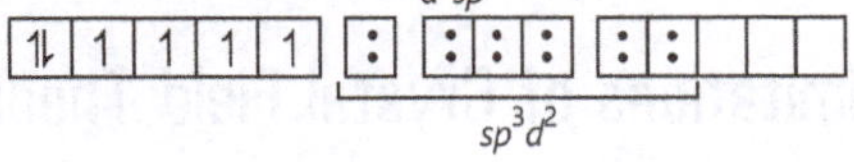	+3	sp^3d^2 (Outer)	Octahedral	4	Paramagnetic

Limitations of Valence Bond Theory

Although, valence bond theory is advantageous to explain formation, structures and magnetic properties of coordination compounds but it suffers with few limitations, listed as follows

- It does not distinguish between weak and strong ligands.
- It does not give quantitative interpretations of magnetic data.
- It does not give a quantitative interpretation of the thermodynamic or kinetic stabilities of coordination compounds and fails to explain relative energies of different shapes.
- It does not explain the colour and spectral properties of the coordination compounds.
- It fails to predict the exact tetrahedral and square planar structures of 4-coordinate complexes.

Crystal Field Theory (CFT)

- It is an electrostatic model which considers the metal-ligand bond to be ionic arising purely from electrostatic interactions between the metal ion and the ligand. The ligands are treated as point charges in case of anions or point dipoles in case of neutral molecules.
- According to CFT, under the influence of ligand field, degeneracy of the *d*-orbital is destroyed and it splits into two or more energy levels.

For Concept Master Video

- Octahedral complexes yield three orbitals of lower energy, t_{2g} set and two orbitals of higher energy, e_g set. This splitting of degenerate levels due to the presence of ligands in a definite geometry is termed as **crystal field splitting** and the energy separation is denoted by Δ_o.
- The splitting of *d*-orbitals in an octahedral crystal field can be seen in following diagram.

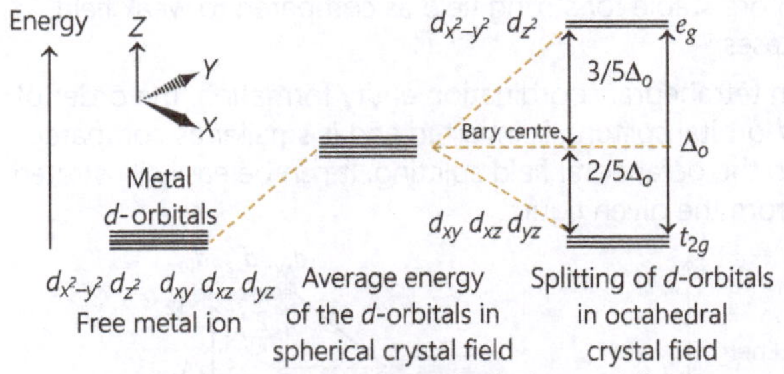

d-orbital splitting in an octahedral crystal field

- Thus, the energy of the two e_g set orbitals will increase by $\left(\frac{3}{5}\right)\Delta_o$ and that of the three t_{2g} will decrease by $\left(\frac{2}{5}\right)\Delta_o$.
- The extent of crystal field splitting depends on the strength of ligand and charge on metal ion. A strong ligand causes greater splitting, while a weak ligand causes smaller splitting.

- Ligands can be arranged in a series in the order of increasing field strength as given below.
  $I^- < Br^- < SCN^- < Cl^- < S^{2-} < F^- < OH^- < C_2O_4^{2-}$
  $< H_2O < NCS^- < EDTA^{4-} < NH_3 < en < NO_2^- < CN^- < CO$
  This series is called **spectrochemical series**.

Mnemonics **Recall Spectrochemical Series**

You can remember the spectrochemical series just by rembering one sentence.

I Bought Some Copies to Study Fundamental of Chemistry
↓ ↓ ↓ ↓ ↓ ↓ ↓ ↓
$I^{\ominus} < Br^{\ominus} < SCN^{\ominus} < Cl^{\ominus} < S^{2-} < F^- < OH^{\ominus} < C_2O_4^{2-}$

He Nurtured Excellence in Necessary Coordination Compounds
↓ ↓ ↓ ↓ ↓ ↓
$H_2O < NCS^- < edta^{4-} < NH_3 < en < CN^- < CO$

- The single *d*-electron of metal ion in octahedral coordination entities occupies one of the lower energy t_{2g} orbitals. In d^2 and d^3 coordination entities, the *d*-electrons occupy the single t_{2g} orbitals in accordance with the Hund's rule. **NEET 2019**
- For metal ion complex, d^4 configuration, *d*-orbital occupancy depends on the relative magnitude of the crystal field splitting, Δ_o and the pairing energy, *P* (It represents the energy required for electron pairing in a single orbital).
  - If $\Delta_o < P$, the fourth electron enters one of the e_g orbitals giving the configuration $t_{2g}^3 e_g^1$. Ligands for which $\Delta_o < P$ are known as **weak field ligands** and form high spin complexes.
  - If $\Delta_o > P$, it becomes more energetically favourable for the fourth electron to occupy t_{2g} orbital with configuration $t_{2g}^4 e_g^0$. Ligands which produce this effect are known as **strong field ligands** and form low spin complexes.
- Calculations show that d^4 to d^7 coordination entities are more stable for strong field as compared to weak field cases.
- In tetrahedral coordination entity formation, the order of *d*-orbital splitting is inverted and is smaller as compared to the octahedral field splitting. It can be easily illustrated from the given figure.

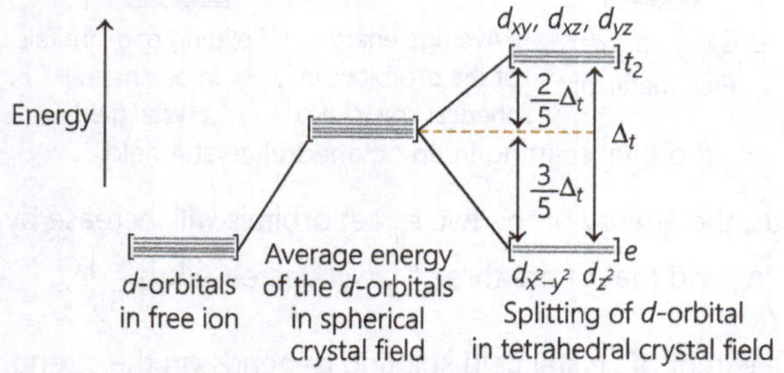

d-orbital splitting in a tetrahedral crystal field

- For the same metal, the same ligands and metal ligand distances, it can be shown as $\Delta_t = 4/9\,\Delta_o$.
- The orbital splitting energies are not sufficiently large for forcing pairing and therefore low spin configurations are rarely observed in tetrahedral complexes.
- The *g* subscript is used for octahedral and square planar complexes which have centre of symmetry. Since, tetrahedral complexes lack symmetry, '*g*' subscript is not used with energy levels.

Colour of Coordination Compounds

- The crystal field theory attributes the colour of the coordination compounds to *d-d* transition of the electron, i.e. electron jump from ground state t_{2g} level to higher state e_g level.
- *d-d* transition takes place in d^1 to d^9 ions, so the ions having d^1 to d^9 configuration are coloured.
- On the other hand, the ions with d^0 and d^{10} configuration do not show *d - d* transition hence colourless.
- In the absence of ligand, crystal field splitting does not occur and hence the substance is colourless.
- The colour of the complex is complementary colour to that which is absorbed. e.g. If green colour is absorbed by the complex, it appears red.

Limitations of Crystal Field Theory

CFT has the following limitations

- As the ligands are point charges, the anionic ligands should exert the greatest splitting effect. Actually, the anionic ligands are found at the low end of the spectrochemical series.
- CFT treats the metal-ligand bond as purely ionic and it does not take into account the covalent character of bonding between the ligand and the central atom.
- It does not consider the formation of π-bonding in the complex.

Bonding in Metal Carbonyls

Most of the transition metals form homoleptic carbonyls (compounds containing carbonyl ligands only). Some of the important characteristics of these compounds are as follows

- In metal carbonyls, the metal carbon bond possesses both σ and π character.
- $M \leftarrow C$ σ-bond is formed by donation of lone pair of electrons of carbonyl carbon to the vacant orbital of the metal.
- $M \rightarrow C$ π-bond is formed by donation of pair of electron from a filled *d*-orbital of metal into vacant antibonding π^*-orbital of carbon monoxide.
- Such type of metal to ligand bonding creates a synergic effect which strengthens the bond between CO and metal.

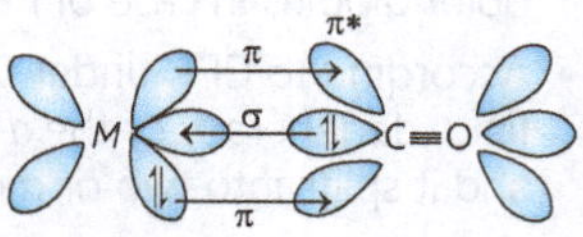

Examples of Mononuclear Carbonyls

(i) $Cr(CO)_6 \rightarrow$ Hexacarbonylchromium (0)

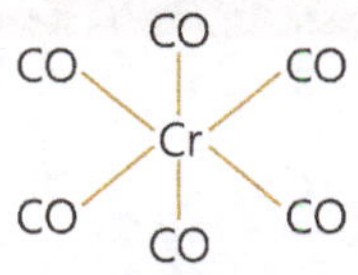

Octahedral

(ii) $Fe(CO)_5 \rightarrow$ Pentacarbonyliron (0)

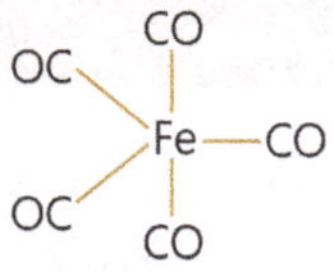

Trigonal bipyramidal

Examples of Polynuclear Carbonyls

(i) $Co_2(CO)_8 \rightarrow$ Octacarbonyldicobalt (0)

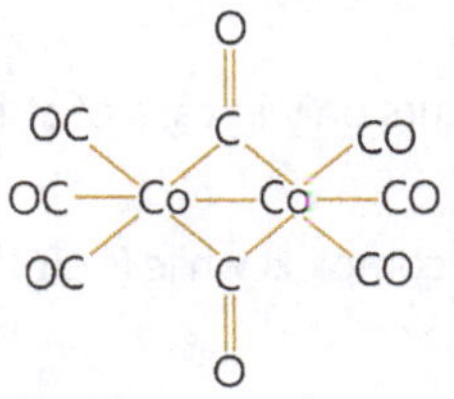

(ii) $Mn_2(CO)_{10} \rightarrow$ Decacarbonyldimanganese (0)

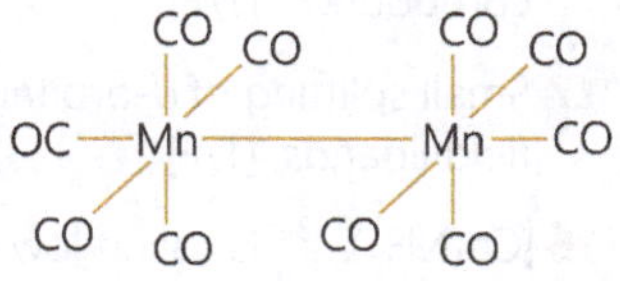

Marks Maximizer

The presence of positive charge on the metal carbonyl, like in $[Mn(CO)_6]^+$, would resist the flow of the metal electron charge to π^* orbitals of CO. This would increase the CO bond order and hence, CO in a metal carbonyl cation would absorb at a higher frequency compared to its absorption in neutral metal carbonyl.

Importance and Applications of Coordination Compounds

The coordination compounds are widely present in the mineral, plant and animal world and are known to play many important functions. Some of them are explain below.

(i) **In qualitative and quantitative analysis** The familier colour reactions given by metal ions with several ligands (especially the chelating ligands) are highly specific and sensitive under controlled experimental conditions. e.g. Nickel is detected and estimated as red dimethyl glyoxime complex (a chelating ligand).

- EDTA is used as ligand for the detection and estimation of many metals.
- Hardness of water is estimated by simple titration with Na_2EDTA. The Ca^{2+} and Mg^{2+} ions form stable complexes with EDTA.

(ii) **Extraction of metals** like gold and silver involves the complex formation. e.g. Gold combines with cyanide in the presence of oxygen and water to form the coordination entity $[Au(CN)_2]^-$ in aqueous solution. Gold can be separated in metallic form from this solution by the addition of zinc.

(iii) **Purification of metals** can be achieved through formation and subsequent decomposition of their coordination compounds.

(iv) In black and white photography, the developed film is fixed by washing with hypo solution which dissolves the undecomposed AgBr to give a complex ion, $[Ag(S_2O_3)_2]^{3-}$.

(v) Coordination compounds are of great importance in **biological system**.

- Haemoglobin, red pigment of blood acts as oxygen carrier is Fe complex.
- Vitamin B_{12}, cyanocobalamine, the antipernicious anaemia factor, is a complex of cobalt.

(vi) **Wilkinson catalyst** $[Rh(PPh_3)_3Cl]$ is used for the hydrogenation of alkenes.

(vii) **In medicinal chemistry** *cis*-platin is used in cancer treatment, EDTA is used for treatment of lead poisoning.

Caution Points

- Particularly compounds with d^0 configuration with CN = 4 undergoes d^3s-hybridisation not sp^3.
- The octahedral complex of Ni(II) will never form an inner orbital complex rather than form an outer orbital complex.
- In square planar complexes, if two bidentate ligand are unsymmetrical then geometrical isomers is possible.

PYQ Notes

1. Cobalt chloride when dissolved in water forms pink coloured complex $[Co(H_2O)_6]^{2+}$ which has octahedral geometry. This solution on treating with conc. HCl forms deep blue complex $[CoCl_4]^{4-}$ which has tetrahedral geometry. **JEE Main 2023**
2. For the complexes, having same oxidation state the order of CFSE will be **JEE Main 2022**
   $3d$-series < $4d$-series < $5d$-series.
3. Identification of Ni^{2+} carried out by dimethyl glyoxime (a bidentate neutral ligand) in the presence of NH_4OH. **JEE Main 2021**
4. Wavelength (λ) of absorption is inversely proportional to CFSE (Δ_o value) of the central metal ion. **NEET 2017**
5. The formula, which is used for the calculation of CFSE of an octahedral coordination compound.
   $$CFSE = -0.4\,\Delta_o \times \text{number of electrons in } t_{2g} \text{ orbital} + 0.6\,\Delta_o \times \text{number of electrons in } e_g \text{ orbital}$$
   NEET 2014

Step by Step

Mastering NCERT

- Concept Builders
- Topical Questions
- Assertion-Reason
- Statement Type
- Matching Type
- Numerical Value
- NCERT Exemplar's
- Past Exams'
- Skill Boosters

Concept Builders

1 The primary valences are .... and are satisfied by .... ions.

2 The .... valency is equal to the coordination number and is fixed for a metal.

3 Write the number of ions given on complete ionisation of one mole of $[Co(NH_3)_3Cl_3]$.

4 The ions or groups bound by the secondary linkages to metal have characteristic spatial arrangement with respect to different coordination number. [T/F]

5 Double salt and complexes are formed by combination of two or more stable compounds in stoichiometric ratio. [T/F]

6 Ni^{2+} and Fe^{3+} in $[NiCl_2(H_2O)_4]$ and $[Fe(CN)_6]^{3-}$, respectively are referred to as .... (Lewis acids/Lewis base)

7 Complex ions like $[Fe(CN)_6]^{4-}$ dissociate into simple ions like Fe^{2+} and CN^- ions when dissolved in water. [T/F]

8 Two compounds having identical empirical formula but different properties. Such compounds are termed as homoleptic compounds. [T/F]

9 Coordination number of Fe and Co in $[Fe(C_2O_4)_3]^{3-}$ and $[Co(en)_3]^{3+}$ is 6. [T/F]

10 Name the geometry exhibit by compounds which has coordination number 5.

11 Name the isomerism arises in heteroleptic complexes due to different possible geometric arrangements of the ligands.

12 Name the compound formed when excess of KCN is added to aqueous solution of copper sulphate.

13 Write the number of geometric isomers that can exist for square planar $[Pt(Cl)(py)(NH_3)(NH_2OH)]^+$.

14 Solvate isomerism is also known as .... isomerism when water is solvent.

15 Name the isomerism exists between $[Cr(H_2O)_6]Cl_2$ and $[Cr(H_2O)_5Cl]Cl_2 \cdot H_2O$ complexes.

16 Valence bond theory does not give quantitative interpretation of kinetic stability of coordination compounds. [T/F]

17 Small splitting of *d*-orbitals occurs only in case of strong field ligands. [T/F]

18 $[Co(NH_3)_6]^{3+}$ is called low spin complex, while $[CoF_6]^{3-}$ is called high spin complex. [T/F]

19 $[Mn(CN)_6]^{3-}$ has magnetic moment of two unpaired electrons, while $[MnCl_6]^{3-}$ has magnetic moment of three unpaired electrons. [T/F]

20 What will be the theoretical value of magnetic moment (μ) when CN^- ligands join Fe^{3+} ion to yield complex?

21 Ligands for which $\Delta_o < P$ are known as .... field ligands and form .... spin complexes.

22 Chelates are more stable than non-chilated complex. [T/F]

23 Name the ligand which has two different donar atoms and either of them participates in the complex.

24 The number of unpaired electrons in $[Cr(H_2O)_6]^{3+}$ is ....

25 On heating $[Ti(H_2O)_6]Cl_3$, violet colour changes to .... while water turns the colour of anhydrous copper sulphate to ....

26 .... and .... are the coordination compounds of magnesium and iron which have biological significance.

27 Name the type of bonding takes place in $Fe(CO)_5$.

28 Impure nickel is converted to $[Ni(CO)_4]$ which is decomposed to yield pure nickel. This is an example of purification of metal with the help of coordination compounds. [T/F]

29 Name the formula of complex ion of Ag is involved in the black and white photography. [T/F]

30 Articles can not be electroplated with silver and gold from $[Ag(CN)_2]^-$ and $[Au(CN)_2]^-$ solution. [T/F]

Topical Questions

Werner's Theory of Coordination Compounds

1 Given, the molecular formula of some hexa coordinated complex. **NCERT Pg 119**

A. $CoCl_3 \cdot 6NH_3$ B. $CoCl_3 \cdot 5NH_3$

C. $CoCl_3 \cdot 4NH_3$

If the number of coordinated NH_3 molecules in *A*, *B* and *C* respectively are 6, 5 and 4, the primary valency, in (*A*), (*B*) and (*C*) respectively.

(a) 6, 5 and 4 (b) 3, 2 and 1
(c) 0, 1 and 2 (d) 3, 3 and 3

2 Which one of the following complexes will consume more equivalents of aqueous solution of $AgNO_3$? **NCERT Pg 119**

(a) $Na_3[CrCl_6]$ (b) $[Cr(H_2O)_5Cl]Cl_2$
(c) $[Cr(H_2O)_6]Cl_3$ (d) $Na_2[CrCl_5(H_2O)]$

3 The primary and secondary valences of chromium in the complex ion, dichlorodioxalato chromium (III) respectively are **NCERT Pg 119**

(a) 3 and 4 (b) 4 and 3 (c) 6 and 3 (d) 3 and 6

4 One mole of $Co(NH_3)_5Br_3$ gives 3 moles of ions on dissolution in water. One mole of this reacts with two moles of $AgNO_3$ to give two moles of AgBr. The complex is **NCERT Pg 119**

(a) $[Co(NH_3)_4Br_2]Br \cdot NH_3$ (b) $[Co(NH_3)_4Br_2]Br_2 \cdot NH_3$
(c) $[Co(NH_3)_5Br]Br_2$ (d) $[Co(NH_3)_3Br_3] \cdot 2NH_3$

5 Coordination complex *X* gives white ppt. with $AgNO_3$ solution while its isomer *Y* gives white ppt. but with $BaCl_2$. Two compounds are isomer of $CuClSO_4 \cdot 5NH_3$. The possible formula of *X* and *Y* are **NCERT Pg 119**

	X	*Y*
(a)	$[Cu(NH_3)_5SO_4]Cl$	$[Cu(NH_3)_5Cl]SO_4$
(b)	$[Cu(NH_3)_5Cl]SO_4$	$[Cu(NH_3)_5SO_4]Cl$
(c)	$[Cu(NH_3)_4ClSO_4]NH_3$	$[Cu(NH_3)_5Cl]SO_4$
(d)	$[Cu(Cl)_5NH_3]SO_4$	$[Cu(Cl)_4(NH_3)SO_4]Cl$

6 Both Co^{3+} and Pt^{4+} have a coordination number of six. Which of the following pairs of complexes will show approximately the same electrical conductance for their 0.001 M aqueous solution? **NCERT Pg 119**

(a) $CoCl_3 \cdot 4NH_3$ and $PtCl_4 \cdot 4NH_3$
(b) $CoCl_3 \cdot 3NH_3$ and $PtCl_4 \cdot 5NH_3$
(c) $CoCl_3 \cdot 6NH_3$ and $PtCl_4 \cdot 5NH_3$
(d) $CoCl_3 \cdot 6NH_3$ and $PtCl_4 \cdot 3NH_3$

7 On the basis of the following observations made with aqueous solutions. **NCERT Pg 119**

Formula	Moles of AgCl precipitated per mole of the compounds with excess $AgNO_3$
I. $PdCl_2 \cdot 4NH_3$	2
II. $NiCl_2 \cdot 6H_2O$	2
III. $PtCl_2 \cdot 4NH_3$	0
IV. $CoCl_3 \cdot 4NH_3$	1
V. $PtCl_2 \cdot 2NH_3$	0

The secondary valencies of I and III is

(a) 4 and 5 respectively (b) 4 and 6 respectively
(c) 6 and 4 respectively (d) 2 and 4 respectively

8 Which of the following complex can be ionised in solution? **NCERT Pg 119**

I. $[CoCl_3(NH_3)_3]$ II. $[Pt(NH_3)_6]Cl_4$
III. $K_2[PtF_6]$ IV. $K_4[Fe(CN)_6]$

Choose the most appropriate answer from the options given below.

(a) I, II and III (b) II, III and IV
(c) I, III and IV (d) I, II, III and IV

Important Terms Pertaining to Coordination Compounds

9 The correct structure of ethylenediaminetetraacetic acid (EDTA) is **NCERT Pg 121**

(a)
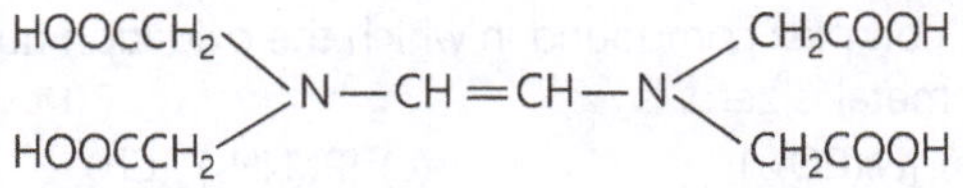

(b)
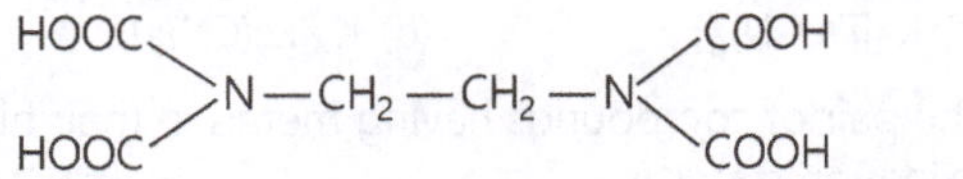

(c)
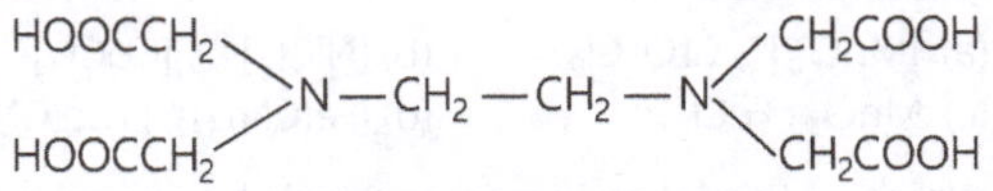

(d)
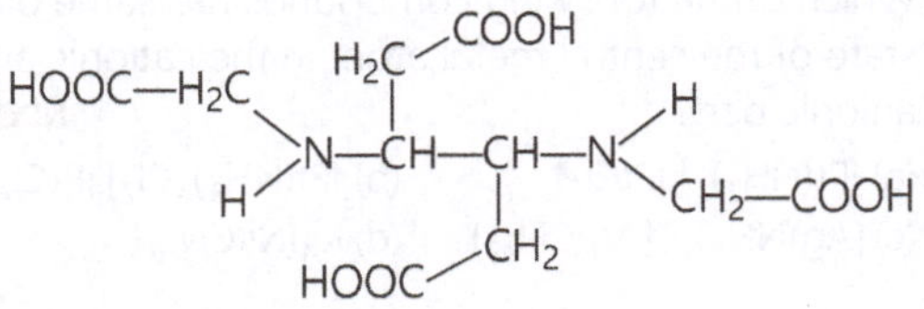

10 Coordination number of Pt and Ni in $[PtCl_6]^{2-}$ and $[Ni(NH_3)_4]^{2+}$ are respectively. **NCERT Pg 121**
(a) 4 and 6 (b) 6 and 4 (c) 4 and 4 (d) 6 and 6

11 In the complex ions, $[Fe(C_2O_4)_3]^{3-}$ and $[Co(en)_3]^{3+}$ the coordination number of Fe and Co is 6. It is because **NCERT Pg 121**
(a) $C_2O_4^{2-}$ and ethane-1,2-diamine are bidentate ligands
(b) $C_2O_4^{2-}$ and ethane-1,2-diamine are ambidentate ligands
(c) $C_2O_4^{2-}$ and ethane-1,2-diamine are polydentate ligands
(d) $C_2O_4^{2-}$ is ambidentate while ethane, 1,2-diamine is polydentate ligand

12 Which of the following statement is incorrect? **NCERT Pg 121**
(a) Coordination entity constitutes a central metal atom or ion bonded to a fixed number of ions or molecules.
(b) Central atom/ions are also referred to as Lewis acids.
(c) Ions or molecules bound to the central atom/ion in the coordination entity are called ligands.
(d) The number of ligating groups is called the ambidentate.

13 The oxidation number of the central atom in a complex is defined as the charge it would carry **NCERT Pg 122**
(a) if all the ligands are removed along with the electron pairs that are donated by the central atom
(b) if all the ligands are removed along with the electron pairs that are shared with the central atom
(c) if only all the ligands are removed from the central metal atom
(d) if only all the electrons pairs are shared with the central atom

14 The oxidation state of Fe in the brown ring complex $[Fe(H_2O)_5NO]SO_4$ is **NCERT Pg 122**
(a) +3 (b) 0 (c) +2 (d) +1

15 A complex compound in which the oxidation number of a metal is zero, is **NCERT Pg 122**
(a) $[Ni(CO)_4]$ (b) $[Pt(NH_3)_4]Cl_2$
(c) $K_3[Fe(CN)_6]$ (d) $K_4[Fe(CN)_6]$

16 The pair of compounds having metals in their highest oxidation states is **NCERT Pg 122**
(a) $[MnO_4]^-$, CrO_2Cl_2 (b) $[NiCl_4]^{2-}$, $[CoCl_4]^-$
(c) MnO_2, $FeCl_3$ (d) $[Fe(CN)_6]^{3-}$, $[Co(CN)_6]^{-3}$

17 Which of the following compounds has same oxidation state of the central metal atom in the cationic and anionic part? **NCERT Pg 122**
(a) $[Pt(NH_3)_4]\ [PtCl_6]$ (b) $[Pt(NH_3)_4Cl_2]\ [PtCl_4]$
(c) $[Ag(NH_3)_2][Ag(CN)_2]$ (d) $K_4[Ni(CN)_6]$

18 Which of the following is correct for $[Co(NH_3)_6]^{3+}$ and $[Co(NH_3)_4Cl_2]^+$ compounds?
(a) Both are homoleptic complexes. **NCERT Pg 122**
(b) Both are heteroleptic complexes.
(c) $[Co(NH_3)_6]^{3+}$ is homoleptic complex; $[Co(NH_3)_4Cl_2]^+$ is heteroleptic complex.
(d) $[Co(NH_3)_6]^{3+}$ is heteroleptic complex; $[Co(NH_3)_4Cl_2]^+$ is homoleptic complex.

19 Which of the following statement is incorrect? **NCERT Pg 122**
(a) Central atom/ion and the ligands attached to it are enclosed in square bracket and is collectively term as coordination sphere.
(b) The ionisable groups are written outside the bracket and are called counter ions.
(c) Most common coordination polyhedra are octahedral, square planar and tetrahedral.
(d) $[Ni(CO)_4]$ is square planar and $[PtCl_4]^{2-}$ is tetrahedral.

Nomenclature of Coordination Compounds

20 If the complex ion is anion, the name of the metal ends with the suffix-ate, for cationic complex ion, **NCERT Pg 123**
(a) the metal is named same as the element
(b) the name of the metal ends with the suffix -ate
(c) the metal is named ends with the suffix-o
(d) the latin name is used

21 The IUPAC name of compound $[Co(en)_2Cl_2]_2SO_4$ is **NCERT Pg 123**
(a) dichloroethylenediamminecobalt (III) sulphate
(b) dichloro*bis*(ethylenediammine)cobalt (III) sulphate
(c) 2-*bis*dichloro(ethylenediammine)cobalt (III) sulphate
(d) dichloro*bis*(ethylenediammine)cobalt (II) sulphate

22 Which among the following will be named as dibromido*bis* (ethylenediammine) chromium (III) bromide ? **NCERT Pg 123**
(a) $[Cr(en)_3]\ Br_3$
(b) $[Cr(en)_2Br_2]Br$
(c) $[Cr(en)Br_4]^-$
(d) $[Cr(en)Br_2]Br$

23 The IUPAC name of the complex $[Pt(NH_3)_3Br(NO_2)Cl]\ Cl$ is **NCERT Pg 123**
(a) triammine chloridobromidonitro platinum (IV) chloride
(b) triammine bromidochloridonitro platinum (IV) chloride
(c) triammine bromidochloridonitro platinum (II) chloride
(d) triammine chloridobromidonitro platinum (II) chloride

24 Ammonia gas does not evolve from the complex $FeCl_3 \cdot 4NH_3$ but it gives white precipitate with aqueous solution of $AgNO_3$. Coordination number of central metal ion in above complex is six. The IUPAC name of the complex is **NCERT Pg 123**

(a) ammonium trichloro triammine iron (III)
(b) tetraammine dichloro iron (III) chloride
(c) dichlorotetraammine ferrate (II) chloride
(d) dichlorotetraammine iron (III) chloride

25 The IUPAC name of the complex $[Pt(NH_3)_2Cl(NH_2CH_3)]Cl$ is **NCERT Pg 123**

(a) diammine (methanamine) chlorido platinum (II) chloride
(b) diamminechlorido (methanamine) platinum (II) chloride
(c) diamminechlorido (aminomethane) platinum (II) chloride
(d) bisammine (methanamine) chlorido platinum (II) chloride

26 According to IUPAC nomenclature sodium nitroprusside is named as **NCERT Pg 123**

(a) sodium pentacyanonitrosyl ferrate (II)
(b) sodium pentacyanonitrosyl ferrate (III)
(c) sodium nitroferricyanide
(d) sodium nitroferrocyanide

27 Consider the following statements. **NCERT Pg 123**

I. The formulas and names adopted for coordination entities are based on recommendations of IUPAC.
II. The charge of cation is balanced by the charge of the anion, while writing the formulas of coordination entities.
III. When ligands are polyatomic their formulas are enclosed in parenthesis.
IV. There should be no space between the ligands and the metal within a coordination sphere.

Choose the correct answer from the options given below.

(a) I and II
(b) II and III
(c) I, II and III
(d) I, II, III and IV

28 Consider the following rules of naming coordination compounds, choose the incorrect option. **NCERT Pg 123**

(a) The cation is named first in both positively and negatively charged coordination entities.
(b) The ligands are named in an alphabetical order after the name of the central atom/ion.
(c) Names of anionic ligands end with o.
(d) Oxidation state of the metal in coordination entity is indicated by roman numerals in parenthesis.

29 Identify the incorrect statement. **NCERT Pg 123**

(a) Molecular formula of tetraamminediaquacobalt (III) chloride is $[Co(NH_3)_4(H_2O)_2Cl_3]$.
(b) $[PtCl_2(en)_2](NO_3)_2$ is the molecular formula of dichlorido*bis*-(ethane-1,2-diammine) platinum (IV) nitrate.
(c) Molecular formula of iron (III) hexacyanoferrate (II) is $Fe_4[Fe(CN)_6]_3$.
(d) If complex name starts with metal, it is an anionic complex.

30 The formula for coordination compound diamminesilver (I) dicyanoargentate (I) is **NCERT Pg 124**

(a) $[Ag(NH_3)_2][Ag(NC)_2]$ (b) $[Ag(NH_3)_3][Ag(CN)_2]$
(c) $[Ag(NH_3)_2][Ag(CN)_3]$ (d) $[Ag(NH_3)_2][Ag(CN)_2]$

31 The formula for coordination compound named as *tris* (ethane-1,2-diammine) cobalt (III) sulphate is **NCERT Pg 124**

(a) $[Co(H_2N\ CH_2CH_2NH_2)_3]_2(SO_4)_3$
(b) $[Co(H_2NCH_2CH_2NH_2)_3]SO_4$
(c) $[Co(H_2NCH_2CH_2NH_3)_2](SO_4)_3$
(d) $[Co(H_2NCH_2CH_2NH_2)_3](SO_4)_3$

32 The name of the complex $[Al(OH)_2(H_2O)_4]SO_4$ is **NCERT Pg 124**

(a) dihydroxotetrahydridealuminium (III) sulphate
(b) tetraaquadihydroxyaluminium (III) sulphate
(c) tetraaquadihydroxyaluminium (IV) sulphate
(d) dihydroxytetrahydridealuminium (IV) sulphate

33 The coordination number of nickel (II) ion is 4.

$$\underset{}{NiCl_2} + \underset{\text{(Excess)}}{KCN} \longrightarrow \underset{\text{(Cyano complex)}}{X}$$

$$X + \underset{\text{(Excess)}}{\text{Conc. HCl}} \longrightarrow \underset{\text{(Chloro complex)}}{Y}$$

The IUPAC name for the complexes X and Y respectively are **NCERT Pg 124**

(a) potassium tetracyanonickel (II) and potassium tetrachloronickel (II)
(b) tetracyanonickel (II) and tetrachloronickel (II)
(c) tetracyano potassium nickelate (II) and tetrachloro potassium nickelate (III)
(d) potassium tetracyanonickelate (II) and potassium tetrachloronickelate (II)

34 Consider the following compound and statements regarding the given coordination compound $[Co(H_2NCH_2CH_2NH_2)_3]_2(SO_4)_3$.

I. Counter anion in the molecule is sulphate.
II. Charge on complex cation must be + 2.
III. Neutral molecule in the compound is ethane-1,2-diammine.

Choose the incorrect statement and marks the correct options given below. NCERT Pg 121, 122
(a) Only II (b) Only III (c) II and III (d) I and III

Isomerism in Coordination Compounds

35 The existence of two different coloured complexes with the composition $[Co(NH_3)_4Cl_2]^+$ is due to NCERT Pg 125
(a) ionisation isomerism (b) linkage isomerism
(c) geometrical isomerism (d) coordination isomerism

36 The complex, $[Pt(py)(NH_3)BrCl]$ will have how many geometrical isomers? NCERT Pg 125
(a) 2 (b) 3 (c) 4 (d) 0

37 Among the following complex ions, the one which shows geometrical isomerism will be NCERT Pg 125
(a) $[Cr(H_2O)_4Cl_2]^+$ (b) $[Pt(NH_3)_3Cl]$
(c) $[Co(NH_3)_6]^{3+}$ (d) $[Co(CN)_5(NC)]^{3-}$

38 The complex that can show *fac*- and *mer*-isomers is NCERT Pg 126
(a) $[Pt(NH_3)_2Cl_2]$ (b) $[Co(NH_3)_3(NO_2)_3]$
(c) $[Co(NH_3)_4Cl_2]^+$ (d) $[CoCl_2(en)_2]$

39 In a coordination entity of the type $[PtCl_2(en)_2]^{2+}$, optical activity is shown by NCERT Pg 126
(a) only *cis*-isomer
(b) only *trans*-isomer
(c) both *cis*- and *trans*-isomers
(d) compound is optically inactive

40 Which one of the following has an optical isomer? (en = ethylenediamine) NCERT Pg 126
(a) $[Zn(en)(NH_3)_2]^{2+}$ (b) $[Co(en)_3]^{3+}$
(c) $[Co(H_2O)_4(en)]^{3+}$ (d) $[Zn(en)_2]^{2+}$

41 Which of the following coordination compounds would exhibit a pair of enantiomer? NCERT Pg 126
(a) Pentaamminenitrocobalt (III) iodide
(b) Diamminedinitroplatinum (II)
(c) *trans*-dicyanobis (ethylenediamine)
(d) *tris*-(ethylenediamine) cobalt (III) bromide

42 Which type of isomerism is associated with the following complex ions ? NCERT Pg 126
I. $[Ni(H_2O)_5NH_3]^{2+}$ II. $[Ni(H_2O)_4(NH_3)_2]^{2+}$
III. $[Ni(H_2O)_3(NH_3)_3]^{2+}$
Choose the most appropriate answer from the options given below.
(a) I and II show geometrical and optical isomerism.
(b) II and III show only optical isomerism.
(c) II and III show only geometrical isomerism.
(d) II and III show geometrical and optical isomerism.

43 In which of the following pairs both the complexes show optical isomerism? NCERT Pg 126
(a) $[Co(NO_3)_3(NH_3)_3]$, *cis*-$[Pt(en)_2Cl_2]$
(b) $[Pt\ Cl(dien)]\ Cl$, $[NiCl_2Br_2]^{2-}$
(c) $[Co(en)_3]Cl_3$, *cis*-$[Co(en)_2Cl_2]Cl$
(d) *cis*-$[Cr(C_2O_4)_2Cl_2]^{3-}$, *cis*-$[Co(NH_3)_4Cl_2]^+$

44 Which type of isomerism arises when bidentate ligands ($L—L$) are present in complexes of formula $[MX_2(L—L)_2]$? NCERT Pg 126
(a) Optical isomerism (b) Geometrical isomerism
(c) Linkage isomerism (d) Solvate isomerism

45 Which type of ligand is contained in linkage isomerism? NCERT Pg 127
(a) Unidentate (b) Bidentate
(c) Polydentate (d) Ambidentate

46 Which of the following pairs represent linkage isomers?
(a) $[Cu(NH_3)_4][PtCl_4]$ and $[Pt(NH_3)_4][CuCl_4]$
(b) $[Pd(PPh_3)_2(SCN)_2]$ and $[Pd(PPh_3)_2(NCS)_2]$
(c) $[Co(NH_3)_5NO_3]SO_4$ and $[Co(NH_3)_5SO_4]NO_3$
(d) $[PtCl_2(NH_3)_4]Br_2$ and $[PtBr_2(NH_3)_4]Cl_2$

47 Coordination isomerism arises NCERT Pg 127
(a) when the counter ion in a complex salt is itself a potential ligand
(b) from the interchange of ligands between cationic and anionic entities of different metal ions present in a complex
(c) when it contains ambidentate ligand
(d) when only water is involved as solvent

48 $[Co(NH_3)_5SO_4]Br$ and $[Co(NH_3)_5Br]SO_4$ are NCERT Pg 127
(a) linkage isomers (b) coordination isomers
(c) ionisation isomers (d) solvate isomers

49 The complexes $[Co(NH_3)_6][Cr(CN)_6]$ and $[Cr(NH_3)_6][Co(CN)_6]$ are the examples of which type of isomerism? NCERT Pg 127
(a) Geometrical isomerism (b) Linkage isomerism
(c) Ionisation isomerism (d) Coordination isomerism

50 Consider the following statements about solvate isomerism NCERT Pg 128
I. It is also known as 'hydrate isomerism' where water is involved as a solvent.
II. It is also similar to ionisation isomerism.
III. Solvate isomers differ by a solvent molecules metal or free molecule in the crystal lattice.
Choose the most appropriate answer from the options given below.
(a) I and II (b) II and III
(c) I and III (d) I, II and III

Bonding in Coordination Compounds

51 When excess of ammonia is added to $CuSO_4$ solution in alkaline medium the deep blue coloured complex is obtained. The complex is **NCERT Pg 128**

(a) tetrahedral and paramagnetic
(b) tetrahedral and diamagnetic
(c) square planar and diamagnetic
(d) square planar and paramagnetic

52 Which one of the following will exhibit minimum paramagnetic behaviour?
(Atomic number of Cr = 24, Mn = 25, Fe = 26, Co = 27)

(a) $[Cr(H_2O)_6]^{2+}$ (b) $[Mn(H_2O)_6]^{2+}$ **NCERT Pg 129**
(c) $[Fe(H_2O)_6]^{2+}$ (d) $[Co(H_2O)_6]^{2+}$

53 Which complex is d^2sp^3-hybridised? **NCERT Pg 129**

(a) $[Co(NH_3)_6]^{3+}$ (b) $[Fe(Cl)_6]^{3-}$
(c) $[Cu(NH_3)_4]^{2+}$ (d) $[CoF_6]^{3-}$

54 Which one of the following is an outer orbital complex and exhibits paramagnetic behaviour? **NCERT Pg 129**

(a) $[Ni(NH_3)_6]^{2+}$ (b) $[Zn(NH_3)_6]^{2+}$
(c) $[Cr(NH_3)_6]^{3+}$ (d) $[Co(NH_3)_6]^{3+}$

55 In an octahedral complex $[Co(NH_3)_6]^{3+}$,

I. the cobalt ion is in +3 oxidation state.
II. it is in $3d^6$ electronic configuration.
III. diamagnetism exists. **NCERT Pg 129**

Choose the most appropriate answer from the options given below.

(a) I and II (b) II and III (c) I and III (d) I, II and III

56 Which of the following statements is true regarding VBT?

I. Metal atom or ion under the influence of ligands can use its $(n-1)$ d, ns, np or ns, np, nd orbitals for hybridisation.
II. Magnetic behaviour of Ti^{3+}, V^{3+} and Cr^{3+} and their coordination entities are similar.
III. Magnetic data agree with maximum spin pairing especially with coordination compounds containing d^6 ions.
IV. $[CoF_6]^{3-}$ is diamagnetic with four electrons, while $[Co(C_2O_4)_3]^{3-}$ is paramagnetic.

Choose the most appropriate answer from the options given below. **NCERT Pg 130**

(a) I and II (b) II and III
(c) I, II and III (d) I, II, III and IV

57 Which among the following ion is paramagnetic in nature? **NCERT Pg 129**

(a) $[Ni(NH_3)_4]^{2+}$ (b) $[Ni(CO)_4]$
(c) $[Co(NH_3)_6]^{3+}$ (d) $[Ni(CN)_4]^{2-}$

58 Select the incorrect statement for $[Co(en)_3]Cl_3$ among the following. **NCERT Pg 129**

(a) Homoleptic complex (b) d^2sp^3-hybridised
(c) Optically active (d) Paramagnetic in nature

59 Which of the following statements are correct for $[Fe(CN)_6]^{3-}$ complex? **NCERT Pg 129**

I. It shows d^2sp^3-hybridisation.
II. It shows high spin complex structure.
III. It is paramagnetic.
IV. It is outer orbital complex.

Choose the most appropriate answer from the options given below.

(a) I and III (b) II and III
(c) III and IV (d) I and II

60 Which of the following complex has square planar geometry? **NCERT Pg 130**

(a) $[CoCl_4]^{2-}$ (b) $[FeCl_4]^{2-}$
(c) $[NiCl_4]^{2-}$ (d) $[PtCl_4]^{2-}$

61 Which of the following is true for the complex $[Ni(CO)_4]$? **NCERT Pg 130**

(a) Hybridisation of Ni is sp^3
(b) High spin complex
(c) Paramagnetic
(d) Square planar

62 What is true about $[MnCl_6]^{3-}$, $[FeF_6]^{3-}$ and $[CoF_6]^{3-}$? **NCERT Pg 130**

I. Each of these are outer orbital complexes.
II. Each of these have sp^3d^2-hybridisation.
III. Each of these are paramagnetic.
IV. $[MnCl_6]^{3-}$, $[FeF_6]^{3-}$ and $[CoF_6]^{3-}$ have four, five and four unpaired electrons respectively.

Choose the most appropriate answer from the options given below.

(a) I, II and III (b) II, III and IV
(c) I, III and IV (d) I, II, III and IV

63 Which of the following descriptions about $[CoF_6]^{3-}$ is correct? **NCERT Pg 130**

(a) sp^3d^2, outer orbital complex, paramagnetic
(b) sp^3d^2, inner orbital complex, diamagnetic
(c) d^2sp^3, inner orbital complex, paramagnetic
(d) d^2sp^3, outer orbital complex, diamagnetic

64 Which of the following facts are related to CFT?

I. The five d-orbitals in an isolated gaseous metal atom/ion have same energy, i.e. they are degenerate.
II. If a spherically symmetrical field of negative charges surrounds the metal atom/ion, the degeneracy is maintained.

III. When this negative field is due to ligands in a complex, it becomes asymmetrical and the degeneracy of the *d*-orbitals is lifted.

IV. This pattern of splitting depends upon the nature of the crystal field.

Choose the correct answer from the options given below. **NCERT Pg 131**

(a) I, II, III and IV (b) II, III and IV
(c) I, II and III (d) I, III and IV

65 Nickel ($Z = 28$) combines with a uninegative monodentate ligand $X^{\ominus}$ to form a paramagnetic complex $[NiX_4]^{2-}$. The number of unpaired electron(s) in the nickel and geometry of this complex ion are respectively. **NCERT Pg 130**

(a) One, tetrahedral (b) Two, tetrahedral
(c) One, square planar (d) Two, square planar

66 Which of the following are the limitations of VBT? **NCERT Pg 131**

I. It does not give quantitative interpretation of magnetic data.

II. It does not distinguish between weak and strong field ligands.

III. It does not explain the colour exhibited by coordination compounds.

IV. It does not give a quantitative interpretation of the thermodynamic or kinetic stabilities of coordination compounds.

Choose the correct answer from the options given below.

(a) I, II, III and IV (b) II, III and IV
(c) I, III and IV (d) I, II and IV

67 $[CoF_6]^{3-}$ is paramagnetic while $[Co(C_2O_4)_3]^{3-}$ is diamagnetic in nature. The reason for the above statement is **NCERT Pg 130**

(a) in $[CoF_6]^{3-}$ four unpaired electrons are present while in $[Co(C_2O_4)_3]^{3-}$ no unpaired electrons are present.
(b) in $[CoF_6]^{3-}$, three unpaired electrons are present while in $[Co(C_2O_4)_3]^{3-}$, no unpaired electrons are present.
(c) $[CoF_6]^{3-}$ shows d^2sp^3-hybridisation hence it is paramagnetic.
(d) $[Co(C_2O_4)_3]^{3-}$ shows sp^3d^2-hybridisation hence it is diamagnetic.

68 The correct order of number of unpaired electrons in the following complexes is

I. $[Cr(H_2O)_6]Br_2$ II. $Na_4[Fe(CN)_6]$
III. $Na_3[Fe(C_2O_4)_3]$ $(\Delta_o > P)$ IV. $(Et_4N)_2[CoCl_4]$

Choose the correct answer from the options given below. **NCERT Pg 132**

(a) (II) ≈ (I) > (IV) > (III) (b) (I) > (IV) > (III) > (II)
(c) (III) > (I) > (IV) > (II) (d) (III) > (I) > (II) > (IV)

69 Among the ligands NH_3, en, CN^- and CO, the correct order of their increasing field strength, is **NCERT Pg 132**

(a) CO < NH_3 < en < CN^- (b) NH_3 < en < CN^- < CO
(c) CN^- < NH_3 < CO < en (d) en < CN^- < NH_3 < CO

70 For d^4 ions, the fourth electron enters one of the e_g orbitals giving the configuration $t_{2g}^3 e_g^1$, when **NCERT Pg 132**

(a) $\Delta_o > P$ (b) $\Delta_o < P$ (c) $\Delta_o = P$ (d) $\Delta_o \geq P$

71 In tetrahedral complexes, low spin complexes are rarely observed. The reason for this observation is **NCERT Pg 133**

(a) $\Delta_o > P$ (b) $\Delta_t < P$ (c) $\Delta_o = P$ (d) $\Delta_t = P$

72 The complex that has highest crystal field splitting energy (Δ), is **NCERT Pg 132**

(a) $[Co(NH_3)_5Cl]Cl_2$ (b) $[Co(NH_3)_5(H_2O)]Cl_3$
(c) $K_3[Co(CN)_6]$ (d) $K_2[CoCl_4]$

73 What is the correct electronic configuration of the central atom in $[Co(ox)_3]^{3-}$ based on crystal field theory? **NCERT Pg 132**

(a) $t_{2g}^4 e_g^2$ (b) $t_{2g}^6 e_g^0$
(c) $e^3 t_2^3$ (d) $e^4 t_2^2$

74 Which of the following complex ions has electrons that are symmetrically filled in both t_{2g} and e_g orbitals? **NCERT Pg 132**

(a) $[FeF_6]^{3-}$ (b) $[Mn(CN)_6]^{4-}$
(c) $[CoF_6]^{3-}$ (d) $[Co(NH_3)_6]^{2+}$

75 The value of the 'spin only' magnetic moment for which of the following ion is 5.9 BM. **NCERT Pg 131**

(a) Ni^{2+} (b) Mn^{2+}
(c) Fe^{2+} (d) Sc^{2+}

76 Choose the correct *d*-orbital configuration in the crystal field of the tetrahedral complex $[NiCl_4]^{2-}$. **NCERT Pg 133**

(a) $e^4 t_2^1$ (b) $e^4 t_2^4$
(c) $e^2 t_2^6$ (d) $e^0 t_2^5$

77 Which of the following complex ion is not expected to absorb visible light? **NCERT Pg 133**

(a) $[Ni(H_2O)_6]^{2+}$ (b) $[Ni(CN)_4]^{2-}$
(c) $[Cr(NH_3)_6]^{3+}$ (d) $[Fe(H_2O)_6]^{2+}$

78 What is the correct order of absorption of wavelength of light in the visible region for the following complexes? **NCERT Pg 133**

(a) $[Ti(H_2O)_6]^{3+} < [Co(NH_3)_6]^{3+} < [Co(CN)_6]^{3-}$
(b) $[Co(CN)_6]^{3-} < [Ti(H_2O)_6]^{3+} < [Co(NH_3)_6]^{3+}$
(c) $[Co(CN)_6]^{3-} < [Co(NH_3)_6]^{3+} < [Ti(H_2O)_6]^{3+}$
(d) $[Ti(H_2O)_6]^{3+} < [Co(CN)_6]^{3-} < [Co(NH_3)_6]^{3+}$

79 The crystal field stabilisation energy (CFSE) is the highest for **NCERT Pg 133**

(a) $[CoF_4]^{2-}$ (b) $[Co(NCS)_4]^{2-}$
(c) $[Co(NH_3)_6]^{3+}$ (d) $[CoCl_4]^{2-}$

80 Ruby, the gemstone **NCERT Pg 134**

I. is aluminium oxide (Al_2O_3).
II. contains 0.5–1% Cr^{3+} ions (d^3).
III. Cr^{3+} ions are randomly distributed in positions normally occupied by Al^{3+}.
IV. Cr^{3+} is incorporated into the alumina lattice as octahedral chromium (III) complex.
V. Metal-Ligand transition gives rise to colour yellow-red

Choose the correct answer from the options given below.

(a) I and II (b) IV and V
(c) II and III (d) I, II, III and IV

Bonding in Metal Carbonyls

81 Which of the following is not true for metal carbonyls? **NCERT Pg 136**

(a) The oxidation state of the metal in the carbonyls is zero.
(b) The secondary carbonyls are obtained from photo-decomposition.
(c) Metal carbonyls are single bonded species.
(d) $d\pi$-$p\pi$ overlap is observed in metal carbonyls.

82 Which of the following statement is true about decacarbonyldimanganese (0)? **NCERT Pg 135**

I. It is made up of two square pyramidal $Mn(CO)_5$ units.
II. It consists a Mn—O—Mn bond.
III. Its structure is

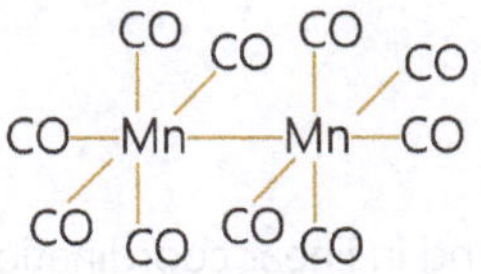

Choose the correct answer from the options given below.

(a) I and II (b) II and III (c) I and III (d) I, II and III

83 In which of the following compound, synergic effect is present? **NCERT Pg 135**

(a) $[Ni(CO)_4]$ (b) $[NiCl_4]^{2-}$
(c) $[CuCl_4]^{2-}$ (d) $[Mn(H_2O)_6]^{2+}$

84 Consider the following figure. **NCERT Pg 136**

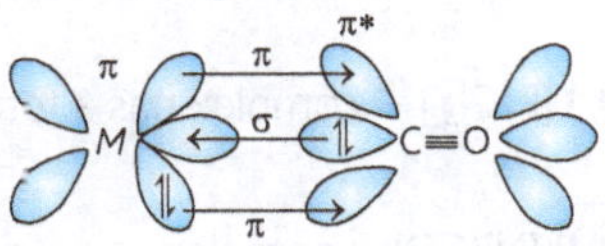

Which type of bond formed between metal and ligand?

(a) Synergic bond
(b) σ-bond only
(c) π-bond only
(d) Covalent bond

Importance and Applications of Coordination Compounds

85 Hardness of water is estimated by simple titration with Na_2EDTA. Which of the following statement is incorrect about it? **NCERT Pg 136**

(a) Ca^{2+} ions form stable complexes with EDTA
(b) Mg^{2+} ions form stable complexes with EDTA
(c) Ca^{2+} and Mg^{2+} ions form unstable complexes with EDTA
(d) The selective estimation of ion is done due to difference of stability complex of Mg and Ca

86 Gold combines with cyanide in the presence of oxygen and water to form coordination entity in aqueous solution. The coordination entity is **NCERT Pg 136**

(a) $[Au(CN)_2]^-$ (b) $[Au(CN)_2]^{2-}$
(c) $[Au(CN)_2]^{3-}$ (d) $[Au(CN)_2]^{4-}$

87 Articles can be electroplated with silver and gold much more smoothly and evenly from solutions of the complexes, respectively are **NCERT Pg 137**

(a) $[Ag(CN)_2]^{2-}$ and $[Au(CN)_2]^{2-}$
(b) $[Ag(CN)_2]^-$ and $[Au(CN)_2]^-$
(c) $[Au(CN)_2]^-$ and $[Ag(CN)_2]^-$
(d) AgCN and AuCN

88 In photography, the use of $Na_2S_2O_3 \cdot 5H_2O$ is **NCERT Pg 137**

(a) for converting AgBr into Ag_2SO_4
(b) for converting AgBr into soluble thiosulphate complex
(c) for converting AgBr into silver thiosulphate
(d) in reduction of Ag metal from AgBr

89 The excess of copper and iron are removed by chelating ligands **NCERT Pg 137**

(a) desferrioxime-B
(b) D-penicillamine
(c) desferrioxime-B and D-penicillamine respectively
(d) D-penicillamine and desferrioxime-B respectively

90 For lead-poisoning, the antidote used is **NCERT Pg 137**

(a) white of an egg
(b) *cis*-platin
(c) nickel
(d) EDTA

Assertion-Reason Questions

Directions (Q. Nos. 1-10) *In the following question Assertion (A) followed by Reason (R) is given below. Choose the correct option out of the choices given below.*

(a) Both A and R are true and R is the correct explanation of A.
(b) Both A and R are true but R is not the correct explanation of A.
(c) A is true but R is false.
(d) A is false but R is true.

1 Assertion (A) $CoCl_3 \cdot 4H_2O$ gives white ppt. with $AgNO_3$.
Reason (R) It contains free chloride ion. NCERT Pg 120

2 Assertion (A) In the coordination compound $[CoCl_2(H_2NCH_2CH_2NH_2)_2]^+$, ethane-1,2-diammine is a neutral molecule.
Reason (R) Oxidation number of Co in the complex ion is +3. NCERT Pg 124

3 Assertion (A) Geometrical isomerism arises in heteroleptic complexes.
Reason (R) Different geometric arrangements of the ligands are possible. NCERT Pg 125

4 Assertion (A) All square planar complexes do not necessarily exhibit geometrical isomerism.
Reason (R) In such complexes metal generally assumes *dsp*^{2}-hybrid state. NCERT Pg 125

5 Assertion (A) Octahedral geometry and diamagnetism exist in $[Co(NH_3)_6]^{3+}$. NCERT Pg 129
Reason (R) It has no unpaired electron.

6 Assertion (A) Linkage isomerism arises in coordination compounds containing ambidentate ligand.
Reason (R) Ambidentate ligand has two different donor atoms. NCERT Pg 127

7 Assertion (A) The coordination complexes $[Ni(CN)_4]^{2-}$ and $[NiCl_4]^{2-}$ have geometries tetrahedral and square planar respectively.
Reason (R) CN^- is a strong ligand and Cl^- is a weak ligand. NCERT Pg 129

8 Assertion (A) $[Cr(H_2O)_6]Cl_2$ and $[Fe(H_2O)_6]Cl_2$ are paramagnetic in nature.
Reason (R) Unpaired electrons are present in their *d*-orbitals. NCERT Pg 129

9 Assertion (A) Potassium ferricyanide is paramagnetic while potassium ferrocyanide is diamagnetic.
Reason (R) Crystal field splitting in ferrocyanide ion is greater than that of ferricyanide ion. NCERT Pg 129, 132

10 Assertion (A) Removal of water from $[Ti(H_2O)_6]Cl_3$ on heating renders it colourless.
Reason (R) In the absence of ligand, crystal field splitting does not occur. NCERT Pg 134

Statement Type Questions

Direction (Q. Nos. 1-6) *In the following questions, two statements (I & II) are given. In the light of the given statements, choose the correct option given below.*

(a) Both Statement I and Statement II are false.
(b) Statement I is true but Statement II is false.
(c) Statement I is false but Statement II is true.
(d) Both Statement I and Statement II are true.

1 Statement I NO_2^- and SCN^- ion are ambidentate ligand.
Statement II SCN^- and NO_2^- ion can coordinate only through N to a central atom or ion. NCERT Pg 121

2 Statement I $[Ag(NH_3)_2][Ag(CN)_2]$ is named as diamminesilver (I) dicyanidoargentate (I).
Statement II In above complex, the silver (I) ion is coordinated by two amine (NH_3) and two cyano (CN) ligands, resulting in linear coordination geometry around silver ion. NCERT Pg 124

3 Statement I The total number of isomers shown by $[Co(en)_2Cl_2]^+$ complex ion is three.
Statement II $[Co(en)_2Cl_2]^+$ complex ion has an octahedral geometry of type $M(AA)_2B_2$. NCERT Pg 126

4 Statement I Optical isomerism is not shown by square planar complexes.
Statement II Square planar complexes are optically active. NCERT Pg 126

5 Statement I $[PtCl_4]^{2-}$ complex has a tetrahedral geometry.
Statement II $[Ni(CO)_4]$ complex has a square planar geometry. NCERT Pg 128

6 **Statement I** The stability of $[Ni(en)_3]Cl_2$ is more than that of $[Ni(NH_3)_6]Cl_2$.

Statement II The geometry of Ni is trigonal bipyramidal in $[Ni(en)_3]Cl_2$. NCERT Pg 131

7 Consider the following statements about these compounds. NCERT Pg 128, 129, 130

$[Mn(CN)_6]^{3-}$, $[Co(NH_3)_6]^{3+}$, $[Cr(H_2O)_6]^{3+}$

I. They have same kind of hybridisation.
II. They have same kind of magnetic behaviour.
III. They form same kind of complexes in reactions.
IV. They have same value of spin only magnetic moment.
V. They have same kind of geometry.

Choose the correct answer from the options given below.
(a) I, II and IV (b) II, III and IV
(c) I, III and V (d) III, IV and V

8 Which of the following statements is/are incorrect? NCERT Pg 122, 123, 125, 136

I. Stereoisomers have different chemical formula, chemical bonds and same spatial arrangement.
II. Homoleptic carbonyls are formed by one kind of donor groups.
III. Impure nickel is converted to $[Ni(CO)_4]$ which is decomposed to yield pure nickel.
IV. Familiar colour reactions given by metal ions with the chelating igands form the basis for their detection and estimation.
V. There should be some space between the ligands and the metal within a coordination sphere.

Choose the correct answer from the options given below.
(a) I and III (b) I, II and III
(c) IV and V (d) I and V

9 Which of the following statements are incorrect? NCERT Pg 132, 133

I. The '*g*' subscript is used for the octahedral complexes which have centre of symmetry.
II. Low spin tetrahedral complexes are not found because CFSE is greater than pairing energy.
III. CFT attributes the colour of coordination compounds to *d*-*d* transition of the electron.
IV. In presence of ligand, crystal field splitting does not occur and, hence the substance is colourless.

Choose the correct answer from the options given below.
(a) I and II (b) I, II and IV
(c) II and IV (d) III and IV

10 Which of the following statements are incorrect? NCERT Pg 132, 133, 137

I. If $\Delta_o < P$, low spin state is more stable.
II. CO is a very weak ligand.
III. Tetrahedral complexes exhibit nearly 50% CFSE value than octahedral complexes.
IV. The colour of a complex depends on the nature of ligands.
V. Wilkinson catalyst is a complex of rhodium metal.

Choose the correct answer from the options given below.
(a) I, II and III (b) I, III and IV
(c) I and II (d) II, III and IV

Matching Type Questions

1 Match the Column I with Column II. NCERT Pg 133

Column I (Complex)		Column II (Colour)	
A.	$[Co(NH_3)_6]^{3+}$	1.	Violet
B.	$[Ni(H_2O)_5]^{3+}$	2.	Pale blue
C	$[Ti(H_2O)_6]^{3+}$	3.	Yellowish orange
D.	$[Ni(H_2O)_4(en)]^{2+}$	4.	Green

Choose the correct option from the codes given below.

	A	B	C	D
(a)	1	2	3	4
(b)	3	4	1	2
(c)	2	3	4	1
(d)	4	2	3	1

2 Match the complex ions given in Column I with the hybridisation and number of unpaired electrons given in Column II. NCERT Pg 128, 129, 130

Column I (Complex ion)		Column II (Hybridisation, number of unpaired electrons)	
A.	$[Cr(H_2O)_6]^{3+}$	1.	dsp^2, 1
B.	$[Co(CN)_4]^{2-}$	2.	sp^3d^2, 5
C.	$[Ni(NH_3)_6]^{2+}$	3.	d^2sp^3, 3
D.	$[MnF_6]^{4-}$	4.	sp^3d^2, 2

Choose the correct option from the codes given below.

	A	B	C	D
(a)	3	1	4	2
(b)	4	3	2	1
(c)	3	2	4	1
(d)	4	1	2	3

3 Match the Column I with Column II. **NCERT Pg 129, 130**

Column I (Complex)	Column II (Structure and magnetic moment)
A. $[Ag(CN)_2]^-$	1. Square planar and 1.73 BM
B. $[Cu(CN)_4]^{3-}$	2. Linear and zero
C. $[Fe(CN)_6]^{3-}$	3. Octahedral and zero
D. $[Cu(NH_3)_4]^{2+}$	4. Tetrahedral and zero
E. $[Fe(CN)_6]^{4-}$	5. Octahedral and 1.73 BM

Choose the correct option from the codes given below.

	A	B	C	D	E
(a)	1	2	3	4	5
(b)	5	3	1	4	2
(c)	2	4	5	1	3
(d)	3	5	4	2	1

4 Match the Column I with Column II. **NCERT Pg 136, 137**

Column I (Coordination compound)	Column II (Uses in medicinal chemistry)
A. *cis*-platin	1. Removal of excess of Cu
B. EDTA	2. Removal of excess of Fe
C. Desferrioxime-B	3. Lead poisoning
D. D-penicillamine	4. Tumour

Choose the correct option from the codes given below.

	A	B	C	D
(a)	1	2	3	4
(b)	2	4	1	3
(c)	3	1	4	2
(d)	4	3	2	1

5 Match Column I with Column II. **NCERT Pg 137**

Column I (Coordination compound)	Column II (Central metal atom)
A. Chlorophyll	1. Rhodium
B. Blood pigment	2. Cobalt
C. Wilkinson catalyst	3. Magnesium
D. Vitamin B_{12}	4. Iron
	5. Calcium

Choose the correct option from the codes given below.

	A	B	C	D
(a)	3	4	1	2
(b)	3	4	5	1
(c)	4	3	2	1
(d)	3	4	2	1

Numerical Value Questions

1 The conductivity of a solution of complex with formula $CoCl_3(NH_3)_5$ corresponds to 1 : 2 electrolyte, then the primary valency of central metal ion is .... **NCERT Pg 119**

2 The number of stereoisomers possible for $[Co(ox)_2Cl(NH_3)]^{2-}$ is .... [ox = oxalato] **NCERT Pg 125**

3 $[Fe(CN)_6]^{4-}$, $[Ti(CN)_6]^{3-}$, $[Ni(CN)_4]^{2-}$, $[Fe(CN)_6]^{3-}$, $[Co(CN)_6]^{3-}$ **NCERT Pg 129**

Among the given complexes, number of diamagnetic complexes is ....

4 The sum of total number of unpaired electrons present in $[Co(CN)_6]^{4-}$ and $[Co(NH_3)_6]Cl_2$ is .... **NCERT Pg 129**

5 The spin only magnetic moment of the compound $[Ru(H_2O)_6]^{2+}$, if $\Delta_o > P$ would be .... **NCERT Pg 130**

NCERT Exemplar's Questions

1 When 0.1 mole of $CoCl_3(NH_3)_5$ is treated with excess of $AgNO_3$, 0.2 mole of AgCl is obtained. The conductivity of solution will correspond to

(a) 1 : 3 electrolyte (b) 1 : 2 electrolyte
(c) 1 : 1 electrolyte (d) 3 : 1 electrolyte

2 When 1 mole of $CrCl_3 \cdot 6H_2O$ is treated with excess of $AgNO_3$, 3 moles of AgCl are obtained. The formula of the complex is

(a) $[CrCl_3(H_2O)_3] \cdot 3H_2O$ (b) $[CrCl_2(H_2O)_4]Cl \cdot 2H_2O$
(c) $[CrCl(H_2O)_5]Cl_2 \cdot H_2O$ (d) $[Cr(H_2O)_6]Cl_3$

3 What kind of isomerism exists between $[Cr(H_2O)_6]Cl_3$ (violet) and $[Cr(H_2O)_5Cl]Cl_2 \cdot H_2O$ (greyish-green)?

(a) Linkage isomerism (b) Solvate isomerism
(c) Ionisation isomerism (d) Coordination isomerism

4 Due to the presence of ambidentate ligands coordination compounds show isomerism. Palladium complexes of the type $[Pd(C_6H_5)_2(SCN)_2]$ and $[Pd(C_6H_5)_2(NCS)_2]$ are

(a) linkage isomers (b) coordination isomers
(c) ionisation isomers (d) geometrical isomers

5 The stabilisation of coordination compounds due to chelation is called the chelate effect. Which of the following is the most stable complex species?
(a) $[Fe(CO)_5]$ (b) $[Fe(CN)_6]^{3-}$
(c) $[Fe(C_2O_4)_3]^{3-}$ (d) $[Fe(H_2O)_6]^{3+}$

6 The CFSE for octahedral $[CoCl_6]^{4-}$ is 18,000 cm^{-1}. The CFSE for tetrahedral $[CoCl_4]^{2-}$ will be
(a) 18000 cm^{-1} (b) 16000 cm^{-1} (c) 8000 cm^{-1} (d) 20000 cm^{-1}

7 The colour of the coordination compounds depends on the crystal field splitting. What will be the correct order of absorption of wavelength of light in the visible region, for the complexes, $[Co(NH_3)_6]^{3+}$, $[Co(CN)_6]^{3-}$ and $[Co(H_2O)_6]^{3+}$?
(a) $[Co(CN)_6]^{3-} > [Co(NH_3)_6]^{3+} > [Co(H_2O)_6]^{3+}$
(b) $[Co(NH_3)_6]^{3+} > [Co(H_2O)_6]^{3+} > [Co(CN)_6]^{3-}$
(c) $[Co(H_2O)_6]^{3+} > [Co(NH_3)_6]^{3+} > [Co(CN)_6]^{3-}$
(d) $[Co(CN)_6]^{3-} > [Co(NH_3)_6]^{3+} > [Co(H_2O)_6]^{3+}$

8 The correct IUPAC name of $[Pt(NH_3)_2Cl_2]$ is
(a) diamminedichloridoplatinum (II)
(b) diamminedichloridoplatinum (IV)
(c) diamminedichloridoplatinum (0)
(d) dichloridodiammineplatinum (IV)

9 A chelating agent has two or more than two donor atoms to bind to a single metal ion. Which of the following is not a chelating agent?
(a) Thiosulphato
(b) Oxalato
(c) Glycinato
(d) Ethane-1, 2-diamine

10 Which of the following species is not expected to be a ligand?
(a) NO (b) NH_4^+
(c) $NH_2CH_2CH_2NH_2$ (d) CO

Past Exams' Questions

NEET Archive

1. Given below are two statements : **NCERT Pg 130, NEET 2024**

Statement I Both $[Co(NH_3)_6]^{3+}$ and $[CoF_6]^{3-}$ complexes are octahedral but differ in their magnetic behaviour.
Statement II $[Co(NH_3)_6]^{3+}$ is diamagnetic whereas $[CoF_6]^{3-}$ is paramagnetic.

In the light of the above statements, choose the correct answer from the options given below:
(a) Both Statement I and Statement II are true.
(b) Both Statement I and Statement II are false.
(c) Statement I is true but Statement II is false.
(d) Statement I is false but Statement II is true.

2 Match List I with List II. **NCERT Pg 125, NEET 2024**

List I (Complex)		List II (Type of isomerism)	
A.	$[Co(NH_3)_5(NO_2)]Cl_2$	I.	Solvate isomerism
B.	$[Co(NH_3)_5(SO_4)]Br$	II.	Linkage isomerism
C.	$[Co(NH_3)_6][Cr(CN)_6]$	III.	Ionisation isomerism
D.	$[Co(H_2O)_6]Cl_3$	IV.	Coordination isomerism

Choose the correct answer from the options given below:
(a) A-II, B-III, C-IV, D-I (b) A-I, B-III, C-IV, D-II
(c) A-I, B-IV, C-III, D-II (d) A-II, B-IV, C-III, D-I

3 Given below are two statements : **NCERT Pg 122, NEET 2024**

Statement I $[Co(NH_3)_6]^{3+}$ is a homoleptic complex whereas $[Co(NH_3)_4Cl_2]^+$ is a heteroleptic complex.

Statement II Complex $[Co(NH_3)_6]^{3+}$ has only one kind of ligands but $[Co(NH_3)_4Cl_2]^+$ has more than one kind of ligands.

In the light of the above statements, choose the correct answer from the options given below.
(a) Both Statement I and Statement II are true.
(b) Both Statement I and Statement II are false.
(c) Statement I is true but Statement II is false.
(d) Statement I is false but Statement II is true.

4 Homoleptic complex from the following complexes is **NCERT Pg 122, NEET 2023**
(a) diamminechloridonitrito-N-platinum (II)
(b) pentaamminecarbonatocobalt (III) chloride
(c) triamminetriaquachromium (III) chloride
(d) potassium trioxalatoaluminate (III)

5 The IUPAC name of the complex $[Ag(H_2O)_2][Ag(CN)_2]$ is **NCERT Pg 124, NEET 2022**
(a) diaquasilver (II) dicyanidoargentate (II)
(b) dicyanidosilver (I) diaquaargentate (I)
(c) diaquasilver (I) dicyanidoargentate (I)
(d) dicyanidosilver (II) diaquaargentate (II)

6 Ethylene diaminetetraacetate (EDTA) ion is **NCERT Pg 123, NEET 2021**
(a) hexadentate ligand with four O and two N donor atoms
(b) unidentate ligand
(c) bidentate ligand with two N donor atoms
(d) tridentate ligand with three N donor atoms

7 Match List-I with List-II. **NCERT Pg 130, NEET 2021**

	List-I		List-II
A.	$[Fe(CN)_6]^{3-}$	1.	5.92 BM
B.	$[Fe(H_2O)_6]^{3+}$	2.	0 BM
C.	$[Fe(CN)_6]^{4-}$	3.	4.90 BM
D.	$[Fe(H_2O)_6]^{2+}$	4.	1.73 BM

Choose the correct answer from the options given below.

	A	B	C	D		A	B	C	D
(a)	4	2	1	3	(b)	2	4	3	1
(c)	1	3	4	2	(d)	4	1	2	3

8 Match the coordination number and type of hybridisation with distribution of hybrid orbitals in space based on valence bond theory. **NCERT Pg 128, NEET 2020**

	Coordination number and type of hybridisation		Distribution of hybrid orbitals in space
A.	4, sp^3	I.	Trigonal bipyramidal
B.	4, dsp^2	II.	Octahedral
C.	5, sp^3d	III.	Tetrahedral
D.	6, d^2sp^3	IV.	Square planar

Select the correct option.

	A	B	C	D		A	B	C	D
(a)	II	III	IV	I	(b)	III	IV	I	II
(c)	IV	I	II	III	(d)	III	I	IV	II

9 What is the correct electronic configuration of the central atom in $K_4[Fe(CN)_6]$ based on crystal field theory? **NCERT Pg 132, NEET 2019**

(a) $t_{2g}^6 e_g^0$ (b) $e^3 t_2^3$
(c) $e^4 t_2^2$ (d) $t_{2g}^4 e_g^2$

10 The type of isomerism shown by the complex $[CoCl_2(en)_2]$ is **NCERT Pg 126, NEET 2018**

(a) ionisation isomerism (b) coordination isomerism
(c) geometrical isomerism (d) linkage isomerism

11 Correct increasing order for the wavelengths of absorption in the visible region for the complexes of Co^{3+} is **NCERT Pg 133, NEET 2017**

(a) $[Co(en)_3]^{3+}$, $[Co(NH_3)_6]^{3+}$, $[Co(H_2O)_6]^{3+}$
(b) $[Co(H_2O)_6]^{3+}$, $[Co(en)_3]^{3+}$, $[Co(NH_3)_6]^{3+}$
(c) $[Co(H_2O)_6]^{3+}$, $[Co(NH_3)_6]^{3+}$, $[Co(en)_3]^{3+}$
(d) $[Co(NH_3)_6]^{3+}$, $[Co(en)_3]^{3+}$, $[Co(H_2O)_6]^{3+}$

12 Which of these statements about $[Co(CN)_6]^{3-}$ is true? **NCERT Pg 128, CBSE-AIPMT 2015**

(a) $[Co(CN)_6]^{3-}$ has no unpaired electrons and will be in a low-spin configuration.
(b) $[Co(CN)_6]^{3-}$ has four unpaired electrons and will be in a low-spin configuration.
(c) $[Co(CN)_6]^{3-}$ has four unpaired electrons and will be in a high-spin configuration.
(d) $[Co(CN)_6]^{3-}$ has no unpaired electrons and will be in a high-spin configuration.

13 Which of the following complexes is used to be as an anticancer agent? **NCERT Pg 137, CBSE-AIPMT 2014**

(a) *mer*-$[Co(NH_3)_3Cl_3]$ (b) *cis*-$[PtCl_2(NH_3)_2]$
(c) *cis*- $K_2[PtCl_2Br_2]$ (d) Na_2CoCl_4

JEE Main Archive

14 The coordination environment of Ca^{2+} ion in its complex with $EDTA^{4-}$ is **NCERT Pg 121, JEE Main 2024**

(a) tetrahedral (b) trigonal prismatic
(c) square planar (d) octahedral

15 Match List I with List II

	List-I		List-II
A.	$K_2[Ni(CN)_4]$	I.	sp^3
B.	$[Ni(CO)_4]$	II.	sp^3d^2
C.	$[Co(NH_3)_6]Cl_3$	III.	dsp^2
D.	$Na_3[CoF_6]$	IV.	d^2sp^3

Choose the correct answer from the options given below : **NCERT Pg 128, 129, JEE Main 2024**

(a) A-III, B-I, C-II, D-IV (b) A-III, B-I, C-IV, D-II
(c) A-I, B-III, C-II, D-IV (d) A-III, B-II, C-IV, D-I

16 Match List-I with List-II.

	List-I (Complex ion)		List-II (Spin only magnetic moment in B.M.)
A.	$[Cr(NH_3)_6]^{3+}$	I.	4.90
B.	$[NiCl_4]^{2-}$	II.	3.87
C.	$[CoF_6]^{3-}$	III.	0.0
D.	$[Ni(CN_4)]^{2-}$	IV.	2.83

Choose the correct answer from the options given below: **NCERT Pg 130, JEE Main 2024**

(a) A-I, B-IV, C-II, D-III (b) A-II, B-III, C-I, D-IV
(c) A-II, B-IV, C-I, D-III (d) A-IV, B-III, C-I, D-II

17 The mismatched combinations are

A. chlorophyll - Co
B. water hardness - EDTA
C. photography -$[Ag(CN)_2]^-$
D. Wilkinson catalyst - $[(Ph_3P)_3RhCl]$
E. chelating ligand -D-penicillamine

Choose the correct answer from the options given below. **NCERT Pg 137, JEE Main 2023**

(a) A and C (b) D and E (c) A, C, and E (d) A and E

18 If Ni^{2+} is replaced by Pt^{2+} in the complex $[NiCl_2Br_2]^{2-}$, which of the following properties are expected to get changed? **NCERT Pg 125, 128, 130, JEE Main 2023**

A. Geometry B. Geometrical isomerism

C. Optical isomerism D. Magnetic properties

Choose the correct answer from the options given below.

(a) A, B and D (b) A and D (c) A, B and C (d) B and C

19 Which of the following complex has a possibility to exist as meridional isomer? **NCERT Pg 126, JEE Main 2023**

(a) $[Pt(NH_3)_2Cl_2]$ (b) $[Co(NH_3)_3(NO_2)_3]$

(c) $[Co(en)_2Cl_2]$ (d) $[Co(en)_3]$

20 The set which does not have any ambidentate ligand(s) is **NCERT Pg 121, JEE Main 2023**

(a) NO_2^-, $C_2O_4^{2-}$, $EDTA^{4-}$

(b) $EDTA^{4-}$, NCS^-, $C_2O_4^{2-}$

(c) $C_2O_4^{2-}$, NO_2^-, NCS^-

(d) $C_2O_4^{2-}$, ethylene diammine, H_2O

21 The correct order of the number of unpaired electrons in the given complexes is

A. $[Fe(CN)_6]^{3-}$ B. $[FeF_6]^{3-}$ C. $[CoF_6]^{3-}$

D. $[Cr(oxalate)_3]^{3-}$ E. $[Ni(CO)_4]$

Choose the correct answer from the options given below : **NCERT Pg 130, JEE Main 2023**

(a) E < A < B < D < C (b) A < E < C < B < D

(c) A < E < D < C < B (d) E < A < D < C < B

22 Match List-I with List-II.

	List-I (Complexes)		List-II (Hybridisation)
A.	$[Ni(CO)_4]$	1.	sp^3
B.	$[Cu(NH_3)_4]^{2+}$	2.	dsp^2
C.	$[Fe(NH_3)_6]^{3+}$	3.	sp^3d^2
D.	$[Fe(H_2O)_6]^{2+}$	4.	d^2sp^3

Codes

(a) A-2, B-1, C-3, D-4 (b) A-2, B-1, C-4, D-3

(c) A-1, B-2, C-4, D-3 (d) A-1, B-2, C-3, D-4

23 Transition metal complex with highest value of crystal field splitting (Δ_o) will be **NCERT Pg 132, JEE Main 2022**

(a) $[Cr(H_2O)_6]^{3+}$ (b) $[Mo(H_2O)_6]^{3+}$

(c) $[Fe(H_2O)_6]^{3+}$ (d) $[Os(H_2O)_6]^{3+}$

24 Given below are two statements.

Statement I $[Ni(CN)_4]^{2-}$ is square planar and diamagnetic complex with dsp^2-hybridisation for Ni but $[Ni(CO)_4]$ is tetrahedral paramagnetic and with sp^3-hybridisation for Ni.

Statement II $[NiCl_4]^{2-}$ and $[Ni(CO)_4]$ both have same *d*-electron configuration have same geometry and are paramagnetic.

In light the above statements, choose the correct answer from the options given below. **NCERT Pg 128, JEE Main 2022**

(a) Both Statement I and Statement II are true.

(b) Both Statement I and Statement II are false.

(c) Statement I is correct but Statement II is false.

(d) Statement I is false but Statement II is true.

25 Given below are two statements. **NCERT Pg 134, JEE Main 2021**

Statement I The identification of Ni^{2+} is carried out by dimethyl glyoxime in the presence of NH_4OH.

Statement II The dimethyl glyoxime is a bidentate neutral ligand.

In the light of the above statements, choose the correct answer from the options given below.

(a) Both Statements I and II are true.

(b) Both Statements I and II are false.

(c) Statement I is true but Statement II is false.

(d) Statement I is false but Statement II is true.

Skill Boosters

1. The complex $[Fe(H_2O)_5NO]^{2+}$ is formed in the brown ring test for nitrates when freshly prepared $FeSO_4$ solution is added to aqueous solution of $NO_3^{\ominus}$ followed by addition of conc. H_2SO_4. Select the incorrect statement about this complex.

(a) Colour change is due to charge transfer.

(b) It has iron in + 1 oxidation state and nitrosyl as $NO^{\oplus}$.

(c) It has magnetic moment of 3.87 BM confirming three unpaired electrons in Fe.

(d) In complex Fe has d^2sp^3-hybridisation.

2. Magnetic moment of a complex, compound can be determined experimentally and theoretically by using spin only formula. The value of spin only magnetic moment for octahedral complex of the following configuration is 2.84 BM. The electronic configuration which shows given magnetic moment is

(a) d^4 (in weak ligand)

(b) d^2 (in weak field and in strong field ligand)

(c) d^3 (in weak field and in strong field ligand)

(d) d^5 (in strong field ligand)

3. When a metal rod M is dipped into an aqueous colourless concentrated solution of compound N, the solution turns light blue. Addition of aqueous NaCl to the compound N gives a white precipitate O. Addition of aqueous NH_3 dissolves O and light blue solution of metal M gives an intense blue solution. The metal rod M is
(a) Fe (b) Cu
(c) Ni (d) Co

4. Cobalt chloride when dissolved in water forms pink coloured complex X which has octahedral geometry. This solution on treating with conc. HCl forms deep blue complex, Y which has a Z geometry. X, Y and Z respectively are
(a) $X = [Co(H_2O)_4Cl_2]^+$, $Y = [CoCl_4]^{2-}$, Z = tetrahedral
(b) $X = [Co(H_2O)_6]^{2+}$, $Y = [CoCl_6]^{3-}$, Z = octahedral
(c) $X = [Co(H_2O)_6]^{2+}$, $Y = [CoCl_4]^{4-}$, Z = tetrahedral
(d) $X = [Co(H_2O)_6]^{3+}$, $Y = [CoCl_6]^{3-}$, Z = octahedral

5. A coordination complex compound of cobalt has the molecular formula containing five ammonia molecules, one nitro group and two chlorine atoms for one cobalt atom. One mole of this compound produces three mole ions in an aqueous solution. On reacting this solution with excess of $AgNO_3$ solution, we get two moles of AgCl precipitate. The ionic formula for this complex would be
(a) $[Co(NH_3)_5(NO_2)]Cl_2$
(b) $[Co(NH_3)_5Cl][Cl(NO_2)]$
(c) $[Co(NH_3)_4(NO_2)Cl][(NH_3)Cl]$
(d) $[Co(NH_3)_5][(NO_2)_2Cl_2]$

6. Dimethyl glyoxime is added to alcoholic solution of $NiCl_2$. When ammonium hydroxide is slowly added to it, a rosy red precipitate of a complex appears given below.

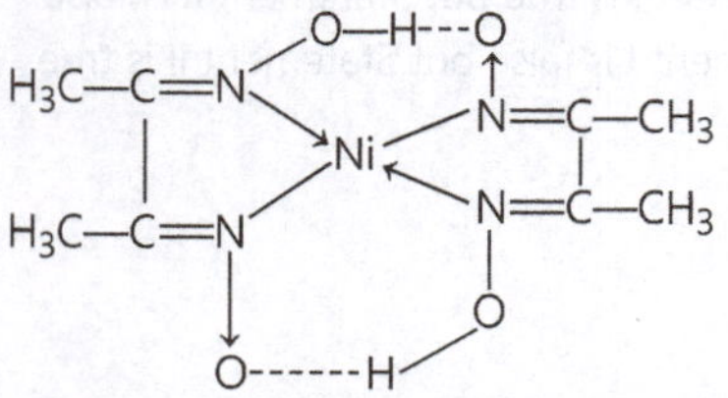

What will be the magnetic behaviour of the above complex?
(a) Paramagnetic (b) Diamagnetic
(c) Ferromagnetic (d) Anti-ferromagnetic

7. In an aqueous solution of $NiBr_2$, if (en) is progressively added in molar ratios such as Ni : en :: 1 : 1, 1 : 2, 1 : 3 then three octahedron complexes x, y, z formed respectively. Select the incorrect statement about x, y and z.
(a) Complex x has minimum value of absorbed wavelength.
(b) Complex y is coloured.
(c) Complex z has maximum number of chelates.
(d) All three are paramagnetic outer orbital complexes.

8. The coordination number of Ni^{2+} is 4.

$$NiCl_2 + 4KCN\ (\text{excess}) \longrightarrow \underset{(P)}{K_2[Ni(CN)_4]} + 2KCl$$

$$K_2[Ni(CN)_4] + \text{Conc. HCl (excess)} \longrightarrow \underset{(Q)}{K_2[Ni(Cl)_4]} + 4HCN$$

Predict the magnetic nature of P and Q.
(a) Both are diamagnetic.
(b) P is diamagnetic and Q is paramagnetic with one unpaired electron.
(c) P is diamagnetic and Q is paramagnetic with two unpaired electrons.
(d) Both are paramagnetic.

9. Simplified absorption spectra of three complexes [I, II and III] of M^{n+} ion are provided below; their λ_{max} values are marked as P, Q and R respectively. The correct match between the complexes and their λ_{max} value is

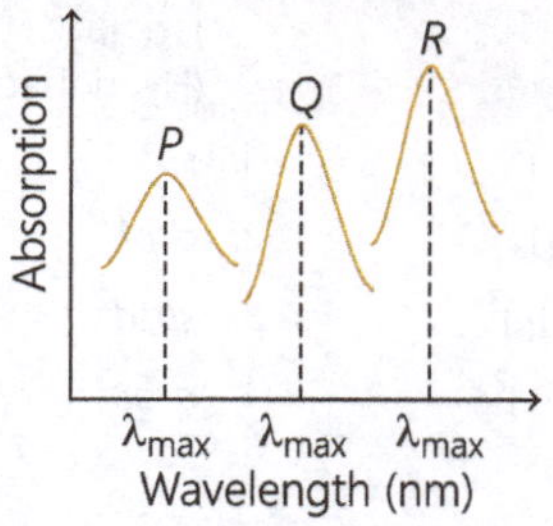

I. $[M(NCS)_6]^{(-6+n)}$ II. $[MF_6]^{(-6+n)}$ III. $[M(NH_3)_6]^{n+}$
(a) P-(III), Q-(I), R-(II)
(b) P-(II), Q-(I), R-(III)
(c) P-(II), Q-(III), R-(I)
(d) P-(I), Q-(II), R-(III)

Correct Codes

Topical Questions

1 (b)	2 (c)	3 (d)	4 (c)	5 (a)	6 (c)	7 (b)	8 (b)	9 (c)	10 (b)
11 (a)	12 (d)	13 (b)	14 (d)	15 (a)	16 (a)	17 (c)	18 (c)	19 (d)	20 (a)
21 (b)	22 (b)	23 (b)	24 (b)	25 (b)	26 (a)	27 (d)	28 (b)	29 (a)	30 (d)
31 (a)	32 (b)	33 (d)	34 (a)	35 (c)	36 (b)	37 (a)	38 (b)	39 (a)	40 (b)
41 (d)	42 (c)	43 (c)	44 (b)	45 (d)	46 (b)	47 (b)	48 (c)	49 (d)	50 (d)
51 (d)	52 (d)	53 (a)	54 (a)	55 (d)	56 (c)	57 (a)	58 (d)	59 (a)	60 (d)
61 (a)	62 (d)	63 (a)	64 (a)	65 (b)	66 (a)	67 (a)	68 (b)	69 (b)	70 (b)
71 (b)	72 (c)	73 (b)	74 (a)	75 (b)	76 (b)	77 (b)	78 (c)	79 (c)	80 (d)
81 (d)	82 (c)	83 (a)	84 (a)	85 (c)	86 (a)	87 (b)	88 (b)	89 (d)	90 (d)

Assertion-Reason

1. (a)	2. (b)	3. (a)	4. (b)	5. (a)	6. (a)	7. (d)	8. (a)	9. (c)	10. (a)

Statement Type

1. (b)	2. (d)	3. (d)	4. (b)	5. (a)	6. (b)	7. (c)	8. (d)	9. (c)	10. (c)

Matching Type

1. (b)	2. (a)	3. (c)	4. (d)	5. (a)

Numerical Value

1. (2)	2. (3)	3. (3)	4. (4)	5. (0)

NCERT Exemplar's

1. (b)	2. (d)	3. (b)	4. (a)	5. (c)	6. (c)	7. (c)	8. (a)	9. (a)	10. (b)

Past Exams'

1. (a)	2. (a)	3. (a)	4. (d)	5. (c)	6. (a)	7. (d)	8. (b)	9. (a)	10. (c)
11. (a)	12. (a)	13. (b)	14. (d)	15. (b)	16. (c)	17. (a)	18. (a)	19. (b)	20. (d)
21. (d)	22. (c)	23. (d)	24. (b)	25. (c)					

Skill Boosters

1. (d)	2. (b)	3. (b)	4. (c)	5. (a)	6. (b)	7. (a)	8. (c)	9. (a)

Step by Step

Decoding the Questions

Concept Builders

1 ionisable, negative
2 secondary 3 One
4 True 5 True
6 Lewis acids 7 False
8 False 9 True
10 Trigonal bipyramidal
11 Geometrical isomerism
12 $K_3[Cu(CN)_4]$
13 Three 14 hydrate
15 Solvate isomerism
16 True 17 False
18 True 19 False
20 1.73 BM 21 weak, high
22 True
23 Ambidentate ligand
24 3
25 Colourless, blue
26 Chlorophyll, haemoglobin
27 Synergic 28 True
29 $[Ag(S_2O_3)_2]^{3-}$ 30 False

Topical Solutions

1 (*b*) The primary valency is always satisfied by anion

A. $\underset{(A)}{[Co(NH_3)_6]Cl_3} \longrightarrow [Co(NH_3)_6]^{3+} + 3Cl^-$

∴ Number of primary valency is 3.

B. $\underset{(B)}{[Co(NH_3)_5Cl]Cl_2} \longrightarrow [Co(NH_3)_5Cl]^{2+} + 2Cl^-$

∴ Number of primary valency is 2.

C. $\underset{(C)}{[Co(NH_3)_4Cl_2]Cl} \longrightarrow [Co(NH_3)_4Cl_2]^+ + Cl^-$

∴ Number of primary valency is 1.

Thus, primary valency in (*A*), (*B*) and (*C*) are 3, 2 and 1 respectively.

2 (*c*) $[Cr(H_2O)_6]Cl_3$ contains maximum number of ionisable anion ($3Cl^-$).
Hence, it will consume more equivalents of aqueous solution of $AgNO_3$ and forms three moles of AgCl (white ppt.).

3 (*d*)

4 (*c*) Since, conductivity corresponds to three ions. Thus, it shows that 2 Br^- ions are ionisable.

$$\therefore [Co(NH_3)_5Br]Br_2 \xrightarrow{H_2O} [Co(NH_3)_5Br]^{2+} + 2Br^-$$

$$2Br^- + 2AgNO_3 \longrightarrow 2AgCl + 2NO_3^-$$

So, the complex is $[Co(NH_3)_5Br]Br_2$.

5 (*a*) As, isomer *X* gives white ppt. with $AgNO_3$ solution this shows that it contains Cl^- as counter ion while isomer *Y* gives white ppt. with $BaCl_2$, this suggest that SO_4^{2-} is present as counter ion.
Thus, possible formula of *X* and *Y* are

$$X = [Cu(NH_3)_5SO_4]Cl$$
$$Y = [Cu(NH_3)_5Cl]SO_4$$

6 (*c*) The pair of complexes that give same number of ions on dissociation will show approximately the same electrical conductance for equimolar 0.001 M aqueous solution.
No. of ions :

$[Co(NH_3)_3Cl_3] = 0$ $[Co(NH_3)_6]Cl_3 = 4$
$[Co(NH_3)_4Cl_2]Cl = 2$ $[Pt(NH_3)_4Cl_2]Cl_2 = 3$
$[Pt(NH_3)_5Cl]Cl_3 = 4$ $[Pt(NH_3)_3Cl_3]Cl = 2$

7 (*b*) Secondary valency means coordination number. As complex I precipitates 2 mole of AgCl.
So, the formula of complex will be $[Pd(NH_3)_4]Cl_2$. Similarly, complex III does not precipitate any AgCl. So, the formula will be $[Pt(NH_3)_4Cl_2]$.
So, the secondary valencies of I and III are 4 and 6 respectively.

8 (*b*) Only $[CoCl_3(NH_3)_3]$ complex does not ionised in solution, as no ion is present outside the coordination sphere. Rest all can be ionised.

9 (*c*) 10 (*b*)

11 (*a*) It is because $C_2O_4^{2-}$ and ethane 1, 2-diamine are bidentate ligand.

12 (*d*) Statement (d) is incorrect.
It's corrected form is as follows
The number of ligating groups is called the denticity of the ligand.

13 (*b*)

14 (*d*) Let the oxidation state of Fe in brown ring complex $[Fe(H_2O)_5NO]SO_4$ be *x*.
$[Fe(H_2O)_5NO]^{2+}$

$$\therefore \quad x + 0 + 1 = 2 \Rightarrow x = +1$$

Here, NO exists as a nitrosyl ion (NO^+).

15 (*a*) CO is a neutral ligand.
$[Ni(CO)_4]$

$$x + (0 \times 4) = 0 \Rightarrow x = 0$$

16 (*a*) In $[MnO_4]^-$ and CrO_2Cl_2 oxidation states of Mn and Cr are +7 and +6 respectively.

17 (*c*) $[Ag(NH_3)_2]$ $[Ag(CN)_2]$
Let the oxidation state of Ag be *x*.
In $[Ag(NH_3)_2]^+$, $x + 0 = +1$
In $[Ag(CN)_2]^-$, $x + 2(-1) = -1$
$\Rightarrow$ $x = +1$
Thus, it is the complex in which the central metal atom in cationic and anionic parts have same oxidation state.

18 (*c*) Homoleptic complexes are those complexes which have one type of ligands. e.g. $[Co(NH_3)_6]^{3+}$, whereas heteroleptic complexes are those which have more than one kind of ligand. e.g. $[Co(NH_3)_4Cl_2]^+$.

19 (*d*) Statement given in option (d) is incorrect. Its correct form is $Ni(CO)_4$ is tetrahedral and $[PtCl_4]^{2-}$ is square planar.

20 (*a*)

21 (*b*) Let the oxidation state of Co in given complex be *x*.

$$\therefore \quad x + 2(0) + 2(-1) = +1$$
$$x = +3$$

Thus, the IUPAC name for $[Co(en)_2Cl_2]_2SO_4$ is dichloro *bis* (ethylenediammine) cobalt (III) sulphate.

22 (*b*) Two Br, two (en) and one Cr are parts of the complex. Charge on the complex is +1.
Thus, complex ion is $[Cr(en)_2Br_2]^+$

23 (*b*)

24 (*b*) As the complex $FeCl_3 \cdot 4NH_3$ gives white precipitate with $AgNO_3$, this suggest that Cl is present as counter ion. Since, the coordination number of Fe is 6, so the formula of complex becomes $[Fe(NH_3)_4Cl_2]Cl$.

Therefore, it's IUPAC name will be tetrammine dichloro iron (III) chloride.

25 (*b*)

26 (*a*) The formula of sodium nitroprusside is $Na_2[Fe(CN)_5NO]$.

Oxidation state of Fe be *x*.

$x + 5(-1) + 1 \times (+1) = -2 \Rightarrow x = +2$

Therefore, the name of the complex is sodium pentacyanonitrosyl ferrate(II).

27 (*d*) Statements given in I, II, III and IV are correct.

28 (*b*) Statement (b) is incorrect. It's correct form is as follows

Ligands are named in a alphabetical order before the name of central metal ion.

29 (*a*) The correct form (a) is

The molecular formula tetrammine diaqua cobalt (III) chloride is $[Co(NH_3)_4(H_2O)_2]Cl_3$.

30 (*d*)

31 (*a*) The charge on complex cation must be +3. Since, ethylene-1,2-diammine is a neutral ligand, it must have 3 sulphate. So, the complex formula is $[Co(H_2NCH_2CH_2NH_2)_3]_2(SO_4)_3$.

32 (*b*)

33 (*d*) $\underset{\text{(excess)}}{NiCl_2 + 4KCN} \longrightarrow \underset{\substack{(X)\\ \text{Potassium tetra cyanonickelate (II)}}}{K_2[Ni(CN)_4]} + 2KCl$

$K_2[Ni(CN)_4] + \underset{\text{(conc.)}}{4HCl} \longrightarrow \underset{\substack{(Y)\\ \text{Potassium tetrachloronickelate(II)}}}{K_2[Ni(Cl)_4]} + 4HCN$

34 (*a*) The statement II is incorrect. It's correct form is as follows

Charge on complex cation in the given compound is +3.

35 (*c*) It is due to geometrical isomerism as *cis* and *trans*-forms are present.

36 (*b*) $[Pt(Py)(NH_3)BrCl]$ type complex have three geometrical isomers as

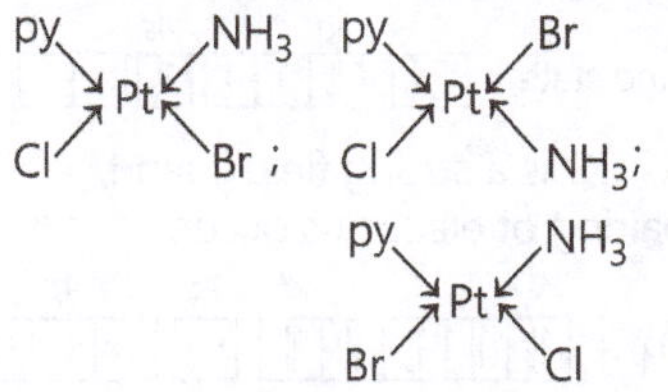

37 (*a*) $[Cr(H_2O)_4Cl_2]^+$ shows geometrical isomerism because it is MA_4B_2 type coordination compound.

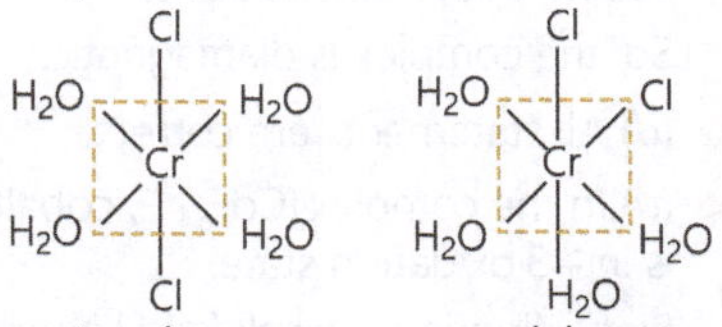

trans-isomer *cis*-isomer

38 (*b*) Octahedral coordination entities with general formula $[Ma_3b_3]$ is $[Co(NH_3)_3(NO_2)_3]$. Thus, it can show *fac* and *mer*-isomers as follows

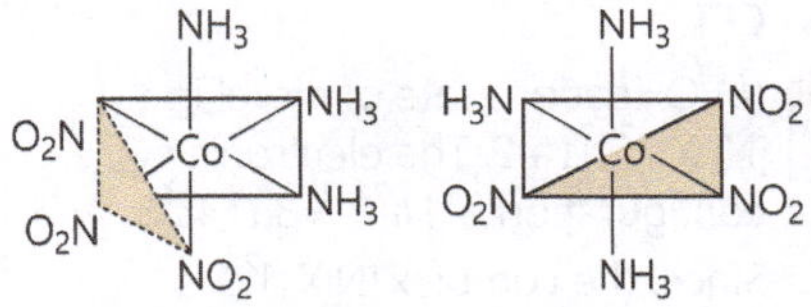

(*fac*) (*mer*)

39 (*a*) In a coordination entity of the type $[PtCl_2(en)_2]^{2+}$, optical activity is shown by *cis*-isomer only.

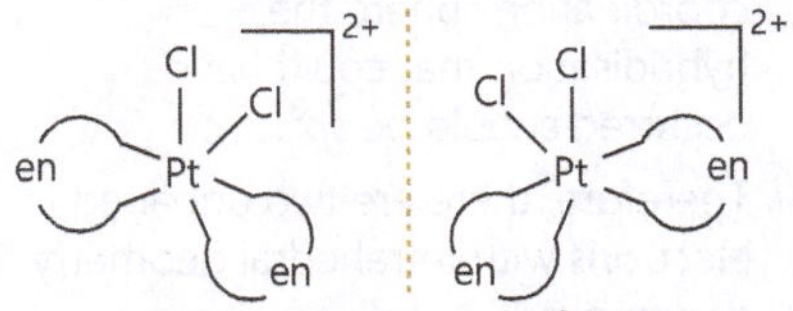

dextro mirror *laevo*

40 (*b*) Complex $[Co(en)_3]^{3+}$ is of type $[M(AA)_3]$ has no plane of symmetry and centre of symmetry, so it is an optical isomer.

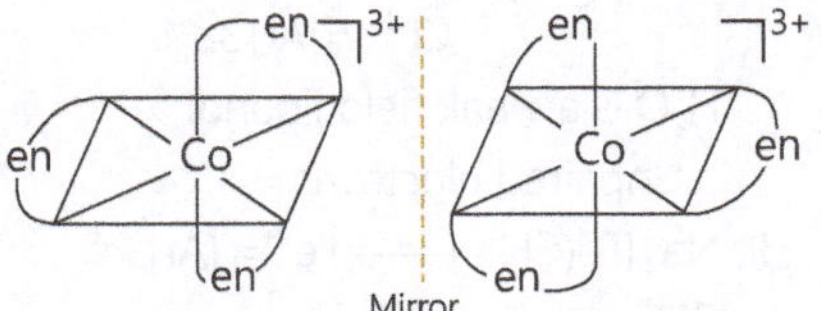

d-form Mirror *l*-form

41 (*d*) *tris*-(ethylenediammine)cobalt (III)bromide, $[Co(en)_3]Br_3$ is of type $M(AA)_3$ exhibits a pair of enantiomers, i.e. optical isomerism.

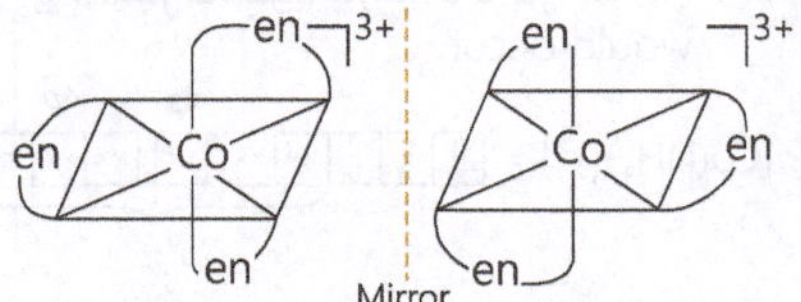

dextro Mirror *laevo*

42 (*c*) (II) and (III) show only geometrical isomerism.

$[Ni(H_2O)_4(NH_3)_2]^{2+}$ show *cis* and *trans*-isomers.

$[Ni(H_2O)_3(NH_3)_3]^{2+}$ show *facial* and *meridional* geometrical isomerism.

43 (*c*)

44 (*b*) Geometrical isomerism arises when bidentate ligands (*L*—*L*) are present in complexes of type $[MX_2(L—L)_2]$.

45 (*d*)

46 (*b*) Linkage isomerism is caused due to presence of ambidentate ligands.

47 (*b*)

48 (*c*) $[Co(NH_3)_5SO_4]Br$ and $[Co(NH_3)_5Br]SO_4$ are ionisation isomers, because there is exchange of Br^- and SO_4^{2-} ions.

49 (*d*) **50** (*d*)

51 (*d*) The reaction involved are

$Cu^{2+} + 2OH^- \longrightarrow Cu(OH)_2$,

$Cu(OH)_2 + 4NH_3 \longrightarrow [Cu(NH_3)_4]^{2+} + 2OH^-$

In $[Cu(NH_3)_4]^{2+}$ oxidation state is +2.

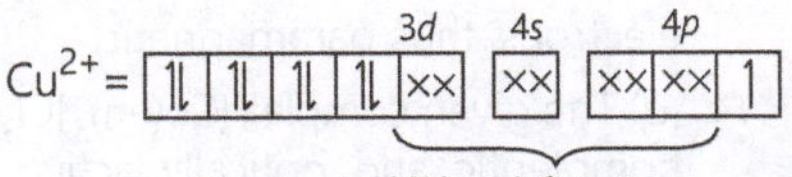

One unpaired $3d\ e^-$ shift to 4p

Thus, the hybridisation is dsp^2, so complex is square planar and paramagnetic.

52 (*d*) Lesser is the number of unpaired electrons, minimum is the paramagnetic behaviour.

$Co^{2+} \longrightarrow 3d^7 4s^0$

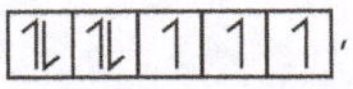

having minimum number of unpaired electrons. (3)

Thus, Co^{2+} in complex $[Co(H_2O)_6]^{2+}$ has minimum paramagnetic behaviour.

53 (*a*) Co is in +3 oxidation state.

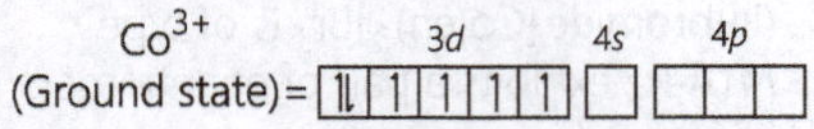

As, NH_3 is a strong ligand, pairing would occur.

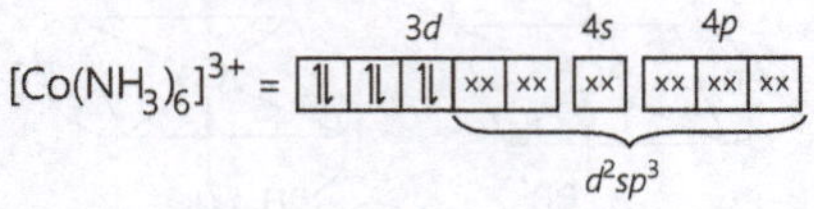

54 (*a*) In $[Ni(NH_3)_6]^{2+}$, $Ni^{2+} = [Ar]3d^8 4s^0$

$[Ni(NH_3)_6]^{2+} =$

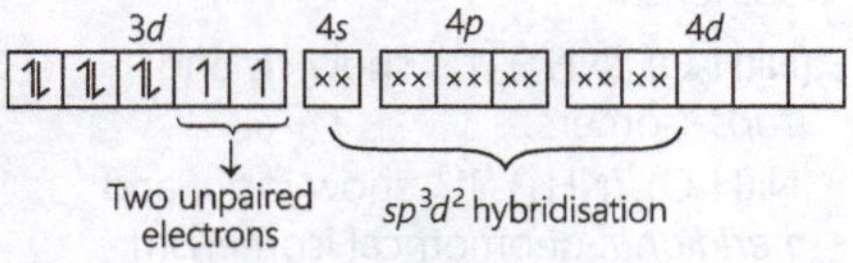

This is an outer orbital complex having paramagnetic character.

55 (*d*) $[Co(NH_3)_6]^{3+}$

Co is in +3 oxidation state, its electronic configuration is $[Ar]3d^6$.

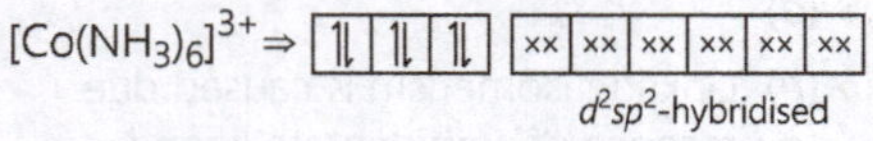

All electrons are paired, hence diamagnetic.

56 (*c*) Among the given statement only IV is incorrect.

$[CoF_6]^{3-}$ is paramagnetic with four unpaired electrons while $[Co(C_2O_4)_3]^{3-}$ is diamagnetic.

57 (*a*) $[Ni(NH_3)_4]^{2+} =$

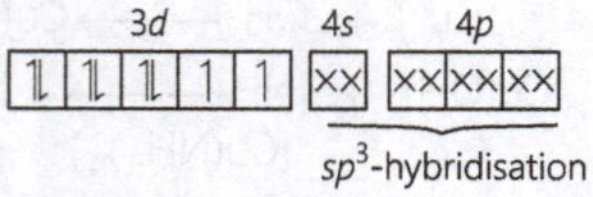

The above complex will be tetrahedral. It has two unpaired electrons, thus paramagnetic.

58 (*d*) The given complex $[Co(en)_3]Cl_3$ is homoleptic and optically active. It does not have any unpaired in Co^{+3}. Thus, it is diamagnetic with d^2sp^3-hybridisation.

59 (*a*) $[Fe(CN)_6]^{3-}$ complex has d^2sp^3 hybridisation, low spin or inner orbital and it is paramagnetic, due to the presence of one unpaired electrons. Thus, Statements I and III are correct.

60 (*d*) Among the given complexes, only $[PtCl_4]^{2-}$ has square planar geometry, while other complexes have tetrahedral geometry.

61 (*a*) The oxidation state of Ni in $[Ni(CO)_4]$ is 0. The electronic configuration of Ni is $3d^8 4s^2$.

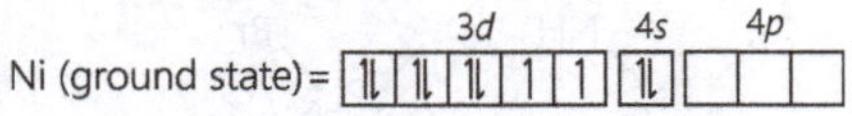

As CO is a strong field ligand, pairing of electrons occur.

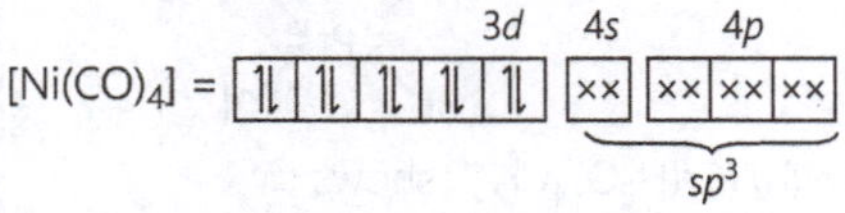

As, it has sp^3 hybridisation, so the geometry is tetrahedral. Since, it has no unpaired electrons.

So, the complex is diamagnetic.

62 (*d*) All statements are correct.

63 (*a*) In the complex $[CoF_6]^{3-}$, cobalt is in +3 oxidation state.

Since, fluorine is weak field ligand, hence no pairing of electron will take place and the complex will be paramagnetic. It will use outer orbital (4*d*) in hybridisation sp^3d^2.

64 (*a*) All statements are correct about CFT.

65 (*b*) Oxidation state of nickel in $[Ni\,X_4]^{2-}$ is +2. The electronic configuration of $Ni^{2+} = 3d^8 4s^0$.

Since, the complex $[NiX_4]^{2-}$ is paramagnetic. So, the ligand must be unable to induce pairing in *d*-orbitals.

To accommodate four ligands in coordination sphere the hybridisation that could have occurred should be sp^3.

Therefore, there are two unpaired electrons with tetrahedral geometry of complex.

66 (*a*) All the given statements explain the limitations of VBT.

67 (*a*)

68 (*b*) I. $[Cr(H_2O)_6]Br_2 \longrightarrow Cr^{2+} = [Ar]3d^4$.

H_2O is a weak field ligand.

$\therefore$ Unpaired electrons = 4

II. $Na_4[Fe(CN)_6] \longrightarrow Fe^{2+} = [Ar]3d^6$

CN^- is a strong field ligand.

Unpaired electrons = 0

III. $Na_3[Fe(C_2O_4)_3] \longrightarrow$

$Fe^{3+} = [Ar]\,3d^5\,\Delta_o > p$ (Given)

Unpaired electrons = 1

IV. $(Et_4N)_2\,[CoCl_4]$

$[CoCl_4]^{2-}$: $Co^{2+} = [Ar]\,3d^7$

$\therefore$ Unpaired electrons = 3

Hence, the correct order of unpaired electrons is I > IV > III > II.

69 (*b*)

70 (*b*) On the basis of crystal field theory, if the configuration is $t_{2g}^3 e_g^1$ then $\Delta_o < P$.

71 (*b*)

72 (*c*) All of the given complex are the octahedral complexes of Co (III) except $K_2[CoCl_4]$, which is a tetrahedral complex of Co (II) (sp^3-hybridised).

We know, $\Delta_t < \Delta_o \quad \left[\because \Delta_t = \frac{4}{9}\Delta_o\right]$

Also, $\Delta_o \propto$ ligand strength, which is based on their positions in the spectrochemical series.

$Cl^- < H_2O < NH_3 < CN^-$

Hence, $K_3[Co(CN)_6]$ will have the highest Δ value.

73 (*b*) In the given complex Co is in +3 oxidation state and oxalate works as strong field ligand.

$\therefore Co^{3+}(d^6) \xrightarrow[\text{SFL}]{\text{OX}} t_{2g}^6 e_g^0$

74 (*a*) $[FeF_6]^{3-}$, oxidation state of Fe = +3

So, $Fe^{3+} = [Ar]3d^5$ where, F^- is a weak field ligand.

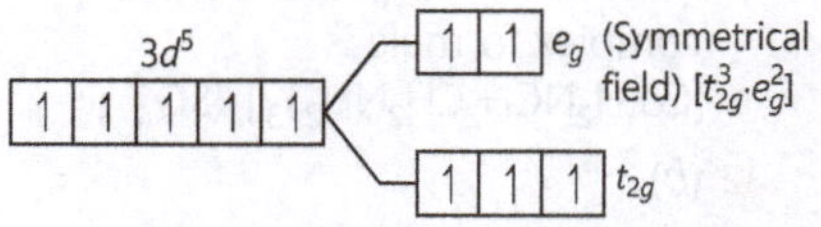

Hence, $[FeF_6]^{3-}$ has symmetrical filled orbitals.

While in other complexes electrons are asymmetrically filled in e_g and t_{2g}.

75 (*b*) The electronic configuration of Mn^{2+} is $3d^5 4s^0$.

So, number of unpaired electron (*n*) = 5.

Therefore, $\mu = \sqrt{n(n+2)} = \sqrt{5 \times 7}$

$= 5.9$ BM

76 (*b*) In tetrahedral complex *e*-orbitals are filled first. It is always high spin. Thus, the configuration is $e^4 t_2^4$.

77 (*b*) In $[Ni(CN)_4]^{2-}$, the oxidation state of Ni is +2. The electronic configuration of Ni^{+2} is $3d^8 4s^0$. As CN^- is a strong field ligand, so pairing will occur.

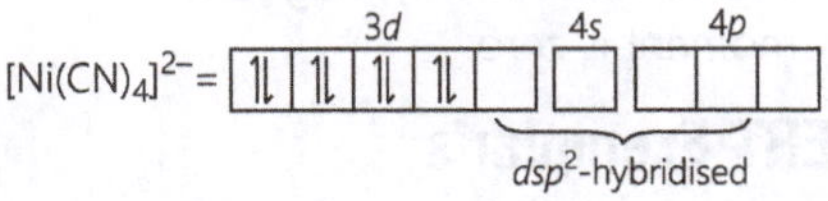

$[Ni(CN)_4]^{2-}$ do not contain unpaired electrons, so no *d*-*d* transition will occur and hence, it will not absorb visible light.

78 (*c*) Weaker the ligand, lesser is the splitting of *d*-orbitals, lesser is the energy and higher is the wavelength of visible light absorbed.

Strength of ligand in the given complexes are $CN^- > NH_3 > H_2O$.

Thus, the correct order is

$[Co(CN)_6]^{3-} < [Co(NH_3)_6]^{3+} < [Ti(H_2O)_6]^{3+}$

79 (*c*) Higher the oxidation state of the metal, greater the crystal field splitting energy. In options (a), (b) and (d), Co is present in + 2 oxidation state and hence in option (c) Co (+3) has a higher value of CFSE.

80 (*d*) Statements I, II, III and IV are correct while V is incorrect. It's correct form is *d*-*d* transition gives rise to the colour.

81 (*d*) Metal carbonyls does not show overlapping.

82 (*c*) Statements I and III are correct but II is incorrect. The correct form is $Mn(CO)_5$ units are joined by a Mn—Mn bond.

83 (*a*)

84 (*a*) The metal-carbon bond in metal carbonyls possess both σ and π-character. The metal to ligand bonding creates a synergic effect which strengthens the bond between CO and the metal.

85 (*c*) Statement given in option (c) is incorrect, while that in (a), (b) and (d) are correct.

86 (*a*) The coordination entity formed is $[Au(CN)_2]^-$.

87 (*b*) The solutions of the complexes are $[Ag(CN)_2]^-$ and $[Au(CN)_2]^-$ respectively for silver and gold.

88 (*b*) $AgBr + 2Na_2S_2O_3 \longrightarrow \underset{\text{Soluble complex}}{Na_3[Ag(S_2O_3)_2]} + NaBr$

89 (*d*)

90 (*d*) The antidote used for lead poisoning is EDTA.

Assertion-Reason

1 (*a*) Both A and R are true and R is the correct explanation of A.

2 (*b*) Ethane-1, 2-diammine is a neutral molecule. As it carries no charge.

Oxidation number of Co in the complex ion is +3.

Thus, both A and R are true but R is not the correct explanation of A.

3 (*a*) Geometrical isomerism arises in heteroleptic complexes because different geometric arrangements of the ligands are possible.

Thus, both A and R are true and R is the correct explanation of A.

4 (*b*) Both A and R are true but R is not the correct explanation of A.

5 (*a*) Both A and R are correct and R is the correct explanation of A.

6 (*a*) Both A and R are true and R is the correct explanation of A.

7 (*d*) $[Ni(CN)]_4^{2-}$ has square planar geometry, while $[NiCl_4]^{2-}$ has tetrahedral geometry because CN^- is a strong ligand whereas Cl^- is a weak ligand.

Thus, A is false but R is true.

8 (*a*) Both A and R are true and R is the correct explanation of A.

9 (*c*) A is true but R is false.

The correct statement of R is that crystal field splitting in ferrocyanide ion is lesser than that of ferricyanide ion.

10 (*a*) Both A and R are true and R is the correct explanation of A.

Statement Type

1 (*b*) Statement I is true but Statement II is false.

The correct form of Statement II is: NO_2^- can coordinate through N and O similarly, SCN^- can coordinate through S and N to a central metal atom/ion.

2 (*d*) Both Statements I and II are true.

3 (*d*) Both Statements I and II is true.

4 (*b*) Statement I is true but statement II is false. The correct form of Statement II is square planar complexes are optical inactive.

5 (*a*) Statements I and II are false. Corrected form are as follows

$[PtCl_4]^{2-}$ complex has a square planar geometry.

$[Ni(CO)_4]$ complex has a tetrahedral geometry.

6 (*b*) Statement I is true but Statement II is false. The correct form of II is

The geometry of Ni is octahedral.

7 (*c*) Statement I, III and V are correct.

These compounds have same hybridisation (d^2sp^3), form same kind of complexes (inner orbital complexes) and also have same kind of geometry (octahedral).

8 (*d*) Statements I and V are incorrect. Their correct form is

- Stereoisomers have same chemical formula, chemical bonds but different spatial arrangement.
- There should not be any space between the ligands and the metals within a coordination sphere.

9 (*c*) Statements II and IV is incorrect.

Their correct form are :

Low spin tetrahedral complexes are not found because CFSE is lower than pairing energy.

In absence of ligand, crystal field splitting does not occur and, hence the substance is colourless.

Rest other statements are correct.

10 (*c*) Statements I and II are incorrect.

Their correct form are as follows

If $\Delta_o < P$, high spin state is more stable and CO is a very strong field ligand.

Rest other statements are correct.

Matching Type

1 (*b*) The correct match is
A-(3), B-(4), C-(1), D-(2).

2 (*a*) The correct match is
A-(3), B-(1) C-(4), D-(2).

A. $[Cr(H_2O)_6]^{3+}$

MOEC (Molecular orbital electronic configuration) of Cr^{3+} in $[Cr(H_2O)_6]^{3+}$ is

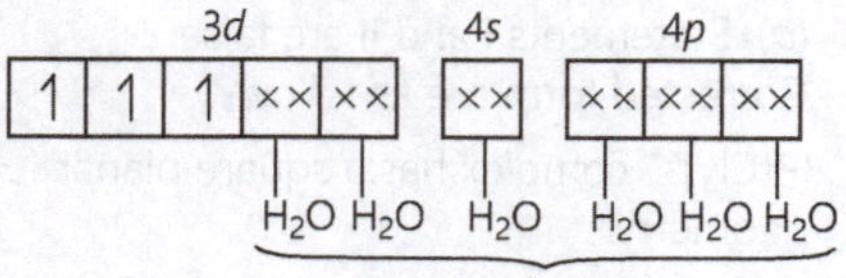

n (number of unpaired electrons) = 3

B. $[Co(CN)_4]^{2-}$

MOEC of Co^{2+} in $[Co(CN)_4]^{2-}$ is

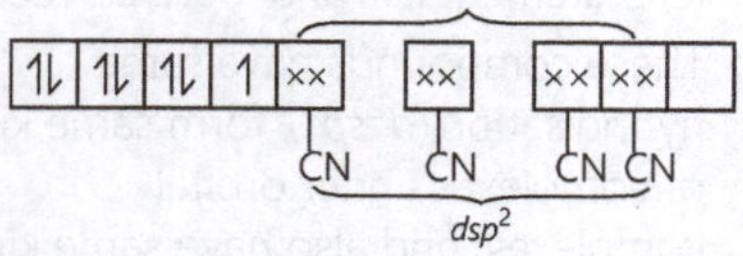

Hybridisation = dsp^2 and $n = 1$

C. $[Ni(NH_3)_6]^{2+}$

MOEC of Ni^{2+} in $[Ni(NH_3)_6]^{2+}$ is

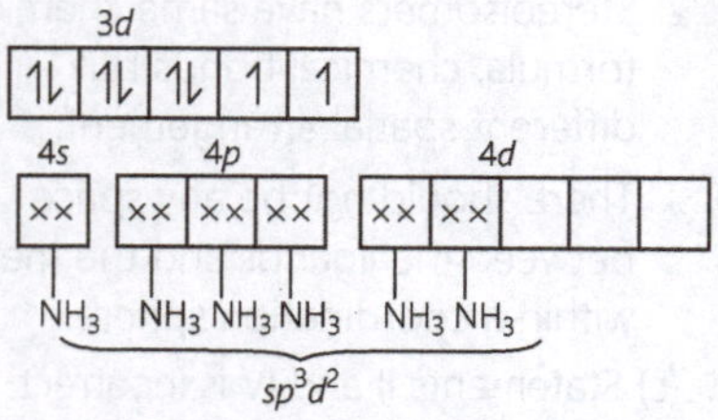

Hybridisation = sp^3d^2 and $n = 2$

D. $[MnF_6]^{4-}$

MOEC of Mn^{2+} in $[MnF_6]^{4-}$ is

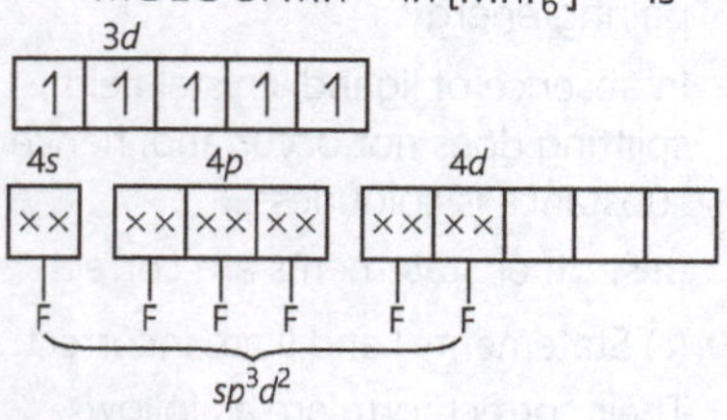

Hybridisation = $sp^3d^2 \Rightarrow n = 5$

3 (*c*) The correct match is
A-(2), B-(4), C-(5), D-(1), E-(3).

4 (*d*) The correct match is
A-(4), B-(3), C-(2), D-(1).

5 (*a*) The correct match is
A-(3), B-(4), C-(1), D-(2).

Numerical Value

1 (2) The complex is
$[CoCl(NH_3)_5]^{2+}2Cl^-$.
Thus, the primary valency is 2.

2 (3) $[Co(ox)_2Cl(NH_3)]^{2-}$ shows geometrical isomerism hence, present in *cis* and *trans* form.

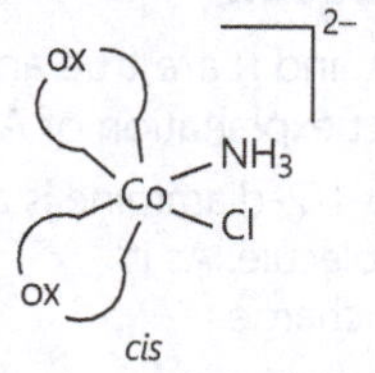

cis

Present in *d*- and *l*- form.

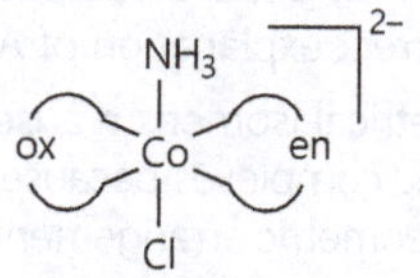

trans

Therefore, total number of stereoisomers possible for $[Co(ox)_2Cl(NH_3)]^{2-}$ is 3.

3 (3)

Complex	Valence shell configuration	Magnetic nature
$[Fe(CN)_6]^{4-}$	$3d^6$ (pairing)	Diamagnetic
$[Ti(CN)_6]^{3-}$	$3d^1$	Paramagnetic
$[Ni(CN)_4]^{2-}$	$3d^8$ (pairing)	Diamagnetic
$[Fe(CN)_6]^{3-}$	$3d^5$ (pairing)	Paramagnetic
$[Co(CN)_6]^{3-}$	$3d^6$ (pairing)	Diamagnetic

4 (4) For the complex $[Co(CN)_6]^{4-}$

Co is in + 2 oxidation state. So,
$Co^{2+} = [Ar]\,3d^7\,(t_{2g}^6 e_g^1)$

Thus, no. of unpaired electron is 1.

Now, for the complex $[Co(NH_3)_6]Cl_2$

Again Co is in + 2 oxidation state.

Thus, $Co^{2+} = [Ar]\,3d^7\,(t_{2g}^5 e_g^2)$

Thus, number of unpaired electron is 3.

So, sum of total number of unpaired electron = 4

5 (0) Oxidation state of Ru in $[Ru(H_2O)_6]^{2+}$ is + 2.

$\therefore$ Ru^{2+} in $[Ru(H_2O)_6]^{2+}$: $4d^6$

$\Rightarrow t_{2g}^6 e_g^0$ since $\Delta_o > P$

As number of unpaired electron is zero.

Therefore, spin only magnetic moment is zero.

NCERT Exemplar's

1 (*b*) In the given reaction, when 0.1 mole of $CoCl_3(NH_3)_5$ is treated with excess of $AgNO_3$, 0.2 mole of AgCl is obtained thus, there must be two free chloride ions in the solution of electrolyte.

So, molecular formula of complex will be $[Co(NH_3)_5Cl]\,Cl_2$ and electrolytic solution must contain $[Co(NH_3)_5Cl]^{2+}$ and two Cl^- as constituent ions. Therefore, it is 1 : 2 electrolyte.

$$[Co(NH_3)_5Cl]Cl_2 \longrightarrow [Co(NH_3)_5Cl]^{2+}(aq) + 2Cl^-(aq)$$

2 (*d*) 1 mole of $AgNO_3$ precipitates one free chloride ion (Cl^-). Here, 3 moles of AgCl are precipitated by excess of $AgNO_3$. Hence, there must be three free Cl^- ions. So, the formula of the complex is $[Cr(H_2O)_6]Cl_3$.

3 (*b*) Coordination compound $[Cr(H_2O)_6]Cl_3$ and $[Cr(H_2O)_5Cl]H_2O \cdot Cl_2$ are solvate isomers, because water is exchanged by chloride ion. This is why both of them show different colour on exposure to sunlight that is $[Cr(H_2O)_6]Cl_3$ shows violet colour, whereas $[Cr(H_2O)_5Cl]Cl_2 \cdot H_2O$ shows greyish green colour.

4 (*a*)

5 (*c*) In the given question only $[Fe(C_2O_4)_3]^{3-}$ is a coordination compound which contains oxalate ion as a chelating ligand. Hence, it stabilises coordination compound by chelating Fe^{3+} ion.

6 (*c*) CFSE for octahedral and tetrahedral complexes are closely related to each other by formula $\Delta_t = \frac{4}{9}\Delta_o$.

where, Δ_o = CFSE for octahedral complex, Δ_t = CFSE for tetrahedral complex

According to question,
$\Delta_o = 18000\ cm^{-1}$

$\therefore \Delta_t = \frac{4}{9}\Delta_o = \frac{4}{9} \times 18000 \text{ cm}^{-1}$
$= 4 \times 2000 \text{ cm}^{-1} = 8000 \text{ cm}^{-1}$

7 (c) As strength of ligand increases crystal field splitting energy increases and wavelength decreases. Thus, the correct order is $[Co(H_2O)_6]^{3+} > [Co(NH_3)_6]^{3+} > [Co(CN)_6]^{3-}$

8 (a)

9 (a) Among the given ligand, thiosulphato ($S_2O_3^{2-}$) is not a chelating ligand because geometrically it is not favourable for ($S_2O_3^{2-}$) to chelate a metal ion.

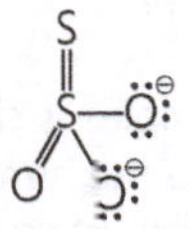

10 (b) Ligand must donate a pair of electron or loosely held electron pair to metal and form a $M—L$ bond.

e.g. $:\ddot{N}=O$, $\ddot{N}H_2CH_2CH_2\ddot{N}H_2$, $:CO$.

Among the given ligands NH_4^+ does not have any pair of electron. Hence, NH_4^+ is not a ligand.

Past Exams'

1. (a) Both Statement I and Statement II are true.
2. (a) The correct match is A-II, B-III, C-IV, D-I.
3. (a) Both Statement I and Statement II are true.
4. (d) Complexes in which a metal is bound to only one kind of donor groups are known as homoleptic complexes. Among the given option potassium trioxalatoaluminate (III) is an example of homoleptic complex.
5. (c) The complex $[Ag(H_2O)_2]$ $[Ag(CN)_2]$ has coordination number 2 and oxidation state of +1 in both cationic and anionic parts. Hence, its IUPAC name is diaquasilver (I) dicyanidoargentate (I).
6. (a) EDTA is a hexadentate ligand with four 'O' and two 'N' donor atoms.
7. (d) The correct match is A-4, B-1, C-2, A-3.

$[Fe(CN)_6]^{3-} \Rightarrow$ Oxidation number of Fe = +3

Electronic configuration of $Fe^{3+} \rightarrow [Ar]3d^5 4s^0$

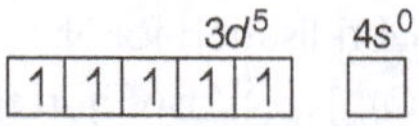

CN^- is a strong field ligand, so pairing of electrons occurs.

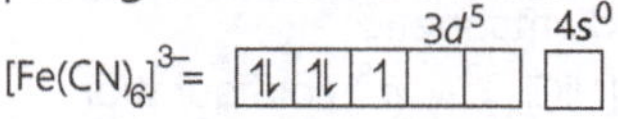

Number of unpaired electrons = 1

$\mu_s = \sqrt{n(n+2)} = \sqrt{1(1+2)} = \sqrt{3}$
$= 1.73$ BM

Similarly, we use can find out the magnetic moment for other given complexes.

8. (b) The correct match is A-III, B-IV, C-I, D-II.
9. (a) In $K_4[Fe(CN)_6]$,
$Fe^{2+} = [Ar]3d^6 4s^0$.

CN^- is a strong field ligand and as it approaches the metal ion, the electrons must pair up. Hence, the electronic configuration of the central atom in $K_4[Fe(CN)_6]$ is $t_{2g}^6 e_g^0$.

10. (c) In $[CoCl_2(en)_2]$, coordination number of Co is 6 with octahedral geometry as $M(AA)_2B_2$ [where, AA is bidentate ligand].

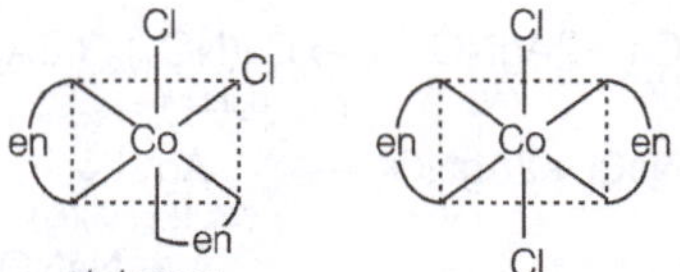

cis-isomer (Optically active) *trans*-isomer (Optically inactive)

Thus, $[CoCl_2(en)_2]$ show geometrical isomerism.

11. (a) According to spectrochemical series the CFSE of ligands attached with Co^{3+} ion is in the order en > NH_3 > H_2O (From spectrochemical series)

$\because$ Wavelength of absorbed light $(\lambda) \propto \frac{1}{\Delta_o}$

$\therefore$ The order of wavelength of absorption in the visible region will be : en < NH_3 < H_2O

or, $[Co(en)_3]^{3+} < [Co(NH_3)_6]^{3+} < [Co(H_2O)_6]^{3+}$

12. (a) $[Co(CN)_6]^{3-}$
$Co^{3+} = [Ar]3d^6$

CN^- is a strong field ligand and as it approaches the metal ion, the electrons must pair up as shown below.

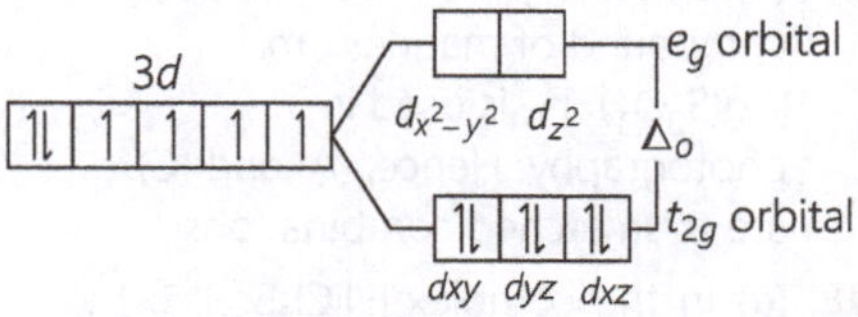

$\therefore [Co(CN)_6]^{3-}$ has no unpaired electron and will be in a low spin configuration.

13. (b) *cis*-platin is known as anti-cancer agent. The formula for *cis*-platin is *cis*-$[PtCl_2(NH_3)_2]$.
14. (d) The coordination environment of Ca^{2+} ion in its complex with $EDTA^{4-}$ is octahedral. As $EDTA^{4-}$ is hexadentate ligand.

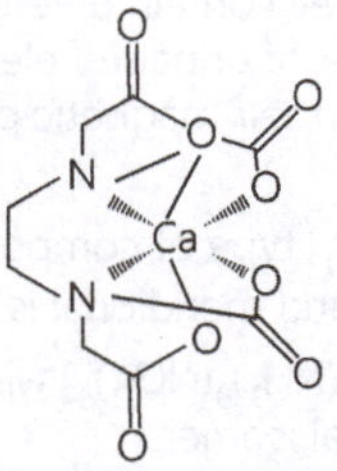

15. (b) The correct match is A-III, B-I, C-IV, D-II.
   - $K_2[Ni(CN)_4]$ is dsp^2 hybridised as Ni is present in +2 oxidation state and CN^- is a strong field ligand.
   - $[Ni(CO)_4]$ is sp^3 hybridised as Ni is present in zero oxidation state.
   - $[Co(NH_3)_6]Cl_3$, Co is d^2sp^3 hybridised as NH_3 acts as strong field ligand for Co^{3+}.
   - $Na_3[CoF_6]$ is sp^3d^3 hybridised act as strong field ligand.

16 (c) The correct match is A-II, B-IV, C-I, D-III

A. $[Cr(NH_3)_6]^{3+} \Rightarrow Cr^{3+}; 3d^3$
unpaired electron, $n = 3$
Using the formula, spin only magnetic moment
$\mu = \sqrt{n(n+2)} = 3.87$ B.M.

B. $[NiCl_4]^{2-} \Rightarrow Ni^{2+} = 3d^8$
unpaired electron, $n = 2$,
$\mu = \sqrt{2(2+2)} = 2.83$ B.M.

C. $[CoF_6]^{3-} \Rightarrow Co^{3+}; 3d^6$
unpaired electron,
$n = 4, \mu = \sqrt{4(4+2)} = 4.90$ B.M.

D. $[Ni(CN)_4]^{2-} \Rightarrow Ni^{2+}; 3d^8$
unpaired electron, $n = 0$,
$\mu = \sqrt{0(0+2)}$ B.M. $= 0$

17. (*a*) Chlorophyll is a coordination compound of magnesium. $[Ag(S_2O_3)_2]^{3-}$ is used in photography. Hence, (A) and (C) are mismatched combinations.

18. (*a*) In the complex $[NiCl_2Br_2]^{2-}$, the geometry is tetrahedral due to presence of weak field ligands and do not show geometrical isomerism.

- However for complex $[PtCl_2Br_2]^{2-}$ the geometry is square planar and it shows two geometrical isomers.
- Both the complex species are optically inactive.
- Also they contain different number of unpaired electron. Hence, their magnetic properties varies.

19. (*b*) $[MA_3B_3]$ type of compound exists as facial and meridional isomer.

Thus, $[Co(NH_3)_3(NO_2)_3]$ will exist as meridional isomer.

20. (*d*) Ambidentate ligand has two different donor atoms and either of the two donor atom is attached to the metal during complex formation. Only NCS^- and NO_2^- are ambidentate ligand while $C_2O_4^{2-}$, ethylene diamine, H_2O and EDTA are not ambidentate ligand.

21. (*d*) The correct order of the number of unpaired electrons in the given complexes is E < A < D < C < B.

(A) $[Fe(CN)_6]^{3-}$ $n = 1$
(B) $[FeF_6]^{3-}$ $n = 5$
(C) $[CoF_6]^{3-}$ $n = 4$
(D) $[Cr(oxalate)_3]^{3-}$ $n = 3$
(E) $[Ni(CO)_4]$ $n = 0$

22. (*c*) The correct match is
A-1, B-2, C-4, D-3.

23. (*d*) For the same oxidation state, CFSE increasing order will be
$3d < 4d < 5d$.
So, $[Os(H_2O)_6]^{3+}$ has maximum CFSE (Δ_o).

24. (*b*) Both the statements I and II are false. Their corrected form is given as

I. $[Ni(CN)_4]^{2-}$ is square planar and diamagnetic with dsp^2-hybridisation for Ni but $[Ni(CO)_4]$ is tetrahedral, diamagnetic and with sp^3-hybridisation for Ni.

II. $[Ni(CO)_4] : d^{10}$ configuration (after excitation), SFL, tetrahedral splitting (sp^3), diamagnetic.
$[NiCl_4]^{2-} : d^8$ configuration, WFL, tetrahedral splitting (sp^3), paramagnetic (2 unpaired e^-)

25. (*c*) Statement I is true but Statement II is false. The correct form of Statement II is given as, DMG is an anionic bidentate ligand.

Skill Boosters

1. (*d*) In complex $[Fe(H_2O)_5NO]^{2+}$, Fe has sp^3d^2 hybridisation.

2. (*b*) In d^2 (in weak field and in strong field ligand)

			e_g^0
1	1		t_{2g}^2

d^2

n(no. of unpaired electron $= 2$)

$\mu_{eff} = \sqrt{n(n+2)} = \sqrt{2(2+2)} = \sqrt{8}$
$= 2.89$ BM

3. (*b*) The reactions involved is represented as

$$\underset{(M)}{Cu} + \underset{(N)}{2AgNO_3} \longrightarrow \underset{\text{Light blue}}{Cu(NO_3)_2} + 2Ag$$

$$NaCl + \underset{(N)}{2AgNO_3} \longrightarrow \underset{\text{(White ppt.)(O)}}{AgCl \downarrow} + NaNO_3$$

$$2AgCl + 2NH_3(aq) \longrightarrow [Ag(NH_3)_2]^+$$

$$Cu(NO_3)_2 + 4NH_3(aq) \longrightarrow \underset{\text{(Deep blue colour)}}{[Cu(NH_3)_4](NO_3)_2}$$

Hence, the metal rod *M* is copper.

4. (*c*) The reaction is represented as

$$CoCl_2 + 6H_2O \longrightarrow [Co(H_2O)_6]Cl_2 \xrightarrow{\text{(conc.) HCl}} [CoCl_4]^{2-}$$

Thus, $X = [Co(H_2O)_6]^{2+}$, $Y = [CoCl_4]^{2-}$
Z = tetrahedral

5. (*a*) As the complex gives 3 ions in aqueous solution thus, complex should be $[Co(NH_3)_5NO_2]Cl_2$.

$$[Co(NH_3)_5(NO_2)]Cl_2 \rightleftharpoons [Co(NH_3)_5NO_2]^{2+} + 2Cl^-$$

$$2Cl^- + 2AgNO_3 \longrightarrow 2AgCl + 2NO_3$$

6. (*b*) The oxidation state of Ni in the given complex $= +2$
Hybridisation of the complex is dsp^2 because it is a planar molecule. The electronic configuration of Ni^{2+} is $3d^8$. There is no unpaired electrons present. Hence, it is diamagnetic in nature.

7. (*a*)

Complex	No. of rings
$x = [Ni(en)(H_2O)_4]^{2+}$	1
$y = [Ni(en)_2(H_2O)_2]^{2+}$	2
$z = [Ni(en)_3]^{2+}$	3

Stability of complex is directly proportional to the number of chelate rings. i.e. Stability of complex $\propto$ No. of chelate rings.

$$\propto \Delta_{absorbed} \propto \frac{1}{\lambda_{absorbed}}$$

So, complex *x* has maximum value of absorbed wavelength.

8. (*c*) The $K_2[Ni(CN)_4]$, complex ion is $[Ni(CN)_4]^{2-}$ Nickel is present as Ni^{2+}. In $[Ni(CN)_4]^{2-}$ ion, Ni^{2+} is present as follows

3d					4d	4p	
⇅	⇅	⇅	⇅	xx	xx	xx	xx

Unpaired electron is not present, so it is diamagnetic in nature. The $K_2[Ni(Cl)_4]$, complex ion is $[Ni(Cl)_4]^{2-}$ Nickel is present as Ni^{2+}. In $[Ni(Cl)_4]^{2-}$ ion, Ni^{2+} is present as follows

3d					4s	4p		
⇅	⇅	⇅	1	1	xx	xx	xx	xx

Due to presence of unpaired electrons, it is paramagnetic in nature.

9. (*a*) As we know, CFSE $(\Delta_o) = \dfrac{hc}{\lambda}$

$$\Delta_o \propto \frac{1}{\lambda}$$

Power of ligand $\propto \Delta_o \propto \dfrac{1}{\lambda}$

According to spectrochemical series, $F^- < NCS^- < NH_3$.

So, for the given complexes, it is evident from the plot

$$\underset{\substack{(R)\\ [F^-]}}{\lambda_{max}} > \underset{\substack{(Q)\\ [NCS^-]}}{\lambda_{max}} > \underset{\substack{(P)\\ [NH_3]}}{\lambda_{max}}$$

06

Scan for Chemistry Through Concept Master Videos

Haloalkanes and Haloarenes

Topicwise No. of Ques asked in 5 Years (NEET)

Topics	No. of Questions				
	2024	2023	2022	2021	2020
Classification, Nomenclature & Nature of C—*X* Bond	–	1	–	–	–
Methods of Preparation of Haloalkanes & Haloarenes	1	–	1	–	–
Physical Properties	–	–	–	1	–
Chemical Reactions	2	–	1	2	1
Polyhalogen Compounds	–	–	–	–	–

Special Type of Ques Asked In 5 Years (NEET)

Types	Years				
	2024	2023	2022	2021	2020
A-R	–	–	–	–	–
Statement Based	–	–	1	–	–
Matching	–	–	–	–	1

Last 5 Years Weightage (NEET)

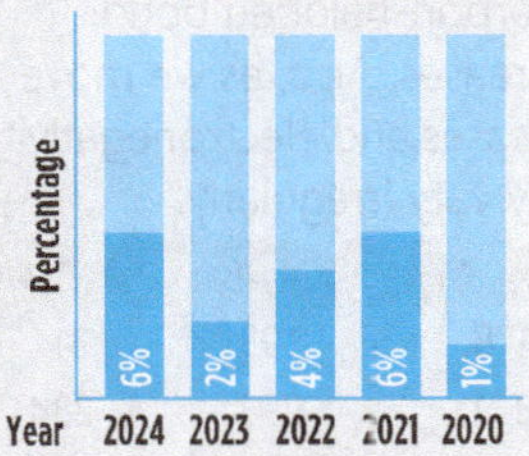

The replacement of hydrogen atom(s) in an aliphatic or aromatic hydrocarbon by halogen atom(s) results in the formation of alkyl halide (haloalkane) or aryl halide (haloarene), respectively.

Haloalkanes contain halogen atom(s) attached to sp^3-hybridised carbon atom of alkyl group, whereas **haloarenes** contain halogen atom(s) attached to sp^2-hybridised carbon atoms of an aryl group.

Classification

Haloalkanes and haloarenes may be classified as follows

On the Basis of Number of Halogen Atoms

They may be classified as mono, di or polyhalogen (tri, tetra etc.) compounds depending on whether they contain one, two or more halogens atoms in their structure. e.g.

C_2H_5X
Monohaloalkane

CH_2X—CH_2X
Dihaloalkane

CH_2X—CHX—CH_2X
Trihaloalkane

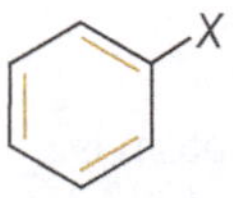

Monohaloarene

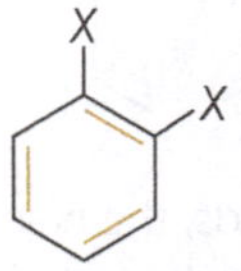

Dihaloarene

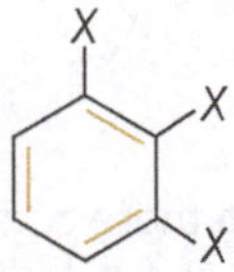

Trihaloarene

On the Basis of Nature of Carbon in C—X Bond

Monohalocompounds may further be classified according to the hybridisation of the carbon atom to which halogen is bonded, as discussed below.

Compounds Containing sp^3 C–X Bond

- **Alkyl halides or haloalkanes** In these compounds, the halogen atom is bonded to an alkyl group. They form a homologous series represented by $C_nH_{2n+1}X$. These are further classified as primary, secondary and tertiary according to the nature of carbon to which halogen is attached.

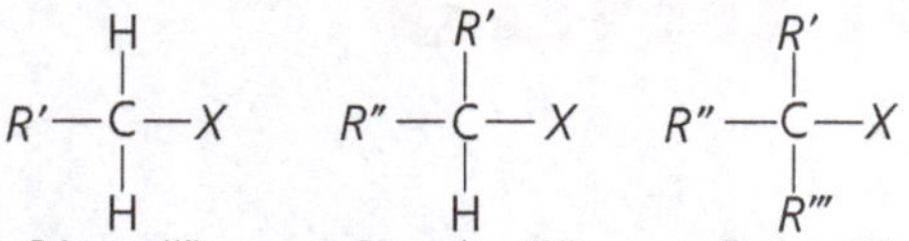

Primary (1°) Secondary (2°) Tertiary (3°)

- **Allylic halides** In these compounds, the halogen atom is bonded to an sp^3-hybridised carbon atom next to carbon-carbon double bond. NEET 2023

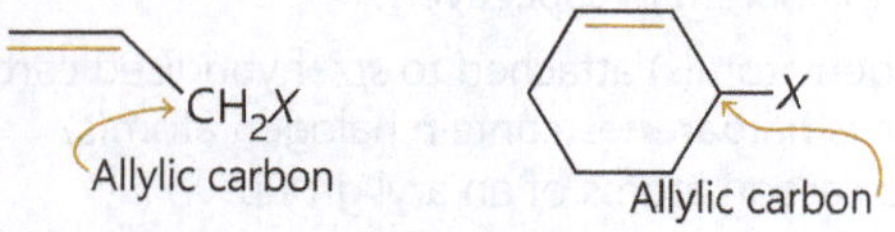

- **Benzylic halides** In these compounds, the halogen atom is bonded to an sp^3-hybridised carbon atom attached to an aromatic ring.

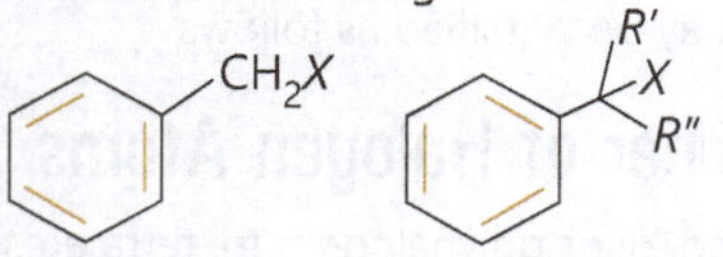

(1°) $R' = CH_3$, $R'' = H$ (2°)
$R' = R'' = CH_3$ (3°)

Compounds Containing sp^2C–X Bond

- **Vinylic halides** In these compounds, the halogen atom is bonded to an sp^2-hybridised carbon atom of carbon-carbon double bond.

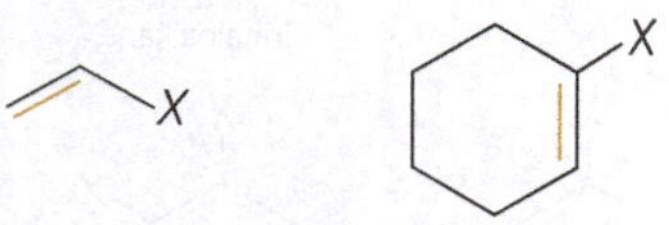

- **Aryl halides** In these compounds, the halogen atom is attached to an sp^2-hybridised carbon atom of an aromatic ring.

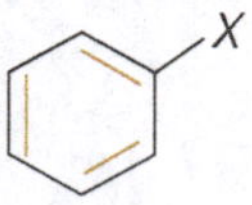

Nomenclature

- The common names of alkyl halides are derived by naming the alkyl group followed by the name of halide.
- In the IUPAC system of nomenclature, alkyl halides are named as halosubstituted hydrocarbons.
- For monohalogen substituted derivatives of benzene, common and IUPAC names are same.
- For dihalogen derivatives, the prefixes *o*-, *m*-, *p*- are used in common system but in IUPAC system, the numerals 1, 2; 1, 3 and 1, 4 are used.

	$CH_3CH_2CH_2Br$	$H_3C—\underset{\displaystyle Cl}{CH}—CH_3$
Common name	*n*-propyl bromide	*Iso*-propylchloride
IUPAC name	1-bromopropane	2-chloropropane

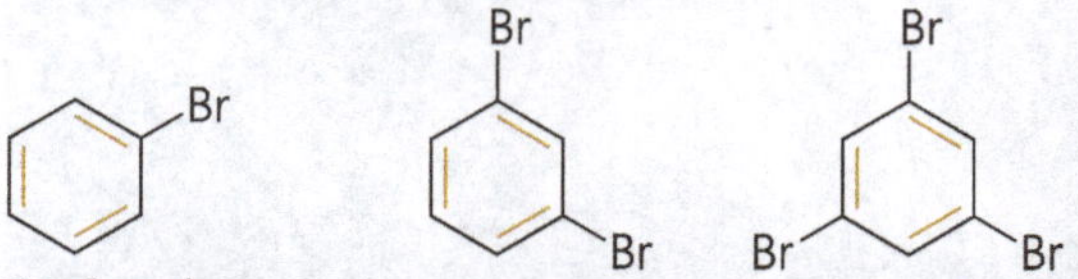

Common name	Bromobenzene	*m*-dibromobenzene	*sym*-tribromobenzene
IUPAC name	Bromobenzene	1,3-dibromobenzene	1,3,5-tribromobenzene

- The dihaloalkanes having the same type of halogen atoms are named as alkylidene or alkylene dihalides. They are further classified as *geminal* halides or *gem*-dihalides (both halogen atoms are present on the same carbon atom) and *vicinal* halides or *vic*-dihalides (halogen atoms are present on the adjacent carbon atoms).

	$H_3C—CHCl_2$	$\underset{\displaystyle Cl}{H_2C}—\underset{\displaystyle Cl}{CH_2}$
Common name	Ethylidene chloride (*gem*-dihalide)	Ethylene dichloride (*vic*-dihalide)
IUPAC name	1, 1-dichloroethane	1, 2-dichloroethane

Nature of C—X Bond

Halogen atoms are more electronegative than carbon, therefore carbon-halogen (C—X) bond of alkyl halide is polarised, i.e. the carbon atom bears a partial positive charge, whereas halogen atom bears a partial negative charge.

$$-\overset{\delta+}{\underset{|}{\overset{|}{C}}}\rightarrow\overset{\delta-}{X}$$

With increase in size of halogen atom, carbon-halogen bond length increases and bond enthalpy decreases. Also, as we move from F to I, the size of halogen atom increases and electronegativity decreases therefore, dipole moment may vary irregularly.

Alkyl halide	$H_3C—F$	$H_3C—Cl$	$H_3C—Br$	$H_3C—I$
Bond length (pm)	139	178	193	214
Bond enthalpy (kJ mol^{-1})	452	351	293	234
Dipole moment (Debye)	1.847	1.860	1.830	1.636

NEET 2021

Methods of Preparation of Haloalkanes

Following method can be used for the preparation of haloalkanes

S.No.		Method	Reaction involved	Important points regarding reaction
1.		**From Alcohol** NEET 2024		
	(i)	1° or 2° alcohol with $HCl + ZnCl_2$	$R—OH + HCl \xrightarrow{ZnCl_2} R—Cl + H_2O$	• With tertiary alcohols catalyst ($ZnCl_2$) is not required. The reaction is conducted by simply shaking the alcohol with conc. HCl at room temperature.
	(ii)	Reaction with $SOCl_2$	$R—OH + SOCl_2 \longrightarrow R—Cl + SO_2 + HCl$	• $SOCl_2$ is preferred because in this reaction alkyl halide is formed along with gases SO_2 and HCl.
	(iii)	Reaction with red P / X_2 where, ($X_2 = Br_2, I_2$)	$R—OH \xrightarrow{\text{Red } P/X_2} R—X$	
	(iv)	Reaction with $NaBr + H_2SO_4$	$R—OH + NaBr + H_2SO_4 \longrightarrow R—Br + NaHSO_4 + H_2O$	
	(v)	Reaction with PX_3	$3R—OH + PX_3 \longrightarrow 3R—X + H_3PO_3$ ($X = Cl, Br$)	
	(vi)	Reaction with PCl_5	$R—OH + PCl_5 \longrightarrow R—Cl + POCl_3 + HCl$	
2.		**From Hydrocarbon**		
	(i)	From alkanes	$CH_3CH_2CH_2CH_3 \xrightarrow[\text{or heat}]{Cl_2/\text{UV light}} CH_3CH_2CH_2CH_2Cl + CH_3CH_2CHClCH_3$	• This reaction occurs through free radical halogenation. The ease of replacement of hydrogen follow the order 3° > 2° > 1°.
	(ii)	From alkene		
	(a)	Addition of hydrogen halide	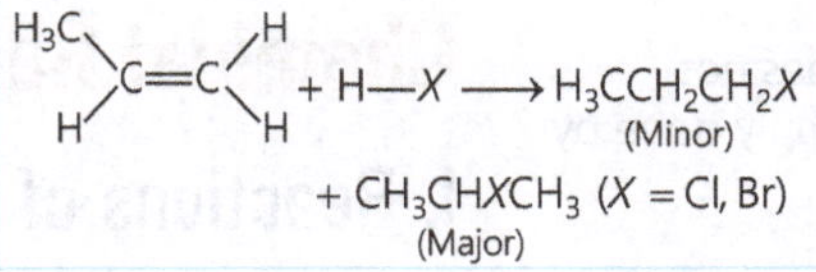	• In two products, only one predominates as per Markovnikov's rule.
	(b)	Addition of halogens	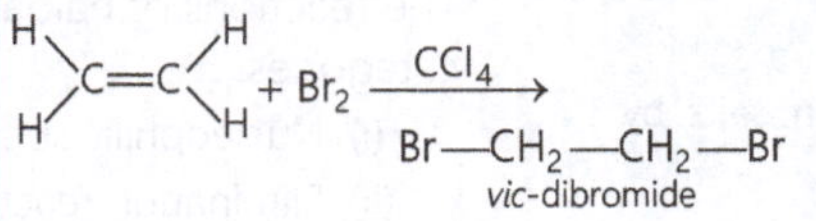	• Addition of bromine in CCl_4 to an alkene resulting in discharge of reddish brown colour of bromine. It is used for detection of double bond.
3.		**Halogen exchange**		
	(a)	Finkelstein reaction	$\underset{(X = Cl, Br)}{R—X} + NaI \xrightarrow[\text{acetone}]{\text{Dry}} R—I + NaX$	• NaCl or NaBr thus formed is precipitated in dry acetone. It facilitates the forward reaction according to Le-Chatelier's principle.
	(b)	Swarts reaction	$\underset{(X = Cl, Br)}{H_3C—X} + \underset{(\text{or } Hg_2F_2 \text{ or } CoF_2 \text{ or } SbF_3)}{AgF} \longrightarrow H_3C—F + AgBr$	

Note
- Good yield of $R—I$ may be obtained by heating alcohols with sodium or potassium iodide in 95% orthophosphoric acid.
- Preparation from alcohols, are not applicable for the preparation of aryl halides because the carbon-oxygen bond in phenols has a partial double bond character.
- Direct iodination is not possible in Finkelstein reaction. It is a reversible reaction, thus it is done in presence of oxidising agents like HNO_3, HIO_3.

Methods of Preparation of Haloarenes

These can be prepared by the following methods.

- **From hydrocarbons by electrophilic substitution** NEET 2022

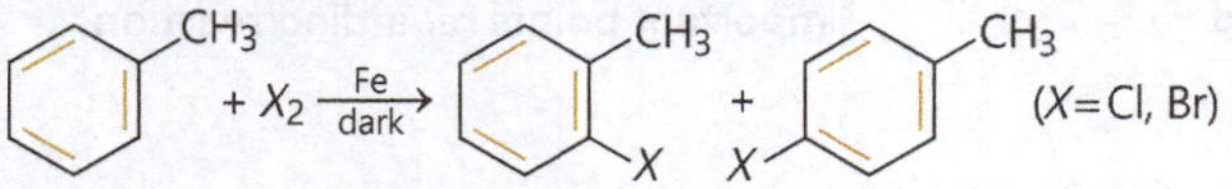

Toluene o-halotoluene p-halotoluene

- The *ortho*-and *para*-isomers can be easily separated due to large difference in their melting points.
- Reactions with iodine are reversible in nature. It requires the presence of an oxidising agent (HNO_3, HIO_4) to oxidise the HI formed during iodination.
- Due to high reactivity of fluorine, fluoro compounds are not prepared by this method.
- **From amines by Sandmeyer's reaction**

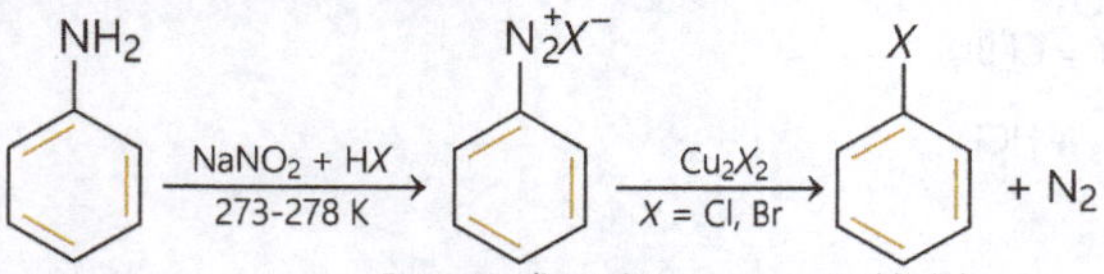

Aniline Benzene diazonium halide Aryl halide

- **From diazonium salt**

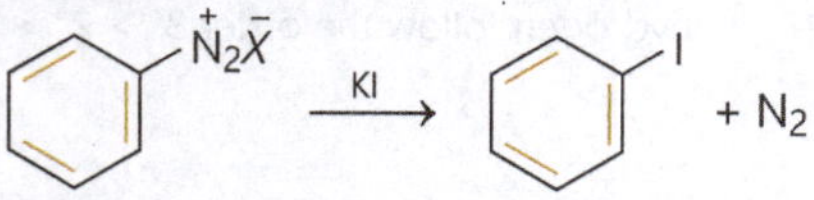

Replacement of diazonium group by iodine does not require the presence of cuprous halide. It is simply done by shaking the diazonium salt with KI.

Marks Maximizer

Fluorobenzene is prepared from arene diazonium salts, by the reaction named as Balz-Schiemann reaction.

$$ArNH_2 \xrightarrow[HBF_4]{HNO_2} Ar\overset{+}{N}_2\overset{-}{B}F_4 \longrightarrow ArF + N_2 + BF_3$$

Physical Properties

- **Colour and odour** Alkyl halides are **colourless**, when pure. Bromides and iodides develop colour when exposed to light. Many volatile halogen compounds have sweet smell.
- **Melting and boiling points** Boiling points of chlorides, bromides and iodides are higher than those of the hydrocarbons of comparable molecular mass. It is due to stronger intermolecular force of attraction.
  - For the same alkyl group, the boiling points of alkyl halides decrease in the order $RI > RBr > RCl > RF$. This is because, with the increase in size and mass of halogen atom, the magnitude of van der Waals' forces increases.
  - The boiling point of isomeric haloalkanes decrease with increase in branching.
  - Boiling point of isomeric dihalobenzenes are very nearly the same. However, the *para*-isomers have high melting point as compared to their *ortho* and *meta*-isomers. It is due to symmetry of *para*-isomers that fits in crystal lattice better as compared to *ortho* and *meta*-isomers.

e.g.

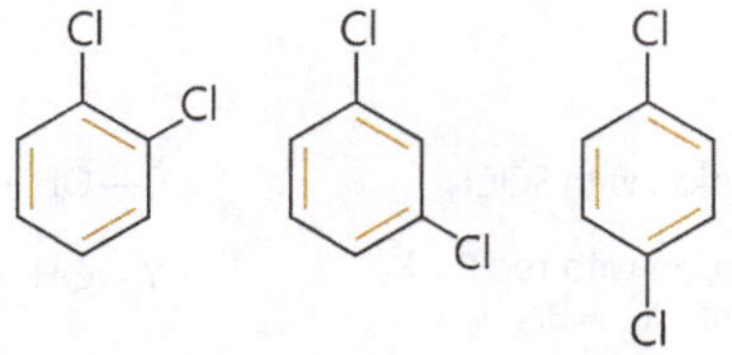

b.p/K	453	446	448
m.p/K	256	249	323

- **Density** Bromo, iodo and polychloro derivatives of hydrocarbons are heavier than water. The density increases with increase in number of carbon atoms, halogen atoms and atomic mass of the halogen atom.

Compound	n-C_3H_7Cl	n-C_3H_7Br	n-C_3H_7I	CH_2Cl_2
Density (g/mL)	0.89	1335	1.747	1.336

- **Solubility** The solubility of haloalkanes in water is low but they tend to **dissolve in organic solvents**.

Chemical Reactions

I. Reactions of Haloalkanes

The reactions of haloalkanes may be divided into three categories.

(i) Nucleophilic substitution reactions
(ii) Elimination reactions
(iii) Reaction with metals

Nucleophilic Substitution Reactions

In these reactions, a nucleophile replaces already existing nucleophile in a molecule.

- A nucleophile reacts with haloalkane (the substrate) having a partial positive charge on the carbon atom bonded to halogen.
- A substitution reaction takes place and halogen atom, called leaving group departs as halide ion.
- Since, the substitution reaction is initiated by a nucleophile, it is called nucleophilic substitution reaction.

$$Nu^- + \overset{\delta+}{C}-\overset{\delta-}{X} \longrightarrow C-Nu + X^-$$

Products formed by the Reaction of Haloalkanes with Some Common Nucleophiles NEET 2024

Reagent	Nucleophile (Nu^-)	Substitution product $(R—Nu)$	Class of main product
NaOH(KOH)	HO^-	ROH	Alcohol
H_2O	H_2O	ROH	Alcohol
$NaOR'$	$R'O^-$	ROR'	Ether
NaI	I^-	$R—I$	Alkyl iodide
NH_3	NH_3	RNH_2	Primary amine
$R'NH_2$	$R'NH_2$	$RNHR'$	*sec*-amine
$R'R''NH$	$R'R''NH$	$RNR'R''$	*tert*-amine
KCN	$\bar{C}\equiv N:$	RCN	Nitrile (cyanide)
AgCN	$Ag—CN:$	RNC (Isocyanide)	Isonitrile
KNO_2	$O=N—O$	$R—O—N=O$	Alkyl nitrite
$AgNO_2$	$Ag—O—\ddot{N}=O$	$R—NO_2$	Nitroalkane
$R'COOAg$	$R'COO^-$	$R'COOR$	Ester
$LiAlH_4$	H	RH	Hydrocarbon
R^-M^+	R^-	RR'	Alkane

Note Groups like cyanides and nitrites possess two nucleophilic centres and are called **ambident nucleophiles**. Therefore, cyanide can act as a nucleophile in two different ways $(^{\ominus}C\equiv N \longleftrightarrow :C=N^{\ominus})$.

Similarly, nitrite ion has two different points of linkage $[\bar{O}—\ddot{N}=O]$.

Mechanism

The two different mechanisms are as follows

1. S_N1 (Substitution Nucleophilic Unimolecular)

NEET 2024

- These reactions follows first order kinetics.
- The reactions are generally carried out in polar protic solvents (like water, alcohol and acetic acid etc).
- It proceeds *via* two steps. i.e.

For Concept Master Video

***Step* I** Formation of carbocation.

***Step* II** Attack of nucleophile on carbocation.

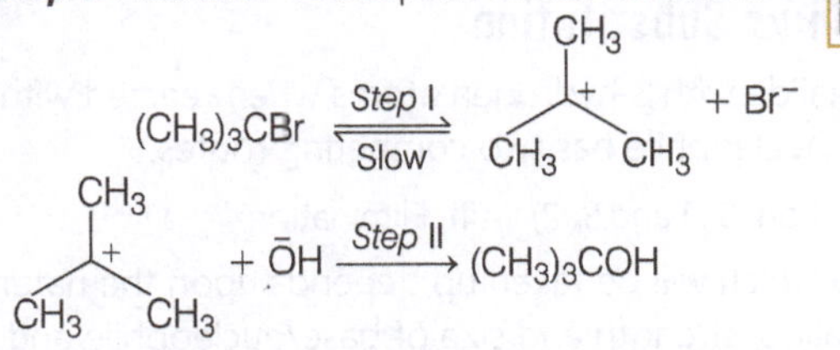

- Here, *step* I is slowest and reversible. Thus, the rate of reaction depends only on the concentration of alkyl halide and not on the concentration of hydroxide ion.
- The reactivity of alkyl halide depends upon the formation of stable carbocation. NEET 2020
- Thus, order of reactivity of alkyl halide towards S_N1 reaction is as follows
  3° halide > 2° halide > 1° halide > methyl halide.
- Primary allylic and benzylic halides show higher reactivity in S_N1 reactions than other primary alkyl halides due to greater stabilisation of allylic and benzylic carbocation intermediates by resonance.
- In these reactions, racemisation occurs due to the possibility of front as well as backside attack on planar carbocation.

2. S_N2 (Substitution Nucleophilic Bimolecular)

- It is a second order reaction. This means that, the rate of reaction depends on the concentration of both the alkyl halide and the incoming nucleophile.
- These reactions takes place in one step through transition state.

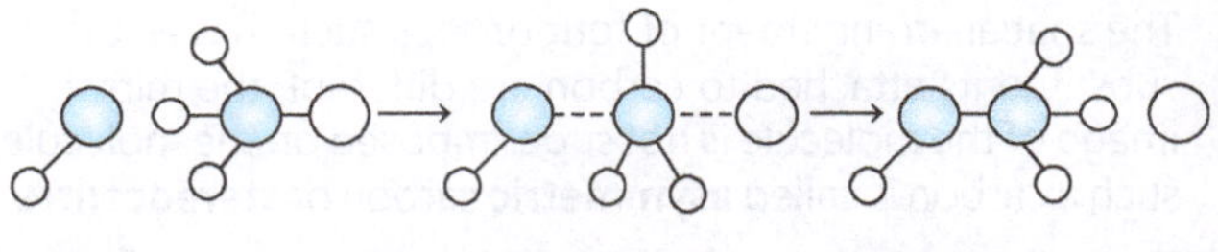

- The order of reactivity of alkyl halides for S_N2 reaction is 3° halide < 2° halide < 1° halide < methyl halide.

For Concept Master Video

Steric effects in S_N2 reaction.

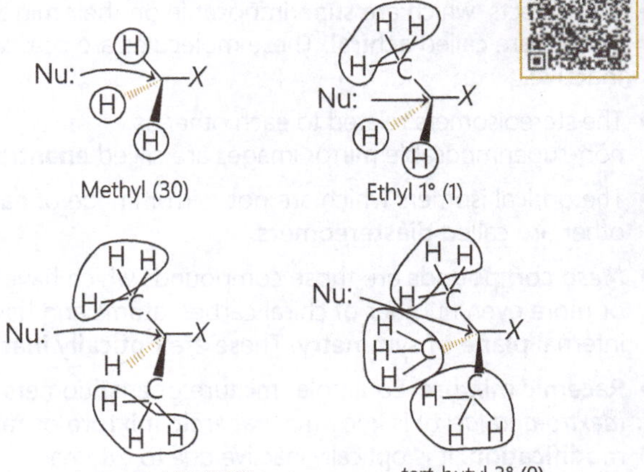

The relative rate of S_N2 reaction is given in parenthesis.

- Lesser the steric hindrance in transition state, faster will be the reaction.
- Rate of reaction in S_N2 mechanism depends on the strength of the attacking nucleophile, which follows the order

$$:OR^- > :OH^- > CH_3COO^- > I^- > F^-$$

- In these reactions, inversion of configuration takes place.

Note For a given alkyl group, the reactivity of the halides $R—X$, follows the same order in both the mechanism.

$$R—I > R—Br > R—Cl >> R—F$$

3. Stereochemical Aspects of Nucleophilic Substitution Reactions

Some basic terms are as follows

- Plane polarised light is produced by passing ordinary light through Nicol prism. When it is passed through the solutions of certain compounds rotates the plane polarised light. Such compounds are called **optically active compounds**.
- If the compound rotates the plane polarised light to the right, it is called *dextrorotatory* or *d*-form. It is indicated by placing (+) sign before the degree of rotation.
- If the light is rotated towards left the compound is said to be *laevorotatory* or *l*-form. It is indicated by placing (–) sign before the degree of rotation. Such (+) and (–) isomers of a compound are called **optical isomers** and phenomenon is termed as **optical isomerism**.

For Concept Master Video

- **Molecular asymmetry, chirality and enantiomers** The spatial arrangement of four groups such that all the substituents attached to carbon are different, the mirror image of the molecule is not superimposed on the molecule, such a carbon is called **asymmetric** carbon or **stereocentre**.
- The objects which are non-superimposable on their mirror image are said to be **chiral** and this property is known as **chirality**. Chiral compounds are **optically active**. NEET 2022
- The objects, which are superimposable on their mirror images are called **achiral**. These molecules are **optically inactive**.
- The stereoisomers related to each other as non-superimposable mirror images are called **enantiomers**.
- The optical isomers which are not mirror image of each other are called **diastereomers**.
- ***Meso* compounds** are those compounds which have two or more even number of chiral carbon atoms and have an internal **plane of symmetry**. These are **optically inactive**.
- **Racemic mixture** Equimolar mixture of enantiomers (*dextro and laevo*) is known as **racemic mixture** or **racemic modification**. It is optically inactive due to external compensation. This phenomenon is known as **racemisation**.
- A racemic mixture is represented by prefixing *dl* or (±) before the name, for example (±) butan-2-ol.

Note The sign of optical rotation is not necessarily related to the absolute (actual) configuration of the molecule.

- **Retention** It is the preservation of the spatial arrangement of bonds to an asymmetric centre during a chemical reaction.
- **Inversion of configuration** 100% inversion of configuration is known as **Walden inversion**.
- The three outcomes, i.e. inversion, retention and racemisation obtained in a reaction are shown in the following reaction.

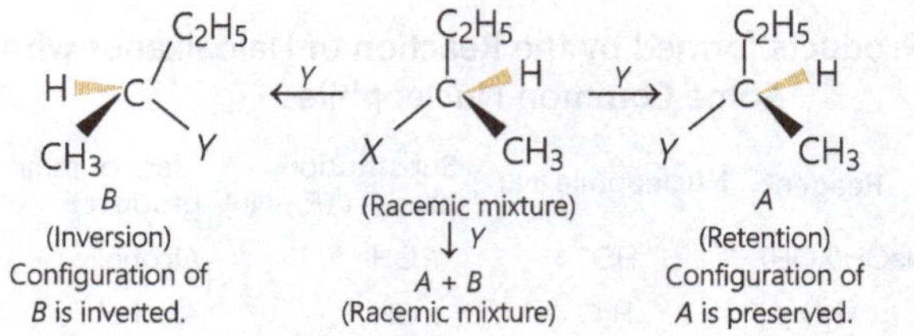

Elimination Reactions

- When haloalkane having β-hydrogen atom is heated with alc. KOH. Then elimination of hydrogen atom from β-carbon and a halogen atom from α-carbon atom takes place.

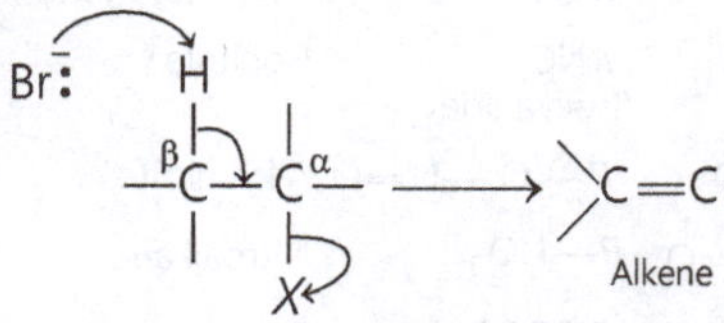

where, B = Base, X = leaving group.

- In the above reaction, alkene is formed as a product. Since, β-hydrogen atom is involved in elimination, it is called **β-elimination**.
- If there is a possibility of formation of more than one alkene due to the availability of more than one β- hydrogen atoms, the usually, one alkene is formed as the major product. The formation of alkene takes place according to **Saytzeff rule**.

It states that, "in dehydrohalogenation reactions, the preferred product is that alkene which has the greater number of alkyl groups attached to the doubly bonded carbon atoms". NEET 2021

e.g.

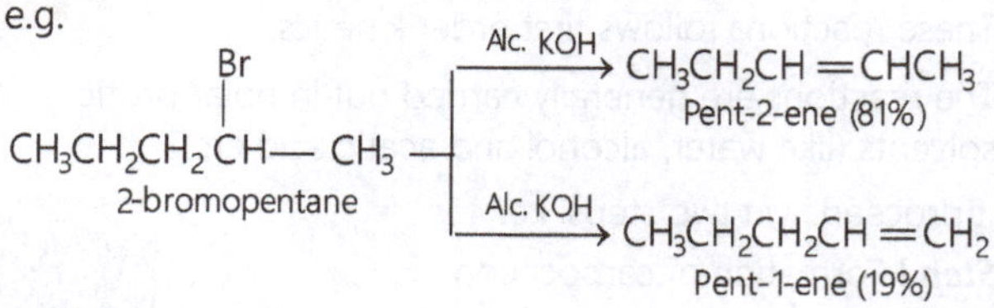

Elimination *vs* Substitution

- An alkyl halide with β-hydrogen atoms when reacted with a base or a nucleophile has two competing routes.
  (i) Substitution (S_N1 and S_N2) (ii) Elimination
- The route which will be taken up depends upon the nature of alkyl halide, strength and size of base/nucleophile and reaction condition.
- A bulkier nucleophile will prefer elimination rather than substitution.
- Generally primary alkyl halide prefers S_N2 reaction.

- Secondary halide follows S_N2 or elimination, depending upon the strength of base/nucleophile.
- Tertiary halide follows S_N1 or elimination depending upon the stability of carbocation or the more substituted alkene.

Reaction with Metals

- Most organic chloride, bromides and iodides react with certain metals to give compounds containing carbon-metal bonds. Such compounds are called **organo-metallic compounds**. Grignard reagents ($RMgX$) is one of its important class.
- Grignard reagents are obtained by the reaction of haloalkanes with magnesium metal in the presence of dry ether.

$$CH_3CH_2X + Mg \xrightarrow{\text{Dry ether}} \underset{\text{Grignard reagent}}{CH_3CH_2MgX} \quad (X = Cl, Br, I)$$

- In Grignard reagent, the carbon-magnesium bond is covalent but highly polar. While magnesium halogen bond is ionic.

$$\overset{\delta-}{R}—\overset{\delta+}{Mg}\overset{\delta-}{X}$$

- They are highly reactive and react with any source of proton to given hydrocarbon.

$$R—MgX + H—G \longrightarrow RH + Mg\begin{matrix} X \\ G \end{matrix}$$

(where, $G = OH, RO, RNH, RC{\equiv}C^-$)

- **Wurtz reaction** This reaction is useful in the preparation of symmetrical alkanes with higher number of carbon atom.

$$2RX + 2Na \xrightarrow{\text{Dry ether}} R—R + 2NaX$$

II. Reactions of Haloarenes

Some important chemical reactions of haloarenes are

Nucleophilic Substitution Reactions

Aryl halides are extremely less reactive towards nucleophilic substitution reactions as compared to alkyl halides. This low reactivity is due to the following reasons.

(i) **Resonance effect** The C—X bond in benzene has a partial double bond character due to resonance with benzene ring. Thus, bond cleavage in haloarene is difficult than haloalkane.

(ii) **Difference in hybridisation of carbon atom in C—X bond.** The C—X bond in aryl halides is less polar as compared to that in alkyl halides. It is because sp^2-hybridised carbon (present on haloarene) is more electronegative than sp^3-hybridised carbon (present in haloalkane).

(iii) **Instability of phenyl cation** In haloarenes, the phenyl cation formed due to self-ionisation is not stabilised by resonance. So, S_N1 mechanism is ruled out.

(iv) For electron rich nucleophile it is difficult to approach electron rich arenes, due to possible repulsion.

Replacement by Hydroxyl Group

Chlorobenzene can be converted into phenol by heating in aqueous sodium hydroxide solution at a temperature of 623 K and a pressure of 300 atm. NEET 2019

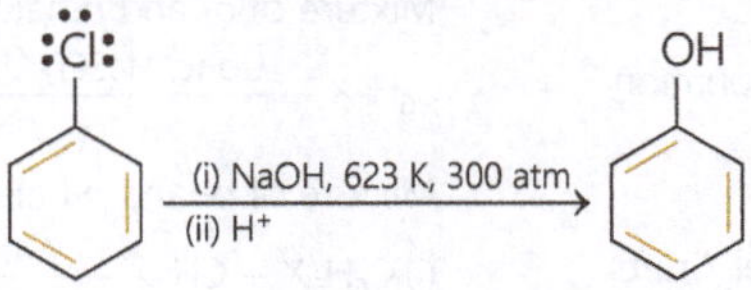

The presence of an electron withdrawing group (—NO_2) at *o*-and *p*-positions increases the reactivity of haloarenes. The presence of electron withdrawing group (—NO_2) at *meta*-position has no effect on reactivity of haloarenes.

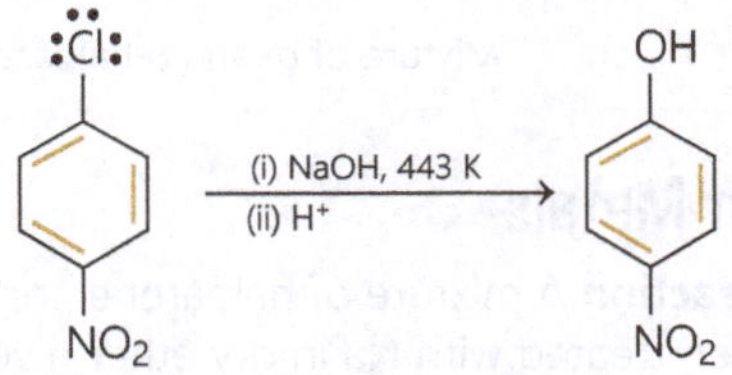

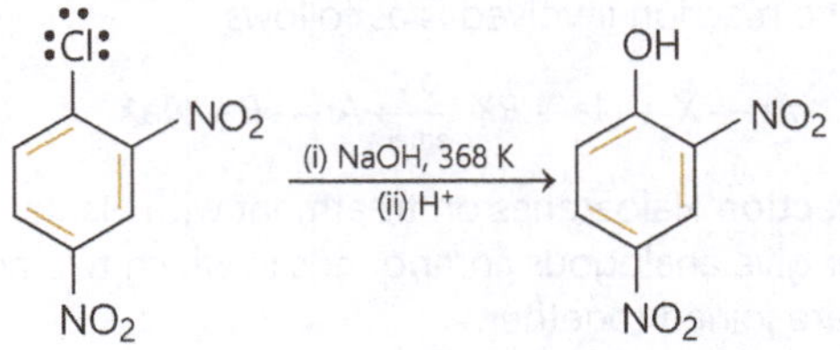

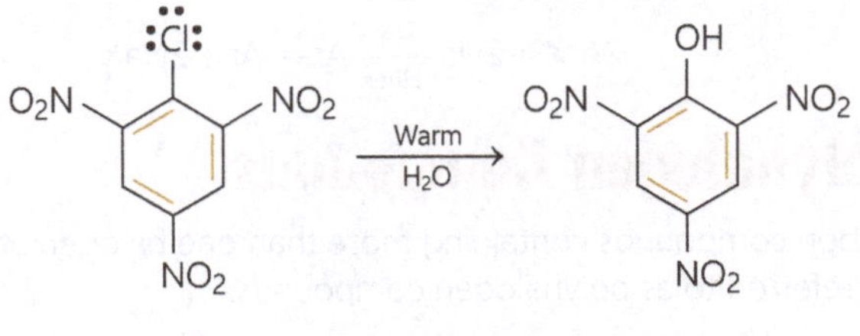

Electrophilic Substitution Reactions

Haloarenes undergo usual electrophilic substitution reactions of benzene ring such as halogenation, nitration, sulphonation and Friedel-Craft alkylation etc.

- $-I$ effect of halogen atom, withdraws electrons from the benzene ring and decrease electron density on benzene ring. As a result, the ring gets deactivated as compared to benzene. So, electrophilic substitution reactions in haloarenes occur slowly. Thus, haloarenes requires more drastic conditions as compared to those in benzene.
- $+M$ effect of halogen increase electron density at *ortho* and *para*-position rather than *meta*-position. That's why haloarenes are *o*, *p*-directing.

These reactions are as follows

S.No.	Methods	Reaction involved	Important points
1.	Halogenation	$C_6H_5X + X_2 \xrightarrow[FeCl_3]{Anhyd.}$ Mixture of *o*- and *p*-dihalobenzene (X = Cl)	1, 4-dihalobenzene is formed as a major product.
2.	Nitration	$C_6H_5X \xrightarrow[Conc.\ H_2SO_4]{HNO_3}$ Mixture of *o*- and *p*-halonitrobenzene (X = Cl)	*p*-halonitrobenzene is formed as a major product.
3.	Sulphonation	$C_6H_5X \xrightarrow[\Delta]{Conc.\ H_2SO_4}$ Mixture of *o*- and *p*-halobenzene sulphonic acid (X = Cl)	*p*-halobenzene sulphonic acid is formed as a major product.
4.	Friedel-Crafts reaction NEET 2022	(i) $C_6H_5X + CH_3X \xrightarrow[AlCl_3]{Anhy.}$ Mixture of *o*- and *p*-halo alkylbenzene (X = Cl)	*p*-haloalkylbenzene is a major product.
		(ii) $C_6H_5X + CH_3-\overset{O}{\overset{\parallel}{C}}-X \xrightarrow[AlCl_3]{Anhyd.}$ Mixture of *o*- and *p*-haloacetophenone (X = Cl)	*p*-haloacetophenone is formed as a major product.

Reaction with Metals

- **Wurtz-Fittig reaction** A mixture of haloarene and haloalkane, when treated with Na in dry ether gives alkyl arene. The reaction involved is as follows

$$Ar-X + Na + RX \xrightarrow[ether]{Dry} Ar-R + NaX$$

- **Fittig reaction** Haloarenes on treatment with Na in dry ether give analogous compounds in which two aryl groups are joined together.

$$2ArX + 2Na \xrightarrow[ether]{Dry} Ar-Ar + 2NaX$$

Polyhalogen Compounds

Carbon compounds containing more than one halogen atom are referred to as polyhalogen compounds.

Some polyhalogen compounds are discussed below

Dichloromethane (Methylene Chloride, CH_2Cl_2)

- It is used as a solvent and paint remover.
- It is used as a metal cleaning and finishing solvent.
- It is used as a propellant in aerosols.

Effects

- It harms the Central Nervous System (CNS).
- Exposure to lower levels of CH_2Cl_2 in air can lead to slightly impaired hearing, vision and high levels causes dizziness, nausea etc.
- Direct-skin contact with methylene chloride causes intense burning and redness in skin and also burns cornea.

Trichloromethane (Chloroform, $CHCl_3$)

- Chemically, chloroform is employed as a solvent for fats, alkaloids, iodine and other substances.
- Earlier it was used as a general anaesthetic but now-a-days, it is replaced by less toxic and safe anaesthetic, like ether.
- It is used in the production of the freon refrigerant *R*-22.

Effects

- Inhaling chloroform vapours depresses the CNS.
- Breathing 900 parts per million of chloroform for a short time can cause dizziness, fatigue and headache.
- Chronic chloroform exposure may cause damage to liver and kidney.
- Chloroform is stored in closed dark coloured bottles, filled completely, so that air is kept out because it is oxidised by air in the presence of light.

$$\underset{\text{Chloroform}}{2CHCl_3} + \underset{\text{(Air)}}{O_2} \xrightarrow{Light} \underset{\substack{\text{Phosgene} \\ \text{(Poisonous gas)}}}{2COCl_2} + 2HCl$$

Triiodomethane (Iodoform, CHI_3)

- It was used as an antiseptic.
- The antiseptic properties are due to the liberation of free iodine and not due to iodoform itself.

Marks Maximizer

Distinction between chloroform and iodoform
Iodoform on heating with $AgNO_3$ gives yellow precipitate of AgI, whereas chloroform does not give this test because of stable nature of chloroform.

Tetrachloromethane (Carbon Tetrachloride, CCl_4)

- It is used in the manufacture of refrigerants and propellants for aerosol cans.
- It is also used as feedstock in the synthesis of chlorofluorocarbons and other chemicals.
- It is widely used as industrial solvent for oils, fats, resins, lacquers, etc.
- It is used as fire extinguisher and as cleaning fluids.

Effects

- Common effects are dizziness, light headedness, nausea and vomiting. It also make the heart beat irregular or stop.
- It can cause permanent damage to nerve cells, which can lead to coma, unconsciousness or even death.
- It may irritate the eyes and depletes the ozone layer.

Freons

The chlorofluorocarbon compounds of methane and ethane are collectively known as freons.

Preparation, Properties

- Freons are manufactured from tetrachloromethane by **Swarts reaction.**
- The reaction involved in the preparation of freon-12 (CCl_2F_2) is as follows

$$CCl_4 + 2AgF_2 \longrightarrow CCl_2F_2 + 2AgCl$$

- They are extremely stable, unreactive, non-toxic, non-corrosive and easily liquefiable gases.
- It is used for aerosol propellants, refrigeration and air conditioning purposes.

Effects

- Freons deplete the protective ozone layer surrounding our planet, so their use has been banned in many countries.
- In stratosphere, it initiates free radical chain reactions with ozone that can disbalance the natural ozone.

DDT (*p*, *p*′-dichlorodiphenyltrichloroethane)

It is a powerful insecticide but not easily biodegradable. Therefore, its long term effects could be potentially dangerous and its use is banned in many countries.

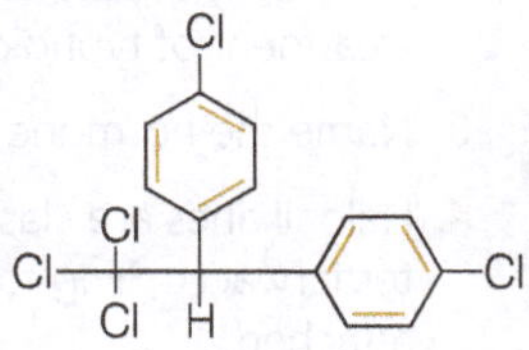

DDT

Effects

- It has high toxicity towards fish.
- It is chemically stable and fat soluble.
- It is not metabolised very rapidly by animals.
- It is deposited and stored in the fatty tissues.
- If ingestion continues at a steady rate, it builds up within the animal over time.

Uses of Halogen Containing Compounds

- Chloramphenicol is effective for the treatment of typhoid.
- Thyroxines deficiency in body causes disease called goiter.
- Chloroquine is used for the treatment of malaria.
- Halothane is used as an anaesthetic during surgery.
- Certain fluorinated compounds are considered as potential blood substitute in surgery.

Caution Points

- While checking the reactivity of S_N1 reaction, keep in mind that the carbocation formed at the bridge head position will be the least reactive.
- Ethyl chloride when treated with alcoholic KOH undergoes dehydrohalogenation reaction whereas with aqueous KOH it undergoes hydrolysis.
- Fluorobenzene and iodobenzene cannot be produced through Sandmeyer's reaction.

PYQ Notes

1. Reaction of 1-methoxy naphthalene with hydroiodic acid will give. **JEE Main 2022**

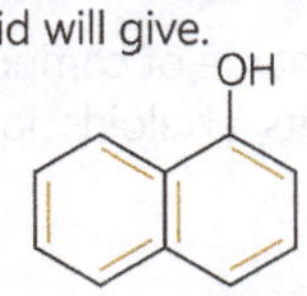

and CH_3I

2. Reaction of $(CH_3)_3CCl$ with $KOC(CH_3)_3$ will give 2-methylprop-1-ene. **JEE Main 2022**
3. PhS^-Na^+ (Sodium phenylthiolate) undergoes S_N2 reaction in presence of DMF. **JEE Main 2022**
4. Wurtz reaction is used for the preparation of higher alkanes containing even number of carbon atoms. **NEET 2020**
5. S_N2 reactions are generally carried out in polar aprotic solvents like acetone DMSO, acetonitrite or DMF. **NEET 2016**

Step by Step

Mastering NCERT

- Concept Builders
- Topical Questions
- Assertion-Reason
- Statement Type
- Matching Type
- Numerical Value
- NCERT Exemplar's
- Past Exams'
- Skill Boosters

Concept Builders

1. Hybridisation of carbon atom to which halogen atom is attached in haloalkanes and haloarenes are .... and .... respectively.
2. Name any antibiotic which is very effective for treatment of typhoid fever.
3. Name the hormone whose deficiency causes goiter.
4. Haloalkanes are classified as primary, secondary or tertiary according to nature of .... to which halogen in attached.
5. Vinylic halides are the compounds in which halogen atom is bonded to sp^3-hybridised carbon atom attached to carbon-carbon double bond. [T/F]
6. The IUPAC name of isopropyl chloride is ....
7. Dihalogen compounds having both halogen atoms present on same carbon atom are called *vic*-dihalide. [T/F]
8. Dihaloalkanes having same type of halogen atoms are called alkylidene or alkylene dihalides. [T/F]
9. Carbon-halogen bond of alkyl halide is polarised because halogen atom is more electronegative than carbon atom. [T/F]
10. Phosphorus chloride (tri and penta) are preferred over thionyl chloride for the preparation of alkyl chloride from alcohol. [T/F]
11. Name the acid in the presence of which *R*—I can be obtained by heating alcohol with KI in a good yield (95% approx).
12. Aryl halide cannot be prepared by replacement of hydroxyl group of phenol with halogen atom. [T/F]
13. Phenols react with halogen acids violently to produce aryl halide. [T/F]
14. Write the number of monochloro structural isomers expected to be formed on free radical monochlorination of $(CH_3)_2CHCH_2CH_3$.
15. Name the product formed when benzene diazonium halide is shaked with potassium iodide.
16. Bromine test is a qualitative test to detect the presence of .... compounds.
17. In Finkelstein reaction, NaCl or NaBr formed, is precipitated which facilitates forward reaction according to Le-Chatelier principle. [T/F]
18. Alkyl fluorides are synthesised by heating an alkyl chloride/bromide in presence of .... [HgF_2/CoF_2]
19. Sulphuric acid is used during the reaction of alcohols with KI because it behaves as reducing agent. [T/F]
20. Name the product formed when 1-methylcyclohexene reacts with hydrogen iodide.
21. Write the product formed when cyclohexane reacts with Br_2 in UV.
22. The boiling points of alkyl halide are higher than those of corresponding alkanes because of ....
23. The reaction in which a nucleophile replaces existing nucleophile in a molecule is called ....
24. If the compound rotates the plane polarised light to the right, i.e .... rotation, then it is called ....
25. In S_N1 reaction, the racemisation takes place due to inversion and retention of configuration. [T/F]
26. Hydrolysis of (–)-2-bromooctane proceeds with inversion of configuration. [T/F]
27. Write the major product formed when 2-bromopentane reacts with nucleophile (OH^-).
28. Haloarenes are less reactive than haloalkanes towards nucleophilic substitution reaction. [T/F]
29. Presence of nitro group at *ortho* or *para*-position increases the reactivity of haloarenes. [T/F]
30. Write the IUPAC name of compound which is employed as a solvent for fats, alkaloids, iodine and other substances.

Topical Questions

Classification, Nomenclature & Nature of C—X Bond

1. Which of the following statements is correct for the alkyl halide? NCERT Pg 159
   (a) These are formed by the replacement of hydrogen atom in hydrocarbon by halogen atom.
   (b) They have no polar bond.
   (c) In haloalkane, halogen is attached to sp^2-hybridised carbon atom.
   (d) Chloroquine is used for the treatment of goiter.

2. Which of the following statements is correct for allylic halide? NCERT Pg 160
   (a) Compound in which halogen atom is bonded to sp^3-hybridised carbon atom next to aromatic ring.
   (b) Compound in which halogen atom is bonded to sp^3-hybridised carbon atom next to carbon-carbon double bond, i.e. (C=C).
   (c) Compound in which halogen atom is bonded to an alkyl group.
   (d) These compounds contain halogen atom directly bonded to sp^2-hybridised carbon atom.

3. Which of the following is not an allylic halide? NCERT Pg 160
   (a) 5-bromopent-1-ene
   (b) 4-bromopent-2-ene
   (c) 3-bromo-2-methylbut-1-ene
   (d) 1-bromobut-2-ene

4. Which of the following is a benzyl halogen compound? NCERT Pg 160
   (a) $Br—C_6H_4CH(CH_3)CH_2CH_3$
   (b) $(CH_3)_3CCH_2CH(Br)C_6H_5$
   (c) $(CH_3)_2CHCH(Cl)CH_3$
   (d) CH_3CH_2Br

5. Which of the following halide is not correct according to the name and classification? NCERT Pg 160, 161
   (a) $(H_3C)_3C—CH_2Cl$, 1-chloro-2, 2-dimethyl propane, primary haloalkane.
   (b) $(H_3C)_2CH—Br$, 2-bromopropane, secondary haloalkane.
   (c) $H_3CC(Cl)(C_2H_5)CH_2CH_3$, 2-chloro-2-ethylbutane, secondary haloalkane.
   (d) $CH_3CH_2C(CH_3)_2CH_2I$, 1-iodo-2, 2-dimethylbutane, primary haloalkane.

6. The IUPAC name of tertiary butyl bromide is NCERT Pg 161
   (a) 3-bromobutane
   (b) 2-bromo-2-methylpropane
   (c) 1,2-bromobutane
   (d) 4-bromobutane

7. Compounds in which the halogen atom is bonded to a sp^2-hybridised carbon atom of a carbon-carbon double bond is known as NCERT Pg 161
   (a) allylic halides
   (b) benzylic halides
   (c) aryl halides
   (d) vinylic halides

8. The common and IUPAC names of the compound

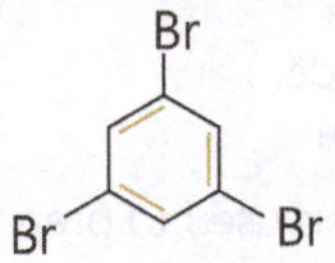

respectively are NCERT Pg 161
   (a) *sym*-tribromobenzene and 1, 2, 5- tribromobenzene
   (b) *sym*-tribromobenzene and 1, 3, 5-tribromobenzene
   (c) *o*, *m*, *p*-tribromobenzene and 1, 3, 5-tribromobenzene
   (d) 1, 3, 5-tribromobenzene, *sym*-tribromobenzene

9. Which of the following is an example of *vic*-dihalide? NCERT Pg 162
   (a) Dichloromethane
   (b) 1,2-dichloroethane
   (c) Ethylidene chloride
   (d) Allyl chloride

10. What is the IUPAC name of the following compound? NCERT Pg 163

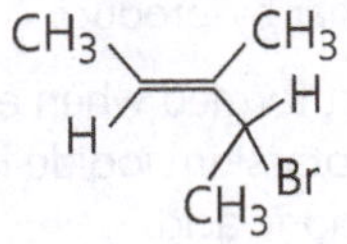

   (a) 3-bromo-3-methyl-1,2-dimethylprop-1-ene
   (b) 3-bromo-1,2-dimethylbut-1-ene
   (c) 2-bromo-3-methylpent-3-ene
   (d) 4-bromo-3-methylpent-2-ene

11. Carbon-halogen bond is polarised because NCERT Pg 163
   (a) halogen atom is less electronegative
   (b) halogen atom is more electronegative than carbon atom
   (c) carbon bears negative charge while halogen bears positive charge
   (d) carbon atom is more electronegative

12. Which of the following has no dipole moment? NCERT Pg 164
   (a) CH_3Cl
   (b) $CHCl_3$
   (c) CH_2Cl_2
   (d) CCl_4

13. Arrange the following compounds in order of increasing dipole moment : Toluene (I), *m*-dichlorobenzene (II), *o*-dichlorobenzene (III), *p*-dichlorobenzene (IV). **NCERT Pg 164**

(a) I < IV < II < III (b) IV < I < II < III
c) IV < I < III < II (d) IV < II < I < III

Methods of Preparation of Haloalkanes and Haloarenes

14. Reaction of red phosphorus with bromine generate **NCERT Pg 164**

(a) phosphorus tribromide
(b) phosphorus diiodide
(c) phosphorus dibromide
(d) phosphorus bromide

15. Which of the following is used to prepare alkyl chloride in presence of alcohol? **NCERT Pg 164**

(a) H_2SO_4
(b) HCl solution (dilute)
(c) Dry HCl gas
(d) Conc. HCl

16. Select the by-product formed in the reaction,

$$ROH + PCl_5 \longrightarrow RCl + 'A'$$

Here, *A* is **NCERT Pg 164**

(a) $POCl_3$ + HCl
(b) H_3PO_3 + No other by-product
(c) H_3PO_3 + HCl
(d) $POCl_3$ +No other by-product

17. Select the product formed when ethyl alcohol is treated with sodium or potassium iodide in the presence of 95% orthophosphoric acid. **NCERT Pg 164**

(a) Methyl iodide (b) Ethyl iodide
(c) Ethane (d) Propyl bromide

18. Methyl chloride reacts with NaI in dry acetone to give methyl iodides. This reaction is called **NCERT Pg 165**

(a) Finkelstein reaction (b) Swarts reaction
(c) Wurtz reaction (d) Fittig reaction

19. Identify the compound *Z* in the reaction, **NCERT Pg 165**

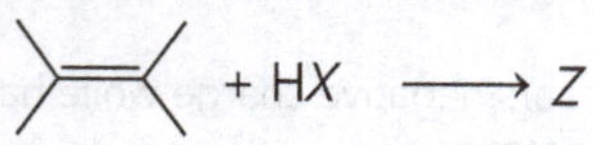

(a) 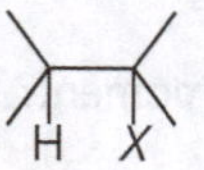 (b) 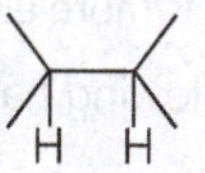

(c) 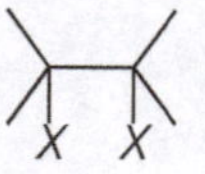 (d) 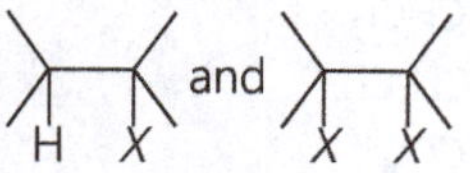

20. Consider the following reaction, **NCERT Pg 165**

$$CH_3CH{=}CH_2 + HI \longrightarrow \underset{(Minor)}{'X'} \text{ and } \underset{(Major)}{'Y'}$$

The products '*X*' and '*Y*' respectively are

(a) $CH_3—CH(CH_3)—I$ (Minor) and $CH_3—CH(CH_3)—CH_3$ (Major)

(b) $CH_3CH_2CH_2I$ (Minor) and $CH_3—CH(I)—CH_3$ (Major)

(c) $CH_3—CH(CH_3)—I$ (Major) and $CH_3—CH(I)—CH_3$ (Minor)

(d) CH_3CHICH_3 (Minor) and $CH_3—CH_2—CH_2—I$ (Major)

21. Major product of the given reaction is

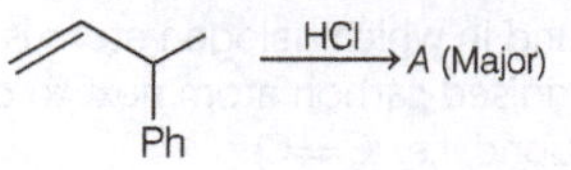

NCERT Pg 165

(a) 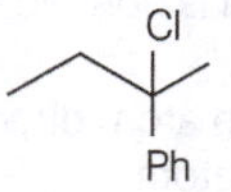 (b) 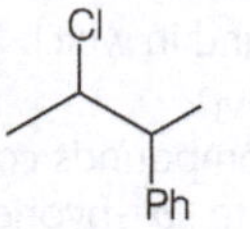

(c) 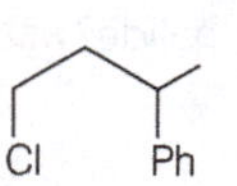 (d) 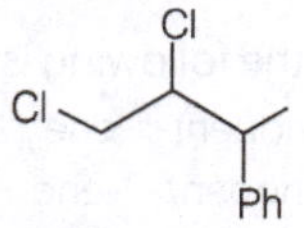

22. Consider the following reaction : **NCERT Pg 166**

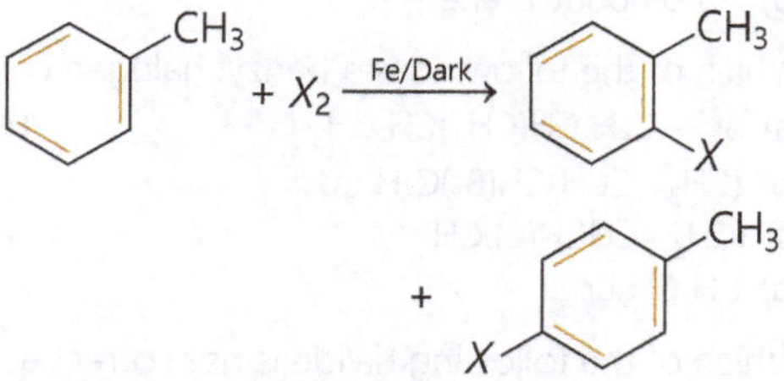

This type of reaction is

(a) nucleophilic substitution
(b) electrophilic substitution
(c) nucleophilic elimination
(d) electrophilic elimination

23. In the following reaction sequence *X* is

$$X \xrightarrow{\text{Bromination}} Y \xrightarrow{NaNO_2/HCl} Z \xrightarrow[C_2H_5OH]{\text{Boiling}} \textit{sym}\text{-tribromobenzene}$$

NCERT Pg 166

(a) Benzoic acid
(b) Salicylic acid
(c) Phenol
(d) Aniline

24. When a primary aromatic amine dissolved in cold aqueous mineral acid (HCl) is treated with sodium nitrite, the product formed is **NCERT Pg 166**

(a) aryl halide
(b) benzene diazonium halide
(c) 2° aromatic amine
(d) 3° aromatic amine

25.

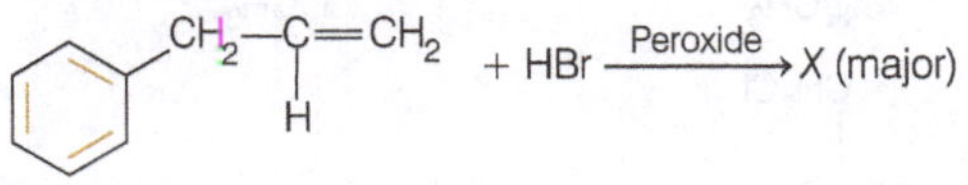

What is *X*? **NCERT Pg 167**

(a) 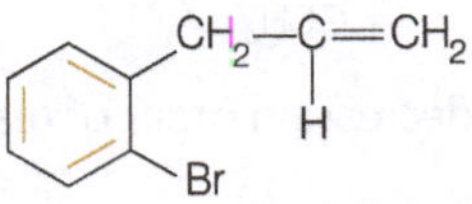 (b) 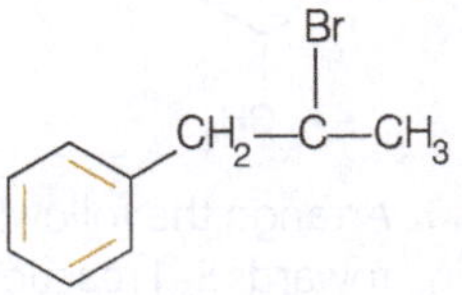

(c) 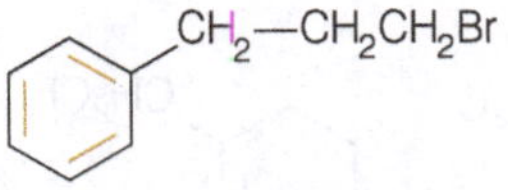 (d) 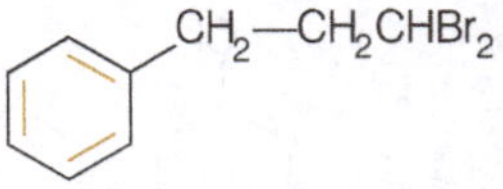

26. The major product in the following conversion is

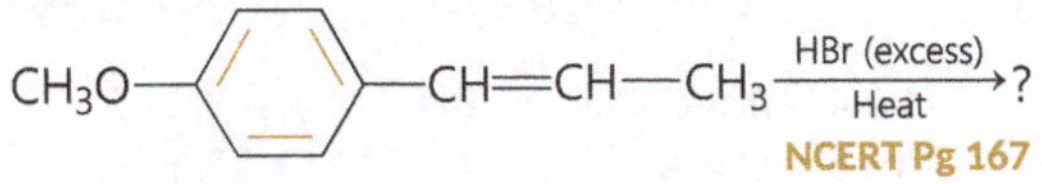

NCERT Pg 167

(a) 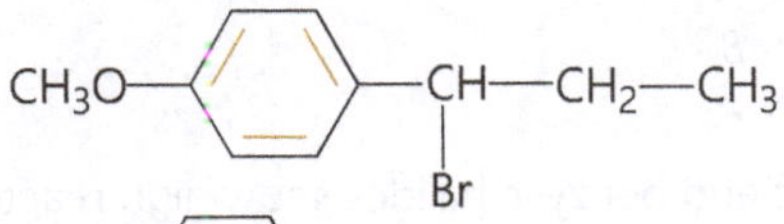

(b) 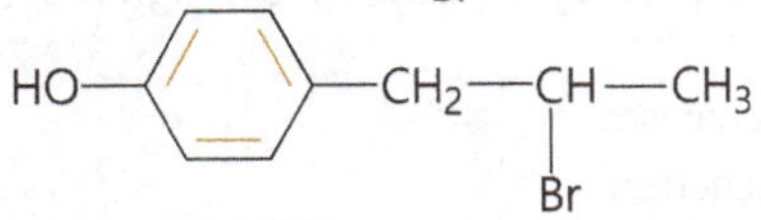

(c) 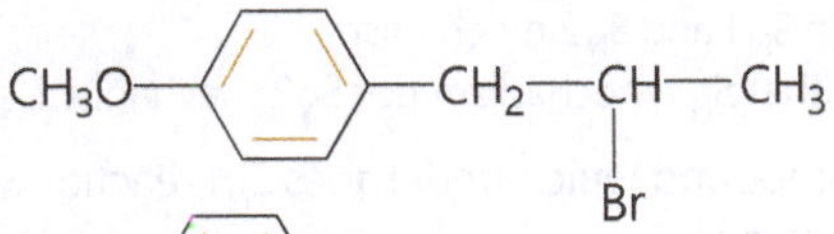

(d) 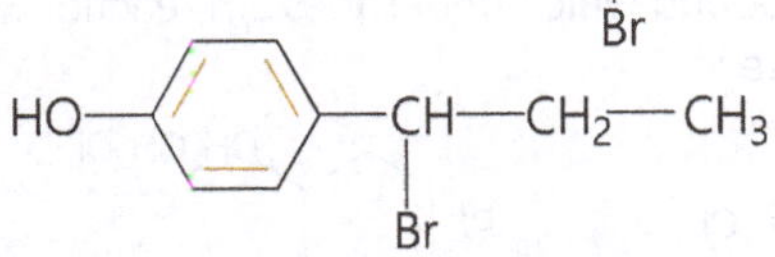

27. Identify the product formed in the given reaction.

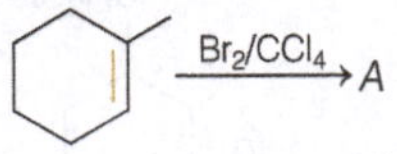

NCERT Pg 165

(a) 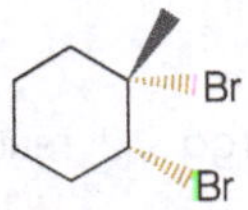 (b) 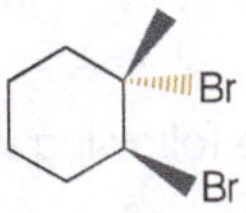

(c) 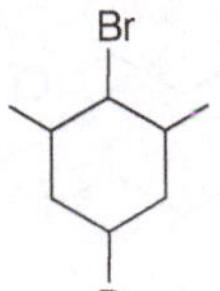 (d) 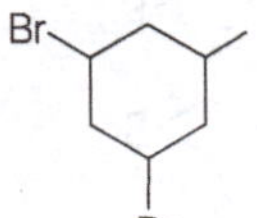

Physical Properties

28. Which of the following alkyl halides has maximum density? **NCERT Pg 169**

(a) C_3H_7I (b) C_2H_5I (c) CH_3Br (d) CH_3I

29. Arrange the following compounds in increasing order of their density. **NCERT Pg 169**

I. CH_2Cl_2 II. $CHCl_3$ III. CCl_4

(a) III < II < I (b) III < I < II (c) III < I = II (d) I < II < III

30. Arrange the following compounds in the decreasing order of their melting points. **NCERT Pg 169**

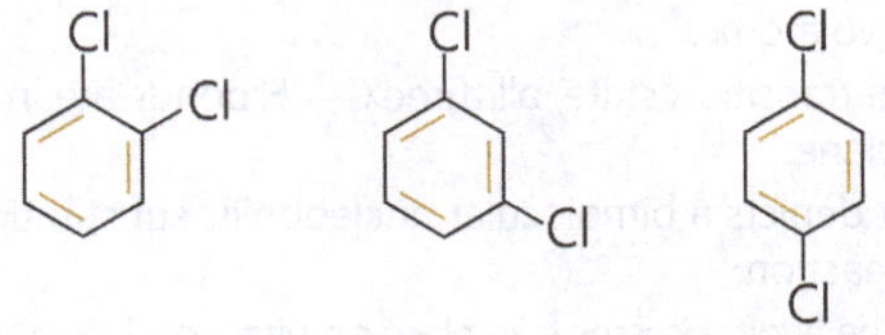

I II III

(a) I > II > III (b) III > I = II
(c) III > I > II (d) III > II > I

31. Which of the following has the highest melting point but least solubility in a given solvent? **NCERT Pg 169**

(a) *o*-dichlorobenzene (b) *p*-dichlorobenzene
(c) *m*-dichlorobenzene (d) Chlorobenzene

Chemical Reactions

32. Cyanide acts as an ambident nucleophile. From which of the following aspects it acts as a stronger nucleophile in aqueous medium? **NCERT Pg 170**

(a) It has same strength from both the ends.
(b) It depends on the nature of alkyl halide.
(c) It acts as a stronger nucleophile from N-end.
(d) It acts as a stronger nucleophile from C-end.

33. Select the incorrect statement regarding S_N2 reaction mechanism. **NCERT Pg 171**

(a) As reaction progress, bond between carbon atom and nucleophile is formed with weakening of carbon atom and the leaving group bond.
(b) There is the inversion of configuration.
(c) The order of reactivity of alkyl halides is 3° < 2° < 1°.
(d) Carbon atom is bonded to four atoms during the transition state.

34.

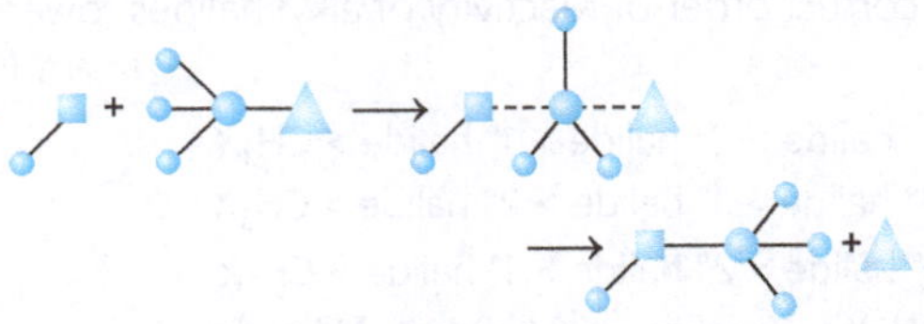

Square dot represents the incoming hydroxide ion, while triangle dot represents the outgoing halide ion.

Which of the following statement is incorrect for the given figure? **NCERT Pg 171**

(a) It is second order kinetics.
(b) Its rate depends upon the concentration of both reactants.
(c) This reaction occur in single step and no intermediate is formed.
(d) It is a first order reaction that proceeds *via* transition state.

35. Which of the following statement is incorrect about S_N2 mechanism? **NCERT Pg 172**

(a) In transition state, carbon is simultaneously bonded to five atoms.
(b) In transition state, all three C—H bonds are in different plane.
(c) It depicts a bimolecular nucleophilic substitution reaction.
(d) The two processes take place simultaneously in a single step.

36. In which case the approach of nucleophile is easy in reaction as shown in figure? **NCERT Pg 173**

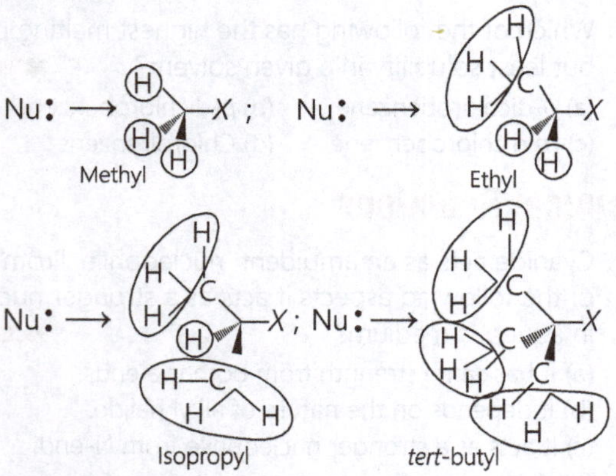

(a) Methyl (b) Ethyl (c) Isopropyl (d) *tert*-butyl

37. Reaction of *tert*-butyl bromide with aqueous sodium hydroxide follows **NCERT Pg 173**

(a) S_N1 mechanism
(b) S_N2 mechanism
(c) Any of the above two depending upon temperature of reaction.
(d) E_1 mechanism

38. The correct order of reactivity of alkyl halides toward S_N1 is **NCERT Pg 174**

(a) 2° halide > 3° halide > 1° halide > CH_3X
(b) 3° halide > 1° halide > 2° halide > CH_3X
(c) 3° halide > 2° halide > 1° halide > CH_3X
(d) CH_3X > 1° halide > 2° halide > 3° halide

39. Which of the following is most reactive towards S_N1 reaction? **NCERT Pg 174**

(a) 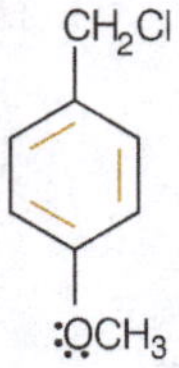

(b) 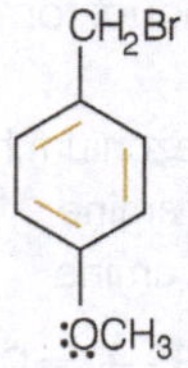

(c) 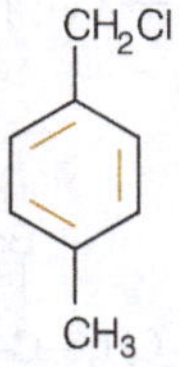

(d) 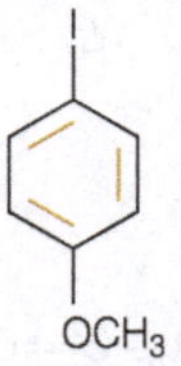

40. Arrange the following in decreasing order of reactivity towards S_N1 reaction. **NCERT Pg 174**

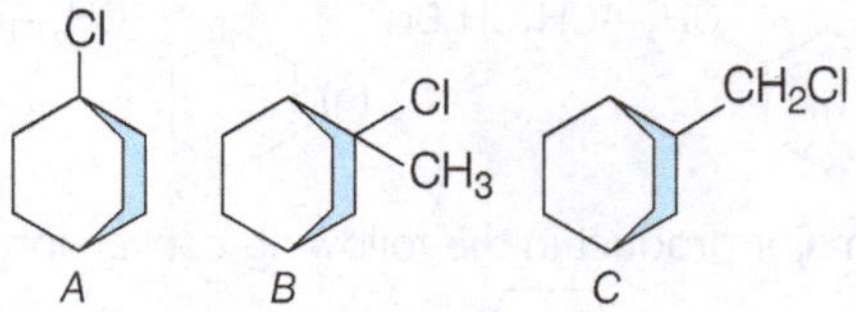

(a) $A > B > C$
(b) $B > C > A$
(c) $A > C > B$
(d) $C > B > A$

41. The allylic and benzylic halides show high reactivity towards **NCERT Pg 174**

(a) S_N1 mechanism
(b) S_N2 mechanism
(c) Both S_N1 and S_N2 mechanism
(d) Neither S_N1 mechanism nor S_N2 mechanism

42. The compound which undergoes S_N1 reaction with fastest rate is **NCERT Pg 174**

(a) 

(b) 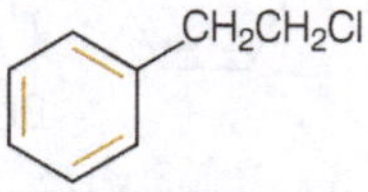

(c) 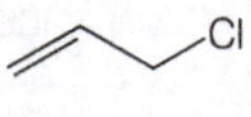

(d) 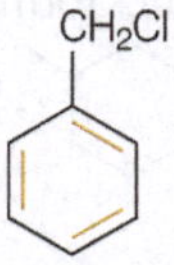

43. Which of the following would undergo S_N2 reaction faster? **NCERT Pg 174**

(a) 

(b) 

(c) 

(d) 

44. The compound which will react fastest by S_N2 mechanism is **NCERT Pg 174**

(a) 

(a) 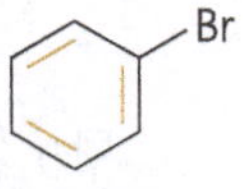

(c) Ph—CH_2—Br (d) $(Ph)_3C$—Br

45. Which of the following is not correct? **NCERT Pg 174**

(a) $PhCH_2Br > PhCHBrCH_3 > PhCBr(CH_3)_2 (S_N1)$
(b) $R—I > R—Br > R—Cl$ (S_N2)
(c) $CH_2{=}CH—Cl < CH_2{=}CH—CH_2—Cl < PhCH_2—Cl$ (S_N1)
(d) $R—Cl < R—Br < R—I$ (S_N1)

46. Which of the following resonating structure of benzyl carbocation is wrong? **NCERT Pg 174**

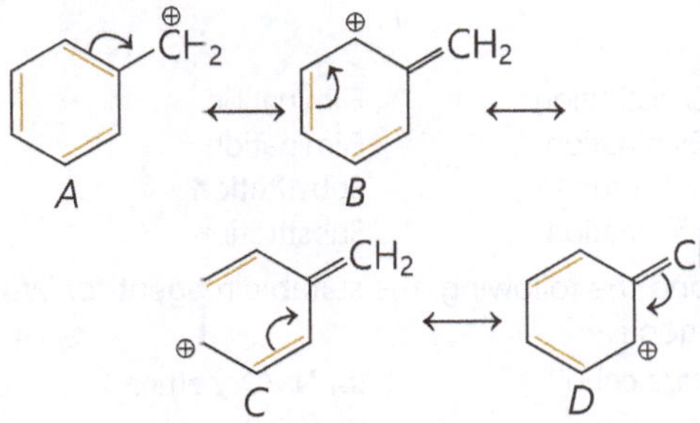

(a) *A* (b) *B* (c) *C* (d) *D*

47. Increasing rate of S_N1 reaction in the following compounds is **NCERT Pg 174**

(A) 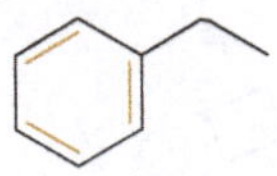

(B) 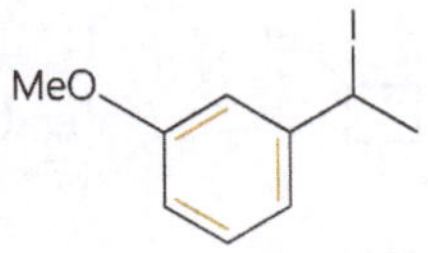

(C) 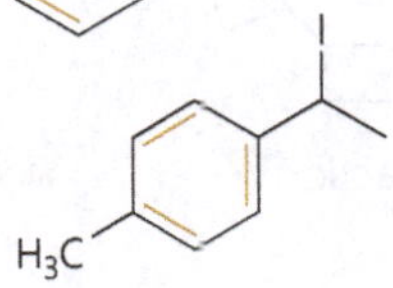

(D) 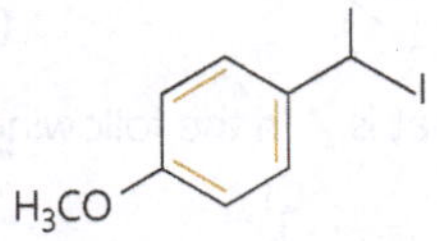

(a) A < B < C < D (b) B < A < C < D
(c) A < B < D < C (d) B < A < D < C

48. Which of the following statements is incorrect? **NCERT Pg 175**

(a) The angle by which plane polarised light is rotated is measured by an instrument called polarimeter.
(b) The compound which rotates the plane polarised light to left is called dextrorotatory and that towards right is called laevorotatory.
(c) Dextrorotatory is indicated by (+) sign and laevorotatory by (–) sign before degree of rotation.
(d) Such (+) and (–) isomers are called optical isomers.

49. Conclude the appropriate term for the molecule in the given figure. **NCERT Pg 177**

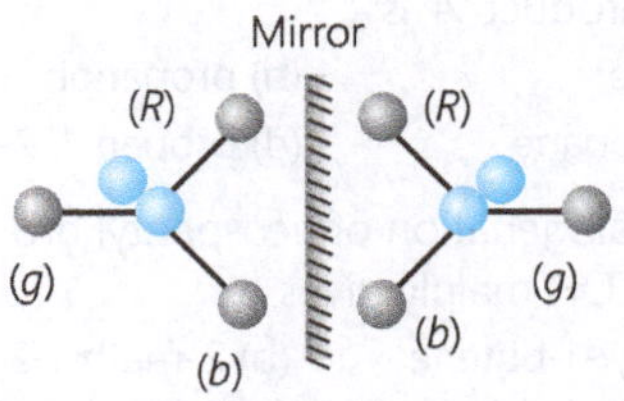

(a) Enantiomers (b) Diastereomers
(c) Racemic mixture (d) *Meso* compounds

50. Consider the following reactions : **NCERT Pg 178**

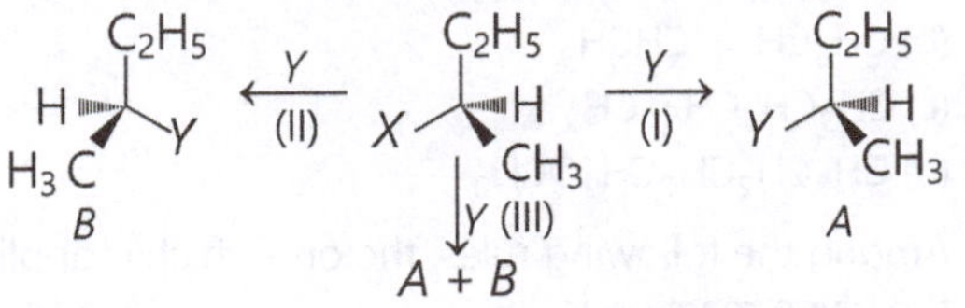

Name the terms that occur in I, II, III equations. Choose the correct option.

	I	II	III
(a)	Retention of configuration	Inversion of configuration	Racemisation
(b)	Retention of configuration	Racemisation	Inversion of configuration
(c)	Inversion of configuration	Retention of configuration	Racemisation
(d)	Racemisation	Inversion of configuration	Retention of configuration

51. If during reaction, no bond of stereocentre is broken, and product has same configuration then such reaction proceeds with **NCERT Pg 178**

(a) inversion of configuration
(b) racemisation
(c) retention of configuration
(d) both racemisation and retention of configuration

52. Correct reactivity order of the given compounds for reaction with alcoholic KOH is **NCERT Pg 179**

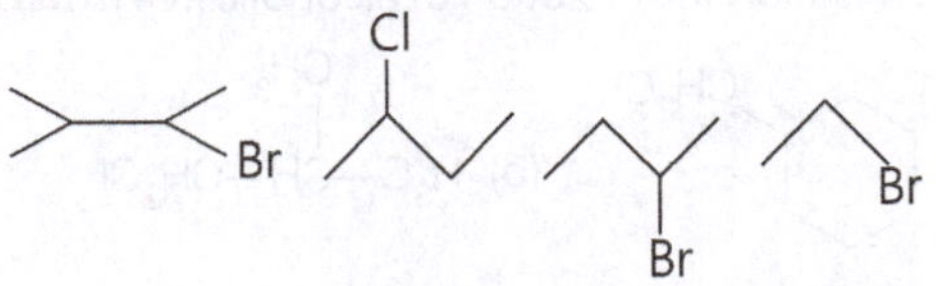

(*A*) (*B*) (*C*) (*D*)

(a) *A* > *B* > *C* > *D* (b) *A* > *C* > *B* > *D*
(c) *D* > *B* > *C* > *A* (d) *A* > *D* > *B* > *C*

53. $CH_3-CH_2-CH_2-Br \xrightarrow[\Delta]{\text{Alc. KOH}} A$

The final product '*A*' is **NCERT Pg 179**

(a) propene (b) propanol

(c) cyclopropane (d) propan-1, 2-diol

54. Dehydrohalogenation of *neo*-pentyl bromide with alcoholic KOH mainly gives **NCERT Pg 174**

(a) 2-methyl-1-butene (b) 2-methyl-2-butene

(c) 2, 2-dimethyl-butene (d) 2-butene

55. Identify the major product that is obtained on treatment of $CH_3CH_2CH(F)CH_3$ with CH_3O^-/CH_3OH is **NCERT Pg 180**

(a) $CH_3CH_2CH(OCH_3)CH_3$

(b) $CH_3CH=CHCH_3$

(c) $CH_3CH_2CH=CH_2$

(d) $CH_3CH_2CH_2CH_2OCH_3$

56. Among the following rules, the one which is applied in the given reaction is **NCERT Pg 180**

$$CH_3CHBrCH_2CH_3 \xrightarrow{\text{Alc. KOH}}$$

I. $CH_3CH=CHCH_3$ (major product)

II. $CH_2=CHCH_2CH_3$ (minor product)

(a) Saytzeff's rule

(b) Hofmann's rule

(c) Markovnikov's rule

(d) Kharasch effect

57. Which of the following is correct order for the ease of dehydrohalogenation of alkyl halide with alc. KOH? **NCERT Pg 180**

(a) 3° < 2° < 1° (b) 3° > 2° < 1°

(c) 3° > 2° > 1° (d) 3° < 2° > 1°

58. Consider the following alkyl halides, **NCERT Pg 180**

C_2H_5I	C_2H_5Cl	C_2H_5Br	C_2H_5F
I	II	III	IV

The correct order of dehydrohalogenation is

(a) I > III > II > IV (b) III > IV > II > I

(c) I > II > III > IV (d) IV > III > II > I

59. Which of the following compounds will undergo racemisation with solution of alcoholic KOH? **NCERT Pg 180**

(a) 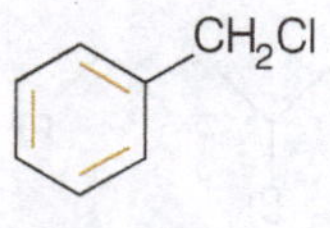

(b) $H_3C-CH(CH_3)-CH_2Cl$

(c) 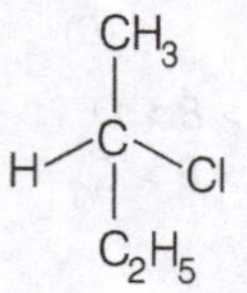

(d) 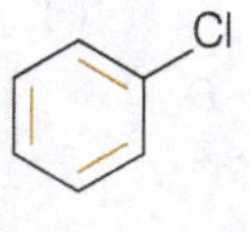

60. What does the figures I and II represent? **NCERT Pg 180**

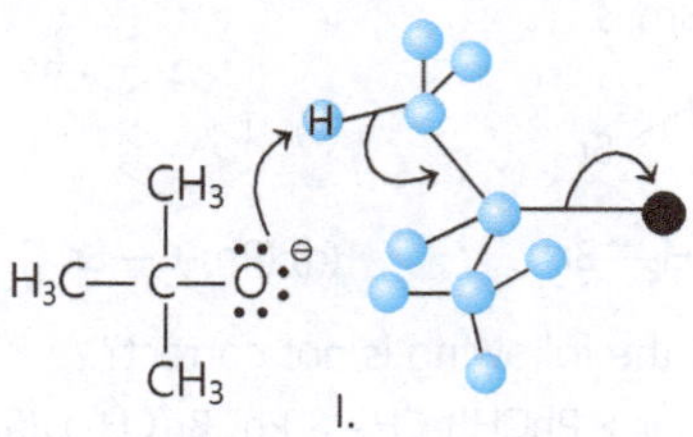

I.

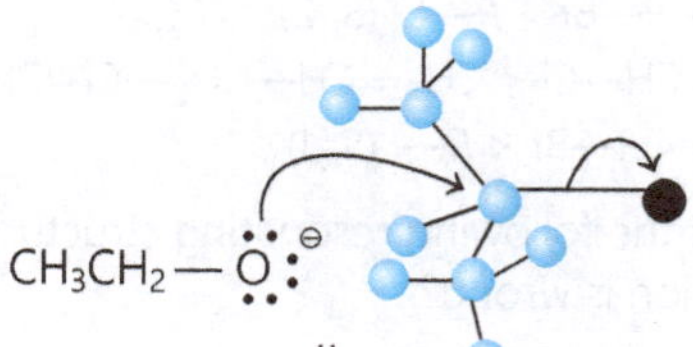

II.

(a) Substitution	Elimination
(b) Elimination	Elimination
(c) Substitution	Substitution
(d) Elimination	Substitution

61. Among the following, the suitable reagent for Wurtz reaction is **NCERT Pg 181**

(a) Na/alcohol (b) Na/Dry ether

(c) Zn/ether (d) Zn/alcohol

62. If 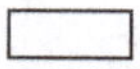 react with Cl_2 in presence of light and then react with Na metal in dry ether, final product is **NCERT Pg 165, 181**

(a) 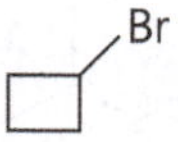 (b) 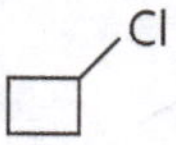

(c)  (d) 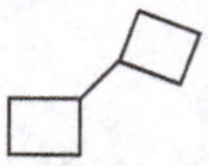

63. What is *A* in the following reaction? **NCERT Pg 182**

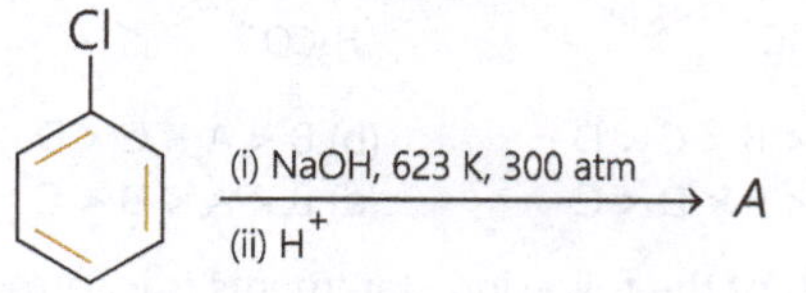

(a) 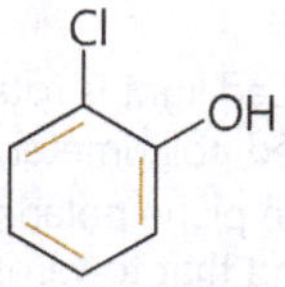 (b) 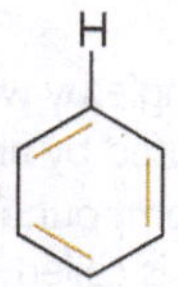

(c) 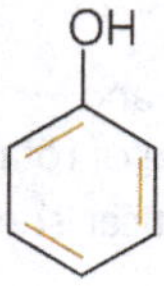 (d) 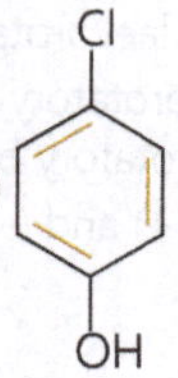

64. Correct order for rate of aromatic nucleophilic substitution reaction for the following compounds: **NCERT Pg 182, 183**

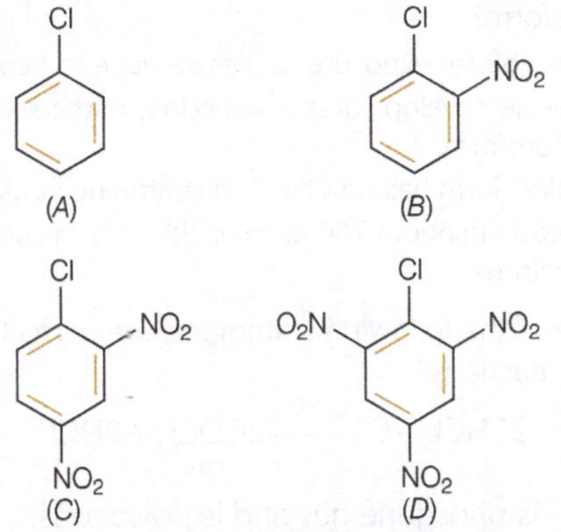

(a) $A > B > C > D$ (b) $D > C > B > A$
(c) $C > D > B > A$ (d) $D > C > A > B$

65. The major product Z obtained in the following reaction scheme is **NCERT Pg 184**

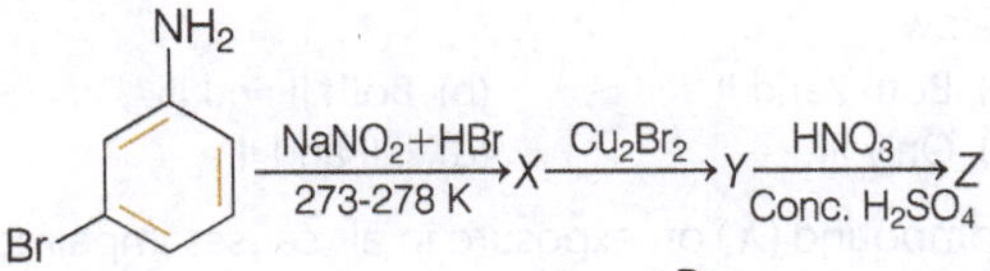

(a) 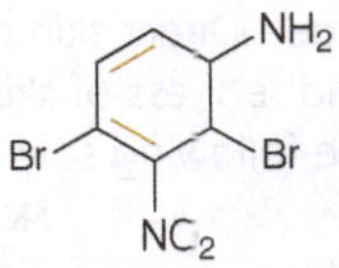

(b) 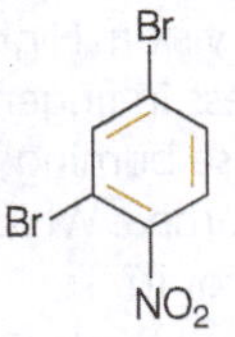

(c) 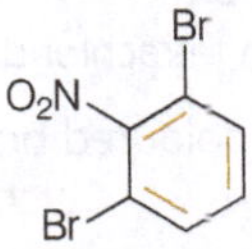

(d) 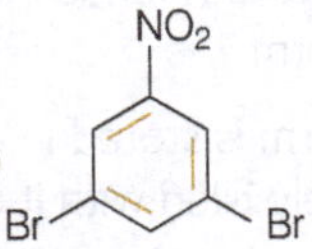

66. Halogenation, sulphonation, Friedel-Crafts reaction of haloarene comes under **NCERT Pg 184**
(a) nucleophilic substitution reaction of benzene
(b) electrophilic substitution reaction of benzene
(c) addition reaction of benzene
(d) elimination reaction of benzene

67. Select the product of the reaction. **NCERT Pg 184**

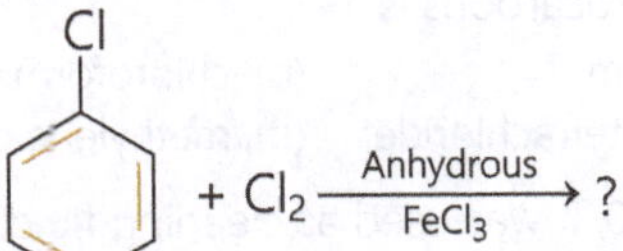

(a) 

(b) 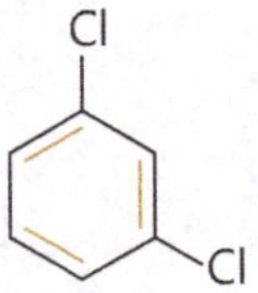

(c) 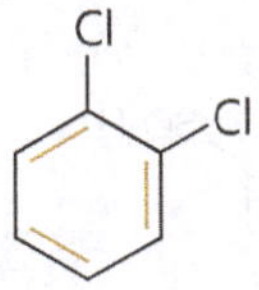

(d) 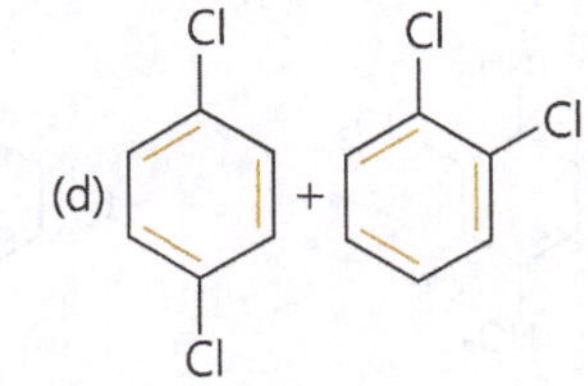

68. 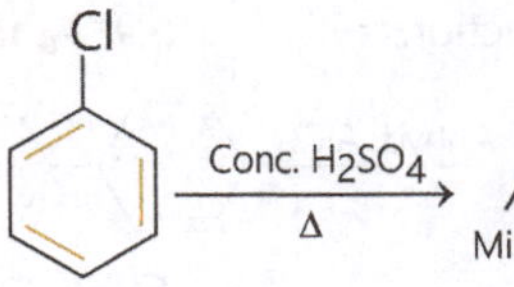

A and B respectively are **NCERT Pg 184**

	A	B
(a)	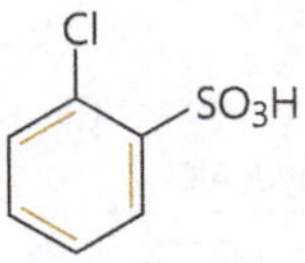	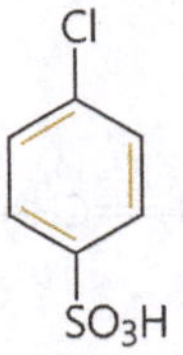
(b)	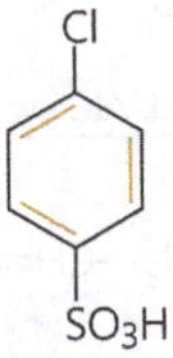	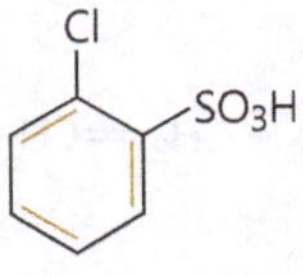
(c)	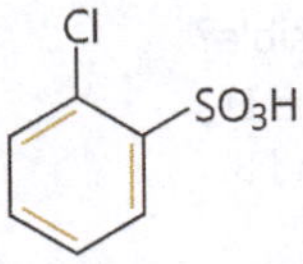	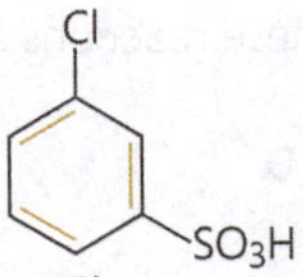
(d)	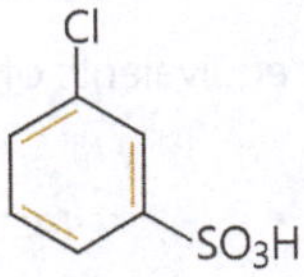	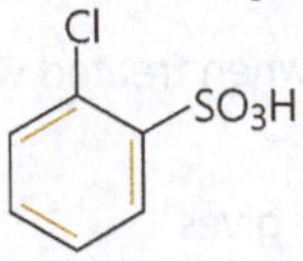

69. 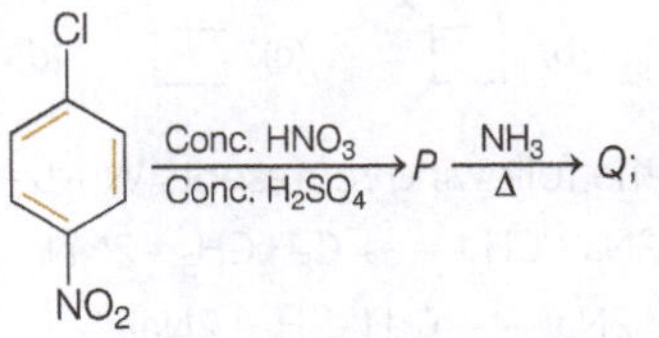

Product Q is **NCERT Pg 184**

(a) 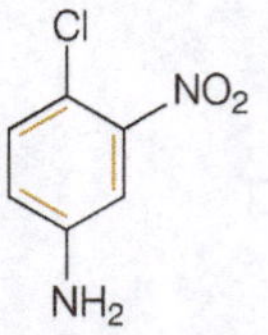 (b) 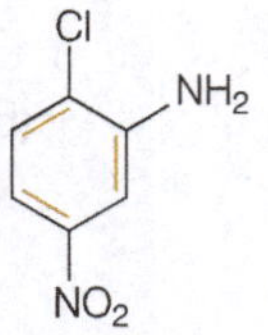

(c) 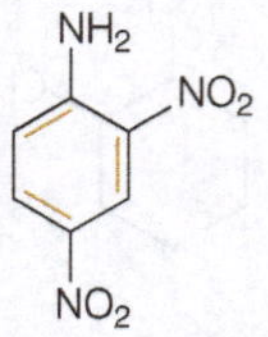 (d) 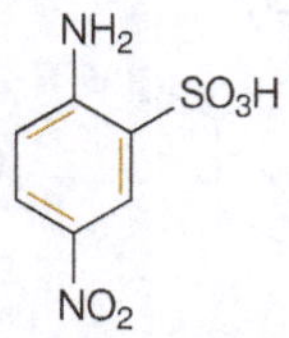

70. Consider the following reactions : **NCERT Pg 184-185**

(A) 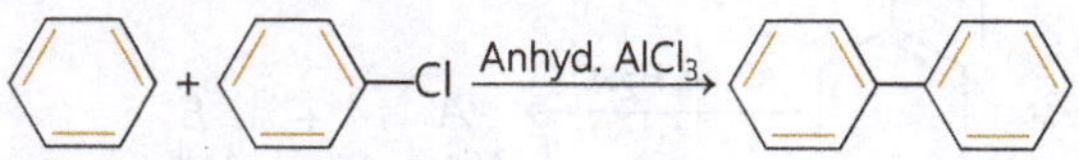

(B) 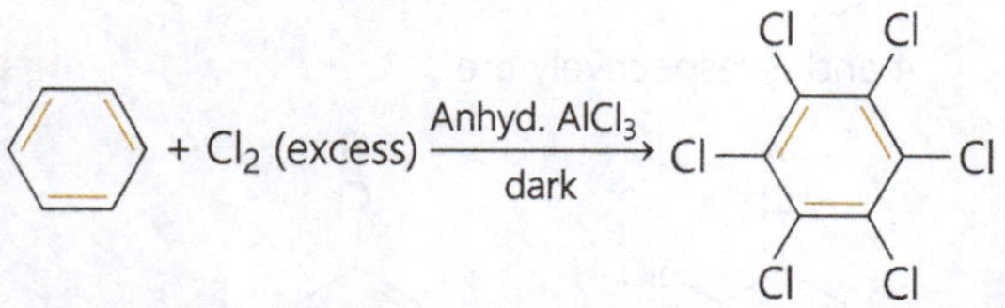

(C) 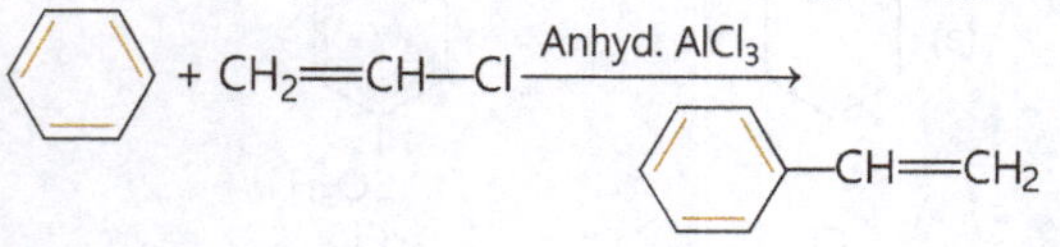

(D) 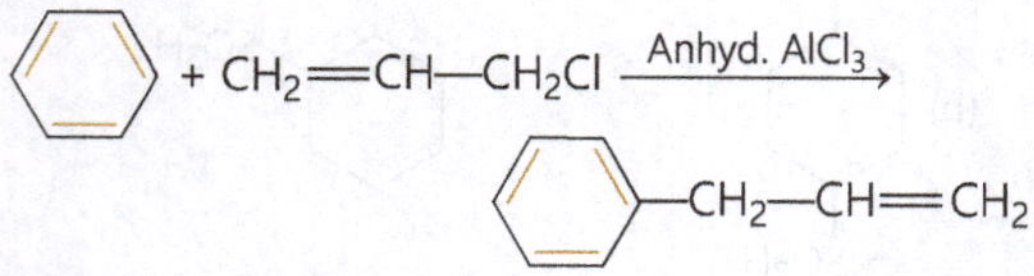

Which of these reactions are possible?

(a) B and D (b) A and D
(c) B, C and D (d) A and B

71. 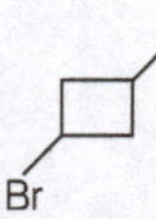 when treated with two equivalents of sodium in dry ether gives **NCERT Pg 186**

(a)  (b)  (c)  (d) 

72. Which of the following represents Wurtz-Fittig reaction? **NCERT Pg 186**

(a) $C_6H_5I + 2Na + CH_3I \longrightarrow C_6H_5CH_3 + 2NaI$
(b) $2C_6H_5I + 2Na \longrightarrow C_6H_5C_6H_5 + 2NaI$
(c) $2CH_3CH_2I + 2Na \longrightarrow CH_3CH_2CH_2CH_3 + 2NaI$
(d) $CH_3Br + AgF \longrightarrow CH_3F + AgBr$

Polyhalogen Compounds

73. Which of the following statements is correct for chloroform? **NCERT Pg 187**

(a) Chloroform exposure causes damage to heart.
(b) People develop sores when skin is immersed in chloroform.
(c) Chloroform has no effect on central nervous system.
(d) Breathing about 700 ppm of chloroform can cause dizziness.

74. Which of the following statements are correct for the given reactions? **NCERT Pg 187**

$$\underset{(A)}{2CHCl_3} + O_2 \xrightarrow{h\nu} \underset{(B)}{2COCl_2} + 2HCl$$

I. B is phosgene gas and is poisonous.
II. A is stored in closed dark coloured bottle.
III. A is used for the production of the freon refrigerant R-22.

Choose the correct answer from the options given below

(a) Both I and II (b) Both II and III
(c) Only III (d) I, II and III

75. Compound (X) on exposure in air causes impaired hearing and vision. Higher level exposure causes nausea and numbness in fingers and toes. Direct skin contact causes intense burning and mild redness of skin and even burn cornea. Which of the following solvents is responsible for it? **NCERT Pg 187**

(a) Methylene chloride (b) Chloroform
(c) Iodoform (d) Carbon tetrachloride

76. Chloroform is stored in closed dark coloured bottles completely filled with it because **NCERT Pg 187**

(a) it is slowly reduced by air in the presence of light to carbonyl chloride
(b) it is slowly oxidised by air in absence of light to carbonyl chloride
(c) it gets slowly reduced by air in absence of light to carbonyl chloride
(d) it gets slowly oxidised by air in the presence of light to carbonyl chloride

77. Solvent which is used in the synthesis of chlorofluorocarbons is **NCERT Pg 187**

(a) iodoform (b) chloroform
(c) carbon tetrachloride (d) methylene chloride

78. In mid 1960, it was used as cleaning fluid, degreasing agent, spot remover, fire extinguisher. The solvent was **NCERT Pg 187**

(a) tetrachloromethane (b) chloroform
(c) iodoform (d) dichloromethane

79. The antiseptic property of triiodomethane is due to
(a) liberation of free iodine **NCERT Pg 187**
(b) liberation of iodoform
(c) formation of chloroform
(d) formation of phosgene

80. Identify the compound which is employed as a solvent for fats, alkaloids, iodine and other substances. **NCERT Pg 187**
(a) Dichloromethane (b) Trichloromethane
(c) Triiodomethane (d) Tetrachloromethane

81. Which of the following statements is/are correct for DDT? **NCERT Pg 188**
I. It is very effective against mosquitoes that spread malaria.
II. It is easily metabolised by animals.
III. It is highly toxic for fish.

Choose the correct answer from the options given below.
(a) Both I and II (b) Both II and III
(c) Only III (d) Both I and III

82. When freon is manufactured by tetrachloromethane, the reaction involved in this process is called **NCERT Pg 188**
(a) Sandmeyer reaction
(b) Swarts reaction
(c) Finkelstein reaction
(d) Wurtz reaction

83. Natural ozone layer is unbalanced due to **NCERT Pg 188**
(a) cloudiness of poisonous gases
(b) presence of rain in the atmosphere
(c) initiation of radical chain by freon
(d) decreased concentration of CCl_4

84. Which of the following compound is used as an organic insecticide? **NCERT Pg 188**
(a) Chloroform (b) Freon-12
(c) Carbon tetrachloride (d) DDT

85. IUPAC name of DDT is **NCERT Pg 188**
(a) 1,1-*bis* (4-chlorophenyl)-2,2,2-trichloroethane
(b) 1,2-*bis* (4-chlorophenyl)-1,1,1-trichloroethane
(c) 2,2-*bis* (4-chlorophenyl)-1,1,1-trichloroethane
(d) 2,1-*bis* (4-chlorophenyl)-1,1,1-trichloroethane

Assertion-Reason Questions

Direction (Q. Nos. 1-10) *In the following question Assertion (A) followed by Reason (R) is given below. Choose the correct option out of the choices given below.*
(a) Both A and R are true and R is the correct explanation of A.
(b) Both A and R are true but R is not the correct explanation of A.
(c) A is true but R is false.
(d) A is false but R is true.

1. Assertion (A) In the preparation of alkyl halides from alcohols, thionyl chloride is preferred over other reagents.
Reason (R) The other two products produced during the reaction of alcohol and thionyl chloride except alkyl halide, are escapable gases. **NCERT Pg 164**

2. Assertion (A) Yield of any single alkyl halide which is formed by the free radical halogenation is low.
Reason (R) Free radical halogenation lead to formation of mixture of isomeric mono and polyhaloalkanes. **NCERT Pg 165**

3. Assertion (A) Boiling points of chlorides, bromides and iodides are considered to be higher than hydrocarbons.
Reason (R) Due to greater polarity and higher molecular mass, the intermolecular forces of attraction are weaker in halogen derivative as compared to hydrocarbon. **NCERT Pg 168**

4. Assertion (A) The boiling points of alkyl halides decrease in the order :
$$RI > RBr > RCl > RF.$$
Reason (R) The boiling points of alkyl chlorides, bromides and iodides are considerably higher than that of the hydrocarbon of comparable molecular mass. **NCERT Pg 168**

5. Assertion (A) Haloalkanes are slightly soluble in water.
Reason (R) Intermolecular attractions between haloalkanes and water molecules have much more strength than intermolecular attraction between water molecules. **NCERT Pg 169**

6. Assertion (A) Vinyl halides do not undergo nucleophilic substitution easily.
Reason (R) Even though the intermediate carbocation is stabilised by loosely held π-electrons the cleavage is difficult because of strong bonding. **NCERT Pg 169**

7. Assertion (A) S_N2 mechanism is accompanied by racemisation.
Reason (R) In S_N2 mechanism, nucleophile attaches itself on opposite side, where halogen atom is present. **NCERT Pg 171**

8. **Assertion** (A) S_N1 reaction is accompanied by racemisation.

Reason (R) Carbocation is formed in this reaction and attack of nucleophile can be from either side of the leaving group. NCERT Pg 173, 179

9. **Assertion** (A) S_N1 mechanism is ruled out in case of haloarene.

Reason (R) Phenyl cation is formed as a result of self ionisation which is not stabilised by resonance. NCERT Pg 182

10. **Assertion** (A) *tert*-butylbromide undergoes Wurtz reaction to give 2, 2, 3, 3-tetramethylbutane.

Reason (R) In Wurtz reaction, alkyl halides react with sodium in dry ether to give hydrocarbon containing double the carbon atoms that are present in the halide. NCERT Pg 181

Statement Type Questions

Directions (Q. Nos. 1-5) *In the following questions, two statements (I & II) are given. In the light of the given statements, choose the correct option given below.*

(a) Both Statement I and Statement II are false.
(b) Statement I is true but Statement II is false.
(c) Statement I is false but Statement II is true.
(d) Both Statement I and Statement II are true.

1. **Statement I** Haloarenes are more reactive towards nucleophilic substitution reaction.

Statement II The C—Cl bond length in haloalkane in less than the bond length of haloarene. NCERT Pg 164

2. **Statement I** Presence of nitro group decrease the nucleophilic substitution reaction in aryl halides.

Statement II The intermediate carbocation is stabilised due to the presence of nitro group. NCERT Pg 181

3. **Statement I** Presence of nitro group at *ortho* or *para*-position increases the reactivity of haloarene towards nucleophilic substitution.

Statement II Nitro group being an electron withdrawing group decreases the electron density over the benzene ring. NCERT Pg 183

4. **Statement I** Electrophilic substitution reactions in haloarene occur slowly and under drastic conditions.

Statement II Haloarenes are highly active as compared to benzene. NCERT Pg 184

5. **Statement I** Chlorine is an *ortho-para* directing group in electrophilic aromatic substitution reaction.

Statement II Chlorine is an electron withdrawing group. NCERT Pg 184

6. Which of the following statements are not correct? NCERT Pg 159, 160, 162, 163

I. Aryl halides are the compounds in which halogen atom is bonded to the sp^2-hybridised carbon atom of a carbon-carbon double bond.

II. Ethylene dichloride is a *vicinal*-dihalide.

III. Carbon-halogen bond length decreases from C—I to C—F.

IV. The position of Cl in the compound $CH_3CH{=}CCl{-}CH_2{-}CH_3$ can be classified as allylic.

V. The common name of $(CH_3)_3CCH_2Br$ is *neo*-pentyl bromide.

Choose the most appropriate answer from the options given below.

(a) I, III and V
(b) I and IV
(c) I, III and II
(d) IV, III and V

7. Which of the following statements are correct?

I. Aryl fluorides can be prepared by electrophilic substitution of arenes.

II. The boiling points of isomeric haloalkanes increase with increase in branching.

III. $C_6H_5CHClC_6H_5$ is more easily hydrolysed by *aq*. KOH than $C_6H_5CH_2Cl$.

IV. Phosphorus tribromide are usually generated *in situ* by the reaction of red phosphorus with bromine.

V. Solution of freshly prepared diazonium salt with cuprous bromide, replaces diazonium group by —Br or —Cl.

Choose the most appropriate answer from the options given below. NCERT Pg 164, 166, 168

(a) III, IV and V
(b) I, IV and V
(c) II, III and IV
(d) I and II

8. Which of the following statements are not correct?

I. In Grignard reagent, the carbon-magnesium bond is ionic and highly polar.

II. Freon-12(CCl_2F_2) can be manufacture from tetrachloromethane by Swarts reaction.

III. Haloarenes are more reactive than haloalkanes towards nucleophilic substitution reaction.

IV. The presence of an electron withdrawing group at *meta*-position increases the reactivity of haloarenes.

V. In stratosphere, freon in able to initiate radical chain reactions that can upset the natural ozone balance.

Choose the most appropriate answer from the options given below: **NCERT Pg 181, 182, 188**

(a) I, II and V only
(b) II and V only
(c) I, III and IV only
(d) II, III and IV only

Matching Type Questions

1. Match the following Column I (statement) to Column II (corresponding halide) and choose the correct option from the codes given below. **NCERT Pg 160, 161**

Column I	Column II
A. Halogen atom is bonded to sp^3-hybridised carbon atom next to an aromatic ring.	1. Aryl halide
B. Halogen atom is bonded to an sp^2-hybridised carbon atom of carbon-carbon double bond.	2. Vinylic halide
C. Halogen atom is bonded to sp^2-hybridised carbon atom of an aromatic ring.	3. Benzylic halide

Codes

	A	B	C
(a)	1	2	3
(b)	3	1	2
(c)	3	2	1
(d)	1	3	2

2. Match the following common name in Column I to the IUPAC name in Column II and choose the correct option from the codes given below. **NCERT Pg 161, 162**

Column I	Column II
A. Bromoform	1. Chloromethylbenzene
B. Vinyl chloride	2. Tribromomethane
C. Benzyl chloride	3. Chloroethene
D. Chloroform	4. Trichloromethane

Codes

	A	B	C	D
(a)	3	1	2	4
(b)	4	1	2	3
(c)	2	3	1	4
(d)	1	2	3	4

3 Match the alkyl halide reacting with reagent given in Column I with their respective substituted product given in Column II and choose the correct option from the codes given below. **NCERT Pg 170**

Column I (Reagent)	Column II (Substituted product)
A. KCN	1. *R*H
B. AgCN	2. *R*CN
C. KNO_2	3. *R*NC
D. $LiAlH_4$	4. *R*—O—N=O

Codes

	A	B	C	D
(a)	2	3	1	4
(b)	3	2	1	4
(c)	2	3	4	1
(d)	3	2	4	1

4. Match the Column I representing alkyl halide with the statement given in Column II and choose the correct option from the codes given below. **NCERT Pg 171, 173**

Column I	Column II
A. Primary alkyl halide	1. S_N2 or elimination depending upon strength of base/ nucleophile.
B. Secondary alkyl halide	2. Prefers S_N2 reaction.
C. Tertiary alkyl halide	3. S_N1 or elimination depending upon stability of carbocation or more substituted alkene.

Codes

	A	B	C
(a)	2	1	3
(b)	1	2	3
(c)	2	3	1
(d)	1	3	2

5. Match the following conditions given in Column I with Column II and choose the correct option from the codes given below. **NCERT Pg 182, 184**

Column I	Column II
A. 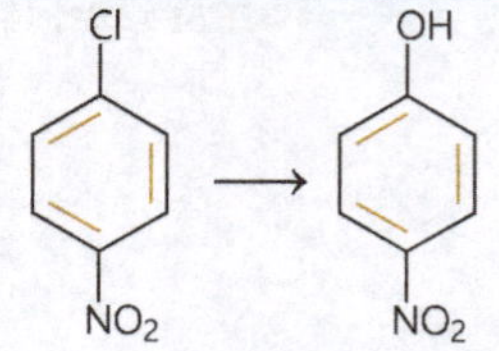	1. NaOH, 443 K, $H^{\oplus}$
B. 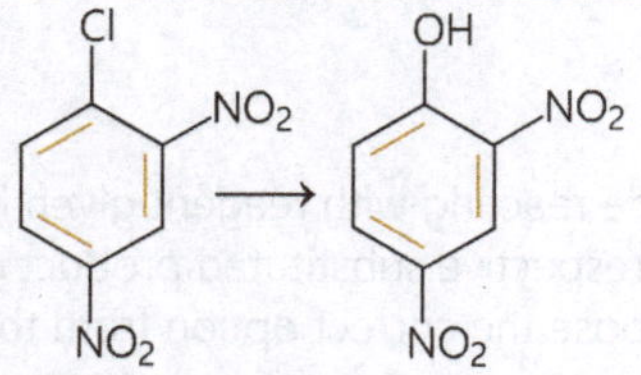	2. NaOH, 368 K, $H^{\oplus}$
C. 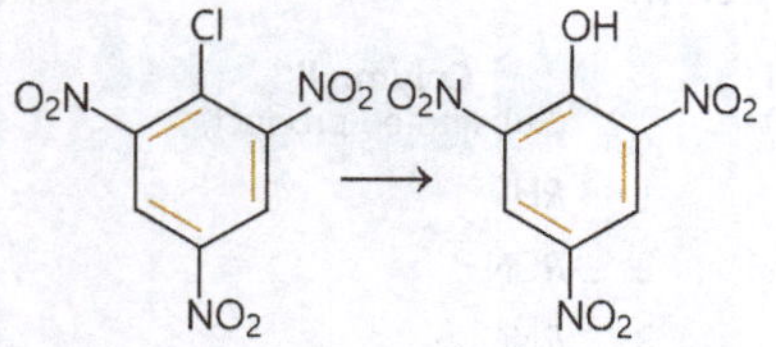	3. Warm H_2O
D. 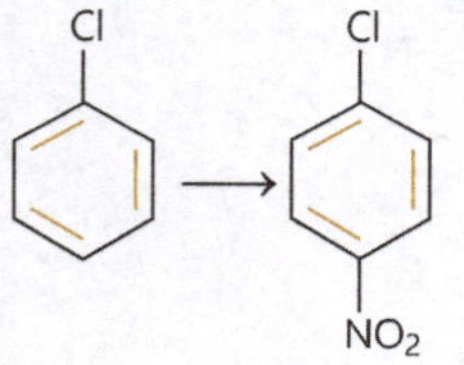	4. HNO_3 Conc. H_2SO_4

Codes

	A	B	C	D		A	B	C	D
(a)	3	4	2	1	(b)	4	3	2	1
(c)	1	2	3	4	(d)	3	2	4	1

6. Match the reactions given in Column I with the types of reactions given in Column II and choose the correct option from the codes given below. **NCERT Pg 180, 182, 184**

Column I	Column II
A. 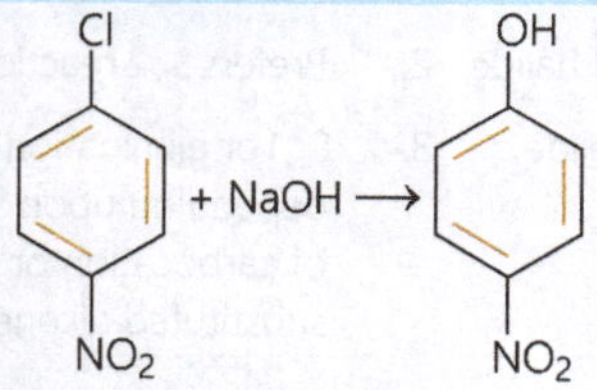	1. Electrophilic addition
B. $CH_3-CH=CH_2 + HBr \longrightarrow CH_3-\underset{\displaystyle Br}{\underset{\vert}{CH}}-CH_3$	2. Electrophilic aromatic substitution
C. 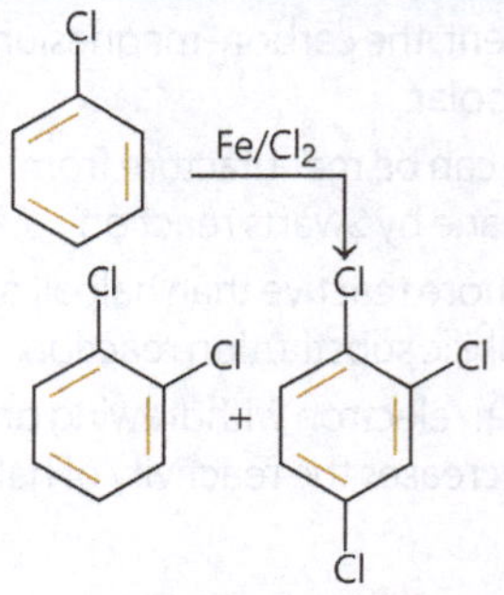	3. Saytzeff elimination
D. $CH_3CH_2\underset{\displaystyle Br}{\underset{\vert}{CH}}CH_3 \xrightarrow{\text{Alc. KOH}} CH_3CH=CHCH_3$	4. Nucleophilic aromatic substitution

Codes

	A	B	C	D
(a)	2	4	1	3
(b)	4	1	2	3
(c)	2	1	4	3
(d)	2	1	3	4

7. Match the reactions given in Column I with the reagents given in Column II. **NCERT Pg 165, 166, 186**

Column I	Column II
A. 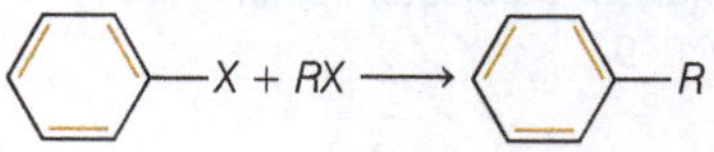	1. Ether
B. 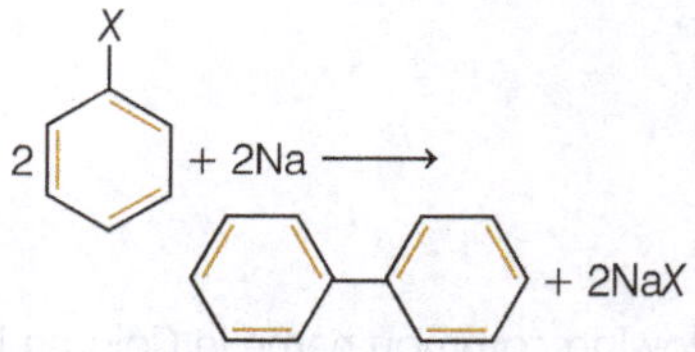	2. Sodium
C. 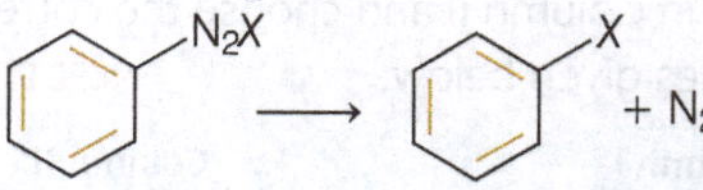	3. Dry acetone
D. $C_2H_5Cl + NaI \longrightarrow C_2H_5I + NaCl$	4. Cu_2X_2

Codes

	A	B	C	D
(a)	2	1	4	3
(b)	1	2	3	4
(c)	4	2	3	1
(d)	3	4	1	2

Numerical Value Questions

1. The major product of the following reaction contains .... bromine atom(s). NCERT Pg 167

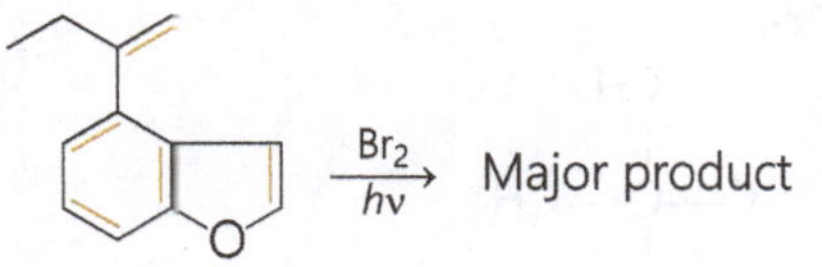

2. 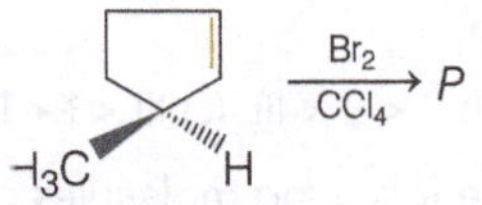

The number of chirаl centres are present in product P is .... NCERT Pg 165

3. 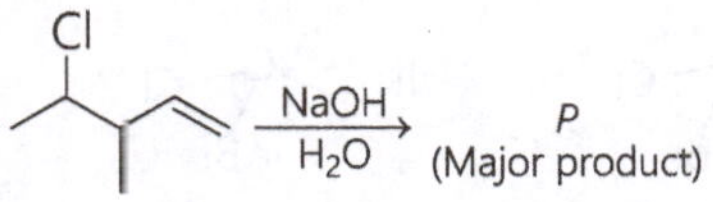

Consider the above reaction. The number of π-electrons present in the product 'P' is .... NCERT Pg 173

4. Observe the structures given below. NCERT Pg 176

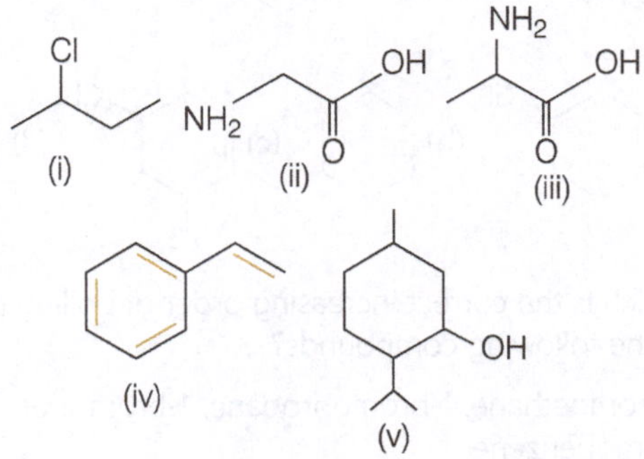

The total number of structures/compounds which possess asymmetric carbon atom is ..... .

5. The number of optically active stereoisomers possible for butane-2, 3-diol are .... NCERT Pg 177

NCERT Exemplar's Questions

1. Which of the following is correct IUPAC name for $CH_3-\underset{\underset{C_2H_5}{|}}{CH}-CH_2-Br$?
(a) 1-bromo-2-ethylpropane
(b) 1-bromo-2-ethyl-2-methylethane
(c) 1-bromo-2-methylbutane
(d) 2-methyl-1-bromobutane

2. What should be the correct IUPAC name for diethylbromomethane?
(a) 1-bromo-1, 1-diethylmethane
(b) 3-bromopentane
(c) 1-bromo-1-ethylpropane
(d) 1-bromopentane

3. Which of the following alcohols will yield the corresponding alkyl chloride on reaction with conc. HCl at room temperature?
(a) $CH_3CH_2-CH_2-OH$
(b) $CH_3CH_2-\underset{\underset{CH_3}{|}}{CH}-OH$
(c) $CH_3CH_2-\underset{\underset{CH_3}{|}}{CH}-CH_2OH$
(d) $CH_3CH_2-\overset{\overset{CH_3}{|}}{\underset{\underset{CH_3}{|}}{C}}-OH$

4. Which of the following is halogen exchange reaction?
(a) $RX + NaI \xrightarrow{\text{Dry acetone}} RI + NaX$
(b) 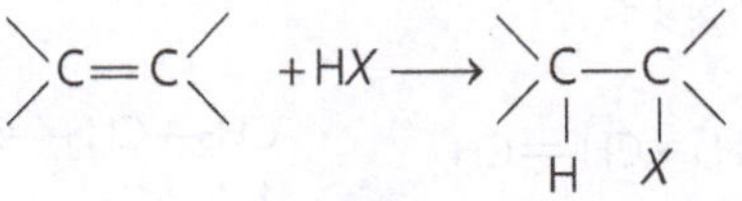

(c) $R-OH + HX \xrightarrow{ZnCl_2} R-X + H_2O$
(d) 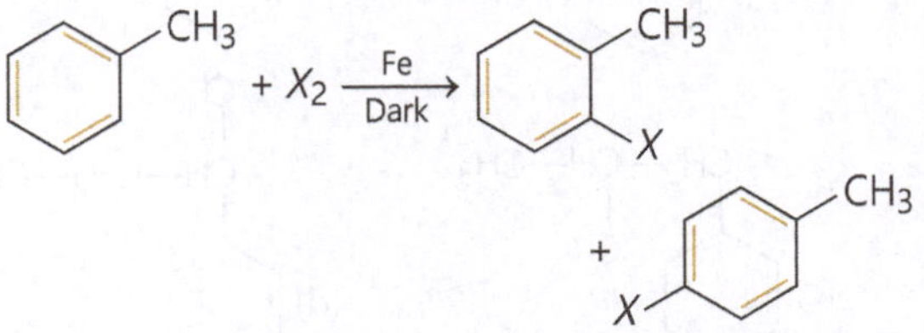

5. Which reagent will you use for the following reaction?

$CH_3CH_2CH_2CH_3 \longrightarrow CH_3CH_2CH_2CH_2Cl + CH_3CH_2CHClCH_3$

(a) Cl_2/UV light
(b) $NaCl + H_2SO_4$
(c) Cl_2 gas in dark
(d) Cl_2 gas in the presence of iron in dark

6. Identify the compound *Y* in the following reaction,

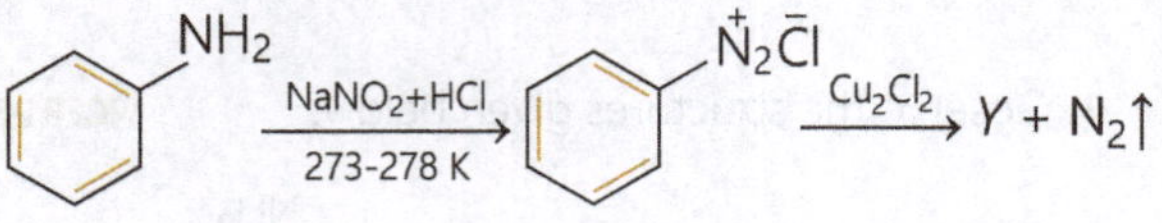

(a) 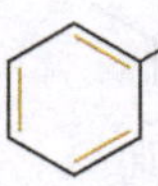 (b)  (c) 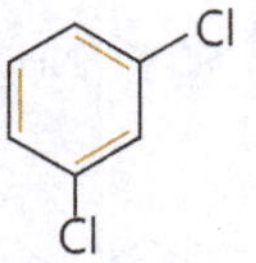 (d) 

7. Which is the correct increasing order of boiling points of the following compounds?

1-bromoethane, 1-bromopropane, 1-bromobutane, bromobenzene

(a) Bromobenzene < 1-bromobutane < 1-bromopropane < 1-bromoethane
(b) Bromobenzene < 1-bromoethane < 1-bromopropane < 1-bromobutane
(c) 1-bromopropane < 1-bromobutane < 1-bromoethane < bromobenzene
(d) 1-bromoethane < 1-bromopropane < 1-bromobutane < bromobenzene

8. What is *A* in the following reaction?

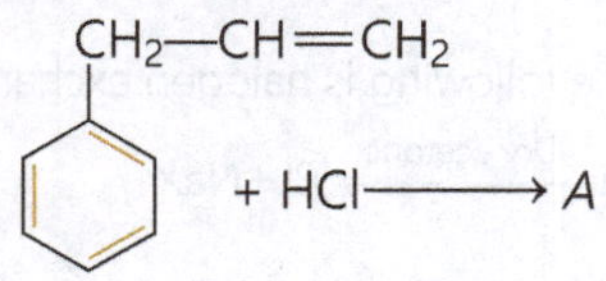

(a) 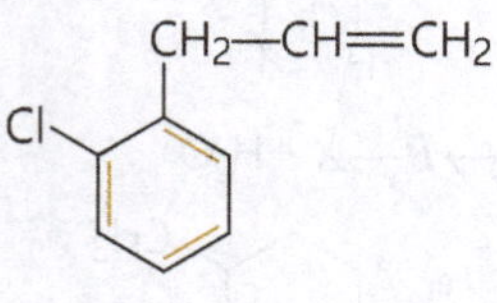 (b) 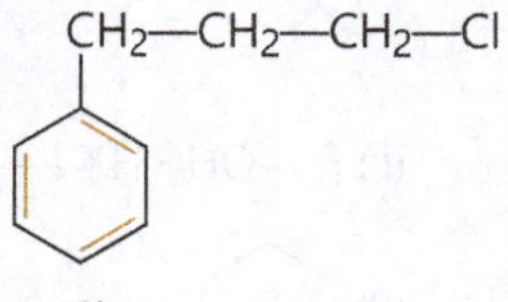

(c) 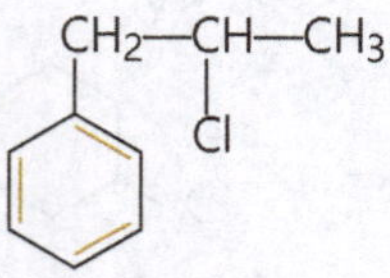 (d) 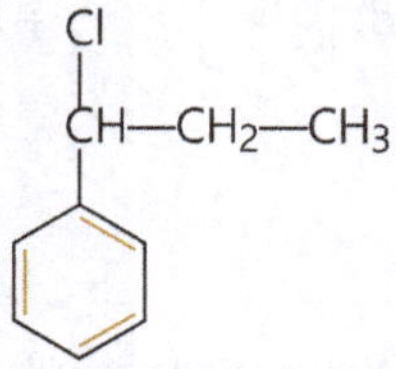

9. Arrange the following compounds in the increasing order of their densities.

I.  II. 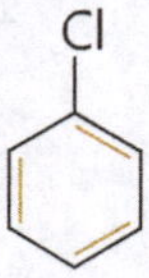 III. 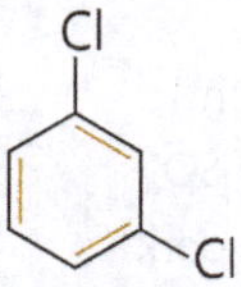 IV. 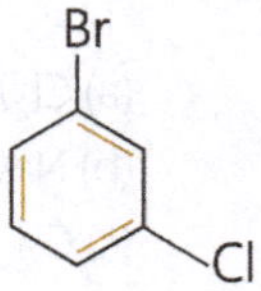

(a) I < II < III < IV (b) I < III < IV < II
(c) IV < III < II < I (d) II < IV < III < I

10. Arrange the following compounds in increasing order of their boiling points.

I. 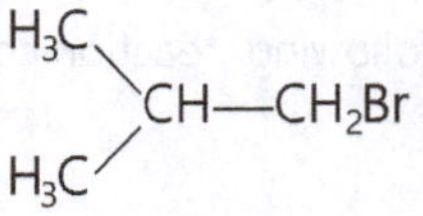 II. $CH_3CH_2CH_2CH_2Br$

III. 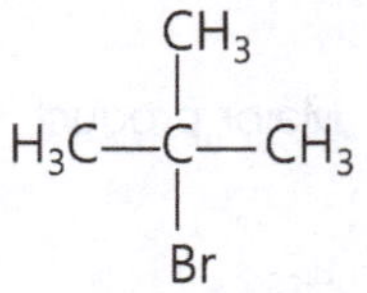

(a) II < I < III (b) I < II < III (c) III < I < II (d) III < II < I

11. In which of the following molecules carbon atom marked with asterisk (*) is asymmetric?

I. 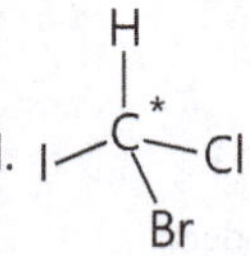 II. 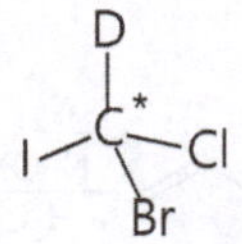

III. 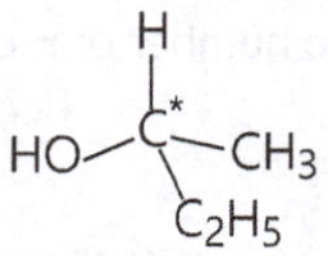 IV. 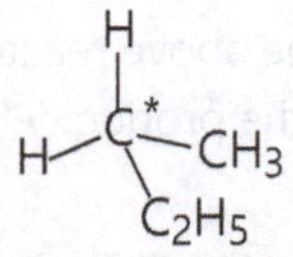

(a) I, II, III and IV (b) I, II and III
(c) II, III and IV (d) I, III and IV

12. Which of the carbon atoms present in the molecule given below are asymmetric?

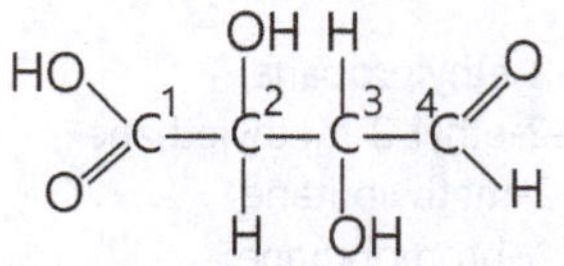

(a) 1, 2, 3, 4 (b) 2, 3 (c) 1, 4 (d) 1, 2, 3

13. Match the structures given in Column I with the names in Column II.

	Column I		Column II
A.	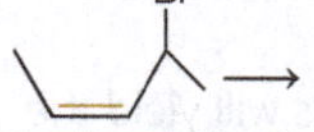	1.	4-bromopent-2-ene
B.	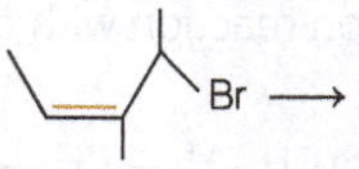	2.	4-bromo-3- methylpent-2-ene
C.	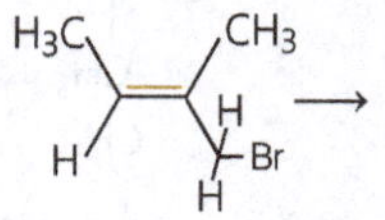	3.	1-bromo-2-methylbut -2-ene
D.	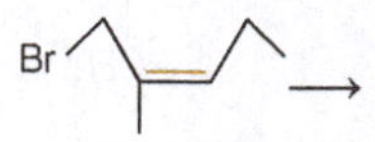	4.	1-bromo-2-methylpent-2-ene

14. Which of the following structures is enantiomeric with the molecule (*A*) given below?

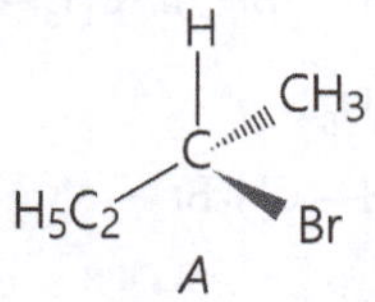

A

(a) 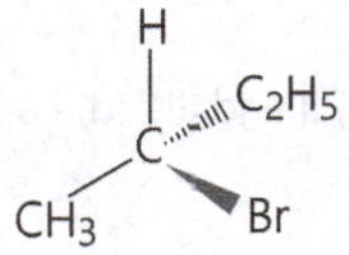 (b) 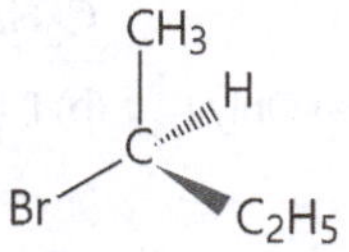

(c) 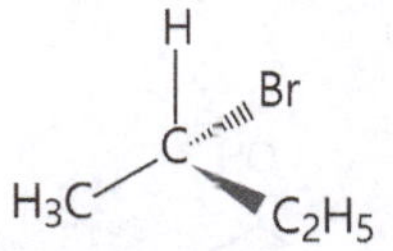 (d) 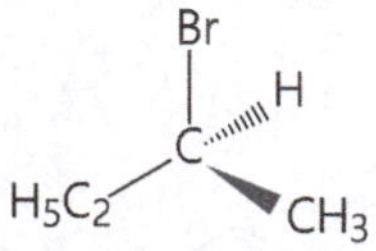

15. (c) Molecule whose mirror image is non-superimposable over them are known as chiral. Which of the following molecule is chiral in nature?

(a) 2-bromobutane (b) 1-bromobutane
(c) 2-bromopropane (d) 2-bromopropan-2-ol

16. Which of the following is an example of *vic*-dihalide?

(a) Dichloromethane (b) 1, 2-dichloroethane
(c) Ethylidene chloride (d) Allyl chloride

17. The position of Br in the given compound $CH_3CH{=}CHC(Br)(CH_3)_2$ can be classified as ....

(a) allyl (b) aryl (c) vinyl (d) secondary

18. Chlorobenzene is formed by reaction of chlorine with benzene in the presence of $AlCl_3$. Which of the following species attacks the benzene ring in this reaction?

(a) Cl^- (b) Cl^+ (c) $AlCl_3$ (d) $[AlCl_4]^-$

19. Ethylidene chloride is a/an ....

(a) *vic*-dihalide (b) *gem*-dihalide
(c) allylic halide (d) vinylic halide

20. The reaction of toluene with chlorine in the presence of iron and in the absence of light yields ....

(a) 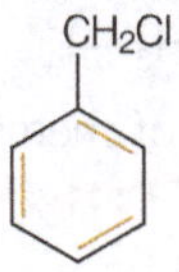 (b) 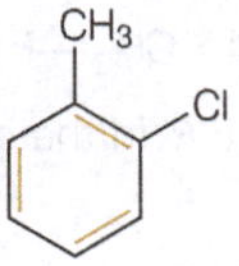

(c)  (d) Mixture of (b) and (c)

21. The order of reactivity of following alcohols with halogen acids is ....

(A) $CH_3CH_2—CH_2—OH$ (B) $CH_3CH_2—CH(CH_3)—OH$

(C) $CH_3CH_2—C(CH_3)_2—OH$

(a) (A) > (B) > (C) (b) (C) > (B) > (A)
(c) (B) > (A) > (C) (d) (A) > (C) > (B)

Directions (Q. Nos. 22-25) *In the questions arrange the compounds in increasing order of rate of reaction towards nucleophilic substitution.*

22. I. 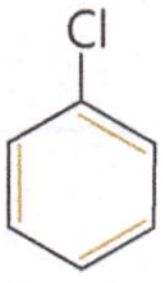 II. 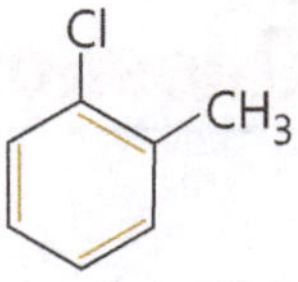 III. 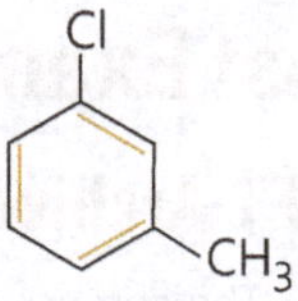

(a) I < II < III (b) I < III < II (c) III < II < I (d) II < III < I

23. I. 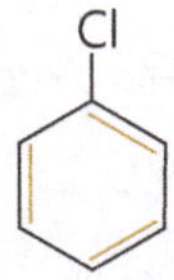 II.  III. 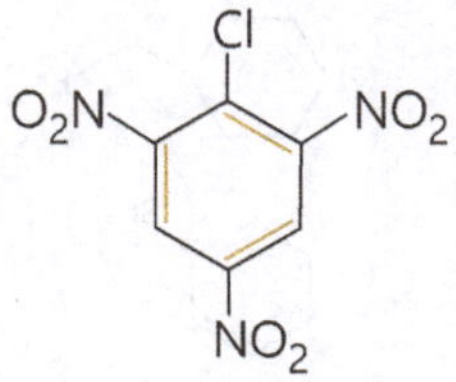

(a) III < II < I (b) II < III < I (c) I < III < II (d) I < II < III

24. I. 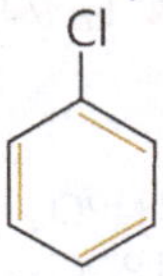 II.  III. 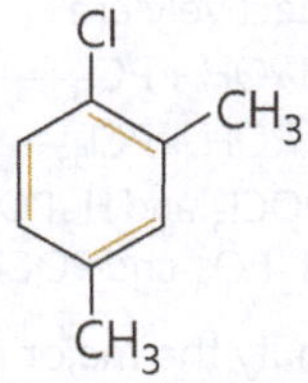

(a) I < II < III (b) II < I < III (c) III < II < I (d) I < III < II

25. I. 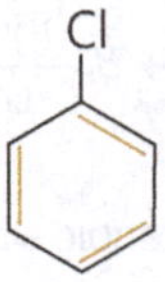 II. 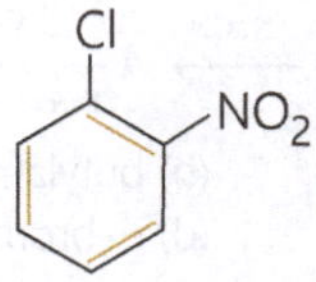 III. 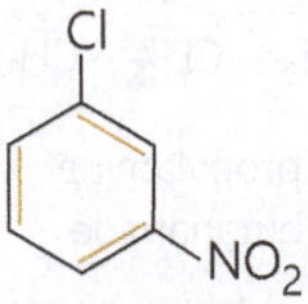

(a) I < II < III (b) III < II < I (c) I < III < II (d) III < I < II

26. Which of the following alkyl halides will undergo S_N1 reaction most readily?

(a) $(CH_3)_3C—F$ (b) $(CH_3)_3C—Cl$
(c) $(CH_3)_3C—Br$ (d) $(CH_3)_3C—I$

27. Match the items of Column I and Column II.

Column I	Column II
A. S_N1 reaction	1. *vic*-dibromides
B. Chemicals in fire extinguisher	2. *gem*-dihalides
C. Bromination of alkenes	3. Racemisation
D. Alkylidene halides	4. Saytzeff rule
E. Elimination of HX from alkyl halide	5. Tetrachloromethane

28. Reaction of $C_6H_5CH_2Br$ with aqueous sodium hydroxide follows

(a) S_N1 mechanism (b) S_N2 mechanism
(c) Any of the above two depending upon the temperature of reaction
(d) Saytzeff rule

29. Which of the following compounds will give racemic mixture on nucleophilic substitution by OH^- ion?

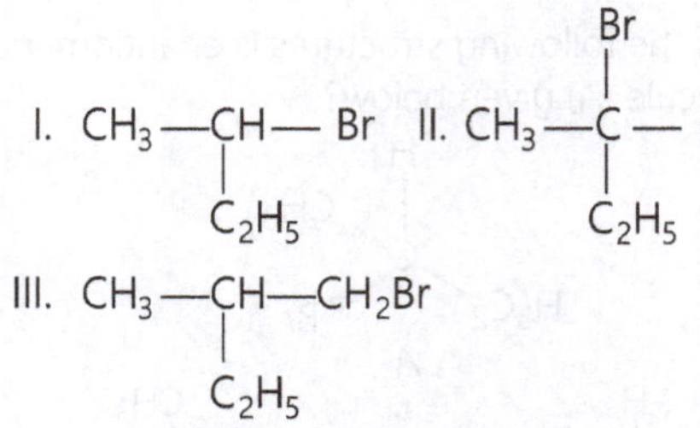

(a) Only I (b) I, II and III (c) II and III (d) I and III

Past Exams' Questions

NEET Archive

1. The compound that will undergo S_N1 reaction with the fastest rate is **NCERT Pg 173, NEET 2024**

(a) 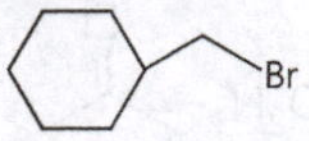

(b) 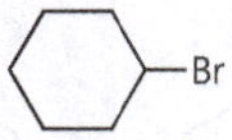

(c) 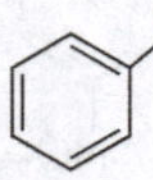

(d) 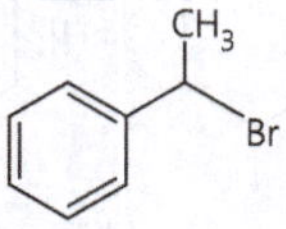

2. The products A and B obtained in the following reactions, respectively are **NCERT Pg 164, NEET 2024**

$3ROH + PCl_3 \longrightarrow 3RCl + A$

$ROH + PCl_5 \longrightarrow RCl + HCl + B$

(a) $POCl_3$ and H_3PO_3 (b) $POCl_3$ and H_3PO_4
(c) H_3PO_4 and $POCl_3$ (d) H_3PO_3 and $POCl_3$

3. Identify the major product C formed in the following reaction sequence: **NCERT Pg 170, NEET 2024**

$$CH_3—CH_2—CH—I \xrightarrow{NaCN} A \xrightarrow[\text{Partial hydrolysis}]{OH^-} B \xrightarrow[Br_2]{NaOH} \underset{(\text{major})}{C}$$

(a) propylamine (b) butylamine
(c) butanamide (d) α-bromobutanoic acid

4. The given compound **NCERT Pg 160, NEET 2023**

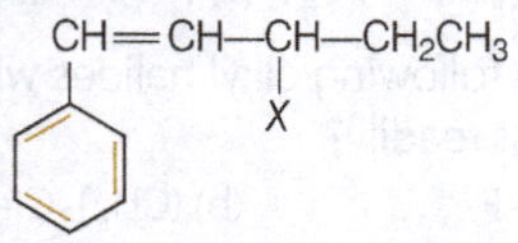

is an example of

(a) aryl halide (b) allylic halide
(c) vinylic halide (d) benzylic halide

5. Identify the product in the following reaction.

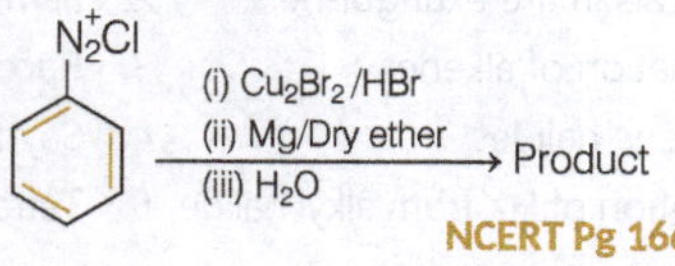

NCERT Pg 166, 181, NEET 2023

(a) 
(b) 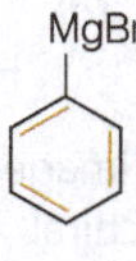

(c) 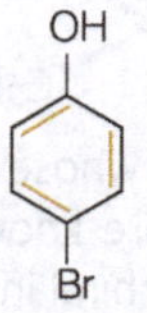

(d) 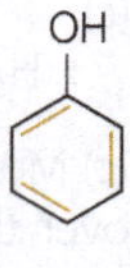

6. The incorrect statement regarding chirality is **NCERT Pg 177, NEET 2022**

(a) The product obtained by S_N2 reaction of haloalkane having chirality at the reactive site shows inversion of configuration.
(b) Enantiomers are superimposable mirror images on each other.
(c) A racemic mixture shows zero optical rotation.
(d) S_N1 reaction yields 1 : 1 mixture of both enantiomers.

7. The major product formed in dehydrohalogenation reaction of 2-bromopentane is pent-2-ene. This product formation is based on **NEET 2021, NCERT Pg 180**

(a) Saytzeff's rule (b) Hund's rule
(c) Hofmann rule (d) Huckel's rule

8. The correct sequence of bond enthalpy of C—X bond is **NCERT Pg 164, NEET 2021**

(a) $CH_3—F < CH_3—Cl < CH_3—Br < CH_3—I$
(b) $CH_3—F > CH_3—Cl > CH_3—Br > CH_3—I$
(c) $CH_3—F < CH_3—Cl > CH_3—Br > CH_3—I$
(d) $CH_3—Cl > CH_3—F > CH_3—Br > CH_3—I$

9. The reagent 'R' in the given sequence of chemical reaction is **NCERT Pg 166, NEET 2021**

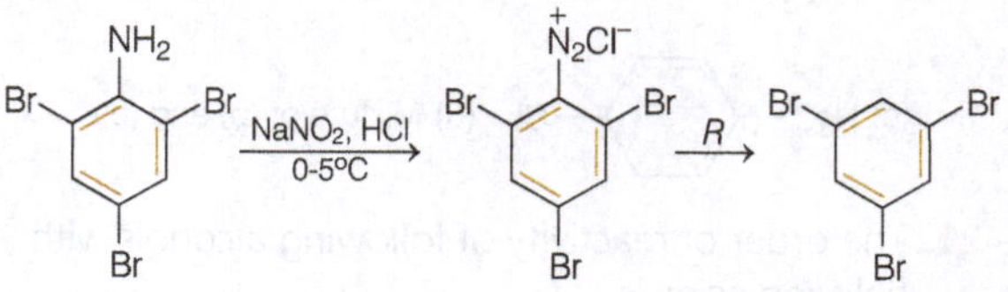

(a) H_2O (b) CH_3CH_2OH
(c) HI (d) CuCN / KCN

10. Which of the following will not undergo S_N1 reaction with $\bar{O}H$? **NCERT Pg 173, NEET 2020**

(a) $CH_2=CH—CH_2Cl$ (b) $(CH_3)_3CCl$

(c) 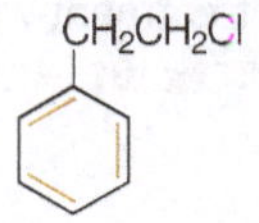 (d) 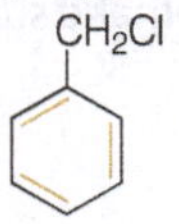

11. Elimination reaction of 2-bromo-pentane to form pent-2-ene is **NCERT Pg 180, NEET 2020**

1. β-elimination reaction.
2. follows Zaitsev rule.
3. dehydrohalogenation reaction.
4. dehydration reaction.

(a) (1), (3), (4) (b) (2), (3), (4) (c) (1), (2), (4) (d) (1), (2), (3)

12. For the following reactions, **NCERT Pg 180, NEET 2016 (Solved)**

(i) $CH_3CH_2CH_2Br + KOH \longrightarrow CH_3CH=CH_2 + KBr + H_2O$

(ii) 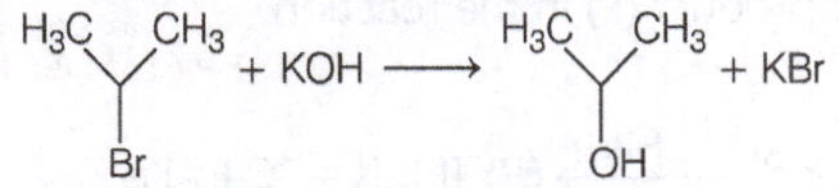

(iii) 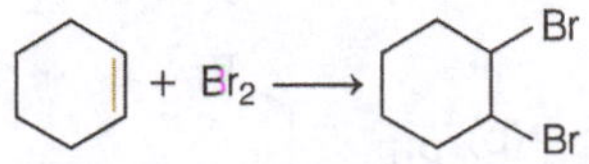

Which of the following statements is correct?

(a) (i) is elimination, reaction, (ii) is substitution and (iii) is addition reaction.
(b) (i) is elimination, (ii) and (iii) are substitution reactions.
(c) (i) is substitution, (ii) and (iii) are addition reactions.
(d) (i) and (ii) are elimination reactions and (iii) is addition reaction.

13. Two possible stereo-strucure of $CH_3CHOHCOOH$, which are optically active, are called **NCERT Pg 177, CBSE-AIPMT 2015**

(a) atropisomers
(b) enantiomers
(c) mesomers
(d) distereomers

14. Which of the following compounds will undergo racemisation when solution of KOH hydrolysis? **NCERT Pg 179, CBSE-AIPMT 2014**

(i) 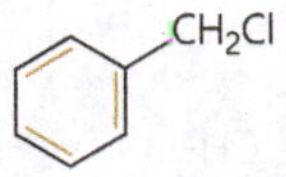 (ii) $CH_3CH_2CH_2Cl$

(iii) $H_3C—\underset{}{\overset{CH_3}{\overset{|}{C}H}}—CH_2Cl$ (iv) 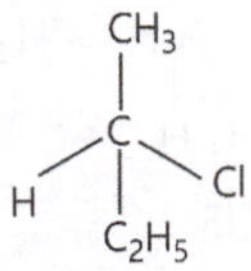

(a) (i) and (ii) (b) (ii) and (iv)
(c) (iii) and (iv) (d) Only (iv)

JEE Main Archive

15 Identify the correct set of reagents or reaction conditions 'X' and 'Y' in the following set of transformation. **NCERT Pg 165, JEE Main 2024**

$$CH_3—CH_2—CH_2—Br \xrightarrow{'X'} \text{Product} \xrightarrow{'Y'} CH_3—\underset{Br}{\underset{|}{C}H}—CH_3$$

(a) X = conc. alc. NaOH, 80°C, Y = HBr/Acetic acid
(b) X = dil. *aq.* NaOH, 20°C, Y = HBr/Acetic acid
(c) X = dil. *aq.* NaOH, 20°C, $Y = Br_2 / CHCl_3$
(d) X = conc. alc. NaOH, 80°C, $Y = Br_2 / CHCl_3$

16 Which among the following halide/s will not show S_N1 reaction? **NCERT Pg 174, JEE Main 2024**

A. $H_2C=CH—CH_2Cl$ B. $CH_3—CH=CH—Cl$

C. 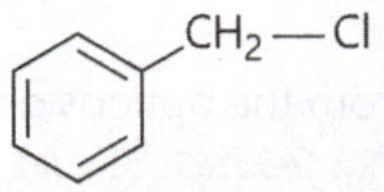 D. 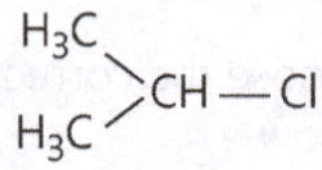

Choose the most appropriate answer from the options given below.

(a) (B) only (b) (A) and (B) only
(c) (A), (B) and (D) only (d) (B) and (C) only

17 Which among the following compounds will undergo fastest S_N2 reaction. **NCERT Pg 171, 172, JEE Main 2024**

(a) 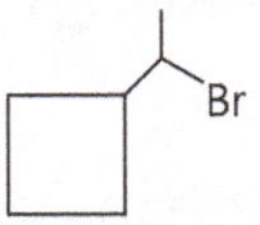 (b) 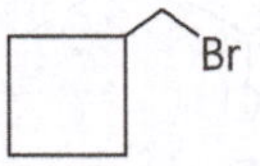

(c) 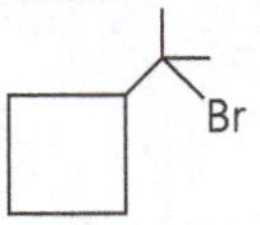 (d) 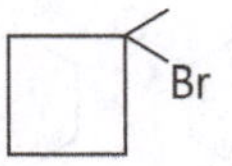

18. 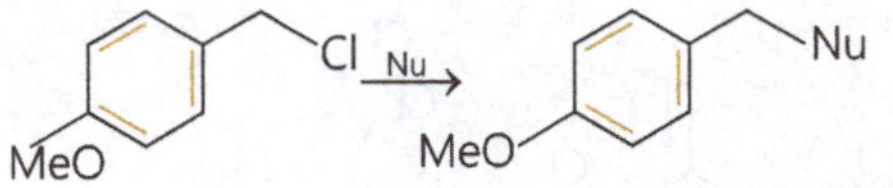 ....(I)

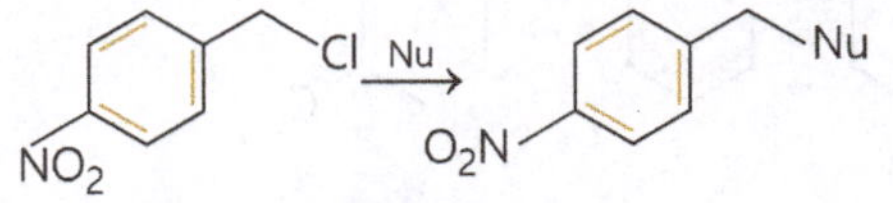 ....(II)

where, Nu = Nucleophile

Find out the correct statement from the options given below for the above 2 reactions. **NCERT Pg 171, 173, JEE Main 2023**

(a) Reaction (I) and (II) both are of 1st order.
(b) Reactions (I) and (II) both are of 2nd order.
(c) Reactions (I) is of 2nd order and reaction (II) is of 1st order.
(d) Reaction (I) is of 1st order and reaction (II) is of 2nd order.

19. Match List-I with List-II.

	List-I		List-II
A.	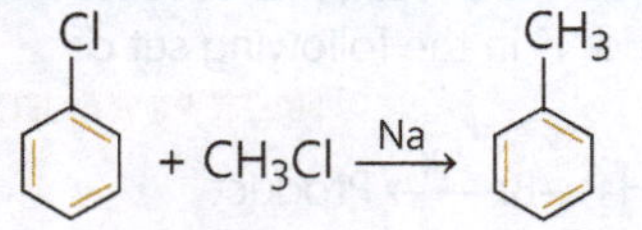	I.	Fittig reaction
B.	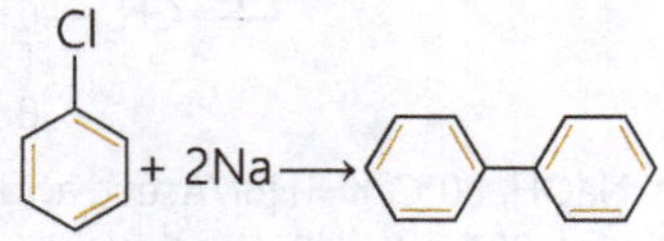	II.	Wurtz-Fittig reaction
C.	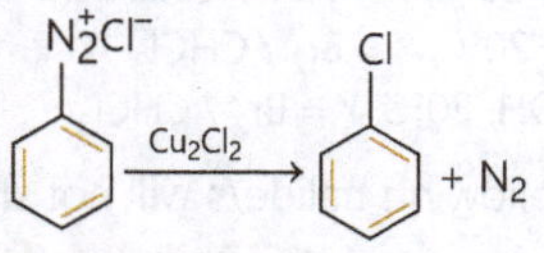	III.	Finkelstein reaction
D.	$C_2H_5Cl + NaI \longrightarrow C_2H_5I + NaCl$	IV.	Sandmeyer reaction

Choose the correct answer from the options given below. **NCERT Pg 166, 165, 186, JEE Main 2023**

(a) A-II, B-I, C-IV, D-III (b) A-III, B-II, C-IV, D-I
(c) A -II, B-I, C-III, D-IV (d) A-IV, B-II, C-III, D-I

20. The correct order of melting points of dichlorobenzenes is **NCERT Pg 169, JEE Main 2023**

(a) 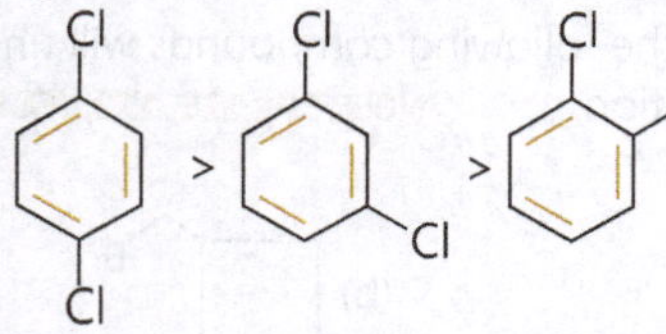

(b) 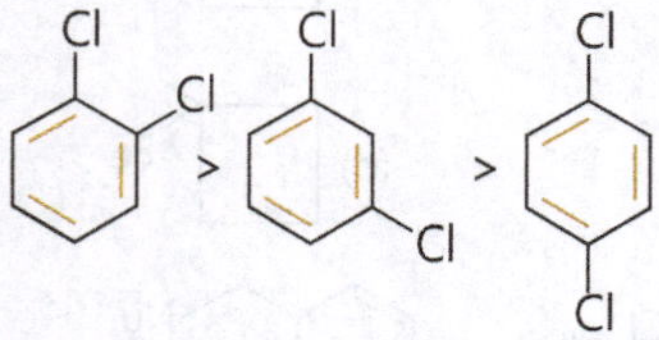

(c) 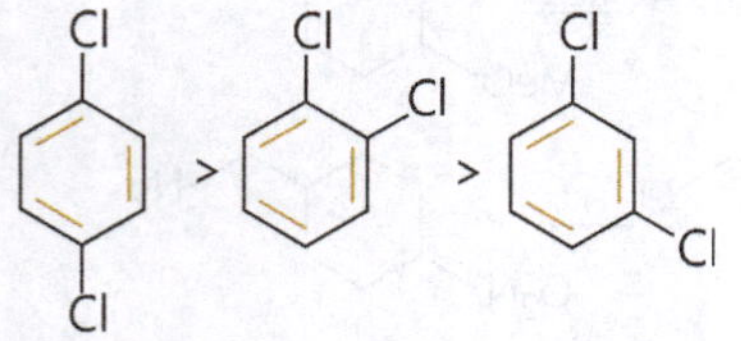

(d) 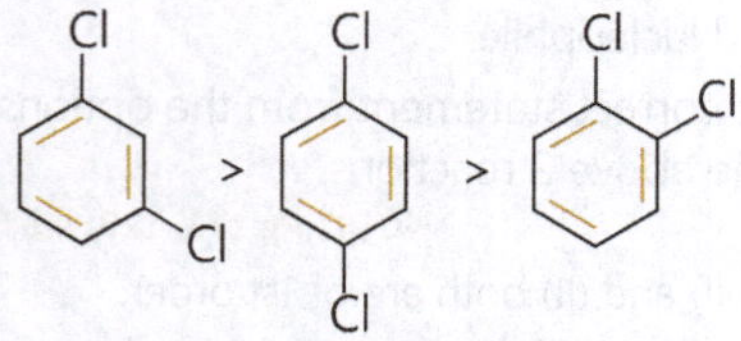

21. The isomeric deuterated bromide with molecular formula C_4H_8DBr having two chiral carbon atoms is

(a) 2-bromo-3-deuterobutane **NCERT Pg 177, JEE Main 2023**
(b) 2-bromo-1-deuterobutane
(c) 2-bromo-1-deutero-2-methylpropane
(d) 2-bromo-2-deuterobutane

22. The compound which will have the lowest rate towards nucleophilic aromatic substitution on treatment with OH^- is **NCERT Pg 182, JEE Main 2023**

(a) 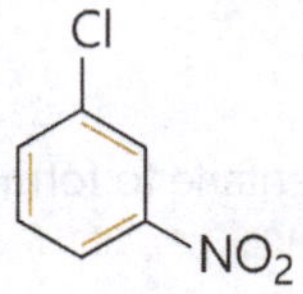 (b) 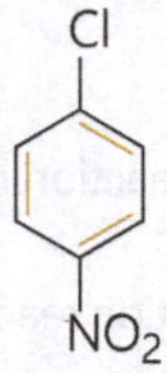

(c) 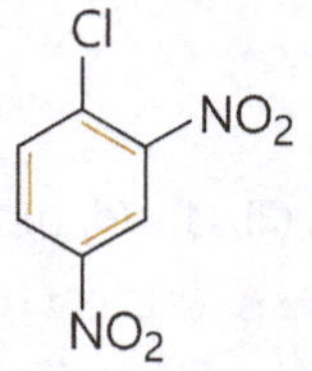 (d) 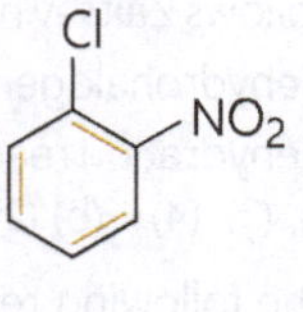

23. The major product (*P*) in the reaction. **NCERT Pg 165, JEE Main 2022**

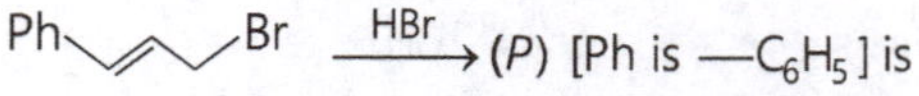

(a) 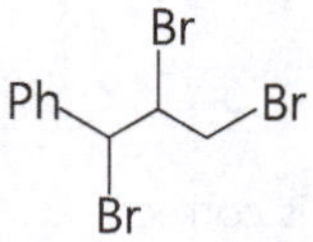 (b) 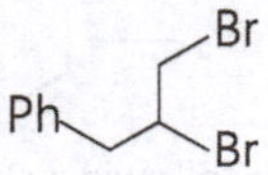

(c) 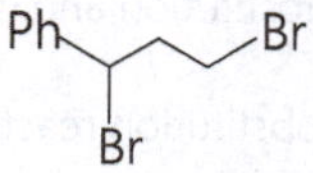 (d) 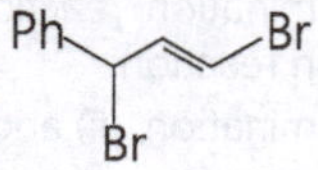

24. The major product in the reaction **NCERT Pg 180, JEE Main 2022**

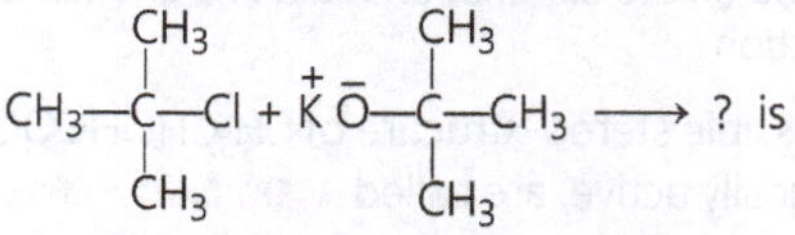

(a) *t*-butyl ethyl ether (b) 2,2-dimethyl butane
(c) 2-methyl pent-1-ene (d) 2-methylprop-1-ene

25. What is the major product formed by HI on reaction with **NCERT Pg 165, JEE Main 2021**

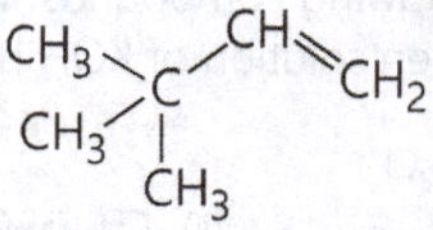

(a) 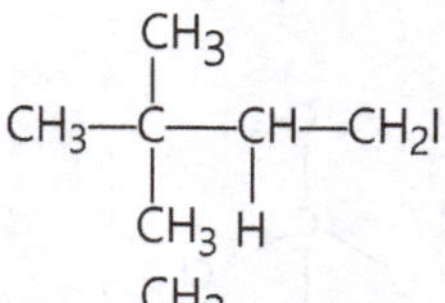 (b) 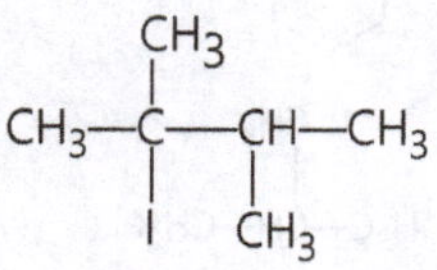

(c) 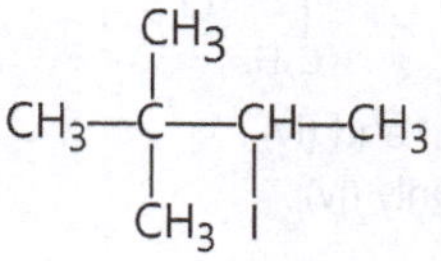 (d) 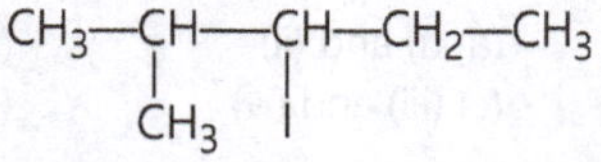

26. For the given reaction,

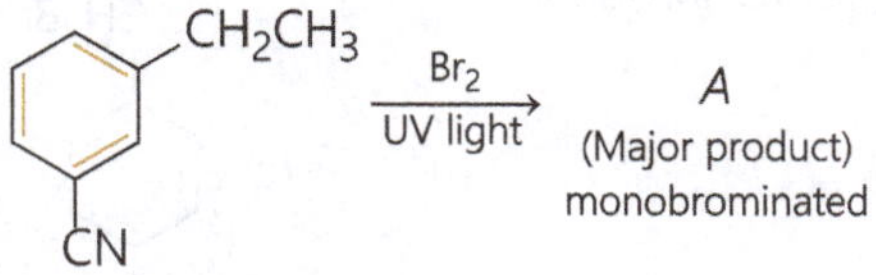

What is *A*?

NCERT Pg 167, JEE Main 2021

(a) 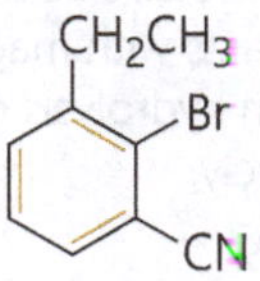

(b) 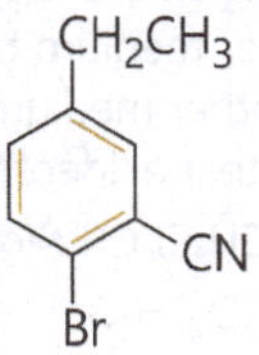

(c) 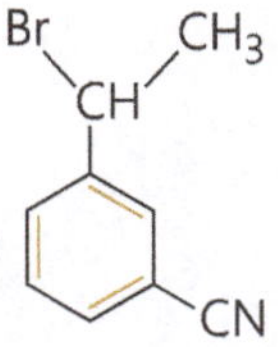

(d) 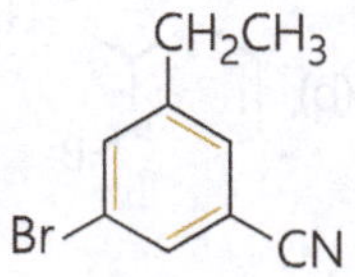

Skill Boosters

1. Bottles containing C_6H_5I and $C_6H_5CH_2I$ lost their original labels. They were labelled as *A* and *B* for testing. *A* and *B* were separately taken in test tubes and boiled with NaOH solution. The end solution in each tube was made acidic with dilute HNO_3 and then some $AgNO_3$ solution was added. Substance *B* gives a yellow precipitate. Which one of the following statements is true for this experiment?

(a) *A* was C_6H_5I

(b) *A* was $C_6H_5CH_2I$

(c) *B* was C_6H_5I

(d) Addition of HNO_3 was unnecessary

2. Anirudh takes a compound whose molecular formula is $C_6H_{13}Br$. On dehydrohalogenation gave two isomeric alkenes *X* and *Y* with molecular formula C_6H_{12}. Further on reductive ozonolysis, *X* and *Y* gave four compounds CH_3COCH_3, CH_3CHO, CH_3CH_2CHO and $(CH_3)_2CHCHO$. Which compound he had taken?

(a) 2-bromohexane

(b) 2, 2-dimethyl-1-bromobutane

(c) 2-bromo-2, 3-dimethylbutane

(d) 3-bromo-2-methylpentane

3. A dihalogen derivative '*X*' of a hydrocarbon with three carbon atoms reacts with alcoholic KOH and produces another hydrocarbon which forms a red precipitate with ammonical Cu_2Cl_2. '*X*' gives an aldehyde on reaction with aqueous KOH. The compound '*X*' is

(a) 1, 3-dichloropropane

(b) 1, 2-dichloropropane

(c) 2, 2-dichloropropane

(d) 1, 1-dichloropropane

4. The mechanism of S_N1 reaction is given as

$$RX \longrightarrow \underset{\text{Ion pair}}{R^+X^-} \longrightarrow \underset{\text{Solvent separated ion pair}}{R^+ || X^-} \xrightarrow{Y^\ominus} RY + X^\ominus$$

Mayank writes general characteristics based on the given mechanism as follows

A. The reaction is favoured by weak nucleophiles.

B. $R^\oplus$ would be easily formed if the substitutents are bulky.

C. The reaction is accompanied by racemisation.

D. The reaction is favoured by non-polar solvents.

Which observations are correct?

(a) A and B (b) A and C (c) A, B and C (d) B and D

5. An alkyl bromide process a single alkene when it reacts with sodium ethoxide and ethanol. This alkene undergoes hydrogenation and produces 2-methylbutane. Then, identify the alkyl bromide.

(a) 1-bromo-2, 2-dimethylpropane

(b) 1-bromobutane

(c) 1-bromo-2-methylbutane

(d) 2-bromo-2-methylbutane

6. When a fire broke out in the lab while doing an experiment, a student used *X* to extinguish the fire. *X* is a well known fire extinguisher. However, after using it to extinguish fire, the room should be will ventilated. Select the most suitable option.

(a) *X* is flammable at higher temperatures.

(b) *X* is toxic.

(c) *X* produces phosgene gas by reaction with water vapours at higher temperatures.

(d) *X* is corrosive.

dicarboxylic acid (*B*), $C_8H_6O_4$ (*B*) easily forms anhydride on heating. Identify the compound *A*.

(a) 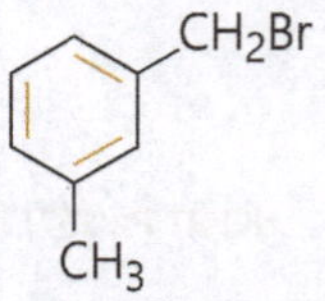

(b) 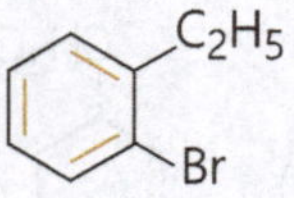

(c) 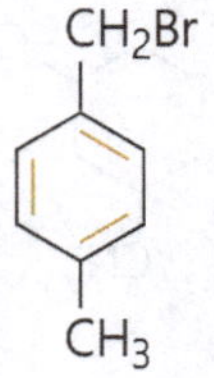

(d) 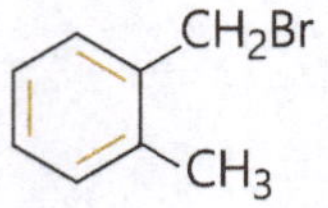

8. A organic compound *A* reacts with metallic sodium in ether medium to form ethane. *A* reacts with magnesium in ether medium to give *B*, which on hydrolysis gives methane. Identify *A* and *B* respectively.

(a) CH_3Cl, CH_3MgCl (b) CH_4, CH_3Cl
(c) CO_2, H_2O (d) CH_3Cl, H_2O

Correct Codes

Topical Questions

1. (a)	2. (b)	3. (a)	4. (b)	5. (c)	6. (b)	7. (d)	8. (b)	9. (b)	10. (d)
11. (b)	12. (d)	13. (b)	14. (a)	15. (c)	16. (a)	17. (b)	18. (a)	19. (a)	20. (b)
21. (a)	22. (b)	23. (d)	24. (b)	25. (c)	26. (d)	27. (a)	28. (a)	29. (d)	30. (c)
31. (b)	32. (d)	33. (d)	34. (d)	35. (b)	36. (a)	37. (a)	38. (c)	39. (b)	40. (b)
41. (a)	42. (d)	43. (d)	44. (a)	45. (a)	46. (c)	47. (b)	48. (b)	49. (a)	50. (a)
51. (c)	52. (b)	53. (a)	54. (b)	55. (b)	56. (a)	57. (c)	58. (a)	59. (c)	60. (d)
61. (b)	62. (d)	63. (c)	64. (b)	65. (b)	66. (b)	67. (d)	68. (a)	69. (c)	70. (a)
71. (d)	72. (a)	73. (b)	74. (d)	75. (a)	76. (d)	77. (c)	78. (a)	79. (a)	80. (b)
81. (d)	82. (b)	83. (c)	84. (d)	85. (c)					

Assertion-Reason

1. (a)	2. (a)	3. (c)	4. (b)	5. (c)	6. (c)	7. (d)	8. (a)	9. (a)	10. (a)

Statement Type

1. (b)	2. (a)	3. (d)	4. (b)	5. (d)	6. (b)	7. (a)	8. (c)

Matching Type

1. (c)	2. (c)	3. (c)	4. (a)	5. (c)	6. (b)	7. (a)

Numerical Value

1. (1)	2. (3)	3. (2)	4. (3)	5. (3)

NCERT Exemplar's

1. (c)	2. (b)	3. (d)	4. (a)	5. (a)	6. (a)	7. (d)	8. (c)	9. (a)	10. (c)
11. (b)	12. (b)	13. A - (1), B - (2), C - (3), D - (4)			14. (a)	15. (a)	16. (b)	17. (a)	18. (b)
19. (b)	20. (d)	21. (b)	22. (d)	23. (d)	24. (c)	25. (c)	26. (d)		
27. A - (3), B - (5), C - (1), D - (2), E- (4)				28. (a)	29. (a)				

Past Exams'

1. (d)	2. (d)	3. (a)	4. (b)	5. (a)	6. (b)	7. (a)	8. (b)	9. (b)	10. (c)
11. (d)	12. (a)	13. (b)	14. (d)	15. (a)	16. (a)	17. (b)	18. (d)	19. (a)	20. (c)
21. (a)	22. (a)	23. (c)	24. (d)	25. (b)	26. (c)				

Skill Boosters

1. (a)	2. (d)	3. (d)	4. (c)	5. (c)	6. (c)	7. (d)	8. (a)

Step by Step

Decoding the Questions

Concept Builders

1. sp^3, sp^2
2. Chloramphenicol
3. Thyroxine
4. Carbon
5. False
6. 2-chloropropane
7. False
8. True
9. True
10. False
11. Orthophosphoric acid
12. True
13. False
14. Four
15. Iodobenzene and dinitrogen
16. unsaturated
17. True
18. CoF_2
19. False
20. 1-iodo-1-methylcyclohexane
21. 1-bromo cyclohexane
22. dipole-dipole interactions
23. nucleophilic substitution reaction
24. clockwise, dextrorotatory
25. True
26. True
27. $H_3C—CH_2—CH = CH—CH_3$
28. True
29. True
30. Trichloromethane

Topical Solutions

1. (*a*) Statement (a) is correct, while statements (b), (c) and (d) are incorrect. Corrected form are as follows
   - The C — *X* bond in the alkyl halide is polar.
   - Haloalkanes contain halogen atom(s) attached to the sp^3-hybridised carbon atom of an alkyl group.
   - Chloroquine is used for the treatment of malaria.
2. (*b*) Statement (b) is correct for allylic halide, while statements (a), (c) and (d) are incorrect.

3 (*a*)

4 (*b*) Benzyl halogen compound are those in which halogen atom is bonded to sp^3-hybridised carbon atom attached to an aromatic ring.
Structural formula of compound (b) is as follows

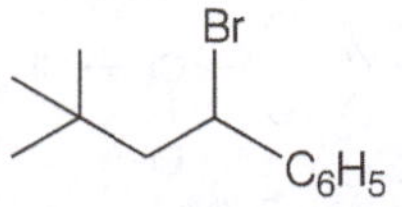

5 (*c*) Option (c) is not correct according to the name and classification.
The IUPAC name of the given compound is 3-chloro-3-methylpentane. It is a tertiary haloalkane.

6 (*b*)

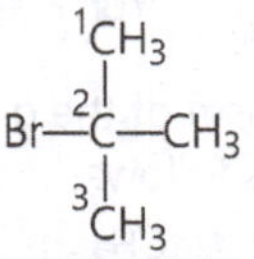

2-bromo-2-methylpropane

7 (*d*) Compounds in which the halogen atom is bonded to a sp^2-hybridised carbon atom of a carbon-carbon double bond is known as vinylic halides.

8 (*b*)

9 (*b*) Among the given compounds, only 1, 2-dichloroethane is an example of *vic*-dihalide.
In *vic*-dihalide, the halogen atoms are present at adjacent C-atoms.

10 (*d*) While naming the compound, alkene gets priority over functional group (—Br) and numbering starts from alkene side. Hence, IUPAC name of the given compound is 4-bromo-3-methyl pent-2-ene.

11 (*b*) Since, halogen atom is more electronegative than carbon atom, carbon-halogen bond (C—*X*) get polarised.

12 (*d*) CCl_4 being symmetrical has no dipole moment.

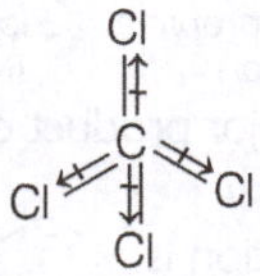

$\mu = 0$

13 (*b*) *p*-dichlorobenzene being symmetrical has zero dipole moment. Toluene due to +*I* effect of the $—CH_3$ group has a small but finite dipole moment. The two dipoles are 60° apart in *o*-dichlorobenzene, while they are 120° apart in *m*-dichlorobenzene. So, *o*-dichlorobenzene has the highest dipole moment followed by *m*-dichlorobenzene.
Hence, the increasing order of dipole moment is, IV < I < II < III.

14 (*a*) Phosphorus tribromide is usually obtained *in situ* by the reaction of red phosphorus with bromine.

15 (*c*)

16 (*a*) The by-product (*A*) formed in the reaction is $POCl_3$ and HCl.
Complete reaction is

$$\underset{\text{Alcohol}}{ROH} + PCl_5 \longrightarrow R — Cl + \underbrace{POCl_3 + HCl}_{(A)}$$

17 (*b*) Reaction involved is as follows

$$\underset{\text{Ethyl alcohol}}{C_2H_5OH} \xrightarrow[95\%\ H_3PO_4]{\text{NaI or KI}} \underset{\text{Ethyl iodide}}{C_2H_5I}$$

18 (*a*) When $H_3C—Cl$ reacts with NaI in dry acetone gives $CH_3—I$. This reaction is called Finkelstein reaction.

19 (*a*) The compound (*Z*) is alkyl halide given in option (a).
Complete reaction is as follows

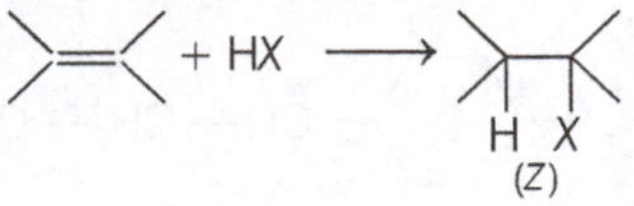

20 (*b*) Propene yields two products, however only one predominates as per Markovnikov's rule as shown below.

$$\underset{\text{Propene}}{CH_3CH{=}CH_2} + HI \longrightarrow \underset{\substack{\text{1-iodopropane}\\ \text{(Minor)}}}{CH_3CH_2CH_2I} + \underset{\substack{\text{2-iodopropane}\\ \text{(Major)}}}{CH_3CHICH_3}$$

21 (*a*) The major product of the given reaction is

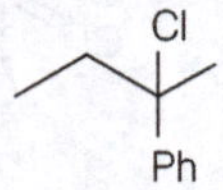

22 (*b*) The given reaction is a type of electrophilic substitution reaction.

23 (*d*) The reaction sequence is as follows

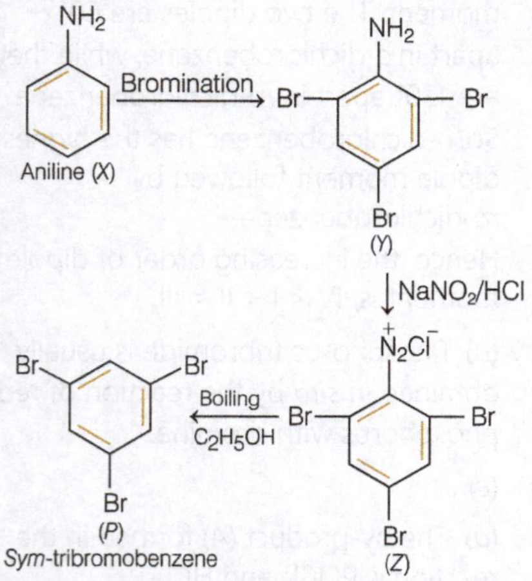

24 (*b*) When a primary aromatic amine, dissolved or suspended in cold aqueous mineral acid (HCl) is treated with sodium nitrite, a diazonium salt is formed.

25 (*c*) According to anti-Markovnikov's addition the major product '*X*' is

$C_6H_5{-}CH_2{-}CH_2{-}CH_2{-}Br$

26 (*d*) The mechanism of complete reaction is as follows

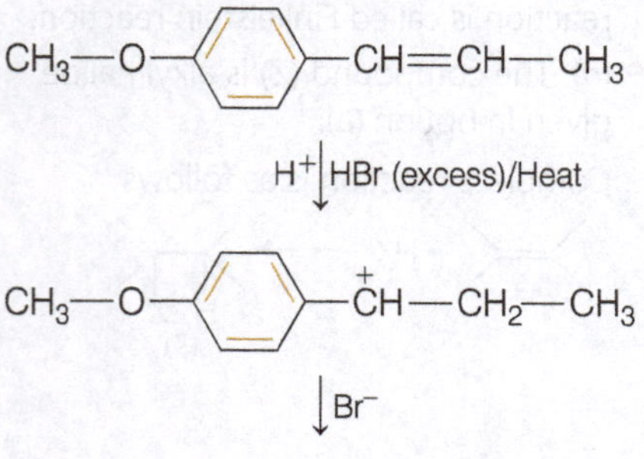

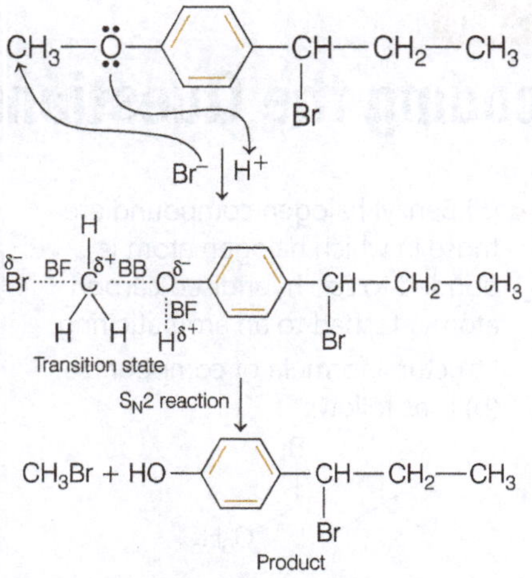

Here, BB = Bond breakage,

BF = Bond formation.

27 (*a*) Among the given options '*A*' is the product formed

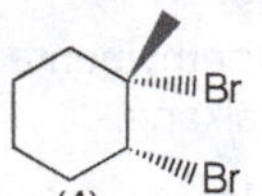

(*A*)

The mechanism of the given reaction is as follows

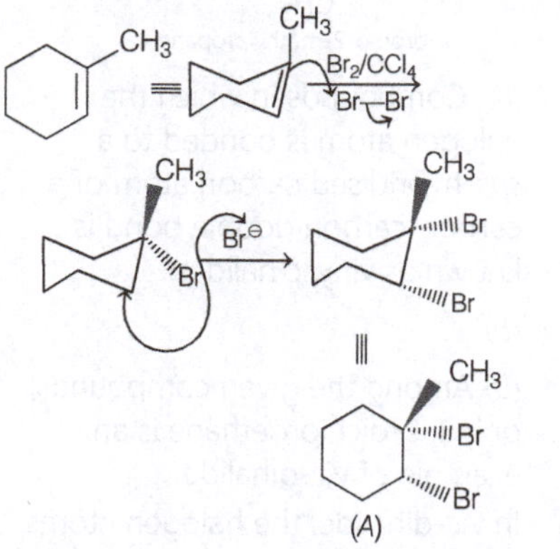

28 (*a*) Among the given options C_3H_7I has maximum density. It is because the density increases with increase in number of carbon atom, halogen atom and atomic mass of halogen atom.

29 (*d*) The correct increasing order is

$$\underset{(I)}{CH_2Cl_2} < \underset{(II)}{CHCl_3} < \underset{(III)}{CCl_4}.$$

30 (*c*) The *para*-isomer III have high melting point as compared to *ortho* and *meta*-isomer. It is due to symmetry of *para*-isomer that fits in crystal lattice better as compared to *ortho* and *meta*-isomers.

Thus, correct order is III > I > II.

31 (*b*) Due to symmetry, the molecule of *p*-dichlorobenzene fit closely in the lattice. As a result, intermolecular forces are strongest in *p*-dichlorobenzene. Hence, it has highest melting point and least solubility.

32 (*d*) Cyanide (CN^-) acts as an ambident nucleophile. It acts as a stronger nucleophile from the carbon end because it will lead to the formation of C—C bond which is more stable than C—N bond.

33 (*d*) Statement (d) is incorrect.

It's correct form is as follows

In S_N2 mechanism, carbon atom is linked with five atoms in transition state which is an unstable form.

Rest other statements are correct.

34 (*d*) Statements given in (a), (b) and (c) are correct while statement (d) is incorrect.

35 (*b*) Statement (b) is incorrect about S_N2 mechanism.

It's correct form is as follows

In transition state, all three C—H bonds are in the same plane and the attacking and leaving nucleophiles are partially attached to the carbon.

Rest other statements are correct.

36 (*a*) For the simple alkyl halides order of reactivity towards S_N2 reaction is methyl halide > primary halide > secondary halide > tertiary halide.

Therefore, in case of methyl halide the approach of nucleophile is easy in S_N2 reaction.

37 (*a*) S_N1 mechanism occurs between *tert*-butyl bromide and aqueous sodium hydroxide ion.

38 (c) The correct order of reactivity of alkyl halides towards S_N1 is as follows

3° halide > 2° halide > 1° halide > CH_3X

39 (*b*) Due to +*I* effect of —OCH_3 here, intermediate will be most stable. Due to this, 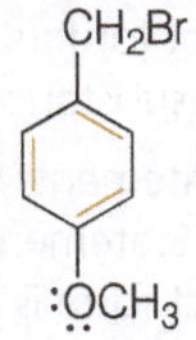 is most reactive towards S_N1 reaction.

40 (*b*) The carbocation formed at bridge-head carbon is unstable. So, I is less reactive. II is more reactive because it forms 3° carbocation which is highly stable. So, correct order is $B > C > A$.

41 (*a*) Allylic and benzylic halides show high reactivity towards S_N1 mechanism because carbocation formed are stable. It get stabilised through resonance.

42 (*d*) The compound 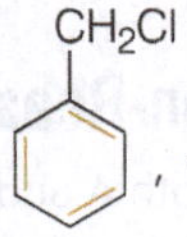, will react faster due to the resonance stabilisation of carbocation. While in CH_3CH_2Cl, $C_6H_5CH_2CH_2Cl$ and CH_2CHCH_2Cl carbocation is stabilised only through hyperconjugation.

43 (*d*) Iodobutane () undergoes S_N2 reaction faster because I^- is a good leaving group.

44 (*a*) Primary alkyl halides undergo S_N2 reaction in a faster rate than secondary and tertiary.

45 (*a*) Trend given in option (a) is incorrect.
In case of halides, 3° halides undergoes S_N1 reaction very fast because of the high stability of 3° carbocation followed by 2° and 1° carbocation
Hence, the correct order is

$$\underset{3°}{Ph\overset{+}{C}(CH_3)_2} > \underset{2°}{Ph\overset{+}{C}HCH_3} > \underset{1°}{Ph\overset{+}{C}H_2}$$

Rest of the other trends are correct.

46 (*c*) Resonating structure (*C*) of benzyl carbocation is incorrect.
The correct structure is

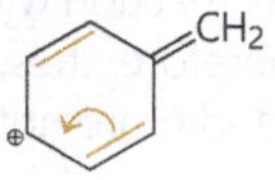

47 (*b*) More stable the carbocation higher will be the rate of S_N1 reaction.
Among the given compounds the stability of intermediates will follow the order.

$$\underset{(-I)}{B} < \underset{(+HPC=3)}{A} < \underset{(+HPC=6)}{C} < \underset{(+HPC=3,\ +R=1)}{D}$$

So, the increasing rate of S_N1 reaction with the given compounds will be $B < A < C < D$.

48. (*b*) Statement (b) is incorrect. It's correct form is as follows
The compound which rotates the plane polarised light to the right, i.e. clockwise is called dextrorotatory.
While, if the light is rotated towards left (anti-clockwise), the compound is said to be laevorotatory.
Rest other statements are correct.

49 (*a*) These are enantiomers which are related to each other as non-superimposable mirror images.

50 (*a*) 51 (*c*)

52 (*b*) When alcoholic KOH reacts with haloalkane, the reaction (rate) depends on the following factor.
(i) Size of halogen $\propto \frac{1}{\text{Strength}}$
(ii) Degree of C-atom to which the halogen atom is bonded, i.e. more the degree of haloalkane, more is its reactivity.
Hence, correct order of reactivity is $A > C > B > D$.
Thus, option (b) is the correct.

53 (*a*) In this reaction, hydrogen is eliminated from β-carbon and the halogen is lost from α-carbon atom. As a result, propene is formed as a final product '*A*'.

54 (*b*) Dehydrohalogenation of *neo*-pentyl bromide with alcoholic KOH mainly gives 2-methyl-2-butene as a major product according to Saytzeff rule.

55 (*b*) The major product obtained on treatment of $CH_3CH_2CH(F)CH_3$ with CH_3O^-/CH_3OH is $CH_3CH{=}CHCH_3$ according to Saytzeff rule.

56 (*a*) In the given reaction, more than one alkene is formed, then according to Saytzeff's rule, the highly substituted alkene formed is the major product.

57 (*c*) The correct order for the ease of dehydrohalogenation of alkyl halide with alc. KOH is 3° > 2° > 1°.

58 (*a*) The correct order of dehydrohalogenation is

$$\underset{(I)}{C_2H_5I} > \underset{(III)}{C_2H_5Br} > \underset{(II)}{C_2H_5Cl} > \underset{(IV)}{C_2H_5F}$$

59 (*c*) Only compound 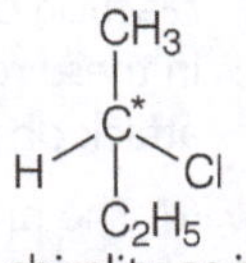 results in formation of racemic product due to chirality as it has one chiral carbon atom *via* S_N1 reaction.

60 (*d*) Figure I represents elimination. Here, the hydrogen atom from β-carbon and a halogen atom from α-carbon atom undergoes elimination. Figure II represents substitution. In this reaction, nucleophile replaces already existing nucleophile in a molecule.

61 (*b*)

62 (*d*) When cyclobutane reacts with Cl_2 in presence of light, substitution reaction takes place as shown below.

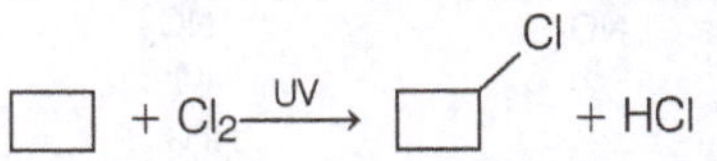

The product obtained reacts with Na metal in dry ether (Wurtz reaction) to give the following reaction :

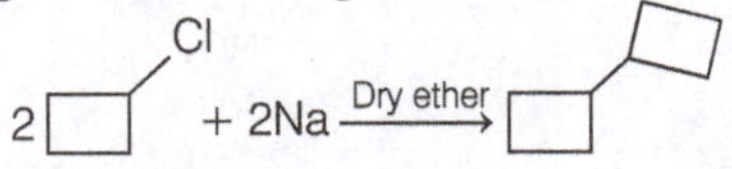

63 (c) The product (*A*) formed is phenol.

64 (*b*) The correct order for the rate of aromatic nucleophilic substitution reaction is *D* > *C* > *B* > *A*.

65 (*b*) The reaction sequence is as follows

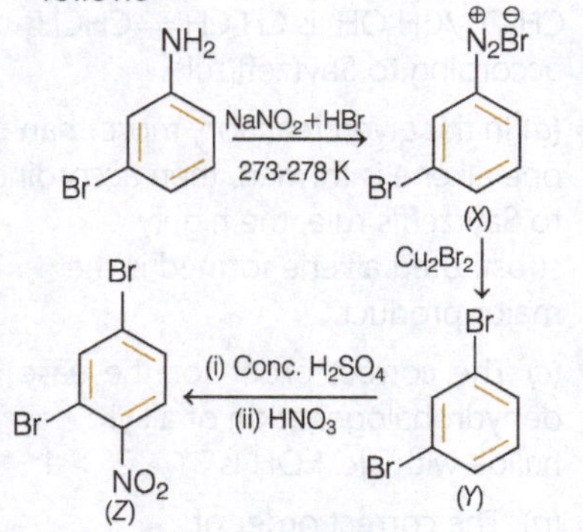

66 (*b*) Halogenation, sulphonation and Friedel-Crafts reaction comes under electrophilic substitution reaction of benzene ring because in these reaction, electrophile attack on benzene ring.

67 (*d*) The product obtained in the given reaction are *o*- and *p*-dichlorobenzene.

68 (*a*) The given reaction is an example of sulphonation reaction. Here, *A* and *B* respectively are 2-chlorobenzene sulphonic acid and 4-chlorobenzene sulphonic acid.

69 (*c*) The reaction proceeds as

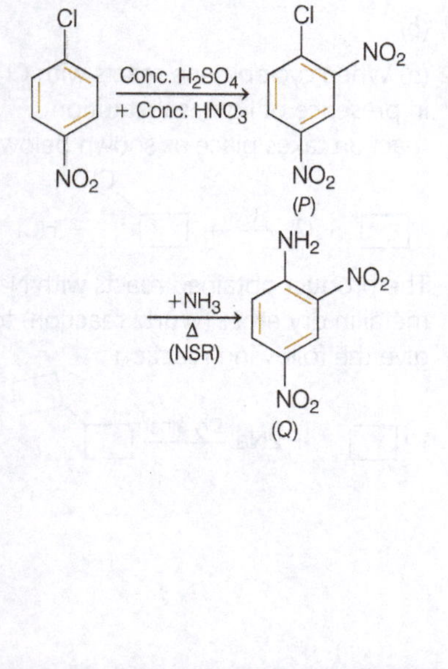

70 (*a*) Aryl halides and vinyl halides in the presence of anhyd. $AlCl_3$ do not act as electrophiles to give Friedel-Crafts reaction with benzene. Therefore, these reactions A and C are not possible.

71 (*d*) When 1-bromo-3-chlorocyclobutane is treated with 2 equivalents of Na in presence of dry ether then bicyclo [1,1,0] butane obtained.

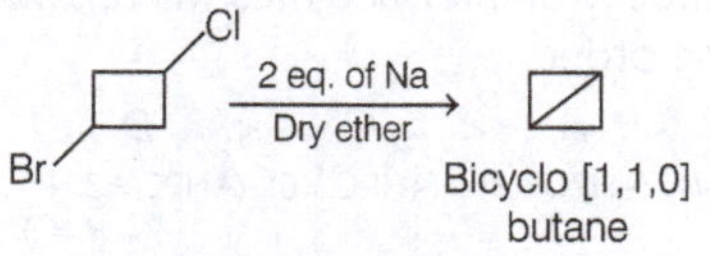

72 (*a*) The Wurtz-Fittig reaction is the reaction of an aryl halide with alkyl halide and sodium metal to give substituted aromatic compound.

73 (*b*) Statement (b) is correct, while other statements (a), (c) and (d) are incorrect. The correct form of these statements are as follows

(a) Chronic chloroform exposure may damage to liver and kidney.

(c) Inhaling chloroform vapours depress the central nervous system.

(d) Breathing about 900 parts per million of chloroform can cause dizziness.

74 (*d*) All the given statements are correct.

75 (*a*)

76 (*d*) Chloroform is stored in closed dark coloured bottles completely filled, so that air is kept out. It readily gets oxidised by air in the presence of light to carbonyl chloride.

77 (*c*) Tetrachloromethane (carbon tetrachloride) is used as feedstock in the synthesis of chlorofluorocarbons.

78 (*a*) **79** (*a*)

80 (*b*) Chemically, chloroform, i.e. trichloromethane is employed as a solvent for fats, alkaloids, iodine and other substances.

81 (*d*) Statements I and III are correct, while Statement II is incorrect. It's correct form is as follows

DDT is not metabolised very rapidly by animals, instead, it is deposited in the fatty tissues.

82 (*b*) **83** (*c*) **84** (*d*)

85 (c) IUPAC name of DDT is 2,2-*bis* (4-chlorophenyl)- 1,1,1-trichloroethane and its structure is

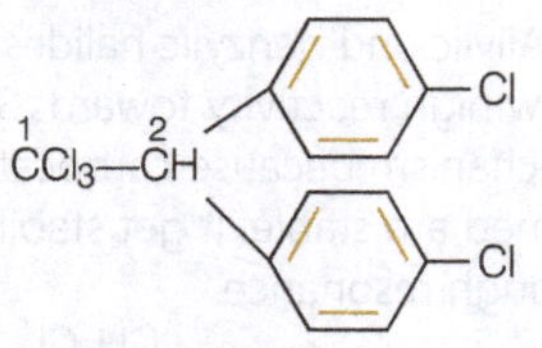

Assertion-Reason

1. (*a*) Both A and R are true and R is the correct explanation of A.

2. (*a*) Both A and R are true and R is the correct explanation of A.

3. (*c*) A is true but R is false. The true form of R is : Due to greater polarity as well as higher molecular mass as compared to the parent hydrocarbon, the intermolecular forces of attraction (dipole-dipole and van der Waals') are stronger in the halogen derivatives.

4. (*b*) Both A and R are true but R is not the correct explanation of A.

5. (*c*) A is true but R is false. The true form of R is : Intermolecular attractions between haloalkanes and water molecules are not strong as than the original hydrogen bonds in water.

6. (*c*) A is true but R is false. This is because it forms highly unstable carbocation ($CH_2 = \overset{\oplus}{C}H$). It cannot delocalise its π-electron.

7. (*d*) A is false but R is true. The true form of A is :

In case of optically active alkyl halides, the product formed as a result of S_N2 mechanism has inverted configuration as a compared to the reactant.

8. (*a*) Both A and R are true and R is the correct explanation of A.
9. (*a*) Both A and R are true and R is the correct explanation of A.
10. (*a*) Both A and R are true and R is the correct explanation of A.

Statement Type

1. (*b*) Statement I is true but Statement II is false. The correct form of Statement II is :

   The C—Cl bond length in haloalkane is more than haloarene.
2. (*a*) Both Statements I and II are false. Their correct form is
   I. Presence of nitro group facilitates nucleophilic substitution reaction in aryl halides.
   II. The intermediate carbanion is stabilised due to the presence of nitro group.
3. (*d*) Both Statements I and II are true.
4. (*b*) Statement I is true but Statement II is false. The correct form of Statement II is :
   Haloarenes are less active as compared to benzene due to $-I$ effect of halogen.
5. (*d*) Both Statement I and Statement II are true.
6. (*b*) Among the given statements, only I and IV are incorrect while the statements II, III and V are correct. The correct form of I and IV are
   I. Aryl halides are the compounds in which halogen atom is bonded to the sp^2-hybridised carbon atom of an aromatic ring.
   IV. The position of Cl in the compound $CH_3CH{=}CCl{-}CH_2{-}CH_3$ can be classified as vinylic.
7. (*a*) Among the given statements, only III, IV and V are correct while the statements I and II are incorrect. Their correct form is :
   I. Due to high reactivity, aryl fluorides cannot be prepared by electrophilic substitution of arenes.
   II. The boiling points of isomeric haloalkanes decrease with increase in branching.
8. (*c*) Among the given statements, I, III and IV are incorrect. Their correct form is :
   I. In Grignard reagent, the carbon-magnesium bond is covalent and highly polar.
   II. Haloarenes are less reactive than haloalkanes towards nucleophilic substitution reaction.
   III. The presence of an electron withdrawing group at *meta*-position has no effect on reactivity of haloarenes.

Matching Type

1. (*c*) The correct match is A-3, B-2, C-1.
2. (*c*) The correct match is A-2, B-3, C-1, D-4.
3. (*c*) The correct match is A-2, B-3, C-4, D-1.
4. (*a*) The correct match is A-2, B-1, C-3.
5. (*c*) The correct match is A-1, B-2, C-3, D-4.
6. (*b*) The correct match is A-4, B-1, C-2, D-3.
7. (*a*) The correct match is A-2, B-1, C-4, D-3.

Numerical Value

1. (*1*) Bromine in presence of sunlight is added to the allylic sp^3-carbon atom.

   This reaction proceeds *via* free radical substitution reaction. As there is only one allylic position(*).

   So, only one Br is present in product.

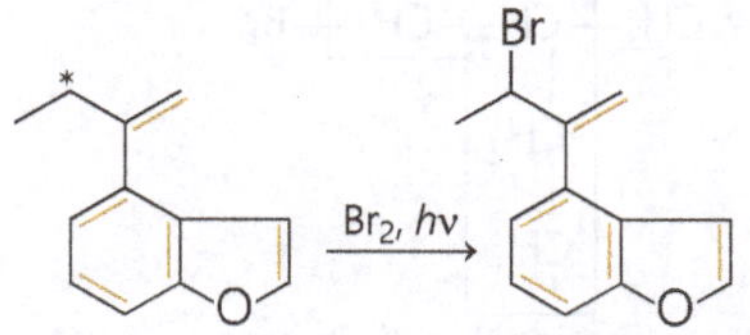

Major product

2. (*3*)

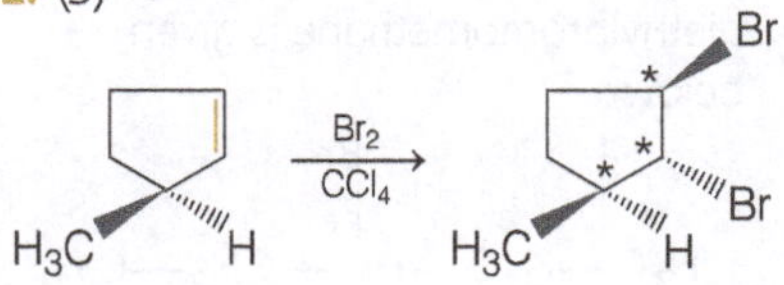

Thus, there are 3 chiral centres present in product *P*.

3. (*2*)

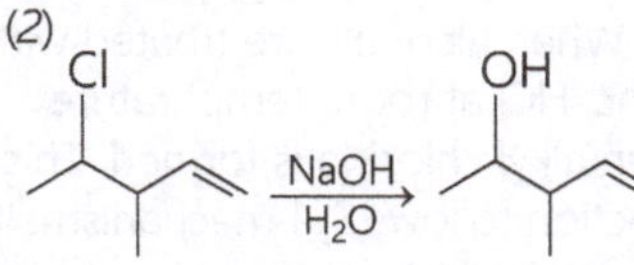

Given reaction is a unimolecular nucleophilic substitution reaction one π-bond is present in the product. So, 2π-electrons are present in this product.

4. (*3*) Among the given compounds, only (i), (iii) and (v) containing asymmetric carbon.
5. (*3*) The stereoisomers of butane-2, 3-diol are three.

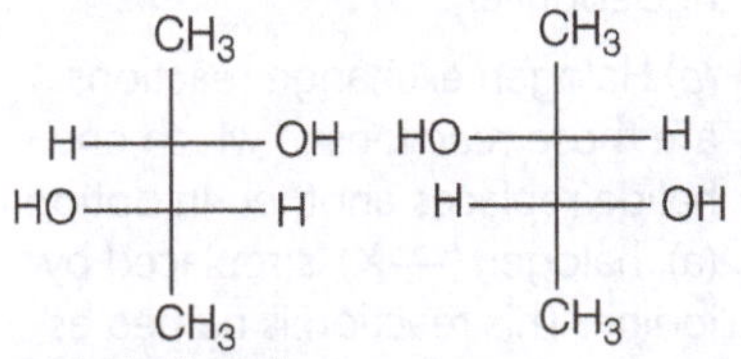

Optically active enantiomers

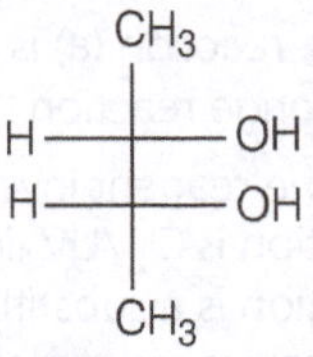

Meso-compound optically inactive

NCERT Exemplar's

1 (c) The correct IUPAC name of the given compound is

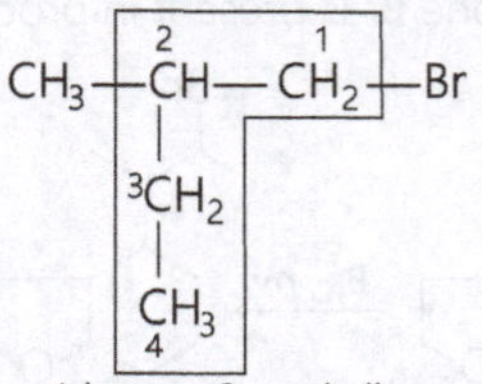

1-bromo-2-methylbutane

2 (b) Structure of diethylbromomethane is given below :

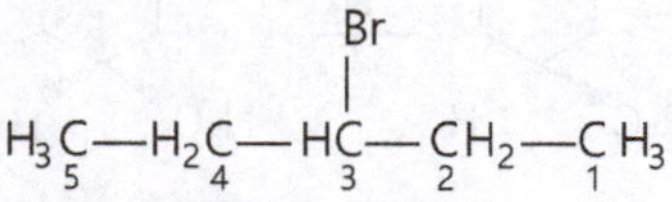

So, the IUPAC name is 3-bromopentane.

3 (d) When alcohols are treated with conc. HCl at room temperature then alkyl chloride is formed. This reaction follows S_N1 mechanism. It completes in two steps.

In first step, a carbocation is formed and this carbocation is attacked by nucleophile in second step.

The attack of nucleophile to the carbocation is possible only if the carbocation is stable. Compound present in option (d) will give tertiary carbocation (in step I). Tertiary carbocation is most stable so it is further attacked by Cl^- nucleophile.

4 (a) Halogen exchange reactions are those reactions in which one halide replaces another. In option (a), halogen (—X) is replaced by iodine. This reaction is named as Finkelstein reaction.

Thus, reaction (a) is halogen exchange reaction.

5 (a) The reagent involved in the reaction is Cl_2/UV light. The given reaction is a substitution reaction. It involves the replacement of 1° and 2° hydrogen atoms of alkanes by chlorine.

6 (a) Product 'Y' is chlorobenzene (C_6H_5Cl). The reaction is proceed as

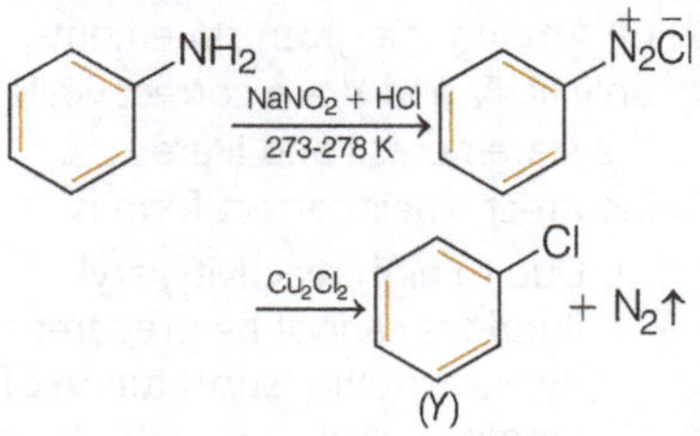

7 (d) Boiling point increases with increase in size of hydrocarbon part for the haloalkanes having same halogen atom.

Thus, the correct increasing order of boiling point is

1-bromoethane < 1-bromopropane < 1-bromobutane < 1-bromobenzene.

8 (c) In the gives reaction, addition of HCl takes place on double bonded carbons in accordance with Markovnikov's rule.

Thus,

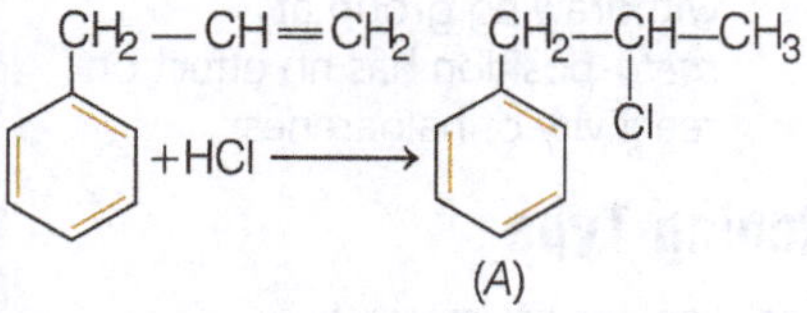

Since, the above reaction involves 2° carbocation, which is less stable than benzylic carbocation.

9 (a) Higher the molecular mass, higher will be the density of the compound.

Therefore, the increasing order of their densities is

benzene (I) < chlorobenzene (II) < dichlorobenzene (III) < bromochlorobenzene (IV)

10 (c) Boiling point of a compound depends upon the surface area. Higher the surface area, higher will be the boiling point of a compound. Surface area decreases with increase in branching. So, a compound having branching have lower boiling point.

Thus, the increasing order of their boiling points is III < I < II.

11 (b) Asymmetric/chiral carbon atom is that in which all the four valencies of carbon are satisfied with four different groups or atoms. So, molecule IV is not an asymmetric carbon atom, while I, II and III molecules have asymmetric carbon.

12 (b) In the given compound, C-2 and C-3 are bonded to four different groups, so these are asymmetric.

13 The correct match is A-1, B-2, C-3, D-4.

14 (a) The stereoisomers which are related to each other as non-superimposable mirror images are called enantiomers.

Hence, the enantiomer of molecule *A* is the molecule given in option (a).

15 (a) The structural formula of the given compounds is

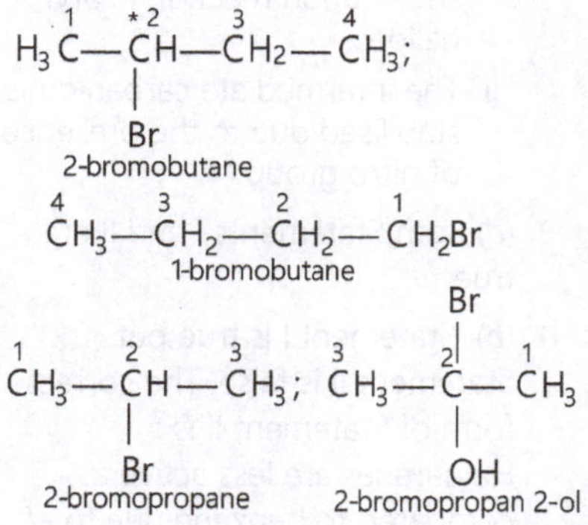

2-bromobutane

1-bromobutane

2-bromopropane

2-bromopropan 2-ol

With the help of these structural formulae it is very clear that only 2-bromobutane in which asterisk marked carbon atom is bonded to four different atoms or groups, is chiral in nature. Other molecules do not contain four different atoms or groups.

16 (b) *vic*-dihalides are those halides in which two halogen atoms are present on the two adjacent carbon atoms. Among the given compounds, only 1, 2-dichloroethane, has two chlorine atoms which are attached to two adjacent carbon atoms.

Hence, option (b) is correct.

17 (*a*) Allyl halides are those compounds in which the halogen atom is bondec to sp^3-hybridised carbon atom next to carbon-carbon double bond.
e.g. $CH_2 = CH - CH_2X$
and $CH_3CH = CHC(Br)(CH_3)_2$.

18 (*b*) In this reaction, Cl^+ electrophile attacks on electron rich benzene ring. The reaction is proceed as

$$AlCl_3 + Cl_2 \longrightarrow [AlCl_4]^- + Cl^+$$

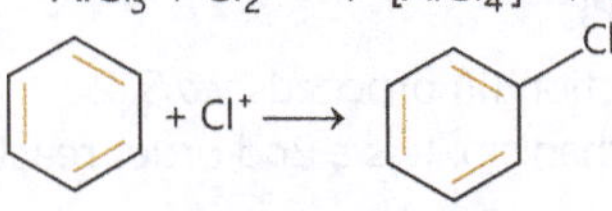

Chlorobenzene

19 (*b*) In ethylidene chloride ($H_3C—CHCl_2$) both halogen atoms are present on same carbon atom so it is a *gem*-dihalide.

20 (*d*) The reaction of toluene with chlorine in the presence of iron and in absence of light, so the substitution occurs in the benzene ring. The $—CH_3$ group of toluene is *o* and *p*-directing then product is the mixture of (b) and (c), i.e. *o*-chlorotoluene and *p*-chlorotoluene.

21 (*b*) Reaction between alcohols and halogen acid follows S_N1 mechanism. In S_N1 mechanism carbocations are formed as intermediates.

So the correct order is $\underset{(3°)}{C} > \underset{(2°)}{B} > \underset{(1°)}{A}$.

22 (*d*) Presence of electron releasing group at *ortho* or *para*-position decreases the rate of nucleophilic substitution reaction.

So, the correct order is II < III < I.

23 (*d*) Presence of electron withdrawing group at *ortho* or *para*-position facilitate the nucleophilic substitution reaction and, hence enhances rate of reaction.

So, the increasing order of rate of reaction towards nucleophilic substitution is I < II < III.

24 (*c*) The rate of nucleophilic substitution reaction is highest in compound I and order is
III < II < I.

25 (*c*) The correct order is
I < III < II.

26 (*d*) All the given compounds are tertiary alkyl halides but the bond formed between carbon and iodine (C—I) is the weakest bond due to large difference in the size of carbon and iodine. So, $(CH_3)_3C—I$ gives S_N1 reaction most readily. Further, iodine is a better leaving group.
Thus, $(CH_3)_3C—I$ will undergo S_N1 reaction most readily.

27 The correct match is
A-(3), B-(5), C-(1), D-(2), E-(4).

(A) If an alkyl halide follows S_N1 mechanism then racemisation takes place while if it follows S_N2 mechanism than inversion takes places.

(B) Tetrachloromethane are used in fire extinguishers.

(C) Bromination of alkenes will give *vicinal* dibromide.

(D) Alkylidene halides are named as *gem*-dihalides.

(E) Elimination of *HX* from alkyl halide follows Saytzeff rule.

28 (*a*) In the given compound, $C_6H_5CH_2Br$, carbocation is $C_6H_5\overset{\oplus}{C}H_2$. This carbocation $C_6H_5\overset{\oplus}{C}H_2$ is a stable carbocation due to resonance, therefore, its shows S_N1 mechanism.

29 (*a*) All those compounds which follow S_N1 mechanism during nucleophilic substitution reaction form racemic mixture.

Order of reactivity of alkyl halides towards S_N1 reactions is as follows

Tertiary halide > secondary halide > primary halide > CH_3X.

Thus, $CH_3—\underset{\underset{C_2H_5}{|}}{CH}—Br$ contains a chiral carbon and gives a racemic product.

Past Exams'

1. (*d*) Reactivity toward $S_N1 \propto$ stability of carbocation, and stability of carbocation depends on number of α-hydrogen.

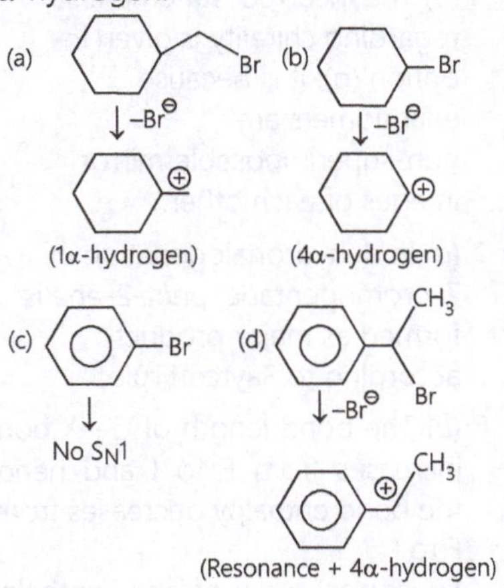

Hence, (d) is correct option.

2 (*d*) The reaction involves are,

$$3R—OH + PCl_3 \longrightarrow 3RCl + H_3PO_3 (A)$$
$$R—OH + PCl_5 \longrightarrow R—Cl + HCl + POCl_3 (B)$$

Hence, products *A* and *B* are
$A = H_3PO_3$; $B = POCl_3$

3 (*a*) The complete reaction is as follow,

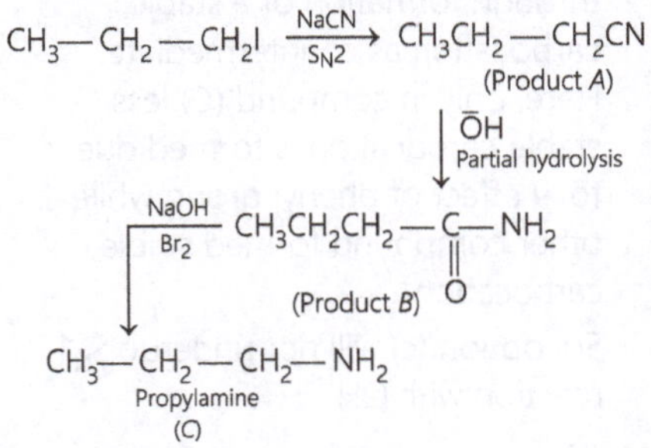

4 (*b*) The given compound is an example of allylic halides.

As in this, the halogen is bonded to the sp^3-hybridised carbon atom next to the carbon-carbon double bond, which is called as allylic halides.

5 (*a*) The reaction is proceed as

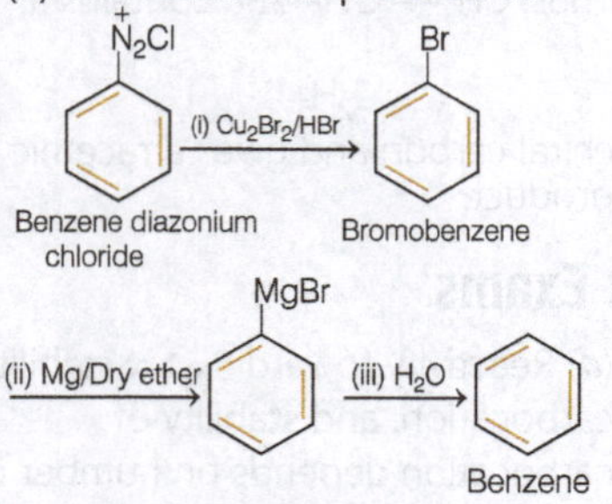

6 (*b*) The incorrect statement regarding chirality is given in option (b). It is because enantiomers are non-superimposable mirror images of each other.

7 (*a*) In dehydrohalogenation of 2-bromopentane, pent-2-ene is formed as major product according to Saytzeff rule.

8 (*b*) The bond length of C—*X* bond increases from F to I and hence, the bond enthalpy decreases from F to I.

So, correct order of bond enthalpy is $H_3C—F > H_3C—Cl > H_3C—Br > H_3C—I$

9 (*b*) Mild reducing agents like alcohol is used to reduce diazonium salts to arene.

Thus, the reagent used is CH_3CH_2OH (ethanol).

10 (*c*) The S_N1 reaction proceeds through formation of a stable carbocation as an intermediate. Here, only in compund (*C*) less stable carbocation is formed due to $-I$ effect of phenyl group while other compound formed stable carbocation.

So, option (c) will not undergo S_N1 reaction with OH^-.

11 (*d*)

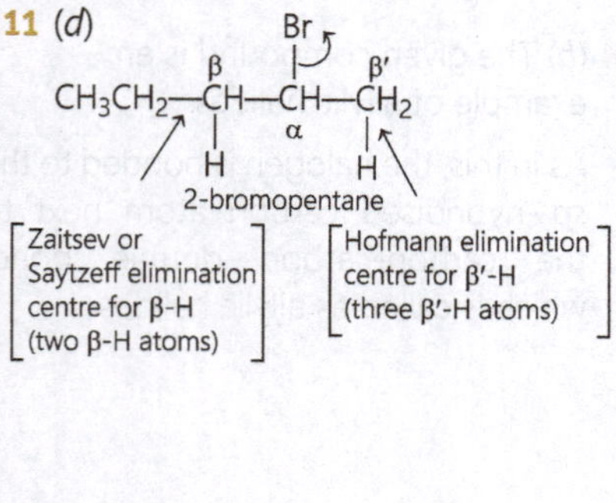

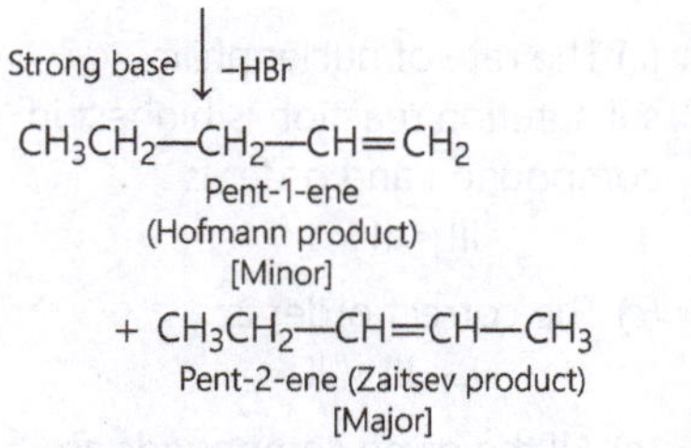

In the above reaction, β-elimination takes place *via* E_2 mechanism (anti-elimination). According to Zaitsev rule, β-carbon carrying lesser number of H-atoms get involved in the elimination to give a more substituted alkene (pent-2-ene) as the major product.

Here, loss of HBr, i.e. dehydrobromination (dehydrohalogenation) takes place.

So, 1, 2 and 3 are correct combination.

12 (*a*)

13 (*b*) Two possible stereo-structure of $CH_3CHOHCOOH$, which are optically active, are called enantiomers.

14 (*d*) Only compound (iv) results in formation of racemic product due to chirality. Other three (i), (ii) and (iii) do not show chirality.

15 (*a*) The complete reaction takes place as follows

$$CH_3—CH_2—CH_2—Br \xrightarrow[80°C\ (X)]{\text{Conc. alc. NaOH}} CH_3—CH=CH_2 \xrightarrow{\text{HBr/Acetic acid }(Y)} CH_3—CHBr—CH_3$$

16 (*a*) Since, $CH_3—CH=\overset{+}{C}H$ is very unstable carbocation thus, $CH_3—CH=CH—Cl$ cannot give S_N1 reaction.

Hence, option (a) is correct.

17 (*b*) Rate of S_N2 reaction depends on steric hindrance, less the steric hindrance more will be rate of reaction, 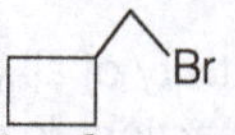 it will undergo S_N2 reaction fastest.

Rate of S_N2 reaction is

$Me—X > 1°—X > 2°—X > 3°—X$

18 (*d*) Reaction (I) proceeds *via* S_N1 mechanism which involves the formation of an intermediate. It is a first order reaction.

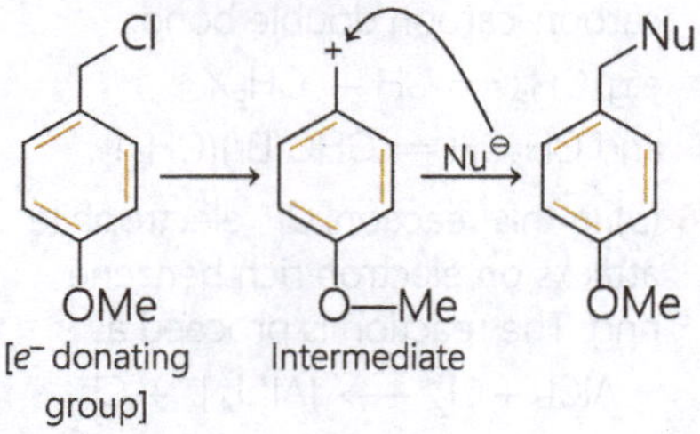

Reaction (II) proceeds *via* S_N2 mechanism. It is a 2nd order reaction.

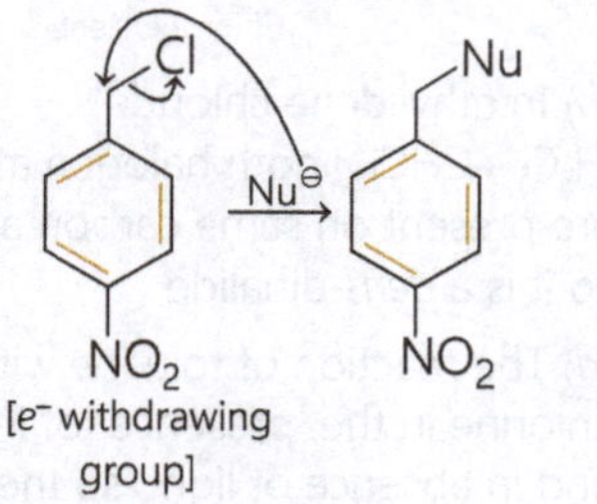

19 (*a*) The correct match is A-II, B-I, C-IV, D-III.

20 (*c*) The correct decreasing order of melting points of dichlorobenzene is

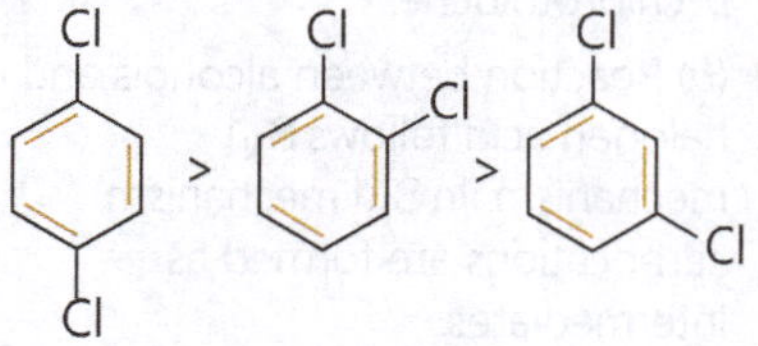

21 (*a*) The isomeric deuterated bromide with molecular formula C_4H_8DBr having two chiral atoms is

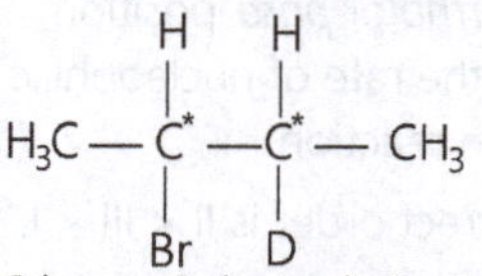

2-bromo-3-deuterobutane

22 (*a*) 3-chloronitrobenzene has weaker electron withdrawing nature of NO_2 ($-I$ only)as compared to other compounds which shows both ($-I$ and $-R$) effect.

So, it gives lowest rate towards nucleophilic aromatic substitution reaction (ArS_N2).

23 (*c*) The given reaction proceeds in two steps:

***Step* 1.** Addition of H^+ or attack of alkene on H^+.

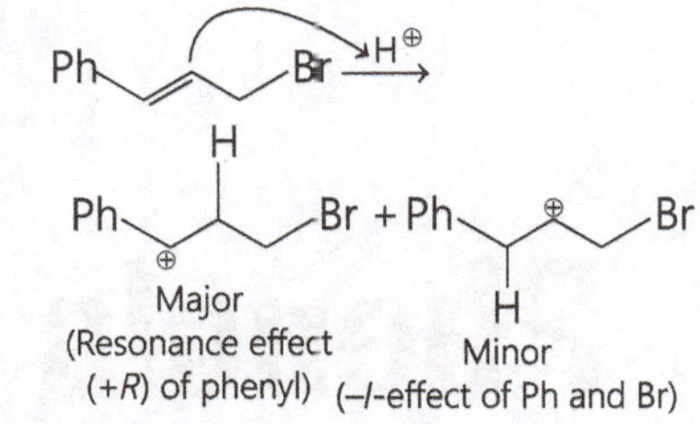

***Step* 2.** Addition of Br^- to carbocation.

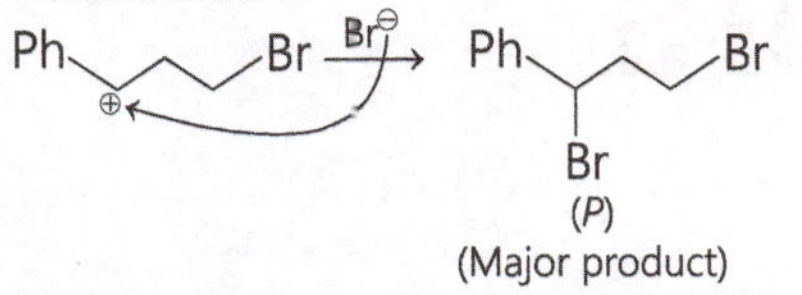

24 (*d*) In 3° alkyl halides E2 elimination will dominate with most nucleophiles (even if they are weak bases).

No S_N2 substitution take place due to sterically hindered butoxide base.

25 (*b*) The major product formed is 2-iodo-2, 3-dimethylbutane.

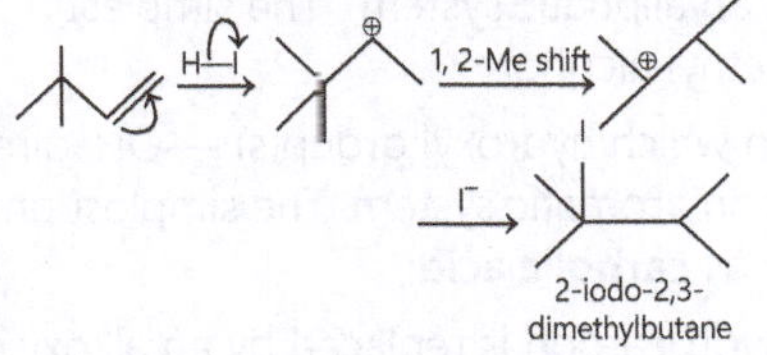

26 (*c*) When 3-ethyl benzonitrile undergoes photochemical reaction (UV) with bromine (1 equivalent), we get a monobrominated product 1 bromo -1 (3-cyanophenyl) ethane (*A*) as the major product.

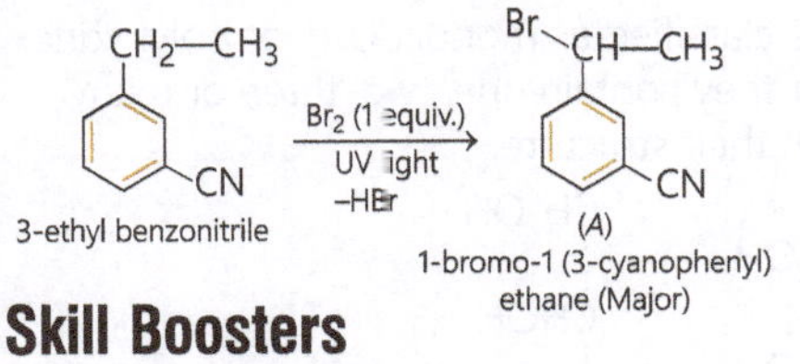

Skill Boosters

1. (*a*) The given reaction is represented as

$$\underset{(A)}{C_6H_5I} \xrightarrow{NaOH} C_6H_5\overset{-}{O}\overset{+}{Na} \xrightarrow{HNO_3/H^+} C_6H_5OH \xrightarrow{AgNO_3} \text{No yellow precipitate}$$

$$\underset{(B)}{C_6H_5CH_2I} \xrightarrow{NaOH} C_6H_5CH_2\overset{-}{O}\overset{+}{Na} \xrightarrow{HNO_3/H^+} C_6H_5CH_2OH \xrightarrow{AgNO_3} \text{Yellow precipitate}$$

Hence, *A* is C_6H_5I and *B* is $C_6H_5CH_2I$.

2. (*d*) Out of CH_3COCH_3, CH_3CHO, CH_3CH_2CHO and $(CH_3)_2CHCHO$, two pairs containing a total of six carbon atoms are

(i) $CH_3COCH_3 + CH_3CH_2CHO$

(ii) $CH_3CHO + (CH_3)_2CHCHO$

The $(CH_3)_2C{=}CHCH_2CH_3$ 2-methyl-2-pentene (I)

and $(CH_3)_2CH{-}CH{=}CHCH_3$

will give above pairs of [(i) and (ii)] of compounds on ozonolysis. There two alkenes can be obtained as dehydrogenation products if the compound is 3-bromo-2-methyl pentane.

3. (*d*) The reaction sequence is as follows

$$\underset{\substack{\text{1, 1-dichloropropane}\\(X)}}{CH_3CH_2CHCl_2} \xrightarrow{\text{Alc. KOH}} CH_3CH_2CHO$$

$$CH_3CH_2CHO \xrightarrow{\text{Alc. KOH}} \underset{\text{Hydrocarbon}}{CH_3{-}C{\equiv}CH} \xrightarrow{Cu_2Cl_2/NH_3} \text{Red ppt.}$$

Hence, the compound *X* is 1, 1-dichloropropane.

4. (*c*) Among the given observations A, B and C are correct while D is incorrect. It is because carbocation ($R^{\oplus}$) formation takes place and $R^{\oplus}$ got stabilised by electronic factors and polar solvent molecules.

5. (*c*) The reaction is represented as

$$\underset{\text{1-bromo-2-methyl butane}}{CH_3{-}CH_2{-}\overset{\overset{\large CH_3}{|}}{C}H{-}CH_2Br} + C_2H_5\overset{-}{O}\overset{+}{Na}$$

$$\xrightarrow{C_2H_5OH} CH_3{-}CH_2{-}\overset{\overset{\large CH_3}{|}}{C}H{=}CH_2 + NaBr + C_2H_5OH \xrightarrow{H_2} CH_3{-}CH_2{-}\underset{\underset{\large H}{|}}{\overset{\overset{\large CH_3}{|}}{C}}{-}CH_3$$

6. (*c*) *X* is CCl_4. It is stable to red heat. Its vapours are highly non-inflammable, i.e. do not catch fire. It is because of this property CCl_4 is used as a fire extinguishes. But now-a-days its use as a fire extinguisher is restricted because with water vapours, it forms highly poisonous phosgene gas.

$$CCl_4 + H_2O \xrightarrow[\text{temp.}]{\text{High}} \underset{\text{Phosgene gas}}{COCl_2} + 2HCl$$

7. (*d*) The complete reaction takes place as follows

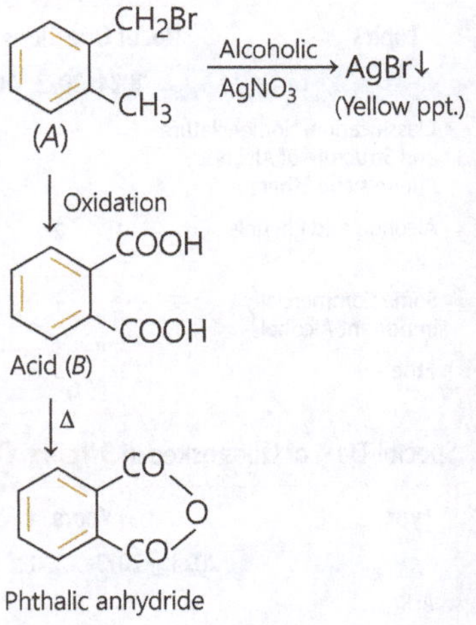

8. (*a*) The reaction is represented as

$$\underset{(A)}{2CH_3Cl} + 2Na \xrightarrow{\text{Dry ether}} CH_3{-}CH_3$$

$$\underset{(A)}{CH_3Cl} + Mg \xrightarrow{\text{Dry ether}} \underset{(B)}{CH_3MgCl} \xrightarrow{H_2O} \underset{\text{(Methane)}}{CH_4} + Mg(OH)Cl$$

Hence, *A* is CH_3Cl and *B* is CH_3MgCl.

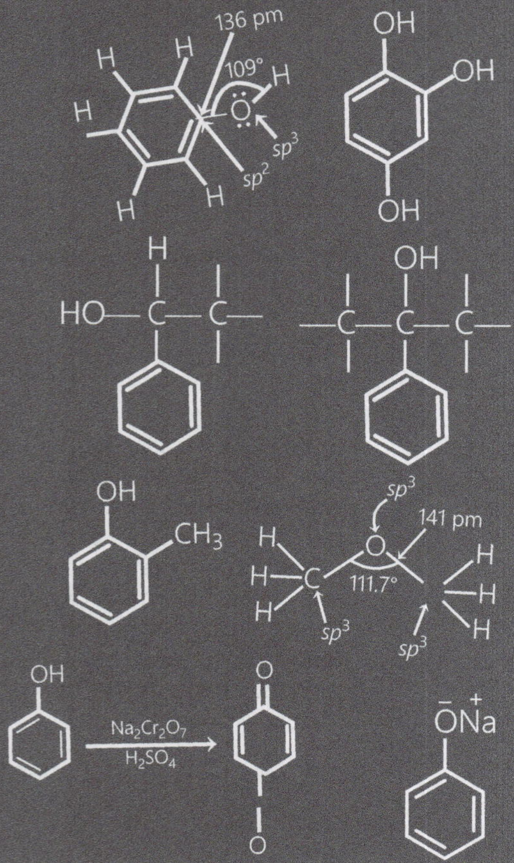

Topicwise No. of Ques asked in 5 Years (NEET)

Topics	No. of Questions				
	2024	2023	2022	2021	2020
Classification, Nomenclature and Structure of Alcohols, Phenols and Ethers	–	–	–	–	–
Alcohols and Phenols	1	2	2	1	3
Some Commercially Important Alcohols	–	–	–	–	–
Ethers	–	–	–	–	–

Special Type of Ques asked in 5 Years (NEET)

Types	Years				
	2024	2023	2022	2021	2020
A-R	–	–	–	–	–
Statement Based	–	–	1	–	–
Matching	–	–	–	–	–

Last 5 Years Weightage (NEET)

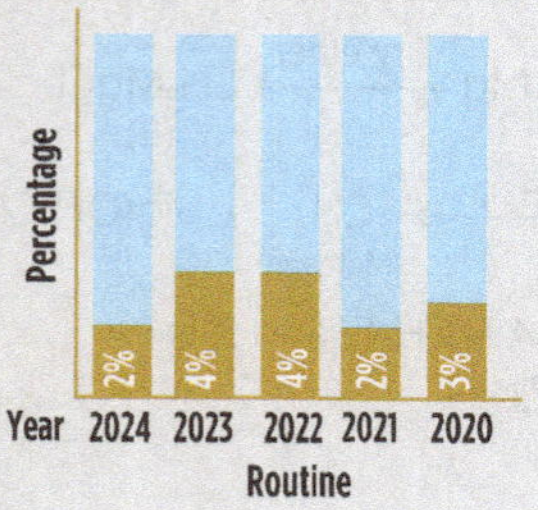

Scan for **Chemistry Through Concept Master** *Videos*

07

Alcohols, Phenols and Ethers

- In an aliphatic or aromatic hydrocarbon, when a hydrogen atom is replaced by the —OH group, then alcohols or phenols are formed respectively.
- The ordinary spirit, sugar and the cotton we use, all are made up of compounds containing —OH groups.
- An **alcohol** contains one or more hydroxyl —OH group(s) directly attached to carbon atom(s) of an aliphatic system. The simplest alcohol is CH_3OH, known as methyl alcohol.
- **Phenols** are the compounds in which hydroxyl group(s) —OH directly attached to carbon atom(s) of an aromatic system. The simplest phenol is C_6H_5OH which is also known as **carbolic acid**.
- When a hydrogen atom in a hydrocarbon is replaced by an alkoxy or aryloxy group (*R*—O/Ar—O), then **ethers** are formed. In another way, they may be visualised as compounds formed by substituting the hydrogen atom of hydroxyl group of an alcohol or phenol by an alkyl or aryl group.

Classification

- **Alcohols and phenols** may be classified as mono, di, tri, or polyhydric compounds based on whether they contain one, two, three or many hydroxyl groups respectively in their structure.

C_2H_5OH (Monohydric), CH_2OH—CH_2OH (Dihydric), CH_2OH—$CHOH$—CH_2OH (Trihydric)

Alcohols

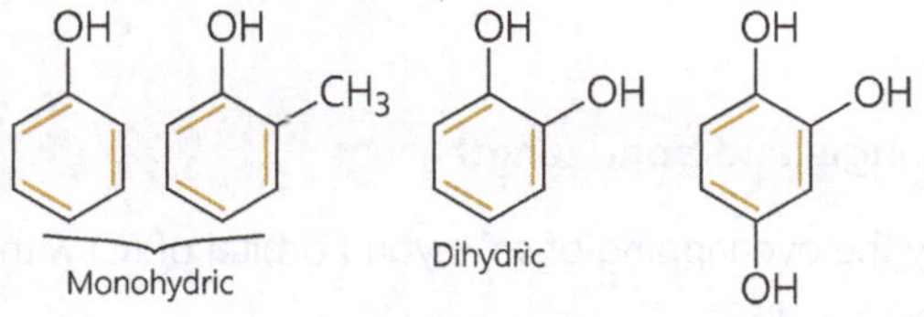

Phenols

In this chapter, we mainly study about preparations and properties with respect to monohydric alcohols. The general formula of monohydric alcohols is $C_nH_{2n+1}OH$.

On the basis of the hybridisation monohydric alcohols may be further classified as following types

I. **Compounds containing C_{sp^3}—OH bonds** In these alcohols —OH group is attached to a sp^3 hybridised carbon atom of an alkyl group. These are further classified as,

(i) **Primary, secondary and tertiary alcohols** In these alcohols, —OH group is attached to 1°, 2° and 3° carbon atom respectively. e.g.

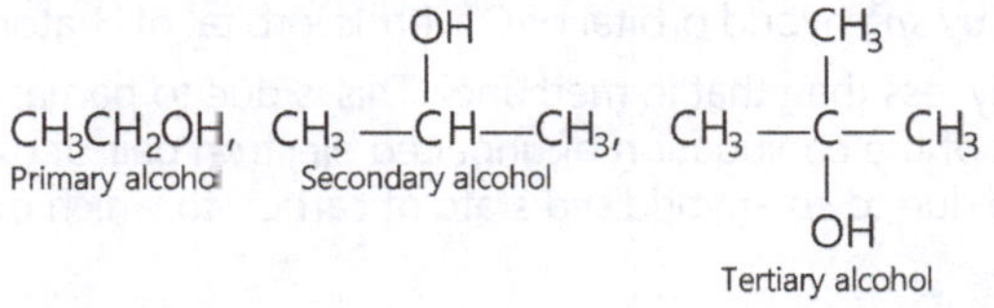

(ii) **Allylic alcohols** In these alcohols, —OH group is attached to a sp^3 hybridised carbon atom adjacent to C=C bond (i.e. allylic carbon).

e.g. $CH_2=CH-CH_2OH$,
(1°)

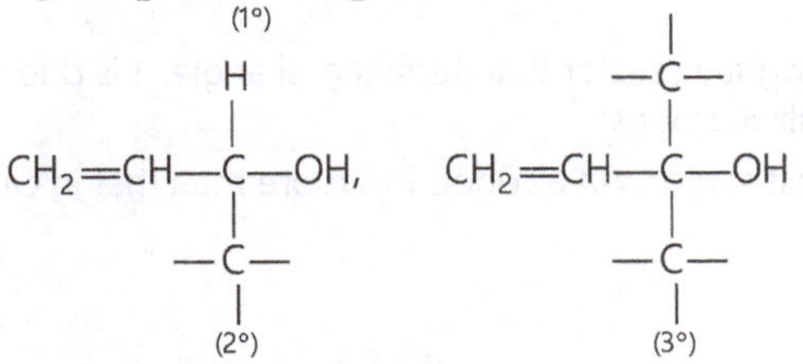

(iii) **Benzylic alcohols** In these alcohols, —OH group is attached to a sp^3 hybridised carbon atom present next to an aromatic ring. e.g.

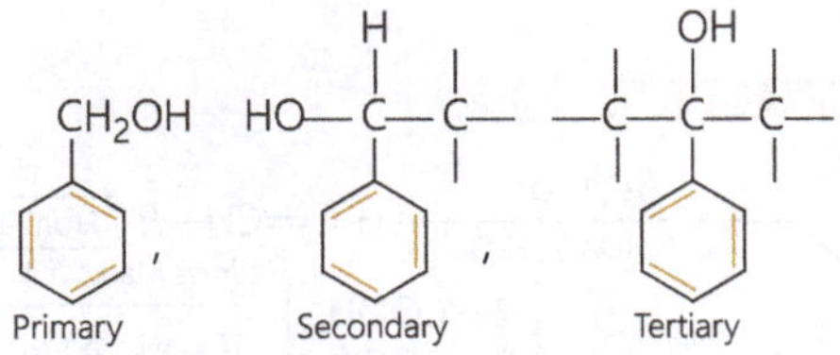

II. **Compounds containing C_{sp^2}—OH bond** These alcohols are also known as **vinylic alcohols**.

In these type of alcohols —OH group is attached to a carbon-carbon double bond, i.e. vinylic carbon or the aryl carbon. e.g. $CH_2=CH-OH$.

- **Phenol** There are classified as monohydric, dihydric and trihydric.
- **Ethers** are classified as **simple** or **symmetrical**, if the alkyl or aryl groups attached to the oxygen atom are same, e.g. CH_3OCH_3 or $C_2H_5OC_2H_5$ and **mixed** or **unsymmetrical**, if the two alkyl or aryl groups are different, e.g. $C_2H_5OCH_3$ or $C_6H_5OC_2H_5$.

Nomenclature

- **Alcohols** In IUPAC system, they are called **'alkanols'**. This name is derived by substituting 'e' of alkane with suffix 'ol'. The position of substituents are indicated by numerals. Cyclic alcohols are named using prefix cyclo by considering —OH group is attached to C-1 of the ring. In common system, alcohols are named as alkyl alcohol.
- **Phenols** The simplest hydroxy derivative of benzene is phenol. This term is accepted a common as well as IUPAC name. In its substituted compound, the term *ortho* (1, 2- disubstituted), *meta* (1, 3-disubstituted) and *para* (1, 4-disubstituted) are used in common names.

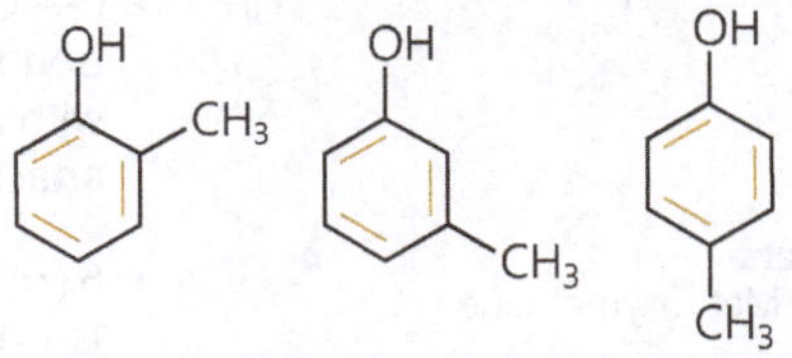

Common name	*o*-cresol	*m*-cresol	*p*-cresol
IUPAC name	2-methyl phenol	3-methyl phenol	4-methyl phenol

Further, the dihydroxy derivatives of benzene are named 1, 2-, 1, 3-and 1, 4-benzenediol. Their common name are catechol, resorcinol and hydroquinone (or quinol) respectively.

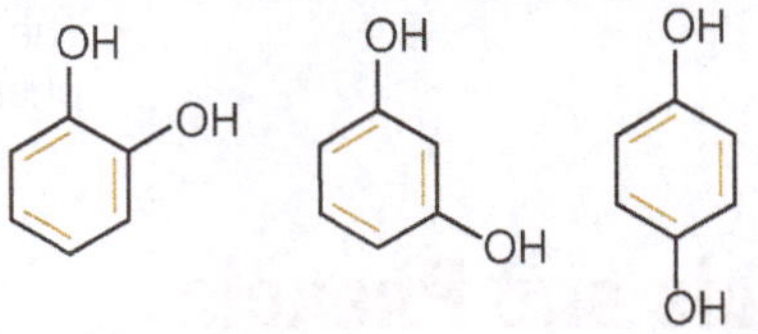

Common name	Catechol	Resorcinol	Quinol or Hydroquinone
IUPAC name	Benzene-1, 2-diol	Benzene-1, 3-diol	Benzene-1,4-diol

- **Ethers** According to IUPAC system of nomenclature, ethers are regarded as hydrocarbon derivatives in which a hydrogen atom is replaced by an —*OR* or —OAr group.
  (i) The larger (*R*) group is chosen as the parent hydrocarbon and smaller one as alkoxy.
  e.g. $CH_3OC_2H_5$ is methoxyethane.
  (ii) Their common names are derived from the names of alkyl, aryl groups written as separate words in alphabetical order and adding word 'ether' at the end, when both the alkyl groups are the same the prefix 'di' is added before alkyl group.

Structures of Functional Group

Compounds	Nature of hybridisation, bond angle and bond length
1. Alcohols e.g. Methanol 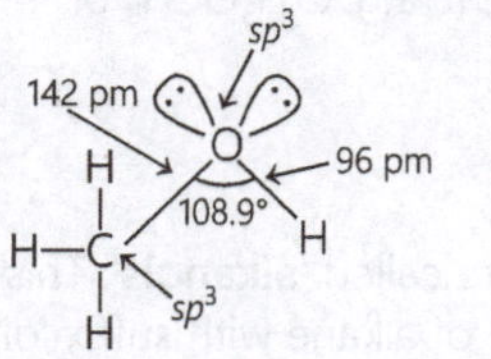	• 3 (σ) C—H bonds are formed by the overlapping of sp^3-hybrid orbital of (C) with 1*s* of (H). • 1 (σ) C—O bonds is formed by overlapping of sp^3-hybrid orbital of (C) with sp^3 of (O). • 1 (σ) O—H bond is formed by the overlapping of sp^3 (O) with 1s orbital of (H). • The (C–Ö–H) bond angle is slightly less than the tetrahedral angle. It is due to the repulsion between *lp* - *lp* of oxygen.
2. Phenols 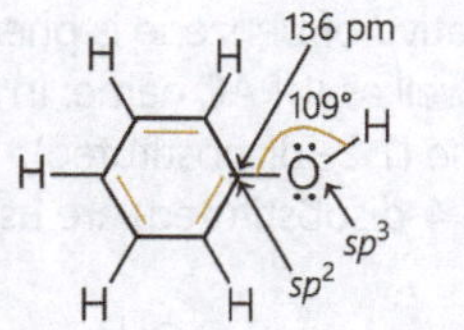	• 5 (σ) C—H bonds in phenyl ring is formed by the overlapping of sp^2-hybrid orbital of C-atom with 1s-orbital of H atom. • 6 (σ) C—C bonds in phenyl ring is formed by overlapping of sp^2-hybrid orbital of C-atom with another sp^2-hybrid orbital of C-atom. • 1 (σ) C—O bond is formed by sp^2-hybrid orbital of C-atom with sp^3-hybrid orbital of O-atom. • 1 (σ) O—H bond is formed by sp^3-hybrid orbital of O with 1*s*-orbital of H-atom. • C—O bond length is slightly less than that in methanol. This is due to partial double bond character on account of the conjugation of unpaired electron pair of oxygen with aromatic ring. It is also due to sp^2-hybridised state of carbon to which oxygen is attached. NEET 2019
3. Ethers e.g. Methoxymethane 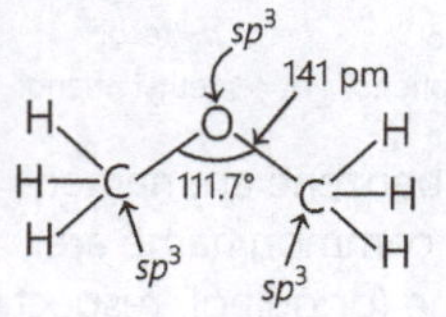	• 6 (σ) C—H bonds are formed by the overlapping of sp^3-hybrid orbital of C with 1*s*-orbital of H-atom. • 2 (σ) C—O bonds are formed by the overlapping of sp^3-hybridised C with sp^3-hydridised O-atom. • The (*R*–Ö–*R*) bond angle is slightly greater than tetrahedral angle. It is due to the repulsion between two bulky alkyl groups. • The C—O bond length is almost same as in alcohols but more than that in case of phenols.

Alcohols and Phenols

Various methods of preparations are as follows

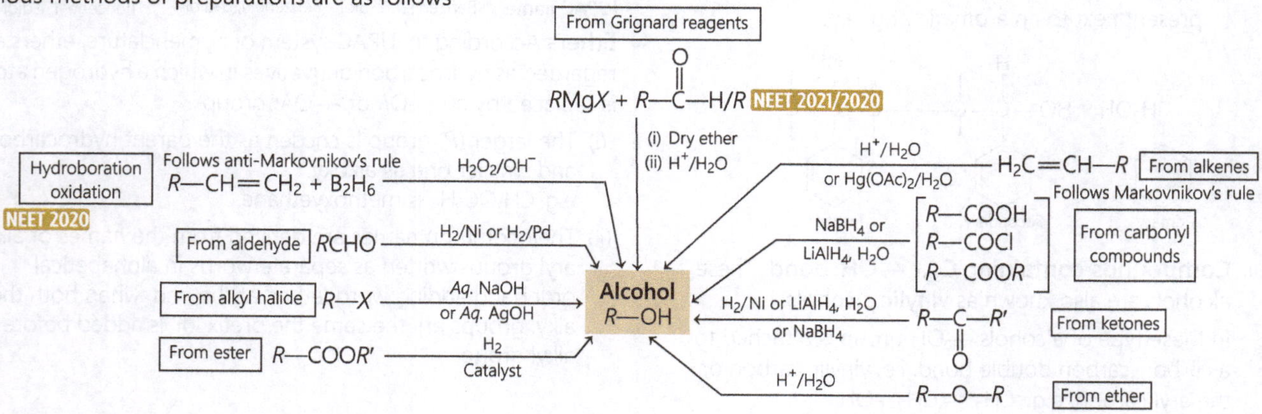

Important points related to behind methods are given below.

- Mechanism of acid catalysed hydration of alkenes is as follows

***Step* I** Protonation of alkene to form a carbocation by electrophilic attack of H_3O^+.

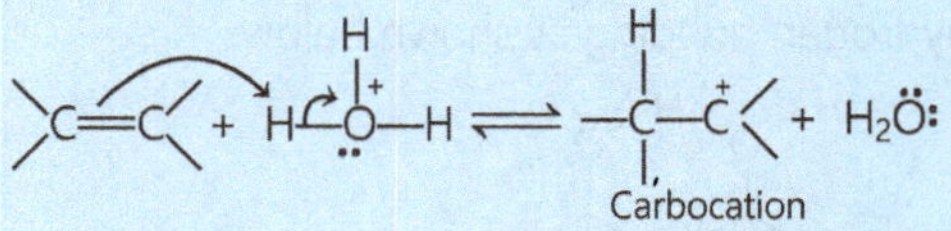

***Step* II** Nucleophilic attack of water on carbocation.

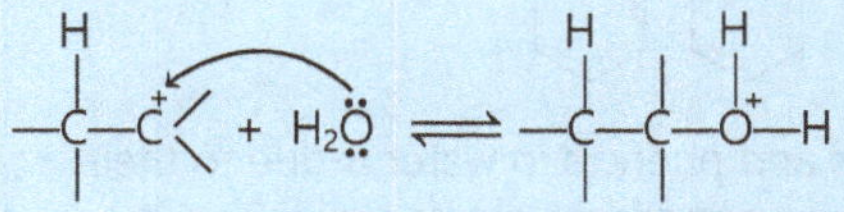

***Step* III** Deprotonation to form an alcohol.

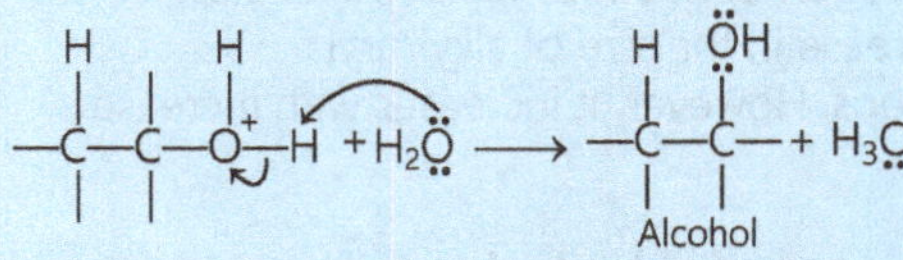

- **Lithium aluminium hydride** ($LiAlH_4$) and **sodium borohydride** ($NaBH_4$) reduces a wide variety of groups without attacking the isolated double bond of the compound if present.
- Catalytic hydrogenation (i.e. H_2 / Ni or H_2 / Pd) reduces carbon-carbon double bond as well as carbonyl group.
- Among **carbonyl compounds** aldehydes give primary alcohols while ketones give secondary alcohols on reduction.
- With **Grignard's reagent** HCHO gives 1° alcohol, aldehydes other than HCHO give 2° alcohols and ketones give 3° alcohols.

Preparation of Phenols

Various methods of preparation for phenols are as follows

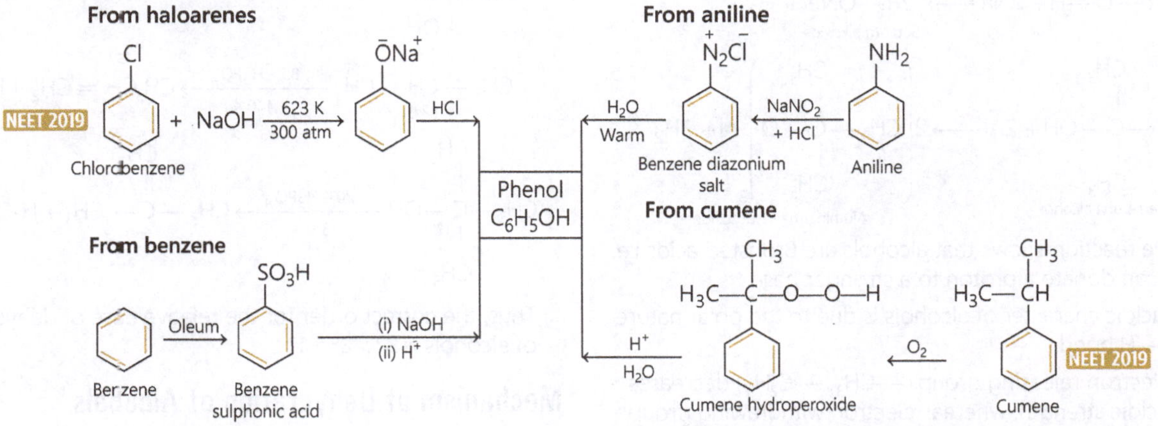

The major advantage of this reaction is that the by product, i.e. acetone, is also an important reagent.

Physical Properties of Alcohols and Phenols

- **Boiling point** In general the boiling point of alcohols increases with increase in the number of carbon atoms. It is due to increase in van der Waals' forces. On the other hand, it decreases with increase of branching in carbon chain. It is due to the decrease in van der Waals' forces with decrease in surface area.
- The boiling point of alcohols are much higher than the corresponding aliphatic hydrocarbons and haloalkanes. It is because of the tendency of —O—H group of alcohol to form intermolecular H-bonding as shown below.

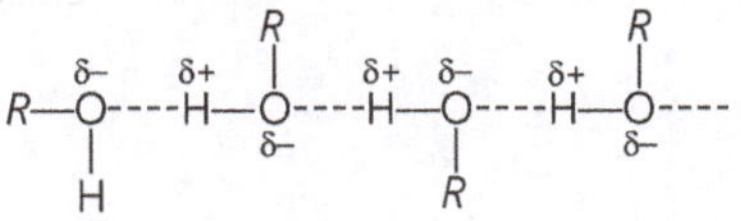

- In phenols, the boiling points are much higher than the corresponding aromatic hydrocarbons and haloarenes of comparable molecular masses due to involvement of intermolecular hydrogen bonding as shown below.

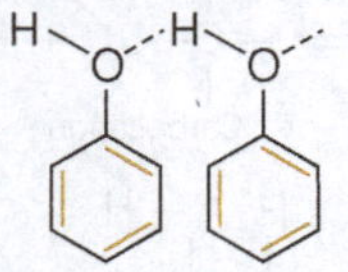

- **Solubility** of alcohols and phenols in water is due to their ability to form hydrogen bonds with water molecules. It decreases with increase in the size of alkyl/aryl (hydrophobic) groups. However, it increases with increase in branching.

Chemical Reactions of Alcohols

Alcohols are versatile compounds as they react both as **nucleophiles** (when bond between O—H is broken) and **electrophile** (when bond between C—O is broken).

The chemical reactions of alcohols are as follows

I. Reactions Involving Cleavage of O—H Bond

- **Acidity of alcohols** These are acidic in nature as they react with active metals such as Na, K and Al to yield corresponding alkoxides/phenoxides along with hydrogen gas.

$$2R\text{—O—H} + 2Na \longrightarrow \underset{\text{Sodium alkoxide}}{2R\text{—}\overset{-}{O}\overset{+}{Na}} + H_2\uparrow$$

$$6\ \underset{\textit{tert}\text{-butyl alcohol}}{(CH_3)_3C\text{—OH}} + 2Al \longrightarrow 2\ \underset{\text{Aluminium } \textit{tert}\text{-butoxide}}{\left((CH_3)_3C\text{—O}\right)_3Al} + 3H_2$$

- Above reaction shows that alcohols are Bronsted acids i.e. they can donate a proton to a stronger base.
- The acidic character of alcohols is due to the polar nature of O—H bond.
- An electron releasing group ($—CH_3$, $—C_2H_5$) decreases the acidic strength, whereas electron withdrawing group ($—NO_2$) increases the acidic strength of alcohol.
- Correct order of acidity of alcohols is 1° > 2° > 3°.
- Alcohols are weaker acids than water or we can say water is a better proton donor than alcohol.

$$\underset{\text{Base}}{R\text{—}\ddot{\underset{..}{O}}:^-} + \underset{\text{Acid}}{H\text{—}\ddot{\underset{..}{O}}\text{—}H} \longrightarrow \underset{\text{Conjugate acid}}{R\text{—OH}} + \underset{\text{Conjugate base}}{:\ddot{\underset{..}{O}}H^{\ominus}}$$

[• Stronger base than sodium hydroxide
• Better proton acceptor than $\bar{O}H$]

- Alcohols act as Bronsted bases (i.e. a proton acceptors) as well. It is due to the presence of unshared electron pair on the oxygen atom.

II. Reactions Involving Cleavage of C—O Bond in Alcohols

- **Reaction with hydrogen halides** NEET 2024

$$ROH + HX \longrightarrow R\text{—}X + H_2O$$

This reaction forms the basis of Lucas test for identification of 1°, 2° and 3° alcohol.

- **Dehydration** Alcohols undergo dehydration to form alkenes on treating with a protic acid like conc. H_2SO_4 or H_3PO_4 or in the presence of catalysts such as anhydrous $ZnCl_2$ or Al_2O_3.

$$\text{—}\underset{H}{\overset{|}{C}}\text{—}\underset{OH}{\overset{|}{C}}\text{—} \xrightarrow[\text{Heat}]{H^+} >C{=}C< + H_2O$$

NEET 2023, 2021

The product formed is in accordance with **Saytzeff's rule**, i.e. the more substituted alkene is the major product.

$$\underset{1°}{C_2H_5OH} \xrightarrow[443K]{\text{Conc. } H_2SO_4} CH_2{=}CH_2 + H_2O$$

Secondary and tertiary alcohols are dehydrated under mild conditions.

$$\underset{(2°)}{CH_3\text{—}\overset{OH}{\overset{|}{CH}}\text{—}CH_3} \xrightarrow[440\text{ K}]{85\%\ H_3PO_4} CH_3CH{=}CH_2 + H_2O$$

$$CH_3\text{—}\underset{CH_3}{\overset{CH_3}{\overset{|}{\underset{|}{C}}}}\text{—OH}\ (3°) \xrightarrow[358\text{ K}]{20\%\ H_3PO_4} CH_3\text{—}\overset{CH_2}{\overset{\|}{C}}\text{—}CH_3 + H_2O$$

Thus, the correct order for the relative ease of dehydration of alcohols is 3° > 2° > 1°.

Mechanism of Dehydration of Alcohols

The mechanism of dehydration of ethanol involves the following steps

Step I Formation of protonated alcohol.

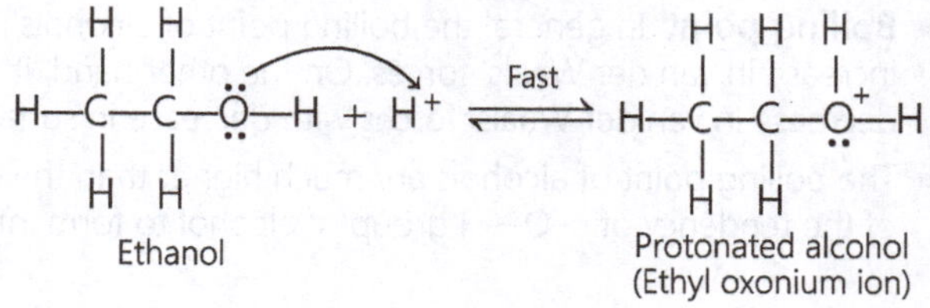

***Step* II** Formation of carbocation

It is the slowest step and hence, it is the rate determining step of the reaction.

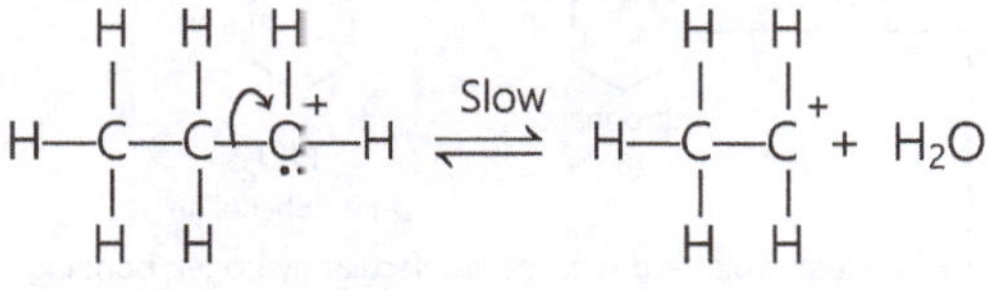

***Step* III** Formation of ethene by the elimination of a proton

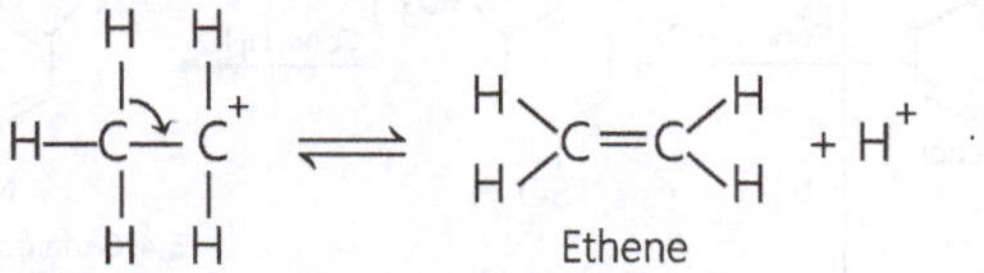

The acid used in step I is released in step III. To drive the equilibrium to the right, ethene is removed as it is formed.

- **Oxidation** In alcohol oxidation involves the formation of a carbon oxygen double bond with cleavage of O—H and C—H bonds.

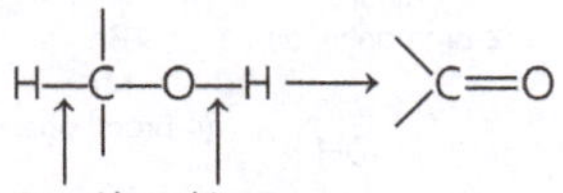

Depending on the oxidising agent used, an alcohol is oxidised as follows

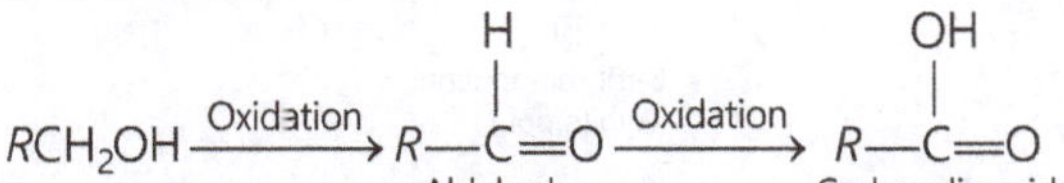

These reaction are also known as **dehydrogenation reaction** as **loss** of dihydrogen from an alcohol molecule is involved.

- **Strong oxidising agent such as $KMnO_4$** (acidified) are used for getting carboxylic acid from alcohols directly.
- CrO_3 in anhydrous medium is used as an oxidising agent for the isolation of aldehydes.
- Pyridinium chlorochromate (PCC), a complex of chromium trioxide with pyridine and HCl, is a better reagent for the conversion of primary alcohols to aldehydes in good yield without affecting the double bonds (if present). NEET 2019
- Secondary alcohols are oxidised to ketones by CrO_3.
- Tertiary alcohols do not undergo oxidation reaction.
- Under strong reaction conditions such as strong oxidising agents ($KMnO_4$) and elevated temperatures, cleavage of various C—C bonds takes place and a mixture of carboxylic acids containing lesser number of carbon atoms are formed.

- **Dehydrogenation** When vapours of a 1° or 2° alcohol are passed over heated copper at 573 K, dehydrogenation takes place and an aldehyde or ketone is formed as shown below.

$$RCH_2OH \xrightarrow[573\text{ K}]{Cu} RCHO$$

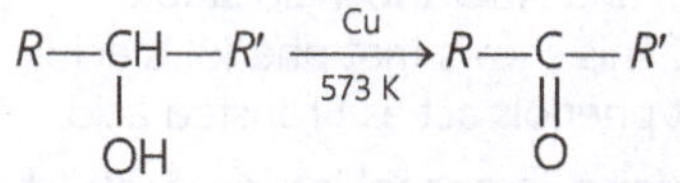

NEET 2019

3° alcohols undergo dehydration under similar conditions to produce alkenes.

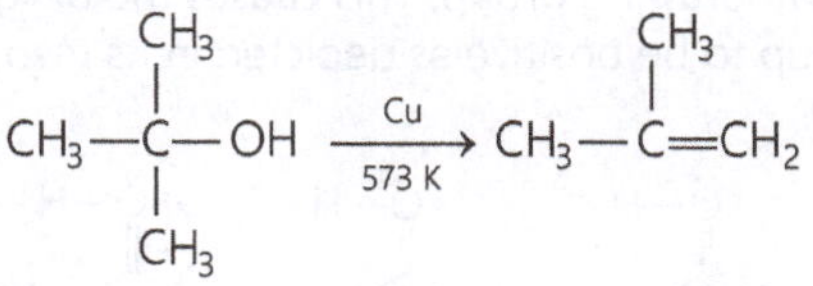

Identification of Primary, Secondary and Tertiary Alcohols

(i) **Dehydrogenation** When the vapours of a 1° or 2° or 3° alcohols are passed over heated copper at 573 K aldehydes, ketones and alkenes are produced respectively.

(ii) **Lucas test** An equimolar mixture of anhydrous $ZnCl_2$ and concentrated HCl is called Lucas reagent.

When alcohols are treated with this reagent following results are observed.

- Tertiary alcohols react and produces turbidity or cloudiness immediately.
- Secondary alcohols react after sometime and accordingly produces turbidity.
- Primary alcohols do not produce turbidity at room temperature. It means their reaction is slowest with Lucas reagent. NEET 2022

For Concept Master *Video*

Marks Maximizer

Victor Meyer's Test

- This test is used to distinguish among primary, secondary and tertiary alcohols it involves some steps as
  (i) reaction of alcohols with (I_2 + P) to give iodoalkane.
  (ii) reaction of iodoalkanes with alcoholic $AgNO_2$ to obtain nitroalkane.
  (iii) reaction of nitroalkane with HNO_2 and final solution become alkaline.
- Now this alkaline solution gives different conclusion with the reaction of different alcohols as
  (i) primary alcohol gives blood red colour.
  (ii) secondary alcohol gives blue colour.
  (iii) tertiary alcohol gives no positive test with alkaline solution so, it does not give any colour.

Chemical Properties of Phenols

For Concept Master Video

- **Acidity of phenols** Just like aliphatic alcohols, phenols reacts with active metals (e.g. Na, Al etc.) and NaOH to yield stable phenoxide ion. This shows that phenol is acidic in nature infact phenols act as Bronsted acid.
- The hydroxyl group, in phenol is directly attached to the sp^2-hybridised carbon of benzene ring which acts as an electron withdrawing group. This causes the oxygen of —OH group to be positive as depicted in its resonance structures.

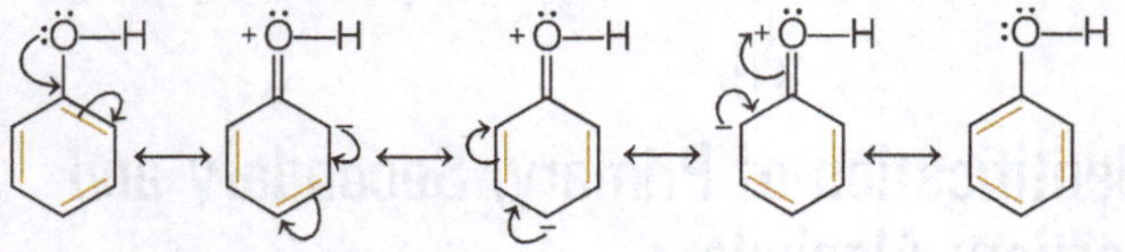

- The decrease in electron density on oxygen increases the polarity of O—H bond and results in an increase in ionisation of phenols than that of alcohols and water.
- Further, the stability of the phenoxide ion is more than the alkoxide ion. It is due to the delocalisation of the negative charge in the phenoxide ion whereas in case of alkoxide it is localised on the O-atom of the alkoxide. This stability of the phenoxide ion favours the ionisation of phenol and makes it more acidic.

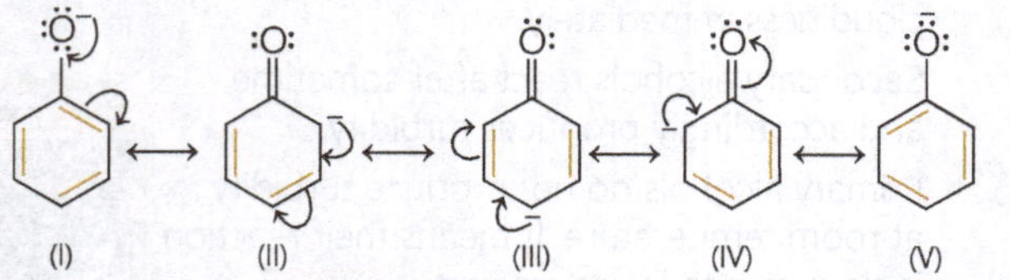

(I) (II) (III) (IV) (V)

- In substituted phenols, the acidity of phenols increase in the presence of the electron withdrawing group. This is due to the stability of the phenoxide ion. The acidity of phenols further increases if these groups are attached at *o*-and *p*-positions.

  Whereas the presence of electron donating group destabilise the phenoxide ion or we can say that the presence of this group do not favour the formation of the phenoxide ion resulting in decrease in the acidic strength.

  e.g. Cresols are less acidic than phenol.

Reactions of Phenol

Phenol readily undergo following reactions.

- **Electrophilic aromatic substitution reactions** The —OH group attached to the benzene ring activates the benzene ring towards electrophilic substitution reaction. It is *ortho* and *para*-directing group.

Important electrophilic substitution reactions of phenols are as follow

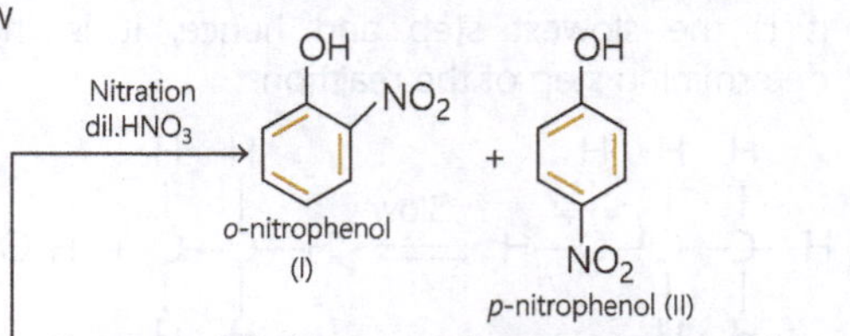

- I is steam volatile due to intramolecular hydrogen bonding.
- Less volatile due to intermolecular hydrogen bonding.

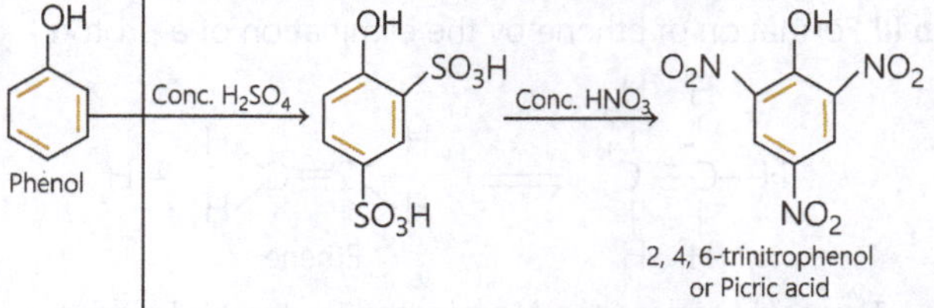

- If we use conc. HNO_3 alone then the yield is poor, hence, we use conc. H_2SO_4 first, followed by conc. HNO_3 to get better yield.

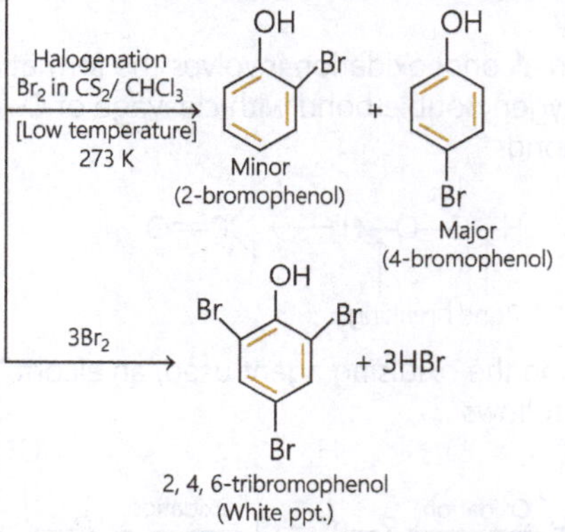

Halogenation of phenols can be carried out even in the absence of Lewis acid because of the highly activating effect of —OH group.

- **Kolbe's reaction**

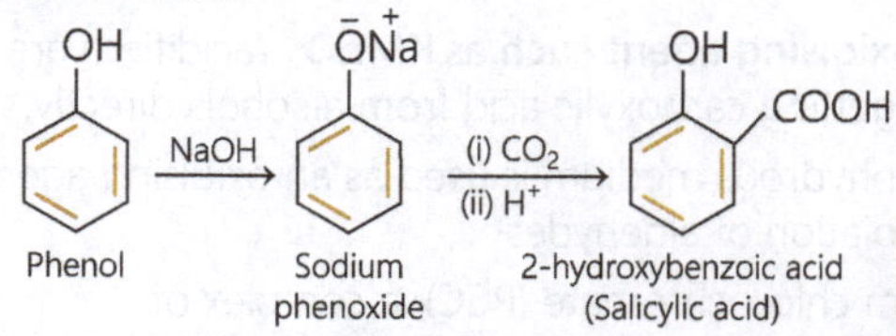

For Concept Master Video

- **Reimer-Tiemann reaction**

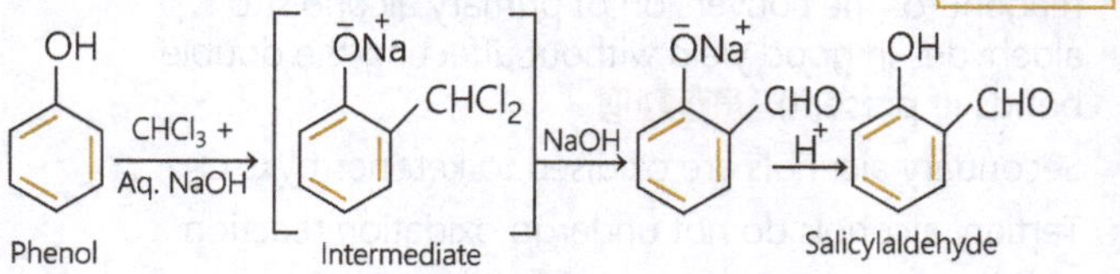

- **Reaction of phenol with zinc dust**

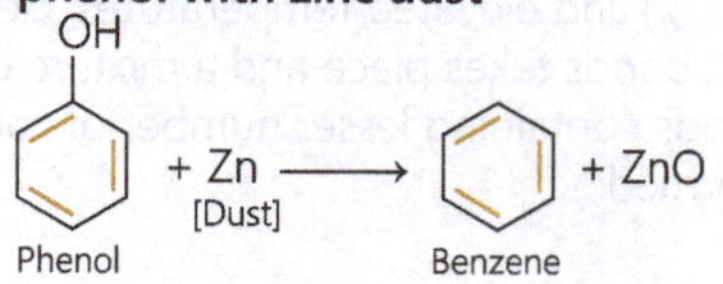

- **Oxidation**

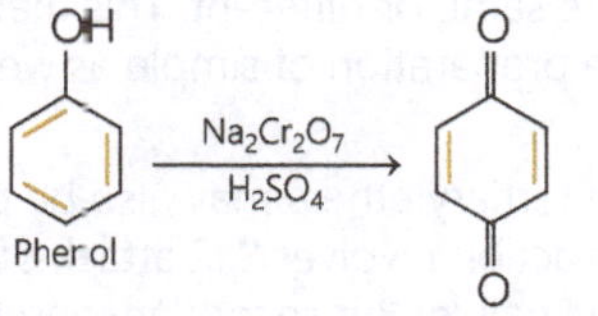

Phenol   Benzoquinone

In the presence of air, phenols are slowly oxidised to dark coloured mixtures containing quinones.

- **Esterification** Alcohols and phenols react with carboxylic acids, acid chlorides and acid anhydrides to form esters.

(i) $Ar/ROH + R'{-}COOH \overset{H^+}{\rightleftharpoons} Ar/ROCOR' + H_2O$

(ii) $Ar/ROH + (R'CO)_2O \overset{H^+}{\rightleftharpoons} Ar/ROCOR' + R'COOH$

(iii) $R/ArOH + R'COCl \overset{\text{Pyridine}}{\rightleftharpoons} R/ArOCOR' + HCl$

Conditions required for above reactions are

- Reactions (i) and (ii) are carried out in the presence of a small amount of concentrated sulphuric acid. Also these reactions are reversible in nature and therefore, water is removed as soon as it is formed.
- Reaction (iii) is carried out in the presence of a base (like pyridine) to neutralise the acid (HCl) formed during the reaction. It also help in shifting the equilibrium to the right side.
- **Acetylation** The introduction of acetyl (i.e. CH_3CO) group in alcohols or phenols is known as acetylation. Acetylation of salicylic acid produces **aspirin**, a pain killer.

e.g.

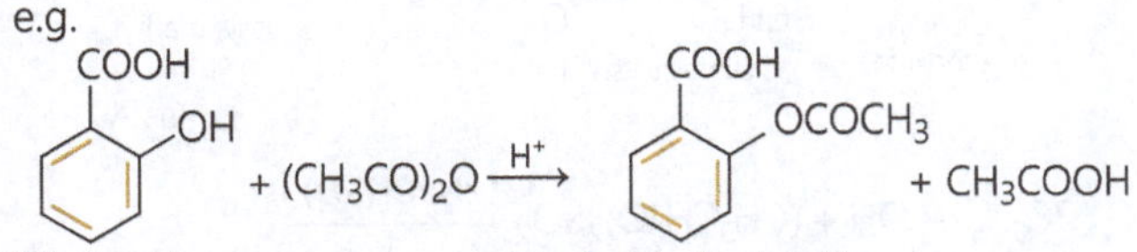

Salicylic acid   Acetyl salicyclic acid (Aspirin)

Some Commercially Important Alcohols

Methanol

- It is also known as **'wood spirit'** and produced by destructive distillation of wood. Generally, it is produced by catalytic hydrogenation of CO at high pressure and temperature in presence of $ZnO - Cr_2O_3$ catalyst.

$$CO + 2H_2 \xrightarrow[200\text{-}300 \text{ atm}, 573\text{-}673 \text{ K}]{ZnO\text{-}Cr_2O_3} CH_3OH$$

- It is **colourless** liquid and boils at **337 K**.
- It is highly poisonous in nature. Ingestion of small quantities of it can cause blindness while large quantities can cause death.
- It is used as a solvent in paints, varnishes and chiefly for making formaldehyde.

Ethanol

- It is obtained commercially by fermentation of sugars. The sugar of molasses, sugarcane or fruits like grapes is converted to glucose and fructose in the presence of an enzyme, invertase.
- Glucose and fructose, further undergo fermentation in the presence of enzyme (zymase) (which is found in yeast) to give ethanol and carbon dioxide. Once the percentage of alcohol formed exceeds 14 percent, the action of zymase is inhibited.
- The fermentation process takes place in anaerobic condition (i.e. in absence of air). This is because if air gets into the process, the oxygen present in air oxidises ethanol to ethanoic acid. This in turn destroys the taste of alcoholic drinks.

$$\underset{\text{Sucrose}}{C_{12}H_{22}O_{11}} + H_2O \xrightarrow{\text{Invertase}} \underset{\text{Glucose}}{C_6H_{12}O_6} + \underset{\text{Fructose}}{C_6H_{12}O_6}$$

$$\underset{\text{Glucose/Fructose}}{C_6H_{12}O_6} \xrightarrow{\text{Zymase}} \underset{\text{Ethanol}}{2C_2H_5OH} + 2CO_2\uparrow$$

- It is a **colourless** liquid with boiling point **351 K**.
- Used as a solvent in paint industry and as reactant in the preparation of a number of carbon compounds.
- In large quantities, ethanol is obtained by hydration of ethene.
- The commercial alcohol is made unfit for drinking by mixing in it some copper sulphate (to give it a colour) and pyridine (a foul smelling liquid). It is known as **denaturation of alcohol**.

Marks Maximizer

List of various kinds of alcohol and its composition

Name of alcohol	**Composition** (in percentage)
• Power alcohol	80% petrol + 20% ethanol
• Methylated spirit	90% ethanol + 9% methanol + 1% other poisonous substances
• Denatured spirit	95% ethanol + 5% methanol
• Rectified spirit	95% alcohol + 5% water
• Absolute alcohol	100% ethanol

Identification Tests for Alcohols and Phenols

- **Litmus test**
  Alcohol → No effect
  Phenol → Turns blue litmus red
- **Reaction with $FeCl_3$**
  Alcohol → No reaction
  Phenol → Blue, violet or green colouration
- **Bromine water test**
  Alcohol → No reaction
  Phenol → A white ppt. of 2, 4, 6 - tribromophenol is formed.
- **Coupling reaction**
  Alcohol → No reaction
  Phenol → Forms yellow or orange coloured azo dyes. [For detailed reaction refer to chapter amines]

Ethers

Preparation of Ethers

By dehydration of alcohols Alcohols undergo dehydration in the presence of protic acids [H_2SO_4, H_3PO_4]. The formation of the reaction product, alkene or ether depends on the reaction conditions.

$$\underset{\text{Ethanol}}{CH_3CH_2OH} \xrightarrow[443\,K]{H_2SO_4} \underset{\text{Ethene}}{CH_2{=}CH_2}$$

$$\underset{\text{Ethanol}}{CH_3CH_2OH} \xrightarrow[413\,K]{H_2SO_4} \underset{\text{Ethoxyethane}}{C_2H_5OC_2H_5}$$

The formation of ether is a nucleophilic bimolecular reaction (S_N2) involving the attack of alcohol molecule on a protonated alcohol, as indicated below.

(i) $CH_3—CH_2—\ddot{O}—H + H^+ \longrightarrow CH_3—CH_2—\overset{+}{\ddot{O}}(H)—H$

(ii) $CH_3CH_2—\ddot{O}(H): + CH_3—CH_2—\overset{+}{O}H_2 \longrightarrow CH_3CH_2—\overset{+}{O}(H)—CH_2CH_3 + H_2O$

(iii) $CH_3CH_2—\overset{+}{O}(H)—CH_2CH_3 \longrightarrow CH_3CH_2—O—CH_2CH_3 + H^+$

- Acidic dehydration of alcohols, to give an alkene is also associated with substitution reaction to give an ether.
- Bimolecular reaction [S_N2] is suitable for the preparation of ethers having primary alkyl group.
- The alkyl group should be unhindered and temperature should be low.
- Otherwise the reaction favours alkene formation. The reaction follows S_N1 pathway when the alcohol is secondary or tertiary.

Williamson synthesis This method is used for the preparation of symmetrical and unsymmetrical ethers.

In this method, an alkyl halide is allowed to react with sodium alkoxide.

For Concept Master Video

$$R—X + R'\overset{-}{\ddot{O}}\overset{+}{Na} \longrightarrow R\ddot{O}R' + NaX$$

- R and R' may be same or different. This method is suitable for the preparation of simple as well as mixed ether.
- Secondary and tertiary ethers may also be prepared by this method. The reaction involves S_N2 attack of an alkoxide ion on primary alkyl halide. But secondary and tertiary alkyl halide cannot be used. In secondary and tertiary alkyl halide, elimination competes over substitution and may give alkene.
- Tertiary alkyl halide gives alkene as the only product and no ether is formed. It is because alkoxides are not only nucleophile but strong bases as well. They abstract proton from the tertiary carbocation leading to elimination reaction.
- Phenols are also converted to ethers by using this method in which phenol is used as the phenoxide moiety.

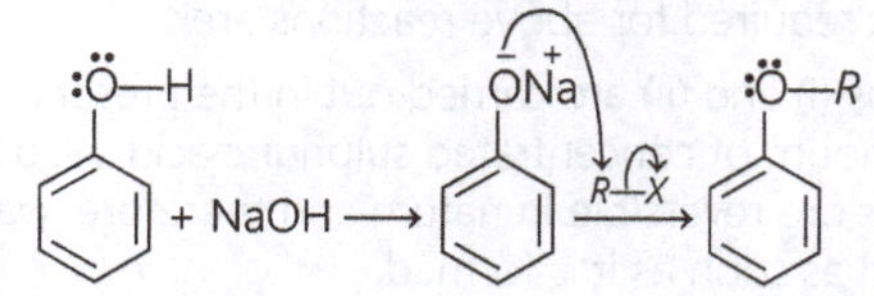

Marks Maximizer

Like halide ions, sulphate ion is a good leaving group. Therefore, in Williamson synthesis, alkyl halides may be replaced by alkyl sulphates. e.g.

$$\underset{\text{Sodium ethoxide}}{2C_2H_5ONa} + \underset{\text{Dimethyl sulphate}}{(CH_3O)_2SO_2} \xrightarrow[\Delta]{2NaOH(aq)} \underset{\text{Ethyl methyl ether}}{2C_2H_5OCH_3} + Na_2SO_4$$

$$\underset{\text{Phenol}}{2C_6H_5—OH} + (CH_3CH_2O)_2SO_2 \xrightarrow[\Delta]{2NaOH(aq)} \underset{\text{Phenetole}}{2C_6H_5OC_2H_5} + Na_2SO_4 + 2H_2O$$

Physical Properties

Various physical properties of ether are as follows

- **Polarity**, the C—O bonds in ethers are polar and thus ethers have a net dipole moment.
- **Boiling points** The alcohols and ethers have large difference in their boiling point due to the presence of hydrogen bonding in alcohols.

- **Solubility** The miscibility of ethers with water resembles those of alcohols of the same molecular mass. This is due to intermolecular hydrogen bonding between ether and water molecules. It generally decreases with increase of molecular mass.
- **Density** Ethers are lighter than water.

Chemical Reactions

These are as follows

Cleavage of C—O Bond in Ethers

It occurs under drastic condition with excess of hydrogen halides as ether are the least reactive of the functional groups.

$$ROR + HX \longrightarrow RX + R\text{—}OH$$
$$R\text{—}OH + HX \longrightarrow RX + H_2O$$

Ethers with two different alkyl groups are also cleaved in the same manner.

$$R\text{—}O\text{—}R' + HX \longrightarrow R\text{—}X + R'\text{—}OH$$

- For a given ether, the reactivity of hydrogen halides follows the order :
  $$HCl < HBr < HI \text{ (strongest acid)}$$
- In case of mixed ethers with different R groups, the product depends on the nature of R groups.
  - When 1° or 2° R groups are present. The smaller R group forms alkyl halide.
    $$CH_3OCH_2CH_3 + HI \longrightarrow CH_3I + CH_3CH_2OH$$ NEET 2019
  - When one of the R group is 3°R group, then tertiary alkyl halide is formed because the reaction then occurs by S_N1 mechanism and 3° carbocation is more stable.

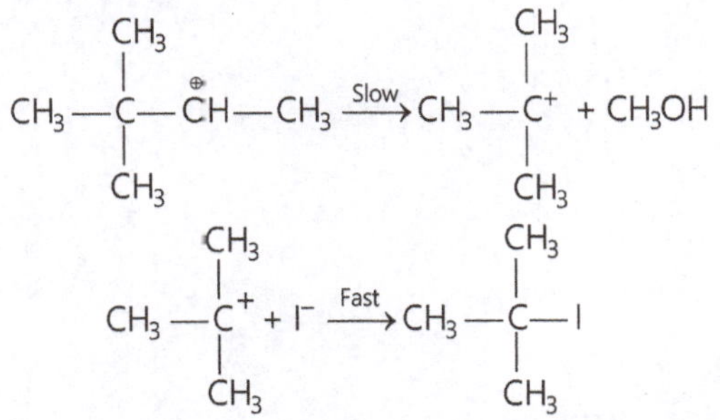

- In case of alkyl aryl ethers, reaction with HX results in the cleavage of R—O bond, Ar—O bond is more stable due to double bond character.

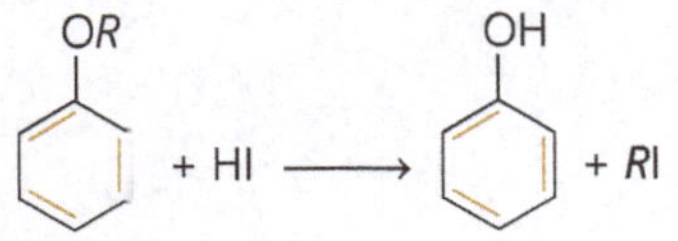

- In case of anisole, methyl phenyloxonium ion, $C_6H_5\text{—}\overset{+}{\underset{|}{O}}\text{—}CH_3$ (with H on O) is formed by protonation of ether. The bond between O—CH_3 is weaker than the bond between O—C_6H_5 because the carbon of phenyl group is sp^2-hybridised and there is a partial double bond character.

Therefore, the attack by I^- ion breaks O—CH_3 bond to form CH_3I. Phenol do not react further to give halide. This is because the sp^2-hybridised carbon of phenol cannot undergo nucleophilic substitution reaction. NEET 2020

Electrophilic Substitution of Aromatic Ethers

The alkoxy group (—OR) activates the aromatic ring towards electrophilic substitution at *ortho* and *para*-positions. The same is observed in the case of phenol.

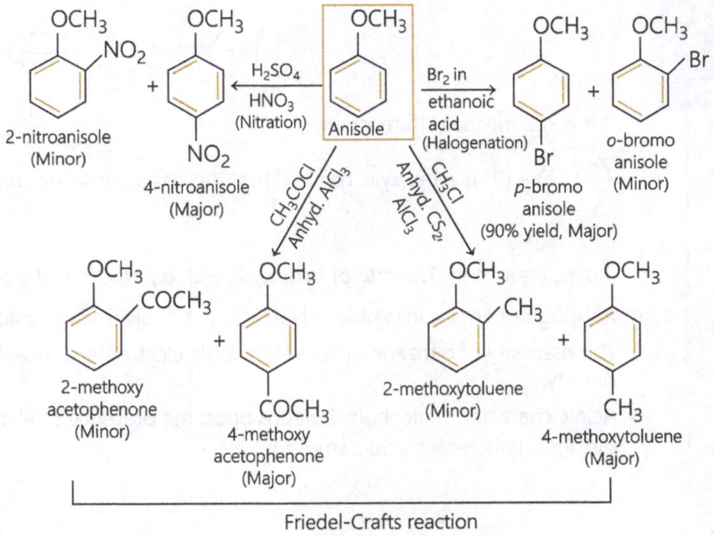

Marks Maximizer

- The large ring ethers with atleast four —OCH_2CH_2— repeating units are named as crown ethers since they have crown like structure.
- The common crown ether is 18-crown-6-ether in which 18 is the ring size and 6 is the number of oxygen atoms.

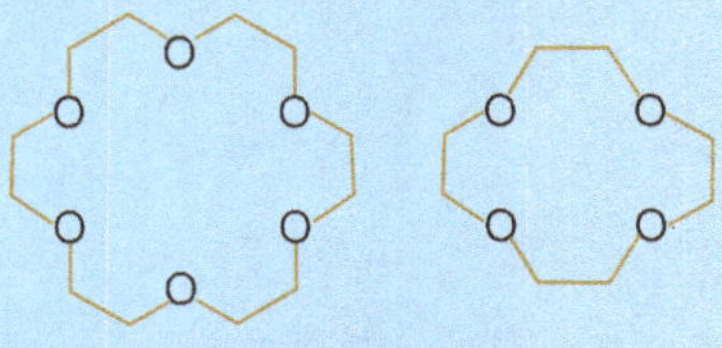

18-crown-6-ether 12-crown-4-ether

Caution Points

- Ether can be formed only by dehydration of primary alcohols. In 2° and 3° alcohol elimination reaction occurs to remove water molecules and to produce corresponding alkene.

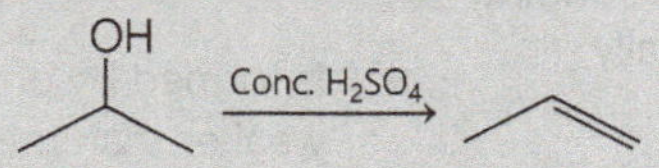

- Bromination of phenol in the absence of a Lewis acid does not produce *p*-substituted product. Although a tri-substituted product can be obtained.
- The temperature should be kept low in the reaction of alcohol with conc. H_2SO_4 to form ether but on high temperature will given alkene.
- Mixed aqueous solutions are preferred for car radiators always. An aqueous mixture containing 50% ethylene glycol is used as anti-freeze for car radiators. It freezes at 34°C and also used as de-icing fluid for aeroplane wings.

PYQ Notes

1. Iodoform reaction is used for the detection of CH_3CO group and also ($CH_3CH(OH)$) group. Compounds containing these groups shows positive iodoform test. **NEET 2018**
2. 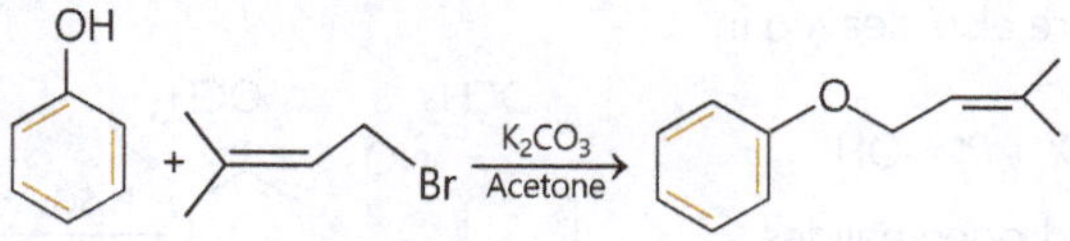

   It is a S_N2 mechanism reaction. **JEE 2021**
3. 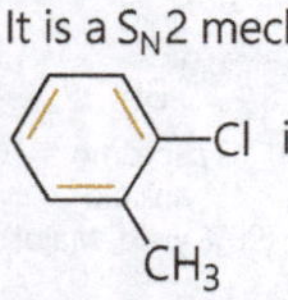 is a benzylic halide. Thus, there is a partial double bond character between sp^3-hybridised C-atom next to an aromatic ring. The rate of hydrolysis with *aq.* NaOH is of slowest rate. **NEET 2019**
4. Although phenol is insoluble in $NaHCO_3$ yet it gives violet colour in neutral $FeCl_3$ solution (Ferric chloride test . **JEE 2022]**
5. The reactivity of benzene increases towards electrophilic substitution reaction when any substituent increases the electron density. **JEE 2023**
6. Acidic character of alcohols depends upon the presence of electron withdrawing group which shows (– *I*)-effect with less distance. It increases acidic strength. **JEE 2023**

Step by Step

Mastering NCERT

- Concept Builders
- Topical Questions
- Assertion-Reason
- Statement Type
- Matching Type
- Numerical Value
- NCERT Exemplar's
- Past Exams'
- Skill Boosters

Concept Builders

1 Name the compound which is an important component of ordinary spirit used for polishing wooden furniture.

2 Compounds containing —OH groups can be used for making alkaloids. [T/F]

3 An alcohol contains one or more (—OH) group directly attached to carbon atom(s) of an ....

4 The substitution of a hydrogen atom in a hydrocarbon by an .... group yields another class of compounds known as ether.

5 The alcohols contains —OH group bonded to an aryl carbon is also known as .... alcohols.

6 $CH_2{=}CH{-}CH_2OH$ is an example of vinylic alcohol. [T/F]

7 Write the IUPAC name of the following compound. $[HOCH_2(CH_2)_3CH_2COCH_3]$

8 The C—O bond length in phenol is less than that of ethers. [T/F]

9 Write the name of the reagent which can be used to reduce carbonyl compounds into alcohols.

10 Write the name of intermediate formed in the preparation of phenol from cumene.

11 With increase of branching in carbon chain, the van der Waals' forces of attraction increase. [T/F]

12 In phenols, electron releasing groups do not favour the formation of phenoxide ion, resulting .... in acidic strength. (increase/decrease)

13 Acetyl salicylic acid possesses analgesic, anti-inflammatory and antipyretic properties also known as ....

14 Tertiary alcohols produces turbidity when reacts with a equimolar mixture of $ZnCl_2$ and conc. HCl. [T/F]

15 Phenyl methanoate on mononitration gives .... product in major amount.

16 What is the name of the reaction in which carbolic acid is treated with chloroform in the presence of sodium hydroxide?

17 In the presence of oxygen, phenols are slowly oxidised to dark coloured mixtures containing ....

18 Glucose and fructose undergo fermentation in the presence of enzyme, invertase, which is found in yeast. [T/F]

19 The commercial alcohol is made unfit for drinking by mixing in it some copper sulphate and pyridine. It is known as .... of alcohol.

20 The .... [S_N1/ S_N2] mechanism path is followed in the formation of ether in a dehydration process.

21 What is the name of the complex that is used in the oxidation of primary alcohols to obtain a good yield of aldehydes?

22 A methanol poisoned patient is treated by giving intravenous infusions of diluted .... (ethanol/propanol)

23 Alcohols and phenols are Bronsted acids. [T/F]

24 Write the name of intermediate product formed in the preparation of picric acid from phenol.

25 .... are slowly oxidised in the presence of air to dark coloured mixtures containing quinones.

26 Write name of the reaction that can be used for the preparation of symmetrical and unsymmetrical ethers.

27 Tertiary alkyl halide is a better compound than secondary alkyl halide in the formation of ether by Williamson synthesis. [T/F]

28 In Williamson reaction primary or secondary alkyl group are present in a ether, it is the .... alkyl group that forms alkyl iodide.

29 In the bromination of anisole, the *para*-bromoanisole is obtained in 90% yield. [T/F]

30 Methoxy benzene reacts with ethanoyl chloride to produce a major product is ....

Topical Questions

Classification, Nomenclature and Structure of Alcohols, Phenols and Ethers

1 In which of the following alcohol the —OH group is attached to sp^3-hybridised carbon atom? NCERT Pg 194
(a) Allylic and vinylic both.
(b) Allylic and benzylic alcohols both.
(c) Vinylic and benzylic alcohols both.
(d) In vinylic only.

2 Vinylic alcohol contains NCERT Pg 195
(a) —OH group attached to an sp^3-hybridised carbon atom.
(b) —OH group attached to an sp-hybridised carbon atom.
(c) —OH group bonded to a carbon-carbon double bond.
(d) —OH group attached to sp^3-hybridised carbon atom next to an aromatic ring.

3 Which of the following is not classified as phenols? NCERT Pg 195

(a) 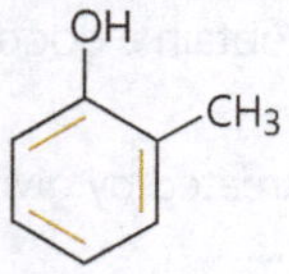
(b) 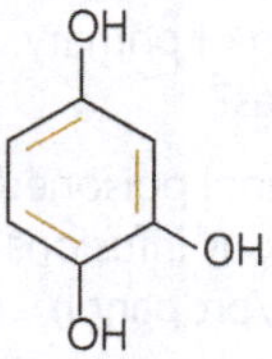
(c) 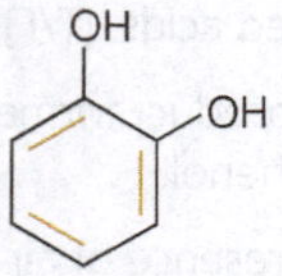
(d) 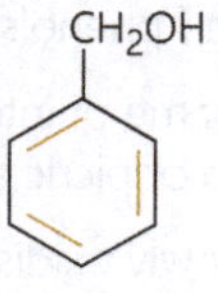

4 Which one of them is an incorrect combination? NCERT Pg 195
(a) $C_2H_5OC_2H_5 \rightarrow$ Simple ether
(b) $C_2H_5OC_6H_5 \rightarrow$ Mixed ether
(c) $C_2H_5OCH_3 \rightarrow$ Unsymmetrical ether
(d) $C_2H_5OC_2H_5 \rightarrow$ unsymmetrical ether

5 The IUPAC name of following structure is NCERT Pg 195, 196

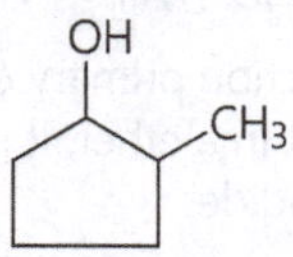

(a) 2-methylhydroxycyclopentane
(b) 2-hydroxy 2-methylcyclopentane
(c) 2-methylcyclopentanol
(d) cyclopentylmethane

6 Observe the following table : NCERT Pg 196

Compound	Common name	IUPAC name
$CH_3—OH$	Methyl alcohol	I
$CH_3—CH(OH)—CH_3$	II	Propan-2-ol
III	*n*-butyl alcohol	Butan-1-ol

Identify I, II and III from the above table.
(a) I → methanol; II → *tert*-propyl alcohol; III → $CH_3CH_2CH_2CH_2OH$
(b) I → methanol; II → propyl alcohol; III → $CH_3CH_2CH_2OH$
(c) I → methanol; II → *iso*-propyl alcohol; III → $CH_3CH_2CH_2CH_2OH$
(d) I → methanol; II → *tert*-propyl alcohol; III → $CH_3CH_2CH_2OH$

7 Select the incorrect match from the following options. NCERT Pg 196
(a) $H_3C—CH_2—CH(OH)—CH_3 \rightarrow$ *sec*-butyl alcohol
(b) $CH_3—CH(CH_3)—CH_2OH \rightarrow$ *iso*-butyl alcohol
(c) $CH_2(OH)—CH(OH)—CH_2(OH) \rightarrow$ Glycerol
(d) $HO—H_2C—CH_2—OH \rightarrow$ Methylene glycol

8 A compound $C_3H_8O_3$ has two primary alcoholic groups and one secondary alcoholic groups. The IUPAC name of this compound is NCERT Pg 196
(a) propane-1, 2-diol (b) propane-1, 3-diol
(c) propane-1, 2, 3-triol (d) 2-methylethane-1-ol

9 IUPAC name of 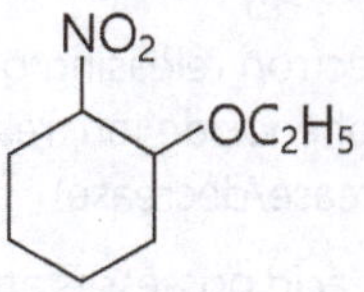 is NCERT Pg 198
(a) ethyl-2-nitrocyclohexane
(b) 1-ethoxy-2-nitrocyclohexane
(c) 1-nitro-2-ethoxycyclohexane
(d) 2-nitro-1-ethoxycyclohexane

10 The C—O—H bond angle in methanol, phenol and methoxymethane respectively are NCERT Pg 198
(a) 108.9°, 109° and 111.7° (b) 109, 108.9° and 111.7°
(c) 111.7, 108.9° and 109° (d) 111.7°, 109° and 108.9°

11 The IUPAC name of $C_6H_{14}O_2$ compound, which has two tertiary alcoho ic groups, is **NCERT Pg 199**
(a) 2-methyl-2, 3-pentandiol
(b) 2,3-dimethyl butane-2,3-diol
(c) 2,3-dimethyl-1,2-butanediol
(d) 2,3-dimethyl-1,2-butanediol

12 In ethers, the two bond pairs and two lone pairs of electrons on oxygen are arranged in a **NCERT Pg 199**
(a) planar arrangement.
(b) tetrahedral arrangement.
(c) trigonal bipyramidal arrangement.
(d) square planar arrangement.

13 Select the incorrect statement regarding ethers. **NCERT Pg 199**
(a) The four electron pairs are arranged approximately in a tetrahedral arrangement.
(b) The C—O—C— bond angle is less than the tetrahedral angle.
(c) The C—O bond length is almost the same as in alcohols.
(d) The C—O bonds in ethers are polar.

Alcohols and Phenols

14 Alkenes react with water in the presence of acid catalyst to form alcohols. **NCERT Pg 199**

$$CH_3CH{=}CH_2 + H_2O \underset{}{\overset{H^+}{\rightleftharpoons}} CH_3-\underset{\displaystyle OH}{\underset{|}{CH}}-CH_3$$

The reaction takes place in accordance with
(a) Hofmann elimination rule
(b) Saytzeff rule
(c) Markovnikov's rule
(d) anti-Markovnikov's addition

15 Consider the following reaction. **NCERT Pg 200**

$$CH_3-CH{=}CH_2 \xrightarrow{X} CH_3-CH_2-CH_2OH$$

The suitable reagent (X) for above reaction is
(a) $H_2 \mid Pt$ (b) (i) B_2H_6 (ii) $H_2O_2 \mid OH^-$
(c) $Br_2 \mid HCl$ (d) $HBr \mid H_2O_2$

16
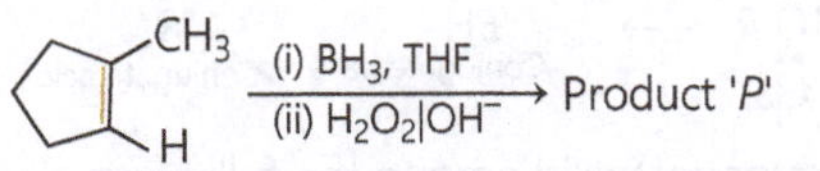

Select the incorrect statement regarding the above reaction. **NCERT Pg 200**
(a) The reaction is known as hydroboration oxidation.
(b) The net addition of —H and —OH occurs with Markovnikov addition.
(c) Hydroboration gives trialkyl boranes as addition product.
(d) The alcohol is obtained in excellent yield.

17 $CH_3CH_2CH_3 \xrightarrow[h\nu]{Br_2} \underset{(Major)}{A} \xrightarrow[\Delta]{alc.KOH} B \xrightarrow[(ii)\ H_2O,\ H_2O_2,\ OH^-]{(i)\ B_2H_6} C$

Here, C is **NCERT Pg 200**
(a) $CH_3CH_2CH_2OH$ (b) $CH_3\underset{\displaystyle OH}{\underset{|}{CH}}-CH_3$
(c) $CH_3CH_2CH_2BH_2$ (d) $CH_3CH_2CH_2Br$

18 The reagents which is not used for the reduction of aldehydes and ketones into alcohols is **NCERT Pg 200**
(a) finely divided metals such as Pt/Pd/Ni
(b) sodium borohydride
(c) lithium aluminium hydride
(d) potassium permanganate

19 Which of the following reagent is used to reduce carboxylic acids to primary alcohols? **NCERT Pg 200**
(a) Pd (b) $KMnO_4$ (c) $LiAlH_4/H_2O$ (d) Ni

20 Consider the following reactions. **NCERT Pg. 200**

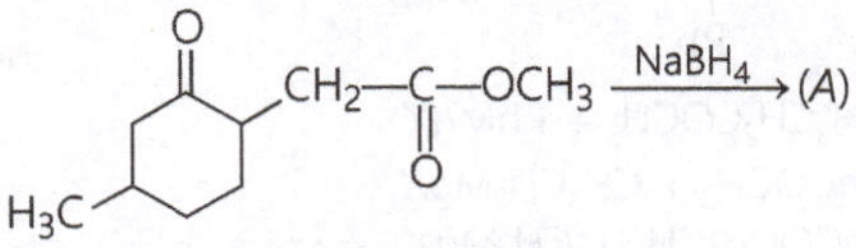

$$CH_3CH_2CH_2\underset{\displaystyle CH_3}{\underset{|}{CH}}-CHO \xrightarrow{NaBH_4} (B)$$

The compound (A) and (B) formed respectively are,

(a)
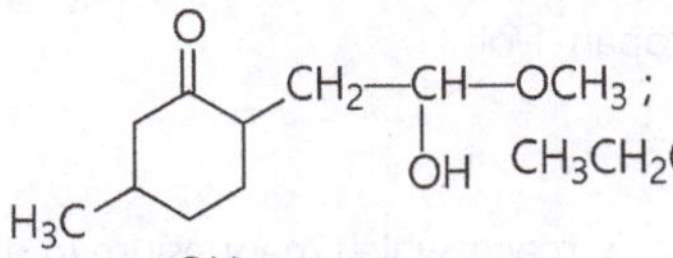

$CH_3CH_2CH_2\underset{\displaystyle CH_3}{\underset{|}{CH}}-CH_2OH$

(b)
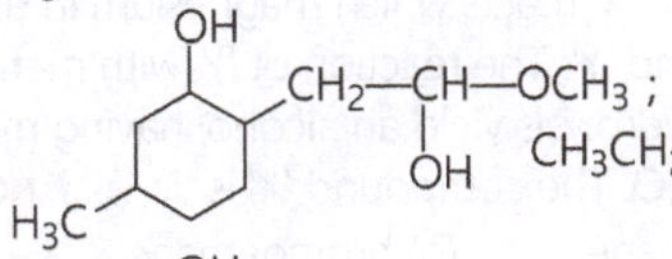

$CH_3CH_2CH_2\underset{\displaystyle CH_2OH}{\underset{|}{CH}}-CH_2OH$

(c)
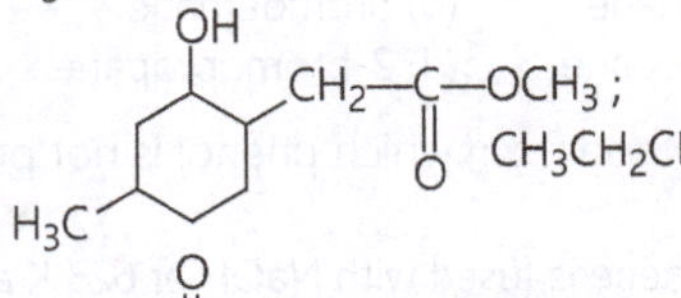

$CH_3CH_2CH_2\underset{\displaystyle CH_3}{\underset{|}{CH}}-CH_2OH$

(d)
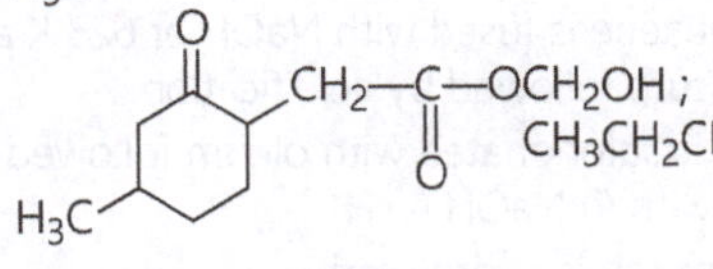

$CH_3CH_2CH_2\underset{\displaystyle CH_3}{\underset{|}{CH}}-CH_2OH$

21 Consider the following sequence of reaction.

$$CH_3COOH \xrightarrow[H^+]{C_2H_5OH} CH_3COOC_2H_5 \xrightarrow[Catalyst]{H_2}$$

The end products formed is/are **NCERT Pg 200**
(a) $CH_3COOH + C_2H_5OH$ (b) $C_2H_5OH + CH_3OH$
(c) $2C_2H_5OH$ (d) $CH_3CH_2CH_2OH$

22 $CH_3CH_2-\overset{\overset{\displaystyle O}{\|}}{C}-OH \xrightarrow{[X]} CH_3CH_2-CH_2-OH$

For the above conversion which of the following reducing agent is/are most suitable? **NCERT Pg 200**

(a) $NaBH_4/EtOH$
(b) $LiAlH_4/H_2O$
(c) B_2H_6/THF
(d) $NaBH_4/EtOH$ or $LiAlH_4/EtOH$

23 The reaction of Grignard reagent with carbonyl compound is a nucleophilic addition reaction. This reaction on hydrolysis produces **NCERT Pg 201**

(a) ester (b) alcohol
(c) carboxylic acid (d) ether

24 $CH_3CH_2-\underset{\underset{\displaystyle Ph}{|}}{\overset{\overset{\displaystyle OH}{|}}{C}}-CH_3$ cannot be prepared by **NCERT Pg 201**

(a) $CH_3CH_2COCH_3 + PhMgX$
(b) $PhCOCH_3 + CH_3CH_2MgX$
(c) $PhCOCH_2CH_3 + CH_3MgX$
(d) $HCHO + PhCH(CH_3)\,CH_2MgX$

25 IUPAC name of the compound formed by the reaction of propanone with methylmagnesiumbromide. **NCERT Pg 201**

(a) 2-methylpropan-2-ol
(b) 2-methylpropan-1-ol
(c) Butan-1-ol
(d) Butan-2-ol

26 A bromoalkane '*X*' reacts which magnesium in dry ether to form compound '*Y*'. The reaction of '*Y*' with methanal followed by hydrolysis yield an alcohol having molecular formula, $C_4H_{10}O$. The compound '*X*' is **NCERT Pg 201**

(a) bromomethane (b) bromoethane
(c) 1-bromopropane (d) 2-bromopropane

27 Select the method from which phenol is not prepared **NCERT Pg 202**

(a) chlorobenzene is fused with NaOH at 623 K and 320 atm pressure followed by acidification.
(b) benzene is sulphonated with oleum followed by reaction with (i) NaOH (ii) H^+.
(c) diazonium salt is hydrolysed.
(d) oxidation of cumene.

28 Which of the following hydrocarbon is used for the bulk production of phenol? **NCERT Pg 202**

(a) *Iso*-butylbenzene
(b) *Iso*-propylbenzene
(c) *Iso*-pentylbenzene
(d) *Iso*-hexylbenzene

29 Identify the major products *P*, *Q* and *R* in the following sequence of reactions : **NCERT Pg 202**

$$C_6H_6 + CH_3CH_2CH_2Cl \xrightarrow[AlCl_3]{\text{Anhy.}} P \xrightarrow[\text{(ii) } H_3O^+]{\text{(i) } O_2} Q + R$$

(a) $C_6H_5CH(CH_3)_2$, C_6H_5OH, $CH_3CH(OH)CH_3$
(b) $C_6H_5CH_2CH_2CH_3$, C_6H_5CHO, C_6H_5COOH
(c) $C_6H_5CH_2CH_2CH_3$, C_6H_5CHO, CH_3CH_2-OH
(d) $C_6H_5CH(CH_3)_2$, C_6H_5OH, $CH_3-CO-CH_3$

30 Which of the following trends is incorrect with properties mentioned? **NCERT Pg 203, 204**

(a) $CH_3CH_2OH > CH_3CH_2CH_2OH > CH_3CH_2CH_2CH_2OH$ (Solubility)
(b) $CH_3CH_2OH < CH_3CH_2CH_2OH < CH_3CH_2CH_2CH_2OH$ (Boiling point)
(c) $CH_3CH_2OH > CH_3-O-CH_3 > CH_3CH_2CH_3$ (Boiling point)
(d) $CH_3-\underset{\underset{\displaystyle CH_3}{|}}{\overset{\overset{\displaystyle CH_3}{|}}{C}}-OH > CH_3-\underset{\underset{\displaystyle CH_3}{|}}{CH}-CH_2OH > CH_3CH_2CH_2CH_2OH$ (Boiling point)

31 Select the correct order of increasing boiling point. **NCERT Pg 204**

(a) Methanol < ethanol < propan-1-ol < butan-2-ol < butan-1-ol < pentan-1-ol
(b) Ethanol < methanol < propan-1-ol < butan-1-ol < butan-2-ol < pentan-1-ol
(c) Methanol < ethanol < propan-1-ol < butan-1-ol < butan-2-ol < pentan-1-ol
(d) Methanol < ethanol < propan-1-ol < butan-1-ol < pentan-1-ol < butan-2-ol

32 Which of the following reaction is correct? **NCERT Pg 205**

(a) $\underset{\text{Acid}}{B^+} + \underset{\text{Base}}{H\ddot{\underset{\cdot\cdot}{O}}R} \longrightarrow \underset{\text{Conjugate base}}{BH} + \underset{\text{Conjugate acid}}{\bar{O}R}$

(b) $\underset{\text{Base}}{B^-} + \underset{\text{Acid}}{H\ddot{\underset{\cdot\cdot}{O}}R} \longrightarrow \underset{\text{Conjugate acid}}{BH} + \underset{\text{Conjugate base}}{\bar{O}R}$

(c) $\underset{\text{Acid}}{B^+} + \underset{\text{Base}}{H\ddot{\underset{\cdot\cdot}{O}}R} \longrightarrow \underset{\text{Conjugate acid}}{BH} + \underset{\text{Conjugate base}}{\bar{O}R}$

(d) $\underset{\text{Base}}{B^-} + \underset{\text{Acid}}{H\ddot{\underset{\cdot\cdot}{O}}R} \longrightarrow \underset{\text{Conjugate base}}{BH} + \underset{\text{Conjugate acid}}{\bar{O}R}$

33 Select the strongest acid among the following compounds. **NCERT Pg 205**

(a) $CH_3CH_2CH_2OH$ (b) $H_3CCH_2CH_2-CH(CH_3)$
(c) CH_3OH (d) $(C_2H_5)_3COH$

34 The most acidic compoud among the following is **NCERT Pg 206**

(a) C_2H_5OH (b) H_2O
(c) C_6H_5OH (d) $HC\equiv CH$

35 Which one is the most acidic compound? **NCERT Pg 207**

(a) 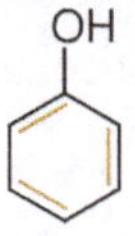

(b) 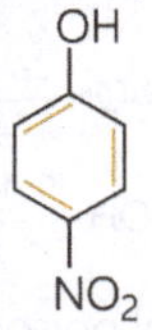

(c) 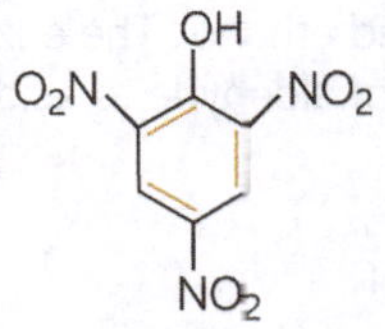

(d) 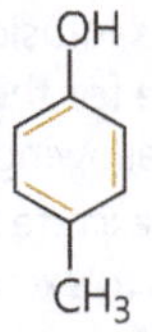

36 Correct increasing order of pK_a values for the following substituted phenol **NCERT Pg 207**

(a) *o*-nitrophenol < *p*-nitrophenol < *m*-nitrophenol < phenol
(b) *p*-nitrophenol < *o*-nitrophenol < *m*-nitrophenol < phenol
(c) *m*-nitrophenol < *o*-nitrophenol < *p*-nitrophenol < phenol
(d) Phenol < *m*-nitrophenol < *o*-nitrophenol < *p*-nitrophenol

37 Cresols are less acidic than phenols because **NCERT Pg 207**

(a) EDGs favour the formation of phenoxide ion resulting in the decrease in acidic strength.
(b) EWGs favour the formation of phenoxide ion resulting in the decrease in acidic strength.
(c) EDGs do not favour the formation of phenoxide ion resulting in the decrease in acidic strength.
(d) EWGs do not favour the formation of phenoxide ion resulting in the decrease in acidic strength.

38 Arrange the following compounds in the decreasing order of acidity. **NCERT Pg 207**

(a) $H_2O > HC\equiv CH > ROH$
(b) $H_2O > ROH > HC\equiv CH$
(c) $HC\equiv CH > ROH > H_2O$
(d) $HC\equiv CH > H_2O > ROH$

39 The reaction of alcohol/phenol with acid chloride is carried out in the presence of pyridine in order to **NCERT Pg 208**

(a) neutralise HCl which is formed during the reaction.
(b) shift the equilibrium to left hand side.
(c) provide catalytic property.
(d) acidic medium for the better yield.

40 Consider the following reaction : **NCERT Pg 208**

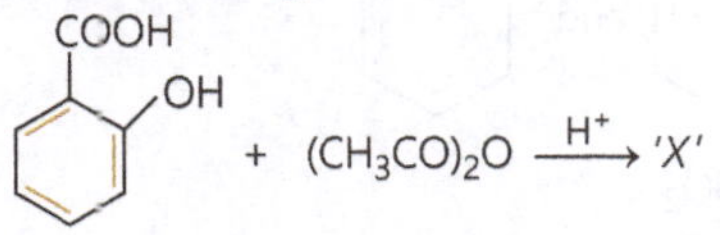

Here, product '*X*' is

(a) 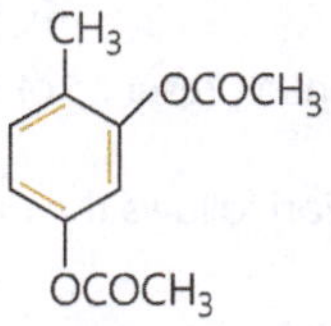

(b) 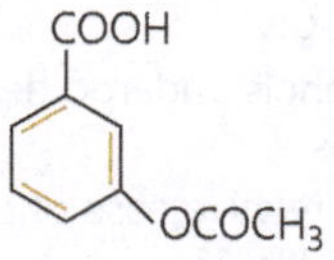

(c) 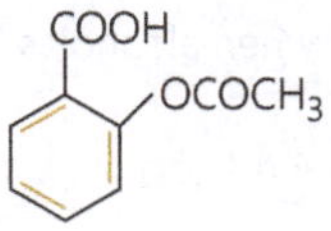

(d) 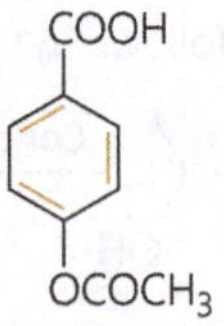

41 The alcohol which reacts fastest with Lucas reagent is **NCERT Pg 208**

(a) 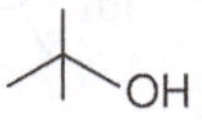

(b) 

(c) 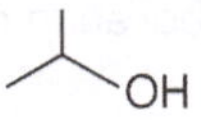

(d) 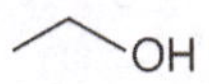

42 Select the alcohol which will not give immediate turbidity on reaction with conc. HCl in presence of anhyd. $ZnCl_2$. **NCERT Pg 208**

(a) $CH_3—CH_2—OH$ (b) $CH_3CH_2CH_2—OH$
(c) $CH_3—CH_2—CH(OH)—CH_3$ (d) $(CH_3)_3C—OH$

43 Consider the following reaction : **NCERT Pg 208**

$$R—OH + HX \longrightarrow R—X + H_2O$$

The correct decreasing order of reactivity of alcohol with HX is

(a) HCl > HBr > HI (b) HI > HBr > HCl
(c) HBr > HCl > HI (d) HI > HCl > HBr

44 Which of the following reagent can be used to distinguish three classes of alcohol? **NCERT Pg 208**

(a) H_2SO_4 or H_3PO_4 (b) Conc. HCl and $ZnCl_2$
(c) $(CH_3CO)_2O$ (d) CH_3COCl

45 An unknown alcohol (*X*) is treated with the "Lucas reagent" to determine whether the alcohol is primary, secondary or tertiary. The type of alcohol that reacts fastest with its mechanism is **NCERT Pg 208**

(a) secondary alcohol by S_N1
(b) tertiary alcohol by S_N2
(c) secondary alcohol by S_N2
(d) tertiary alcohol by S_N1

46 Which of the following product is formed by the dehydration of 2-methylcyclohexanol and butan-1-ol? **NCERT Pg 208**

(a) 1-methylcyclohexene and but -2-ene
(b) 2-methylcyclohexene and butane
(c) 2-methylcyclohexene and but-2-ene
(d) 1-methylcyclohexene and but-1-ene

47 Choose the incorrect statements regarding dehydration of alcohols. **NCERT Pg 208**

(a) Alcohols undergo dehydration in presence of protic acids.

(b) The relative ease of dehydration follows the order $3° > 2° > 1°$.

(c) The temperature should be low.

(d) Reaction follows S_N1 pathway when alcohol is 2° and 3°.

48 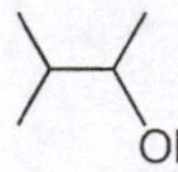 $\xrightarrow[\Delta]{\text{Conc. } H_2SO_4}$ A (Major)

Product A in the given reaction is **NCERT Pg 208**

(a) 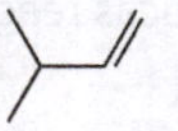 (b) 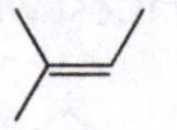 (c) 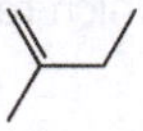 (d) 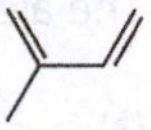

49 Alcohol that will give most stable carbocation during dehydration is **NCERT Pg 209**

(a) butan-1-ol (b) 2-methylpropan-1-ol

(c) 2-methylpropan-2-ol (d) butan-2-ol

50 Alcohol which get dehydrated easily, **NCERT Pg 209**

(a) 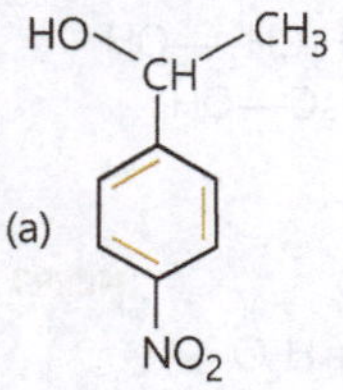

(b) 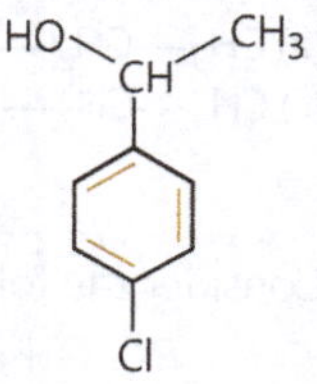

(c) 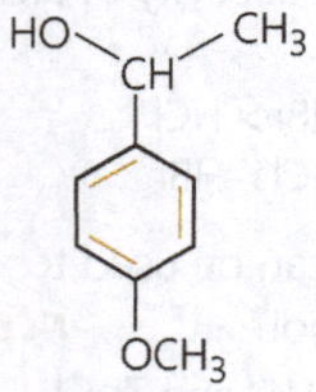

(d) 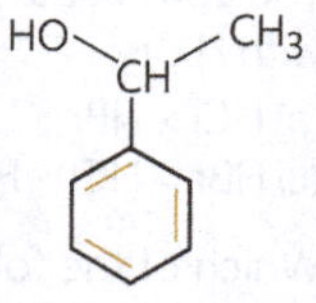

51 PCC is the **NCERT Pg 210**

(a) complex of chromium trioxide with pyridine and HCl.

(b) complex of chromium trioxide with ammonia and HCl.

(c) complex of chromium dioxide with pyridine and HCl.

(d) complex of chromium dioxide with ammonia and HCl.

52 Identify an appropriate reagent for the conversion of alcohol to carboxylic acid. **NCERT Pg 210**

(a) PCC (b) Anhydrous CrO_3

(c) Cu/573 K (d) $KMnO_4$

53 Choose incorrect option. **NCERT Pg 210**

(a) $CH_3-C(OH)(CH_3)-CH_3 \xrightarrow[300°C]{Cu} (CH_3)_2C=CH_2 + H_2O$

(b) $2CH_3CH_2OH \xrightarrow[140°C]{\text{Conc. } H_2SO_4} CH_3CH_2OCH_2CH_3 + H_2O$

(c) $2CH_3CH_2OH \xrightarrow[250°C]{Al_2O_3} C_2H_5OC_2H_5 + H_2O$

(d) $CH_3CH_2OH \xrightarrow[100°C]{\text{Conc. } H_2SO_4} CH_2=CH_2$

54 A methanol poisoned patient is treated by giving intravenous infusions of diluted ethanol. The enzyme responsible for the oxidation of aldehyde to acid is swamped allowing time for **NCERT Pg 210**

(a) liver to excrete methanol

(b) kidneys to excrete methanol

(c) liver to excrete methanal

(d) kidneys to excrete methanal

55 Which of the following is not correct in case of dehydrogenation reaction of 1°, 2° alcohol with over heated copper at 573 K? **NCERT Pg 210**

(a) Tertiary alcohol → Alkene

(b) Primary alcohol → Aldehyde

(c) Secondary alcohol → Ketone

(d) Phenol → Phenyl methanol

56 Consider the following reaction, **NCERT Pg 211**

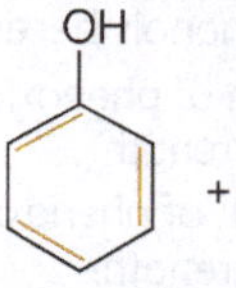

+ Dil. $HNO_3 \xrightarrow{298\text{ K}}$?

Select the product(s) formed in the given reaction.

(a) 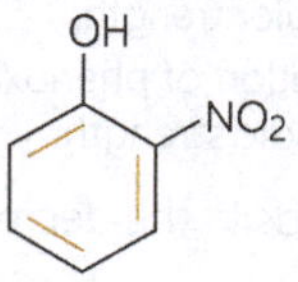

only

(b) 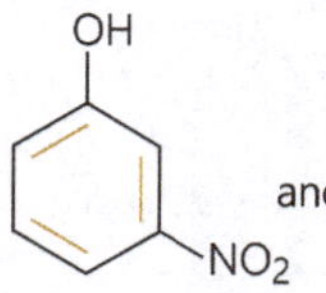

and 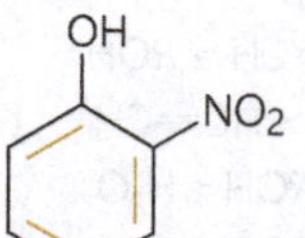

(c) 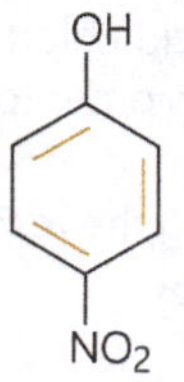

only

(d) 

and 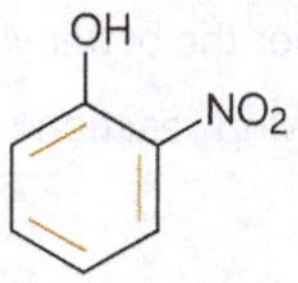

57 Phenol on reaction with conc. HNO_3 produces
(a) *o*-nitrophenol (b) *p*-nitrophenol **NCERT Pg 211**
(c) 2, 4, 6-trinitrophenol (d) *m*-nitrophenol

58 Phenol on treatment with dil. HNO_3 at 298 K gives two products *P* and *Q*. Out of them, only *P* is steam volatile. Here, *P* and *Q* respectively are. **NCERT Pg 211**

(a) 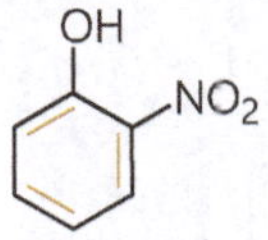 and 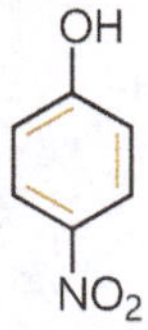

(b)  and 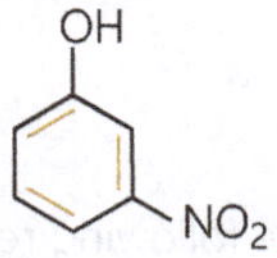

(c) 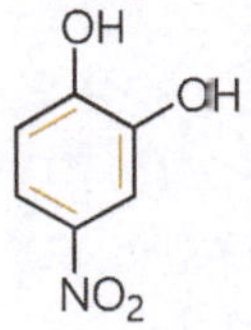 and 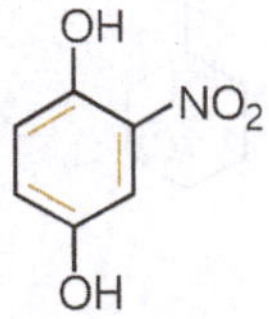

(d) 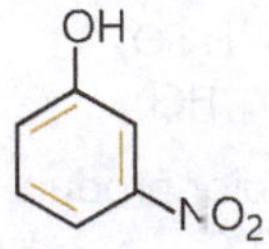 and 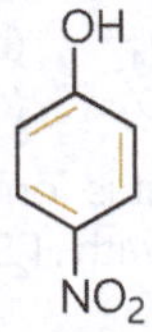

59 The major product(s) formed by the mononitration of 3-methylphenol is **NCERT Pg 212**

(a) 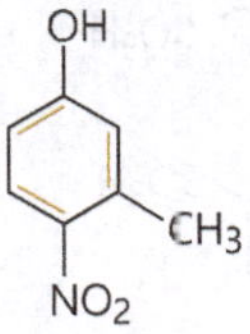

(b) 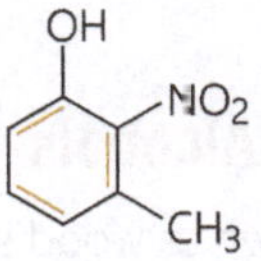 and 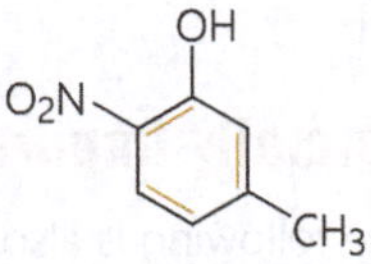

(c) 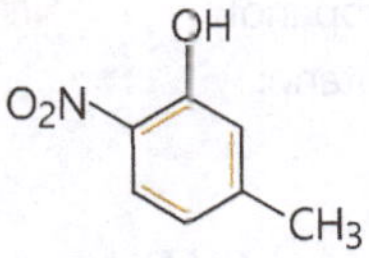

(d) 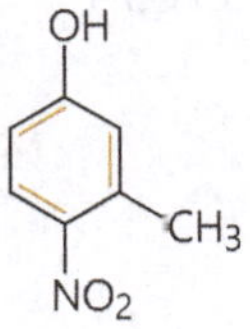 and 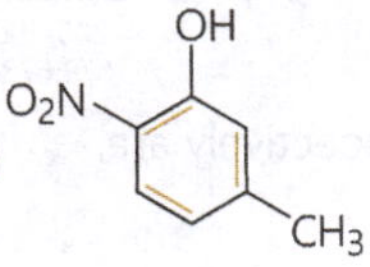

60 Which of the following name reaction is involved in the conversion of phenol to salicylic acid and to salicylaldehyde respectively? **NCERT Pg 212, 213**
(a) Kolbe's reaction and Reimer-Tiemann reaction
(b) Kolbe's reaction and Williamson's synthesis
(c) Williamson's synthesis and hydroboration oxidation
(d) Reimer-Tiemann reaction and Kolbe's reaction

61 Choose the incorrect reaction, **NCERT Pg 212, 213**

(a) 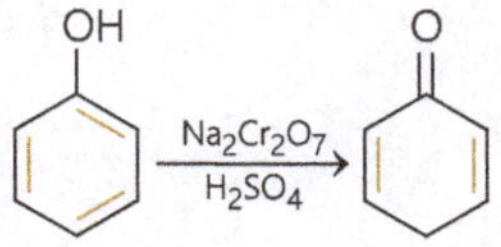

(b) 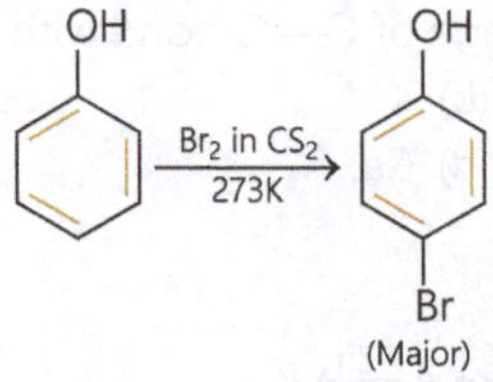

(c) 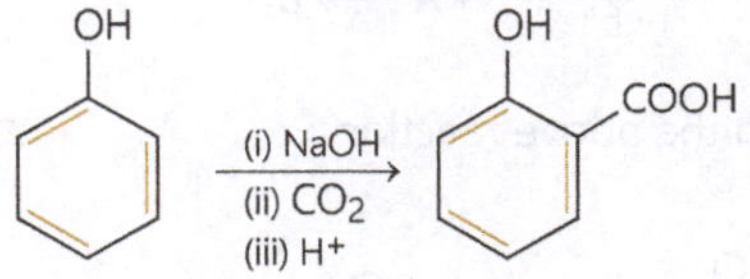

(d) 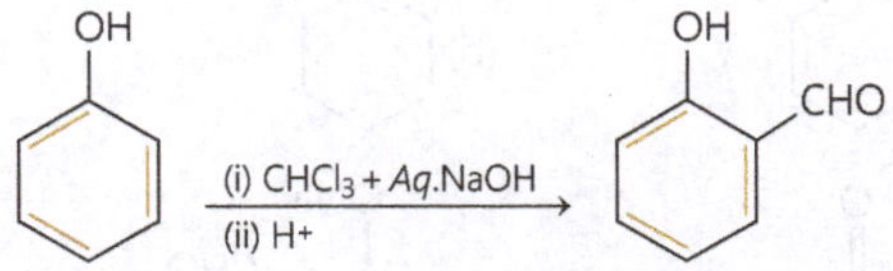

62 Consider the following reaction. **NCERT Pg 213**

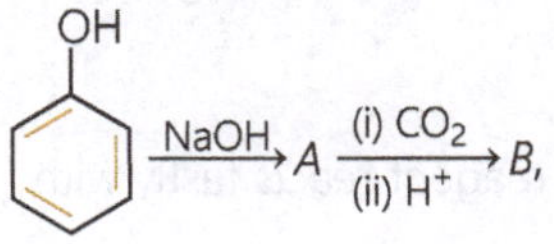

The major product (*B*) obtained in the above reaction is,
(a) salicylaldehyde
(b) salicylic acid
(c) benzoic acid
(d) phthalic acid

63 When phenol is treated with $CHCl_3$ and NaOH followed by acidification, salicylaldehyde is obtained. Which of the following species is involved in the above mentioned reaction as intermediates? **NCERT Pg 213**

(a) 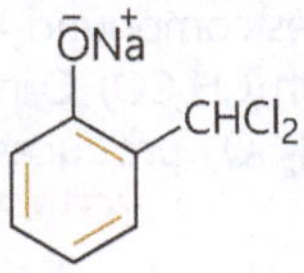 (b) 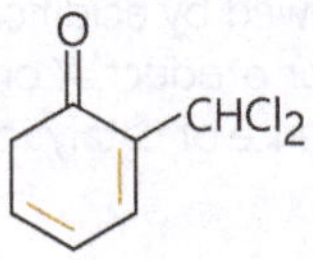

(c) 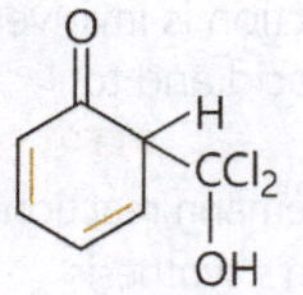
(d) 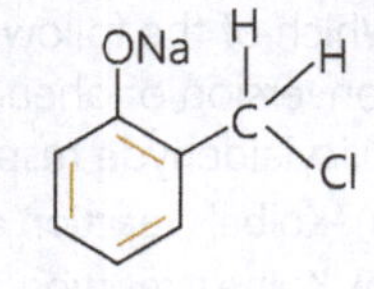

64 Phenol on reaction with Zn dust followed by heating gives '*X*' as which on further reaction with CH_3COCl and anhy. $AlCl_3$ and gives *Y* as final product. Here, *Y* is **NCERT Pg 213**

(a) acetophenone
(b) benzophenone
(c) diphenyl
(d) methyl salicylate

65 Phenols show the cleavage of C—O bond with **NCERT Pg 213**

(a) Na (b) K
(c) Zn (d) Ca

66 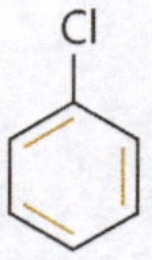 $\xrightarrow[\text{HCl}]{\text{NaOH, 623K, 300atm}} A \xrightarrow[\Delta]{\text{Zn}} B$

Product *B* in the above reaction. **NCERT Pg 213**

(a) 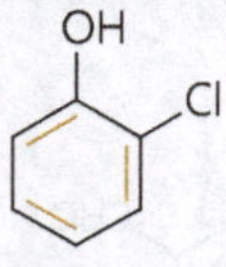
(b) 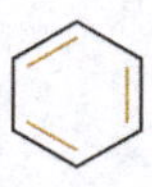
(c) 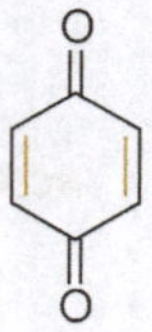
(d) 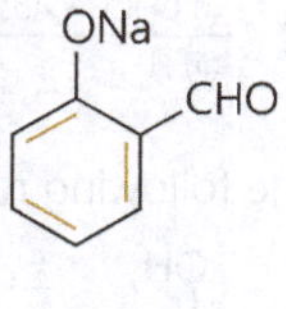

67 Electrophilic reagent reacts fastly with **NCERT Pg 213**

(a) 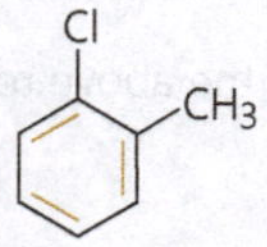
(b) 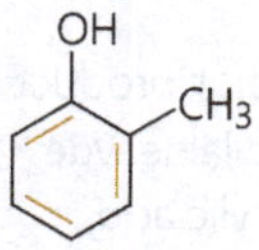
(c) 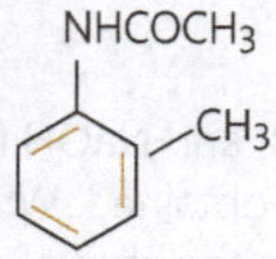
(d) 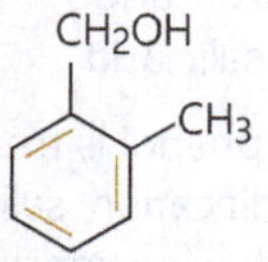

68 Phenol on treatment with CO_2 in the presence of NaOH followed by acidification produces compound *X* as the major product. *X* on treatment with $(CH_3CO)_2O$ in the presence of catalytic amount of H_2SO_4 produces: **NCERT Pg 208, 213**

(a) 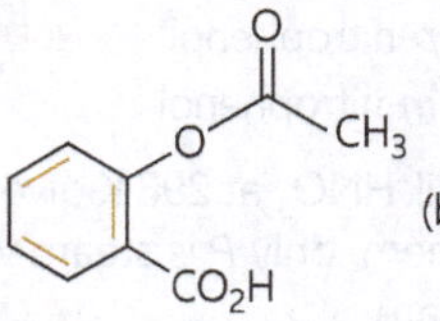
(b) 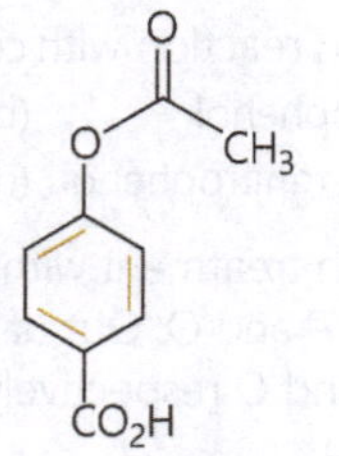
(c) 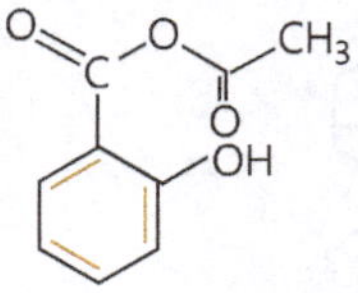
(d) 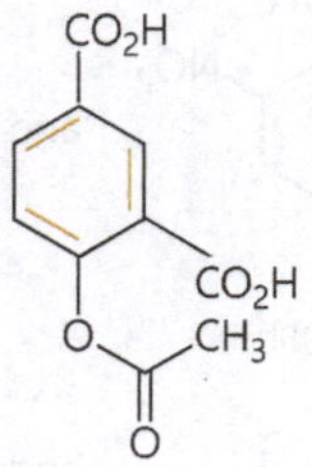

69 Consider the following reaction, **NCERT Pg 213**

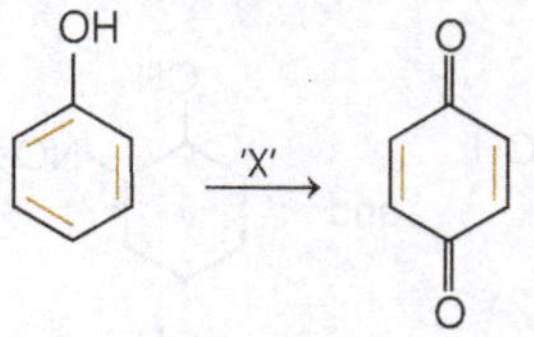

Here, '*X*' is

(a) K_2MnO_4, H_2SO_4 (b) $KMnO_4$, H_2SO_4
(c) $Na_2Cr_2O_7$, H_2SO_4 (d) Na_2CrO_4, HCl

70 Select the one that is formed as major product when phenol is heated with H_2SO_4 at 100°C. **NCERT Pg 213**

(a) 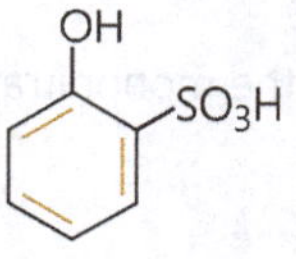
(b) 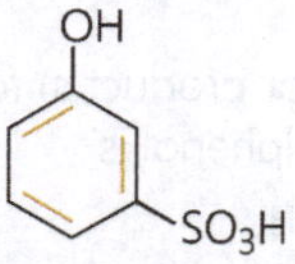
(c) 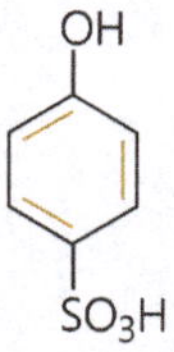
(d) 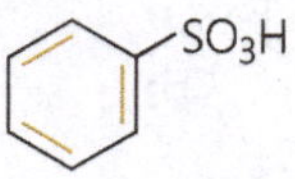

Some Commercially Important Alcohols

71 Which of the following is also known as wood spirit? **NCERT Pg 214**

(a) Ethanol (b) Propanol
(c) Methanol (d) Butanol

72 In the reaction,

$$X + H_2 \xrightarrow[\text{200-300 atm, 573-673 K}]{Y} CH_3OH$$

X and *Y* respectively are, **NCERT Pg 214**

	X	*Y*
(a)	CO_2,	$ZnO—CrO_3$
(b)	CO,	$ZnO—Cr_2O_3$
(c)	CO_2,	$ZnO—Cr_2O_3$
(d)	CO,	$ZnO—CrO_3$

73 Consider the following reaction, **NCERT Pg 214**

$$\underset{\text{(found in molasses)}}{\text{Sugar}} + H_2O \xrightarrow{X} \text{Glucose} + \text{Fructose}$$

$$\underset{\text{(found in yeast)}}{\text{Glucose / Fructose}} \xrightarrow{Y} \text{Ethanol} + CO_2$$

Select the enzymes used in the above reactions.
(a) $X \rightarrow$ Invertase, $Y \rightarrow$ Zymase
(b) $X \rightarrow$ Zymase, $Y \rightarrow$ Invertase
(c) X and $Y \rightarrow$ Invertase
(d) X and $Y \rightarrow$ Zymase

74 The action of zymase is inhibited during fermentation if the percentage of alcohol formed exceeds **NCERT Pg 214**
(a) 5% (b) 7%
(c) 10% (d) 14%

75 Denaturation of alcohol is the **NCERT Pg 214**
(a) mixing of $CuSO_4$ (a foul smelling solid) and pyridine (to give the colour) to make the commercial alcohol unfit for drinking.
(b) mixing of $CuSO_4$ (to give the colour) and pyridine (a foul smelling liquid) to make the commercial alcohol unfit for drinking.
(c) mixing of $Cu(OAc)_2$ and ammonia to make the commercial alcohol unfit for drinking.
(d) mixing of $Cu\ (OAc)_2$ and pyridine to make the commercial alcohol unfit for drinking.

Ethers

76 Identify the condition I and II for the reaction to occur.

$$CH_3CH_2OH \begin{cases} \xrightarrow{\text{I}} CH_2{=}CH_2 \\ \xrightarrow{\text{II}} C_2H_5OC_2H_5 \end{cases}$$

NCERT Pg 215

(a) $I \rightarrow H_2SO_4$, 443 K ; $II \rightarrow H_2SO_4$, 443 K
(b) $I \rightarrow H_2SO_4$, 413 K ; $II \rightarrow H_2SO_4$, 413 K
(c) $I \rightarrow H_2SO_4$, 443 K ; $II \rightarrow H_2SO_4$, 413 K
(d) $I \rightarrow H_2SO_4$, 413 K ; $II \rightarrow H_2SO_4$, 443 K

77 The alcohols that give best yield of dialkyl ether on being heated with a trace of sulphuric acid? **NCERT Pg 215**
(a) Pentan-2-ol
(b) 2-methyl butan-2-ol
(c) Pentan-1-ol
(d) Propen-2-ol

78 Williamson's synthesis involves which of the following type of mechanism when attack of an alkoxide ion on primary alkyl halide takes place? **NCERT Pg 215**
(a) S_N1 (b) S_N2
(c) E1 (d) E2

79 $CH_3—C(CH_3)_2—O—CH_3$ can be produced by which of the following pair selectively? **NCERT Pg 215, 216**

(a) $CH_3—C(CH_3)(O^-Na^+)—CH_3$, CH_3I (b) $CH_3—CH(CH_3)—CH_2I$, $CH_3O^-Na^+$
(c) $CH_3—C(CH_3)(I)—CH_3$, CH_3I, Ag_2O (d) CH_3CH_2I, $NaOH(CH_3)_2$

80 The major product of the following reaction,

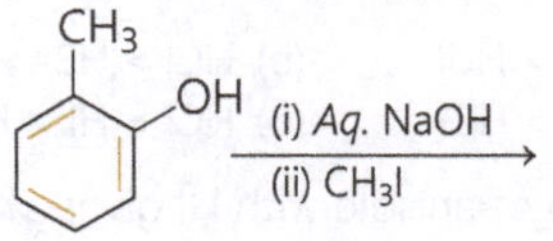

NCERT Pg 216

is

(a) 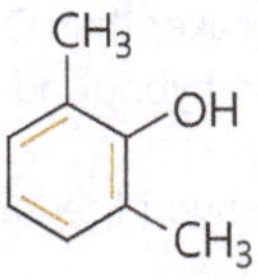

(b) 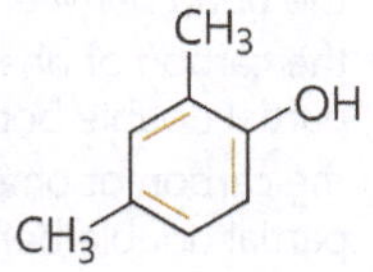

(c) 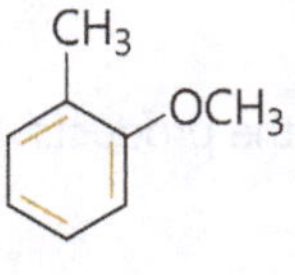

(d) 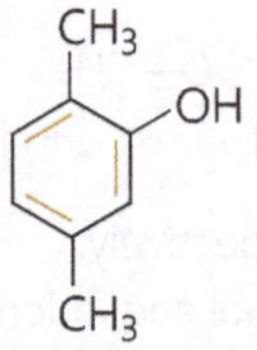

81 2-chloro-2-methylpentane on reaction with sodium methoxide in methanol yields **NCERT Pg 217**

I. $C_2H_5CH_2C(CH_3)_2—OCH_3$ II. $C_2H_5CH_2C(CH_3){=}CH_2$

III. $C_2H_5CH{=}C(CH_3)—CH_3$

(a) Both I and III
(b) Only III
(c) Both I and II
(d) I, II and III

82 Consider the following reaction. **NCERT Pg 216**

$$CH_3CHBrCH_3 \xrightarrow{\text{Alc. KOH}} A \xrightarrow[\text{Peroxide}]{\text{HBr}} B \xrightarrow{CH_3ONa} C$$

Here, *A*, *B* and *C* respectively are,

(a) $CH_3CH{=}CH_2$, $CH_3CH_2CH_2Br$, $CH_3CH_2CH_2OCH_3$

(b) $CH_3\underset{\underset{OH}{|}}{C}H—CH_3$, $CH_3CHBrCH_3$, $CH_3CH_2OCH_2CH_3$

(c) $CH_3\underset{\underset{OH}{|}}{C}H—CH_3$, $CH_3CH_2CH_2Br$, $CH_3CH_2OCH_2CH_3$

(d) $CH_3CH{=}CH_2$, $CH_3CHBrCH_2Br$, $CH_3CH(OH)CH_3$

83 Select the correct increasing order of boiling point. **NCERT Pg 217**

(a) *n*-pentane, ethoxyethane, butan-1-ol

(b) Ethoxyethane, *n*-pentane, butan-1-ol

(c) Butan-1-ol, *n*-pentane, ethoxyethane

(d) Ethoxyethane, butan-1-ol, *n*-pentane

84 The order of reactivity of hydrogen halides with ether is as follows **NCERT Pg 217**

(a) HBr > HI > HCl (b) HCl > HBr > HI

(c) HI > HBr > HCl (d) HCl > HI > HBr

85 The reaction of anisole with HI gives phenol rather than iodobenzene because **NCERT Pg 217**

(a) the bond between $O—CH_3$ is weaker than $O—C_6H_5$.

(b) the carbon of phenyl group is sp^3-hybridised and has a partial double bond character.

(c) the carbon of phenyl group is *sp*-hybridised and has a partial double bond character.

(d) the bond between $O—C_6H_5$ is weaker than $O—CH_3$.

86 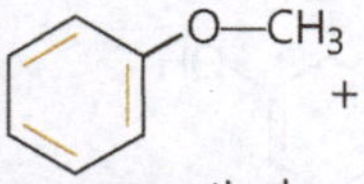

+ HI ⟶ *A* + *B*, the products *A* and *B* are respectively. **NCERT Pg 217**

(a) Phenol and iodomethane

(b) Methanol and iodobenzene

(c) Methoxy methane and phenol

(d) Phenol and benzyl alcohol

87 Select the incorrect statement. **NCERT Pg 217**

(a) Ethers have lower boiling points than the isomeric alcohols.

(b) Ethers are less water soluble than isomeric alcohols.

(c) Ether used as a solvent in Grignard reactions.

(d) Ethers are more polar in nature than alcohol.

88 An organic compounds with molecular formula $C_6H_{14}O$ does not react with sodium, whereas when it is reacted with excess of HI it gives only one type of alkyl halides. The compound is, **NCERT Pg 217**

(a) $CH_3CH_2CH_2OCH_2CH_2CH_3$ (b) $CH_3\underset{\underset{OCH_3}{|}}{C}HCH_2CH_2CH_3$

(c) $CH_3CH_2CH_2CH_2CH_2OCH_3$ (d) $CH_3CH_2CH_2CH_2CH_2CH_2OH$

89 The major product of the following reaction is, **NCERT Pg 217**

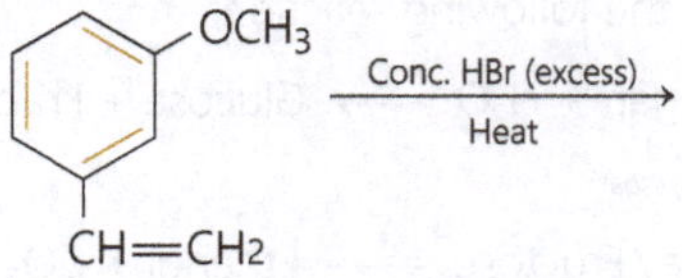

(a) 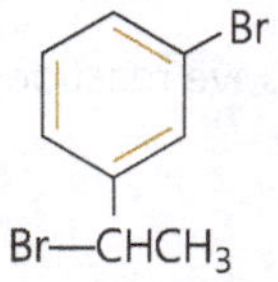

(b) 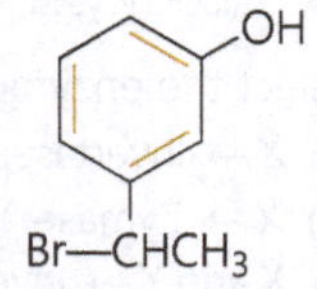

(c) 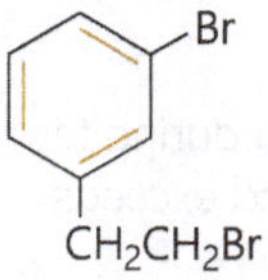

(d) 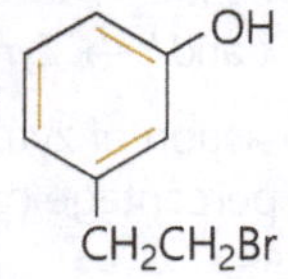

90 Which of the following ether undergo electrophilic substitution reaction? **NCERT Pg 219**

(a) CH_3OCH_3 (b) $CH_3OC_2H_5$

(c) $C_6H_5OCH_3$ (d) $C_2H_5OC_2H_5$

91 Which of the following resonating structure for $C_6H_5—O—R$ is incorrect? **NCERT Pg 219**

(a) 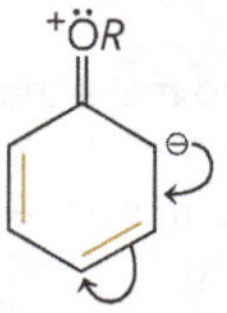

(b) 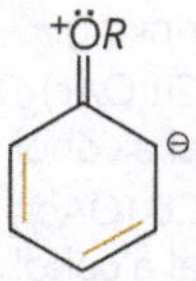

(c) 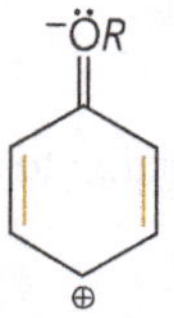

(d) 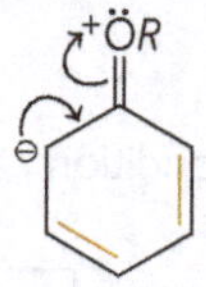

92 Anisole undergo bromination with bromine in ethanoic acid to give. **NCERT Pg 219**

(a) 20% *p*-bromoanisole and 80% *o*-bromoanisole

(b) 10% *p*-bromotoluene and 90% *o*-bromotoluene

(c) 90% *p*-bromoanisole and 10% *o*-bromoanisole

(d) 20% *p*-bromotoluene and 80% *o*-bromotoluene

93 Anisole on reaction with ethanoyl chloride in presence of anhydrous $AlCl_3$ gives **NCERT Pg 220**

(a) 2-methylacetophenone and 4-methoxyacetophenone

(b) 4-methylacetophenone and 4-methoxyacetophenone

(c) 2-methoxyacetophenone and 4-methylacetophenone

(d) 2-methoxyacetophenone and 4-methoxyacetophenone

Assertion-Reason Questions

Direction (Q. Nos. 1-10) *In the following question Assertion (A) followed by Reason (R) is given below. Choose the correct option out of the choices given below.*

(a) Both A and R are true and R is the correct explanation of A.
(b) Both A and R are true but R is not the correct explanation of A.
(c) A is false but R is true.
(d) A is true but R is false.

1 **Assertion** (A) The bond angle in alcohol is slightly more than the tetrahedral angle.
Reason (R) Variation in bond angle of alcohol is due to the repulsion between the unshared electron pair of oxygen. **NCERT Pg 199**

2 **Assertion** (A) Commercially acids are reduced to alcohols by converting them to the esters followed by their reduction using catalytic hydrogenation.
Reason (R) $LiAlH_4$ can reduce carboxylic acids to primary alcohols but $LiAlH_4$ is an expensive reagent and used for preparing special chemicals only. **NCERT Pg 200**

3 **Assertion** (A) Methanol poisoned patients are prone to blindness and death.
Reason (R) In body, methanol is oxidised first to methanoic acid which may cause blindness and death. **NCERT Pg 200**

4 **Assertion** (A) Lower alcohols and phenols are soluble in water.
Reason (R) There occurs a dipole-dipole interaction of —OH group of alcohol and phenol with water molecules, which is responsible for their solubility in water. **NCERT Pg 204**

5 **Assertion** (A) Increasing order of acid strength of alcohol is 1° alcohol > 2° alcohol > 3° alcohol.
Reason (R) An electron releasing group increases the electron density on oxygen which tends to decrease the polarity of O—H bond. **NCERT Pg 205**

6 **Assertion** (A) *o*-nitrophenol is less volatile than *p*-nitrophenol.
Reason (R) There occur intramolecular hydrogen bonding in *o*-nitrophenol and intermolecular hydrogen bonding in *p*-nitrophenol. **NCERT Pg 211**

7 **Assertion** (A) Phenols give *o*- and *p*-nitrophenol on nitration with conc. HNO_3 and H_2SO_4 mixture.
Reason (R) —OH group in phenol is *o*, *p*-directing. **NCERT Pg 211**

8 **Assertion** (A) Ethers are not obtained during the dehydration of secondary and tertiary alcohols.
Reason (R) In the secondary and tertiary alcohols, substitution occurs during dehydration. **NCERT Pg 215**

9 **Assertion** (A) In the presence of air, phenol mixture becomes dark in colour.
Reason (R) Phenols are slowly oxidised to the dark coloured mixture containing quinones. **NCERT Pg 213**

10 **Assertion** (A) The cleavage of C—O bond in ethers take place under unfavourable condition with excess of hydrogen halides.
Reason (R) Ethers are the most reactive among all the functional groups. **NCERT Pg 217**

Statement Type Questions

Direction (Q. Nos. 1-6) *In the following questions, two statements (I & II) are given. In the light of the given statements, choose the correct option given below.*

(a) Both Statement I and Statement II are false.
(b) Statement I is true but Statement II is false.
(c) Statement I is false but Statement II is true.
(d) Both Statement I and Statement II are true.

1 **Statement I** Diborane reacts with alkanes to give trialkyl boranes as addition product which is oxidised to alcohol by H_2O_2 in the presence of aqueous NaOH.
Statement II The alcohol obtained by hydroboration oxidation is an example of Markovnikov's addition. **NCERT Pg 200**

2 **Statement I** Hydroxyketones can be used in Grignard reaction.
Statement II Ketones on reaction with Grignard reagent are used to obtained tertiary alcohols. **NCERT Pg 201**

3 **Statement I** Benzene diazonium chloride on boiling with water gives phenol.
Statement II Benzene diazonium salts can be formed by primary, secondary and tertiary aromatic amines. **NCERT Pg 202**

4 **Statement I** The acidic strength of monosubstituted chlorophenol is higher than phenol due to the presence of electron withdrawing chloro group.

Statement II *o*-chlorophenol, *m*-chlorophenol and *p*-chlorophenol will have same acidic strength as they have one chloro group attached to the phenolic ring.
NCERT Pg 206, 207

5 Statement I In Lucas test, primary, secondary and tertiary alcohols are distinguished on the basis of their reactivity with conc. HCl and $ZnCl_2$, known as Lucas reagent.
Statement II Secondary and tertiary alcohol produces turbidity at normal conditions and take same time.
NCERT Pg 208

6 Statement I Methyl bromide reacts with sodium methoxide by S_N2 reaction and dimethyl ether is formed.
Statement II Tertiary butyl chloride in presence of sodium ethoxide gives substitution reaction.
NCERT Pg 215, 216

7 Select the correct statements from the following.
I. Solubility of alcohol decreases with increase in size of alkyl/aryl groups.
II. Alcohols and phenols react with active metals like Na, K etc., to produce corresponding alkoxides or phenoxides.
III. Alcohols act as Bronsted acid in the presence of strong acid.
IV. Alcohols react with both nucleophiles and electrophiles.
V. Acetylation of salicyaldehyde produces is known as aspirin.
Choose the correct answer from the options given below.
(a) II and V NCERT Pg 204, 205, 206, 208
(b) II and III
(c) I, II and IV
(d) II, III and IV

8 Consider the following statements.
I. The reactions of phenol with metals and sodium hydroxide indicate its basic nature.
II. The hydroxyl group in phenol is directly attached to sp^2-hybridised carbon of benzene ring.
III. The charge distribution in phenol causes the oxygen of —OH group to be positive.
IV. A compound in which hydroxyl group attached to an aromatic ring is more acidic than the one in which hydroxyl group is attached to an alkyl group.
V. In substituted phenols, the presence of electron donating group enhances the acidic strength of phenols.
Choose the correct answer from the options given below.
(a) I, II and III (b) I and II NCERT Pg 205, 206, 207
(c) II, III and IV (d) III and V

9 Which of the following statements are correct?
I. Methanol is a colourless liquid and highly poisonous in nature.
II. Ingestion of small quantities of methanol can cause blindness and its large quantities causes the death.
III. Methanol is used as a solvent in paints, varnishes and chiefly for making formaldehyde.
IV. *o*-nitrophenol is steam volatile due to intermolecular hydrogen bonding.
V. In presence of air phenols are slowly reduced to dark coloured mixture containing quinones.
Choose the correct answer from the options given below. NCERT Pg 211, 213, 214
(a) I and II (b) II and V
(c) III, IV and V (d) I, II and III

10 Which of the following statements are incorrect?
I. Alkyl aryl ethers are cleaved at the alkyl-oxygen bond due to the more stable aryl-oxygen bond.
II. The alkoxy group is *o*-, *p*-directing and activates the aromatic ring towards nucleophilic substitution reaction.
III. Aryl ether can undergo Friedel-Craft reaction in the presence of a Lewis acid.
IV. Phenols can give aryl halide by nucleophilic substitution reaction.
V. In the presence of electron releasing group, phenols undergo electrophilic substitution to give *para*-substituted (major) product.
Choose the correct answer from the options given below.
NCERT Pg 218, 219, 220
(a) I, II and IV
(b) Only I and III
(c) Only II and IV
(d) I, III and IV

Matching Type Questions

1 Match the Column I with Column II and choose the correct option from the codes given below.

Column I (Distinguish)	Column II (Reagent)
A. Methanol and diethyl ether	1. Lucas reagent
B. Methanol and ethanol	2. Sodium metal
C. Phenol and cyclohexanol	3. Iodoform test
D. *n*-propyl alcohol and *tert*-butyl alcohol	4. Ferric chloride

Codes NCERT Pg 205, 208

	A	B	C	D		A	B	C	D
(a)	2	4	3	1	(b)	2	3	4	1
(c)	2	3	1	4	(d)	3	2	1	4

2 Match Column I with Column II.

Column I	Column II
A. Kolbe's reaction	1. 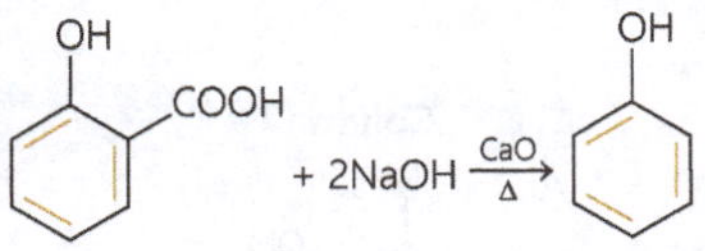
B. Reimer-Tieman n reaction	2. 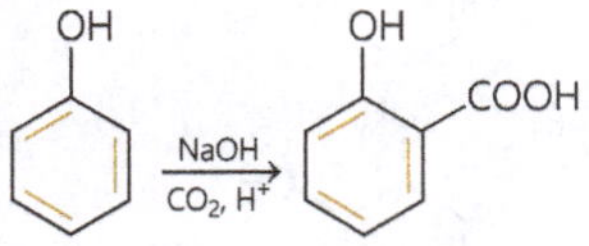
C. Friedel-Crafts reaction	3. 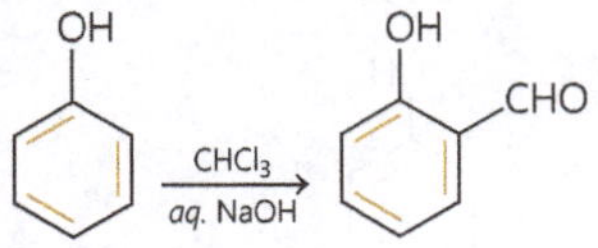
D. Decarboxylation	4. 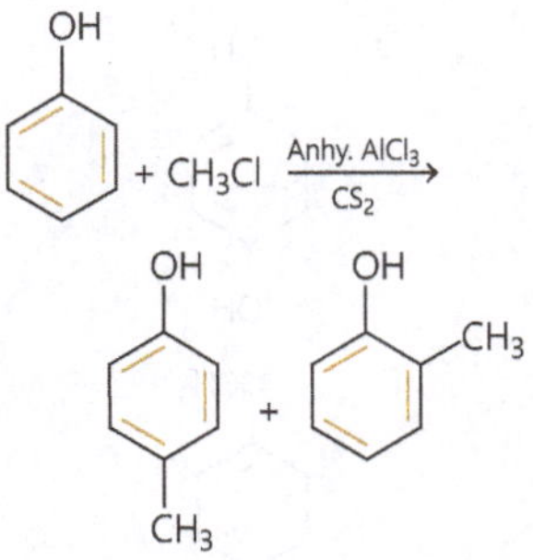

Codes NCERT Pg 212, 220

	A	B	C	D		A	B	C	D
(a)	2	3	4	1	(b)	3	2	4	1
(c)	4	3	2	1	(d)	1	3	2	4

3 Match the following compounds given in Column I with their names given in Column II and choose the correct option from the codes given below.

Column I (Compound)	Column II (Name)
A. $C_6H_5OCH_3$	1. 2-ethoxy-1,1-dimethyl cyclohexane
B. $C_6H_5O(CH_2)_6CH_3$	2. Anisole
C. $C_6H_5OCH_2CH_2-\underset{CH_3}{\underset{\mid}{C}H}-CH_3$	3. 3-methyl butoxybenzene
D. 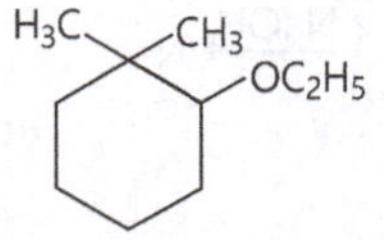	4. 1-phenoxyheptane

Codes NCERT Pg 197

	A	B	C	D		A	B	C	D
(a)	1	2	3	4	(b)	4	3	2	1
(c)	2	3	4	1	(d)	2	4	3	1

4 Match the following reactants and reagents given in Column I with the products given in Column II and choose the correct option from the codes given below. NCERT Pg 213

Column I (Reactant)	Column II (Product)
A. 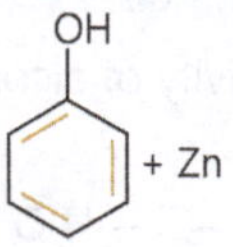	1. Benzene
B. 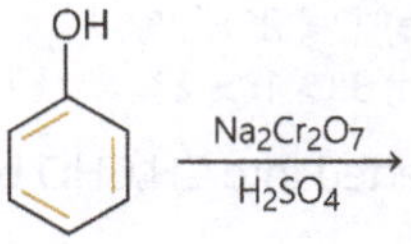	2. Salicylaldehyde
C. 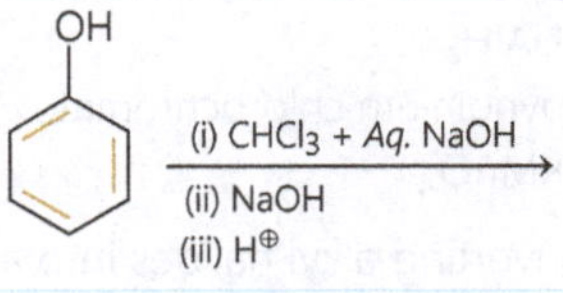	3. Benzoquinone
D. 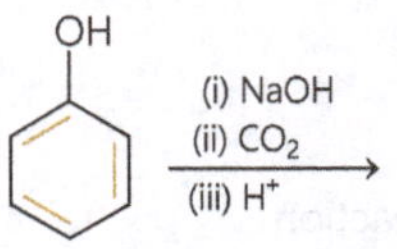	4. Salicylic acid

Codes

	A	B	C	D		A	B	C	D
(a)	3	1	2	4	(b)	1	3	2	4
(c)	1	2	3	4	(d)	3	2	1	4

Numerical Value Questions

1 In the following reactions,

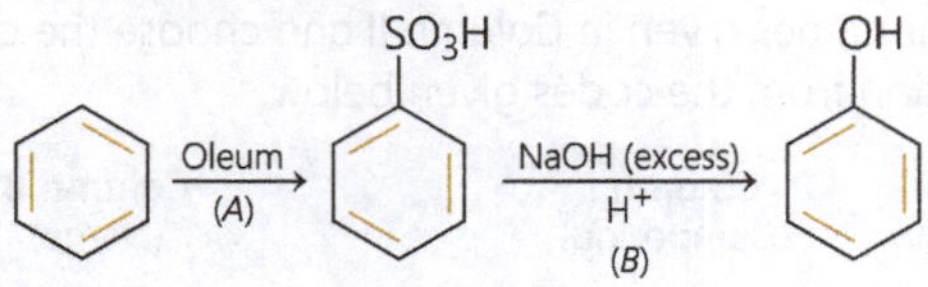

the percentage yield for reaction *A* is 60% and that of reaction *B* is 50%. The overall yield of the complete reaction is .... %. (Nearest integer) **NCERT Pg 202**

2 The number of resonance structure for N is

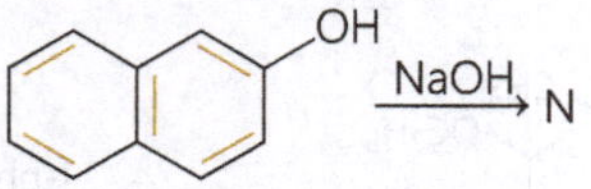

NCERT Pg 205

3 Among the following compounds, the number of compounds that will given instant turbidity when react with Lucas reagent is .... **NCERT Pg 208**

I. 2-methyl butan-2-ol II. 2-butanol
III. 2-methyl propan-2-ol IV. ethanol
V. pentan-3-ol

4 Compound (*X*) on nitration with dil. HNO_3 yield two isomers (*A*) and (*B*). There isomers can be separated by steam distillation. Isomers (*A*) and (*B*) shown the intramolecular and intermolecular hydrogen bonding respectively. Compound (*X*) on reaction with concentrated. HNO_3 yields a yellow compound (*Y*), a strong acid. The number of oxygen atoms present in compound (*Y*) is .... **NCERT Pg 211**

5 The total number of structural isomers for ether having molecular formula $C_4H_{10}O$ is .... **NCERT Pg 215**

NCERT Exemplar's Questions

1 Monochlorination of toluene in sunlight followed by hydrolysis with *aq*. NaOH yields
(a) *o*-cresol (b) *m*-cresol
(c) 2, 4- dihydroxytoluene (d) benzyl alcohol

2 How many alcohols with molecular formula $C_4H_{10}O$ are chiral in nature?
(a) 1 (b) 2 (c) 3 (d) 4

3 What is the correct order of reactivity of alcohols in the following reaction?

$$R\text{—}OH + HCl \xrightarrow{ZnCl_2} R\text{—}Cl + H_2O$$

(a) 1° > 2° > 3° (b) 1° < 2° > 3°
(c) 3° > 2° > 1° (d) 3° > 1° > 2°

4 CH_3CH_2OH can be converted into CH_3CHO by
(a) catalytic hydrogenation
(b) treatment with $LiAlH_4$
(c) treatment with pyridinium chlorochromate
(d) treatment with $KMnO_4$

5 The process of converting alkyl halides into alcohols involves
(a) addition reaction
(b) substitution reaction
(c) dehydrohalogenation reaction
(d) rearrangement reaction

6 Match the structures of the compounds given in Column I with the name of the compounds given in Column II.

	Column I		Column II
A.	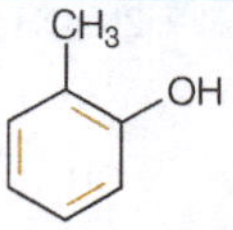	1.	Hydroquinone
B.	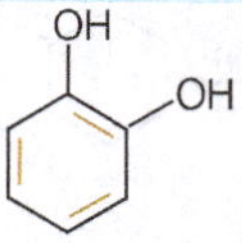	2.	Phenetole
C.	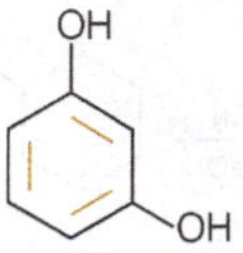	3.	Catechol
D.		4.	*o*-cresol
E.	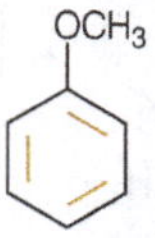	5.	Quinone
F.	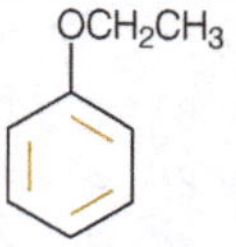	6.	Resorcinol
		7.	Anisole

7 Which of the following compounds is aromatic alcohol?

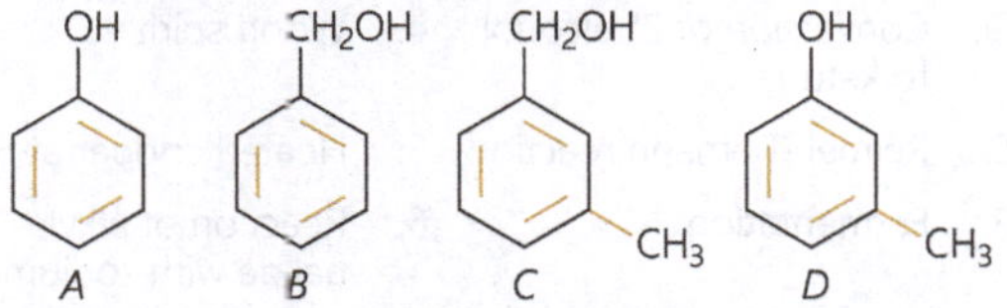

A B C D

(a) *A*, *B*, *C* and *D* (b) *A* and *D* (c) *B* and *C* (d) Only *A*

8 IUPAC name of *m*-cresol is

(a) 3-methylphenol (b) 3-chlorophenol
(c) 3-methoxyphenol (d) benzene-1, 3-diol

9 Match the starting material given in Column I with the products formed by these (Column II) in the reaction with HI.

Column I	Column II
A. CH_3-O-CH_3	1. 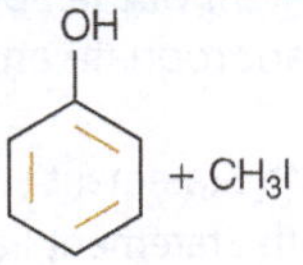
B. $(CH_3)_2CH-O-CH_3$	2. $(CH_3)_3C-I + CH_3OH$
C. $H_3C-C(CH_3)_2-O-CH_3$	3. 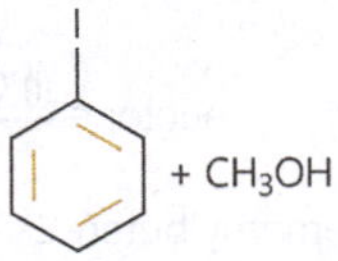
D. 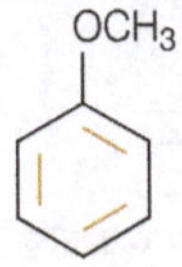	4. $CH_3-OH + CH_3I$
	5. $(CH_3)_2CH-OH + CH_3I$
	6. $(CH_3)_2CH-I + CH_3OH$
	7. $(CH_3)_3C-OH + CH_3I$

10 Which of the following species can act as the strongest base?

(a) $^{\ominus}OH$ (b) $^{\ominus}OR$
(c) $^{\ominus}OC_6H_5$ (d) 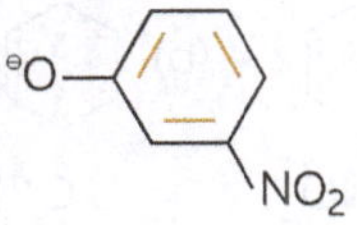

11 Which of the following compounds will react with sodium hydroxide solution in water?

(a) C_6H_5OH (b) $C_6H_5CH_2OH$ (c) $(CH_3)_3COH$ (d) C_2H_5OH

12 Phenol is less acidic than

(a) ethanol (b) *o*-nitrophenol
(c) *o*-methylphenol (d) *o*-methoxyphenol

13 Match the items of Column I with items of Column II.

Column I	Column II
A. Antifreeze used in car engine	1. Neutral ferric chloride
B. Solvent used in perfumes	2. Glycerol
C. Starting material for picric acid	3. Methanol
D. Wood spirit	4. Phenol
E. Reagent used for detection of phenolic group	5. Ethylene glycol
F. By product of soap industry used in cosmetics	6. Ethanol

14 Which of the following is most acidic?

(a) Benzyl alcohol (b) Cyclohexanol
(c) Phenol (d) *m*-chlorophenol

15 Mark the correct order of decreasing acid strength of the following compounds.

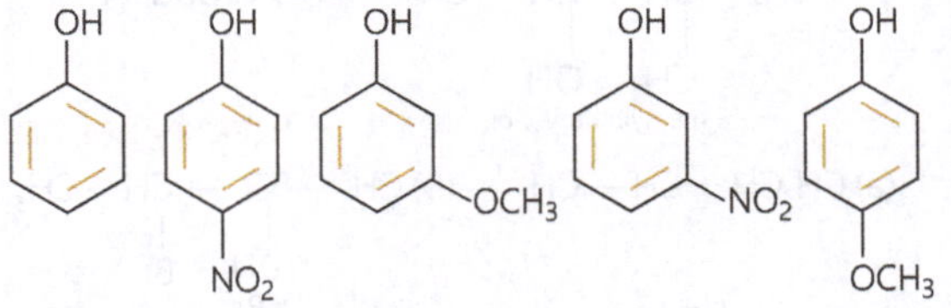

(I) (II) (III) (IV) (V)

(a) V > IV > II > I > III (b) II > IV > III > I > V
(c) IV > V > III > II > I (d) V > IV > III > II > I

16 Mark the correct increasing order of reactivity of the following compounds with HBr/HCl.

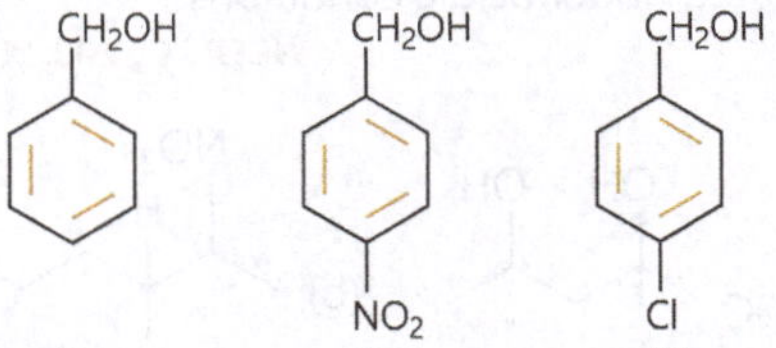

(I) (II) (III)

(a) I < II < III (b) II < I < III (c) II < III < I (d) III < II < I

17 Arrange the following compounds in increasing order of boiling point.

Propan-1-ol, butan-1-ol, butan-2-ol, pentan-1-ol

(a) Propan-1-ol, butan-2-ol, butan-1-ol, pentan-1-ol
(b) Propan-1-ol, butan-1-ol, butan-2-ol, pentan-1-ol
(c) Propan-1-ol, butan-2-ol, pentan-1-ol, butan-1-ol
(d) Propan-1-ol, butan-1-ol, pentan-1-ol, butan-2-ol

18 Match the items of Column I with items of Column II.

Column I	Column II
A. Methanol	1. Conversion of phenol to o-hydroxysalicylic acid
B. Kolbe's reaction	2. Ethyl alcohol
C. Williamson's synthesis	3. Conversion of phenol to salicylaldehyde
D. Conversion of 2° alcohol to ketone	4. Wood spirit
E. Reimer-Tiemann reaction	5. Heated copper at 573K
F. Fermentation	6. Reaction of alkyl halide with sodium alkoxide

Past Exams' Questions

NEET Archive

1 Which one of the following alcohols reacts instantaneously with Lucas reagent? **NCERT Pg 208, NEET 2024**

(a) $CH_3CH_2CH_2CH_2OH$ (b) $CH_3—CH_2—CH(CH_3)—OH$

(c) $CH_3—CH(CH_3)—CH_2OH$ (d) $CH_3—C(CH_3)_2—OH$

2 Consider the following reaction and identify the product (*P*).

$$CH_3—CH(CH_3)—CH(OH)—CH_3 \xrightarrow{HBr} \text{Product } (P)$$

3-methylbutan-2-ol

NCERT Pg 224, NEET 2023

(a) $CH_3CH=CH—CH_3$ (b) $CH_3—CH(CH_3)—CH(Br)—CH_3$

(c) $CH_3—C(CH_3)_2—CH_2Br$ (d) $CH_3—C(Br)(CH_3)—CH_2—CH_3$

3 Which amongst the following will be most readily dehydrated under acidic conditions? **NCERT Pg 208, 209, NEET 2023**

(a) 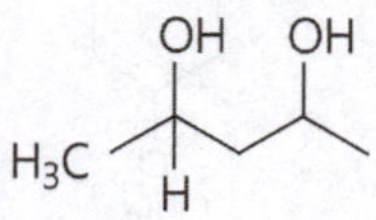

(b) 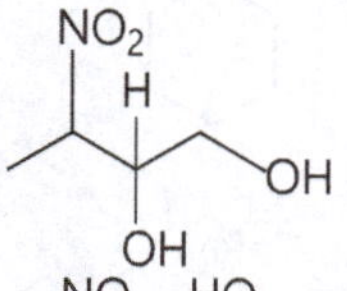

(c) 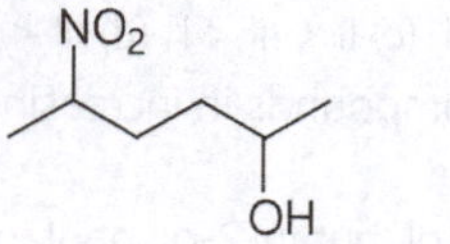

(d) 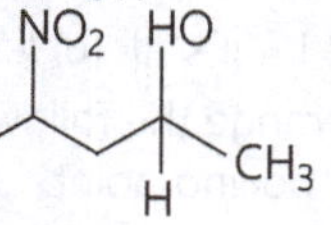

4 Given below are two statements.

Statement I The acidic strength of monosubstituted nitrophenol is higher than phenol because of electron withdrawing nitro group.

Statement II *o*-nitrophenol, *m*-nitrophenol and *p*-nitrophenol will have same acidic strength as they have one nitro group attached to the phenolic ring.

In the light of the above statements, choose the most appropriate answer from the options given below. **NCERT Pg 207, NEET 2022**

(a) Both Statement I and Statement II are true.
(b) Both Statement I and Statement II are false.
(c) Statement I is true but Statement II is false.
(d) Statement I is false but Statement II is true.

5 What is the IUPAC name of the organic compound formed in the following chemical reaction? **NCERT Pg 201, NEET 2021**

$$\text{Acetone} \xrightarrow[\text{(ii) } H_2O,\ H^+]{\text{(i) } C_2H_5MgBr,\ \text{Dry ether}} \text{Product}$$

(a) 2-methylbutan-2-ol (b) 2-methylpropan-2-ol
(c) pentan-2-ol (d) pentan-3-ol

6 $CH_3CH_2CH=CH_2 \xrightarrow[H_2O, H_2O_2, OH^-]{B_2H_6} Z$

What is *Z*? **NCERT Pg 200, NEET (Oct.) 2020**

(a) $CH_3CH_2CH_2CH_2OH$ (b) $CH_3CH_2CH(OH)CH_3$
(c) $CH_3CH_2CH_2CHO$ (d) $CH_3CH_2CH_2CH_3$

7 Reaction between acetone and methyl magnesium chloride followed by hydrolysis will give **NCERT Pg 201, NEET 2020**

(a) *iso*-propyl alcohol (b) *sec*-butyl alcohol
(c) *tert*-butyl alcohol (d) *iso*-butyl alcohol

8 Which of the following substituted phenols is the strongest acid? **NCERT Pg 207, NEET (Oct.) 2020**

(a) 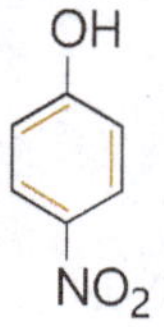

(b) 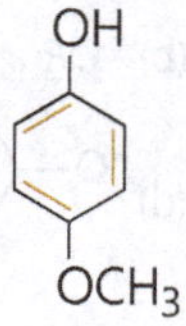

(c) 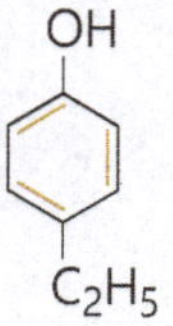

(d) 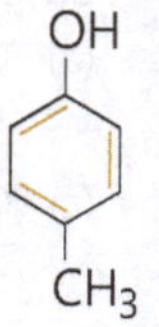

9 Anisole on cleavage with HI gives:
NCERT Pg 217, NEET (Sep.) 2020

(a) 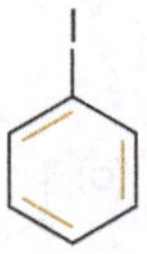 + CH_3OH (b) 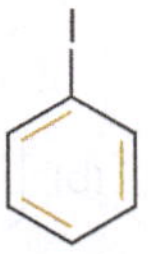 + C_2H_5I

(c) 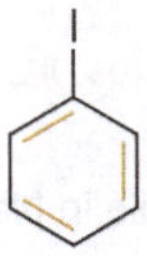 + C_2H_5OH (d) 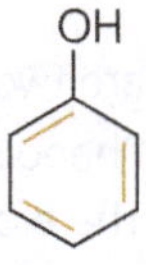 + CH_3I

10 In the reaction,

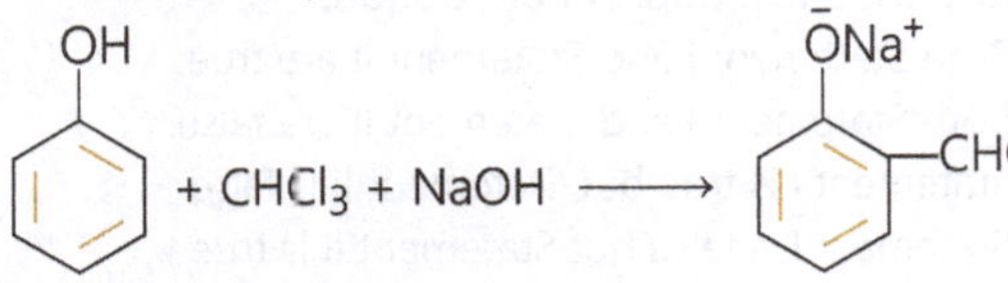

the electrophile involved is NCERT Pg 213, NEET 2018
(a) dichloromethyl cation ($\overset{+}{C}HCl_2$)
(b) formyl cation ($\overset{+}{C}HO$)
(c) dichloromethyl anion ($\overset{-}{C}HCl_2$)
(d) dichlorocarbene ($:CCl_2$)

11 The heating of phenyl-methyl ethers with HI produces.
NCERT Pg 217, NEET 2017
(a) ethyl chlorides
(b) iodobenzene
(c) phenol
(d) benzene

12 The reaction

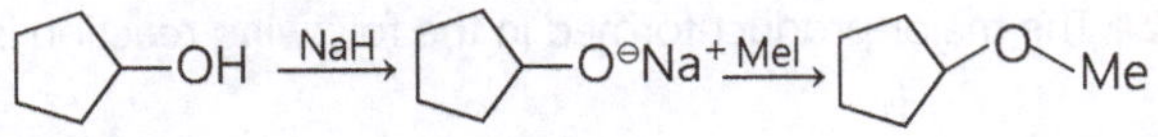

can be classified as NCERT Pg 205, 215, NEET 2016, Phase I
(a) Alcohol formation reaction
(b) Dehydration reaction
(c) Williamson's alcohol synthesis reaction
(d) Williamson's ether synthesis reaction

13 Which of the following is not the product of dehydration of

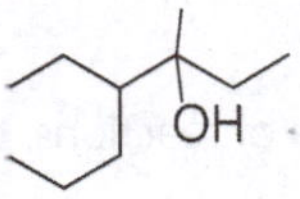

NCERT Pg 208, CBSE-AIPMT 2015

(a) 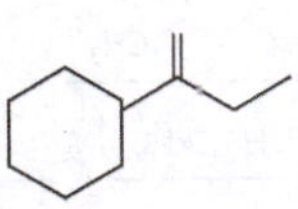 (b) 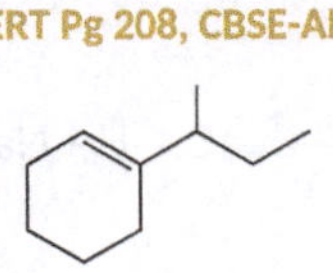

(c) 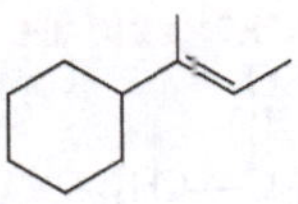 (d) 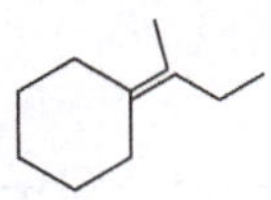

14 Identity Z in the sequence of reactions,
NCERT Pg 215, CBSE-AIPMT 2014

$$CH_3CH_2CH{=}CH_2 \xrightarrow{HBr/H_2O_2} Y \xrightarrow{C_2H_5ONa} Z$$

(a) $CH_3—(CH_2)_3—O—CH_2CH_3$
(b) $(CH_3)_2CH_2—O—CH_2CH_3$
(c) $CH_3(CH_2)_4—O—CH_3$
(d) $CH_3\ CH_2—CH(CH_3)—O—CH_2CH_3$

15 Among the following ethers which one will produce methyl alcohol on treatment with hot concentrated HI?
NCERT Pg 218, CBSE-AIPMT 2013

(a) $CH_3—CH_2—CH_2—CH_2—O—CH_3$
(b) $CH_3—CH_2—\underset{|}{\overset{}{C}}H—O—CH_3$ with CH_3 on the CH: $CH_3—CH_2—CH(CH_3)—O—CH_3$
(c) $CH_3—C(CH_3)_2—O—CH_3$
(d) $CH_3—CH(CH_3)—CH_2—O—CH_3$

JEE Main Archive

16 Match List-I with List-II. NCERT Pg 213, JEE Main 2024

List-I (Reactions)		List-II (Products)	
A.	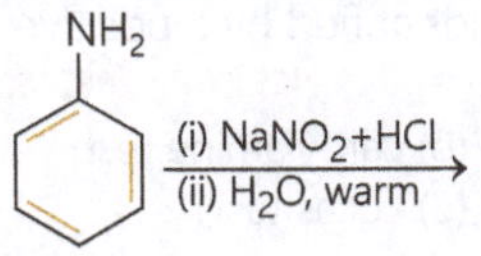	I.	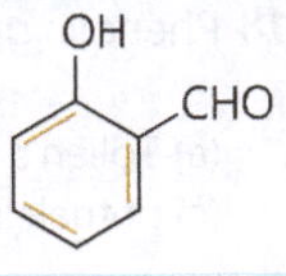
B.	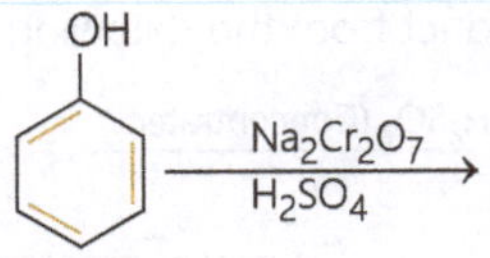	II.	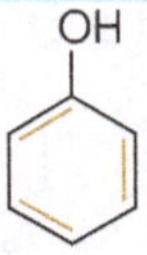
C.	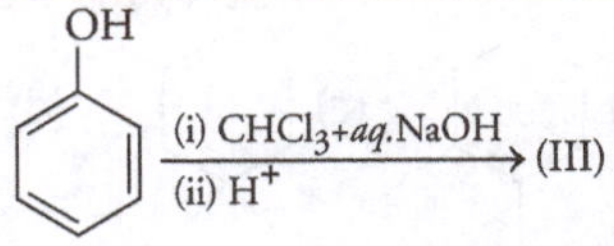	III.	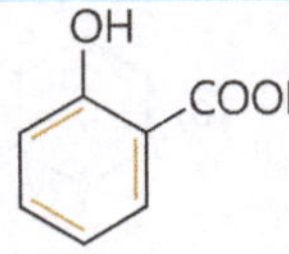
D.	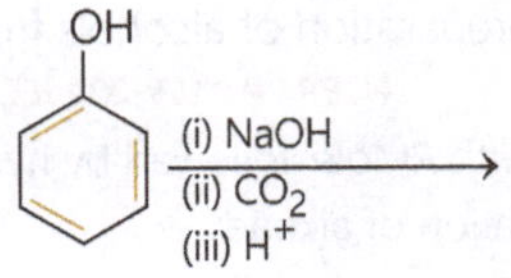	IV.	

Choose the correct answer from the options given below.
(a) A-I, B-IV, C-II, D-III (b) A-III, B-II, C-I, D-IV
(c) A-IV, B-II, C-III, D-I (d) A-II, B-IV, C-I, D-III

17 Match List-I with List-II. NCERT Pg 213, JEE Main 2024

List-I (Reaction)	List-II (Reagents)
A. 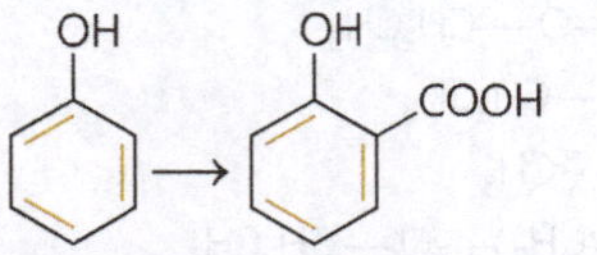	I. $Na_2Cr_2O_7$, H_2SO_4
B. 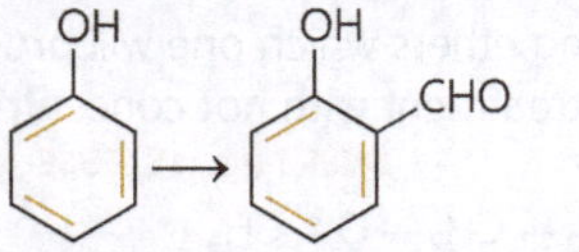	II. (i) NaOH (ii) CH_3Cl
C. 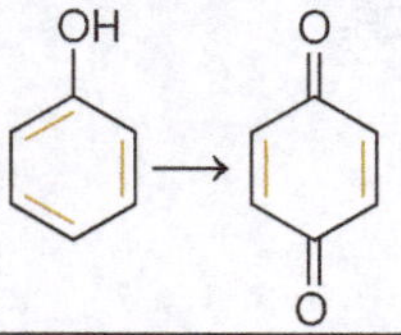	III. (i) NaOH, $CHCl_3$ (ii) NaOH (iii) HCl
D. 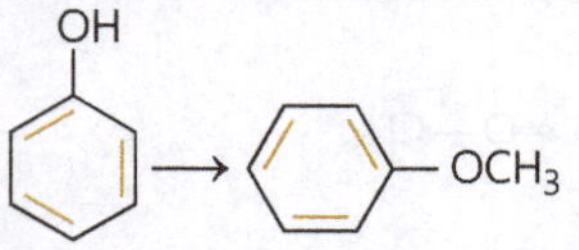	IV. (i) NaOH (ii) CO_2 (iii) HCl

Choose the correct answer from the options given below.

	A	B	C	D		A	B	C	D
(a)	II	III	I	IV	(b)	II	I	III	IV
(c)	IV	I	III	II	(d)	IV	III	I	II

18 Phenolic group can be identified by a positive NCERT Pg 208, JEE Main 2024

(a) Tollen's test (b) carbylamine test
(c) phthalein dye test (d) Lucas test

19 Find out the major product from the following reaction.

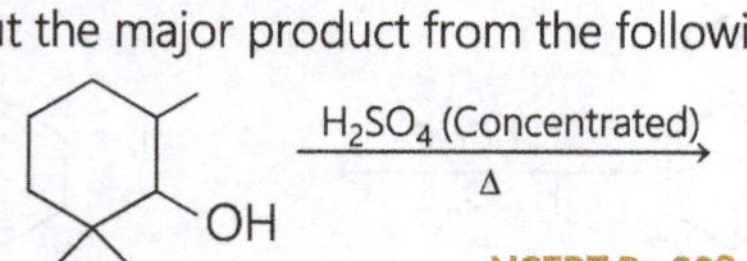

NCERT Pg 208, JEE Main 2023

(a) 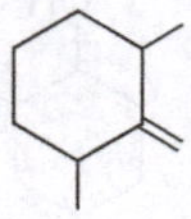 (b) 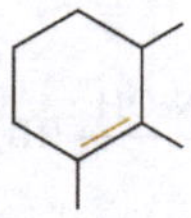 (c) 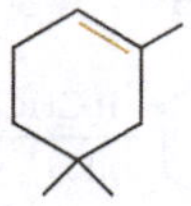 (d) 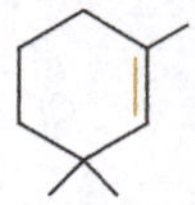

20 Incorrect method of preparation of alcohols from the following is NCERT Pg 199-202 JEE Main 2023

(a) reaction of ketone with *R*MgBr followed by hydrolysis
(b) hydroboration-oxidation of alkene
(c) ozonolysis of alkene
(d) reaction of alkyl halide with aqueous NaOH

21 A compound '*X*' is acidic and it is soluble in NaOH solution, but insoluble in $NaHCO_3$ solution. Compound '*X*' also gives violet colour with neutral $FeCl_3$ solution. The compound '*X*' is NCERT Pg 206, JEE Main 2022

(a) 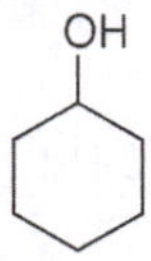 (b) 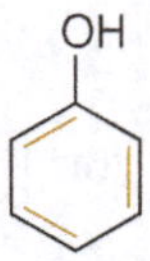 (c) 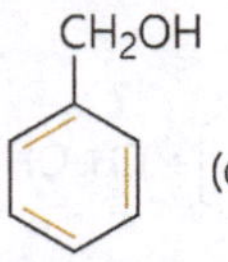 (d) 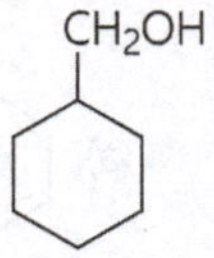

22 Given below are two statements. NCERT Pg 206, JEE Main 2022

Statement I Phenols are weakly acidic.

Statement II Therefore they are freely soluble in NaOH solution and are weaker acids than alcohols and water.

Choose the most appropriate option.

(a) Both Statement I and Statement II are true.
(b) Both Statement I and Statement II are false.
(c) Statement I is true but Statement II is false.
(d) Statement I is false but Statement II is true.

23 Which reactant will give the following alcohol on reaction with one mole of phenyl magnesium bromide (PhMgBr) followed by acidic hydrolysis? NCERT Pg 201, JEE Main 2022

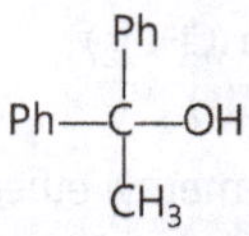

(a) $CH_3-C\equiv N$ (b) $Ph-C\equiv N$
(c) $CH_3-\overset{O}{\overset{\|}{C}}-O-Ph$ (d) $Ph-\underset{O}{\underset{\|}{C}}-CH_3$

24 The major product formed in the following reaction is

$$CH_3-\overset{CH_3}{\overset{|}{\underset{CH_3}{\underset{|}{C}}}}-\underset{OH}{\underset{|}{CH}}-CH_3 \xrightarrow[\text{a few drops}]{\text{Conc.}H_2SO_4} \text{Major product}$$

NCERT Pg 208, JEE Main 2021

(a) $CH_3-\underset{CH_3}{\underset{|}{C}}=CH-CH_2CH_3$ (b) 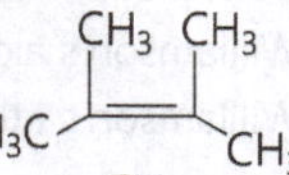

(c) $(CH_3)_2C=CH-CH_3$ (d) $CH_3-\overset{CH_3}{\overset{|}{\underset{CH_3}{\underset{|}{C}}}}-CH=CH_2$

25 In the following sequence of reactions, the final product *D* is.

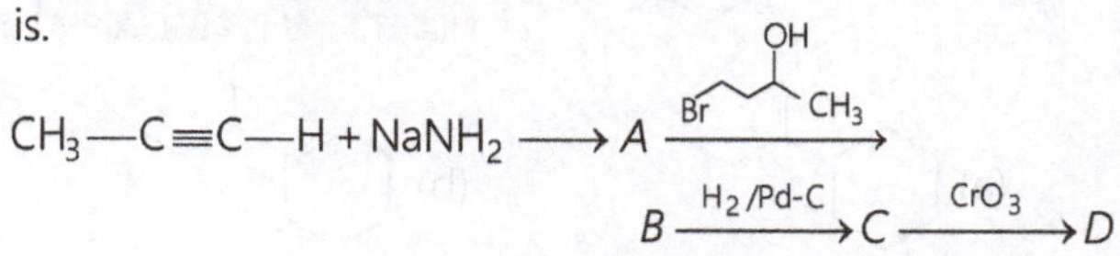

NCERT Pg 210, JEE Main 2021

(a) $CH_3-CH_2-CH_2-CH_2-CH_2-\overset{O}{\overset{\|}{C}}-CH_3$
(b) $H_3C-CH=CH-CH(OH)-CH_2-CH_2CH_3$

(c) $CH_3—CH=CH—CH_2—CH_2—CH_2—COOH$

(d) $H_3C—CH_2—CH_2—CH_2—CH_2—\overset{O}{\overset{||}{C}}—H$

26 Given below are two statements one is labelled as Assertion (A) and the other is labelled as Reason (R).

Assertion (A) Synthesis of ethyl phenyl ether may be achieved by Williamson's synthesis.

Reason (R) Reaction of bromobenzene with sodium ethoxide yields ethyl phenyl ether.

In the light of the above statements, choose the most appropriate answer from the options given below.

NCERT Pg 216, JEE Main 2021

(a) Both (A) and (R) are correct and (R) is the correct explanation of (A).
(b) (A) is correct but (R) is incorrect.
(c) (A) is incorrect but (R) is correct.
(d) Both (A) and (R) are correct but (R) is not the correct explanation of (A).

Skill Boosters

1 Compound (*A*) reacts with $SOCl_2$ to give compound (*B*) which reacts with Mg, ether to form Grignard reagent then treated with acetone and the product obtained is further hydrolysed to give 2-methyl butan-2-ol. Compounds *A* and *B* are

	A	*B*
(a)	$CH_3CH_2CH_3$	CH_3CH_2Cl
(b)	$CH_3CH_2CH_2OH$	$CH_3CH_2(Cl)CH_3$
(c)	$CH_3CH(OH)CH_3$	$CH_3CH(Cl)CH_3$
(d)	CH_3CH_2OH	CH_3CH_2Cl

2 An organic compound (*A*) with molecular formula C_6H_6O gives a characteristic colour with aqueous $FeCl_3$ solution. When (*A*) is treated with CO_2 and NaOH at 410 K under pressure, it gives compound (*B*) which upon acidification gives compound (*C*). Compound (*C*) reacts with acetyl chloride to give (*D*) which is popular pain killer. Identify the structure of *D*.

(a) 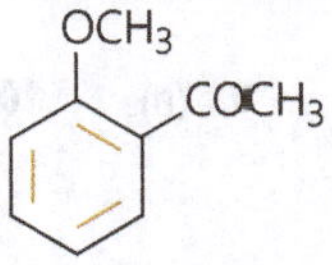

(b) 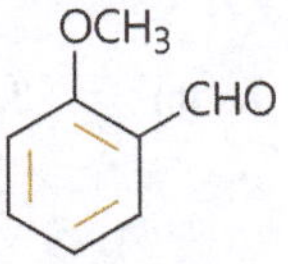

(c) 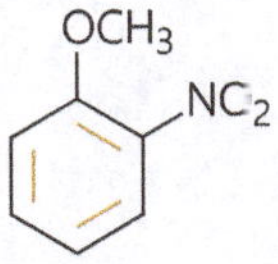

(d) 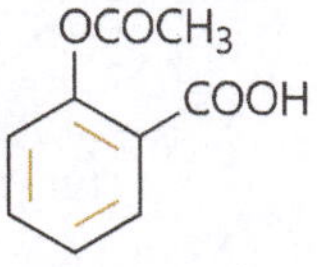

3 An alcoholic person has mistakenly ingested denatured alcohol which was produced by mixing ethanol with a compound (*A*). *A* is produced by catalytic hydrogenation of carbon monoxide at high pressure and temperature. When the compound *A* is oxidised by chromic acid it produces a carboxylic acid. The name of the carboxylic acid formed is

(a) methanoic acid (b) benzoic acid
(c) acetic acid (d) salicylic acid

4 A student carried out an experiment in laboratory in this experiment he took a compound (*X*) which gives pink colour on reaction with phthalic anhydride in conc. H_2SO_4 followed by treatment with NaOH. Identify the compound *X*.

(a) 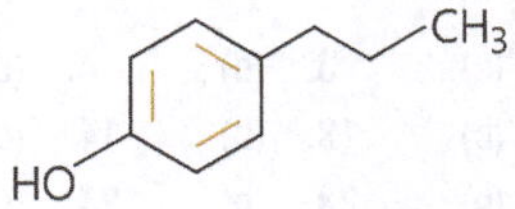

(b) 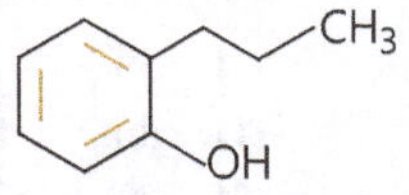

(a) 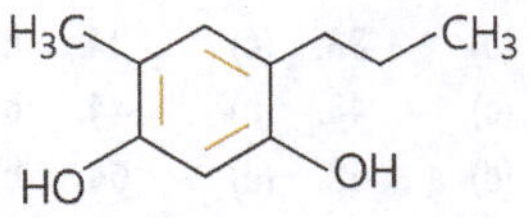

(b) 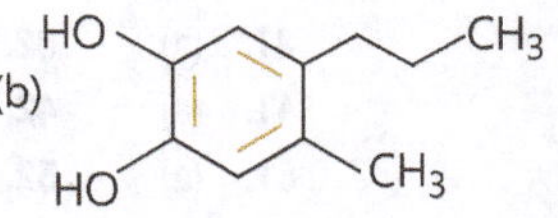

5 The sugar found in fruits undergo reaction with a catalyst A which turn it into two different sugars. One of them when undergo action of a catalyst *B* produces an alcohol. When this alcohol reacts with a protic acid at 413 K it produces a compound *X* having molecular formula of $C_4H_{10}O$. The compound *X* and catalyst, *B* respectively are

(a) methoxymethane, amylase (b) anisole, convertase
(c) ethylmethyl ether, invertase (d) ethoxyethane, zymase

6 In a laboratory, 3 containers are filled with 3 liquids *A*, *B* and *C*. When these liquids reacted with an equimolar mixture of conc. HCl and $ZnCl_2$ some observations were taken. It was observed that in liquid (*A*) no change happens, in liquid (*B*) some turbidity was observed in about 4-5 minutes and in liquid (*C*) turbidity was appeared instantly. A sample of liquid (*B*) was taken out and reacted with conc. H_2SO_4 to produce an alkene.

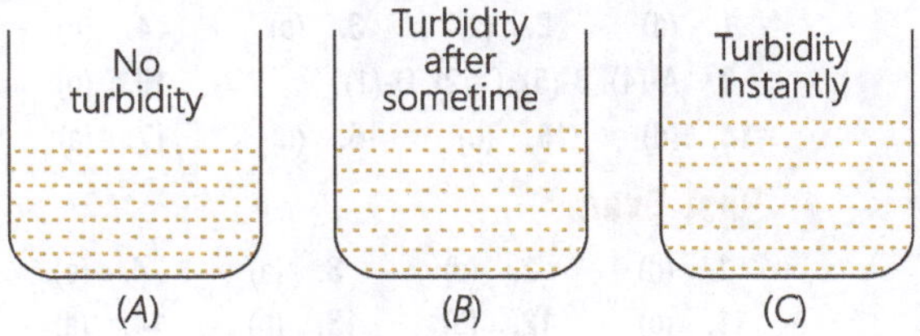

NCERT Pg 206

Identify the liquid *B* and the mechanism by which the alkene formed respectively.

(a) Primary alcohol, S_N1 substitution

(b) Secondary alcohol, S_N2 substitution
(c) Tertiary alcohol, addition
(d) Secondary alcohol, elimination

7 An ether (*A*), $C_5H_{12}O$, when heated with excess of hot concentrated HI, produced two alkyl halides which on treatment with NaOH yielded compounds (*B*) and (*C*), oxidation of (*B*) and (*C*) gave a propanone and an ethanoic acid respectively. The IUPAC name of the ether (*A*) is

(a) 2-ethoxypropane (b) ethoxypropane
(c) methoxybutane (d) 2-methoxybutane

8 Sunil takes a sample of phenol and react it with a dilute nitric acid at low temperature to obtain a mixture of products. To separate them out he used steam distillation so one of the product comes out in the vapour form.

Name of the product that form vapours and the reason behind this process respectively are

(a) 2, 4, 6-trinitrophenol, van der Waals' forces
(b) *p*-nitrophenol, intermolecular hydrogen bonding
(c) *o*-nitrophenol, intramolecular hydrogen bonding
(d) *m*-nitrophenol, intramolecular hydrogen bonding

Correct Codes

Topical Questions

1. (b) 2. (c) 3. (d) 4. (d) 5. (c) 6. (c) 7. (d) 8. (c) 9. (b) 10. (a)
11. (b) 12. (b) 13. (b) 14. (c) 15. (b) 16. (b) 17. (a) 18. (d) 19. (c) 20. (c)
21. (c) 22. (b) 23. (b) 24. (d) 25. (a) 26. (c) 27. (d) 28. (b) 29. (d) 30. (d)
31. (a) 32. (b) 33. (c) 34. (c) 35. (c) 36. (d) 37. (c) 38. (b) 39. (a) 40. (c)
41. (a) 42. (c) 43. (b) 44. (b) 45. (d) 46. (d) 47. (c) 48. (b) 49. (c) 50. (c)
51. (a) 52. (d) 53. (d) 54. (b) 55. (d) 56. (d) 57. (c) 58. (a) 59. (d) 60. (a)
61. (a) 62. (b) 63. (a) 64. (a) 65. (c) 66. (b) 67. (b) 68. (a) 69. (c) 70. (c)
71. (c) 72. (b) 73. (a) 74. (d) 75. (b) 76. (c) 77. (c) 78. (b) 79. (a) 80. (c)
81. (d) 82. (a) 83. (b) 84. (c) 85. (a) 86. (a) 87. (d) 88. (a) 89. (b) 90. (c)
91. (c) 92. (c) 93. (d)

Assertion-Reason

1. (c) 2. (b) 3. (d) 4. (d) 5. (a) 6. (c) 7. (c) 8. (d) 9. (a) 10. (d)

Statement Type

1. (b) 2. (c) 3. (b) 4. (b) 5. (b) 6. (b) 7. (c) 8. (c) 9. (d) 10. (c)

Matching Type

1. (b) 2. (a) 3. (d) 4. (b)

Numerical Value

1. (30) 2. (9) 3. (2) 4. (7) 5. (3)

NCERT Exemplar's

1. (d) 2. (a) 3. (c) 4. (c) 5. (b) 6. A-(4), B-(3), C-(6), D-(1), E-(7), F-(2) 7. (c) 8. (a)
9. A-(4), B-(5), C-(2), D-(1) 10. (b) 11. (a) 12. (b) 13. A-(5), B-(6), C-(4), D-(3), E-(1), F-(2)
14. (d) 15. (b) 16. (c) 17. (a) 18. A-(4), B-(1), C-(6), D-(5), E-(3), F-(2)

Past Exams'

1. (d) 2. (d) 3. (a) 4. (c) 5. (a) 6. (a) 7. (c) 8. (a) 9. (d) 10. (d)
11. (c) 12. (d) 13. (b) 14. (a) 15. (c) 16. (d) 17. (d) 18. (c) 19. (b) 20. (c)
21. (b) 22. (c) 23. (d) 24. (b)

Skill Boosters

1. (d) 2. (d) 3. (a) 4. (b) 5. (d) 6. (d) 7. (a) 8. (c)

Step by Step

Decoding the Questions

Concept Builders

1 Ethyl alcohol 2 True
3 aliphatic system 4 alkoxy
5 vinylic 6 False
7 7-hydroxy heptan-2-one
8 True
9 Sodium borohydride/Lithium aluminium hydride
10 Cumene hydroperoxide
11 False 12 decrease
13 aspirin 14 True
15 4-nitrophenyl ethanoate
16 Reimer-Tiemann reaction
17 quinones 18 False
19 denaturation 20 S_N2
21 Pyridinium chlorochromate
22 ethanol 23 True
24 Phenol-2, 4-disulphonic acid
25 Phenol
26 Williamson synthesis
27 False 28 Primary
29 True
30 4-methoxy acetophenone

Topical Solutions

1 (*b*) In allylic and benzylic alcohols, the —OH group is attached to sp^3-hybridised carbon atom.

2 (*c*) Vinylic alcohols contain —OH group bonded to a carbon-carbon double bond, i.e to a vinylic carbon.

3 (*d*) $C_6H_5CH_2OH$ is not classified as phenols because in this molecule —OH group is directly attached to alkyl group not with aryl group.

4 (*d*) If the alkyl or aryl groups attached to the oxygen atom are different, then it is unsymmetrical or mixed ether.

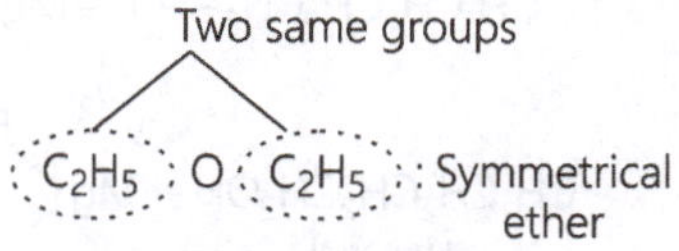

5 (*c*) The IUPAC name of the given structure is 2-methyl cyclopentanol.

6 (*c*) I is methanol, II is *iso*-propyl alcohol and III is $CH_3CH_2CH_2CH_2OH$.

7 (*d*) The incorrect match is (d).

$$HO—CH_2—CH_2—OH$$
Ethylene glycol

8 (*c*) The IUPAC name of the compound is propane-1, 2, 3-triol and it has two primary alcoholic groups and one secondary alcoholic groups. It structure is as follows

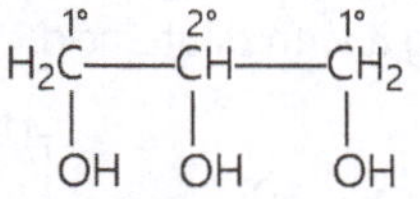

Propane-1, 2, 3-triol

9 (*b*) The IUPAC name of given compound is 1-ethoxy-2-nitrocyclohexane.

10 (*a*) The C—O—H bond angle in methanol, phenol and methoxymethane are 108.9°, 109° and 111.7° respectively.

11 (*b*) The $C_6H_{14}O_2$ compound having two tertiary alcoholic group is

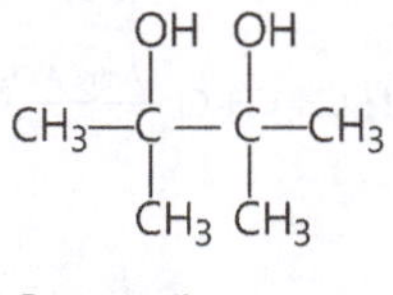

Its IUPAC name is 2,3-dimethylbutane-2, 3-diol.

12 (*b*) Tetrahedral arrangement.

e.g.

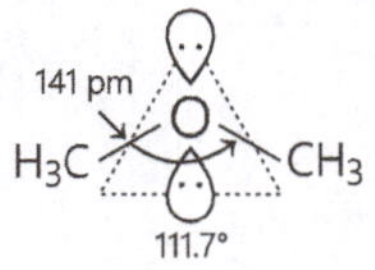

13 (*b*) The statements (a), (c) and (d) are correct. The correct form of statement (b) is :

The C—O—C bond angle is more than tetrahedral angle.

14 (*c*) In case of unsymmetrical alkenes, the addition reaction takes place in accordance with Markovnikov's rule.

15 (*b*) The suitable reagent *X* for the given conversion is
(i) B_2H_6 , (ii) H_2O_2/OH^-

$$CH_3CH=CH_2 + (H—BH_2)_2 \longrightarrow$$

$$\underset{\displaystyle H}{CH_3—CH}—\underset{\displaystyle BH_2}{CH_2} \xrightarrow{2CH_3—CH=CH_2}$$

$$(CH_3—CH_2—CH_2)_3B \xrightarrow{H_2O, 3H_2O_2, \bar{O}H} \underset{\text{Propan-1-ol}}{3CH_3CH_2CH_2—OH} + B(OH)_3$$

This reaction is known as hydroboration-oxidation reaction.

16 (*b*) The correct form of statement (b) is

The net addition of —H and —OH occurs in a way opposite to the Markovnikov's rule.

17 (*a*)

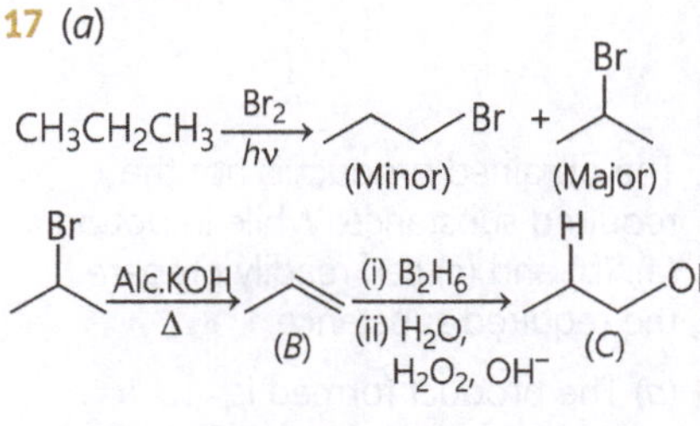

18 (*d*) Among the given reagents potassium permanganate is not used for the reduction of aldehydes and ketone into alcohols. $KMnO_4$ is an oxidising agent.

19 (*c*) Carboxylic acids are reduced to primary alcohols in excellent yields by ($LiAlH_4$), a strong reducing agent. The reaction is as follows

$$RCOOH \xrightarrow[\text{(ii) } H_2O]{\text{(i) } LiAlH_4} RCH_2OH$$

20 (c) The product formed are,

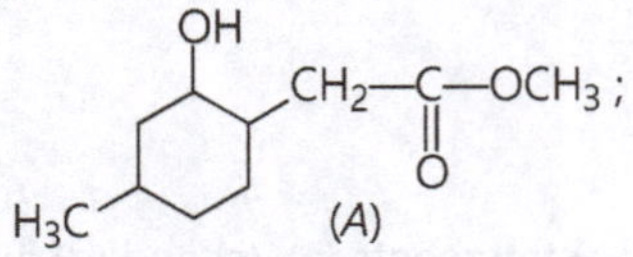

(A)

$CH_3CH_2CH_2\,CH(CH_3)—CH_2OH$

(B)

$NaBH_4$ reduce only aldehyde and ketone not esters.

21 (c) Complete sequence of reaction is as follows

$$\underset{\text{Ethanoic acid}}{CH_3COOH} \xrightarrow[H^+]{C_2H_5OH} CH_3COOC_2H_5 \xrightarrow[\text{Catalyst}]{H_2} \underset{\text{Ethanol}}{2C_2H_5OH}$$

22 (b)

$$CH_3CH_2—\overset{O}{\overset{\|}{C}}—OH \xrightarrow{LiAlH_4/H_2O} CH_3CH_2CH_2OH$$

23 (b) This reaction on hydrolysis produces an alcohol.

24 (d)

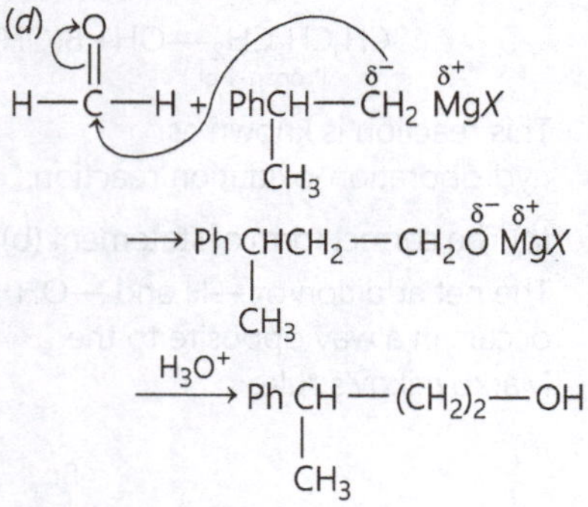

The obtained product is not the required substance. While in option (a), (b) and (c) can readily prepare the required substance.

25 (a) The product formed is,

$$CH_3—\underset{CH_3}{\overset{CH_3}{C}}—OH.$$ Its IUPAC name is

2-methylpropan-2-ol.

26 (c)

$$\underset{\substack{\text{1-bromopropane}\\(X)}}{CH_3CH_2CH_2Br} + Mg \xrightarrow{\text{Dry ether}} \underset{(Y)}{CH_3CH_2CH_2MgBr}$$

$$\xrightarrow{HCHO} CH_3CH_2CH_2CH_2—O—MgBr \xrightarrow{H_2O} \underset{\text{1-butanol}}{CH_3CH_2CH_2CH_2OH} + Mg(Br)(OH)$$

Hence, compound '*X*' is 1-bromopropane.

27 (d) Cumene is first oxidised in the presence of air to cumene hydroperoxide, then it is converted to phenol and acetone by treating with dilute acid.

28 (b) Phenol is manufactured from the hydrocarbon, cumene.

Cumene (*iso*-propylbenzene) is oxidised in the presence of air to cumene hydroperoxide. It is converted to phenol and acetone by treating it with dilute acid.

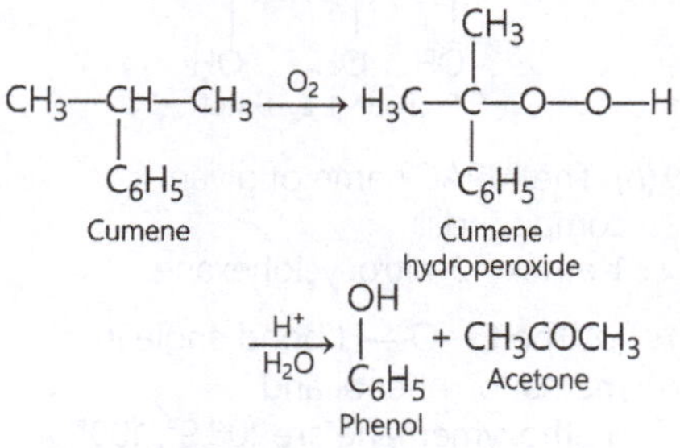

29 (d) The major products *P*, *Q* and *R* in the given reaction are as follows

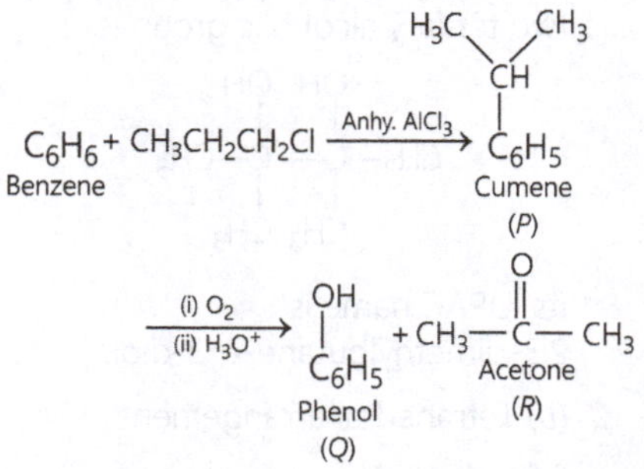

30 (d) Boiling points of alcohols increases with increase in the number of carbon atoms and decrease with increase of branching in carbon chain.

Hence, the correct trends of boiling point is

$$CH_3—\underset{CH_3}{\overset{CH_3}{C}}—OH < CH_3—\underset{CH_3}{CH}—CH_2OH < CH_3CH_2CH_2CH_2OH$$

31 (a) The boiling points of alcohols increases with increase in the number of carbon atom as there is a increase in van der Waals' forces. The correct order is (a).

32 (b) Alcohols (*R*OH) are Bronsted acids, i.e. they can donate a proton to a stronger base (B**:**).

The reaction takes place as follows

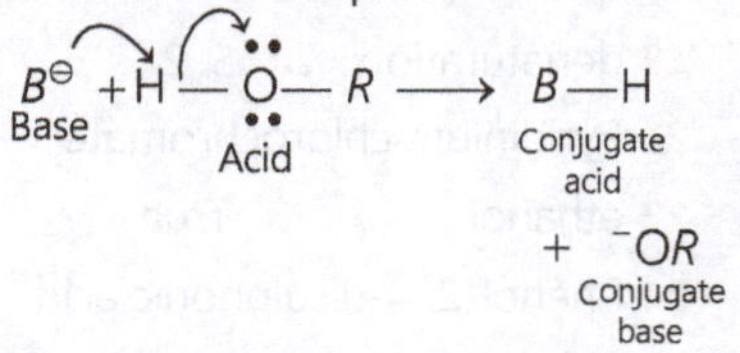

33 (c) Methanol is more acidic among all compounds. Because of lower number of alkyl group and +*I* effect.

34 (c) Among the given compounds phenol is the most acidic as it can lose a hydrogen ion to give a stable phenoxide ion.

35 (c) In the substituted phenols, the presence of electron withdrawing groups like $—NO_2$, enhances the acidic strength of phenol.

Picric acid have 3-nitro group which makes it a very strong acid.

36 (d) Higher is the acidic strength, lower is the pK_a value. Thus, the increasing order of acidic strength is option (d).

37 (c) The correct option is (c).

38 (*b*) A stronger acid displaces a weaker acid from its salt.
Since, H_2O displaces *R*OH from $R\overset{-}{O}\overset{+}{N}a$ and both H_2O and alcohol displace acetylene from sodium acetylide.
Therefore, water is the strongest acid followed by alcohol, while acetylene is the weakest acid.
Their acidic order is shown below.

$$H_2O > ROH > HC\equiv CH$$

39 (*a*) To neutralise HCl which is formed during the reaction.
It shifts the equilibrium to the right hand side.

40 (*c*)

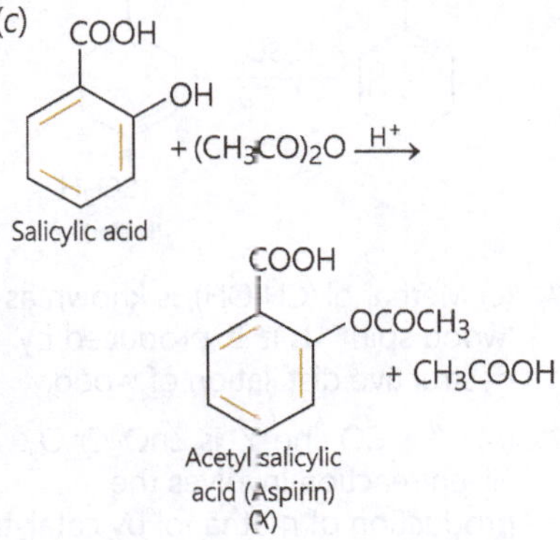

41 (*a*) Tertiary alcohol reacts readily with Lucas reagent.

42 (*c*) $CH_3CH_2\underset{|}{C}H{-}CH_3$ (OH) is a 2° alcohol.
Thus, it will not give immediate turbidity on reaction with Lucas test.

43 (*b*) The correct decreasing order of reactivity of alcohol with *HX* is

$$HI > HBr > HCl.$$

44 (*b*) Conc. HCl and $ZnCl_2$, (i.e. Lucas reagent) can be used to distinguish three classes of alcohols.

45 (*d*) The reaction of alcohol with Lucas reagent is S_N1 reaction and the rate of reaction is directly proportional to the stability of carbocation formed in the reaction.
Since, 3° alcohol forms 3° carbocation (most stable), hence it will react fastest.

46 (*d*)

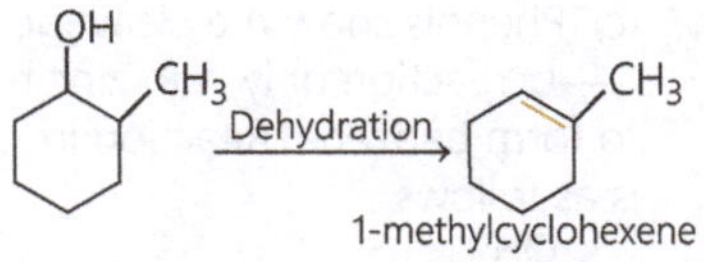

$$CH_3CH_2CH_2CH_2OH \xrightarrow{\text{Dehydration}} \underset{\text{But-1-ene}}{CH_3CH_2{-}CH{=}CH_2}$$

47 (*c*) The incorrect statement is (c). Its correct form is :
The temperature should be high.

48 (*b*)

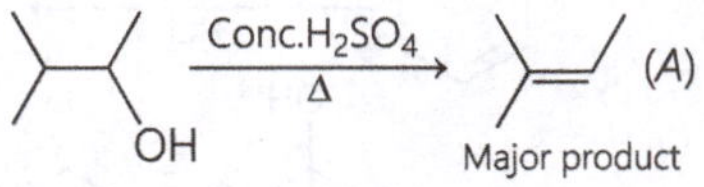

49 (*c*) 2-methylpropan-2-ol because it gives tertiary carbocation during dehydration.
Reaction involved is shown below.

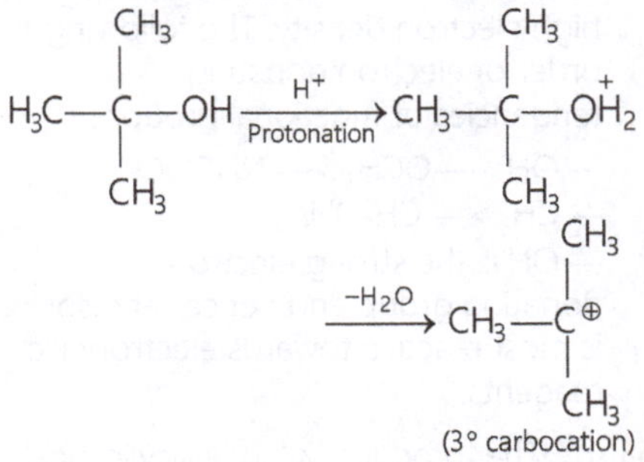

50 (*c*) Compound III, i.e. p-$CH_3OC_6H_4CH(OH)CH_3$ alcohol get dehydrated easily. Presence of electron releasing group, i.e. $-OCH_3$ facilitates the protonation of alcohol that involve in dehydration.

51 (*a*) PCC (Pyridinium Chlorochromate) is the complex of chromium trioxide with pyridine and HCl.

52 (*d*) Strong oxidising agent such as acidified $KMnO_4$ is used for conversion of alcohol to carboxylic acid.

53 (*d*) Among the given reactions (d) is incorrect.
The correct reaction is given as,

$$CH_3CH_2OH \xrightarrow[170\,°C]{\text{Conc. } H_2SO_4} CH_2{=}CH_2$$

54 (*b*) Kidneys to excrete methanol.

55 (*d*) The reaction in option (d) is incorrect as this conversion cannot be takes place by using copper at 573 K.

56 (*d*) Nitration of phenol with dilute nitric acid at low temperature (298 K), yield a mixture of *ortho* and *para*-nitrophenols.

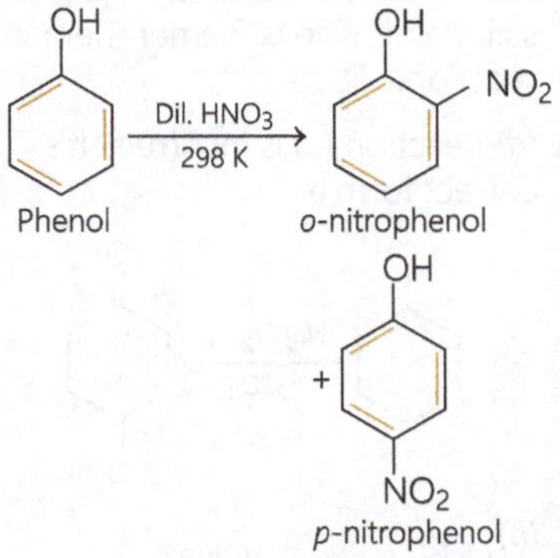

57 (*c*) Phenol on reaction with conc. HNO_3 produces 2,4,6-trinitrophenol (picric acid).

58 (*a*)

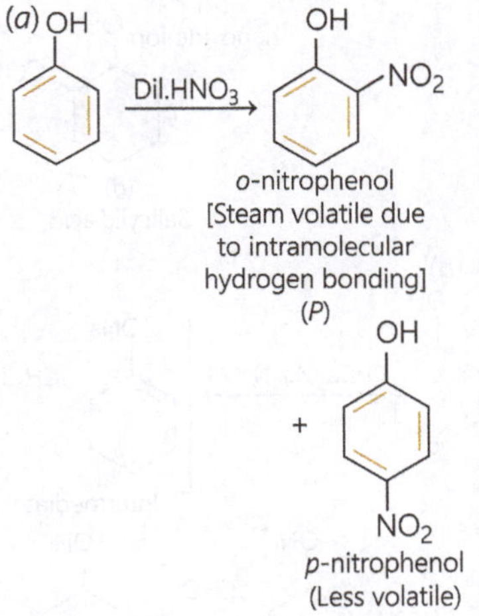

59 (*d*) Since, —OH and $-CH_3$ groups are *ortho* and *para*-directing. The major product obtained in the given reaction are as follows

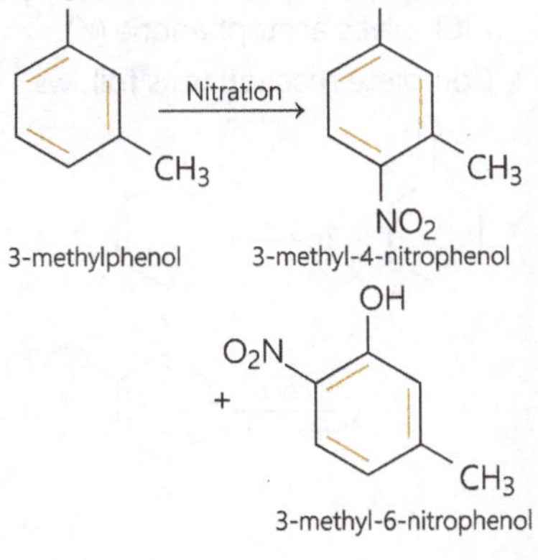

60 (*a*) The conversion of phenol to salicylic acid is called Kolbe's reaction.

The conversion of phenol to salicylaldehyde is Riemer-Tiemann reaction.

61 (*a*) Reaction (a) is incorrect. It's correct form is

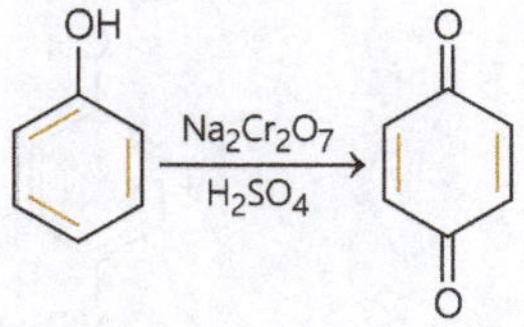

62 (*b*)

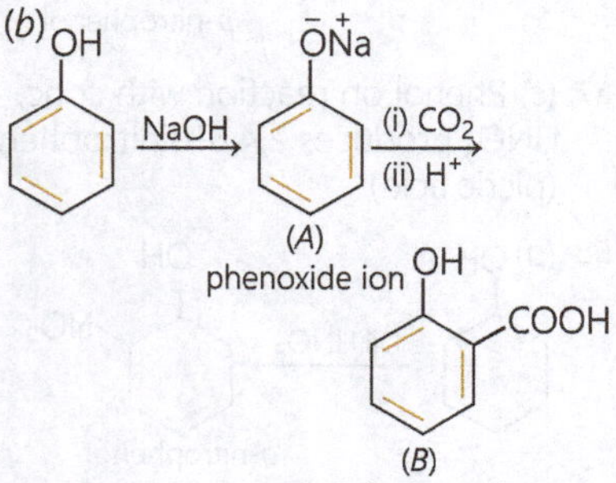

63 (*a*)

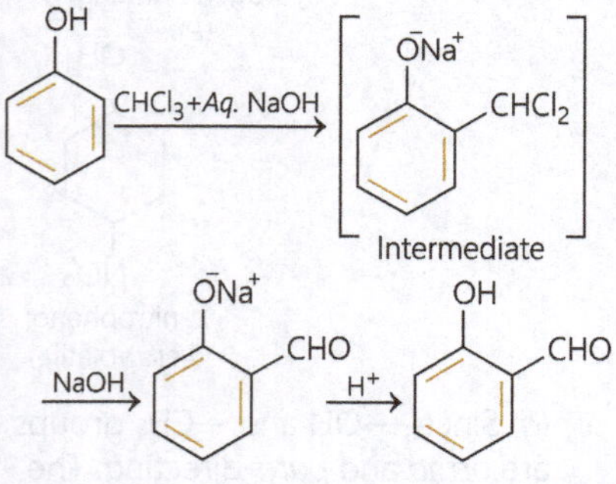

64 (*a*) Phenol on reaction with zinc form benzene (*X*) which on further reaction with CH_3COCl and anhyd. $AlCl_3$ gives acetophenone (*Y*).

Complete reaction is as follows

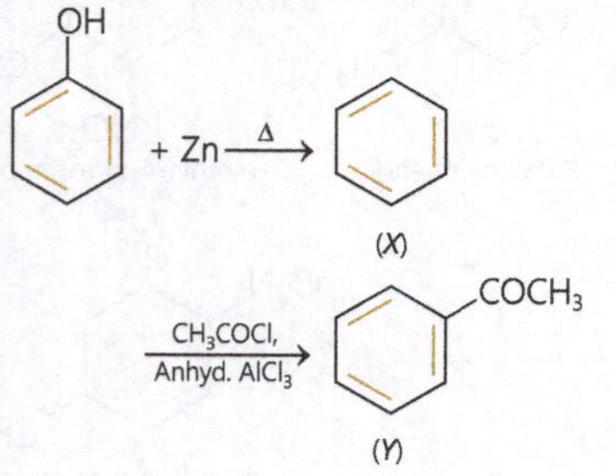

65 (*c*) Phenols show the cleavage of C—O reaction only with zinc metal to form benzene. Reaction involved is as follows

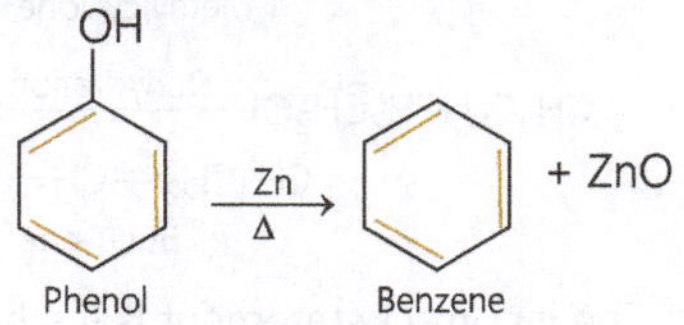

66 (*b*)

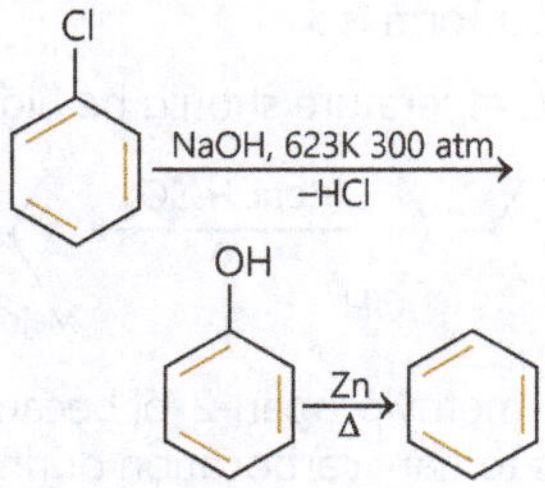

67 (*b*) Electrophilic reagent readily attacks on the benzene ring having high electron density. The following order of electron donating tendencies of functional groups :

—OH > —OCH_3 > —$NHCOCH_3$ > —CH_3 > —CH_2OH.

—OH is the strong electron donating group and hence *o*-cresol is most reactive towards electrophilic reagents.

68 (*a*) The product '*X*' is salicylic acid which is produced by Kolbe's reaction.

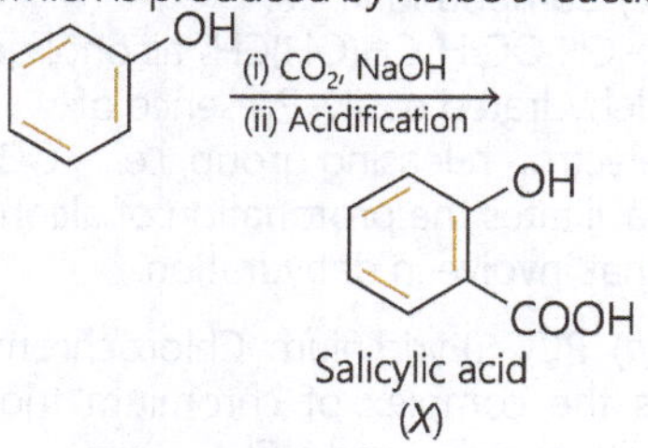

The salicylic acid undergoes acetylation to produce aspirin as

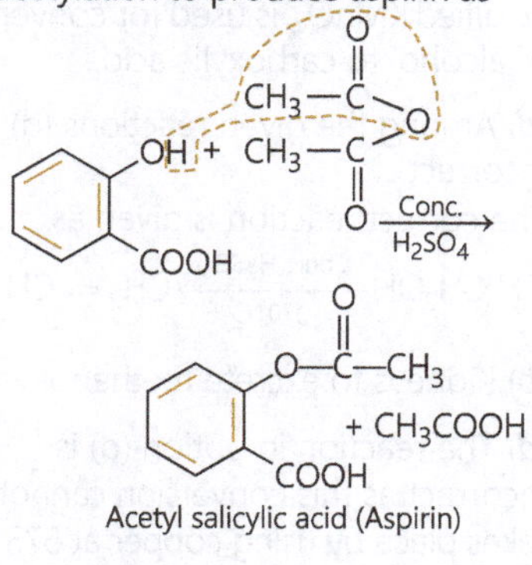

Aspirin is a non-narcotic analgesic (Pain killer).

69 (*c*) '*X*' in the given reaction is $Na_2Cr_2O_7, H_2SO_4$. Complete reaction involves the oxidation of phenol to benzoquinone as shown below.

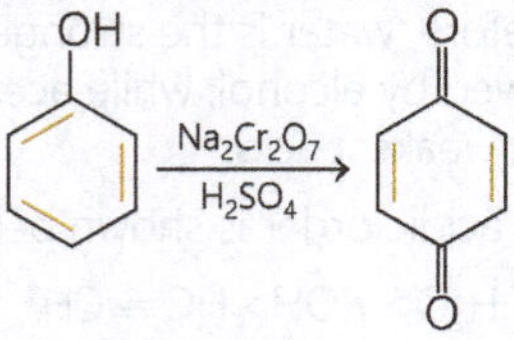

70 (*c*) When phenol is reacted with H_2SO_4 at 100°C *para*-substituted product is formed.

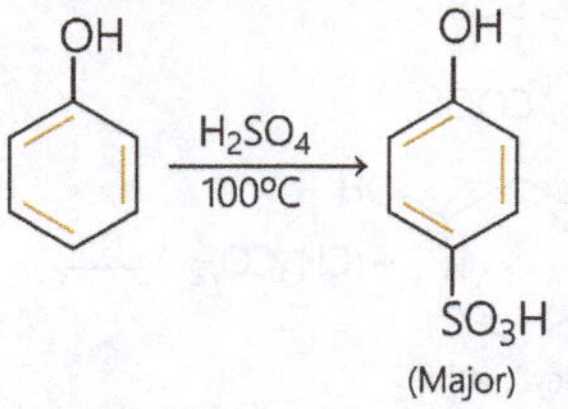

71 (*c*) Methanol (CH_3OH), is known as 'wood spirit' as it is produced by destructive distillation of wood.

72 (*b*) '*X*' is CO and '*Y*' is $ZnO\text{-}Cr_2O_3$. Given reaction involves the production of methanol by catalytic hydrogenation of carbon monoxide at high pressure and temperature in the presence of $ZnO\text{-}Cr_2O_3$ catalyst.

73 (*a*) $\underset{\text{(Molasses / Sugarcane / fruits)}}{C_{12}H_{22}O_{11}} + H_2O \xrightarrow{\text{Invertase }(X)} \underset{\text{Glucose}}{C_6H_{12}O_6} + \underset{\text{Fructose}}{C_6H_{12}O_6}$

$\underset{\text{Glucose / Fructose}}{C_6H_{12}O_6} \xrightarrow{\text{Zymase }(Y)} 2C_2H_5OH + 2CO_2\uparrow$

Here, *X* is invertase and *Y* is zymase.

74 (*d*) The action of zymase is inhibited once the percentage of alcohol formed exceeds 14 percents.

75 (*b*) The mixing of copper sulphate ($CuSO_4$) (to give it colour) and pyridine (a foul smelling liquid) to make commercial alcohol unfit for drinking. It is known as denaturation of alcohol.

76 (*c*) Ethanol is dehydrated to ethene in the presence of H_2SO_4 at 443 K. At 413 K, ethoxyethane is the main product. The reactions are as follows

$$CH_3CH_2OH \xrightarrow[443\,K]{H_2SO_4} CH_2{=}CH_2(I) \text{ (Ethene)}$$
Ethanol
$$CH_3CH_2OH \xrightarrow[413\,K]{H_2SO_4} C_2H_5OC_2H_5\,(II) \text{ (Ethoxyethane)}$$

77 (*c*) Pentan-1-ol give best yield of dialkyl ether on being heated with a trace of sulphuric acid. It is a primary alcohol and readily undergoes substitution reaction to give ether.

78 (*b*) Williamson's synthesis involves S_N2 mechanism when attack of an alkoxide ion on primary alkyl halide takes place.

79 (*a*)

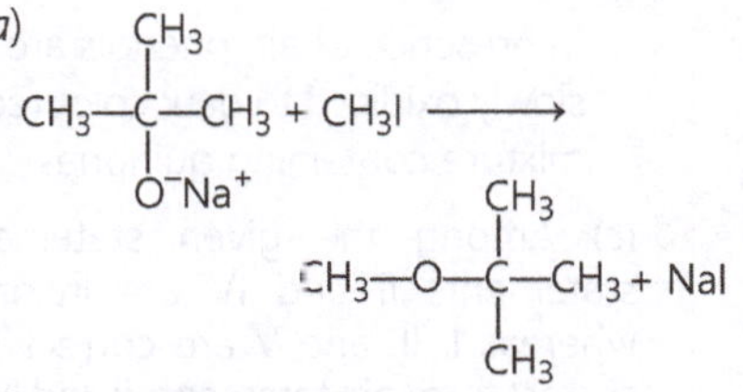

80 (*c*) Substituted phenols react with *aq.* NaOH to form sodium phenoxides which on reaction with CH_3I undergoes S_N2 reaction to give 2-methoxytoluene.

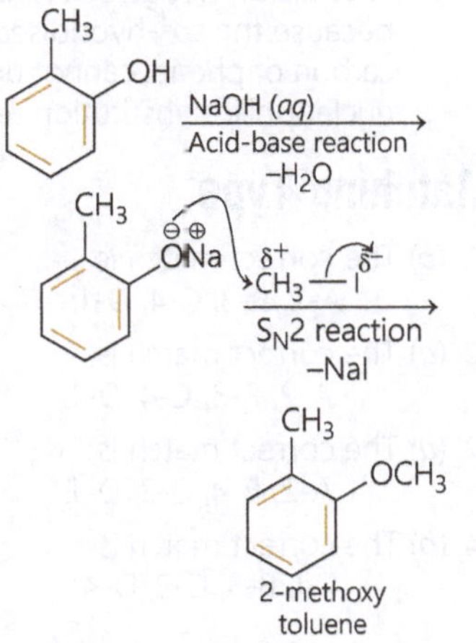

81 (*d*)

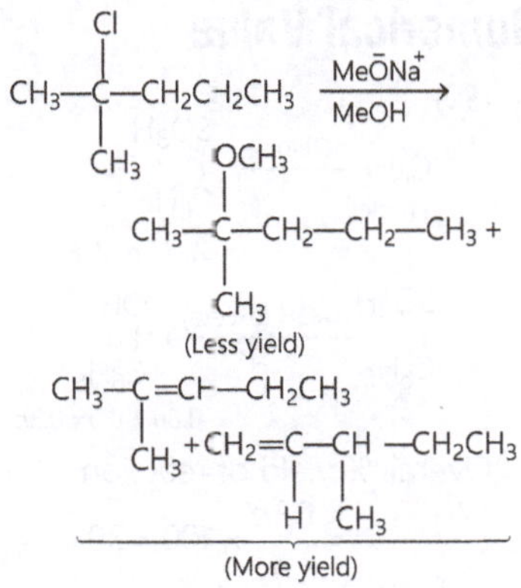

82 (*a*) $CH_3CHBrCH_3 \xrightarrow{Alc.KOH} CH_3CH{=}CH_2\,(A) \xrightarrow[Peroxide]{HBr} CH_3CH_2CH_2Br\,(B) \xrightarrow{CH_3ONa} CH_3CH_2CH_2OCH_3\,(C)$

83 (*b*) The correct increasing order of boiling point is

	Ethoxyethane	<	*n*-pentane	<	Butan-1-ol
B.P.	307.6	<	309.1	<	390

84 (*c*) The order of reactivity of hydrogen halides with ether is as follows

HI > HBr > HCl.

85 (*a*) The reaction of anisole with HI gives phenol rather than iodobenzene because the bond between O—CH_3 is weaker than the bond between O—C_6H_5.

86 (*a*)

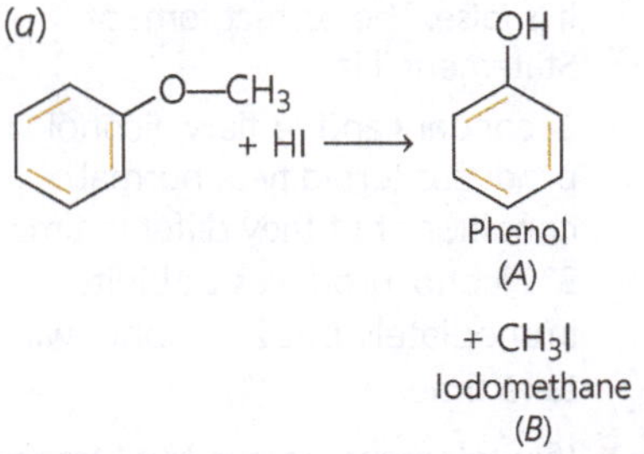

87 (*d*) Among the given statements (d) is incorrect.

Ethers are less polar than alcohols.

88 (*a*) As, the given compound $C_6H_{14}O$ does not react with Na, thus it is not an alcohol. The compound give only one type of halide that means it is a symmetrical ether, i.e. $CH_3CH_2CH_2OCH_2CH_2CH_3$.

89 (*b*) The major product obtained in the reaction is as follows

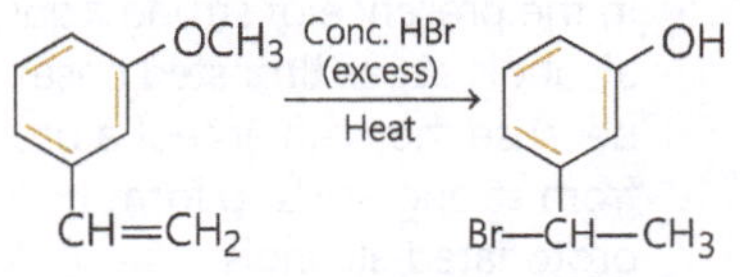

As conc. HBr is in excess.

So, reaction will take place at both the substituents.

90 (*c*) Among the given compound $C_6H_5OCH_3$ undergo electrophilic substitution reaction.

91 (*c*) Resonating structure in option (c) is incorrect.

92 (*c*)

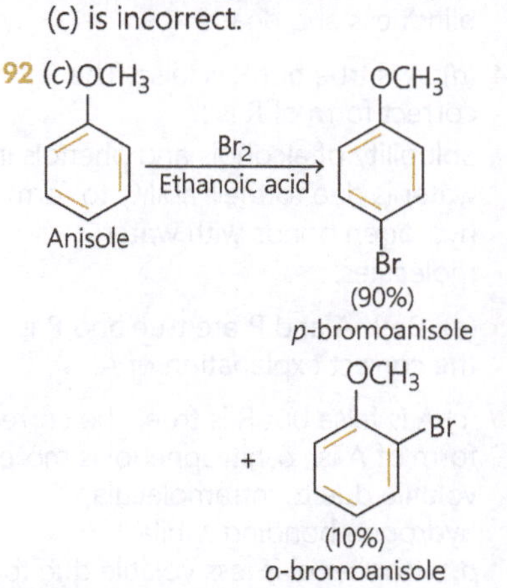

93 (*d*)

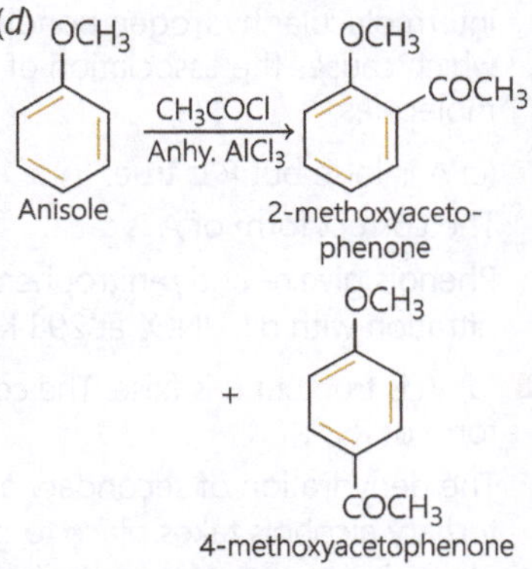

Assertion-Reason

1 (*c*) A is false but R is true. The correct form of A is :

The bond angle in alcohols is slightly less than the tetrahedral angle (109°28′). It is due to the repulsion between the unshared electron pair of oxygen.

2 (*b*) Both A and R are true but R is not the correct explanation of A. The correct explanation of A is :

Commercially, acids are reduced to alcohols by converting them to esters followed by their reduction using hydrogen in the presence of catalyst. This is done for higher yield and purity of alcohol formed. Besides reaction conditions are milder in hydrogenation.

3 (*c*) A is true but R is false. The correct form of R is :

In the body, methanol is oxidised first to methanal and then to methanoic acid which may cause blindness and death.

4 (*d*) A is true but R is false. The correct form of R is :

Solubility of alcohols and phenols in water is due to their ability to form hydrogen bonds with water molecules.

5 (*a*) Both A and R are true and R is the correct explanation of A.

6 (*c*) A is false but R is true. The correct form of A is : *o*-nitrophenol is more volatile due to intramolecular hydrogen bonding, while *p*-nitrophenol is less volatile due to intermolecular hydrogen bonding which causes the association of molecules.

7 (*c*) A is false but R is true.

The correct form of A is :

Phenols give *o*- and *p*-nitrophenol on nitration with dil. HNO_3 at 298 K.

8 (*d*) A is true but R is false. The correct form of R is :

The dehydration of secondary and tertiary alcohols takes place to give ethers is unsuccessful as elimination competes over substitution and as a consequence alkene are easily formed.

9 (*a*) Both A and R are true and R is the correct explanation of A.

10 (*d*) A is true but R is false. The correct form of R is :

Ethers are the least reactive among all the functional groups.

Statement Type

1 (*b*) Statement I is true but Statement II is false.

The correct form at II is :

The alcohol obtained by hydroboration oxidation in a way opposite to the Markovnikov's rule.

2 (*c*) Statement I is false but Statement II is true. The correct form of I is :

Hydroxyketones are not directly used in Grignard reagent. Grignard reagents are very reactive. Therefore, they react with hydroxyl group.

3 (*b*) Statement I is true but Statement II is false.

The correct form of II is :

Benzene diazonium salts can be only formed by primary aromatic amines.

e.g.

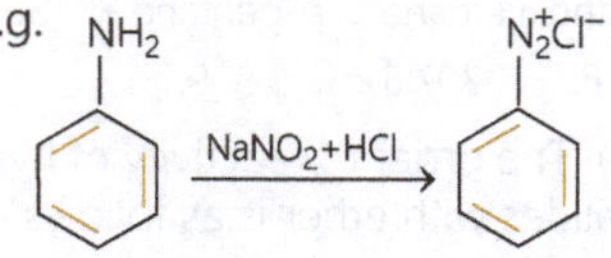

4 (*b*) Statement I is true but Statement II is false. The correct form of II is :

The position of Cl group present on the ring shows different, acidic strength.

5 (*b*) Statement I is true and Statement II is false. The correct form of Statement II is :

Secondary and tertiary alcohol produces turbidity at normal conditions but they differ in time 3° alcohol produces turbidity immediately but 2° alcohol will take time.

6 (*b*) Statement I is true but Statement II is false. The correct form of Statement II is :

Tertiary butyl chloride in presence of sodium ethoxide gives elimination reaction because sodium ethoxide is a strong nucleophile as well as a strong base.

7 (*c*) Statements I, II and IV are correct, whereas Statements III and V are incorrect.

Their correct form is

- In the presence of strong acids, alcohols act as Bronsted bases because they can accept a proton from strong acids to form protonated alcohols.
- Acetylation of salicylic acid produces aspirin.

8 (*c*) Statements II, III and IV are correct while I and V are incorrect. Their correct form is :

- The reaction of phenol with metals and sodium hydroxide indicate its acidic nature.
- In substituted phenols, the presence of electron withdrawing group enhances the acidic strength of phenol.

9 (*d*) Among the given statements I, II and III are correct while IV and V are incorrect. Their correct form is

- *o*-nitrophenol is steam volatile due to intramolecular hydrogen bonding.
- In presence of air, phenols are slowly oxidised to dark coloured mixture containing quinones.

10 (*c*) Among the given statements, statements II and IV are incorrect whereas I, III and V are correct. The correct form of Statements II and IV is :

II. The alkoxy group is *o*-, *p*-directing and activates the aromatic ring towards electrophilic substitution reaction.

IV. Phenols do not give aryl halide because the sp^2-hybridised carbon of phenol cannot undergo nucleophilic substitution reaction.

Matching Type

1 (*b*) The correct match is A-2, B-3, C-4, D-1.

2 (*a*) The correct match is A-2, B-3, C-4, D-1.

3 (*d*) The correct match is A-2, B-4, C-3, D-1.

4 (*b*) The correct match is A-1, B-3, C-2, D-4.

Numerical Value

1 (30)

$$\underset{n \text{ moles}}{C_6H_5} \xrightarrow{\text{Oleum}} \underset{60\% \text{ of } n = 0.6n}{C_6H_5SO_3H}$$

$$\underset{0.6n}{C_6H_5SO_3H} \xrightarrow[H^+]{\text{NaOH (excess)}} \underset{0.6n \times 0.5 = 0.3n}{C_6H_5OH}$$

Overall % yield of reaction

$$= \frac{0.3n}{n} \times 100 = 30$$

2 (*9*) The number of resonance structure for N is 9.

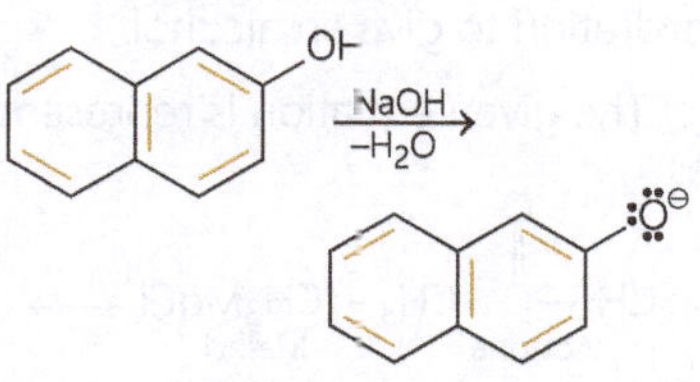

3 (*2*) The compounds I and III are tertiary alcohols that produces turbidity instantly reacts with Lucas reagent.

4 (*7*) Phenol on reaction with mixed acid forms picric acid. Picric acid contain seven oxygen atoms.

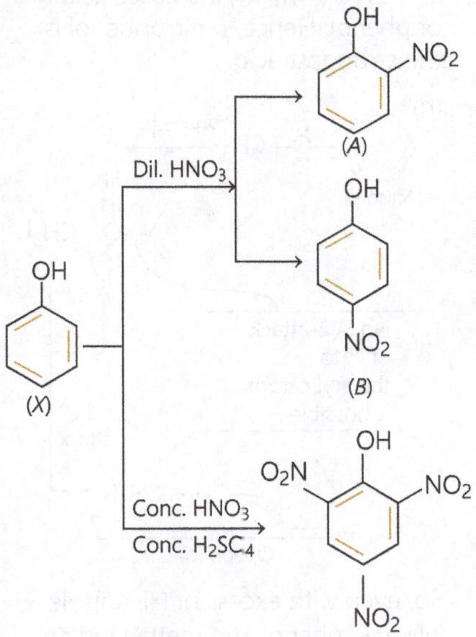

Picric acid (*Y*)

5 (*3*) There are three structural isomers for ether $C_4H_{10}O$.

1. $CH_3CH_2OCH_2CH_3$
Ethoxyethane

2. $CH_3OCH_2CH_2CH_3$
1-methoxypropane

3. $CH_3—O—CH(CH_3)—CH_3$
2-methoxypropane

NCERT Exemplar's

1 (*d*) Monochlorination of toluene in sunlight gives benzyl chloride.

Reaction is as follows

$$C_6H_5CH_3 \xrightarrow[\text{Sunlight}]{Cl_2} C_6H_5CH_2Cl \xrightarrow{\text{Aq. NaOH}} C_6H_5CH_2OH$$

Toluene → Benzyl chloride → Benzyl alcohol

2 (*a*) The three isomers of butanol ($C_4H_{10}O$) are given below.

(i) $CH_3CH_2—CH_2—CH_2OH$
Butan-1-ol

(ii) $CH_3—CH_2—\overset{*}{C}H(OH)—CH_3$ (→ Chiral carbon)
Butan-2-ol

(iii) $H_3C—C(CH_3)(OH)—CH_3$
2-methylpropan-2-ol

3 (*c*) Higher the stability of intermediate, higher will be the reactivity of reactant molecule. So, the order of reactivity of alcohols in the given reaction is 3° > 2° > 1°.

4 (*c*) Treatment with pyridinium chlorochromate ($C_5H_5\overset{+}{N}HCl\overset{-}{Cr}O_3$) oxidises CH_3CH_2OH to CH_3CHO. Strong oxidising agents such as $KMnO_4$ are used for getting carboxylic acid from alcohols.

5 (*b*) The process of converting alkyl halides into alcohols involve substitution reaction.

6 A-4, B-3, C-6, D-1, E-7, F-2

7 (*c*) Compounds *B* and *C* are aromatic alcohols. In compounds (*B*) and (*C*), —OH group is bonded to sp^3-hybridised carbon which in turn is bonded to benzene ring.

8 (*a*) IUPAC name of *m*-cresol is 3-methylphenol because —OH is the functional group and methyl is a substituent.

9 A-(4), B-(5), C-(2), D-(1)

10 (*b*) Among all the given acids, the strongest base is RO^- because its conjugate is a weak acid *ROH*.

11 (*a*) Phenol (C_6H_5OH) react with sodium hydroxide solution in water because it is more acidic in nature.

Phenol readily lose one proton and gives phenoxide ion. This phenoxide ion is resonance stabilised. As phenoxide ion is a stable intermediate. So, the tendency to give proton is more in phenol than others.

12 (*b*) In *o*-nitrophenol, nitro group is present at *ortho*-position. Presence of electron withdrawing group at *ortho*-position increases the acidic strength.

13 A-(5), B-(6), C-(4), D-(3), E-(1), F-(2)

14 (*d*) In *m*-chlorophenol electron withdrawing group (—Cl) is present at *meta*-position.

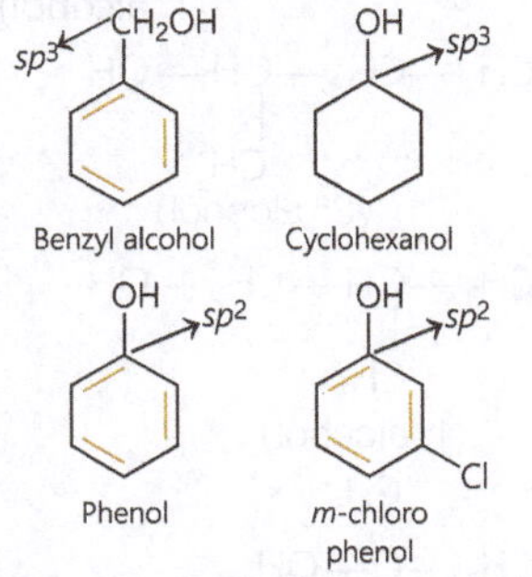

Presence of electron withdrawing group increases the acidic strength. So, *m*-chlorophenol is most acidic among all the given compounds.

15 (*b*) Presence of electron withdrawing group on phenols, increases its acidic strength.

On the other hand, presence of electron releasing group on phenol, decreases its acidic strength.

Hence, the correct order is

II > IV > III > I > V.

16 (*c*) Presence of electron withdrawing group decreases the stability of carbocation.

Since, $—NO_2$ group is a stronger EWG than —Cl.

So, $NO_2—C_6H_5—\overset{+}{C}H_2$ carbocation will be less stable than

$Cl—C_6H_5—\overset{+}{C}H_2$ carbocation.

Thus, the order of stability of carbocation is

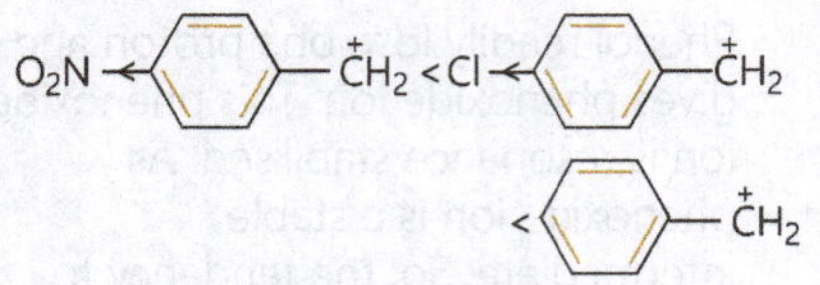

So, the correct order is II < III < I.

17 (*a*) Propan-1-ol < butan-2-ol < butan-1-ol < pentan-1-ol.

18 A-(4), B-(1), C-(6), D-(5), E-(3), F-(2)

Past Exams'

1 (*d*) The reactivity order of alcohols toward Lucas' reagent is 3° alcohols > 2° alcohols > 1° alcohol.

(a) $CH_3—CH_2—CH_2—CH_2—OH$ (1° alcohol)

(b) $CH_3—CH_2—CH(CH_3)—OH$ (2° alcohol)

(c) $CH_3—CH(CH_3)—CH_2—OH$ (1° alcohol)

(d) $CH_3—C(CH_3)_2—OH$ (3° alcohol)

Hence, option (d) is correct.

2 (*d*) $CH_3CH(CH_3)—CH(OH)—CH_3 \xrightarrow{H^+}$
3-methylbutan-2-ol

$CH_3—CH(CH_3)—\overset{+}{C}H—CH_3 \xrightarrow{\text{Hydride shift}}$
2° carbocation (Less stable)

$CH_3—\overset{+}{C}(CH_3)—CH_2—CH_3 \xrightarrow{Br^-}$
3° carbocation (More stable)

$CH_3—C(Br)(CH_3)—CH_2—CH_3$
2-bromo-2-methylbutane

3 (*a*) Among the given alcohols,

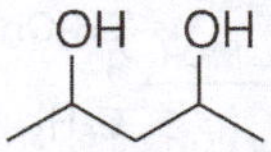

will be most readily dehydrated under acidic conditions to give

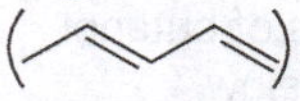

1, 3-butadiene as a product, in which double bonds are present in conjugation.

4. (*c*) Statement I is true but Statement II is false because, the order of acidic strength is as follows

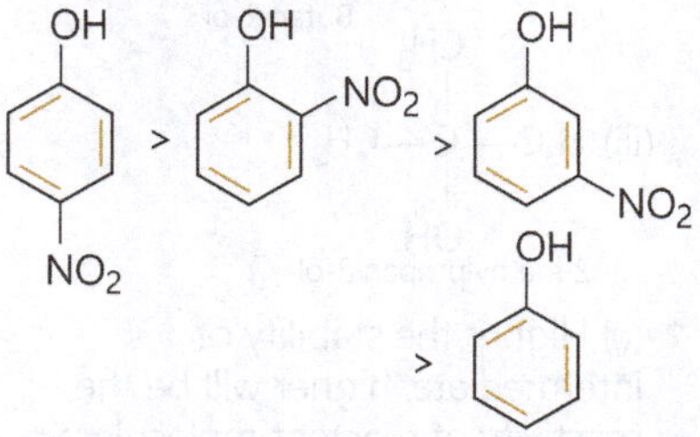

—NO_2 group at *ortho* and *para*-position withdraws electrons of the O—H bonds towards itself by the stronger –*R*-effect while the NO_2 group at *meta*-position withdraws electrons of O—H bond by the weaker –*I*-effect.

Thus, *ortho* and *para*-nitrophenol are more acidic than *meta*-nitrophenol.

5. (*a*) $CH_3—CO—CH_3$ (Acetone) $\xrightarrow[\text{Dry ether}]{\text{(i) } C_2H_5MgBr}$ $CH_3—C(\overset{\ominus}{O}\overset{\oplus}{M}gBr)(C_2H_5)—CH_3 \xrightarrow{\text{(ii) } H_2O/H^+} CH_3—C(OH)(C_2H_5)—CH_3$
2-methylbutan-2-ol

6. (*a*)

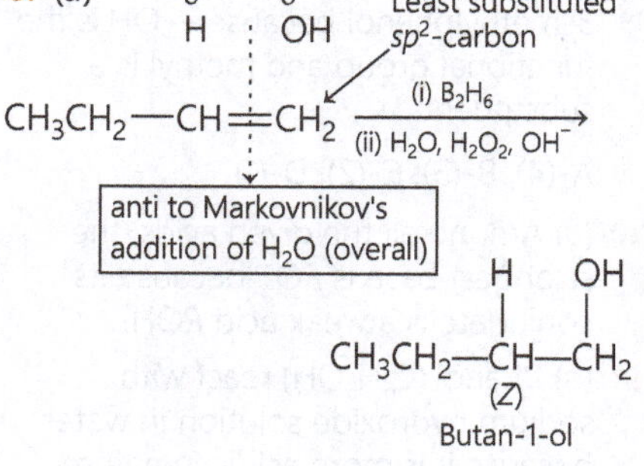

It is hydroboration-oxidation reaction of an alkene which undergoes hydration to give an alcohol.

7. (*c*) The given equation is represented as

$CH_3—CO—CH_3$ (Acetone) $+ CH_3MgCl$ (Methyl magnesium chloride) $\longrightarrow CH_3—C(\overset{\ominus}{O}\overset{\oplus}{M}gCl)(CH_3)—CH_3 \xrightarrow{H_2O} H_3C—C(OH)(CH_3)—CH_3$
tert-butyl alcohol

8. (*a*) EDG (+ *R*, + *I*) decreases acidity and EWG (– *R*, – *I*) increases acidity of phenol. Hence, *p*-nitrophenol is the strongest acid.

9. (*d*)

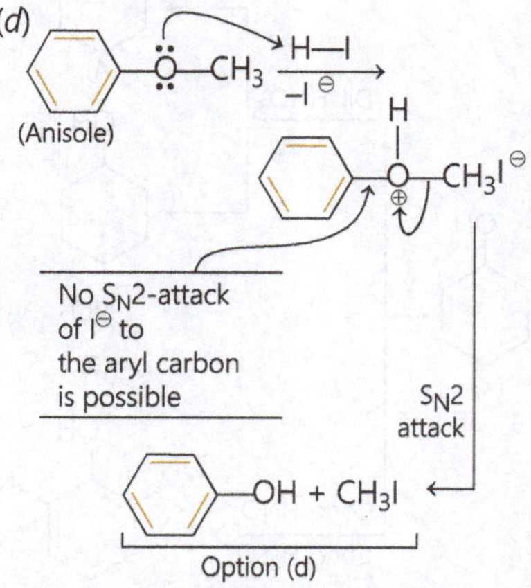

So, even with excess of HI, anisole will give phenol and methyl iodide.

10. (*d*) It is Reimer-Tiemann reaction. The electrophile formed is dichlorocarbene ($:CCl_2$). The mechanism is as follows

$$CHCl_3 + OH^- \rightleftharpoons \overset{-}{C}Cl_3 + H_2O$$

$$\downarrow -Cl^- \ (\alpha\text{-elimination})$$

$$:CCl_2$$

Dichlorocarbene (electrophile)

11. (*c*) The reaction of phenylmethyl ether with HI produces yields phenol and alkyl halide.

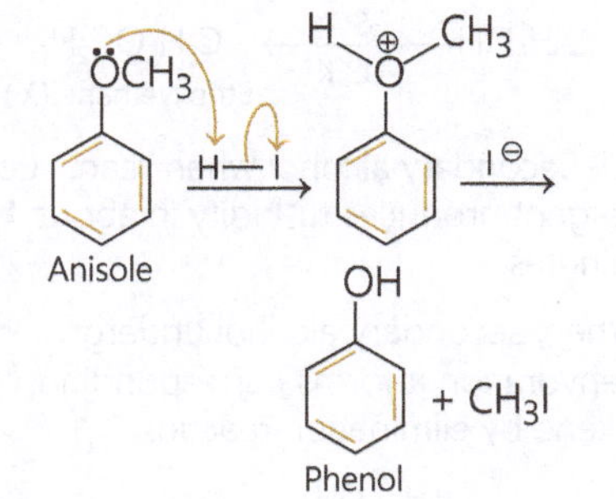

12. (*d*) The formation of ether from alcohol in the presence of base followed by alkylation is known as Williamson's ether synthesis reaction.

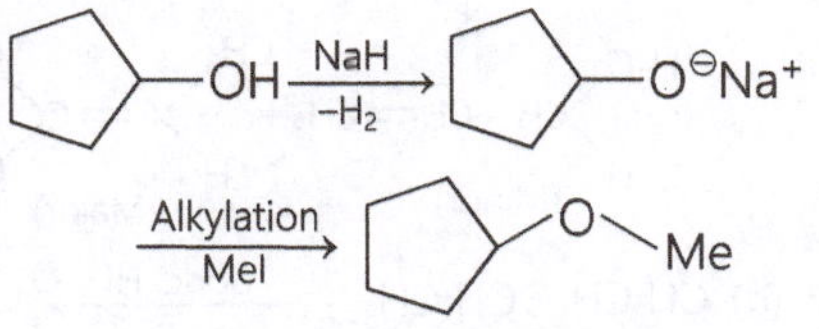

13. (*b*) The reaction is represented as,

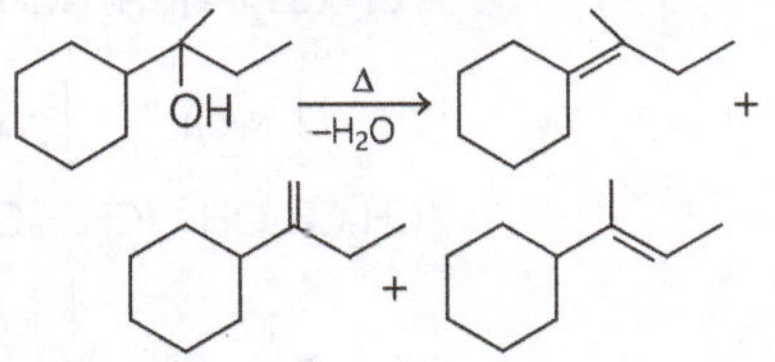

14. (*a*)

$$CH_3CH_2CH{=}CH_2 \xrightarrow[\text{Anti-Markovnikov's rule}]{HBr/H_2O_2} CH_3CH_2CH_2CH_2Br$$

Bromobutane (1° product)

$$\underset{\text{(Williamson's synthesis)}}{CH_3CH_2CH_2CH_2Br} \xrightarrow[S_N2\text{ reaction}]{C_2H_5ONa} CH_3CH_2CH_2CH_2OC_2H_5$$

Ethoxybutane

15. (*c*) The ether which gives more stable carbocation, forms CH_3OH as one of the product with hot conc. HI. The order of stability of carbocation is $3° > 2° > 1°$

Thus, (c) gives CH_3OH as one of the product.

16 (*d*) Use elimination technique as time saver. As preparation of phenol from aniline, i.e. A-II is given is option (d) only.

The correct match is

A-II, B-IV, C-I, D-III.

17. (*d*) The correct match is

A-IV, B-III, C-I, D-II.

(A)

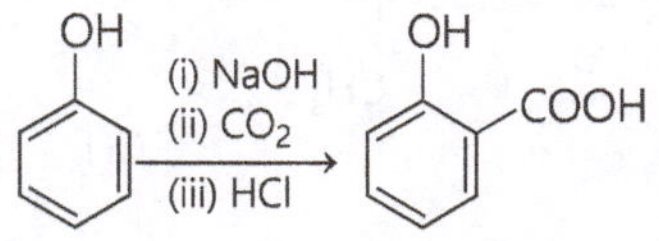

Kolbe-Schmidt reaction

(B)

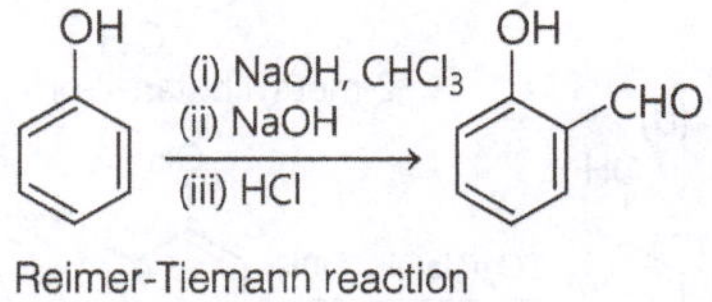

Reimer-Tiemann reaction

(C)

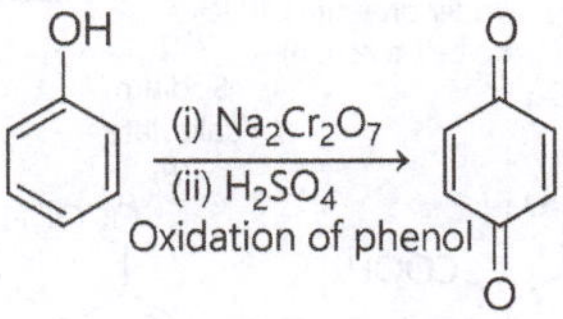

Oxidation of phenol

(D)

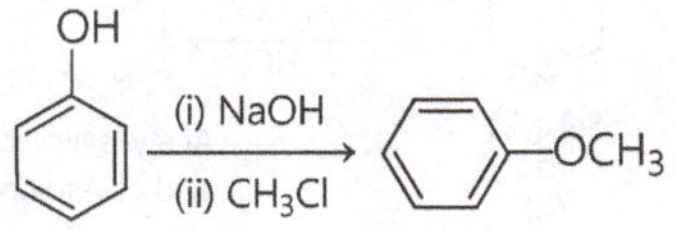

Hence, option (d) is correct.

18. (c) Phenolic group can be identified by a positive phthalein dye test by giving pink colour solution. The complete reaction is as follows

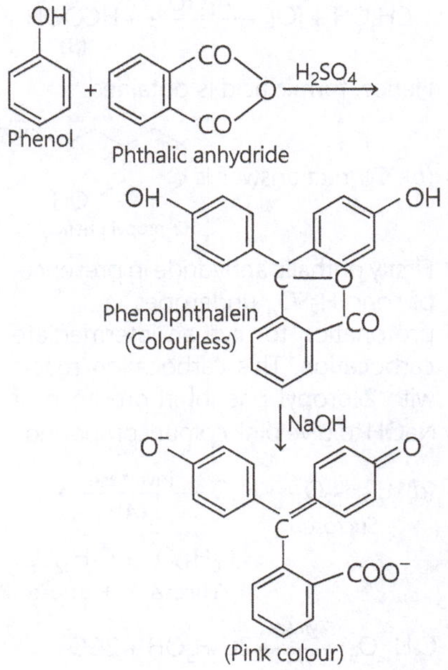

19 (*b*) The major product from the following reaction is given in option (b).

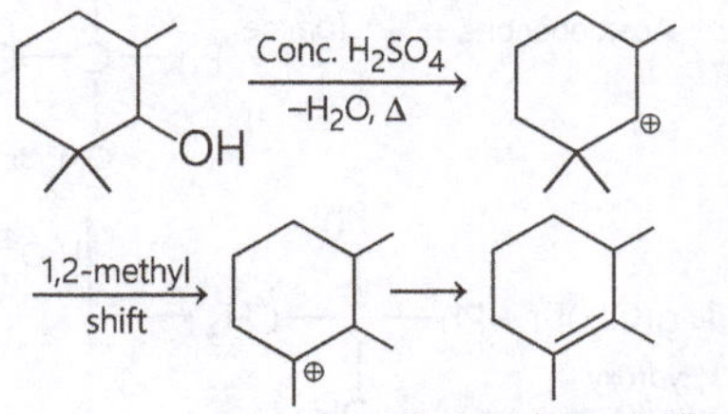

Thermodynamically controlled product

20 (*c*) Among the given options, the incorrect method of preparation of alcohols is from ozonolysis of alkene. It is because on ozonolysis, alkenes gives aldehyde, ketones and carboxylic acids instead of alcohol.

21 (*b*) Phenol is acidic in nature as after removing H^+ ion, phenoxide ion is stabilised by resonance.

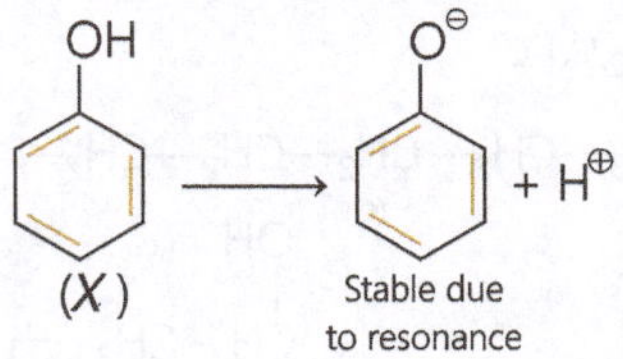

Phenol is although acidic but it is not soluble in $NaHCO_3$ solution. However, it gives violet colour with neutral $FeCl_3$ solution.

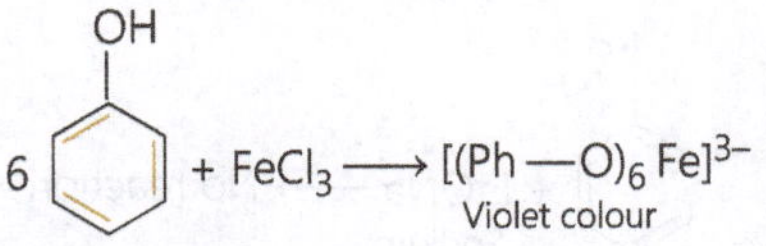

Hence, compound '*X*' is phenol.

22 (*c*) Statement I is true but Statement II is false. The correct form of Statement II is :

II. Phenols are freely soluble in NaOH solution and are stronger acids than alcohols and water.

23 (*d*) Diphenylethanol can be obtained from acetophenone and phenyl magnesium bromide as shown below.

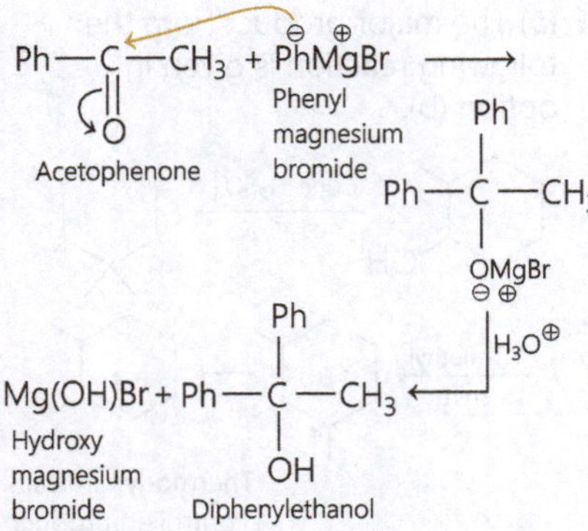

24 (*b*)

25 (*a*) In the given reaction sequence compounds involved are :

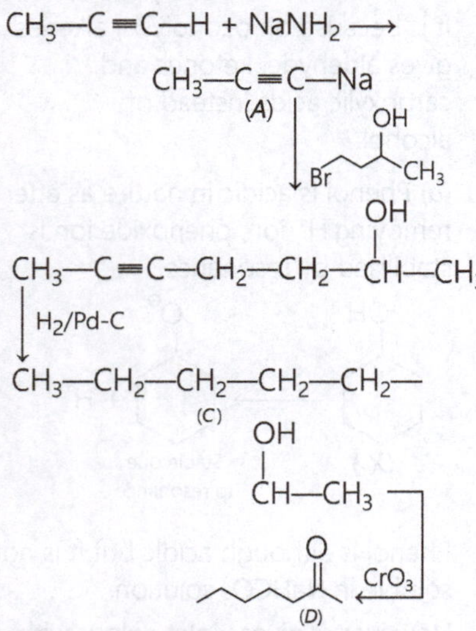

26 (*b*) A is correct but R is incorrect. The correct form of R is :

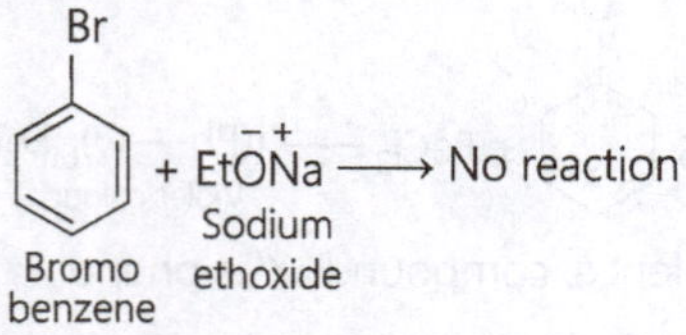

This reaction is not possible as bromine has partial double bond character with benzene ring, so it cannot be dissociated.

Skill Boosters

1 (*d*) $\underset{\text{(Ethanol) (A)}}{CH_3CH_2OH} \xrightarrow{SOCl_2} \underset{\text{(Ethyl chloride) (B)}}{CH_3CH_2Cl} \xrightarrow[\text{Ether}]{Mg} \underset{\text{(Grignard) reagent}}{CH_3\overset{\ominus}{C}H_2\overset{\oplus}{Mg}Cl}$

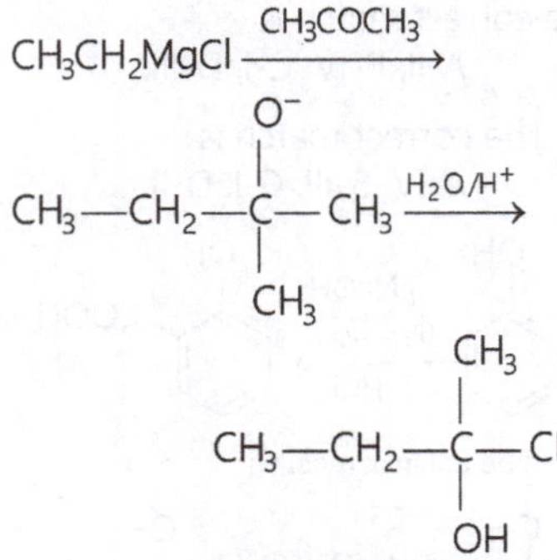

2-methyl butan-2-ol

2 (*d*)

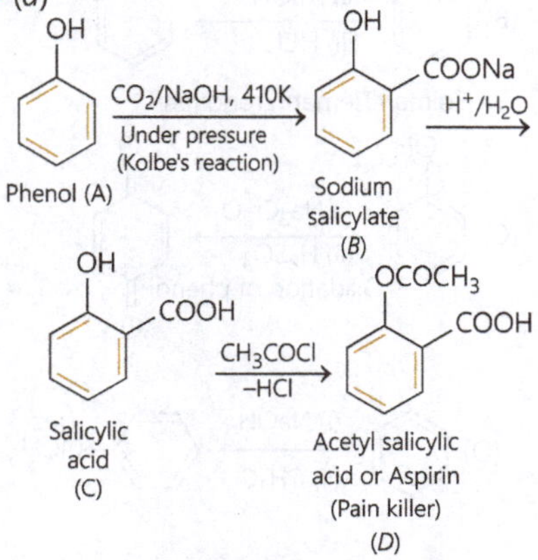

3 (*a*) The denatured alcohol is produced by mixing ethanol with methanol.

$$CO + 2H_2 \xrightarrow[\substack{200\text{-}300 \text{ atm} \\ 573\text{-}673 \text{ K}}]{ZnO\text{-}Cr_2O_3} \underset{(A)}{CH_3OH}$$

$$CH_3OH + [O] \xrightarrow{H_2CrO_4} \underset{(B)}{HCOOH}$$

Hence, formic acid is obtained.

4 (*b*) Correct answer is

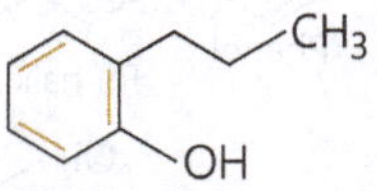

(2-propyl phenol)

Firstly phthalic anhydride in presence of conc. H_2SO_4 undergoes protonation to give an intermediate carbocation. This carbocation reacts with 2-propyl phenol in presence of NaOH to give pink colour compound.

5 (*d*) $\underset{\text{Sucrose}}{C_{12}H_{22}O_{11}} + H_2O \xrightarrow[(A)]{\text{Invertase}} \underset{\text{Glucose}}{C_6H_{12}O_6} + \underset{\text{Fructose}}{C_6H_{12}O_6}$

$$\underset{\text{Glucose}}{C_6H_{12}O_6} \xrightarrow[(B)]{\text{Zymase}} \underset{\text{Ethanol}}{2C_2H_5OH} + 2CO_2$$

$$C_2H_5OH \xrightarrow[413 \text{ K}]{H_2SO_4} \underset{\text{Ethoxyethane } (X)}{C_2H_5OC_2H_5}$$

6 (*d*) Secondary alcohol when react Lucas reagent produces turbidity in about 4-5 minutes.

When, secondary alcohol undergo dehydration it forms corresponding alkene by elimination reaction S_N1.

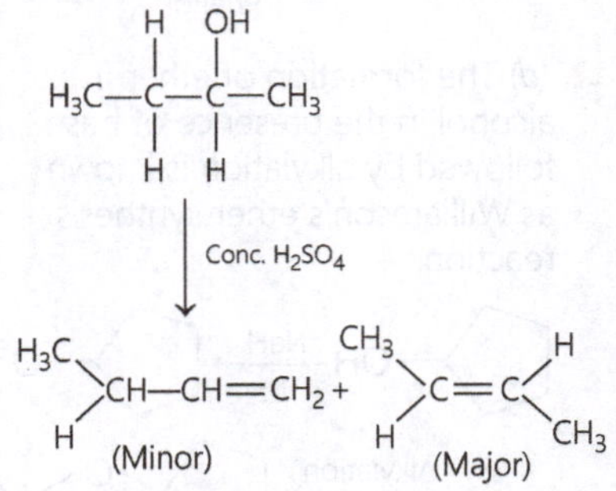

7 (*a*)

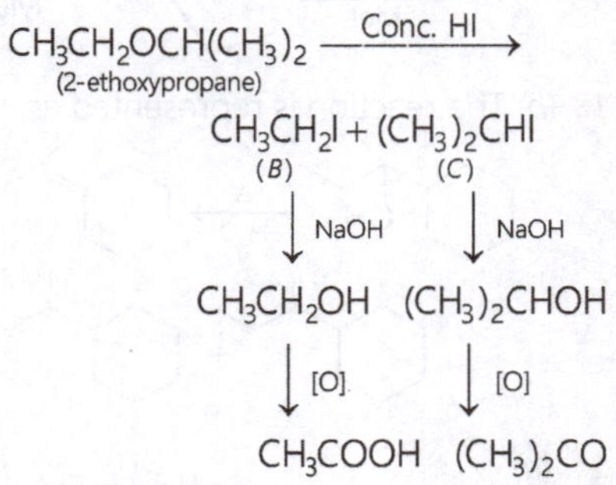

The IUPAC name at the ether (*A*) is 2-ethoxypropane.

8 (*c*)

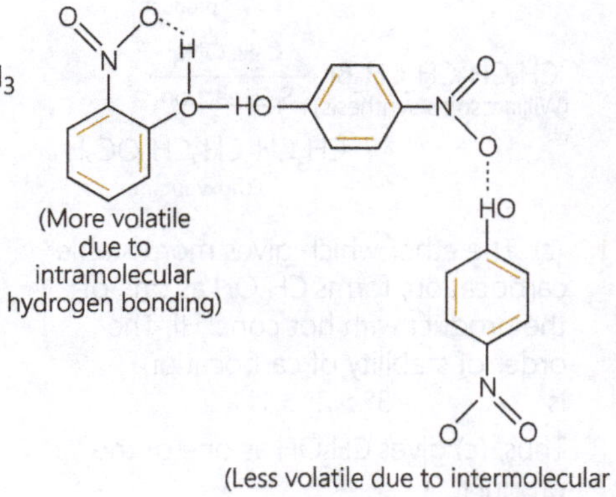

The name of the product formed is *o*-nitrophenol and due to intramolecular hydrogen bonding it is more volatile and form vapours on steam distillation.

Scan for Chemistry Through Concept Master Videos

08

Aldehydes, Ketones and Carboxylic Acids

Topicwise No. of Ques asked in 5 Years (NEET)

Topics	No. of Questions				
	2024	2023	2022	2021	2020
Nomenclature and Structure of Carbonyl Group	–	–	–	1	–
Preparation of Aldehydes and Ketones	1	1	1	1	2
Properties and Uses of Aldehydes and Ketones	–	1	2	2	1
Nomenclature, Structure and Preparation of Carboxylic Acids	1	1	1	–	–
Properties and Uses of Carboxylic Acids	–	–	–	–	1

Special Type of Ques Asked In 5 Years (NEET)

Types	Years				
	2024	2023	2022	2021	2020
A-R	–	–	–	–	–
Statement Based	–	–	1	–	–
Matching	–	–	1	1	–

Last 5 Years Weightage (NEET)

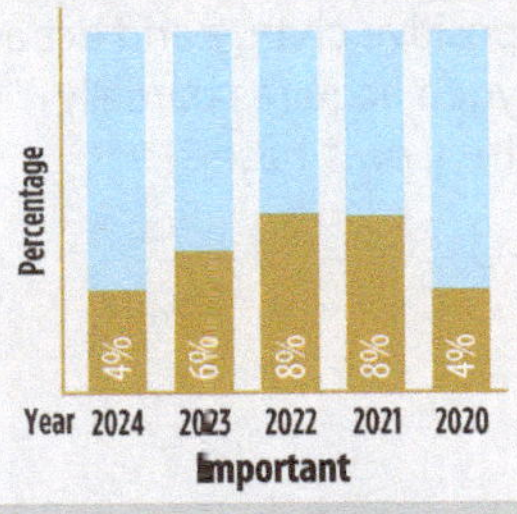

- The organic compounds containing carbon-oxygen double bond, i.e. $(\gt C{=}O)$ are known as **carbonyl compounds** and the group present is known as **carbonyl group**.
- In **aldehydes**, the carbonyl group is bonded to either two H-atoms or a carbon and a hydrogen while in **ketones**, it is bonded to two carbon atoms.
- The carbonyl compounds in which carbonyl group is bonded to carbon or hydrogen and oxygen of hydroxyl moiety (—OH) are known as **carboxylic acids**. Esters and anhydrides are derivatives of carboxylic acids.

The general formulas of these classes of compounds are as follows

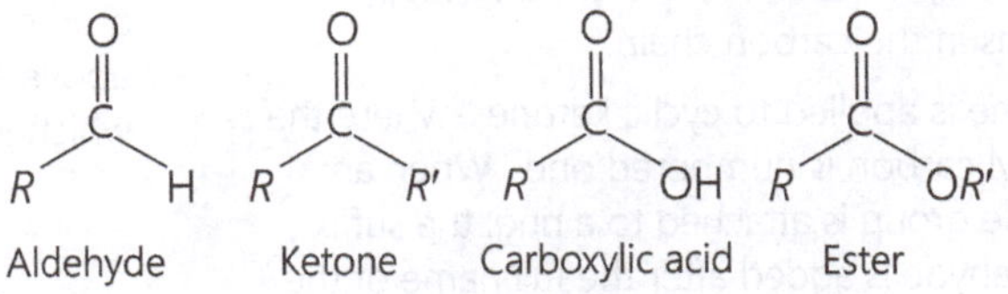

Nomenclature and Structure of Carbonyl Group

Nomenclature

- **Common names of most of the aldehydes** are derived from the common name of corresponding carboxylic acids by replacing the ending -ic of acid with aldehyde. The location of substituent in the carbon chain is indicated by Greek letters $\alpha, \beta, \gamma, \delta$, etc.

- The α-carbon being the one directly linked to the aldehyde group , β-carbon the next and so on.

e.g.

CH_3CHO — Acetaldehyde

C_6H_5-CHO — Benzaldehyde

$\underset{\gamma}{H_3C}-\underset{\beta}{CH(Br)}-\underset{\alpha}{CH_2}-C(=O)-H$

β-bromobutyraldehyde

- **Common names of ketones** are derived by naming two alkyl or aryl groups bonded to the carbonyl group.
- The locations of substituents are indicated by Greek letters αα′, ββ′ and so on beginning with the carbon atoms next to the carbonyl group, indicated as αα′.

e.g.

$CH_3-C(=O)-CH_3$ — Acetone

$CH_3CH(OCH_3)CHO$ — α-methoxy propionaldehyde

- **IUPAC names of open chain aliphatic aldehydes and ketones** are derived from the names of the corresponding alkanes by replacing the ending -'e' with -'al' and -'one', respectively.
In case of aldehydes, the longest carbon chain is numbered starting from the carbon of the aldehyde group while in case of ketones, the numbering begins from the end nearer to the carbonyl group.
- The substituents are prefixed in alphabetical order along with numerals indicating their positions in the carbon chain.
- The same is applied to cyclic ketones, where the carbonyl carbon is numbered one. When an aldehyde group is attached to a ring, the suffix carbaldehyde is added after the full name of the cycloalkane.
- The numbering of the ring carbon atoms start from the carbon atom attached to the aldehyde group.

$CH_3-C(=O)-H$

Ethanal

$H_3C-CH_2-C(=O)-CH_2-C(=O)-H$

3-oxopentanal

Common and IUPAC name of some aldehydes and ketones

Structure	Common name	IUPAC name
Aldehydes		
$(CH_3)_2CHCHO$	*Iso*-butyraldehyde	2-methylpropanal
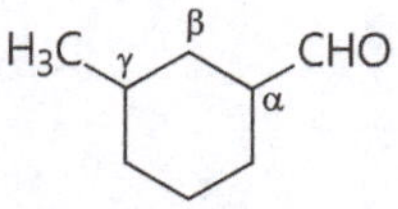	γ-methylcyclohexane carbaldehyde	3-methylcyclohexanecarbaldehyde
$CH_3CH(OCH_3)CHO$	α-methoxy-propionaldehyde	2-methoxypropanal
$CH_3CH_2CH_2CH_2CHO$	Valeraldehyde	Pentanal
$CH_2{=}CHCHO$	Acrolein	Prop-2-enal
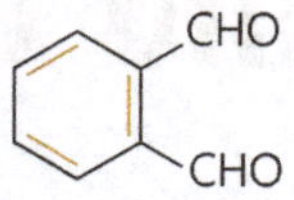	Phthaldehyde	Benzene-1, 2-dicarbaldehyde
Ketones		
$CH_3COCH_2CH_2CH_3$	Methyl *n*-propyl ketone	Pentan-2-one
$(CH_3)_2CHCOCH(CH_3)_2$	Di-*iso*-propyl ketone	2, 4-dimethylpentan-3-one
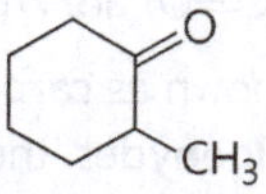	α-methylcyclohexan one	2-methylcyclohexanone
$(CH_3)_2C{=}CHCOCH_3$	Mesityl oxide	4-methylpent -3-en-2-one

Structure of the Carbonyl Group

- The C-atom of carbonyl group is ***sp*²-hybridised** and forms 3σ-bonds and 1π-bond with O-atom. In addition to it, oxygen atom also has two non-bonding electron pairs. Thus, the carbonyl carbon and the three atoms attached to it lie in the same plane and the π-electron cloud lies above and below this plane. The bond angles are approximately 120° which is same as in case of trigonal coplanar structure.

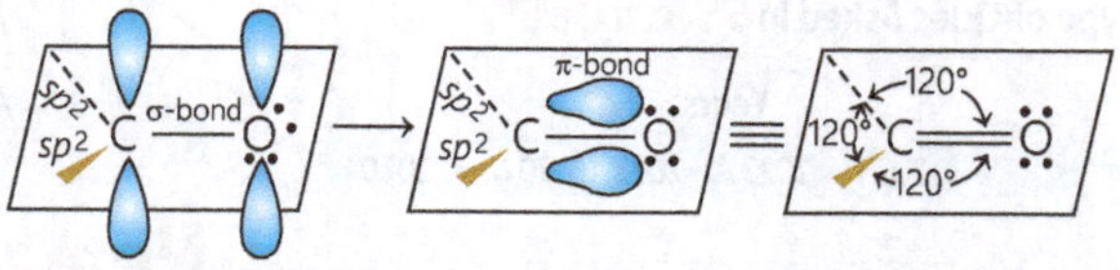

Orbital diagram for the formation of carbonyl group

- The carbon-oxygen bond is polarised due to higher electronegativity of oxygen atom relative to carbon and shows net dipole moment.
- As a result of this, carbon acquires partially positive charge and act as electrophilic centre (Lewis acid), whereas oxygen acquires partially negative charge and act as nucleophilic centre [Lewis base].

$$\underset{(I)}{>C{=}O} \longleftrightarrow \underset{(II)}{>\overset{+}{C}-O^-}$$

Preparation of Aldehydes and Ketones

Some important methods for the preparation of aldehydes and ketones are as follows

Preparation of Aldehydes

Some of the important preparation reactions of aldehydes are as follows

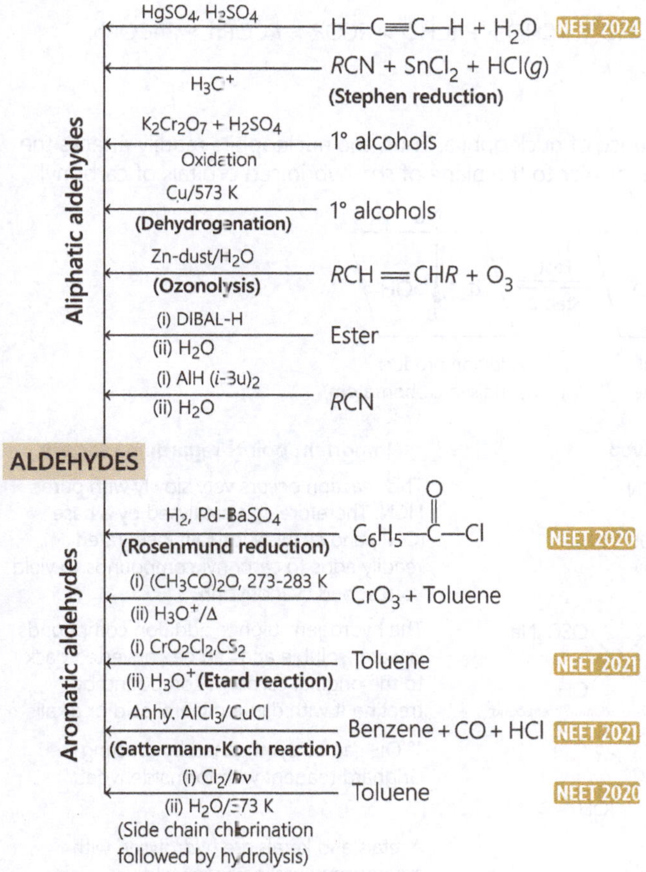

Note • The intermediate formed in the reactions (a) and (b) are

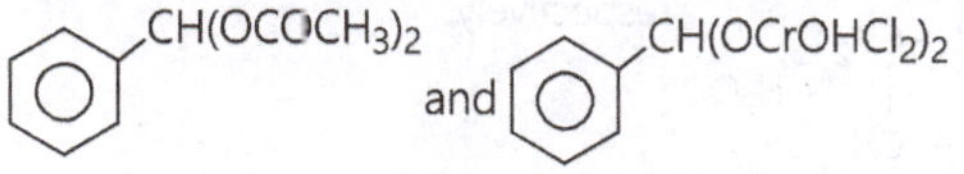

respectively.

- Formaldehyde cannot be prepared by Rosenmund's reaction since formyl chloride is unstable at room temperature.

Preparation of Ketones

Some of the important preparation reactions of ketones are as follows

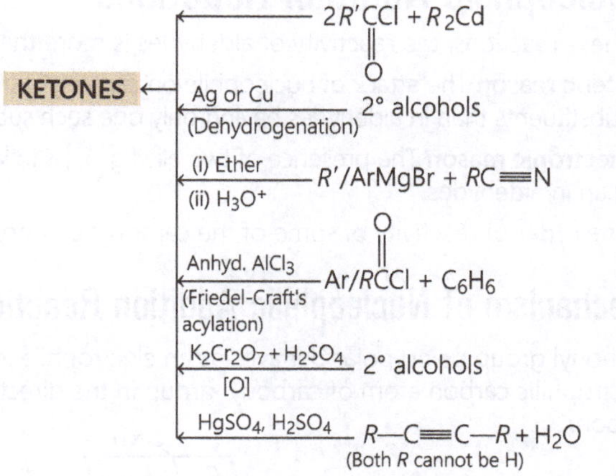

Physical Properties

- **Physical state** Lower member of aldehydes and ketones (upto C_{10}) are **colourless, volatile liquid**, while formaldehyde is a gas at ordinary temperature. Lower ketones have pleasant smell while aldehydes possess sharp pungent odour. As the size of aldehydes, increases the odour becomes less pungent and more fragrant.
- **Boiling points** Boiling points of carbonyl compounds are higher than hydrocarbons and ethers of comparable molecular masses. It is due to weak molecular association in aldehydes and ketones which is arising out of the **dipole-dipole interactions.** NEET 2022

  However, their boiling points are lower than those of corresponding alcohols. It is due to absence of intermolecular hydrogen bonding.
- **Solubility** (upto C_3) Lower members of aldehydes and ketones are soluble in water because they form H-bonding between polar carbonyl group and water as shown.

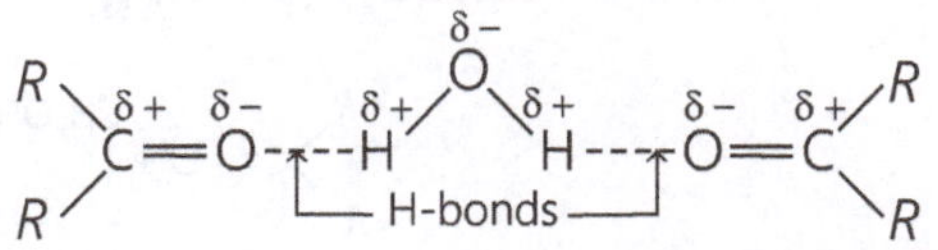

The solubility of aldehydes and ketones decreases rapidly on increase in molecular weight. All aldehydes and ketones are fairly soluble in organic solvents like benzene, ether, etc.

Chemical Reactions

Since, aldehydes and ketones both possess the carbonyl functional group, they undergo nucleophilic addition reactions.

Nucleophilic Addition Reactions

In these reactions, the reactivity of aldehydes is more than that of ketones due to the following reasons.

- **Steric reason** The attack of nucleophile on carbonyl carbon of ketones is hindered by the presence of two relatively large size of substituents than in aldehydes having only one such substituent.
- **Electronic reason** The presence of two alkyl groups in ketones reduce the electrophilicity of carbonyl carbon more effectively than in aldehydes.

  The order of reactivity of some of the carbonyl compounds is HCHO > *R*CHO > PhCHO > *R*CO*R* > *R*COPh > PhCOPh.

Mechanism of Nucleophilic Addition Reactions

Carbonyl group being polar behaves as an electrophile in the presence of nucleophile. Thus, the nucleophile readily attacks the electrophilic carbon atom of carbonyl group in the direction perpendicular to the plane of sp^2-hybridised orbitals of carbonyl carbon.

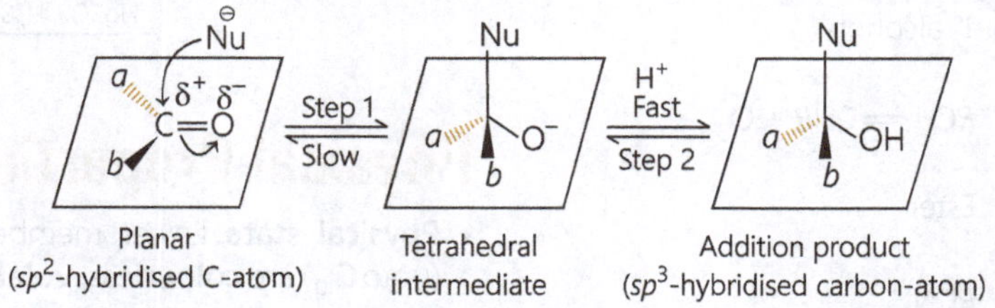

S. No.	Methods	Reaction involved	Important points regarding reaction
1.	Addition of hydrogen cyanide NEET 2023, 2022	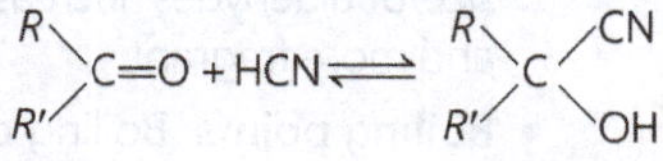 (Cyanohydrin)	This reaction occurs very slowly with pure HCN. Therefore, it is catalysed by a base (OH^-) and cyanide ion CN^- generated readily adds to carbonyl compounds to yield correspond cyanohydrin.
2.	Addition of sodium hydrogen sulphite	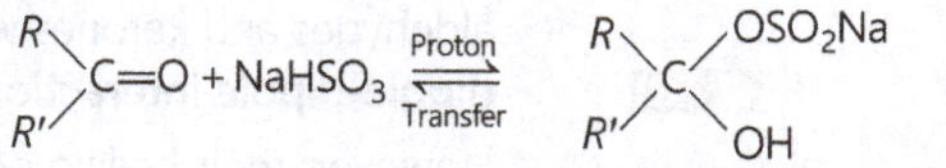 (Bisulphite addition compound)	The hydrogen sulphite addition compounds is water soluble and can be converted back to the original carbonyl compound by treating it with dilute mineral acid or alkali.
3.	Addition of Grignard reagent NEET 2021, 2020	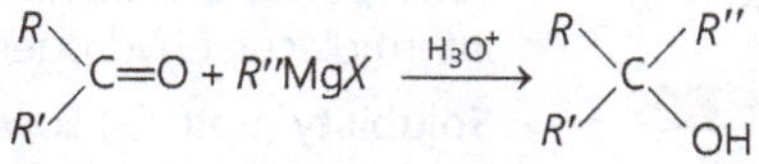	1° OH can be synthesised by reacting the Grignard reagent with formaldehyde.
4.	Addition of alcohols NEET 2022	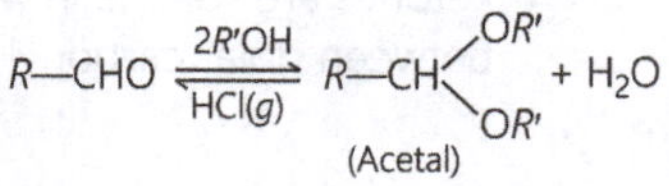 (Acetal) 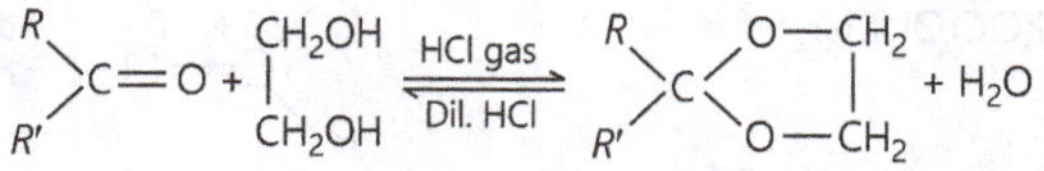 (Ethylene glycol ketal)	Acetals and ketals are hydrolysed with aqueous mineral acids to yield corresponding aldehydes and ketones respectively.

Nucleophilic Addition Elimination Reaction

Aldehydes and ketones react with ammonia and a number of its derivatives, $H_2N—Z$ in weakly acidic medium to form compounds containing $>C=N$ group. These reactions are reversible and catalysed by acid. The equilibrium favours the product formation due to rapid dehydration of the intermediate to form $>C=N—Z$ type compounds.

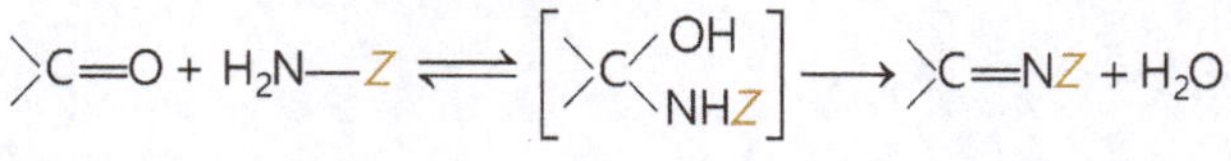

Some N-substituted Derivatives of Aldehydes and Ketones [$>C=N-Z$]

Z	Reagent name	Carbonyl derivative	Product name
—H	Ammonia	$>C=NH$	Imine
—*R*	Amine	$>C=NR$	Substituted imine (Schiff's base)
—OH NEET 2022	Hydroxylamine	$>C=N-OH$	Oxime
$-NH_2$	Hydrazine	$>C=N-NH_2$	Hydrazone
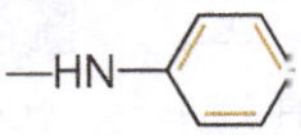	Phenylhydrazine	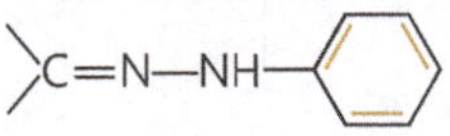	Phenylhydrazone
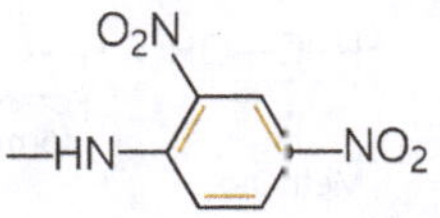	2, 4-dinitrophenylhydrazine	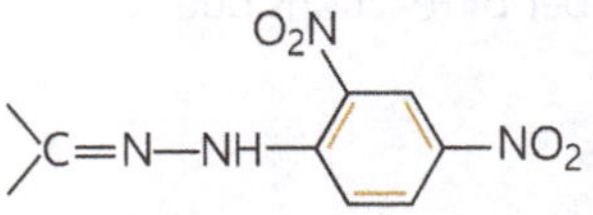	2, 4-dinitrophenylhydrazone
$-NH-\overset{O}{\overset{\|\|}{C}}-NH_2$	Semicarbazide	$>C=N-NH-\overset{O}{\overset{\|\|}{C}}-NH_2$	Semicarbazone

Note 2, 4-DNP-derivatives are yellow, orange or red solids useful for characterisation of aldehydes and ketones.

Reduction and Oxidation

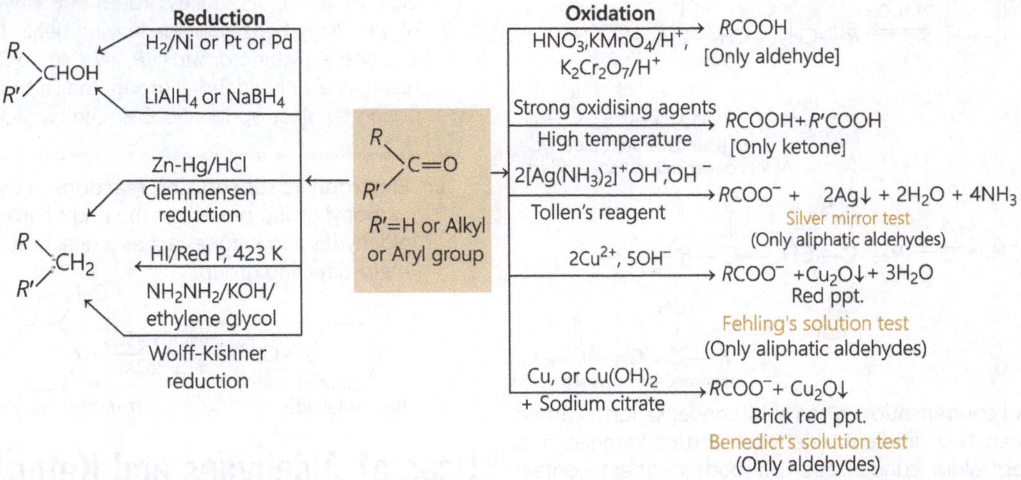

- **Haloform reaction** This test is given by the compounds having CH_3CO- group or $CH_3CH(OH)$ group.

$$NaOH + X_2 \longrightarrow NaX + NaOX + H_2O \ (X = Cl, \ Br, \ I)$$

$$RCOCH_3 + 3\,NaOX \longrightarrow RCO\bar{O}Na^+ + \underset{\text{(Haloform)}}{CHX_3\downarrow} + 2\,NaOH$$

Marks Maximizer

- Usually, ketones does not reduce Tollen's reagent but the ketones present in the form 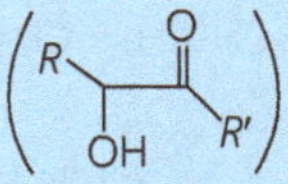 reduces Tollen's reagent. It is due to the oxidation of OH group present in them.
- Distinction between aldehydes of ketones

Tests	Aldehydes	Ketones
Schiff's reagent	Pink colour	No colour
Fehling's solution	Red precipitate	No precipitate
Tollen's reagent	Silver mirror	No silver mirror
2, 4-dinitrophenyl hydrazine	Formation of a yellow, orange or orange-red precipitate	Orange-yellow crystal formed

Reactions due to α-hydrogen

The strong electron withdrawing effect of carbonyl group and resonance stabilisation of the conjugate base are responsible for the **acidity of α-hydrogen atom**.

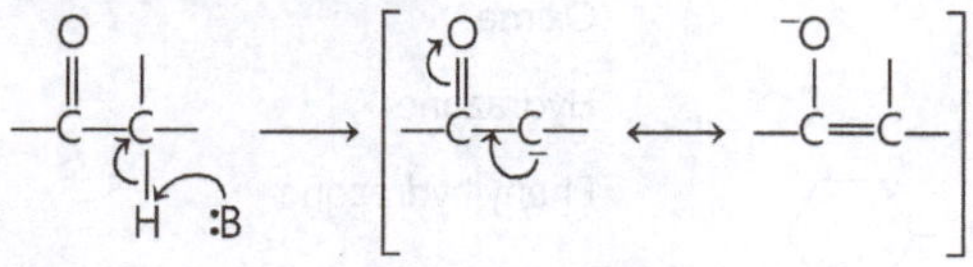

Aldehydes and ketones undergo a number of reactions due to acidic nature of α-hydrogen.

Some important reactions are as follows

(i) **Aldol condensation** Aldehydes and ketones having at least one α-hydrogen undergo a reaction in presence of dilute alkali (catalyst) to form β-hydroxy aldehydes (aldol) or β-hydroxy ketones (ketol) respectively. The aldol and ketol readily lose water to give α,β-unsaturated carbonyl compounds.

For Concept Master Video

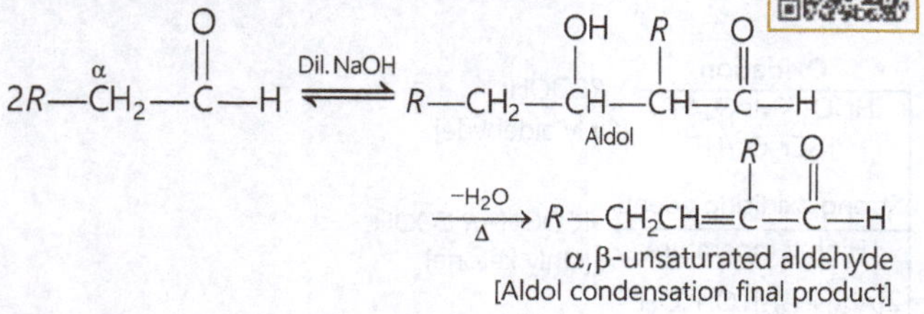

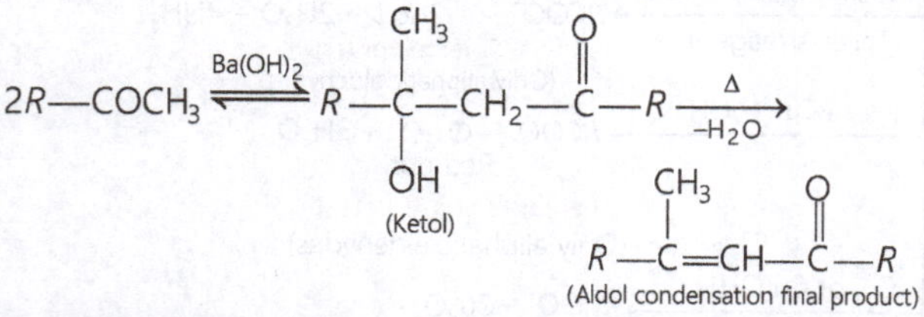

(ii) **Cross aldol condensation** When aldol condensation is carried out between two different aldehydes and/or ketones, it is called cross aldol condensation. If both of them contain α-hydrogen atoms, it gives a mixture of four products. e.g.

NEET 2022, 2020

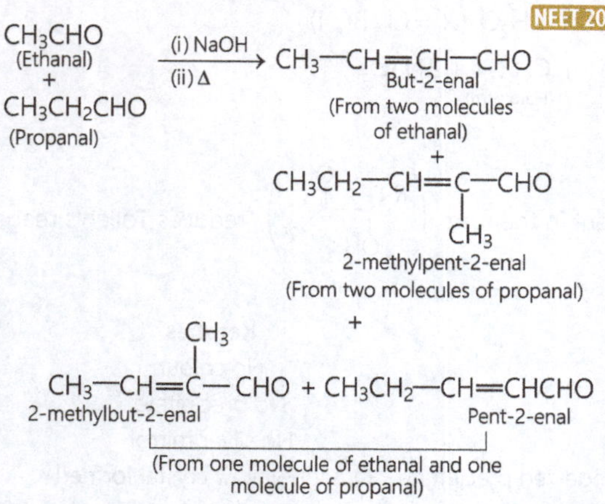

Other Reactions

(i) **Cannizzaro reaction** Those aldehydes which **do not have an α-hydrogen atom** undergo self oxidation and reduction (disproportionation) reaction on heating with concentrated alkali. In this reaction, one molecule of the aldehyde is reduced to alcohol while another is oxidised to carboxylic acid salt.

For Concept Master Video

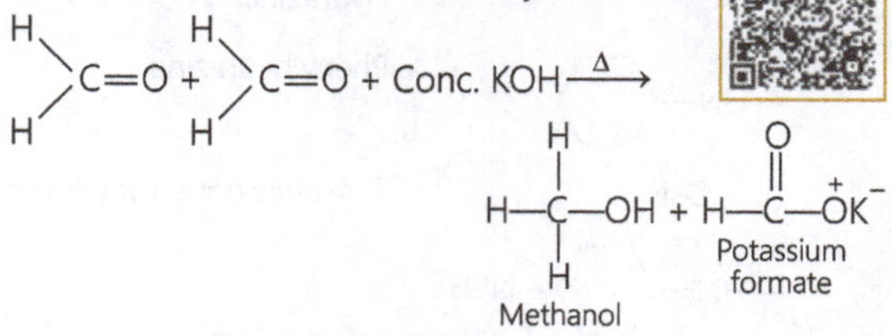

Marks Maximizer

- **Intramolecular Cannizzaro reaction** is given by dialdehydes having no α-hydrogen atoms.
- $HO—C_6H_5—CHO$ does not contain any α-hydrogen but still fails to undergo Cannizzaro reaction. Because in basic medium, OH^- takes proton of the hydroxy group of *p*-hydroxy benzaldehyde leaving behind O^-, which is a strong activating group (+*R*, + *I*). When O^- come in resonance with aldehdye group, the carbonyl carbon is no longer electrophilic. So, OH^- can't attack there.

(ii) **Electrophilic substitution reactions** In these reactions carbonyl group present at the ring of aromatic aldehydes and ketones act as a deactivating and *meta*-directing group.

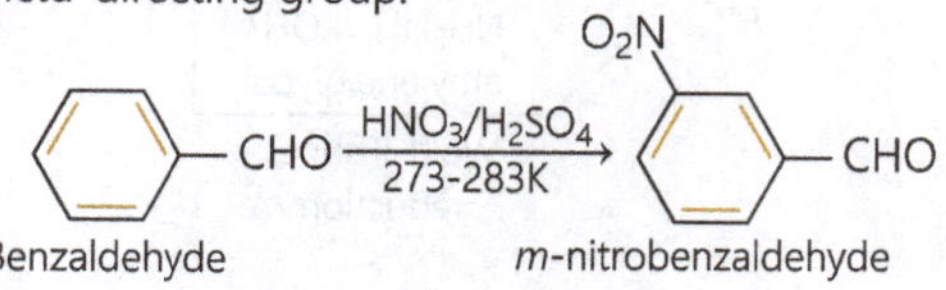

Uses of Aldehydes and Ketones

Some of the important uses of aldehydes and ketones are as follows

- These are used as solvents, starting material and reagent for the synthesis of other organic compounds in chemical industry.
- Formalin (40% solution of formaldehyde) is used to preserve biological specimens.
- Formaldehyde is used to prepare bakelite (a phenol-formaldehyde resin), urea-formaldehyde glues and other polymeric products.
- Acetaldehyde is used as a starting material in the manufacture of acetic acid, ethyl acetate, vinyl acetate, polymers and drugs.
- Benzaldehyde is used in perfumery and in dye industries.

- These are also used to add odours and as flavouring agent, e.g. butyraldehyde, vanillin, acetophenone, camphor etc.

Carboxylic Acids

The carboxyl group consists of a carbonyl group attached to a hydroxyl group. Carbon compounds containing a carboxyl functional group called carboxylic acids.

They may be aliphatic (*R*COOH) or aromatic (ArCOOH) depending on the group, alkyl or aryl, attached to carboxylic carbon.

Some higher members of aliphatic carboxylic acids (C_{12} - C_{18}) known as **fatty acids**.

Nomenclature and Structure of Carboxyl Group

Nomenclature

- The **common name** of carboxylic acids end with the suffix '-ic acid'. These names have been derived from Latin or Greek names of their natural sources (see table).
- In **IUPAC system**, aliphatic carboxylic acids are named by replacing the ending '-e' in the name of the corresponding alkane with '-oic' acid.
- For naming compounds containing more than one carboxyl group, the alkyl chain leaving carboxyl groups is numbered and the number of carboxyl groups are indicated by adding multiplicative prefix (like dicarboxylic, tricarboxylic acid etc.) to the name of parent alkyl chain.

Some of the carboxylic acid along with their common and IUPAC names

Structure	Common name	IUPAC name
HCOOH	Formic acid	Methanoic acid
CH_3COOH	Acetic acid	Ethanoic acid
$(CH_3)_2CHCOOH$	Isobutyric acid	2-methylpropanoic acid
HOOC—COOH	Oxalic acid	Ethanedioic acid
HOOC—CH_2—COOH	Malonic acid	Propanedioic acid
HOOC—$(CH_2)_2$—COOH	Succinic acid	Butanedioic acid
HOOC—$(CH_2)_3$—COOH	Glutaric acid	Pentanedioic acid
HOOC—CH_2—CH(COOH)—CH_2—COOH	Tricarballylic acid or Carballylic acid	Propane-1, 2, 3-tricarboxylic acid
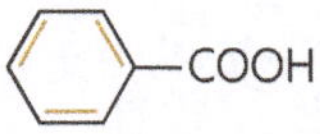	Benzoic acid	Benzenecarboxylic acid (Benzoic acid)
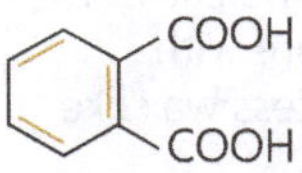	Phthalic acid	Benzene-1, 2-dicarboxylic acid

Structure of Carboxyl Group

In carboxylic acids, the bonds to the carboxyl carbon lie in one plane, these bonds are separated by an angle of about 120°. The carboxylic carbon is less electrophilic than carbonyl carbon because of the possible resonance structure shown below

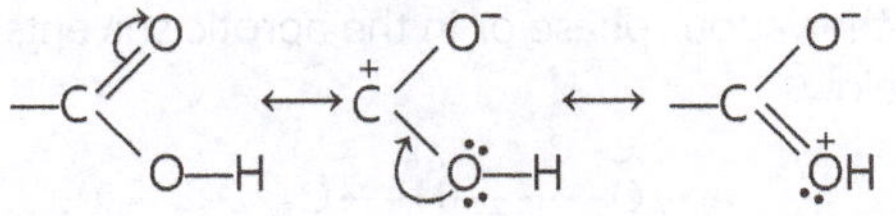

Method of Preparation of Carboxylic Acids

S.No.	Methods	Reactions involved	Important points regarding reaction
1.	From primary alcohol and aldehydes	$\underset{(1°OH)}{RCH_2OH} \xrightarrow[(ii)\,H_3O^+]{(i)\,Alk.\,KMnO_4} RCOOH$ NEET 2019, 2024 $\underset{(1°OH)}{RCH_2OH} \xrightarrow[\text{Jones reagent}]{CrO_3\text{-}H_2SO_4} RCOOH$ $RCHO \xrightarrow[\text{agents}]{\text{Mild oxidising}} RCOOH$	
2.	From alkyl benzene	$C_6H_5—CH_3 \xrightarrow[\Delta]{KMnO_4\text{-}KOH} C_6H_5COOH$	The entire side chain is oxidised to the carboxyl group irrespective of length of the side chain.
3.	From nitriles and amide NEET 2023	$Ar/R—CN \xrightarrow[H_2O]{H^+ \text{ or } OH^-} Ar/R—\overset{O}{\overset{\parallel}{C}}—NH_2 \xrightarrow[\Delta]{H^+ \text{ or } OH^-} Ar/R—COOH$	Mild reaction conditions are used to stop the reaction at the amide stage.
4.	From Grignard reagent NEET 2022	$R—MgX + O{=}C{=}O \xrightarrow[H_3O^+]{\text{Dry ether}} RCOOH$	This method is useful for converting alkyl halide into corresponding carboxylic acids having one carbon atom more than that present in alkyl halides.

S.No.	Methods	Reactions involved	Important points regarding reaction
5.	From acyl halides and anhydrides	$RCOCl \xrightarrow{H_2O} RCOOH + Cl^-$ $\downarrow HO^-/H_2O$ $RCOO^- + Cl^- \xrightarrow{H_3O^+} RCOOH$ $\underset{\text{Acid anhydride}}{(RCO)_2O} \xrightarrow{H_2O} 2RCOOH$ (R = alkyl or aryl group or both)	Acid chlorides when hydrolysed with water give carboxylic acids or more readily with aqueous base to give carboxylate ion which on acidification provide corresponding acids. Anhydride are hydrolysed to corresponding acid(s) with water.
6.	From esters	**Acidic hydrolysis,** $RCOOR' \underset{}{\overset{H_3O^+}{\rightleftharpoons}} RCOOH + R'OH$ **Basic hydrolysis,** $RCOOR' \overset{NaOH}{\rightleftharpoons} RCOONa + R'OH$ $\downarrow H_3O^+$ $RCOOH$ [R, R' = aryl or alkyl group]	Acidic hydrolysis of esters gives directly carboxylic acids while basic hydrolysis gives carboxylates, which on acidification give corresponding carboxylic acids.

Physical Properties

- **Physical state** Aliphatic carboxylic acids upto nine carbon atoms are colourless liquids at room temperature with unpleasant odours. The higher acids are odourless wax like solids and low volatile.
- **Boiling points** Carboxylic acid have higher boiling points as compared to the aldehyde, ketones and alcohols of comparable molecular masses. It is due to the extensive association of their molecules through strong intermolecular hydrogen bonding.
- The H-bond are not broken completely even in the vapour phase. Moreover, most of the carboxylic acids exists as dimer in the vapour phase or in the aprotic solvents as shown below.

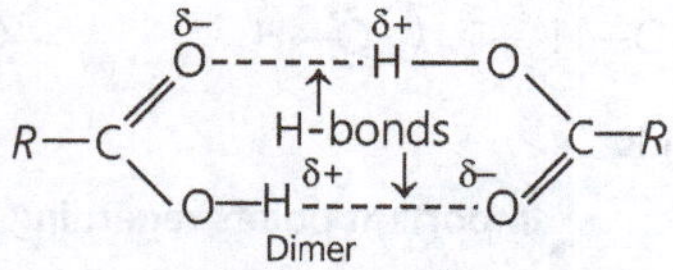

In vapour state or in aprotic solvent

- **Solubility** Simple aliphatic carboxylic acids having upto four carbon atoms are soluble in water. It is due to the formation of the H-bonds with water.

  The solubility decreases with increase in number of C-atoms.
  - Higher carboxylic acids are practically insoluble in water. This is due to the increased hydrophobic interaction of hydrocarbon part.
  - The simplest aromatic carboxylic acid, i.e. benzoic acid is nearly insoluble in cold water.

Chemical Reactions

The reaction of carboxylic acids are classified as follows

I. Reactions Involving Cleavage of O—H Bond

Reactions with Metals and Alkalies

- Like alcohols, carboxylic acids evolve hydrogen with electropositive metals.
- Like phenols, they form salts with alkalies.
- Unlike phenols they react with weaker bases such as carbonates and hydrogen carbonates to evolve CO_2. This reaction is used to detect the presence of —COOH group in an organic compounds.

$$R\text{—}COOH \xrightarrow{2Na} 2RCO\overset{-}{O}\overset{+}{Na} + H_2$$
$$R\text{—}COOH \xrightarrow{NaOH} RCO\overset{-}{O}\overset{+}{Na} + H_2O$$
$$R\text{—}COOH \xrightarrow{NaHCO_3} RCO\overset{-}{O}\overset{+}{Na} + H_2O + CO_2$$

Acidic Strength of Carboxylic Acids

The acidity of the carboxylic group is due to the presence of positive charge on oxygen. As a result of which it can easily liberates the hydronium ion along with carboxylate ion. The carboxylate ion so formed is resonance stabilised.

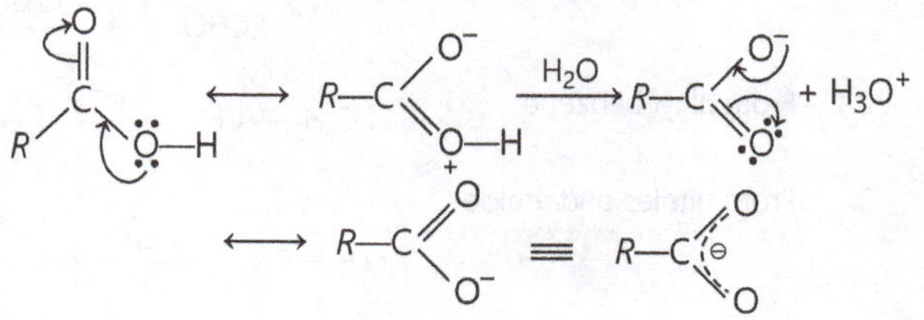

$$K_{eq} = \frac{[RCOO^-][H_3O^+]}{[RCOOH][H_2O]} \text{ or } K_a = K_{eq}[H_2O]$$

$$\Rightarrow \frac{[RCOO^-][H_3O^+]}{[RCOOH]} = K_a$$

where, K_{eq} = Equilibrium constant

K_a = Disscciation constant of acid

- Smaller the numerical value of pK_a, stronger is the carboxylic acid.
- Carboxylic acids are stronger acids than alcohols and many simple phenols but weaker than mineral acids.
- Carboxylic acids are stronger acids than phenols. This is because the carboxylate ion (i.e. conjugate base of carboxylic acid) is stabilised by two equivalent resonance structures.
- In these two resonance structure, the negative charge is delocalised over two more electronegative oxygen atom as shown below.

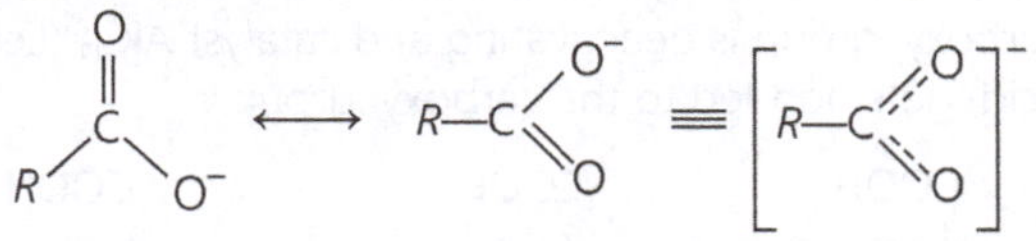

Whereas, phenoxide ion (i.e. conjugate base of phenol) has non-equivalent resonance structure in which the negative charge is less effectively delocalised over one oxygen atom and ess electronegative carbon atoms in phenoxide ion.

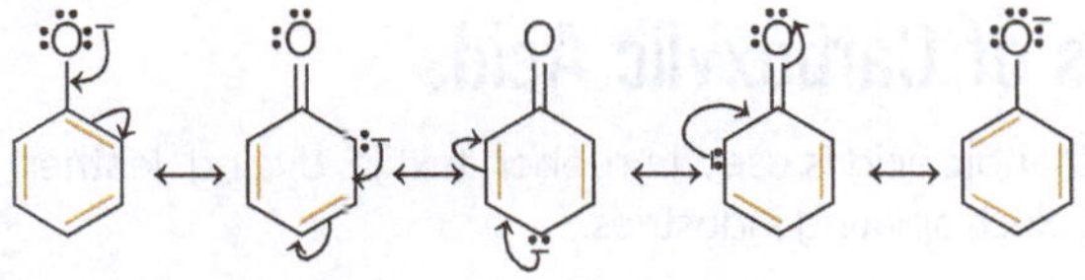

Effect of the different Substituents on the Acidity of Carboxylic Acids

- The presence of the electron withdrawing groups increase the acidity of carboxylic acids, as they stabilises the conjugate base through delocalisation of the negative charge by inductive and/or resonance effects.
- Acidity also increases as the electronegativity of substituents increases.

e.g.

CF_3CH_2COOH (Trifluoroethanoic acid) > Cl_3CH_2COOH (Trichloroethanoic acid)

$HC{\equiv}C{-}COOH$ (Propiolic acic) > CH_3CH_2COOH (Propanoic acid)

- However, the electron donating groups decreases the acidity by destabilising the conjugate base.
- The effect of some groups in increasing acidic order is

$$Ph < I < Br < Cl < F < CN < NO_2 < CF_3.$$

e.g. $CF_3COOH > CCl_3COOH > CHCl_2COOH > NO_2CH_2COOH > NC{-}CH_2COOH > FCH_2COOH > ClCH_2COOH > BrCH_2COOH > HCOOH > ClCH_2CH_2COOH > C_6H_5COOH > C_6H_5CH_2COOH > CH_3COOH > CH_3CH_2COOH$

- Acidity increases with decreasing the distance of EWG from the carboxyl group, whereas it is reverse in case when EDG is attached.
- Electron withdrawing group attached to phenyl ring of aromatic carboxylic acid increases their acidity while electron releasing group decreases their acidity.

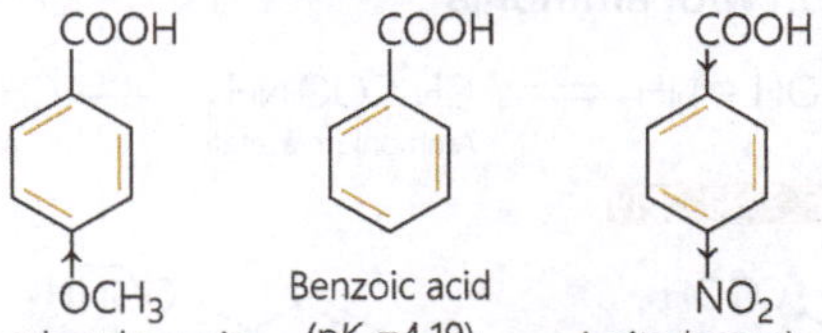

4-methoxybenzoic acid (pK_a=4.46) | Benzoic acid (pK_a=4.19) | 4-nitrobenzoic acid (pK_a=3.41)

II. Reactions Involving Cleavage of C — OH Bond

(i) **Formation of anhydride**

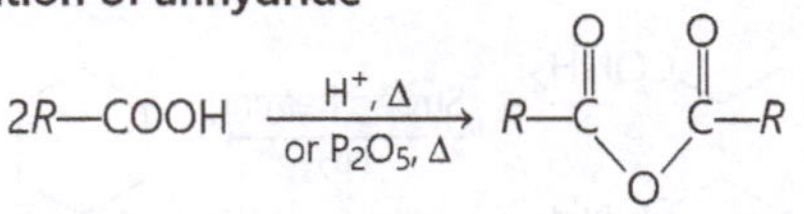

(ii) **Esterification** NEET 2021, 2020

$$RCOOH + R'OH \overset{H^+}{\rightleftharpoons} RCOOR' + H_2O$$

Mechanism of Esterification

This reaction is a kind of nucleophilic acyl substitution. The steps involves are as follows

***Step* I Protonation of carbonyl oxygen**

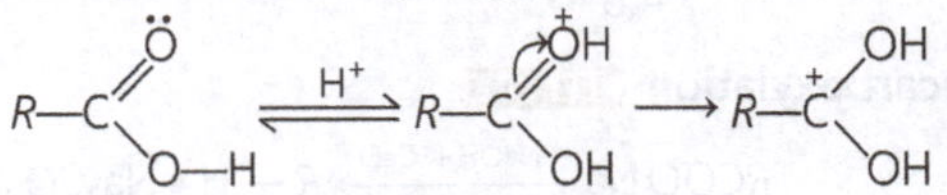

***Step* II Nucleophilic addition of alcohol**

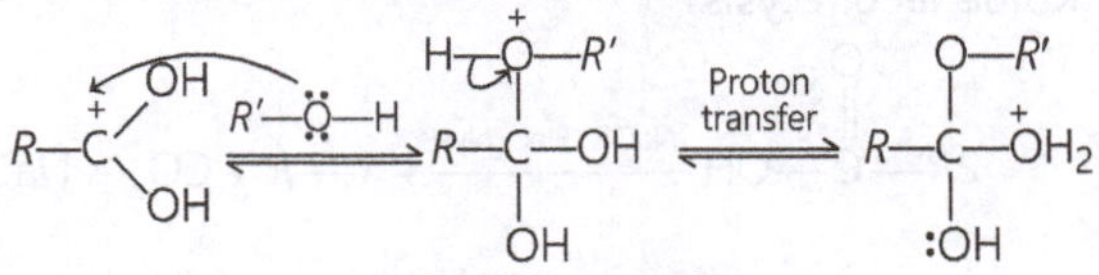

Tetrahedral intermediate

***Step* III Elimination of water molecule**

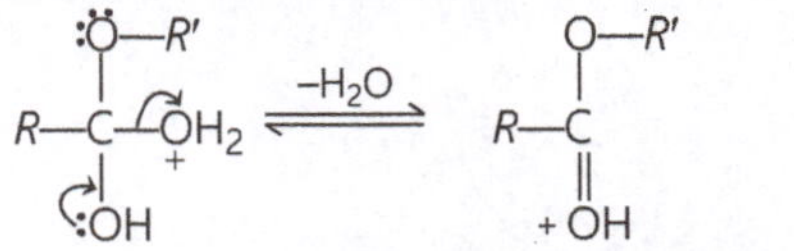

Protonated ester

***Step* IV Protonated ester loses a proton to give ester**

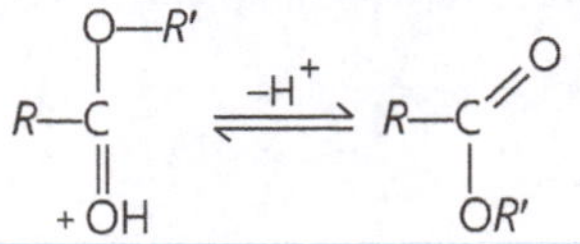

(iii) **Reaction with PCl_5, PCl_3 and $SOCl_2$**

$$R\text{—}COOH \begin{cases} \xrightarrow{PCl_5} RCOCl + POCl_3 + HCl \\ \xrightarrow{PCl_3} 3RCOCl + H_3PO_3 \\ \xrightarrow{SOCl_2} RCOCl + SO_2 + HCl \end{cases}$$

In the formation of acyl chloride from carboxylic acid, thionyl chloride ($SOCl_2$) is preferred because the other two products are gaseous which makes the purification of the products easier.

(iv) **Reaction with ammonia**

$$CH_3COOH + NH_3 \rightleftharpoons \underset{\text{Ammonium acetate}}{CH_3CO\overset{-}{O}\overset{+}{N}H_4} \xrightarrow[-H_2O]{\Delta} \underset{\text{Acetamide}}{CH_3CONH_2}$$

e.g. NEET 2020, 2019

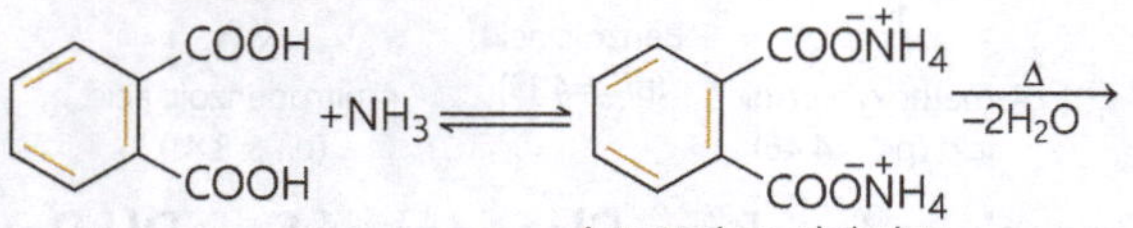

Ammonium phthalate

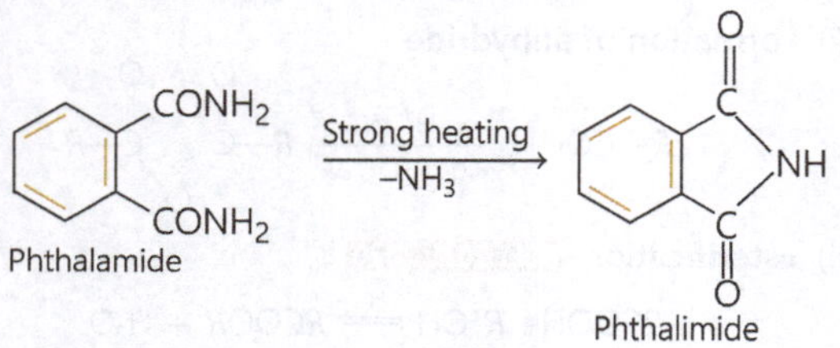

Phthalamide

Phthalimide

III. Reactions Involving —COOH Group

(i) **Reduction**

$$RCOOH \xrightarrow[2.\ H_3O^+]{1.\ LiAlH_4/\text{ether or } B_2H_6} RCH_2OH$$

(ii) **Decarboxylation** NEET 2023

$$RCO\overset{-}{O}\overset{+}{N}a \xrightarrow[\text{Heat}]{NaOH + CaO} R\text{—}H + Na_2CO_3$$

(iii) **Kolbe electrolysis**

$$2R\text{—}\overset{\overset{\large O}{\|}}{C}\text{—}OH \xrightarrow{\text{NaOH, Electrolysis}} R\text{—}R + CO_2 + NaOH$$

IV. Substitution Reactions in the Hydrocarbon Part

(i) **Hell-Volhard Zelinsky reaction** Carboxylic acids having an α-hydrogen are halogenated at the α-position on treatment with chlorine or bromine in the presence of small amount of red phosphorus to give α-halocarboxylic acids. NEET 2021

$$RCH_2COOH \xrightarrow[2.\ H_2O]{1.\ X_2/\text{Red P}} R\text{—}\underset{\underset{X}{|}}{C}HCOOH$$

(X=Cl, Br)

(ii) **Ring substitution** Aromatic carboxylic acids undergo electrophilic substitution reactions in which the carboxyl group acts as a **deactivating** and ***meta*-directing group.**

They do not undergo Friedel-Craft's reaction because carboxyl group is deactivating and catalyst $AlCl_3$ (Lewis acid) gets bonded to the carboxyl group.

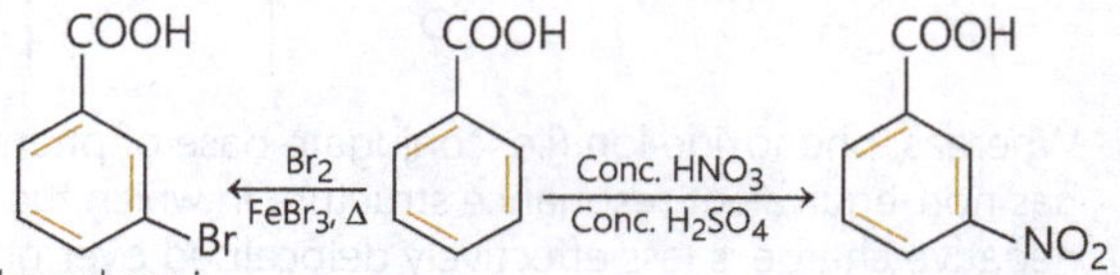

m-bromobenzoic acid

m-nitrobenzoic acid

Uses of Carboxylic Acids

- Methanoic acid is used in rubber, textile, dyeing, leather and electroplating industries.
- Ethanoic acid is used as a solvent, hexanedioic acid is used in the manufacture of nylon-6, 6.
- Sodium benzoate is used as a food preservative.
- Ester of benzoic acid are used in perfumery.
- Higher fatty acids are used for the manufacture of soaps and detergents.

Marks Maximizer

- $LiAlH_4$ *vs* $NaBH_4$

Characteristics	$LiAlH_4$	$NaBH_4$
Molar mass	37.95 g/mol	37.83 g/mol
Reducing power	A strong reducing agent that can reduce many compounds such as esters, amides, acids, aldehydes, ketones, nitro compounds etc.	A mild reducing agent that can reduce aldehydes and ketones, acyl chlorides but not esters, amides and acids.
Reaction with α, β-unsaturated aldehydes and ketones	It reduces only C=O group.	It reduces both C=O and C=C group.
Reaction with water	Reacts violently with water.	It gets dissolved in water slowly.

- Distinction test between phenol and carboxylic acid

Test	Phenol	Carboxylic acid
$NaHCO_3$ test	No reaction	Brisk effervescence of CO_2 gas
$FeCl_3$ test	Violet colour	Buff coloured ppt.

- Abnormal behaviour of formic acid :
  - It is due to the presence of aldehydic group.

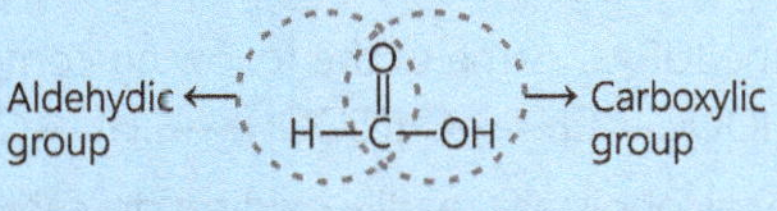

  - Formic acid reduces Tollen's reagent and Fehling solution like, aldehydes.
- Reduces mercuric chloride to mercurous chloride which is further converted to grey precipitate of mercury.

$$HCOOH + 2HgCl_2 \longrightarrow CO_2 + Hg_2Cl_2 \downarrow + 2HCl$$
$$HCOOH + Hg_2Cl_2 \longrightarrow CO_2 + 2Hg \downarrow + 2HCl$$

- Its boiling point is 373.8 K which is very near to that of H_2O, i.e. 373 K.

Caution Points

- Ketones have slightly higher boiling points in comparison to isomeric aldehydes.
- It is possible to stop the oxidation at the aldehyde stage with suitable reagents such as chromyl chloride and chromic oxide.
- Aromatic aldehyde do not give to Fehling's test.
- Sodium borohydride does not reduce the carboxyl group.
- Since, formyl chloride is unstable at room temperature, thus formaldehyde cannot be prepared by Rosenmund's reaction.
- P_2O_5 is dehydrating agent, thus upon heating it removes water from $—CONH_2$ to form cyanide group.

PYQ Notes

1. Salicylic acid on reacting with $CH_3OH / H^+, \Delta$ gives methyl -2- hydroxy benzoate, while on reacting with $(CH_3CO)_2O / H^+$ gives aspirin. **JEE Main 2023**
2. 3-methyl -2-cyclohexenone on reacting with MeMgBr / CuI followed by *n*-propyl iodide to give 3, 3-dimethyl -2- propylcyclohexanone as final product. **JEE Main 2023**
3. In keto-enol tautomerism, a carbonyl compound with a hydrogen atom on its alpha-carbon rapidly equilibrates with its corresponding enol. **NEET 2016**

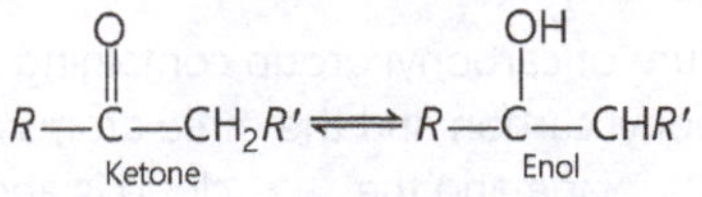

It is the basis of aldol condensation.

4. In presence of Pd-catalyst, selective reduction α,β-unsaturated carbonyl is observed as hydrogenation takes places at carbon-carbon double bond only. **NEET 2016**

e.g.

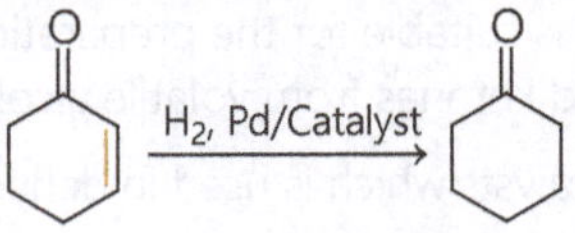

5. Primary alcohol on reacting with PCC gives aldehyde and secondary alcohol gives ketone. **NEET 2019**
6. Treatment of cyclopentanone with methyl lithium gives lithium cyclopentanoyl anion and methane. **NEET 2015**

Step by Step

Mastering NCERT

- Concept Builders
- Topical Questions
- Assertion-Reason
- Statement Type
- Matching Type
- Numerical Value
- NCERT Exemplar's
- Past Exams'
- Skill Boosters

Concept Builders

1 In aldehydes, the carbonyl group is bonded to two carbon atoms whereas in ketones, the carbonyl is bonded to a carbon and one or more hydrogen atoms. [T/F]

2 Ester and anhydrides are derivatives of ....

3 Name the ketone which is used as solvent to prepare materials like adhesives, paints, resins, perfumes, plastics, fabrics etc.

4 The simplest aromatic aldehyde carrying $\mathrm{H}\underset{\underset{\mathrm{O}}{\|}}{\mathrm{C}}—$ group on a benzene ring is benzene carbaldehyde. [T/F]

5 Alkyl phenyl ketones are usually named by adding the name of .... as prefix to the word phenone.

6 Write the common name of the compound. $CH_2{=}CHCHO$

7 In structure of carbonyl group containing compounds, the carbonyl carbon and the three atoms attached to it lie on .... plane and the .... cloud is above and below this plane.

8 The carbon-oxygen double bond is polarised due to higher electronegativity of oxygen relative to carbon. [T/F]

9 .... method is suitable for the preparation of aldehydes and ketones from volatile alcohols.

10 Name the catalysts which is used in dehydrogenation of alcohols.

11 Addition of water to ethyne in the presence of H_2SO_4 and $HgSO_4$ gives ketones. [T/F]

12 Nitriles are selectively reduced by .... to imines followed by hydrolysis to ....

13 Name the reagent which is used in Etard reaction.

14 Side chain chlorination of toluene gives benzal chloride, which on hydrolysis gives benzaldehyde. [T/F]

15 Name the carbonyl compound which is used for preserving biological specimens.

16 The solubility of aldehydes and ketones .... rapidly on increasing the length of alkyl chain.

17 Ketones are generally more reactive than aldehydes in nucleophilic addition reactions due to steric and electronic reasons. [T/F]

18 The reduction in which the carbonyl group of aldehydes and ketones is reduced to CH_2 group on treatment with Zn—Hg and conc. HCl.

19 The name aldol is derived from the names of the two functional groups .... and .... present in the products.

20 Name the reaction, in which one molecule of the aldehyde is reduced to alcohol while another is oxidised to carboxylic acid salt.

21 Some lower members of aliphatic carboxylic acids known as fatty acids. [T/F]

22 .... was first obtained from red ants and .... obtained from rancid butter.

23 Write the IUPAC name of the following compound.

$$HOOC—CH_2—CH(COOH)—CH_2—COOH$$

24 Primary alcohols are readily oxidised to carboxylic acids with chromium trioxide in basic medium. [T/F]

25 Tertiary alkyl benzenes undergo vigorous oxidation to give carboxylic acids. [T/F]

26 The solubility of carboxylic acids decreases with increase the number of carbon atom. [T/F]

27 Name the simplest aromatic carboxylic acid which is nearly insoluble in cold water.

28 Direct attachment of groups such as phenyl or vinyl to the carboxylic acid, ... the acidity of corresponding carboxylic acid.

29 Diborane does not reduce the carboxylic acid to primary alcohol. [T/F]

30 Name a carboxylic acid which is used in the manufacture of nylon-6, 6.

Topical Questions

Nomenclature and Structure of Carbonyl Group

1 When the aldehyde group is attached to a non-aromatic ring, which of the following suffix is added after the full name of the cycloalkane? **NCERT Pg 229**
(a) Aldehyde (b) Carbaldehyde
(c) Carboxyaldehyde (d) Cycloaldehyde

2 Write IUPAC name of the following **NCERT Pg 229**

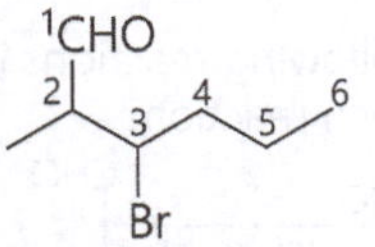

(a) 2-bromo-2-ethyl hexanal
(b) 3-bromo-2-methyl hexanal
(c) 2-methyl-3-bromo hexanal
(d) 3-bromo-2-formyl hexane

3 IUPAC names of $H_3C—CH_2—\underset{\underset{O}{\|}}{C}—CH_2—CHO$ (I)

and $OHC—CH_2—\underset{\underset{CHO}{|}}{CH}—CH_2—CHO$ (II)

respectively are **NCERT Pg 230**

	I	II
(a)	3-onepentanal	β-aldehydepentan-1,2-dial
(b)	3-onepentanal	Pentane-1,2,3-tricarbaldehyde
(c)	3-oxopentanal	Propane-1,2,3-tricarbaldehyde
(d)	3-oxopentanal	Pentane-1,2,3-tricarbaldehyde

4 Which of the following names of the organic compounds is not correctly matched? **NCERT Pg 230**

(a) 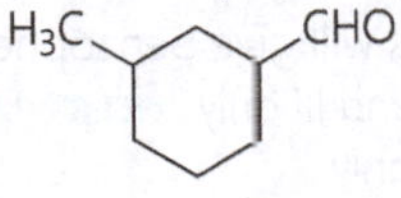

→ 2-methylcyclohexanecarbaldehyde

(b) $OHC—CH_2—\underset{\underset{CHO}{|}}{CH}—CH_2—CHO$ → Propane-1, 2, 3-tricarbaldehyde

(c) $CH_3—\underset{\overset{|}{CH_3}}{CH}—\overset{\overset{O}{\|}}{C}—\underset{\overset{|}{CH_3}}{CH}—CH_3$ → 2, 4-dimethylpentan-3-one

(d) $(CH_3)_2CHCHO$ → Isobutyraldehyde

5 What is the IUFAC names of mesityl oxide and acrolein respectively? **NCERT Pg 230**
(a) Pentan-2-one, Pentanal
(b) 2, 4-dimethyl pentan-3-one, 2-methoxypropanal
(c) 4-methylpent-3-en-2-one, prop-2-enal
(d) 2-methylcyclohexanone, prop-2-enal

6 The bond angle and structure of carbonyl compounds respectively are **NCERT Pg 231**
(a) 120° and trigonal planar
(b) 109°28′ and tetrahedral
(c) 120° and tetrahedral
(d) 109°28′ and trigonal planar

7 The most polar compound among the given carbonyl compounds is **NCERT Pg 231**
(a) propanone (b) formaldehyde
(c) propanal (d) hexan-3-one

8 Choose the incorrect statements regarding carbonyl group. **NCERT Pg 231**
I. Carbonyl carbon atom is sp^3-hybridised.
II. The carbonyl carbon and three atoms attached to it lie perpendicular to the plane.
III. The bond angle is 120° approx.
IV. The carbon-oxygen bond is polarised.
Choose the correct answer from the options given below :
(a) I and II (b) I and III
(c) II and IV (d) I and IV

Preparation of Aldehydes and Ketones

9 Alcohol vapours are passed over which of the following catalysts to give aldehydes and ketones? **NCERT Pg 231**
(a) S or Pd (b) Ag or Cu
(c) F or Cl (d) Li or K

10 During the ozonolysis of organic compound *X* formaldehyde is formed as one of the product. This shows that **NCERT Pg 231**
(a) an acetylenic triple bonds is present
(b) two ethylenic double bonds are present
(c) a vinyl group is present
(d) an acetylenic triple bonds is present

11 On ozonolysis, which of the following compound will give 5-keto-2-methyl hexanal? **NCERT Pg 231**

(a) 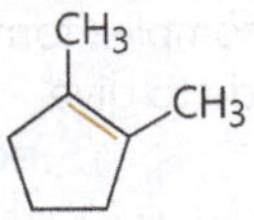

(b) 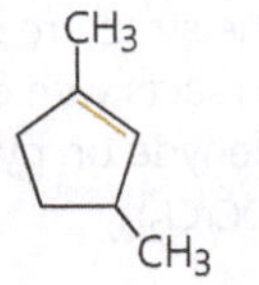

(c) 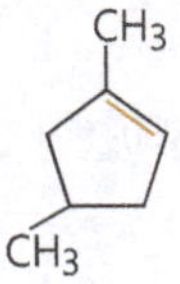

(d) 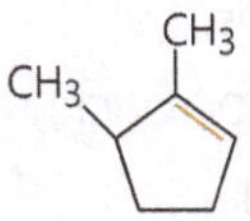

12 Consider the following.

$$\text{Ethyne} + H_2O \xrightarrow[H_2SO_4]{HgSO_4}$$

Product formed in the given reaction is **NCERT Pg 232**

(a) benzaldehyde (b) acetaldehyde
(c) ethanoic acid (d) ethanoyl chloride

13 Acetone can be prepared by **NCERT Pg 232**

(a) treating ethyne with iodine and NaOH
(b) boiling propyne with mercuric sulphate and dilute H_2SO_4 at 333 K
(c) passing a mixture of propane and ethanol over a catalyst zinc chromite
(d) passing a mixture of ethyne and steam over a catalyst, magnesium at 420°C

14 Consider the following reaction.

$$R-\overset{\overset{O}{\|}}{C}-Cl \xrightarrow[Pd/BaSO_4]{H_2} P$$

Here, P is **NCERT Pg 232**

(a) $RCHO$ (b) RCH_3
(c) $RCOOH$ (d) RCH_2OH

15 The reaction,

$$RCN + SnCl_2 + HCl \longrightarrow RCH{=}NH \xrightarrow{H_3O^+} RCHO$$

is known as **NCERT Pg 232**

(a) Etard reaction (b) Haloform reaction
(c) Gattermann-Koch reaction (d) Stephen reaction

16 The major product of following reaction is

$$R-C{\equiv}N \xrightarrow[\text{(ii)}\, H_2O]{\text{(i)}\, AlH(i\text{-}Bu)_2} ?$$

NCERT Pg 232

(a) $RCHO$ (b) $RCONH_2$
(c) $RCOOH$ (d) RCH_2NH_2

17 Which of the following substrates give the same product on the reduction with DIBAL-H? **NCERT Pg 232**

(a) $CH_3-(CH_2)_9-CN$ and $CH_3(CH_2)_9-COOH$
(b) $CH_3-(CH_2)_9-CN$ and $CH_3(CH_2)_9-COOC_2H_5$
(c) $CH_3-(CH_2)_9-COOH$ and $CH_3(CH_2)_9-CHO$
(d) $CH_3(CH_2)_9-COOH$ and $CH_3(CH_2)_9COOC_2H_5$

18 Select the structure of chromium complex formed when toluene reacts with chromyl chloride to give benzaldehyde on hydrolysis. **NCERT Pg 233**

(a) $C_6H_5-CH(OCrCl_2)_2$ (b) $C_6H_5-CH_2(OCrOHCl_2)$
(c) $C_6H_5-CH(OCrOHCl_2)_2$ (d) $C_6H_5-CH(OCrOH_2Cl)_2$

19 Consider the following reaction. **NCERT Pg 233**

$$C_6H_5-CH_3 \xrightarrow{Cl_2/h\nu} \text{'X'} \xrightarrow[373\,K]{H_2O} \text{'Y'}$$

Here 'X' and 'Y' respectively are

(a) $C_6H_5-CH_2Cl$, C_6H_5-COOH (b) $C_6H_5-CHCl_2$, C_6H_5-CHO
(c) $C_6H_5-CH_2Cl$, C_6H_5-CHO (d) $C_6H_5-CHCl_2$, C_6H_5-COOH

20 Which of the following reactions is called Gattermann-Koch reaction? **NCERT Pg 233**

(a) $C_6H_6 \xrightarrow[\text{Anhyd. } AlCl_3/CuCl]{CO,\, HCl} C_6H_5-CHO$

(b) $C_6H_5-CH_3 \xrightarrow{Cl_2/h\nu} C_6H_5-CHCl_2 \xrightarrow[373\,K]{H_2O} C_6H_5-CHO$

(c) $C_6H_5-CH_3 + CrO_3 + (CH_3CO)_2O \xrightarrow{273\text{-}278\,K} C_6H_5-CH(OCOCH_3)_2 \xrightarrow[\Delta]{H_3O} C_6H_5-CHO$

(d) $C_6H_5-CH_3 + CrO_2Cl_2 \xrightarrow{CS_2} C_6H_5-CH(OCrOHCl_2)_2 \xrightarrow{H_3O^+} C_6H_5-CHO$

21 Consider the following reactions.

I. Benzoyl chloride + Diphenyl cadmium.
II. Benzoyl chloride + Benzene + Anhydrous $AlCl_3$.
III. Benzonitrile + Phenyl magnesium bromide + Ether, H_3O^+

Which of the above reactions will give benzophenone?

(a) II, and III (b) I and III only **NCERT Pg 233, 234**
(c) I, II and III (d) I only

22 Which of the following reactions is not correct regarding the preparation of ketone? **NCERT Pg 232, 233, 234**

(a) Treatment of acyl chlorides with dialkyl cadmium, prepared by the reaction of cadmium chloride with Grignard reagent, gives ketones.
(b) When benzene or substituted benzene is treated with acid chloride in the presence of anhydrous aluminium chloride, it gives the corresponding ketone. This reaction is known as Friedel-Crafts acylation reaction.
(c) Treating a nitrile with Grignard reagent followed by hydrolysis yields a ketone.
(d) Treatment of acyl chlorides with H_2, Pd-$BaSO_4$ gives ketones.

Properties and Uses of Aldehydes and Ketones

23 Arrange the following compounds in the increasing order of their boiling points.

$CH_3CH_2CH_2CHO$ (I), $CH_3CH_2CH_2CH_2OH$ (II),

$H_5C_2O - C_2H_5$ (III), $CH_3CH_2CH_2CH_2CH_3$ (IV)

NCERT Pg 235

(a) IV < I < II < III (b) IV < III < II < I

(c) IV < III < I < II (d) IV < II < III < I

24 Which of the following is the correct increasing order of the reactivity towards nucleophilic addition reactions? NCERT Pg 236

(a) Ethanal < Propanal < Propanone < Butanone

(b) Propanal < Ethanal < Propanone < Butanone

(c) Propanone < Butanone < Propanal < Ethanal

(d) Butanone < Propanone < Propanal < Ethanal

25 Study the mechanism given below carefully.

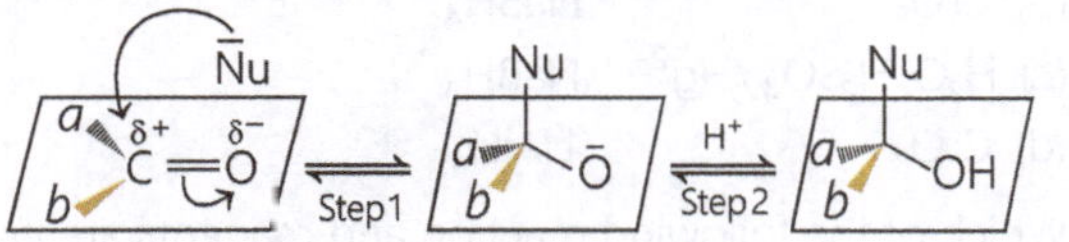

Select the incorrect statement for the above diagram from the options given below. NCERT Pg 236

(a) A nucleophile attacks the electrophilic carbon of the polar carbonyl group from a direction approximately perpendicular to the plane of sp^2-hybridised orbitals of carbonyl carbon.

(b) The hybridisation of carbon changes from *sp* to sp^2 in this process.

(c) The net result is the addition of $Nu^{\ominus}$ and $H^{\oplus}$ across the carbon oxygen double bond.

(d) The rate determining step is step 1 (i.e. addition of $Nu^{\ominus}$).

26 Which of the following reaction can be used to get purified form of acetone? NCERT Pg 237

(a) $CH_3COCH_3 + HCN \xrightarrow{H_3O^+} CH_3COCH_3$

(b) $CH_3COCH_3 + HCl \xrightarrow{\Delta} CH_3COCH_3$

(c) $CH_3COCH_3 + NaHSO_3 \xrightarrow{Na_2CO_3} CH_3COCH_3$

(d) $CH_3COCH_3 + H_2SO_4 \xrightarrow{\Delta} CH_3COCH_3$

27 Consider the reaction given below.

$$R\text{—}CHO \underset{\text{HCl gas}}{\overset{R'OH}{\rightleftharpoons}} \text{I} \underset{H^+}{\overset{R'OH}{\rightleftharpoons}} \text{II} + H_2O$$

Identify the I and II in the given reaction. NCERT Pg 237

	I	II
(a)	Acetal or *gem*-dialkoxy	Hemiacetal or alkoxyalcohol
(b)	Acetal or alkoxy alcohol	Hemiacetal or *gem*-dialkoxy compound
(c)	Hemiacetal or alkoxy alcohol	Acetal or *gem*-dialkoxy compound
(d)	Hemiacetal or *gem*-dialkoxy	Acetal or alkoxy alcohol

28 The addition of sodium hydrogen sulphite to carbonyl compounds is an example of NCERT Pg 237

(a) nucleophilic addition reaction

(b) nucleophilic substitution reaction

(c) electrophilic addition reaction

(d) elimination addition reaction

29 Choose the correct reaction among the given options in which nucleophilic addition followed by elimination reaction occur respectively with the carbonyl compound. NCERT Pg 238

(a) Addition of Grignard reagent

(b) Addition of sodium sulphide

(c) Addition of HCN

(d) Addition of NH_3

30 Which of the following is not correctly matched? NCERT Pg 238

	Carbonyl derivative	Product name
(a)	$>C{=}NH$	Imine
(b)	$>C{=}N\text{—}NH\text{—}Ph$	Phenylhydrazone
(c)	$>C{=}N\text{—}NH\text{—}\overset{O}{\overset{\Vert}{C}}\text{—}NH_2$	Carbazone
(d)	$>C{=}NR$	Schiff's base

31 For the reaction,

$CH_3CH{=}CH\text{—}CHO + \text{semicarbazide} \xrightarrow{H^+} X$

The product formed *X* is NCERT Pg 238

(a) $CH_3CH{=}CH\text{—}\overset{OH}{\overset{|}{C}H}\text{—}NHCONHNH_2$

(b) $CH_3CH{=}CH\text{—}\underset{OH}{\underset{|}{C}H}\text{—}NHCOCH{=}NNH_2$

(c) $CH_3\text{—}CH{=}NCONH_2$

(d) $CH_3CH{=}CH\text{—}CH{=}N\text{—}NH\text{—}\overset{O}{\overset{\Vert}{C}}\text{—}NH_2$

32 Consider the reaction given below,

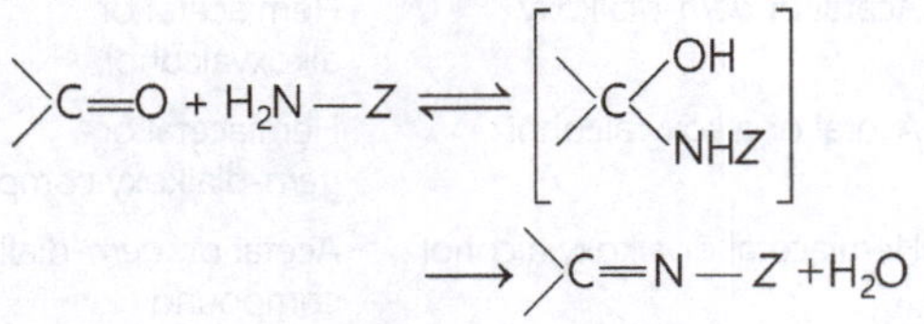

Which of the following statements is not correct about the above reaction? **NCERT Pg 238**

(a) $H_2N—Z$ add to the carbon of carbonyl group of aldehydes and ketones.
(b) The reaction is reversible and catalysed by acid.
(c) The equilibrium favours the product formation.
(d) The reaction is due to α-hydrogens.

33 Consider the reaction given below.

$$CH_2{=}CH—CHO \longrightarrow CH_2{=}CH—CH_2—OH$$

Which of the following is the suitable reagent for the conversion of following reaction? **NCERT Pg 238**

(a) $NaBH_4$
(b) $K_2Cr_2O_7$
(c) Zn—Hg / HCl
(d) Red P + HI

34

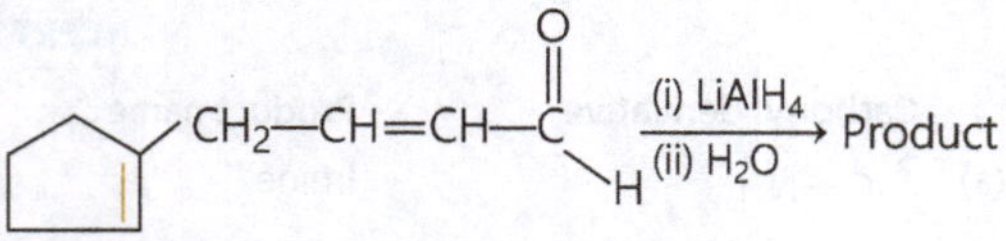

Product of the reaction will be **NEET Pg 238**

(a) 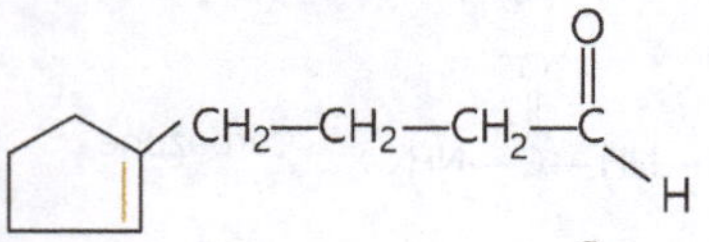

(b) 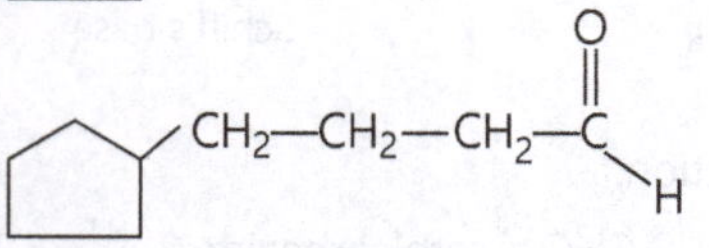

(c) 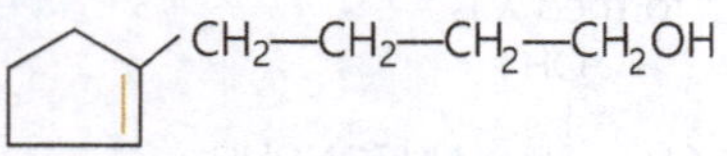

(d) 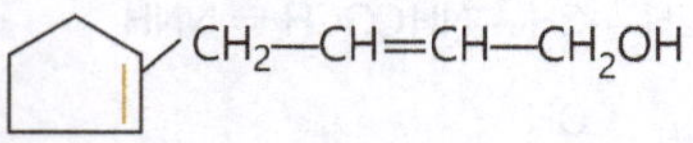

35 The major product of the following reaction is

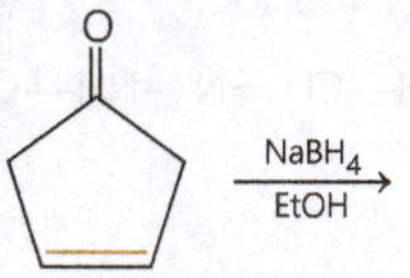

NCERT Pg 238

(a) 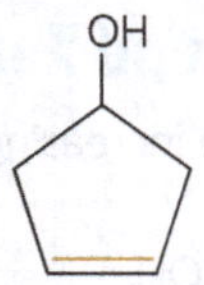
(b) 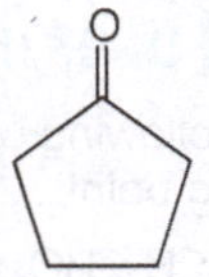

(c) 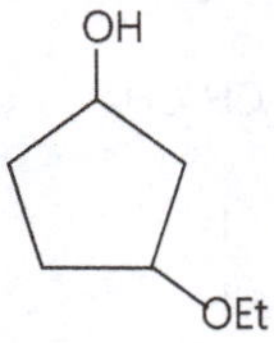
(d) 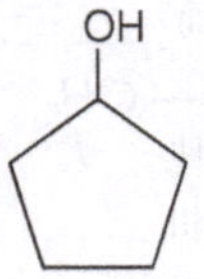

36 Identify X and Y in the given reaction sequence.

$$CH_3—C{\equiv}CH \xrightarrow{X} CH_3—\overset{O}{\overset{\|}{C}}—CH_3 \xrightarrow{Y} CH_3—\overset{OH}{\overset{|}{C}H}—CH_3$$

NCERT Pg 232, 238

	X	Y
(a)	$H_2O, H_2SO_4/Hg^{2+}$	CrO_3
(b)	CrO_3	$NaBH_4$
(c)	$H_2O, H_2SO_4/Hg^{2+}$	$NaBH_4$
(d)	CrO_3	$LiAlH_4$

37 Which of the following reaction and reagents are not correctly matched? **NCERT Pg 238**

(a) $CH_3CH{=}CHCHO \longrightarrow CH_3CH{=}CHCH_2OH$; H_2/Pt
(b) $R—CHO \longrightarrow R—CH_2OH$; $NaBH_4$
(c) $CH_3CH_2COCl \longrightarrow CH_3CH_2CHO$; $H_2, Pd/BaSO_4$
(d) $CH_3CH{=}CHCHO \longrightarrow CH_3CH{=}CHCOOH$; Tollen's reagent

38 When aldehydes and ketones are reacted with Zn—Hg and conc. HCl, hydrocarbons are formed. The reaction is called as **NCERT Pg 239**

(a) Wolff-Kishner reduction (b) Clemmensen reduction
(c) Rosenmund reduction (d) Cannizzaro reaction

39 The correct sequence to convert acetyldehyde to acetone is **NCERT Pg 239**

(a) EtMgBr, H_2O, oxidation
(b) oxidation, $Ca(OH)_2$, heat
(c) reduction, KCN, hydrolysis
(d) oxidation, EtONa, heat

40 Composition of Fehling's solution A and Fehling's solution B is **NCERT Pg 239**

(a) an aqueous copper sulphate and alkaline sodium potassium tartarate (Rochelle salt) respectively
(b) an alkaline sodium potassium tartarate (Rochelle salt) and aqueous copper sulphate respectively
(c) an aqueous copper sulphate (Rochelle salt) and acidic sodium potassium tartarate respectively
(d) an acidic sodium potassium tartarate (Rochelle salt) and aqueous copper sulphate respectively

41 Which of the following compound does not give a silver mirror with ammonical silver nitrate solution but give an oxime with hydroxylamine? NCERT Pg 239

(a) $CH_2=CH—OCH_3$ (b) CH_3CH_2CHO

(c) $CH_3CO\ CH_3$ (d) $CH_2=CH—CH_2—OH$

42 Which of the following oxidising agent is used for oxidation of $CH_3CH=CH—CHO$ to $CH_3CH=CH—COOH$? NCERT Pg 239

(a) Schiff's reagent (b) Tollen's reagent

(c) Baeyer's reagent (d) Acidified dichromate

43 On heating an aliphatic aldehyde with Fehling's reagent, a reddish brown precipitate is obtained due to the formation of NCERT Pg 239

(a) CuO (b) Cu_2O (c) $CuSO_4$ (d) $Cu(OH)_2$

44 Reaction by which benzaldehyde cannot be prepared is NCERT Pg 232, 233, 239

(a) $C_6H_5—CH_3$ + CrO_2Cl_2 in CS_2 followed by H_3O^+

(b) $C_6H_5—COCl$ + H_2 in the presence of Pd-$BaSO_4$

(c) C_6H_5 + CO + HCl in the presence of anhyd. $AlCl_3$

(d) $C_6H_5—COCH_3$ + Zn/Hg and conc. HCl

45 Which of the following test is not correct for the differentiation of the mentioned compounds? NCERT Pg 240

(a) Benzoic acid and acetone –Sodium bicarbonate test

(b) Acetophenone and benzophenone– Iodoform test

(c) Propanal and propanone–Silver mirror test

(d) Ethanal and propanal–Fehling's test

46 Identify the product formed in the given reaction.

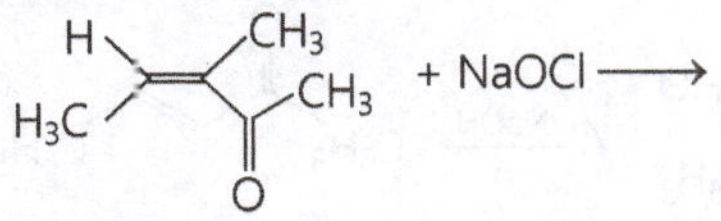

NCERT Pg 240

(a) 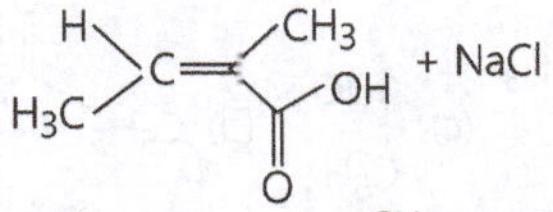

(b) 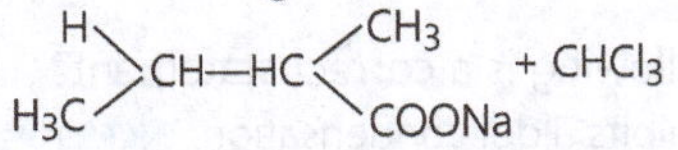

(c) 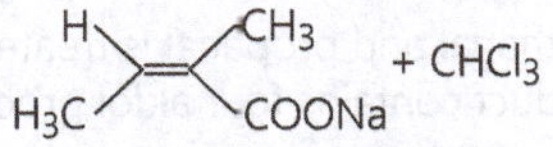

(d) 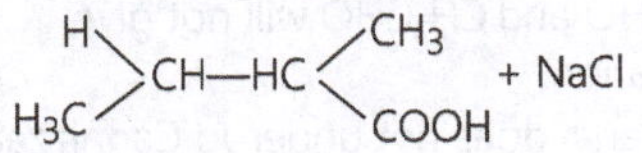

47 The compound which does not give yellow precipitate on reaction with NaOI is NCERT Pg 240

(a) acetone (b) acetaldehyde

(c) isopropanol (d) formaldehyde

48 Which of the following compounds produces an orange-red precipitate with 2, 4-DNP reagent? NCERT Pg 240

(a) Acetamide

(b) Dimethyl ether

(c) Butanone

(d) Propyl butanoate

49 Compound *A*, with molecular formula C_8H_8O, is found to react with NaOI (produced by reacting *B* with NaOH) and yields a yellow precipitate with characteristics smell. *A* and *B* respectively are NCERT Pg 240

(a) 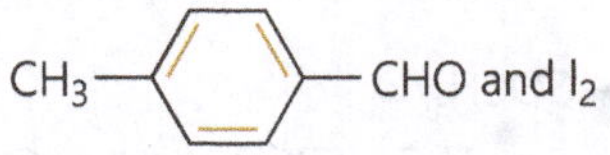

(b) 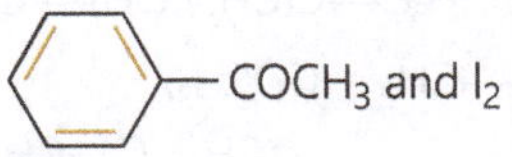

(c) 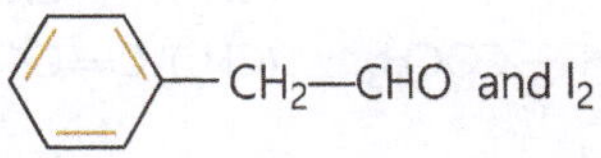

(d) 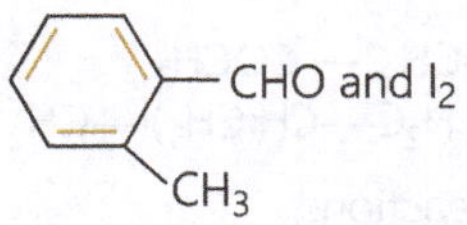

50 Select the correct statement for haloform reaction. NCERT Pg 240

(a) $CH_3—O$ group undergoes this reaction.

(b) CH_3CO and $CH_3CH(OH)$ groups are detected in this reaction.

(c) Sodium hypohalite is not used as a reagent in this reaction.

(d) In this reaction, methane is obtained as a side product.

51 Which one is most reactive towards nucleophilic addition reaction? NCERT Pg 236

(a) 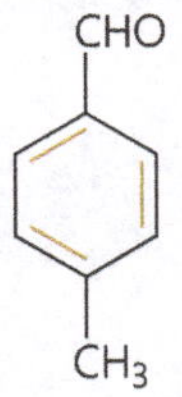

(b) 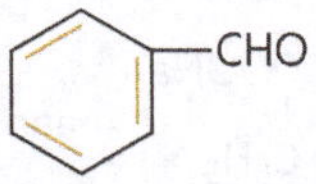

(c) 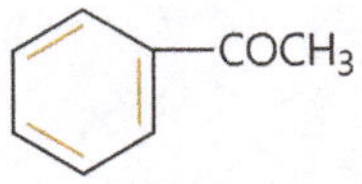

(d) 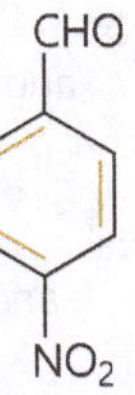

52 Which of the following compounds do not undergo aldol condensation? NCERT Pg 241

(a) $CH_3-C(CH_3)_2-CHO$ (b) CH_3-CHO

(c) $CH_3-CO-CH_3$ (d) CH_3CH_2CHO

53 Consider the reaction given below.

$$2CH_3COCH_3 \underset{}{\overset{Ba(OH)_2}{\rightleftharpoons}} X \xrightarrow[-H_2O]{\Delta} Y$$

Identify *X* and *Y* in the given reaction. NCERT Pg 241

	X	Y
(a)	$(CH_3)_2C{=}CH-COCH_3$,	$H_3C-C(CH_3)(OH)-CH_2COCH_3$
(b)	$H_3C-C(CH_3)(OH)-CH_2-COCH_3$,	$(CH_3)_2C{=}CH-COCH_3$
(c)	$(CH_3)_2CH-CH(OH)-COCH_3$,	$(CH_3)_2C{=}C-COCH_3$
(d)	$H_3C-C(CH_3)(OH)-CH_2-COCH_3$,	$H_2C-CH(CH_3)-CH_2-COCH_3$

54 Consider the following reactions,

$$CH_3COCl \xrightarrow{(X)} CH_3CHO \underset{}{\overset{(Y)}{\rightleftharpoons}} CH_3-CH(OH)-CH_2CHO \xrightarrow{(Z)} CH_3CH{=}CHCHO$$

Here, *X*, *Y* and *Z* respectively are NCERT Pg 232, 241

(a) $Pd/BaSO_4$; Dil. NaOH; Heat (b) NaOH; Hydrolysis ; Heat

(c) $I_2/NaOH$; $LiAlH_4$; H_3O^+ (d) CrO_3; Warm; CO_2

55 $C_6H_6 \xrightarrow[\text{Anhyd. } AlCl_3/CuCl]{CO + HCl} A \xrightarrow[\Delta]{\text{Conc. NaOH}} B + C$

Products *B* and *C* are NCERT Pg 233, 242

(a) $C_6H_5CH_2COOH$ and $C_6H_5CH_2-OH$

(b) $C_6H_5CO\bar{O}Na^+$ and $C_6H_5CH_2-OH$

(c) $C_6H_5CO\bar{O}Na^+$ and $CHCl_3$

(d) $C_6H_5CO\bar{O}Na^+$ and C_6H_5CHO

56 Major products of the following reaction are

$$C_6H_5CHO + HCHO \xrightarrow[\text{(ii) } H_3O^+]{\text{(i) 50\% NaOH}}$$

NCERT Pg 242

(a) CH_3OH and HCO_2H

(b) CH_3OH and C_6H_5COOH

(c) HCOOH and $C_6H_5CH_2OH$

(d) $C_6H_5CH_2OH$ and C_6H_5COOH

57 Which of the following does not give Cannizzaro reaction? NCERT Pg 242

(a) C_6H_5-CO-H (b) $Cl_3C-CO-H$

(c) CH_3-CO-H (d) $(CH_3)_3C-CO-H$

58 Cinnamaldehyde can be obtained by cross aldol condensation of NCERT Pg 242

(a) $C_6H_5-CHO + CH_3COCH_3$

(b) $CH_3CHO + CH_3COCH_3$

(c) $C_6H_5-CHO + C_6H_5-COCH_3$

(d) $C_6H_5-CHO + CH_3CHO$

59 Which of the following is the correct formula of the compound *A* used with benzaldehyde in order to synthesise the product given in the reaction? NCERT Pg 242

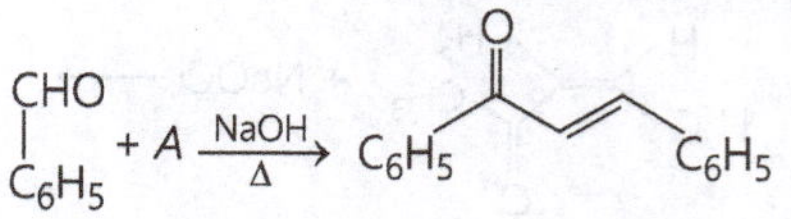

(a) C_6H_5COOH (b) $C_6H_5COOCH_3$ (c) C_6H_5CHO (d)

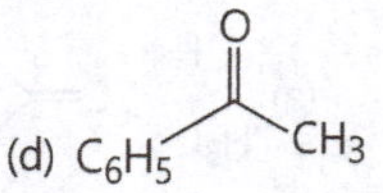

60 Which of the following is a correct statement?

(a) CCl_3CHO exhibits aldol condensation. NCERT Pg 241, 242

(b) When mixture of ethanal and propanal is treated with *aq*. NaOH, the product contains four aldol products.

(c) Mixture of HCHO and CH_3CHO will not give aldol condensation.

(d) 2-methyl propanal does not undergo Cannizzaro reaction.

61 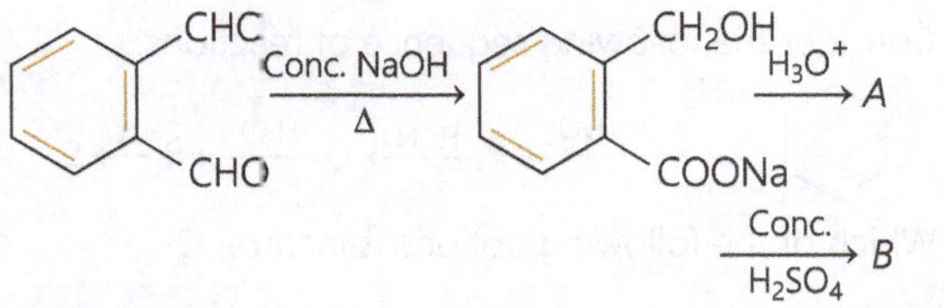

Here, *B* is NCERT Pg 242

(a) 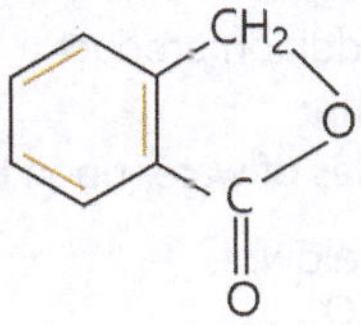

(b) 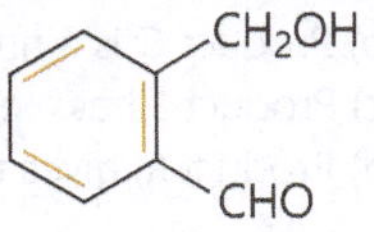

(c) 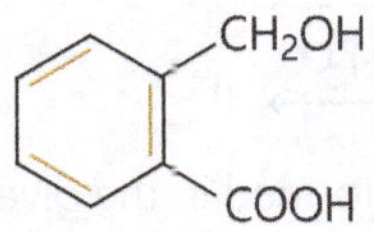

(d) 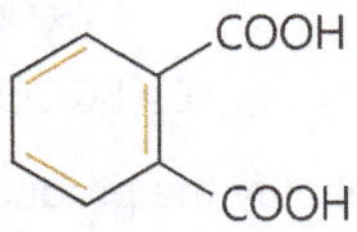

62 In the given reaction,

Benzaldehyde + HNO_3(conc.) $\xrightarrow{\text{Conc. } H_2SO_4}$ *P* (Major)

The product *F* is NCERT Pg 243

(a) *m*-nitrobenzaldehyde (b) *o*-nitrobenzaldehyde
(c) *p*-nitrobenzaldehyde (d) Nitrobenzene

Nomenclature, Structure and Preparation of Carboxylic Acids

63 Which of the following is the common name of 2-methylpropanoic acid? NCERT Pg 244

(a) Adipic acid
(b) Malonic acid
(c) Isobutyric acid
(d) Carballylic acid

64 IUPAC name of α-acetyl succinic acid is NCERT Pg 244

(a) 2-(1-oxoethyl) butan-1,4-dioic acid
(b) 3-(2-oxoethyl) butan-1,4-dioic acid
(c) Hexane-1,6-dioic acid
(d) Butane-1,4-dicarboxylic acid

65 Structure of the compound whose IUPAC name is 3-ethyl-2-hydroxy-4-methylhex-3-en-5-ynoic acid is NCERT Pg 244

(a) 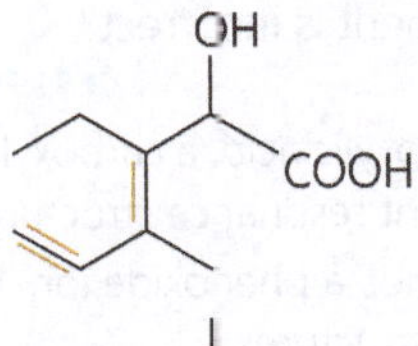

(b) 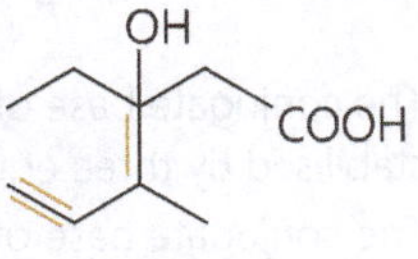

(c) 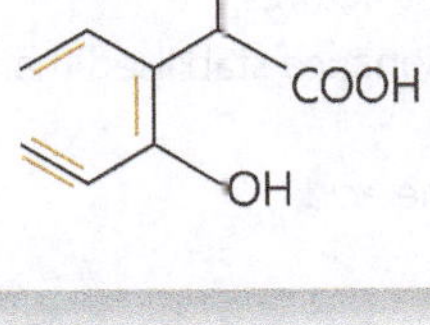

(d) 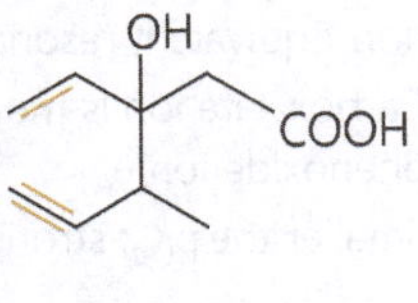

66 Choose the option in which IUPAC name is not correctly matched? NCERT Pg 245

(a) Ph—CH_2CH_2COOH → 1-phenylpropanoic acid

(b) 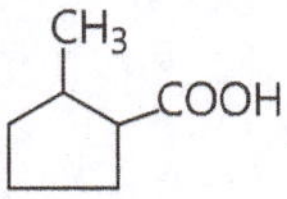

→ 2-methylcyclopentanoic acid

(c) 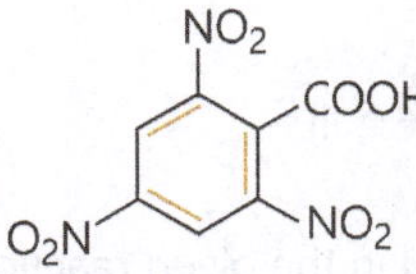

→ 2,4,6-trinitrobenzoic acid

(d) $(CH_3)_2$—C=CHCOOH → 3-methylbut-2-enoic acid

67 Which of the following statements is correct? NCERT Pg 239, 245

(a) Aldehydes are generally oxidised under vigorous conditions.
(b) Ketones are easily oxidised to carboxylic acids even under mild oxidising agents.
(c) Oxidation of ketone involves carbon-carbon bond cleavage to give a mixture of carboxylic acids having lesser number of C-atoms than the parent ketones.
(d) In carboxylic acids, the entire molecule is planar with sp^3-hybridised carbon atom and square planar geometry.

68 Consider the following reaction sequence.

C_6H_5—$CH_2CH_2CH_3$ $\xrightarrow[\text{KOH},\Delta]{KMnO_4}$ *A* $\xrightarrow{H_3O^+}$ *B*

Identify (*A*) and (*B*) formed in the given reaction sequence. NCERT Pg 246

	A	*B*		*A*	*B*
(a)	C_6H_5—CH_2OH	C_6H_5—CH=CH_2	(b)	C_6H_5—COOK	C_6H_5—COOH
(c)	C_6H_5—CH_2OH	C_6H_5—CHO	(a)	C_6H_5—COOH	C_6H_5—CHO

69 Select the incorrect statement(s) from the following. NCERT Pg 245, 246

(a) Nitriles are hydrolysed to amides and then to acids in the presence of H^+ or OH^- as catalyst.
(b) Mild reaction conditions are used to stop the reaction at the amide stage during the hydrolysis of nitriles.
(c) Grignard reagents react with dry ice to form salts of carboxylic acids which in turn give corresponding carboxylic acids after acidification with mineral acid.
(d) Primary alcohols can not oxidised by CrO_3 in acidic medium to carboxylic acid.

70 Consider the following reactions. **NCERT Pg 246**

$$C_6H_5\text{—}CH_3 \xrightarrow[\text{(ii) } H_3O^+]{\text{(i) } KMnO_4\text{ - }KOH/\Delta} I$$

$$C_6H_5\text{—}CH_2CH_2CH_3 \xrightarrow[\text{(ii) } H_3O^+]{\text{(i) } KMnO_4\text{ - }KOH/\Delta} II$$

$$C_6H_5\text{—}C(CH_3)_3 \xrightarrow[\text{(ii) } H_3O^+]{\text{(i) } KMnO_4\text{ - }KOH/\Delta} III$$

Identify the products formed in the given reaction.

	I	II	III
(a)	$C_6H_5\text{—}COOH$	$C_6H_5\text{—}CH_2CH_2CH_2OH$	$HO\text{—}C(CH_3)_2\text{—}C_6H_5$
(b)	$C_6H_5\text{—}COOH$	$C_6H_5\text{—}COOH$	No reaction will occur
(c)	$C_6H_5\text{—}COOH$	$C_6H_5\text{—}CH_2CH_2COOH$	$HOOC\text{—}C(CH_3)_2\text{—}C_6H_5$
(d)	$C_6H_5\text{—}CH_2OH$	$C_6H_5\text{—}CH_2OH$	No reaction will occur

71 Consider the following reaction sequence.

$$\text{Phenol} \xrightarrow{\text{Zn dust}} A \xrightarrow[\text{Anhydrous } AlCl_3]{(CH_3)_2CHCOCl} B \xrightarrow[\text{(ii) } H_3O^+]{\text{(i) Alk. } KMnO_4/\Delta} C$$

The product '*C*' is **NCERT Pg 246**

(a) $C_6H_5\text{—}CHO$ (b) $C_6H_5\text{—}COOH$

(c) $C_6H_5\text{—}CH_2CHO$ (d) $C_6H_5\text{—}CH_2COOH$

72 Consider the following reaction, **NCERT Pg 246**

$$C_6H_5\text{—}MgBr \xrightarrow[\text{(ii) } H_3O^+]{\text{(i) } CO_2\text{, Dry ether}} (P)$$

In the above reaction product '*P*' is

(a) $C_6H_5\text{—}CHO$ (b) $C_6H_5\text{—}COOH$ (c) $C_6H_5\text{—}OH$ (d) $C_6H_5\text{—}\overset{O}{\overset{\|}{C}}\text{—}C_6H_5$

73 Select the acid which cannot be prepared by Grignard reagent? **NCERT Pg 246**

(a) Acetic acid (b) Pentanoic acid

(c) Formic acid (d) Butanoic acid

74 Consider the following sequence of reactions.

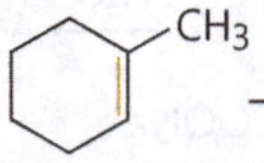 $\xrightarrow{O_3/H_2O_2} P \xrightarrow{HCN} Q \xrightarrow{H_3O^+} R \xrightarrow{\Delta} S$

Which of the following options is incorrect? **NCERT Pg 231, 237, 246**

(a) Product *P* has both carbonyl and carboxyl group.

(b) Product *Q* is a nucleophilic addition product.

(c) Product *S* has a carboxyl group.

(d) Product *R*, gives two molecules of water upon heating.

75 Consider the reactions given below.

$$(C_6H_5CO)_2O \xrightarrow{H_2O} I$$

$$C_6H_5COOCOCH_3 \xrightarrow{H_2O} II$$

Identify the products I and II formed in the given reactions. **NCERT Pg 247**

	I	II
(a)	2 molecules of benzoic acid	2 molecules of ethanoic acid
(b)	2 molecules of benzoic acid	1 molecule of benzoic acid and 1 molecule of ethanoic acid
(c)	1 molecule of ethanoic acid	1 molecule of benzoic acid
(d)	1 molecule of benzoic acid	1 molecule of butanoic acid

76 3-nitrobenzoic acid can be prepared from 3-nitrobromobenzene by treatment with **NCERT Pg 248**

(a) Mg/ether and CO_2 followed by acid hydrolysis

(b) Mg/ether followed by reaction with $KMnO_4$/KOH dil. H_2SO_4

(c) KCN and heating following by acid hydrolysis

(d) Jones reagent

Properties and Uses of Carboxylic Acids

77 The compound which does not react with $NaHCO_3$ is **NCERT Pg 249**

(a) CH_3COOH (b) 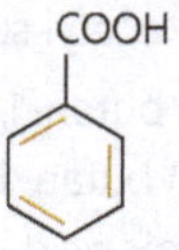

(c) HCOOH (d) 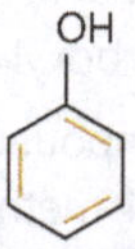

78 Which of the following statement is incorrect? **NCERT Pg 249, 250**

(a) The conjugate base of carboxylic acid, a carboxylate ion, is stabilised by three equivalent resonance structures.

(b) The conjugate base of phenol, a phenoxide ion, has non-equivalent resonance structures.

(c) Carboxylate ion is more resonance stabilised than phenoxide ion.

(d) Smaller the pK_a, stronger the acid.

79 The correct decreasing order for acid strength is **NCERT Pg 250, 251**

(a) $FCH_2COOH > NCCH_2COOH > NO_2CH_2COOH > ClCH_2COOH$

(b) $NCCH_2COOH > O_2NCH_2COOH > FCH_2COOH > ClCH_2COOH$

(c) $NO_2CH_2COOH > NCCH_2COOH > FCH_2COOH > ClCH_2COOH$

(d) $NO_2CH_2COOH > FCH_2COOH > NCCH_2COOH > ClCH_2COOH$

80 Arrange the following derivative of carboxylic acid in the increasing order of their acidity. **NCERT Pg 251**

(a) *p*-methoxybenzoic acid < Benzoic acid < *p*-nitrobenzoic acid

(b) *p*-methoxybenzoic acid > Benzoic acid > *p*-nitrobenzoic acid

(c) *p*-methoxybenzoic acid > Benzoic acid < *p*-nitrobenzoic acid

(d) *p*-methoxybenzoic acid ≃ Benzoic acid < *p*-nitrobenzoic acid

81 Arrange the following acids in the decreasing order of acidic strength. **NCERT Pg 251**

$HC\equiv C—COOH$ (I) $\quad C_6H_5COOH$ (II)

$CH_2=CH—COOH$ (III) $\quad CH_3COOH$ (IV)

Choose the correct option.

(a) I > II > III > IV (b) I < II < III < IV

(c) I > III > II > IV (d) I > IV > III > II

82 I. $F_3C—COOH$ II. CH_3COOH **NCERT Pg 251**

III. C_6H_5COOH IV. CH_3CH_2COOH

Correct order of pK_a value is

(a) I > III > II > IV

(b) IV > II > III > I

(c) IV > III > II > I

(d) I > II > IV > III

83 Which of the following reagents is/are used for the conversion of ethanoic acid to ethanoic anhydride? **NCERT Pg 251**

(a) $SOCl_2, \Delta$ (b) PCl_3, Δ

(c) P_2O_5, Δ (d) NH_3, Δ

84 Consider the following reactions. **NCERT Pg 252**

I. $RCOOH + PCl_5 \longrightarrow RCOCl$

II. $RCOOH + PCl_3 \longrightarrow RCOCl$

III. $RCOOH + SOCl_2 \longrightarrow RCOCl$

Which of the above reactions is/are preferred for the synthesis of $RCOCl$?

(a) Only I (b) II and III

(c) Only III (d) I, II and III

85 In a set of reactions, *m*-bromobenzoic acid gave a product *B*. Identify the product *B*. **NCERT Pg 252**

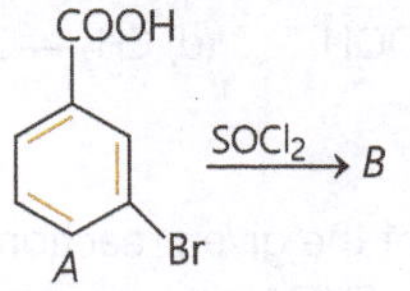

(a) 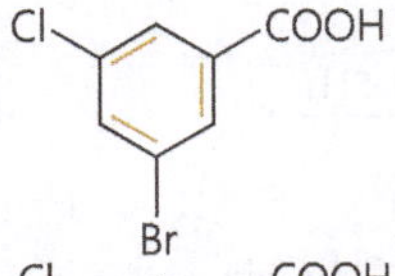

(b) 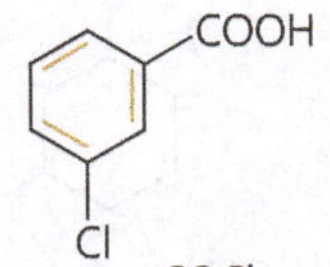

(c) 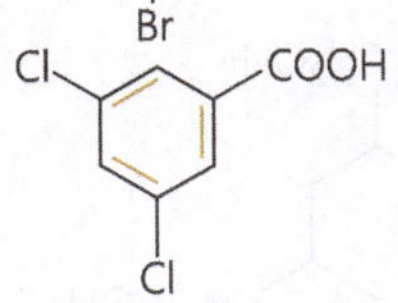

(d) 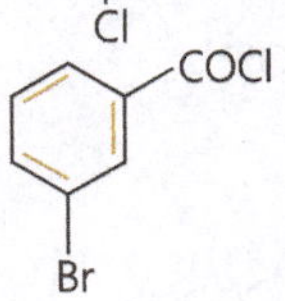

86 $Ph—\overset{O}{\overset{\|}{C}}—OH + CH_3—\overset{18}{O}—H \xrightarrow{\text{Conc. } H_2SO_4} P$

Product (*P*) is **NCERT Pg 251, 252**

(a) $Ph—\overset{O}{\overset{\|}{C}}—\overset{18}{O}—CH_3$ (b) $Ph—\overset{O}{\overset{\|}{C}}—O—CH_3$

(c) $Ph—\overset{^{18}O}{\overset{\|}{C}}—O—CH_3$ (d) $Ph—\overset{^{18}O}{\overset{\|}{C}}—\overset{18}{O}—CH_3$

87 In a set of the given reactions, acetic acid yielded a product *C*.

$CH_3COOH + PCl_5 \longrightarrow A \xrightarrow[\text{Anhy. } AlCl_3]{C_6H_6} B \xrightarrow[\text{Ether}]{C_2H_5MgBr} C$

Product *C* would be **NCERT Pg 252**

(a) $CH_3CH(OH)C_2H_5$ (b) $CH_3COC_6H_5$

(c) $CH_3CH(OH)C_6H_5$ (d) $CH_3C(C_2H_5)(OH)C_6H_5$

88 Which of the following will be most easily decarboxylate on heating? **NCERT Pg 253**

(a) 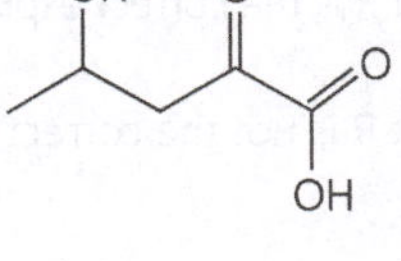

(b) 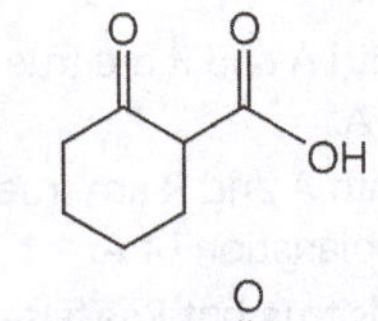

(c) 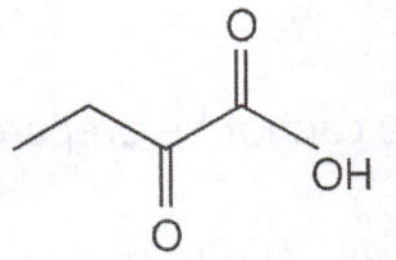

(d) 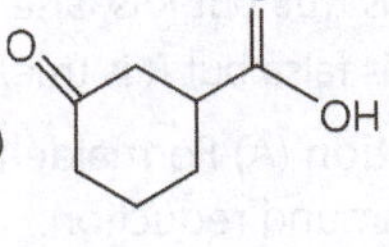

89 Which one of the following compounds will give HVZ reaction? NCERT Pg 253

(a) C_6H_5-COOH (b) HCOOH

(c) $CH_3-C(CH_3)_2-COOH$ (d) $CH_3-CH(CH_3)-COOH$

90 Major product of the given reaction is

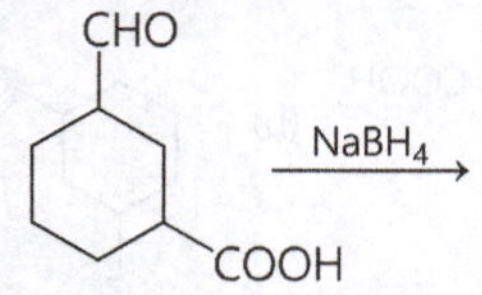

NCERT Pg 253

(a) 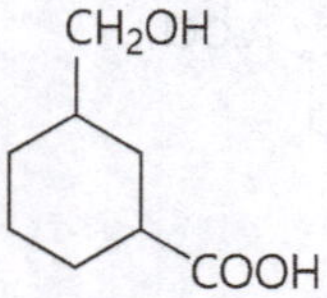 (b) 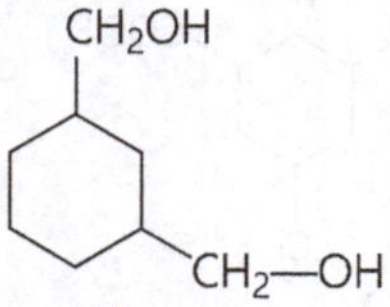

(c) 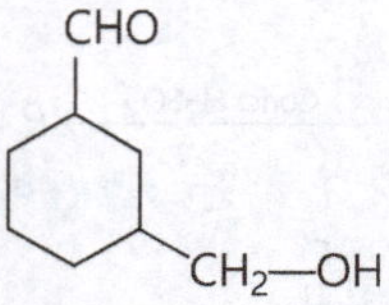 (d) 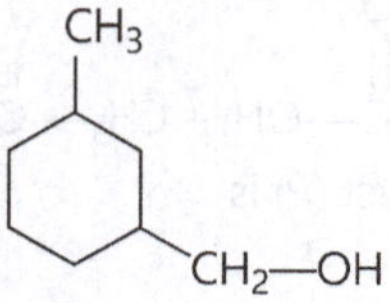

91 Diborane can reduce the functional group such as

(a) acid (b) ester (c) nitro (d) halo NCERT Pg 253

92 Which of the following product is formed during the decarboxylation of malonic acid? NCERT Pg 253

(a) Acetic acid (b) Benzophenone

(c) Propanone (d) Formic acid

93 Alkali metal salts of carboxylic acids undergo decarboxylation on electrolysis of their aqueous solutions and form hydrocarbons having twice the number of C-atoms present in the alkyl group of the acid. The reaction is known as NCERT Pg 253

(a) Kolbe electrolysis (b) decarboxylation

(c) HVZ-reaction (d) Friedel-Crafts reaction

94 Aromatic carboxylic acids do not undergo Friedel-Crafts reaction because NCERT Pg 254

(a) carboxyl group acts as an activating and *meta*-directing group.

(b) carboxyl group act as a deactivating and *ortho* and *para*-directing group.

(c) carboxyl group act as an activating and *ortho*-directing group.

(d) carboxyl group acts as deactivating and the catalyst aluminium chloride (Lewis acid) gets bonded to the carboxyl group.

95 Consider the following : NCERT Pg 254

$$\text{Benzoic acid} \xrightarrow[\text{Conc. } H_2SO_4]{\text{Conc. } HNO_3} X$$

$$\text{Benzoic acid} \xrightarrow{Br_2/FeBr_3} Y$$

Identify *X* and *Y* for the above reaction.

	X	*Y*
(a)	*o*-nitrobenzoic acid	*o*-bromobenzoic acid
(b)	*m*-nitrobenzoic acid	*p*-bromobenzoic acid
(c)	*p*-nitrobenzoic acid	*o*-bromobenzoic acid
(d)	*m*-nitrobenzoic acid	*m*-bromobenzoic acid

96 Which of the following acid is used in rubber, textile, dyeing, leather and electroplating industries? NCERT Pg 254

(a) Hexanedioic acid (b) Ethanoic acid

(c) Methanoic acid (d) Sodium benzoate

Assertion-Reason Questions

Directions (Q. Nos. 1-6) *In the following question Assertion (A) followed by Reason (R) is given below. Choose the correct option out of the choices given below.*

(a) Both A and R are true and R is the correct explanation of A.

(b) Both A and R are true but R is not the correct explanation of A.

(c) A is true but R is false.

(d) A is false but R is true.

1 Assertion (A) Formaldehyde cannot be prepared by the Rosenmund reduction.

Reason (R) Formyl chloride is unstable at room temperature. NCERT Pg 232

2 Assertion (A) Benzaldehyde is less reactive towards nucleophilic addition reactions than propanal.

Reason (R) The carbon atom of the carbonyl group of benzaldehyde is less electrophilic than carbon atom of the carbonyl group present in propanal. NCERT Pg 236

3 Assertion (A) The reaction of aldehydes and ketones with pure HCN is very slow to yield cyanohydrin.

Reason (R) The addition reaction is catalysed by a base to generate cyanide ion, CN^- being a strong nucleophile, adds to carbonyl compounds to yield corresponding cyanohydrin. NCERT Pg 237

4 Assertion (A) The addition of sodium hydrogen sulphite to aldehydes and ketones is the useful method for separation and the purification of aldehydes.

Reason (R) The hydrogen sulphite addition compound is water soluble and can be converted back to the original carbonyl compound by treating it with dilute mineral acid or alkali. NCERT Pg 237

5 **Assertion** (A)

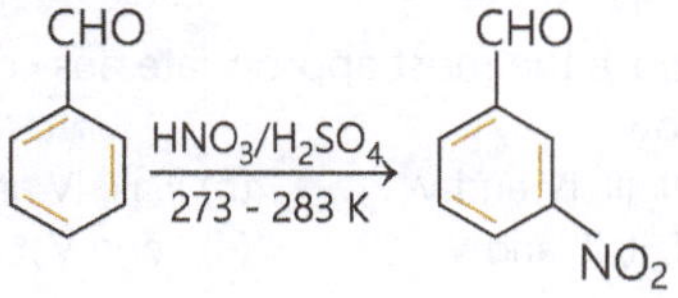

Reason (R) Aldehydic group acts as a deactivating and *meta*-directing group. NCERT Pg 243

6 **Assertion** (A) Ester hydrolysis is fast in the beginning and becomes slow after sometime.

Reason (R) The rate of ester hydrolysis increases with the increase in the amount of carboxylic acid produced. NCERT Pg 251

Statement Type Questions

Direction (Q.Nos. 1-5) *In the following questions, two statements (I & II) are given in the light of the given statements, choose the correct option given below.*

(a) Both Statement I and Statement II are true.
(b) Statement I is false but Statement II is true.
(c) Statement I is true but Statement II is false.
(d) Both Statement I and Statement II are false.

1. **Statement I**

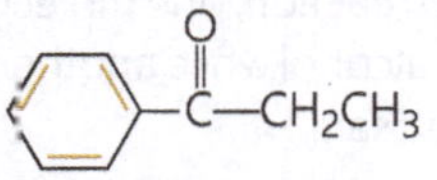

and $CH_3CH_2CH_2CH(Br)CH(CH_3)CH_2CHO$ are named as phenylpropan-1-one and 4-bromo-3-methyl-heptanal.

Statement II In case of aldehydes, the numbering of longest carbon chain starts from the carbon of the aldehyde group, while in case of ketones the numbering begins from the end nearer to the carbonyl group. NCERT Pg 229

2 **Statement I** Addition of water to propyne in the presence of H_2SO_4 and $HgSO_4$ gives propanone.

Statement II Toluene is treated with acetyl chloride in the presence of anhydrous aluminium chloride, gives 4-methyl acetophenone. NCERT Pg 232, 234

3 **Statement I** The nucleophilic addition of sodium hydrogen sulphite to an aldehyde or a ketone involves proton transfer to form a stable ion.

Statement II The nucleophilic addition of hydrogen cyanide to an aldehyde or a ketone yields amine as final product. NCERT Pg 237

4 **Statement I** Aldehydes and ketones do not have any methyl group linked to the carbonyl carbon atom when oxidised by sodium hypohalite in a haloform reaction.

Statement II In haloform reaction, the oxidation (methyl to ha oform) does not affect carbon-carbon double bond, if present in the molecule. NCERT Pg 240

5 **Statement I** Ethanoic acid on heating with P_2O_5 gives ethanoic anhydride.

Statment II Ethanoic acid is used in the manufacture of nylon-6,6. NCERT Pg 251, 254

6 Which of the following statements are correct?

I. In the carbonyl group, carbonyl carbon is an electrophilic and carbonyl oxygen is a nucleophilic centre.
II. In Rosenmund reduction, acyl chloride is hydrogenated over catalyst, palladium on barium sulphate.
III. Nitriles are reduced to corresponding imine with $SnCl_2$ in the presence of HCl, which on hydrolysis gives corresponding ketone.
IV. Strong oxidising agents oxidise toluene and its derivatives to benzoic acids.
V. In Friedel-Crafts acylation reaction, when benzene is treated with acid chloride in the presence of anhy. $AlCl_3$ gives corresponding aldehyde.

Choose the most appropriate answer from the options given below: NCERT Pg 231, 232, 234

(a) I, III and IV (b) II, IV and V
(c) I, II and IV (d) I, III and V

7 Select the incorrect statements from the following.

I. The boiling points of aldehydes and ketones are lower than hydrocarbons and ethers of comparable molecular masses.
II. Acetone and benzaldehyde on heating wih Fehling's reagent oxidises to corresponding carboxylate anion.
III. The carbonyl group of aldehydes and ketones is reduced to —CH_2 group on treatment with hydrazine followed by heating with KOH in ethylene glycol.
IV. Aldehydes are generally more reactive than ketones in nucleophilic addition reactions.
V. Formalin is used to prepare bakelite (a phenol-formaldehyde resin).

Choose the most appropriate answer from the options given below: NCERT Pg 235, 236, 239, 243

(a) I and II (b) II, III and IV
(c) I, III and IV (d) II and III

8 Which of the following statements are not correct?

I. Some higher members aliphatic carboxylic acids ($C_{12} - C_8$) known as fatty acids.
II. IUPAC name of glutaric acid is butanedioic acid.
III. Nitriles are hydrolysed to amides and then to acids in the presence of H^+ or OH^- as catalyst.
IV. In carboxylic acids, the bonds to the carboxyl carbon lie in one plane and are separated by about 108°.
V. Jones reagent is chromium oxide (Cr_2O_3) in acidic media.

Choose the most appropriate answer from the options below: NCERT Pg 244, 245, 246

(a) IV and V (b) I and IV
(c) III and V (d) II, IV and V

9 Select the correct statements from the following:

I. Higher carboxylic acids are practically insoluble in water due to the increased hydrophobic interaction of hydrocarbon part.
II. Carboxylic acids react with weaker bases such as carbonates and hydrogen carbonates to evolve carbon dioxide.
III. Carboxylic acids are esterified with alcohols or phenols in the presence of conc. H_2SO_4 or HCl gas as a catalyst.
IV. Carboxylic acids react with ammonia to give ammonium salt which on further heating at low temperature give amides.
V. Sodium benzoate is used as food preservative.

Choose the most appropriate answer from the options below NCERT Pg 249, 251, 252, 254

(a) II, III, IV and V (b) II, III, IV and V
(c) I, II, III and V (d) I and V

10 Which of the following statements are not correct?

I. Aromatic carboxylic acids undergo electrophilic substitution reactions in which the carboxyl group acts as an activating and meta-directing group.
II. In Hell-Volhard-Zelinsky reaction, the carboxylic acids having an α-hydrogen are halogenated at the α-position on treatment with Cl_2 or Br_2 in the presence of red P.
III. The solubility of carboxylic acids decreases with increasing the number of carbon atoms.
IV. In Cannizzaro reaction, one molecule of the aldehyde is reduced to alcohol while another is oxidised to carboxylic acid salt.
V. The hydrogen sulphite addition compound is insoluble in water.

Choose the most appropriate answer from the options below. NCERT Pg 237, 242, 249, 254

(a) I and V (b) II and IV
(c) II and V (d) III and IV

Matching Type Questions

1 Match the following structure given in Column I with their common name given in Column II and choose the correct option from the codes given below. NCERT Pg 230

Column I (Structure)	Column II (Common name)
A. HCHO	1. Valeraldehyde
B. $CH_3CH_2CH_2CH_2CHO$	2. Phthaldehyde
C. $H_2C{=}CH{-}CHO$	3. Acrolein
D. 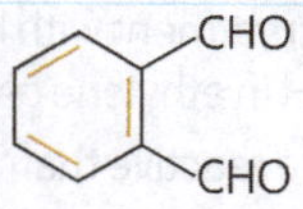	4. Formaldehyde

Codes

	A	B	C	D		A	B	C	D
(a)	2	1	3	4	(b)	2	3	1	4
(c)	4	3	1	2	(d)	4	1	3	2

2 Match the following names of reagents given in Column II to bring about the conversions given in Column I and choose the correct option from the codes given below. NCERT Pg 232, 233

Column I (Conversion)	Column II (Reagents)
A. Hexan-1-ol to hexanal	1. PCC
B. Cyclohexanol to cyclohexanone	2. CrO_3 in the presence of acetic anhydride
C. *p*-fluorotoluene to *p*-fluorobenzaldehyde	3. $K_2Cr_2O_7$ in acidic medium
D. Ethanenitrile to ethanol	4. (DIBAL-H)

Codes

	A	B	C	D		A	B	C	D
(a)	1	4	3	2	(b)	4	3	1	2
(c)	1	3	2	4	(d)	2	1	3	4

3 Match the reagents given in (Column I) with the correct product name (Column II). Choose the correct option from the codes given below. NCERT Pg 238

Column I (Reagent)		Column II (Product)	
A.	Hydroxylamine	1.	Semicarbazone
B.	Hydrazine	2.	2, 4-dinitrophenyl hydrazone
C.	2, 4-DNP	3.	Hydrazone
D.	Semicarbazide	4.	Oxime

Codes

	A	B	C	D
(a)	1	2	3	4
(b)	4	3	2	1
(c)	3	2	1	4
(d)	2	1	3	4

4 Match the following carbonyl compounds given in Column I with their uses given in Column II and choose the correct option from the codes given below. NCERT Pg 243

Column (Carbonyl compounds)		Column II (Uses)	
A.	Formaldehyde	1.	Perfumery and dye industries
B.	Acetaldehyde	2.	Preparation of bakelite
C.	Benzaldehyde	3.	Odours and flavours
D.	Butyraldehyde	4.	Manufacture of vinyl acetate and ethyl acetate

Codes

	A	B	C	D
(a)	1	2	3	4
(b)	2	3	4	1
(c)	1	3	4	2
(d)	2	4	1	3

5 Match the acids given in Column I with their correct IUPAC names given in Column II and choose the correct option from the codes given below. NCERT Pg 244

Column I (Acids)		Column II (IUPAC names)	
A.	Oxalic acid	1.	Hexanedioic acid
B.	Succinic acid	2.	Pentanedioic acid
C.	Adipic acid	3.	Butanedioic acid
D.	Glutaric acid	4.	Ethanedioic acid

Codes

	A	B	C	D
(a)	1	2	3	4
(b)	4	3	1	2
(c)	4	2	1	3
(d)	4	1	2	3

6 Match the following compounds given in Column I with their uses given in Column II and choose the correct option from the codes given below. NCERT Pg 254

Column I (Compounds)		Column II (Uses)	
A.	Ethanoic acid	1.	Soaps and detergents
B.	Hexanedioic acid	2.	Nylon-6, 6
C.	Sodium benzoate	3.	Food preservative
D.	Fatty acids	4.	Vinegar

Codes

	A	B	C	D
(a)	4	2	3	1
(b)	1	2	3	4
(c)	1	3	2	4
(d)	4	3	2	1

Numerical Value Questions

1 The total number of C—C sigma bond is in mesityl oxide ($C_6H_{10}O$) is .... NCERT Pg 230

2 In Tollen's test for aldehyde, the overall number of electrons transferred to the Tollen's reagent formula $[Ag(NH_3)_2]^+$ per aldehyde group to form silver mirror is .... (Round off to the nearest integer). NCERT Pg 239

3 The number of molecules which gives haloform test among the following molecules is .... NCERT Pg 240

(i) 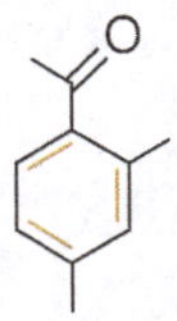

(ii) 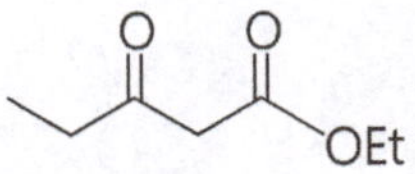

(iii) 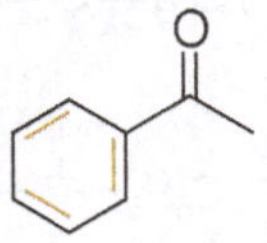

(iv) 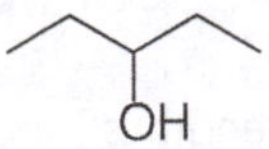

(v) 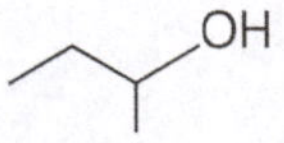

(vi) 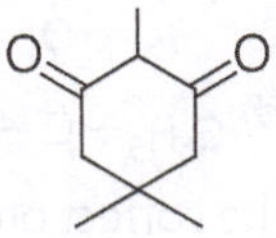

4 In the given reaction,

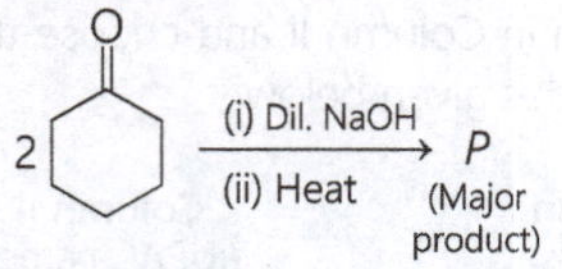

The number of π-electrons present in the product P is ....

NCERT Pg 241

5 Number of compounds from the following which will not dissolve in cold $NaHCO_3$ and NaOH solutions but will dissolve in hot NaOH solution is ....

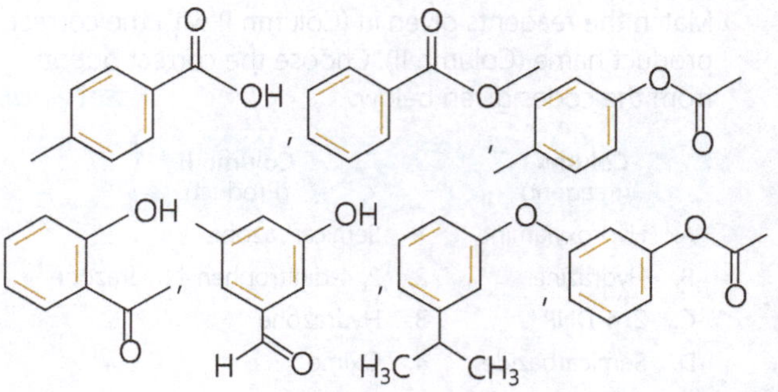

NCERT Pg 249, 253

NCERT Exemplar's Questions

1 Addition of water to alkynes occurs in acidic medium and in the presence of Hg^{2+} ions as a catalyst. Which of the following products will be formed on addition of water to but-1-yne under these conditions?

(a) $CH_3—CH_2—CH_2—\overset{O}{\overset{\|}{C}}—H$

(b) $CH_3—CH_2—\overset{O}{\overset{\|}{C}}—CH_3$

(c) $CH_3—CH_2—\overset{O}{\overset{\|}{C}}—OH + CO_2$

(d) $CH_3—\overset{O}{\overset{\|}{C}}—OH + H—\overset{O}{\overset{\|}{C}}—H$

2 Which of the following compounds is most reactive towards nucleophilic addition reactions?

(a) $CH_3—\overset{O}{\overset{\|}{C}}—H$

(b) $CH_3—\overset{O}{\overset{\|}{C}}—CH_3$

(c) $C_6H_5—\overset{O}{\overset{\|}{C}}—H$

(d) $C_6H_5—\overset{O}{\overset{\|}{C}}—CH_3$

3 The correct order of increasing acidic strength is

(a) phenol < ethanol < chloroacetic acid < acetic acid
(b) ethanol < phenol < chloroacetic acid < acetic acid
(c) ethanol < phenol < acetic acid < chloroacetic acid
(d) chloroacetic acid < acetic acid < phenol < ethanol

4 Compound $Ph—O—\overset{O}{\overset{\|}{C}}—Ph$ can be prepared by the reaction of

(a) phenol and benzoic acid in the presence of NaOH
(b) phenol and benzoyl chloride in the presence of pyridine
(c) phenol and benzoyl chloride in the presence of $ZnCl_2$
(d) phenol and benzaldehyde in the presence of palladium

5 Match the reactions given in Column I with the suitable reagents given in Column II.

Column I (Reactions)	Column II (Reagents)
A. Benzophenone → Diphenylmethane	1. $LiAlH_4$
B. Benzaldehyde → 1-phenylethanol	2. DIBAL-H
C. Cyclohexanone → Cyclohexanol	3. Zn(Hg)/Conc. HCl
D. Phenyl benzoate → Benzaldehyde	4. CH_3MgBr

6 The reagent which does not react with both acetone and benzaldehyde is

(a) sodium hydrogen sulphite
(b) phenyl hydrazine
(c) Fehling's solution
(d) Grignard reagent

7 Cannizzaro's reaction is not given by ....

(a) 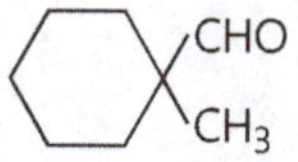

(b) 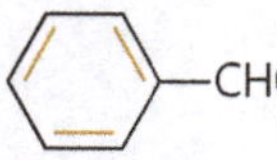

(c) HCHO

(d) CH_3CHO

8 Which products is formed, when the compound 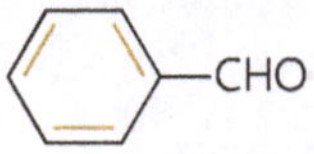 is treated with conc. KOH solution?

(a) 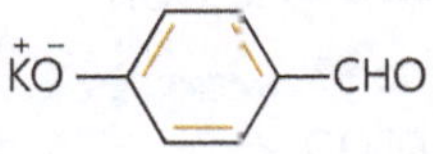

(b) 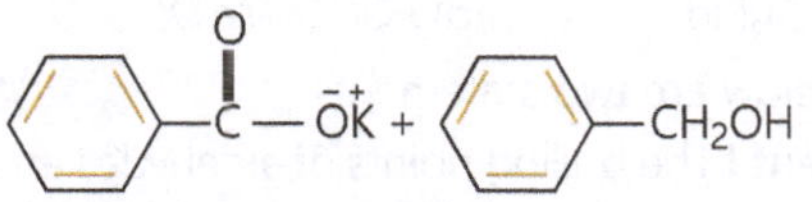

(c) 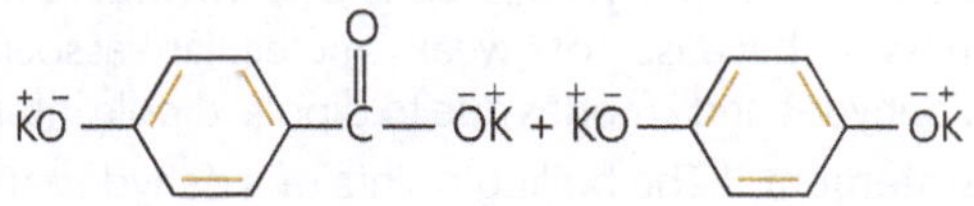

(d) 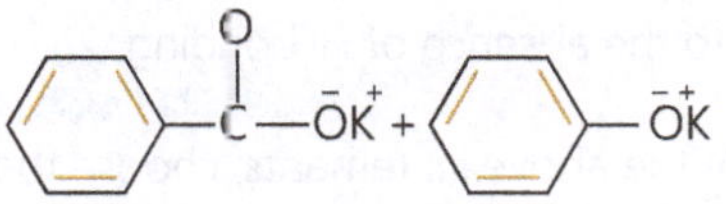

9 $CH_3-C\equiv CH \xrightarrow[1\%\ HgSO_4]{40\%\ H_2SO_4} A \xrightarrow{\text{Isomerisation}} CH_3-\overset{\overset{\large O}{\|}}{C}-CH_3$

Structure of *A* and type of isomerism in the above reaction respectively are

(a) prop-1-en-2-ol and metamerism
(b) prop-1-en-1-ol and tautomerism
(c) prop-2-en-2-ol and geometrical isomerism
(d) prop-1-en-2-ol and tautomerism

10 Compounds *A* and *C* in the following reaction are

$CH_3CHO \xrightarrow[\text{(ii) } H_2O]{\text{(i) } CH_3MgBr} A \xrightarrow[\Delta]{H_2SO_4,\ \text{Dehydration}} B \xrightarrow{\text{Hydroboration oxidation}} C$

(a) Identical
(b) Positional isomers
(c) Functional isomers
(d) Optical isomers

11 Match the reactions given in Column I with the suitable reagents given in Column II.

Column I (Reactions)	Column II (Reagents)
A. $CH_3-\overset{\overset{O}{\|}}{C}-Cl + H_2 \xrightarrow{Pd/BaSO_4} CH_3-\overset{\overset{O}{\|}}{C}-H$	1. Friedel-Crafts acylation
B. 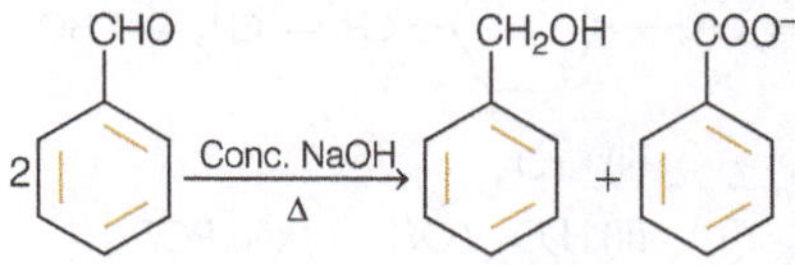	2. HVZ reaction
C. 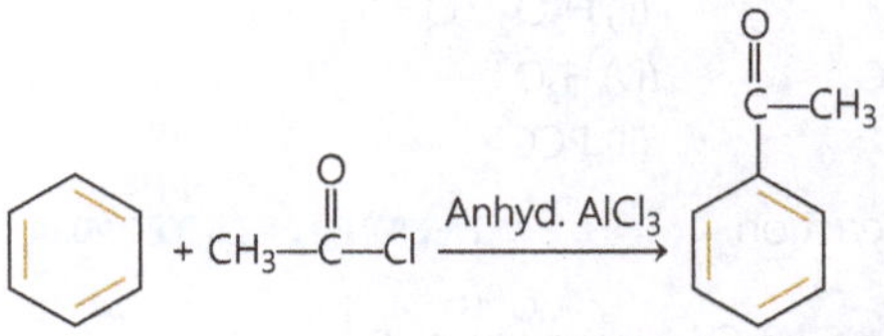	3. Rosenmund's reduction
D. $R-CH_2-COOH \xrightarrow[\text{(ii)} H_2O]{\text{(i) } Br_2/\text{Red P}} R-\underset{\underset{Br}{\|}}{CH}-COOH$	4. Cannizzaro's reaction

12 Which is the most suitable reagent for the following conversion?

$$CH_3-CH=CH-CH_2-\overset{\overset{O}{\|}}{C}-CH_3 \longrightarrow CH_3-CH=CH-CH_2-\overset{\overset{O}{\|}}{C}-ONa$$

(a) Tollen's reagent
(b) Benzoyl peroxide
(c) I_2 and NaOH solution
(d) Sn and NaOH solution

13 Which of the following compounds will give butanone on oxidation with alk. $KMnO_4$ solution?

(a) Butan-1-ol
(b) Butan-2-ol
(c) Butan-3-ol
(d) Butan-4-ol

14 In Clemmensen's reduction, carbonyl compound is treated with

(a) zinc amalgam + HCl
(b) sodium amalgam + HCl
(c) zinc amalgam + nitric acid
(d) sodium amalgam + HNO_3

Past Exams' Questions

NEET Archive

1. Identify the correct reagents that would bring about the following transformation. NCERT Pg 231, NEET 2024

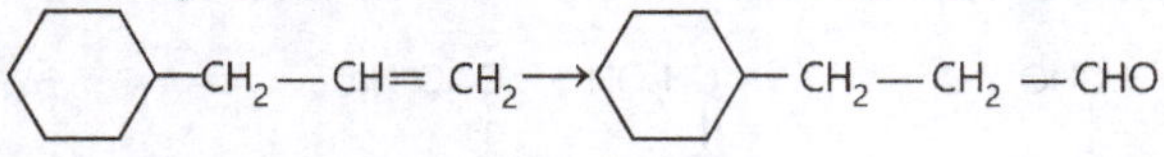

(a) (i) $H_2O / H^{\oplus}$ (ii) CrO_3
(b) (i) BH_3 (ii) $H_2O_2 / \overset{\ominus}{O}H$ (iii) PCC
(c) (i) BH_3 (ii) $H_2O_2 / \overset{\ominus}{O}H$ (iii) Alk. $KMnO_4$ (iv) $H_3O^{\oplus}$
(d) (i) $H_2O / H^{\oplus}$ (ii) PCC

2. For the given reaction NCERT Pg 245, NEET 2024

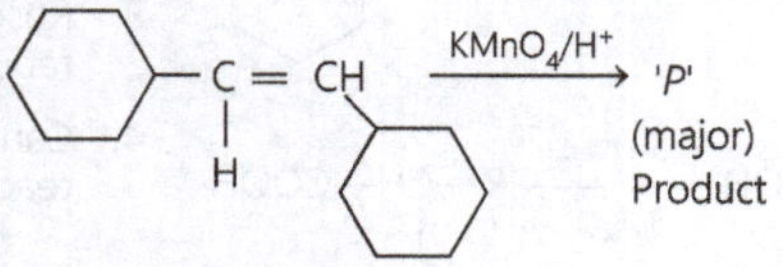

'P' is

(a) 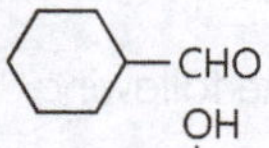 (b) 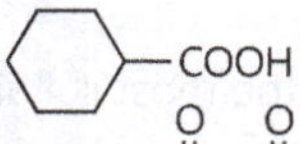
(c) 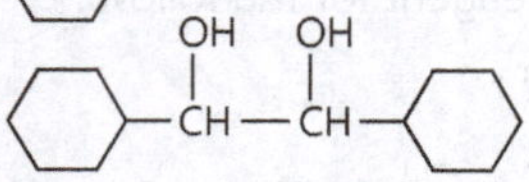 (d) 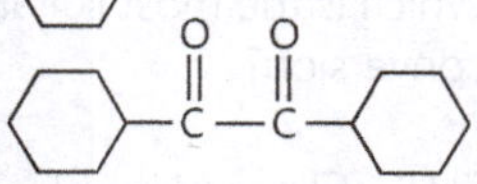

3. Complete the following reaction.

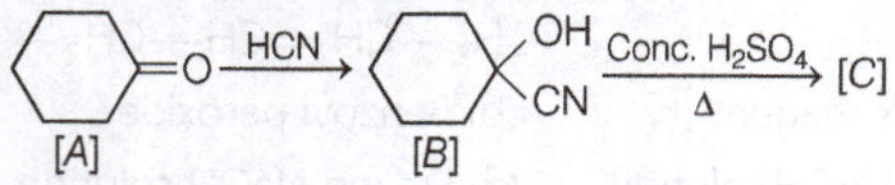

is .... NCERT Pg 237, NEET 2023

(a) 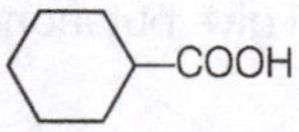 (b) 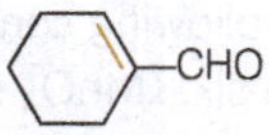
(c) 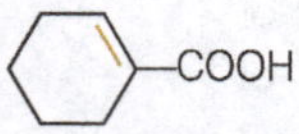 (d) 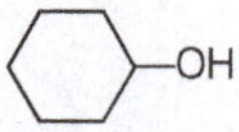

4. Identify the major product obtained in the following reaction

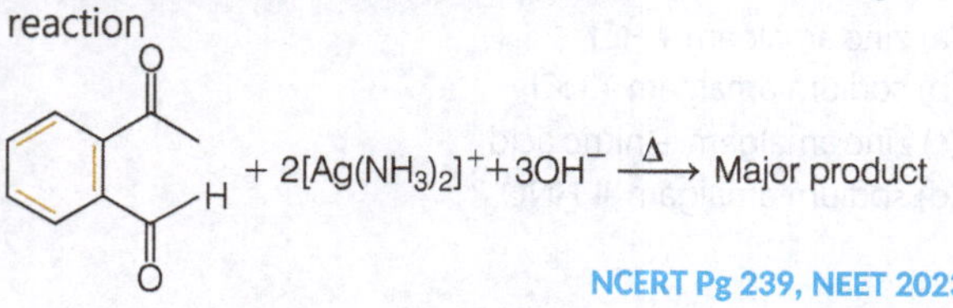

NCERT Pg 239, NEET 2023

(a) 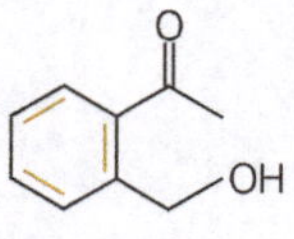 (b) 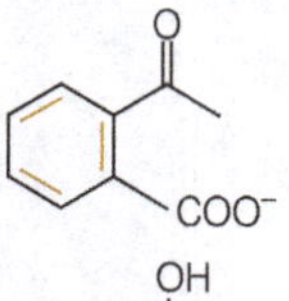
(c) 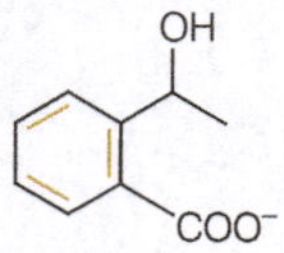 (d) 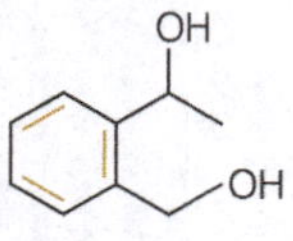

5. $RMgX + CO_2 \xrightarrow[\text{ether}]{\text{Dry}} Y \xrightarrow{H_3O^+} RCOOH$

What is Y in the above reaction ? NCERT Pg 246, NEET 2022

(a) $R_3CO^-Mg^+X$ (b) $RCOO^-X^+$
(c) $(RCOO)_2Mg$ (d) $RCOO^-Mg^+X$

6. Given below are two statements.

Statement I The boiling points of aldehydes and ketones are higher than hydrocarbons of comparable molecular masses because of weak molecular association in aldehydes and ketones due to dipole-dipole interactions.

Statement II The boiling points of aldehydes and ketones are lower than the alcohols of similar molecular masses due to the absence of H-bonding. NCERT Pg 235, NEET 2022

In the light of the above statements, choose the most appropriate answer from the options given below

(a) Both Statement I and Statement II are incorrect.
(b) Statement I is correct but Statement II is incorrect.
(c) Statement I is incorrect but Statement II is correct.
(d) Both Statement I and Statement II are correct.

7. The intermediate compound 'X' in the following chemical reaction is NCERT Pg 233 NEET 2021

$C_6H_5CH_3 + CrO_2Cl_2 \xrightarrow{CS_2} X \xrightarrow{H_3O^+} C_6H_5CHO$

(a) $C_6H_5CH(OCrOHCl_2)_2$ (b) $C_6H_5CH(OCOCH_3)_2$
(c) $C_6H_5CHCl_2$ (d) $C_6H_5CH_2Cl$

8. Match List-I with List-II. NCERT Pg 233, 240, 253, 251, NEET 2021

	List-I		List-II
A.	$C_6H_6 \xrightarrow[\text{Anhyd. AlCl}_3/\text{CuCl}]{\text{CO, HCl}}$	1.	Hell-Volhard-Zelinsky reaction
B.	$R-\overset{O}{\overset{\Vert}{C}}-CH_3 + NaOX \longrightarrow$	2.	Gattermann-Koch reaction
C.	$R-CH_2-OH + R'COOH \xrightarrow{\text{Conc. }H_2SO_4}$	3.	Haloform reaction
D.	$R-CH_2-COOH \xrightarrow[\text{(ii) }H_2O]{\text{(i) }X_2/\text{Red P}}$	4.	Esterification

Choose the correct answer from the options given below.

	A	B	C	D		A	B	C	D
(a)	4	1	2	3	(b)	3	2	1	4
(c)	1	4	3	2	(d)	2	3	4	1

9. Which of the following acid will form an (i) anhydride on heating and (ii) acetamide on strong heating with ammonia? **NCERT Pg 253, NEET 2020**

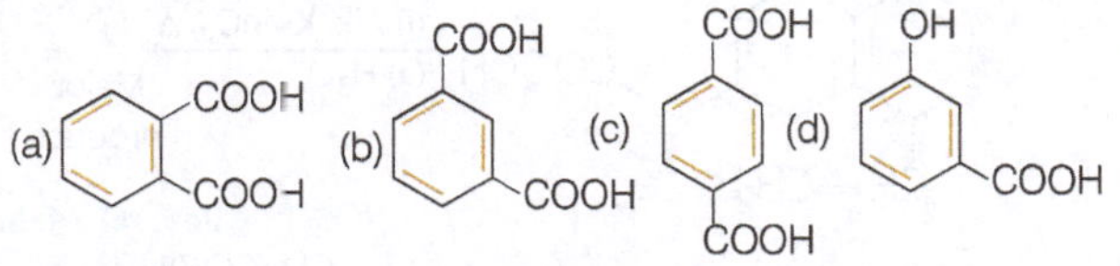

10. Identify compound (*A*) in the following reaction.

$$A \xrightarrow{H_2/Pd/BaSO_4} C_6H_5CHO$$

NCERT Pg 232, NEET 2020

(a) Benzoyl chloride (b) Toluene
(c) Acetophenone (d) Benzoic acid

11. Identify compound *X* in the following sequence of reactions.

$$C_6H_5CH_3 \xrightarrow{Cl_2/h\nu} X \xrightarrow[373\ K]{H_2O} C_6H_5CHO$$

NCERT Pg 233, NEET 2020

(a) $C_6H_5CH_2Cl$ (b) $C_6H_5CHCl_2$ (c) $C_6H_5CCl_3$ (d) C_6H_5Cl

12. Carboxylic acids have higher boiling points than aldehydes, ketones and even alcohols of comparable molecular mass. It is due to their **NCERT Pg 249, NEET 2018**

(a) more extensive association of carboxylic acid *via* van der Waals' force of attraction
(b) formation of carboxylate ion
(c) formation of intramolecular H-bonding
(d) formation of intermolecular H-bonding

13. Of the following which is the product formed when cyclohexanone undergoes aldol condensation followed by heating? **NCERT Pg 241, NEET 2017**

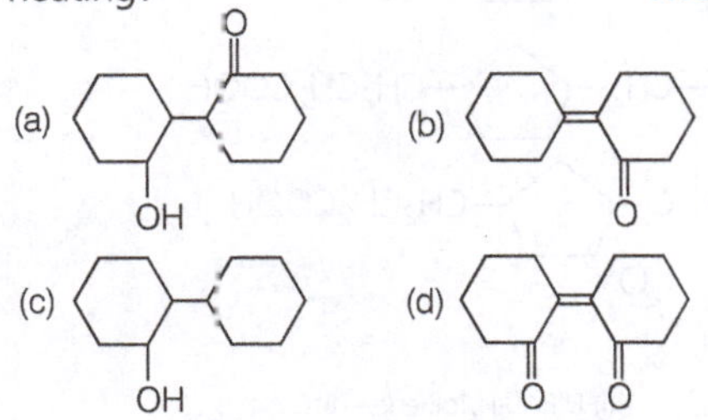

14. The IUPAC name of the compound

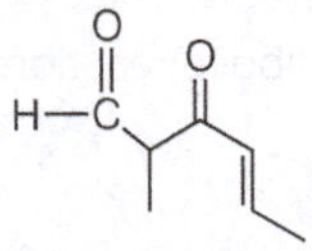

is ....

NCERT Pg 229, NEET 2017

(a) 3-keto-2-methylhex-4-enal (b) 5-formylhex-2-en-3-one
(c) 5-methyl-4-oxohex-2-en-5-al (d) 3-keto-2-methylhex-5-enal

15. The correct order of strengths of the carboxylic acids **NCERT Pg 250, NEET 2016**

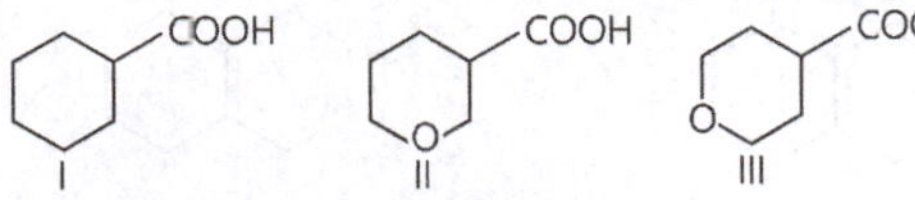

is

(a) I > II > III (b) II > III > I (c) III > II > I (d) II > I > III

JEE Main Archive

16. Identify the name reaction. **NCERT Pg 233, JEE Main 2024**

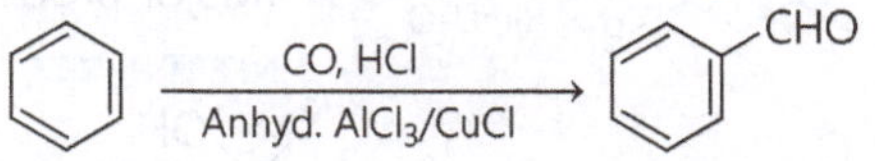

(a) Etard reaction
(b) Gattermann-Koch reaction
(c) Stephen reaction
(d) Rosenmund reduction

17. The molecular formula of second homologue in the homologous series of monocarboxylic acids is .... **NCERT Pg 244 JEE Main 2024**

(a) CH_2O (b) $C_3H_6O_2$
(c) $C_2H_2O_2$ (d) $C_2H_4O_2$

18. Given below are two statements. **NCERT Pg 241, 242 JEE Main 2024**

Statements I Acidity of α-hydrogens of aldehydes and ketones is responsible for aldol reaction.

Statements II Reaction between benzaldehyde and ethanal will not give cross-aldol product.

In the light of the above statements, choose the most appropriate answer from the options given below:

(a) Both Statement I and Statement II are incorrect.
(b) Both Statement I and Statement II are correct.
(c) Statement I is incorrect but Statement II is correct.
(d) Statement I is correct but Statement II is incorrect.

19.

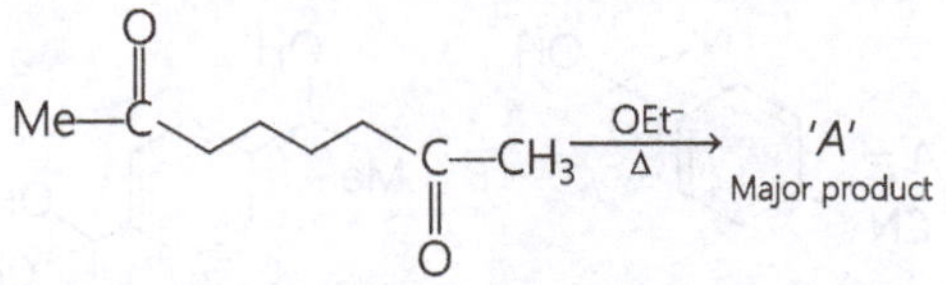

A in the above reaction is **NCERT Pg 241, JEE Main 2023**

(a)

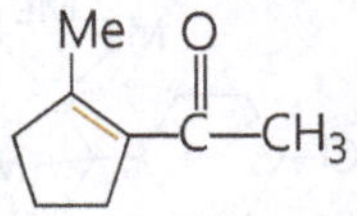

(b)

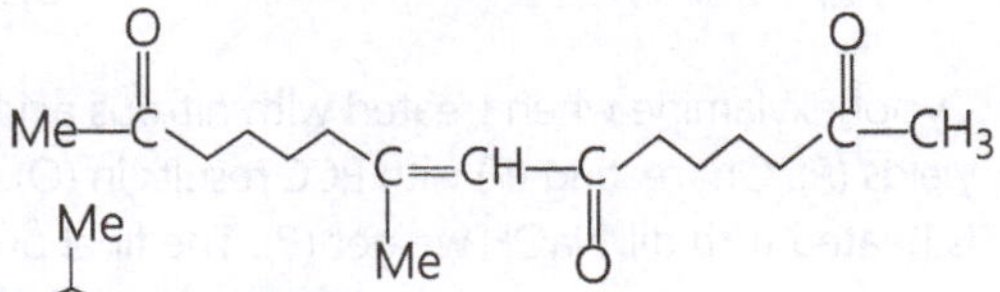

(c)

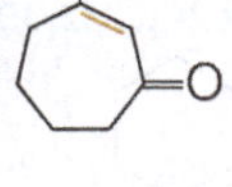

(d)

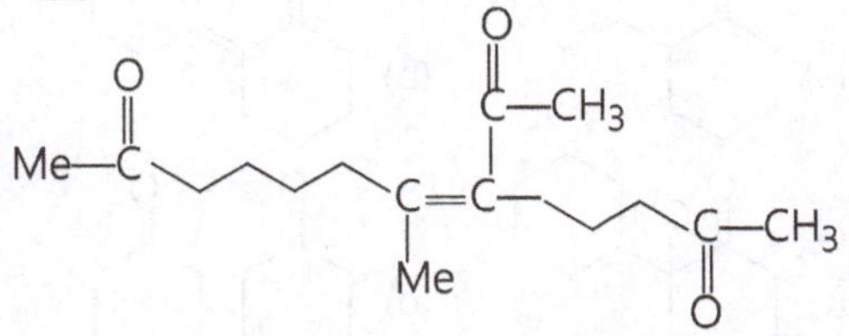

20. In the following reaction

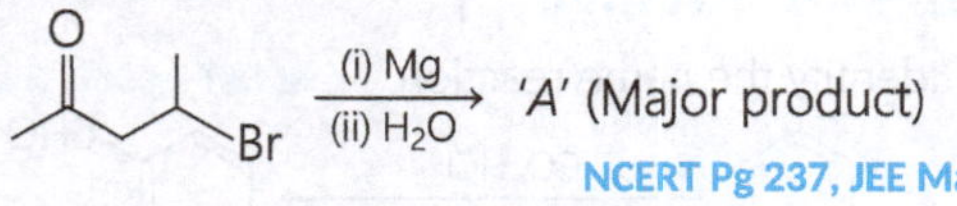

A is,

NCERT Pg 237, JEE Main 2023

(a) 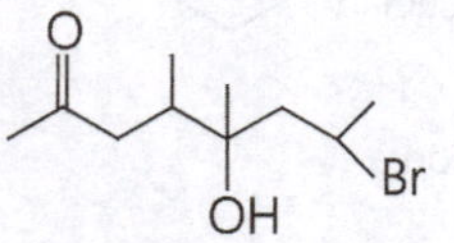 (b) 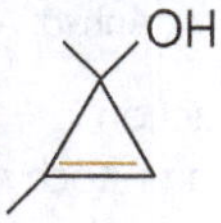

(c) 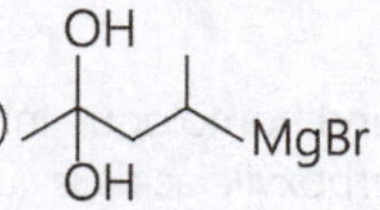 (d) 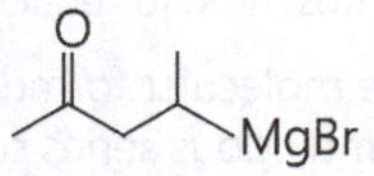

21. Find out the major products from the following reaction sequence.

NCERT Pg 237, JEE Main 2023

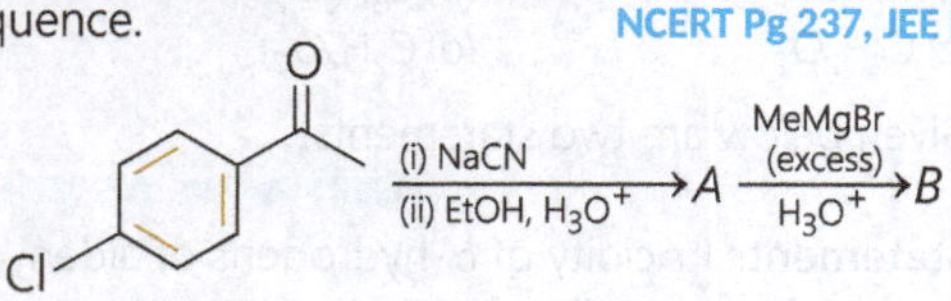

(a) 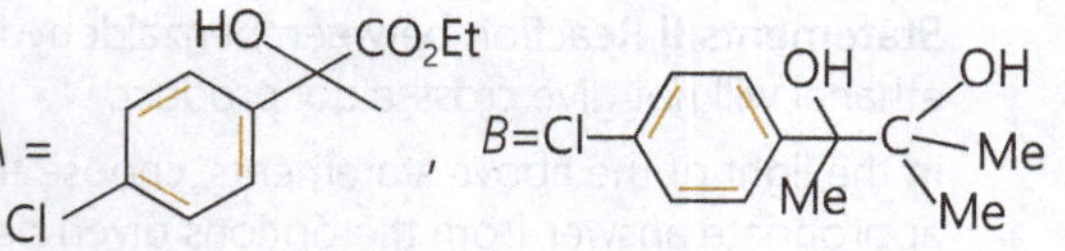

(b) 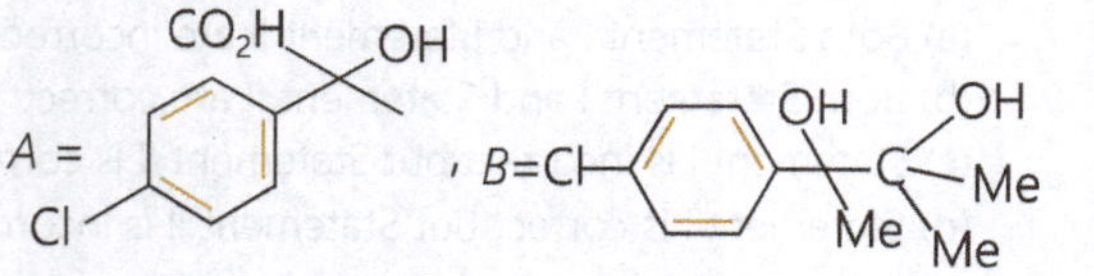

(c) 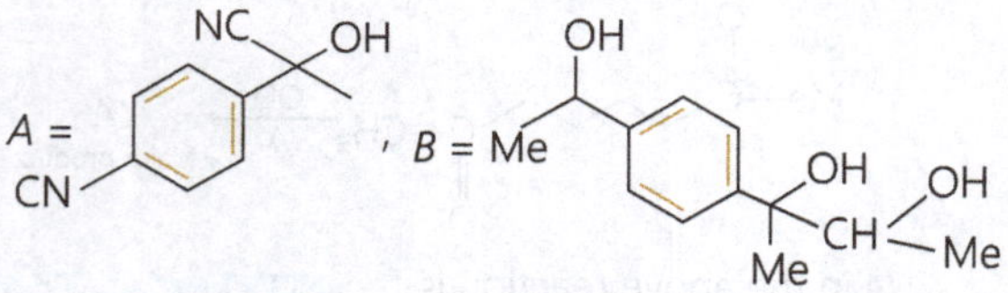

(d) 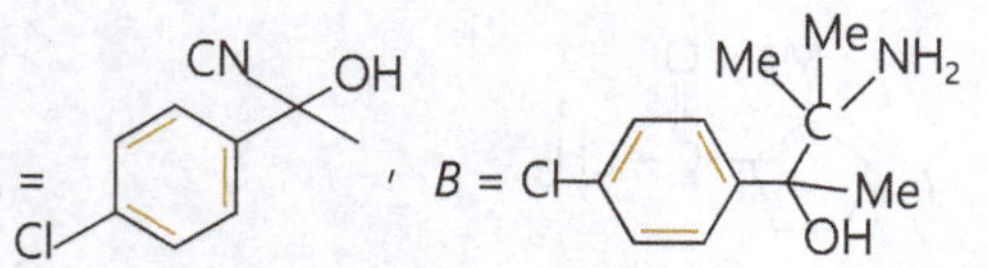

22. Cyclohexylamine when treated with nitrous acid yields (*P*). On treating (*P*) with PCC results in (*Q*). When (*Q*) is heated with dil. NaOH we get (*R*). The final product (*R*) is

NCERT Pg 241, 242, JEE Main 2023

(a) 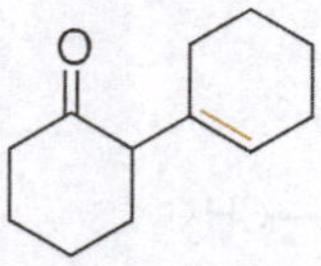 (b) 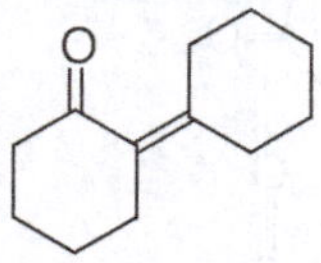

(c) 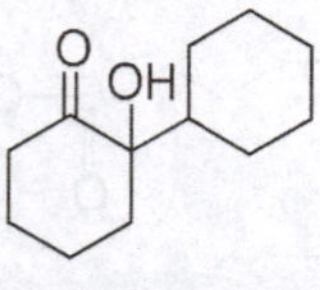 (d) 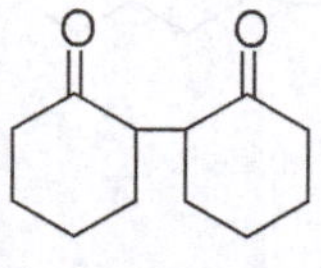

23. The major product '*P*' formed in the given reaction is

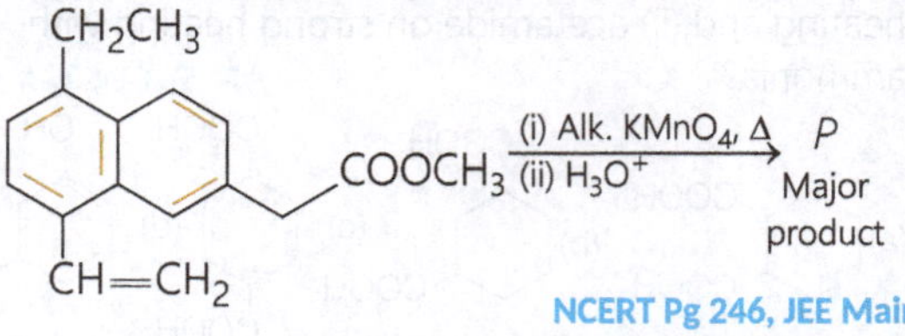

NCERT Pg 246, JEE Main 2023

(a) 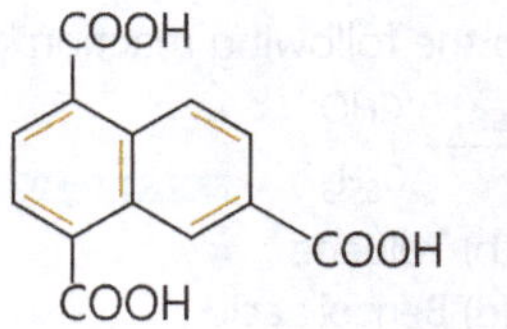 (b) 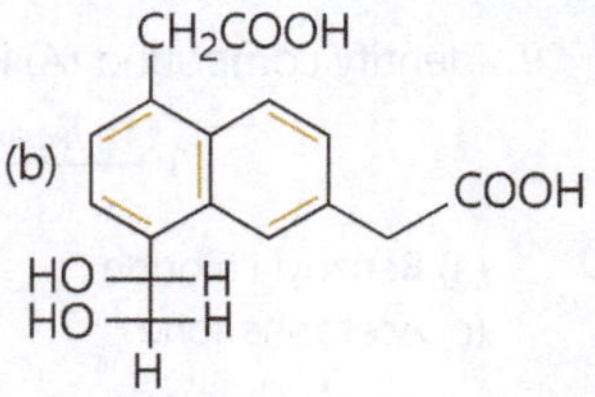

(c) 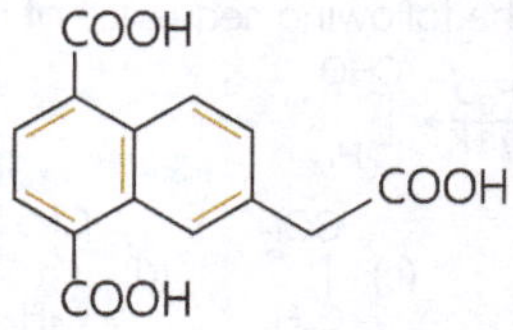 (d) 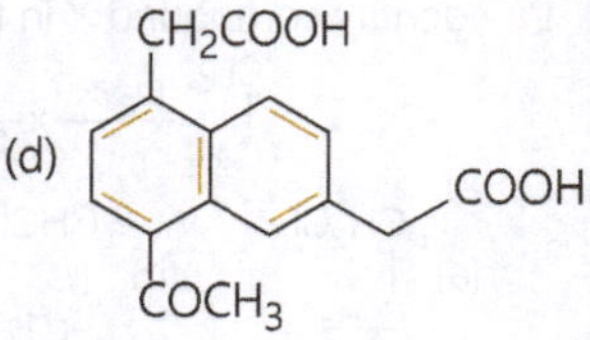

24.

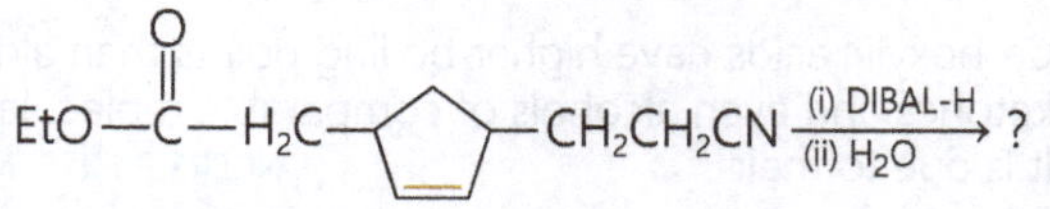

[Et is $-C_2H_5$]

Consider the above reaction and predict the major product.

NCERT Pg 232, JEE Main 2022

(a) 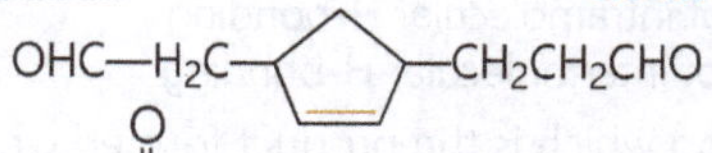

(b) 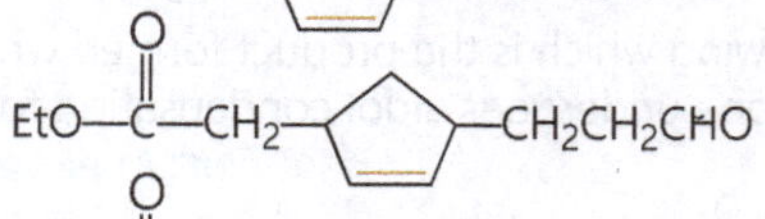

(c) 

(d) 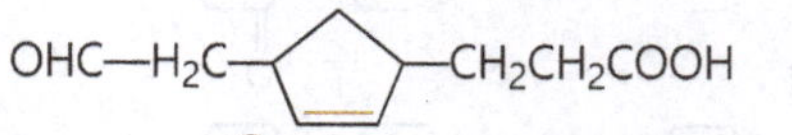

25.

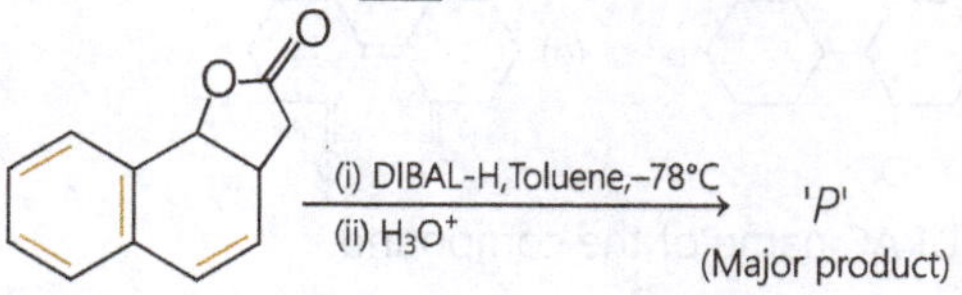

The product *P* in the above reaction is

NCERT Pg 232, JEE Main 2021

(a) 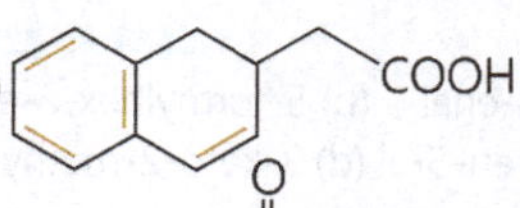 (b) 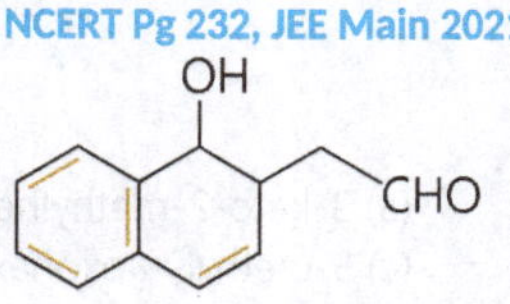

(c) 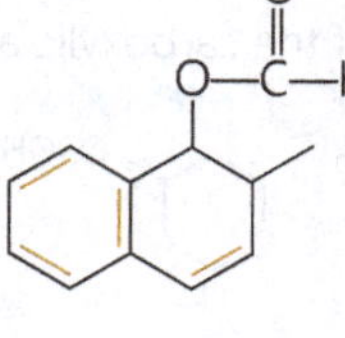 (d) 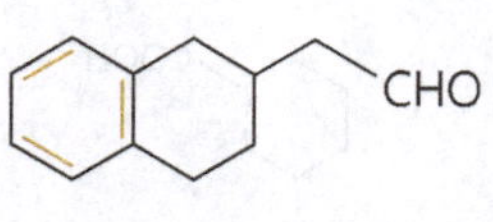

Skill Boosters

1. Anu takes a compound 'X' whose molecular formula is C_8H_8O. It forms an orange-red precipitate on reacting with 2,4-DNP reagent and gives yellow precipitate on heating with iodine in the presence of sodium hydroxide. It neither reduces Tollen's or Fehling's reagent, nor does it decolourise bromine water or Baeyer's reagent. Which compound she had taken?

(a) 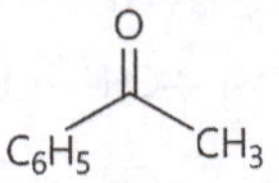
(b) $C_6H_5-CH_2CHO$
(c) $CH_3C{\equiv}C-CH{=}CH-CH{=}CH-CHO$
(d) $CH_3-CH{=}CH-C{\equiv}C-CH{=}CH-CHO$

2. Ankur takes a aldehyde compound with molecular formula A ($C_{11}H_8O$). The compound do not undergo aldol condensation and it gives benzaldehyde and two moles of compound B on ozonolysis. Compound B, on oxidation with silver ion gives oxalic acid. Identify the compound A and B respectively.

(a) $C_6H_5CH_2CH_2CH_2CH_2CHO$, $CHO-CH_2COOH$
(b) $C_6H_5-CH{=}CH-C{\equiv}C-CHO$, $CHO-COOH$
(c) $C_6H_5CH_2CHO$, $C_6H_5-CH_2-CH_2-OH$
(d) $C_6H_5-CH_2-CH_2-COOH$, CH_3-CH_2-COOH

3. Consider the following reactions.

Unknown aldehyde (A) + Unsaturated aldehyde (B)

(A) + (B) → β-hydroxy butyraldehyde $\xrightarrow{-H_2O}$ But-2-enal

(B) $\xrightarrow{\text{Conc. alkali}}$ C + D; Alcohol (C_7H_8O)

What is A and B in the above reaction sequence?

	A	B
(a)	Benzaldehyde	Acetaldehyde
(b)	Acetaldehyde	Benzaldehyde
(c)	Formaldehyde	Acetaldehyde
(d)	Acetaldehyde	Formaldehyde

4. A dialkyl carbonyl compound 'A' with three carbon atoms is not readily oxidised but on reduction gives $C_3H_8O(B)$. B on reaction with HBr gives a bromide (C) which is converted to Grignard reagent. This Grignard reagent reacts with (A) to give 2, 3-dimethylbutan-2-ol. Here A, B and C respectively are

(a) CH_3CH_2CHO, $CH_3CH_2CH_2OH$, $CH_3CH_2CH_2Br$
(b) CH_3COCH_3, $CH_3CH(OH)CH_3$, $CH_3CH(Br)CH_3$
(c) CH_3CH_2CHO, $CH_3CH{=}CH_2$, $CH_3CCH(Br)CH_3$
(d) CH_3COCH_3, $CH_3CH(OH)CH_3$, $CH_3CH(Br)CH_3$

5. Compound 'A' (molecular formula C_3H_8O) is treated with acidified potassium dichromate to form a product 'B' (molecular formula C_3H_6O). 'B' forms a shining silver mirror on warming with ammoniacal silver nitrate. 'B' when treated with an aqueous solution of $H_2NCONHNH_2$, HCl and sodium acetate gives a product 'C'. The structure of the compound 'C' will be

(a) $CH_3CH_2CH{=}NNHCONH_2$
(b) $CH_3-CH{=}N(CH_3)NHCONH_2$
(c) $CH_3CH{=}N(CH_3)CONHNH_2$
(d) $CH_3CH_2CH-NCONHNH_2$

6. An organic compound 'A' (C_4H_8O) is resistant to oxidation but forms compound 'B' ($C_4H_{10}O$) on reduction. 'B' reacts with HBr to form the compound 'C'. 'C' with Mg forms Grignard's reagent 'D' which reacts with 'A' to form a product which on hydrolysis gives 'E'. Identify E.

(a) Butan-2-ol
(b) 2, 3-dimethylpentan-3-ol
(c) 3, 3-dimethyl butanal
(d) 3, 3-dimethyl pantanal

7. Riya takes two test tubes A and B. In both test tubes she takes a compound 'X'.

In test tube A, she performed 2, 4-DNP test and she observed a coloured ppt. formed. Similarly, in test tube B, she performed a iodoform test and she observed a yellow ppt. On the basis of the given observations identify the compound 'X'.

(a) 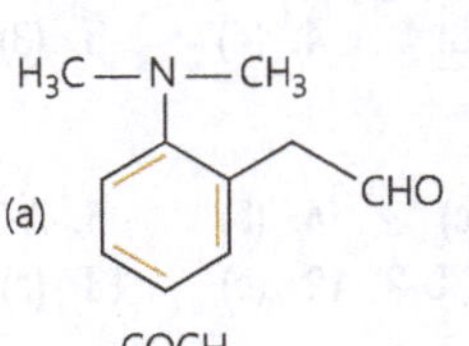

(b) 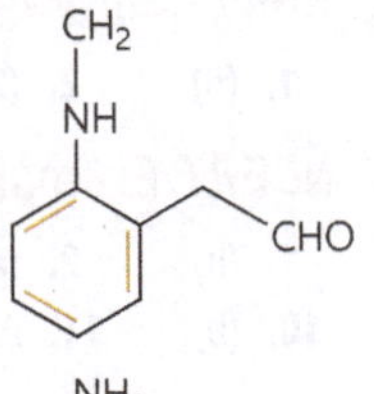

(c) 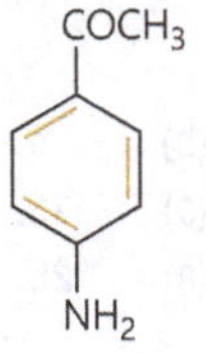

(d) 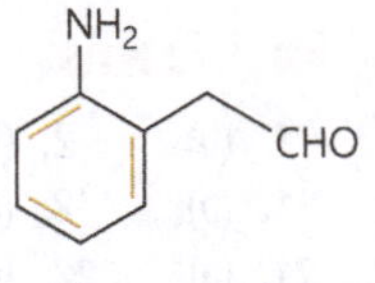

8. An organic compound $X(C_8H_{16}O_2)$ undergo hydrolysis with dil. H_2SO_4 to give carboxylic acid Y and alcohol Z. Oxidation of Z with chromic acid produce Y. Z upon dehydration gives but-1-ene. What are the compound X, Y and Z?

(a) $X \rightarrow H_3CCH_2-CH_2-CH_2-\underset{\underset{O}{\|}}{C}-OCH_2CH_2CH_3,$

$Y \rightarrow CH_3CH_2CH_2COOH,\ Z \rightarrow CH_3CH_2CH_2OH$

(b) $X \rightarrow CH_3CH_2-\underset{\underset{CH_3}{|}}{CH_2}-\underset{\underset{O}{\|}}{C}-OCH_2CH_2CH_3$

$Y \rightarrow CH_3-CH_2-\underset{\underset{CH_3}{|}}{CH}-COOH,\ Z \rightarrow CH_3CH_2CH_2OH$

(c) $X \rightarrow CH_3-CH_2-CH_2-\underset{\underset{O}{\|}}{C}-O-CH_2CH_2CH_2CH_3,$

$Y \rightarrow CH_3CH_2CH_2-COOH,\ Z \rightarrow CH_3CH_2CH_2CH_2OH$

(d) $X \rightarrow CH_3CH_2CH_2-\underset{\underset{O}{\|}}{C}-O-CH_2-\underset{\underset{CH_3}{|}}{CH}-CH_3,$

$Y \rightarrow CH_3CH_2CH_2-COOH,\ Z \rightarrow CH_3-\underset{\underset{CH_3}{|}}{CH}-CH_2OH$

✔ Correct Codes

Topical Questions

1. (b)	2. (b)	3. (c)	4. (a)	5. (c)	6. (a)	7. (b)	8. (a)	9. (b)	10. (c)
11. (b)	12. (b)	13. (b)	14. (a)	15. (d)	16. (a)	17. (b)	18. (c)	19. (b)	20. (a)
21. (c)	22. (d)	23. (c)	24. (d)	25. (b)	26. (c)	27. (c)	28. (a)	29. (d)	30. (c)
31. (d)	32. (d)	33. (a)	34. (c)	35. (a)	36. (c)	37. (a)	38. (b)	39. (b)	40. (a)
41. (c)	42. (b)	43. (b)	44. (d)	45. (d)	46. (c)	47. (d)	48. (c)	49. (b)	50. (b)
51. (d)	52. (a)	53. (b)	54. (a)	55. (b)	56. (c)	57. (c)	58. (d)	59. (d)	60. (b)
61. (a)	62. (a)	63. (c)	64. (a)	65. (a)	66. (a)	67. (c)	68. (b)	69. (d)	70. (b)
71. (b)	72. (b)	73. (c)	74. (d)	75. (b)	76. (a)	77. (d)	78. (a)	79. (c)	80. (a)
81. (a)	82. (b)	83. (c)	84. (c)	85. (d)	86. (a)	87. (d)	88. (b)	89. (d)	90. (a)
91. (a)	92. (a)	93. (a)	94. (d)	95. (d)	96. (c)				

Assertion-Reason

1. (a)	2. (a)	3. (b)	4. (a)	5. (a)	6. (d)

Statement Type

1. (b)	2. (a)	3. (c)	4. (b)	5. (c)	6. (c)	7. (a)	8. (d)	9. (c)	10. (a)

Matching Type

1. (d)	2. (c)	3. (b)	4. (d)	5. (b)	6. (a)

Numerical Value

1. (5)	2. (2)	3. (3)	4. (4)	5. (3)

NCERT Exemplar's

1. (b)	2. (a)	3. (c)	4. (b)	5. A-3, B-4, C-1, D-2	6. (c)	7. (d)	8. (b)	9. (d)
10. (b)	11. A-3, B-4, C-1, D-2	12. (c)	13. (b)	14. (a)				

Past Exams'

1. (b)	2. (b)	3. (c)	4. (b)	5. (d)	6. (d)	7. (a)	8. (d)	9. (a)	10. (a)
11. (b)	12. (d)	13. (b)	14. (a)	15. (b)	16. (b)	17. (d)	18. (b)	19. (a)	20. (a)
21. (a)	22. (b)	23. (a)	24. (a)	25. (b)					

Skill Boosters

1. (a)	2. (b)	3. (b)	4. (d)	5. (a)	6. (b)	7. (c)	8. (c)

Step by Step
Decoding the Questions

Concept Builders

1. False
2. carboxylic acid
3. Acetone
4. True
5. acyl group
6. Acrolein
7. same, π-electron
8. True
9. Dehydrogenation
10. Ag or Cu
11. False
12. DIBAL-H, aldehydes
13. Chromyl chloride in CS_2 solvent
14. True
15. Formaldehyde (formalin 40% solution)
16. decrease
17. False
18. Clemmensen reduction
19. aldehyde, alcohol
20. Cannizzaro reaction
21. False
22. Formic acid, butyric acid
23. Propane-1, 2, 3-tricarboxylic acid
24. False
25. False
26. True
27. Benzoic acid
28. increases
29. False
30. Hexanedioic acid

Topical Solutions

1 (*b*) When the aldehyde group is attached to a ring, the suffix carbaldehyde is added after the full name of the cycloalkane.

2 (*b*) The priority order of functional group is —CHO > Br. Therefore, IUPAC name of the given compound is 3-bromo-2-methylhexanal.

3 (*c*) The name of the compound I is 3-oxopentanol and the name of compound II is propane-1, 2, 3-tricarbaldehyde

4 (*a*) Among the given option (a) is incorrectly matched. The correct IUPAC name is 3-methylcyclohexanecarbaldehyde

5 (*c*) The IUPAC name of the given compounds is

(i) Mesityl oxide-4-methylpent-3-en-2-one

(ii) Acrolein-prop-2-enal

6 (*a*) The bond angles are approximately 120° as expected of a trigonal planar structure in the carbonyl compounds.

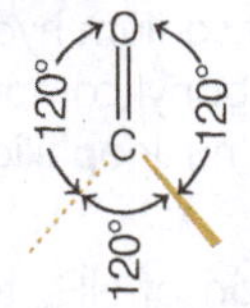

Trigonal planar

7 (*b*) Among the given compounds, formaldehyde is the most polar due to lowest electron density on C of carbonyl group, whereas in all other cases, the electron density on C is high due to +*I*-effect of alkyl groups.

8 (*a*) Among the given statements I and II are incorrect while rest are correct. Their correct form are :

- Carbonyl carbon atom is sp^2-hybridised.
- The carbonyl carbon and three atoms attached to it lie in the same plane.

9 (*b*) Alcohol vapours are passed over heavy metal catalysts (Ag or Cu) to give aldehydes and ketones.

10 (*c*)

$$CH_2{=}C\begin{smallmatrix}H\\R\end{smallmatrix} \xrightarrow{O_3} HCHO + RCHO$$

Vinyl group ($CH_2{=}CH{-}$) on ozonolysis gives formaldehydes.

11 (*b*) Among the given compounds, only (b) give 5-keto-2-methyl hexanal.

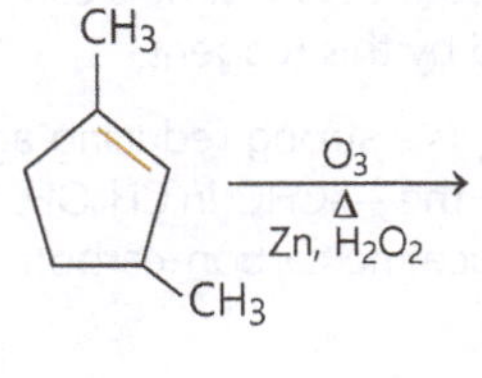

$$CH_3{-}\overset{O}{\overset{\|}{C}}{-}CH_2{-}CH_2{-}\overset{CH_3}{\overset{|}{CH}}{-}CHO$$

5-keto-2-methyl hexanal

12 (*b*) Addition of water to ethyne in the presence of H_2SO_4 and $HgSO_4$ gives acetaldehyde.

13 (*b*) $\underset{\text{Propyne}}{CH_3{-}C{\equiv}CH} + H{-}OH \xrightarrow[333\,K]{Hg^{2+}/H^+}$

$$CH_3\underset{\underset{O-H}{|}}{C}{=}CH_2 \xrightarrow{\text{Tautomerism}} \underset{\text{Propanone}}{CH_3{-}\overset{O}{\overset{\|}{C}}{-}CH_3}$$

14 (*a*) The product formed is *R*—CHO. The name of this reaction is Rosenmund reduction.

15 (*d*) The given reaction is called Stephen reaction.

16 (*a*) The reaction is proceed as

$$R{-}C{\equiv}N \xrightarrow[\text{(ii)}H_2O]{\text{(i)} AlH(i\text{-Bu})_2} RCHO$$

So, *R*CHO is the major product.

17 (*b*) Among the given substrates, only (b) give the same product, i.e. aldehyde on the reduction with DIBAL-H. Nitriles are selectively reduced by DIBAL-H to imines followed by hydrolysis to aldehyde. Esters are also reduced to aldehydes by DIBAL-H.

18 (*c*) The complete reaction is shown below.

$$\underset{\text{Toluene}}{\overset{CH_3}{\underset{C_6H_5}{|}}} + CrO_2Cl_2 \xrightarrow{CS_2}$$

$$\underset{\text{Chromium complex}}{\underset{C_6H_5}{\overset{CH(OCrOHCl_2)_2}{|}}} \xrightarrow{H_3O^+} \underset{\text{Benzaldehyde}}{\underset{C_6H_5}{\overset{CHO}{|}}}$$

This reaction is called Etard reaction.

19 (*b*) The complete reaction is shown below :

$$C_6H_5CH_3 \xrightarrow{Cl_2/h\nu} \underset{\text{Benzal chloride 'X'}}{C_6H_5CHCl_2} \xrightarrow[373\,K]{H_2O} \underset{\text{Benzaldehyde 'Y'}}{C_6H_5CHO}$$

20 (*a*) Among the given reactions, option (a) is the Gattermann-Koch reaction.

21 (*c*) Among the given reactions I, II and III gives benzophenone as main product.

22 (*d*) Among the given statements, statement (d) is not correct. The correct form is :

Treatment of acyl chloride with H_2, Pd-$BaSO_4$ gives aldehyde not ketone.

23 (*c*) The boiling point of butan-1-ol (II) would be the highest, due to extensive intermolecular hydrogen bonding. Butanal (I) is more polar than ethoxyethane (III).

n-pentane (IV) have only weak van der Waals' forces and thus will have the lowest boiling point. Therefore, the correct increasing order is (c).

24 (*d*) Aldehydes are generally more reactive than ketones in nucleophilic addition reactions due to steric and electronic reasons.

The additional carbon in butanone increases steric hindrance, making it less reactive than propanone, which is also the case in propanal and ethanal Thus, the correct order is (d).

25 (*b*) Statement (b) is incorrect, while the other statements are correct. Corrected form are as follows

The hybridisation of carbon changes from sp^2 to sp^3 in this process and a tetrahedral alkoxide intermediate is produced.

26 (*c*) Sodium hydrogen sulphite adds to ketones to form addition product (bisulphite addition compound).

The hydrogen sulphite addition compound is water soluble and can be converted backs to the original carbonyl compound by treating it with dilute mineral acid or alkali.

$$CH_3COCH_3 + NaHSO_3 \longrightarrow \underset{\text{(Bisulphite addition compound)}}{CH_3-C(OH)(CH_3)-SO_3Na} \xrightarrow{Na_2CO_3} CH_3COCH_3$$

27 (*c*) I and II are Hemiacetal and acetal respectively.

28 (*a*) Addition of sodium hydrogen sulphite to carbonyl compounds is an example of nucleophilic addition reaction.

29 (*d*) The addition of NH_3 to carbonyl compound is an example in which nucleophilic addition is followed by elimination reaction occur respectively.

30 (*c*) The correct match is

$$>C{=}N-NH-\overset{\overset{O}{\|}}{C}-NH_2 \longrightarrow \text{Semicarbazone}$$

31 (*d*) The complete reaction is,

$$CH_3CH{=}CH-CHO + NH_2-\overset{\overset{O}{\|}}{C}-NHNH_2 \xrightarrow{H^+} CH_3CH{=}CH-CH{=}N-NH-\overset{\overset{O}{\|}}{C}-NH_2$$

32 (*d*) Statements (a), (b), and (c) are correct but the statement (d) is not correct. The correct form is

The given reaction is a nucleophilic-addition reaction and thus, there is no role of α-hydrogens.

33 (*a*) The suitable reagent for the given conversion is $NaBH_4$.

It is a selective reagent and does not reduce carbon-carbon double bond. Thus, unsaturated alcohols can be prepared by this reagent.

34 (*c*) $LiAlH_4$ is a strong reducing agent, it reduce the —CHO in CH_2OH. It also reduce the carbon-carbon double bond when, C = C will be in conjugation with carbonyl group. The reaction is proceed as

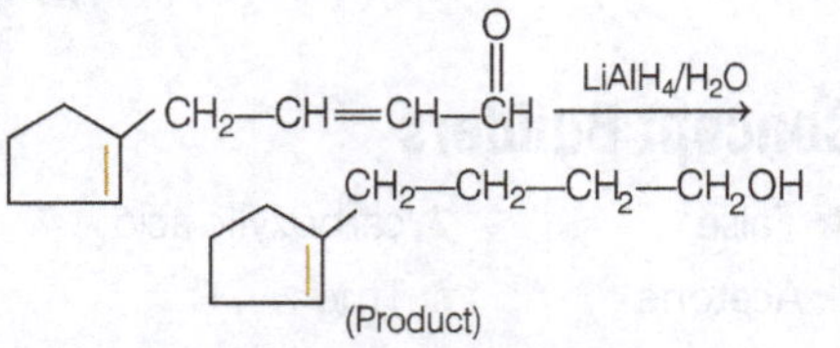

35 (*a*) Reducing agents like $LiAlH_4$, $NaBH_4$, i.e. complex hydrides usually does not affect π-bonds.

Thus, option (a) is correct answer.

36 (*c*) *X* and *Y* in the given reaction are H_2O, H_2SO_4/Hg^{2+} and $NaBH_4$ respectively.

37 (*a*) $CH_3CH{=}CHCHO \xrightarrow[Pt]{H_2} CH_3CH_2CH_2CHO$

38 (*b*) The given reaction is Clemmensen reduction.

$$>C{=}O \xrightarrow[HCl]{Zn\text{-}Hg} >CH_2 + H_2O$$

39 (*b*) The correct sequence is

$$CH_3CHO \xrightarrow[{[O]}]{K_2Cr_2O_7/H^+} CH_3COOH \xrightarrow{Ca(OH)_2} (CH_3COO)_2Ca \xrightarrow{\Delta} CH_3COCH_3$$

40 (*a*) Composition of Fehling's solution *A* is an aqueous copper sulphate and Fehling's solution *B* is alkaline sodium potassium tartarate (Rochelle salt) respectively.

41 (*c*) Among the given compounds CH_3COCH_3 does not give a silver mirror with ammonical silver nitrate but gives oxime with hydroxylamine.

42 (*b*) Tollen's reagent

43 (*b*) On heating an aliphatic aldehyde with Fehling's reagent, a reddish brown precipitate is obtained due to the formation of Cu_2O.

44 (*d*) Among the given reactions only (d) will not give benzaldehyde.

$$C_6H_5COCH_3 + Zn/Hg \xrightarrow{\text{Conc. HCl}} \underset{\text{Ethyl benzene}}{C_6H_5CH_2CH_3} + H_2O$$

This reaction is known as Clemmensen's reduction.

45 (*d*) Ethanal and propanal is distinguished by iodoform test. Ethanal has one methyl group linked to the carbonyl carbon atom and therefore, responds to this test. Propanal does not respond to this test.

46 (*c*) The complete reaction is shown below.

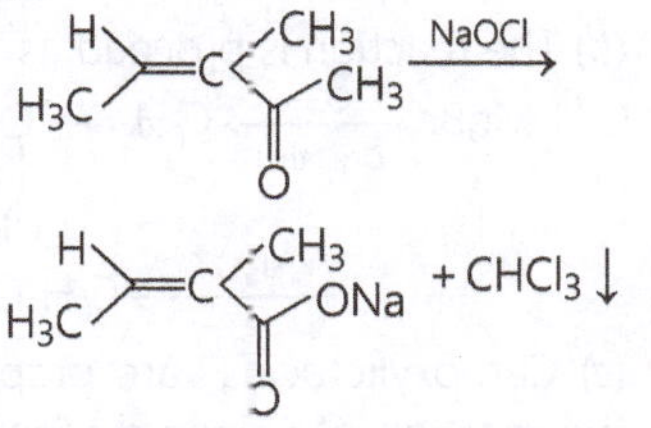

This reaction is an example of haloform reaction.
In this oxidation the carbon-carbon double bond is not affected, if present in the molecule.

47 (*d*) Among the given compounds, formaldehyde is the only one which does not give haloform test.

48 (*c*) 2, 4-DNP reagent reacts with carbonyl compounds (aldehydes and ketones) to produce orange-red precipitate.

Among the given compounds, butanone is a carbonyl compound and, thus can react with 2, 4-DNP reagent.

49 (*b*) Compounds, *A* and *B* are

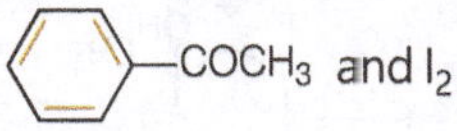

and I_2 respectively.

The reaction is proceed as

$2NaOH + \underset{(B)}{I_2} \longrightarrow NaOI + NaI + H_2O$

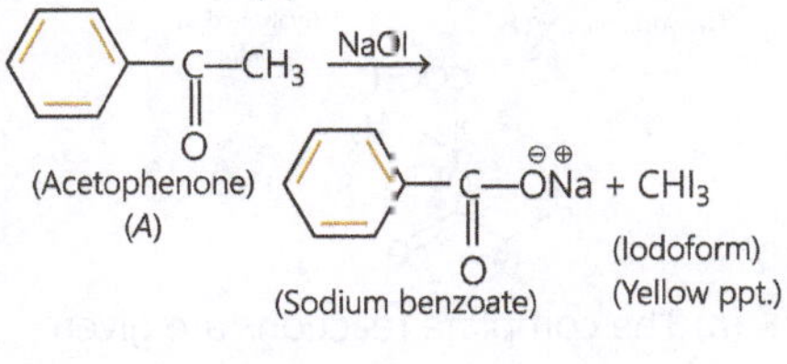

50 (*b*) Statement (b) is correct, while the statements (a), (c), (d) are incorrect. Their correct form are as follows

(a) CH_3—O group does not undergo haloform reaction.

(c) Sodium hypohalite (Na*OX*) is used as a reagent in this reaction.

(d) In this reaction, the methyl group is converted to haloform (CHX_3).

51 (*d*) Reactivity of carbonyl compounds towards nucleophilic addition reaction depends on steric and electronic effects.

Reactivity ∝ E.W.G. (Electron withdrawing group)

$$\propto \frac{1}{\text{Steric hindrance}}$$

Thus, (d) is most reactive towards nucleophilic substitution.

52 (*a*) The necessary condition for aldol condensation is the presence of atleast one α-H atom in aldehydes and ketones. Thus, among the given options, (a) does not undergo aldol condensation as it does not contains any α-hydrogen atom.

53 (*b*) The compounds *X* and *Y* are,

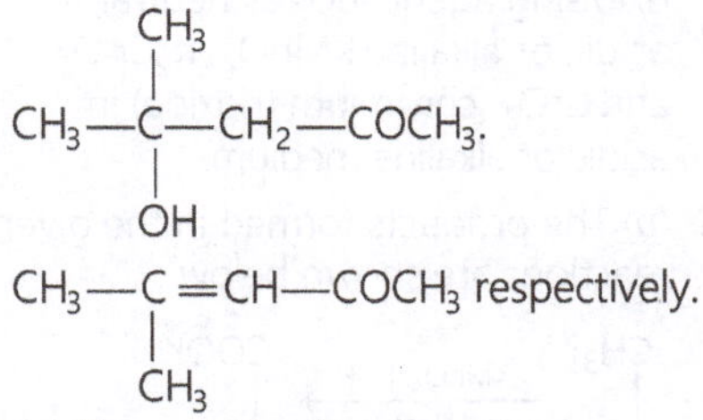

54 (*a*) The reaction is proceed as

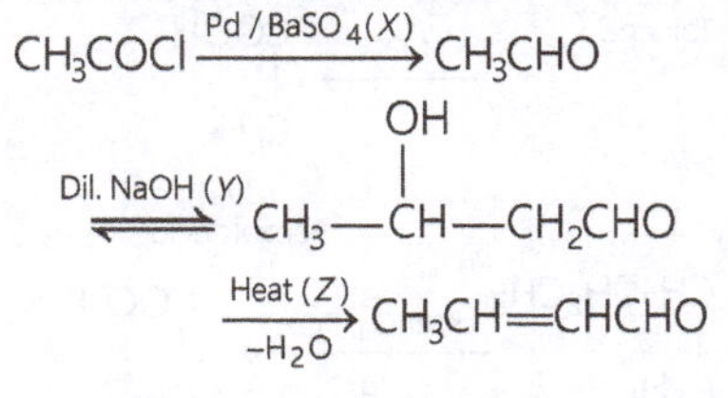

55 (*b*) The reaction is proceed as

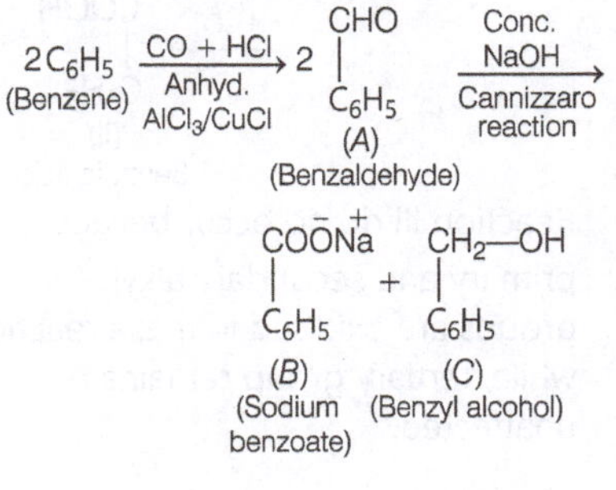

56 (*c*) The given reaction is a crossed Cannizzaro reaction which is a redox reaction too. Oxidation number of carbon atom of the —CHO groups of Ph—CHO and H—CHO are +1 and zero respectively.

So, HCHO is the stronger reducing agent than PhCHO. As a result, HCHO is oxidised to HCOONa (by donation of hydride, H^-) and PhCHO (H^- acceptor) is reduced to $PhCH_2OH$.

The reaction is proceed as

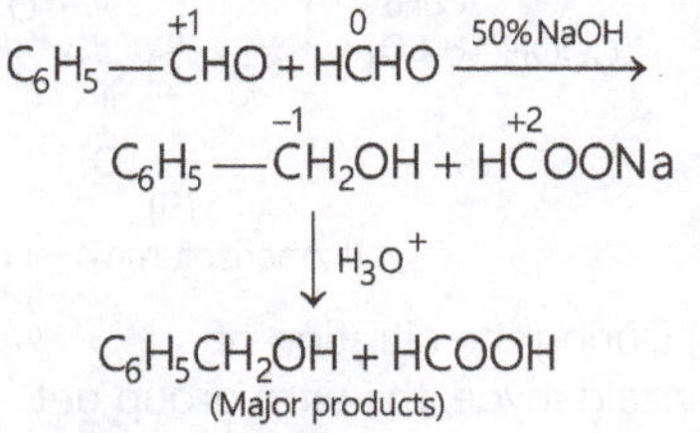

57 (*c*) Aldehydes that do not have α-hydrogen, undergo Cannizzaro reaction.

Among the given options, acetaldehyde does not give Cannizzaro reaction because it has 3 α-hydrogen.

58 (*d*) The reaction is proceed as

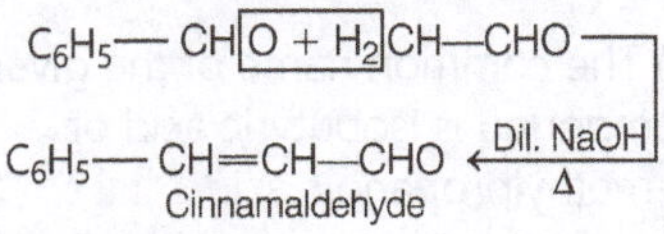

59 (*d*) The compound *A* is acetophenone.

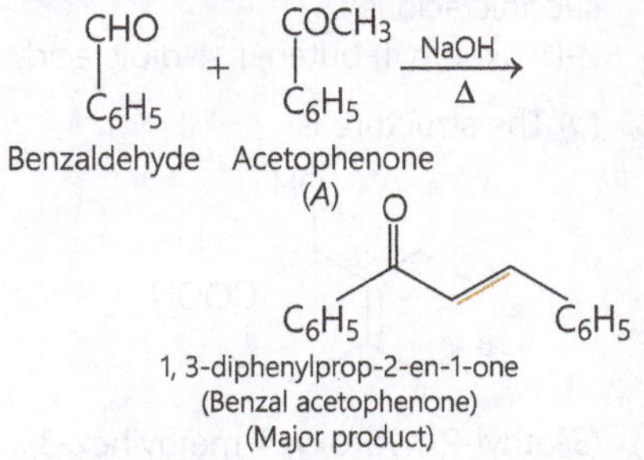

60 (*b*) Statement (b) is correct, while the other statements are incorrect. Their corrected form are as follows

(a) Due to absence of α-hydrogen, CCl_3CHO does not exhibit aldol condensation.

(c) Mixture of HCHO and CH_3CHO will give self aldol as well as cross-aldol condensation.

(d) 2-methyl propanal undergoes Cannizzaro reaction although it contains α-H-atom. It is due to the formation of less stable carbanion.

61 (*a*) The reaction is proceed as

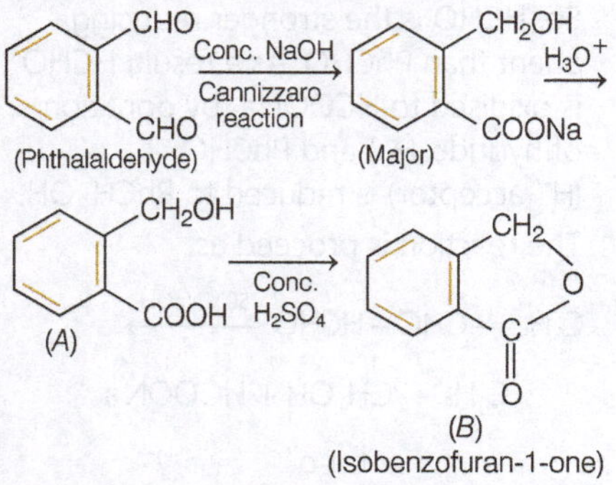

62 (*a*) During the nitration of benzaldehyde, the nitro group get attached to the *meta*-position forming *m*-nitrobenzaldehyde. The reaction is as follows

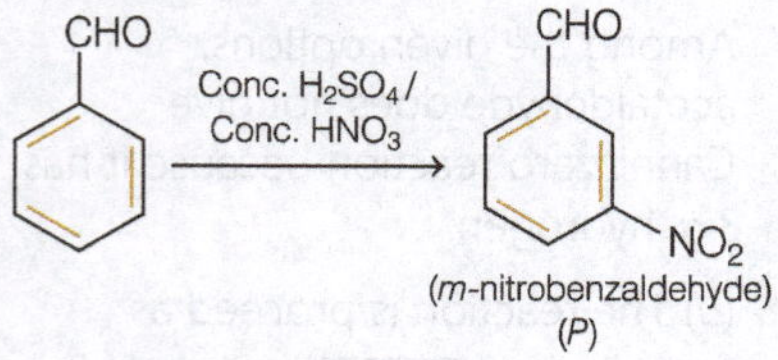

63 (*c*) The common name of the given compound is isobutyric acid or α-methylpropanoic acid.

64 (*a*) The IUPAC name of the α-acetyl succinic acid is 2-(1-oxoethyl) butan-1, 4-dioic acid.

65 (*a*) The structure is

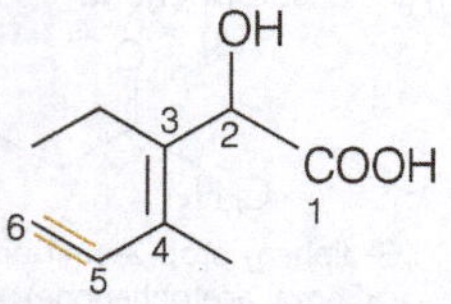

(3-ethyl-2-hydroxy-4-methylhex-3-en-5-ynoic acid).

66 (*a*) Among the given option (a) is incorrectly matched.

$PhCH_2CH_2COOH \rightarrow$ 3-phenylpropanoic acid.

67 (*c*) Statement (c) is correct, while the other statements are incorrect.

Their correct form as follows

- Aldehydes are easily oxidised to carboxylic acids on treatment with mild oxidising agents.
- Ketones are oxidised to carboxylic acids under vigorous conditions, i.e. strong oxidising agents and at elevated temperatures.
- In carboxylic acids, the bonds to the carboxyl carbon are planar with sp^2-hybridised carbon atom and trigonal planar geometry.

68 (*b*)

$$\underset{C_6H_5}{CH_2CH_2CH_3} \xrightarrow[\text{Heat}]{KMnO_4,\ KOH} \underset{(A)}{\underset{C_6H_5}{COOK}} \xrightarrow{H_3O^+} \underset{(B)}{\underset{C_6H_5}{COOH}}$$

69 (*d*) Statements (a), (b) and (c) are correct while the statement (d) is incorrect. The corrected form is as follows

Primary alcohols are readily oxidised to carboxylic acids with common oxidising agent such as neutral, acidic or alkaline $KMnO_4$, $K_2Cr_2O_7$ and CrO_3 (chromium trioxide) in acidic or alkaline medium.

70 (*b*) The products formed in the given reactions are shown below :

$$\underset{\text{Toluene}}{\underset{C_6H_5}{CH_3}} \xrightarrow[\text{Heat}]{KMnO_4,\ KOH} \underset{C_6H_5}{CO\overset{-}{O}\overset{+}{K}} \xrightarrow{H_3O^+} \underset{\text{Benzoic acid}}{\underset{(I)}{\underset{C_6H_5}{COOH}}}$$

$$\underset{C_6H_5}{CH_2CH_2CH_3} \xrightarrow[\Delta]{KMnO_4,\ KOH} \underset{C_6H_5}{COO^-K^+} \xrightarrow{H_3O^+} \underset{\text{Benzoic acid}}{\underset{(II)}{\underset{C_6H_5}{COOH}}}$$

Reaction III do no occur because primary and secondary alkyl groups are oxidised in these reaction while, tertiary group remains unaffected.

71 (*b*) The reaction is proceed as

$$\underset{\text{(Phenol)}}{\underset{C_6H_5}{OH}} \xrightarrow[\text{dust}]{Zn} \underset{(A)}{\underset{\text{(Benzene)}}{C_6H_6}} \xrightarrow[\text{Anhy. } AlCl_3]{(CH_3)_2CHCOCl} \underset{(B)}{\underset{C_6H_5}{H_3C-\overset{H}{C}-CH_3}} \xrightarrow[\text{(ii) } H_3O^+]{\text{(i) Alk. } KMnO_4} \underset{\text{(Benzoic acid)}}{\underset{(C)}{\underset{C_6H_5}{COOH}}}$$

72 (*b*) The reaction is proceed as

$$C_6H_5MgBr \xrightarrow[\text{Dry ether}]{CO_2} C_6H_5-\underset{O^-MgBr^+}{C}=O \xrightarrow{H_3O^+} C_6H_5COOH$$

73 (*c*) Carboxylic acids are prepared by the reaction of Grignard reagent with CO_2.

∵ Formic acid (HCOOH) has only one carbon-atom hence cannot be prepared from Grignard reagent.

74 (*d*) Statement (d) is incorrect.

It's correct form is as follows

After heating *R*, only one water molecule is removed. This can be shown in the given mechanism.

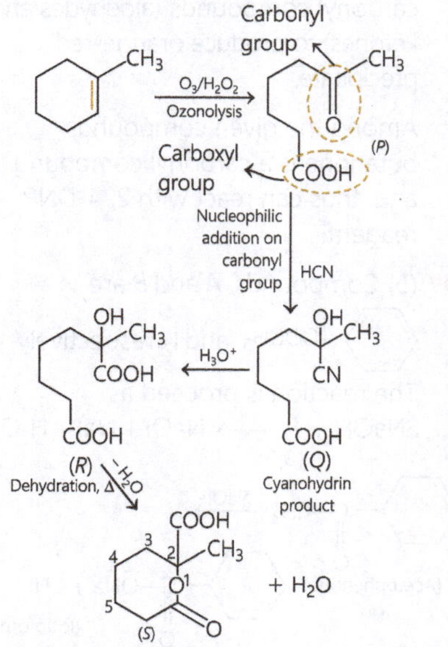

75 (*b*) The complete reactions are given below.

- $\underset{\text{Benzoic anhydride}}{(C_6H_5CO)_2O} \xrightarrow{H_2O} \underset{\text{Benzoic acid (I)}}{2C_6H_5-COOH}$

Thus, two molecules of benzoic acid are formed in the above reaction.

- $\underset{\text{Benzoyl ethanoic anhydride}}{C_6H_5COOCOCH_3} \xrightarrow{H_2O} \underset{\text{Benzoic acid}}{C_6H_5COOH} + \underset{\text{Ethanoic acid (II)}}{CH_3COOH}$

Thus, option (b) is correct.

76 (*a*)

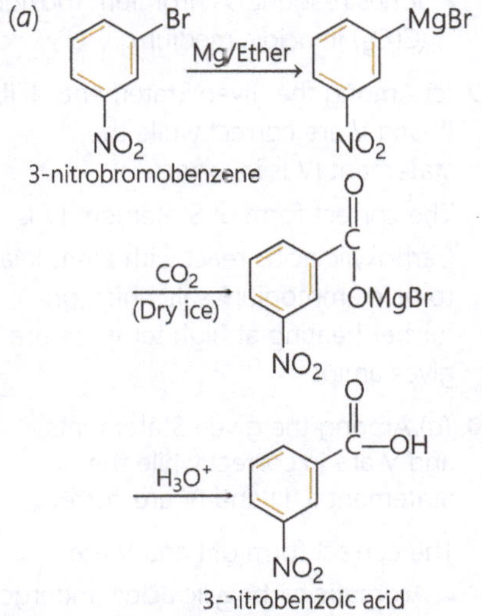

77 (*d*) Phenol does not react with $NaHCO_3$, whereas carboxylic acids react.

78 (*a*) Statement (a) is incorrect. It's correct form is as follows
The conjugate base of carboxylic acid, a carboxylate ion, is stabilised by two equivalent resonance structures.

79 (*c*) All the given compounds are α-monosubstituted acetic acid derivatives and the α-substitutions have been made by strong –*I*-groups/atoms. More powerful the –*I*-group, stronger will be the acid. –*I*-power of different groups is as follows

$$—NO_2 > —CN > —F > —Cl.$$

Thus, the correct decreasing order for acid strength is (c).

80 (*a*) The presence of electron withdrawing group on the benzene ring of aromatic carboxylic acid increases its acidity, while electron donating group decreases its acidity. Therefore, the correct increasing order of acidity is (a).

81 (*a*) Acidity increases as the electronegativity of the C-atom directly attached to —COOH group or the hybridisation of the C-atom directly attached to COOH changes from $sp^3 \rightarrow sp^2 \rightarrow sp$.
Hence, the acidic strength decreases in the order I > II > III > IV.

82 (*b*) As, $pK_a \propto \frac{1}{\text{acidic strength}}$

Hence, correct order of pK_a values is IV > II > III > I.

83 (*c*) Reagents that are used for the conversion of ethanoic acid to ethanoic anhydride are mineral acids such as H_2SO_4 or with P_2O_5.

84 (*c*) The reaction III is preferred for the preparation of *R*COCl because the side two products obtained in chemical reaction are gaseous and escape from the reaction mixture making the purification of the products easier.

85 (*d*) The complete reaction is as follows

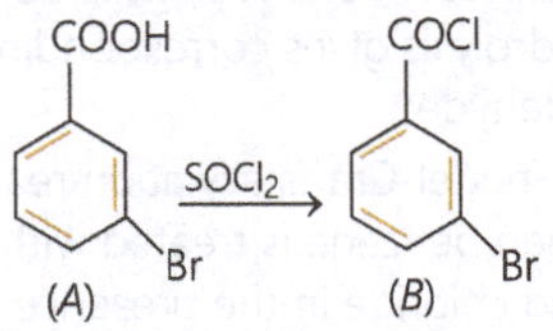

86 (*a*) The reaction is proceed as

$$\underset{\text{Benzoic acid}}{C_6H_5—\overset{O}{\overset{\|}{C}}—OH} + \underset{\text{Methanol}}{H—\overset{18}{O}—CH_3} \xrightarrow{H^+} \underset{(P)\ \text{Methyl benzoate}}{C_6H_5—\overset{O}{\overset{\|}{C}}—\boxed{\overset{18}{O}—CH_3}}$$

87 (*d*) $CH_3COOH + PCl_5 \longrightarrow \underset{(A)}{CH_3COCl} \xrightarrow[\text{Anhy. AlCl}_3]{C_6H_6} \underset{(B)}{C_6H_5COCH_3} \xrightarrow[\text{Ether}]{C_2H_5MgBr} \underset{(C)}{C_6H_5C(OH)(C_2H_5)CH_3}$

88 (*b*) Among the given options, compound (b) will go fastest decarboxylation as it is a β-keto acid. β-keto acid on slight heating undergo decarboxylation and gives ketone.

89 (*d*) Among the given options, compound (d) has an alpha-carbon present along with an alpha-hydrogen. Therefore, this compounds will undergo an HVZ reaction.

90 (*a*) $NaBH_4$ is a good reducing agent, but it is not as powerful as $LiAlH_4$. It can reduce aldehydes, ketones, acid chlorides but can not reduce carboxylic acids.
Hence, the major product of the above reaction is (a).

91 (*a*) Diborane does not easily reduce functional groups such as ester, nitro, halo etc. Carboxylic acids are reduced to primary alcohols by lithium aluminium hydride or with diborane.

92 (*a*) The decarboxylation of malonic acid is shown below.

$$\underset{\text{Malonic acid}}{HO—\overset{\beta}{\underset{\underset{O}{\|}}{C}}—\overset{\alpha}{CH_2}—COOH} \xrightarrow[\text{Decarboxylation}]{\Delta} \underset{\text{Acetic acid}}{H_3C—COOH} + CO_2\uparrow$$

Therefore, acetic acid is formed by the decarboxylation of malonic acid.

93 (*a*) Alkali metal salts of carboxylic acids undergo decarboxylation on electrolysis and form hydrocarbons, with twice the number of carbon present in alkyl group of the acid. This is known as Kolbe's electrolysis.

94 (*d*) Aromatic carboxylic acids do not undergo Friedel-Crafts reaction because the carboxyl group is deactivating and the catalyst aluminium chloride (Lewis acid) gets bonded to the carboxyl group.

95 (*d*) The reactions are as follows

$$\text{Benzoic acid} \xrightarrow[\text{Conc. } H_2SO_4]{\text{Conc. } HNO_3} m\text{-nitrobenzoic acid}$$

$$\text{Benzoic acid} \xrightarrow{Br_2/FeBr_3} m\text{-bromobenzoic acid}$$

96 (*c*) Methanoic acid is used in rubber, textile, dyeing, leather and electroplating industries.

Assertion-Reason

1 (a) Both A and R are true and R is the correct explanation of A.

2 (a) Both A and R are true and R is the correct explanation of A.

3 (b) Both A and R are true but R is not the correct explanation of A. The correct explanation of A is :
HCN is mainly a covalent compound and cannot provides CN^- ion readily for the nucleophilic attack on the carbonyl compound. The reaction is carried in the presence of base which helps in the ionisation of the acid to liberate CN^- ion.

4 (a) Both A and R are true and R is the correct explanation of A.

5 (a) Both A and R are true and R is the correct explanation of A.

6 (d) A is false but R is true.
The correct form of A is :
Ester hydrolysis is slow in the beginning and becomes fast after sometime because a small amount of dilute sulphuric acid is added in the beginning to start the reaction.

Statement Type

1 (b) Statement I is false but Statement II is true.
The correct form of Statement I is :

$$Ph{-}\overset{\overset{\displaystyle O}{\|}}{C}{-}CH_2{-}CH_3 \text{ and}$$

$CH_3CH_2CH_2{-}CH(Br)CH(CH_3)CH_2CHO$ are named as 1-phenylpropan-1-one and 4-bromo-3-methylheptanal.

2 (a) Both Statements I and II are true.

3 (c) Statement I is true but Statement II is false.
The correct form Statement II is :
Nucleophilic addition of HCN (hydrogen cyanide) to an aldehyde/ketone yield cyanohydrin as final product.

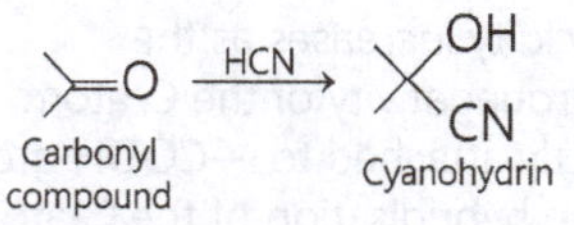

4 (b) Statement I is false but Statement II is true.
The correct form of Statement I is:
Aldehydes and ketones have atleast one methyl group linked to the carbonyl carbon atom when oxidised by sodium hypohalite.

5 (c) Statement I is true but Statement II is false.
The correct form of Statement II is :
Ethanoic acid is used as solvent and as vinegar in food industry.
Hexanedioic acid is used in the manufacture of nylon-6, 6.

6 (c) Among the given statements, only I, II and IV are correct while III and V are incorrect.
Their correct form is :

- Nitriles are reduced to corresponding imine with $SnCl_2$ in the presence of HCl, which on hydrolysis gives corresponding aldehyde.
- In Friedel-Crafts acylation reaction, when benzene is treated with acid chloride in the presence of anhy. $AlCl_3$ gives corresponding ketone.

7 (a) Among the given statements, only I and II are incorrect while the other statements III, IV and V are correct.
The correct form of I and II is:

- The boiling points of aldehydes and ketones are higher than hydrocarbons and ethers of comparable molecular masses.
- Acetone and benzaldehyde do not respond to Fehling's test because benzaldehyde does not have α-hydrogen and ketone does not respond to Fehling test.

8 (d) Among the given statements, II, IV and V are incorrect, while the statements I and III are correct.
The correct form of II, IV and V are

- IUPAC name of glutaric acid is pentanedioic acid.
- In carboxylic acids, the bonds to the carboxyl carbon lie in one plane and are separated by about 120°.
- Jones reagent is chromium trioxide (CrO_3) in acidic medium.

9 (c) Among the given Statements, I, II, III and V are correct while the statement IV is incorrect.
The correct form of Statement IV is:
Carboxylic acids react with ammonia to give ammonium salt which on further heating at high temperature gives amide.

10. (a) Among the given Statements, I and V are in correct while the Statement II, III and IV are correct.
The correct form of I and V are:

- Aromatic carboxylic acids undergo electrophilic substitution reaction in which the carboxyl group acts as a deactivating and *meta*-directing group.
- The hydrogen sulphite addition compound is water soluble and can be converted back to the original carbonyl compound by treating it with dilute mineral acid or alkaline

Matching Type

1 (d) The correct match is
A-4, B-1, C-3, D-2.

2 (c) The correct match is
A-1, B-3, C-2, D-4.

3 (b) The correct match is
A-4, B-3, C-2, D-1.

4 (d) The correct match is
A-2, B-4, C-1, D-3.

5 (b) The correct match is
A-4, B-3, C-1, D-2.

6 (a) The correct match is
A-4, B-2, C-3, D-1.

Numerical Value

1 (5) Structure of mesityl oxide is

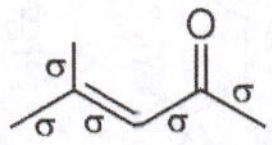

Hence, number of C—C sigma bond is 5.

2 (2) Two half reactions are

$$[Ag(NH_3)_2]^+ + e^- \longrightarrow Ag + 2NH_3$$

$$RCHO + 3OH^- \longrightarrow RCO_2^- + 2H_2O + 2e^-$$

Thus, overall reaction is

$$2[Ag(NH_3)_2]^+ + RCHO + 3OH^- \longrightarrow 2Ag + RCO_2^- + 4NH_3 + 2H_2O$$

Therefore, for 1 mole of R—CHO, 2 mole of $[Ag(NH_3)_2]^+$ is reduced.

3 (3) Haloform test is given by molecules with

$$-\overset{O}{\overset{\|}{C}}-CH_3 \text{ and } -\overset{OH}{\overset{|}{C}H}-CH_3 \text{ group}$$

present in them thus total three compounds with this functional group will give haloform test, i.e. (i), (iii) and (v) give haloform test.

4 (4) Given reaction is an example of aldol condensation as a ketone with α-H is reacting in presence of base.

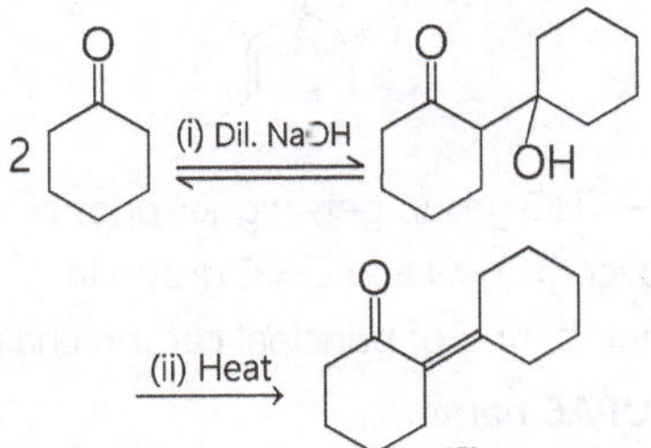

Major product

∴Number of π-electrons present in the product 'P' is 4.

5 (3)

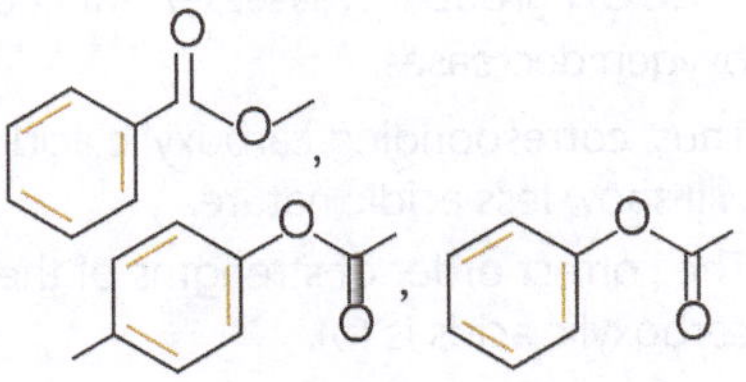

Those compounds dissolved in cold $NaHCO_3$ and NaOH solution contain carboxylic acid and phenol group. But the compounds containing an ester functional group will only dissolve in hot NaOH solution.

NCERT Exemplar's

1 (b) But-1-yne on reaction with water in the presence of Hg^{2+} ions as a catalyst produces butan-2-one.

Mechanism

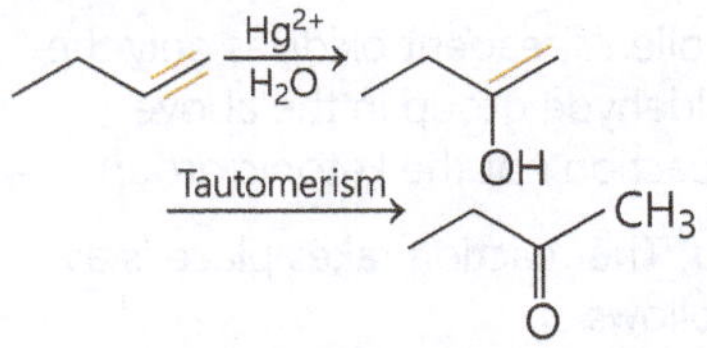

2 (a) CH_3—CHO is most reactive towards nucleophilic addition reaction due to steric and electronic reasons.

3 (c) Phenol is more acidic than ethanol due to the formation of more stable conjugate base, phenoxide ion after the removal of H^+ from phenol.

On the other hand, carboxylic acid is more acidic than phenol due to formation of more stable conjugate base after removal of H^+ as compared to that of phenol.

Chloroacetic acid is more acidic than acetic acid due to the presence of electron withdrawing chlorine group attached to α-carbon of carboxylic acid. Thus, the correct order is (c).

4 (b) Compound Ph—COO—Ph can be prepared by the reaction of phenol and benzoyl chloride in the presence of pyridine. The reaction involved is as shown below.

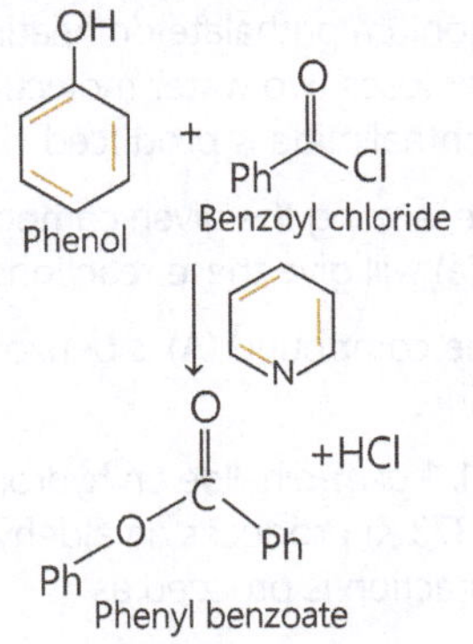

This is an example of Schotten-Baumann reaction.

5 The correct match is A-(3), B-(4), C-(1), D-(2).

6 (c) Acetone and benzaldehyde both do not react with Fehling's solution. This is because, acetone is a ketone while benzaldehyde is an aromatic aldehyde having no α-hydrogen.

7 (d) Necessary condition for Cannizzaro reaction is absence of α-hydrogen atom.

So, CH_3CHO will not give Cannizzaro reaction as there is α - H, while other three compounds have no α-hydrogen.

8 (b) The reaction is as follows

$$\underset{\text{Benzaldehyde}}{C_6H_5CHO} \xrightarrow{\text{Conc. KOH}} \underset{\text{Benzyl alcohol}}{C_6H_5CH_2OH} + \underset{\text{Potassium benzoate}}{C_6H_5COO^-K^+}$$

9 (d) Chemical reaction can be shown as

$$\underset{\text{Propyne}}{CH_3-C\equiv CH} \xrightarrow[\text{1\% } HgSO_4]{\text{40\% } H_2SO_4} \underset{\substack{\text{Prop-1- en-2-ol}\\(A)}}{CH_3-\overset{OH}{\overset{|}{C}}=\overset{H}{\overset{|}{C}H}} \xrightarrow{\text{Keto-enol tautomerism}} \underset{\text{Acetone}}{CH_3-\overset{O}{\overset{\|}{C}}-CH_3}$$

10 (b) Chemical reaction can be shown as

$$\underset{\text{Ethanal}}{CH_3CHO} \xrightarrow[\text{(ii) } H_2O]{\text{(i) } CH_3MgBr} \underset{\substack{(A)\\\text{Propan-2- ol}}}{CH_3-\underset{CH_3}{\underset{|}{CH}}-OH}$$

$$\xrightarrow[\text{Dehydration}]{H_2SO_4,\ \Delta} \underset{\substack{(B)\\\text{Propene}}}{CH_3-\underset{H}{\underset{|}{C}}=CH_2} \xrightarrow[\text{(Hydroboration -oxidation)}]{\text{(i) } BH_3,\ \text{(ii) } H_2O_2/\overline{O}H} \underset{\substack{(C)\\\text{Propan-1-ol}}}{CH_3-CH_2-CH_2OH}$$

Thus, $CH_3-\underset{CH_3}{\underset{|}{CH}}-OH$ (A) and $CH_3-CH_2-CH_2OH$ (C) are positional isomers.

11 The correct match is A-(3), B-(4), C-(1), D-(2).

12 (c) The most suitable reagent is I_2 and NaOH solution.

$$\underset{\text{Hex-4-en-2-one}}{CH_3CHCHCH_2COCH_3} \xrightarrow[\text{(Iodoform reaction)}]{I_2/NaOH \text{ solution}} CH_3CHCHCH_2COONa$$

13 (b) Among the given compounds, only butan-2-ol on oxidation with alk. $KMnO_4$ solution produces butanone as follows

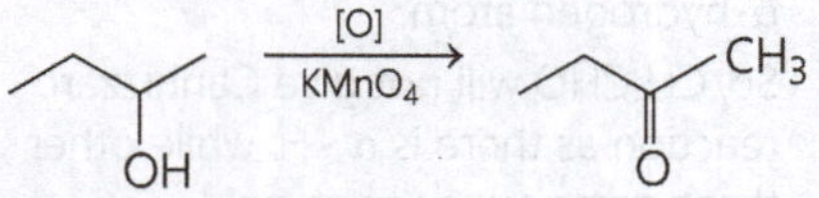

Butan-2-ol (2° alcohol) Butan-2-one

14 (a) In Clemmensen's reduction carbonyl group is treated with zinc amalgam and HCl to convert carbonyl group into CH_2 group.

Past Exams'

1 (b) The complete reaction is as follows,

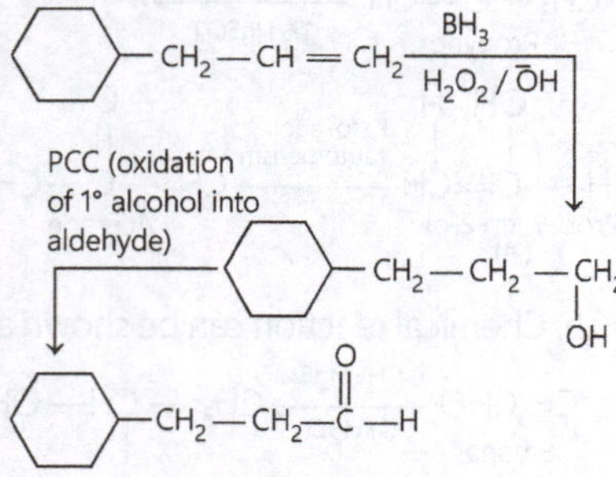

2 (b) The complete reaction is as follows

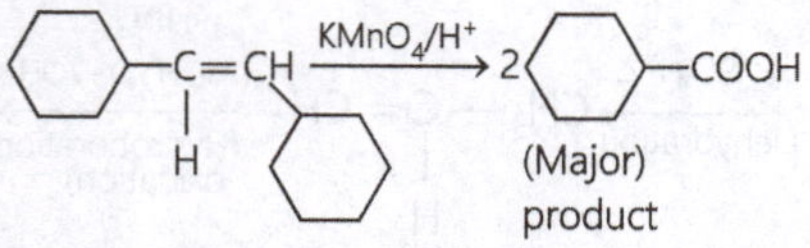

3 (c) The reaction is proceed as

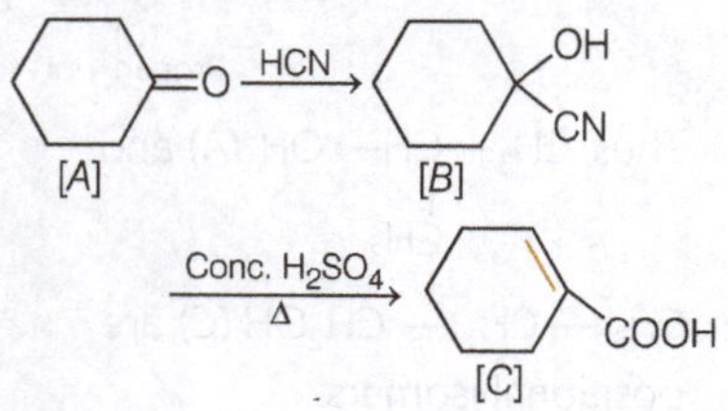

4 (b) The complete given reaction is as follows

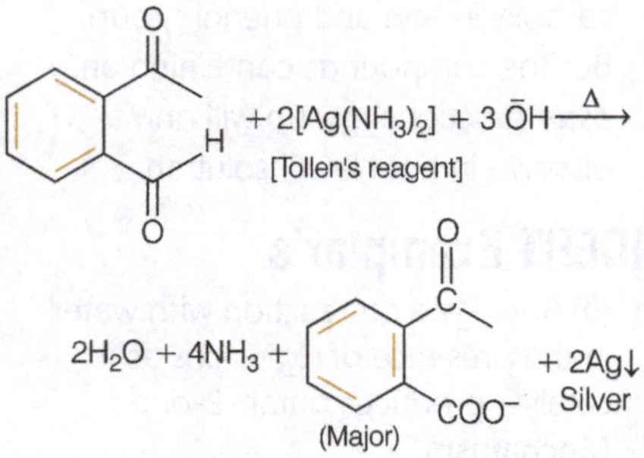

Tollen's reagent oxidises only the aldehyde group in the above reaction not the ketonic group.

5 (d) The reaction takes place is as follows

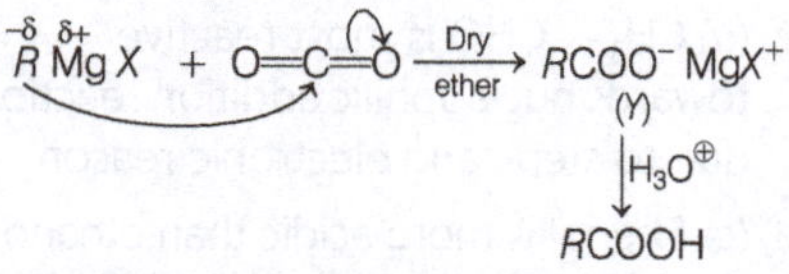

6 (d) Both Statement I and Statement II are correct.

7 (a)

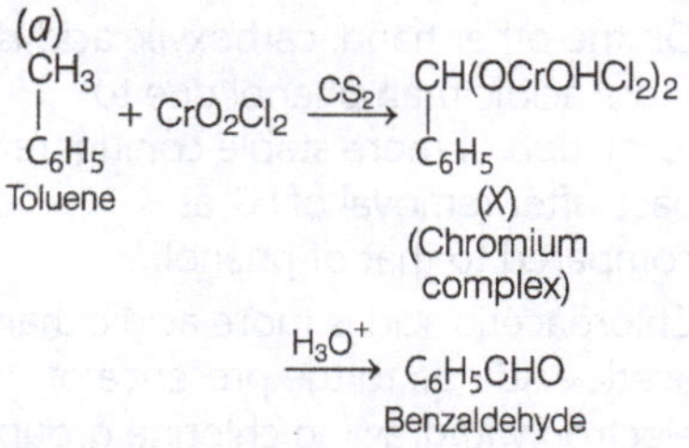

8 (d) The correct match is A - (2), B - (3), C - (4), D - (1).

9 (a) Phthalic acid on simple heating gives an anhydride. Phthalic acid in reaction with ammonia gives an ammonium salt.

Ammonium phthalate on heating further loses two water molecules and phthalimide is produced.

Hence, among the given compounds, only (a) will give these reactions.

10 (a) The compound (A) is benzoyl chloride.

11 (b) A 1, 1-*gem*-dihalide on hydrolysis (H_2O/373 K) produces an aldehyde. The reaction is proceed as

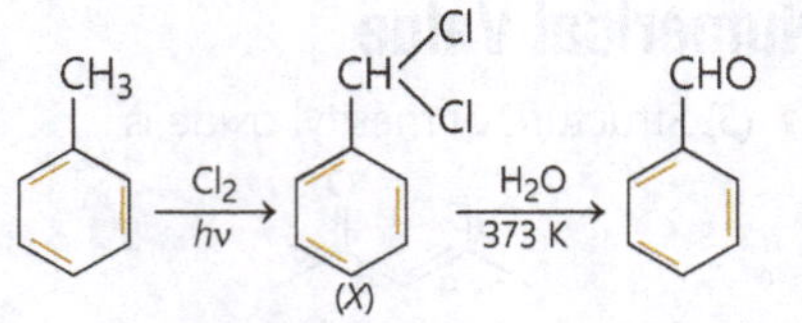

12 (d) Carboxylic acids have higher boiling points than aldehyde, ketones and even alcohols of comparable molecular mass because of the extent of intermolecular-hydrogen bonding with water, due to which they exist as associated molecules.

13 (b)

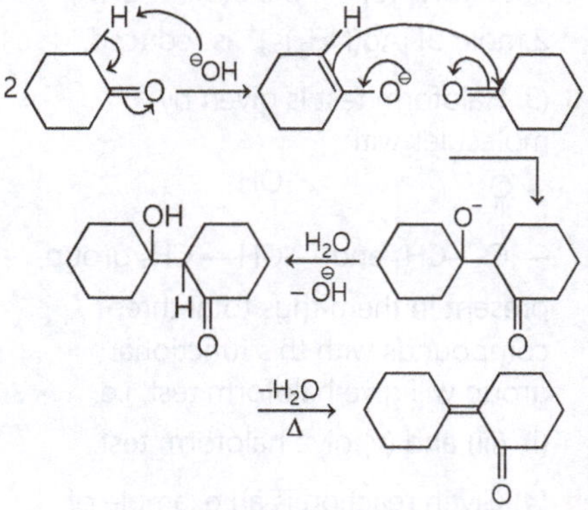

(α, β- unsaturated compound)

14 (a)

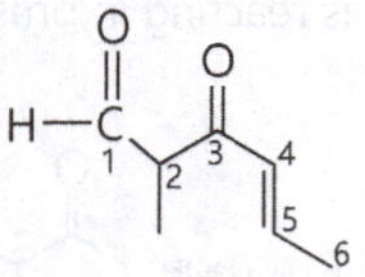

—CHO group gets higher priority over >C=O and C=C group in numbering of principal carbon chain.

IUPAC name

3-keto-2-methylhex-4-enal.

15 (b) The oxygen atom present in the ring shows *I*-effect.

As the distance between oxygen and —COOH group increases, –*I*-effect of oxygen decreases.

Thus, corresponding carboxylic acid will show less acidic nature.

The correct order of strengths of the carboxylic acids is (b).

16. (*b*) The given reaction is : Gattermann-Koch reaction. In this reaction, benzene is treated with carbon monoxide in the acidic medium in presence of anhydrous aluminium chloride to give benzaldehyde. The complete reaction is as follow,

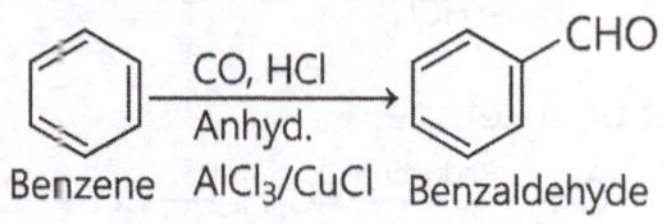

17 (*d*) The molecular formula of second homologue in the homologous series of mono-carboxylic acid is CH_3COOH i.e., $C_2H_4O_2$.

18 (*b*)

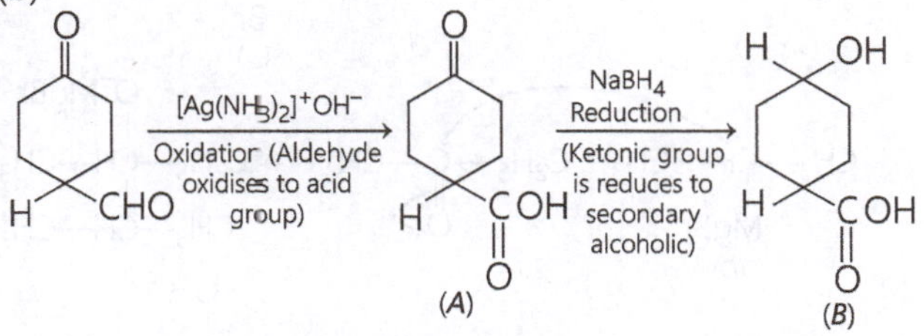

19 (*a*) The mechanism of given reaction is

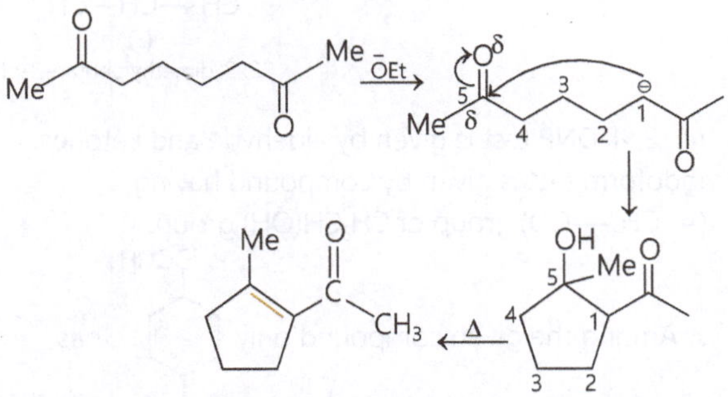

20 (*a*) The structure of product (*A*) is given in option (a). The mechanism of the given reaction is

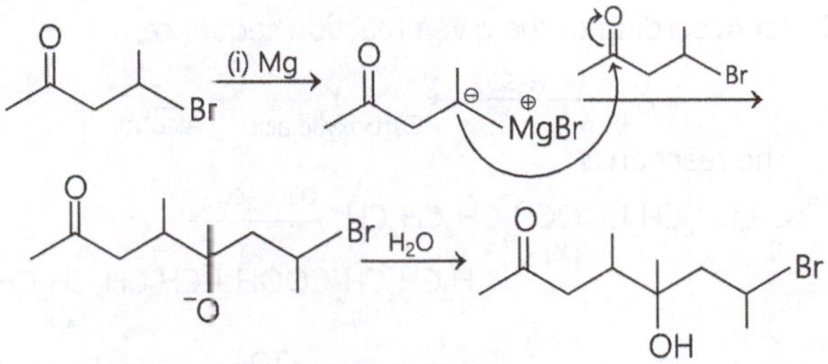

21 (*a*) The mechanism of the given reaction is:

In step (i), nucleophile CN^- of NaCN will attack the electrophilic centre (δ^+) group of $>C=O$ and form cyanohydrin. In presence of water (polar solvent) cyanide converts into acid.

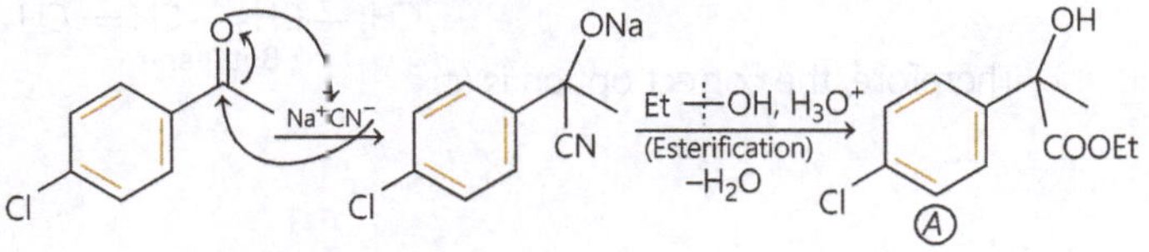

(*A*) on reacting with methyl magnesium bromide in excess shows following reaction.

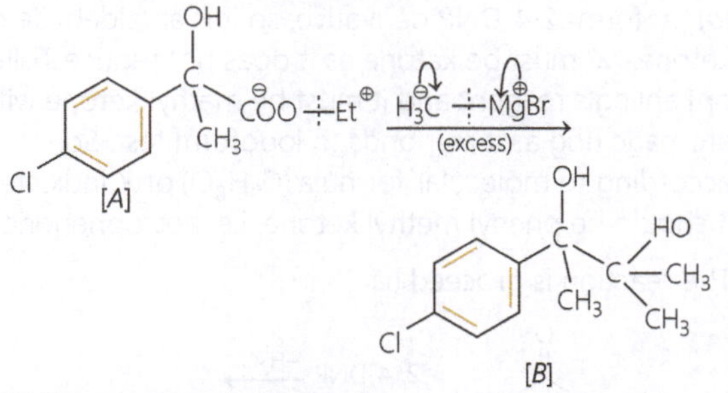

22 (*b*) The reaction is proceed as

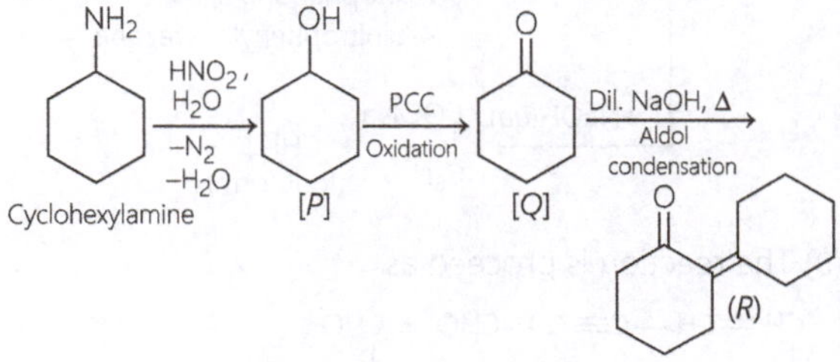

23 (*a*)

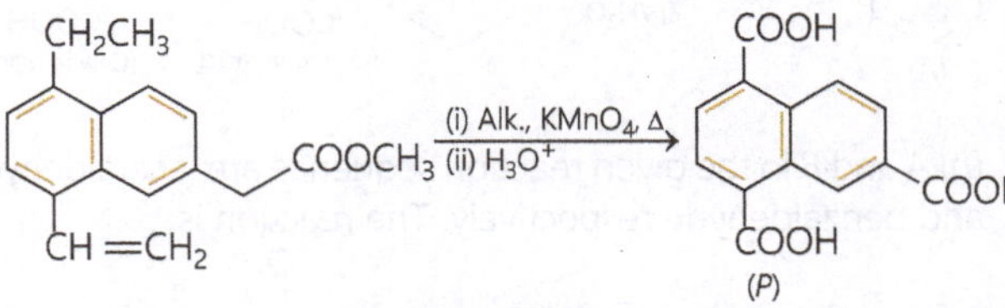

In the above reaction $KMnO_4$ oxidises benzylic carbon containing at least one α-hydrogen atom to —COOH.

24 (*a*) DIBAL-H reduces both the cyanides and esters to aldehydes without affecting the double bond.

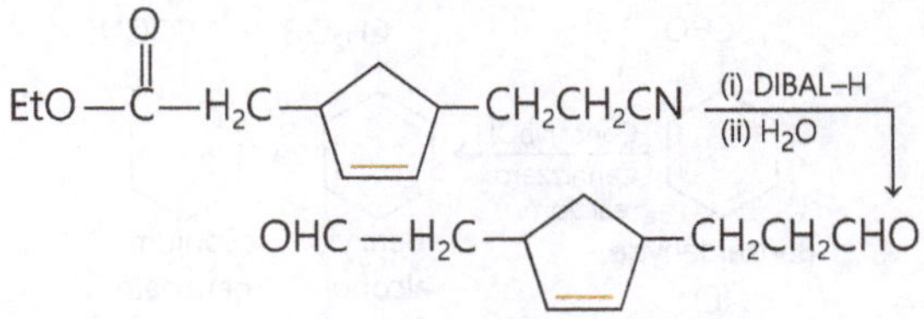

25 (*b*) DIBAL-H is added to produce aldehyde from ester by keeping the temperature low while at higher temperature it can perform different conversions. Complete reaction is as follows

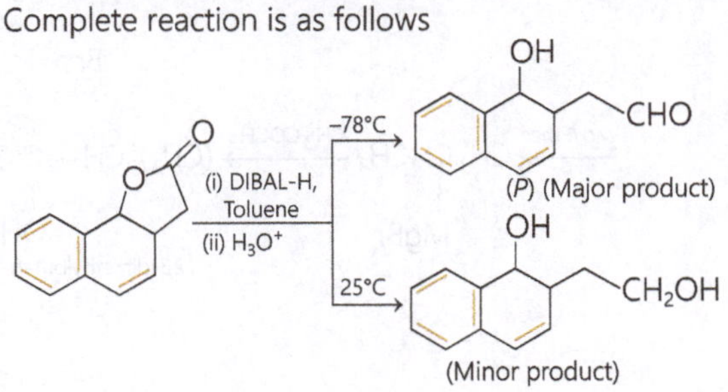

Skill Boosters

1. (*a*) '*X*' forms 2,4-DNP derivative, so it is an aldehyde or ketone. '*X*' must be ketone as it does not reduce Tollen's or Fehling's reagent and it must be methyl ketone with aromatic ring as it responds to iodoform test. So, according to molecular formula (C_8H_8O) of *X* indicates that it should be phenyl methyl ketone, i.e. acetophenone.

The reaction is proceed as

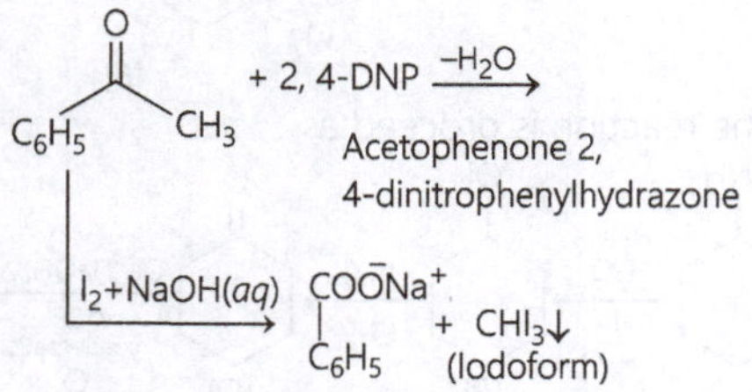

2. (*b*) The reaction is proceed as

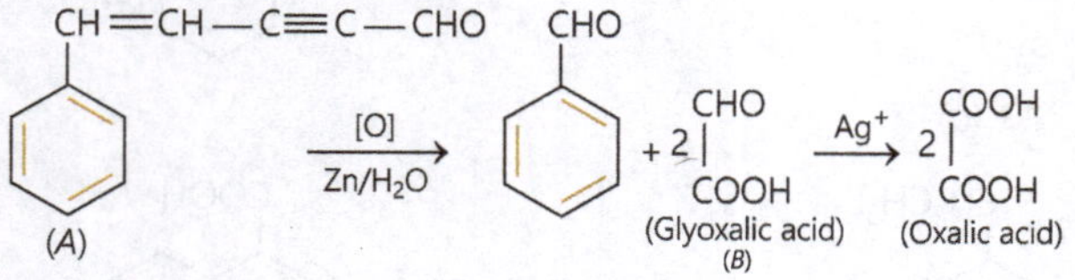

3. (*b*) *A* and *B* in the given reaction sequence are acetaldehyde and benzaldehyde respectively. The reaction is

$$\underset{\underset{(A)}{\text{Acetaldehyde}}}{2CH_3CHO} \xrightarrow[\text{Aldol condensation}]{\text{Dil. alkali}} \underset{\beta\text{-hydroxy butyraldehyde}}{H_3C-\overset{\overset{OH}{|}}{CH}-CH_2CHO}$$

$$\xrightarrow[-H_2O]{\Delta} \underset{\text{But-2-enal}}{CH_3-CH=CH-CHO}$$

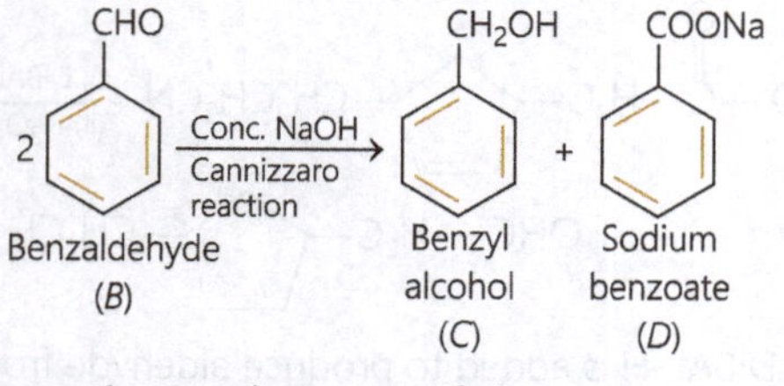

4. (*d*) The reaction involves are as follow

$$\underset{(A)}{CH_3COCH_3} \xrightarrow{\text{Reduction}} \underset{(B)}{CH_3CH(OH)CH_3} \xrightarrow{HBr} \underset{(C)}{CH_3\underset{\underset{Br}{|}}{CH}CH_3}$$

$$\xrightarrow{\text{Mg/Ether}} CH_3\underset{\underset{MgBr}{|}}{CH}CH_3 \xrightarrow{CH_3COCH_3} \underset{\text{(2,3-dimethylbutan-2-ol)}}{(CH_3)_2CH-\underset{\underset{OH}{|}}{C}(CH_3)_2}$$

5. (*a*)The reaction is proceed as:

$$\underset{(A)}{CH_3-CH_2-CH_2OH} \xrightarrow{[O]} \underset{(B)}{CH_3-CH_2-CHO}$$

$$\xrightarrow[+ HCl]{H_2NNHCONH_2} \underset{(C)}{CH_3CH_2CH=N-NHCONH_2}$$

6. (*b*) '*A*' must be a ketone.

$$\underset{(A)}{C_2H_5-\overset{\overset{}{}}{\underset{\underset{O}{\|}}{C}}-CH_3} \xrightarrow{\text{Reduction}} \underset{(B)}{C_2H_5-\underset{\underset{OH}{|}}{CH}-CH_3} \xrightarrow{HBr}$$

$$\underset{(C)}{C_2H_5-\underset{\underset{Br}{|}}{CH}-CH_3} + Mg \xrightarrow{\text{Ether}}$$

$$\underset{(D)}{CH_3-\underset{\underset{MgBr}{|}}{CH}-CH_3} + \underset{(A)}{C_2H_5-\underset{\underset{O}{\|}}{C}-CH_3} \longrightarrow C_2H_5-\overset{\overset{O^-\overset{+}{M}gBr}{|}}{\underset{\underset{CH_3-CH-CH_3}{|}}{CH}}-CH_3$$

$$\xrightarrow[H^+]{HOH} \underset{\text{2, 3-dimethylpentan-3-ol}}{\underset{(E)}{C_2H_5-\overset{\overset{OH}{|}}{\underset{\underset{CH_3-CH-CH_3}{|}}{CH}}-CH_3}}$$

7. (*c*) 2, 4-DNP test is given by aldehyde and ketones. Iodoform test is given by compound having (—CH_3—CO) group or $CH_3CH(OH)$ group.

∴ Among the given compound only 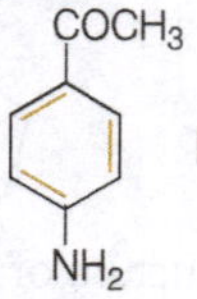 has (—$COCH_3$) group. So, it is the compound *X*.

8. (*c*) According to the given reaction sequence,

$$X \xrightarrow{\text{Dil. } H_2SO_4} \underset{\text{Carboxylic acid}}{Y} + \underset{\text{Alcohol}}{Z}$$

The reaction is

$$\underset{(X)}{CH_3CH_2CH_2COOCH_2CH_2CH_2CH_3} \xrightarrow{\text{Dil. } H_2SO_4}$$

$$\underset{(Y)}{CH_3CH_2CH_2COOH} + \underset{(Z)}{CH_3CH_2CH_2CH_2OH}$$

$$\underset{(Z)}{CH_3-CH_2-CH_2-CH_2-OH} \xrightarrow[H_2SO_4]{CrO_3} \underset{(Y)}{CH_3CH_2CH_2COOH}$$

$$\underset{(Z)}{CH_3-CH_2-CH_2-CH_2-OH} \xrightarrow[-H_2O]{\Delta} \underset{\text{But-1-ene}}{CH_3-CH_2-CH=CH_2}$$

Therefore, the correct option is (c).

09

Scan for **Chemistry Through Concept Master** *Videos*

Amines

Amines are the derivatives of ammonia obtained by replacing either one, two or three H-atoms of ammonia by alkyl or aryl groups.

e.g. CH_3-NH_2, $C_6H_5-NH_2$, $CH_3-NH-CH_3$, $CH_3-N\begin{matrix} CH_3 \\ CH_3 \end{matrix}$

In nature, they occur among proteins, vitamins, alkaloids and hormones.

Structure of Amines

Like ammonia, nitrogen atom of amines is trivalent and carries an unshared pair of electrons. In amines, N is sp^3-hybridised and the geometry is **pyramidal**. Due to the presence of unshared pair of electrons, the angle C—N—*E*, (where, *E* is C or H) is less than 109.5°. For instance it is 108° in case of trimethylamine as shown in figure.

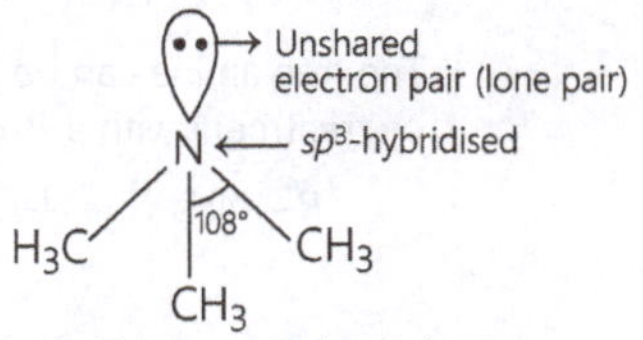

Pyramidal shape of trimethylamine

Classification

Amines are classified as primary (1°), secondary (2°) and tertiary (3°) depending upon the number of hydrogen atoms replaced by alkyl or aryl groups in ammonia molecule.

- Amines containing $-NH_2$ group, are called **primary amines**.
  e.g. CH_3NH_2, $C_6H_5NH_2$.
- Amines containing $-\overset{|}{N}H$ group, are called **secondary amines**.
  e.g. $CH_3-NH-CH_3$, $C_6H_5-NHC_2H_5$.
- Amines containing $-\overset{|}{\underset{|}{N}}$ group, are called **tertiary amines**.
  e.g. $CH_3-\underset{\underset{CH_3}{|}}{N}-CH_3$, $H_5C_6-\underset{\underset{CH_3}{|}}{N}-C_2H_5$.

Topicwise No. of Ques asked in 5 Years (NEET)

Topics	No. of Questions				
	2024	2023	2022	2021	2020
Structure, Classification and Nomenclature of Amines	–	–	–	–	–
Preparation of Amines	–	1	–	–	1
Physical Properties and Chemical Reactions of Amines	1	–	3	1	2
Methods of Preparation of Diazonium salt	–	–	–	–	–
Physical Properties and Chemical Reactions of Diazonium Salt	–	1	1	1	–

Special Type of Ques asked in 5 Years (NEET)

Types	Years				
	2024	2023	2022	2021	2020
A-R	–	–	–	–	–
Statement Based	1	–	1	–	–
Matching	–	–	–	–	–

Last 5 Years Weightage (NEET)

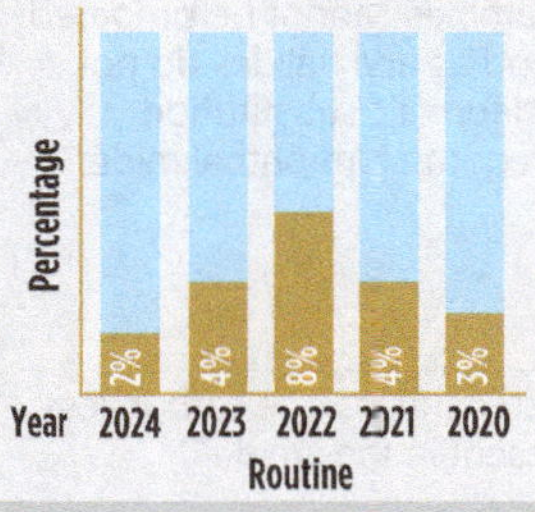

- Amines are said to be 'simple' when all the alkyl or aryl groups are the same and 'mixed' when they are different.

Nomenclature

- In common system, an aliphatic amine is named by prefixing alkyl group to amine, i.e. alkylamine. e.g. CH_3NH_2 (methylamine).
- In secondary and tertiary amines, when two or more groups are same, the prefix di or tri is added before the name of alkyl group. e.g. $N(CH_3)_3$ (trimethylamine).
- In IUPAC system, primary amines are named as **alkanamines.** To name 2° and 3° amines, we use locant 'N' to designate substituent attached to a nitrogen atom, while naming aryl amines, suffix 'e' of arene is replaced by 'amine'.

e.g.

CH_3NH_2 ,
Methanamine

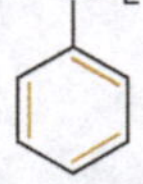

Benzenamine or aniline

$CH_3CH_2NHCH_3$,
N-methylethanamine

$CH_3CH_2—N(CH_3)—CH_2CH_2CH_3$
N-ethyl-N-methylpropanamine

Preparation of Amines

Following methods can be used for the preparation of amines

S.No.	Methods	Reactions involved	Important points regarding reaction
1.	**By reduction of** (i) **Alkyl nitrile**	$R—C\equiv N \xrightarrow[Na(Hg)/C_2H_5OH]{H_2/Ni} R—CH_2—NH_2$ NEET 2023,2022	• It is used for ascent of amine series, i.e. for preparation of amines containing one C-atom more than starting amine.
	(ii) **Nitro compounds**	$R/ArNO_2 + H_2 \xrightarrow[Ethanol]{Ni/Pt/Pd} R/ArNH_2$ $R/ArNO_2 \xrightarrow[\text{or Fe + HCl}]{\text{Sn + HCl}} R/ArNH_2$	• Reduction with Fe scrap and HCl is preferred because $FeCl_2$ formed gets hydrolysed to release HCl during reaction. Thus, only a small amount of HCl is required to initiate the reaction.
	(iii) **Amides**	$R—\overset{O}{\overset{\parallel}{C}}—NH_2 \xrightarrow[\text{(ii) } H_2O]{\text{(i) } LiAlH_4} RCH_2NH_2$	• Reduction of amides give amine with same number of carbons.
2.	**From alkyl halide** (Hofmann ammonolysis method)	• $\ddot{N}H_3 + R—X \xrightarrow{373\ K} R—\overset{+}{N}H_3X^-$ (Substituted ammonium salt) • $R\ddot{N}H_2 \xrightarrow{RX} R_2NH \xrightarrow{RX} R_3N \xrightarrow{RX} R_4\overset{+}{N}X^-$ (1°) (2°) (3°) (Quaternary ammonium salt) • The free amine can be obtained from the ammonium salt by treatment with a strong base. $R—\overset{+}{N}H_3X^- + NaOH \longrightarrow RNH_2 + H_2O + \overset{+}{Na}\overset{-}{X}$	• It yields a mixture of 1°, 2° and 3° amines and also quaternary ammonium salt. • 1° amine is obtained as a major product, when excess of NH_3 is taken. • If excess of alkyl halide is used, tertiary amine is obtained as main product. • Tertiary butyl bromide on treatment with NH_3 prefers to undergo elimination rather than substitution. • Order of reactivity of halides with amines is $RI > RBr > RCl$. • This reaction is a nucleophilic substitution reaction.
3.	**Gabriel phthalimide synthesis** For Concept Master Video	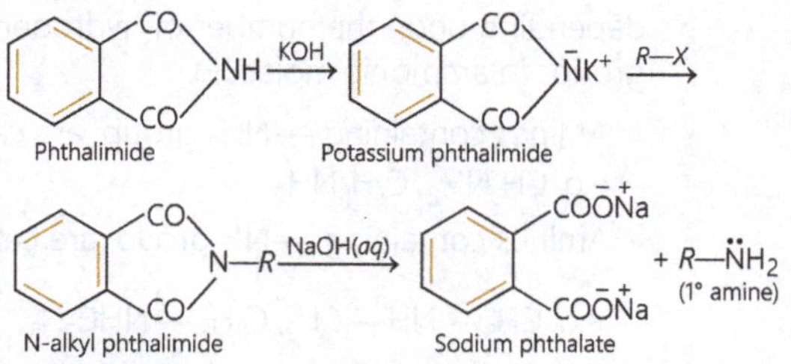	• Only 1° aliphatic amines can be synthesised by this method. • Aromatic 1° amines cannot be prepared by this method as aryl halides do not undergo nucleophilic substitution reaction with potassium phthalimide.
4.	**Hofmann bromamide degradation**	$RCONH_2 + Br_2 + 4NaOH \xrightarrow{\Delta} \underset{(1^\circ \text{ amine})}{RNH_2} + 2NaBr + Na_2CO_3 + 2H_2O$	• Amine formed contains one carbon less than that present in the amide.

Physical Properties

- **Physical state** Lower aliphatic amines are gases with ammoniacal smell. Primary amines with three or more carbon atoms are liquids with fishy odour. Lower aromatic amines are liquids with characteristic unpleasant odour but higher ones are solids which are odourless.
- **Colour** Aniline and other aryl amines are usually colourless but get coloured on storage due to atmospheric oxidation.
- **Solubility** Lower aliphatic amines are soluble in water as they can form hydrogen bonds with water molecules and their solubility decreases as the size of the hydrophobic alkyl group increases. Higher amines and aromatic amines are insoluble in water but soluble in organic solvents.
- **Boiling point** Primary and secondary amines are engaged in intermolecular association due to hydrogen bonding, while tertiary amines do not have intermolecular association (due to absence of H-atom). Therefore, the order of boiling points of isomeric amines is as follows
$$1° > 2° > 3°$$

Chemical Reactions

Some of the reactions of amines are described below.

Basic Character of Amines

For Concept Master Video

- The reaction of amines with mineral acids to form ammonium salts show that, they are basic in nature.

$$R—\ddot{N}H_2 + HX \rightleftharpoons R—\overset{\oplus}{N}H_3X^- \text{ (salt)}$$

- Their basicity is due to **lone pair of electrons** on N-atom and behave as **Lewis base**.
- Basic character of amines can be better understood by their K_b and pK_b values.
- Larger the value of K_b or smaller the value of pK_b, stronger is the base, i.e. $pK_b = -\log K_b$.

Structure-Basicity Relationship of Amines

Alkanamines *vs* Ammonia

- Alkyl amines are stronger bases than NH_3.
- Basic nature of aliphatic amines increases with increase in the number of alkyl groups, i.e. +*I*-effect of alkyl group increases their basicity.
- The order of basicity of amines in **gaseous phase** is
$$3° \text{ amine} > 2° \text{ amine} > 1° \text{ amine} > NH_3.$$
- In **aqueous phase**, solvation effect and steric hindrance, besides **inductive effect** of alkyl group decides the basic strength of alkyl amines.
- In gaseous phase or in non-aqueous phase, the solvation effects, i.e. stabilisation of the conjugate acid due to H-bonding are absent and hence basicity depends only on the + *I* effect of the alkyl groups.
- In aqueous phase when the alkyl group is bigger than —CH_3 group, there will be some steric hindrance to H-bonding. As a result, stability due to +*I* effect predominates over the stability due to H-bonding and hence, 3° amines becomes more basic than 1° amines in aqueous solution.
- The order of basicity of amines, when alkyl group is ethyl group is,

Amines : $(C_2H_5)_2NH > (C_2H_5)_3N > C_2H_5NH_2 > NH_3$
pK_b : 3.00   3.25   3.29   4.75

- The order of basicity of amines, when alkyl group is methyl group is,

Amines : $(CH_3)_2NH > CH_3NH_2 > (CH_3)_3N > NH_3$
pK_b : 3.27   3.38   4.22   4.75 NEET 2019

Arylamines *vs* Ammonia

- Aniline is more stable than anilinium ion. Hence, the proton acceptability (basic nature) of aniline or aryl amines would be less than that of ammonia.
- Anilinium ion formed after protonation of amines is less stable than aniline because it has only two resonating structures.

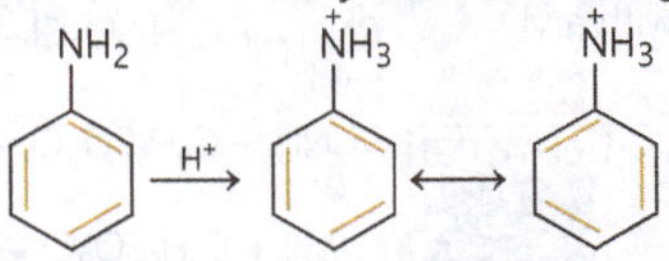

- The less basicity of aniline as compared to NH_3 is attributed to – *I*-effect of benzene (sp^2-hybridised) ring and delocalisation of lone pair of N. It has five resonating structures.

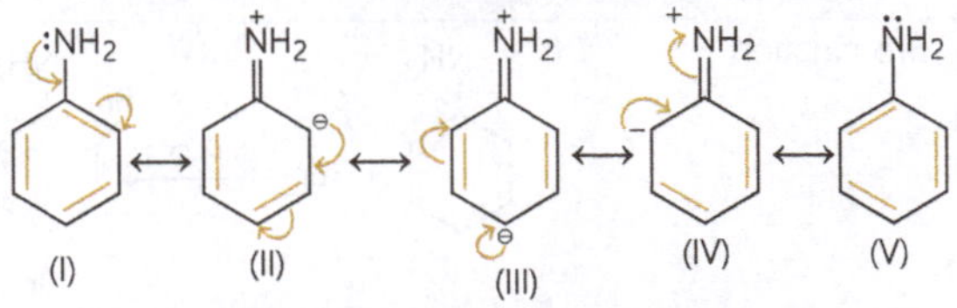

- In substituted aniline, electron releasing groups (—OCH_3, —CH_3) increase basic strength, whereas electron withdrawing group (—NO_2, —SO_3H) decrease it.
- In aromatic amines, basic strength increases in the order

primary < secondary < tertiary
$C_6H_5NH_2 < C_6H_5NHCH_3 < C_6H_5N(CH_3)_2$
pK_b : 9.38   9.30   8.92

Marks Maximizer

For N-substituted aniline basicity order is

- N, N-dimethyl aniline > N-methyl aniline >aniline (If substituent is alkyl).
- Aniline > diphenylamine > triphenylamine (If substituent is phenyl).

Some Important Reactions of Amines

S.No.	Method	Reaction involved	Important points related to reaction
I.	**Aliphatic/Aromatic amines**		
1.	Acylation	$R/Ar\text{—}\ddot{N}H\text{—}H \xrightarrow[\text{Base}]{CH_3COCl} R/Ar\text{—}\ddot{N}(H)\text{—}C(=O)\text{—}CH_3 + HCl$ $R/Ar\text{—}\ddot{N}H\text{—}H \xrightarrow[\text{Base}]{(CH_3CO)_2O} R/Ar\text{—}\ddot{N}(H)\text{—}C(=O)\text{—}CH_3 + CH_3COOH$ N-alkyl/aryl ethanamide	• The reaction is carried out in presence of a base stronger than amine (e.g. pyridine) which removes HCl so formed and shifts the equilibrium to the right hand side. • Activating effect of —NH_2 group in aniline can be controlled by protecting the —NH_2 group by acetylation with acetic anhydride and then carrying out the desired substitution followed by hydrolysis.
2.	Benzoylation	$Ar/RNH_2 + C_6H_5COCl \longrightarrow Ar/RNHCOC_6H_5 + HCl$ Benzoyl chloride; Benzamide	• Substituted aryl amides are obtained by this method.
3.	Carbylamine reaction	$Ar/RNH_2 + CHCl_3 + 3KOH \xrightarrow{\Delta} Ar/R\text{—}NC + 3KCl + 3H_2O$ Isocyanide (Foul smelling substance)	• It is also known as **isocyanide test** and is used as a test for aliphatic and aromatic 1° amine. • Secondary and tertiary amines do not show this reaction. NEET 2020
4.	Reaction with $NaNO_2$ and HCl (Nitrous acid test)	$R\text{—}NH_2 + HNO_2 \xrightarrow{NaNO_2+HCl} [R\text{—}\overset{+}{N_2}Cl^-]$ Unstable diazonium salt $\xrightarrow{H_2O} ROH + N_2 + HCl$ $Ar\text{—}NH_2 \xrightarrow[273-278\ K]{NaNO_2 + 2HCl} Ar\text{—}N_2^+Cl^- + NaCl + 2H_2O$ Aryl diazonium salt NEET 2021	• Reaction is used to distinguish three classes of amines, i.e. 1°, 2° and 3° amines. • Primary aliphatic amines react with nitrous acid to form aliphatic diazonium salts which being unstable, liberate nitrogen gas and alcohols. • Aromatic amines react with nitrous acid at low temperature (273-278 K) to form diazonium salts.
5.	Reaction with aryl sulphonyl chloride (Hinsberg's reagent, $C_6H_5SO_2Cl$) For Concept Master Video	$RNH_2\ (1°) + C_6H_5SO_2Cl \xrightarrow{-HCl} C_6H_5SO_2NH\text{—}R$ (Soluble in alkali) $R_2NH\ (2°) + C_6H_5SO_2Cl \xrightarrow{-HCl} C_6H_5SO_2NR_2$ (Insoluble in alkali) $R_3N\ (3°) + C_6H_5SO_2Cl \longrightarrow$ No reaction NEET 2021,2019	• Reaction is used to distinguish three classes of amines, i.e. 1°, 2° and 3° amines. • Primary amine gives N-alkyl sulphonamide which is soluble in alkali. 2° amine gives N, N-dialkyl sulphonamide which is insoluble in KOH, whereas 3° amines does not give this test.
II.	**Only aromatic amines**		
	Electrophilic substitution reactions		
1.	Bromination	I. 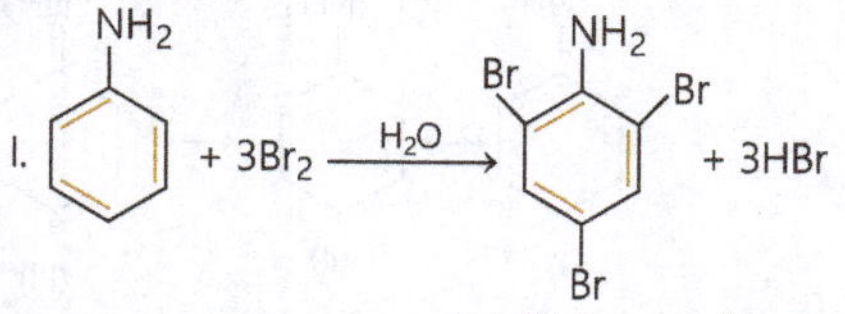 2, 4, 6-tribromoaniline II. $C_6H_5NH_2 \xrightarrow[\text{Base}]{(CH_3CO)_2O} C_6H_5NHCOCH_3 \xrightarrow[CH_3COOH]{Br_2}$ N-phenylethanamide (Acetanilide) 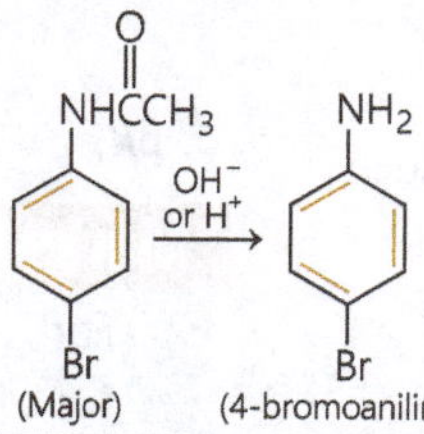 (Major) (4-bromoaniline)	• To get monosubstituted aniline derivative, path II can be followed. • The lone pair on nitrogen of acetanilide is less available for conjugation with benzene ring. Therefore, activating effect of —$NHCOCH_3$ group is less than that of amino group.

S.No.	Method	Reaction involved	Important points related to reaction
2.	Nitration	I. 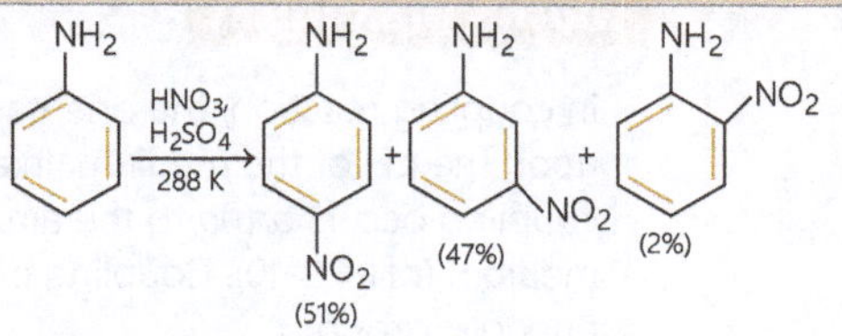 II. 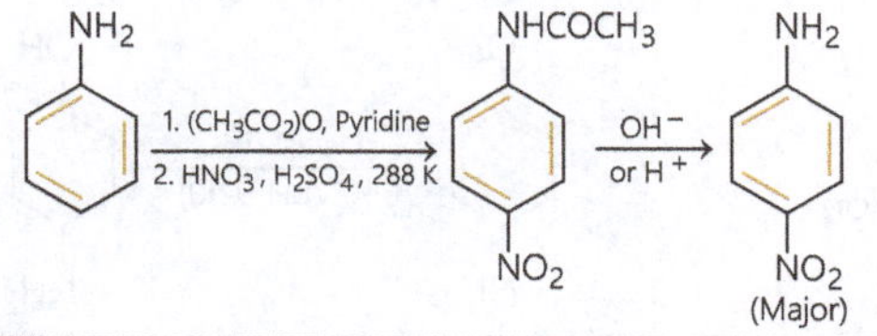	• Direct nitration of aniline in strongly acidic medium produces *ortho*, *para* and *meta*-derivative because anilinium ion formed by protonation is *meta*-directing. • To get monosubstituted *p*-nitroderivatives, path II is followed.
3.	Sulphonation	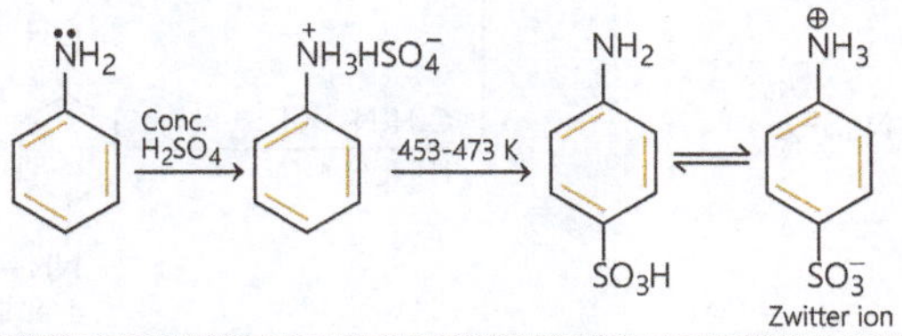	• *p*-aminobenzene sulphonic acid is the major product because distance between $—NH_2$ and $—SO_3H$ is maximum. • Sulphanilic acid exist in Zwitter ion form as shown.

Note Aniline is a Lewis base, while $AlCl_3$ is a Lewis acid. They combine with each other form salt ($C_6H_5\overset{+}{N}H_2AlCl_3^-$). The positively charged nitrogen of the salt which acts as a strong deactivating group hence, aniline does not undergo Friedel-Crafts reaction. NEET 2024

> **Marks Maximizer**
> Aromatic amines on oxidation with a mixture of sulphuric acid and $K_2Cr_2O_7$ forms a black dye of complex known as aniline black and controlled oxidation forms *p*-benzoquinone.

Diazonium Salts

- **General formula** $R\overset{+}{N}_2\overset{-}{X}$; R = aryl group, $\overset{\ominus}{X}$ ion may be Cl^-, Br^-, HSO_4^-, $B\bar{F}_4$, etc.
- **Nomenclature** Benzene diazonium salts are named by suffixing diazonium to the name of the parent hydrocarbon from which they are formed followed by the name of anion.

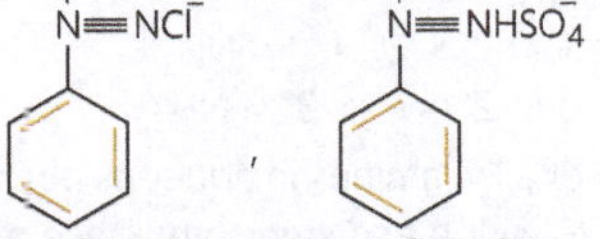

Benzene diazonium chloride, Benzene diazonium hydrogen sulphate

- **Stability** Primary aliphatic amines form highly unstable alkyl diazonium salts.

  On the other hand, primary aromatic amines form arene diazonium salt which are stable for a short time in solution at low temperatures (273 - 278 K).

The stability is explained on the basis of resonance.

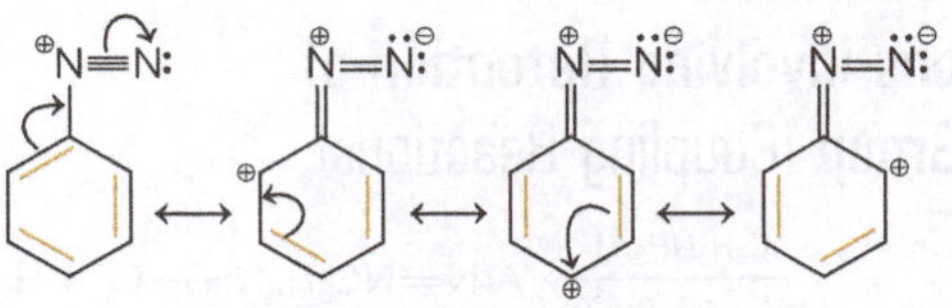

Method of Preparation of Diazonium Salts

- Benzene diazonium chloride is prepared by the reaction of aniline with nitrous acid at 273-278 K.
- The conversion of primary aromatic amines into diazonium salts is known as **diazotisation**.
- Due to its instability, the diazonium salt is not generally stored and is used immediately after its preparation.

$$C_6H_5NH_2 + NaNO_2 + 2HCl \xrightarrow{273\text{-}278\ K} C_6H_5N_2^+Cl^- + NaCl + 2H_2O$$

Physical Properties

- Benzene diazonium chloride is a colourless crystalline solid. It is readily soluble in water and is stable in cold but reacts with water when warmed.
- It decomposes easily in the dry state.
- Benzene diazonium fluoroborate is water insoluble and stable at room temperature.

Chemical Reactions

Chemical reactions involving displacement of nitrogen (diazo group; a good leaving group) are as follows

$ArN_2^+X^-$:

- $\xrightarrow{Cu_2Cl_2/HCl} ArCl + N_2$ (Sandmeyer reaction)
- $\xrightarrow{Cu_2Br_2/HBr} ArBr + N_2$ (Sandmeyer reaction)
- $\xrightarrow{CuCN/KCN} ArCN + N_2$ (Sandmeyer reaction)
- $\xrightarrow{Cu/HCl} ArCl + N_2 + CuX$ (Gattermann reaction)
- $\xrightarrow{Cu/HBr} ArBr + N_2 + CuX$ (Gattermann reaction)
- $\xrightarrow{KI} ArI + KX + N_2$
- $\xrightarrow{HBF_4} ArN_2^+BF_4^- \xrightarrow{\Delta} ArF + BF_3 + N_2$
  - $ArN_2^+BF_4^- \xrightarrow[\Delta]{NaNO_2,\ Cu} ArNO_2 + N_2\uparrow + NaBF_4$
- $\xrightarrow[283\ K]{H_2O} ArOH + N_2 + HX$
- $\xrightarrow{H_3PO_2 + H_2O} ArH + N_2 + H_3PO_3 + HX$
- $\xrightarrow{CH_3CH_2OH} Ar—H + N_2 + CH_3CHO + HX$

Reactions Involving Retention of Diazo Group (Coupling Reactions)

$$ArN_2^+X^- \xrightarrow[pH\ =\ 4\text{-}5,\ 0\text{-}5°C]{C_6H_5NH_2/H^+} ArN{=}NC_6H_4NH_2 + Cl^- + H_2O$$
p-aminoazobenzene (Yellow dye)

$$ArN_2^+X^- \xrightarrow[pH\ =\ 9\text{-}10,\ 0\text{-}5°C]{C_6H_5OH/OH^-} ArN{=}NC_6H_4OH + Cl^- + H_2O$$
p-hydroxyazobenzene (Orange dye)

Note Only 1° aromatic amines give coloured azo-dyes. This test is known as **azo-dye test**.

Marks Maximizer

In coupling reaction, the orientation of coupling depends upon the pH of the medium. In acidic medium (pH = 4-5), coupling occurs *ortho* to the amino group but in basic medium (pH = 9-10). Coupling occurs *ortho* to the phenolic group.

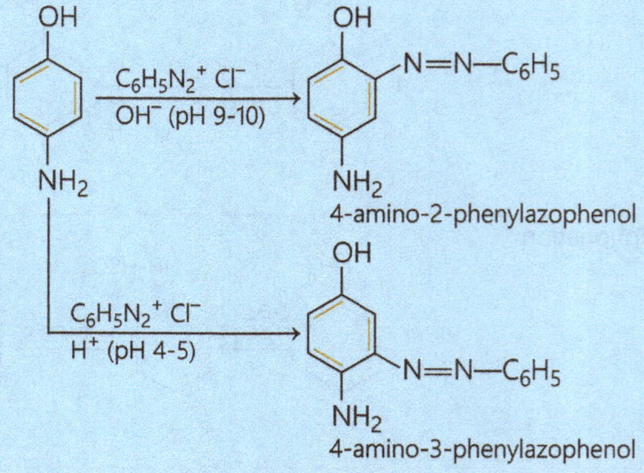

Importance of Diazonium Salts in Synthesis of Aromatic Compounds

- The diazonium salts are very good intermediates for the introduction of —F,—Cl, —Br, —I, —CN, —OH, $—NO_2$ group into the aromatic ring.
- It is used as intermediates in the preparation of dyes.
- Aryl fluorides and iodides cannot be prepared by direct halogenation. The cyano group cannot be introduced by nucleophilic substitution of chlorine in chlorobenzene but cyanobenzene can be easily obtained from diazonium salt.
- The replacement of diazo group by other groups is helpful in preparing those substituted compounds which cannot be prepared by direct substitution in benzene or substituted benzene.

Caution Points

- Amines are soluble in organic solvents like alcohol, ether and benzene. Alcohols are more polar than amines and form stronger intermolecular hydrogen bonds than amines, whereas amines form weaker hydrogen bonds with water.
- Direct nitration can't be carried out due to activating effect of $(—NH_2)$ group. To deactivate the activating effect of $(—NH_2)$ acetylation is introduced. Then, the major *para*-derivative aniline products can be formed.
- Keep in mind that primary amines react with nitrous acid to form aliphatic diazonium salts which is unstable. So, it can be hydrolysed to corresponding alcohols.
- The trend of basicity of amines in gaseous phase is different than that in liquid phase.

  In gaseous, 3° > 2° > 1° > NH_3

  In aqueous, 2° > 1° > 3° > NH_3

  Basic strength of alkyl amines in aqueous phase changes due to the + *I*-effect, solvation and steric hindrance of the alkyl group.

PYQ Notes

1. Reduction of isocyanide by $LiAlH_4$ gives secondary amines. **NEET 2023**
2. Aniline is more basic than acetamide. **JEE Main 2021**
3. If large amount of $KHSO_4$ is added to the mixture of H_2SO_4 and HNO_3 in the nitration of benzene, more HSO_4^- ion is furnished and the concentration of NO_2^+, i.e. electrophile decreases and hence rate of nitration decreases. **NEET 2016 Phase I**
4. In Hofmann hypobromamide reaction, amide with no substituent on nitrogen is converted to an amine containing one carbon less, due to action of alkaline hypobromide. **NEET 2017**

Step by Step

Mastering NCERT

- Concept Builders
- Topical Questions
- Assertion-Reason
- Statement Type
- Matching Type
- Numerical Value
- NCERT Exemplar's
- Past Exams'
- Skill Boosters

Concept Builders

1 Synthetic example of amine containing substances are alkaloids and hormones. [T/F]

2 Adrenaline and ephedrine are biologically active compounds containing secondary amino group. [T/F]

3 The geometry of amines is .... and the orbitals of nitrogen are ...... hybridised.

4 Name an aliphatic amine in common system containing one carbon atom.

5 In secondary and tertiary amines, when two or more groups are the same, prefix .... or ...... is used before the name of alkyl group.

6 Reduction of nitroalkanes to amines using iron scrap requires small amount of hydrochloric acid for initiation of reaction. [T/F]

7 An alkyl or benzyl halide on reaction with an ethanolic solution of .... undergoes .... substitution reaction.

8 During ammonolysis reaction, primary amine obtained in first step behaves as an electrophile and further reacts with alkyl halide to form secondary and tertiary amines. [T/F]

9 Butanamide on treatment with bromine in ethanolic solution of sodium hydroxide gives amine '*A*'. Identify '*A*'.

10 Phenyl ethane nitrile on reduction with H_2/Ni gives the product ....

11 Aniline and other aryl amines are colourless and are stable towards atmospheric oxidation. [T/F]

12 Solubility of amines in water increase with increase in molar mass. [T/F]

13 Tertiary amines show .... intermolecular association due to the absence of hydrogen atom.

14 Primary, secondary and tertiary amines show difference in reactivity due to difference in number of hydrogen atoms attached to their nitrogen atom. [T/F]

15 Amines have an unshared pair of electrons on nitrogen atom which makes them to acts as ....

16 Which effect is responsible for making aliphatic amines much stronger bases than ammonia?

17 Acidic character of an amine depends upon ease of formation of cation by accepting proton from the acid. [T/F]

18 In aqueous phase, ammonium cations get stabilised due to electron releasing effect of alkyl group and destabilised due to solvation with water molecules. [T/F]

19 The product obtained by acylation of amines is ....

20 Anilinium ion have only two resonating structures. [T/F]

21 Primary aliphatic amines on reaction with nitrous acid liberates .... gas which is used in estimation of .... and proteins.

22 Write the formula of Hinsberg's reagent.

23 Hydrogen attached to nitrogen in sulphonamide is strongly basic due to the presence of strong electron withdrawing sulphonyl group. [T/F]

24 Name the product formed on reaction of benzene sulphonyl chloride with N, N-diethyl amine.

25 .... does not undergo Friedel-Crafts reaction due to the formation of salt with aluminium chloride.

26 Primary aliphatic amines form highly unstable alkyl diazonium salts. [T/F]

27 Name the aryl halides which cannot be prepared by direct halogenation.

28 Name the compound which will not undergo coupling reaction with benzene diazonium chloride.

29 .... are very good intermediates for the introduction of —F, —Cl, —CN, —OH, groups into the aromatic ring.

30 Write the product formed when 3-methylaniline reacts with $NaNO_2$, HCl (at 273-278 K) followed by reaction with HBF_4.

Topical Questions

Structure, Classification and Nomenclature of Amines

1 The hybridisation and geometry of amines are sp^3 and pyramidal respectively due to the presence of
(a) divalent N-atom (b) trivalent N-atom **NCERT Pg 259**
(c) monovalent N-aom (d) tetravalent N-atom

2 Which of the following statements is not correct for amines? **NCERT Pg 259**
(a) Amines are derived by replacing one or more H-atoms of ammonia molecule by alkyl/aryl group(s).
(b) In nature, they occur among proteins, vitamins, alkaloids and hormones.
(c) Synthetic amines are polymers, dye stuffs and drugs.
(d) Quaternary ammonium salts are used to increase blood pressure.

3 Which of the following compounds contain secondary amino group? **NCERT Pg 259**
(a) Adrenaline (b) Novocain
(c) Benadryl (d) Pyridine

4 The structure of trimethylamine is given below. **NCERT Pg 260**

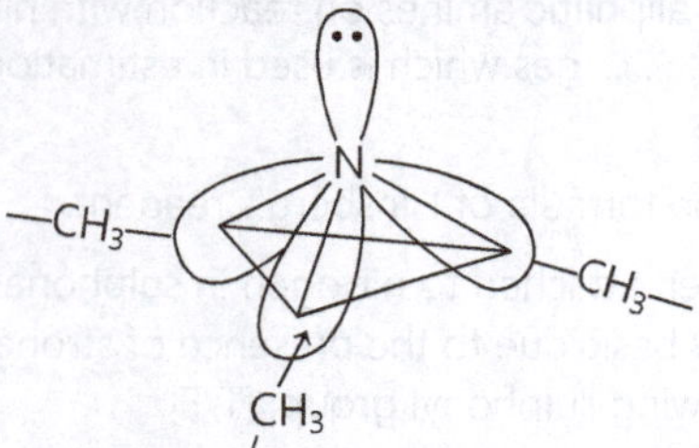

Select the correct statements regarding above structure.
I. Three sp^3-hybridised orbitals of nitrogen overlap with orbitals of hydrogen or carbon depending upon the composition of the amines.
II. The fourth orbital of nitrogen in amines contain an unshared pair of electrons.
III. The shape of this compound is tetrahedral.
IV. The bond angle C—N—C is 109.5°.
Choose the correct answer from the options given below.
(a) I and II (b) I and III (c) III and IV (d) II and IV

5 Which one of the following is a secondary amine?
(a) Ethylmethylamine (b) Isobutylamine **NCERT Pg 261**
(c) *Iso*-propylamine (d) Trimethylamine

6 C_2H_7N can represent **NCERT Pg 261**
(a) 1° amine (b) 2° amine
(c) 3° amine (d) 1° and 2° amine

7 IUPAC name of the compound trimethylamine is
(a) N, N-dimethylmethanamine **NCERT Pg 261**
(b) N-methylethanamine
(c) propanamine
(d) propan-2-amine

8 Which of the following IUPAC name of the corresponding compound is incorrect? **NCERT Pg 261**

(a) 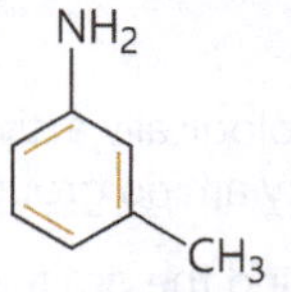

— 1-aminotoluene

(b) $NH_2—CH_2—CH{=}CH_2$ — Prop-2-en-1-amine

(c) $CH_3—CH(NH_2)—CH_3$ — Propan-2-amine

(d) 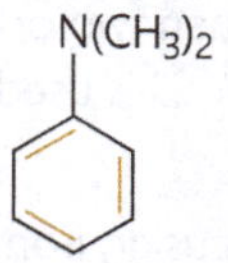

— N,N-dimethylbenzen-amine

9 The IUPAC name of the compound **NCERT Pg 261**

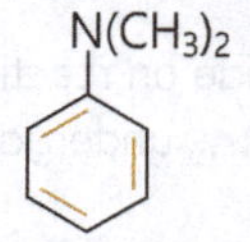

is

(a) N-phenyl-N-propene
(b) N, N-methylbenzene
(c) N, N-dimethylbenzenamine
(d) N, N-dimethylbenzene

10 Choose the incorrect statement regarding the isomeric form of amine having molecular formula $C_4H_{11}N$.
(a) It has only one tertiary amine. **NCERT Pg 262**
(b) It forms four primary amines.
(c) It forms three secondary amines.
(d) It shows only three primary amines.

Preparation of Amines

11 Which of the following reagents is/are not used in the given reaction? **NCERT Pg 262**

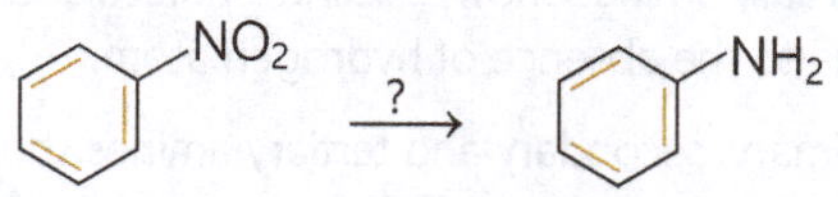

(a) H_2/Pd, ethanol (b) Sn + HCl
(c) Fe + HCl (d) CuCN, $LiAlH_4$

12 Select the correct statements regarding ammonolysis. **NCERT Pg 262, 263**

(a) It is the process of cleavage of the C—X bond by ammonia molecule.
(b) This reaction is carried out in an open tube at 373 K.
(c) Benzyl halide on reaction with an ethanolic solution of ammonia undergoes electrophilic substitution.
(d) Free amine is obtained from the ammonium salt by treatment with strong acid.

13 Consider the following reaction, **NCERT Pg 262, 263**

$$NH_3 + RX \longrightarrow R\text{—}\overset{\oplus}{N}H_3 X^{\ominus} \xrightarrow[-HX]{NaOH} \underset{(1°)}{RNH_2} + H_2O + NaX$$

$$RNH_2 \xrightarrow{RX} \underset{(2°)}{R_2NH} \xrightarrow{RX} \underset{(3°)}{R_3N} \xrightarrow{RX} R_4N^{\oplus}X^{-}$$

Select the incorrect statement(s) regarding the above reaction.

(a) RI is most reactive towards primary amine.
(b) In this reaction, RX is the nucleophile.
(c) $R_4N^{\oplus}X^{-}$ is called quaternary ammonium salt.
(d) Primary amine is obtained as a major product by taking large excess of ammonia.

14 The disadvantage of ammonolysis is that, **NCERT Pg 263**

(a) it produce toxic products
(b) it give very less yield of primary amine
(c) it produce tertiary amines only
(d) it yields a mixture of primary, secondary and tertiary amines

15 What is the correct order of reactivity of halides with amines? **NCERT Pg 263**

(a) $RCl > RBr > RI$
(b) $RI > RBr > RCl$
(c) $RCl > RI > RBr$
(d) $RI > RCl > RBr$

16 Which of the following reagent(s) is/(are) required for the following conversion? **NCERT Pg 263**

$$C_6H_5CH_2Cl \longrightarrow C_6H_5CH_2\text{—}\underset{\displaystyle CH_3}{\underset{|}{N}}\text{—}CH_3$$

(a) $(CH_3)_2NH, CH_3OH$
(b) CH_3Cl, RNH_2
(c) $NH_3, 2CH_3Cl$
(d) $CH_3CH_2NH_2$

17 Which of the following reaction is used for the preparation of amine having one C-atom more than the starting amine? **NCERT Pg 263**

(a) Reduction of nitriles
(b) Reduction of amides
(c) Reduction of nitro compounds
(d) Ammonolysis of alkyl halide

18 Select the correct statement for the conversion.

$$RCN \longrightarrow RCH_2NH_2$$ **NCERT Pg 263**

(a) It is an oxidation reaction.
(b) Reagents used in this reaction are $LiAlH_4$, H_2/Ni, $Na(Hg)/C_2H_5OH$.
(c) $LiAlH_4$ reduces CH_3CN into CH_3NH_2.
(d) This reaction produce primary and secondary amine.

19 Which of the following product is formed in the given reaction? **NCERT Pg 263**

$$R\text{—}CONH_2 \xrightarrow[\text{(ii) } H_2O]{\text{(i) } LiAlH_4}$$

(a) RNH_2 (b) RCH_2NH_2
(c) $RCH_2CH_2NH_2$ (d) RCN

20 Which one of the following reagent is used for conversion of alkyl cyanide to primary amine? **NCERT Pg 263**

(a) R—MgX/H_2O (b) H_2/Ni
(c) $SnCl_2$ + Conc. HCl (d) $H_2O/\bar{O}H$

21 Consider the following sequence of reaction :

$$CH_3CH_2COOH \xrightarrow{A} X \xrightarrow{B} Y \xrightarrow{C} CH_3CH_2NH_2$$

Here, A, B and C respectively are **NCERT Pg 263, 264**

	A	B	C
(a)	HCN	NH_3	Br_2/KOH
(b)	HNO_2	PtI_2	$LiAlH_4$
(c)	$SOCl_2$	NH_3	Br_2/KOH
(d)	$Ca(OH)_2$	Heat	Pt/H_2

22 Which of the following reaction will give primary amine?

(i) $CH_3CONH_2 \xrightarrow{KOH+Br_2}$

(ii) $CH_3CN \xrightarrow{LiAlH_4}$

(iii) $(C_2H_5)_2NH \xrightarrow{C_2H_5\text{—}Cl}$

(iv) $CH_3CONH_2 \xrightarrow{LiAlH_4}$

Choose the most appropriate answer from the options given below. **NCERT Pg 263, 264**

(a) (i) and (ii) (b) (ii) and (iv)
(c) (i), (ii) and (iii) (d) (i), (ii) and (iv)

23 Which of the following statements is/are correct regarding Hofmann bromamide reaction? **NCERT Pg 264**

(a) In this reaction, migration of an alkyl or aryl group takes place from nitrogen atom of amide to the carbonyl carbon.
(b) The amine, so formed contains one carbon more than that present in the amide.
(c) It is a degradation reaction.
(d) Hofmann bromamide method is used for preparation of secondary amines.

24 Identify X in the given reaction. NCERT Pg 264

Ethanamide + $X \longrightarrow$ Methanamine

(a) PCl_5 (b) $NaOH + Br_2$
(c) HNO_3 (d) NaOH + water

25 Which of the following can be prepared using Gabriel phthalimide synthesis? NCERT Pg 264

(a) Primary aromatic amines
(b) Secondary amines
(c) Primary aliphatic amines
(d) Tertiary amines

26 Consider the following reaction, NCERT Pg 264

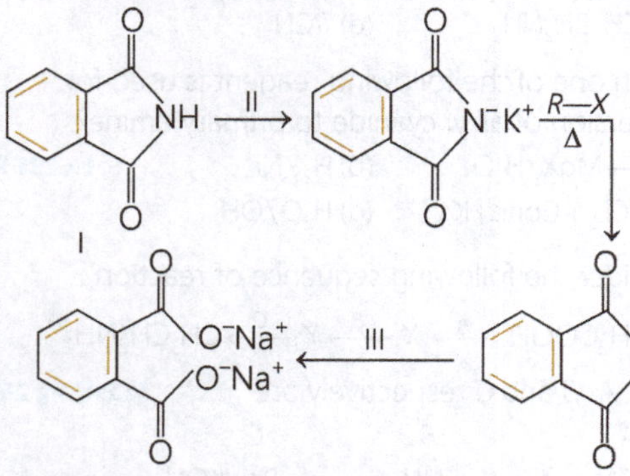

What is I, II and III in the above reaction?

	I	II	III
(a)	Phthalimide;	Ethanolic KOH	NaOH(*aq*)
(b)	Phthalamide;	Ethanolic KOH	NaOH(alc.)
(c)	Phthalimide;	HCl	NaOH(alc.)
(d)	Phthalamide;	HCl	NaOCl

27 Ethylamine ($C_2H_5HN_2$) can be obtained from N-ethylphthalimide on treatment with NCERT Pg 264

(a) $NaBH_4$ (b) NaOH (c) H_2O (d) CaH_2

28 Which of the following reactions is appropriate for the conversion of acetamide to methanamine? NCERT Pg 264

(a) Carbylamine reaction
(b) Hofmann bromamide reaction
(c) Stephen's reaction
(d) Gabriel's phthalimide synthesis

Physical Properties and Chemical Reactions of Amines

29 Choose the incorrect statement from the following. NCERT Pg 265

(a) Lower aliphatic amines are soluble in water.
(b) Solubility decreases with increase in molar mass of amine.
(c) Higher aliphatic amines are insoluble in water.
(d) Aryl amines are colourful in nature.

30 The correct order of increasing boiling points for the bases, CH_3NH_2, $(CH_3)_2NH$, $(CH_3)_3N$ is NCERT Pg 266

(a) $CH_3NH_2 < (CH_3)_2NH < (CH_3)_3N$
(b) $CH_3NH_2 < (CH_3)_3N < (CH_3)_2NH$
(c) $(CH_3)_3N < (CH_3)_2NH < CH_3NH_2$
(d) $(CH_3)_3N < CH_3NH_2 < (CH_3)_2NH$

31 Which of the following statements is/are incorrect?

(a) Higher amines are insoluble in water. NCERT Pg 265, 266
(b) Electronegativity of nitrogen in amine and that of oxygen in alcohol is 3.5 and 3.0 respectively.
(c) Amines are soluble in organic solvents.
(d) Boiling point of 3° amine is less than that of 2° amine.

32 Observe the given figure, NCERT Pg 265, 266

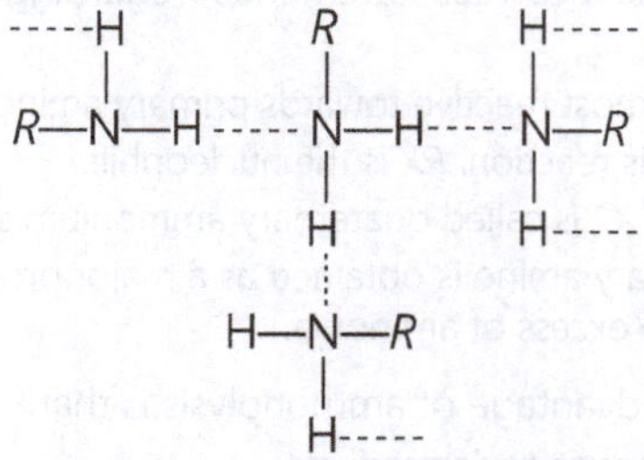

Which of the following statement is correct?

(a) Intramolecular hydrogen bonding present in primary aliphatic amines.
(b) Intermolecular hydrogen bonding present in primary amines.
(c) Intermolecular hydrogen bonding is not present in secsondary amines.
(d) Intermolecular hydrogen bonding present in tertiary amines.

33 Amines on treatment with acids yield salt because they are NCERT Pg 266

(a) basic in nature (b) acidic in nature
(c) amphoteric in nature (d) neutral in nature

34 Amines behave as a nucleophile because of NCERT Pg 266

(a) the presence of unshared pair of electrons on N-atom
(b) the absence of unshared pair of electrons on N-atom
(c) the vacant *p*-orbital of N-atom
(d) having vacant *d*-orbital in N-atom

35 Which of the following statements is/are correct about amines? NCERT Pg 267

(a) Amine salts are soluble in ether but insoluble in water.
(b) Amines have an unshared pair of electrons on nitrogen atom due to which they behave as Lewis acid.
(c) Methanamine is a strong base than benzenamine.
(d) Larger tha value of K_b, weaker is the base.

36 For the reaction, NCERT Pg 267

$$RNH_2 + H_2O \rightleftharpoons R\text{—}\overset{+}{N}H_3 + \overset{-}{O}H$$

Select the incorrect expression(s) for the above reaction.

(a) $K[H_2O] = \dfrac{[R\overset{+}{N}H_3][\overset{-}{O}H]}{[RNH_2]}$ (b) $K_b = \dfrac{[R\overset{+}{N}H_3][\overset{-}{O}H]}{[RNH_2]}$

(c) $pK_b = \log K_b$ (d) $K_b = 10^{-pK_a}$

37 Consider the following amines alongwith their pK_b values : NCERT Pg 267

Amines	pK_b
Methanamine	3.38
N-methylmethanamine	3.27
Benzenamine	9.38
Phenylmethanamine	4.70

Which one is the strongest base?

(a) Benzenamine
(b) Phenyl methanamine
(c) Methanamine
(d) N-methylmethanamine

38 Select the correct statements from the following.

I. Primary amines have high boiling point than tertiary amine. NCERT Pg 265, 266, 267, 278
II. Aliphatic amines are stronger base than ammonia.
III. Tertiary amines are used as insect attractants.
IV. Primary amines are not soluble in water.

Choose the correct answer from the options given below.

(a) Only I (b) Only II
(c) I, II and III (d) II, III and IV

39 Choose the incorrect statement from the following. NCERT Pg 268

(a) Basic character of amine depends upon the ease of formation of cation.
(b) More stable is the cation, more basic is the amine.
(c) Alkylamines are weaker base than ammonia.
(d) Greater is the size of the ion, lesser will be the solvation.

40 Identify the correct statements from the following. NCERT Pg 268

(i) $C_2H_5NH_2$ is a weaker base than $(C_2H_5)_3N$ in gaseous phase.
(ii) NH_3 is a weaker base than $C_2H_5NH_2$ in gaseous phase.
(iii) Methylamine is a weaker base than ammonia in gaseous phase.
(iv) Methyl amine is basic in nature.
(v) Ethylamine contains a basic —NH_2 group.

(a) (i) and (ii) (b) (i), (ii), (iv) and (v)
(c) (iv) and (v) (d) (iii) and (iv)

41 The increasing order of basicity of the following compounds in aqueous solution. NCERT Pg 268

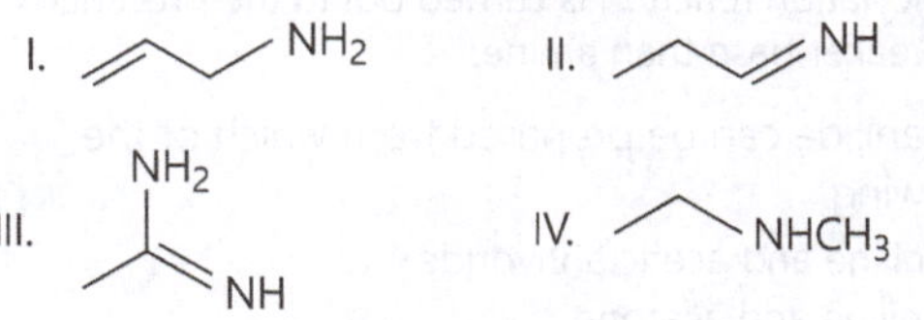

(a) I < II < III < IV (b) II < I < III < IV
(c) II < I < IV < III (d) IV < II < I < III

42 The correct order of the basic strength of methyl substituted amines in aqueous solution is NCERT Pg 269

(a) $(CH_3)_3N > CH_3NH_2 > (CH_3)_2NH$
(b) $(CH_3)_3N > (CH_3)_2NH > CH_3NH_2$
(c) $CH_3NH_2 > (CH_3)_2NH > (CH_3)_3N$
(d) $(CH_3)_2NH > CH_3NH_2 > (CH_3)_3N$

43 The decreasing order of basicity of the following amines is NCERT Pg 269

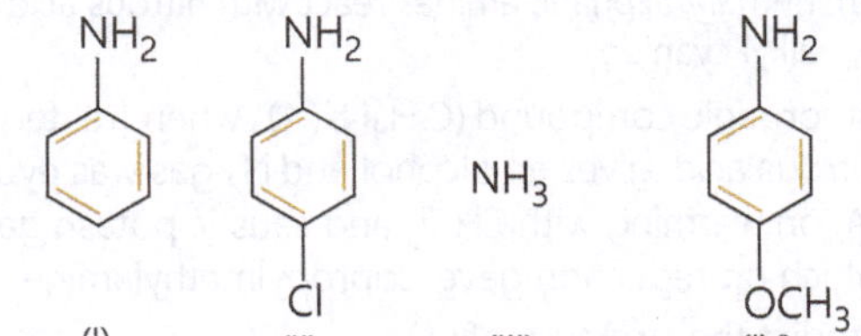

(I) (II) (III) (IV)

(a) (III) > (IV) > (I) > (II) (b) (III) > (II) > (I) > (IV)
(c) (I) > (III) > (IV) > (II) (d) (II) > (III) > (IV) > (I)

44 Consider the following reaction : NCERT Pg 270

$$C_6H_5\text{—}\ddot{N}(H)\text{—}H + CH_3\underset{\underset{O}{\|}}{C}\text{—}O\text{—}\underset{\underset{O}{\|}}{C}CH_3 \xrightarrow{\text{Base}} 'X' + CH_3COOH$$

Here, 'X' is

(a) N-phenyl-N-ethylmethanamine
(b) N, N-ethylphenylmethanamide
(c) N-phenylethanamide
(d) N-phenylmethanamide

45 N-methylbenzamide is formed when methanamine reacts with benzoyl chloride. This reaction is known as NCERT Pg 270

(a) Benzoylation (b) Hinsberg test
(c) Schmidt reaction (d) Curtius reaction

46 Which of the following statements is/are not correct? NCERT Pg 270

(a) Primary and secondary amines reacts with acid chlorides, anhydrides and esters by nucleophilic substitution reaction.
(b) In the acylation reaction of amines there is replacement of hydrogen atom of NH_2 or NH group by the acyl group.

(c) The products obtained in acylation reaction of amines are amides.
(d) Acylation reaction is carried out in the presence of weaker base than amine.

47 Acetanilide can be prepared from which of the following. NCERT Pg 270
(a) Aniline and acetic anhydride
(b) Aniline and acetone
(c) Aniline and ethanol
(d) Aniline and acetaldehyde

48 Which of the following statements is/are correct? NCERT Pg 271
(a) Aromatic amines react with nitric acid to form diazonium salts.
(b) Formation of diazonium salts occur at high temperature.
(c) Side products formed during the formation of benzene diazonium chloride are NaCl and H_2O molecules.
(d) Primary aliphatic amines react with nitrous acid to form alkyl cyanide.

49 An organic compound (C_3H_9N) (*A*), when treated with nitrous acid, gives an alcohol and N_2 gas was evolved. (*A*) on warming with $CHCl_3$ and caustic potash gave (*C*) which on reduction gave isopropylmethylamine. Predict the structure of (*A*). NCERT Pg 271
(a) $(H_3C)_2CH—NH_2$
(b) $CH_3CH_2—NH—CH_3$
(c) $CH_3—N(CH_3)—CH_3$
(d) $CH_3CH_2CH_2—NH_2$

50 Name the product(s) formed during the reaction of primary aliphatic amines with nitrous acid at room temperature? NCERT Pg 271
(a) RNO_2
(b) ROH
(c) NaOCl
(d) ROH and NaCl

51 An amine (*X*) react with nitrous acid at low temperatures to form stable diazonium salts. The structure of amine (*X*) is NCERT Pg 271
(a) CH_3NH_2
(b) $CH_3CH_2NH_2$
(c) $CH_3(CH_2)NH_2$
(d) $C_6H_5—NH_2$

52 Consider the following reaction: NCERT Pg 271

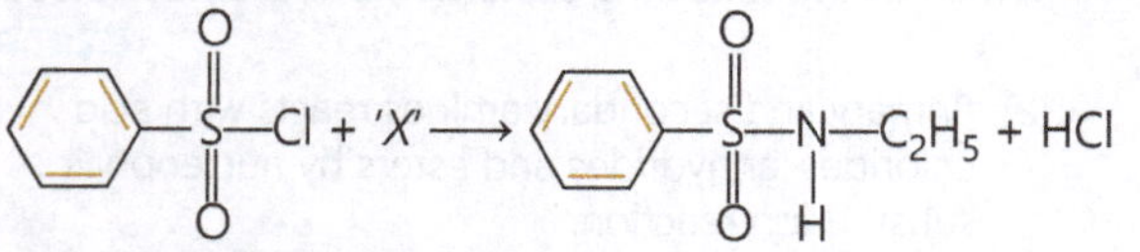

Here, substance '*X*' is
(a) $C_2H_5NH_2$
(b) $(C_2H_5)_2NH$
(c) $(C_2H_5)_3N$
(d) $(C_2H_5)_4N^+$

53 The amine that reacts with Hinsberg's reagent to give an alkali insoluble product is NCERT Pg 271
(a) $(CH_3)_2CH—NH—CH(CH_3)_2$
(b) $N(CH_2CH_3)_3$
(c) $CH_3—C(NH_2)(CH_3)—CH_2CH_2CH_3$
(d) $CH_3—C(CH_3)_2—CH(CH_3)—NH_2$

54 N, N-diethylbenzene sulphonamide is not acidic because NCERT Pg 272
(a) it does not contain unshared pair of electron on N-atom
(b) it does not have H-atom attached with the N-atom
(c) it contains —OH group with N-atom
(d) it is insoluble in alkali

55 $—NH_2$ group in aniline is an activating group and hence reaction occurs at NCERT Pg 272
(a) *para* position only
(b) *ortho* position only
(c) *meta* position only
(d) *ortho* and *para* position

56 In the following reaction sequence,

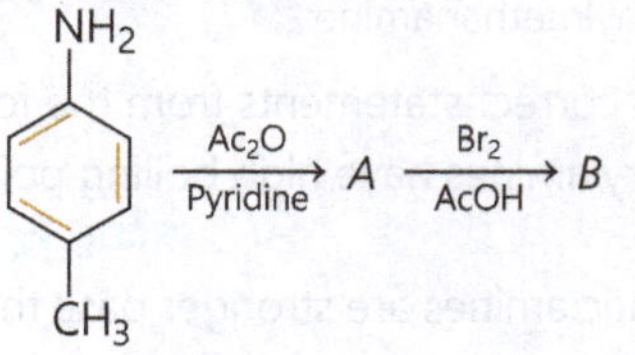

The major product *B* is NCERT Pg 272

(a)
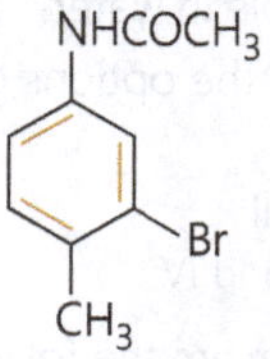

(b)
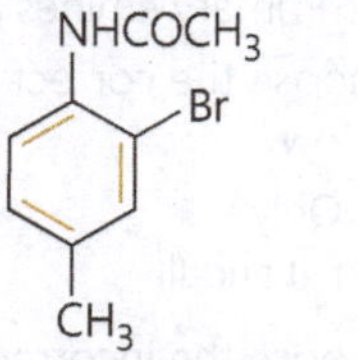

(c)
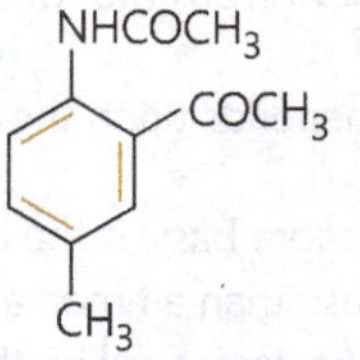

(d)
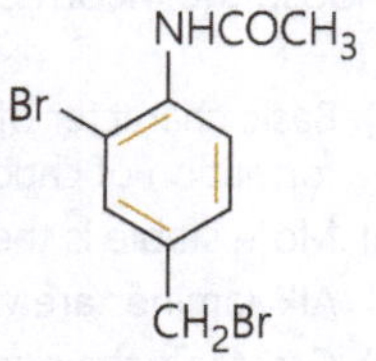

57
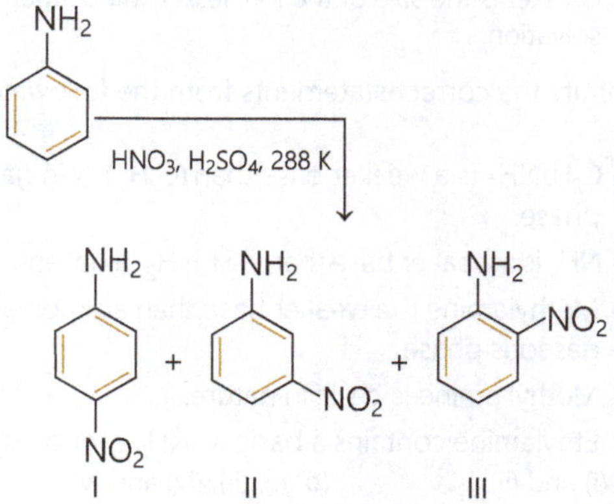

I II III

Select the percentage in which these amine derivatives are formed in the reaction mixture along with the reason. NCERT Pg 273

(a) I $\rightarrow$ 2%, II $\rightarrow$ 47%, III $\rightarrow$ 51%
In the acidic medium, aniline is protonated to form the anilinium ion which is *ortho*-directing.

(b) I $\rightarrow$ 51%, II $\rightarrow$ 2%, III $\rightarrow$ 47%
In the acidic medium, aniline is protonated to form the anilinium ion which is *para*-directing.

(c) I $\rightarrow$ 51%, II $\rightarrow$ 47%, III $\rightarrow$ 2%
In the acidic medium, aniline is protonated to form the anilinium ion which is *meta*-directing.

(d) I $\rightarrow$ 50%, II $\rightarrow$ 20%, III $\rightarrow$ 20%
In acidic medium aniline is protonated to form the anilinium ion which is *ortho*-directing.

58 Nitration of aniline in strong acidic medium also gives *m*-nitroaniline because NCERT Pg 273

(a) in absence of substituents nitro group always goes to *m*-position
(b) in electrophilic substitution reactions amino group is *meta* directive
(c) in spite of substituents nitro group always goes to only *m*-position
(d) in strong acidic medium aniline is present as anilinium ion

59 Under which of the following conditions, aniline gives *p*-nitroderivative as the major product? NCERT Pg 273

I. Acetyl chloride/pyridine followed by reaction with conc. H_2SO_4 + conc. HNO_3.
II. Acetic anhydride/pyridine followed by conc. H_2SO_4 + conc. HNO_3, 288 K
III. Dil. HCl followed by reaction with conc. H_2SO_4 + conc. HNO_3.
IV. Reaction with conc. HNO_3 + conc. H_2SO_4, 288 K

Choose the correct answer from the options given below.

(a) I, II and IV
(b) II and III
(c) III and IV
(d) I and IV

60 Which of the following statement is not correct? NCERT Pg 271, 272, 273

(a) Aromatic amines are stronger base than ammonia.
(b) Ammonia are weaker base than aliphatic amines.
(c) Aniline is dentified by carbylamine reaction.
(d) Aniline does not undergo Friedel-Crafts reaction.

61 Select the correct order of the reagent to carry out the following reaction. NCERT Pg 273

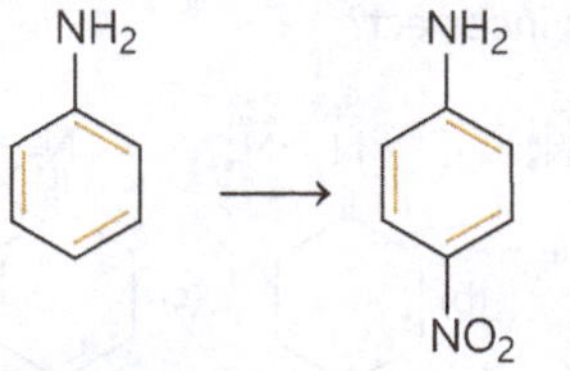

(a) (i) $(CH_3CO)_2O$, pyridine
(ii) OH^- or H^+
(iii) HNO_3, H_2SO_4, 288 K

(b) (i) $(CH_3CO)_2O$, pyridine
(ii) HNO_3, H_2SO_4, 288 K
(iii) OH^- or H^+

(c) (i) HNO_3, H_2SO_4, 288 K
(ii) OH^- or H^+

(d) (i) OH^- or H^+
(ii) HNO_3, H_2SO_4, 288 K

62 In the following reaction the intermediate is NCERT Pg 273

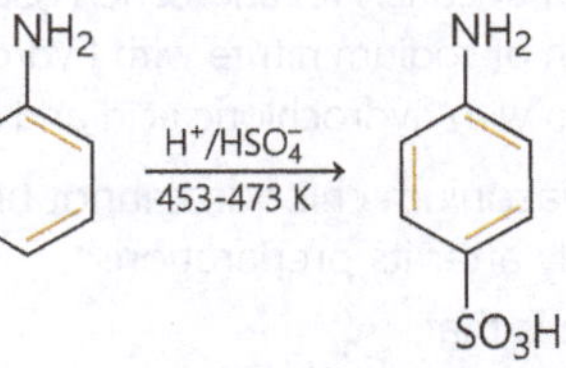

(a) 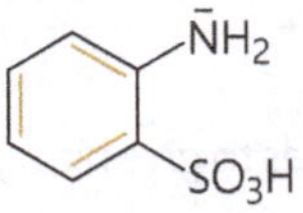

(b) 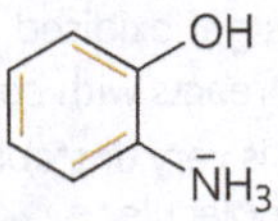

(c) 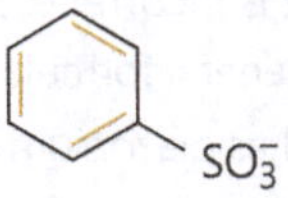

(d) 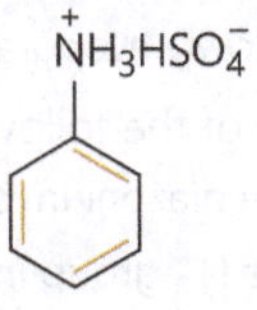

63 Aniline does not undergo Friedel-Crafts reaction due to NCERT Pg 273

(a) less reactivity of aniline
(b) salt formation with $AlCl_3$
(c) electron accepting effect of —NH_2 group present in aniline
(d) $AlCl_3$ act as Lewis base

Methods of Preparation of Diazonium Salts

64 Which of the following will be most stable? NCERT Pg 274

(a) $CH_3N_2^+X$
(b) $C_6H_5N_2^+X^-$
(c) $CH_3CH_2N_2^+X^-$
(d) $CH_3CH_2CH_2N_2^+X^-$

65 The stability of arene diazonium ion is explained on the basis of resonance. Which of the following resonating structure is incorrect? NCERT Pg 274

(a) 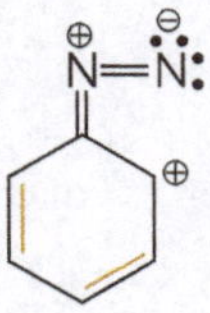 (b) 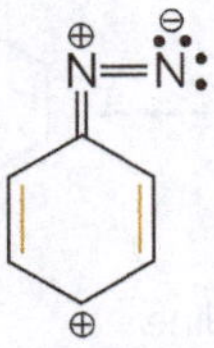 (c) 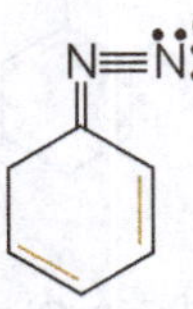 (d) 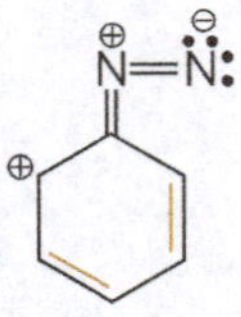

66 Which of the following amine will form stable diazonium salt at 273-278 K? NCERT Pg 274

(a) $C_2H_5NH_2$
(b) $C_6H_5NH_2$
(c) $CH_3CH_2NHCH_3$
(d) $C_6H_5N(CH_3)_2$

67 Which of the following is correct preparation of nitrous acid? NCERT Pg 274

(a) Reaction of conc. HNO_3 and conc. H_2SO_4.
(b) Reaction of conc. HCl and conc. H_2SO_4.
(c) Reaction of sodium nitrite with hydrochloric acid.
(d) Reaction with hydrochloric acid and nitric acid.

68 Benzene diazonium chloride cannot be stored and is used immediately after its preparation.
The reason is that, NCERT Pg 274

(a) its get oxidised
(b) it reacts with containers
(c) it is very unstable and dissociates to give nitrogen molecule.
(d) it slowly evaporates on storage.

69 Which of the following statement is incorrect? NCERT Pg 274

(a) The diazonium salts have the general formula $R\overset{+}{N}_2\overset{-}{X}$.
(b) The N_2^+ group in $R\overset{+}{N}_2\overset{-}{X}$ is called as diazonium group.
(c) The stability of arene diazonium ion is explained on the basis of inductive effect.
(d) Primary aliphatic amines form highly unstable alkyl diazonium salts.

70 Identify *A*, *B*, *C*, *D*, *E* in the given sequence of reaction. NCERT Pg 262, 271, 275

$$C_6H_5NO_2 \xrightarrow{H_2/Pd} A \xrightarrow[0\text{-}5°C]{NaNO_2+HCl} B \xrightarrow{CuCN/KCN} C$$

	A	B	C
(a)	C_6H_5Cl	C_6H_5CN	$C_6H_5CH_2NH_2$
(b)	C_6H_5N—NO	C_6H_5NC	$C_6H_5NO_2$
(c)	$C_6H_5NH_2$	$C_6H_5N_2Cl^-$	C_6H_5NC
(d)	$C_6H_5NH_2$	$C_6H_5\overset{+}{N}_2\overset{-}{Cl}$	C_6H_5CN

Physical Properties and Chemical Reactions of Diazonium Salts

71 Which of the following statement is correct regarding the property of benzene diazonium chloride?

(a) It is readily soluble in water. NCERT Pg 275
(b) It is yellowish crystalline solid in nature.
(c) It does not react with water when warmed.
(d) It does not decompose in dry state.

72 Among the following, which reaction is not a Sandmeyer reaction? NCERT Pg 275

(a) $Ar\overset{+}{N}_2\overset{-}{X} \xrightarrow{Cu_2Cl_2/HCl} ArCl + N_2$
(b) $Ar\overset{+}{N}_2\overset{-}{X} \xrightarrow{Cu_2Br_2/HBr} ArBr + N_2$
(c) $Ar\overset{+}{N}_2\overset{-}{X} \xrightarrow{CuCN/KCN} ArCN + N_2$
(d) $Ar\overset{+}{N}_2\overset{-}{X} \xrightarrow{Cu/HBr} ArBr + N_2 + CuX$

73 Which of the following reagent is responsible for converting aniline to chlorobenzene? NCERT Pg 274, 275

(a) $K_2Cr_2O_7$, $SOCl_2$ (b) $LiAlH_4$
(c) $NaNO_2 + HCl$, Cu_2Cl_2/HCl (d) KOH, $CuCl_2$

74 Phenyl cyanide is prepared by which of the following reaction? NCERT Pg 274, 275

(a) Rosenmund's reduction (b) Carbylamine reaction
(c) Reimer-Tiemann reaction (d) Sandmeyer reaction

75 In the chemical reaction. NCERT Pg 274, 275

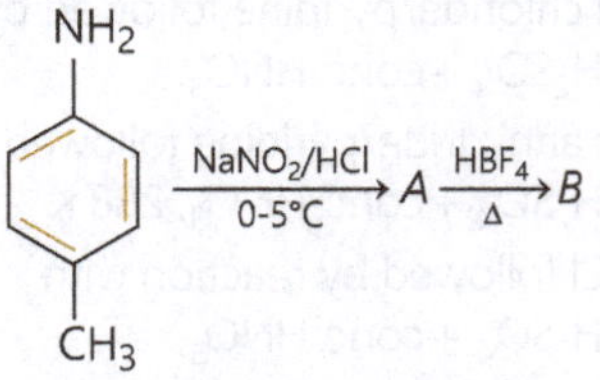

The compounds *A* and *B* respectively are

(a) nitrobenzene and chlorobenzene
(b) phenol and benzene
(c) diazonium salt and *p*-fluorotoluene
(d) Benzene diazonium chloride and fluorobenzene

76 Benzene diazonium salt on reaction with KI gives ArI alongwith some side products. The side products are

(a) KNO_2 (b) $KCl + N_2$ NCERT Pg 275
(c) KCl (d) K_2Cl_3

77 The reagent used to form aryl fluoride from arene diazonium chloride is NCERT Pg 276

(a) HF (b) KF (c) HBF_4 (d) CuF

78 In the reaction.

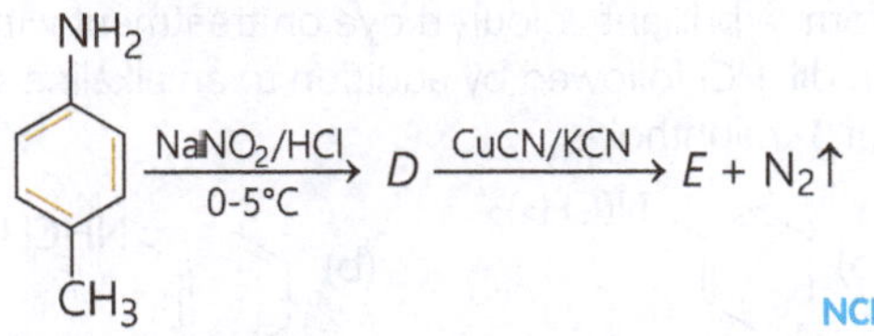

NCERT Pg 275

The product E is

(a) 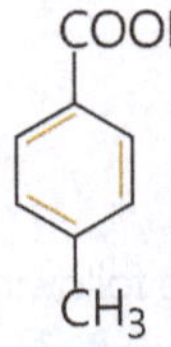

(b) 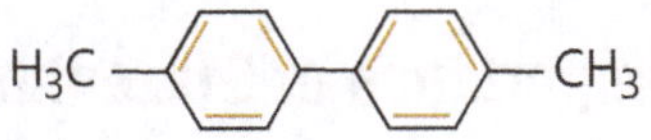

(c) 

(d) 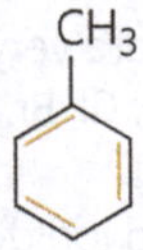

79 Benzene diazonium chloride on reaction with hypophosphorus acid produces NCERT Pg 276

(a) benzene (b) phenol

(c) phenol isocyanide (d) phenyl phosphate

80 Identify the reagents X, Y and Z for the following products. NCERT Pg 275, 276

(i) $C_6H_5\overset{+}{N}_2\overset{-}{Cl} \xrightarrow{X} C_6H_5F$ (ii) $C_6H_5\overset{+}{N}_2\overset{-}{Cl} \xrightarrow{Y} C_6H_5OH$

(iii) $C_6H_5\overset{+}{N}_2\overset{-}{BF_4} \xrightarrow{Z} C_6H_5NO_2$

	X	Y	Z
(a)	HBF_4, Δ	H_2O, 283 K	$NaNO_2$, Cu, Δ
(b)	CuI	NaCN	KOH
(c)	KI, warm	CuCN	H_2O, warm
(d)	AgF, warm	AgCN, warm	KOH, boil

81 The structure of product X in the following reaction is NCERT Pg 275, 276

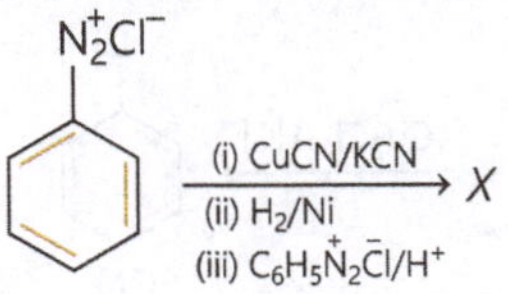

(a) 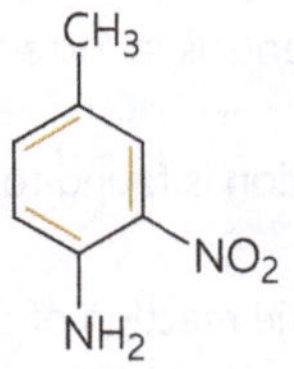

(b) 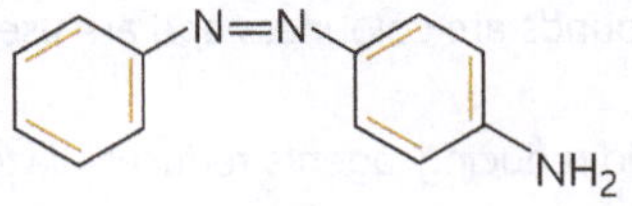

(c) 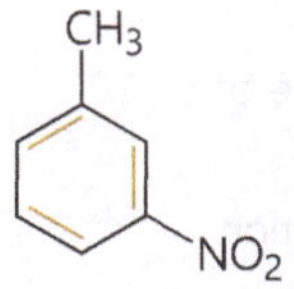

(d) 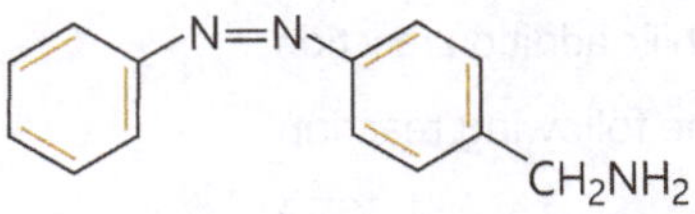

82 Mark the correct route for the conversion of aniline to *p*-nitrofluorobenzene. NCERT Pg 273, 275

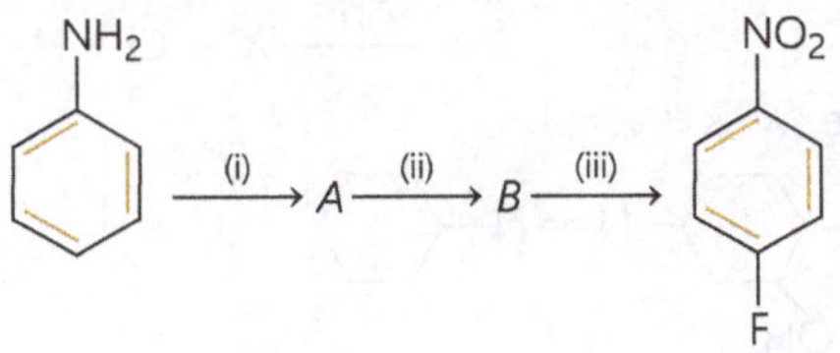

	(i)	(ii)	(iii)
(a)	Nitration	$NaNO_2 + HCl$, 0 – 5°C	HBF_4/Δ
(b)	Nitration	H_2/Pt	Hydrolysis
(c)	Diazotisation	H_2O/H^+	Sn/HCl
(d)	Diazotisaiton	CuCN	HBF_4

83 Which of the following statement/reaction is correct? NCERT Pg 271, 274, 276

(a) Nitrous acid is produced by the reaction of aniline with HCl.

(b) 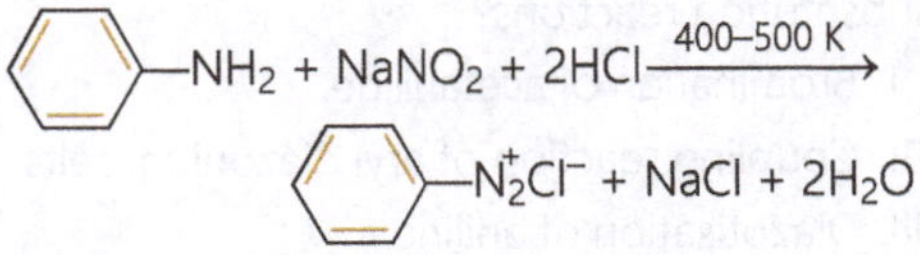

(c) Coupling of diazonium salt with amines occur in strongly basic medium.

(d) Diazonium salt is not generally stored and it is used immediately after its preparation.

84 Which of the following statements is incorrect? NCERT Pg 274, 275, 276

(a) The yield in Sandmeyer reaction is found to be better than Gattermann reaction.

(b) Nitrobenzene is formed by the reaction of diazonium fluoroborate with in presence of copper sodium nitrites.

(c) Azo compounds are colourless and are used as antiseptics.

(d) Certain mild reducing agents reduces diazonium salts to arenes.

85 Coupling reaction is an example of NCERT Pg 276

(a) nucleophilic addition reaction

(b) nucleophilic substitution reaction

(c) electrophilic substitution reaction

(d) electrophilic addition reaction

86 Consider the following reaction. NCERT Pg 276

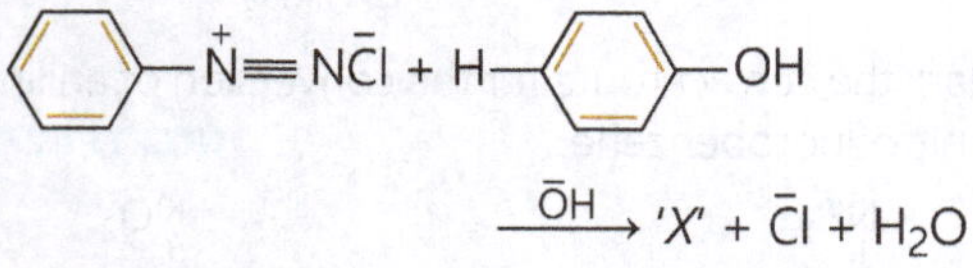

Here, 'X' is

(a) 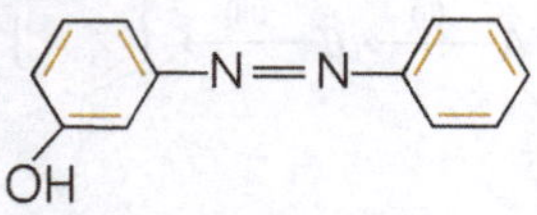

(b) 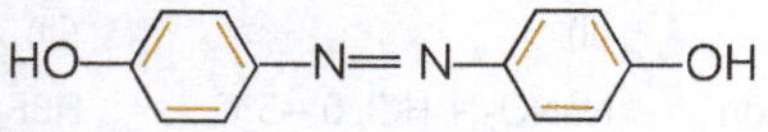

(c) 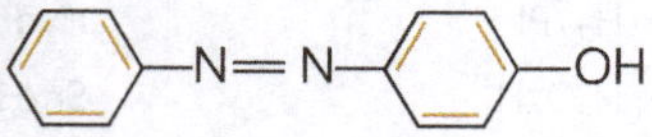

(d) 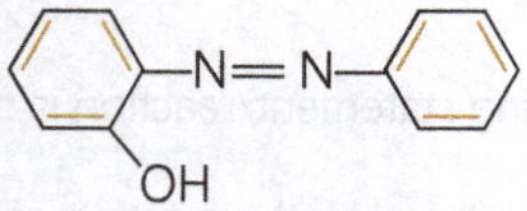

87 Which of the following reactions are electrophilic substitution reactions?

I. Bromination of acetanilide.

II. Coupling reaction of aryl diazonium salts.

III. Diazotisation of aniline.

IV. Acylation of aniline.

Choose the correct answer from the options given below.

(a) I and II NCERT Pg 272, 273, 276

(b) I, II and III

(c) III and IV

(d) I and IV

88 Among the given compounds, the one that would form a brilliant coloured dye on treatment with $NaNO_2$ in dil. HCl followed by addition to an alkaline solution of β- naphthol is NCERT Pg 276

(a) 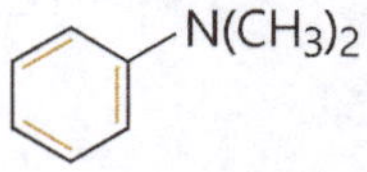

(b) 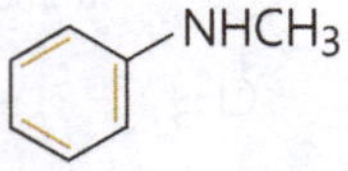

(c) 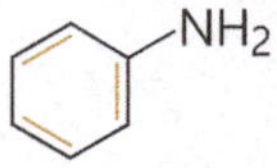

(d) 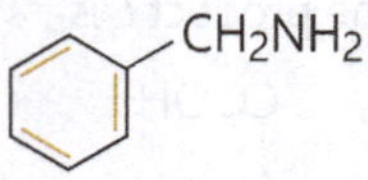

Importance of Diazonium Salt

89 Select the incorrect statements from the following. NCERT Pg 271, 276, 277

I. Diazonium salts are very good intermediates for the introduction of F, Cl, Br, I, CN, OH, NO_2 groups into the aromatic ring.

II. Aryl fluorides and iodides can be prepared by direct halogenation.

III. The reaction of benzenesulphonyl chloride with 2° amine yield N-alkyl benzene sulphonyl amide.

IV. The replacement of diazo group by other groups is helpful in preparing those substituted aromatic compounds which cannot be prepared by direct substitution in benzene or substituted benzene.

Choose the correct answer from the options given below.

(a) I and II (b) II and III (c) III and IV (d) I and IV

90 Which of the following group that cannot be introduced to aromatic ring by diazonium salt? NCERT Pg 276

(a) —F (b) —Cl

(c) $—OCH_3$ (d) $—NO_2$

91 Which of the following reactions is incorrect? NCERT Pg 276, 275

(a) 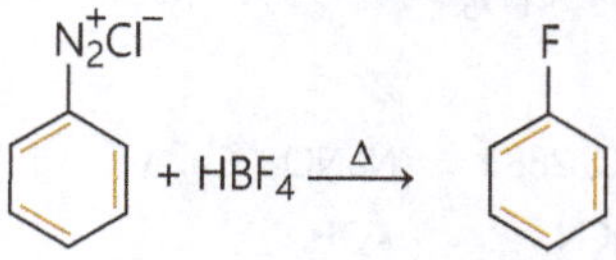

(b) 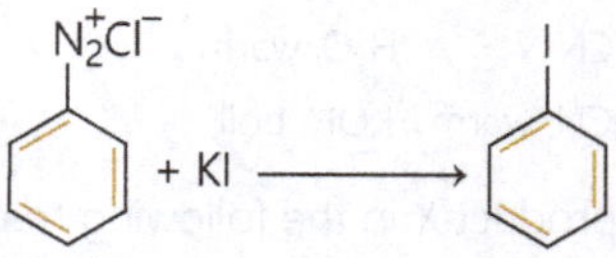

(c) 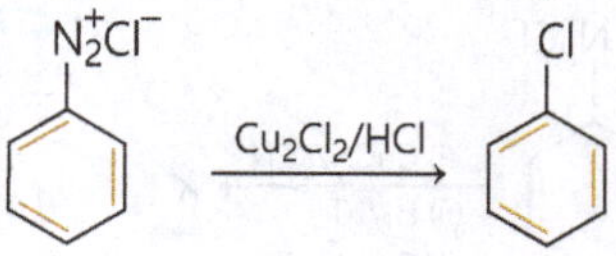

(d) 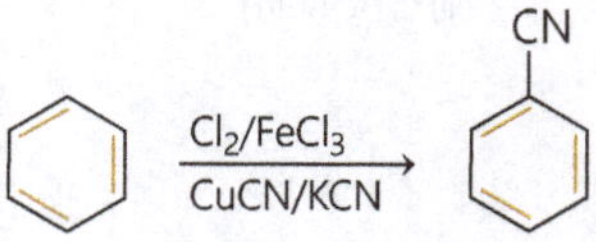

Assertion-Reason Questions

Directions Q. Nos. (1-10) *In the following question Assertion (A) followed by Reason (R) is given below. Choose the correct option out of the choices given below.*

(a) Both A and R are true and R is the correct explanation of A.
(b) Both A and R are true but R is not the correct explanation of A.
(c) A is true but R is false.
(d) A is false but R is true.

1 Assertion (A) The angle of C—N—C in trimethylamine is 108°.
Reason (R) There is unshared pair of electron in trimethylamine which makes the angle less than 109.5°. NCERT Pg 259, 260

2 Assertion (A) Tertiary butylamine can be prepared by the action of NH_3 on *tert*-butylbromide.
Reason (R) Tertiary butylbromide being 3° alkylhalide prefers to undergo elimination on the treatment with a base. NCERT Pg 262

3 Assertion (A) Aromatic primary amines cannot be prepared by Gabriel phthalimide synthesis.
Reason (R) Aryl halides do not undergo electrophilic substitution with anion formed by phthalimide. NCERT Pg 264

4 Assertion (A) Substituted ammonium ion formed from the amine is stable.
Reason (R) There is dispersal of the positive charge on substituted ammonium ion by the + *I*-effect of the alkyl group. NCERT Pg 268

5 Assertion (A) Order of basicity of amines in gaseous phase is NH_3 > primary amine > secondary amine > tertiary amine.
Reason (R) In gaseous phase, the basic nature of aliphatic amine increases with the increase in number of alkyl groups. NCERT Pg 268

6 Assertion (A) Aliphatic amines are weaker bases than ammonia.
Reason (R) +*I*-effect of alkyl groups on aliphatic amines increase the electron density on nitrogen atom. NCERT Pg 268

7 Assertion (A) $MeNH_2$ is the weaker base than MeOH.
Reason (R) N is less electronegative than O, lone pair of electrons on N is more easily available for donation in $MeNH_2$. NCERT Pg 268

8 Assertion (A) In acylation reaction of amines, equilibrium shifts to the right hand side in the presence of pyridine.
Reason (R) In the presence of strong base, HCl is removed and reaction shifts towards the right hand side. NCERT Pg 270

9 Assertion (A) Aniline does not undergo Friedel-Craft's alkylation and acetylation.
Reason (R) Nitrogen of aniline acquires positive charge and acts as a strong deactivating group for further reaction. NCERT Pg 273

10 Assertion (A) Benzene diazonium salts are soluble in water.
Reason (R) They are covalent in nature, so they are soluble in water. NCERT Pg 275

Statement Type Questions

Direction (Q. Nos. 1-5) *In the following questions, two statements (I & II) are given. In the light of the given statements, choose the correct option given below.*

(a) Both Statement I and Statement II are false.
(b) Statement I is true but Statement II is false.
(c) Statement I is false but Statement II is true.
(d) Both Statement I and Statement II are true.

1 Statement I Reduction of nitro compound with iron scrap and HCl is preferred over H_2/Pd and ethanol.
Statement II Nitriles on reduction with lithium aluminium hydride or catalytic hydrogenation produce tertiary amines. NCERT Pg 262, 263

2 Statement I Primary aromatic amines reacts with HNO_2 to form diazonium salts which are stable at low temperature (273-278 K).
Statement II Primary aliphatic amines do not react with HNO_2. NCERT Pg 271

3 Statement I Carbylamine reaction involves the reaction between primary aniline and chloroform in basic medium.
Statement II In carbylamine reaction, —NH_2 group is converted into CN group. NCERT Pg 271

4 **Statement I** Aniline reacts with concentrated sulphuric acid to form sulphanilic acid. NCERT Pg 273

Statement II Sulphanilic acid can act as a Zwitter ion.

5 **Statement I** Benzene diazonium chloride reacts with phenol to give *p*-hydroxy azobenene. NCERT Pg 276

Statement II This reaction occur in the acidic medium.

6 Which of the following statement is not correct?

I. H_2/Pd in ethanol is used for the reduction of nitrobenzene to aniline.

II. Aromatic primary amine is prepared by Gabriel phthalimide synthesis.

III. Solubility of amines in water decreases with decrease in molar mass..

IV. Ammonia are stronger base than aromatic amines.

V. Carbylamine reaction is used as a test for 1° amines.

Choose the most appropriate answer from the options given below. NCERT Pg 262, 264, 265, 267, 271

(a) I, II, III and IV
(b) II and III
(c) I and V
(d) I, IV and V

7 Select the incorrect statements from the following.

I. N, N-dimethylaniline has a higher pK_b value than N-methylaniline.

II. Aniline reacts with bromine water at room temperature to give a yellow precipitate of *p*-bromoaniline.

III. The lone pair of electrons on nitrogen of acetanilide interacts with oxygen atom due to resonance.

IV. Direct nitration of aniline yields tarry oxidation products.

V. Azo-dyes formed by the Coupling reaction of aryl diazonium salts with phenols.

Choose the most appropriate answer from the options given below. NCERT Pg 267, 272, 273, 276

(a) I, III and IV
(b) I and II
(c) III, IV and V
(d) II, III and IV

8 Which of the following statement is/are correct?

I. *Iso*-propylamine and ethyl methylamine both show carbylamine reaction.

II. Primary aromatic amine not be prepared by Gabriel phthalimide synthesis.

III. Lower aliphatic amines are gases but higher amines are solid.

IV. Amines are trigonal planar in shape.

Choose the most appropriate answer from the options given below. NCERT Pg 259, 264, 265, 271

(a) I, II and III
(b) II and IV
(c) II and III
(d) II, III and IV

9 Select the correct statements from the following.

I. Dimethylamines gives carbylamine test.

II. Primary amines with Hinsberg's reagent yields N-alkyl benzene sulphonyl amide.

III. Aryl amines generally less basic than alkylamines.

IV. Anilinium ion is resonance stabilised.

Choose the most appropriate answer from the options given below. NCERT Pg 268, 269, 271

(a) I and III (b) II and III
(c) I and IV (d) III and IV

10 Which of the following statement are not correct?

I. Arene diazonium fluoroborate can be converted to nitrobenzene by using $NaNO_2$ and Cu-metal/Δ.

II. Chloroform when treated with aniline and alcoholic KOH gives phenyl cyanide.

III. Diazo coupling is useful to prepare some pesticides.

IV. In basic medium, nitrobenzene is reduced to aniline.

V. In diazotisation of aniline, an excess of HCl is used primarily to suppress the concentration of free aniline available for coupling.

Choose the most appropriate answer from the options given below. NCERT Pg 262, 271, 276

(a) I and II (b) III, IV and V
(c) II, III and IV (d) III and IV

Matching Type Questions

1 Match the amines given in Column I with their uses in Column II and choose the correct option from the codes given below.

Column I	Column II
A. Novocain	1. Surfactants
B. Benadryl	2. As an anaesthetic in dentistry
C. Quaternary ammonium salts	3. Preparation of aromatic compounds
D. Diazonium salts	4. Antihistaminic drug

NCERT Pg 259

Codes

	A	B	C	D
(a)	1	2	3	4
(b)	2	4	1	3
(c)	4	3	2	1
(d)	3	1	2	4

2 Match the amines given in Column I with their classification in the Column II and choose the correct option from the codes given below.

Column I	Column II
A. 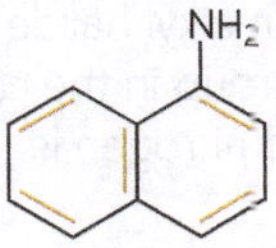	1. Primary amine
B. 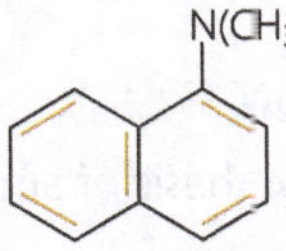	2. Secondary amine
C. $(C_2H_5)_2NH$	3. Tertiary amine

NCERT Pg 260

Codes

	A	B	C
(a)	1	2	3
(b)	1	3	2
(c)	2	1	3
(d)	2	3	1

3 Match the following structures of amine given in Column I with their common names given in Column II and choose the correct option from the codes given below.

Column I (Amines)	Column II (Common name)
A. 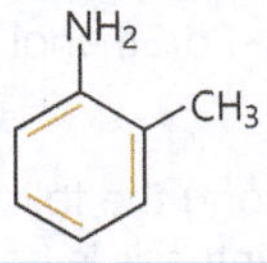	1. Hexamethylenediamine
B. $H_2N—CH_2—CH=CH_2$	2. Allylamine
C. $H_2N—(CH_2)_6—NH_2$	3. N,N-dimethylaniline
D. 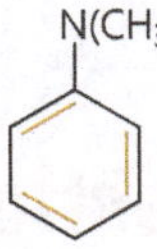	4. *o*-toluidine

Codes NCERT Pg 261

	A	B	C	D
(a)	1	2	3	4
(b)	4	2	1	3
(c)	2	4	3	1
(d)	2	3	4	1

4 Match the following Column I (reactants) with their (products) given in Column II and choose the correct option from the codes given below. NCERT Pg 270, 273

Column I (Reactants)	Column II (Products)
A. $H_5C_2NH_2 + H_3CCOCl$	1. Acetanilide
B. $H_5C_2—NH—C_2H_5 + H_3CCOCl$	2. N,N-diethylethanamide
C. $C_6H_5—NH_2 + (H_3CCO)_2O$	3. N-ethylethanamide
D. $C_6H_5—NH_2 + H_2SO_4$	4. Anilinium hydrogen sulphate

Codes

	A	B	C	D		A	B	C	D
(a)	1	3	2	4	(b)	3	4	2	1
(c)	1	2	4	3	(d)	3	2	1	4

Numerical Value Questions

1 Among the possible aliphatic, acyclic isomers corresponding to the molecular formula, $C_4H_{11}N$, the total number of 1° amines is .... NCERT Pg 260

2 The total number of reagents from those given below, that can convert nitrobenzene into aniline is ....

I. Sn-HCl   II. Sn-NH_4OH
III. Zn-HCl   IV. H_2-Pd/Ethanol
V. H_2-Ni/Ethanol

NCERT Pg 262

3 The total number of amines among the following which can be synthesised by Gabriel synthesis is

A. 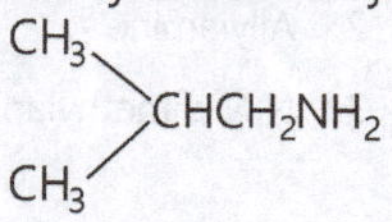

B. $CH_3CH_2NH_2$

C. 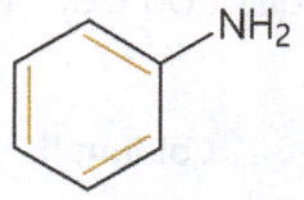

NCERT Pg 264

4 An organic compound $P(C_7H_9N)$ on reaction with nitrous acid give benzyl alcohol. Number of structural isomers of P is .... NCERT Pg 271

5 The total number of following compounds that will given positive carbylamine test is ....

I. N, N-dimethylaniline   II. 2, 4-dimethyl aniline
III. 4-methyl benzylamine   IV. Diphenylamine
V. 1-naphthylamine

NCERT Pg 271

NCERT Exemplar's Questions

1 Which of the following is a 3° amine?
(a) 1-methylcyclohexylamine (b) Triethylamine
(c) *tert*-butylamine (d) N-methylaniline

2 The correct IUPAC name for $CH_2{=}CHCH_2NHCH_3$ is
(a) allylmethylamine
(b) 2-amino-4-pentene
(c) 4-aminopent-1-ene
(d) N-methylprop-2-en-1-amine

3 Amongst the following, the strongest base in aqueous medium is
(a) CH_3NH_2 (b) $NCCH_2NH_2$
(c) $(CH_3)_2NH$ (d) $C_6H_5NHCH_3$

4 Which of the following is the weakest Bronsted base?

(a) 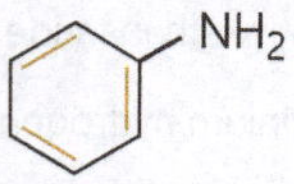
(b) 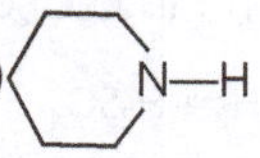
(c) 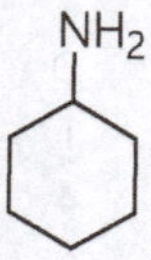
(d) CH_3NH_2

5 Benzylamine may be alkylated in following manner :

$$C_6H_5CH_2NH_2 + R{-}X \longrightarrow C_6H_5CH_2NHR$$

Which of the following alkyl halides is best suited for this reaction through S_N1 mechanism?
(a) CH_3Br (b) C_6H_5Br
(c) $C_6H_5CH_2Br$ (d) C_2H_5Br

6 Which of the following reagents would not be a good choice for reducing an aryl nitro compound to an amine?
(a) H_2(excess)/Pt (b) $LiAlH_4$ in ether
(c) Fe and HCl (d) Sn and HCl

7 In order to prepare 1° amine from an alkyl halide with simultaneous addition of one CH_2 group in the carbon chain, the reagent used as source of nitrogen is
(a) sodium amide ($NaNH_2$)
(b) sodium azide (NaN_3)
(c) potassium cyanide (KCN)
(d) potassium phthalimide ($C_6H_4(CO)_2N^-K^+$)

8 The source of nitrogen in Gabriel synthesis of amines is
(a) sodium azide, (NaN_3)
(b) sodium nitrite, ($NaNO_2$)
(c) potassium cyanide, (KCN)
(d) potassium phthalimide ($C_6H_4(CO)_2N^-K^+$)

9 Match the reactions given in Column I with the statements given in Column II.

Column I	Column II
A. Ammonolysis	1. Amine with lesser number of carbon atoms.
B. Gabriel phthalimide synthesis	2. Detection test for primary amines.
C. Hofmann bromamide reaction	3. Reaction of phthalimide with KOH and $R{-}X$.
D. Carbylamine reaction	4. Reaction of alkylhalides with NH_3.

10 Amongst the given set of reactants, the most appropriate for preparing 2° amine is

(a) $2^{\circ} R—Br + NH_3$
(b) $2^{\circ} R—Br$ + NaCN followed by H_2/Pt
(c) $1^{\circ} R—NH_2 + RCHO$ followed by H_2/Pt
(d) $1^{\circ} R—Br$(2 mol) + potassium phthalimide followed by H_3O^+/ Heat

11 Which of the following is the best reagent for converting 2-phenylpropanamide into 2-phenyl propanamine?

(a) Excess H_2
(b) Br_2 in *aq.* NaOH
(c) Iodine in the presence of red phosphorus
(d) $LiAlH_4$ in ether

12 Which of the following is the best reagent for converting 2-phenyl propanamide to 1-phenyl ethanamine?

(a) Excess H_2/Pt
(b) $NaOH/Br_2$
(c) $NaBH_4$ /Methanol
(d) $LiAlH_4$/ Ether

13 Hofmann bromamide degradation reaction is shown by

(a) $ArNH_2$ (b) $ArCONH_2$
(c) $ArNO_2$ (d) $ArCH_2NH_2$

14 The correct increasing order of basic strength for the following compounds are

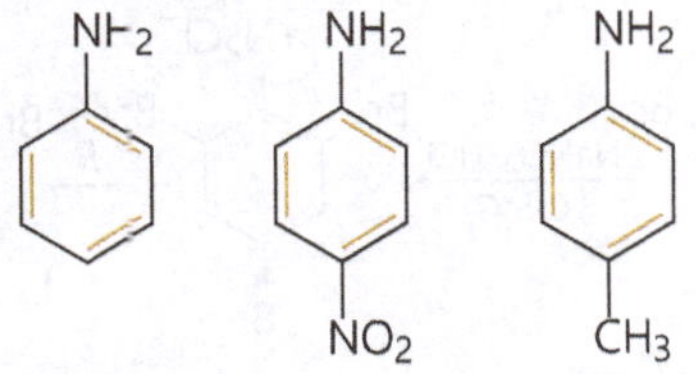

I II III

(a) II < III < I (b) III < I< II
(c) III < II < I (d) II < I < III

15 Methylamine reacts with HNO_2 and H_2O to form

(a) $CH_3—O—N=O$ (b) $CH_3—O—CH_3$
(c) CH_3OH (d) CH_3CHO

16 The gas evolved when methylamine reacts with nitrous acid is

(a) NH_3 (b) N_2 (c) H_2 (d) C_2H_6

17 In the nitration of benzene using a mixture of conc. H_2SO_4 and conc. HNO_3, the species which initiates the reaction is

(a) NO_2 (b) NO^+ (c) NO_2^+ (d) NO_2^-

18 Match the compounds given in Column I with the items given in Column II.

	Column I	Column II
A.	Benzene sulphonyl chloride	1. Zwitter ion
B.	Sulphanilic acid	2. Hinsberg reagent
C.	Alkyl diazonium salts	3. Dyes
D.	Aryl diazonium salts	4. Conversion to alcohols

19 Reduction of aromatic nitro compounds using Fe and HCl gives

(a) aromatic oxime
(b) aromatic hydrocarbon
(c) aromatic primary amine
(d) aromatic amide

20 The most reactive amine towards dilute hydrochloric acid is

(a) $CH_3—NH_2$ (b) 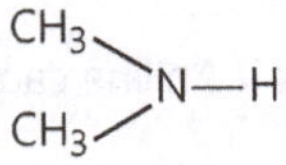

(c) 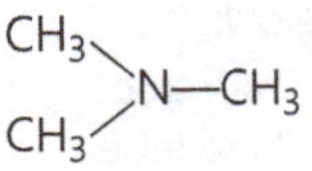 (d) 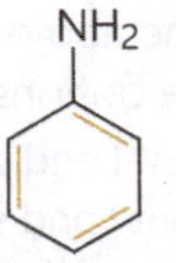

21 Best method for preparing primary amines from alkyl halides without changing the number of C-atoms in the chain is

(a) Hofmann bromamide reaction
(b) Gabriel phthalimide synthesis
(c) Sandmeyer reaction
(d) reaction with NH_3

22 Which of the following compounds will not undergo azo coupling reaction with benzene diazonium chloride?

(a) Aniline (b) Phenol
(c) Anisole (d) Nitrobenzene

23 Which of the following compounds is the weakest Bronsted base?

(a) 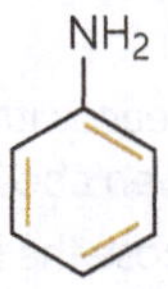 (b) 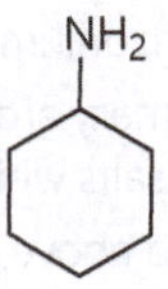

(c) 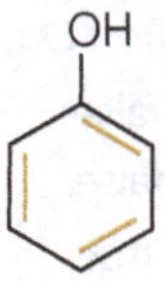 (d) 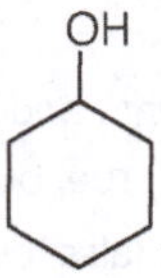

24 The correct decreasing order of basic strength of the following species is, H_2O, NH_3, OH^-, NH_2^-.

(a) $NH_2^- > OH^- > NH_3 > H_2O$ (b) $OH^- > NH_2^- > H_2O > NH_3$
(c) $NH_3 > H_2O > NH_2^- > OH^-$ (d) $H_2O > NH_3 > OH^- > NH_2^-$

25 Which of the following should be most volatile?

I. $CH_3CH_2CH_2NH_2$
II. $(CH_3)_3N$
III. $(CH_3CH_2)(CH_3)NH$
IV. $CH_3CH_2CH_3$

(a) II (b) IV (c) I (d) III

26 The reaction $Ar\overset{+}{N_2}Cl^- \xrightarrow{Cu/HCl} ArCl + N_2 + CuCl$ is named as ....

(a) Sandmeyer reaction (b) Gattermann reaction
(c) Claisen reaction (d) Carbylamine reaction

Past Exams' Questions

NEET Archive

1 Given below are two statements. NCERT Pg 273, NEET 2024

Statement I Aniline does not undergo Friedel-Crafts alkylation reaction.

Statement II Aniline cannot be prepared through Gabriel synthesis.

In the light of the above statements, choose the correct answer from the options given below:

(a) Both statement I and statement II are true.
(b) Both statement I and statement II are false.
(c) Statement I is true but statement II is false.
(d) Statement I is false but Statement II is true.

2 Which of the following reactions will not give primary amine as the product? NCERT (New) Pg 263, 272 NEET 2023

(a) $CH_3CN \xrightarrow[\text{(ii) } H_3O^+]{\text{(i) } LiAlH_4}$ Product

(b) $CH_3NC \xrightarrow[\text{(ii) } H_3O^+]{\text{(i) } LiAlH_4}$ Product

(c) $CH_3CONH_2 \xrightarrow[\text{(ii) } H_3O^+]{\text{(i) } LiAlH_4}$ Product

(d) $CH_3CONH_2 \xrightarrow{Br_2/KOH}$ Product

3 Given below are two statements.

Statement I Primary aliphatic amines react with HNO_2 to give unstable diazonium salts.

Statement II Primary aromatic amines react with HNO_2 to form diazonium salts which are stable even above 300 K.

In the light of the above statements, choose the most appropriate answer from the options given below.
NCERT (New) Pg 271, NEET 2022

(a) Both Statement I and Statement II are false.
(b) Statement I is true, but Statement II is false.
(c) Statement I is false, but Statement II is true.
(d) Both Statement I and Statement II are true.

4 The product formed from the following reaction sequence is NCERT Pg 263, 274, NEET 2022

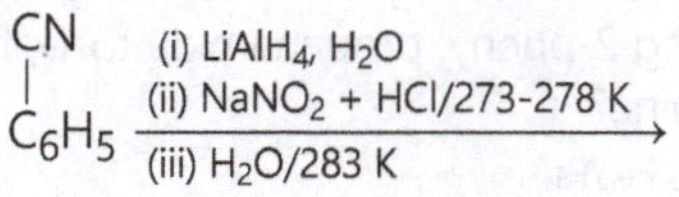

(a) 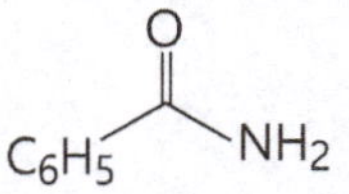

(b) 

(c) 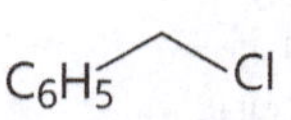

(d) 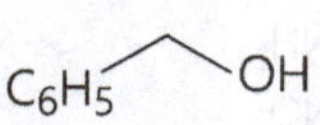

5 The reagent in 'R' in the given sequence of chemical reaction is NCERT (New) Pg 276, NEET 2021

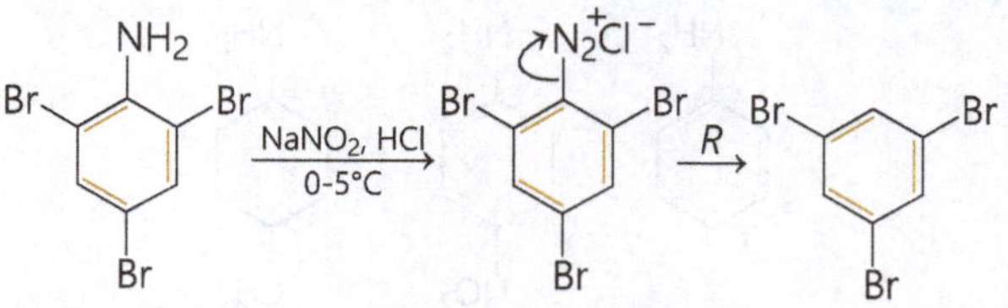

(a) CuCN/KCN
(b) H_2O
(c) CH_3CH_2OH
(d) HI

6 Which of the following amine will give the carbylamine test? NCERT (New) Pg 271, NEET (Sep.) 2020

(a) 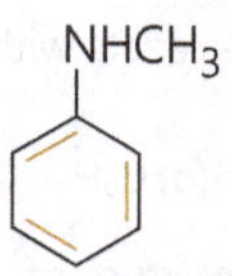

(b) 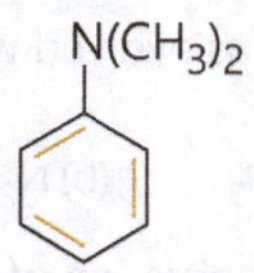

(c) 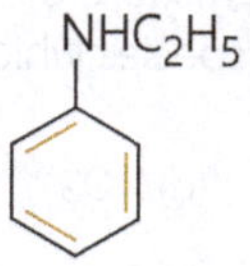

(d) 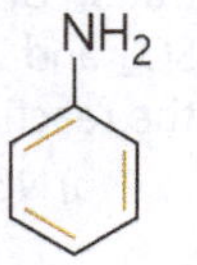

7 The amine that reacts with Hinsberg's reagent to give an alkali insoluble product is NCERT (New) Pg 271, NEET (Odisha) 2019

(a) $CH_3-CH(CH_3)-NH-CH(CH_3)CH_3$

(b) $CH_3-CH_2-N(CH_2CH_3)-CH_2CH_3$

(c) $CH_3-C(NH_2)(CH_3)-CH_2CH_2CH_3$ (d) $CH_3-C(CH_3)_2-CH(CH_3)-NH_2$

8 A nitrogen-containing aromatic compound '*A*' reacts with Sn/HCl, followed by HNO_2 to give an unstable compound '*B*', '*B*', on treatment with phenol, forms a beautiful coloured compound '*C*' with the molecular formula $C_{12}H_{10}N_2O$. The structure of compound '*A*' is NCERT (New) Pg 262, 274, 276, NEET 2016

(a) 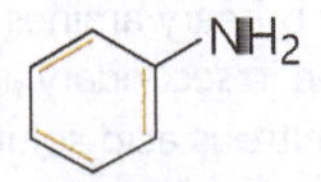
(b) 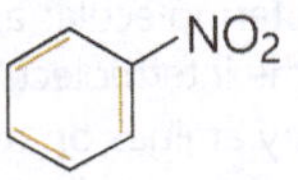

(c) 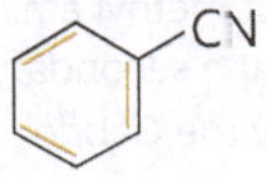
(d) 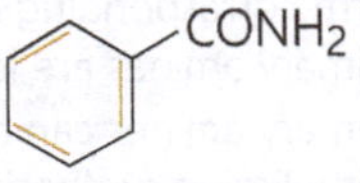

9 The correct statement regarding the basicity of arylamines is NCERT (New) Pg 269, NEET 2016, Phase I

(a) Arylamines are generally more basic than alkylamines because the nitrogen lone-pair electrons are not delocalised by interaction with the aromatic ring π-electron system.
(b) Arylamines are generally more basic than alkylamines because of aryl group.
(c) Arylamines are generally more basic than alkylamines, because the nitrogen atom in arylamines is *sp*-hybridised.
(d) Arylamines are generally less basic than alkylamines because the nitrogen lone-pair electrons are delocalised by interaction with the aromatic ring π-electron system.

10 The number of structural isomers possible from the molecular formula C_3H_9N is NCERT Pg 262, CBSE-AIPMT 2015

(a) 4 (b) 5 (c) 2 (d) 3

11 In the following reaction, the product (*A*) is

$$C_6H_5\overset{+}{N_2}\overset{-}{Cl} \quad C_6H_5NH_2 \xrightarrow{H^+} \underset{\text{Yellow dye}}{(A)}$$

NCERT (New) Pg 276, CBSE-AIPMT 2014

(a) 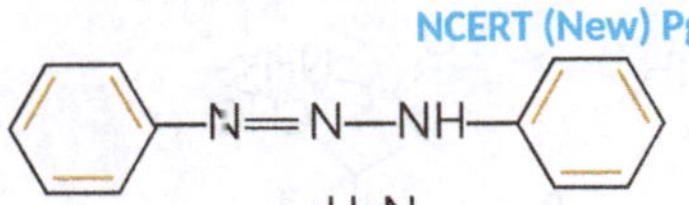

(b) 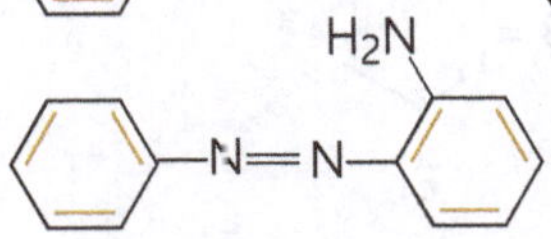

JEE Main Archive

12 Given below are two statements : NCERT Pg 271, JEE Main 2024

Statement I All the following compounds react with *p*-toluenesulphonyl chloride.

$C_6H_5NH_2$ $(C_6H_5)_2NH$ $(C_6H_5)_3N$

Statement II Their products in the above reaction are soluble is aqueous NaOH.

In the light of the above statements, choose the correct answer from the options given below:
(a) Statement I is true but statement II is false.
(b) Both statement I and statement II are true
(c) Both statement I and statement II are false.
(d) Statement I is false but statement II is true.

13 The major products formed

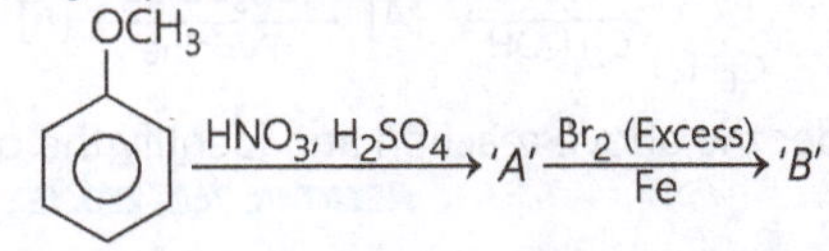

A and *B* respectively are NCERT Pg 273, JEE Main 2024I

(a) 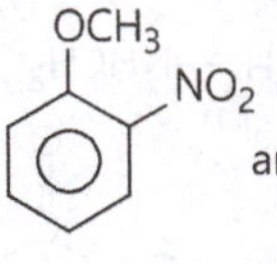 and 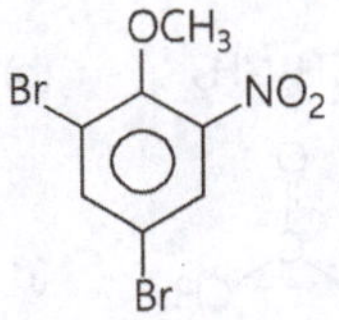

(b) 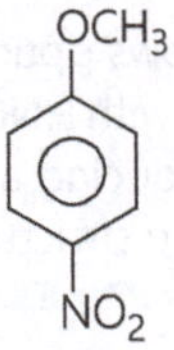 and 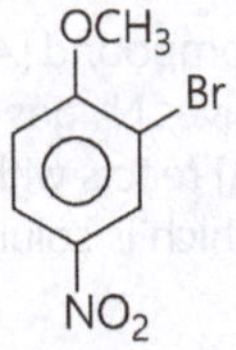

(c) 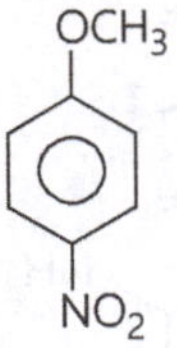 and 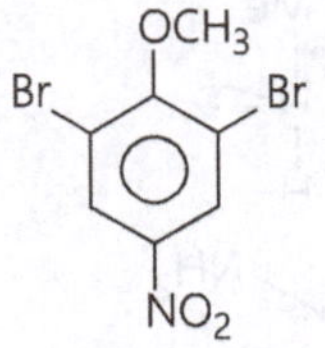

(d) 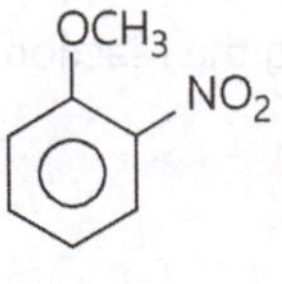 and 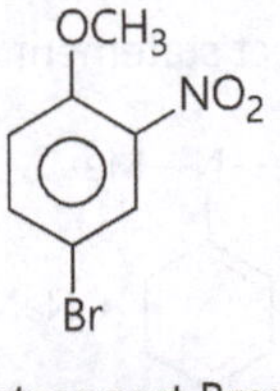

14 Which of the following is strongest Bronsted base? NCERT Pg 266, 267, JEE Main 2024

(a) 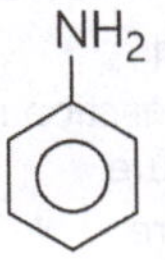
(b) 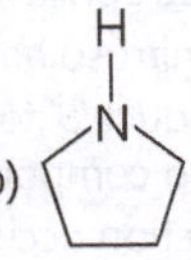

(c) 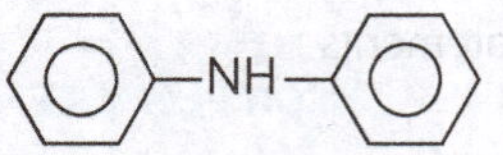 (d) 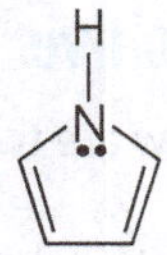

15 o-phenylenediamine $\xrightarrow{HNO_2}$ '*X*' (Major)

Product '*X*' is **NCERT Pg 271, 274, JEE Main 2023**

(a) 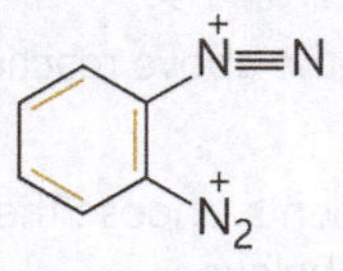 (b) 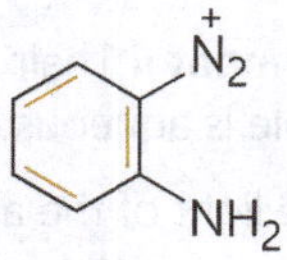

(c) 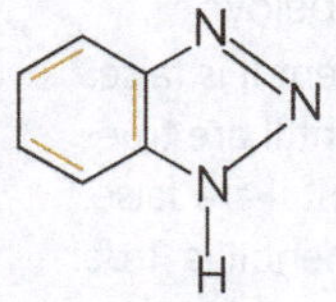 (d) 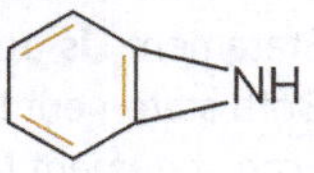

16 $\underset{C_6H_5}{NO_2} \xrightarrow[C_2H_5OH]{H_2/Pd} [A] \xrightarrow[\text{Pyridine}]{(CH_3CO)_2O} [B]$

Consider the above reaction and identify the product *B*.

NCERT Pg 262, 270, JEE Main 2023

(a) 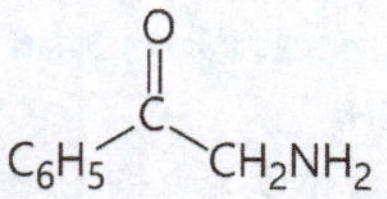 (b) 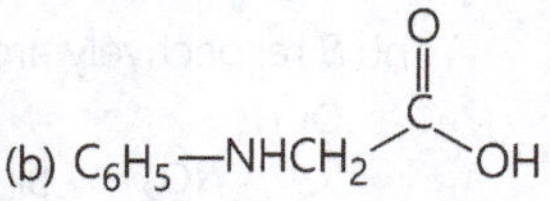

(c) 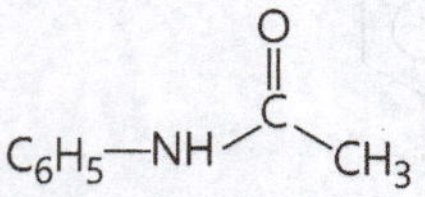 (d) 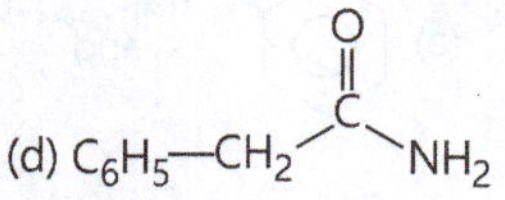

17 An organic compound [*A*] ($C_4H_{11}N$), shows optical activity and gives N_2 gas on treatment with HNO_2. The compound [*A*] reacts with $PhSO_2Cl$ producing a compound which is soluble in KOH. The structure of *A* is **NCERT Pg 271, JEE Main 2023**

(a) 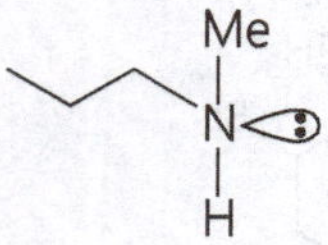 (b) 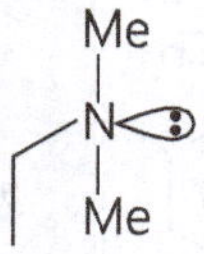

(c)  (d) 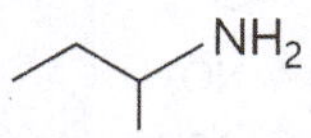

18 The incorrect statement regarding the reaction given below is

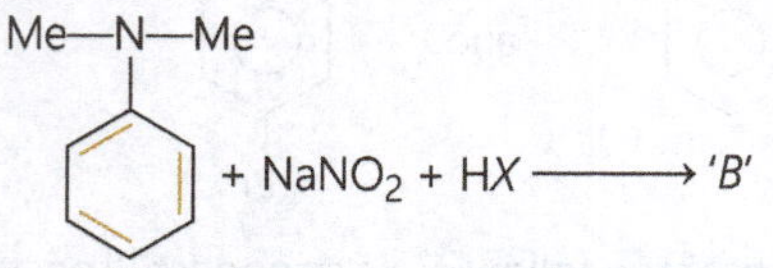

'*A*' **NCERT Pg 271, JEE Main 2023**

(a) The electrophile involved in the reaction is NO^+.

(b) '*B*' is N-nitroso ammonium compound.

(c) The product '*B*' formed in the above reaction is *p*-nitroso compound at low temperature.

(d) The reaction occurs at low temperature.

19 Given below are two statements, one is labelled as Assertion (A) and the other is labelled as Reason (R).

Assertion (A) Experimental reaction of CH_3Cl with aniline and anhydrous $AlCl_3$ does not give *o* and *p*-methylaniline. **NCERT Pg 273, JEE Main 2022**

Reason (R) The —NH_2 group of aniline becomes deactivating because of salt formation with anhydrous $AlCl_3$ and hence yields *m*-methyl aniline as the product.

In the light of the above statements, choose the most appropriate answer from the options given below

(a) Both (A) and (R) are true and (R) is the correct explanation of (A).

(b) Both (A) and (R) are true but (R) is not the correct explanation of (A).

(c) (A) is true, but (R) is false.

(d) (A) is false, but (R) is true.

20 Which of the following is not a correct statement for primary aliphatic amines? **NCERT Pg 265, JEE Main 2021**

(a) The intermolecular association in primary amines is less than the intermolecular association in secondary amines.

(b) Primary amines on treating with nitrous acid solution form corresponding alcohols except methyl amine.

(c) Primary amines are less basic than the secondary amines.

(d) Primary amines can be prepared by the Gabriel phthalimide synthesis.

21 Hofmann bromamide degradation of benzamide gives product *A*, which upon heating with $CHCl_3$ and NaOH gives product *B*. The structures of *A* and *B* are **NCERT Pg 264, JEE Main 2021**

(a) *A* = 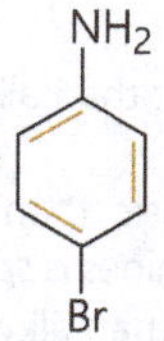 *B* = 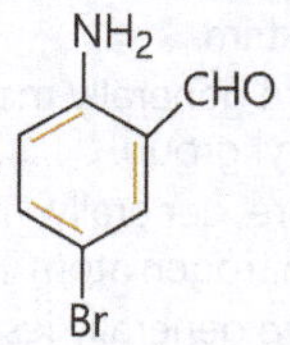

(b) *A* = 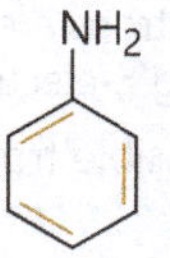 *B* = 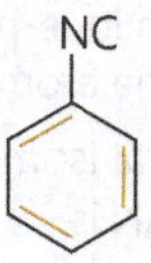

(c) *A* = 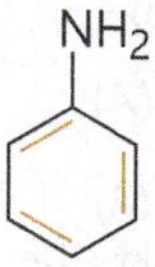 *B* = 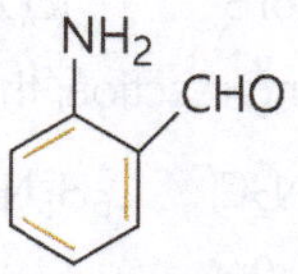

(d) *A* = 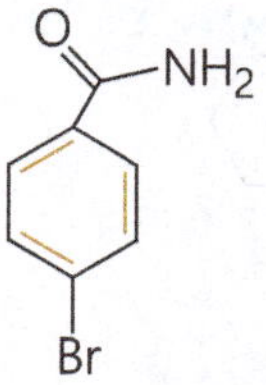 *B* = 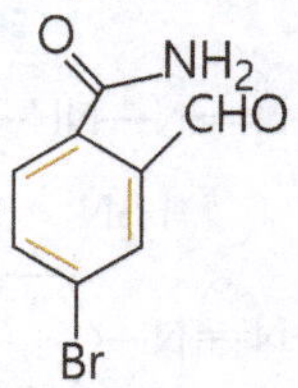

Skill Boosters

1 Toluene is nitrated and the resulting product is reduced with tin and hydrochloric acid. The product obtained is diazotised and then heated with cuprous bromide. The reaction mixture formed is
(a) mixture of *o*- and *p*-dibromobenzenes
(b) mixture of *o*- and *p*-bromoanilines
(c) mixture of *o*- and *m*-bromotoluenes
(d) mixture of *o*-and *p*-bromotoluenes

2 Reaction of cyclohexanone with dimethylamine in the presence of catalytic amount of an acid forms a compound if water during the reaction is continuously removed. The compound formed is generally known as
(a) Schiff's base
(b) an enamine
(c) an imine
(d) an amine

3 Three isomers *A*, *B* and *C* (molecular formula $C_8H_{11}N$) give the following results.

$$A \text{ and } C \xrightarrow{\text{Diazotisation}} P \text{ and } Q \xrightarrow[\text{(ii) Oxidation}]{\text{(i) Hydrolysis}} R$$

and *S* (product of *A*) and *S* (product of *C*)
(*R* has lower boiling point than *S*)

$$B \xrightarrow{C_6H_5SO_2Cl} \text{alkali-insoluble product}$$

A, *B* and *C*, respectively are

(a) 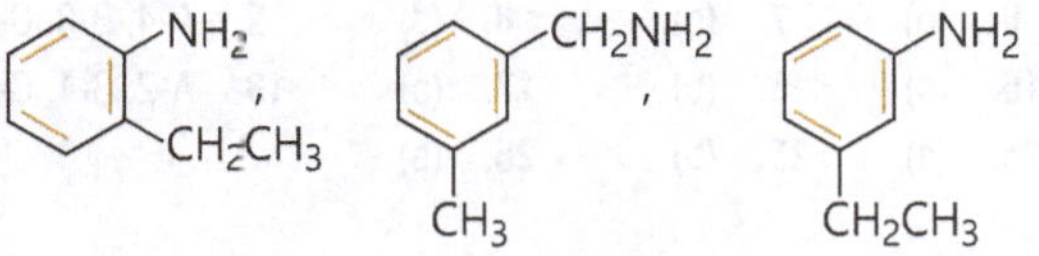

(b) 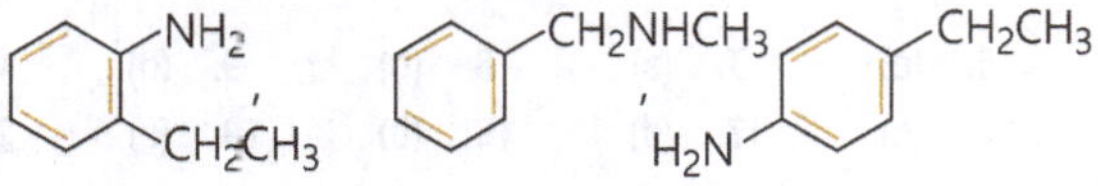

(c) 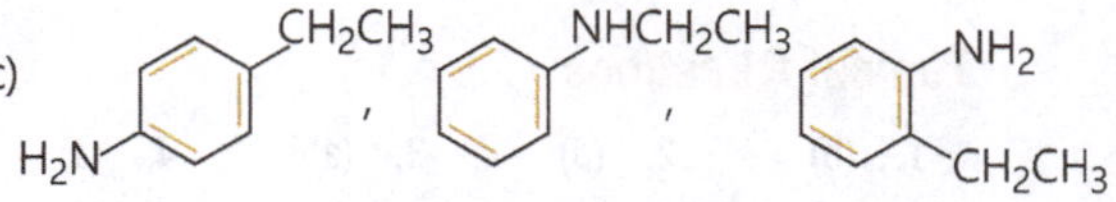

(d) 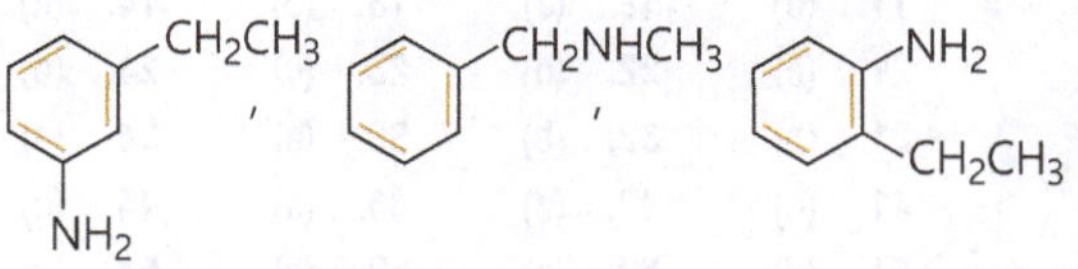

4 Ethanoic acid on heating with ammonia forms compound *A* which on treatment with bromine and sodium hydroxide gives compound *B*. Compound *B* on treatment with $NaNO_2$/dil. HCl gives compound *C*. The compounds *A*, *B* and *C* respectively are
(a) ethanamide, methanamine, methanol
(b) propanamide, ethanamine, ethanol
(c) ethanamine, bromoethane, ethane diazonium chloride
(d) methanamine, ethanamide, methanol

5 A nitrogen containing organic compound give an oily liquid on heating with bromine and potassium hydroxide solution. On shaking the product with acetic anhydride an antipyretic drug was obtained. The reaction indicate that the starting compound is
(a) aniline
(b) benzamide
(c) acetamide
(d) nitrobenzene

6 Aniline is reacted with bromine water and the resulting product is treated with an aqueous solution of sodium nitrite in presence of dilute HCl. The compound so formed is converted into tetrafluoroborate which is subsequently heated. The final product is
(a) *p*-bromofluorobenzene
(b) *p*-bromoaniline
(c) 2, 4, 6-tribromofluorobenzene
(d) 1, 3, 6-tribromobenzene

7 A substance '*A*' ($C_6H_5NO_2$) is reduced to '*B*' by passing hydrogen gas in the presence of Ni in acidic medium. *B* on reacting with $CHCl_3$ and alc. potash produces an obnoxious smell due to the formation of compound '*C*'. Further *B* on reacting with $NaNO_2$ with HCl at 0-5°C produces '*D*' which reacts with ethyl alcohol produces *E*. Identify the compounds from '*A*' to '*E*'.

Choose the correct answer from the options given below.

	A	*B*	*C*	*D*	*E*
(a)	Benzene	Phenyl isocyanide	Aniline	Nitrobenzene	Benzene diazonium chloride
(b)	Nitrobenzene	Aniline	Phenyl isocyanide	Benzene diazonium chloride	Benzene
(c)	Aniline	Nitrobenzene	Phenyl isocyanide	Benzene	Benzene diazonium chloride
(d)	Nitrobenzene	Aniline	Benzene diazonium chloride	Phenyl isocyanide	Benzene

Correct Codes

Topical Questions

1. (b)	2. (d)	3. (a)	4. (a)	5. (a)	6. (d)	7. (a)	8. (a)	9. (c)	10. (d)
11. (d)	12. (a)	13. (b)	14. (d)	15. (b)	16. (c)	17. (a)	18. (b)	19. (b)	20. (b)
21. (c)	22. (d)	23. (c)	24. (b)	25. (c)	26. (a)	27. (b)	28. (b)	29. (d)	30. (c)
31. (b)	32. (b)	33. (a)	34. (a)	35. (c)	36. (c)	37. (d)	38. (c)	39. (c)	40. (b)
41. (c)	42. (d)	43. (a)	44. (c)	45. (a)	46. (d)	47. (a)	48. (c)	49. (a)	50. (b)
51. (d)	52. (a)	53. (a)	54. (b)	55. (d)	56. (b)	57. (c)	58. (d)	59. (a)	60. (a)
61. (b)	62. (d)	63. (b)	64. (b)	65. (c)	66. (b)	67. (c)	68. (c)	69. (c)	70. (d)
71. (a)	72. (d)	73. (c)	74. (d)	75. (c)	76. (b)	77. (c)	78. (c)	79. (a)	80. (a)
81. (d)	82. (a)	83. (d)	84. (c)	85. (c)	86. (c)	87. (a)	88. (c)	89. (b)	90. (c)
91. (d)									

Assertion-Reason

1. (a)	2. (d)	3. (c)	4. (a)	5. (d)	6. (d)	7. (d)	8. (a)	9. (a)	10. (c)

Statement Type

1. (b)	2. (b)	3. (b)	4. (c)	5. (b)	6. (b)	7. (b)	8. (c)	9. (b)	10. (c)

Matching Type

1. (b)	2. (b)	3. (b)	4. (d)

Numerical Value

1. (4)	2. (3)	3. (2)	4. (5)	5. (3)

NCERT Exemplar's

1. (b)	2. (d)	3. (c)	4. (a)	5. (c)	6. (b)	7. (c)	8. (d)	9. A-4, B-3, C-1, D-2
10. (c)	11. (d)	12. (b)	13. (b)	14. (d)	15. (c)	16. (b)	17. (c)	18. A-2, B-1, C-4, D-3
19. (c)	20. (b)	21. (b)	22. (d)	23. (c)	24. (a)	25. (b)	26. (b)	

Past Exams'

1. (a)	2. (b)	3. (b)	4. (d)	5. (c)	6. (d)	7. (a)	8. (b)	9. (d)	10. (a)
11. (d)	12. (c)	13. (c)	14. (b)	15. (c)	16. (c)	17. (d)	18. (b)	19. (c)	20. (a)
21. (b)									

Skill Boosters

1. (d)	2. (d)	3. (b)	4. (a)	5. (b)	6. (c)	7. (b)

Step by Step

Decoding the Questions

Concept Builders

1 False 2 True

3 pyramidal, sp^3 4 Methylamine

5 di, tri 6 True

7 ammonia, nucleophilic

8 False

9 $CH_3—CH_2—CH_2—NH_2$

10 2-phenylethanamine

11 False 12 False

13 no 14 True

15 Lewis base

16 + *I* effect of alkyl group

17 False 18 False

19 amides

20 True

21 nitrogen, amino acids

22 $C_6H_5SO_2Cl$ 23 False

24 N,N-diethylbenzene sulphonamide

25 Aniline 26 True

27 Aryl fluoride and aryl iodide

28 Nitrobenzene

29 Diazonium salts

30 3-methylbenzene diazonium fluoroborate

Topical Solutions

1 (*b*) Due to the presence of trivalent N-atom and unshared pair of electrons in amines, hybridisation and geometry become sp^3 and pyramidal respectively.

2 (*d*) Statement (d) is not correct for amines. Its correct form is quaternary ammonium salts are used as surfactants.

3 (*a*) Adrenaline contains secondary amino group, whereas novocain, pyridine and benadryl contains tertiary amino group.

4 (*a*) Statements given in I and II are correct while III and IV are incorrect. Their correct form is :

- The shape of the given compound is pyramidal.
- The bond angle C—N—C is 108°.

5 (*a*) Among the given amines, ethylmethylamine is a secondary amine.

6 (*d*) C_2H_7N can represent 1° and 2° amines.

(i) $\underset{\text{(1° amine)}}{CH_3—CH_2—NH_2}$

(ii) $\underset{\text{(2° amine)}}{CH_3—NH—CH_3}$

7 (*a*) IUPAC name of the compound trimethylamine is N,N-dimethylmethanamine.

8 (*a*) The correct IUPAC name of the given compound is 3-aminotoluene.

9 (*c*) The IUPAC name of the compound $C_6H_5—N—(CH_3)_2$ is N, N-dimethylbenzenamine.

10 (*d*) The isomers of $C_4H_{11}N$ are :

Primary amine

n-butylamine, *sec*-butylamine, *iso*-butyl amine and tertiary butyl amine.

Secondary amine

N-methylpropan-1-amine, N-methyl isopropyl amine, N, N-diethyl amine.

Tertiary amine

N, N-dimethyl ethamamine

11 (*d*) The reagent CuCN, $LiAlH_4$ cannot be used in the given reaction.

12 (*a*) Statement (a) is correct, while other statements are incorrect. Their correct form are as follows

- The reaction is carried out in a sealed tube at 373 K.
- Benzyl halide on reaction with ethanolic solution of ammonia undergoes nucleophilic substitution.
- Free amine is obtained from the ammonium salt by treatment with strong base.

13 (*b*) Statements (a), (c) and (d) are correct, while statement (b) is incorrect. It's correct form is :

In the given reaction, NH_3 acts as a nucleophile.

14 (*d*) 15 (*b*)

16 (*c*) For the given reaction, the reagent required is NH_3, $2CH_3Cl$.

17 (*a*)

18 (*b*) Among the given statements, only (b) is correct while statements (a), (c) and (d) are incorrect. Their correct form are

(a) It is a reduction reaction.

(b) $LiAlH_4$ reduces CH_3CN to $CH_3CH_2NH_2$.

(d) This reaction produces primary amines only.

19 (*b*) The amide on reduction with $LiAlH_4/H_2O$ yields amine.

$$\underset{\text{Alkyl amide}}{R—CONH_2} \xrightarrow[\text{(ii) } H_2O]{\text{(i) } LiAlH_4} \underset{\text{Alkyl amine}}{RCH_2NH_2}$$

20 (*b*) H_2/Ni reagent is used to convert alkyl cyanide into alkylamine.

21 (*c*) The reaction proceeds as

$$\underset{\text{Propanoic acid}}{CH_3CH_2COOH} \xrightarrow{SOCl_2\ (A)} \underset{\substack{\text{Propanoyl chloride}\\(X)}}{CH_3CH_2COCl} \xrightarrow{NH_3 (B)} \underset{\substack{\text{Propanamide}\\(Y)}}{CH_3CH_2CONH_2} \xrightarrow{Br_2/KOH\ (C)} \underset{\text{Propanamine}}{CH_3CH_2NH_2}$$

22 (*d*) Reactions (i), (ii) and (iv) will give primary amine while reaction (iii) will give tertiary amine.

23 (*c*) Statement (c) is correct while the other statements (a), (b) and (d) are incorrect. Their correct form are as follows

(a) In this reaction, migration of an alkyl or aryl group takes place from carbonyl carbon of the amide to the N-atom.

(b) The amine so formed contains one carbon less than that present in the amide.

(d) Hofmann developed a method for preparation of primary amines.

24 (*b*) The reaction is proceed as

$$\underset{\text{Ethanamide}}{CH_3CONH_2} + 4NaOH + Br_2 \longrightarrow \underset{\text{Methanamie}}{CH_3NH_2} + 2NaBr + Na_2CO_3 + 2H_2O$$

25 (*c*) Primary aliphatic amines can be prepared by Gabriel phthalimide synthesis.

26 (*a*) Phthalimide (I), ethanolic KOH (II) and NaOH(*aq*) (III) are in the given reaction.

27 (*b*) The reaction for the production of ethylamine from N-ethylphthalimide can be takes place as follows

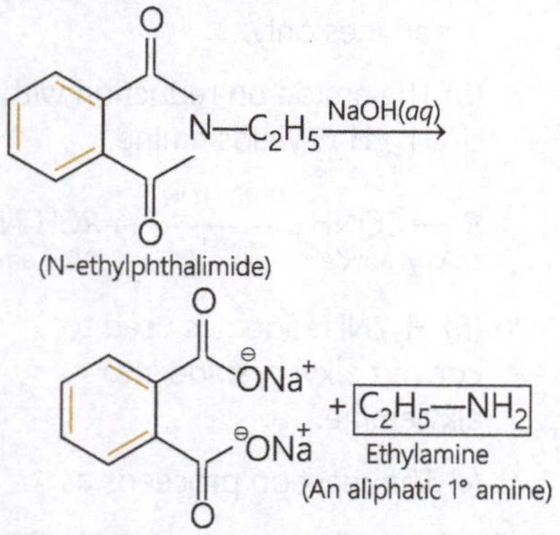

28 (*b*) The conversion of acetamide to methanamine can be achieved by Hofmann bromamide reaction.

29 (*d*) Statement (d) is incorrect while the other statements are correct. The correct form of statement (d) is :

Aryl amines are usually colourless but get coloured on storage due to atmospheric oxidation.

30 (*c*) The correct order of increasing boiling point is

$(CH_3)_3N < (CH_3)_2NH < CH_3NH_2$.

31 (*b*) Statement (b) is incorrect. While other statements are correct. The correct form of statement (b) is :

The electronegativity of nitrogen of amine and that of oxygen of alcohol are 3.0 and 3.5 respectively.

32 (*b*) Statements (a), (c) and (d) are incorrect. Their correct form is

- Intermolecular hydrogen bonding is present in 1° and 2° amines.
- There is no H-bonding in 3° amines, due to absence of hydrogen atom.

33 (*a*) **34** (*a*)

35 (*c*) Statement (c) is correct, while the other statements (a), (b) and (d) are incorrect. Their correct form is :

(a) Amine salts are soluble in water but insoluble in organic solvents like ether.

(b) Amines have an unshared pair of electrons on nitrogen atom due to which they behave as Lewis base.

(d) Larger the value of K_b, stronger is the base.

36 (*c*) Among the given relations, the incorrect relation is (c). It's correct form is $pK_b = -\log K_b$.

37 (*d*) Among the given amines N-methylmethanamine has the lowest pK_b value, i.e. 3.27. Hence, it is the strongest base.

38 (*c*) Statements I, II and III are correct, while statement IV is incorrect. The correct form of statement IV is :

IV. Primary amines are soluble in water.

39 (*c*) The statement (c) is incorrect while statements (a), (b) and (d) are correct. The correct form of (c) is :

Alkylamines are stronger base than ammonia.

40 (*b*) Among given statements, the correct statements are (i), (ii), (iv) and (v). The incorrect statement is (iii). It's correct form is methylamine is stronger base than ammonia due to electron releasing inductive effect of methyl group.

41 (*c*) The correct increasing order of basicity in aqueous solution is

II < I < IV < III.

42 (*d*) The correct order of basic strength of methyl substituted amines in aqueous medium will be

$$\underset{(2°)}{(CH_3)_2NH} > \underset{(1°)}{CH_3NH_2} > \underset{(3°)}{(CH_3)_3N}$$

43 (*a*) The correct decreasing order of basicity of the given amines is as follows

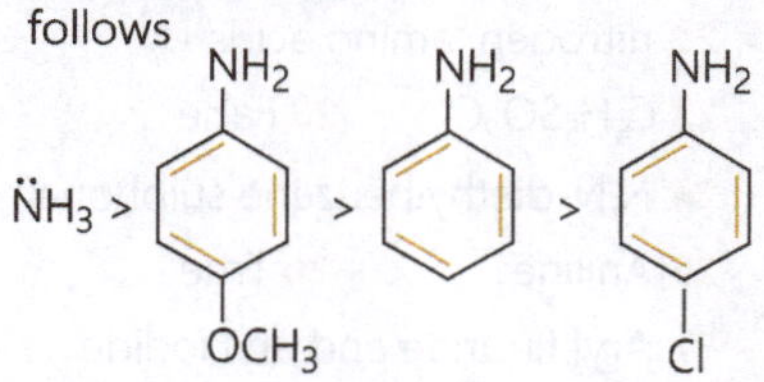

44 (*c*) The reaction involved is as follows

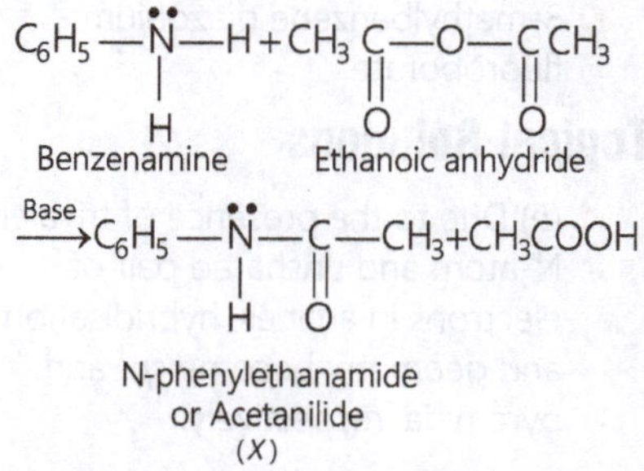

The product '*X*' obtained is N-phenylethanamide.

45 (*a*) Methanamine reacts with benzoyl chloride to give N-methylbenzamide. This reaction is known as benzoylation.

46 (*d*) Among the given statements (a), (b) and (c) are correct while statement (d) incorrect. The correct form of statement (d) is as follows :

Acylation reaction is carried out in the presence of a base stronger than amine like pyridine.

47 (*a*) Acetanilide can be prepared from aniline and acetic anhydride.

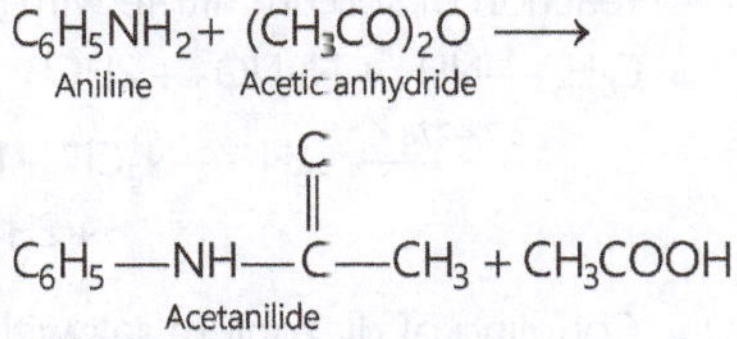

48 (*c*) Among the given statements, only (c) is correct while statements (a), (b) and (d) are incorrect. Their correct form are

(a) Aromatic amines react with nitrous acid to form diazonium salts.

(b) Formation of diazonium salts occur at low temperatures (273 K- 278 K).

(d) Primary aliphatic amines react with nitrous acid to form alcohols because alkyl diazonium salt is unstable and it hydrolysed to alcohol.

49 (*a*) On treatment with nitrous acid, primary amine gives an alcohol and N_2 gas. So, *A* should be primary amine.

Only 1° amines give carbylamine reaction. So, the steps are as follows

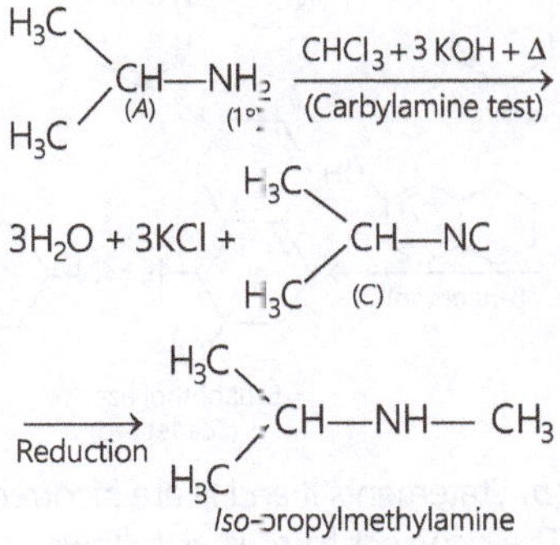

50 (*b*) Primary aliphatic amines react with nitrous acid to form aliphatic diazonium salts which being unstable, form alcohol and liberate nitrogen gas quantitatively.

So, the product formed is *R*—OH.

51 (*d*) Structure of amine (*X*) is $C_6H_5—NH_2$.

52 (*a*) The substance '*X*' in the given reaction is ethanamine ($C_2H_5NH_2$).

53 (*a*) Secondary amine given in option (a), i.e. $[(CH_3)_2CH—NH—CH(CH_3)_2]$ react with Hinsberg's reagent to yeild N,N-di*iso*propylbenzene sulphonamide which is insoluble in alkali while the remaining options are 1° and 3° amines.

1° amines react with Hinsberg's reagent to yield N-alkylbenzene sulphonamide which is soluble in alkali and 3° amines do not react with $C_6H_5SO_2Cl$.

54 (*b*) N, N-diethylbenzene sulphonamide does not contain any H-atom attached to N-atom, thus it is not acidic and, hence insoluble in alkali.

55 (*d*) —NH_2 group in aniline is an activating group and the reaction occurs at *ortho* and *para*-position.

56 (*b*) The major product *B* is 2-bromo-4-methylacetanilide.

The reaction takes place as follows

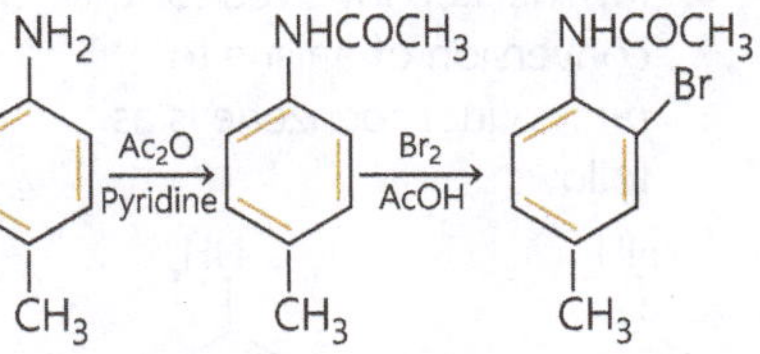

57 (*c*) In strongly acidic medium, aniline is protonated to form the anilinium ion which is *meta*-directing. That is why, besides the *ortho* and *para*-derivatives, significant amount of *meta*-derivative is also formed. Hence, the percentage of the given amines derivates will be I (51%), II (47%) and III (2%).

58 (*d*) Nitration of aniline in strong acidic medium also gives *m*-nitroaniline because in strongly acidic medium, aniline is protonated to form the anilinium ion, which is *meta* directing. Thus, besides *ortho* and *para* derivatives, significant amount of *meta*-derivative is also formed.

59 (*a*) Aniline gives *p*-nitroderivative as the major product by I, II and IV under given conditions.

60 (*a*) Among the given statements, the incorrect statement is (a) while (b), (c) and (d) are correct. The correct form of (a) is :

Aromatic amines are weaker base than ammonia.

61 (*b*) The correct order of the reagent to carry out the given reaction is

(i) $(CH_3CO)_2O$, Pyridine

(ii) HNO_3, H_2SO_4, 288 K

(iii) OH^- or H^+

62 (*d*) In the given reaction the intermediate is 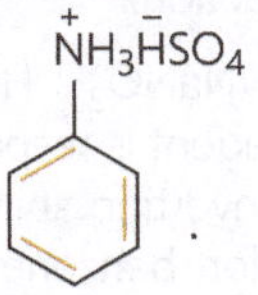 .

63 (*b*)

64 (*b*) $C_6H_5\overset{+}{N}_2\overset{-}{X}$ (aryl diazonium salt) is most stable than other options (aliphatic diazonium salts) due to resonance.

65 (*c*) The incorrect resonating structure is (c). It's correct form is

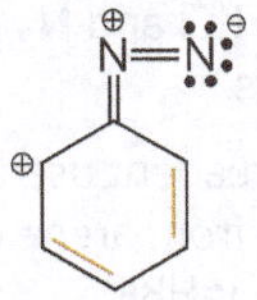

66 (*b*) Primary aromatic amines ($C_6H_5NH_2$) form arenediazonium salts which are stable for a short time in solution at low temperatures (273-278 K).

67 (*c*) Nitrous acid is prepared by the reaction of sodium nitrite with hydrochloric acid.

68 (*c*) The reason is that, it is very unstable and dissociates to give nitrogen molecule.

69 (*c*) Statement (c) is incorrect.

It's correct form is :

The stability of arene diazonium ion is explained on the basis of resonance effect.

70 (*d*) In this reaction *A*, *B* and *C* are; aniline, benzene diazonium chloride and benzene nitrile respectively.

71 (*a*) Statements (b), (c) and (d) are incorrect. Their correct form

(b) It is a colourless crystalline solid.

(c) It react with water when warmed.

(d) It decomposes easily in the dry state.

72 (*d*) Reaction (d) is not a Sandmeyer reaction.

73 (*c*) $(NaNO_2 + HCl, Cu_2Cl_2/HCl)$ reagent is responsible for converting aniline to chlorobenzene.

74 (*d*) Phenyl cyanide can be prepared by Sandmeyer reaction.

75 (*c*) The compounds *A* and *B* are diazonium salt and *p*-fluorotoluene respectively.

76 (*b*) Benzene diazonium salt on reaction with KI forms ArI, KCl and N_2. KCl and N_2 are side products.

77 (*c*) The reagent used to form aryl fluoride from arene diazonium chloride is HBF_4.

78 (*c*) The product *E* is 4-methyl cyanobenzene, i.e.

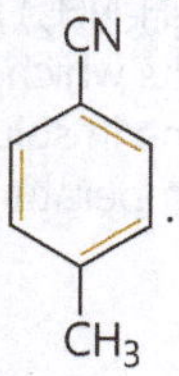

79 (*a*) Benzene diazonium chloride on reaction with hypophosphorus acid produces benzene

80 (*a*)

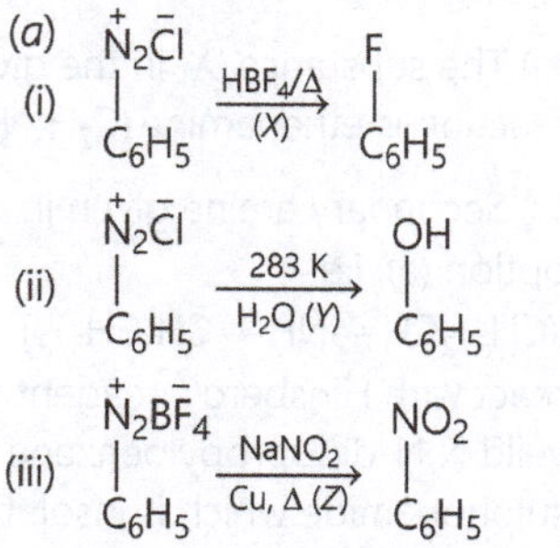

81 (*d*) The reaction takes place as follows

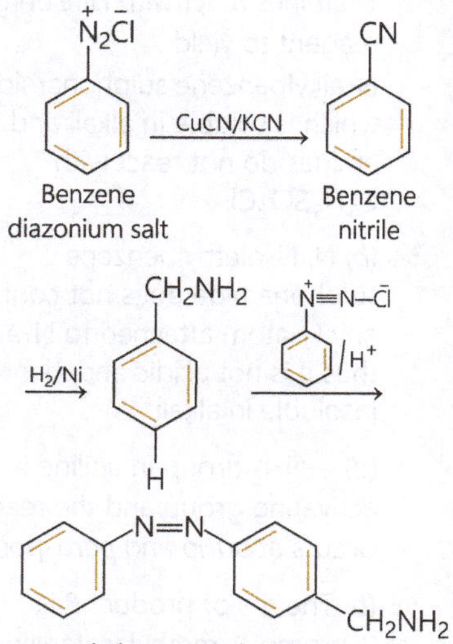

p-methylamine azobenzene

82 (*a*) The step involved for the conversion of aniline to *p*-nitrofluorobenzene is as follows

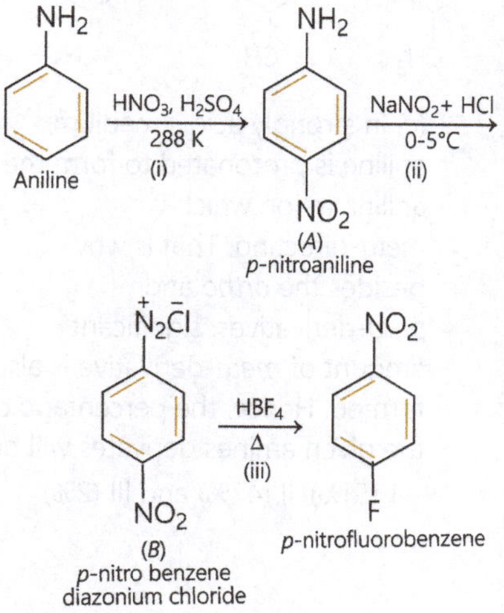

Thus, option (a) is the correct route for this conversion.

83 (*d*) Statements (a), (b) and (c) are incorrect. Their correct form is as follows

- Nitrous acid is produced by the reaction of sodium nitrite with HCl.
- $C_6H_5—NH_2 + NaNO_2 + 2HCl \xrightarrow{273\text{-}278\ K} C_6H_5—\overset{+}{N_2}Cl^- + NaCl + 2H_2O$
- Coupling of diazonium salt with amines occur in mild acidic/basic medium.

84 (*c*) Statement (c) is incorrect.

It's correct form is :

Azo compounds are often coloured and are used as dyes.

85 (*c*)

86 (*c*) The given reaction is a coupling reaction.

$$C_6H_5—\overset{+}{N}{\equiv}N\overset{-}{Cl} + C_6H_5—OH \xrightarrow{\overset{\ominus}{O}H} C_6H_5—N{=}N—C_6H_4—OH + \overset{-}{Cl} + H_2O$$

p-hydroxy azobenzene (*X*)

Therefore, *X* is *p*-hydroxyazobenzene.

87 (*a*) Reactions I and II are electrophilic substitution reaction but III and IV are nucleophilic substitution reactions.

88 (*c*)

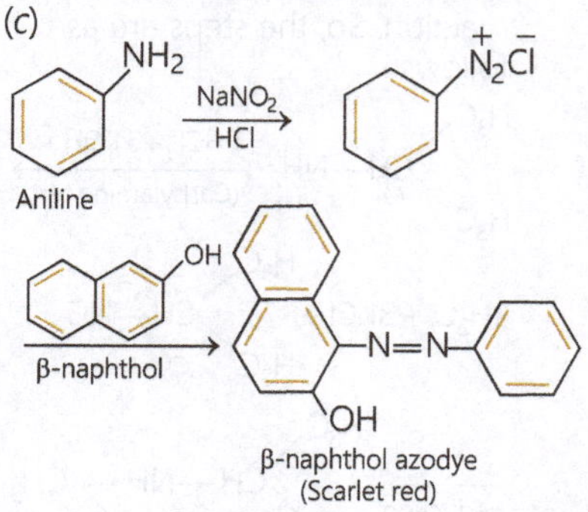

89 (*b*) Statements II and III are incorrect. Their correct form is as follows

II. Aryl fluorides and iodides cannot be prepared by direct halogenation.

III. The reaction of benzene sulphonyl chloride with 1° amine yield N-alkyl benzene sulphonyl amide.

90 (*c*) The group which is not introduced to the aromatic ring by diazonium salt is —OCH_3 (methoxy group).

91 (*d*) The reaction (d) is incorrect.

Because the introduction of —F, —Cl, —I, —CN can be done only by diazonium salts. In reaction (d) cyanobenzene can be prepared by diazonium salt only.

Assertion-Reason

1 (*a*) Both A and R are true and R is the correct explanation of A.

2 (*d*) A is false but R is true. The correct form of A is :

tert-butylamine cannot be prepared by the reaction of *tert*-butylbromide with NH_3.

3 (*c*) A is true but R is false. The correct form of R is :

Aryl halides do not undergo nucleophilic substitution reaction with the anion formed by phthalimide.

4 (*a*) Both A and R are true and R is the correct explanation of A.

5 (*d*) A is false But R is true The correct form of A is :

Order of basicity of amines in gaseous phase follows the order: 3° amine > 2° amine >1° amine > NH_3.

6 (*d*) A is false but R is true . The correct form of A is

Aliphatic amines are stronger bases than ammonia.

7 (*d*) A is false but R is true. The correct form of A is :

$MeNH_2$ is the stronger base than MeOH.

8 (*a*) Both A and R are true and R is the correct explanation of A.

9 (*a*) Both A and R are true and R is the correct explanation of A.

10 (*c*) A is true but R is false. The correct form of R is :

Benzene diazonium salts are soluble in water because they are polar in nature.

Statement Type

1 (*b*) Statement I is true but Statement II is false.

The correct form of Statement II is :

Nitriles on reduction with lithium aluminium hydride or catalytic hydrogenation produces primary amines.

2 (*b*) Statement I is true but Statement II is false.

The correct form of Statement II is :

Primary aliphatic amines reacts with HNO_2 to give unstable diazonium salts.

3 (*b*) Statements I is true but Statement II is false.

The correct form of Statement II is :

In carbylamine reaction, —NH_2 group is converted into —NC group.

4 (*c*) Statement I is false but Statement II is true.

The correct form of Statement I is :

Aniline reacts with conc. H_2SO_4 to form anilinium hydrogen sulphate.

5 (*b*) Statement I is true but Statement II is false.

The correct form of Statement II is :

The given reaction occur in the basic medium.

6 (*b*) Statements II and III are incorrect while I, IV and V statements are correct. The correct form of II and III are

II. Aromatic primary amines can not be prepared by Gabriel phthalimide synthesis because aryl halides do not undergo nucleophilic substitution with the anion formed by phthalimide.

III. Solubility of amines in water decreases with increase in molar mass of amines.

7 (*b*) Among the given statements, I and II are incorrect while III, IV and V are correct. The correct form of I and II are

- N, N-dimethylaniline has lower pK_b value (8.92) than N-methylaniline (9.30).
- Aniline reacts with bromine water at room temperature to give a white precipitate of 2,4,6-tribromoaniline.

8 (*c*) Among the given statements, only II and III are correct while statements I and IV are incorrect. Their correct form are

- In *iso*-propylamine and ethyl methylamine only *iso*-propylamine shows carbylamine reaction because only primary aliphatic and aromatic amines shows carbylamine reaction.
- Amines are in pyramidal shape.

9 (*b*) Among the given statements, only II and III are correct while statements I and IV are incorrect. Their correct are

- Dimethylamines does not give carbylamine test because carbylamine test is only given by primary amines.
- Anilinium ion is not resonance stabilised because charge dispersion at ring may involve pentavalent nitrogen structure.

10 (*c*) Among the given statements II, III and IV are incorrect while the statements I and V are correct. The correct form of II, III and IV are

- Chloroform when treated with aniline and alcoholic KOH gives phenyl isocyanide.
- Diazo coupling is useful to prepare some azo dyes.
- Nitrobenzene is reduced to aniline in acidic medium.

Matching Type

1 (*b*) The correct match is A-2, B-4, C-1, D-3.

2 (*b*) The correct match is A-1, B-3, C-2.

3 (*b*) The correct match is A-4, B-2, C-1, D-3.

4 (*d*) The correct match is A - 3, B - 2, C - 1, D-4.

Numerical Value

1 (*4*) Primary amines are

(i) *n*-butyl amine $CH_3CH_2CH_2CH_2NH_2$

(ii) *sec*-butyl amine $(CH_3)_2CHCH_2NH_2$
(iii) *iso*-butyl amine $CH_3CH_2CH(CH_3)NH_2$
(iv) *tert*-butyl amine $C(CH_3)_2NH_2$

2 (3) The nitrobenzene can be reduced to aniline *via* following reagents.
I. Sn—HCl
IV. H_2—Pd/Ethanol
V. H_2—Ni/Ethanol

3 (2) Only aniline $(C_6H_5NH_2)$ which is an aromatic amine cannot undergo nucleophilic substitution.
Hence, cannot be prepared by Gabriel synthesis.

4 (5) The given reaction is represented as

$$\underset{(P)}{C_6H_5—CH_2—NH_2} + HNO_2 \xrightarrow[\text{(ii) } H_2O]{\text{(i) } NaNO_2 + HCl} C_6H_5—CH_2—OH + HCl + N_2\uparrow$$

The number of possible isomers for compound *P* is 5. It is represented as

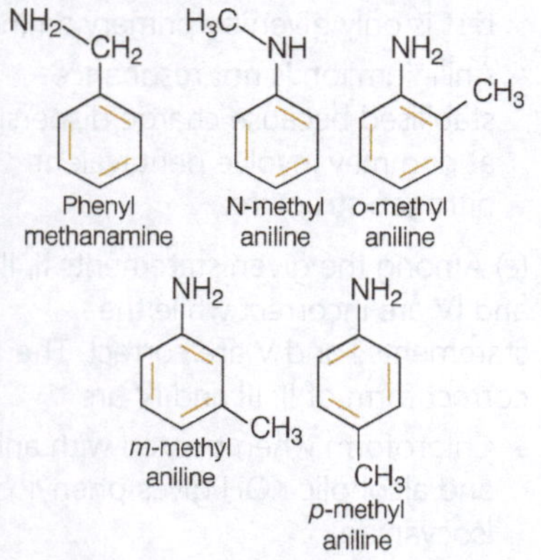

5 (3) Carbylamine test are for primary aliphatic and aromatic amines. Hence, among the given compounds, only II, III and V give positive carbylamine test.

NCERT Exemplar's

1 (*b*) Among the given compounds, only triethylamine is the tertiary (3°) amine while (a) and (c) 1° and (d) is 2° amines.

2 (*d*) IUPAC name of
$\overset{3}{C}H_2 = \overset{2}{C}H\overset{1}{C}H_2NHCH_3$ is
N-methylprop-2-en-1-amine.

3 (*c*) As + *I*-effect and solvation effect increases, basic character increases while –*I*-effect and resonance effect decreases, basic character decreases, hence $(CH_3)_2NH$ is the strongest base in aqueous medium.

4 (*a*) Aniline is the weakest Bronsted base among the given four compounds due to resonance present in the case of aniline.

5 (*c*) More is the stability of carbocation more is the reactivity towards S_N1 mechanism.
Since, $C_6H_5CH_2Br$ gives a resonance stabilised carbocation $(C_6H_5\overset{+}{C}H_2)$, it is best suited for the reaction through S_N1 mechanism.

6 (*b*) Aryl nitro compound cannot be converted into amine using $LiAlH_4$ in ether. Other given reagents can be used to reduce aryl nitro compounds.

7 (*c*) **8** (*d*)

9 The correct match is
A-(4), B-(3), C-(1), D-(2).

10 (*c*) Chemical transformation can be shown as,

$$\underset{(1°\text{amine})}{R—NH_2} + RCHO \longrightarrow [R—N{=}\underset{\substack{|\\H}}{C}—R] \xrightarrow{H_2/Pt} \underset{(2°\text{amine})}{R—\underset{\substack{|\\H}}{N}—\overset{\substack{H\\|}}{\underset{\substack{|\\H}}{C}}—R}$$

While, other given set of reactants give primary amine only.

11 (*d*) The best reagent for converting 2-phenylpropanamide into 2-phenylpropanamine is $LiAlH_4$ in ether.

12 (*b*) The best reagent for converting 2-phenylpropan-amide into 1-phenylethanamine is $NaOH/Br_2$.

13 (*b*) Hofmann bromamide degradation is shown by amide, i.e. $Ar—\overset{\overset{O}{\|}}{C}—NH_2$.

14 (*d*) The correct increasing order of basic strength is as follows
II < I < III.
Greater the electron density towards ring, greater will be basic strength of $—NH_2$.

15 (*c*) Methylamine reacts with HNO_2 (nitrous acid) to form methanol.

16 (*b*)

17 (*c*) In the nitration of benzene, the species which initiates the reaction is NO_2^+.

18 The correct match is A-(2), B-(1), C-(4), D-(3).

19 (*c*)

20 (*b*) Greater the strength of base, greater is its reactivity towards dil. HCl. Since, $(CH_3)_2NH$ has highest basic strength, so it has highest reactivity.

21 (*b*) **22** (*d*)

23 (*c*) Among the given compounds, phenol is the weakest Bronsted base as after losing, its positive charge it produces least stable conjugate acid among the compounds.

24 (*a*) The correct decreasing order is
$NH_2^- > OH^- > NH_3 > H_2O$.

25 (*b*) Due to weak dipole-dipole interactions, amines have higher boiling point (i.e. less volatile) than hydrocarbons. Hence, hydrocarbon $(CH_3CH_2CH_3)$ is the most volatile among given compounds.

26 (*b*)

Past Exams'

1 (*a*) Both statement I and statement II are true.

2 (*b*) Among the given reactions, primary amine will not form in case of (b) reaction.

$$CH_3NC \xrightarrow[H_2O]{LiAlH_4} \underset{(2°\text{ amine})}{CH_3—\underset{\substack{|\\H}}{N}—CH_3}$$

3 (*b*) Statement I is true but Statement II is false. Correct form of Statement II is :

Primary aromatic amines form arenediazonium salts which are stable for a short time in solution at low temperature (273-278 K).

4 (*d*) The given reaction is represented as

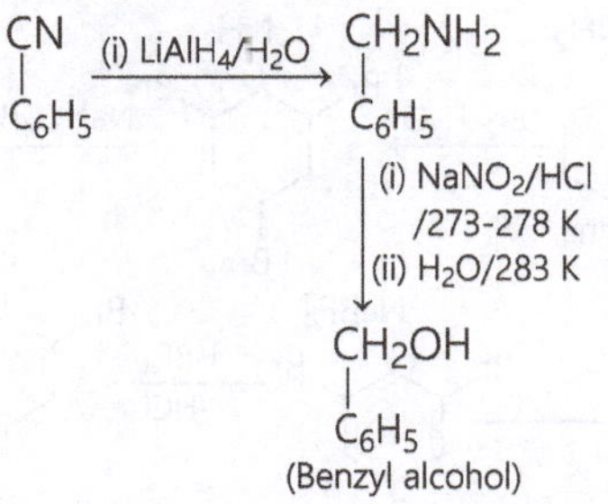

5 (*c*) The reagent *R* is the given reactions is CH_3CH_2OH.

6 (*d*) Carbylamine test is responded by primary (aliphatic or aromatic) amine only.

7 (*a*) Secondary amines on reaction with Hinsberg's reagent (benzene sulphonyl chloride) forms N,N-dialkylbenzenesulphonamide which is insoluble in alkali.

8 (*b*) The reaction is proceed as

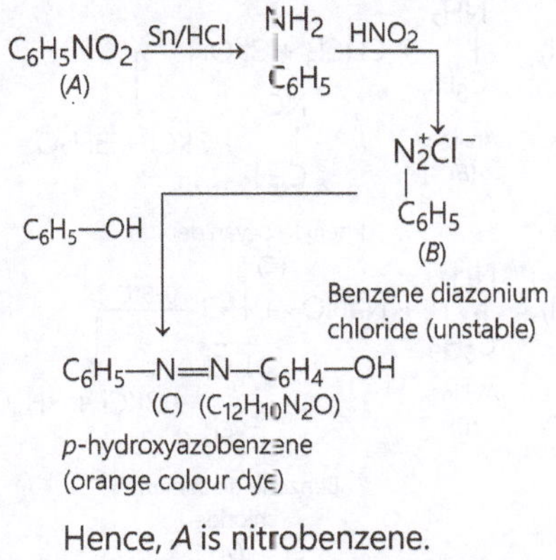

Hence, *A* is nitrobenzene.

9 (*d*) Among the given statements, only (d) is correct regarding arylamines.

10 (*a*) Structural isomers of C_3H_9N are

$CH_3CH_2CH_2NH_2$, $CH_3—CH(NH_2)—CH_3$ (1° amine)

$CH_3—CH_2—NH—CH_3$ (2° amine), $CH_3—N(CH_3)—CH_3$ (3° amine)

11 (*d*) The given reaction is represented as

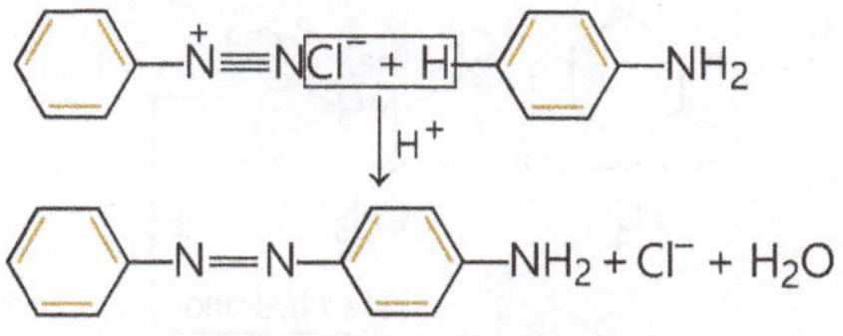

p-aminoazobenzene (yellow dye) (*A*)

12 (*c*) Both statement I and statement II are false. The reason is that, 1° and 2° amines only reacts with *p*-toluenesulphonyl chloride and product of 1° amine only is soluble in aqueous NaOH.

13 (*c*) The complete reaction is as follows

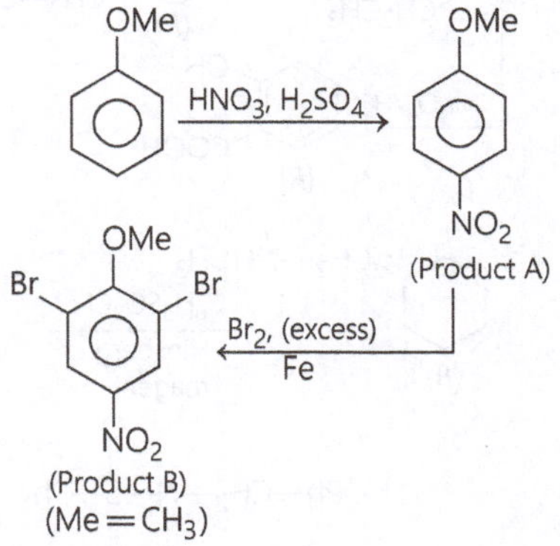

14 (*b*) In options (a), (c) and (d) lone pairs is delocalised due to resonance. While option (b) has highest availability of lone pair due to absence of resonance. Thus, it act as best proton acceptor or strongest bronsted base.

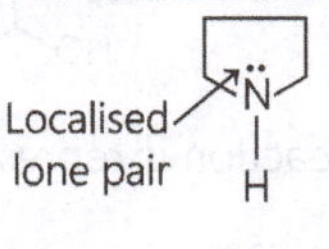

15 (*c*)

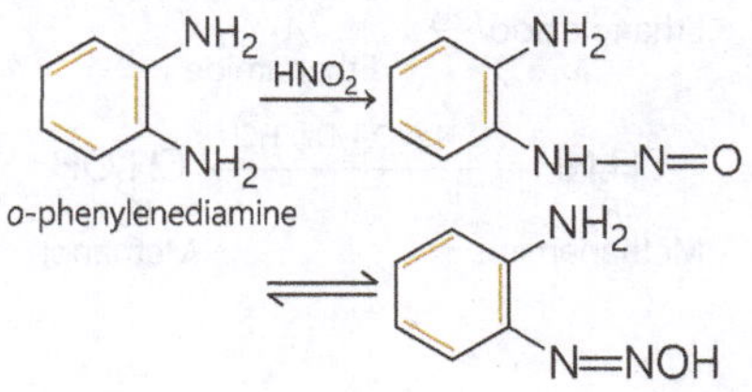

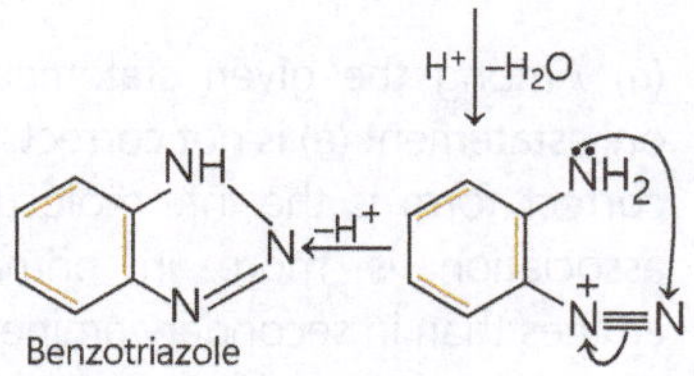

16 (*c*) The reaction or proceeds as

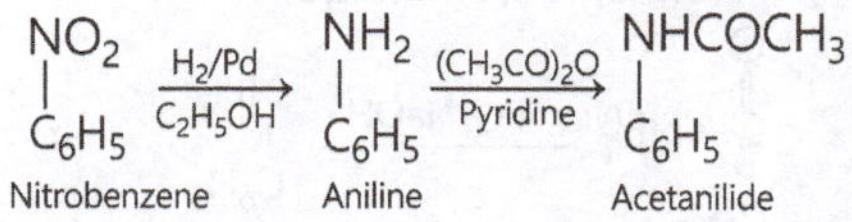

17 (*d*) The reaction proceeds as

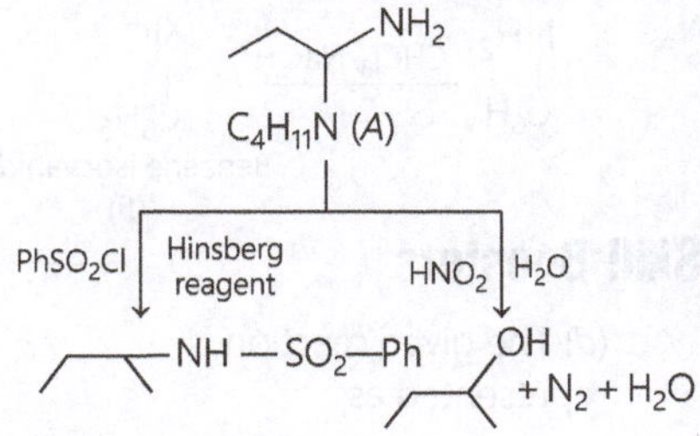

$C_4H_{11}N$ since it releases N_2 with HNO_2, it is a primary amine.

After reacting with Hinsberg reagent it forms a compound which is soluble in KOH.

18 (*b*) Among the given options, incorrect statement is given in option (b). It is because '*B*' is *p*-nitroso ammonium compound. The product formation will takes place as follows

$$NaNO_2 + HX \longrightarrow HNO_2 + NaX$$

$$H—O—N{=}O \xrightarrow[-\,H_2O]{H^{\oplus}} NO^+ \text{ (Nitrosonium ion)}$$

$$C_6H_5—N(Me)_2 \xrightarrow[273\text{-}278\ K]{NO^+} C_6H_4(NO)N(Me)_2$$

p-nitrosoammonium compound *B*

19 (*c*) A is true but R is false. The correct form of R is :

Aniline does not show Friedel-Craft reaction as it is a weak base and reacts with $AlCl_3$ (electron deficient) which act as Lewis acid forming salt instead of *o*- or *p*-substituted product.

20 (*a*) Among the given statements, only statement (a) is not correct. It's correct form is the intermolecular association is more in primary amines than in secondary amines.

21 (*b*) The reaction is proceed as Hofmann bromamide

$$\underset{\text{Benzamide}}{C_6H_5CONH_2} \xrightarrow{Br_2/NaOH} \underset{\text{Aniline (A)}}{C_6H_5NH_2}$$

$$C_6H_5NH_2 \xrightarrow{CHCl_3/NaOH} \underset{\text{Benzene isocyanide (B)}}{C_6H_5NC}$$

Skill Boosters

1 (*d*) The given reaction is represented as

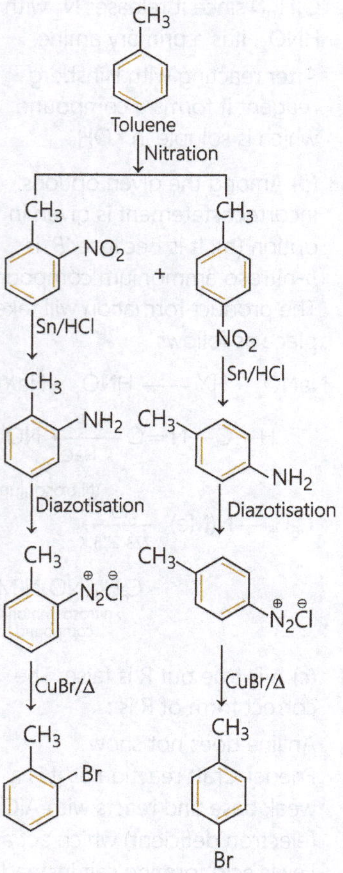

2 (*b*) When cyclohexanone reacts with dimethylamine in presence of acid a hydroxyl amine is formed, further when water is removed an enamine is formed as a product.

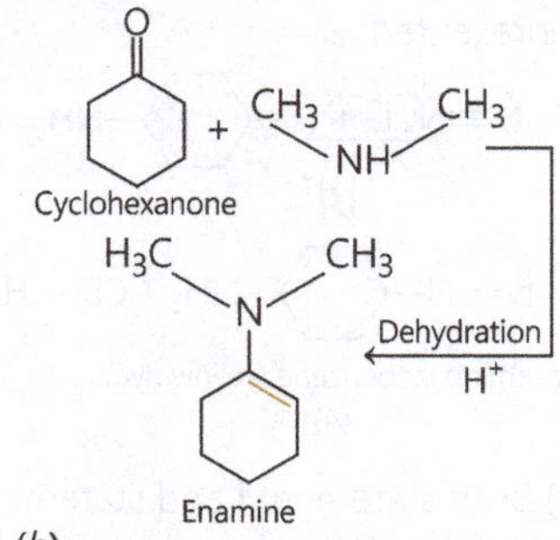

3 (*b*)

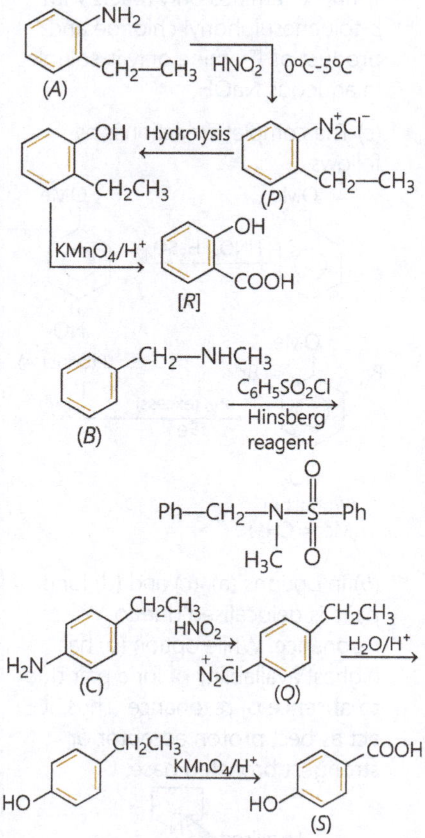

4 (*a*) The reaction is represented as

$$\underset{\text{Ethanoic acid}}{CH_3COOH} \xrightarrow[\Delta]{NH_3} \underset{\text{Ethanamide}}{\underset{(A)}{CH_3CONH_2}} \xrightarrow{Br_2/NaOH}$$

$$\underset{\text{Methanamine}}{\underset{(B)}{CH_3NH_2}} \xrightarrow{NaNO_2/\text{Dil. HCl}} \underset{\text{Methanol}}{\underset{(C)}{CH_3OH}}$$

5 (*b*) The reaction is represented as

$$\underset{\text{Benzamide}}{C_6H_5CONH_2} + Br_2 + KOH \longrightarrow C_6H_5NH_2$$

$$C_6H_5NH_2 + (CH_3CO)_2O \longrightarrow \underset{\text{Acetanilide (antipyretic)}}{CH_3CONHC_6H_5} + CH_3COOH$$

6 (*c*) The reaction is represented as

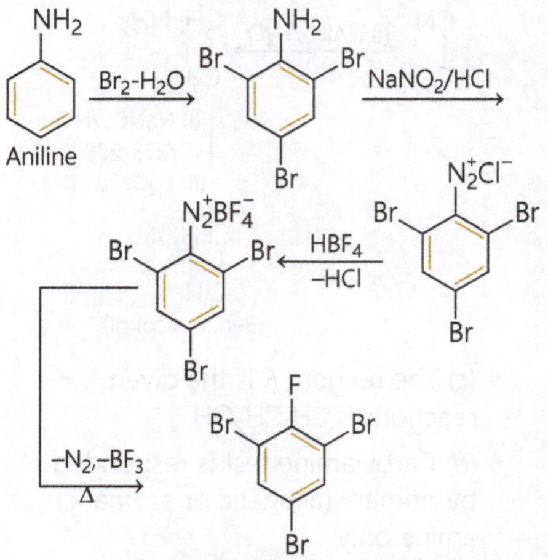

2, 4, 6-tribromofluorobenzene

7 (*b*)

(i) $\underset{\text{Nitrobenzene (A)}}{C_6H_5NO_2} \xrightarrow[HCl]{H_2/Ni} \underset{\text{Aniline (B)}}{C_6H_5NH_2}$

(ii) $\underset{\text{Aniline (B)}}{C_6H_5NH_2} + CHCl_3 + 3KOH \longrightarrow \underset{\text{Phenyl isocyanide (C)}}{C_6H_5NC} + 3KCl + 3H_2O$

(iii) $\underset{\text{Aniline (B)}}{C_6H_5NH_2} + NaNO_2 + HCl \xrightarrow{0\text{-}5°C} \underset{\text{Benzene diazonium chloride (D)}}{C_6H_5\overset{+}{N_2}\overset{-}{Cl}} + 3KCl + 3H_2O$

(iv) $\underset{\text{Aniline (D)}}{C_6H_5\overset{+}{N_2}\overset{-}{Cl}} + CH_3CH_2OH \longrightarrow \underset{\text{Benzene (E)}}{C_6H_6} + N_2 + CH_3CHO + HCl$

Thus, the compounds from '*A*' to '*E*' are nitrobenzene, aniline, phenyl isocyanide, benzene diazonium chloride and benzene.

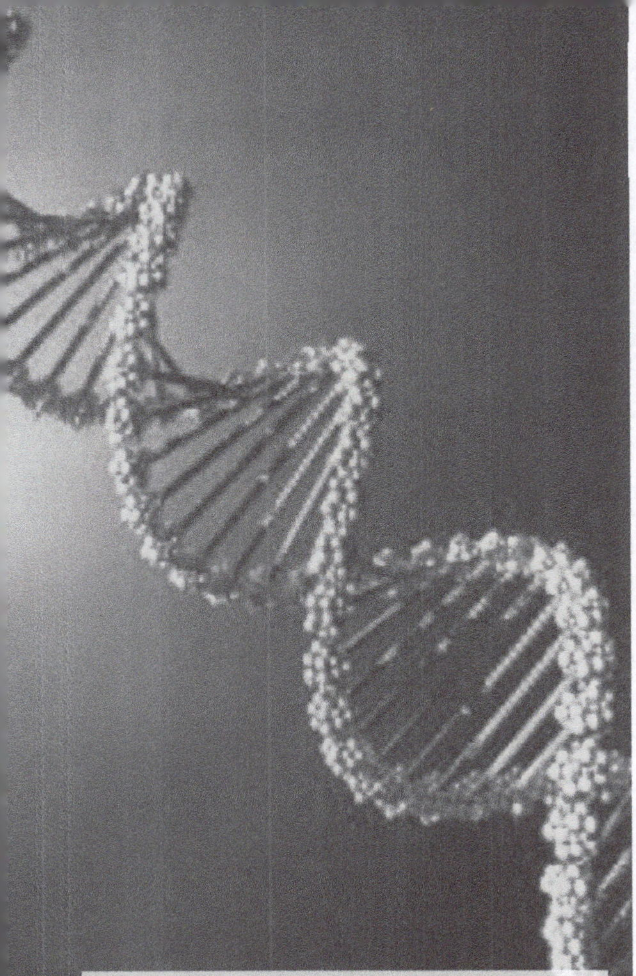

Scan for **Chemistry Through Concept Master** Videos

10

Biomolecules

The branch of chemistry, which studies the chemical changes within the living system is called **biochemistry**.

Living systems are made up of various complex molecules like carbohydrates, proteins, nucleic acids, lipids etc. These molecules are called **biomolecules**. They interact with each other and constitute the molecular logic of life processes.

In addition to these, vitamins and mineral salts (simple molecules) also play an important role in the functions of organisms.

Topicwise No. of Ques asked in 5 Years (NEET)

Topics	No. of Questions				
	2024	2023	2022	2021	2020
Carbohydrates	1	–	–	–	3
Proteins	–	–	–	–	1
Enzymes and Vitamins	–	–	1	1	1
Nucleic Acid	–	1	1	–	–
Hormones	–	–	–	–	–

Special Type of Ques Asked In 5 Years (NEET)

Types	Years				
	2024	2023	2022	2021	2020
A-R	–	–	–	–	–
Statement Based	–	1	1	–	–
Matching	–	–	–	–	–

Last 5 Years Weightage (NEET)

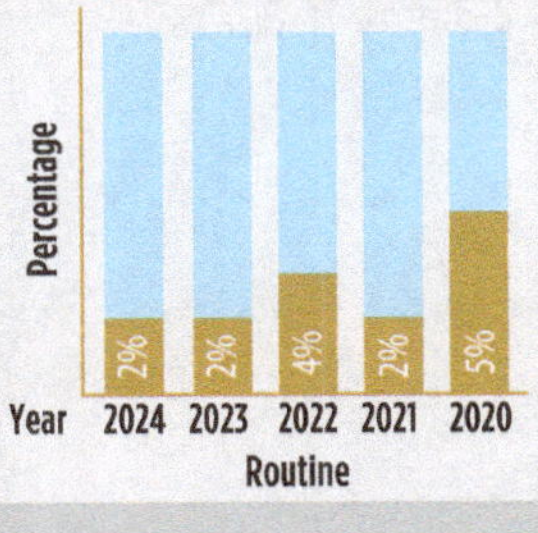

Carbohydrates

- These are primarily produced by plants and form a very large group of naturally occurring organic compounds.
- Most of carbohydrates have a general formula, $C_x(H_2O)_y$ and word considered as hydrates of carbon. The molecular formula of glucose ($C_6H_{12}O_6$) fits into the given general formula, $C_6(H_2O)_6$.
  But all the compounds which fit into this formula may not be classified as carbohydrates, e.g. acetic acid (CH_3COOH).
  Similarly, all the carbohydrates do not fit into this formula. e.g. Rhamnose ($C_6H_{12}O_5$) is a carbohydrate but does not fit in this formula.
- Carbohydrates are **optically active** polyhydroxy aldehydes or ketones or the compounds which produce such units on hydrolysis. Some common examples of carbohydrates are cane sugar, glucose, starch etc.
- Some of the carbohydrates which are sweet in taste are called **sugars**. The most common sugar, used in our homes is known as **sucrose** whereas the sugar present in milk is known as **lactose**. These are also called **saccharides** (Greek : Sakcharon means sugar).

Classification of Carbohydrates

Group	Definition	Examples
1. On the basis of their behaviour on hydrolysis		
Monosaccharides	• They cannot be hydrolysed to give simpler unit of polyhydroxy aldehyde or ketone. • These contain single unit of saccharide and about 20 monosaccharides are known to occur in nature.	• Glucose, fructose, ribose etc.
Oligosaccharides	• They yield two to ten monosaccharide units on hydrolysis. • These are further classified as disaccharides, trisaccharides, tetrasaccharides etc.	• Disaccharide-sucrose (glucose + fructose) maltose (glucose + glucose).
Polysaccharides	• They yield a large number of monosaccharide units on hydrolysis. • These are not sweet in taste, hence are also called non-sugars.	• Starch, cellulose, glycogen, gums etc.
2. On the basis of reducing property		
Reducing sugars	• These carbohydrates reduce Fehling's solution and Tollen's reagent. • All monosaccharides whether aldose or ketose are reducing sugars. • These sugars contain free ketone or aldehyde group.	• Monosaccharides like glucose, fructose, ribose etc.
Non-reducing sugars	• These carbohydrates are not capable of reducing Fehling's solution or Tollen's reagent. • In these sugar aldehydic or ketonic group are bonded.	• Disaccharides like sucrose and polysaccharides like starch, cellulose etc.

Monosaccharides

These are classified on the basis of the functional group present in them i.e. an **aldose** (monosaccharide containing an aldehyde group) and **ketose** (monosaccharide containing a keto group).

Monosaccharides can be further classified into different categories depending upon the number of carbon atoms.

For example, monosaccharides with three carbon atoms are called trioses, with four carbon atoms as tetroses and so on.

Glucose

It is an aldohexose (also known as dextrose) with molecular formula, $C_6H_{12}O_6$.

It occurs freely as well as in combined form in nature.

It is present in sweet fruits, ripe grapes and honey.

Preparation of Glucose

It can be prepared as follows

(i) **From sucrose** (cane sugar) Glucose can be easily obtained in a laboratory by the hydrolysis of alcoholic solution of cane sugar, i.e. sucrose is boiled with dilute HCl or H_2SO_4 at 50°C to give glucose and fructose in equal amounts.

$$\underset{\text{Sucrose}}{C_{12}H_{22}O_{11}} + H_2O \xrightarrow{H^+} \underset{\text{Glucose}}{C_6H_{12}O_6} + \underset{\text{Fructose}}{C_6H_{12}O_6}$$

(ii) **From starch** Commercially, glucose is obtained by the hydrolysis of starch by boiling it with dilute H_2SO_4 at 393 K, under 2-3 standard atmospheric pressure.

$$\underset{\text{Starch or Cellulose}}{(C_6H_{10}O_5)_n} + nH_2O \xrightarrow[\text{393 K, 2-3 atm}]{H^+} \underset{\text{Glucose}}{nC_6H_{12}O_6}$$

Structure of Glucose

Based on the following evidences given below the **open chain** structure was assigned : NEET 2024

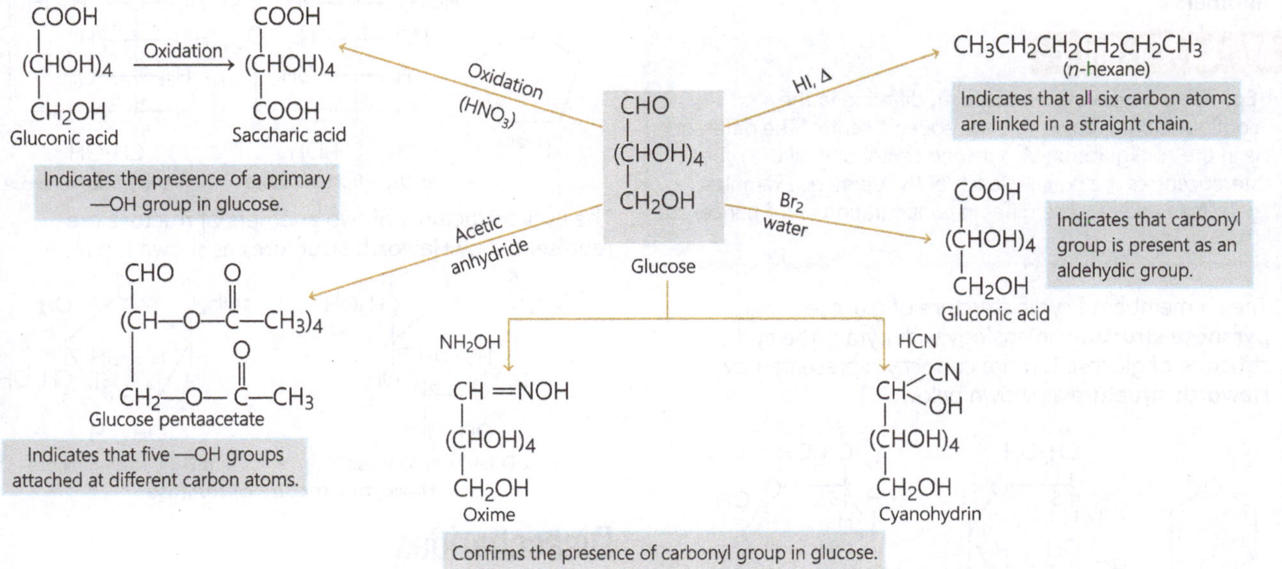

D and L Notations

- 'D' and 'L' have no relation with the optical activity of the compound.
- To assign D and L-configurations to monosaccharides the simplest carbohydrate, glyceraldehyde is chosen as the standard. It contain one chiral carbon atom and hence exist in two enantiomeric forms as shown below.

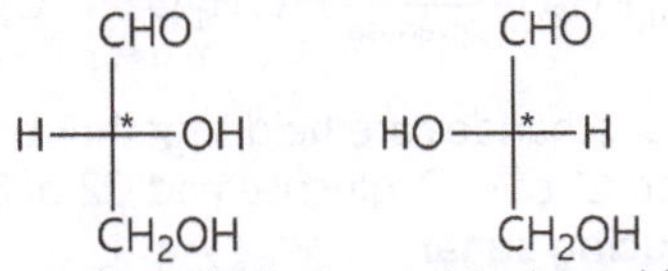

D-(+)-glyceraldehyde L-(−)-glyceraldehyde

- The letters 'D' or 'L' before a molecule indicate the relative configuration of a particular stereoisomer of a compound with respect to configuration of a particular isomer of glyceraldehyde.
- In 'L' isomer, —OH group is on left hand side while in 'D' isomer, —OH group is on right hand side.

Configuration of Glucose

The exact spatial arrangement of different —OH groups was given by Fischer.

'D' represents the configuration whereas '(+)' represent the dextrorotatory nature.

For assigning the configuration of monosaccharides, always remark the lowest asymmetric carbon atom, which is compared as shown in the structure.

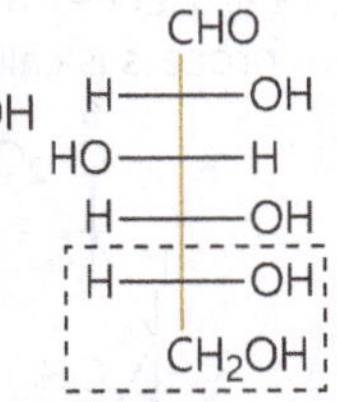

D-(+)-glucose

Cyclic Structure of Glucose

Following reactions and facts are not explained by open chain structure of glucose. So, it was proposed that, glucose form a cyclic hemiacetal structure. These are summarised as follows

- It does not give **Schiff's test** and does not form hydrogen sulphite addition product with $NaHSO_3$, despite having the aldehyde group.
- Pentaacetate of glucose does not react with **hydroxylamine** indicating the absence of free —CHO group.
- It is found to exist in two different crystalline forms which are named as α and β.
- α-form of glucose (m.p. 419 K) is obtained by crystallisation from concentrated solution of glucose at 303 K, while the β-form (m.p. 423K) is obtained by crystallisation from hot and saturated aqueous solution at 371 K.

The two cyclic forms exist in equilibrium with open chain structure is as follows

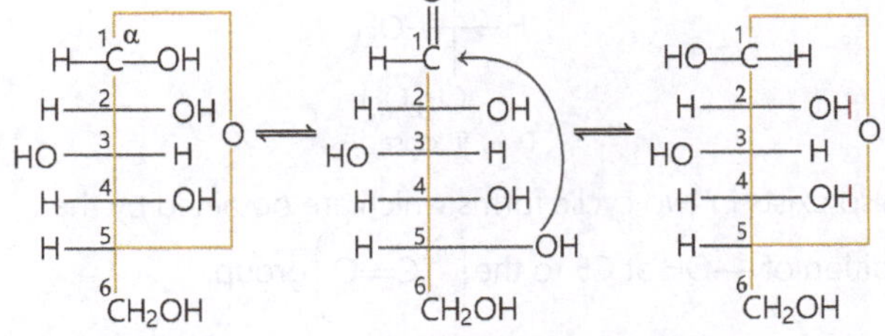

α-D-(+)-glucose D-(+)-glucose (open chain structure) β-D-(+)-glucose

- The two cyclic hemiacetal forms of glucose differ only in the configuration of hydroxyl group at C1 called **anomeric carbon** and isomers, i.e. α-form and β-form are called **anomers**.

Marks Maximizer

Epimer is a type of stereoisomer, differing in the configuration of any single stereogenic centre. The difference is in the configuration of only one center and all the other stereocentres are equal in each of the epimers. Examples: galactose and glucose differ in configuration at C4 hence, are C4 epimers.

- The six membered cyclic structure of glucose is called **pyranose structure**, in analogy with pyran. The cyclic structure of glucose is more correctly represented by **Haworth structure** as shown below

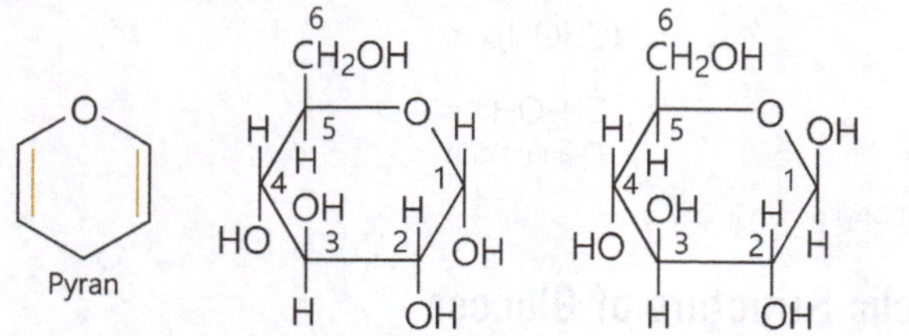

Pyran α-D-(+)-glucopyranose β-D-(+)-glucopyranose

Haworth structure of glucose

Fructose

It is an important ketohexose. It is obtained along with glucose by the hydrolysis of disaccharide, sucrose. In its pure form it is used as a sweetener.

Structure of Fructose

It has molecular formula $C_6H_{12}O_6$. It belongs to D-series and is a laevorotatory compound and written as D-(–)- fructose. Its open chain structure is as shown below :

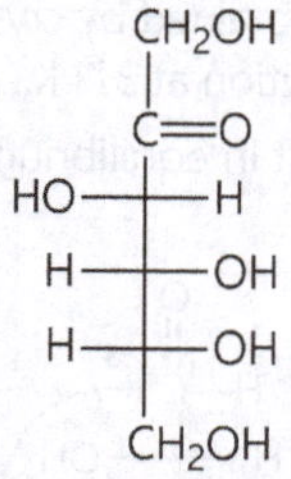

D-(–)-fructose

It also exists in two cyclic forms which are obtained by the addition of —OH at C5 to the $\left(>C=O\right)$ group.

The ring, thus formed is a five membered ring and is named as **furanose** with analogy to the compound furan.

Furan is a five membered cyclic compound with one oxygen and four carbon atoms.

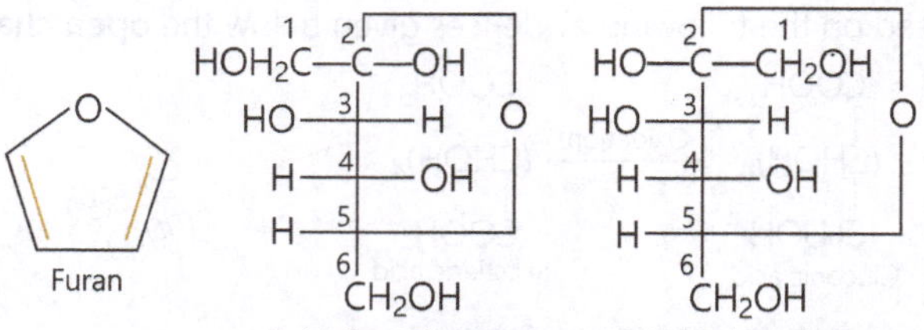

Furan α-D-(–)-fructofuranose β-D-(–)-fructofuranose

The cyclic structures of two anomers of fructose are represented by **Haworth structures** as shown below.

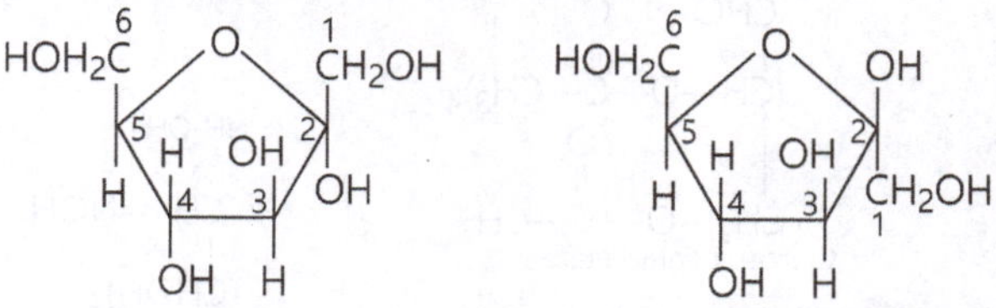

α-D-(–)-fructofuranose β-D-(–)-fructofuranose

Haworth structure of fructose

Disaccharides

These compounds on hydrolysis with dilute acids or enzymes, yield two molecules of either the same or different monosaccharides. The two monosaccharides unit are joined together by an oxide linkage formed by loss of a water molecule is known as **glycosidic linkage.** Some important disaccharides are

- **Sucrose** (cane sugar) hydrolyse to give an equimolar mixture of D-(+)-glucose and D-(–)-fructose.

$$\underset{\text{Sucrose}}{C_{12}H_{22}O_{11}} + H_2O \xrightarrow[\text{Invertase}]{\text{Hydrolysis}} \underset{\text{D-(+)-glucose}}{C_6H_{12}O_6} + \underset{\text{D-(–)-fructose}}{C_6H_{12}O_6}$$

The two monosaccharides are held together by a glycosidic linkage between C1 of α-D-glucose and C2 of β-D-fructose. It is a **non-reducing sugar.**

Sucrose is dextrorotatory with specific rotation of +66.5°. However, after hydrolysis, it gives dextrorotatory glucose and laevorotatory fructose.

The mixture is laevorotatory because laevorotation of fructose (–92.4°) is more than dextrorotation of glucose (+ 52.5°). Therefore, hydrolysis of sucrose brings about a change in the sign of rotation, i.e. from *dextro* (+) to *laevo* (–). Hence, the product is known as **invert sugar** and the process is called **inversion of sugar.**

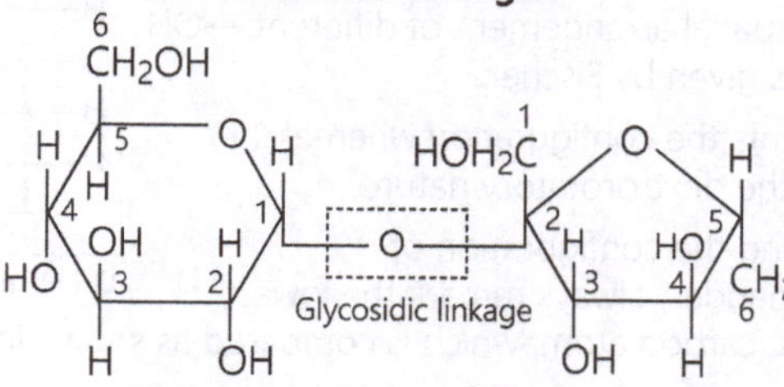

α-D-glucose **Sucrose** β-D-fructose

- **Maltose** (malt sugar) is composed of two α-D-glucose units in which C1 of one glucose is linked to C4 of another glucose unit. The free aldehyde group can be produced at C1 of second glucose in solution and it shows reducing properties. So, it is a reducing sugar.

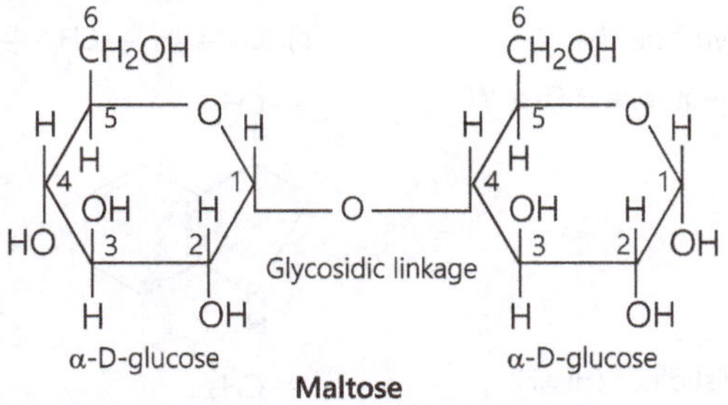

Maltose

- **Lactose** (milk sugar) is composed of β-D-galactose and β-D-glucose. The linkage is between C1 of galactose and C4 of glucose. It is also a reducing sugar.

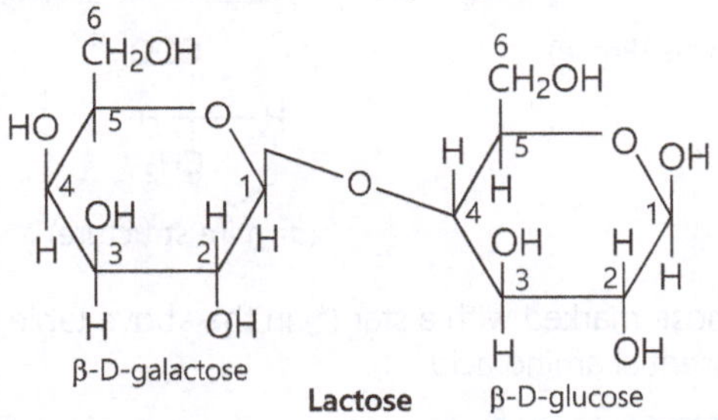

Lactose

*Polysaccharides

These contain a large number of monosaccharide units joined together by glycosidic linkages. e.g.

(i) **Starch** is the main storage polysaccharide of plants. High content of starch is formed in cereals, roots, tubers and some vegetables. It is a polymer of α-glucose and consists of two components **amylose** and **amylopectin.**

- **Amylose** is water soluble component that constitutes about 15-20% of starch. It is a long unbranched chain with 200-1000 α-D-(+) - glucose units held together by C1-C4 glycosidic linkage.

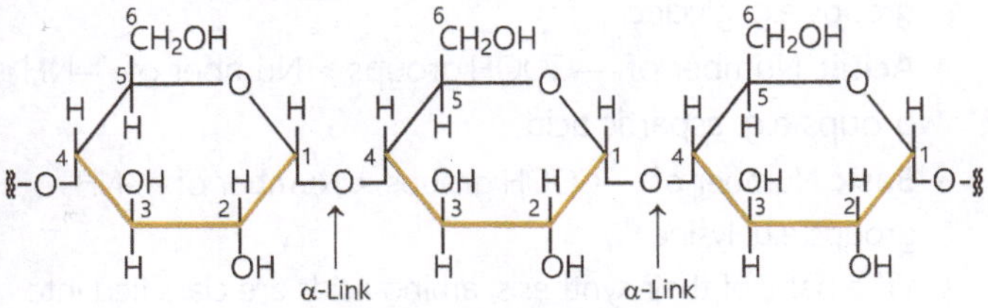

Structure of amylose

- **Amylopectin** is insoluble in water and constitutes about 80-85% of starch. It is a branched chain polymer of α-D-glucose units in which chain is formed by C1-C4 linkage and branching occurs by at C1-C6 glycosidic linkage.

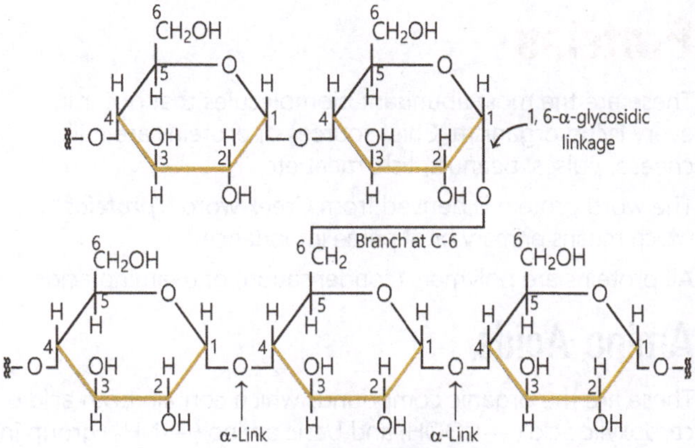

Structure of amylopectin

(ii) **Cellulose** occurs in plants and a predominant constituent of cell wall of plant cells. It is a straight chain polysaccharide composed only of β-D-glucose units which are joined by glycosidic linkage between C1 of one glucose unit and C4 of next glucose unit.

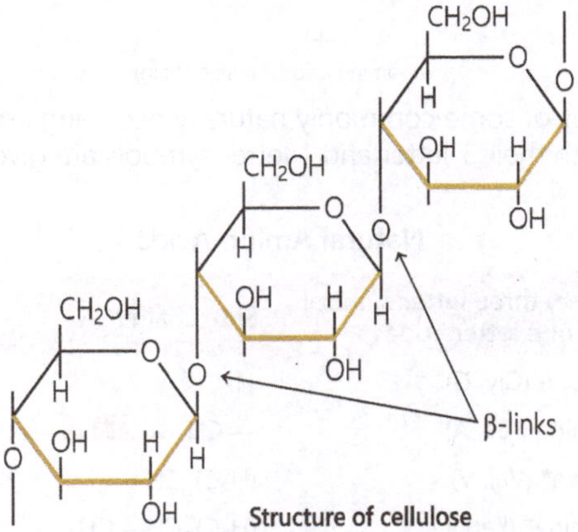

Structure of cellulose

(iii) **Glycogen** is known to be the storage material of animal. It is also known as animal starch because its structure is similar to amylopectin and is rather more highly branched. It is present in liver, muscles and brain. It is also found in yeast and fungi.

* *This topic not include in latest NEET syllabus, but it is given in latest rationalised NCERT.*

Importance of Carbohydrates

- Carbohydrates are essential for life in both plants and animals.
- They are used as storage molecules.
- They provide raw materials for many important industries like textiles, paper, lacquers and breweries.
- It is found in biosystem in combination with many proteins and lipids.

Proteins

These are the most abundant biomolecules that occur in every living organism. Chief sources of proteins are milk, cheese, pulses, peanuts, fish, meat etc.

The word protein is derived from Greek word, ***"proteios"*** which means primary or of prime importance.

All proteins are polymers (condensation) of α-amino acids.

Amino Acids

These are the organic compounds which contain both acidic carboxylic acid (—COOH) and basic amino (—NH_2) group in their molecules. Amino acids can be classified on the basis of relative position of amino group with respect to carboxyl group as α, β, γ .... and so on. Only α-amino acids are obtained on hydrolysis of proteins.

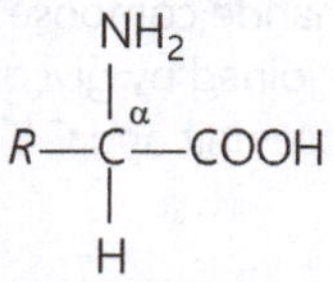

α-amino acid (*R* = side chain)

Structures of some commonly naturally occurring amino acids along with their 3-letter and 1-letter symbols are given below in table.

Natural Amino Acids

Name, three letter symbol and one letter code	Side chain *R*
1. Glycine (Gly, G)	H
2. Alanine (Ala, A)	—CH_3 NEET 2019
3. Valine* (Val, V)	$(H_3C)_2CH$—
4. Leucine* (Leu, L)	$(H_3C)_2CH—CH_2$—
5. Isoleucine* (Ile, I)	$H_3C—CH_2—CH(CH_3)$—
6. Arginine* (Arg, R)	$HN{=}C(NH_2)—NH—(CH_2)_3$—
7. Lysine* (Lys, K)	$H_2N—(CH_2)_4$— NEET 2020
8. Glutamic acid (Glu, E)	$HOOC—CH_2—CH_2$—
9. Aspartic acid (Asp, D)	$HOOC—CH_2$—
10. Glutamine (Gln, Q)	$H_2N—C(=O)—CH_2—CH_2$—
11. Asparagine (Asn, N)	$H_2N—C(=O)—CH_2$—
12. Threonine* (Thr, T)	$H_3C—CHOH$—
13. Serine (Ser, S)	$HO—CH_2$—
14. Cysteine (Cys, C)	$HS—CH_2$—
15. Methionine* (Met, M)	$H_3C—S—CH_2—CH_2$—
16. Phenylalanine* (Phe, F)	$C_6H_5—CH_2$—
17. Tyrosine (Tyr, Y)	$(p)HO—C_6H_4—CH_2$—
18. Tryptophan* (Trp, W)	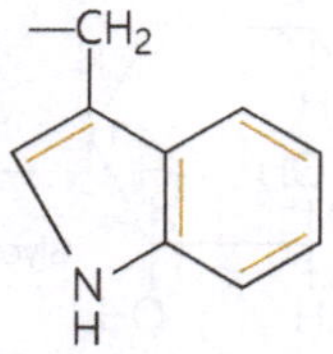
19. Histidine* (His, H)	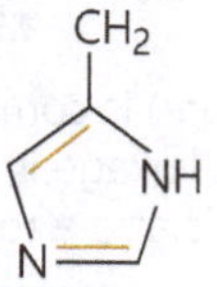
20. Proline (Pro, P)	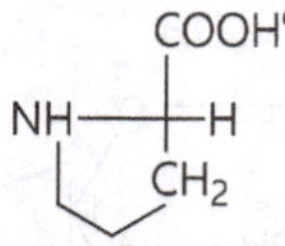 (*a*=ntire structure)

Note Those marked with a star (*) in the above table are all essential amino acid.

Mnemonics (Recall the name of essential amino acids)

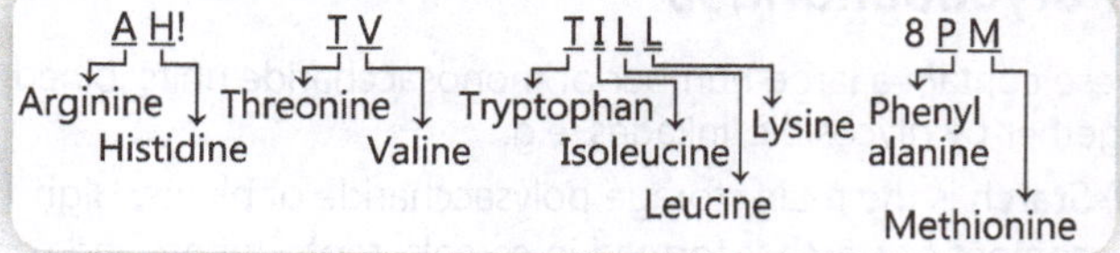

Classification of Amino Acids

For Concept Master Video

Depending upon the relative number of amino (—NH_2) and carboxyl (—COOH) groups present in their molecules, amino acids are classified as follows

- **Neutral** Number of —COOH groups = Number of —NH_2 groups e.g. glycine.
- **Acidic** Number of —COOH groups > Number of —NH_2 groups e.g. aspartic acid.
- **Basic** Number of —COOH groups < Number of —NH_2 groups e.g. lysine.

On the basis of their synthesis, amino acids are classified into two classes

- **Essential amino acids** cannot be synthesised in the body and must be obtained through diet. e.g. valine, lysine, etc.
- **Non-essential amino acids** can be synthesised in the body, e.g. alanine, aspartic acid etc.

Properties of Amino Acids

- These are usually colourless, crystalline solids, water soluble and high melting solids.
- They behave like salts rather than simple amines or carboxylic acids due to the presence of both acidic (carboxyl group) and basic (amino group) groups in the same molecule.
- In aqueous solution, the carbonyl group can lose a proton and amino group can accept a proton giving rise to a dipolar ion known as **Zwitter ion**. This is neutral but contains both positive and negative charges.

For Concept Master Video

$$R{-}\underset{\underset{\ddot{N}H_2}{|}}{CH}{-}\overset{\overset{O}{||}}{C}{-}OH \rightleftharpoons R{-}\underset{\underset{+NH_3}{|}}{CH}{-}\overset{\overset{O}{||}}{C}{-}O^-$$

(Zwitter ion)

- The pH at which dipolar ion, i.e. Zwitter ion exist as neutral ion, i.e. positive and negative charge are equal and it does not migrate to either electrode is called **isoelectric point.** At this point, amino acids have least solubility in water which helps in their separation.
- Amino acids in Zwitter ionic form show amphoteric behaviour as they react both with acids and bases.
- Except glycine, all other naturally occurring α-amino acids are optically active, since the α-carbon atom is asymmetric. These exist both in 'D' and 'L' forms. Most naturally occurring amino acids have L-configuration. L-amino acids are represented by writing $—NH_2$ group on left hand side.

Structure of Proteins

- Proteins are the polymers of α-amino acids and they are connected to each other by **peptide bond** or **peptide linkage.**
- Chemically, peptide linkage is an amide formed between —COOH group and $—NH_2$ group.
- **Peptide linkages** can be of various types i.e. **dipeptide** (combination of amino group of one molecule with carboxyl group of other), **tripeptide** (three amino acids linked by two peptide linkages), **tetrapeptide, pentapeptide, hexapeptide** and so on.

e.g. $H_2N{-}CH_2{-}COOH + H_2N{-}\underset{\underset{CH_3}{|}}{CH}{-}COOH \xrightarrow{-H_2O}$

$$H_2N{-}CH_2{-}\boxed{CO{-}NH}{-}\underset{\underset{CH_3}{|}}{CH}{-}COOH$$

Peptide linkage

Glycylalanine (Gly–Ala)

- When number of amino acids is between 2-10 then the products are called **oligopeptides** and more than ten are known as **polypeptides**.
- A **polypeptide** with more than hundred amino acids residues having molecular mass higher than 10,000 u is called a **protein**.

Classification of Proteins

I. On the basis of their molecular shape proteins are classified as:

- **Fibrous proteins** have thread like structures in which polypeptide chains run parallel and are held together by hydrogen and disulphide bonds. These proteins are **insoluble** in water. e.g. Keratin (present in hair, wool, silk), myosin (present in muscles).
- **Globular proteins** have spherical shape in which chains of polypeptides coil around. They are usually water **soluble**, e.g. insulin and albumins.

II. On the basis of structure and shape proteins can be studied at different levels as shown below:

- **Primary structure** simply reveals the sequence of amino acids which are held together by peptide bonds.
- **Secondary structure** refers to the shape in which a long polypeptide chain can exist.

It is mainly of two types

(i) **α-helix** Polypeptide chain forms all possible hydrogen bonds by twisting into a right handed screw (helix) with the—NH group of each amino acid residue hydrogen bonded to the $\rangle C{=}O$ of an adjacent turn of the helix.

(ii) **β-pleated sheet structure** Peptide chains are stretched out to nearly maximum extension and then laid side by side which are held together by intermolecular hydrogen bonds.

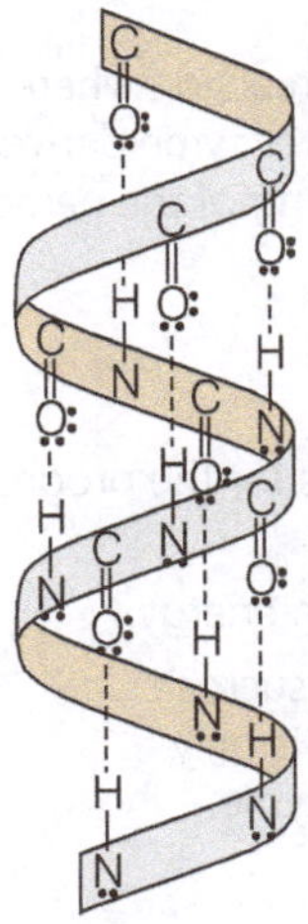

α-helix

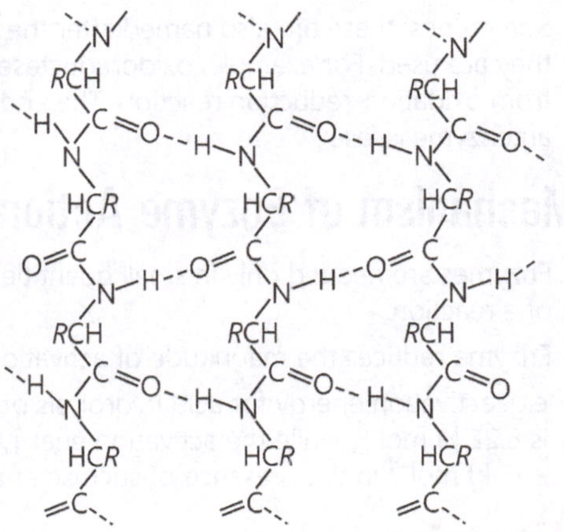

β-pleated sheet structure of proteins

- **Tertiary structure** It represents overall folding of the polypeptide chains, i.e. further folding of the secondary structure. It gives rises to two major molecular shapes of proteins, i.e. fibrous and globular. The forces which stabilise the structure of proteins are hydrogen bonds, disulphide linkages, van der Waals' and electrostatic forces of attraction.

- **Quaternary structure** Some of the proteins are composed of two or more polypeptide chains referred to as sub-units. The spatial arrangement of these subunits with respect to each other is known as quaternary structure.

Denaturation of Proteins

- When a protein in its native form is subjected to physical change like change in temperature or chemical change like change in pH, the hydrogen bonds are disturbed. Due to this, globules unfold and helix get uncoiled and protein loses its biological activity. This process is called denaturation of proteins.
- The denaturation causes change in 2° and 3° structures but 1° structure remains intact, NEET 2019 e.g. curdling of milk which is caused due to the formation of lactic acid by the bacteria present in milk.

Enzymes

- These are essential biological catalysts (or biocatalysts) which are needed to catalyse biochemical reactions. Almost all the enzymes are globular proteins. NEET 2022
- These are very specific for a particular reaction and for a particular substrate.
- They are generally named after the compounds or class of compounds upon which they work, e.g. the enzyme that catalyses hydrolysis of maltose into glucose is named as maltase.

$$\underset{\text{Maltose}}{C_{12}H_{22}O_{11}} \xrightarrow{\text{Maltase}} \underset{\text{Glucose}}{2C_6H_{12}O_6}$$

- Sometimes, these are also named after the reaction where they are used. For example, oxidoreductase enzyme derived from oxidation-reduction reaction. The ending of the name of an enzyme is 'ase'.

Mechanism of Enzyme Action

- Enzymes are needed only in small quantities for the progress of a reaction.
- Enzyme reduces the magnitude of activation energy.

  e.g. activation energy for acid hydrolysis of sucrose is 6.22 kJ mol^{-1}, while the activation energy is only 2.15 kJ mol^{-1} in the presence of sucrase enzyme.

Vitamins

These are certain organic compounds required in our diet in small amounts to perform specific biological functions for normal maintenance of optimum growth and health of an organism. These are classified into two groups depending upon their solubility in water or fat.

- **Fat soluble** Vitamins, which are soluble in fat and oils but insoluble in water. These are vitamins A, D, E, K. They are stored in liver and adipose tissues.
- **Water soluble** Vitamins, which are soluble in water, these include B group vitamins and vitamin C. They must be supplied in diet because they are readily excreted in urine and cannot be stored (except vitamin B_{12}) in our body.

Some Important Vitamins, their Sources and their Deficiency Diseases

Name of vitamins	Sources	Deficiency diseases
Vitamin A (Retinol)	Fish liver oil, carrots, butter and milk	Xerophthalmia (hardening of cornea of eye) or night blindness
Vitamin B_1 (Thiamine)	Yeast, milk, green vegetables and cereals	*Beri-beri* (loss of appetite, retarded growth)
Vitamin B_2 (Riboflavin)	Milk, egg white, liver, kidney	Cheilosis (fissuring at corners of mouth and lips), digestive disorders and burning sensation of the skin
Vitamin B_6 (Pyridoxine)	Yeast, milk, egg yolk, cereals and grams	Convulsions
Vitamin B_{12} (Cyanocobalamine)	Meat, fish, egg and curd	Pernicious anaemia (RBC deficient in haemoglobin) NEET 2021
Vitamin C (Ascorbic acid)	Citrus fruits, amla and green leafy vegetables	Scurvy (bleeding gums)
Vitamin D (Calciferol)	Exposure to sunlight, fish and egg yolk	Rickets (bone deformities in children) and osteomalacia (soft bones and joint pain in adults) NEET 2020
Vitamin E (α-Tocopherol)	Wheat germ oil, sunflower oil	Increased fragility of RBCs and muscular weakness
Vitamin K (Phylloquinone)	Green leafy vegetables	Increased blood clotting time

Marks Maximizer

- The conditions of vitamin deficiency is known as **avitaminosis** while the condition where the consumption of vitamins is beyond the requirement is called **hypervitaminosis**.
- Vitamin H commonly known as biotin is neither soluble in water nor in fats.

Nucleic Acids

These are the biomolecules, which are found in the nuclei of all living cells and play an important role in transmission of heredity, characteristics and protein synthesis.

Since, nucleic acids are long chain polymers of **nucleotides**, so they are also called polynucleotides.

These are of two types i.e. Deoxyribonucleic acid (DNA) and Ribonucleic acid (RNA).

Chemical Composition of Nucleic Acids

Complete hydrolysis of nucleic acids give following three different compounds.

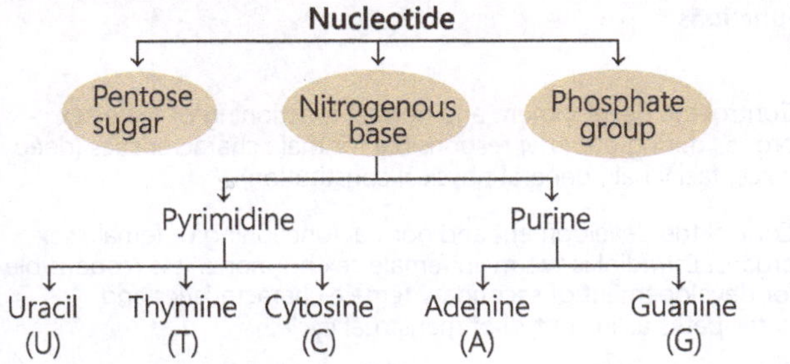

- **Pentose sugar** DNA molecules contain β-D-2-deoxyribose, a sugar moiety, whereas RNA molecules contain β-D-ribose.

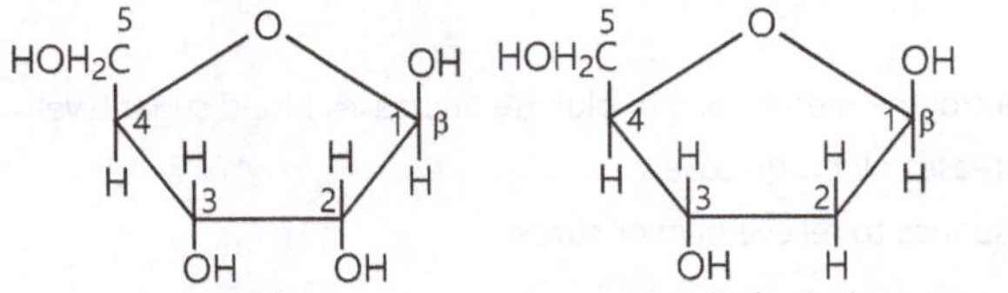

β-D-ribose β-D-2-deoxyribose

- **Phosphoric acid** It is the common product for both DNA and RNA hydrolysis.
- **Nitrogenous base** Nitrogen containing heterocyclic compounds are called nitrogenous base.
- DNA and RNA both contain three common bases; adenine (A), guanine (G) and cytosine (C). Thymine (T) is present in DNA but in place of thymine, RNA contains uracil (U).

  So, there are four bases in each DNA and RNA.

  i.e. DNA = A, G, C, T or RNA = A, G, C, U

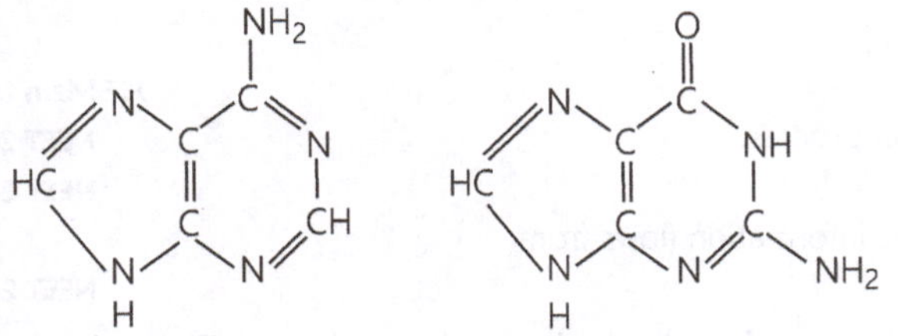

Adenine (A) Guanine (G)

Structures of purines

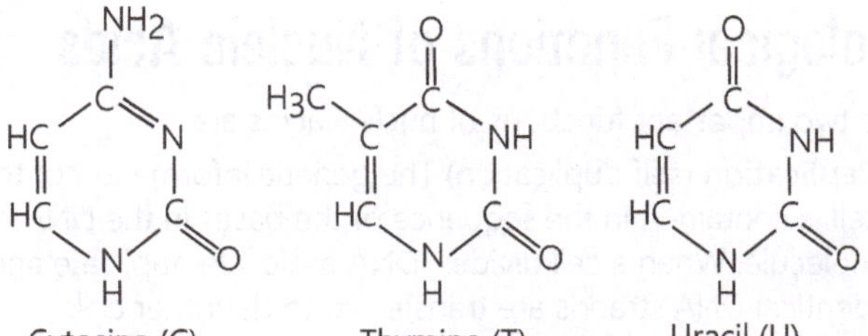

Cytosine (C) Thymine (T) Uracil (U)

Structures of pyramidines

Structure of Nucleic Acids

- A unit formed by the attachment of base to 1′ position of sugar is known as **nucleoside.** When nucleoside is linked to phosphoric acid at 5′-position of sugar moiety, **nucleotide** is formed. NEET 2023

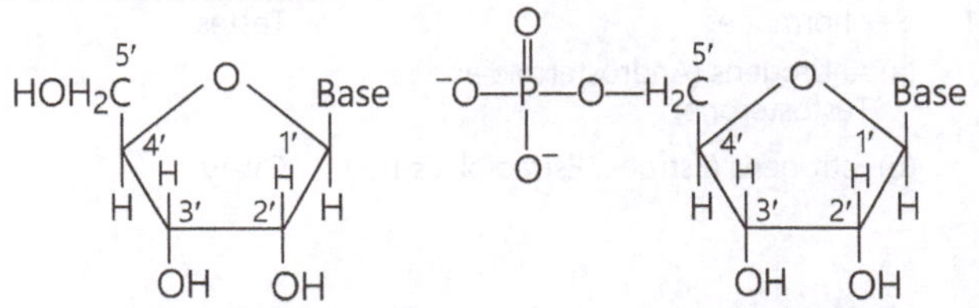

Nucleoside (sugar + base) Nucleotide (sugar + base + phosphate)

- **Nucleotides** are joined together by phosphodiester linkage between 5′ and 3′ carbon atoms of the pentose sugar.
- **Primary structure** gives the information regarding the sequence of nucleotides in the chain of a nucleic acid.
- **Secondary structure** Two strands of polynucleotides coil around each other in the form of double helix. The backbone of each strand consist of sugar phosphate units and base units of each strand are pointed into the interior of helix and are linked through H-bonds.
  - **DNA** has double stranded α-**helix structure** given by *James Watson* and *Francis Crick*. The two strands are complementary to each other because the hydrogen bonds are formed between specific pairs.
  - Unlike DNA, RNA is a single stranded which sometime foldsback on themselves to form a double bond helix structure.
  - Adenine forms 2 hydrogen bonds with thymine, whereas cytosine forms 3 hydrogen bonds with guanine.

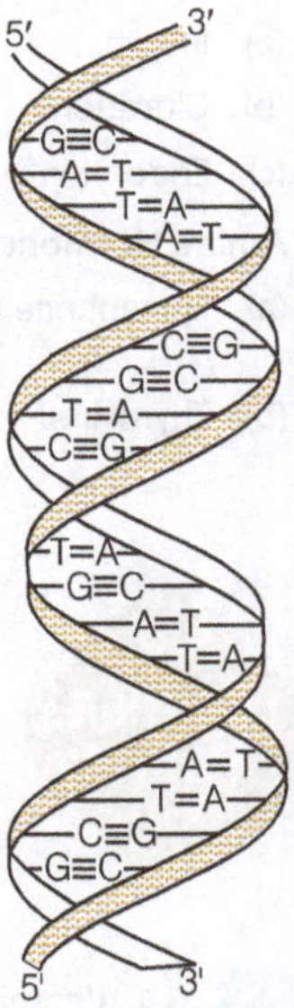

Double strand helix structure for DNA

- **RNA** molecules are of three types, i.e. **messenger RNA** (*m* - RNA), **ribosomal RNA** (*r* - RNA) and **transfer RNA** (*t* - RNA).

Biological Functions of Nucleic Acids

The two important functions of nucleic acids are

- **Replication** (self duplication) The genetic information of the cell is contained in the sequence of the bases in the DNA molecule. When a cell divides, DNA molecule duplicate and identical DNA strands are transferred to daughter cells.
- **Protein synthesis** The protein are synthesised by the RNA molecule in the cell but the message for the synthesis of a particular protein is present in DNA.

Hormones

- These are the molecules that act as intercellular messengers.
- These are produced by endocrine glands in the body and are poured directly in the blood stream which transports them to the site of action.
- Various types of hormones are **steroids** (estrogen and androgens), **polypeptide** (insulin and endorphins), **amino acid derivative** (epinephrine and norepinephrine). They help to maintain the balance of biological activities in the body.

For Concept Master Video

Name, Sources and Functions of Some Hormones

Name	Organ of secretion	Functions
Steroid Hormones		
1. Sex hormones (a) Androgens (Androsterone and Testosterone)	Testes	Control the development and normal functioning of male sex organs during puberty; responsible for male characteristics (deep voice, facial hair, general physical constitution).
(b) Estrogens (Estrone, Estradiol, Estriol)	Ovary	Control the development and normal functioning of female sex organs. Estradiol is the main female sex hormone. It is responsible for developement of secondary female characteristics and participates as in control of menstrual cycle.
(c) Progesterone	Corpus luteum	Prepare uterus for implantation of the fertilized egg.
2. Adrenal cortex hormones or corticoids (glucocorticoids, mineralocorticoides)	Adrenal cortex	Regulate the metabolism of fats, proteins and carbohydrates. Control the balance of water and mineral in the body.
Peptide Hormones		
(a) Insulin	Pancreas	Control the metabolism of glucose decreases blood sugar level.
(b) Glucagon	Pancreas	Increases blood glucose.
(c) Endorphin	Pituitary gland	Response to relieve pain or stress.
Amine Hormones		
(a) Epinephrine and norepinephrine	Adrenal medulla, nervous system	Regulate the body's nervous system by raising the pulse rate, blood pressure etc during emergency.
(b) Thyroxine	Thyroid gland	Controls metabolism of carbohydrates, lipids and proteins.

Caution Points

- Only α-amino acids are obtained on hydrolysis of proteins.
- Most naturally occurring sugars have D-form.
- At isoelectric point, the amino group do not migrate under the influence of electric field.
- In double helix structure of DNA, adenine forms hydrogen bonds with thymine whereas cytosine forms hydrogen bonds with guanine.
- The secondary structure of RNA comprises of single stranded helix which sometimes folds back on itself.

PYQ Notes

1. Vitamin B_{12} can be stored in human body. **JEE Main 2024**
2. Primary structure of proteins remains intact during denaturation process. **NEET 2019**
3. Denaturation of protein makes the protein inactive. **NEET 2017**
4. The central dogma of molecular genetics states that the genetic information flows from DNA $\xrightarrow{\text{Transcription}}$ RNA $\xrightarrow{\text{Translation}}$ Protein. **NEET 2016**
5. Adrenal gland produces adrenaline hormone after receiving a message from the brain under stressful situation. **NEET 2014**

Step by Step

Mastering NCERT

- Concept Builders
- Topical Questions
- Assertion-Reason
- Statement Type
- Matching Type
- Numerical Value
- NCERT Exemplar's
- Past Exams'
- Skill Boosters

Concept Builders

1 Write the name of any two complex biomolecules present in living organisms.

2 Carbohydrates are optically active polyhydroxy aldehydes or ketones. [T/F]

3 On oxidation with HNO_3, glucose yield .... which indicates the presence of primary alcoholic (—OH) group in glucose.

4 Mention the linkage between two monosaccharides units bonded through oxygen atom to form a disaccharide.

5 Glucose is a ketohexose carbohydrate. [T/F]

6 Write the name of the monomer of starch.

7 .... (Amylose/Amylopectin) is a long branched polymer of α-D-glucose units.

8 Biomolecule, which present in milk, cheese, pulses, peanuts etc., are ....

9 Write the name of any basic amino acid.

10 Aspartic acid is a .... amino acid, while glycine is a .... amino acid.

11 Amino acids exists in .... form in aqueous medium.

12 Give any two examples of fibrous proteins present in our body.

13 On hydrolysis of proteins, the α-amino acids are obtained. [T/F]

14 Amino acids which can be synthesised in the body are called essential amino acids. [T/F]

15 During denaturation, primary and secondary structure are destroyed but tertiary structure remain intact. [T/F]

16 Enzymes are .... which reduces the magnitude of ....

17 The conversion of maltose into glucose is possible by enzyme ....

18 Sucrose is a disaccharide which involves glycosidic linkage between C1 of β-glucose and C2 of α-fructose. [T/F]

19 Write the name of any vitamin which can be stored in human body.

20 Complete the following analogy and recognise *X*.
Ascorbic acid : Vitamin C : : Pyridoxine : *X*

21 Which vitamin is helpful in the blood clotting?

22 Deficiency of riboflavin causes cheilosis. [T/F]

23 Write the name of the vitamin which can help in the treatment of osteomalacia.

24 Particles in nucleus of the cell, responsible for heredity are called .... which are made up of proteins and ....

25 The presence or absence of hydroxy group on which carbon atom of sugar differentiates RNA and DNA?

26 Write the name of linkage through which nucleotides are joined together with 5′ and 3′ carbon atoms of pentose sugars.

27 The bond which holds two nucleic acid chains together is ....

28 Identify *X* and complete the following analogy.
Adenine : Thymine : : Cytosine : *X*

29 .... (Thyroid/Glucagon) is a peptide hormone.

30 Name the hormone which is responsible for development of secondary female characteristics?

Topical Questions

Carbohydrates

1 Which of the following statement(s) is incorrect about carbohydrates? NCERT Pg 281

(a) Most carbohydrates have general formula, $C_x(H_2O)_y$.
(b) They were considered hydrates of carbon.
(c) They are stored in animal body as glycogen.
(d) They are generally optically inactive.

2 What will be produced, if a disaccharide molecule, i.e. sucrose is hydrolysed? NCERT Pg 282

(a) Two molecules of fructose.
(b) Two molecules of glucose.
(c) One molecule of glucose and fructose.
(d) One molecule of glucose and maltose.

3 Which of the following is not an example of polysaccharide? NCERT Pg 282

(a) Starch (b) Cellulose (c) Glycogen (d) Maltose

4 Polysaccharides are called non-sugars because NCERT Pg 282

(a) they yield large number of monosaccharide on hydrolysis.
(b) they do not taste sweet.
(c) they are reducing sugars.
(d) they are non-reducing sugars.

5 Two monosaccharides containing aldehydic group and keto group having 5C-atoms respectively are known as NCERT Pg 282

(a) aldopentose, ketonpentose
(b) aldopentose, ketopentose
(c) aldopentose, aldohexose
(d) ketopentose, aldopentose

6 If sucrose is boiled with dilute HCl or H_2SO_4 in alcoholic solution, then NCERT Pg 282

(a) glucose occur in lower form and fructose in excess.
(b) glucose form in excess and fructose in lower form.
(c) glucose and fructose are obtained in equal amount.
(d) both glucose and fructose have very low yield.

7 Which of the following properties of glucose cannot be explained by its open chain structure? NCERT Pg 283, 284

A. Glucose does not form hydrogen sulphite with $NaHSO_3$.
B. On oxidation with HNO_3 glucose give saccharic acid.
C. Glucose is found to exist in two different crystalline forms which are named as α and β.

(a) Only B (b) A and C
(c) A and D (d) Only C

8 Which of the following reagent and condition required for carrying out the following reaction. [NCERT Pg 283]

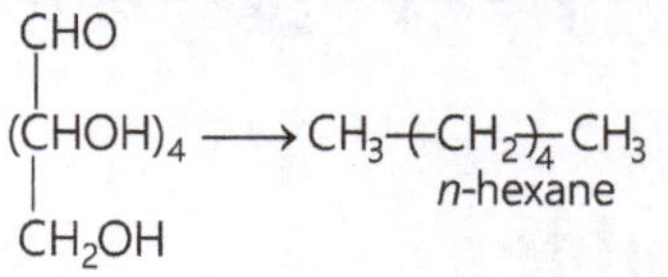

(a) HF, Δ (b) HCl, Δ (c) HBr, Δ (d) HI, Δ

9 Consider the following reaction,

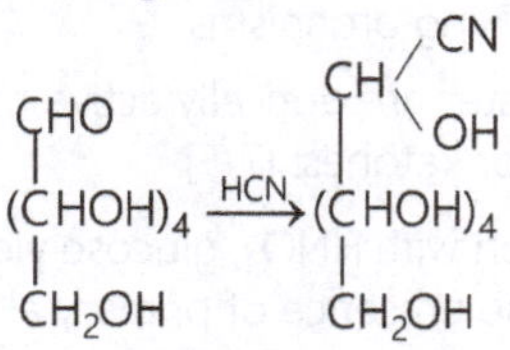

The given reaction confirms the NCERT Pg 283

(a) presence of primary alcoholic group.
(b) five —OH groups attached to different carbon atoms.
(c) all six carbon atoms are linked in a straight chain.
(d) presence of a carbonyl group in glucose.

10 Which product is formed when D-glucose is treated with Br_2 water? NCERT Pg 283

(a) Saccharic acid (b) Gluconic acid
(c) Valeric acid (d) Nucleic acid

11 Glucose react with acetic anhydride, form is NCERT Pg 283

(a) glucose triacetate (b) glucose tetracetate
(c) glucose pentaacetate (d) glucose pentaformate

12 Which product is formed by the oxidation of glucose and gluconic acid with nitric acid? NCERT Pg 284

(a) Rhamnose (b) Saccharic acid
(c) Citric acid (d) Oxalic acid

13 The spatial arrangement of different —OH groups in the molecules is given as NCERT Pg 284

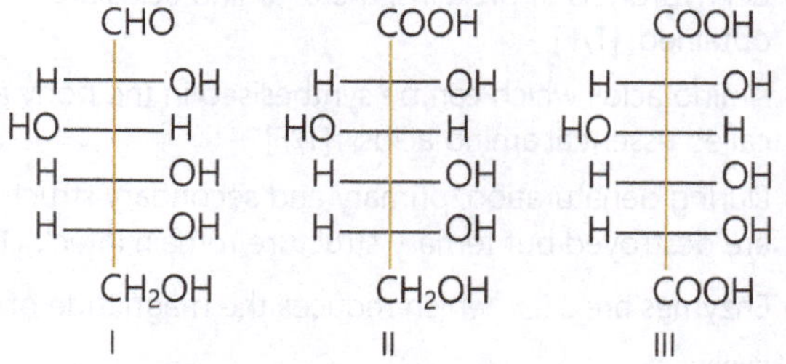

Choose the correct option with names for I, II and III.

(a) I → Gluconic acid II → Glucose, III → Saccharic acid
(b) I → Saccharic acid, II → Glucose, III → Gluconic acid
(c) I → Glucose, II → Gluconic acid, III → Saccharic acid
(d) I → Glucose, II → Saccharic acid, III → Gluconic acid

14 What does 'D' and (+) signifies in D-(+)-glucose? **NCERT Pg 284**

(a) D represents conformation and (+) represents the laevorotatory nature of molecule.
(b) D represents configuration and (+) represents the dextrorotatory nature of molecule.
(c) D represents conformation and (+) represents the dextrorotatory nature of molecule.
(d) D represents configuration and (+) represents the laevorotatory nature of molecule.

15 Glucose $\xrightarrow{\text{HCN}} X \xrightarrow{\text{Hydrolysis}} Y \xrightarrow{\text{HI, }\Delta} Z$

IUPAC name of Y and Z respectively are, **NCERT Pg 283**
(a) hexahydroxyl heptanoic acid, heptane
(b) 2, 3, 4, 5, 6, 7-hexahydroxy hexanoic acid, hexane
(c) pentahydroxyl hexanoic acid, hexane
(d) 2, 3, 4, 5, 6, 7-hexahydroxy heptanoic acid, heptane

16 Assign the configuration to glyceraldehyde (I) and glucose (II). **NCERT Pg 285**

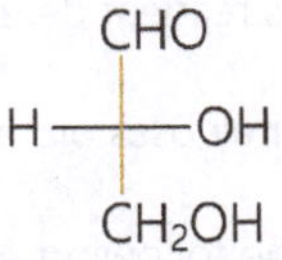

Glyceraldehyde
I

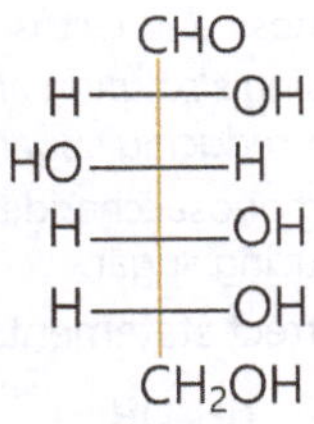

Glucose
II

Choose the correct option.
(a) I → D; II → D
(b) I → L; II → L
(c) I → L; II → D
(d) I → D; II → L

17 At which step, α-form of glucose is obtained? **NCERT Pg 285**

(a) It is obtained by the crystallisation from concentrated solution of glucose at 317 K.
(b) It is obtained by the crystallisation from concentrated solution of glucose at 303 K.
(c) It is obtained by the crystallisation from hot saturated aqueous solution at 303 K.
(d) It is obtained by the crystallisation from hot and saturated aqueous solution at 371 K.

18 At what temperature, the β-form of glucose is obtained by crystallisation from hot and saturated aqueous solution? **NCERT Pg 285**

(a) 303 K (b) 423 K
(c) 371 K (d) 419 K

19 Which of the following statement is not true for glucose? **NCERT Pg 285**

(a) The pentaacetate of glucose does not react with hydroxylamine to give oxime.
(b) It exists in two crystalline forms α and β.
(c) It gives Schiff's test for aldehyde.
(d) It reacts with hydroxylamine to form oxime.

20 Which of the following statement is incorrect about the given structure? **NCERT Pg 285**

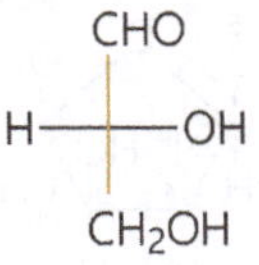

(I)

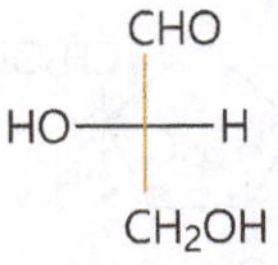

(II)

(a) These are the isomers of glyceraldehyde.
(b) Both contain one asymmetric carbon atom.
(c) Both exist in the two enantiomeric form.
(d) I → (–)-glyceraldehyde said to have D-configuration.
II → (+)-glyceraldehyde said to have L-configuration.

21 Which of the following statement(s) is/are true?
I. Pyran is a cyclic organic compound with one oxygen atom and five carbon atoms.
II. The cyclic structure of glucose is more correctly represented by Haworth structure rather than by open chain structure.
III. Five membered cyclic structure of glucose is called pyranose structure.

Choose the correct answer from the options given below. **NCERT Pg 286**
(a) I and III (b) I and II (c) Only III (d) I, II and III

22 Which set of terms correctly identifies the carbohydrate shown? **NCERT Pg 286**

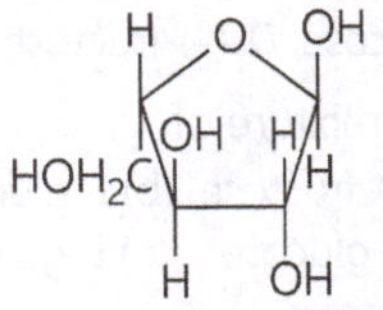

I. Pentose II. Hexose III. Ketose
IV. Aldose V. Furanose VI. Pyranose
(a) I, IV and V (b) I, III and V
(c) II, IV and VI (d) I, IV and V

23 Which of the following statement is correct about fructose? **NCERT Pg 286**
(a) It is dextrorotatory compound.
(b) It exists in the two cyclic forms which is obtained by the addition of —OH at C5 to the $\rangle C{=}O$ group.
(c) It exists as six membered ring.
(d) It is named as furanose as it contain one oxygen and six carbon-atom.

24 Identify the α-D-(–)-fructofuranose and β-D-(–)-fructofuranose from the following structure. NCERT Pg 286

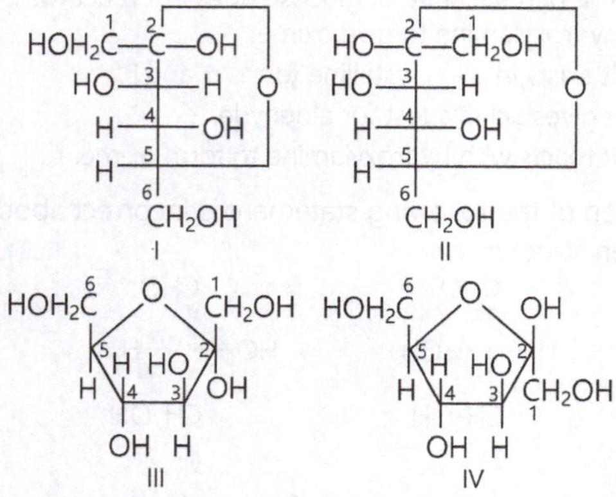

Choose the correct option.

	α-D-(–)-fructofuranose	β-D-(–)-fructofuranose
(a)	I and II	III and IV
(b)	I and III	II and IV
(c)	II and III	I and IV
(d)	II and IV	I and III

25 In sucrose, the two monosaccharides are held together by a glycosidic linkage. The linkage is between NCERT Pg 287
(a) C1 of α-D-glucose and C2 of β-D-fructose
(b) C2 of α-D-glucose and C1 of β-D-fructose
(c) C1 of β-D-glucose and C2 of β-D-fructose
(d) C1 of β-D-glucose and C2 of α-D-fructose

26 Hydrolysis of sucrose with dilute aqueous sulphuric acid yields NCERT Pg 287
(a) 1 : 2 D-(+)-glucose; D-(–)-fructose
(b) 1 : 2 D-(–)-glucose; D-(+)-fructose
(c) 1 : 1 D-(–)-glucose; D-(+)-fructose
(d) 1 : 1 D-(+)-glucose; D-(–)-fructose

27 Invert sugar is a mixture of NCERT Pg 287
(a) D-glucose + D-fructose (b) L-glucose + D-fructose
(c) L-glucose + D-glucose (d) L-glucose + L-glucose

28 Identify the constituents and type of linkage present in maltose. NCERT Pg 287
(a) One α-D-glucopyranose unit and one β-D-glucopyranose unit with 1, 2-glycosidic linkage.
(b) Two α-D-glucopyranose unit with 1, 2-glycosidic linkage.
(c) Two β-D-glucopyranose units with 1, 4-glycosidic linkage.
(d) Two α-D-glucopyranose units with 1, 4-glycosidic linkage.

29 Two monomers in maltose are NCERT Pg 287
(a) α-D-glucose and α-D-glucose
(b) α-D-glucose and α-D-galactose
(c) α-D-glucose and β-D-glucose
(d) α-D-glucose and α-D-fructose

30 Which of the following statement is not true about sucrose? NCERT Pg 287
(a) It is a disaccharide.
(b) The glycosidic linkage is present between C1 of α-glucose and C1 of β-fructose.
(c) It is a non-reducing sugar.
(d) On hydrolysis, it produces glucose and fructose.

31 Which one of the following statements is not true regarding (+)- lactose? NCERT Pg 288
(a) (+)-lactose, $C_{12}H_{22}O_{11}$ contains 8 —OH groups.
(b) On hydrolysis (+)-lactose gives equal amount of D-(+) glucose and D-(+) galactose.
(c) (+)-lactose is a β-glycoside formed by the union of molecule of D-(+)-glucose and a molecule of D-(+)-galactose.
(d) (+)-lactose is not a reducing sugar.

32 Find out the correct option among the following statements. NCERT Pg 287
(a) In reducing sugars, aldehydic and ketonic group are bonded.
(b) Maltose and lactose are non-reducing sugar.
(c) Fehling's solution and Tollen's reagent detect non-reducing sugar.
(d) All monosaccharides, whether aldoses or ketoses are reducing sugar.

33 The correct statements about the following A and B are NCERT Pg 287

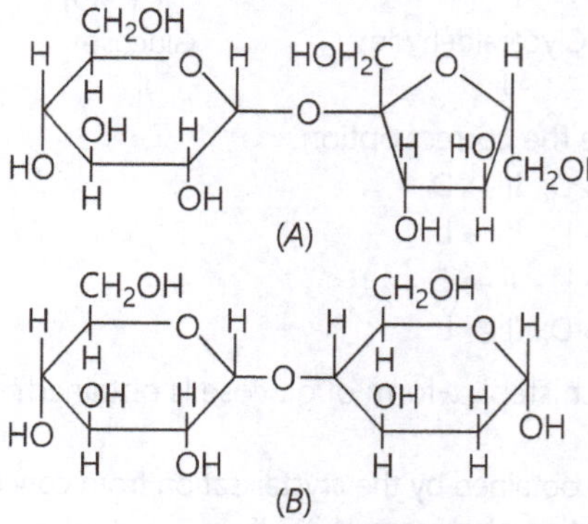

(a) *A* is reducing sugar and *B* is a non-reducing sugar.
(b) *A* is a non-reducing sugar and *B* is a reducing sugar.
(c) The glycosidic linkage in both *A* and *B* are β.
(d) The glycosidic linkage in *A* and *B* are β-and α-respectively.

34 Which of the following statements is incorrect about amylose? NCERT Pg 288
(a) It is soluble in water.
(b) It constitutes about 15-20% of starch.
(c) In amylose α-D-(+)-glucose units are held by C1-C4 glycosidic linkage.
(d) It constitute 85% of starch.

35 Amylopectin is composed of NCERT Pg 288

(a) β-D-glucose, C_1- C_4 and C_2- C_6 linkages
(b) α-D-glucose, C_1- C_4 and C_2- C_6 linkages
(c) β-D-glucose, C_1-C_4 and C_1 - C_6 linkages
(d) α-D-glucose, C_1- C_4 and C_1- C_6 linkages

36 Which of the following polysaccharide is composed only of β-D-glucose units that are joined by glycosidic linkage between C1 of one glucose unit and C4 of the next glucose unit? NCERT Pg 289

(a) Amylose (b) Cellulose
(c) Amylopectin (d) Glycogen

37 Which one of the following is correct description about the structure of cellulose? NCERT Pg 289

(a) Branched, α-(1, 4) and β-(1, 6)-glucose
(b) Unbranched, α-(1, 6)-glucose
(c) Branched, α-(1, 4)-glucose
(d) Unbranched, β-(1, 4)-glucose

38 Which of the following is known as animal starch?

(a) Amylose (b) Amylopectin NCERT Pg 289
(c) Glycogen (d) Cellulose

Proteins

39 Which of the following product is obtained when hydrolysis of protein occurs? NCERT Pg 290

(a) Only β-amino acids (b) Only α-amino acids
(c) Only β-carboxylic acids (d) Only α-carboxylic acids

40 Which one of the following amino acid has (P) $HO—C_6H_4—CH_2$ group? NCERT Pg 291

(a) Lysine (b) Arginine
(c) Proline (d) Tyrosine

41 Among the following compounds, most basic amino acid is NCERT Pg 291

(a) serine (b) asparagine
(c) lysine (d) histidine

42 Which of the following is non essential amino acid? NCERT Pg 291

(a) Histidine (b) Methionine
(c) Isoleucine (d) Tyrosine

43 The essential amino acid among the following is

(a) glycine (b) tyrosine NCERT Pg 291
(c) glutamine (d) leucine

44 Which of the following amino acids can be synthesised in the body? NCERT Pg 291

(a) Valine (b) Leucine (c) Lysine (d) Glycine

45 Which of the following is the incorrect statement?

(a) There are 10 essential amino acids. NCERT Pg 291
(b) L-amino acids are represented by writing the $—NH_2$ group on the left side.
(c) Only β-amino acids are obtained on hydrolysis of proteins.
(d) The amino acids which are synthesised in the body are known as non-essential amino acids.

46 Consider the following amino acids. NCERT Pg 291

I. Histidine
II. Proline
III. Threonine
IV. Aspartic acid

Select the essential amino acids from the above given amino acids and choose the appropriate option.

(a) II and III (b) I and IV
(c) I and III (d) I and II

47 Which of the following amino acids is not optically active?

(a) Lysine (b) Glycine NCERT Pg 292
(c) Leucine (d) Glutamine

48 How many number of water molecules are removed from the *n* number of amino acids during the formation of peptide bond? NCERT Pg 292

(a) $(n-1)$ (b) n
(c) $(n/2)$ (d) $(n+1)$

49 In the given reaction,

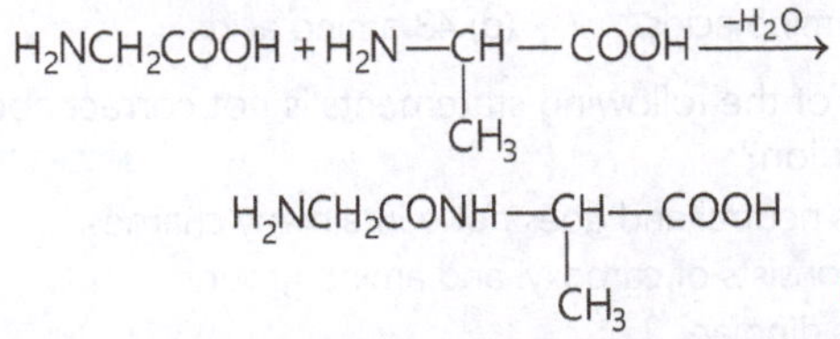

NCERT Pg 292

Choose the correct dipeptide formed in the above reaction.

(a) Alanglycine
(b) Glycylalanine
(c) Alaninglycine
(d) Glycinalanine

50 Select the correct option from the examples of fibrous proteins given below. NCERT Pg 292

I. Insulin II. Keratin
III. Albumin IV. Myosin

(a) I and II (b) II and IV
(c) III and I (d) I and III

51 Which one of the following is the correct representation of tripeptide, i.e. (alanine-glycine- alanine)? NCERT Pg 292

(a) 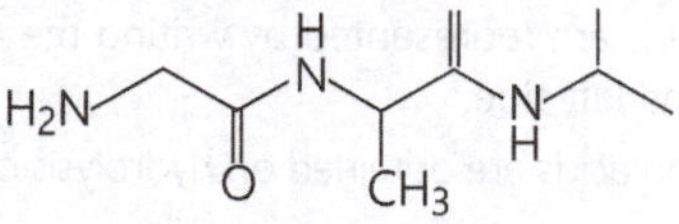

(b) 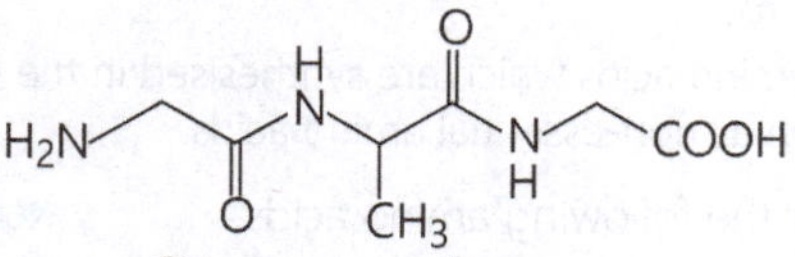

(c) 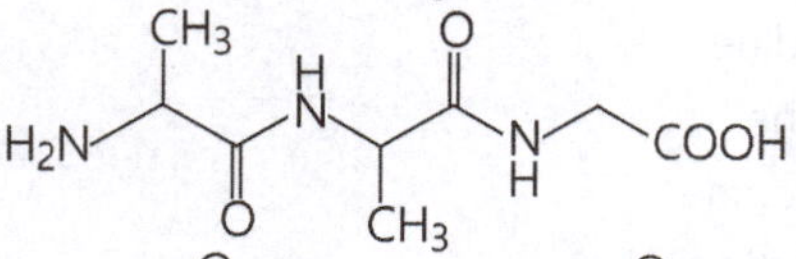

(d) 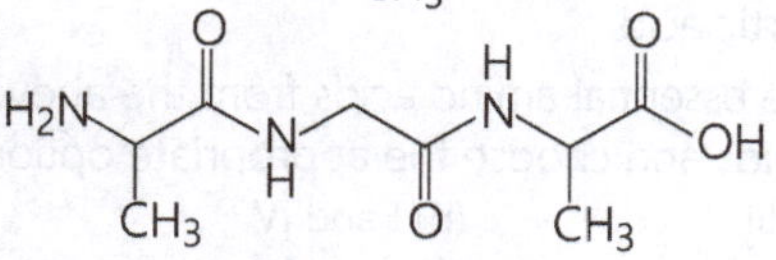

52 "When the polypeptide chains run parallel are held together by hydrogen and disulphide bonds, then fibre like structure is formed. Such proteins are generally insoluble in water." NCERT Pg 292

Which protein satisfy the above information?

(a) Fibrous protein (b) Globular protein
(c) Primary protein (d) Tertiary protein

53 A protein which is responsible for keeping the blood glucose level within the narrow unit is a polypeptide of

(a) 36 amino acids (b) 27 amino acids
(c) 51 amino acids (d) 43 amino acids

54 Which of the following statements is not correct about a Zwitter ion? NCERT Pg 292

(a) It is neutral and does not contain any charges.
(b) It consists of carboxyl and amino groups.
(c) It is dipolar.
(d) Many amino acids exist as Zwitter ions.

55 Which of the following is incorrect about amino acids? NCERT Pg 292

(a) Glycine is the only naturally occurring amino acid which is optically inactive.
(b) Most of naturally occurring amino acids have D-configuration.
(c) Alanine has one amino and one carboxylic group.
(d) Amino acids are the constituents of all proteins.

56 Which of the following statements is incorrect about the secondary structure of protein? NCERT Pg 292, 293

(a) It refers to the shape in which long polypeptide chain can exist.
(b) It exists in two different type of structures, i.e. α-helix and β-pleated sheet structure.
(c) Its structure arises due to regular folding of the backbone of the polypeptide chain.
(d) There is covalent bonding between $>C{=}O$ and —NH groups of the peptide bond.

57 Which of the following statements is incorrect about globular proteins? NCERT Pg 293

(a) Globular proteins are usually soluble in water.
(b) In these proteins, chains of polypeptides coil around each other to give a spherical shape.
(c) Insulin is an example of globular protein.
(d) Keratin is an example of globular protein.

58 The spatial arrangement of the two or more polypeptide chains with respect to each other is known as NCERT Pg 293

(a) primary structure
(b) secondary structure
(c) tertiary structure
(d) quaternary structure

59 Which of the following is incorrect? NCERT Pg 293, 295

(a) The coagulation of egg white on boiling is an example of peptisation.
(b) β – pleated structure arises due to the regular folding of the backbone of the polypeptide chain due to the hydrogen bonding between $(-\underset{\underset{O}{\|}}{C}-)$ and —NH— groups of the peptide bond.
(c) Tryptophan is an essential amino acids.
(d) Except glycine, all other naturally occurring of amino acids are optically active.

60 The correct statement about the denaturation of protein is NCERT Pg 294

(a) during denaturation, 1° and 2°structures of proteins are destroyed but 3° structure remains intact.
(b) during denaturation, 2° and 3°structures of proteins are destroyed but 1° structure remains intact.
(c) during denaturation, 1° and 3°structures of proteins are destroyed but 2° structure remains intact.
(d) during denaturation, 1° structures of proteins is destroyed but 2° and 3° structure remains intact.

Enzymes and Vitamins

61 Which of the following statement is incorrect regarding enzymes? NCERT Pg 295

(a) They are mostly proteinous in nature.
(b) They are essential as biocatalysts.
(c) They have a very large turnover number.
(d) Their action is not specific.

62 What is the common name given to the enzyme which catalyse the oxidation of one substrate with simultaneous reduction of another substrate? **NCERT Pg 295**

(a) Reductioxidase (b) Oxidonductase
(c) Oxidoreductase (d) Reductoxides

63 $\underset{\text{(Maltose)}}{C_{12}H_{22}O_{11}} \xrightarrow{X} 2C_6H_{12}O_6$

The above reaction is forwarded by the catalyst '*X*'. What is the nature of '*X*'? **NCERT Pg 295**

(a) It is an amino acid.
(b) It is a polysaccharide.
(c) It is a globular protein.
(d) It is a nucleic acid.

64 Which one of the following statements is incorrect about enzyme catalysts? **NCERT Pg 295**

(a) They are mostly globular proteins.
(b) Their action is specific.
(c) They are denatured by ultraviolet rays and at high temperature.
(d) They are least reactive at optimum temperature.

65 Which of the following statements regarding vitamins is/are incorrect? **NCERT Pg 295**

I. They are the organic compounds required in small amounts in the diet but their deficiency causes specific disease.
II. Their synthesis can not takes place in plants but human body can synthesise them.
III. They are necessary to perform the specific biological functions for the normal maintenance of optimum growth and health of the organism.

Choose the correct answer from the given options given below.

(a) Only I (b) Only II
(c) I and II (d) II and III

66 Why vitamin C must be supplied regularly in diet? **NCERT Pg 296**

(a) It is fat soluble vitamin, hence stored in the body and cannot be used on regular basis.
(b) It is water soluble vitamin, hence excreted in urine and cannot be stored in the body.
(c) It is required in a large amount by the body, hence supplied regularly.
(d) It is a water soluble vitamin hence used by the body on daily basis and is to be supplied regularly.

67 Pyridoxine is also known as **NCERT Pg 296**

(a) vitamin B_2 (b) vitamin B_6
(c) vitamin B_{12} (d) vitamin B_1

68 Which of the following acids is a vitamin? **NCERT Pg 296**

(a) Aspartic acid (b) Ascorbic acid
(c) Adipic acid (d) Saccharic acid

69 Which of the following disease is caused by the deficiency of vitamin E? **NCERT Pg 297**

(a) *Beri-beri* (b) Rickets
(c) Scurvy (d) Muscular weakness

70 Deficiency of which vitamin causes convulsions **NCERT Pg 296**

(a) vitamin B_{12} (b) vitamin D
(c) vitamin B_6 (d) vitamin K

71 Cheilosis is caused by the deficiency of which vitamin? **NCERT Pg 296**

(a) Thiamine (b) Riboflavin
(c) Pyridoxine (d) Ascorbic acid

72 Choose the correct match **NCERT Pg 296**

(a) Vitamin B_2- Fish liver oil
(b) Vitamin B_{12} - Dark green leafy vegetables
(c) Vitamin A-Sunlight exposure
(d) Vitamin E- Germ oil

Nucleic Acids

73 Which of the following combination is correct between nucleic acid and its respective sugar base? **NCERT Pg 297**

(a) DNA $\rightarrow$ β-D-3-deoxyribose
(b) DNA $\rightarrow$ β-D-1-deoxyribose
(c) RNA $\rightarrow$ β-D-ribose
(d) RNA $\rightarrow$ β-D-3-deoxyribose

74 Select the base which is not common between DNA and RNA. **NCERT Pg 298**

(a) Adenine (A) (b) Guanine (G)
(c) Cytosine (C) (d) Uracil (U)

75 Which of the following bases is absent in RNA? **NCERT Pg 298**

(a) 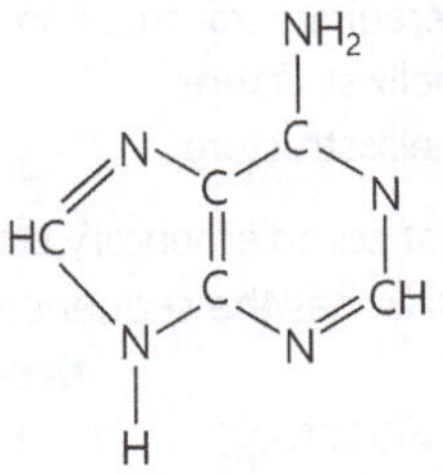

(b) 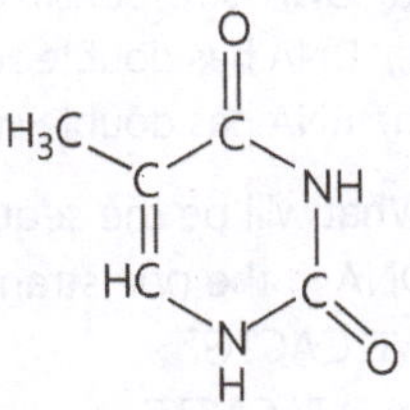

(c) 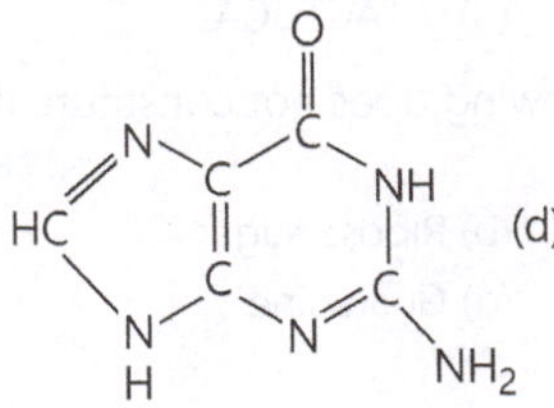

(d) 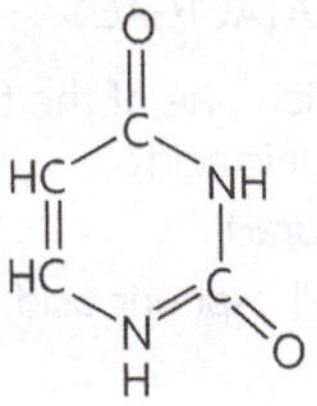

76 Consider the following reaction,

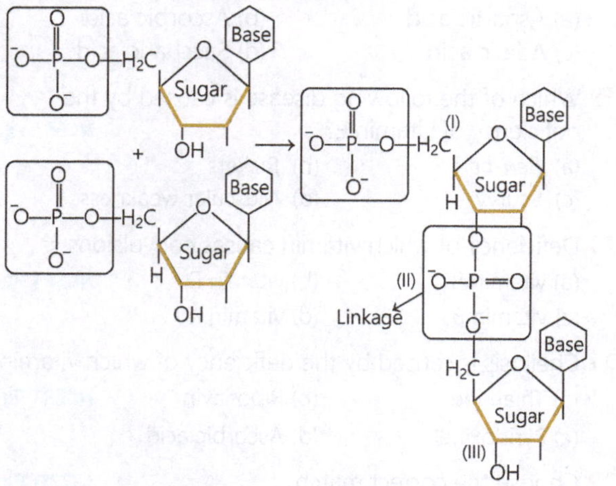

Identify I, II and III in the above figure and mark the correct option : NCERT Pg 299

(a) I → 3′ end of chain,
II → Phosphodiester linkage,
III → 5′ end of chain

(b) I → 3′ end of chain,
II → Phosphate linkage,
III → 5′ end of chain

(c) I → 5′ end of chain,
II → Phosphodiester linkage,
III → 3′ end of chain

(d) I → 5′ end of chain,
II → Phosphate linkage,
III → 3′ end of chain

77 Which of the following was discovered by the J. D. Watson and F. Crick? NCERT Pg 299

(a) Chromosome is made up of protein and nucleic acid.
(b) DNA is responsible for hereditary transmission.
(c) DNA has double strand helix structure.
(d) RNA has double strand helix structure.

78 What will be the sequence of complementary strand of DNA, if the one strand of DNA has the sequence of TATGACTG? NCERT Pg 299

(a) ATACACTC (b) ACGTTGAC
(c) ATACTGAC (d) ATACTGCA

79 Which one of the following does not constitute the nucleic acid? NCERT Pg 299

(a) Uracil (b) Ribose sugar
(c) Phosphoric acid (d) Guanidine

80 Which of the following statement is not true about RNA? NCERT Pg 299

(a) Synthesis of protein is regulated by RNA.
(b) It has always double stranded α-helix structure.
(c) It can not replicate.
(d) It is present in the nucleus of the cell.

81 Which of the following is incorrect about DNA fingerprinting? NCERT Pg 300

(a) It is used in forensic laboratories for identification of criminals.
(b) It is same for every cell and can be altered by any known treatment.
(c) It is used to identify the dead bodies in any accident by comparing the DNA's of parents.
(d) It is used to identify racial groups to rewrite biological evolution.

Hormones

82 Which of the following is not a hormone? NCERT Pg 300

(a) Insulin
(b) Endorphins
(c) Norepinephrine
(d) Thymine

83 The major role of insulin is NCERT Pg 300

(a) to decrease the glucose level in human body.
(b) to keep the blood glucose level within the narrow limit.
(c) to regulate growth.
(d) to transport minerals.

84 Choose the incorrect statement about hormones from the given options. NCERT Pg 300

(a) They are molecules that act as intercellular messengers.
(b) They are produced by endocrine gland in the body and are poured directly in the blood stream.
(c) They help to maintain the balance of biological activities in the body.
(d) Insulin is a steroid hormone.

85 Choose the correct statement about steroid hormone. NCERT Pg 301

(a) Epinephrine is an example of steroid hormone.
(b) They are produced by adrenal cortex and gonads.
(c) Glucocorticoids control the level of excretion of water and salt by kidney.
(d) Mineralocorticoids control the carbohydrate metabolism.

86 Choose the incorrect statements about sex hormones. NCERT Pg 301

(a) Sex hormones are released by gonads and are responsible for the development of secondary sex characters.
(b) Testosterone is the major sex hormone produced in males.
(c) Estradiol is the main male sex hormone which is responsible for deep voice and facial hair in males.
(d) Progesterone is responsible for preparing uterus for implantation of fertilised egg.

87 If adrenal cortex does not function properly then one of the results may be NCERT Pg 301

(a) hypothyroidism (b) hypoglycemia
(c) deep voice, facial hair (d) menstrual cycle

88 Which of the following hormone is an iodinated derivate of amino acid tyrosine and abnormally low level of it leads to hypothyroidism? NCERT Pg 301

(a) Epinephrine (b) Estrogen
(c) Thyroxine (d) Estradiol

89 Addison's disease is treated by NCERT Pg 301

(a) glucocorticoids
(b) norepinephrine
(c) epinephrine
(d) thyroxin

90 The hormone responsible for preparing the uterus for implantation of fertilised egg is NCERT Pg 301

(a) estroadiol (b) testosterone
(c) glucocorticoid (d) progesterone

Assertion-Reason

Directions (Q. Nos. 1-13) *In the following question Assertion (A) followed by Reason (R) is given below. Choose the correct option out of the choices given below.*

(a) Both A and R are true and R is the correct explanation of A.
(b) Both A and R are true but R is not the correct explanation of A.
(c) A is true but R is false.
(d) A is false but R is true.

1 Assertion (A) Acetic acid is not a carbohydrate.
Reason (R) Acetic acid fits into general formula of carbohydrate, i.e. $C_x(H_2O)_y$. NCERT Pg 281

2 Assertion (A) Rhamnose is a carbohydrate.
Reason (R) Rhamnose does not fit into the general formula of carbohydrate, i.e. $C_x(H_2O)_y$. NCERT Pg 281

3 Assertion (A)

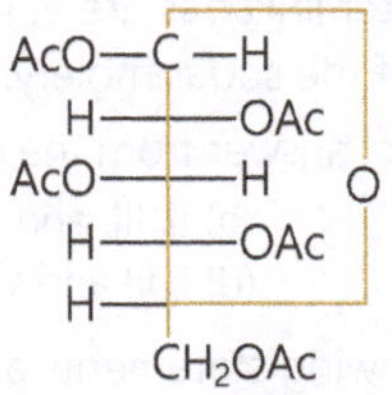

NCERT Pg 283

This compound does not form oxime.
Reason (R) Glucose pentaacetate does not have a free —OH group at C1 and so it cannot be converted to the open chain form to give —CHO group. Hence, it does not form the oxime.

4 Assertion (A) Glucose does not form the hydrogen bisulphite addition product.
Reason (R) Glucose is not so reactive to form the product with $NaHSO_3$. NCERT Pg 285

5 Assertion (A) Glucose does not give 2, 4-DNP test.
Reason (R) Glucose exists in cyclic hemiacetal form. NCERT Pg 285

6 Assertion (A) Two sugar units are joined by 1, 2-glycosidic bond in sucrose. NCERT Pg 287
Reason (R) It contains C1-glucose and C2-fructose glycosidic bond.

7 Assertion (A) Sucrose is dextrorotatory. NCERT Pg 287
Reason (R) Sucrose on hydrolysis gives dextrorotatory glucose (+52.5°) and laevorotatory fructose (– 92.4°).

8 Assertion (A) Sucrose is called invert sugar. NCERT Pg 287
Reason (R) On hydrolysis of sucrose, a change in the sign of rotation from *dextro* (+) to *laevo* (–) takes place.

9 Assertion (A)Tryptophan is an example of non-essential amino acid. NCERT Pg 291
Reason (R) The amino acids that are not synthesised in human body are essential amino acids.

10 Assertion (A) α-helix structure of proteins is in the shape of right handed screw. NCERT Pg 293
Reason (R) There is hydrogen bond between the >NH group of each amino acid to the >C=O of an adjacent turn of the helix.

11 Assertion (A) Vitamins B and C must be supplied regularly in the diet. NCERT Pg 296
Reason (R) Vitamins B and C are soluble in water which are readily excreted through urine and cannot be stored (except vitamin B_{12}) in our body.

12 Assertion (A) The two strands of DNA are complementary to each other. NCERT Pg 299

Reason (R) In DNA, adenine forms hydrogen bonds with cytosine and thymine forms hydrogen bonds with guanine.

13 Assertion (A) DNA is responsible for maintaining the identity of different species of organisms over millions of years. NCERT Pg 300

Reason (R) DNA molecule is capable of self duplication during cell division and identical DNA strands are transferred to daughter cells.

Statement Type Questions

Directions (Q. Nos. 1-5) *In the following questions, two statements (I & II) are given. In the light of the given statements, choose the correct option given below.*

(a) Both Statement I and Statement II are false.
(b) Statement I is true but Statement II is false.
(c) Statement I is false but Statement II is true.
(d) Both Statement I and Statement II are true.

1 Statement I Lactose sugar is present in the milk.

Statement II There are two monosaccharide units present in the lactose, i.e. glucose and galactose. NCERT Pg 288

2 Statement I At isoelectric point, the amino acids does not migrate under the influence of electric field.

Statement II At isoelectric point, amino acid exists as a Zwitter ion. NCERT Pg 292

3 Statement I Protein with a unique 3-D structure and biological activity is called a native protein.

Statement II Protein denaturation occurs when a protein in its native form is remain unchanged. NCERT Pg 293, 294

4 Statement I Vitamin D cannot be stored in our body.

Statement II Vitamin D is fat soluble vitamin and is excreted from the body in urine. NCERT Pg 296

5 Statement I Hormones are molecules that act as intercellular messengers.

Statement II Insulin is released in response to the rapid rise in blood glucose level. NCERT Pg 300

6 Which of the following statement(s) is/are incorrect? NCERT Pg 283, 288, 291, 297

I. The product obtained when glucose is reacted with acetic anhydride confirms the presence of five —OH group.

II. Hydrolysis of sucrose brings, about a change in the sign of rotation from *dextro* (+) to *laevo* (–) and the product named is invert sugar.

III. The following chain of amino acid can be synthesised in body.

Gly — Leu — Asp — Pro — His — Met — Ser — Tyr

IV. An increase in blood clotting time is due to lack of vitamin K is the body.

V. The activation energy change in hydrolysis of sucrose is due to enzyme, glucose.

Choose the correct answer from the options given below.

(a) I and III (b) III and V
(c) II , III and V (d) IV and V

7 Which of the following statement(s) is/are correct? NCERT 284, 287, 292, 299

I. A solution of sucrose in water is dextrorotatory but on hydrolysis in presence of dil. HCl, it becomes laevorotatory.

II. Carbohydrates can be classified on the basis of optical activity .

III. Serine is an example of a polar but uncharged amino acid.

IV. Monomer of sucrose can be classified as a oligosaccharides.

V. In both DNA and RNA, heterocyclic base and phosphate ester linkages are at C1 and C5 respectively of the sugar moiety.

Choose the correct answer from the options given below.

(a) I and IV (b) II, III, and V
(c) II and IV (d) I, III and V

8 Which of the following statements are correct? NCERT Pg 285, 293, 299, 301

I. The α- form of glucose (m. p. 419 K) is obtained by crystallisation from hot and saturated aqueous solution at 371 K.

II. β- pleated structure is further folding of polypeptide chains of amino acids.

III. The following pairs can be seen in a RNA molecule.

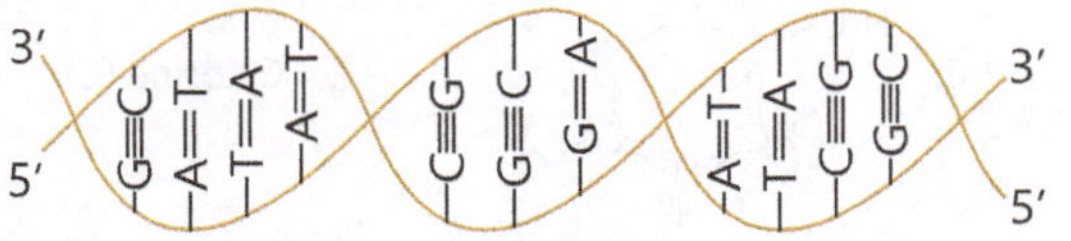

IV. Lethargic person is suggested to take iodised salt.

Choose the correct answer from the options given below.

(a) I, II and IV (b) III and IV

(c) Only IV (d) I, III and IV

9 Which of the following statements are incorrect? NCERT Pg 286, 287, 299

I. Complete hydrolysis of DNA (or) RNA yields a pentose sugar, phosphoric acid and nitrogen containing heterocyclic compounds. The sugar derived in RNA is

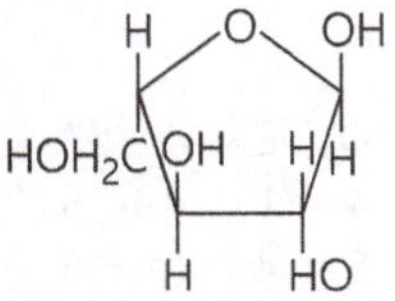

II. DNA molecule is capable of self duplication during cell division and identical DNA strands are transferred to daughter cells.

III. Unfolding of globules and uncoiled helix of a protein is due to physical or a chemical change and due to this protein loses its biological activity.

IV. RNA is responsible for hereditary transmission.

V. In both pyranose and furanose, the (—OH) group at the C5 carbon is involved in the ring formation.

Choose the correct answer from the options given below.

(a) I and IV

(b) II, IV and III

(c) III and IV

(d) I and V

10 Which of the following statements is correct? NCERT Pg 292, 297

I. DNA molecule consists of alternating units of phosphate and the sugar deoxyribose. Each unit has a pair of pentose / hexose bases.

II. Protein found in a biological system with a unique three - dimensional structure and biological activity is called a native protein.

III. To replenish the loss of energy we can use glucose as an instant source of energy.

IV. 'D' and 'L' can be written as 'd' and 'l', as it is only use for the identification of the compounds.

V. Chronic consumption of pyridoxine causes ataxia.

Choose the correct answer from the options given below.

(a) II and V (b) IV and V

(c) I, II and III (d) II, III and V

Matching Type Questions

1 Match the following reactants in Column I with product given in the Column II and select the correct option from the codes given below. NCERT Pg 283

Column I	Column II
A. $CHO-(CHOH)_4-CH_2OH \xrightarrow{NH_2OH}$	1. $COOH-(CHOH)_4-CH_2OH$
B. $CHO-(CHOH)_4-CH_2OH \xrightarrow{HCN}$	2. $CH{=}NOH-(CHOH)_4-CH_2OH$
C. $CHO-(CHOH)_4-CH_2OH \xrightarrow{Br_2\ water}$	3. $CH(CN)(OH)-(CHOH)_4-CH_2OH$

Codes

	A	B	C		A	B	C
(a)	1	2	3	(b)	1	3	2
(c)	2	3	1	(d)	2	1	3

2 Match the following amino acids in Column I with their characteristic feature of side chain are given in the Column II and select the correct option from the codes given below. NCERT Pg 291

Column I	Column II
A. Asparagine (Asn, N)	1. 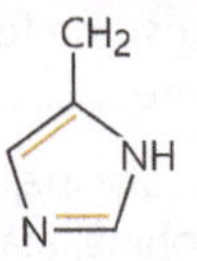
B. Histidine (His, H)	2. $HOOC-CH_2-CH_2-$
C. Glutamic acid (Glu, E)	3. $HO-CH_2-$
D. Serine (Ser, S)	4. $H_2N-COCH_2-$

Codes

	A	B	C	D		A	B	C	D
(a)	4	1	2	3	(b)	4	2	1	3
(c)	4	3	1	2	(d)	4	1	3	2

3 Match the following vitamins given in Column I with their deficiency diseases in Column II and select the option from the codes given below. NCERT Pg 296

Column I	Column II
A. Riboflavin	1. *Beri-beri*
B. Thiamine	2. Scurvy
C. Pyridoxine	3. Cheilosis
D. Ascorbic acid	4. Convulsions

Codes

	A	B	C	D		A	B	C	D
(a)	3	4	1	2	(b)	3	1	4	2
(c)	4	2	1	3	(d)	1	4	3	2

4 Match the following structure of base given in Column I with their name given in the Column II and select the correct option from the codes given below. NCERT Pg 298

Column I	Column II
A. 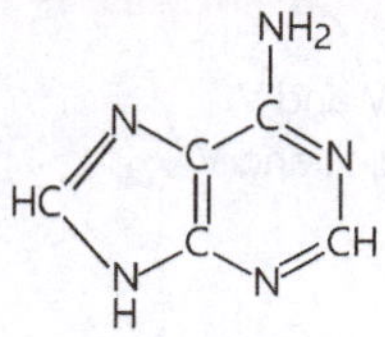	1. Thymine (T)
B. 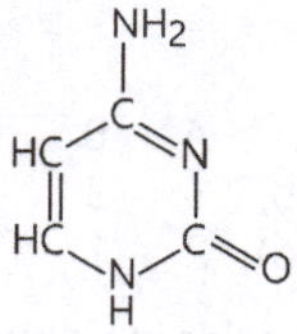	2. Guanine (G)
C. 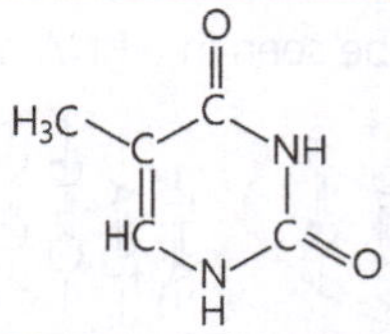	3. Cytosine (C)
D. 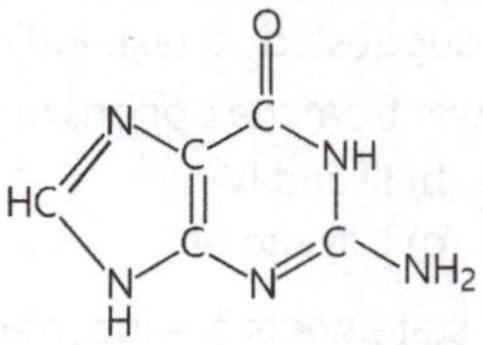	4. Uracil (U)
E. 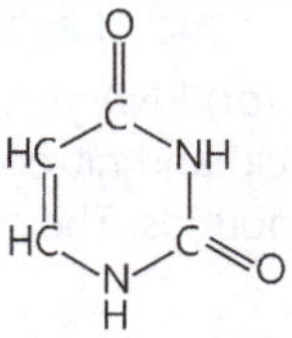	5. Adenine (A)

Codes

	A	B	C	D	E		A	B	C	D	E
(a)	5	3	2	4	1	(b)	5	1	2	4	3
(c)	2	3	1	5	4	(d)	5	3	1	2	4

5 Match the type of hormones given in Column I with their example given in Column II and select the correct option from the codes given below.. NCERT Pg 300, 301

Column I (Type of hormone)	Column II (Example)
A. Steroid	1. Progesterone
B. Polypeptide	2. Norepinephrine
C. Amino acid derivative	3. Glucocorticoids
D. Sex	4. Endorphin

Codes

	A	B	C	D		A	B	C	D
(a)	3	4	2	1	(b)	1	2	3	4
(c)	2	3	1	3	(d)	4	2	1	3

Numerical Value Questions

1 Amongst the following, total number of essential amino acids are......... . NCERT Pg 291

Valine, glycine, phenylalanine, lysine, leucine, isoleucine, methionine, alanine, threonine.

2 The number of $>C{=}O$ groups present in a tripeptide Asp-Glu-Lys is .... NCERT Pg 291

3 Total number of fat soluble vitamins are.... . NCERT Pg 296

4 Number of common pyrimidine present in DNA and RNA is...... . NCERT Pg 298

5 The number of hydrogen bonds present in between DNA base pairs-adenine-thymine and guanine-cytosine is *x* and *y* respectively. The sum of *x* and *y* is .... NCERT Pg 299

NCERT Exemplar's Questions

1 Glycogen is a branched chain polymer of α-D-glucose units in which chain is formed by C1-C4 glycosidic linkage, whereas branching occurs by the formation of C1-C6 glycosidic linkage. Structure of glycogen is similar to

(a) amylose (b) amylopectin
(c) cellulose (d) glucose

2 Which of the following polymer is stored in the liver of animals?

(a) Amylose (b) Cellulose
(c) Amylopectin (d) Glycogen

3 Which of the following statements is not true about glucose?

(a) It is an aldohexose.
(b) On heating with HI it forms *n*-hexane.
(c) It is present in furanose form.
(d) It does not give 2, 4-DNP test.

4 Which of the following reactions of glucose can be explained only by its cyclic structure?

(a) Glucose forms pentaacetate.
(b) Glucose reacts with hydroxylamine to form an oxime.
(c) Pentaacetate of glucose does not react with hydroxyl amine.
(d) Glucose is oxidised by nitric acid to saccharic acid.

5 In disaccharides, if the reducing groups of monosaccharides, i.e. aldehydic or ketonic groups are bonded, these are non-reducing sugars. Which of the following disaccharide is a non-reducing sugar?

(a)
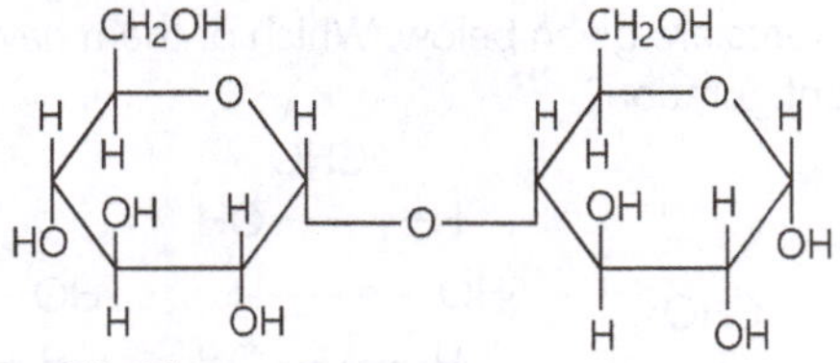

(b)
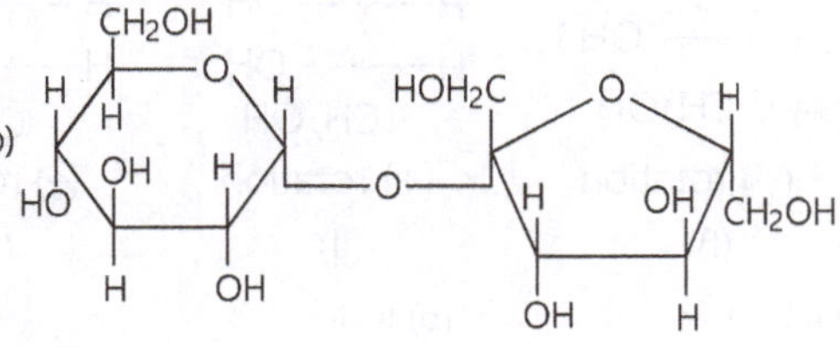

(c)
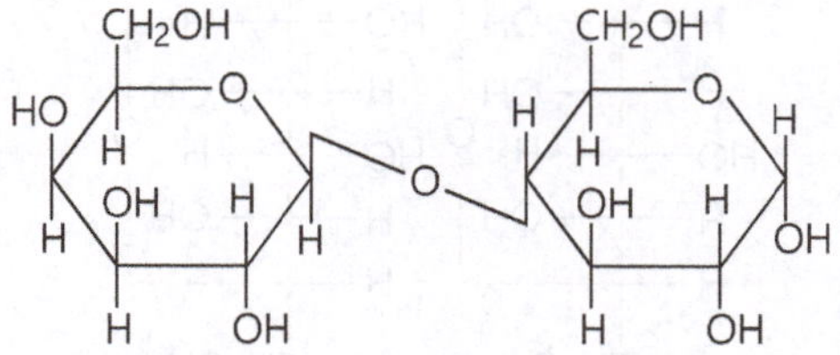

(d)
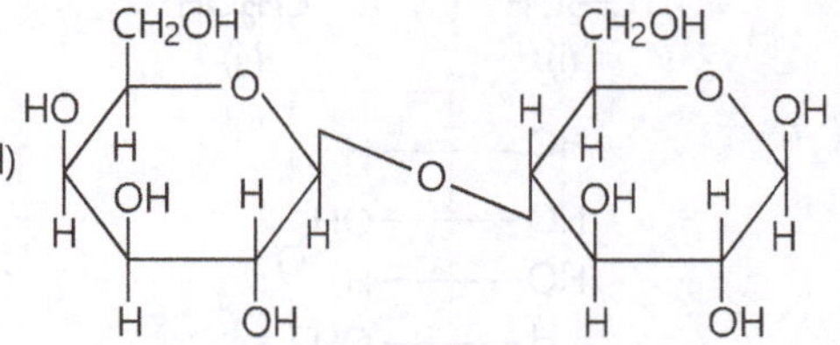

6 Which of the following pairs represents anomers?

(a)
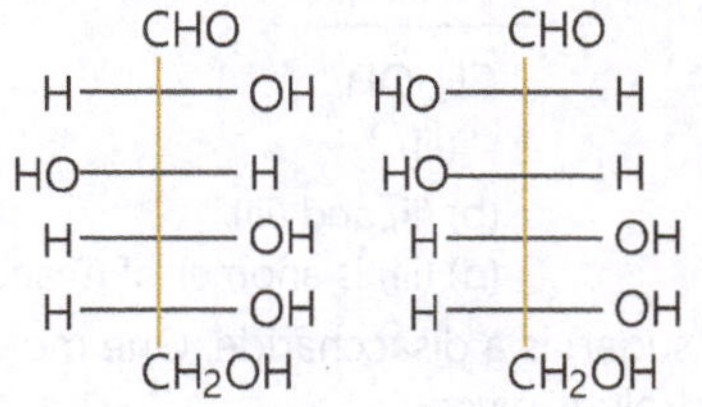

(b)
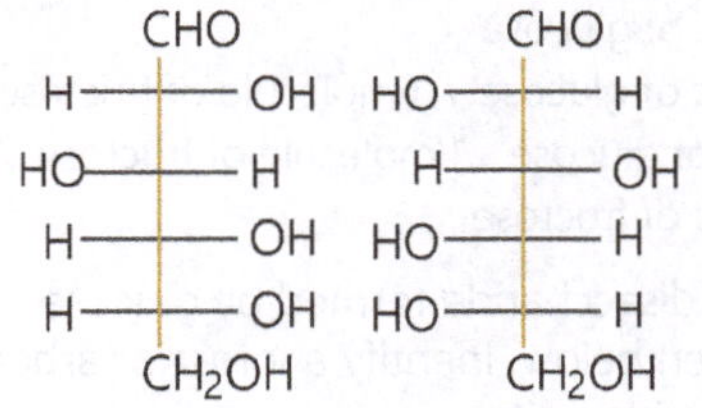

(c)
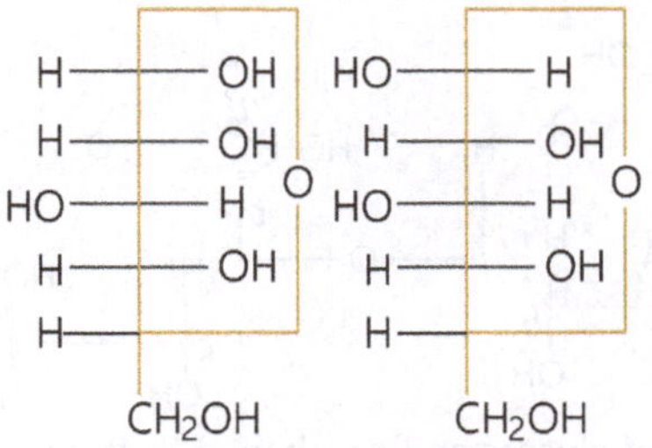

(d)
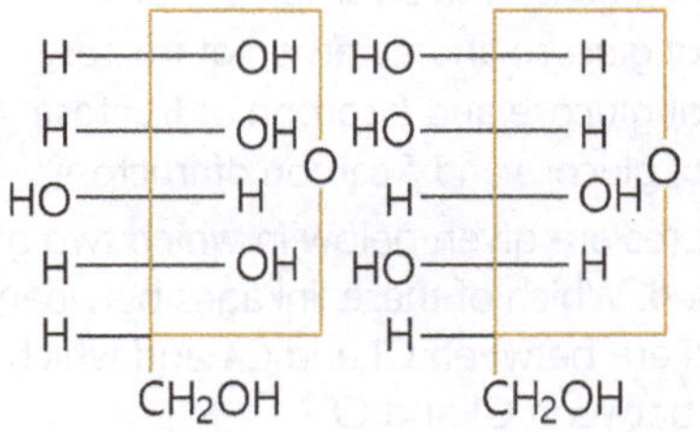

7 Three cyclic structures of monosaccharides are given below. Which of these are anomers?

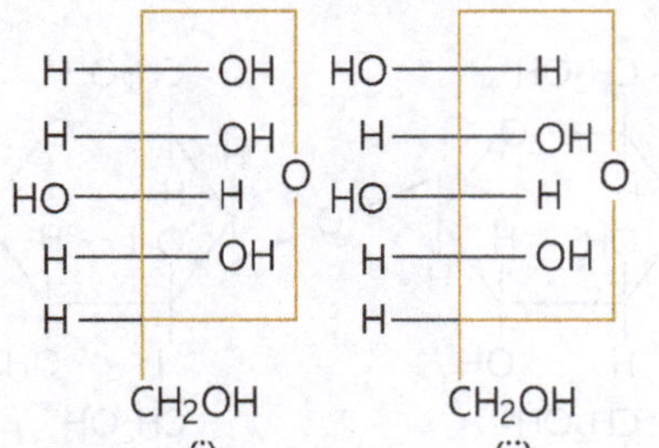

(i) (ii)

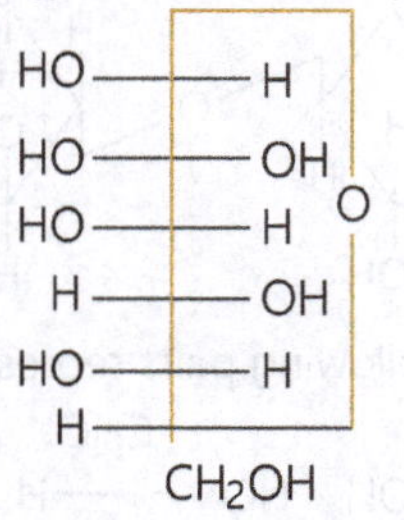

(iii)

(a) (i) and (ii) (b) (ii) and (iii)
(c) (i) and (iii) (d) (iii) is anomer of (i) and (ii)

8 Sucrose (cane sugar) is a disaccharide. One molecule of sucrose on hydrolysis gives
(a) 2 molecules of glucose
(b) 2 molecules of glucose + 1 molecule of fructose
(c) 1 molecule of glucose +1 molecule of fructose
(d) 2 molecules of fructose

9 A structure of disaccharide formed by glucose and fructose is given below. Identify anomeric carbon atoms in monosaccharide units.

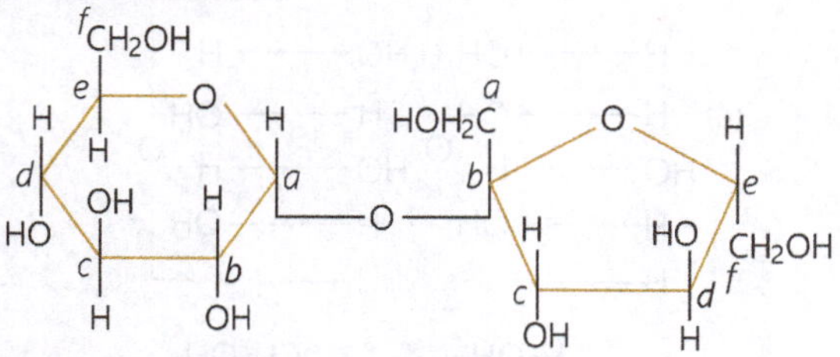

(a) *a* carbon of glucose and *a* carbon of fructose
(b) *a* carbon of glucose and *e* carbon of fructose
(c) *a* carbon of glucose and *b* carbon of fructose
(d) *f* carbon of glucose and *f* carbon of fructose

10 Three structures are given below in which two glucose units are linked. Which of these linkages between glucose units are between C1 and C4 and which linkages are between C1 and C6?

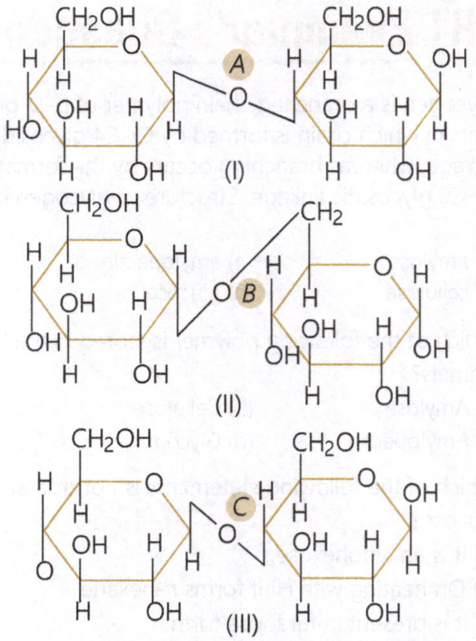

(I) (II) (III)

(a) *A* is between C1 and C4, *B* and *C* are between C1 and C6.
(b) *A* and *B* are between C1 and C4, *C* is between C1 and C6.
(c) *A* and *C* are between C1 and C4, *B* is between C1 and C6.
(d) *A* and *C* are between C1 and C6, *B* is between C1 and C4.

11 Dinucleotide is obtained by joining two nucleotides together by phosphodiester linkage. Between which carbon atoms of pentose sugars of nucleotides are these linkages present?
(a) 5′ and 3′ (b) 1′ and 5′ (c) 5′ and 5′ (d) 3′ and 3′

12 Nucleic acids are the polymers of
(a) nucleosides (b) nucleotides
(c) bases (d) sugars

13 Optical rotations of some compounds alongwith their structures are given below. Which of them have D-configuration?

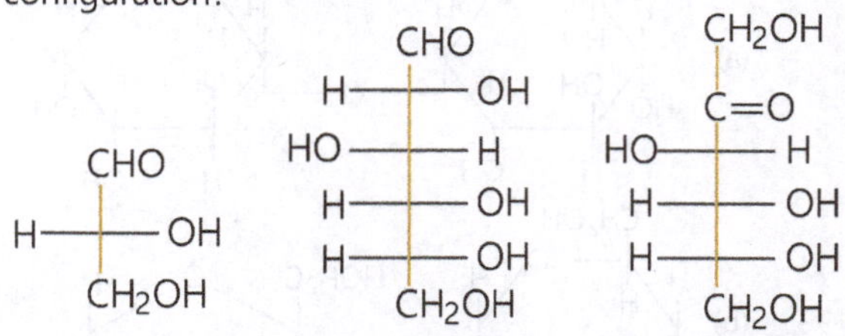

(+) rotation (I) (+) rotation (II) (–) rotation (III)

(a) I, II, III (b) II, III
(c) I, II (d) III

14 Proteins are found to have two different types of secondary structures *viz* α-helix and β-pleated sheet structure. α-helix structure of protein is stabilised by
(a) peptide bonds (b) van der Waals' forces
(c) hydrogen bonds (d) dipole-dipole interactions

15 Each polypeptide in a protein has amino acids linked with each other in a specific sequence. This sequence of amino acids is said to be
(a) primary structure of proteins
(b) secondary structure of proteins
(c) tertiary structure of proteins
(d) quaternary structure of proteins

16 Which of the following B group vitamins can be stored in our body?
(a) Vitamin B_1 (b) Vitamin B_2
(c) Vitamin B_6 (d) Vitamin B_{12}

17 DNA and RNA contain four bases each. Which of the following bases is not present in RNA?
(a) Adenine (b) Uracil
(c) Thymine (d) Cytosine

18 Which of the following bases is not present in DNA?
(a) Adenine (b) Thymine
(c) Cytosine (d) Uracil

Past Exams' Questions

NEET Archive

1 The reagents with which glucose does not react to give the corresponding tests/products are
NCERT Pg 283, 284, NEET 2024
A. Tollen's reagent B. Schiff's reagent
C. HCN D. NH_2OH E. $NaHSO_3$
Choose the correct options from the given below:
(a) B and C (b) A and D (c) B and E (d) E and D

2 Given below are two statements.
Statement I A unit formed by the attachment of a base to 1′-position of sugar is known as nucleoside.
Statement II When nucleoside is linked to phosphoric acid at 5′-position of sugar moiety, we get nucleotide.
NCERT Pg 298, NEET 2023
In the light of the above statements, choose the correct answer from the options given below
(a) Both Statement I and Statement II are false.
(b) Statement I is true but Statement II is false.
(c) Statement I is false but Statement II is true.
(d) Both Statement I and Statement II are true.

3 The incorrect statement regarding enzymes is
NCERT Pg 295, NEET 2022
(a) like chemical catalysts enzymes reduce the activation energy of bio processes.
(b) enzymes are polysaccharides.
(c) enzymes are very specific for a particular reaction and substance.
(d) enzymes are biocatalysts.

4 The RBC deficiency is deficiency disease of
NCERT Pg 296, NEET 2021
(a) vitamin-B_{12} (b) vitamin-B_6
(c) vitamin-B_1 (d) vitamin-B_2

5 Deficiency of which vitamin causes osteomalacia?
NCERT Pg 296, NEET 2020 Phase II
(a) Vitamin A (b) Vitamin D
(c) Vitamin K (d) Vitamin E

6 Which of the following is a basic amino acid?
NCERT Pg 291, NEET 2020
(a) Alanine (b) Tyrosine
(c) Lysine (d) Serine

7 Which structure(s) of proteins remain(s) intact during denaturation process? **NCERT Pg 295, NEET 2019**
(a) Both secondary and tertiary structures
(b) Primary structure
(c) Secondary structure
(d) Tertiary structure

8 The non-essential amino acid among the following is
NCERT Pg 291, NEET National 2019
(a) leucine (b) alanine (c) lysine (d) valine

9 Which of the following compounds can form a Zwitter ion? **NCERT Pg 292, NEET 2018**
(a) Benzoic acid (b) Acetanilide
(c) Aniline (d) Glycine

10 Which of the following statements is not correct?
NCERT Pg 294, 300, NEET 2017
(a) Insulin maintains sugar level in the blood of a human body.
(b) Ovalbumin is a simple food reserve in egg white.
(c) Blood proteins thrombin and fibrinogen are involved in blood clotting.
(d) Denaturation makes the proteins more active.

11 In a protein molecule various amino acids are linked together by **NCERT Pg 292, NEET 2016**
(a) β-glycosidic bond (b) peptide bond
(c) dative bond (d) α-glycosidic bond

12 The correct statement regarding RNA and DNA respectively, is **NCERT Pg 297, NEET 2016**

(a) The sugar component in RNA is ribose and the sugar component in DNA is 2′-deoxyribose.
(b) The sugar component in RNA is arabinose and the sugar component in DNA is ribose.
(c) The sugar component in RNA is 2′-deoxyribose and the sugar component in DNA is arabinose.
(d) The sugar component in RNA is arabinose and the sugar component in DNA is 2′-deoxyribose.

JEE Main Archive

13 Which of the following is the correct structure of L-glucose? **NCERT Pg 285, JEE Main 2024**

(a) 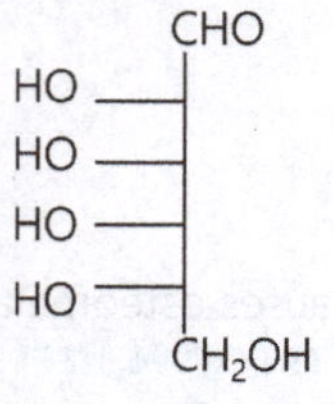

(b) 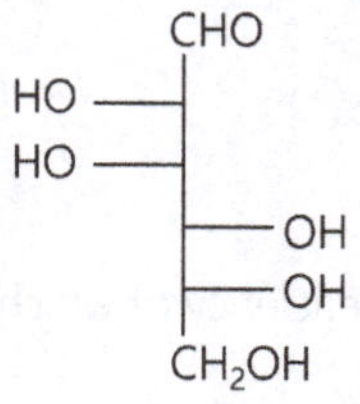

(c) 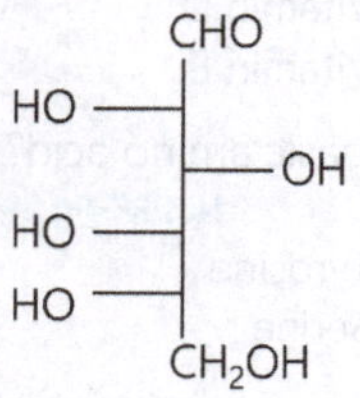

(d) 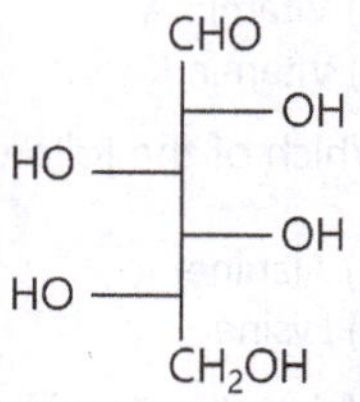

14 Match items of Row-I with those of Row-II.

Row I

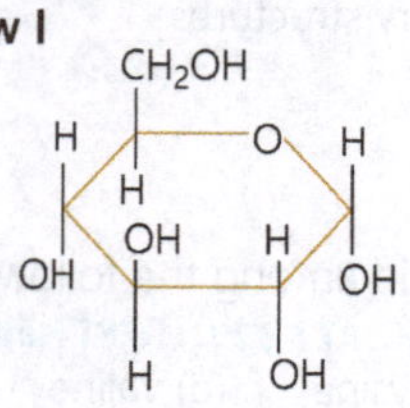

(A)

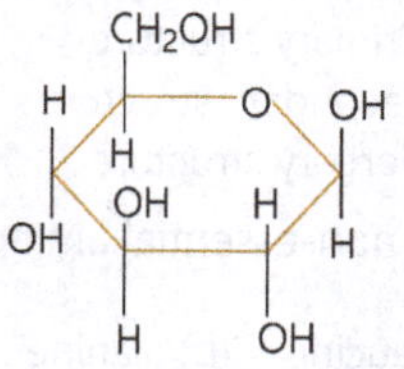

(B)

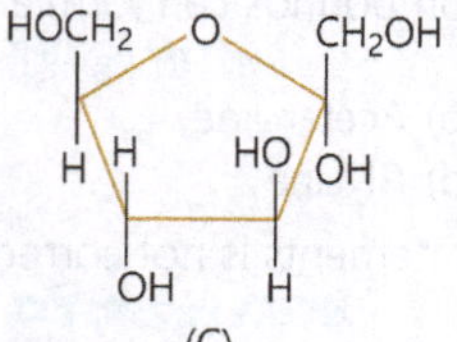

(C)

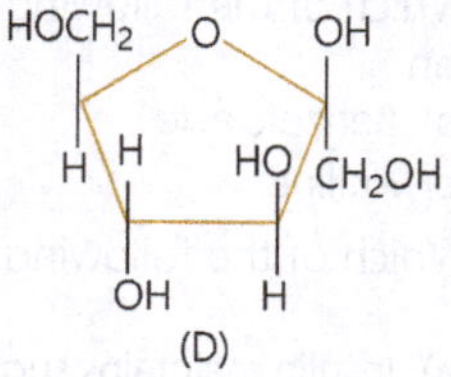

(D)

Row II

(i) α-D-(–)-fructofuranose
(ii) β-D-(–)-fructofuranose
(iii) α-D-(–) glucopyranose
(iv) β-D-(–)-glucopyranose

Correct match is **NCERT Pg 286 ,JEE Main 2023**

(a) A-(iv), B-(iii), C-(i), D-(ii) (b) A-(iii), B-(iv), C-(i), D-(ii)
(c) A-(i), B-(ii), C-(iii), D-(iv) (d) A-(iii), B-(iv), C-(ii), D-(i)

15 Following tetrapeptide can be represented as

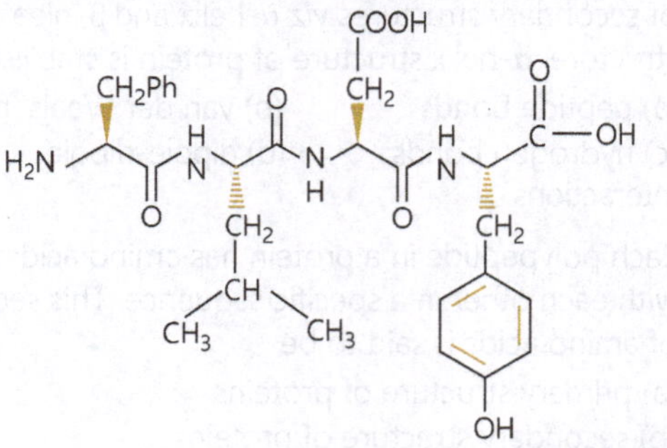

(*F, L, D, Y, I, Q, P* are one letter codes for amino acids) **NCERT Pg 291, JEE Main 2023**

(a) *FLQY* (b) *YQLF*
(c) *FLDY* (d) *PLDY*

16 The correct representation in six membered pyranose form for the following sugar [*X*] is **NCERT Pg 286, JEE Main 2023I**

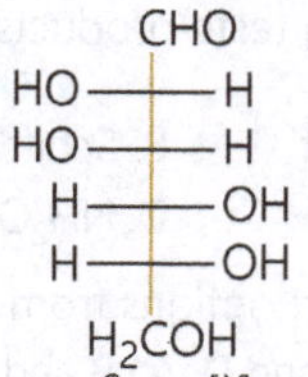

Sugar [*X*]

(a) 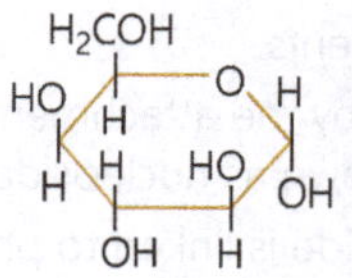

(b) 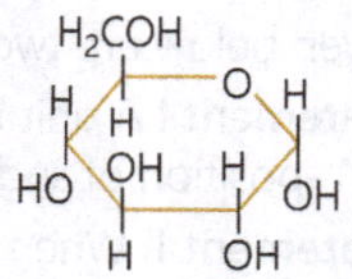

(c) 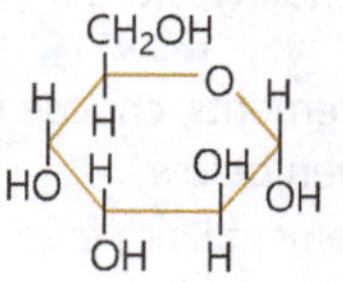

(d) 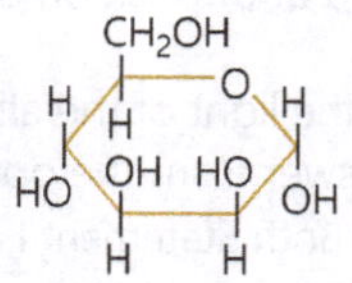

17 Match List-I with List-II.

List-I (Natural amino acid)		List-II (One letter code)
A. Arginine	I.	D
B. Aspartic acid	II.	N
C. Asparagine	III.	A
D. Alanine	IV.	R

Choose the correct answer from the options given below. **NCERT Pg 291, JEE Main 2023**

(a) A-III, B-I, C-II, D-IV
(b) A-IV, B-I, C-III, D-II
(c) A-I, B-III, C-IV, D-II
(d) A-IV, B-I, C-II, D-III

18 Sulphur (S) containing amino acids from the following are
NCERT Pg 291, JEE Main 2023

I. Isoleucine II. Cysteine III. Lysine IV. Methionine
V. Glutamic acid

(a) I, II, III (b) II, III, V (c) II, IV (d) I, IV

19 Given below are two statements.

Statments I Maltose has two α-D-glucose units linked at C1 and C4 and is a reducing sugar.

Statement II Maltose has two monosaccharides: α-D-glucose and β-D-glucose linked at C1 and C6 and it is a non-reducing sugar.

In the light of the above statements, choose the correct answer from the options given below.
NCERT Pg 287, JEE Main 2022

(a) Both Statement I and Statement II are true.
(b) Both Statement I and Statement II are false.
(c) Statement I is true but Statement II is false.
(d) Statement I is false but Statement II is true.

20 Sugar moiety in DNA and RNA molecules respectively are
NCERT Pg 297, JEE Main 2022

(a) β-D-2-deoxyribose, β-D-deoxyribose
(b) β-D-2-deoxyribose, β-D-ribose
(c) β-D-ribose, β-D-2-deoxyribose
(d) β-D-deoxyribose, β-D-2-deoxyribose

21 Which of the following vitamin is helpful in delaying the blood clotting?
NCERT Pg 297, JEE Main 2021

(a) Vitamin C (b) Vitamin B
(c) Vitamin E (d) Vitamin K

22 A non-reducing sugar "A" hydrolysis to give two reducing monosaccharides. Sugar *A* is
NCERT Pg 287, JEE Main 2021

(a) fructose (b) galactose
(c) glucose (d) sucrose

23 Which of the following is not an example of fibrous protein?
NCERT Pg 292,JEE Main 2021

(a) Keratin (b) Albumin
(c) Collagen (d) Myosin

Skill Boosters

1 When a disaccharide '*A*' is boiled with dilute sulphuric acid in alcoholic solution, the formation of two isomers '*x*' and '*y*' takes place. '*x*' on oxidation with nitric acid gives saccharic acid while '*y*' is laevorotatory. The compound '*A*' is

(a) sucrose (b) ribose (c) maltose (d) lactose

2 A sugar '*S*' dehydrates carefully under acidic condition to give furfural which on further reaction with resorcinol gives the product (coloured) after same duration. Identify the sugar '*S*'

(a) aldotetrose (b) ketoterose
(c) aldopentose (d) ketopentose

3 A polysaccharide (*S*) on boiling with dil. H_2SO_4 at 393 K under 2-3 atm pressure yield '*P*'. '*P*' on treatment with bromine water gives gluconic acid. '*S*' contains β-glycosidic linkages only. Compound '*S*' is

(a) cellulose (b) starch (c) amylose (d) amylopectin

4 *L*-isomer of a compound '*A*' ($C_4H_8O_4$) gives a positive test with $[Ag(NH_3)_2]^+$. Treatment of '*A*' with acetic anhydride yields triacetate derivative. Compound (*A*) produces on optically active compound (*B*) and an optically inactive compound (*C*) on treatment with bromine water and HNO_3 respectively. Compound (*A*) is

(a) 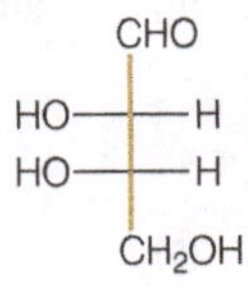

(b) 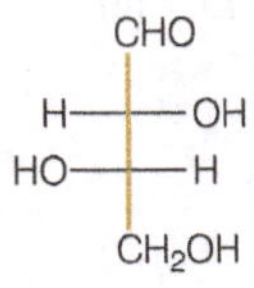

(c) 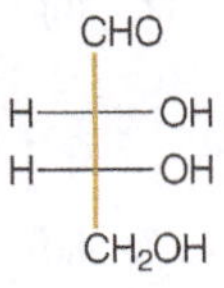

(d) 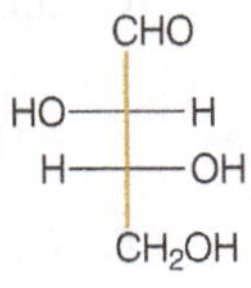

5 Amino acids are the building blocks of proteins. Some amino acids are acidic some basic and some neutral in nature because every amino acid contains amino and carboxyl group simultaneously. So, the amino acids which are showing salt like character in aqueous solution may have composition like.

(a) $—NH_2$ group > —COOH group
(b) $—NH_2$ group < —COOH group
(c) $—NH_2$ group = —COOH group
(d) Only $—NH_2$ group

6 An optically active compound having molecular formula $C_6H_{12}O_6$ is found in two isomeric form (*P*) and (*Q*) in nature. When (*P*) and (*Q*) are dissolved in water, they shows the following equilibrium.

$$\underset{[\alpha]_D = 111°}{(P)} \rightleftharpoons \underset{52.5°}{\text{Equilibrium mixture}} \rightleftharpoons \underset{[\alpha]_D = 19.2°}{(Q)}$$

These isomers are known as

(a) anomers (b) epimers (c) enantiomers (d) homomers

7 During the process of digestion, the proteins present in food material are hydrolysed in the presence of '*X*' which convert it to polypeptides, further involvment of '*Y*' accelerate the process to convert polypeptides into amino acids.

$$\text{Proteins} \xrightarrow{'X'} \text{Polypeptides} \xrightarrow{'Y'} \text{Amino acids}$$

(a) Pepsin and Trypsin (b) Invertase and Zymase
(c) Amylase and Maltase (d) Lipase and Amylase

8 A protein 'X' with molecular weight of 70,000 u, on hydrolysis gives amino acid. One of these amino acid is

(a) $NH_2—CH_2—CH(CH_3)—CH_2CH_2COOH$

(b) $CH_3—CH(CH_3)—CH_2—CH(NH_2)—COOH$

(c) $CH_3—C(CH_3)(NH_2)—CH_2—COOH$

(d) $CH_3—C(CH_3)(NH_2)—CH_2—COOH$

9 When sucrose undergoes hydrolysis, the glycosidic bond is cleaved and two products are formed *a* and *b*, then these products are reacted with Seliwanoff's reagent to form *X*. The correct observation in the above reaction is

(a) formation of blue colour

(b) formation of violet colour

(c) formation of red colour

(d) formation of yellow colour

Correct Codes

Topical Questions

1. (d) 2. (c) 3. (d) 4. (b) 5. (b) 6. (c) 7. (b) 8. (d) 9. (d) 10. (b)
11. (c) 12. (b) 13. (c) 14. (b) 15. (d) 16. (a) 17. (b) 18. (c) 19. (c) 20. (d)
21. (b) 22. (a) 23. (b) 24. (b) 25. (a) 26. (d) 27. (a) 28. (d) 29. (a) 30. (b)
31. (d) 32. (d) 33. (b) 34. (d) 35. (d) 36. (b) 37. (d) 38. (c) 39. (b) 40. (d)
41. (c) 42. (d) 43. (d) 44. (d) 45. (c) 46. (c) 47. (b) 48. (a) 49. (b) 50. (b)
51. (d) 52. (a) 53. (c) 54. (a) 55. (b) 56. (d) 57. (d) 58. (d) 59. (a) 60. (b)
61. (d) 62. (c) 63. (c) 64. (d) 65. (b) 66. (b) 67. (b) 68. (b) 69. (d) 70. (c)
71. (b) 72. (d) 73. (c) 74. (d) 75. (b) 76. (c) 77. (c) 78. (c) 79. (d) 80. (b)
81. (b) 82. (d) 83. (b) 84. (d) 85. (b) 86. (c) 87. (b) 88. (c) 89. (a) 90. (d)

Assertion-Reason

1. (b) 2. (b) 3. (a) 4. (c) 5. (a) 6. (a) 7. (b) 8. (a) 9. (d) 10. (a)
11. (a) 12. (c) 13. (a)

Statement Type

1. (d) 2. (d) 3. (b) 4. (a) 5. (d) 6. (b) 7. (d) 8. (c) 9. (a) 10. (d)

Matching Type

1. (c) 2. (a) 3. (b) 4. (d) 5. (a)

Numerical Value

1. (7) 2. (5) 3. (4) 4. (1) 5. (5)

NCERT Exemplar's

1. (b) 2. (d) 3. (c) 4. (c) 5. (b) 6. (c) 7. (a) 8. (c) 9. (c) 10. (c)
11. (a) 12. (b) 13. (a) 14. (c) 15. (a) 16. (d) 17. (c) 18. (d)

Past Exams'

1. (c) 2. (d) 3. (b) 4. (a) 5. (b) 6. (c) 7. (b) 8. (b) 9. (d) 10. (d)
11. (b) 12. (a) 13. (c) 14. (b) 15. (c) 16. (d) 17. (d) 18. (c) 19. (c) 20. (b)
21. (d) 22. (d) 23. (b)

Skill Boosters

1. (a) 2. (c) 3. (a) 4. (a) 5. (c) 6. (a) 7. (a) 8. (b) 9. (c)

Step by Step

Decoding the Questions

Concept Builders

1 Carbohydrates and proteins.

2 True 3 saccharic acid

4 Glycosidic linkage

5 False 6 α-glucose

7 Amylopectin 8 proteins

9 Arginine 10 acidic, neutral

11 Zwitter ionic 12 Keratin, myosin

13 True 14 False 15 False

16 biocatalyst, activation energy

17 Maltase

18 False 19 Vitamin B_{12}

20 Vitamin B_6 21 Vitamin K

22 True 23 Vitamin D

24 chromosomes, nucleic acids

25 Second

26 Phosphodiester

27 hydrogen bond

28 Guanine 29 Glucagon

30 Estradiol

Topical Solutions

1 (*d*) Carbohydrates are generally optically active because they have one or more chiral carbon atoms.

2 (*c*) Sucrose on hydrolysis gives one molecule each of glucose and fructose.

3 (*d*) Maltose is not an example of polysaccharide.

4 (*b*) Polysaccharides are called non-sugars as they do not taste sweet.

5 (*b*) Monosaccharide containing 5 carbon-atoms for aldehyde group is known as aldopentose and keto group is known as ketopentose.

6 (*c*) If sucrose is boiled with dil. HCl or H_2SO_4 in alcoholic solution, glucose and fructose are obtained in equal amounts. Reaction is as follows

$$\underset{\text{Sucrose}}{C_{12}H_{22}O_{11}} + H_2O \xrightarrow{H^+} \underset{\text{Glucose}}{C_6H_{12}O_6} + \underset{\text{Fructose}}{C_6H_{12}O_6}$$

7 (*b*) 8 (*d*) 9 (*d*)

10 (*b*) The product formed is gluconic acid. The reaction involved is as follows

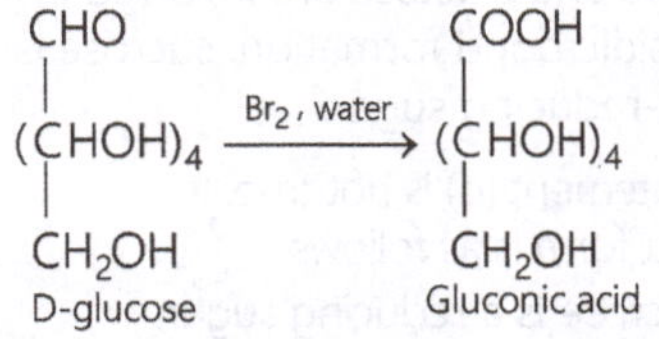

11 (*c*) The given reaction is represented as

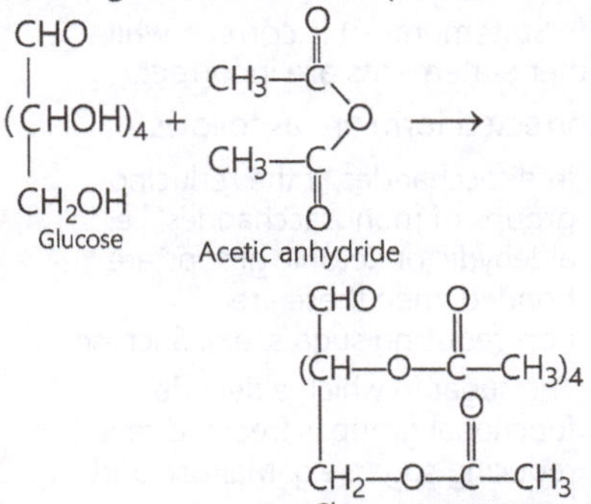

12 (*b*) Glucose and gluconic acid, both on oxidation yields a dicarboxylic acid or saccharic acid. This indicates the presence of primary alcohol (OH) group in glucose.

13 (*c*) 14 (*b*)

15 (*d*) The reaction that takes place are as follows

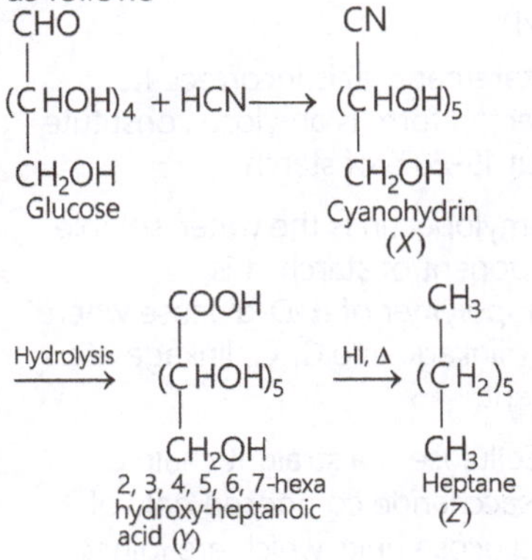

16 (*a*) I represents D-form of glyceraldehyde. II represents D-(+) glucose, —OH on the lowest asymmetric carbon is on the right side which is comparable to (+) glyceraldehyde, so it is assigned as D-configuration.

17 (*b*)

18 (*c*) β-form of glucose (m.p. 423 K) is obtained by crystallisation from hot and saturated aqueous solution at 371 K.

19 (*c*) The incorrect statement is (c). It can be corrected as follows

Glucose does not give Schiff's test due to absence of free —CHO in cyclic form.

20 (*d*) Statement (d) is incorrect. It's correct form is as follows

The letter 'D' or 'L' before the name of any compound indicate the relative configuration of particular stereoisomer.

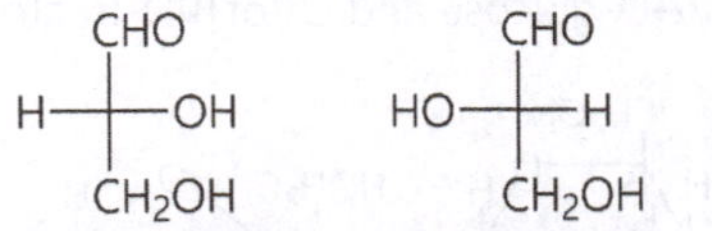

D(+)-glyceraldehyde [I] L(–)-glyceraldehyde [II]

21 (*b*) Statements I and II are correct, while the statement III is incorrect. It's correct form is as follows

The six membered cyclic structure of glucose is called pyranose structure (α or β),in analogy with pyran.

22 (*a*) It is a pentose sugar, it contains 5 carbon atoms.

The ring formed is a five membered ring and is named as furanose with analogy to the compound furan.

The Fischer projection of the ring is

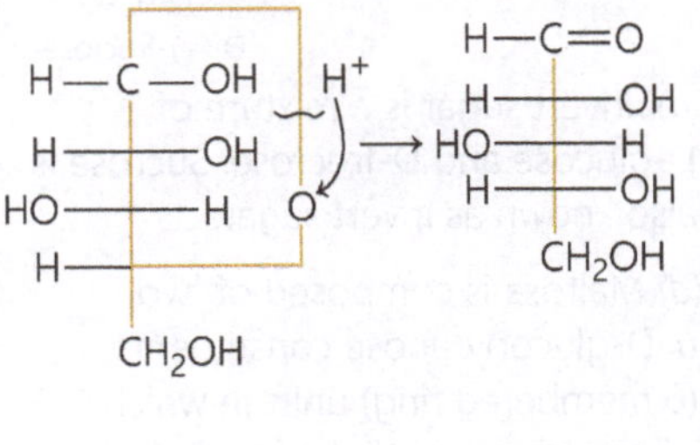

It is an aldose because it contains an aldehyde group in its open chain structure.

23 (*b*) Statement (b) is correct while the other statements are incorrect. Corrected form are as follows

Fructose has the molecular formula $C_6H_{12}O_6$. It belongs to D-series and is a laevorotatory compound. It also exists in two cyclic forms which are obtained by the addition of —OH at C–5 to the $\left(\rangle C{=}O\right)$ group.

The ring, thus formed is a five membered ring and is named as furanose with analogy to the compound furan. Furan is a five membered cyclic compound with one oxygen and four carbon atoms.

24 (*b*)

25 (*a*) In sucrose, the two monosaccharides are held together by a glycosidic linkage. The linkage is between C_1 of α-D-glucose and C_2 of β-D-fructose.

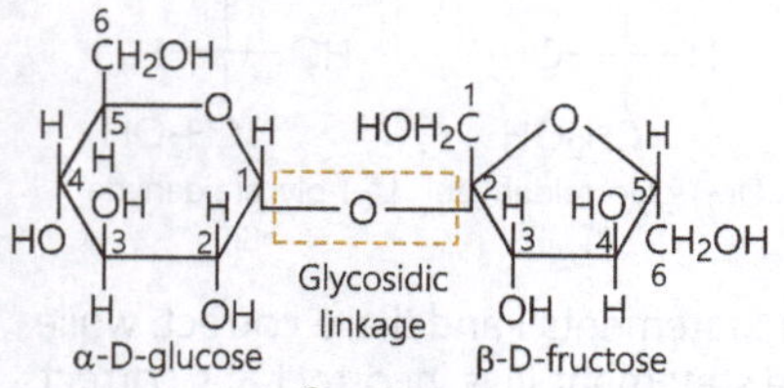

26 (*d*) On hydrolysis of sucrose with dilute aqueous sulphuric acid, it forms an equimolar mixture of D-(+)-glucose and D-(–)-fructose. The reaction for the hydrolysis of sucrose is as follows

$$\underset{\text{Sucrose}}{C_{12}H_{22}O_{11}} + H_2O \xrightarrow{H_2SO_4} \underset{\text{D-(+)-glucose}}{C_6H_{12}O_6} + \underset{\text{D-(–)-fructose}}{C_6H_{12}O_6}$$

27 (*a*) Invert sugar is a mixture of D-glucose and D-fructose. Sucrose is also known as invert sugar.

28 (*d*) Maltose is composed of two α-D-glucopyranose constituents (6 membered ring) units in which C-1 of one glucose is linked to C-4 of another glucose unit. Hence, type of linkage is 1, 4-glycosidic linkage.

29 (*a*) Maltose is a disaccharide formed from monosaccharides α-D- glucose and α-D-glucose *via* $C_1 — C_4$ glycosidic linkage.

30 (*b*) Statement (b) is not true for sucrose. It is linked through a glycosidic linkage between C_1 of α-glucose and C_2 of β-fructose. Since, the reducing groups of glucose and fructose are involved in glycosidic bond formation, sucrose is a non-reducing sugar.

31 (*d*) Statement (d) is not true. It's correct form is as follows

(+)-lactose is a reducing sugar.

Rest other statements are true.

32 (*d*) Statement (d) is correct, while other statements are incorrect.

Corrected form are as follows

- In disaccharides, if the reducing groups of monosaccharides, i.e. aldehydic or ketonic groups are bonded, then these are non-reducing sugars. e.g. Sucrose.
- The sugar in which aldehyde functional group is free, are called reducing sugar. e.g. Maltose and lactose.
- Fehling's solution and Tollen's reagent are used to detect reducing sugars.

33 (*b*) *A* is sucrose it is not a reducing sugar because it doesn't contain hemiacetal group.

B is maltose it is a reducing sugar because it contains a hemiacetal group.

34 (*d*) Statement (d) is incorrect. Its corrected form is amylose constitute about 15-20% of starch.

35 (*d*) Amylopectin is the water-soluble component of starch. It is homopolymer of α-D-glucose where C_1-C_4 linkage and C_1-C_6 linkage are present.

36 (*b*) Cellulose is a straight chain of polysaccharide composed only of β-D-glucose units which are joined by the glycosidic linkage between C_1 of one glucose unit and C_4 of the next glucose unit.

37 (*d*) Cellulose has a straight chain polysaccharide composed only of β-D-glucose units. These β-D-glucose units are linked together by C_1-C_4 glycosidic linkage.

38 (*c*) Glycogen is also known as animal starch because its structure is similar to amylopectin and is rather more highly branched. The carbohydrates get stored in animal body as glycogen.

39 (*b*) Only α-amino acids are obtained on the hydrolysis of protein.

40 (*d*) Tyrosine has (*p*) HO—C_6H_4—CH_2 group. The molecular structure of tyrosine is as follows

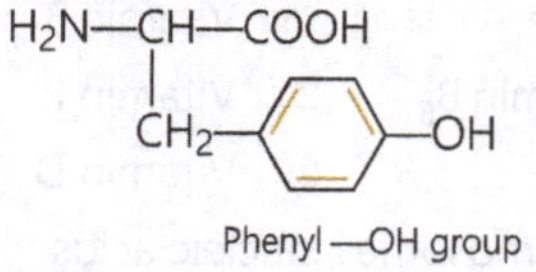

41 (*c*) The most basic amino acid is lysine. There are only two basic amino acids (amino acids with two basic nitrogen containing groups). These are lysine and arginine.

42 (*d*) Tyrosine is non-essential amino acid.

43 (*d*) Leucine is an essential amino acid.

44 (*d*) Valine, leucine and lysine are among the amino acids that cannot be synthesised in body, whereas glycine can be synthesised in the body as it is non-essential amino acid.

45 (*c*) Statement (c) is incorrect. It's correct form is as follows

All proteins are polymers of α-amino acids, hence on hydrolysis give α-amino acids.

Rest other statements are correct.

46 (*c*) Histidine (I) and threonine (III) amino acids are essential amino acids.

47 (*b*) Glycine (Gly) is not optically active amino acid. It does have a chiral carbon due to the presence of two identical groups.

48 (*a*) $(n-1)$ number of water molecules are removed from the *n* number of amino acids during the formation of peptide bond.

49 (*b*) When carboxyl group of glycine combines with the amino group of alanine we get dipeptide, glycylalanine.

50 (*b*) Some common examples of fibrous proteins are keratin (present in hair, wool, silk) and myosin (present in muscles). Insulin and albumin are the examples of globular proteins.

51 (*d*) The correct representation of tripeptide, i.e alanine-glycine-alanine.

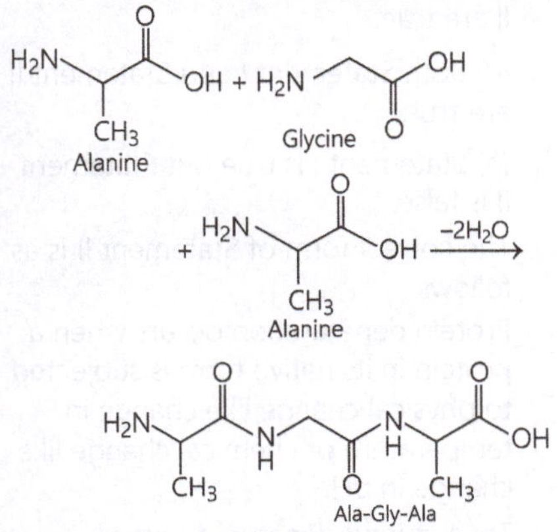

52 (*a*) When the polypeptide chains run parallel and are held together by hydrogen and disulphide bonds, then fibre-like structure is formed. These are called fibrous proteins. Such proteins are generally insoluble in water.

53 (*c*) Insulin is responsible for controlling blood sugar level. Insulin is a polypeptide of 51 amino acids. It consists of two polypeptide chains of 30 and 21 amino acids.

54 (*a*) Statement (a) is incorrect. It's correct form is as follows
It contains both positive and negative charges, but due to cancellation of charge it appears neutral at isoelectric point.
Rest other statements are correct.

55 (*b*) Statement (b) is incorrect. It's correct form is as follows
Most of the naturally occurring amino acids have L-configuration.
Rest other statements are correct.

56 (*d*) Statement (d) is incorrect. It's correct form is as follows
The secondary structure of proteins arises due to the regular folding of the backbone of the polypeptide chain due to hydrogen bonding between $-\overset{\overset{O}{\|}}{C}-$ and —NH group of the peptide bond.
Rest other statements are correct.

57 (*d*) Statement (d) is incorrect. It's correct form is as follows
Keratin is an example of fibrous protein. It is present in hair, wool, silk.
Rest other statements are correct.

58 (*d*) The spatial arrangement of the two or more polypeptide chains with respect to each other is known as quaternary structure.

59 (*a*) The coagulation of egg white on boiling is an example of denaturation of protein.

60 (*b*)

61 (*d*) Enzymes are very specific for a particular reaction and for a particular substrate.

62 (*c*)

63 (*c*) This '*X*' is an enzyme called maltase. It is a globular protein. It is used in the hydrolysis of maltose into glucose.

64 (*d*) Statement (II) is incorrect. It's correct form is as follows
At optimum temperature, which is generally in between 25°C-35°C, enzyme activity is maximum.
Rest other statements are correct.

65 (*b*) Statement (II) is incorrect. It's correct form is as follows
Most of the vitamins cannot be synthesised in our body but plants can synthesise almost all of them.
Rest other statements are correct.

66 (*b*) 67 (*b*)

68 (*b*) Ascorbic acid is the chemical name of vitamin C. The other compounds are not vitamins.
Aspartic acid is an amino acid.
Adipic acid is a dicarboxylic acid having 6 carbon chains. Saccharic acid is a dicarboxylic acid obtained by oxidation of glucose using HNO_3.
Therefore, ascorbic acid is a vitamin.

69 (*d*) Muscular weakness is caused by the deficiency of vitamin E. To remove deficiency, vegetable oil like wheat germ oil, sunflower oil etc., should be included in the diet.

70 (*c*) 71 (*b*)

72 (*d*) The correct match pairs are

Vitamin B_2	–	Milk, egg white
Vitamin B_{12}	–	Meat, fish
Vitamin A	–	Carrots, butter
Vitamin E	–	Germ oil

73 (*c*) Option (c) is the correct combination. In DNA molecule, the sugar moiety is β-D-2-deoxyribose, whereas in RNA molecule, it is β-D-ribose.

74 (*d*) DNA contains four bases, i.e. adenine (A), guanine (G), cytosine (C) and thymine (T). RNA also contains four bases, the first three bases are same as in DNA, but the fourth one is uracil (U). So, uracil is not common between DNA and RNA.

75 (*b*) RNA also contains four bases as same as DNA. But RNA contains uracil in place of thymine.

76 (*c*) Nucleotides are joined together by phosphodiester linkage between 5′and 3′ C-atoms of the pentose sugar. So, I is 5′end of chain, II is phosphodiester linkage and III is 3′end of chain.

77 (*c*) J.D. Watson and F. Crick discovered that, the DNA has a double strand helix structure that resembles with a twisted ladder.

78 (*c*) Complementary strand of DNA is ATACTGAC. As two strands are complementary to each other. So, adenine forms hydrogen bonds with thymine, whereas cytosine forms hydrogen bonds with guanine.

79 (*d*) Guanidine does not constitute the nucleic acid. Uracil is a base present in RNA. Ribose sugar and phosphoric acid are a part of DNA or RNA.

80 (*b*) RNA does not have double stranded α-helix structure. Helixes present in RNA are single-stranded but sometimes they fold back on themselves to form a double helix structure.

81 (*b*) It is same for every cell and cannot be altered by any known treatment.

82 (*d*) Thymine is not a hormone. It is a nitrogenous base. All other three options are hormone.

83 (*b*)

84 (*d*) Statement (d) is incorrect. It's correct form is as follows
Insulin is a polypeptide hormone which helps in keeping the blood glucose level within the narrow limit. It is released in response to the rapid rise in the blood glucose level.
Rest other statements are correct.

85 (*b*) Statement (b) is correct, while the other statements are incorrect. Their are corrected form are as follows
(a) Epinephrine is an example of amino acid derivative hormone.
(c) Glucocorticoids control the carbohydrate metabolism and modulate the inflammatory reactions.
(d) The mineralocorticoids control the level of excretion of water and salt by the kidney.

86 (*c*) Statement III is incorrect. It's correct form is as follows
Estradiol is the main female sex hormone which is responsible for the development of secondary characteristics and participitates in the control of menstrual cycle.
Rest other statements are correct.

87 (*b*) Abnormal function of adrenal cortex resulting in Addison's disease characterised by hypoglycemia, weakness and increased susceptiblity to stress. The disease is fatal unless, it is treated by glucocorticoids and minerals corticoids.

88 (*c*)

89 (*a*) Addison's disease is treated by glucocorticoids and mineralocorticoids. Glucocorticoids control the carbohydrate metabolism, modulate inflammatory reactions and are involved in reactions to control stress. Mineralocorticoids control the level of excretion of water and salt by the kidney.

90 (*d*)

Assertion-Reason

1 (*b*) Acetic acid (CH_3COOH) fits into the general formula $C_x(H_2O)_y$ but is not classified as a carbohydrate.
Therefore, both A and R are true but R is not the correct explanation of A.

2 (*b*) Rhamnose ($C_6H_{12}O_5$) is a carbohydrate but does not fit into the definition of carbohydrate.
Therefore, both A and R are true but R is not the correct explanation of A.
It correct explanation is
Rhamnose is optically active and gives positive Molisch's test.

3 (*a*) Both A and R are true and R is the correct explanation of A.

4 (*c*) Glucose does not form the hydrogen bisulphite addition product because it has cyclic structure in which —CHO group is not free to react.
Therefore, A is true but R is false.

5 (*a*) Both A and R are true and R is the correct explanation of A.

6 (*a*) Both A and R are true and R is the correct explanation of A.

7 (*b*) Sucrose is dextrorotatory but after hydrolysis gives dextrorotatory glucose and laevorotatory fructose. Since, the laevorotation of fructose (–92.4°) is more than dextrorotation of glucose (+52.5°),the mixture is laevorotatory.
Therefore, both A and R are correct but R is not the correct explanation of A.

8 (*a*) Both A and R are true and R is the correct explanation of A.

9 (*d*) Tryptophan is an example of essential amino acids.
Therefore, A is false but R is true.

10 (*a*) Both A and R are true and R is the correct explanation of A.

11 (*a*) Both A and R are true and R is the correct explanation of A.

12 (*c*) Two strands of DNA are complementary to each other because the hydrogen bonds are formed between specific pairs of bases. Adenine forms hydrogen bonds with thymine, whereas cytosine forms hydrogen bonds with guanine.
Therefore, A is true but R is false.

13 (*a*) Both A and R are true and R is the correct explanation of A.

Statement Type

1 (*d*) Both Statements I and Statement II are true.

2 (*d*) Both Statement I and Statement II are true.

3 (*b*) Statement I is true but Statement II is false.
The correct form of Statement II is as follows
Protein denaturation occurs when a protein in its native form is subjected to physical change like change in temperature or chemical change like change in pH.
Thus, during denaturation the secondary and tertiary structures are destroyed but the primary.

4 (*a*) Both Statement I and Statement II are false. Vitamin D is a fat soluble vitamin and can be stored in the body since it is not excreted out of the body.

5 (*d*) Both Statement I and Satement II are true.

6 (*b*) Except III and V and all the statements are correct. The correct statements of III and V is
III. The given chain of amino acids can't be synthesised in body because some of the amino acids are essential amino acids.
V. Activation energy for acid hydrolysis of sucrose is 6.22 kJ mol^{-1} while the activation energy is only 2.15 kJ mol^{-1} when hydrolysed by the enzyme, sucrase.

7 (*d*) The statements I, III and V are correct but statements II and IV are incorrect. The correct form of II and IV are

II. Carbohydrates can be classified on the basis of reducing character, hydrolysis (complexity of structure) and nature (sugars and non-sugars).

IV. Oligosaccharides (carbohydrates) that yield two to ten monosaccharides units on hydrolysis. Monomers of sucrose (glucose and fructose) are monosaccharide.

8 (*c*) The statement IV is correct whereas I, II and III are incorrect statements their correct form is

I. The β-form of glucose (m.p 423 K) is obtained by crystallisation from hot and saturated aqueous solution at 371 K.

II. In β-pleated structure all peptide chains stretched out to nearly maximum extension and laid side by side which are held together by hydrogen bonds.

III. In RNA, all nitrogenous bases are same except thymine, uracil is present in place of thymine in RNA molecule.

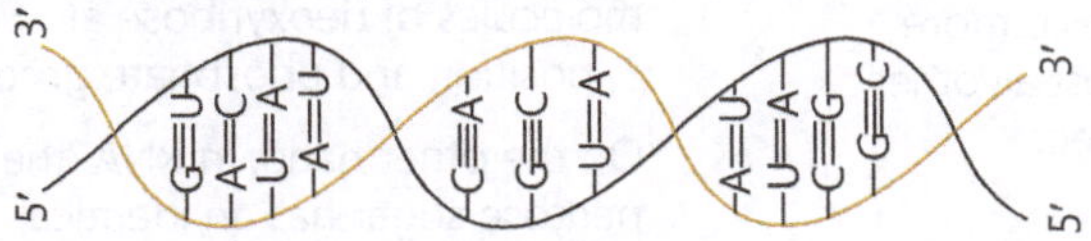

9 (*a*) Except I and IV all statements are correct. The correct form of I and IV is as follows:

I. The sugar derived in RNA is β-D-ribose

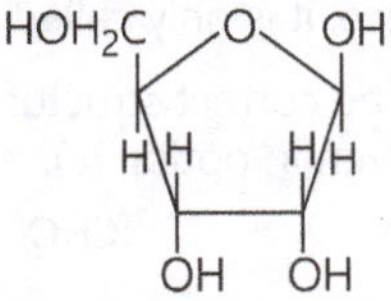

β-D-ribose

IV. DNA is responsible for hereditary transmission.

10 (*d*) Except I and IV all statements are incorrect, the correct form of I and IV is as follows:

I. DNA molecule consists of alternating units of phosphate and the sugar deoxyribose. Each unit has a pair of purine (A, G)/ pyrimidine (C, T) bases.

IV. 'D' and 'L' represents the relative configuration of a particular stereoisomer of a compound with respect to configuration of some other compound. The *d*- and *l*- are synonymous with (+) and (–) respectively the sign of optical rotation.

Matching Type

1 (*c*) The correct match is A-2, B-3, C-1.

2 (*a*) The correct match is A-4, B-1, C-2, D-3.

3 (*b*) The correct match is A-3, B-1, C-4, D-2.

4 (*d*) The correct match is A-5, B-3, C-1, D-2, E-4.

5 (*a*) The correct match is A-3, B-4, C-2, D-1.

Numerical Value

1 (7) Except glycine and alanine, the remaining 7 are essential amino acids.

2 (5) The amino acids present in the given tripeptide Asp-Glu-Lys are

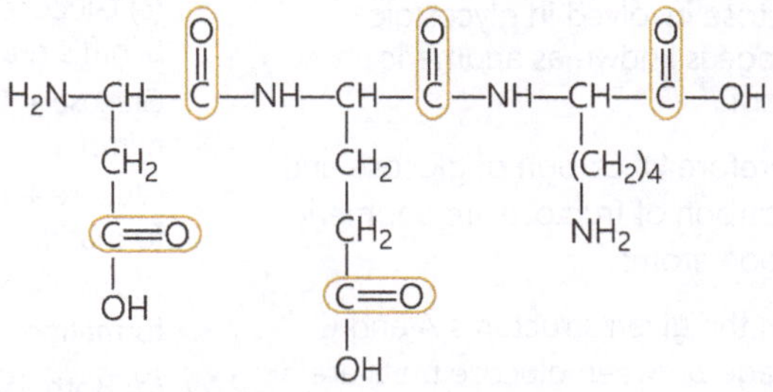

So, number of carbonyl group present in tripeptide = 5.

3 (4) A, D, E and K are fat soluble vitamins.

4 (1) Only cytosine is the only pyrimidine base present both in DNA and RNA.

5 (5) Adenine forms 2 hydrogen bonds with thymine.

Thus, $x = 2$

Cytosine forms 3 hydrogen bonds with guanine. Thus, $y = 3$

Hence, $x + y = 5$

NCERT Exemplar's

1 (*b*) Structure of glycogen is similar to amylopectin.

2 (*d*) Glycogen is a polymer of α-D-glucose stored in the liver, brain and muscles of animals and is also known as animal starch. It is present in pyranose form.

3 (*c*) Statement (c) is not true.

It does not exist in furanose form, exists in pyranose form as shown below :

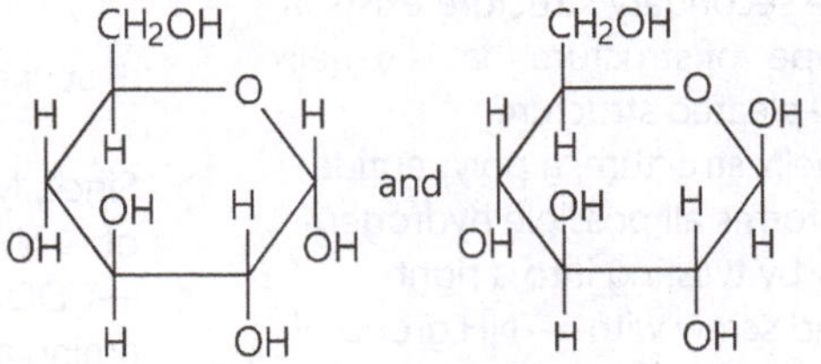

α-D-(+)-glucopyranose β-D-(+)-glucopyranose

4 (*c*) Pentaacetate of glucose does not react with hydroxylamine showing absence of free —CHO group. This cannot be explained by open structure of glucose.

5 (*b*) Structure given in option (b) is a non-reducing sugar.

6 (*c*) Anomers have different configuration at C-1.

7 (*a*) Here, (i) and (ii) are anomer because they differ from each other at carbon-1 only.

8 (*c*) Sucrose (cane sugar) is a disaccharide. One molecule of sucrose on hydrolysis gives one molecule of glucose and one molecule of fructose.

$$\underset{\text{Cane sugar}}{C_{12}H_{22}O_{11}} \xrightarrow[H^+]{H_2O} \underset{\text{D-(+)-glucose}}{C_6H_{12}O_6} + \underset{\text{D-(–)-fructose}}{C_6H_{12}O_6}$$

9 (c) Carbon adjacent to oxygen atom in the cyclic structure of glucose or fructose involved in glycosidic linkage is known as anomeric carbon.

Therefore '*a*' carbon of glucose and '*b*' carbon of fructose are anomeric carbon atoms.

10 (c) In the given structures *A* and *C* linkage between glucose units are between C_1 and C_4 and B is between C_1 and C_6.

11 (*a*) Dinucleotides are formed by phosphodiester linkage between 5′ and 3′carbon atoms of the pentose sugar.

12 (*b*) Nucleic acids are polymers of nucleotides in which nucleic acids are linked together by phosphodiester linkage. e.g. DNA, RNA etc.

13 (*a*) D and L-configurations are relative configuration decided by relating structure of given saccharide with D or L-isomer of glyceraldehyde.

Therefore, all the given structures have D-configuration.

14 (c) The secondary structure exists in two types of structure that is α-helix and β-pleated structure.

In α-helix structure, a polypeptide chain forms all possible hydrogen bonds by twisting into a right handed screw with —NH group of each amino acid residue hydrogen bonded to >C=O of adjacent amino acid, which form a helix.

15 (*a*) In primary structure of proteins, each polypeptide in a protein has amino acids linked with each other in a specific sequence.

16 (*d*) Vitamin B_{12} can be stored in our body because it is water insoluble.

17 (c) DNA contains four bases that is adenine, guanine, thymine and cytosine, while RNA contains four bases adenine, uracil, guanine and cytosine. Thus, RNA does not contain thymine.

18 (*d*) It does not contain uracil (U).

Past Exams'

1 (c) Glucose does not react with Schiff's reagent and $NaHSO_3$.

Glucose + Tollen's reagent ⟶ Silver mirror

Glucose + HCN ⟶ Cyanohydin formation

Glucose + NH_2OH ⟶ Oxime formation

2 (*d*) Both Statement I and statement II are true.

3 (*b*) The incorrect statement about enzymes is option (b) because enzymes are protein in nature and comprised of amino acids that are linked together in one or more polypeptide chains. Rest all other given options are correct.

4 (*a*) 5 (*b*)

6 (c)

(a) Alanine ⇒ $CH_3-CH\begin{smallmatrix}NH_2\\COOH\end{smallmatrix}$

(b) Tyrosine

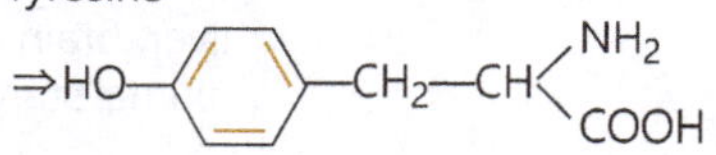

(c) Lysine ⇒ $H_2N-(CH_2)_4-CH\begin{smallmatrix}NH_2\\COOH\end{smallmatrix}$

(d) Serine ⇒ $HO-CH_2-CH\begin{smallmatrix}NH_2\\COOH\end{smallmatrix}$

Since, lysine contains more number of $-NH_2$ groups as compared to $-COOH$ groups, hence it is a basic amino acid.

7 (*b*) During the denaturation, primary structure remains intact but secondary and tertiary structures are destroyed.

8 (*b*) The amino acids that can be synthesised in our body are not essentially required in our diet are called non-essential amino acids. e.g. glycine, alanine, serine, proline, cysteine, glutamine, tyrosine, aspartic acid, glutamic acid, asparagine.

9 (*d*) Among the given options, only glycine (H_2N-CH_2-COOH) is an amino acid which contains both acidic (acquiring negative charge) and basic group (acquiring positive charge). Thus, glycine can form a Zwitter ion.

10 (*d*) When protein is subjected to physical change like change in temperature or chemical change like change in pH, the hydrogen bonds are disturbed.

Hence, the denaturation of protein makes the protein inactive.

11 (*b*) Two amino acids in a protein are linked by a peptide bond.

12 (*a*) In DNA, two helically twisted strands connected together by steps. Each strand consists of alternating molecules of deoxyribose at 2′-position and phosphate groups.

On the other hand, in RNA, the pentose sugar has an identical structure with deoxyribose sugar except that there is an —OH group instead of —H on carbon atom at 2′.

Hence, it is only called ribose.

13 (c) The correct structure of L-glucose is given in option (c).

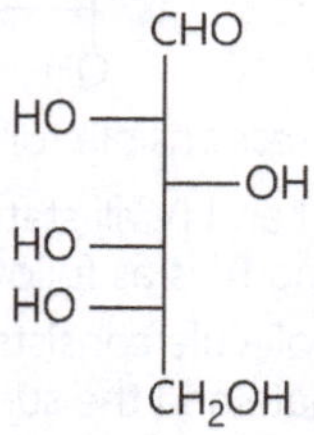

14 (*b*) The correct match is A-(iii), B-(iv), C-(i), D-(ii).

15 (c) Different codes of amino acids are

F = Phenylalanine =

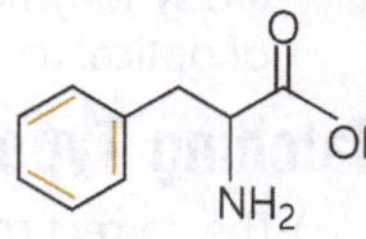

L = Leucine

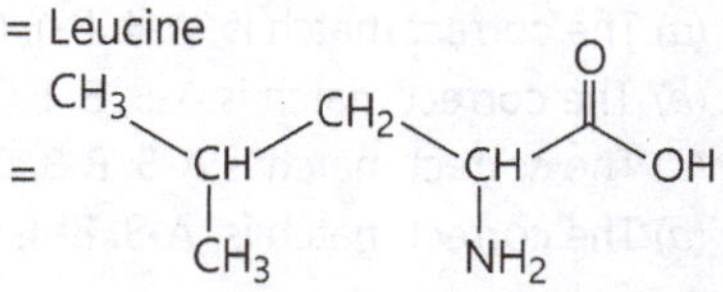

D = Aspartic acid

$= HO-\overset{O}{\overset{\|}{C}}-CH_2-\overset{NH_2}{\overset{|}{CH}}-\overset{O}{\overset{\|}{C}}-OH$

Y = Tyrosine =

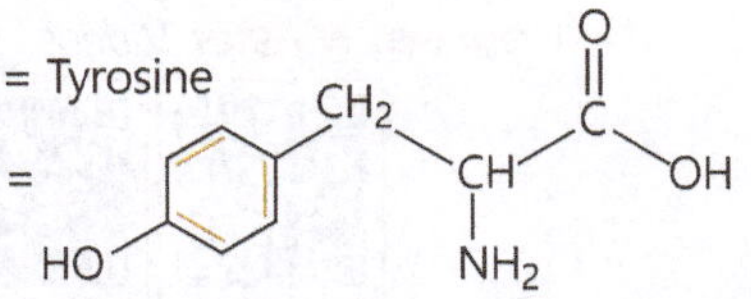

So, the correct code for given representation is *FLDY*.

16 (*d*) The Haworth projection is cyclic representation of monosaccharides with simple three dimensional perspective. D-mannose Haworth structure is in the α-pyranose configuration.

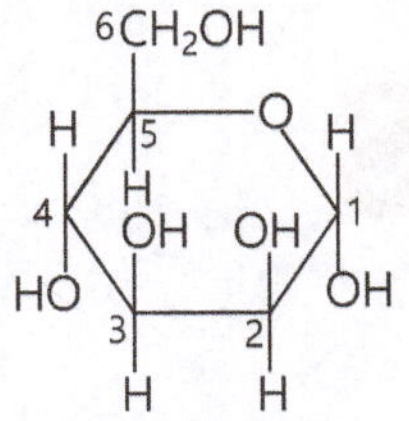

17 (*d*) The correct match is A-IV, B-I, C-II, D-III.

18 (*c*) Sulphur containing amino acids are cysteine (II) and methionine (IV). Their structures are as follows

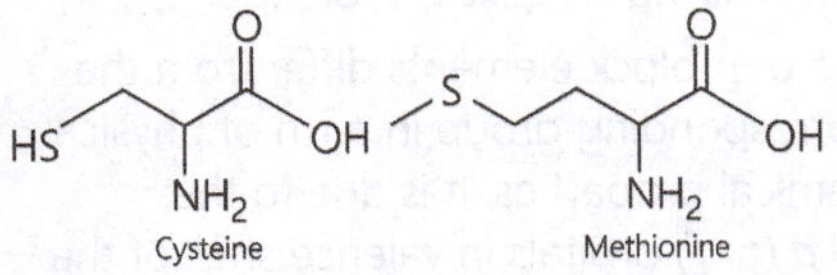

19 (*c*) Statement I is true but statement II is false. Maltose has two α-D-glucose units linked at C_1 and C_4 and is a reducing sugar as free aldehyde is formed by using opening and can react with Fehling's solution.

20 (*b*) The sugar found in polynucleotides is either ribose (a monosaccharide pentose) or 2-deoxyribose. A nucleic acid containing β-D-2-deoxyribose is called deoxyribonucleic acid (DNA) while that which contains β-D-ribose is called ribonucleic acid (RNA).

21 (*d*)

22 (*d*) Sucrose is non-reducing sugar. Since the reducing groups of two monosaccharide (glucose and fructose) are involved in glycosidic bond formation and these are not free.

While all others, i.e. glucose, fructose and galactose are reducing sugar.

23 (*b*)

Skill Boosters

1 (a) Sucrose is the compound, which is disaccharide boiled with dil. H_2SO_4 in alcoholic solution to give glucose and fructose (two isomers) in equal amount.

$$\underset{(A)}{C_{12}H_{22}O_{11}} + H_2O \xrightarrow{H^+} \underset{\substack{\text{Glucose}\\(x)}}{C_6H_{12}O_6} + \underset{\substack{\text{Fructose}\\(y)}}{C_6H_{12}O_6}$$

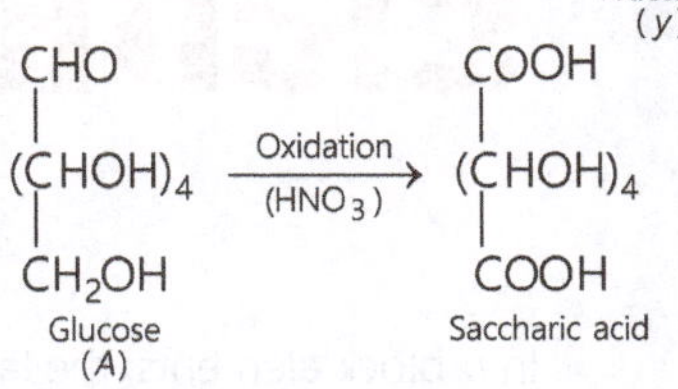

Fructose is laevorotatory.

2 (*c*) It is aldopentose which give furfural under acidic condition on dehydration.

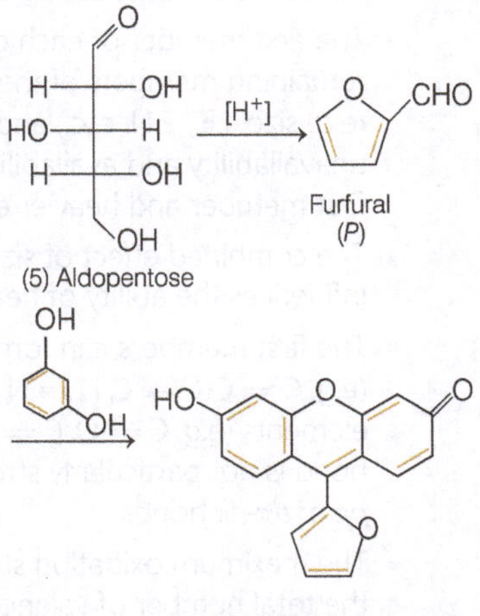

3 (*a*) $\underset{(S)}{\text{Cellulose}} \xrightarrow[\substack{393\text{ K}\\(2\text{-}3\text{ atm})}]{\text{Dil. }H_2SO_4} \underset{(P)}{\text{Glucose}} \xrightarrow{Br_2\text{ water}} \text{Gluconic acid}$

4 (*a*) When *A* is heated with acetic anhydride, acetylation occurs and —OH group is replaced by $-O-\overset{\overset{O}{\|}}{C}-CH_3$ and hence triacetate is formed.

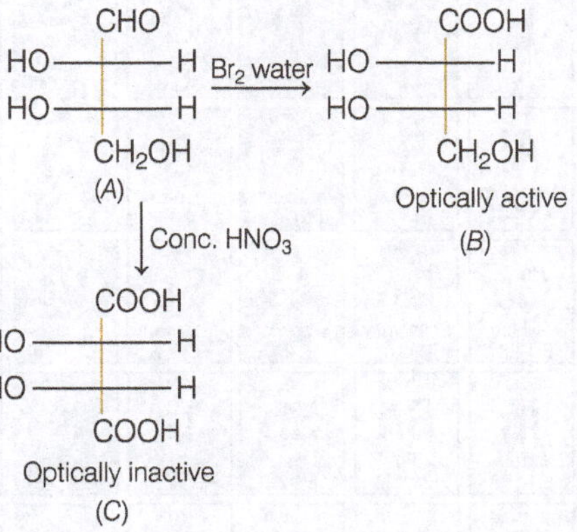

5 (*c*) For behaving like salt any compound should have to build the nature of neutralised compound, so if there a condition like below should be present.

$$-NH_2 \text{ group} = -COOH \text{ group}$$

6 (*a*) The optically active compound having molecular formula $C_6H_{12}O_6$ is called glucose. It exist in two isomeric form α-D-glucopyranose and β-D-pyranose. These isomers of glucose differ in configuration at carbon one (1). Such isomers are referred as anomers.

7 (*a*) Digestion is a biological process which is completed in many step. Each step consists different kind of enzymes. In the conversion of protein to amino acid the two enzymes involved in the process are pepsin and trypsin.

$$\text{Proteins} \xrightarrow{\text{Pepsin }(X)} \text{Polypeptides} \xrightarrow{\text{Trypsin }(Y)} \text{Amino acids}$$

8 (*b*) On hydrolysis, proteins give a mixture of α-amino acids. The α-carbon in α-amino acids is obtained by hydrolysis of proteins has 'L' configuration.

Only in option (b) α-amino acid is given all the other options are not α-amino acid.

9 (*c*) The given reaction is represented as

$$\text{Sucrose} \xrightarrow[\text{Hydrolysis}]{} \underset{(a)}{\text{Glucose}} + \underset{(b)}{\text{Fructose}} \xrightarrow[\text{reagent}]{\text{Seliwanoff's}} \text{Red colour}$$

Seliwanoff's test is used to distinguish between aldose and ketose sugars, when added to a solution containing ketose, red colour is formed rapidly.

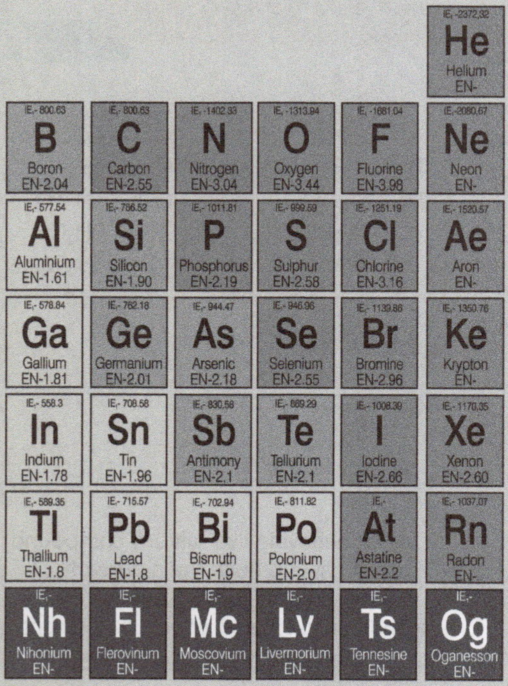

Scan for **Chemistry Through Concept Master** *Videos*

11

p-Block Elements

Topicwise No. of Ques asked in 5 Years (NEET)

Topics	No. of Questions				
	2024	2023	2022	2021	2020
Introduction					
Group-13 Elements : The Boron Family	–	2	1	1	1
Group-14 Elements : The Carbon Family	–	1	1	–	3
Group 15 Elements	–	–	–	–	–
Group 16 Elements	2	1	1	1	1
Group 17 Elements	–	–	1	1	–
Group 18 Elements	–	–	–	1	1

Special Type of Ques Asked In 5 Years (NEET)

Types	Years				
	2024	2023	2022	2021	2020
A-R	–	–	1	–	–
Statement Based	1	–	3	2	2
Matching	–	2	–	–	2

Last 5 Years Weightage (NEET)

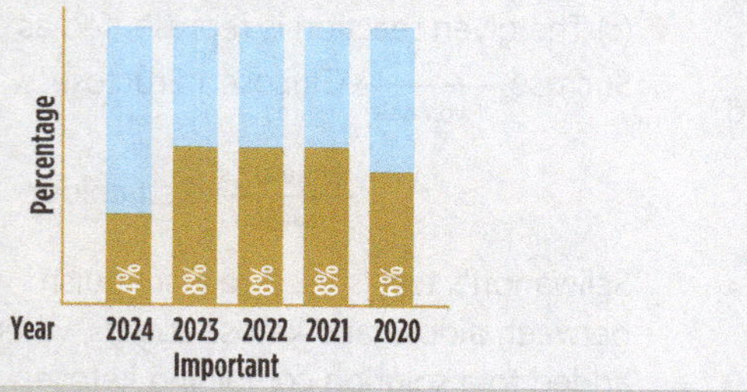

- In *p*-block elements, the last electron enters in the outermost *p*-orbital.
- As the maximum number of electrons that can be accommodated in a set of *p*-orbitals is six. Thus, there are six groups of *p*-block elements in the periodic table numbering from 13 to 18.
- General electronic configuration is ns^2np^{1-6} (except for He).
- The first member of each group of *p*-block elements differ from the remaining members of their corresponding group in term of physical (e.g. size, I.E., E.N. etc.) and chemical properties. It is due to the unavailability and availability of *d* (or *f*) orbitals in valence shell of the first member and heavier elements respectively.
- The combined effect of size and availability of *d*-orbitals considerably influences the ability of heavier elements to form π-bonds.
- The first members can form $p\pi$-$p\pi$ multiple bonds with itself (e.g. $C=C$, $C\equiv C$, $N\equiv N$, $O=O$) and with other second row elements (e.g. $C=O$, $C=M$, $C\equiv M$, $N=O$), whereas this type of bond is not particularly strong for heavier elements, thus they form $d\pi$-$p\pi$ or $d\pi$-$d\pi$ bonds.
- The maximum oxidation state shown by a *p*-block element is equal to the total number of valence electrons.
- The number of possible oxidation states increases towards the right of the periodic table.
- *p*-block elements may show other oxidation states along with group oxidation state.
- The oxidation state two unit less than the group oxidation state becomes progressively more stable for the heavier elements in each group. The occurrence of oxidation states two unit less than the group oxidation states is called **inert pair effect**.
- It includes metals, metalloids and non-metals which brings the diversification in chemistry of these elements.

- Non-metal oxides are **acidic** or **neutral**, whereas metal oxides are **basic** in nature.

General Electronic Configuration and Oxidation States of p-Block Elements

Group	13	14	15	16	17	18
General electronic configuration	ns^2np^1	ns^2np^2	ns^2np^3	ns^2np^4	ns^2np^5	ns^2np^6 ($1s^2$ for He)
Group oxidation state	+3	+4	+5	+6	+7	+8
Other oxidation states	+1	+2, −4	+3, −3	+4, +2, −2	+5, +3, +1, −1	+6, +4, +2

Group 13 Elements : The Boron Family

- There are total six elements in group-13; boron (B), aluminium (Al), gallium (Ga), indium (In), and thallium (Tl) and nihonium (Nh). These are collectively known as **Boron Family**.
- Group 13 is a very discrepant group on the basis of properties. Among all, boron is a typical semi-metal due to its high ionisation enthalpy.
- Boron is a fairly rare element mainly occurs as orthoboric acid (H_3BO_3), borax ($Na_2B_4O_7 \cdot 10H_2O$) and kernite ($Na_2B_4O_7 \cdot 4H_2O$). There are two isotopic forms of boron, i.e. ^{10}B(19%) and ^{11}B(81%).
- Aluminium is a metal but it shows so many common trends of chemical properties with boron, likewise gallium, indium and thallium are also metals.
- Aluminium is the most abundant metal and third most abundant element in earth's crust, after oxygen and silicon.
- **Bauxite**, $Al_2O_3 \cdot 2H_2O$ and **cryolite**, Na_3AlF_6 are the important minerals of aluminium. Gallium, indium and thallium are also occur insufficiently in nature.

Electronic Configuration

Their electronic configuration is [inert gas] ns^2np^1.

Atomic Radii

- It increases on moving down the group from B to Tl.
- However, the atomic radius of Ga (135 pm) is less than that of Al (143 pm).
- It follows the trend as B < Ga < Al < In < Tl.

Atomic radius of Ga is less than that of Al because the presence of additional 10 d-electrons offer only poor screening effect for the outer electrons from the increased nuclear charge in gallium (Ga).

Ionisation Enthalpy

- It does not follow a regular or general trend in this group.
- There is a discontinuity in the ionisation enthalpy values between Ga and Tl due to inability of d-and f-electrons, having low screening effect to compensate the increased nuclear charge.
  - It follows the trend given below :
    I.E. order – In < Al < Ga < Tl < B
  - This group has first ionisation enthalpies less than their corresponding s-block elements of group 2. It is due to the less penetration and shielding effect of p-electrons than s-electrons.
- The order of ionisation enthalpies is $IE_1 < IE_2 < IE_3$ or $\Delta_i H_1 < \Delta_i H_2 < \Delta_i H_3$. Sum of the first three I.E. for all elements to give M^{+3} ions is very high.

Electronegativity

It first decreases from B to Al and then increases marginally. This is due to the poor shielding effect. It shows the following trends

Elements (Pauling scale value) B > Tl > In > Ga > Al
(2.0) (1.8) (1.7) (1.6) (1.5)

These elements are more electronegative than s-block elements.

Physical Properties

- Boron is non-metallic, extremely hard and has high melting point. Its high melting point is due to its existence in strong crystalline lattice.
- Rest of the members are soft metals with low melting point and high electrical conductivity.
- Gallium can exist in liquid state during summer due to its unusual low melting point (303 K). However, its boiling point (2676 K) is very high which makes it a useful material for measuring high temperatures.
- Density of the elements increases down the group from boron to thallium.

Chemical Properties

- According to valence electronic configuration, i.e. ns^2np^1, the expected oxidation state shown by these elements are +1 and +3.
- Boron prevents to form +3 ions, it is because its sum of first three ionisation enthalpies ($\Delta_i H_3$) is very high. However, Al form Al^{3+} ion as its $\Delta_i H_3$ is less. Infact Al is highly electropositive metal.
- On moving down the group, the stability of +3 oxidation state decrease and +1 oxidation state increases. It is due to poor shielding effect of intervening d and f-orbitals, the

increased effective nuclear charge hold *ns*-electrons tightly. This restrict the participation of *ns*-electrons (inert pair effect) which result, that only *p*-orbital electron may be involved in the bonding.

The trend is as follows

$$Al^+ < Ga^+ < In^+ < Tl^+$$
$$Al^{3+} > Ga^{3+} > In^{3+} > Tl^{3+}$$

- The compounds in +1 oxidation state are more ionic in nature.
- In trivalent state (+ 3), there are only six electrons around the central atom in a molecules of the compounds of these elements (e.g boron in BF_3) NEET 2023. Therefore, they are called **electron deficient molecule** and behave as Lewis acids. They have tendency to accept a pair of electrons to achieve stable electronic configuration. This tendency to behave as Lewis acids decreases with increase in the size, i.e. down the group.

Both BCl_3 and $AlCl_3$ are electron deficient as well as **Lewis acids**. BCl_3 easily accepts a lone pair of electrons from base like ammonia to form $BCl_3 \cdot NH_3$ while $AlCl_3$ form dimer to achieve stability.

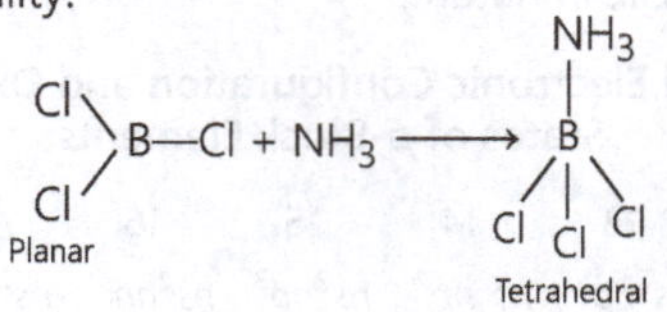

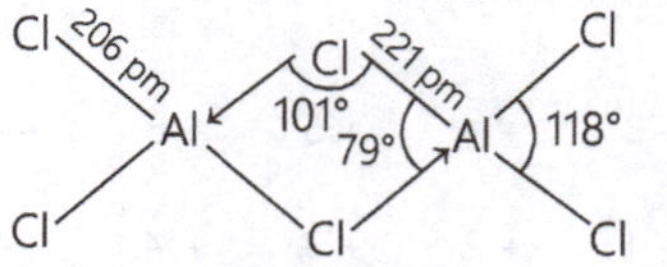

Tetrahedral

- In + 3 state, most of the compounds being covalent are hydrolysed in water. e.g. The trichlorides on hydrolysis form species like $[M(OH)_4]^-$ (tetrahedral, sp^3 hybridised). Aluminium chloride in acidified aqueous solution forms $[Al(H_2O)_6]^{3+}$ (octahedral sp^3d^2-hybridised). NEET 2019

Important Chemical Reactions of Group 13

Reactions	Properties
Reactivity towards air With oxygen of air $4E(s) + 3O_2(g) \xrightarrow{\Delta} 2E_2O_3(s)$ (E = group-13 element)	• Crystalline boron is unreactive. • Aluminium forms a very thin oxide layer on the surface which protects the metal from further attack. • B_2O_3 is **acidic** and react with basic (metallic) oxides forming metal borates. Oxides of Al and Ga are **amphoteric** and those of In and Tl are **basic**.
With nitrogen of air $2E(s) + N_2(g) \xrightarrow{\Delta} 2EN(s)$	• With dinitrogen at high temperature they form nitrides.
Reactivity towards acids and alkalies $2Al(s) + 6HCl(aq) \longrightarrow 2Al^{3+}(aq) + 6Cl^-(aq) + 3H_2\uparrow(g)$ (Exception boron) $2Al(s) + 2NaOH(aq) + 6H_2O(l) \longrightarrow 2Na^+[Al(OH)_4]^-(aq) + 3H_2(g)$ (Exception In and Tl)	• Boron does not react with acids and alkalies even at moderate temperature. • Al dissolves in mineral acids and aqueous alkalies and liberate hydrogen. Thus, shows **amphoteric** character. • Concentrated nitric acid renders aluminium passive by forming a protective oxide layer on the surface.
Reactivity towards halogen $2E(s) + 3X_2(g) \longrightarrow 2EX_3(s)$ (where, X = F, Cl, Br, I) (Exception TlI_3)	• The covalent trihalides, (e.g. BF_3) being electron deficient are strong Lewis acids and the tendency to behave as Lewis acids decreases with increase in size down the group. Anhydrous aluminium chloride is partially hydrolysed with atmospheric moisture to liberate white fumes of HCl gas.

Important Trends and Anomalous Properties of Boron

Due to its extremely small size, high electron density, high electronegativity and non-availability of *d*-electrons boron exhibits following anomalous behaviour.

- Boron is a typical semi-metal, while other members of the group are metals.
- Due to the absence of *d*-orbital it cannot expand its covalency above four, e.g. boron form only $[BF_4]^-$, whereas aluminium can form $[AlF_6]^{3-}$ ions.
- Only boron exhibits allotropy and exists in crystalline as well as amorphous forms.
- It forms only covalent compounds, while other members can form covalent as well as ionic compounds.
- Its melting and boiling points are higher than other members of the group.

- Boron combines with metals and forms borides, while other elements do not combine.
- Except boron all other halides of the group elements are hydrolysed in water and exist as $[M(OH)_4]^-$ and $[M(H_2O)_6]^{3+}$ species in aqueous medium.
- Boron forms only monomeric trihalides while other element can dimerised.

$$F_3B + :NH_3 \longrightarrow F_3B \longleftarrow NH_3$$

Diborane (B_2H_6)

- It is the simplest electron deficient hydride of boron NEET 2020. It is colourless, highly toxic gas with b.p. of 180 K. It is inflammable in nature.

$$3B_2H_6 + 6NH_3 \longrightarrow 3[BH_2(NH_3)_2]^+[BH_4]^- \xrightarrow{\text{Heat}} \underset{\text{Borazine}}{2B_3N_3H_6} + 12H_2$$

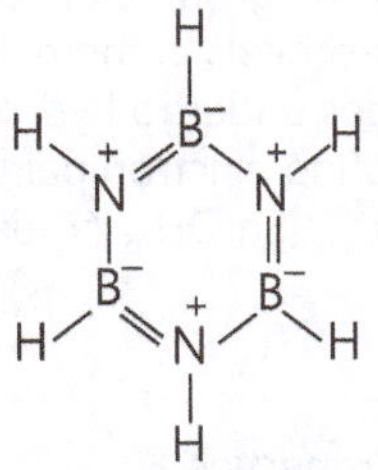

Borazine

For Concept Master Video

- Borazine is also known as inorganic benzene because it contains alternate BH and NH groups and also similar in some physical and chemical properties.

Marks Maximizer

- **Diborane** has non-planar structure, each B-atom uses sp^3-hybrids for bonding [NEET 2022]. Out of the four sp^3-hybrids on each B-atom, one is without an electron shown in broken lines.
- The four terminal B—H bonds (2C—2e) lie in same plane while the two bridge B----H----B bonds (3C—2e) lie above and below the plane of 4 B—H bonds as shown below :

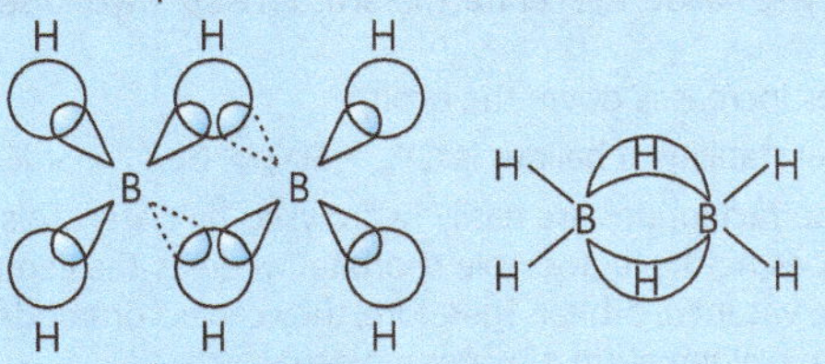

Bonding in diborane

The (3C— 2e) bridge bonds are also referred to as banana bonds.

- Boranes having general formula B_nH_{n+6} are called **arachno-boranes** while boranes having general formula B_nH_{n+4} are called **nido-boranes**.

Group 14 Elements : The Carbon Family

- This group includes carbon (C), silicon (Si), germanium (Ge), tin (Sn), lead (Pb) and flerovium (Fl) elements.
- Carbon is 17th most abundant element by mass in the earth crust.
- It is available as coal, graphite and diamond in element state, while in combined state it is present as metal carbonates, hydrocarbons and CO_2 gas.
- Naturally occurring carbon contains two stable isotopes, i.e. ^{12}C and ^{13}C. In addition to these, third isotope ^{14}C is a radioactive isotope with half-life 5770 years, it is used for radiocarbon dating.
- Silicon is the second most abundant element on the earth's crust after oxygen.
- Germanium exists only in traces. Tin mainly occurs as cassiterite (SnO_2) and lead as galena (PbS).
- Ultrapure form of Ge and Si are used to make transistors and semiconductor devices.

Electronic Configuration

The general electronic configuration of these elements is ns^2np^2.

Covalent Radius

It increases considerably from C to Si thereafter from Si to Pb a small increase in radius is observed. This is due to the presence of completely filled *d* and *f*-orbitals in heavier members.

Ionisation Enthalpy

- In general, the value of ionisation enthalpy decreases down the group. However, this decrease in value is not in the regular order.
- As, there is small decrease in $\Delta_i H$ from Si to Ge to Sn and slight increase in $\Delta_i H$ from Sn to Pb is observed. It is due to the consequence of poor shielding effect of intervening *d* and *f*-electrons and increase in size of the atom. Thus, the order is

$$C > Si > Ge > Sn < Pb$$

- The first ionisation enthalpy of group 14 elements is higher than the corresponding elements of group 13. This is due to their higher nuclear charge and smaller size.

Electronegativity

- The electronegativity values for elements from Si to Pb are almost the same.
- Due to small size, the elements of this group are slightly more electronegative than group 13 elements.

Physical Properties

- All members of this group are solid in nature.
- Carbon and silicon are non-metals, germanium is a metalloid, whereas tin and lead are soft metals with low melting points. Melting points and boiling points of group 14 elements are much higher than those of corresponding group 13 elements.

Chemical Properties

- The common **oxidation states** exhibited by these elements are + 4 and + 2. However, carbon also exhibits negative oxidation states as C^{4-} or C_2^{2-} in some carbides. e.g. Be_2C, CaC_2 etc.
- The compounds of this group element in + 4 oxidation state are generally covalent in nature. It is because, the sum of first four ionisation enthalpies of these elements is very high.
- Carbon and silicon mostly show + 4 oxidation state. Thus, the order of stability of ions of this group are as follows

$$\underset{\text{(Reducing agent; less stable)}}{Ge^{2+}} < Sn^{2+} < \underset{\text{(More stable)}}{Pb^{2+}};$$

$$\underset{\text{(More stable)}}{Ge^{4+}} > Sn^{4+} > \underset{\text{(Oxidising agents less stable)}}{Pb^{4+}}$$

- On going down the group the tendency to show + 2 oxidation state increases and that of the (+4) decreases (i.e. due to the inert pair effect).
- In tetravalent state, the octet of element of group 14 is complete, i.e. their compounds act as electron precise molecules. Hence, in general, they neither accept nor lose electrons.
- Carbon cannot exceed its covalence more than 4, while other elements of the group can do so. It is because of the presence of *d*-orbitals in them. Because of this reason, their halides undergo hydrolysis and form complex by accepting electron pairs from donor species, e.g. SiF_6^{2-}, $[GeCl_6]^{2-}$, $[Sn(OH)_6]^{2-}$ exist.

Important Chemical Reactions of Group 14

Reactions	Properties
Reactivity towards oxygen $M(s) + \frac{1}{2}O_2(g) \longrightarrow MO$ (Limited supply) $M(s) + O_2(g) \longrightarrow MO_2$ (Excess)	• Forms two types of oxides, i.e. monoxide (MO) and dioxide (MO_2). – SiO only exists at high temperature. – Oxides in higher oxidation states of elements are generally more acidic than lower one. • Nature of monoxide is CO-neutral, GeO-acidic, SnO and PbO-amphoteric. • Nature of dioxides is $\underbrace{CO_2, SiO_2, GeO_2}_{\text{Acidic}}$, $\underbrace{SnO_2 \text{ and } PbO_2}_{\text{Amphoteric}}$
Reactivity towards water $Sn(s) + 2H_2O(l) \xrightarrow{\Delta} SnO_2 + 2H_2(g)$	• C, Si, Ge are not affected by water. • Sn decomposes steam to form dioxide and H_2 gas. • Pb is unaffected by H_2O due to the formation of protective oxide film.
Reactivity towards halogen $M + X_2 \longrightarrow MX_2$ [where, X = F, Cl, Br, I] $M + 2X_2 \longrightarrow MX_4$ [**Exception**-PbI_4 (does not exist)]	• These elements can form halides of formula MX_2 and MX_4. • Except carbon, all other members react directly with halogen. • Most of the MX_4 are covalent in nature (exception are SnF_4 and PbF_4 which are ionic in nature). In these halide, the central metal atom is sp^3-hybridised and have tetrahedral shape. • Stability of dihalides increases down the group. • The order of thermal stability of halides is $CX_4 > SiX_4 > GeX_4 > SnX_4 > PbX_4$. • Except CCl_4, other tetrachlorides are easily hydrolysed by water. This is because the carbon atom does not have available *d*-orbital whereas the central atom of other elements have vacant *d*-orbital. Therefore, they can accommodate the lone pair of electron from oxygen atom of water molecule. • $SiCl_4$ undergoes hydrolysis by initially accepting lone pair of electrons from water molecule in *d*-orbitals of Si. Finally, leading to the formation of $Si(OH)_4$. $SiCl_4 + H_2O \xrightarrow[-HCl]{} Si(OH)Cl_3 \xrightarrow[-3HCl]{+3H_2O} \underset{\text{Silicic acid}}{Si(OH)_4}$

Anomalous Behaviour of Carbon

Carbon shows following anomalous behaviour due to its small size, higher electronegativity, higher ionisation enthalpy, property of catenation and unavailability of *d*-orbitals.

- Carbon is a typical non-metal forming covalent bonds employing all its four valence electrons.
- The melting and boiling points of carbon are very high.
- CO_2 is a gas, while dioxides of all other members are solids.
- Carbon also has unique ability to form $p\pi$-$p\pi$ multiple bonds with itself and with other atoms of small size and high electronegativity.
  e.g. $C=C$, $C\equiv C$, $C=O$, $C=S$ and $C\equiv N$.
  However, heavier elements do not form $p\pi$-$p\pi$ bonds because their atomic orbitals are too-large and diffuse to have effective overlapping.
- Carbon have the remarkable property of catenation (i.e. the ability of like atoms to link together through covalent bond). The tendency of catenation depends upon the strength of element-element bond which in turn depends upon the size and electronegativity of the element.
- On moving down the group the size increases and electronegativity decreases and thereby tendency to show catenation decreases (C >> Si > Ge ≈ Sn). Lead does not show catenation.
- Due to the absence of *d*-orbital the maximum covalency of C is 4, while other members can expand their covalence due to the presence of *d*-orbitals, e.g. $[SiF_6]^{2-}$ etc.
- Carbon is able to show allotropic forms (due to property of catenation and $p\pi$-$p\pi$ bond formation) while other do not.

Allotropes of Carbon

Carbon exhibits many allotropic forms, both crystalline as well as amorphous.

Crystalline Allotropes of Carbon

Diamond

- It has rigid 3-D crystalline lattice network of sp^3-hybridised C-atoms **NEET 2022, 2023**. It is the hardest known substance on earth.
- It is an insulator of electricity, but a conductor of heat.

Graphite

- It has layered structure. Each layer has sp^2-hybridised carbon atoms in hexagonal ring and adjacent layers are held together by van der Waals' forces, thus graphite shows lubricating properties at high temperature. **NEET 2023**

It is a good conductor of electricity, so used in making electrodes. Graphite is thermodynamically most stable allotrope of carbon.

Fullerenes

- These are only pure form of carbon because they have smooth structure without having dangling bonds.
- C_{60} molecule has a shape, like soccer balls and called **Buckminster fullerene**.
- It contains 20, six-membered and 12, five-membered rings.
- Each carbon atoms is sp^2-hybridised and forms 3σ-bonds with other three carbon atoms. The remaining electron at each carbon is delocalised in molecular orbitals, which in turn give aromatic character to molecule.

Amorphous Allotropes of Carbon

- Carbon black is obtained by burning hydrocarbons in a limited supply of air.
- Charcoal and coke are obtained by heating wood or coal respectively at high temperatures in the absence of air.

Group 15 Elements

- The group 15 includes nitrogen (N), phosphorus (P), arsenic (As), antimony (Sb), bismuth (Bi) and moscovium (Mc).
- As we go down the group, there is a shift from non-metallic to metallic through metalloid character.

$$\underbrace{N\ ,\ P}_{\text{Non-metals}}\ ,\ \underbrace{As\ ,\ Sb}_{\text{Metalloids}}\ ,\ \underbrace{Bi\ ,\ Mc}_{\text{Typical metals}}$$

Electronic Configuration

The general electronic configuration of these elements is ns^2np^3.

Occurrence

- Molecular nitrogen constitutes about 78% by volume of atmosphere. In combined state, it is found as nitrates [$NaNO_3$ (Chile saltpetre), KNO_3 (Indian saltpetre)], as proteins and amino acids in plants and animals. Phosphorus is found as phosphates. The rest elements occur as sulphides or oxides.
- Moscovium is a synthetic radioactive element. It is because its half-life is very short and also present in very little amount.

Atomic/Ionic Radii

- Ionic radii as well as covalent radii increases with increase in size down the group. There is a considerable increase in covalent radius from N to P.
- However, from As to Bi only a small increase in covalent radius is observed. This is due to the presence of completely filled *d* and/or *f*-orbitals in heavier members.

Ionisation Enthalpy

- It decreases down the group due to gradual increase in atomic size. Because of the extra stable half-filled *p*-orbitals electronic configuration and smaller size, $IE_{15} > IE_{14}$.
- The order of successive ionisation enthalpies of this group as expected is $\Delta_i H_1 < \Delta_i H_2 < \Delta_i H_3$.

Electronegativity

It decreases down the group with increasing atomic size. But amongst the heavier elements, the difference is not that much noticeable.

Physical Properties

- Metallic character increases down the group.
- Boiling point increases from top to bottom due to increase in their atomic size, whereas melting point first increases from N to As and then decreases from Sb to Bi due to their tendency to form three covalent bonds instead of five due to inert pair effect.
- Except nitrogen, all the elements show allotropy.

Chemical Properties

These are some chemical properties given below.

Oxidation State

- Elements of group 15 exhibit a number of oxidation states which are as follows

Element	N	P	Ar	Sb	Bi
Oxidation state	−3 to +5	+5, +3, −3, +1	+5, +3	+5, +3	+3

- On going down the group, stability of +3 oxidation state increases and that of +5 decreases due to **inert pair effect**.
- The stability of −3 oxidation state decreases down the group. It is due to increase in size and metallic character.

Anomalous Properties of Nitrogen

- It shows anomalous behaviour due to its small size, high electronegativity, high ionisation energy and absence of *d*-orbitals.
- It has unique ability to form $p\pi$-$p\pi$ multiple bonds with itself and with other elements because small size and high electronegativity whereas heavier elements of this group do not from $p\pi$-$p\pi$ bonds due to ineffective overlapping.
- Nitrogen exists as diatomic molecule as $N \equiv N$, whereas phosphorus, arsenic and antimony form single bond as P—P, As—As and Sb—Sb. Bi form metallic bonds in elemental state.
- Due to the absence of *d*-orbitals in the valence shell of N, its covalency is restricted to four and cannot form $d\pi$-$p\pi$ bond, whereas heavier elements have vacant *d*-orbitals in their valence shell thus they can expand their covalency beyond four and form $d\pi$-$p\pi$ bond. e.g. $R_3P = O$ or $R_3P = CH_2$ (R = alkyl group).
- P and As can form $d\pi$-$d\pi$ bond with transition metals when their compounds act as a ligand. e.g. $P(C_2H_5)_3$ and $As(C_6H_5)_3$.
- N—N bond is weaker than the single P—P bond due to high interelectronic repulsion of non-bonding electrons in N_2 molecule which is due to small bond length.

Trends in Chemical Reactivity

Hydrides	General formula, MH_3
Bond angle	$NH_3 > PH_3 > AsH_3 > SbH_3 > BiH_3$
Basicity	$NH_3 > PH_3 > AsH_3 > SbH_3 \geq BiH_3$
*Boiling point	$PH_3 < AsH_3 < NH_3 < SbH_3 < BiH_3$
*Melting point	$PH_3 < AsH_3 < SbH_3 < NH_3$ (due to H-bonding)
Thermal stability	$NH_3 > PH_3 > AsH_3 > SbH_3 > BiH_3$
Reducing character	$NH_3 < PH_3 < AsH_3 < SbH_3 < BiH_3$
Halides	**General formula, MX_3 or MX_5**
Stability	$NF_3 > NCl_3 > NBr_3$
Lewis acid strength	$PCl_3 > AsCl_3 > SbCl_3$ and $PF_3 > PCl_3 > PBr_3 > PI_3$
Lewis base strength	$NI_3 > NBr_3 > NCl_3 > NF_3$
Bond angle	$PF_3 < PCl_3 < PBr_3 < PI_3$
Oxides	**General formula, M_2O_3 and M_2O_5**
Acidic strength of trioxides	$N_2O_3 > P_4O_6 > As_4O_6 > Sb_4O_6$
Acidic strength of oxides of nitrogen	$N_2O < NO < N_2O_3 < N_2O_4 < N_2O_5$ (oxidation number increases)

Reactivity towards metals All these elements react with metals to form binary compounds exhibiting −3 oxidation state such as Ca_3N_2, Ca_3P_2, Na_3As_2, Zn_3Sb_2, Mg_3Bi_2.

Oxides of Nitrogen

Nitrogen forms a number of oxides in different oxidation states. Some important information regarding these oxides are as follows

Name	Oxidation state of nitrogen	Properties	Resonance structures (Lewis dot form)	Bond parameters
Dinitrogen monoxide or dinitrogen oxide [Nitrogen (I) oxide] (N_2O)	+1	Colourless gas, neutral	$\ddot{N}=N=\ddot{O} \leftrightarrow :N\equiv N-\ddot{O}:$	N — N — O 113 pm 119 pm (Linear)
Nitrogen monoxide [Nitrogen (II) oxide] (NO)	+2	Colourless gas, neutral, paramagnetic.	$:N=\ddot{O}: \leftrightarrow :\dot{N}=\ddot{O}:$	N—O 115 pm (Linear)
Dinitrogen trioxide [Nitrogen (III) oxide] (N_2O_3)	+3	Blue solid, acidic	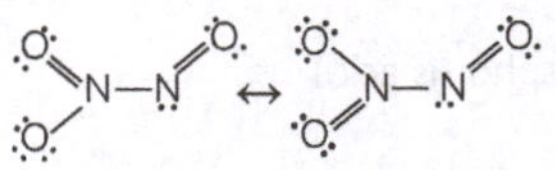	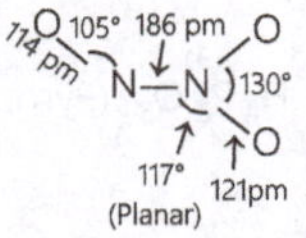
Nitrogen dioxide [Nitrogen (IV) oxide] (NO_2)	+4	Brown gas, reactive, paramagnetic, acidic	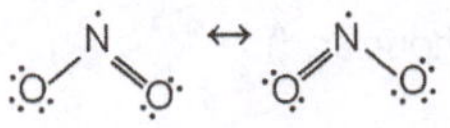	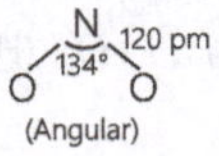
Dinitrogen tetraoxide [Nitrogen (IV) oxide] (N_2O_4)	+4	Colourless exists both in solid and liquid state with NO_2 in equilibrium, acidic.	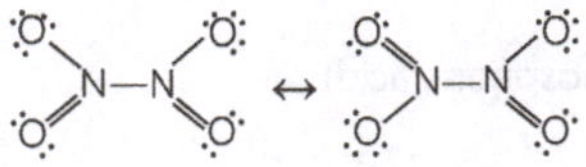	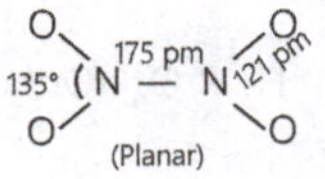
Dinitrogen pentaoxide [Nitrogen (V) oxide] (N_2O_5)	+5	Unstable as gas. In the solid state exists as $[NO_2]^+ [NO_3]^-$, colourless, acidic.	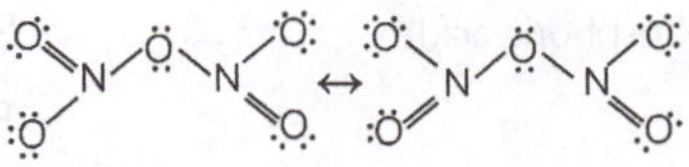	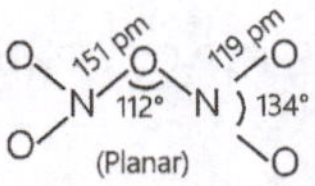

Note NO_2 behaves as a typical odd molecule as it contains odd number of valence electrons. Thus, it get dimerised and converted to stable N_2O_4 molecule with even number of electrons. The covalence of N in N_2O_4 is 4.

Phosphorus-Allotropic Forms

Phosphorus is found in many allotropic forms, the important ones are white, red and black.

- **White phosphorus** is a translucent white waxy solid, which is poisonous in nature. It is insoluble in water but soluble in CS_2. It consist of discrete tetrahedral molecule as shown below.

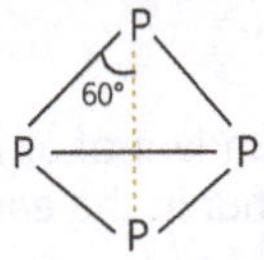

It readily catches fire in air to give the following reaction.

$$P_4 + 5O_2 \longrightarrow \underset{\text{(Dense white fume)}}{P_4O_{10}}$$

- **Red phosphorus** is obtained by heating white phosphorus at 573 K in an inert atmosphere for several days. It is odourless, non-poisonous and insoluble in water as well as in CS_2.
- It is less reactive than white phosphorus. It is polymeric, consisting of chains of P_4 tetrahedra unit. Its structure is as follows

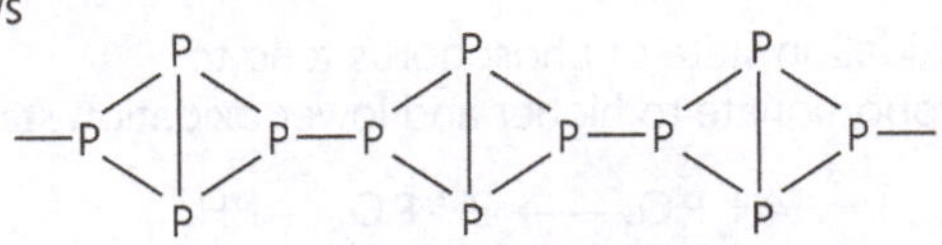

- When red phosphorus is heated under high pressure, a series of phases of **black phosphorus** is formed.
- **Black phosphorus** has two forms α-black and β-black phosphorus. α-black phosphorus is formed, when red phosphorus is heated in a sealed tube at 803 K.
- It has opaque monoclinic or rhombohedral crystals and can be sublimed in air. It does not oxidise in air.
- β-black phosphorus is prepared by heating white phosphorus at 473 K under high pressure. It does not burn in air upto 673 K.

Oxoacids of Phosphorus

For Concept Master Video

Phosphorus forms a number of oxoacids which are as follows

Oxoacids	Structure	Basicity	Preparation
$H_3\overset{(+1)}{P}O_2$ (Hypophosphorus acid or Phosphorus acid) NEET 2019	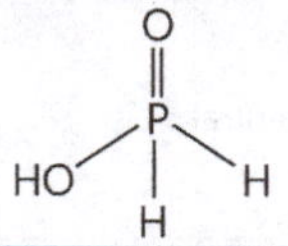	Monobasic	White P_4 + Alkali
$H_3\overset{(+3)}{P}O_3$ (Orthophosphorus acid or Phosphonic acid)	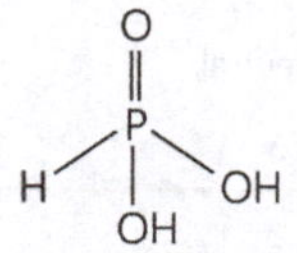	Dibasic	$P_2O_3 + H_2O$
$H_4\overset{(+3)}{P_2}O_5$ (Pyrophosphorus acid)	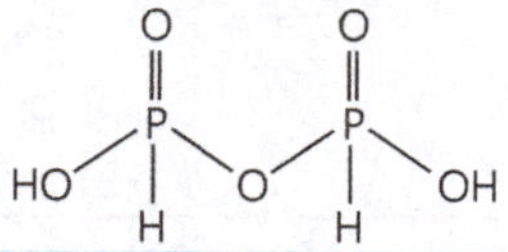	Dibasic	$PCl_3 + H_3PO_3$
$H_4\overset{(+4)}{P_2}O_6$ (Hypophosphoric acid)	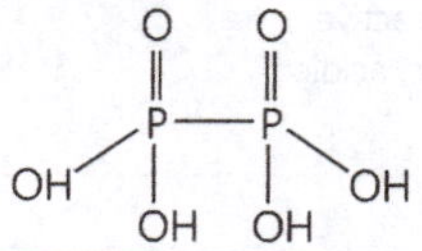	Tetrabasic	Red P_4 + Alkali
$H_3\overset{(+5)}{P}O_4$ (Orthophosphoric acid)	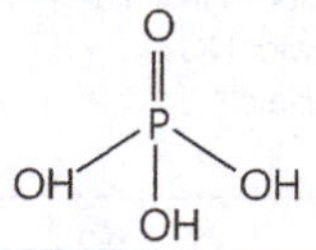	Tribasic	$P_4O_{10} + H_2O$
$H_4\overset{(+5)}{P_2}O_7$ (Pyrophosphoric acid)	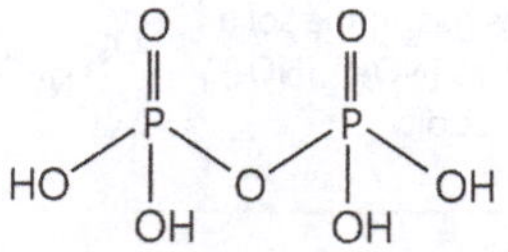	Tetrabasic	Phosphoric acid + Heat
$(H\overset{+5}{P}O_3)_n$ (Metaphosphoric acid exists in polymeric form)	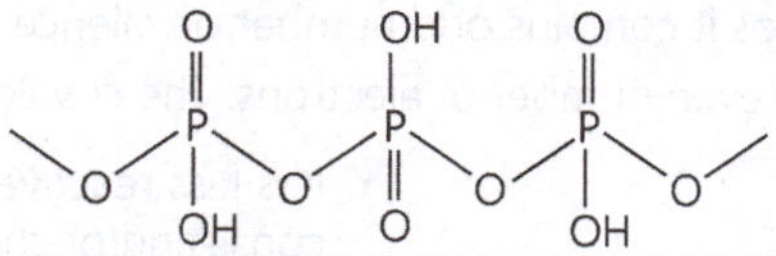		Phosphorus acid + Br_2, heat in a sealed tube.

- + 3 oxidation state of phosphorus tend to disproportionate to higher and lower oxidation states.

e.g. $$4H_3\overset{+3}{P}O_3 \longrightarrow 3H_3\overset{+5}{P}O_4 + \overset{-3}{P}H_3$$

- Those acids which contains P—H bond have strong reducing properties, e.g. hypophosphorus.
- Only those H-atoms which are attached with oxygen in P—OH form are ionisable and cause the basicity. P—H bonds are not ionisable to give H^+ ions. Thus, H_3PO_4 and H_3PO_3 are tribasic and dibasic respectively.

Group 16 Elements

Oxygen (O), sulphur (S), selenium (Se), tellurium (Te), polonium (Po) and livermorium (Lv) are the elements of group 16 in the periodic table. They are also known as group of **chalcogens.**

Electronic Configuration

The general electronic configuration of these elements is ns^2np^4.

Occurrence

- Oxygen is the most abundant of all elements on earth. The abundance of sulphur in the earth's crust is only 0.03 - 0.1%.
- Se and Te are found as metal selenides and tellurides in sulphide ores.
- Po occurs in nature as a decay product of Th and U minerals. Lv is a synthetic radioactive element. It has been produced only in a very small amount and has very short half-life. This limit the study of properties of Lv.

Atomic/Ionic radii

Due to increase in number of shells, atomic/ionic radii increase from top to bottom in a group. The size of oxygen atom is however exceptionally small.

Ionisation Enthalpy

- It decreases down the group due to increase in size.
- Ionisation enthalpy of elements of this group is lower as compared to those of group 15 elements in the corresponding periods. Because of the fact that group 15 elements have extra stable half-filled *p*-orbital configurations.

Electron Gain Enthalpy

Because of the compact nature of oxygen atom, it has less negative electron gain enthalpy than sulphur. But from sulphur onwards, the value again becomes less negative upto polonium.

Electronegativity

Oxygen has the highest electronegativity value amongst the elements after fluorine. Within the group, electronegativity decreases from top to bottom.

Physical Properties

- **Metallic character** increases from top to bottom.

  Oxygen, Sulphur (Non-metal), Selenium, Tellurium (Metalloids), Polonium (Metal) [Radioactive and short lived]

- With an increase in atomic number down the group, the **melting** and **boiling points** increases.
- The melting and boiling point of oxygen is very much greater than sulphur. This is because oxygen exists as diatomic molecules (O_2) whereas sulphur as polyatomic molecule (S_8).
- All the elements of this group exhibit allotropy.

Chemical Properties

Oxidation State

- Elements of group 16 exhibit a number of oxidation states which are as follows

Elements	O	S	Se	Te	Po
Oxidation state	−2, −1, 1, 2	−2, 2, 4, 6	−2, 2, 4, 6	−2, 2, 4, 6	2, 4

- The stability of −2 oxidation state decreases down the group. Oxygen mainly exhibit −2 oxidation state (except in OF_2, where it shows +2), as its electronegativity is very high.
- Stability of +4 oxidation state increases and that of +6 oxidation state decreases down the group due to inert pair effect. Compounds of these elements in +4 and +6 oxidation states are primarily covalent.

Anomalous Behaviour of Oxygen

Due to small size, high electronegativity and absence of *d*-orbital oxygen show anomalous behaviour. Some of them are as follows

- H_2O shows hydrogen bonding while hydrides of other members do not show same behaviour.
- The absence of *d*-orbitals in oxygen limits its covalency to 4 and in practice, rarely exceeds two. Whereas, other members of the group can exceeds their covalence beyond four.

Trends in Chemical Reactivity

Reactivity with Hydrogen

Some of the properties of these halides are discussed below.

- The acidic character of these hydrides decreases as $H_2Te > H_2Se > H_2S > H_2O$. It is because bond enthalpy for the dissociation of H—*E* bond decreases down the group as H—O > H—S > H—Se > H—Te.
- As the H—*E* bond dissociation energy decreases down the group thus, the thermal stability also decreases as $H_2O > H_2S > H_2Se > H_2Te$. NEET 2019
- All the hydrides (except H_2O) have reducing character and this character increases as $H_2S < H_2Se < H_2Te$.
- Melting and boiling point of H_2O is expectedly very high it is due to hydrogen bonding. Thus, the order is as follows

  B.P and M.P: $H_2O > H_2Te > H_2Se > H_2S$ NEET 2022

  Bond angle : $H_2O > H_2S > H_2Se > H_2Te$

Reactivity with Oxygen

- The elements of group-16 form oxides of the EO_2 and EO_3 types. Both type of oxides are acidic in nature and this nature decreases in the order as

  $SO_2 > SeO_2 > TeO_2$ and $SO_3 > SeO_3 > TeO_3$

- The acidic nature of a particular element increases with increase in oxidation number of the central element, e.g. $SO < SO_2 < SO_3$.
- O_3 and SO_2 are gases while SeO_2 is solid.

Reactivity with Halogens

- All the elements of group 16 form the halides of types EX_2, EX_4 and EX_6, where, *E* is an element of the group and *X* is a halogen.
- The stability of halide decreases in the order

  $F^- > Cl^- > Br^- > I^-$.

- Amongst hexahalides, hexafluorides are the only stable halides.
- All the hexafluorides are gaseous in nature.

- Their stability decreases in the following order $SF_6 > SeF_6 > TeF_6$ but ease of hydrolysis increases in the reverse order. NEET 2019
- SF_6 is exceptionally stable for steric reason.
- Hexafluorides have octahedral structure, tetrafluorides have trigonal bipyramidal structure (sp^3d-hybridised) (*see-saw* geometry) and dihalides have tetrahedral structure.
- $\underbrace{SF_4}_{\text{Gas}}, \underbrace{SeF_4}_{\text{Liquid}}, \underbrace{TeF_4}_{\text{Solid}}$
- All elements except oxygen form dichlorides and dibromides having tetrahedral structure and sp^3-hybridised.
- Known monohalides are dimeric in nature, e.g. S_2F_2, S_2Cl_2, S_2Br_2, Se_2Cl_2 and Se_2Br_2.
- Dimeric halides of this group undergo disproportionation as shown below.

$$2Se_2Cl_2 \longrightarrow SeCl_4 + 3Se$$

Sulphur Allotropic Forms

Sulphur forms numerous allotropes of which the **yellow rhombic** (α-sulphur) and **monoclinic** (β-sulphur) are the most important.

(i) **Rhombic sulphur** (α-sulphur)

- It is yellow in colour.
- It is formed on evaporating the solution of roll sulphur in CS_2.
- It is insoluble in water but dissolves in benzene, alcohol and ether (to some extent). It is readily soluble in CS_2.

(ii) **Monoclinic sulphur** (β-sulphur)

- It is prepared by melting rhombic sulphur above 369 K.
- It is soluble in CS_2.
- It is stable above 369 K.

(iii) The stable form at room temperature is rhombic sulphur which transforms to monoclinic sulphur when heated above 369 K. At 369 K, both the forms are stable. This temperature is called **transition temperature.**

(iv) The S_8 ring in both forms is puckered and has a crown shape. In cyclo S_6, the ring adopts the chair form :

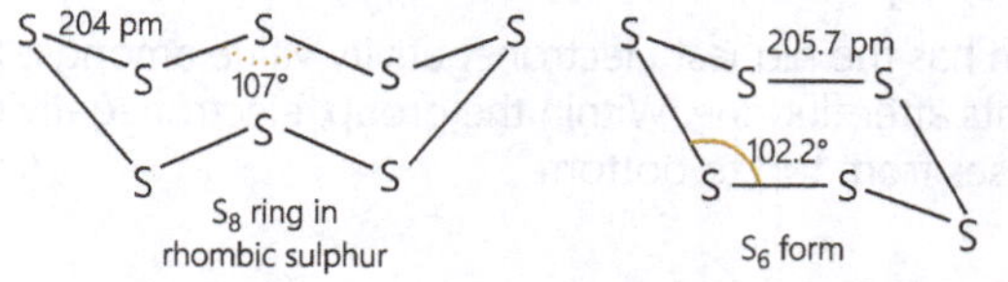

(v) At elevated temperature (~1000 K). S_2 is the dominant species and is paramagnetic.

Oxoacids of Sulphur

Sulphur forms a number of oxoacids structures of some important oxoacids are given in following table. NEET 2023

Oxoacids	Sulphurous acid (H_2SO_3)	Sulphuric acid (H_2SO_4)	Pyrosulphuric or Oleum ($H_2S_2O_7$)	Peroxodisulphuric acid Marshall's acid ($H_2S_2O_8$)
Structure	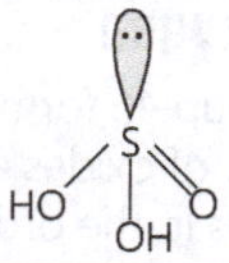	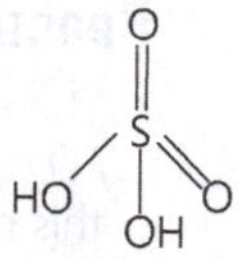	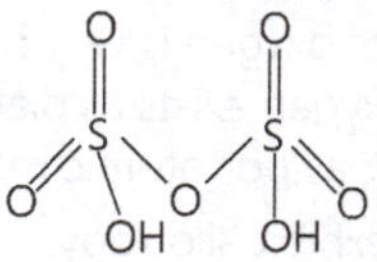	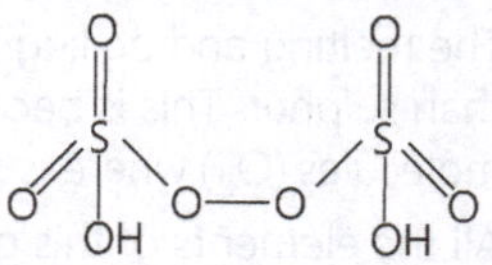
Oxidation state of sulphur	+4	+6	+6	+6

Group 17 Elements

- Fluorine (F), chlorine (Cl), bromine (Br), iodine (I), astatine (At) and tennessine (Ts) are the members of group 17 (halogen family). These are collectively known as the **halogens.**
- (In Greek *halo* means salt and genes means born, i.e. salt producers). These are highly reactive non-metallic elements.
- Astatine and tennessine are radioactive elements.

Electronic Configuration

General electronic configuration of these elements is ns^2np^5.

Occurrence

- Out of all halogen element, F and Cl are much abundant while Br and I are not that much. At and Ts are very limited in amount as they are radioactive elements.
- Fluorides occur in soil, river water, bones and teeth of animals. Chlorides, bromides and iodides are persent in sea water.

Atomic/Ionic Radii

Halogens have the smallest radii in their respective periods. From top to bottom, atomic/ionic radii increases with increase in number of shells. Fluorine is exceptionally small.

Ionisation Enthalpy

Halogens have very high value of ionisation enthalpy and on moving down the group, it decreases due to increase in atomic size.

Electron Gain Enthalpy

- Halogens have maximum negative electron gain enthalpy in the corresponding periods. This is because atoms of these elements have only one electron less than stable noble gas configurations. It is due to the small size of fluorine atom because of which there are strong inter electronic repulsions in the small 2*p*-orbitals of fluorine. Thus, incoming electron does not encounter much attraction.
- Electron gain enthalpies of elements of group becomes less negative down the group. However, the negative electron gain enthalpy of F is less than that of Cl due to small size of fluorine atom.

Electronegativity

Halogens have maximum electronegativity in whole periodic table. F is the most electronegative element.

Physical Properties

- Fluorine and chlorine are gases, bromine is a liquid and iodine is a solid.
- Their **melting** and **boiling points** steadily increase with atomic size due to increase in van der Waals' forces of attraction.
- Due to small size of F-atom and large electron-electron repulsion among the lone pairs of fluorine, the bond dissociation enthalpy of F_2 is smaller as compared to that of Cl_2, whereas the **bond dissociation enthalpies** from Cl_2 onwards show the expected trend as follows

$$Cl—Cl > F—F > Br—Br > I—I$$

Chemical Properties

Oxidation States

- The most common oxidation state of halogen is –1. However, Cl, Br and I exhibit +1, + 3, + 5 and +7 oxidation states as well.
- Order of oxidising power of halogens is $F_2 > Cl_2 > Br_2 > I_2$.
- In general, a halogen oxidises halide ions of higher atomic number.

$$F_2 + 2X^- \longrightarrow 2F^- + X_2 \quad (X = Cl, Br \text{ or } I)$$

$$Cl_2 + 2X^- \longrightarrow 2Cl^- + X_2 \quad (X = Br \text{ or } I)$$

$$Br_2 + 2I^- \longrightarrow 2Br^- + I_2$$

- The relative oxidising power of halogens can be further illustrated by their reactions with water.

$$2F_2(g) + 2H_2O(l) \longrightarrow 4H^+(aq) + 4F^-(aq) + O_2(g)$$

$$X_2(g) + H_2O(l) \longrightarrow HX(aq) + HOX(aq)$$

$$(X = Cl \text{ or } Br)$$

$$4I^-(aq) + 4H^+(aq) + O_2(g) \longrightarrow 2I_2(s) + 2H_2O(l)$$

Anomalous Behaviour of Fluorine

- Due to the small size, highest electronegativity, low F—F bond dissociation enthalpy and non-availability of *d*-orbital. Fluorine shows following anomalous behaviour.
- Ionisation enthalpy, electronegativity and electrode potential are higher for fluorine than expected from other halogens, whereas ionic and covalent radii, melting and boiling points and electron gain enthalpy are quite low than expected.

Trends in Chemical Reactivity

Reactivity towards Hydrogen

- They all react with H_2 to give hydrogen halides.

  $F_2 > Cl_2 > Br_2 > I_2$; order of reactivity to form *HX*.
- Hydrides of halogens are covalent in the gaseous state and behave as acids in the aqueous solution.

  (a) HI > HBr > HCl > HF, acidic strength

  (b) HI > HBr > HCl > HF, reducing character

  (c) HF > HI > HBr > HCl, boiling points

  (d) HF > HCl > HBr > HI, thermal stability

  (e) HI > HBr > HCl > HF, bond length

  (f) HF > HCl > HBr > HI, bond dissociation enthalpy

  (g) HI > HF > HBr >HCl, melting point

Reactivity towards Oxygen

- Halogens form many oxides with oxygen but most of them are unstable. Fluorine forms two oxides OF_2 and O_2F_2, while other halogens form oxides in which the oxidation states of these halogens range from +1 to +7.
- O_2F_2 oxidises Pu to PuF_6. This reaction is used to remove plutonium as PuF_6 from spent nuclear fuel.
- A combination of kinetic and thermodynamic factors lead to the generally decreasing order of stability of oxides formed by halogens, I > Cl > Br.
- Due to greater polarisibility of the bond between iodine and oxygen, oxides of iodine are more stable. In case of chlorine, multiple bond formation between chlorine and oxygen takes place (due to availability of *d*-orbitals) which leads to increase in stability of its oxides as compare to bromine oxides.
- Bromine lacks both the characteristics, hence stability of oxides of bromine is least. In general the lower oxides of halogens are less stable than higher ones.
- Chlorine oxides (Cl_2O, ClO_2, Cl_2O_6 and Cl_2O_7) are highly reactive oxidising agents and tend to explode. ClO_2 is commonly used as bleaching agent.

- Bromine oxides (Br_2O, BrO_2, BrO_3) exist only at low temperature and are powerful oxidising agents. Iodine oxides (I_2O_4, I_2O_5, I_2O_7) are insoluble solids and decompose on heating. I_2O_5 is a very good oxidising agent and is used in the estimation of CO.

Reactivity towards Metals

- Halogens react with metals to form metal halides. The ionic character of the halides decreases in the order $MF > MCl > MBr > MI$, where M is a monovalent metal.

- Halides in higher oxidation state will be more covalent than the one in lower oxidation state. e.g. $SnCl_4$, $PbCl_4$, $SbCl_5$ and UF_6 are more covalent than $SnCl_2$, $PbCl_2$, $SbCl_3$ and UF_4 respectively.

Reactivity towards other Halogens

- Halogens combine amongst themselves to form a number of compounds known as interhalogens of the type XX', XX'_3, XX'_5 and XX'_7, where X is larger size halogen and X' is smaller size halogen.

Oxoacids of Halogens

Different oxoacids of halogens are as follows

Halic (I) acid (Hypohalous acid)	**HOF** (Hypofluorous acid)	**HOCl** (Hypochlorous acid)	**HOBr** (Hypobromous acid)	**HOI** (Hypoiodous acid)
Halic (III) acid (Halous acid)	—	HOClO (Chlorous acid)	—	—
Halic (V) acid (Halic acid)	—	$HOClO_2$ (Chloric acid)	$HOBrO_2$ (Bromic acid)	$HOIO_2$ (Iodic acid)
Halic (VII) acid (Perhalic acid)	—	$HOClO_3$ (Perchloric acid)	$HOBrO_3$ (Perbromic acid)	$HOIO_3$ (Periodic acid)

Thermal stability, covalent character of X—O bond → Oxidising power, Acidity increases

← E.M thermal stability, Acidic strength decreases

Structure

The structure of oxoacids of chlorine are

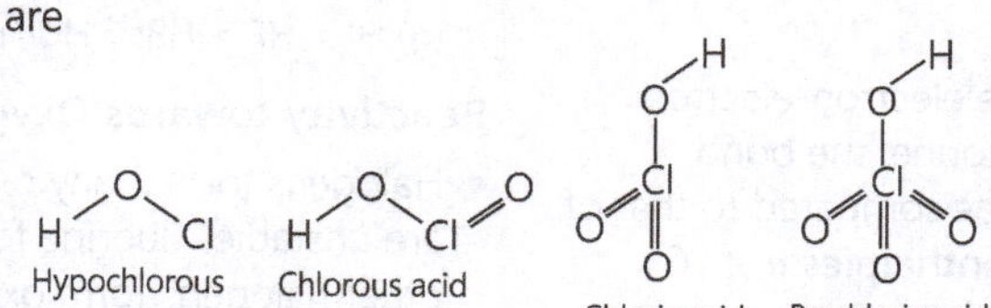

Hypochlorous acid   Chlorous acid   Chloric acid   Perchloric acid

Interhalogen Compounds

- Two different halogens may react to form interhalogen compounds of the type XX', XX'_3, XX'_5, XX'_7. where, X = higher molecular mass (or more electropositive) halogen, X' is smaller molecular mass halogen.
- Their physical properties are intermediate between those of constituent halogens except that their m.p. and b.p. are a little higher than expected.
- In all interhalogen compounds, X—X' bond is weaker than X—X bond (except F—F bond). So, these compounds are more reactive than individual halogens (except fluorine).
- These are all covalent molecule and are diamagnetic in nature.

Properties

Some of the important interhalogen compounds with their properties are tabulated below.

Types of interhalogen compounds	Hybridisation	Formula and name	Physical state and colour at ordinary temperatures	Structure and shape
XX'	sp^3	ClF-Chlorine fluoride	Gas, colourless	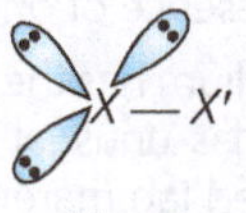 (Linear)
		BrF-Bromine fluoride	Liquid below 293 K, pale-brown gas above 293 K	
		BrCl-Bromine chloride	Gas, reddish yellow	
		ICl-Iodine chloride	Solid, ruby red (α-form)	
		IBr-Iodine bromide	Solid, brown like iodine	
XX'_3	sp^3d	ClF_3-Chlorine trifluoride	Liquid below 261 K, colourless gas above 261 K	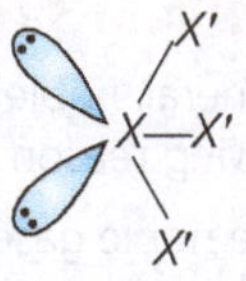 (Bent T-shaped)
		BrF_3-Bromine trifluoride	Liquid, yellow green	
		ICl_3-Iodine trichloride	Solid, orange	
		IF_3-Iodine trifluoride	Yellow powder	
XX'_5	sp^3d^2	ClF_5-Chlorine pentafluoride	Liquid, colourless	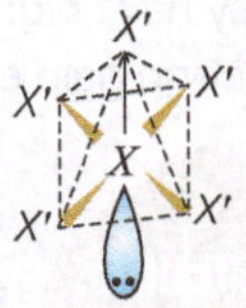 (Square pyramidal)
		BrF_5-Bromine pentafluoride	Liquid, colourless	
		IF_5-Iodine pentafluoride	Gas, colourless but solid below 77 K	
XX'_7	sp^3d^3	IF_7-Iodine heptafluoride	Gas, colourless	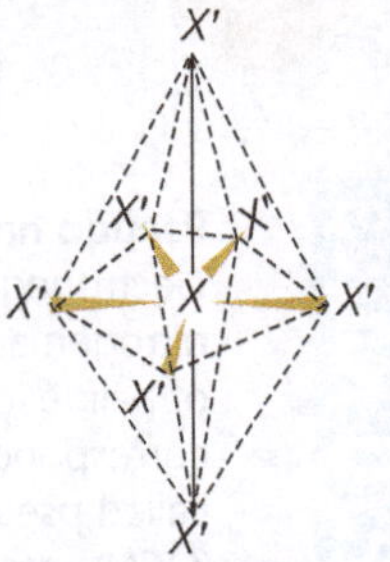 (Pentagonal bipyramidal)

Group 18 Elements

- The group 18 includes helium (He), neon (Ne), argon (Ar), krypton (Kr), xenon (Xe), radon (Rn) and oganesson (Og). Og and Rn is radioactive. These are known as **rare gas** or **inert gases**.
- All there are gases and chemically unreactive. They form very few compounds, because of this they are termed as **noble gases**.

Occurrence

All these gases except radon and oganesson occur in the atmosphere. In dry air their abundance is ~1% by volume of which argon is major constituent. Helium and sometime neon are found in minerals of radioactive origin, e.g. pitch blende, monazite, cleveite. Radon and oganesson can be obtained as

$$^{226}_{88}Ra \longrightarrow ^{222}_{86}Rn + ^{4}_{2}He$$

$$^{249}_{98}Cf + ^{48}_{20}Ca \longrightarrow ^{294}_{118}Og + 3n$$

Electronic Configuration

The general electronic configuration of these elements is ns^2np^6 (except He whose electronic configuration is $1s^2$).

Atomic Radii

It increases down the group with increase in atomic number.

Ionisation Enthalpy

Due to stable electronic configuration, these gases exhibit very high ionisation enthalpy and it goes on decreasing down the group due to increase in atomic size.

Electron Gain Enthalpy

They have large positive values of electron gain enthalpy due to no tendency to accept the electron.

Physical Properties

- All the noble gases are monoatomic and sparingly soluble in soluble in water.
- They have very low melting and boiling points due to presence of only weak dispersion forces NEET 2020.
- Helium has the lowest boiling point of any known substance. It has unusual diffusing property through most commonly used lab materials, e.g. rubber, glass, plastics etc.

Chemical Properties

In general, noble gases are least reactive. This is due to following reason

- The noble gases (except helium) have completely filled ns^2np^6 electronic configuration in their valence shell.
- They have high ionisation enthalpy and more positive electron gain enthalpy.
- Neil Bartlett prepared a compound of a noble gas which was $Xe^+ [PtF_6]^-$.
- Structure of important xenon compound NEET 2020 are represented as

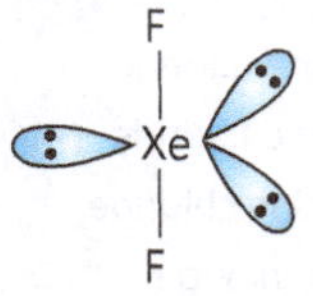

(a) XeF_2 (Linear, sp^3d)

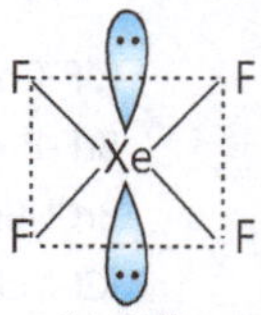

(b) XeF_4 (Square planar, sp^3d^2)

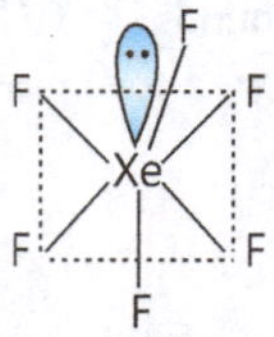

(c) XeF_6 (Distorted octahedral, sp^3d^3)

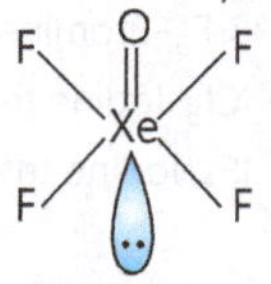

(d) $XeOF_4$ (Square pyramidal, sp^3d^2)

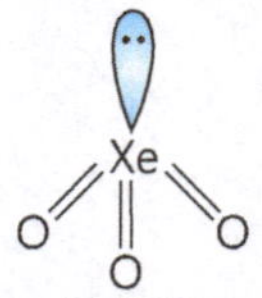

(e) XeO_3 (Pyramidal, sp^3)

Caution Points

- Generally, group 13 elements form only E_2O_3 type oxides except thallium (Tl), it forms two oxides Tl_2O (more stable) and Tl_2O_3 (less stable).
- Oxides in higher oxidation state of an element are more acidic than that of the lower oxidation state.
- Lead does not shown catination property.
- Stability of +1 oxidation state progressively increases from Al to Tl while +3 oxidation state follows the reverse order.

PYQ Notes

1. **Pseudo halide** ions consists of two or more electronegative atoms of which atleast one is nitrogen and have properties similar to those of halide ions (e.g. CN^-, SCN^-, OCN^- etc). The corresponding dimeric molecules are called pseudo halogens. (e.g. $(CN)_2$, $(SCN)_2$, $(OCN)_2$ etc.) **NEET 2021**
2. Dinitrogen is a robust compound, but reacts at high altitude to form oxides. Higher concentration of NO_2 damage the leaves of the plant and retard the rate of photosynthesis. **JEE Main 2022**
3. PCl_5 forms five bonds using the vacant *d*-orbitals to expand the octet. NCl_5 does not exist. It has only *s* and *p*-orbitals and no *d*-orbitals in the second energy level. **JEE Main 2022**
4. Nitrous acid (HNO_2) is unstable and exists in solution only. **NEET 2020**
5. Nitrogen forms three different hydrides, i.e. ammonia (NH_3), hydrazine ($NH_2—NH_2$) and hydrazoic acid (N_3H).
6. Tooth enamel is made up of calcium phosphate and fluoride ions which combines with calcium and phosphate in enamel. **JEE Main 2022**
7. Polar stratospheric clouds provide surface for the hydrolysis of chlorine nitrate gives HOCl and HNO_3 while its reaction with HCl produces HNO_3 and Cl_2. **JEE Main 2022**
8. The elements present in 15th group are collectively called '**pnictogens, pnicogens or pnictides**' drived from Greek word which means "to choke" referring to the chocking property of nitrogen gas. **NEET 2020**
9. Flerovium (Fl) has been prepared in small amount and its half-life is short, thus its chemistry has not been established. **NEET 2019**
10. In gas phase, XeF_6 has distorted octahedral structure while in solid, XeF_6 contains tetrameric and hexameric units in which square pyramidal XeF_5^+ units are linked by bent F^- pyramidal bridges.
11. Nh has been prepared in small amounts and its half-life of most stable isotope is 20 seconds. Due to these reasons, its chemistry has not been established yet. **NEET 2019**

Step by Step

Mastering NCERT

- Concept Builders
- Topical Questions
- Assertion-Reason
- Statement Type
- Matching Type
- Numerical Value
- NCERT Exemplar's
- Past Exams'
- Skill Boosters

Concept Builders

1. Boron is a semi-metal due to its high ionisation enthalpy. [T/F]
2. Write the molecular formula of cryolite from which aluminium can be obtained.
3. There is a discontinuity in the ionisation enthalpy values between Al and .... that between .... and Tl.
4. Boron is unable to form BF_6^{3-} ion, while Al can form AlF_6^{6-}. [T/F]
5. In the bonding of diborane, the (3C—2e) bridge bonds are also referred to as ....
6. Tendency of catenation follows the order $C \leq Si \leq Ge \leq Sn$. [T/F]
7. Name the one allotrope of carbon which is thermodynamically most stable.
8. Carbon black, coke and charcoal are all pure forms of diamond. [T/F]
9. Write the name of that allotrope of carbon, which contain 'dangling bond'.
10. Stability of dihalides of group-14 .... (increases/decreases) down the group.
11. Nitrogen in the earth crust occurs as chile saltpetre and Indian saltpetre. [T/F]
12. Write the name of the group-15 element present in bones as well as in living cells.
13. Stability of (+ 5) oxidation state ..... (increases/decreases) and (+ 3) state .... (increases/decreases) as we go down in the group 15 due to inert pair effect.
14. Write the name of the strongest reducing agent of group 15 hydrides.
15. Name the nitrogen oxide having two nitrogen atoms that does not contain N—N bond.
16. Oxygen has less negative electron gain enthalpy than sulphur due to its compact nature. [T/F]
17. .... effect is the cause of decreasing the stability of (+ 6) oxidation state and increasing the stability of (+ 4) oxidation state down the group-in group-16.
18. Write the name of two important allotropes of sulphur.
19. Write the number of P—O—P bond(s) in $H_4P_2O_5$ (oxoacids of P).
20. H_3PO_3 is a tribasic acid. [T/F]
21. Fluorine is present in cryolite. [T/F]
22. Standard electrode potential of halogens are dependent on the dissociation enthalpy, electron gain enthalpy and ....
23. Write the name of the halogen acid having highest bond dissociation enthalpy.
24. ClF_3 is a colourless gas having .... shape.
25. In interhalogen compounds, as the ratio between radii of X and X' increases, number of atoms per molecule also increases. [T/F]
26. Noble gases exhibit very high ionisation energy and very small positive value of electron gain enthalpy. [T/F]
27. The hybridisation and geometry of $XeOF_4$ are .... and .... respectively.
28. Name the compound of Xe, having same number of lone pair as in XeO_3 and $XeOF_4$.
29. Noble gases have large values of electron gain enthalpy. [T/F]
30. XeF_2 and XeF_4 have .... and .... structures respectively.

Topical Questions

Introduction

1 The number of possible oxidation states of *p*-block elements NCERT Pg 307

(a) first decrease and then increase in a period
(b) increases towards the right of the periodic table
(c) first increases then decreases down the group
(d) first decreases then increases down the group

2 The second period elements of *p*-block starting from boron, are restricted to a maximum covalency of NCERT Pg 308

(a) four (using 1*s*, 2*s* and two 2*p*-orbitals)
(b) six (using 1*s* and 2*s* -orbitals)
(c) four (using one 2*s* and three 2*p*-orbitals)
(d) six (using 1*s* and three 2*p*-orbitals)

3 The third period elements of *p*-block with the electronic configuration $3s^2 3p^n$ have the vacant 3*d* orbitals lying between the NCERT Pg 308

(a) 3*p* and 4*s* levels of energy
(b) 3*s* and 3*p* levels of energy
(c) 3*s* and 4*s* levels of energy
(d) 2*p* and 3*s* levels of energy

4 Which orbitals are used by third period of *p*-block elements in order to expand their covalency beyond four? NCERT Pg 308

(a) 3*d* (b) 4*s*
(c) 3*p* (d) 4*d*

5 The element that shows greater ability to form $p\pi$-$p\pi$ multiple bonds, is NCERT Pg 309

(a) Ge (b) Si
(c) Sn (d) C

Group-13 Elements : The Boron Family

6 Boron forms only $[BF_4]^-$. Which one of the following is formed by aluminium? NCERT Pg 308

(a) $[AlF_4]^-$ (b) $[AlF_6]^{3-}$
(c) $[AlF_4]^{3-}$ (d) $[AlF_6]^-$

7 Boron is not found in the form of the compounds given below. NCERT Pg 309

(a) Borax (b) Kernite
(c) Carnallite (d) Orthoboric acid

8 Which of the following element is the most abundant metal and the third most abundant element in the earth's crust? NCERT Pg 309

(a) Al (b) B
(c) Ga (d) In

9 Between which of the following elements is the discontinuity in the ionisation enthalpy values observed? NCERT Pg 309

(a) Al and Ga (b) In and Al
(c) B and Al (d) Ga and Tl

10 Atomic radius of Ga (135 pm) is less than that of Al (143 pm) because NCERT Pg 309

(a) of the small variation in the inner core of the electronic configuration
(b) of poor screening effect of *d*-electrons for the outer electrons from the increased nuclear charge in gallium
(c) of the large difference in *d*-electrons
(d) of the inert pair effect

11 Among the elements of group-13, boron possesses a high melting point due to NCERT Pg 310

(a) very high electronegativity
(b) very high ionisation energy
(c) small size
(d) strong bonding between individual atoms in the solid state

12 Which of the following oxidation state(s) is/are shown by Ga, In and Tl? NCERT Pg 310

(a) Only +1 (b) Only +3
(c) +3 as well as +1 (d) Only +2

13 The relative stability of +1 oxidation state of group 13 elements follows the order NCERT Pg 310

(a) Al < Ga < Tl < In
(b) Al < Ga < In < Tl
(c) Tl < In < Ga < Al
(d) Ga < Al < In < Tl

14 The correct statements regarding the possible reason for the trend of electronegativity in group-13 elements is NCERT Pg 310

(a) similarities in density of the elements
(b) discrepancies in atomic size of the elements
(c) discrepancies in atomic number of the elements
(d) similarities in atomic mass of the elements

15 Consider the given statements regarding the properties of boron. NCERT Pg 310

I. It is a hard refractory solid.
II. It has low melting point and high density.
III. It shows high electrical conductivity.

Choose the correct answer from the options given below.

(a) Only I (b) I and III
(c) II and III (d) I and II

16 Which of the following statements is/are correct regarding gallium? **NCERT Pg 310**

I. It has unusually low melting point (303 K).
II. It exists in liquid state during summer.
III. It has a high boiling point (2676 K).

Choose the correct answer from the options given below

(a) I and II (b) I and III
(c) II and III (d) I, II and III

17 Which of the following statements is correct regarding group 13 elements? **NCERT Pg 310**

(a) Density increases down the group from B to Ga and then decreases upto Tl.
(b) Boiling point of gallium is very high (2676 K).
(c) Boron is a soft non-metal.
(d) Boron has high electrical conductivity.

18 Which of the following statements is/are incorrect ?

I. Compounds of group 13 elements in +1 oxidation state is predominant.
II. Compounds of group 13 elements in, +3 oxidation state is oxidising in nature.
III. Compounds of group 13 elements in +1 oxidation state are less ionic than those in +3 oxidation state.

Choose the correct answer from the options given below. **NCERT Pg 310**

(a) Only I (b) II and III (c) I and II (d) Only III

19 Standard electrode potential values, $E^{\ominus}$ for Al^{3+}/Al is –1.66 V and that of Tl^{3+}/Tl is +1.26 V. Which of the following is incorrect regarding the given information? **NCERT Pg 310**

(a) Tl^{3+} is a powerful reducing agent.
(b) Tl^{+} is more stable in solution than Tl^{3+}.
(c) Al is more electropositive than thallium.
(d) Al is able to form +3 ion easily.

20 In trivalent state, the number of electrons around the central atom in a molecule of the compounds of group 13 elements will be **NCERT Pg 310, 311**

(a) three (b) six (c) eight (d) nine

21 Consider the following reaction. **NCERT Pg 311**

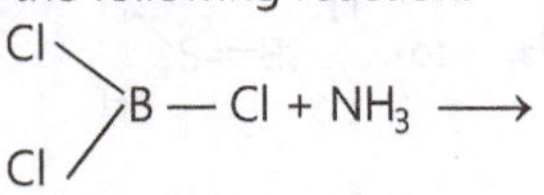

The product formed will be

(a) $\overset{+}{N}H_3Cl$ and $\overset{-}{B}Cl_2$ (b) 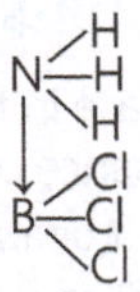

(c) 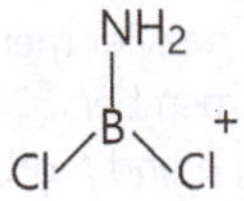 + HCl (d) 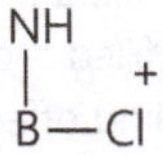 + 2HCl

22 $AlCl_3$ achieves stability by forming a dimer. Structure of this dimer is **NCERT Pg 311**

(a) 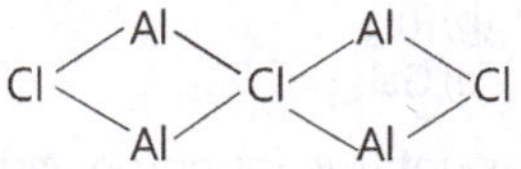

(b) 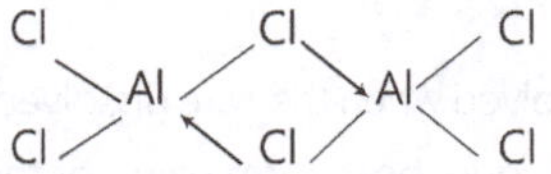

(c) 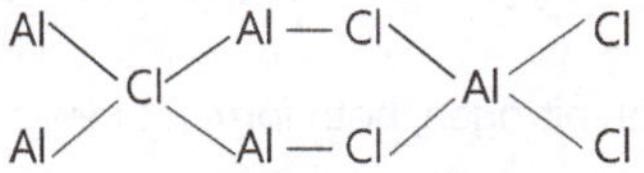

(d) 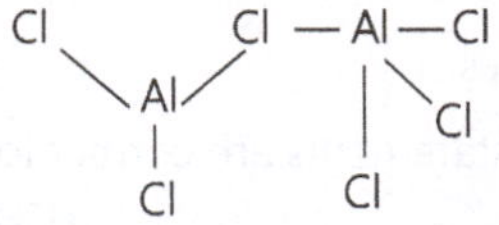

23 Consider the following reactions. **NCERT Pg 311**

$$4B(s) + 3O_2(g) \xrightarrow{\Delta} I$$
$$2Al(s) + N_2(g) \xrightarrow{\Delta} II$$

Identify the products I and II.

(a) $I \rightarrow B_2O_3(s)$, $II \rightarrow AlN(g)$
(b) $I \rightarrow B_2O_3(g)$, $II \rightarrow AlN(s)$
(c) $I \rightarrow B_2O_3(g)$, $II \rightarrow AlN(g)$
(d) $I \rightarrow B_2O_3(s)$, $II \rightarrow AlN(s)$

24 Boron trioxide is acidic and reacts with metal oxides to form **NCERT Pg 311**

(a) metal borates (b) metal boroxides
(c) metal hydroxide (d) metal dioxide

25 In the reaction,

$$2Al(s) + 2NaOH(aq) + 6H_2O(l) \longrightarrow 2A + 3H_2(g)$$

A is **NCERT Pg 311**

(a) $Na^{+}[Al(OH)_4]^{-}$ (*aq*) Sodium tetrahydroxoaluminate (III)
(b) $Na_2[Al(OH)_4]^{-}$ (*aq*) Sodium tetrahydroxoaluminate (III)
(c) $Na^{+}[Al(OH)_6]^{-}$ (*aq*) Sodium hexahydroxoaluminate (II)
(d) $Na[Al(OH)_6]^{-}$ (*aq*) Sodium hexahydroxoaluminate (III)

26 Which of the following statement is incorrect? **NCERT Pg 311**

(a) The trichlorides of group 13 elements, on hydrolysis form $[M(OH)_4]^{-}$.
(b) $AlCl_3$ in acidified aqueous solution forms $[Al(H_2O)_6]^{3+}$.
(c) Boron is unreactive in crystalline form.
(d) Boron forms a very thin hydroxide layer on its surface.

27 Which of the following is correct statement? **NCERT Pg 311**

(a) Aluminium dissolves in dilute mineral acids but is made passive by concentrated nitric acid.
(b) Aluminium vessel can be used to storage of NaOH.
(c) Aluminium chloride does not dissociate in water.
(d) AlF_3 is soluble in anhydrous HF.

28 The group 13 elements react with halogens to form trihalides except NCERT Pg 311

(a) BCl_3 (b) TlI_3
(c) $AlCl_3$ (d) GaI_3

29 Which of the following is not true for boron and aluminium? NCERT Pg 311

(a) Hydrogen gas is evolved when they are dissolved in alkali.
(b) On heating with oxygen, both form oxide of the type M_2O_3.
(c) On heating with nitrogen, both form nitrides of the type MN.
(d) Both form acidic oxides

30 Which of the following statements are correct for the compound Al_2Cl_6? NCERT Pg 311

I. Six Al—Cl bonds are of same length.
II. The terminal Cl—Al—Cl is 118°.
III. Four Al—Cl bonds are of same length and two of different length.
IV. The angle Cl—Al—Cl is 79° and Al—Cl—Al is 101°.

Choose the correct answer from the options given below.

(a) I, II and III
(b) II, III and IV
(c) I, III and IV
(d) I, II and IV

31 Boron is unable to form BF_6^{3-} ion due to NCERT Pg 312

(a) unavailability of d-orbitals
(b) small size of boron atom
(c) strong reducing agent
(d) less reactivity towards halogen

32 The similarities among the trichlorides, tribromides and triiodides of all group 13 elements is/are : that they are NCERT Pg 312

(a) covalent in nature
(b) hydrolysed in non-aqueous solution
(c) not hydrolysed
(d) ionic in nature

33 Which of the following elements does not exist in aqueous medium, as species like tetrahedral $[M(OH)_4]^-$ and octahedral $[M(H_2O)_6]^{3+}$? NCERT Pg 312

(a) Boron (b) Thallium
(c) Gallium (d) Indium

34 BF_3 easily reacts with a Lewis base such as NH_3 to complete octet around boron. This can be expressed as NCERT Pg 312

(a) $F_3B + :NH_3 \longrightarrow F_3B \leftarrow NH_3$
(b) $F_3B + :NH_3 \longrightarrow F_3B \rightarrow NH_3$
(c) $:BF_3 + NH_3 \longrightarrow BF_3 \rightarrow NH_3$
(d) $:BF_3 + NH_3 \longrightarrow BF_3 \leftarrow NH_3$

35 Which of the following reaction is not shown by diborane? NCERT Pg 313

(a) $B_2H_6 + 2NMe_3 \longrightarrow 2BH_3 \cdot NMe_3$
(b) $B_2H_6 + 6H_2O \longrightarrow 2B(OH)_3 + 6H_2$
(c) $B_2H_6 + 2CO \longrightarrow 2BH_3 \cdot CO$
(d) $B_2H_6 + H_2 \longrightarrow 2BH_4$

36 In the given reaction, NCERT Pg 313

$$B_2H_6 + NH_3 \xrightarrow[\text{ratio}]{(1:2)\text{ molar}} A \xrightarrow{\Delta} B + H_2(g)$$

Identify the 'A' and 'B' respectively.

(a) H_3BO_3, B_2O_3
(b) H_3BO_3, HBO_2
(c) $[BH_2(NH_3)_2]^+ [BH_4]^-$, B_2O_3
(d) $[BH_2(NH_3)_2]^+ [BH_4]^-$, $B_3N_3H_6$

37 Diborane (B_2H_6) reacts independently with O_2 and H_2O to produce, respectively. NCERT Pg 313

(a) B_2O_3 and H_3BO_3
(b) B_2O_3 and $[BH_4]^-$
(c) H_3BO_3 and B_2O_3
(d) HBO_2 and H_3BO_3

38 Which of the following statement is correct regarding diborane? NCERT Pg 313

(a) The two bridged hydrogen atoms and the one boron atoms lie in one plane.
(b) Out of six B—H bonds, two bonds can be described in terms of 2-centre-2-electron bonds.
(c) Out of six B—H bonds, four B—H bonds can be described in terms of 3-centre-2-electron bonds.
(d) The four terminal B—H bonds are 2-centre-2-electron regular bonds.

39 Identify the correct structure of diborane, B_2H_6. NCERT Pg 313

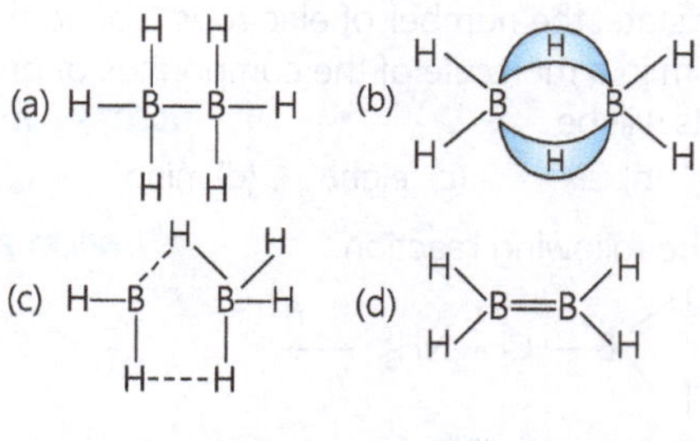

Group-14 Elements : The Carbon Family

40 The small increase in the covalent radii from Si to Pb is due to the presence of NCERT Pg 315

(a) half-filled d-orbitals in heavier members
(b) completely filled d and f-orbitals in heavier members
(c) completely filled d-orbitals in lighter members
(d) poor shielding effect of intervening d and f-orbitals

41 Which of the following is the correct order of first ionisation enthalpy of group 14 elements? NCERT Pg 315

(a) Si > Ge > Sn > Pb
(b) Si > Ge > Sn < Pb
(c) Si < Ge < Sn < Pb
(d) Si < Ge < Sn > Pb

42 Which of the following statement is incorrect about group 14 elements? NCERT Pg 315, 316

(a) All members of group 14 are solids.
(b) Carbon and silicon are non-metals whereas germanium, tin and lead are metals
(c) Melting and boiling points of group 14 elements are higher than those of corresponding elements of group 13
(d) The general electronic configuration of group 14 is ns^2np^2

43 The tendency of group 14 elements to show +2 oxidation state increases in the sequence of NCERT Pg 316

(a) Ge = Sn < Pb < C < Si
(b) C < Si < Ge < Sn < Pb
(c) C > Si > Ge > Sn > Pb
(d) C < Si < Ge > Sn = Pb

44 Which of the following option is correct about the following oxides?

GeO, CO_2, CO, GeO_2, SiO_2, SnO_2, SnO NCERT Pg 316

(a) Acidic — GeO_2, CO, SiO_2; Neutral— GeO Amphoteric— CO_2, SnO, SnO_2
(b) Acidic—SnO_2, GeO_2, CO_2; Neutral— CO, SnO, SiO_2 Amphoteric— GeO
(c) Acidic— CO_2, GeO_2, SiO_2; Neutral— CO Amphoteric— SnO_2, SnO
(d) Acidic— GeO, SiO_2, SnO; Neutral— CO, CO_2 Amphoteric — SnO_2, GeO_2

45 Which of the following statements is incorrect about group-14 elements? NCERT Pg 316

(a) These can form halides of formula MX_2 and MX_4.
(b) Except carbon, all other members can react directly with halogen under suitable conditions.
(c) Most of the tetrahalides are ionic in nature.
(d) SnF_4 and PbF_4 are ionic in nature.

46 Consider the following statements. NCERT Pg 316

I. Sn in +2 oxidation state is an oxidising agent.
II. Pb compounds are stable in +2 state.
III. Pb compounds act as reducing agent in +4 state.

Choose the correct answer from the options given below.

(a) Only I
(b) Only II
(c) Only III
(d) I, II and III

47 Which of the following molecule does not exist? NCERT Pg 316

(a) PbI_4
(b) PbF_4
(c) CCl_4
(d) CBr_4

48 Consider the following reaction. NCERT Pg 317

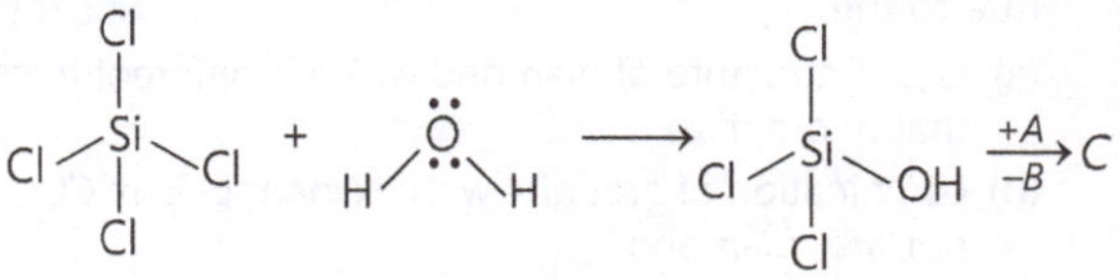

Identify the A, B and C.

(a) $A \longrightarrow 3H_2O$; $B \longrightarrow 3HCl$; $C \longrightarrow$
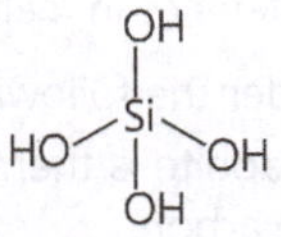

(b) $A \longrightarrow 2H_2O$; $B \longrightarrow 2HCl$; $C \longrightarrow$
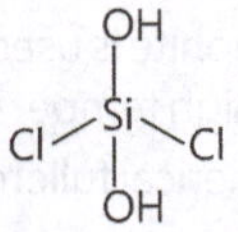

(c) $A \longrightarrow H_2O$; $B \longrightarrow HCl$; $C \longrightarrow$
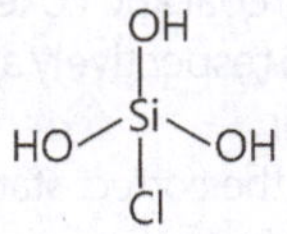

(d) $A \longrightarrow \frac{1}{2}H_2O$; $B \longrightarrow HCl$; $C \longrightarrow$
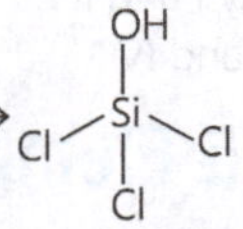

49 Which of the following property is incorrect regarding anomalous behaviour of carbon? NCERT Pg 317

(a) It forms compounds with $p\pi$-$p\pi$ multiple bonds.
(b) It shows catenation property.
(c) Its ionisation enthalpy is lower.
(d) It can accommodate only four pair of electrons.

50 Which of the following statement is incorrect?

NCERT Pg 317

(a) Sn do not form $p\pi$-$p\pi$ bonds.
(b) The order of catination is C >> Si > Ge ≈ Sn.
(c) Lead does not show catenation.
(d) Si—Si bond enthalpy is less than Ge—Ge bond enthalpy.

51 In which of the following allotropes of carbon, each carbon atom undergoes sp^3-hybridisation and linked to four other carbon atoms by using hybridised orbitals in tetrahedral manner? NCERT Pg 317

(a) Diamond
(b) Graphite
(c) Fullerene
(d) C_{60}

52 Graphite conducts electricity due to highly NCERT Pg 318

(a) delocalised nature of π-electrons
(b) localised nature of π-electrons
(c) polarised nature of π-electrons
(d) demobilised nature of π-electrons

53 The major difference between diamond and graphite is due to the NCERT Pg 318
(a) crystal structure of diamond which is different from that of graphite
(b) combination of graphite with oxygen to form CO_2 but not with diamond
(c) different masses of atoms
(d) difference in melting point

54 Consider the following statements. NCERT Pg 318, 319
I. Graphite is thermodynamically most stable allotrope of carbon.
II. Graphite is used as a dry lubricant in machines running at high temperature.
III. Spherical fullerenes are also called bucky sphere.
IV. Charcoal and coke are obtained by heating wood or coal respectively at high temperatures in the absence of air.
Choose the correct statements and select the correct option.
(a) Only I and II (b) Only III and IV
(c) I, II and IV (d) II, III and IV

Group-15 Elements

55 Which of the following statements is incorrect for group 15 elements? NCERT Pg 165
(a) It contains nitrogen, phosphorus, arsenic, antimony, bismuth and moscovium elements.
(b) As we go down the group, there is shift from non-metallic to metallic character.
(c) Nitrogen and phosphorus are non-metals, arsenic and antimony are metalloids, bismuth and moscovium are typical metals.
(d) Ionisation enthalpy increase down the group.

56 The synthetic radioactive element having very short half-life among group 15 elements is NCERT Pg 166
(a) antimony (b) moscovium
(c) livermorium (d) tellurium

57 An element M belongs to group 15 and it occurs as the founder of the apatite family. It is an essential constituent of animal and plant matter. It is also present in bones as well as in living cells. Identify M. NCERT Pg 166
(a) Calcium (b) Magnesium
(c) Nitrogen (d) Phosphorus

58 Ionic radii (Å) of Sb^{3+}, Bi^{3+} and As^{3+} follow the order NCERT Pg 166
(a) $Sb^{3+} > Bi^{3+} > As^{3+}$ (b) $Bi^{3+} > As^{3+} > Sb^{3+}$
(c) $Bi^{3+} > Sb^{3+} > As^{3+}$ (d) $As^{3+} > Sb^{3+} > Bi^{3+}$

59 The correct order of melting point for group 15 elements is NCERT Pg 167
(a) N < P < As > Sb > Bi (b) N < P < As < Sb < Bi
(c) N > P > As > Sb > Bi (d) N > P > As < Sb < Bi

60 Nitrogen forms N_2 but phosphorus is converted into P_4 from P_2. The reason is NCERT Pg 167
(a) weak $p\pi$-$p\pi$ bonding
(b) weak $d\pi$-$p\pi$ bonding
(c) strong $p\pi$-$p\pi$ bonding
(d) triple bond is present in phosphorus atoms

61 Nitrogen lacks d-orbital in its valence shell and hence, it cannot NCERT Pg 167
(a) exhibit orbital hybridisation
(b) exhibit the oxidation state of + 5
(c) forms oxides with oxidation state greater than +3
(d) have covalency greater than three

62 Which of the following pair behaves as strongest and weakest base hydride respectively NH_3, PH_3, AsH_3, SbH_3, BiH_3 ? NCERT Pg 168
(a) NH_3, PH_3
(b) NH_3, BiH_3
(c) PH_3, BiH_3
(d) BiH_3, AsH_3

63 Which of the following hydrides has largest bond angle? NCERT Pg 168
(a) PH_3 (b) NH_3
(c) SbH_3 (d) AsH_3

64 Which of the following hydrides has the lowest boiling point? NCERT Pg 168
(a) PH_3 (b) AsH_3
(c) SbH_3 (d) NH_3

65 The correct order of melting point hydrides of group 15 elements is NCERT Pg 168
(a) $NH_3 > SbH_3 > PH_3 < AsH_3$
(b) $NH_3 > PH_3 > AsH_3 > SbH_3$
(c) $NH_3 < PH_3 < AsH_3 < SbH_3$
(d) $NH_3 < PH_3 > AsH_3 > SbH_3$

66 Which of the following statements is incorrect regarding group 15 elements? NCERT Pg 168
(a) Oxides of type E_2O_3 of nitrogen and phosphorus are acidic.
(b) Oxides of type E_2O_3 of arsenic, antimony are amphoteric.
(c) Oxides of type E_2O_3 of bismuth is predominantly basic.
(d) Trihalides except BiF_3 are predominantly ionic in nature.

67 Which of the following statements are correct? NCERT Pg 168
I. Covalency of N is restricted to four.
II. N cannot form $d\pi$-$p\pi$ bond as the heavier element.
III. P and As cannot form $d\pi$-$d\pi$ bond with transition elements when their compounds like $P(C_2H_5)_3$ and As $(C_6H_5)_3$ act as ligands.
Choose the correct answer from the options given below.
(a) I and II (b) II and III
(c) I and III (d) I, II and III

68 Which of the following are the applications of dinitrogen gas? NCERT Pg 170

(a) Preservation of biological materials and food items.
(b) Production of inert atmosphere in copper and steel industry.
(c) In the preparation of explosives.
(d) Etching of metals.

69 The correct order of the oxidation states of nitrogen in NO, NO_2, N_2O and N_2O_3 is NCERT Pg 172, 173

(a) $NO_2 < NO < N_2O_3 < N_2O$
(b) $N_2O < NO < N_2O_3 < NO_2$
(c) $NO_2 < N_2O_3 < NO < N_2O$
(d) $N_2O > N_2O_3 > NO > NO_2$

70 Which of the following statements regarding phosphorus is incorrect? NCERT Pg 175

(a) White phosphorus dissolves in boiling NaOH solution in an inert atmosphere giving PH_3.
(b) Red phosphorus is obtained by heating black phosphorus at 573K.
(c) White phosphorus readily catches fire in air to give dense white fumes of P_4O_{10}.
(d) Red phosphorus is polymeric consisting of chains of P_4.

71 α and β-black phosphorus are obtained, respectively by heating NCERT Pg 176

(a) red and white phosphorus
(b) white and red phosphorus
(c) red and red phosphorus
(d) white and white phosphorus

72 Which of the following reaction does not give H_3PO_3 as a product? NCERT Pg 177

(a) $PCl_3 + 3H_2O \longrightarrow$
(b) $P_4 + SO_2Cl_2 \longrightarrow$
(c) $PCl_3 + CH_3COOH \longrightarrow$
(d) $PCl_3 + C_2H_5OH \longrightarrow$

73 PCl_5 is prepared by the action of excess of Cl_2 on NCERT Pg 178

(a) P_4 (b) PCl_3 (c) P (d) $POCl_3$

74 Among the following, the number of compounds that can react with PCl_5 to give $POCl_3$ is

I. O_2 II. CO_2 III. CH_3COOH IV. H_2O V. C_2H_5OH

(a) 1 (b) 2 (c) 3 (d) 4 NCERT Pg 178

75 In which of the following, oxidation state of phosphorus is + 3? NCERT Pg 179, 180

(a) Orthophosphoric acid
(b) Pyrophosphoric acid
(c) Orthophosphorus acid
(d) Cyclotrimetaphosphoric acid

76 The pair that contains two P—H bonds in each of the oxoacids is NCERT Pg 180

(a) $H_4P_2O_5$ and $H_4P_2O_6$ (b) H_3PO_3 and H_3PO_2
(c) $H_4P_2O_5$ and H_3PO_3 (d) H_3PO_2 and $H_4P_2O_5$

77 Which of the following is a tetrabasic acid? NCERT Pg 180

(a) Hypophosphorus acid (b) Pyrophosphoric acid
(c) Orthophosphoric acid (d) Orthophorus acid

78 In cyclo trimetaphosphate ion, the number of O-atoms, P—O—P bonds and unit negative charges respectively are NCERT Pg 180

(a) 3, 6, 3 (b) 9, 6, 3 (c) 6, 6, 3 (d) 9, 3, 3

Elements of Group-16

79 Arrange the following elements in the correct order of increasing ionic radii: NCERT Pg 181

Se, Te, Po, O, S

(a) O < S < Se < Te < Po
(b) Po < Te < Se < S < O
(c) S < O < Se < Te < Po
(d) S < O < Po < Se < Te

80 Which of the following statements is/are correct?

I. Atomic and ionic radii of group 16 elements decrease from top to bottom.
II. Ionisation enthalpy decreases down the group 16.
III. Oxygen has less negative electron gain enthalpy than sulphur.

Choose the correct answer from the given options.

(a) Only I (b) Only II NCERT Pg 181
(c) II and III (d) I and II

81 Which of the following statements is/are incorrect about group 16 ?

I. Oxygen, sulphur, selenium, tellurium, polonium and livermorium are known as chalcogens.
II. Livermorium is a synthetic radioactive element with electronic configuration, $[Rn]5f^{14}6d^{10}7s^27p^4$.
III. Metallic character decreases from oxygen to polonium.
IV. There is a large difference between melting and boiling points of oxygen and sulphur due to their atomicity.

Choose the correct answer from the options given below.

(a) Only II (b) Only III NCERT Pg 181, 182
(c) I and III (d) I, II, III and IV

82 Water is much less volatile than H_2S because NCERT Pg 182

(a) H_2O has a bond angle of nearly 150°
(b) hydrogen is loosely bonded with the sulphur
(c) S-atom is less electronegative than O-atom
(d) S-atom is more electronegative than O-atom

83 Which of the following statements regarding sulphur is incorrect? NCERT Pg 182

(a) SO_2 molecule is paramagnetic.
(b) The vapour at 200°C consists mostly of S_8 rings.
(c) At 600°C the gas mainly consists of S_2 molecules.
(d) The oxidation state of sulphur is never less than + 4 in its compounds.

84 Oxygen shows anomalous behaviour from other members of its family because NCERT Pg 182

I. oxygen shows maximum valency of two.
II. among chalcogens, oxygen is of the smallest size.
III. oxygen exhibits allotropy.
IV. oxygen has no vacant *d*-orbital.

Choose the correct answer from the options given below.

(a) I, II and III
(b) I, II and IV
(c) I, III and IV
(d) I, II, III and IV

85 Sulphur exhibits valencies of 2, 4 and 6, whereas oxygen has a valency of 2 due to NCERT Pg 183

(a) being less electronegative than S
(b) presence of *d*-orbitals in S
(c) S is bigger atom
(d) S has higher ionisation potential

86 All the hydrides (of group 16 elements) except one possess reducing property. Identity the hydride NCERT Pg 183

(a) H_2Se (b) H_2O
(c) H_2S (d) H_2Te

87 The stability of the halides of group 16 elements decreases in the order. NCERT Pg 183

(a) $Br^- > I^- > Cl^- > F^-$
(b) $F^- > I^- > Cl^- > Br^-$
(c) $F^- > Cl^- > Br^- > I^-$
(d) $I^- > Cl^- > Br^- > F^-$

88 The correct order of increasing stability of group 16 hydrides. NCERT Pg 183

(a) $H_2S < H_2O < H_2Te < H_2Se$
(b) $H_2O < H_2Te < H_2Se < H_2S$
(c) $H_2O < H_2S < H_2Se < H_2Te$
(d) $H_2Te < H_2Se < H_2S < H_2O$

89 Which of the following statement(s) is/are correct?

I. Sulphur forms only two types of allotropes. NCERT Pg 187
II. Rhombic and monoclinic sulphur are the types of allotropic sulphur.
III. The stable form of sulphur at room temperature is monoclinic sulphur.

Choose the correct answer from the options given below.

(a) Only I (b) Only II
(c) I, II and III (d) I and III

90 At elevated temperatures, the dominant species of sulphur is NCERT Pg 188

(a) Cyclo S_6 (b) α-sulphur
(c) β-sulphur (d) S_2

91 Peroxoacids of sulphur are NCERT Pg 189

(a) $H_2S_2O_8$ and H_2SO_5 (b) $H_2S_2O_8$ and $H_2S_2O_7$
(c) $H_2S_2O_7$ and $H_2S_2O_6$ (d) H_2SO_5 and $H_2S_2O_7$

92 The number of bonds between sulphur and oxygen atoms in $S_2O_8^{2-}$ and the number of bonds between sulphur and sulphur atoms in rhombic sulphur, respectively, are NCERT Pg 188, 189

(a) 4 and 6 (b) 8 and 8
(c) 4 and 8 (d) 8 and 6

Elements of Group-17

93 Which of the following halogen is a synthetic radioactive element? NCERT Pg 192

(a) Bromine (b) Iodine
(c) Astatine (d) Tennessine

94 In the periodic table, on moving down the group 17 NCERT Pg 193

(a) ionic radius increases
(b) electronegativity increases
(c) ionisation energy increases
(d) reactivity increases

95 Which of the following statements are correct?

I. Due to maximum effective nuclear charge, the halogens have the smallest atomic radii in their respective periods.
II. These have low ionisation enthalpy.
III. Halogens have maximum negative electron gain enthalpy.
IV. Fluorine is the most electronegative element in the periodic table.

Choose the correct answer from the options given below NCERT Pg 193

(a) I, II, III and IV (b) I, II and III
(c) I, III and IV (d) II, III and IV

96 Which of the following statements are correct? NCERT Pg 194

I. Fluorine and chlorine react with water. Bromine and iodine are only sparingly soluble in water.
II. Enthalpy of dissociation of Cl_2 is smaller as compared to F_2.
III. Fluorine atom has no *d*-orbitals in its valence shell and exhibits only −1 oxidation state.
IV. F_2 is the strongest reducing halogen.

Choose the correct answer from the options given below.

(a) I and II (b) II and III
(c) II and IV (d) I and III

97 Which of the following is not reason of anomalous behaviour of fluorine? NCERT Pg 195

(a) Its small size.
(b) Its highest electronegativity.
(c) Low F—F bond dissociation enthalpy and non-availability of *d*-orbitals in valence shell.
(d) Its highest electron gain enthalpy.

98 Arrange the following acids in the correct increasing order of their acidic strength:

HCl, HBr, HI and HF NCERT Pg 196

(a) HI < HBr < HCl < HF
(b) HF < HCl < HBr < HI
(c) HCl < HBr < HI < HF
(d) HBr < HI < HF < HCl

99 The ionic character of the metal halides, *M*Cl, *M*I, *M*Br, *M*F decreases in the order: NCERT Pg 197

(a) *M*F > *M*Br > *M*I > *M*Cl
(b) *M*I > *M*Br > *M*F > *M*Cl
(c) *M*F > *M*Cl > *M*Br > *M*I
(d) *M*Br > *M*F > *M*I > *M*Cl

100 Choose the incorrect statement regarding interhalogen compounds. NCERT Pg 201

(a) Interhalogen compounds are more reactive than the parent halogens but less reactive than F_2.
(b) All interhalogens are covalent molecules.
(c) The boiling points decreases with the increase in the electronegativity difference between *A* and *B*.
(d) More polar is the *A*—*B* bond more is the thermal stability of interhalogen compound (*AB*).

Elements of Group 18

101 Which of the following rare gas is the abundant in air? NCERT Pg 203

(a) He (b) Ne
(c) Ar (d) Kr

102 What is the correct order of atomic radii for noble gases? NCERT Pg 204

(a) He < Ne < Ar < Kr < Xe
(b) He > Ne > Ar > Kr > Xe
(c) He < Ne < Ar > Kr > Xe
(d) He < Ne > Ar > Kr < Xe

103 The first noble gas compound obtained was NCERT Pg 204

(a) $Xe^+PtF_6^-$ (b) XeF_4 (c) XeF_2 (d) $XeOF_4$

104 The type of hybridisation and number of lone pair(s) of electrons of Xe in $XeOF_4$, respectively, are NCERT Pg 205

(a) sp^3d^2 and 1 (b) sp^3d and 2
(c) sp^3d and 1 (d) sp^3d^2 and 2

105 Which of the following reaction is incorrect? NCERT Pg 205

(a) $\underset{\text{(Excess)}}{Xe(g)} + F_2(g) \xrightarrow{673\text{K}, 1\text{ bar}} XeF_2(s)$

(b) $\underset{\text{(1:5 ratio)}}{Xe(g) + 2F_2(g)} \xrightarrow{873\text{K}, 7\text{bar}} XeF_4(s)$

(c) $\underset{\text{(1 : 40 ratio)}}{Xe(g) + 2F_2(g)} \xrightarrow{573\text{K}, 60\text{-}70\text{ bar}} XeF_6(s)$

(d) $XeF_4 + O_2F_2(g) \longrightarrow XeF_6 + O_2$

106 Among $XeOF_4$, XeO_4 and XeF_6, the molecules having same number of lone pairs on Xe are NCERT Pg 205

(a) XeO_3 and $XeOF_4$ (b) XeO_3 and XeF_6
(c) XeO_4 and XeF_6 (d) XeO_3, $XeOF_4$ and XeF_6

Assertion-Reason Questions

Directions (Q. Nos. 1-26) *In the following question Assertion (A) followed by Reason (R) is given below. Choose the correct option out of the choices given below.*

(a) Both A and R are true and R is the correct explanation of A.
(b) Both A and R are true but R is not the correct explanation of A.
(c) A is true but R is false.
(d) A is false but R is true.

1 Assertion (A) The heaviest element in each *p*-block group is most metallic in nature.

Reason (R) The metallic character increases down the group. NCERT Pg 308

2 Assertion (A) Boron always forms covalent bond.

Reason (R) The small size of B^{3+} favours formation of covalent bond. NCERT Pg 309

3 Assertion (A) Boron has unusually high melting point.

Reason (R) Boron has very strong crystalline lattice. NCERT Pg 310

4 Assertion (A) On going down the group-13, inert pair effect increases.

Reason (R) On going down the group, there is poor shielding effect of intervening *d* and *f*-orbitals. Due to this, the effective nuclear charge increases which holds *ns*-electrons tightly. NCERT Pg 310

5 Assertion (A) Aluminium shows amphoteric behaviour.

Reason (R) Aluminium does not react with acids and alkalies even at moderate temperature. NCERT Pg 311

6 **Assertion** (A) $AlCl_3$ is dimerised through halogen bridging.

Reason (R) Metal species, Al in $AlCl_3$ completes its octet by accepting electrons from bridged halogens and forms, Al_2Cl_6. NCERT Pg 311

7 **Assertion** (A) The elements of the group 14 are slightly more electronegative than group 13 elements.

Reason (R) Group 14 elements are larger in size than group 13 elements. NCERT Pg 315

8 **Assertion** (A) The common oxidation states exhibited by the group-14 elements is +2 only.

Reason (R) Carbon exhibits both positive and negative oxidation states. NCERT Pg 316

9 **Assertion** (A) PbI_4 is an unstable compound.

Reason (R) +2 oxidation state of Pb is more stable than +4 state. NCERT Pg 316

10 **Assertion** (A) From As to Bi, there is only a small increase in covalent radius.

Reason (R) *d* and/or *f*-orbitals are completely filled in heavier elements. NCERT Pg 166

11 **Assertion** (A) The electronegativity value of group 15 elements, in general, decreases down the group with increasing atomic size.

Reason (R) Amongst the heavier elements, the difference in electronegativity values is prominent. NCERT Pg 167

12 **Assertion** (A) The stability of +5 oxidation state decreases and that of +3 state increases down the group 15.

Reason (R) Inert pair effect is more prone in case of heavier members of *p*-block. NCERT Pg 167

13 **Assertion** (A) Heavier elements of group 15 do not form $p\pi$-$p\pi$ bonds.

Reason (R) Atomic orbitals of heavier elements of group 15 cannot have effective overlapping due to their large size. NCERT Pg 167

14 **Assertion** (A) PH_3 forms bubbles, when passed slowly in water but NH_3 dissolves.

Reason (R) NH_3 is water soluble. NCERT Pg 168

15 **Assertion** (A) In group 15 elements, their pentahalides are more covalent than trihalides.

Reason (R) All the group 15 elements react with metals to form their binary compounds exhibiting −3 oxidation states. NCERT Pg 168

16 **Assertion** (A) H_3PO_2 is a dibasic acid.

Reason (R) Two H-atoms are directly attached to P. NCERT Pg 180

17 **Assertion** (A) Oxygen has a covalency of four.

Reason (R) *d*-orbitals are absent in oxygen. NCERT Pg 182

18 **Assertion** (A) SF_6 is known but SCl_6 is not.

Reason (R) The size of fluorine is less than that of chlorine. NCERT Pg 183

19 **Assertion** (A) Acidic character increases from H_2O to H_2Te.

Reason (R) There is a decrease in bond enthalpy for the dissociation of H—*E* bond down the group. NCERT Pg 183

20 **Assertion** (A) SF_6 cannot be hydrolysed but SF_4 can be.

Reason (R) Six F-atoms in SF_6 prevent the attack of H_2O on sulphur atom of SF_6. NCERT Pg 183

21 **Assertion** (A) Sulphur shows paramagnetism.

Reason (R) In vapour state sulphur partly exists as S_2 molecule which has two unpaired electrons in the antibonding π^*-orbitals. NCERT Pg 188

22 **Assertion** (A) Electron gain enthalpy of fluorine is less negative as compared to the chlorine.

Reason (R) F—F bond has low dissociation enthalpy and F has high hydration enthalpy. NCERT Pg 193

23 **Assertion** (A) All the halogens exhibit −1 oxidation state.

Reason (R) Chlorine, bromine and iodine exhibit +1, + 3, + 5 and +7 oxidation states. NCERT Pg 194

24 **Assertion** (A) Most of the oxoacids of halogens cannot be isolated in pure state.

Reason (R) Oxoacids of halogens are stable only in aqueous solutions or in the form of their salts. NCERT Pg 200

25 **Assertion** (A) Interhalogen compounds are more reactive than halogens (except fluorine).

Reason (R) *X*—*X*′ bond in interhalogens is weaker than *X*—*X* bond in halogens. NCERT Pg 201

26 **Assertion** (A) ClF_3 exists but FCl_3 does not exist.

Reason (R) F is more electronegative than Cl. NCERT Pg 202

Statement Type Questions

Directions (Q. Nos. 1-6) *In the following questions, a statement (I and II) in the light of the above statements, choose the correct answer from the options given below.*

(a) Both Statement I and Statement II are false.
(b) Statement I is true but Statement II is false.
(c) Statement I is false but Statement II is true.
(d) Both Statement I and Statement II are true.

1 Statement I Compounds formed by non-metals with metals are covalent in nature.

Statement II Compounds formed between non-metals themselves are largely covalent. NCERT Pg 308

2 Statement I The tetrahalides of carbon are not hydrolysed water under normal conditions.

Statement II Carbon cannot expand its coordination number beyond 4 because of the absence of *d*-orbitals. NCERT Pg 316

3 Statement I E_2O_3 type oxides of nitrogen and phosphorus are purely acidic.

Statement II The N—N single bond is stronger than the P—P single bonds. NCERT Pg 168

4 Statement I The pentavalent oxide of group-15 element, E_2O_5, is less acidic than trivalent oxide, E_2O_3 of the same element.

Statement II The acidic character of trivalent oxide of group 15 elements, E_2O_3, decreases down the group. NCERT Pg 168

5 Statement I Brown ring test for nitrates depends on the ability of Fe^{2+} to reduce nitrates to nitric oxide.

Statement II Reaction of nitric oxide with Fe^{2+} to form a brown coloured complex. NCERT Pg 175

6 Statement I In interhalogen compounds, the central atom will be the smaller one.

Statement II These compounds can be formed only between two halogen and not more than two halogens. NCERT Pg 201

7 Which of the following statements are correct? NCERT Pg 317, 179, 180, 313, 193

I. F_2 has higher dissociation energy than Cl_2.
II. Oxidation number of P is +2 in H_3PO_2.
III. The group 16 family is also called as chalcogens.
IV. Carbon's allotropes are diamond, graphite and fullerene.
V. The structure of diborane is planar.

Choose the correct answer from the options given below.

(a) I and II (b) I, II and III
(c) III and IV (d) III, IV and V

8 Which of the following statements are incorrect? NCERT Pg 314, 319, 166, 183

I. Aluminium vessels should not be washed with washing soda because it reacts with Al to form soluble aluminate.
II. Diamond is the thermodynamically most stable form of the carbon.
III. The ionisation enthalpies of group 15 elements are higher than those of corresponding elements of group 14 and 16.
IV. O is more electronegative than sulphur, yet H_2S is acidic, while H_2O is neutral.
V. C_{60} is radioactive with very short half-life.

Choose the correct answer from the options given below.

(a) I, II and III (b) II and III
(c) III, IV and V (d) II and V

9 Which of the following statement(s) are incorrect?

I. Boron forms diborane involving banana bonding.
II. Carbon has allotropic nature.
III. Nitrogen cannot form oxides due to absence of *d*-orbital.
IV. Sulphur atom is more electronegative than oxygen atom.
V. The ionic character of the metal halides decreases down the group.

Choose the correct answer from the options given below. NCERT Pg 314, 317, 172, 181

(a) I, II and III (b) II and III
(c) III and IV (d) I, III and V

10 Which of the following statements are correct? NCERT Pg 310, 311, 315, 166, 183

I. Lewis acid nature of $BX_3 \rightarrow BF_3 < BCl_3 < BBr_3 < BI_3$
II. Stability of +1 oxidation of group 13 → Al < Ga < In < Tl
III. First ionisation enthalpy of group 14 → Si < Ge < Sn < Pb
IV. Ionic radii (Å) of (+3) oxidation state of group 15 → $As^{3+} > Sb^{3+} > Bi^{3+}$
V. Stability of halides of group 16 → $I^- > Br^- > Cl^- > F^-$

Choose the correct answer from the options given below.

(a) I, II and III (b) II, III and IV
(c) III, IV and V (d) I, II, III, IV and V

Matching Type Questions

1 Match the following columns and choose the correct option from the codes given below. NCERT Pg 309

Column I (Element)		Column II (Electronic configuration)
A.	In	1. [He]$2s^2 2p^1$
B.	Tl	2. [Ne]$3s^2 3p^1$
C.	B	3. [Ar] $3d^{10} 4s^2 4p^1$
D.	Ga	4. [Kr]$4d^{10} 5s^2 5p^1$
E.	Al	5. [Xe]$4f^{14} 5d^{10} 6s^2 6p^1$

Codes

	A	B	C	D	E		A	B	C	D	E
(a)	1	2	3	4	5	(b)	4	5	1	3	2
(c)	2	3	5	1	4	(d)	5	4	3	2	1

2 Match the species given in Column I with the properties mentioned in Column II and choose the correct options from the codes given below. NCERT Pg 311, 316

Column I	Column II
A. BF_4^-	1. Oxidation state of central atom is +4
B. $AlCl_3$	2. Lewis acid
C. SnO	3. Can be further oxidised
D. PbO_2	4. Tetrahedral shape

Codes

	A	B	C	D
(a)	4	2	3	1
(b)	1	3	2	4
(c)	1	2	3	4
(d)	3	1	2	4

3 Match the terms of Column I with the terms of Column II and choose the correct option from the codes given below. NCERT Pg 179

Column I (Molecular formula)	Column II (Oxidation state of P)
A. H_3PO_2	1. +1
B. H_3PO_3	2. +3
C. $H_4P_2O_6$	3. +4
D. H_3PO_4	4. +5

Codes

	A	B	C	D
(a)	1	2	3	4
(b)	2	3	4	1
(c)	3	4	1	2
(d)	4	1	2	3

4 Match the Column I with Column II and choose the correct option from the codes given below. NCERT Pg 180

Column I (Structure of acid)	Column II (Name of acid)
A. 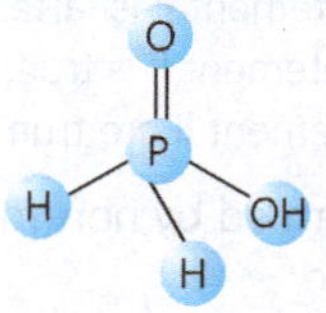	1. Orthophosphorus acid
B. 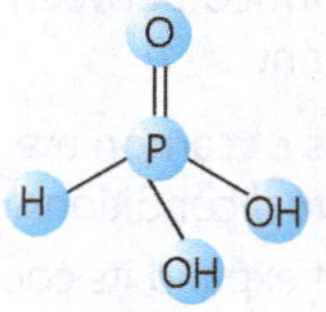	2. Hypophosphorus acid
C. 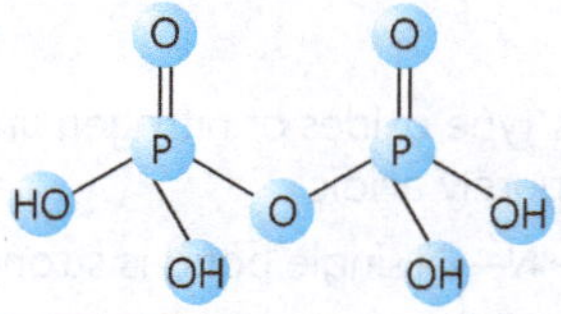	3. Orthophosphoric acid
D. 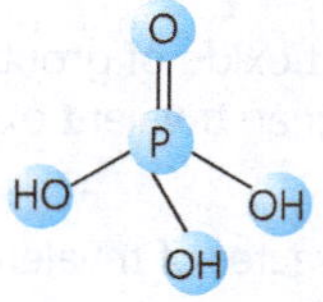	4. Pyrophosphoric acid

Codes

	A	B	C	D		A	B	C	D
(a)	2	1	4	3	(b)	4	2	3	1
(c)	3	4	1	2	(d)	1	3	2	4

5 Match the following columns and choose the correct option from the codes given below. NCERT Pg 200

Column I (Structures)	Column II (Oxoacids of halogens)
A. 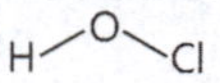	1. Perchloric acid
B. 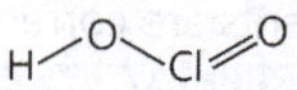	2. Chloric acid
C. 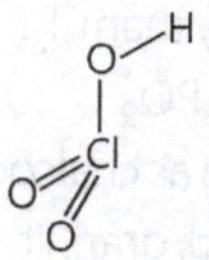	3. Chlorous acid
D. 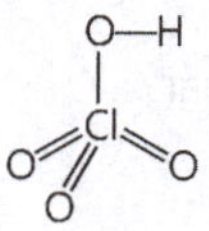	4. Hypochlorous acid

Codes

	A	B	C	D
(a)	1	2	3	4
(b)	3	2	4	1
(c)	4	3	2	1
(d)	2	1	4	3

6 Match the following columns and choose the correct option from the codes given below. NCERT Pg 201

	Column I (Formula)		Column II (Colour and physical state)
A.	ClF_3	1.	Colourless gas but solid below 77 K with square pyramidal
B.	IF_5	2.	Colourless gas with bent T-shaped
C.	IF_7	3.	Orange solid with bent T-shaped
D.	ICl_3	4.	Colourless gas with pentagonal bipyramidal

Codes

	A	B	C	D		A	B	C	D
(a)	1	2	3	4	(b)	1	4	2	1
(c)	2	1	4	3	(d)	4	3	2	1

7 Match the compounds given in Column I with the hybridisation and shape given in Column II and mark the correct option. NCERT Pg 205

	Column I		Column II
A.	XeF_6	1.	sp^3d^3-distorted octahedral
B.	XeO_3	2.	sp^3d^2-square planar
C.	$XeOF_4$	3.	sp^3-pyramidal
D.	XeF_4	4.	sp^3d^2-square pyramidal

Codes

	A	B	C	D		A	B	C	D
(a)	1	3	4	2	(b)	1	2	4	3
(c)	4	3	1	2	(d)	4	1	2	3

Numerical Value Questions

1 The coordination number of Al in the crystalline state of $AlCl_3$ is .... NCERT Pg 311

2 The total number of acidic oxides among the following are .... NCERT Pg 316

CO_2, SiO_2, GeO_2, SnO_2, PbO_2

3 Total number of acidic oxides among NCERT Pg 173, 196
N_2O_3, NO_2, N_2O, Cl_2O_7, CO, CaO, Na_2O and NO is ....

4 A xenon compound '*P*' upon partial hydrolysis gives XeO_2F_2. The number of lone pair of electrons present in compound *P* is .... NCERT Pg 205

5 XeF_4 reacts with SbF_5 to form $[XeF_x]^y\ [SbF_z]^w$ −

$w + x + y + z =$....... NCERT Pg 205

NCERT Exemplar's Questions

1 The element which exists in liquid state for a wide range of temperature and can be used for measuring high temperature is

(a) B (b) Al (c) Ga (d) In

2 Ionisation enthalpy ($\Delta_i H$ kJ mol^{-1}) for the elements of group 13 follows the order

(a) B > Al > Ga > In > Tl (b) B < Al < Ga < In < Tl
(c) B < Al > Ga < In > Tl (d) B > Al < Ga > In < Tl

3 The exhibition of highest coordination number depends on the availability of vacant orbitals in the central atom. Which of the following elements is not likely to act as central atom in MF_6^{3-}?

(a) B (b) Al (c) Ga (d) In

4 The geometry of a complex species can be understood from the knowledge of type of hybridisation of orbitals of central atom. The hybridisation of orbitals of central atom in $[B(OH_4)]^-$ and the geometry of the complex are respectively

(a) sp^3, tetrahedral (b) sp^3, square planar
(c) sp^3d^2, octahedral (d) dsp^2, square planar

5 In the structure of diborane,

(a) all hydrogen atoms lie in one plane and boron atoms lie in a plane perpendicular to this plane.
(b) 2 boron atoms and 4 terminal hydrogen atoms lie in the same plane and 2 bridging hydrogen atoms lie in the perpendicular plane.
(c) 4 bridging hydrogen atoms and boron atoms lie in one plane and two terminal hydrogen atoms lie in a plane perpendicular to this plane.
(d) all the atoms are in the same plane.

6 Catenation, i.e. linking of similar atoms depends on size and electronic configuration of atoms. The tendency of catenation in group 14 elements follows the order

(a) C > Si > Ge > Sn (b) C >> Si > Ge ≈ Sn
(c) Si > C > Sn > Ge (d) Ge > Sn > Si > C

7 Quartz is extensively used as a piezoelectric material, it contains ....
(a) Pb (b) Si (c) Ti (d) Sn

8 Which of the following elements does not show allotropy?
(a) Nitrogen (b) Bismuth (c) Antimony (d) Arsenic

9 Bond dissociation enthalpy of E—H (E = element) bonds is given below. Which of the compounds will act as strongest reducing agent?

Compound	NH_3	PH_3	AsH_3	SbH_3
$\Delta_{diss}(E—H)/kJ\ mol^{-1}$	389	322	297	255

(a) NH_3 (b) PH_3 (c) AsH_3 (d) SbH_3

10 Which of the following elements can be involved in $p\pi$ - $d\pi$ bonding?
(a) Carbon (b) Nitrogen
(c) Phosphorus (d) Boron

11 Which of the following statements is wrong?
(a) Single N—N bond is stronger than the single P—P bond.
(b) PH_3 can act as a ligand in the formation of coordination compound with transition elements.
(c) NO_2 is paramagnetic in nature.
(d) Covalency of nitrogen in N_2O_5 is four.

12 A brown ring is formed in the ring test for NO_3^- ion. It is due to the formation of
(a) $[Fe(H_2O)_5(NO)]^{2+}$ (b) $FeSO_4 \cdot NO_2$
(c) $[Fe(H_2O)_4(NO)_2]^{2+}$ (d) $FeSO_4 \cdot HNO_3$

13 Which of the following acids forms three series of salts?
(a) H_3PO_2 (b) $H_4P_2O_5$ (c) H_3PO_4 (d) H_3PO_3

14 Strong reducing behaviour of H_3PO_2 is due to
(a) low oxidation state of phosphorus
(b) presence of two —OH groups and one P—H bond
(c) presence of one —OH group and two P—H bonds
(d) high electron gain enthalpy of phosphorus

15 The oxidation state of central atom in the anion of compound NaH_2PO_2 will be
(a) + 3 (b) + 5 (c) + 1 (d) − 3

16 In a cyclotrimetaphosphoric acid molecule, how many single and double bonds are present?
(a) 3 double bonds and 9 single bonds
(b) 6 double bonds and 6 single bonds
(c) 3 double bonds and 12 single bonds
(d) Zero double bond and 12 single bonds

17 Which of the following are peroxoacids of sulphur?
(a) H_2SO_5 and $H_2S_2O_8$ (b) H_2SO_5 and $H_2S_2O_7$
(c) $H_2S_2O_7$ and $H_2S_2O_8$ (d) $H_2S_2O_6$ and $H_2S_2O_7$

18 Which of the following is not tetrahedral in shape?
(a) NH_4^+ (b) $SiCl_4$ (c) SF_4 (d) SO_4^{2-}

19 Affinity for hydrogen decreases in the group from fluorine to iodine. Which of the following halogen acids should have highest bond dissociation enthalpy?
(a) HF (b) HCl (c) HBr (d) HI

20 Maximum covalency of nitrogen as ....
(a) 3 (b) 5 (c) 4 (d) 6

Past Exams' Questions

NEET Archive

1 Given below are two statements: NCERT Pg 182, NEET 2024
Statement I The boiling point of hydrides of group 16 elements follow the order $H_2O > H_2Te > H_2Se > H_2S$.
Statement II On the basis of molecular mass, H_2O is expected to have lower boiling point than the other members of the group but due to the presence of extensive H-bonding in H_2O, it has higher boiling point.
In the light of the above statements, choose the correct answer from the options given below.
(a) Both Statement I and Statement II are true.
(b) Both Statement I and Statement II are false.
(c) Statement I is true but Statement II is false.
(d) Statement I is false but Statement II is true.

2 Among group 16 elements, which one does not show −2 oxidation state? NCERT Pg 182, NEET 2024
(a) O (b) Se (c) Te (d) Po

3 Match List-I with List-II. NCERT Pg 317, 318, NEET 2023

	List-I		List-II
A.	Coke	1.	Carbon atoms are sp^3-hybridised.
B.	Diamond	2.	Used as a dry lubricant.
C.	Fullerene	3.	Used as a reducing agent.
D.	Graphite	4.	Cage like molecules.

Choose the correct answer from the options given below.
(a) A-4, B-1, C-2, D-3 (b) A-3, B-1, C-4, D-2
(c) A-3, B-4, C-1, D-2 (d) A-2, B-4, C-1, D-3

4 Which of the following statement is not correct about diborane? NCERT Pg 313, NEET 2022
(a) The four terminal B—H bonds are 2-centre-2 electron bonds.
(b) The four terminal hydrogen atoms and the two boron atoms lie in one plane.
(c) Both the boron atoms are sp^2-hybridised.
(d) There are two 3-centre-2-electron bonds.

5 Choose the correct statement. NCERT Pg 317, NEET 2022
(a) Diamond is covalent and graphite is ionic.
(b) Diamond is sp^3-hybridised and graphite is sp^2-hybridised.
(c) Both diamond and graphite are used as dry lubricants.
(d) Diamond and graphite have two dimensional network.

6 Which of the following compounds is used in cosmetic surgery? NCERT Pg 322, NEET (Odisha) 2019
(a) Silica (b) Silicates (c) Silicones (d) Zeolites

7 The correct order of atomic radii in group 13 elements is NCERT Pg 309, NEET 2018
(a) B < Ga < Al < Tl < In (b) B < Al < Ga < In < Tl
(c) B < Al < In < Ga < Tl (d) B < Ga < Al < In < Tl

8 The stability of +1 oxidation state among Al, Ga, In and Tl increases in the sequence. NCERT Pg 310, NEET AIPMT 2015
(a) Ga < In < Al < Tl (b) Al < Ga < In < Tl
(c) Tl < In < Ga < Al (d) In < Tl < Ga < Al

9 Match List-I with List-II.

List-I (Oxoacids of sulphur)	List-II (Bonds)
A. Peroxodisulphuric acid	1. Two S—OH, four S=O, one S—O—S
B. Sulphuric acid	2. Two S—OH, one S=O
C. Pyrosulphuric acid	3. Two S—OH, Four S=O, one S—O—O—S
D. Sulphurous acid	4. Two S—OH, two S=O

Choose the correct answer from the options given below. NCERT Pg 189, NEET 2023
(a) A-3, B-4, C-1, D-2 (b) A-1, B-3, C-4, D-2
(c) A-3, B-4, C-2, D-1 (d) A-1, B-3, C-2, D-4

10 Noble gases are named because of their inertness towards reactivity. Identify an incorrect statement about them. NCERT Pg 203, NEET 2021
(a) Noble gases are sparingly soluble in water.
(b) Noble gases have very high melting and boiling points.
(c) Noble gases have weak dispersion forces.
(d) Noble gases have large positive values of electron gain enthalpy.

11 Match the compounds of Xe in Column I with the molecular structure in Column II. NCERT Pg 205, 206, NEET 2020

Column I	Column II
A. XeF_2	1. Square planar
B. XeF_4	2. Linear
C. XeO_3	3. Square pyramidal
D. $XeOF_4$	4. Pyramidal

Codes

	A	B	C	D		A	B	C	D
(a)	2	1	3	4	(b)	2	4	3	1
(c)	2	3	1	4	(d)	2	1	4	3

12 Which is the correct thermal stability order for H_2E (E = O, S, Se, Te and Po)? NCERT Pg 183, NEET 2019
(a) $H_2O < H_2S < H_2Se < H_2Te < H_2Po$
(b) $H_2Po < H_2Te < H_2Se < H_2S < H_2O$
(c) $H_2Se < H_2Te < H_2Po < H_2O < H_2S$
(d) $H_2S < H_2O < H_2Se < H_2Te < H_2Po$

13 In the structure of ClF_3, the number of lone pairs of electrons on central atom 'Cl' is NCERT Pg 201. NEET 2018
(a) four (b) two (c) one (d) three

14 Match the interhalogen compounds of Column I with the geometry in Column II and assign the correct code. NCERT Pg 201, NEET 2017

	Column I	Column II
A.	XX'	1. T- shape
B.	XX'_3	2. Pentagonal bipyramidal
C.	XX'_5	3. Linear
D.	XX'_7	4. Square-pyramidal
		5. Tetrahedral

Codes

	A	B	C	D		A	B	C	D
(a)	3	4	1	2	(b)	3	1	4	2
(c)	5	4	3	2	(d)	4	3	2	1

15 Strong reducing behaviour of H_3PO_4 is due to NCERT Pg 180, NEET 2015
(a) presence of one —OH group and two P—H bonds
(b) high electron gain enthalpy of phosphorus
(c) high oxidation state of phosphorus
(d) presence of two —OH groups and one P—H bond

JEE Main Archive

16 Given below are two statements. NCERT Pg 182, JEE Main 2024
Statement I Oxygen being the first member of group 16 exhibits only −2 oxidation state.
Statement II Down the group 16 stability of + 4 oxidation state decreases and + 6 oxidation state increases.
In the light of the above statements, choose the most appropriate answer from the options given below.
(a) Statement I is correct but Statement II is incorrect.
(b) Both Statement I and Statement II are incorrect.
(c) Statement I is incorrect but Statement II is correct.
(d) Both Statement I and Statement II are correct.

17 Given below are two statements. NCERT Pg 311, JEE Main 2024
Statement I Group 13 trivalent halides get easily hydrolysed by water due to their covalent nature.
Statement II $AlCl_3$ upon hydrolysis in acidified aqueous solution forms octahedral $[Al(H_2O)_6]^{3+}$ ion.

In the light of the above statements, choose the correct answer from the options given below
(a) Both statement I and statement II are false.
(b) Both statement I and statement II are true.
(c) Statement I is false but statement II is true.
(d) Statement I is true but statement II is false.

18 Choose the correct statements from the following. NCERT Pg 182, JEE Main 2024

A. All group 16 elements form oxides of general formula EO_2 and EO_3, where E = S, Se, Te and Po. Both the types of oxides are acidic in nature.
B. TeO_2 is an oxidising agent while SO_2 is reducing in nature.
C. The reducing property decreases from H_2S to H_2Te down the group.
D. The ozone molecule contains five lone pairs of electrons.

Choose the correct answer from the options given below.
(a) A and B only (b) B and C only
(c) C and D only (d) A and D only

19 The Lewis acid character of boron trihalides follows the order NCERT Pg 311, JEE Main 2023
(a) $BBr_3 > BI_3 > BCl_3 > BF_3$
(b) $BF_3 > BCl_3 > BBr_3 > BI_3$
(c) $BI_3 > BBr_3 > BCl_3 > BF_3$
(d) $BCl_3 > BF_3 > BBr_3 > BI_3$

20 The incorrect statement from the following for borazine is NCERT Pg 313, JEE Main 2023
(a) it is a cyclic compound.
(b) it contains banana bonds.
(c) it has electronic delocalisation.
(d) it can react with water.

21 Group 13 elements react with O_2 in amorphous form to form oxides of type M_2O_3 (M = element). Which among the following is the most basic oxide? NCERT Pg 311, JEE Main 2023
(a) Ga_2O_3 (b) B_2O_3 (c) Al_2O_3 (d) Tl_2O_3

22 The geometry around boron in the product 'B' formed from the following reaction is NCERT Pg 314, JEE Main 2022

$$BF_3 + NaH \xrightarrow{450\text{ K}} A + NaF$$
$$A + NMe_3 \longrightarrow B$$

(a) trigonal planar (b) tetrahedral
(c) pyramidal (d) square planar

23 Identify the correct statement for B_2H_6 from those given below: NCERT Pg 313, 314, JEE Main 2022
(A) In B_2H_6, all B—H bonds are equivalent.
(B) In B_2H_6 there are four 3-centre-2-electron bonds.
(C) B_2H_6 is a Lewis acid.
(D) B_2H_6 can be synthesised from both BF_3 and $NaBH_4$.
(E) B_2H_6 is a planar molecule.

Choose the most appropriate answer from the options given below.
(a) (A) and (E)
(b) (B), (C) and (E)
(c) (C) and (D)
(d) (C) and (E)

24 The correct statements about B_2H_6 is NCERT Pg 313, JEE Main 2021
(a) all B—H—B angles are of 120°.
(b) the two B—H—B bonds are not of same length.
(c) terminal B—H bonds have less *p*-character when compared to bridging bonds.
(d) Its fragment, BH_3, behaves as a Lewis base.

25 The number of P—O—P bonds in $H_4P_2O_7$, $(HPO_3)_3$ and P_4O_{10} are respectively NCERT Pg 179, JEE Main 2023
(a) 1, 2, 4 (b) 0, 3, 4
(c) 0, 3, 6 (d) 1, 3, 6

26 The oxidation states of nitrogen in NO, NO_2, N_2O and NO_3^- are in the order of NCERT Pg 172, JEE Main 2022
(a) $NO_3^- > NO_2 > NO > N_2O$
(b) $NO_2 > NO_3^- > NO > N_2O$
(c) $N_2O > NO_2 > NO > NO_3^-$
(d) $NO > NO_2 > N_2O > NO_3^-$

27 The correct order of melting point of hydrides of group 16 elements is NCERT Pg 183, JEE Main 2022
(a) $H_2S < H_2Se < H_2Te < H_2O$
(b) $H_2O < H_2S < H_2Se < H_2Te$
(c) $H_2S < H_2Te < H_2Se < H_2O$
(d) $H_2Se < H_2S < H_2Te < H_2O$

28 $A \xrightarrow{573\text{ K}}$ Red phosphorus $\xrightarrow[\text{Under pressure}]{\text{Heat; 803 K}} B$

Red phosphorus is obtained by heating "A" at 573 K, and can be converted to "B" by heating at 803 K under pressure. A and B, respectively, are NCERT Pg 176, JEE Main 2022
(a) β-black phosphorus and white phosphorus
(b) White phosphorus and β-black phosphorus
(c) α-black phosphorus and white phosphorus
(d) White phosphorus and α-black phosphorus

29 The number of S=O bonds present in sulphurous acid, peroxodisulphuric acid and pyrosulphuric acid, respectively are NCERT Pg 189, JEE Main 2021
(a) 2, 3 and 4
(b) 1, 4 and 3
(c) 2, 4 and 3
(d) 1, 4 and 4

30 Given below are two statements.

Statement I α and β-forms of sulphur can change reversibly between themselves with slow heating or slow cooling.

Statement II At room temperature, the stable crystalline form of sulphur is monoclinic sulphur.

In the light of the above statements, choose the correct answer from the options given below.
NCERT Pg 187, JEE Main 2021

(a) Both statements I and II are true.
(b) Both statements I and II are false.
(c) Statement I is true but statement II is false.
(d) Statement I is false but statement II is true.

31 Match List-I with List-II. NCERT Pg 179, JEE Main 2021

List-I (Name of oxo acid)		List-II (Oxidation state of 'P')	
A.	Hypophosphorus acid	1.	+5
B.	Orthophosphoric acid	2.	+4
C.	Hypophosphoric acid	3.	+3
D.	Orthophosphorus acid	4.	+2
		5.	+1

Choose the correct answer from the options given below :
(a) A-4, B-5, C-2, D-3 (b) A-4, B-4, C-2, D-3
(c) A-5, B-1, C-2, D-3 (d) A-4, B-1, C-2, D-3

Skill Boosters

1. Roasting of sulphides gives the gas *P* as a by product. This is colourless gas with choking smell of burnt sulphur and causes great damage to respiratory organs as a result of acid rain. If aqueous solution is acidic, acts as reducing agent and its acid has never been isolated. The gas *P* is
(a) sulphur trioxide (b) hydrogen sulphide
(c) sulphur dioxide (d) chlorine

2. Boron reacts with oxygen at 700°C to give (*A*). Compound *A* reacts with carbon and dry chloride to give (*B*) and carbon monoxide. (*B*) on reduction with $LiAlH_4$ gives (*C*) along with LiCl and $AlCl_3$. *C* on reaction with ammonia gives *D* having sp^2-hybridised central atom, which on heating gives an inorganic benzene.

The correct statement about compound *B* is
(a) Boron is sp^3 hybridised.
(b) The boron atoms are linked through hydrogen bridges.
(c) It is a Lewis base.
(d) It is a trigonal planar molecule.

3. A metal *A* reacts with aqueous NaOH solution to form *B* and a highly inflammable gas. Solution *B* is heated and CO_2 is poured through it. *C* precipitates out and Na_2CO_3 is formed. *C* on heating gives Al_2O_3. Identify *A*, *B* and *C*.

	A	*B*	*C*
(a)	Al	$NaAlO_2$	$Al(OH)_3$
(b)	Al_2O_3	$NaAlO_2$	Al_2CO_3
(c)	Al_2O_3	$[Na_2AlO_2]^+OH^-$	$Al(OH)_3$
(d)	Al	$Al(OH)_3$	Al_2O_3

4. When metal '*M*' is treated with NaOH, a white gelatinous precipitate '*A*' is obtained which is soluble in excess of NaOH. The precipitate '*A*' when heated strongly gives an oxide which is used as an adsorbent in chromatography. The metal '*M*' is
(a) Al (b) Ga (c) B (d) Ca

5. The number of P—O—P bridges in the structure of phosphorus pentoxide and phosphorus trioxide are six in both cases. Which of the following acid is obtained when phosphorus pentoxide is heated with water?
(a) Hypophosphorus acid (b) Orthophosphorus acid
(c) Hypophosphoric acid (d) Orthophosphoric acid

6. Soldiers of Napolean army while at Alps during freezing winter suffered a serious problem as regards to the tin buttons of their uniforms. While metallic tin buttons got converted to grey powder. This transformation is related to
(a) a change in the partial pressure of oxygen in the air
(b) a change in the crystalline structure of tin
(c) an interaction with water vapour contained in the humid air
(d) an interaction with N_2 gas of the air at very low temperature

7 Consider the following reactions,

I. $ZnSO_4(aq) + 2NH_4OH(aq) \longrightarrow \underset{(A)}{Zn(OH)_2(s)} + (NH_4)_2SO_4(aq)$

II. $FeCl_3(aq) + NH_4OH(aq) \longrightarrow \underset{(B)}{Fe_2O_3 \cdot xH_2O(s)} + NH_4Cl(aq)$

The colour of compounds *A* and *B* respectively are
(a) brown and white (b) brown and brown
(c) white and brown (d) white and white

8 Swati does an experiment for which she takes three test tubes *X*, *Y* and *Z*. Then, she pours NaF, NaCl and NaI in these test tubes respectively.
Select the correct observation, when Br_2 is added in *X*, *Y* and *Z*?

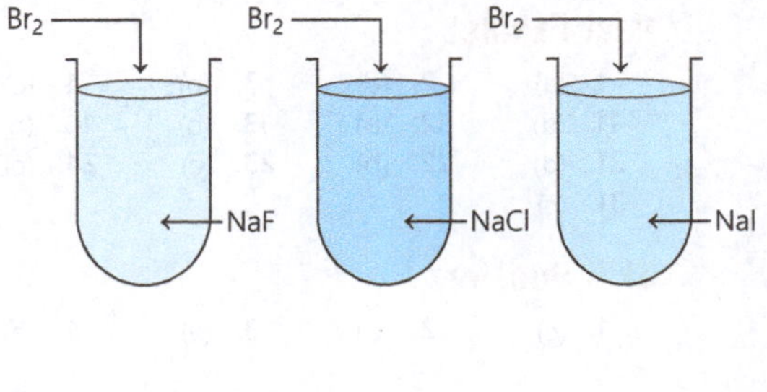

(a) F_2 is liberated in (*X*) and Cl_2 in (*Y*)
(b) Only I_2 is liberated in (*Z*)
(c) Only Cl_2 is liberated in (*Y*)
(d) Only F_2 is liberated in (*X*)

9 Gas *X* is obtained by the reaction of copper with dilute nitric acid. The obtained gas is oxidised to brown gas *Y*, when reacts with oxygen. The gas *Y* is soluble in water and its aqueous solution is *Z*. *X*, *Y* and *Z* respectively are
(a) NO, NO_2 and HNO_3
(b) NO_2, NO and HNO_3
(c) N_2O, NO and HNO_2
(d) NO, N_2O and HNO_3

10. An interhalogen compound (AX_n) is a molecule which contains two or more different halogen atoms. These are essentially covalent and more reactive than the halogen since the bond *A*—*X* is weaker than *A*—*A* or *X*—*X* bond. The incorrect statement for interhalogen compounds is
(a) the value of *n* in AX_n (interhalogen) can be 1, 3, 5 or 7.
(b) the value of *n* in AX_n (interhalogen) can be 2, 4 or 6.
(c) *A* can never be fluorine as it is most electronegative halogen.
(d) *X* can never be iodine as it is electronegative halogen.
(e) *X* can never be iodine as it is least electronegative halogen.

Correct Codes

Topical Questions

1. (b)	2. (c)	3. (a)	4. (a)	5. (d)	6. (b)	7. (c)	8. (a)	9. (a)	10. (b)
11. (d)	12. (c)	13. (b)	14. (b)	15. (a)	16. (d)	17. (b)	18. (d)	19. (a)	20. (b)
21. (b)	22. (b)	23. (d)	24. (a)	25. (a)	26. (d)	27. (a)	28. (b)	29. (d)	30. (b)
31. (a)	32. (a)	33. (a)	34. (a)	35. (d)	36. (d)	37. (a)	38. (d)	39. (b)	40. (b)
41. (b)	42. (b)	43. (b)	44. (c)	45. (c)	46. (b)	47. (a)	48. (a)	49. (c)	50. (d)
51. (a)	52. (a)	53. (a)	54. (c)	55. (d)	56. (b)	57. (d)	58. (c)	59. (a)	60. (a)
61. (b)	62. (b)	63. (b)	64. (a)	65. (a)	66. (d)	67. (d)	68. (a)	69. (b)	70. (b)
71. (a)	72. (b)	73. (a)	74. (c)	75. (c)	76. (d)	77. (b)	78. (d)	79. (a)	80. (c)
81. (b)	82. (c)	83. (d)	84. (d)	85. (b)	86. (b)	87. (c)	88. (d)	89. (b)	90. (d)
91. (a)	92. (b)	93. (d)	94. (a)	95. (c)	96. (d)	97. (d)	98. (b)	99. (c)	100. (c)
101. (c)	102. (a)	103. (a)	104. (a)	105. (c)	106. (d)				

Assertion-Reason

1. (a)	2. (c)	3. (a)	4. (a)	5. (c)	6. (a)	7. (c)	8. (d)	9. (a)	10. (a)
11. (c)	12. (a)	13. (a)	14. (a)	15. (b)	16. (d)	17. (a)	18. (a)	19. (a)	20. (a)
21. (a)	22. (a)	23. (b)	24. (a)	25. (a)	26. (a)				

Statement Type

1. (c)	2. (d)	3. (b)	4. (c)	5. (d)	6. (c)	7. (c)	8. (d)	9. (c)	10. (a)

Matching Type

1. (b)	2. (a)	3. (a)	4. (a)	5. (c)	6. (c)	7. (a)

Numerical Value

1. (6)	2. (3)	3. (3)	4. (19)	5. (11)

NCERT Exemplar's

1. (c)	2. (d)	3. (a)	4. (a)	5. (b)	6. (b)	7. (b)	8. (a)	9. (d)	10. (c)
11. (a)	12. (a)	13. (c)	14. (c)	15. (c)	16. (c)	17. (a)	18. (c)	19. (a)	20. (c)

Past Exams'

1. (a)	2. (d)	3. (b)	4. (c)	5. (b)	6. (c)	7. (d)	8. (b)	9. (a)	10. (b)
11. (d)	12. (b)	13. (b)	14. (b)	15. (a)	16. (b)	17. (b)	18. (a)	19. (c)	20. (b)
21. (d)	22. (b)	23. (c)	24. (c)	25. (d)	26. (a)	27. (a)	28. (d)	29. (d)	30. (c)
31. (c)									

Skill Boosters

1. (c)	2. (d)	3. (a)	4. (a)	5. (d)	6. (b)	7. (c)	8. (b)	9. (a)	10. (b)

Step by Step

Decoding the Questions

Concept Builders

1. True
2. Na_3AlF_6
3. Ga, In
4. True
5. banana bond
6. False
7. Graphite
8. False
9. Fullerene
10. increase
11. True
12. Phosphorus (P)
13. decreases, increases
14. BiH_3
15. N_2O_5
16. True
17. Inert pair effect
18. (i) Rhombic sulphur
    (ii) Monoclinic sulphur
19. One (1) [P—O—P bond]
20. False
21. True
22. hydration enthalpy
23. HF (Hydrogen fluoric acid)
24. Bent T
25. True
26. False
27. sp^3d^2, square pyramidal
28. XeF_6
29. True
30. linear, square planar

Topical Solutions

1 (*b*) The number of possible oxidation states of *p*-block elements increases towards the right of the periodic table.

2 (*c*) The second period elements of *p*-block starting from boron are restricted to a maximum covalency of four.

3 (*a*) The third period elements of *p*-block with the electronic configuration $3s^2 3p^n$ have the vacant 3*d*-orbitals lying between the 3*p* and 4*s* levels of energy.

4 (*a*) 3*d*- orbitals are used by third period of *p*-block elements in order to expand their covalency beyond four.

5 (*d*) The element, C, shows greater ability to form $p\pi$-$p\pi$ multiple bonds.

6 (*b*) Boron forms $[BF_4]^-$, while aluminium forms $[AlF_6]^{3-}$ as it expands its covalency beyond four by utilising 3*d*-orbitals for bond formation.

7 (*c*) Carnallite is $KCl \cdot MgCl_2 \cdot 6H_2O$. It is not a mineral of boron.

8 (*a*) Aluminium is the most abundant metal and the third most abundant element in the earth's crust (8.3% by mass) after oxygen (45.5%) and Si (27.7%).

9 (*a*) The observed discontinuity in the ionisation enthalpy values between Al and Ga, and that between In and Tl are due to the inability of *d*-and *f*-electrons, which have low screening effect, to compensate the increase in nuclear charge down the group.

10 (*b*) The electrons in *d*-orbitals cannot screen the nucleus effectively and hence effective nuclear charge of Ga (It contains 10 electrons) is greater in magnitude than that of Al. So, electrons of Ga experience greater force of attraction than Al.

11 (*d*) Strong bonding between individual atoms in the solid state having very strong crystalline lattice.

12 (*c*) Ga, In and Tl shows the oxidation state(s) of + 3 as well as + 1.

13 (*b*) The stability order of + 1 oxidation states of group 13 elements will be

$$B << Al < Ga < In < Tl$$
(order of + 1 oxidation state)

14 (*b*) Electronegativity in group 13 elements first decreases from B to Al and then increases marginally. It is due to discrepancies in atomic size of the elements.

15 (*a*) Statement I is correct regarding the properties of boron, while the Statements II and III are incorrect.

Corrected form are as follows :

II. Boron has high melting point and low density.

III. Boron shows low electrical conductivity.

16 (*d*) Gallium usually has low melting point and high boiling point. It exists in liquid state during summer.

17 (*b*) Statement (b) is correct, while other Statements are incorrect. Corrected form are as follows :

(a) Density of the group-13 elements increases down the group from boron to thallium.

(c) Boron is a hard non-metal.

(d) Boron has low electrical conductivity.

18 (*d*) Statement III is incorrect. It's correct form is as follows

The compounds of group-13 elements in +1 oxidation state, as expected from energy considerations, are more ionic than those in +3 oxidation state.

Rest other statements are correct.

19 (*a*) Statement (a) is incorrect. It's correct form is as follows

Tl^{3+} is a powerful oxidising agent. Thus, Tl^+ is more stable in solution than Tl^{3+}.

Rest other statements are correct.

20 (*b*) The number of electrons will be only six because sharing of only three electrons is possible.

21 (*b*) BCl_3 (Lewis acid) reacts with NH_3 (Lewis base) to form an addition product.

The complete reaction is shown below.

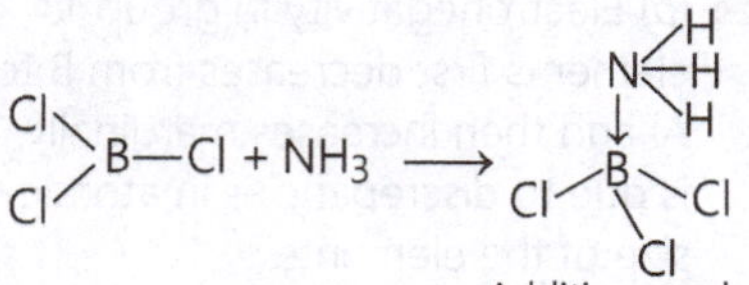

Addition product

22 (*b*) $AlCl_3$ achieves stability by forming a dimer and the correct structure is

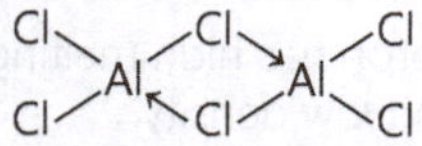

23 (*d*) $4B(s) + 3O_2(g) \xrightarrow{\Delta} 2B_2O_3(s)$ (I)

$2Al(s) + N_2(g) \xrightarrow{\Delta} 2AlN(s)$ (II)

24 (*a*) Boron trioxide is acidic and reacts with metal oxides to form metal borates.

25 (*a*) $2Al(s) + 2NaOH(aq) + 6H_2O(l) \longrightarrow 2Na^+[Al(OH)_4]^-(aq) + 3H_2(g)$

26 (*d*) Statement (d) is incorrect. It's correct form is as follows

Aluminium forms a very thin oxide layer on its surface which protects the metal from further attack by oxygen.

Rest other statements are correct.

27 (*a*) Statement (a) is correct, Corrected form of rests are as follows

(b) NaOH cannot be stored in a vessel made of Al.

(c) Aluminium chloride dissociates in water.

(d) AlF_3 is insoluble in anhydrous HF.

28 (*b*) The elements of group 13 react with halogens to form trihalides (except TlI_3). Tl forms TlI instead of TlI_3.

29 (*d*) Boron forms acidic oxide B_2O_3, while Al forms amphoteric oxide Al_2O_3.

30 (*b*) Statements II, III and IV are correct, while Statement I is incorrect. It's correct form is as follows

The structure of Al_2Cl_6 is shown below :

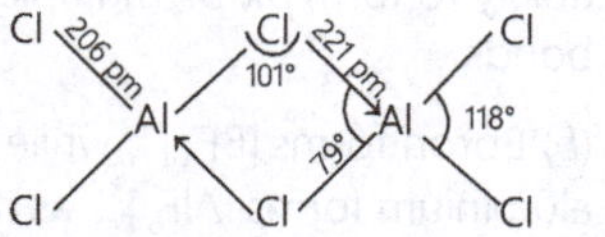

The six Al—Cl bonds are not of the same length.

31 (*a*) Boron form BF_4^- in which boron atom extends its coordination number to 4 by utilising empty *p*-orbital. It cannot expands its octet due to non-availability of *d*-orbitals.

32 (*a*) The trichlorides, tribromides and triiodides of all the group-13 elements are covalent in nature and they are hydrolysed in water.

33 (*a*) Species like tetrahedral $[M(OH)_4]^-$ and octahedral $[M(H_2O)_6]^{3+}$ does not exist in case of boron due to non-availability of *d*-orbitals for expanding its covalency.

34 (*a*) The monomeric trihalides of elements of group 13, being electron deficient, are strong Lewis acids. Boron trifluoride (BF_3) easily reacts with Lewis base such as NH_3 to complete its octet around boron. This can be expressed as shown below :

$$F_3B + :NH_3 \longrightarrow F_3B \longleftarrow NH_3$$

35 (*d*)

36 (*d*) $B_2H_6 + NH_3 \xrightarrow[\text{ratio}]{1:2\text{ molar}} \underset{(A)}{[BH_2(NH_3)_2]^+[BH_4]^-} \xrightarrow{\Delta} \underset{(B)}{B_3N_3H_6} + H_2(g)$

37 (*a*) $B_2H_6 + 3O_2 \longrightarrow B_2O_3 + 3H_2O$

It gets hydrolysed readily to give boric acid.

$$\underset{\text{Borane}}{B_2H_6} + 6H_2O \longrightarrow \underset{\text{Orthoboric acid}}{2H_3BO_3} + \underset{\text{Dihydrogen}}{6H_2\uparrow}$$

38 (*d*) Statement (d) is correct, while other statements are incorrect. Corrected form are as follows

(a) The four terminal hydrogen atoms and the two boron atoms lie in one plane.

Above and below this plane, there are two bridging hydrogen atoms.

(b) The four terminal B—H bonds are regular 2-centre-2-electron bonds.

(c) The two bridged (B—H—B) bonds are different and can be described in terms of 3-centre-2-electron bonds.

39 (*b*) The correct structure of diborane is given in option (b).

40 (*b*) There is a considerable increase in covalent radius from C to Si, thereafter from Si to Pb a small increase in radius is observed. This is due to the presence of completely filled *d* and *f*-orbitals in heavier members.

41 (*b*) There is a small decrease in $\Delta_i H$ from Si to Ge to Sn and slight increase in $\Delta_i H$ from Sn to Pb. This is the consequence of poor shielding effect of intervening *d* and *f*-orbitals and an increase in size of the atom.

42 (*b*) Statement (b) is incorrect. It's correct form is as follows :

Carbon and silicon are non-metals, germanium is metalloid, whereas tin and lead are soft metals with low melting points.

43 (*b*) Thus, the correct sequence is $C < Si < Ge < Sn < Pb$. It is because of inert pair effect, due to which ns^2 electrons of valence shell are unable to participate in bonding.

44 (*c*) $CO_2, GeO_2, SiO_2 \longrightarrow$ Acidic

$CO \longrightarrow$ Neutral

$SnO_2, SnO \longrightarrow$ Amphoteric

45 (*c*) Statement (c) is incorrect.

It's correct form is as follows

Most of the tetrahalides are covalent in nature.

46 (*b*) Statement II is correct, while Statements I and III are incorrect. Corrected form are as follows

I. Sn in +2 oxidation state is a reducing agent.

III. Pb compounds act as oxidising agent in +4 state.

47 (*a*) PbI_4 does not exist because Pb—I bond, initially formed during the reaction, does not release enough energy to unpair $6s^2$ electrons and excite one of them to higher orbital to have four unpaired electrons around lead (Pb) atom.

48 (*a*) The complete reaction is given below.

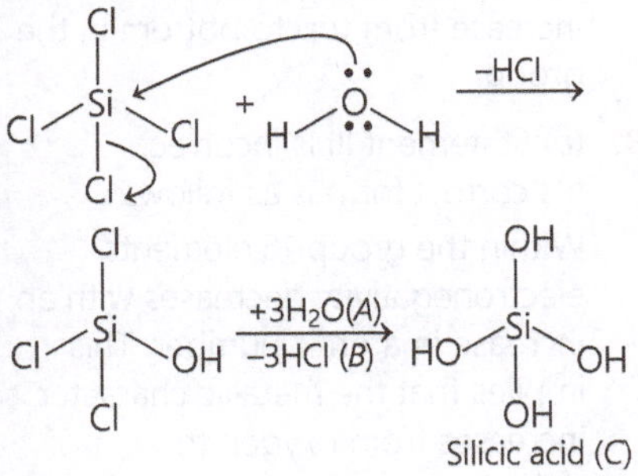

Silicic acid (*C*)

Hence, *A* is $3H_2O$, *B* is 3HCl and *C* is silicic acid.

49 (*c*) The incorrect statement is (c). Its correct form is :

Carbon has higher ionisation ethalpy.

50 (*d*) The bond enthalpy of Si—Si (297 kJ/mol) is greater than Ge—Ge (260 kJ/mol).

51 (*a*)

52 (*a*) Graphite conducts electricity due to highly delocalised nature of π-electrons.

53 (*a*) The major difference between diamond and graphite is due to the crystal structure of diamond which is different from that of graphite.

54 (*c*) Statements I, II and IV are correct, while Statement III is incorrect. It's correct form is as follows

Spherical fullerenes are also called bucky balls in short.

55 (*d*)

56 (*b*) Moscovium, the element of group 15 is a synthetic radioactive element with electronic configuration $[Rn]5f^{14}6d^{10}7s^27p^3$. Due to very short half-life and availability in very little amount, its chemistry is yet to be established.

57 (*d*) Phosphorus belongs to group 15 and it also occur as the founder of the apatite family which are the main components of phosphate rocks. Thus, element *M* is phosphorus.

58 (*c*) Ionic radii (Å) of Sb^{3+}, Bi^{3+} and As^{3+} follow the order :

$Bi^{3+} > Sb^{3+} > As^{3+}$ because ionic and atomic radii increases on moving down the group due to addition of extra shells.

59 (*a*) Melting point of group 15 elements first increases upto arsenic and then decreases upto bismuth. Thus, the correct order of melting point for group 15 elements is

$$N < P < As > Sb > Bi$$

60 (*a*) $p\pi$-$p\pi$ bonding is weak in P than N, so it does not form P_2 like N_2. Heavier elements of group 15 do not form $p\pi$ -$p\pi$ bonds as their atomic orbitals are so large and diffuse that they cannot have effective overlapping.

61 (*b*) Nitrogen lacks *d*-orbitals in its valence shell. It cannot form compounds with + 5 oxidation state such as nitrogen pentahalides.

62 (*b*) The basic strength of given hydrides decreases in the following order :

$$NH_3 > PH_3 > AsH_3 > SbH_3 > BiH_3$$

This is due to the decrease in the availability of the lone pair of electrons which decreases with increase in the size of central atom from N to Bi.

63 (*b*) Bond angle gradually decreases down the group as bond pair-lone pair repulsion decreases.

Thus, NH_3 has largest bond angle.

64 (*a*) PH_3 has the lowest boiling point because boiling point increases with increase in size of central atom and NH_3 has more boiling point than that of PH_3 due to hydrogen bonding.

65 (*a*) The melting point of group 15 elements increases down the group but due to hydrogen bonding in NH_3, it has higher melting point than PH_3.

	NH_3	PH_3	AsH_3	SbH_3
Melting point/K	195.2	139.5	156.7	185

66 (*d*) Statement (d) is incorrect. It's correct form is as follows

Trihalides except BiF_3 are predominantly covalent in nature.

Rest other statements are correct.

67 (*d*) All the given statements are correct.

68 (*a*) Liquid N_2 is used as refrigerant to preserve biological materials, food items and in cryosurgery.

It also finds use where an inert atmosphere is required (e.g. in iron and steel industry, inert diluent for reactive chemicals).

69 (*b*) The correct increasing order of oxidation state of nitrogen for nitrogen oxides is

$$\overset{+1}{N_2}O < \overset{+2}{N}O < \overset{+3}{N_2}O_3 < \overset{+4}{N}O_2$$

70 (*b*) Statement (b) is incorrect. It's correct form is as follows

Red phosphorus is obtained by heating white phosphorus at 573 K in an inert atmosphere for several days. When red phosphorus is heated under high pressure, a series of phases of black phosphorus is obtained.

Rest other statements are correct.

71 (*a*) α - black phosphorus is formed when red phosphorus is heated in a sealed tube at 803 K. On the other hand, β-black phosphorus is prepared by heating white phosphorus at 473 K under a high pressure.

72 (*b*) The complete reactions are given as

$$PCl_3 + 3H_2O \longrightarrow H_3PO_3 + 3HCl$$

$$P_4 + 8SO_2Cl_2 \longrightarrow 4PCl_3 + 4SO_2 + 2S_2Cl_2$$

$$3CH_3COOH + PCl_3 \longrightarrow 3CH_3COCl + H_3PO_3$$

$$3C_2H_5OH + PCl_3 \longrightarrow 3C_2H_5Cl + H_3PO_3$$

Thus, the reaction given in option (b) does not produces H_3PO_3.

73 (*a*) PCl_5 is prepared by the action of Cl_2 on P_4. The reaction is given as below.

$$P_4 + 10Cl_2 \longrightarrow 4\,PCl_5$$

74 (*c*) Among the given compounds, the three compounds, i.e. CH_3COOH, H_2O and C_2H_5OH can react with PCl_5 to give $POCl_3$. The reactions are given as below.

$$PCl_5 + CH_3COOH \longrightarrow CH_3COCl + POCl_3 + HCl$$

$$PCl_5 + H_2O \longrightarrow POCl_3 + 2HCl$$

$$PCl_5 + C_2H_5OH \longrightarrow POCl_3 + C_2H_5Cl + HCl$$

75 (*c*) The structure and oxidation state of oxoacids of phosphorus are as follows

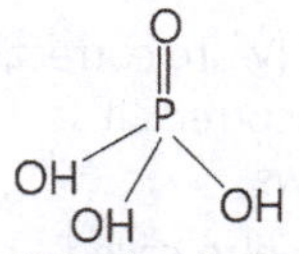

Orthophosphoric acid (H_3PO_4) (O.S + 5)

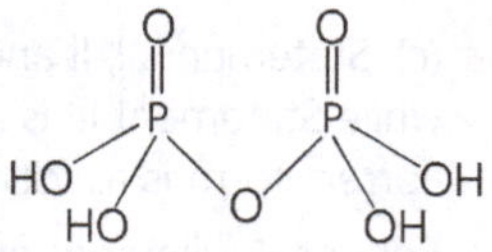

Pyrophosphoric acid (O.S + 5)

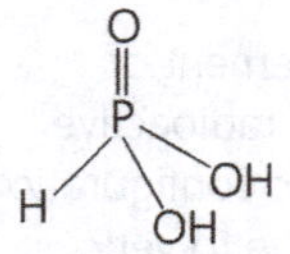

Orthophosphorus acid (H_3PO_3) (O.S + 3)

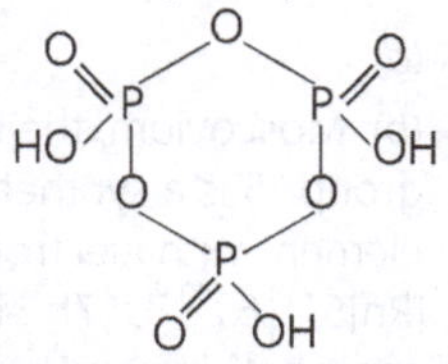

Cyclotrimetaphosphoric acid $(HPO_3)_3$ (O.S + 5)

Thus, in orthophosphorus acid oxidation state of phosphorus is +3.

76 (*d*) Let us consider the structure of the phosphorus oxyacids.

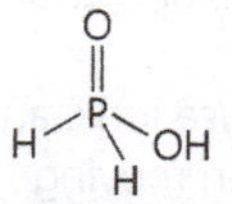

H_3PO_2 Hypophosphorus acid (P—H bonds=2)

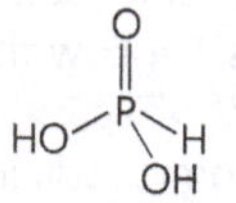

H_3PO_3 Orthophosphorus acid (P—H bond =1)

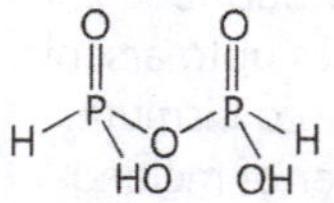

$H_4P_2O_5$ Pyrophosphorus acid (P—H bonds=2)

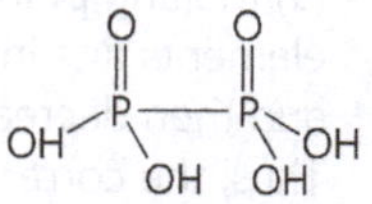

$H_4P_2O_6$ Hypophosphoric acid (P—H bond = 0)

77 (*b*) Among the given options, pyrophosphoric acid is tetrabasic. Its structure is

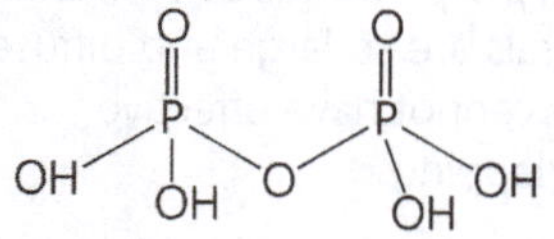

78 (*d*) The structure of cyclotrimetaphosphate ion is,

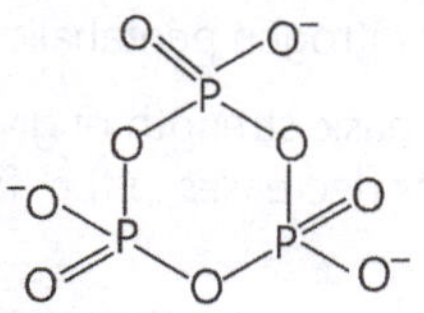

Therefore, in cyclotrimetaphosphate ion, the number of O-atoms, P—O—P bonds and unit negative charges respectively are 9, 3, 3.

79 (*a*) Due to increase in the number of shells, atomic and ionic radii increases from top to bottom in the group. The size of oxygen atom is, exceptionally small. The correct order of increasing ionic radii is,

$$O < S < Se < Te < Po$$

80 (*c*) Statements II and III are correct, while I is incorrect. It's correct form is as follows

The elements of group-16 have ns^2np^4 general electronic configuration.

Due to increase in the number of shells, atomic and ionic radii increase from top to bottom in the group.

81 (*b*) Statement III is incorrect. It's correct form is as follows

Within the group 16 elements, electronegativity decreases with an increase in atomic number. This implies that the metallic character increases from oxygen to polonium.

Rest other statements are correct.

82 (*c*) Water (H_2O) is much less volatile than H_2S because sulphur atom is less electronegative than O-atom and, hence does not form H-bonding like water.

83 (*d*) Statement (d) is incorrect. It's correct form is as follows :

Oxidation states of sulphur in some important compounds are as follows

− 2	in	H_2S
0	in	S_8
+ 2	in	$S_2O_3^{2-}$
+ 4	in	SO_2
+ 6	in	SO_3

Rest other statements are correct.

84 (*d*) All statements are correct.

85 (*b*) Due to presence of *d*-orbitals, sulphur can expand its valencies from 2 to 6, while oxygen has only one valency (2) due to the absence of *d*-orbital.

86 (*b*) All the hydrides of group 16 elements except H_2O possess reducing property and this character increases from H_2S to H_2Te.

87 (*c*) Elements of group 16 form a large number of halides of the type EX_6, EX_4 and EX_2 where E is an element of these group 16 and X is a halogen. The stability of these halides decreases in the order :

$$F^- > Cl^- > Br^- > I^-$$

88 (*d*) As the size of the element increases on moving down the group the bond enthalpy decreases. Hence, the stability decreases.

89 (*b*) Statement II is correct, while statements I and III are incorrect. Corrected form are as follows

I. Sulphur forms numerous allotropes of which the yellow rhombic (α-sulphur) and monoclinic (β-sulphur) forms are the most important.

III. The stable form at room temperature is rhombic sulphur, which transforms to monoclinic sulphur, when heated above 369 K.

90 (*d*) At elevated temperatures (~ 1000 K), S_2 is the dominant species of S and it is paramagnetic like O_2.

91 (*a*) $H_2S_2O_8$ (peroxodisulphuric acid) and H_2SO_5 (peroxomonosulphuric acid) are peroxoacids of sulphur.

92 (*b*) $S_2O_8^{2-}$ is

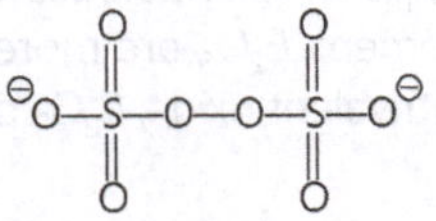

Total number of S—O or S=O bond = 8

Rhombic sulphur is

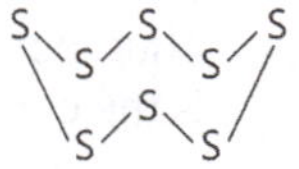

Total number of S—S bond = 8

Thus, the correct answer is (b).

93 (*d*) Tennessine (Ts) is a synthetic radioactive element with electronic configuration $[Rn]5f^{14}6d^{10}7s^27p^5$.

94 (*a*) Electronegativity, ionisation enthalpy and reactivity decreases but ionic radius increases on moving down the group of halogen family.

Thus option (a) is correct.

95 (*c*) Statements I, III and IV are correct. Statement II is incorrect. It's correct form is as follows

Halogens have high ionisation enthalpies, due to their little tendency to lose electron.

96 (*d*) Statements I and III are correct, while the statements II and IV are incorrect.

Corrected form are as follows

II. Enthalpy of dissociation of F_2 is smaller as compared to Cl_2. It is due to relatively large electron-electron repulsion among the lone pairs in F_2 molecule.

IV. F_2 is the strongest oxidising halogen and it oxidises other halide ions in solution or even in the solid phase.

97 (*d*) The anomalous behaviour of fluorine is due to its small size, highest electronegativity, low F — F bond dissociation enthalpy and non-availability of *d*-orbitals in its valence shell.

So, (d) is not the correct reason.

98 (*b*) On moving down the group, H—*X* bond length increases. So correct increasing order of their acidic strength is

$$HF < HCl < HBr < HI.$$

99 (*c*) The ionic character of the metal halides decreases in the order : $MF > MCl > MBr > MI$ because size increases from F to I.

100 (*c*) The boiling points increases with the increase in the electronegativity difference between *A* and *B*.

101 (*c*) The compositions of rare gases in air are

	% by volume
He	5.24×10^{-4}
Ne	1.82×10^{-3}
Ar	0.934
Kr	1.14×10^{-4}
Xe	8.7×10^{-6}

So, Ar is most abundant noble gas in air.

102 (*a*) Atomic radii increase down the group with increase in atomic number. Thus, the correct order of atomic radii of noble gases is

$$He < Ne < Ar < Kr < Xe.$$

103 (*a*) The first noble gas compound obtained by mixing PtF_6 and xenon, $Xe^+PtF_6^-$.

104 (*a*) In $XeOF_4$, Xe is sp^3d^2-hybridised. Geometry of the molecule is octahedral, but shape of the molecule is square pyramidal. According to VSEPR theory, it has one π bond. Remaining six electron pairs form an octahedron with one position occupied by a lone pair.

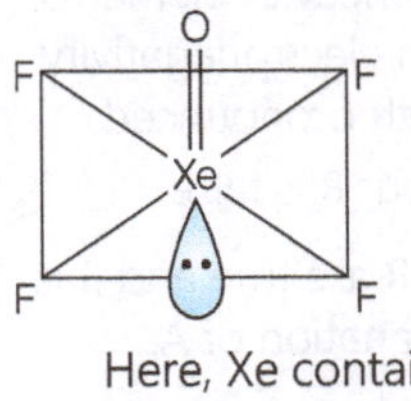

[Number of *bp* = 5
Number of *lp* = 1]

Here, Xe contains one lone pair of electrons.

105 (*c*) The reaction given in option (c) is incorrect and can be corrected as follows

$$\underset{(1:20 \text{ ratio})}{Xe(g) + 3F_2(g)} \xrightarrow{573K,\ 60\text{-}70 \text{ bar}} XeF_6(s)$$

106 (*d*) Among XeO_3, $XeOF_4$ and XeF_6, all the molecules have one lone pair of electrons on Xe.

Assertion-Reason

1 (*a*) Both A and R are true and R is the correct explanation of A.

2 (*c*) Boron always forms covalent bond because of its small size. B never forms B^{3+} ion.

Thus, A is true but R is false.

3 (*a*) Both A and R are true and R is the correct explanation of A.

4 (*a*) Both A and R are true and R is the correct explanation of A.

5 (*c*) A is true and R is false. The correct form R is : Aluminium dissolves in mineral acids and aqueous alkalies.

6 (*a*) Both A and R are true and R is the correct explanation of A.

7 (*c*) Group 14 elements are actually smaller in size than group 13 elements.

Thus, A is true but R is false.

8 (*d*) The common oxidation states exhibited by the group-14 elements are +4 and +2.

Thus, A is false but R is true.

9 (*a*) Both A and R are true and R is correct explanation of A.

10 (*a*) Both A and R are correct and R is correct explanation of A.

11 (*c*) Amongst the heavier elements, the difference in electronegativity value is not much pronounced.

Thus, A is true but R is false.

12 (*a*) Both A and R are true and R is the correct explanation of A.

13 (*a*) Both A and R are true and R is the correct explanation of A.

14 (*a*) NH_3 forms hydrogen bond with water. Thus, it is soluble in it but PH_3 cannot form hydrogen bond with water so it escapes as gas.

Thus, both A and R are true and R is the correct explanation of A.

15 (*b*) Pentahalides are more covalent than trihalides This is due to the fact that in pentahalides +5 oxidation state exists while in case of trihalides +3 oxidation state exists. Since, elements in +5 oxidation state will have more polarising power than in +3 oxidation state, the covalent character is more in pentahalides. Thus, both A and R are true but R is not the correct explanation of A.

16 (*d*) H_3PO_2 is not a dibasic acid. It is a monobasic acid because of the presence of only one —OH group.

Thus, A is false but R is true.

17 (*a*) Both A and R are true and R is correct explanation of A.

18 (*a*) SF_6 is known but SCl_6 is not. It is due to the small size of fluorine. Six F^- ions can be accommodated around sulphur while chloride ion is comparatively larger in size, thus, there will be interatomic repulsion.

Thus, both A and R are true and R is the correct explanation of A.

19 (*a*) Elements of group-16 form hydrides of the type H_2E (E = O, S, Se, Te and Po). Their acidic character increases from H_2O to H_2Te due to decrease in bond enthalpy for the dissociation of H—E bond down the group.

Thus, both A and R are true and R is correct explanation of A.

20 (*a*) Both A and R are true and R is the correct explanation of A.

21 (*a*) Both A and R are true and R is the correct explanation of A.

22 (*a*) Both A and R are true and R is the correct explanation of A.

23 (*b*) All the halogens exhibit –1 oxidation state because these require only one electron to complete their octet. However, chlorine, bromine and iodine exhibit +1, +3, +5 and +7 oxidation states when they form compounds with even more electronegative elements like oxygen and fluorine. Thus, both A and R are true but R is not the correct explanation of A.

24 (*a*) Both A and R are true and R is the correct explanation of A.

25 (*a*) Both A and R are true and R is the correct explanation of A.

26 (*a*) Both A and R are true and R is the correct explanation of A.

Statement Type

1 (*c*) Statement I is false but Statement II is true. The correct form of statement I is as follows : Compounds formed by non-metals with metals are generally ionic in nature due to the view of larger differences in their electronegativities.

2 (*d*) Both Statement I and Statement II are true.

3 (*b*) Statement I is true but Statement II is false. The correct form of statement II is as follows

Due to small size of nitrogen, in N—N single bond, 2*p*-2*p* repulsion is more than P—P single bond therefore N—N single bond is weaker than the P—P single bond.

4 (*c*) Higher the oxidation state of the central atom means higher will be the acidic nature of their oxides.

Thus, pentavalent oxides of group 15 element, E_2O_5 are more acidic than trivalent oxide, E_2O_3 of same element. On moving down the group, metallic character increases that means the acidic nature of the oxides of group 15 elements decreases down the group. Hence, given Statement I is false but Statement II is true.

5 (*d*) Both the given statements are true.

6 (*c*) Statement I is false but Statement II is true.

The correct form of Statement I is as follows

The central atom must be the more electropositive and bigger element in interhalogen compounds.

7 (*c*) Statements III and IV are correct I, II and V are incorrect. Their correct statements are

I. F_2 has lower dissociation energy than Cl_2.

II. Oxidation state of P is +1 is H_3PO_2.

V. The structure of diborane is non-planar.

8 (*d*) Statements II and V are incorrect. Their correct forms are

I. Graphite is the thermodynamically most stable form of carbon.

V. C_{60} is the only pure form of carbon, it is not radioactive.

9 (*c*) Statements II and IV are incorrect. Their correct form are

III. Nitrogen forms a number of oxides.

IV. Oxygen is more electronegative than sulphur.

10 (*a*) Statements I, II and III are correct while IV and V are incorrect. Their correct form are

IV. The correct order of ionic radii of +3 oxidation state is $Bi^{3+} > Sb^{3+} > As^{3+}$.

V. The increase in halogen size decreases stability. Thus, the correct order is $F^- > Cl^- > Br^- > I^-$.

Matching Type

1 (*b*) The correct match of electronic configuration is
A-4, B-5, C-1, D-3, E-2.

2 (*a*) The correct match is
A-4, B-2, C-3, D-1.

3 (*a*) The correct match is
A-1, B-2, C-3, D-4.

4 (*a*) The correct match is
A-2, B-1, C-4, D-3.

5 (*c*) The correct match is
A-4, B-3, C-2, D-1.

6 (*c*) The correct match is
A-2, B-1, C-4, D-3.

	Formula	Physical state and colour	Structure
A.	ClF_3	Colourless gas	Bent T-shaped
B.	IF_5	Colourless gas but solid below 77 K	Square pyramidal
C.	IF_7	Colourless gas	Pentagonal bipyramidal
D.	ICl_3	Orange solid	Bent T-shaped

7 (*a*) The correct match is
A-1, B-3, C-4, D-2.

Numerical Value

1 (6) In liquid state, $AlCl_3$ exists as a dimer. Aluminium is surrounded by 6 chlorine. So, the coordination number of Al in $AlCl_3$ is 6.

2 (3) CO_2, SiO_2, GeO_2—Acidic, SnO_2, PbO_2—Amphoteric.

3 (3) An oxide which combines with water to form an acid generally, the oxides of non-metals are acidic in nature. Hence, N_2O_3, NO_2, Cl_2O_7 are acidic except N_2O, NO, CO, which are neutral oxides and CaO, Na_2O are basic oxides.

4 (19) Xenon hexafluoride (*A*) on partial hydrolysis gives XeO_2F_2 as a product.

$$\underset{(P)}{XeF_6} + 2H_2O \longrightarrow XeO_2F_2 + 4HF$$

Structure of XeF_6 is given as

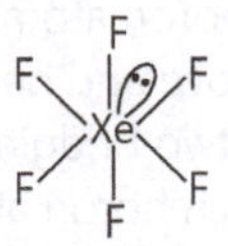

∴ Thus, total no. of lone pair = lone pair on Xe + 6 × lone pair on F
$= 1 + 6 \times 3 = 19$

5 (11) When XeF_4 reacts with SbF_5

$$XeF_4 + SbF_5 \longrightarrow [XeF_3]^+ [SbF_6]^-$$

$x = 3, y = 1, z = 6, w = 1$

$w + x + y + z = 6 + 3 + 1 + 1 = 11$

NCERT Exemplar's

1 (*c*) Ga exists as liquid from 30°C upto 2403°C and hence, it is used in high temperature thermometry.

2 (*d*) B > Al < Ga > In < Tl

3 (*a*) Boron has atomic number 5 and does not have vacant *d*-orbital. The element *M* in the complex ion MF_6^{3-} has a coordination number of six. Boron can show maximum coordination number of 4 due to absence of *d*-orbitals.

Thus, B cannot form complex of the type MF_6^{3-}.

4 (*a*) Structure of $B(OH)_4^-$ is

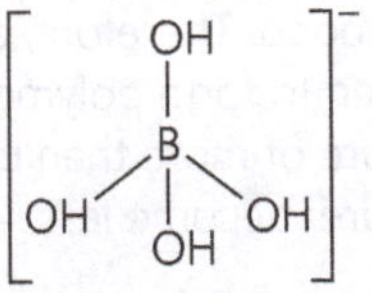

It contains four bond pairs and no lone pairs. Thus, the hybridisation of central atom is sp^3 and the geometry of the complex is tetrahedral.

5 (*b*) The geometry of B_2H_6 can be represented as shown below

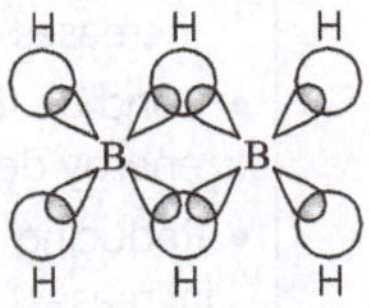

Bonding in diborane

The four terminal hydrogen atoms and two boron atoms lie in one plane. Above and below the plane, there are two bridging hydrogen atoms. Each boron atom forms four bonds even though it has only three electrons. The terminal B—H bonds are regular bonds but the bridge B—H bonds are different.

Each bridge hydrogen is bonded to the two boron atoms only by sharing of two electrons. Such covalent bond is called 3-centre-2-electron bond or a multicentre bond or banana bond.

6 (*b*) The catenation is maximum in carbon and decreases down the group as shown below :

$$C >> Si > Ge \approx Sn > Pb$$

This is due to high bond energy of C—C bonds. Down the group, size increases and electronegativity decreases, thereby, the tendency to show catenation decreases.

7 (*b*) Quartz (crystalline form of silica, SiO_2) is extensively used as a piezo-electric material as it contains Si.

8 (*a*) Nitrogen does not show allotropy due to its weak N—N single bond. Therefore, ability of nitrogen to form polymeric structure of more than one structure become less.

9 (*d*) On moving top to bottom, size of central atom increases. Bond length of *E*—H bond increases and bond dissociation energy decreases.

Hence, reducing nature increases.

NH_3
PH_3 • Bond length increases
AsH_3 • Bond dissociation energy decreases
SbH_3 • Reducing character increases
↓

Hence, SbH_3 acts as strongest reducing agent among these.

10 (*c*) Among given four elements, i.e. carbon, nitrogen, phosphorus and boron, only phosphorus has vacant *d*-orbitals. Thus, only phosphorus has ability to form $p\pi$ - $d\pi$ bonding.

11 (*a*) Option (a) in an incorrect statement. Correct statement is that single N—N bond is weaker than single P—P bond. That is why, phosphorus shows allotropy but nitrogen does not.

Rest other statements are correct.

12 (*a*) When freshly prepared solution of $FeSO_4$ is added in a solution containing NO_3^- ion, it leads to formation of a brown coloured complex. This is known as brown ring test of nitrate.

$$NO_3^- + 3Fe^{2+} + 4H^+ \longrightarrow NO + 3Fe^{3+} + 2H_2O$$

$$[Fe(H_2O)_6]^{2+} + NO \longrightarrow \underset{\text{Brown ring}}{[Fe(H_2O)_5(NO)]^{2+}} + H_2O$$

13 (*c*) Structure of H_3PO_4 is,

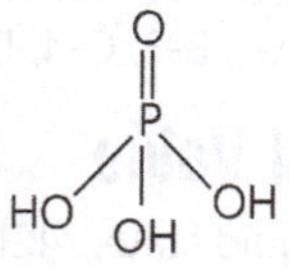

H_3PO_4 has 3 —OH groups, i.e. has three ionisable H-atoms and hence forms three series of salts.

NaH_2PO_4, Na_2HPO_4 and Na_3PO_4

14 (*c*) Strong reducing behaviour of H_3PO_2 is due to presence of two P—H bonds and one P—OH bond.

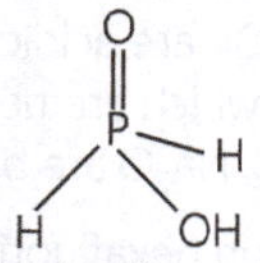

Hypophosphorus acid

15 (*c*) The anion of compound NaH_2PO_2 is $H_2PO_2^-$. Let oxidation state of P in $H_2PO_2^-$ is *x*.

$$\therefore 2 \times 1 + x + 2 \times (-2) = -1$$
$$2 + x - 4 = -1$$
$$x - 2 = -1$$
$$\Rightarrow x = +1$$

16 (*c*) Cyclotrimetaphosphoric acid contains 3 double bonds and 12 single bonds as shown below.

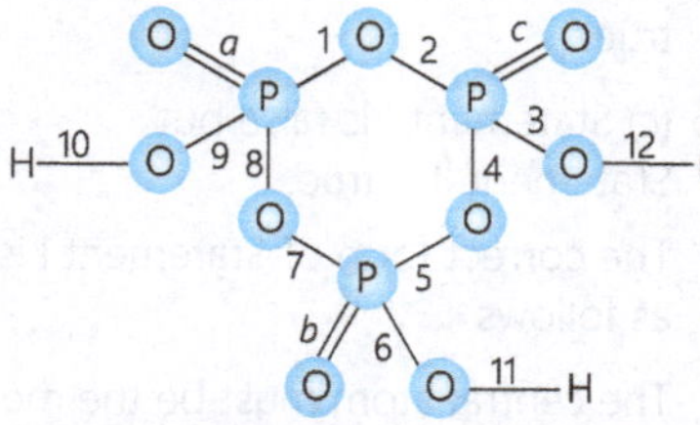

Cyclotrimetaphosphoric acid $(HPO_3)_3$

a, *b*, *c* are three π-bonds and numerics 1 to 12 are σ-bonds.

17 (*a*) H_2SO_5 and $H_2S_2O_8$ are peroxoacids of sulphur because peroxoacids of sulphur must contain one —O—O— bond as shown below.

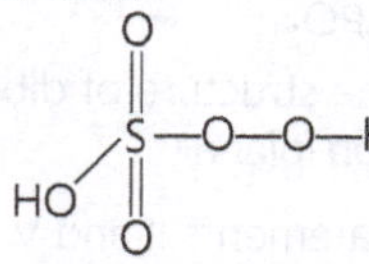

H_2SO_5

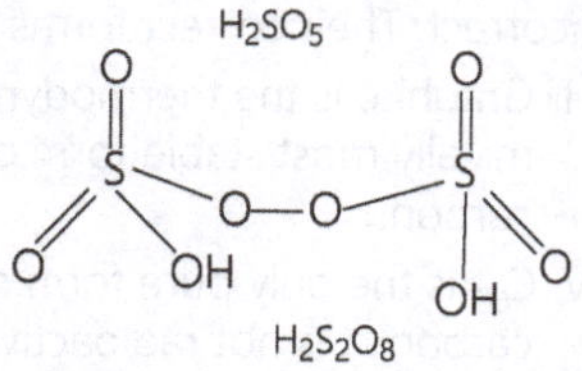

$H_2S_2O_8$

18 (*c*) SF_4 is not tetrahedral in shape. It has *see-saw* shaped due to presence of a lone pair of electrons, as shown below.

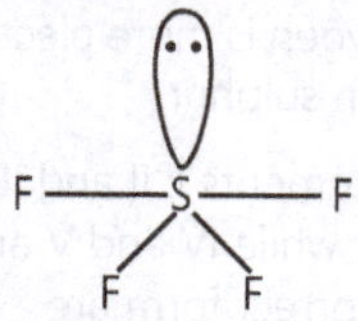

It has trigonal bipyramidal geometry having sp^3d-hybridisation.

19 (*a*) On moving top to bottom.

- Size of halogen atom increases
- H—*X* bond length increases

- Bond dissociation enthalpy decreases in the following order:
  HF > HCl > HBr > HI

Thus, HF has highest value of bond dissociation enthalpy.

20 (*c*) Covalency of an atom in a covalent compound is the number of covalent bonds formed by an atom. Maximum covalency of nitrogen is 4. e.g. In ammonium ions (NH_4^+).

Past Exams'

1 (*a*) Both Statement I and Statement II are true.

2 (*d*) Among the given elements, only Po does not show –2 oxidation state due to its highly metallic nature.

3 (*b*) The correct match is
A-3, B-1, C-4, D-2.

4 (*c*) The incorrect statement about diborane is option (c) because boron has sp^3-hybridisation and it is non-planar.

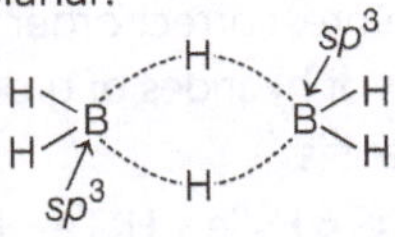

5 (*b*) The correct statement is option (b). It is because in diamond, each carbon is bonded with four other carbon atoms. So, hybridisation of carbon atom is sp^3. In graphite each carbon atom is bonded with three other carbon atoms.
So, hybridisation of carbon atom in graphite is sp^2.

6 (*c*) Silicones are synthetic organo-silicon polymers contaning repeated R_2SiO units. It is used in surgical and cosmetic implants. They are also used as low temperature lubricants, in making waterproof clothes and paper, etc.

7 (*d*) The atomic radii as well as ionic radii increases on moving down the group 13 elements because of the successive addition of one extra shell of electrons.

However, there is an anomaly at gallium in case of atomic radii. Atomic radii of Ga is lesser as compared to Al.
Thus, the increasing order of atomic radii of the group 13 elements is B (85 pm) < Ga (135 pm) < Al (143 pm) < In (167 pm) < Tl (170 pm).

8 (*b*) Al < Ga < In < Tl
This is due to inert pair effect or tendency of ns^2 *d*-electrons do not participate in bond formation. This tendency decreases on moving down group.

9 (*a*) The correct match is
A-3, B-4, C-1, D-2.
Structure of given oxoacids of sulphur are as follows

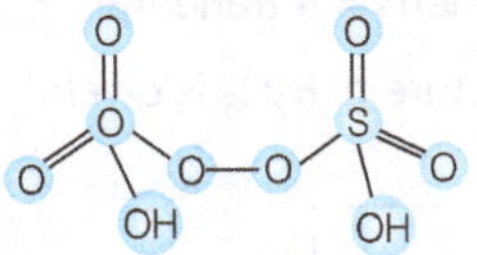

Peroxodisulphuric acid
[Two S—OH,
Four S═O
One S—O—O—S bonds.]

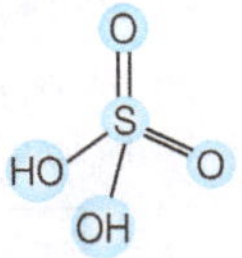

Sulphuric acid
[Two S═O,
Two S—OH]

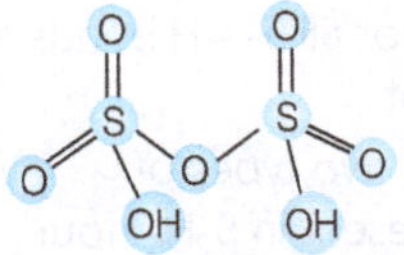

Peroxodisulphuric acid
[Four S═O,
Two S—OH
One S—O—S]

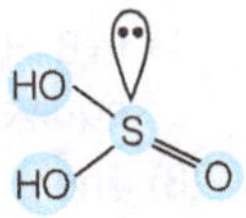

Sulphurous acid
[One S═O,
Two S—OH]

10 (*b*) Statement (b) is incorrect. Its correct form is :
Nobles gases have weak interatomic forces (van der Waals' forces). So, they have low melting and boiling points.

11 (*d*) The correct match is
A-2, B-1, C-4, D-3.

(A) $\ddot{X}eF_2$

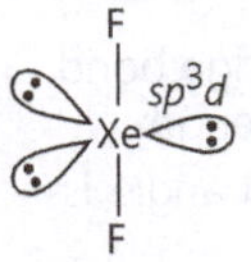

Linear (2)

(B) $\ddot{X}eF_4$

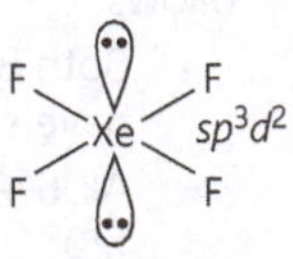

Square planar (1)

(C) $\ddot{X}eO_3$

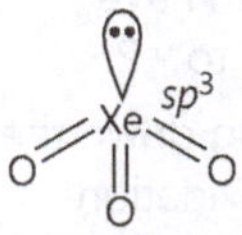

Pyramidal (4)

(D) $\ddot{X}eOF_4$

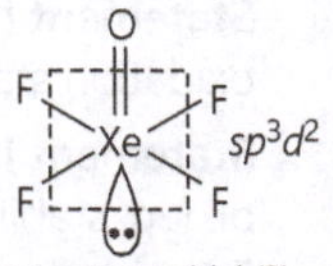

Square pyramidal (3)

Hence, option (d) is correct match.

12 (*b*) For group 16 elements, the hydrides with high molar mass (e.g. H_2Po) are less thermally stable than hydride with lower molar mass (e.g. H_2O). This is due to the increase in size of central atom which results to the weakening of *M*—H bond due to increased bond length.
Thus, the correct order of thermal stability for H_2E(E = O, S, Se, Te and Po) is as follows
$H_2Po < H_2Te < H_2Se < H_2S < H_2O$

13 (*b*)The central atom Cl has seven electrons in the valence shell. Three of these will form electron pair bonds with three fluorine atoms leaving behind four electrons.

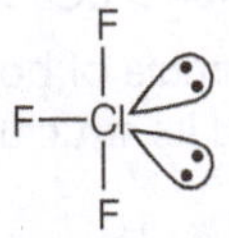

Thus, there are three bond pairs and two lone pairs of electrons.

14 (*b*) Two different halogens may react to form interhalogen compounds as

XX'(ClF, BrF, BrCl, IF, ICl)	Linear
XX'_3 (ClF_3, BrF_3, IF_3, ICl_3)	Bent T-shaped
XX'_5 (ClF_5, $BrCl_5$, IF_5)	Square pyramidal
XX'_7 (IF_7)	Pentagonal bipyramidal

15 (*a*) The oxy acid of phosphorus which contain P—H bond act as a reducing agent or reductant.

In H_3PO_4 one —OH group and two P—H bonds are present.

16 (*b*) Both Statement I and Statement II are incorrect.

Their correct forms are as follows.

Statement I Oxygen can have oxidation state from –2 to +2.

Statement II On moving down the group, stability of + 4 oxidation state increases whereas stability of + 6 oxidation state decreases due to inert pair effect.

17 (*b*) Both Statement I and Statement II are true.

18 (*a*) Statements given in option (a), i.e. A and B are correct, while other two statements are incorrect.

Their correct form are :

The reducing property increases from H_2S to H_2Te down the group.

The ozone molecules contains 6 lone pairs of electrons.

19 (*c*) Extent of back bonding, reduces down the group leading to more Lewis acidic strength.

Extent of back bonding

$$\underset{2p-2p}{BF_3} > \underset{2p-3p}{BCl_3} > \underset{2p-4p}{BBr_3} > \underset{2p-5p}{BI_3}$$

Lewis acid character order

$$BI_3 > BBr_3 > BCl_3 > BF_3$$

20 (*b*) The formula of borazine is $B_3N_3H_6$ and its structure is as follows

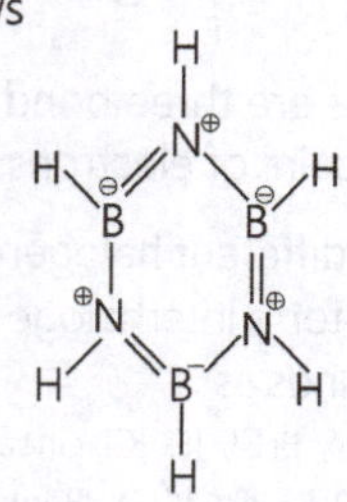

$$B_3N_3H_6 + 9H_2O \longrightarrow 3NH_3 + 3H_3BO_3 + 3H_2$$

But it does not contain banana bond. Hence, option (b) is an incorrect statement.

21 (*d*) As the metallic character increases, the basicity also increases and *vice-versa.*

On moving down the group the atomic radius of element increases that means tendency to release electron from outermost shell increases which will increase basicity of oxides.

Therefore, Tl_2O_3 is the most basic oxide in group 13.

22 (*b*) Complete and balanced reaction is

$$2BF_3 + 6NaH \xrightarrow{450\text{ K}} \underset{\substack{\text{(Diborane)}\\(A)}}{B_2H_6} + 6NaF$$

$$\underset{(A)}{B_2H_6} + 2NMe_3 \longrightarrow \underset{(B)}{2BH_3 \cdot NMe_3}$$

BH_3 is electron deficient, so NMe_3 forms a coordinate bond with it.

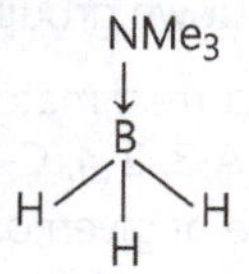

Shape/geometry = tetrahedral

23 (*c*) The structure of B_2H_6 is given below.

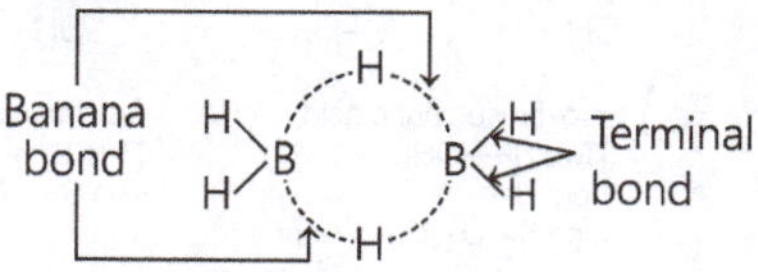

(A) In B_2H_6, not all B—H bonds are equivalent.

(B) There are two types of bonds present in B_2H_6, four normal covalent bonds and two 3-centres-2-electrons bonds.

(E) B_2H_6 is a non-planar molecule.

24 (*c*) Statement (c) is correct, whereas all other statements are incorrect.

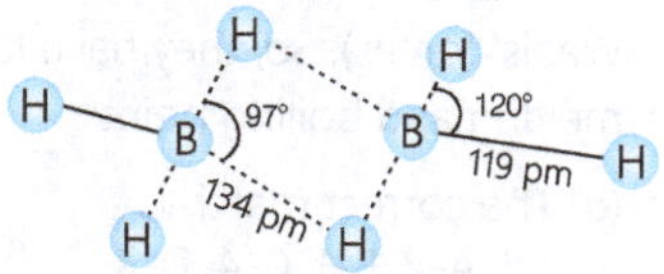

Other correct statements are as follows

- Both B—H—B bridge bond have same bond length.
- All B—H—B bond angle is not 120°.
- BH_3 is electron deficient species and therefore act as Lewis acid.

25 (*d*) $H_4P_2O_7 \rightarrow$ One P—O—P bond.
$(HPO_3)_3 \rightarrow$ Three P—O—P bond.
$P_4O_{10} \rightarrow$ Six P—O—P bond.

26 (*a*) Oxidation states of 'N' in the given compounds are as follows

$$NO \rightarrow x + 1(-2) = 0$$
$$x = +2$$
$$NO_2 \rightarrow x + 2 \times (-2) = 0$$
$$x = +4$$
$$N_2O \rightarrow 2x + (-2) = 0$$
$$x = +1$$
$$NO_3^- \rightarrow x + 3(-2) = -1$$
$$x = +5$$

Thus, $NO_3^- > NO_2 > NO > N_2O$.

27 (*a*) As we move down the group, molecular size and surface area increase and also van der Waals' forces increase.

Therefore, correct order of melting points of hydrides of group 16 element is

$$H_2S < H_2Se < H_2Te < H_2O.$$

28 (*d*) Red phosphorus is produced by heating white phosphorus at 573 K in inert atmosphere.

When red phosphorus is heated in a sealed tube at 803 K, we get α-black phosphorus.

29 (*d*)

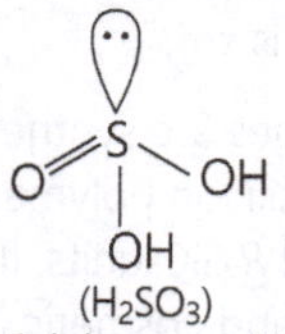

(H_2SO_3)
Sulphurous acid
No. of S=O bond = 1

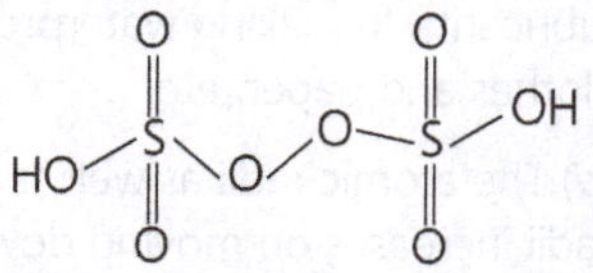

($H_2S_2O_8$)
Peroxodisulphuric acid
No. of S=O bond = 4

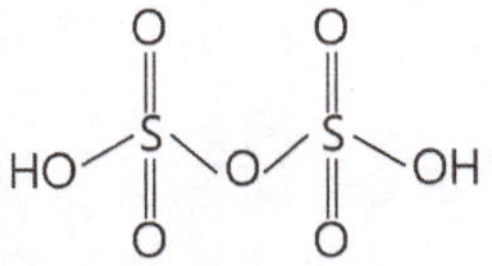

$H_2S_2O_7$
Pyrosulphuric acid
No. of S=O bond = 4

30 (c) Two crystalline allotropic forms of sulphur (S_α and S_β) can change reversibly between themselves with slow heating (above 369 K) or cooling.

$$\underset{\text{(Rhombic)}}{S_\alpha} \underset{\text{Cooling}}{\overset{> 369\text{ K}}{\rightleftharpoons}} \underset{\text{(Monoclinic)}}{S_\beta}$$

So, Statement I is true.

At room temperature or at standard conditions of pressure and temperature, rhombic sulphur is the thermodynamically most stable crystalline allotrope of sulphur ($\Delta_f H^\circ = 0$).

So, Statement II is false.

31 (c) The correct match is
A-5, B-1, C-2, D-3.

Skills Boosters

1. (c) Roasting of sulphides gives the gas SO_2 as a by product.

$$2ZnS + 3O_2 \longrightarrow 2ZnO + 2SO_2$$

$$4FeS_2 + 11O_2 \longrightarrow 2Fe_2O_3 + 8SO_2$$

Sulphur dioxide dissolves in water forming sulphurous acid.

$$H_2O + SO_2 \rightleftharpoons H_2SO_3$$

It reduces chlorine to HCl.

$$SO_2 + Cl_2 + 2H_2O \longrightarrow H_2SO_4 + 2HCl$$

Therefore, P is SO_2 gas.

2. (d) $4B + 3O_2 \xrightarrow{700°C} \underset{(A)}{2B_2O_3}$

$$B_2O_3 + 3C + 3Cl_2 \longrightarrow \underset{(B)}{2BCl_3} + 3CO$$

$$\underset{(B)}{4BCl_3} + 3LiAlH_4 \longrightarrow \underset{(C)}{2B_2H_6} + 3\,LiCl + 3AlCl_3$$

$$B_2H_6 + 2NH_3 \xrightarrow{120°C} [H_2B(NH_3)_2]^{\oplus}[BH_4]^{\ominus}$$

$$3[H_2B(NH_3)_2]^+[BH_4]^- \xrightarrow{200°C,\Delta} \underset{\text{Inorganic benzene}}{2B_3N_3H_6} + 12H_2$$

$\therefore$ BCl_3 is a triangular planar molecule having sp^2-hybridised boron atom.

3. (a) $\underset{(A)}{2Al} + 2NaOH + 2H_2O \longrightarrow \underset{(B)}{2NaAlO_2} + 12H_2$

$$\underset{(B)}{2NaAlO_2} + CO_2 + 3H_2O \xrightarrow{328-353\text{ K}} \underset{(C)}{2Al(OH)_3} + Na_2CO_3$$

$$\underset{(C)}{2Al(OH)_3} \xrightarrow{1200°C} Al_2O_3 + 3H_2O$$

4. (a) $\underset{(M)}{Al^{3+}} \xrightarrow{NaOH} Al(OH)_3$

$$\underset{\substack{\text{White gelatinous ppt}\\(A)}}{Al(OH)_3} \xrightarrow[\text{NaOH}]{\text{Excess of}} \underset{\text{soluble}}{NaAlO_2}$$

$$\downarrow \Delta$$

$$\underset{\text{(used as adsorbent in chromatography)}}{Al_2O_3}$$

5. (d) The involves is

$$P_2O_5 + 3H_2O \xrightarrow{\Delta} \underset{\text{(Orthophosphoric acid)}}{2H_3PO_4}$$

6. (b) As temperature decreases, white tin (β-form) changes to grey tin (α-form).

7 (c) The colour of compounds *A* and *B* are white and brown respectively. The reactions are given as below.

I. $ZnSO_4(aq) + 2NH_4OH(aq) \longrightarrow \underset{\text{'A' (White ppt.)}}{Zn(OH)_2(s)} + (NH_4)_2SO_4(aq)$

II. $FeCl_3(aq) + NH_4OH(aq) \longrightarrow \underset{\text{'B' (Brown ppt.)}}{Fe_2O_3 \cdot xH_2O(s)} + NH_4Cl(aq)$

8 (b) More reactive halogen can displace less reactive halogen from its salt solution. F_2 can displace Cl_2, Br_2, I_2 from their salt solutions while Cl_2 can displace Br_2 and I_2 from NaBr and NaI. Br_2 can displace only I_2 from NaI.

$$2NaI + Br_2 \longrightarrow 2NaBr + I_2\uparrow$$

9 (a) The complete road map for the given reaction is as below.

$$3Cu + 8HNO_3(\text{dil.}) \longrightarrow 3Cu(NO_3)_2 + \underset{(X)}{2NO} + 4H_2O$$

$$2NO + O_2 \rightleftharpoons \underset{(Y)}{2NO_2}$$

$$3NO_2 + H_2O \longrightarrow \underset{(Z)}{2HNO_3} + NO$$

Thus, *X*, *Y* and *Z* are respectively NO, NO_2 and HNO_3.

10 (b) The value of *n* in AX_n (interhalogen) can be 1, 3, 5, 7 not 2, 4 or 6.

12

Principles Related to Practical Chemistry

Experimental (practical) chemistry is concerned with the methods of producing chemical products under specific experimental conditions.

Topicwise No. of Ques asked in 5 Years (NEET)

Topics	No. of Questions				
	2024	2023	2022	2021	2020
Organic Chemistry Related Principles	2	–	–	–	–
Physical Chemistry Related Principles	1	–	–	–	–
Inorganic Chemistry Related Principles	–	–	–	–	–

Special Type of Ques Asked In 5 Years (NEET)

Types	Years				
	2024	2023	2022	2021	2020
A-R	–	–	2	–	–
Statement Based	–	–	1	–	–
Matching	–	1	–	–	1

Last 5 Years Weightage

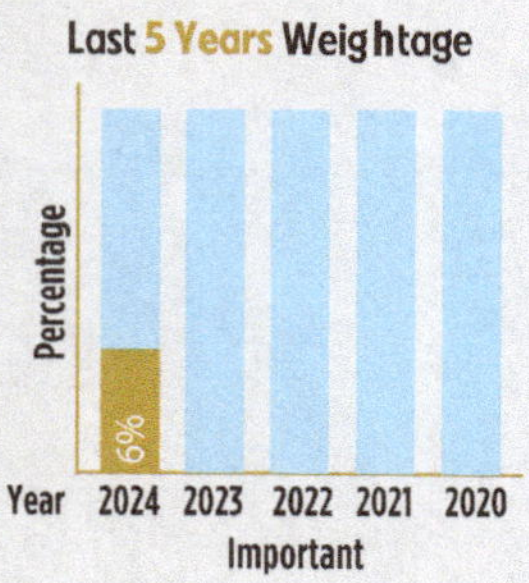

Organic Chemistry Related Principles

Qualitative Analysis of Organic Compounds

The qualitative analysis of an organic compound implies the detection of all the major elements other than C and H which are present in it, with the help of suitable chemical tests. Two major steps involved in the characterisation of an organic compound are

(i) Detection of extra elements (ii) Detection of functional groups

Detection of Extra Elements (Using Lassaigne's Test)

Nitrogen, sulphur and halogens present in an organic compound are detected by Lassaigne's test. It involves two steps which are as follows

(i) Preparation of Lassaigne's extract.

(ii) Detection of elements using Lassaigne's extract. **JEE Main 2023**

In preparation of Lassaigne's extract, the organic substance is fused with small quantity of Na pieces in a fusion tube. The red hot tube is plunged into distilled water contained in a China dish. The contents of dish are boiled for couple of minutes, then cooled and filtered. The filtered liquid, i.e. alkaline solution is called sodium extract or Lassaigne's extract.

The elements like N, S, C, F, Cl, Br, I, etc., which are present in the organic compound, get fused with Na and convert into their ionic form.

e.g.

$$Na + C + N \xrightarrow{\text{Fusion}} \underset{\text{Sodium cyanide}}{NaCN}$$

$$2Na + S \xrightarrow{\text{Fusion}} \underset{\text{Sodium sulphide}}{Na_2S}$$

$$Na + C + N + S \longrightarrow \underset{\substack{\text{(Sodium sulphocyanide)} \\ \text{(when N and S both are present)}}}{NaSCN}$$

$$Na + \underset{\text{Halogen}}{X} \longrightarrow \underset{\text{Sodium halide}}{NaX}$$

Note Li and K both cannot be used for the preparation of Lassaigne's extract in place of Na as the former reacts very slowly and forms covalent compounds while later reacts vigorously and thus cannot be handled properly.

Detection of Nitrogen

The Lassaigne's extract (NaCN) is boiled with $FeSO_4$ solution. After that a few drops of $FeCl_3$ is added and then acidified with concentrated sulphuric acid. The acid helps in the oxidation of ferrous ions to ferric ions. The formation of prussian blue colour confirms the presence of nitrogen.

$$Fe^{2+} + 6CN^- \longrightarrow [Fe(CN)_6]^{4-}$$

$$Fe^{2+} + H^+ \longrightarrow Fe^{3+} + e^-$$

$$3[Fe(CN)_6]^{4-} + 4Fe^{3+} \xrightarrow{xH_2O} \underset{\text{(Prussian blue)}}{Fe_4[Fe(CN)_6]_3 \cdot xH_2O}$$ JEE Main 2022

Note If Fe^{3+} ions are in excess, green colour appears instead of blue. This test fails in case of compounds which contain nitrogen but no carbon, e.g. hydrazine (NH_2NH_2), hydroxylamine (NH_2OH) etc.

Detection of Sulphur

- Lassaigne's extract (Na_2S) is acidified with few drops of sodium nitroprusside solution. The appearance of violet colouration confirms the presence of sulphur.

$$Na_2S + Na_2[Fe(CN)_5NO] \longrightarrow \underset{\text{Violet colour}}{Na_4[Fe(CN)_5NOS]}$$

- Lassaigne's extract is acidified with acetic acid and then lead acetate solution is added to the solution. Formation of black precipitate confirms the presence of sulphur in the compound.

$$Na_2S + (CH_3COO)_2Pb \longrightarrow \underset{\text{Black ppt.}}{PbS \downarrow} + 2CH_3COO^-Na^+$$

- If the compound contains both sulphur and nitrogen, then Lassaigne's extract, i.e. sodium sulphocyanide, gives blood red colouration of $Fe(SCN)_3$ with $FeCl_3$.

$$Na + C + N + S \longrightarrow \underset{\text{Sodium sulphocyanide}}{NaSCN} \xrightarrow{FeCl_3} \underset{\text{Ferric sulphocyanide (Blood red)}}{Fe(SCN)_3} + 3NaCl$$

Detection of Halogens JEE Main 2021

Lassaigne's extract (Na*X*) is acidified with conc. HNO_3 and then treated with $AgNO_3$. After that cooling it, the precipitates formed by this reaction can be used to detect the presence of halogen.

- White ppt. soluble in NH_4OH, indicates the presence of chlorine.

$$NaCl + AgNO_3 \longrightarrow \underset{\text{(White ppt.)}}{AgCl \downarrow} + NaNO_3$$

$$AgCl + 2NH_4OH \longrightarrow \underset{\text{Diammine silver (I) chloride}}{[Ag(NH_3)_2]Cl} + 2H_2O$$

- Pale yellow precipitate partially soluble in NH_4OH solution, indicates the presence of bromine.

$$NaBr + AgNO_3 \longrightarrow \underset{\text{(Pale yellow ppt.)}}{AgBr \downarrow} + NaNO_3$$

- Yellow precipitates insoluble in NH_4OH solution, indicates the presence of iodine.

$$AgNO_3 + NaI \longrightarrow \underset{\text{(Yellow ppt.)}}{AgI \downarrow} + NaNO_3$$

Beilstein Test for Halogens

Organic compound taken on copper wire, burning with coloured flame (blue or green) show the presence of halogens.

This test is not given by fluorine since CuF_2 is non-volatile.

Layer Test for Bromine and Iodine

Take a small portion of sodium extract and acidify with dil. HNO_3 or dil. H_2SO_4. Then add $CHCl_3$ or CCl_4 and excess of chlorine water with constant shaking. An orange and violet layer confirms the presence of bromine and iodine respectively

Marks Maximizer

Lassaigne's extract is boiled with dil. HNO_3 to decompose sodium cyanide or sodium sulphide if present to avoid any interference with the test.

$$NaCN + HNO_3 \longrightarrow NaNO_3 + HCN \uparrow$$

$$Na_2S + 2HNO_3 \longrightarrow 2NaNO_3 + H_2S \uparrow$$

Otherwise NaCN and Na_2S react with $AgNO_3$ and will create interference in the test.

Detection of Functional Groups

Element detection shows the presence or absence of different elements. On the basis of element present, the test of corresponding functional group is performed.

An atom or group of atoms that largely determine the properties of a compound is known as functional group. Tests for different functional groups are given below.

Tests for Alcoholic (–OH) Group

(i) **Sodium test** In a test tube, take some organic compound and add a thin piece of sodium metal to it. A brisk effervescence due to the formation of hydrogen gas takes place.

$$\underset{\text{Alcohol}}{2ROH} + 2Na \longrightarrow \underset{\text{Sodium alkoxide}}{2R\overset{-}{O}\overset{+}{Na}} + H_2 \uparrow$$

(ii) **Ester test** Heat the given compound with acetic acid in the presence of sulphuric acid.

A fruity smell indicates the formation of ester.

$$ROH + \underset{\text{Acetic acid}}{CH_3COOH} \underset{}{\overset{\text{Conc. } H_2SO_4}{\rightleftharpoons}} \underset{\text{Ester (Fruity smell)}}{RCOOCH_3} + H_2O$$

Alcohols give crystalline esters with 3,5-dinitrobenzoyl chloride. These esters have sharp melting points and can be used for testing a given alcohol.

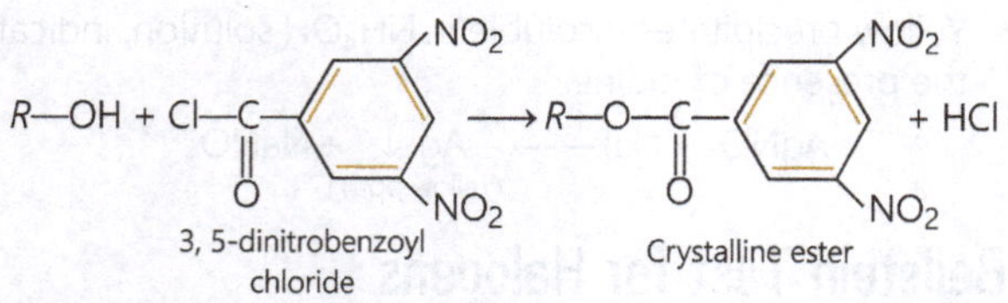

(iii) **Ceric ammonium nitrate test** To small amount of organic compound or its aqueous solution, add a few drops of ceric ammonium nitrate. A red colour indicates the presence of alcoholic hydroxy group.

$$\underset{\text{Alcohol}}{3ROH} + \underset{\substack{\text{Ceric ammonium}\\\text{nitrate}}}{(NH_4)_2Ce(NO_3)_6} \longrightarrow \underset{\text{Red colour}}{Ce(NO_3)_4 \cdot (ROH)_3} + 2NH_4NO_3$$

(iv) **Acetyl chloride test** Alcohols react with acid chlorides to produce ester and hydrochloric gas. If a glass rod dipped in ammonia is brought near the reaction mixture, white dense fumes of ammonium chloride are produced.

$$\underset{\text{Alcohol}}{R—OH} + \underset{\text{Acetyl chloride}}{CH_3COCl} \longrightarrow CH_3COOR + HCl$$

$$HCl + \underset{\text{Ammonia}}{NH_3} \longrightarrow \underset{\substack{\text{Ammonium chloride}\\\text{(White fumes)}}}{NH_4Cl}$$

Distinction between Primary, Secondary and Tertiary Alcohols

Lucas test This test is used to distinguish between primary, secondary and tertiary alcohols. Alcohols react with Lucas reagent (equimolar mixture of concentrated HCl and anhydrous $ZnCl_2$) to produce alkyl halides which being insoluble results in cloudiness (turbidity) in solution.

$$R—OH + HCl \xrightarrow{ZnCl_2} R—Cl + H_2O$$

Following observations indicates the presence of 1°, 2° and 3° alcohols as follows

- Immediate formation of turbidity indicates the presence of **tertiary alcohol.**
- Formation of turbidity after 4-5 min shows the presence of **secondary alcohols.**
- If solution remains clear, then **primary alcohol** is present.

Victor Meyer's test The reactions performed in this test are

$$\underset{(1° \text{ alcohol})}{R\,CH_2OH} \xrightarrow{HI} RCH_2I \xrightarrow{AgNO_2} R\,CH_2NO_2 \xrightarrow{HONO} \underset{\substack{\|\\ NOH \\ \text{Nitrolic acid}}}{R—C—NO_2} \xrightarrow{NaOH} \text{Blood red colour}$$

$$\underset{(2° \text{ alcohol})}{R_2CHOH} \xrightarrow{HI} R_2CHI \xrightarrow{AgNO_2} R_2CHNO_2 \xrightarrow{HONO} \underset{\substack{| \\ NO \\ \text{Pseudonitrole}}}{R_2C—NO_2} \xrightarrow{NaOH} \text{Blue colour}$$

$$\underset{(3° \text{ alcohol})}{R_3C—OH} \xrightarrow{HI} R_3C—I \xrightarrow{AgNO_2} R_3C—NO_2 \xrightarrow{HONO} \text{No reaction} \xrightarrow{NaOH} \text{Colourless}$$

Catalytic dehydrogenation It involves the passing of vapours of alcohol over hot copper at 300°C and the product thus formed is identified.

(i) Primary alcohols give aldehydes by dehydrogenation.

$$CH_3CH_2OH \xrightarrow{Cu, 300°C} \underset{\text{Ethanal}}{CH_3CHO} + H_2$$

(ii) Secondary alcohols give ketones by dehydrogenation.

$$CH_3—\overset{\overset{OH}{|}}{CH}—CH_3 \xrightarrow{Cu, 300°C} \underset{\text{Acetone}}{CH_3—\overset{\overset{O}{\|}}{C}—CH_3} + H_2$$

(iii) Tertiary alcohols form olefins (alkenes) by dehydration.

$$(CH_3)_3C—OH \xrightarrow{Cu, 300°C} \underset{\text{2-methyl prop-1-ene}}{CH_3—\overset{\overset{CH_3}{|}}{C}{=}CH_2} + H_2O$$

Tests for Phenolic Group

(i) **Litmus test** Phenols being acidic convert blue litmus paper (or solution) to red. Since, phenols are weak acids they do not give effervescence with sodium carbonate solution.

(ii) **Ferric chloride test** Phenols with freshly prepared ferric chloride solution forms coloured complexes. Appearance of violet colour shows the presence of phenol. The reaction is as follows

$$\underset{\text{Phenol}}{6C_6H_5OH} + \underset{\text{Ferric chloride}}{FeCl_3} \longrightarrow 3H^+ + \underset{\text{Violet}}{[Fe(OC_6H_5)_6]^{3-}} + 3HCl$$

This test is also given by enols.

(iii) **Liebermann's nitroso test** Phenols on reaction with sodium nitrite and conc. H_2SO_4 give a blue colouration which changes to red on dilution. In alkaline medium the blue colour is restored.

$$\underset{\text{Sodium nitrite}}{2NaNO_2} + \text{Conc.}\,H_2SO_4 \longrightarrow \underset{\text{Nitrous acid}}{2HNO_2} + Na_2SO_4$$

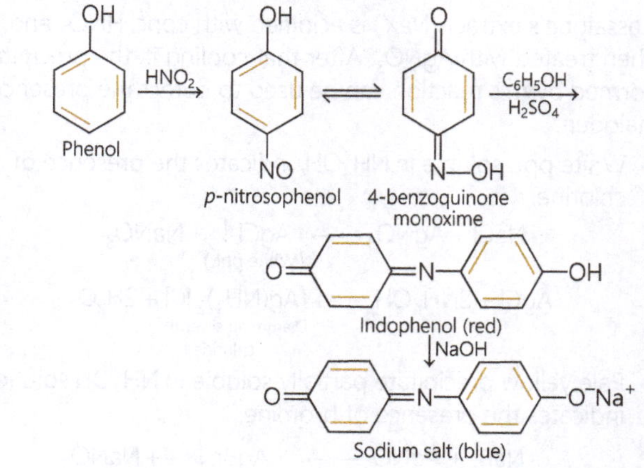

Test for Carbonyl Group (Aldehydes and Ketones)

(i) **2, 4-dinitrophenyl hydrazine test** Carbonyl compounds on mixing with 2, 4-dinitrophenyl hydrazine produce yellow- orange crystals of 2, 4-dinitrophenyl hydrazone. Appearance of yellow-orange precipitate in reaction mixture confirms presence of carbonyl group.

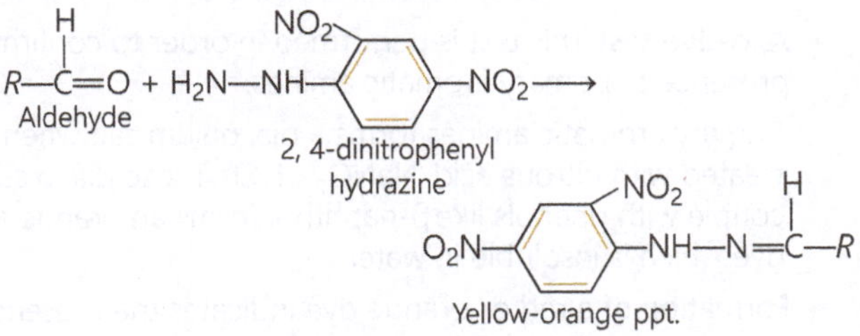

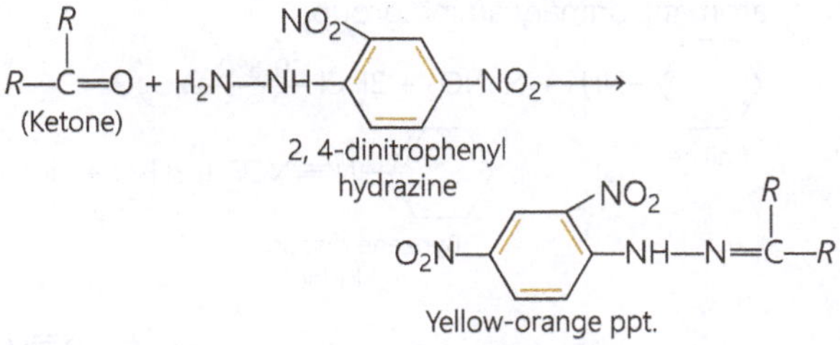

(ii) **Sodium bisulphite test** Aldehydes and ketones on treatment with sodium bisulphite forms well-crystallised water soluble products known as aldehyde bisulphite and ketone bisulphite.

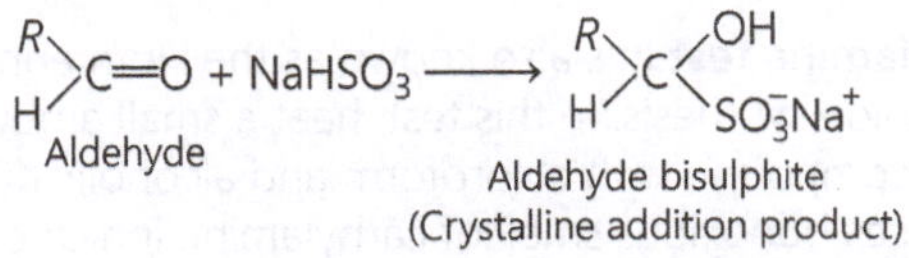

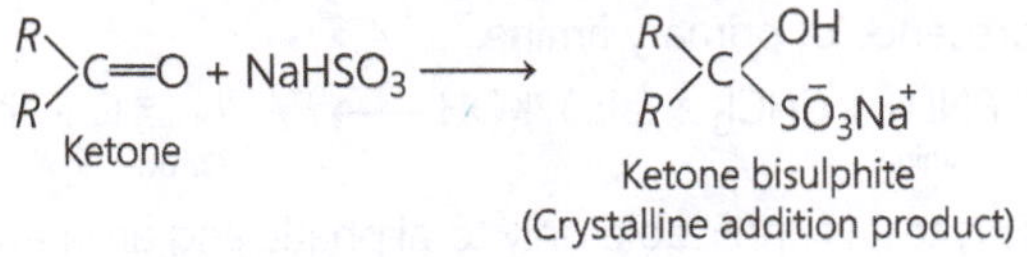

Marks Maximizer

- Amongst aromatic carbonyl compounds, benzaldehyde gives sodium bisulphite test but acetophenone and benzophenone do not give this test.
- Amongst ketones only methyl ketones which are not sterically hindered give this test.

Distinction between Aldehydes and Ketones

Test for Aldehydes

(i) **Tollen's test** (silver mirror test) It is a test used to distinguish between an aldehyde and a ketone. Take a little quantity of the compound and warm it with freshly prepared ammonical silver nitrate solution (Tollen's reagent). Shake and allow the contents to stand for few minutes.

Formation of silver mirror or a grey ppt. indicates the presence of an **aldehydic group**. Ketones do not give this test.

$$2[Ag(NH_3)_2]OH + RCHO \longrightarrow \underset{\text{Silver mirror or Grey ppt.}}{2Ag\downarrow} + RCO\overset{-}{O}\overset{+}{N}H_4 + 3NH_3\uparrow + H_2O$$

This reaction occurs in alkaline medium.

(ii) **Fehling's solution test** Fehling's solution is **NEET 2024** an aqueous solution of copper sulphate (Fehling solution *A*) containing an alkaline solution of sodium potassium tartarate (Rochelle salt) (Fehling solution *B*) as a complexing agent. The two solutions are mixed in equal amount to get the final Fehling solution which is deep blue. The deep blue ingredient is the *bis* (tartarate) complex of Cu^{2+}.

The aldehyde group oxidises to acid and copper (II) ions get reduced to Cu(I) ions. After dehydration, $Cu(OH)_2$ changes into copper (I) oxide and forms red precipitate.

$$RCHO + 2Cu(OH)_2 + NaOH \longrightarrow RCOONa + \underset{\text{Red ppt.}}{Cu_2O} + 3H_2O$$

Formation of a red ppt. shows the presence of an aldehyde group. Aromatic aldehyde do not respond to this test.

Note Benzaldehyde does not reduce Fehling's solution (a distinction from other aldehydes). Benzaldehyde is confirmed by **malachite green test.**

- Both the above tests are also given by **reducing sugars.**
- Formic acid also gives this test.

(iii) **Schiff's test** This test is performed by a reagent called schiff's reagent which is a colourless solution formed by passing sulphur dioxide through dilute solution of *p*-rosaniline hydrochloride (pink in colour). On addition of small amount of aldehyde, pink, magneta, red or violet colour appears which confirms aldehyde group.

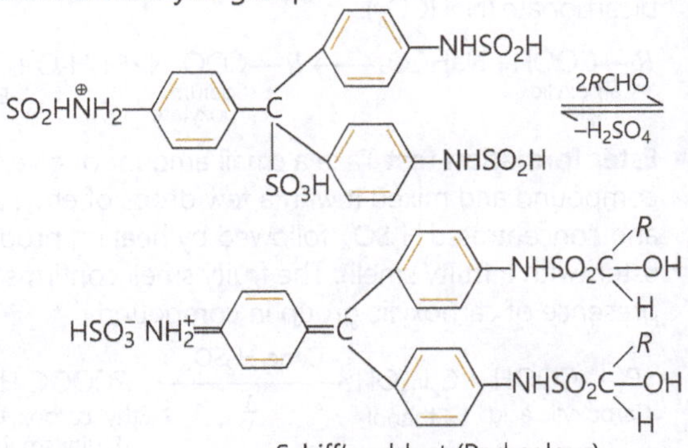

Schiff's adduct (Red colour)

Ketones do not respond to this test.

Marks Maximizer

Schiff's reagent should not be treated with alkali, otherwise pink colour would develop even in absence of aldehydes.

(iv) **Benedict's test** It is a chemical test that can be used to detect the presence of reducing sugars in a given analyte. Benedict's test is done by a reagent, which is a complex mixture of sodium citrate, sodium carbonate, and the pentahydrate of copper (II) sulphate.

It is based on the principle that reducing sugars (having —CHO group) when reacts with Benedict's reagent, it reduce Cu^{2+} ion to Cu^{+} ions.

$$\underset{\text{Cupric ions}}{Cu^{2+}} + \underset{\text{Aldehyde}}{RCHO} \longrightarrow \underset{\text{Carboxylic acid}}{RCOOH} + \underset{\text{Cuprous oxide (brick-red precipitate)}}{Cu_2O}$$

Note This test is usually given by only aliphatic aldehydes, thus used to differentiate between aliphatic and aromatic aldehydes.

Test for Ketones

- ***m*-dinitrobenzene test** The organic compound is mixed with finely powder *m*-dinitrobenzene and the solution is made alkaline. A violet colour is formed which slowly fades confirms ketonic group. Benzophenone and aldehydes do not give this test.
- **Sodium nitroprusside test** Alkaline solution of ketones react with nitroprusside to form coloured ion.
- $\underset{\text{Nitroprusside ion}}{[Fe(CN)_5NO]^{2-}} + CH_3COCH_2^- \longrightarrow \underset{\text{(Red coloured ppt.)}}{[Fe(CN)_5NO \cdot CH_3COCH_2]^{3-}}$

Test for Carboxylic Group

- **Litmus paper test** Carboxylic acids are acidic in nature and turns blue litmus to red. Phenols also gives this test.
- **Sodium bicarbonate test** A small amount of organic compound which contains carboxyl group produces brisk effervescence (due to CO_2) with a pinch of sodium bicarbonate ($NaHCO_3$).

$$\underset{\text{Carboxylic acid}}{R\text{—}COOH} + NaHCO_3 \longrightarrow \underset{\text{Sodium carboxylate}}{R\text{—}COO^-Na^+} + H_2O + \underset{\text{Effervescence}}{CO_2\uparrow}$$

- **Ester formation test** Take a small amount of given organic compound and mixed it with a few drops of ethyl alcohol and concentrated H_2SO_4 followed by heating produces ester (with a fruity smell). The fruity smell confirms the presence of carboxylic group in compound.

$$\underset{\text{Carboxylic acid}}{R\text{—}COOH} + \underset{\text{Ethanol}}{C_2H_5OH} \xrightarrow[\Delta]{\text{Conc. } H_2SO_4} \underset{\text{Ethyl carboxylate (Fruity smell)}}{RCOOC_2H_5} + H_2O$$

Test for Amino Group

- **Litmus test** Amines are basic in nature and thus, turn red litmus to blue.
- **Solubility test** Amines are basic in nature and thus, they dissolve in mineral acids.

$$RNH_2 + HCl \longrightarrow RNH_3^+Cl^-$$

- **Azo-dye test** This test is performed in order to confirm the presence of primary aromatic amines.

Primary aromatic amines forms a diazonium salt when treated with nitrous acid ($NaNO_2 + HCl$). These diazo salt couple with phenols like β-naphthol forms an orange azo dye which is insoluble in water.

- Formation of a red or orange dye indicates the presence of aromatic primary amino group.

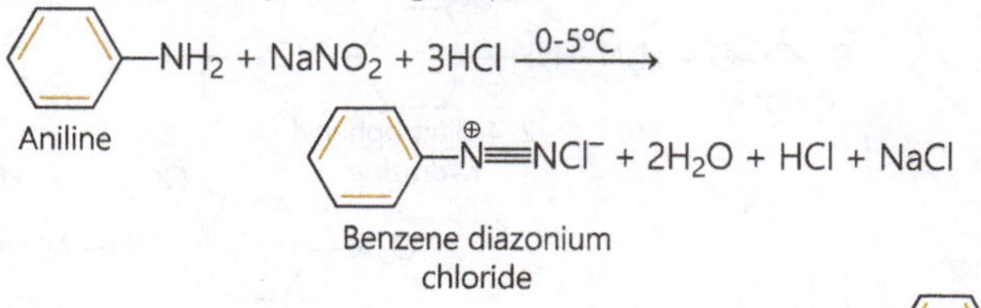

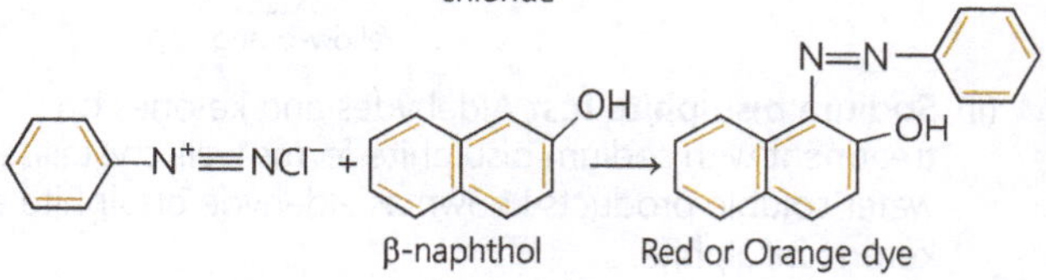

- **Carbylamine test** It is also known as the Hofmann isocyanide synthesis. In this test, heat a small amount of given compound with chloroform and alcoholic KOH, produces obnoxious smell of carbylamine indicates the presence of primary amine.

$$\underset{(1^\circ\text{ amine})}{RNH_2} + CHCl_3 + (\text{alc.})3KOH \longrightarrow \underset{\text{(Carbylamine)}}{R\text{—}N \equiv C} + 3KCl + 3H_2O$$

- This test is applicable only to aliphatic and aromatic primary amines.

Test to Distinguish between Primary, Secondary and Tertiary Amines

Nitrous acid test This test can be used to identify primary, secondary and tertiary amines.

- Primary aliphatic amines react with nitrous acid to give nitrogen gas. Appearance of bubbles of N_2 gas confirms primary aliphatic amines.

$$\underset{\text{Primary amine}}{R\text{—}NH_2} + HNO_2 \longrightarrow \underset{\text{Alcohol}}{ROH} + H_2O + \underset{\text{Nitrogen}}{N_2\uparrow}$$

- Secondary amines react with nitrous acid to form a yellow coloured oily N-nitrosoamines.

$$\underset{\text{Secondary amine}}{R_2NH} + HNO_2 \longrightarrow \underset{\text{Nitroso compound (oily)}}{R_2N\text{=}NO} + H_2O$$

- Aliphatic tertiary amines react with nitrous acid to form soluble nitrite salts.

$$R_3N + HONO \longrightarrow [R_3NH]^+ONO^-$$

- On reaction with HNO_2, amines produce green or brown colour indicates the presence of aromatic tertiary amines.

Hinsberg's test Primary and secondary amines react with Hinsberg's reagent ($C_6H_5SO_2Cl$) to form sulphonamides.

- Primary amines react with Hinsberg reagent usually forms an amide called N-alkyl benzene sulphonamide.

$$C_6H_5SO_2Cl + RNH_2 \longrightarrow \underset{\text{N-alkyl benzene sulphonamide (Yellow colour)}}{C_6H_5SO_2—NHR} + HCl$$

- The product formed is soluble in alkali (NaOH).
- Secondary amines react with Hinsberg reagent to form an amide (N,N-dialkyl benzene sulphonamide)

$$C_6H_5SO_2Cl + R_2NH \longrightarrow \underset{\text{(N,N-dialkyl benzene sulphonamide) (Orange colour)}}{C_6H_5SO_2—NR_2} + HCl$$

  The product so formed is insoluble in alkali (NaOH) due to absence of acidic hydrogen on N-atom.
- Tertiary amines do not react with $C_6H_5SO_2Cl$. They are insoluble in NaOH but dissolve by addition of HCl.

Preparation of Organic Compounds

1. Acetanilide

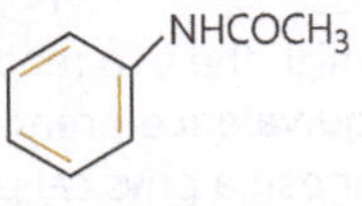

Anilides are N-phenyl derivatives of amide of an acid.

Theory

Acetanilide is prepared by direct acetylation of aniline by using the mixture of equal volumes of acetic anhydride and glacial acetic acid.

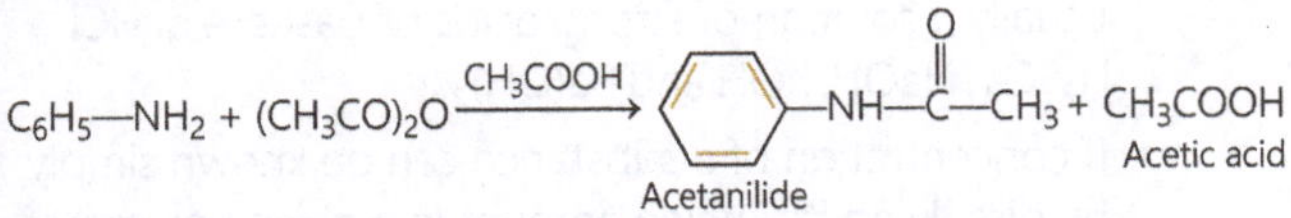

- The prepared mixture is cooled in ice cold water so that white precipitate of crude acetanilide separates out.
- Pure acetanilide can be obtained from the mixture by recrystallisation.

Chemistry Involved

- Acetylation of aniline can be carried out either with acetic anhydride or acetyl chloride, but both processes require a catalyst. Reaction with acetic anhydride requires glacial acetic acid and with acetyl chloride requires pyridine.

$$\underset{\text{Aniline}}{C_6H_5—NH_2} + \underset{\text{Acetyl chloride}}{CH_3COCl} \xrightarrow{\text{Pyridine}} \underset{\text{Acetanilide}}{C_6H_5NHCOCH_3} + HCl$$

- In this experiment small amount of zinc should be added to the reaction mixture. It protects aniline from oxidation and also reduces its coloured impurities.
- The prepared mixture after boiling should be cooled before pouring to ice-cold pack otherwise it may lead to hydrolysis of acetanilide to aniline.
- In acetanilide the acetamido group is predominantly *p*-directing. So, acetanilide is a useful intermediate for formation of major *p*-substituted products.

$$\text{Acetanilide} \xrightarrow{HNO_3} \underset{\text{(Major)}}{p\text{-nitroacetanilide}} + \underset{\text{(Minor)}}{o\text{-nitroacetanilide}}$$

2. *p*-nitroacetanilide

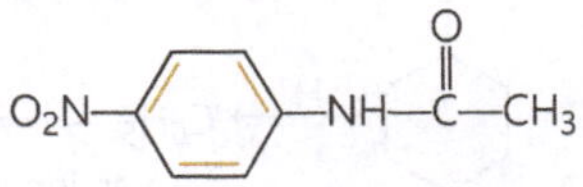

Theory

It is prepared from acetanilide through nitration. When acetanilide is treated with nitrating mixture that is a mixture of nitric acid and sulphuric acid, so that *p*-nitroacetanilide is formed.

Along with *p*-nitroacetanilide, *o*-nitroacetanilide is also formed as a minor product. Since, *o*-nitroacetanilide is very much soluble in alcohol it is very easy to isolate *p*-nitroacetanilide through crystallisation.

Chemistry Involved

Direct nitration of aniline with nitric acid is impractical because nitric acid is a strong oxidising agent and it oxidises $—NH_2$ group of aniline. So, $—NH_2$ group is protected by acetylation.

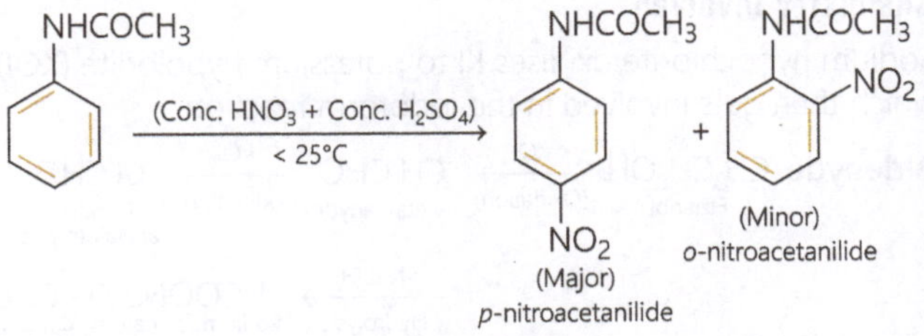

Note The above process should be performed under temperature of less than 25°C.

3. Aniline Yellow

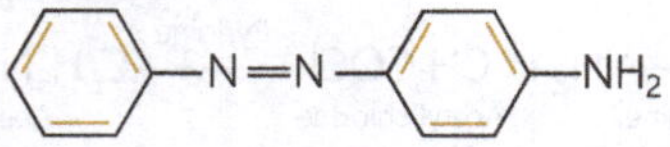

It is a yellow compound and basic azodye due to the presence of —N=N— (azo) group in it.

Theory

Aniline yellow (*p*-aminoazobenzene) is prepared by the coupling reaction between benzene diazonium chloride and aniline in slightly acidic medium.

Chemistry Involved

Aniline is reacted with sodium nitrite in the presence of acid. Diazonium salt is formed which, further couple with aniline to form azo dye *p*-aminoazobenzene (aniline yellow).

$$C_6H_5NH_2 \xrightarrow{NaNO_2 + HCl} C_6H_5N_2^+Cl^-$$

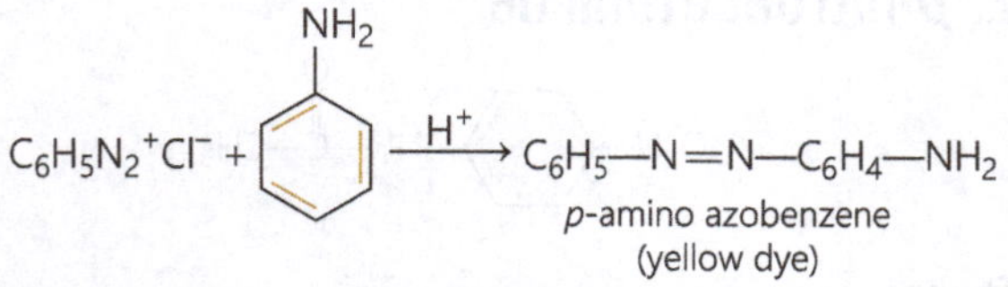

- The reaction take place between the two latter compounds under weakly acidic conditions.
- It is quite sensitive to acids, hence it is not used as a dye.

4. Iodoform, CHI_3: Triiodomethane

Theory

The iodoform test is used to determine whether a given unknown chemical compound contains carbonyl compounds with an α-methyl group with the structural formula ($RCOCH_3$) or alcohols with the formula $R — CH(OH) — CH_3$.

Iodine and aqueous sodium hydroxide (NaOH) solution or potassium iodide (KI) and sodium hypochlorite (NaOCl) solution can also be used.

Chemistry Involved

Sodium hypochlorite oxidises KI to potassium hypoiodite (KOI) which then gets involved in the iodoform reaction.

Aldehyde $\underset{\text{Ethanol}}{CH_3CH_2OH} \xrightarrow[\text{(Oxidation)}]{KOI} \underset{\text{Acetaldehyde}}{CH_3CHO} \xrightarrow[\text{Iodination}]{KOI} \underset{\text{Triiodo acetaldehyde}}{Cl_3CHO}$

$$\xrightarrow[\text{Hydrolysis}]{NaOH} \underset{\text{Sodium formate}}{HCOONa} + \underset{\text{Iodoform}}{CHI_3}$$

Ketone $\underset{\text{Ketone}}{CH_3COCH_3} \xrightarrow[\text{Iodination}]{NaOH} \underset{\text{Triiodoacetone}}{Cl_3COCH_3} \xrightarrow[\text{Hydrolysis}]{NaOH} \underset{\text{Sodium acetate}}{CH_3COONa} + \underset{\text{Iodoform}}{CHI_3}$

With acetone no initial oxidation takes place and a better yield of iodoform is obtained. Iodoform is used as an antiseptic.

Physical Chemistry Related Principles

Titrimetric Exercises

Volumetric Analysis (Quantitative Analysis)

- It involves the measurement of the volume of a known solution required to bring about the completion of the reaction with a measured volume of the unknown solution.
- **Titration** The main process of volumetric analysis is called titration. Typically, the **titrant** (the known solution) is added from a burette to a known quantity of the analyte (the unknown solution) until the reaction is complete.

Some Important Terms Related to Volumetric Analysis

- The substance whose chemical constituents are being identified and measured is known as **analyte**.
- The solution taken in the burette is called the titrant, while that taken in the titration flask is called the analyte.
- The titration is carried out till the reagents present in both the solutions react completely.
- The stage at which the two reagents react completely is called the **equivalence point**. At this point there is a sudden change in a physical property. Such as indicator colour, pH conductivity or absorbance. It is also known as end point.
- The end point is usually detected by the change in the colour of a suitable **indicator**.
- A **standard solution** used for acid-base titration is usually a solution of strong acids or bases, e.g. HCl, H_2SO_4, NaOH, KOH and $Ba(OH)_2$.
- If concentration of a substance can be known simply by dissolving its known amount in a given volume of solution, then the substance is called **primary standard** and the solution formed as **primary standard solutions.** e.g. Oxalic acid, potassium dichromate.
- In most cases, concentration can be determined by standardisation against primary standard solution. Such solutions are called **secondary standard solutions.** e.g. Ferrous sulphate, mineral acids (H_2SO_4, HNO_3).

Theory

- Known volume (generally 20 mL) of one solution is taken in a conical flask. Few drops of a suitable indicator are added to this solution.
- Another solution is taken in burette and added to the solution in conical flask.
- A sudden change in some property (usually colour) of the solution (in conical flask) reflects end point of reaction. At this point, volume of titrant used can be marked from burette reading.

General Calculations

- We apply law of chemical equivalence to each titration.

$$\underset{\text{(Solution-1)}}{N_1V_1} = \underset{\text{(Solution-2)}}{N_2V_2} \quad \text{[Normality equation]}$$

Volume of two solutions in the titration is known. By knowing normality of one solution, normality of another solution can be calculated.

On applying molarity equation as $\underset{\text{(Solution-1)}}{M_1V_1n_1} = \underset{\text{(Solution-2)}}{M_2V_2n_2}$

Strength of a solution can be calculated as

Strength (g/L) = Normality × Eq. wt.

or Strength (g/L) = Molarity × Mol. mass

Percentage purity of a sample can also be calculated

$$\text{Percentage purity} = \frac{\text{Strength of pure sample}}{\text{Strength of given sample}} \times 100$$

Acid-Base Titration

(Neutralisation Method of Analysis)

Acid-base titrations involves a neutralisation reaction between an acid and a base in which acid reacts with an equivalent amount of base.

The reaction is characterised by a rapid change in pH near the equivalence point, which is detected by the colour change of indicator that occur at the end point. It is a common method of determining the amount of acids, bases or salt of weak bases or acids in an unknown sample.

The analysis can be done by neutralisation method may be grouped in two general classes

- Determination of acid or base or their anhydride in a sample by titrating with a standard solution of base or acid.
- Determination of salts of weak acids or bases by titrating with a standard solution of a strong base or acid.

In either weak acid or weak base and a strong acid or strong base, the **titration curve** is irregular and pH shifts less with small addition of titrant near equivalence point.

The titration curve for the titration of oxalic acid with NaOH can be depicted as:

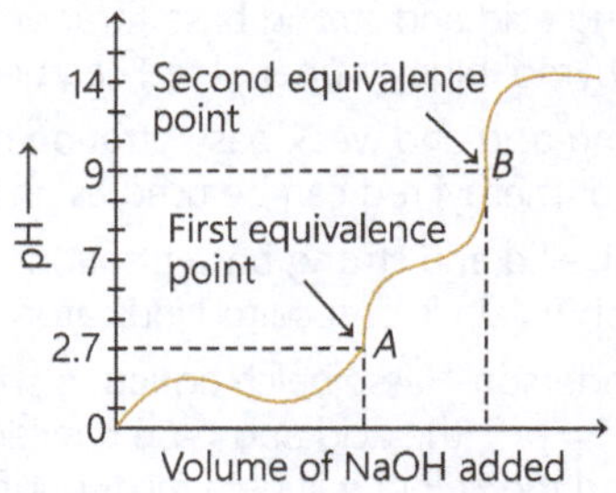

This reaction takes place in two stages and thus consists of two equivalence points. First and second equivalence point appears at pH of about 2.7 and 9 respectively.

Usually, when acid is too weak to be titrated with a standard base, a salt of acid can be titrated with standard base solution. e.g. Carbonic acid cannot be titrated by sodium hydroxide quantitatively, but sodium carbonate can be titrated by hydrochloric acid or sulphuric acid.

$$CO_3^{2-} + 2H^+ \longrightarrow H_2O + CO_2$$

e.g. Na_2CO_3 (Strong base) *vs* HCl (Strong acid)

Acid-Base Indicators

They basically indicates the end point of the titration by changing colour. For acid-base titration, a weak acid or weak base is used as an indicator.

Some common indicators with their colours and the pH range in which they change colour are given in the following table.

An indicator show change in colour in the same pH range as developed around the equivalence point.

pK_a (indicator) = pH at the half-equivalence point

pH Range and Colours of Some Common Indicators

Indicators	pH range	Colour in acid solution	Colour in alkaline solution
Thymol blue	1.2-2.8	Red	Yellow
Bromophenol blue	3.1-4.6	Yellow	Purple
Methyl orange	3.1-4.5	Red	Yellow
Methyl red	4.2-6.3	Red	Yellow
Bromothymol blue	6.0-7.5	Orange	Blue
Phenol red	6.4-8.2	Yellow	Red
Thymol blue (base)	8.1-9.6	Yellow	Blue
Phenolphthalein	8.0-9.8	Colourless	Pink
Thymophthalein	9.3-10.5	Colourless	Blue
Alizarin yellow R	10.1-12.1	Yellow	Lilac

Marks Maximizer

- For strong acid and strong base titration bromothymol blue or phenol red can be used.
- For strong acid and weak base titration methyl orange or methyl red can be used as an indicator.
- For weak acid and strong base titration phenolphthalein is best suited indicator.
- The Henderson-Hasselbalch equation shows that when $pH = pK_a$ the acid and base concentration are equal and the colour will be a mixture of both acid and base forms.

  At $pH < pK_a - 1.0 \rightarrow$ The acid form predominate.

  At $pH > pK_a + 1.0 \rightarrow$ The base form predominate.

Redox Titrations

Redox reactions are based on reduction-oxidation reaction between an oxidising and reducing agent. Thus, the concentration of reducing agents like Fe, Fe^{2+}, H_2O_2, $CaOCl_2$, MnO_2 can be determined by using suitable oxidising agents like $KMnO_4$, $K_2Cr_2O_7$ in acidic, basic or neutral medium.

- **Indicator** In these titrations, $KMnO_4$ acts as self indicator. In acidic medium, $KMnO_4$ reacts with reducing agent (like oxalic acid or Mohr's salt), when whole of the reducing agent has been oxidised the remaining $KMnO_4$ is not decomposed and imparts pink colour to the solution and thus acts as an indicator.
- **End point** In $KMnO_4$ titration end point is from colourless to permanent light pink colour.

$KMnO_4$ Titrations

Redox titration involving $KMnO_4$ as oxidising agent are called **permanganometric titrations.**

In these titrations $KMnO_4$ is reduced to $MnSO_4 (MnO_4^- \rightarrow Mn^{2+})$ and the reducing agent is oxidised to its respective higher oxidation state, e.g. during the titration of Mohr's salt with $KMnO_4$ the ionic equation taking place can be represented as : Fe^{2+} is oxidised to Fe^{3+} by MnO_4^- which in turn is reduced to Mn^{2+} in acidic medium.

$$5Fe^{2+} + MnO_4^- + 8H^+ \longrightarrow Mn^{2+} + 5Fe^{3+} + 4H_2O$$

In all cases, $N_1V_1 = N_2V_2$,

But $M_1V_1 \neq M_2V_2$

$$\text{Equivalent weight} = \frac{\text{molecular weight}}{\text{total change in ON (oxidation number)}} \text{ or}$$

$$= \frac{\text{molecular weight}}{\text{number of electrons gained or lost}}$$

Redox Titrations (Excluding Iodometric/Iodimetric Titrations)

Estimation of	By titrating with	Reactions	Relations between O.A and R.A
Fe^{2+}	MnO_4^-	$Fe^{2+} \longrightarrow Fe^{3+} + e^-$ $MnO_4^- + 8H^+ + 5e^- \longrightarrow Mn^{2+} + 4H_2O$	$5Fe^{2+} \equiv MnO_4^-$ Eq. wt. $Fe^{2+} = \frac{M}{1}$; Eq. wt. $MnO_4^- = \frac{M}{5}$
Fe^{2+}	$Cr_2O_7^{2-}$	$Fe^{2+} \longrightarrow Fe^{3+} + e^-$ $Cr_2O_7^{2-} + 14H^+ + 6e^- \longrightarrow 2Cr^{3+} + 7H_2O$	$6Fe^{2+} \equiv Cr_2O_7^{2-}$; Eq. wt. $Cr_2O_7^{2-} = \frac{M}{6}$
$C_2O_4^{2-}$	MnO_4^-	$Cr_2O_4^{2-} \longrightarrow 2CO_2 + 2e^-$ $MnO_4^- + 8H^+ + 5e^- \longrightarrow Mn^{2+} + 4H_2O$ JEE Main 2022	$5C_2O_4^{2-} \equiv 2MnO_4^-$ Eq.wt. $C_2O_4^{2-} = \frac{M}{2}$; Eq. wt. $MnO_4^- = \frac{M}{5}$
H_2O_2	MnO_4^-	$H_2O_2 \longrightarrow 2H^+ + O_2 + 2e^-$	$5H_2O_2 \equiv 2MnO_4^-$ Eq. wt. $H_2O_2 = \frac{M}{2}$; Eq. wt. $MnO_4^- = \frac{M}{5}$
As_2O_3	MnO_4^-	$As_2O_3 + 5H_2O \longrightarrow 2AsO_4^{3-} + 10H^+ + 4e^-$	Eq.wt. $As_2O_3 = \frac{M}{4}$
AsO_3^{3-}	BrO_3^-	$AsO_3^{3-} + H_2O \longrightarrow AsO_4^{3-} + 2H^+ + 2e^-$ $BrO_3^- + 6H^+ + 6e^- \longrightarrow Br^- + 3H_2O$	Eq.wt. $AsO_3^{3-} = \frac{M}{2}$ Eq.wt. of $BrO_3^- = \frac{M}{6}$

Titration of Oxalic Acid *vs* $KMnO_4$

Indicator $KMnO_4$ is a self indicator.

End point Colourless to permanent pink colour ($KMnO_4$ in burette).

Theory

- Titration is experimented generally by taking 20 mL of oxalic acid solution in a conical flask. Oxalic acid may be of known concentration or unknown concentration.
- To this oxalic acid solution, equal volume of dil. H_2SO_4(~ 4N) is added to make the solution acidic.
- The solution is heated to 60-70°C and then titrated against $KMnO_4$ solution taken in burette till a permanent pink colour is imparted to the solution. $KMnO_4$ solution used may be of known concentration or unknown concentration but its volume used is observed from reading of burette.
- Same steps are repeated for 3-4 times to take a concordant set of readings.

Chemistry Involved

- This is a redox titration in which the concentration of oxalic acid (reducing agent) is determined by titrating it with a standard solution of an oxidising agent, $KMnO_4$.
- Such reactions are accompanied by the change in valency of ions. In these titrations oxidation and reduction takes place simultaneously.

$$\underset{\text{Oxidising agent}}{2KMnO_4} + 3H_2SO_4 \longrightarrow K_2SO_4 + 2MnSO_4 + 3H_2O + 5[O]\,; \quad \left(E_{KMnO_4} = \frac{M}{5}\right)$$

$$\underset{\text{Reducing agent}}{5\begin{array}{c}COOH\\|\\COOH\end{array}} + 5[O] \xrightarrow{60\text{-}70^\circ C} 5H_2O + 10CO_2\uparrow\,; \left(E_{H_2C_2O_4} = \frac{M}{2}\right)$$

- Oxalic acid is heated to 60-70°C before titrating with $KMnO_4$ because in cold, reaction is very slow due to the slow formation of Mn^{2+}.
- This titration is carried out in the presence of H_2SO_4 but not in the presence of HCl because chlorine is formed as a consequence of oxidation of HCl. JEE Main 2022
- We can also apply molarity equation to this titration. Since, two moles of $KMnO_4$ react with 5 moles of oxalic acid.

Calculation : $$\frac{M_{KMnO_4} \times V_{KMnO_4}}{M_{\text{Oxalic acid}} \times V_{\text{Oxalic acid}}} = \frac{2}{5}$$

$$\text{Equivalent mass of oxalic acid} = \frac{\text{Molecular mass}}{2} = \frac{126}{2} = 63$$

$$\text{Equivalent mass of } KMnO_4 = \frac{\text{Molecular mass}}{5} = \frac{158}{5} = 31.6$$

Titration of Mohr's Salt *vs* $KMnO_4$

Indicator $KMnO_4$ is a self indicator.

End point Colourless to permanent light pink ($KMnO_4$ in burette).

Theory

This titration is same as of oxalic acid *vs* $KMnO_4$, but in case of Mohr's salt titre is not required to be heated.

Chemistry Involved

- The titration of Mohr's salt ($FeSO_4 \cdot (NH_4)_2SO_4 \cdot 6H_2O$) *versus* $KMnO_4$ (acts as an oxidising agent) is also a redox titration.
- In this titration, the active constituent of ferrous ammonium sulphate (Mohr's salt) is ferrous sulphate, which is oxidised to ferric sulphate by acidified potassium permanganate as follows

$$2KMnO_4 + 3H_2SO_4 \longrightarrow K_2SO_4 + 2MnSO_4 + 3H_2O + 5\,[O]; \quad \left(E_{KMnO_4} = \frac{M}{5}\right)$$

$$\underline{[2FeSO_4 + H_2SO_4 + [O] \longrightarrow Fe_2(SO_4)_3 + H_2O] \times 5}$$

$$2KMnO_4 + 8H_2SO_4 + 10FeSO_4 \longrightarrow K_2SO_4 + 2MnSO_4 + 5Fe_2(SO_4)_3 + 8H_2O \quad \left(E_{FeSO_4} = \frac{M}{1}\right)$$

- This titration is carried out at room temperature because Mohr's salt is oxidised by air on heating. Sulphuric acid should be present in excess otherwise a brown precipitate due to the formation of MnO_2 will be formed.

Calculations

- Molarity equation can also be applied to this titration.

$$\frac{M_{KMnO_4} \times V_{KMnO_4}}{M_{\text{Mohr's salt}} \times V_{\text{Mohr's salt}}} = \frac{1}{5}$$

- $\text{Eq. mass of Mohr's salt} = \dfrac{\text{Molecular mass}}{1} = 392$

$$\text{Eq. mass of } KMnO_4 = \frac{158}{5} = 31.6$$

Enthalpy of Solution of $CuSO_4$

- **Heat of dissolution** may be defined as the amount of heat change when 1 mol of a substance is dissolved in large excess of solvent so that further dilution does not bring any heat change. It is also known as heat of solution or enthalpy of solution.
- Heat of solution may be positive or negative, i.e. dissolution of salt may be an endothermic or exothermic process.

Theory

- It can be determined by putting a known volume of water in a thermally insulated vessel and then, finding out its change in temperature on adding a known weight of the given substance ($CuSO_4$) into it. From the change in temperature, heat absorbed or evolved can be calculated.

$$CuSO_4 \cdot 5H_2O + H_2O(l) \longrightarrow CuSO_4(aq) + \Delta H$$

- **Calculation** Enthalpy of solution/dissolution

$$= \frac{(W + m) \times \Delta t \times 4.2 \times M}{w} \text{ J mol}^{-1}$$

$$= \frac{(W + m) \times \Delta t \times M}{w} \text{ cal mol}^{-1}$$

where, W = water equivalent of calorimeter
m = mass of water taken in calorimeter
Δt = change in temperature = $(t_{final} - t_{initial})$
M = molecular mass of solute
w = mass of solute

- **Water equivalent of calorimeter** It is defined as the amount of water that requires same quantity of heat to raise the temperature through one degree as it is required by the calorimeter.

Chemical Principle Involved in the Experiment

- During electrolysis, when $CuSO_4$ is introduced to water, it dissolves $CuSO_4$ splits into Cu^{2+} and SO_4^{2-} ions and moves freely in the solution since it is an electrolyte.
- Two copper electrodes are immersed in the solution.
- Cu^{2+} ions will be drawn to the cathode and attached to – ve terminal of battery and SO_4^{2-} ions will be drawn to anode and attached to + ve terminal.
- As the result, SO_4^{2-} ions will migrate to the anode and form SO_4 radical.
- However, the sulphate radical can't exist in an electrically neutral state, it will attack the copper anode and produce copper sulphate.
- $CuSO_4$ can not exist as a single molecule in water, thus it splits into Cu^{2+} and SO_4^{2-} and dissolves in water. As a result, copper is deposited on cathode during electrolysis using copper electrodes and the same quantity of copper is removed from the anode.

Note The enthalpy of solution of $CuSO_4$ is –16 K cal.

Enthalpy of Neutralisation of Strong Acid and Strong Base

- Heat of neutralisation is defined as the change in enthalpy that takes place when 1 gram equivalent of an acid is neutralised by 1 gram equivalent of a base or *vice-versa* in the dilute aqueous solutions.

$$HCl(aq) + NaOH(aq) \longrightarrow NaCl(aq) + H_2O, \Delta H = -ve$$

- Neutralisation reactions are exothermic in nature, i.e. ΔH is always negative.

Theory

- Enthalpy of neutralisation of strong acid and strong base is measured using simple calorimeter consisting of polythene bottle. Known volumes of standard solution of an acid and alkali are mixed and change in temperature is recorded.
- **Calculation** Heat of neutralisation

$$= \frac{(W + m) \times \Delta t \times 4.2}{N \times V_{(mL)}} \text{ kJ} = \frac{(W + m) \times \Delta t}{N \times V_{(mL)}} \text{ cal}$$

where, W = water equivalent of calorimeter
m = mass of mixture of solution after neutralisation
Δt = change in temperature
N = normality of acid or base under investigation
V = volume of acid or base under investigation in mL.

Chemical Principle Involved in the Experiment

- Heat is evolved during neutralisation of an acid with alkali.
- The average enthalpy of neutralisation of any strong acid by a strong base is found to be –57.3 kJ (–13.7 kcal) irrespective of the nature of the acid or the base.

$$H^+(aq) + OH^-(aq) \longrightarrow H_2O(l); \Delta H = -13.7 \text{ kcal}$$

$$H^+(aq) + Cl^-(aq) + Na^+(aq) + OH^-(aq) \longrightarrow Na^+(aq) + Cl^-(aq) + H_2O(l); \Delta H = -13.7 \text{ kcal}$$

13.7 kcal of heat is liberated out and is the heat of neutralisation for all strong acids and bases.

- Enthalpy of neutralisation is always constant. For a strong acid and a strong base as they completely ionised in dil. solution.

Preparation of Lyophilic and Lyophobic Sols

Colloids

- Colloidal state is an intermediate state between true solutions and suspensions. Colloidal particle size range is between 1-1000 nm. Colloidal solution is heterogeneous in nature and consists of two phases :

(i) **Dispersed phase** Equivalent to solute in true solution.

(ii) **Dispersion medium** Equivalent to solvent in true solution.

- Dispersed phase is distributed in dispersion medium.
- Depending upon the interaction between dispersed phase and dispersion medium the colloidal solutions are of two types.

- **Lyophilic sols** In this type of colloidal solution, dispersed phase has great affinity for the dispersion medium. These are easy to prepare just by mixing, shaking or heating substance with the dispersion medium. These are highly stable and do not coagulate easily on adding electrolytes. These are reversible sols and can be reconstituted back by adding the dispersion medium, e.g. starch, protein, gum, gelatin. If water is used as dispersion medium, the sol is called hydrophilic sol.
- **Lyophobic sols** In this type of colloidal solution, dispersed phase has little or no affinity for the dispersion medium. They are solvent repelling colloids. These colloids require special methods to prepare and an electrolyte for stabilisation. These are unstable and can easily be coagulated by electrolytes. These are irrversible sols and once precipitated, they can not be reconstituted back just by adding the dispersion medium, e.g. metals, metal sulphides and oxides.

  e.g. Sol of aluminium hydroxide, ferric hydroxide, arsenic sulphide etc.

Theory of Preparation of Sols

Lyophilic sols like starch, gum-arabic, gelatin, etc., can be easily prepared by warming these substances with suitable solvent. However, lyophobic sols can be prepared in the laboratory by any one of the following two methods.

(i) **Condensation method** This method involves the increase in size of the solute particle in solution up to the colloidal size. This may be affected by hydrolysis, oxidation, reduction or double decomposition.

All these reactions are performed in such a way that these result in the formation of insoluble products. Arsenic sulphide, ferric hydroxide, aluminium hydroxide sols are prepared by this method.

In the preparation of ferric hydroxide sol, ferric chloride is added dropwise to boiling water.

$$FeCl_3(aq) + 3H_2O(l) \xrightarrow{\text{Boil}} Fe(OH)_3(s) + 3HCl(aq)$$

(ii) **Dispersion method** This method involves crushing of coarse (bigger) particles in a suspension to the colloidal size. Reduction in size of the coarse particle to colloidal size may be reduced by the use of an electric arc, mechanical method such as grinding, shaking or homogenising. Gold and starch sols are prepared by this method.

Marks Maximizer

Arsenic sulphide sol is formed by double decomposition reaction of arsenious oxide with H_2S gas.

$$As_2O_3 + 3H_2S \longrightarrow \underset{\text{(Sol)}}{As_2S_3} + 3H_2O$$

Purification of Sols

Sols can be prepared by various methods may contain impurities of soluble electrolyte. These impurities cause precipitation of sols on standing. Therefore, it becomes essential to remove these unwanted impurities. The method is most commonly used in dialysis.

Dialysis

This method is based on the fact that a semipermeable membrane allows the passage of only electrolytes through it and not of colloidal particles. (Semipermeable membrane is made of parchment or cellophane paper or thin animal skin).

The sol is taken in a parchment paper or thin animal skin bag which is placed in running water in a trough the impurities gradually diffuse out of the bag leaving a pure sol inside it.

Kinetic Study of the Reaction of Iodide Ions with Hydrogen Peroxide

- **Rate of reaction** It is defined as rate of change of concentration, i.e. change in concentration per unit time of any one or the reactants or products.

  For a general reaction, $A + B \longrightarrow C + D$

  $$\text{Rate of reaction} = -\frac{\Delta[A]}{\Delta t} = -\frac{\Delta[B]}{\Delta t}$$

  $$= \frac{+\Delta[C]}{\Delta t} = \frac{+\Delta[D]}{\Delta t} = \text{mol L}^{-1}\text{ s}^{-1}$$

- Negative sign in rate expression indicates decrease in concentration whereas +ve sign represents increase in concentration.

Theory of Reaction

- Hydrogen peroxide is an oxidising agent that oxidises iodide ions to iodine in acidic medium.

  $$H_2O_2 + 2I^- + 2H^+ \xrightarrow{\text{Slow}} 2H_2O + I_2$$

- The reaction is monitered by adding a known volume of sodium thiosulphate solution and starch solution to the reaction mixture.
- The liberated iodine reacts with sodium thiosulphate and is reduced to iodide ions.

  $$I_2 + 2S_2O_3^{2-} \xrightarrow{\text{Fast}} S_4O_6^{2-} + 2I^-$$

- When thiosulphate ions are completely consumed, the liberated iodine reacts with starch solution and give a blue colour.

  $$I_2 + \text{Starch} \longrightarrow \text{Blue complex}$$

- The time elapsed before the appearance of blue colour gives an idea about rate of reaction.
- This reaction is also called clock reaction because time for the appearance of colour shows the accuracy of clock.

Chemistry Principle Involved in the Experiment

- For a general reaction, $xX + yY \longrightarrow$ Product

According to law of mass action,

$$\text{Rate} \propto [X]^x[Y]^y \text{ or Rate} = k[X]^x[Y]^y$$

where, x and y are stoichiometric coefficients.

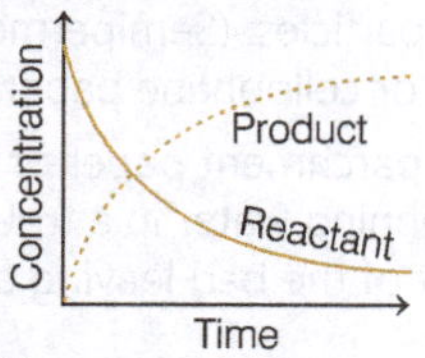

According to rate law,

$$\text{Rate} \propto [X]^a[Y]^b \text{ or Rate} = k[X]^a[Y]^b$$

where, $[X]$ and $[Y]$ are molar concentration of X and Y respectively. k is called rate constant or velocity constant, a and b are experimentally known coefficients of $[X]$ and $[Y]$.

$(a + b)$ is known as order of reaction whereas $(x + y)$ is known as molecularity of reaction for an elementary reaction. Greater the concentration of reactant, faster is the reaction.

Besides concentration of reactant, rate of reaction depends on nature of reactants, temperature, catalyst, surface area, light etc.

Inorganic Chemistry Related Principles

Mohr's Salt $[FeSO_4 \cdot (NH_4)_2SO_4 \cdot 6H_2O]$

NEET 2024

It is a double salt. When solutions of ferrous sulphate and ammonium sulphate are mixed together, evaporated and cooled, light green crystals of Mohr's salt are obtained.

$$(NH_4)_2SO_4 + FeSO_4 \cdot 7H_2O \longrightarrow \underset{\substack{\text{Mohr's salt} \\ \text{(light green)}}}{FeSO_4 \cdot (NH_4)_2SO_4 \cdot 6H_2O} + H_2O$$

During the preparation of ferrous sulphate solution in hot water, dilute H_2SO_4, (in small amount), is also added in hot water to prevent the hydrolysis of ferrous sulphate, i.e. to prevent conversion of ferrous sulphate into ferrous hydroxide.

Chemistry

Double salts are obtained by dissolving equimolar mixture of constituent salt in water so that they crystallise together as a single substance.

Water used in the preparation of Mohr's salt is boiled for 5 minutes in advance to expel dissolved oxygen which can oxidise ferrous salt to ferric salt.

Applications

In analytical chemistry, this salt is the preferred source of ferrous ions.

It is a common laboratory reagent because it is readily crystallised and crystals resist oxidation by air.

Potash Alum, $K_2SO_4Al_2(SO_4)_3 \cdot 24H_2O$

It is also a double salt. Potash alum is prepared by dissolving K_2SO_4 and $Al_2(SO_4)_3$ in equimolar ratio in small amount of water containing some drops of conc. H_2SO_4. On cooling potash alum separates as colourless crystals.

$$K_2SO_4 + Al_2(SO_4)_3 + 24H_2O \longrightarrow K_2SO_4 \cdot Al_2(SO_4)_3 \cdot 24H_2O$$

Alums are isomorphous crystalline solids. Their aqueous solution is acidic in nature due to hydrolysis.

Chemistry

A little sulphuric acid is added during preparation of potash alum or Mohr's salt to avoid hydrolysis.

Applications

- It is used for purification of impure water, stops bleeding and mordant for dyeing industry.
- It is also used as a deodrant, after shave treatment.

Qualitative Analysis or Salt Analysis

Identification of basic and acidic radicals in a salt can be carried out by performing various tests.

(i) **Dry tests** It involve following tests

- Physical observation
- Effect of heating
- Smell of compound
- Solubility of salts
- Flame tests
- Charcoal cavity test
- Cobalt nitrate test
- Borax bead test
- Microcosmic salt bead test
- Sodium carbonate bead test

(ii) **Wet tests** Dry tests tells us about the presence of possible radicals in the mixture but these are confirmed by wet tests.

Dry Tests

Physical Observation of Salt or Mixture

In physical examination, colour, smell and density of a given mixture are observed.

Observation	Inference
A. If colour of the substance is	
blue, its aqueous solution is also blue.	Cupric salt
green, its aqueous solution is also green.	Salts of nickel
light pink, its aqueous solution is colourless.	Salts of manganese
reddish brown	Fe_2O_3
red	Pb_3O_4, Cu_2O
black	CuO, NiO, FeS, CuS, PbS, FeO, Ni_2O_3, Cu_2S, $CuBr_2$, NiS etc.
yellow	CdS, PbI_2, chromates etc.
yellow-green, aqueous solution is light green or almost colourless.	Salts of Fe^{2+}
yellow-brown, aqueous solution is yellow	Salts of Fe^{3+}
colourless	Transition metals absent except some salts of Mn^{2+}
B. Odour of the substance	
Vinegar like smell	Acetates
Rotten egg like smell	Sulphides
Ammoniacal smell	Ammonia salts mainly $(NH_4)_2CO_3$ Some ammonium salts and sulphides do not give smell.
C. Density	
Mixture or salt is light	Salts of Zn, Al, Ba, Ca and Mg.
Mixture of salts is heavy	Salts of Pb.

Effect of Heating

Take the given substance in a clear, dry test tube and heat it first gently and then strongly. As a result, there occurs a change in the colour of the salts.

Observation	Inference
Substance melts	Pb and their salts having water of crystallisation.
Substance cracks	$Pb(NO_3)_2$, $Ba(NO_3)_2$, NaCl and KI
Substance sublimes on heating and the colour of sublimate is	
• White	$AlCl_3$
• Blue, yellow or violet vapours	Iodides
Colour of residue obtained after heating (Residue mainly contains metallic oxide)	
• White and non-fusible	Oxides of Ca, Ba, Mg, Zn and Al.
• Red-brown	Fe_2O_3
• Black and infusible	NiO, MnO_2 and CuO
• White, infusible, becomes yellow on heating	ZnO
• Initially, it is blue or green but becomes white on heating	$CuSO_4 \cdot 5H_2O$
Observations of gases evolved	
(i) Colourless, odourless gas	
• CO_2, which turns lime water milky	Carbonates and oxalates
(ii) Colourless, odorous gas	
• H_2S, smell of rotten eggs	Sulphides.
• HCl, Pungent smell and forms white fumes with NH_3	Hydrated chloride salts
(iii) Coloured, odorous gas	
• Cl_2, yellow-green pungent smelling gas.	Chloride
• I_2, violet gas	Iodides
• Br_2, red-brown gas	Bromides
• NO_2, brown gas	Nitrates or nitrites of heavy metals

Flame Test

- This test is based upon the fact that in a state of high ionisation of chloride some of the cations impart characteristic colour to the flame, as the cation absorbs energy from the flame and transmit the same as light of characteristic colour.
- In this method, paste of the salt and conc. HCl is taken into the lower oxidising zone and colour imparted to the flame by salts is observed.
- Salts particularly of group V (Ba^{2+}, Ca^{2+}, Sr^{2+}) are identified by colours of the flame.

Colour in Flame Test

Colour	Cation
Brick red	Ca^{2+}
Apple-green	Ba^{2+}
Green	Cu^{2+}
Blue	Cu^{2+}
Crimson red	Sr^{2+}
Golden yellow	Na^{+}

Marks Maximizer

Platinum metal preferred over other metals for flame test because platinum does not react with acids and does not itself impart any characteristic colour to the flame.

Borax Bead Test

Borax, $Na_2B_4O_7 \cdot 10H_2O$ is heated on the platinum loop, a transparent colourless glass like bead of sodium metaborate ($NaBO_2$) and boric anhydride (B_2O_3) is formed.

$$Na_2B_4O_7 \xrightarrow{\Delta} 2NaBO_2 + B_2O_3$$

Characteristics coloured beads are produced with salts of Cu, Fe, Cr, Mn, Co and Ni. The colour of the bead depends upon the flame in which it has been heated.

$$CuSO_4 + B_2O_3 \longrightarrow \underset{\substack{\text{Copper (II) metaborate} \\ \text{(green when hot and} \\ \text{blue when cold)}}}{Cu(BO_2)_2} + SO_3 \quad \text{(Oxidising flame)}$$

$$2Cu(BO_2)_2 + C \longrightarrow 2CuBO_2 + B_2O_3 + CO\uparrow \quad \text{(Reducing flame)}$$

$$2CuBO_2 + C \longrightarrow \underset{\text{Red}}{2Cu\downarrow} + B_2O_3 + CO\uparrow$$

Colours of some ions shown is borax bead test.

Colour in Borax Bead Test

Oxidising flame		Reducing flame		Metal
Hot	Cold	Hot	Cold	
Green	Blue	Colourless	Opaque red-brown	Cu
Yellowish-brown	Yellow	Green	Green	Fe
Violet	Amethyst	Colourless	Colourless	Mn
Violet	Reddish-brown	Grey	Grey	Ni

Wet Tests

- In wet analysis, the substance is first dissolved in water to bring it in solution form and is analysed for acid and basic radicals.
- In the analysis of inorganic salt mixture, first acid radicals are analysed and then basic radicals.

Analysis of Acid Radicals

1. Analysis of First Group Anions (CO_3^{2-}, S^{2-}, NO_2^-)

- The Group reagent is dilute sulphuric acid.
- Anions of first group, when treated with dil. H_2SO_4 evolve gases with characteristic colour and smell.
- On the basis of gases released, anions are identified.

(i) Reactions Involved in the Test of Carbonate (CO_3^{2-})

- $Na_2CO_3 + 2HCl \longrightarrow 2NaCl + H_2O + \underset{\substack{\text{Colourless,} \\ \text{odourless gas}}}{CO_2\uparrow}$
- $Ca(OH)_2 + CO_2 \longrightarrow \underset{\substack{\text{Calcium carbonate} \\ \text{(milky)}}}{CaCO_3\downarrow} + H_2O$
- $\underset{\text{White ppt.}}{CaCO_3} + H_2O + CO_2\text{(excess)} \longrightarrow \underset{\substack{\text{Calcium bicarbonate} \\ \text{(colourless)}}}{Ca(HCO_3)_2}$

I. Test for CO_3^{2-}

Experiment	Observation	Inference
Take mixture in a dry test tube and add dil. HCl or H_2SO_4. Warm gently	Brisk effervescence with the evolution of colourless and odourless gas (CO_2)	may be CO_3^{2-}
Pass the evolved gas into lime water [$Ca(OH)_2$]	Lime water turns milky	CO_3^{2-} confirmed

(ii) Reactions Involved in the Test of Sulphide (S^{2-})

- $Na_2S + H_2SO_4 \longrightarrow H_2S + Na_2SO_4$
- $(CH_3COO)_2Pb + H_2S \longrightarrow \underset{\text{Black}}{PbS\downarrow} + 2CH_3COOH$

II. Tests for S^{2-}

Experiment	Observation	Inference
Take mixture in a dry test tube and add dil. HCl or H_2SO_4 and warm gently	A colourless gas (H_2S) with smell of rotten eggs evolved	may be S^{2-}
Bring filter paper dipped in lead acetate over the mouth of test tube	Filter paper turns black due to formation of PbS	S^{2-} confirmed

(iii) Reactions Involved in the Test of Nitrite (NO_2^-)

- $2NaNO_2 + H_2SO_4 \longrightarrow Na_2SO_4 + 2HNO_2$

$$3HNO_2 \longrightarrow HNO_3 + 2NO\uparrow + H_2O$$

$$2NO + O_2 \longrightarrow \underset{\text{(Brown)}}{2NO_2\uparrow}$$

- $2KI + 2NO_2 \longrightarrow 2KNO_2 + I_2$

$$I_2 + \text{Starch} \longrightarrow \text{Blue colour}$$

Tests for Nitrate (NO_2^-)

Experiment	Observation	Inference
Take mixture in a dry test tube and add dil. HCl. Warm gently	Brown fumes (NO_2) with pungent odour are evolved	May be NO_2^-
Take filter paper dipped in (starch + KI) solution, on the mouth of test tube	Evolved gas turns filter paper blue	NO_2^- confirmed

2. Analysis of Second Group Anions (Cl^-, Br^-, I^-, NO_3^-)

Acidic radicals or anions of second group give no response with dil. acids. However, with conc. acids (conc. H_2SO_4 group reagent), they evolve gases with characteristic colour and smell, thus can be identified by using conc. acids.

(i) Reactions Involved in the Test of Chloride (Cl^-)

- $NaCl + H_2SO_4 \longrightarrow NaHSO_4 + \underset{\text{Pungent smelling gas}}{HCl\uparrow}$
- $HCl + NH_4OH \longrightarrow \underset{\text{White fumes}}{NH_4Cl\uparrow} + H_2O$
- $2NaCl + MnO_2 + 3H_2SO_4 \longrightarrow 2NaHSO_4 + MnSO_4 + 2H_2O + \underset{\text{Yellowish-green}}{Cl_2\uparrow}$
- **Chromyl chloride test**

$$4NaCl + K_2Cr_2O_7 + \underset{(Conc.)}{3H_2SO_4} \longrightarrow \underset{\text{Chromyl chloride (orange yellow gas)}}{2CrO_2Cl_2} + 2Na_2SO_4 + K_2SO_4 + 3H_2O$$

$$CrO_2Cl_2 + 4NaOH \longrightarrow \underset{\text{Yellow solution}}{Na_2CrO_4} + 2NaCl + 2H_2O$$

$$(CH_3COO)_2Pb + Na_2CrO_4 \longrightarrow \underset{\text{Yellow ppt.}}{PbCrO_4\downarrow} + 2CH_3COONa$$

Note If a mixture contains chlorates, chromyl chloride test for chloride anion should not be performed because chlorates on reaction with H_2SO_4 form chlorine dioxide gas which dissolves in H_2SO_4 and form highly explosive orange yellow solution.

$$3KClO_3 + 3H_2SO_4 \longrightarrow 2ClO_2\uparrow + ClO_4^- + 3SO_4^{2-} + 4H^+ + 3K^+ + H_2O$$

I. Tests for Chloride (Cl^-)

Experiment	Observation	Inference
Heat the mixture with 1-2 mL conc. H_2SO_4 in a dry test tube.	A colourless, pungent gas (HCl) is evolved.	May be Cl^-
Bring a glass rod dipped in NH_4OH near the mouth of test tube.	White dense fumes of NH_4Cl is evolved.	Cl^- confirmed
Heat the mixture with conc. H_2SO_4 and MnO_2 in a dry test tube.	Greenish-yellow (Cl_2) pungent gas is evolved.	Cl^- confirmed
Chromyl chloride test • Heat the mixture with solid $K_2Cr_2O_7$ and conc. H_2SO_4.	Orange-yellow vapours of chromyl-chloride (CrO_2Cl_2) are evolved.	Cl^- confirmed
• Collect evolved vapours in a test tube containing NaOH. Acidified it with acetic acid and add lead acetate solution.	A yellow ppt. or solution of lead chromate is formed.	Cl^- confirmed

(ii) Reactions Involved in the Test of Bromide (Br^-)

- $NaBr + \underset{\text{Conc.}}{H_2SO_4} \longrightarrow NaHSO_4 + HBr\uparrow$

  $2HBr + H_2SO_4(\text{conc.}) \longrightarrow 2H_2O + SO_2\uparrow + \underset{\text{Reddish brown}}{Br_2\uparrow}$
- $2NaBr + MnO_2 + 3H_2SO_4 \longrightarrow 2NaHSO_4 + MnSO_4 + 2H_2O + \underset{\text{Reddish brown}}{Br_2\uparrow}$
- $NaBr + AgNO_3 \xrightarrow{\text{Dil. }HNO_3} \underset{\text{Pale yellow}}{AgBr\downarrow} + NaNO_3$
- $AgBr + 2NH_4OH \longrightarrow \underset{\text{Diammine silver (I) bromide (hardly soluble)}}{[Ag(NH_3)_2]Br} + 2H_2O$

II. Test for Bromide (Br^-)

Experiment	Observation	Inference
Heat the mixture with 1-2 mL conc. H_2SO_4 in a dry test tube.	A colourless, pungent gas (HBr) or sometimes brown fumes are evolved.	May be Br^-
Heat the mixture with MnO_2 and conc. H_2SO_4.	Red brown vapour of Br_2 evolved.	Br^- confirmed
To the solution of mixture in dil. HNO_3, add $AgNO_3$ solution.	A pale yellow ppt. of AgBr is formed (sparingly soluble in NH_4OH).	Br^- confirmed

(iii) Reactions Involved in the Test of Iodide (I^-)

- $NaI + \underset{\text{Conc.}}{H_2SO_4} \longrightarrow HI + NaHSO_4$
- $H_2SO_4 + 2HI \longrightarrow \underset{\text{Violet vapours}}{I_2\uparrow} + SO_2 + 2H_2O$
- $2NaI + MnO_2 + 3H_2SO_4 \longrightarrow I_2\uparrow + 2NaHSO_4 + MnSO_4 + 2H_2O$
- $I_2 + \text{Starch} \longrightarrow \text{Blue colour}$
- $NaI + AgNO_3 \longrightarrow \underset{\text{Yellow}}{AgI\downarrow} + NaNO_3$
- $\underset{\text{Yellow ppt. insoluble}}{AgI} + NH_4OH \longrightarrow [Ag(NH_3)_2]I + H_2O$

III. Test for Iodide (I^-)

Experiment	Observation	Inference
Heat the mixture with 1-3 mL conc. H_2SO_4 in a dry test tube.	Dark violet fumes (I_2) are evolved.	May be I^-
Heat the mixture with MnO_2 and conc. H_2SO_4.	Violet vapours in excess are evolved.	May be I^-
Bring a paper dipped in starch solution on the mouth of test tube.	Paper turns blue.	I^- confirmed
To the solution of mixture in dil. HNO_3, add $AgNO_3$ solution.	A yellow ppt. of AgI is formed (insoluble in NH_4OH).	I^- confirmed

(iv) Reactions Involved in the Test of Nitrate (NO_3^-)

- $NaNO_3 + H_2SO_4 \longrightarrow NaHSO_4 + HNO_3$ (Conc.)
- $4HNO_3 \longrightarrow 4NO_2\uparrow + O_2\uparrow + 2H_2O$ (NO_2: Brown)
- $3Cu + 8HNO_3 \longrightarrow 3Cu(NO_3)_2 + 2NO\uparrow + 4H_2O$
  $2NO + O_2 \longrightarrow 2NO_2\uparrow$
- **Brown ring test** JEE Main 2023
  $6FeSO_4 + 2HNO_3 + 3H_2SO_4 \longrightarrow 3Fe_2(SO_4)_3 + 4H_2O + 2NO\uparrow$
  $FeSO_4 + 5H_2O + NO \longrightarrow [Fe(H_2O)_5NO]SO_4$ (Brown ring) Ferrous nitroso sulphate

JEE Main 2020

IV. Tests for Nitrate (NO_3^-)

Experiment	Observation	Inference
Heat the mixture with 1-2 mL conc. H_2SO_4 in a dry test tube.	Pungent light brown gas (NO_2) is evolved.	May be NO_3^-
Heat the mixture with copper turnings and conc. H_2SO_4.	Deep brown fumes (NO_2) in excess are evolved.	May be NO_3^-
Brown ring test To the solution of mixture in dil. HCl, add freshly prepared solution of $FeSO_4$. Shake well gradually and add conc. H_2SO_4 by the sides of test tube.	A brown ring of $FeSO_4 \cdot NO$ is formed at the junction of two liquids.	NO_3^- confirmed

Analysis of Third Group Anion (SO_4^{2-})

- Third group radical is identified on the basis of precipitate obtained.
- Reactions involved in the test of sulphate (SO_4^{2-})

$$Na_2SO_4 + BaCl_2 \longrightarrow \underset{\text{White}}{BaSO_4}\downarrow + 2NaCl$$

$$(CH_3COO)_2Pb + Na_2SO_4 \longrightarrow \underset{\text{White}}{PbSO_4}\downarrow + 2CH_3COO\overset{+}{Na}$$

Tests for Sulphate (SO_4^{2-})

Radical or anion	Experiment	Observation	Inference
Sulphate (SO_4^{2-})	In the solution of mixture, add $BaCl_2$ solution.	A curdy white ppt. ($BaSO_4$) is formed (insoluble in all conc acids).	May be SO_4^{2-}
	In the solution of mixture, add lead acetate solution.	White ppt. of $PbSO_4$ is formed.	SO_4^{2-} confirmed

Analysis of Basic Radicals (Cations)

Basic radicals have been classified into six groups on the basis of the solubility products of their salts with group reagent. The radicals have been grouped in the order of increasing solubility product.

Basic radicals are classified into following groups

Classification of Basic Radicals into Groups NEET 2024

Group	Basic radicals	Group reagent	Precipitate as	Observation
(I)	Pb^{2+}	Dil. HCl	Chlorides ($PbCl_2$) (White)	Chloride insoluble in cold dil. HCl.
(II)	Cu^{2+}, Pb^{2+}	H_2S gas in presence of dil. HCl	Sulphides (black) CuS and PbS	Sulphides insoluble in dil. HCl.
(III)	Al^{3+}, Fe^{3+}	NH_4OH in presence of NH_4Cl	Hydroxides [$Al(OH)_3$] (White)	Hydroxides are insoluble in NH_4OH.
(IV)	Zn^{2+}, Ni^{2+}	H_2S in ammoniacal medium	Sulphides (ZnS; Greenish white) NiS; (Black)	Sulphides are insoluble in NH_4OH.
(V)	Ca^{2+}, Ba^{2+}	$(NH_4)_2CO_3 + NH_4Cl$	Carbonates ($CaCO_3$, $BaCO_3$) (White)	Carbonates are insoluble.
(VI)	Mg^{2+}	$NH_4OH + Na_2HPO_4$	White precipitate ($MgHPO_4$)	
Zero	NH_4^+	Dilute NaOH	NH_3 gas is evolved.	

Preparation of Original Solutions

To prepare transparent solution of salt, following solvents are used strictly in the order given below.

(i) Cold water (ii) Hot water (iii) Dilute HCl (iv) Conc. HCl

Note HNO_3 or H_2SO_4 cannot be used to prepare original solution because both are oxidising agents.

Analysis of Group I Cations

The basic radicals of this group is Pb^{2+}.

Reactions Involved in the Tests of Cation (Pb^{2+})

- $\underset{\text{(Cold O.S)}}{Pb^{2+}} + \underset{\text{from HCl}}{2Cl^-} \longrightarrow \underset{\text{White ppt.}}{PbCl_2 \downarrow}$
- $\underset{\text{Soluble in hot water}}{PbCl_2} + K_2CrO_4 \longrightarrow \underset{\text{Yellow ppt.}}{PbCrO_4 \downarrow} + 2KCl$
- $PbCrO_4 + 4NaOH \longrightarrow \underset{\text{(Sodium plumbite) soluble}}{Na_2PbO_2} + Na_2CrO_4$
- $PbCl_2 + 2KI \longrightarrow \underset{\text{Yellow}}{PbI_2} + 2KCl$
- $PbCl_2 + H_2SO_4 \longrightarrow \underset{\text{White ppt.}}{PbSO_4 \downarrow} 2HCl$

$PbSO_4 + 2CH_3COONH_4 \longrightarrow \underset{\text{Soluble}}{(CH_3COO)_2Pb} + (NH_4)_2SO_4$

Test for Lead (Pb^{2+})

Experiment	Observation	Inference
Hot filtrate is taken in the test tube and add K_2CrO_4.	Yellow ppt. of $PbCrO_4$ is obtained which is soluble in NaOH but insoluble in CH_3COOH.	Indicates the presence of Pb^{2+}.
Hot filtrate is taken in the test tube and add KI.	Yellow ppt. of PbI_2 is formed.	Pb^{2+} confirmed
Dilute H_2SO_4 is added to hot filtrate and mixture is cooled.	White precipitate of $PbSO_4$ is obtained which is soluble in CH_3COONH_4 solution.	Pb^{2+} confirmed

Analysis of Group II Cations

The basic radicals of this group are Pb^{2+} and Cu^{2+}.

Reactions Involved in the Test of Cation (Cu^{2+})

- $\underset{\text{Black ppt.}}{3CuS} + 8HNO_3 \longrightarrow \underset{\text{Soluble blue}}{3Cu(NO_3)_2} + 2NO + 3S + 4H_2O$
- $Cu(NO_3)_2 + 2CH_3COOH \longrightarrow (CH_3COO)_2Cu + 2HNO_3$

$2(CH_3COO)_2Cu + K_4[Fe(CN)_6] \longrightarrow \underset{\text{Chocolate brown ppt.}}{Cu_2[Fe(CN)_6]} + 4CH_3CO\overset{-}{O}\overset{+}{K}$

- $Cu^{2+} + 4NH_3(\text{excess}) \longrightarrow \underset{\text{Deep blue}}{[Cu(NH_3)_4]^{2+}}$
- $Cu(NO_3)_2 + 2KSCN \longrightarrow \underset{\text{Black ppt.}}{Cu(SCN)_2} + 2KNO_3$

Tests for Copper (Cu^{2+})

Experiment	Observation	Inference
Take black ppt. of CuS in the test tube and add HNO_3.	Blue coloured solution is obtained	It indicates the presence of Cu^{2+}
Divide blue solution obtained into three parts.		
(i) Add CH_3COOH and $K_4[Fe(CN)_6]$ to first part.	Chocolate brown ppt. is formed	Cu^{2+} confirmed
(ii) Add aqueous NH_3 (excess) in second part of blue solution.	Deep blue solution is obtained	Cu^{2+} confirmed
(iii) Add KSCN in the third part of blue solution.	Black ppt. is obtained	Cu^{2+} confirmed

Analysis of Group III Cations

The basic radicals of this group are Al^{3+} and Fe^{3+}.

(i) Reactions Involved in the Test of Cation (Al^{3+})

- $\underset{\text{White ppt.}}{Al(OH)_3} + NaOH \longrightarrow \underset{\text{Sodium meta-aluminate (soluble)}}{NaAlO_2} + 2H_2O$
- $NaAlO_2 + NH_4Cl + H_2O \xrightarrow{\Delta} NaCl + \underset{\text{White gelatinous}}{Al(OH)_3} + NH_3$

I. Tests for Aluminium (Al^{3+})

Experiment	Observation	Inference
Add NaOH solution in excess to white gelatinous ppt.	White gelatinous ppt. dissolves due to the formation of sodium meta-aluminate.	It indicates the presence of Al^{3+}
In soluble meta-aluminate add NH_4Cl and boil	White gelatinous ppt. of $Al(OH)_3$ reappears	Al^{3+} confirmed

(ii) Reactions Involved in the Test of Cation (Fe^{3+})

- $\underset{\text{Reddish brown ppt.}}{Fe(OH)_3} + 3HCl \longrightarrow \underset{\text{Soluble}}{FeCl_3} + 3H_2O$
- $4FeCl_3 + 3K_4[Fe(CN)_6] \longrightarrow \underset{\text{Ferric ferrocyanide (dark blue colour)}}{Fe_4[Fe(CN)_6]_3} + 12KCl$
- $FeCl_3 + \underset{\text{Potassium sulphocyanide}}{KCNS} \longrightarrow \underset{\text{Ferrithiocyanate (blood red colour)}}{[Fe(CNS)]Cl_2} + KCl$

II. Tests for Iron (Fe^{3+})

Experiment	Observation	Inference
Add dilute HCl in red brown ppt. and divide it into two parts.	Precipitate dissolves	Fe^{3+} confirmed
• Add $K_4[Fe(CN)_6]$ in the first part of the above solution.	Dark blue colour is obtained	Fe^{3+} confirmed
• Add KCNS in the second part of the solution.	Dark (Blood) red colour is obtained	Fe^{3+} confirmed

Analysis of Group IV Cations

The basic radicals in this group are Zn^{2+} and Ni^{2+}.

(i) Reactions Involved in the Test of Cation (Ni^{2+})

- $\underbrace{3NiS + 6HCl + 2HNO_3}_{\text{Aqua-regia}} \longrightarrow 3NiCl_2 + 2NO + 3S + 4H_2O$
- $NiCl_2 + 2DMG \longrightarrow$

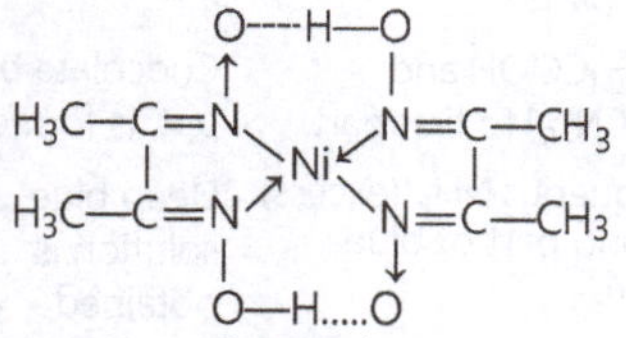

Cherry red ppt.
(Dimethyl glyoxime)

- $2K_2[Ni(CN)_4] + NaOBr + 4NaOH \longrightarrow Ni_2O_3 + 4KCN + 4NaCN + NaBr + 2H_2O$

I. Tests for Nickel (Ni^{2+})

Experiment	Observation	Inference
Dissolve black ppt of NiS in *aqua-regia* (3 part conc. HCl + 1 part conc. HNO_3) and divide it into two parts.	Soluble chloride is formed.	It indicates the presence of Ni^{2+}
• Add NH_4OH and dimethyl glyoxime to the solution	Cherry red ppt.	Ni^{2+} confirmed
• Add potassium cyanide solution and heat and add NaOH/Br_2 water and again heat.	Black ppt. is obtained.	Ni^{2+} confirmed

(ii) Reactions Involved in the Test of Cation (Zn^{2+})

- $ZnS + 2HCl \longrightarrow ZnCl_2 + H_2S$
- $ZnCl_2 + 2NaOH \longrightarrow \underset{\text{White ppt.}}{Zn(OH)_2\downarrow} + 2NaCl$
- $Zn(OH)_2 + 2NaOH \longrightarrow \underset{\text{Sodium zincate (Soluble)}}{Na_2ZnO_2} + 2H_2O$
- $Na_2ZnO_2 + H_2S \longrightarrow 2NaOH + \underset{\text{White ppt.}}{ZnS\downarrow}$
- $2ZnCl_2 + K_4[Fe(CN)_6] \longrightarrow \underset{\text{Bluish white ppt.}}{Zn_2[Fe(CN)_6]\downarrow} + 4KCl$

II. Tests for Zinc (Zn^{2+})

Experiment	Observation	Inference
Dissolve white ppt. of ZnS in dil. HCl and divide it into two parts.	Soluble chloride is formed.	It indicates the presence of Zn^{2+}.
(i) Add NaOH in the solution. White ppt. is obtained which is soluble in excess of NaOH.	White ppt. of ZnS reappears on passing H_2S into soluble sodium zincate solution.	Zn^{2+} confirmed
(ii) Solution is acidified with acetic acid and add $K_4[Fe(CN)_6]$	Bluish white ppt. is obtained.	Zn^{2+} confirmed

Analysis of Group V Cations

The basic radicals in this group are Ca^{2+} and Ba^{2+}.

(i) Reactions Involved in the Test of Cation (Ba^{2+})

- $\underset{\text{White ppt.}}{BaCO_3} + 2CH_3COOH \xrightarrow{\Delta} (CH_3COO)_2Ba + H_2O + CO_2$
- $(CH_3COO)_2Ba + K_2CrO_4 \longrightarrow \underset{\text{Barium chromate (yellow ppt.)}}{BaCrO_4\downarrow} + 2CH_3COOK$

II. Tests for Barium (Ba^{2+})

Experiment	Observation	Inference
Dissolve the ppt. in acetic acid and heat it gently and add potassium chromate solution and again heat.	Yellow ppt. appears.	Ba^{2+} confirmed

(ii) Reactions Involved in the Test of Cation (Ca^{2+})

- $\underset{\text{White ppt.}}{CaCO_3} + 2CH_3COOH \xrightarrow{\Delta} (CH_3COO)_2Ca + H_2O + CO_2$
- $(CH_3COO)_2Ca + (NH_4)_2C_2O_4 \longrightarrow \underset{\text{White ppt.}}{CaC_2O_4\downarrow} + 2CH_3COONH_4$
- $5CaC_2O_4 + \underset{\text{Pink}}{2KMnO_4} + 16HCl \longrightarrow 5CaCl_2 + \underset{\text{Colourless}}{2MnCl_2} + 10CO_2 + 8H_2O + 2KCl$

II. Tests for Calcium (Ca^{2+})

Experiment	Observation	Inference
Dissolve the ppt. in acetic acid ,add ammonium oxalate solution (excess) and heat.	White ppt. appears.	Ca^{2+} confirmed
Acidified white ppt. obtained by adding dilute CH_3COOH and add $KMnO_4$ solution drop wise and add HCl.	Pink colour of $KMnO_4$ disappears.	Ca^{2+} confirmed

Analysis of Group VI Cation (Mg^{2+})

Reactions Involved in the Test of Cation Mg^{2+}

$MgCl_2 + \underset{\text{Disodium hydrogen phosphate}}{Na_2HPO_4} + NH_4OH \longrightarrow \underset{\text{Magnesium ammonium phosphate (white ppt.)}}{Mg(NH_4)PO_4} + 2NaCl + H_2O$

Tests for Magnesium (Mg^{2+})

Experiment	Observation	Inference
Filtrate of group V is heated with NH_4OH and Na_2HPO_4.	A fine crystalline ppt. on scratching the side of the test tube.	Mg^{2+} confirmed

Analysis of Zero Group Cation (NH_4^+)

Ammonium salts are decomposed by alkali and NH_3 is liberated which can be identified by a number of methods.

Reaction Involved in Test of Cation (NH_4^+)

- $\underset{\text{(From mixture)}}{NH_4Cl} + NaOH \xrightarrow{\Delta} NH_3(g) + NaCl + H_2O$
- $NH_3(g) + HCl \longrightarrow \underset{\substack{\text{Ammonium chloride}\\\text{(white fumes)}}}{NH_4Cl}$
- $NH_3 + 3\,NaOH + \underset{\substack{\text{Nessler's}\\\text{reagent}}}{2K_2[HgI_4]} \longrightarrow$

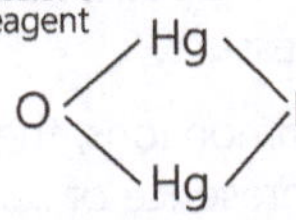

$NH_2I + 4KI + 3NaI + 2H_2O$

Iodide of Million's base
(brown ppt.)

Tests for Ammonium (NH_4^+)

Experiment	Observation	Inference
Take small amount of mixture in the test tube and heat it with NaOH solution.	Smell of ammonia.	NH_4^+ confirmed
Bring the moistened glass rod with conc. HCl near the mouth of the test tube.	White fumes are formed.	NH_4^+ confirmed
Take small amount of salt in the test tube and add NaOH and heat. Add Nessler's reagent to the solution.	Brown ppt. is obtained.	NH_4^+ confirmed

Caution Points

- In the preparation of aniline yellow, keep the diazotisation reaction temperature below 5°C to prevent undesirable side reactions.
- For kinetic study of reaction of iodide ion with hydrogen peroxide, maintain a constant temperature throughout the experiment, as temperature can significantly influence reaction rates.
- In qualitative analysis of NH_4^+ cation, if a precipitate is formed, add NaOH drop by drop, **shake the tube after each drop**, until the precipitate dissolves or until no more precipitate is formed.
- It is essential to add dil. HCl before proceeding to the test for the basic radicals of group II.

PYQ Notes

1. In Lassaigne's test for detection of phosphorus the reagent used is ammonium molybdate $(NH_4)_2MoO_4$. **JEE Main 2023**
2. In acid base titration, at the end point methyl orange is present as quinonoid form which is red in colour. **JEE Main 2022**
3. 1-naphthylamine and sulphanilic acid is used for the detection of NO_2^- with help of acetic acid. **JEE Main 2021**
4. In indirect iodometric titration, Cu^{2+} salt react with potassium iodide to give Cu_2I_2. **JEE Main 2021**
5. Seliwanoff's test is used to distinguish between ketoses and aldoses. The Seliwanoff's reagent contains resorcinol and HCl. **JEE Main 2021**

Step by Step

Mastering NCERT

- Concept Builders
- Topical Questions
- Assertion-Reason
- Statement Type
- Matching Type
- Numerical Value
- Past Exams'
- Skill Boosters

Concept Builders

1. When sodium nitroprusside is added to Lassaigne's extract a violet colour ppt. is formed. It indicates the presence of ....

2. An organic compound with alcoholic group when reacts with sodium metal produces effervescence of nitrogen gas. [T/F]

3. Which alcohol gives blue colouration in Victor Meyer test?

4. Carbonyl compounds on mixing with .... produce yellow-orange crystals.

5. Formation of black ppt. in Tollen's test confirms the presence of an aldehyde group. [T/F]

6. The name of the test in which brisk effervescence of CO_2 shows the presence of —COOH group.

7. Secondary amines react with Hinsberg's reagent to form an amide which is .... in sodium hydroxide.

8. Zinc is added to prevent the oxidation of aniline during the preparation of acetanilide. [T/F]

9. In volumetric analysis, name the stage at which two reagents react completely.

10. Phenolphthalein shows .... colour in alkaline medium.

11. Titration of oxalic acid *vs* $KMnO_4$ is a redox titration [T/F].

12. The average enthalpy of neutralisation of any strong acid by a strong base is found to be .... kJ/mol.

13. What type of colloids that are reversible in nature?

14. The reaction between iodide ions and hydrogen peroxide takes place in basic medium. [T/F]

15. What is the chemical formula of Mohr's salt?

16. Chemical reaction that absorbs heat from the surroundings is said to be .... and has a .... ΔH value at constant pressure.

17. In flame test for common ions, the apple-green colour flame confirms the presence of .... ion.

18. Which coloured bead is formed when oxidising flame is hot in borax bead test to detect Cu^{2+} ?

19. CO_3^{2-} is a group II acid radical [T/F]

20. In wet test for acid radicals, the presence of NO_2^- is confirmed by turning filter paper blue when dipped in starch and potassium iodide solution. [T/F]

21. Orange-yellow vapours of CrO_2Cl_2 confirms the presence of .... ion which is a group .... anion.

22. In silver nitrate test for bromide ion, a pale yellow precipitate of .... is formed which is sparingly soluble in ....

23. Brown ring test is performed to confirmed the presence of NO_3^- ion. [T/F]

24. The group reagent for group-I cations is ....

25. What is the name of the product obtained by the reaction of lead ion with potassium chromate solution?

26. In the confirmatory test for group-IV cations, cherry red ppt. of DMG confirms the presence of Ni^{2+} cation. [T/F]

27. NH_4OH in the presence of NH_4Cl is the group reagent for group .... basic radicals.

28. White ppt. of $BaCrO_4$ in the analysis of Ba^{2+} ion confirms its presence. [T/F]

29. The confirmatory test for magnesium ion, group V filtrate is heated with NH_4OH and ....

30. The common name for the compound $NaBO_2$ is ....

Topical Questions

Organic Chemistry Related Principles

1. In organic analysis, the reagent 2, 4-dinitrophenyl hydrazine is used for the detection of which of the following functional groups ?

(a) Alcohol (b) Acid
(c) Aldehyde (d) Amines

2. The sodium extract on acidification with acetic acid and then adding lead acetate solution, gives a black precipitate. The organic compound contains

(a) nitrogen (b) halogen
(c) sulphur (d) phosphorus

3. Aniline on heating with conc. HNO_3 + conc. H_2SO_4 mixture yields

(a) *o*- and *p*- nitroanilines
(b) *m*-nitroaniline
(c) a black tarry matter
(d) no reaction

4. The test performed on compound *X* and their inferences are

Test	Inference
(i) 2,4-DNP test	Coloured precipitate
(ii) Iodoform test	Yellow precipitate
(iii) Azo-dye test	No dye formation

Compound '*X*' is

(a) 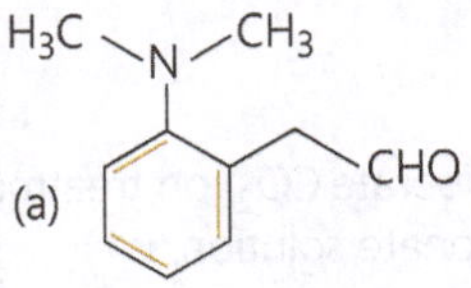 (b) 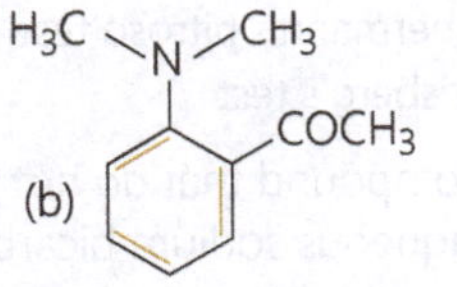

(c) 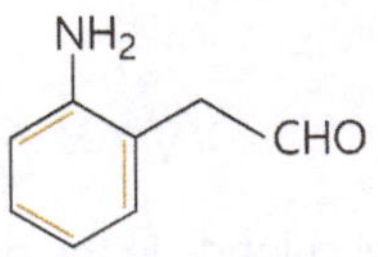 (d) 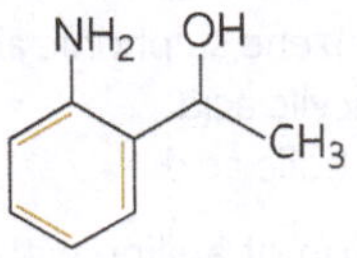

5. During the preparation of acetanilide from aniline a small amount of zinc is added to the reaction mixture because

(a) zinc induces the precipitation
(b) zinc prevents the reduction of aniline during the reaction
(c) zinc reduces the coloured impurities in the aniline and also prevents its oxidation during the reaction
(d) zinc forms a white crystalline complex with aniline

6. The organic compound which can give positive iodoform and Tollen's tests is

(a) CH_3CH_2OH (b) $CH_3CH_2CH_2CHO$
(c) CH_3CHO (d) CH_3COCH_3

7. An organic compound *X* showing the following solubility profile is

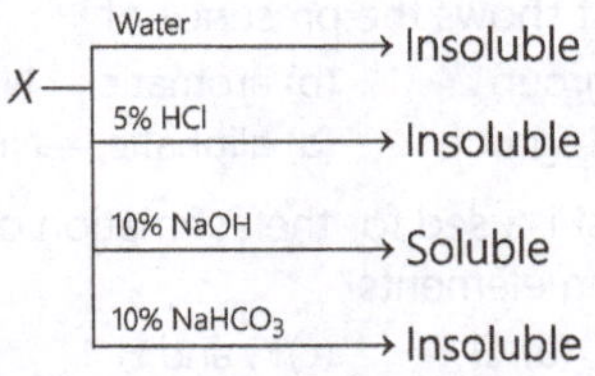

(a) *o* -toluidine (b) oleic acid
(c) *m*-cresol (d) benzamide

8. Lucas reagent is used to

(a) distinguish between 1°, 2° and 3° alcohols
(b) distinguish between 1°, 2° and 3° amines
(c) distinguish between alcohols and phenols
(d) distinguish between aldehydes and ketones

9. In Lassaigne's test sodium extract is heated with concentrated HNO_3 before testing for halogens because

(a) Ag_2S and AgCN are soluble in acidic medium
(b) silver halides are totally insoluble in nitric acid
(c) S^{2-} and CN^-, if present, are decomposed by conc. HNO_3 and hence do not interfere in the test
(d) Ag reacts faster with halides in acidic medium

10. The compound formed in the positive test for nitrogen with Lassaigne's solution of an organic compound is

(a) $Na_4[Fe(CN)_5NOS]$
(b) $Na_3[Fe(CN)_6]$
(c) $Fe(CN)_3$
(d) $Fe_4[Fe(CN)_6]_3$

11. In the preparation of *p*-nitroacetanilide from aniline, nitration is not done by nitrating mixture (a mixture of conc. H_2SO_4 and conc. HNO_3) because

(a) on nitration it gives *o*-nitroacetanilide
(b) it gives a mixture of *o*-and *p*-nitroaniline
(c) $—NH_2$ group gets oxidised
(d) it forms a mixture of *o*-and *p*-nitroacetanilide

12. In Duma's method for determining the nitrogen content of an organic compound, the nitrogen content is determined in the form of

(a) gaseous NH_3 (b) NaCN
(c) gaseous N_2 (d) $(NH_4)_2SO_4$

13. Compound '*A*' reacts with $CHCl_3$ and KOH gives offensive smelling compound. Compound '*A*' can be
(a) quaternary aliphatic amine
(b) primary aromatic amine
(c) secondary amine
(d) tertiary amine

14. An organic compound is treated with $NaNO_2$ and dil. HCl at 0°C. The resulting solution is added to an alkaline solution of β-naphthol where by a brilliant red dye is produced. It shows the presence of
(a) $—NO_2$ group (b) aromatic $—NH_2$ group
(c) $—CONH_2$ group (d) aliphatic $—NH_2$ group

15. Beilstein test is used for the estimation of which one of the following elements?
(a) S (b) Cl (c) C and H (d) N

16. The ammonia evolved from the treatment of 0.30 g of an organic compound for the estimation of nitrogen was passed in 100 mL of 0.1 mL of 0.1 M sulphuric acid. The excess of acid required 20 mL of 0.5 M NaOH solution for complete neutralisation. The organic compound is
(a) thiourea (b) benzamide (c) urea (d) acetamide

17. The presence of carbon in an organic compound can be shown by
(a) heating with copper that goes black
(b) burning it to produce green edge flame
(c) heating it with copper oxide to convert it into CO_2
(d) heating with iron that goes blue

18. Small amount of zinc dust is added to reaction mixture during preparation of acetanilide because
(a) zinc catalyses the reaction
(b) zinc helps in crystallisation
(c) zinc protects aniline from oxidation
(d) zinc hydrolyses acetic anhydride

19. Which one of the following compounds will produce a water-insoluble yellow oily liquid of nitrosoamine on reaction with $NaNO_2$ and dilute HCl at 0°C?
(a) Ethylamine (b) Methylamine
(c) Diethylamine (d) Triethylamine

20. Which of the following reagents may be used to distinguish between phenol and benzoic acid?
(a) Aqueous NaOH (b) Tollen's reagent
(c) Molisch reagent (d) Neutral $FeCl_3$

21. The reagent neutral ferric chloride is used to detect the presence of ....
(a) sulphide ion and alcoholic —OH group
(b) acetate ion and phenolic —OH group
(c) sulphide ion and phenolic —OH group
(d) acetate ion and alcoholic —OH group

22. Which of the following compounds cannot used in preparation of iodoform?
(a) CH_3CHO (b) CH_3COCH_3
(c) HCHO (d) 2-propanol

23. A compound liberates CO_2 with $NaHCO_3$ and also gives colour with neutral $FeCl_3$ solution. The compound can be

(a) 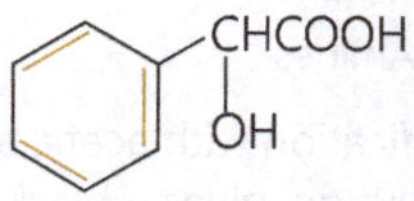

(b) 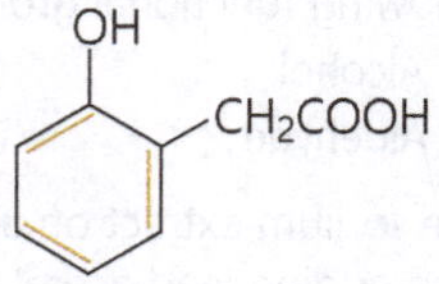

(c) 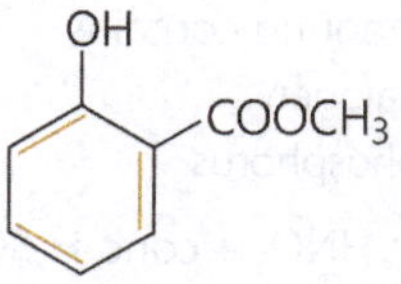

(d) 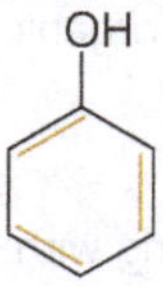

24. Some organic compounds are purified by distillation at low pressure because the compounds are
(a) low boiling liquids
(b) high boiling liquids
(c) highly volatile
(d) dissociated before reaching their boiling points

25. The offensive smell produced in carbylamine reaction is due to the formation of
(a) nitrile (b) chloro compound
(c) nitrosoamine (d) isocyanide

26. Presence of phenolic group can be confirmed by
(a) litmus test
(b) Fehling's test
(c) Liebermann's nitroso test
(d) Hinsberg's test

27. The compound that do not liberate CO_2, on treatment with aqueous sodium bicarbonate solution, is
(a) benzoic acid
(b) benzene sulphonic acid
(c) salicylic acid
(d) carbolic acid

28. Reaction of aniline with acetyl chloride in the presence of NaOH gives
(a) acetanilide (b) *p*-chloroaniline
(c) a red dye (d) aniline hydrochloride

29. Which of the following tests would you perform to identify the functional groups present in *p*-aminoacetophenone?
(a) Azodye test and $NaHCO_3$ test
(b) $FeCl_3$ test and azo dye test
(c) Carbylamine test and Brady's reagent test
(d) Carbylamine test and azo dye test

30. The formula of the purple colour formed in Lassaigne's test for sulphur using sodium nitroprusside is
(a) $NaFe[Fe(CN)_6]$ (b) $Na[Cr(NH_3)_2(NCS)_4]$
(c) $Na_2[Fe(CN)_5(NO)]$ (d) $Na_4[Fe(CN)_5(NOS)]$

31. Which of the following test cannot be used for identifying amino acids?
(a) Biuret test (b) Barfoed test
(c) Ninhydrin test (d) Xanthoproteic test

32. Which of the following statement is wrong about aniline yellow?
(a) It is carcinogenic.
(b) It is also called *p*-aminoazobenzene.
(c) It is an acid dye.
(d) It is also called 4-phenylazoaniline.

Physical Chemistry Related Principles

33. In an acid-base titration, 0.1 M HCl solution was added to the NaOH solution of unknown strength. Which of the following correctly shows the change of pH of the titration mixture in this experiment? [*V* is the volume of the acid added].

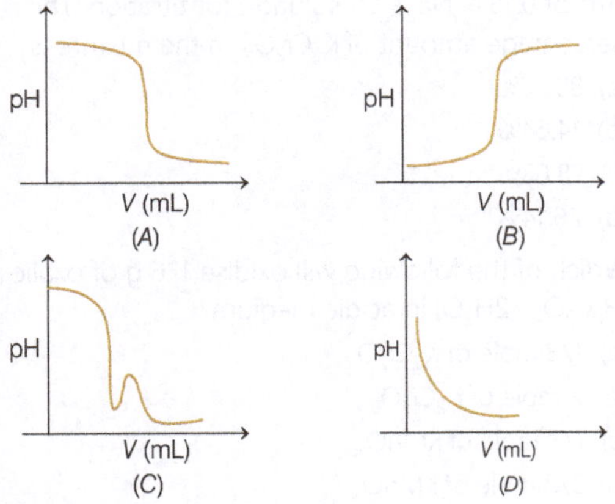

(a) (*D*) (b) (*A*) (c) (*B*) (d) (*C*)

34. If during experiment to calculate enthalpy of copper sulphate temperature is recorded for every half minute of $2\frac{1}{2}$ minute then zinc powder should be added in cup at
(a) precisely 3 minutes (b) anytime after $2\frac{1}{2}$ minutes
(c) after 3 minutes (d) None of these

35. During experiment to calculate heat of neutralisation of strong acid and strong base, temperature should by recorded till.
(a) Constant temperature is achieved
(b) Maximum temperature is achieved
(c) Minimum temperature is achieved
(d) None of the above

36. Phenolphthalein is an indicator for acid-base titration, it exists as
(a) benzenoid form in acid and quinonoid form in basic solution
(b) quinonoid form in acid and benzenoid form in basic solution
(c) quinonoid form in both
(d) benzenoid form in both

37. Why are strong acids generally used as standard solution in acid-base titration?
(a) The pH at equivalence point is always.
(b) They can be used to titrate both strong and weak bases.
(c) Strong acids form more stable solution the weak acids.
(d) The salts of strong acid do not hydrolyse.

38. The difference between titrant and titrate is
(a) that titrant is a solution of an accurately known concentration whereas a titrate is the substance whose concentration is to be determined by titration
(b) that titrant is a solution of unknown concentration whereas titrate is a solution of known concentration
(c) that one is titrated against the other
(d) that one is the reactant and the other is the product

39 For standardising NaOH solution, which of the following is used as a primary standard?
(a) Oxalic acid (b) Ferrous ammonium sulphate
(c) Sodium tetraborate (d) Dil. HCl

40. When arsenic sulphide sol is prepared by dissolving arsenic oxide in water and then passing H_2S through it. Which reaction takes place?
(a) Arsenic oxide directly reacts with H_2S and it is a double decomposition reaction.
(b) Arsenic oxide first forms arsenious acid which then reacts with H_2S.
(c) Both (a) and (b) take place.
(d) Excess H_2S is removed by boiling it off.

41. Which of the following statements is not true ?
(a) An acidified solution of $K_2Cr_2O_7$ liberates iodine from iodides
(b) In acidic solution, dichromate ions are converted to chromate ions
(c) $(NH_4)_2Cr_2O_7$ on heating undergo exothermic decomposition to give Cr_2O_3
(d) Potassium dichromate is used as a titrant for estimation of Fe^{2+} ions

42. In the titration of oxalic acid *vs* potassium permanganate, potassium permanganate acts as
(a) external indicator (b) self indicator
(c) reductant (d) catalyst

43. Which of the following is true in case of titration of Mohr's salt with $KMnO_4$?

(a) $M_{KMnO_4} \times V_{KMnO_4} = 5 \times M_{Mohr's\ salt} \times V_{Mohr's\ salt}$
(b) $M_{KMnO_4} \times V_{KMnO_4} = M_{Mohr's\ salt} \times V_{Mohr's\ salt}$
(c) $M_{KMnO_4} \times V_{Mohr's\ salt} = M_{Mohr's\ salt} \times V_{KMnO_4}$
(d) $5 \times M_{KMnO_4} \times V_{KMnO_4} = M_{Mohr's\ salt} \times V_{Mohr's\ salt}$

44. Consider a titration of potassium dichromate solution with acidified Mohr's salt solution using diphenylamine as indicator. The number of moles of Mohr's salt required per mole of dichromate is

(a) 3 (b) 4 (c) 5 (d) 6

45. While titrating dilute HCl solution with aqueous NaOH, which of the following will not be required?

(a) Pipette and distilled water
(b) Burette and porcelain tile
(c) Bunsen burner and measuring cylinder
(d) Clamp and phenolphthalein

46. In the kinetic study of reaction of iodide ion with hydrogen peroxide, a known volume of sodium thiosulphate solution is added to

(a) oxidise iodide ion to iodine
(b) reduce iodine to iodide ion
(c) from a soluble blue complex
(d) induce the reaction rate

47. 100 mL of HCl + 35 mL of NaOH, colour of methyl orange in the solution will be

(a) red (b) yellow
(c) can't be predicted
(d) methyl orange is not suitable indicator

48. In the reaction of $KMnO_4$ with an oxalate in acidic medium, MnO_4^- is reduced to Mn^{2+} and $C_2O_4^{2-}$ is oxidised to CO_2. Hence, 50 mL of 0.04 M $KMnO_4$ is equivalent to

(a) 100 mL of 0.1 M $H_2C_2O_4$ (b) 50 mL of 0.2 M $H_2C_2O_4$
(c) 50 mL of 0.1 M $H_2C_2O_4$ (d) 25 mL of 0.1 $H_2C_2O_4$

49.

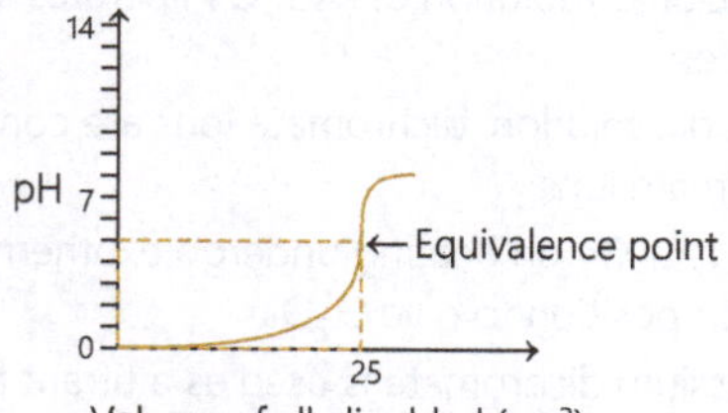

The graph represents titration curve for

(a) strong acid with strong base
(c) weak acid with strong base
(c) strong acid with weak base
(d) weak acid with weak base

50. Which is incorrect about primary standard?

(a) They are hygroscopic and deliquescent.
(b) They are stable in air.
(c) They exist in highly pure state.
(d) They readily dissolve in water.

51. While preparing $Fe(OH)_3$ sol, we should

(a) add $FeCl_3$ solution slowly into boiling water
(b) add boiling water slowly into $FeCl_3$ solution
(c) mix equal amounts of $FeCl_3$ solution and boiling water
(d) mix $FeCl_3$ with water and then boil the mixture.

52. Why is HCl not used to make the medium acidic in oxidation reaction of $KMnO_4$ in acidic medium?

(a) Both HCl and $KMnO_4$ act as oxidising agent
(b) $KMnO_4$ oxidises HCl into Cl_2 which is also an oxidising agent
(c) $KMnO_4$ is a weaker oxidising agent than HCl
(d) $KMnO_4$ acts as a reducing agent in the presence of HCl

53. 0.5 g mixture of $K_2Cr_2O_7$ and $KMnO_4$ was treated with excess of KI in acidic medium. I_2 liberated required 100 cm^3 of 0.15 N $Na_2S_2O_3$ solution for titration. The percentage amount of $K_2Cr_2O_7$ in the mixture is

(a) 85.36%
(b) 14.64%
(c) 58.63%
(d) 26.14%

54. Which of the following will oxidise 126 g of oxalic acid ($H_2C_2O_4 \cdot 2H_2O$) in acidic medium?

(a) 1/3 mole of $K_2Cr_2O_7$
(b) 2 mole of $K_2Cr_2O_7$
(c) 1/3 mole of $KMnO_4$
(d) 5/2 mole of $KMnO_4$

55. The titration of Mohr's salt *vs* $KMnO_4$ is an example of redox titration. In this titration, $KMnO_4$ oxidises only ferrous salt to the ferric salt (no effect on other ions) but we cannot use ferrous sulphate in place of Mohr's salt because

(a) it is less stable than Mohr's salt
(b) in air it is oxidised to ferric sulphate
(c) in air it loses water of crystallisation
(d) All of the above

56. Preparation of lyophobic sols by chemical method involves

(a) double decomposition
(b) oxidation and reduction
(c) hydrolysis
(d) All of the above

57. When $KMnO_4$ solution is added to oxalic acid solution, the decolourisation is slow in the beginning but becomes instantaneous after sometime because
(a) CO_2 is formed as the products
(b) reaction is exothermic
(c) MnO_4^- catalyses the reaction
(d) Mn^{2+} acts as auto-catalyst

58. 3.92 g of ferrous ammonium sulphate (Mohr's salt) react completely with 50 mL $\frac{N}{10}$ $KMnO_4$ solution. The percentage purity of the sample is
(a) 50 (b) 78.4 (c) 80 (d) 39.2

Inorganic Chemistry Related Principles

59. On the addition of a solution *A* to a strongly acidified solution of barium nitrate, a white precipitate was obtained which did not dissolve even after large addition of water.
Solution *A* contains
(a) sodium phosphate (b) sodium carbonate
(c) sodium sulphate (d) sodium chloride

60. Borax on heating strongly above its melting point melts to a liquid, which then solidifies to a transparent mass commonly known as borax-bead. The transparent glassy mass consists of
(a) sodium pyroborate (b) boric anhydride
(c) sodium metaborate
(d) boric anhydride and sodium metaborate

61. Formation of which complex, among the following, is not a confirmatory test of Pb^{2+} ions
(a) lead chromate (b) lead nitrate
(c) lead sulphate (d) lead iodide

62. Nitrite (NO_2^-) interferes in the 'ring-test' of nitrate (NO_3^-). Some of the following reagents can be used for the removal of nitrite.
I. NH_4Cl II. $(NH_2)_2CS$ (Thiourea)
III. NH_2SO_3H (Sulphamic acid)
IV. Sulphanilic acid
Correct choice is
(a) I, II (b) I, II, IV (c) I, II, III (d) I, III, IV

63. *X* is a colourless salt gives following reactions.

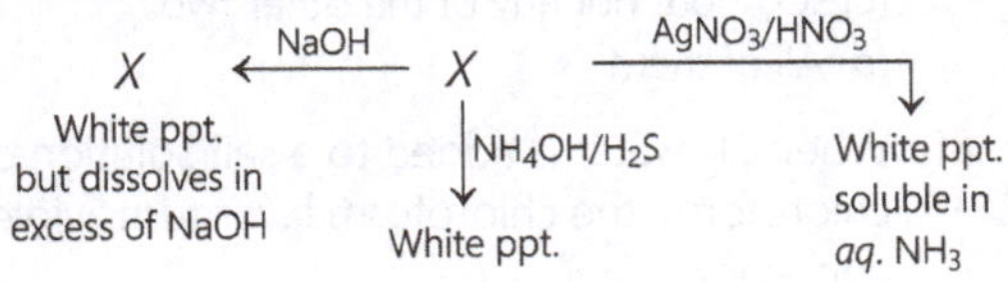

X can be
(a) $AlCl_3$ (b) $ZnCl_2$
(c) $Zn(CH_3COO)_2$ (d) $ZnBr_2$

64. In the detection of group II acid radicals, the salt containing chloride is treated with concentrated sulphuric acid, a colourless gas is liberated. The name of the gas is
(a) hydrogen chloride gas
(b) chlorine gas
(c) sulphur dioxide gas
(d) hydrogen gas

65. Microcosmic salt and borax are used in the identification of cations by dry tests. They are respectively
(a) $NaBO_2$ and $NaPO_3$
(b) $NaNH_4HPO_4 \cdot 4H_2O$ and $Na_2B_4O_7 \cdot 10H_2O$
(c) $NaPO_3$ and $NaBO_2$
(d) $Na_2B_4O_7$ and $NaNH_4HPO_4$

66. Which of the following compounds are partially soluble or insoluble in NH_4OH solution?
1. $Fe(OH)_3$ 2. Ag_2CrO_4
3. $Al(OH)_3$ 4. $Ni(OH)_2$
Correct choice is
(a) 1, 2 (b) 2, 3, 4
(c) 1, 3 (d) 2, 3

67. If NaOH is added to an aqueous solution of zinc ions, a white precipitate appears and on adding excess NaOH, the precipitate dissolves. In the solution, zinc exists in the
(a) cationic part
(b) anionic part
(c) both the cationic and anionic part
(d) None of the above

68. Black precipitate form in many metal ion solutions, then which anion is used as a precipitating agent?
(a) Cl^- (b) S^{2-} (c) PO_4^{3-} (d) CO_3^{2-}

69. Aqueous solution of a mixture contains Br^- and I^-. On passing Cl_2 gas and adding $CHCl_3$, then organic layer will be
(a) violet (b) reddish brown
(c) colourless (d) blue

70. A mixture contains Cu^{2+}, Al^{3+} and Co^{2+}. Following steps have been adopted but written in disorder :
I. Filter, boil off H_2S gas and add NH_4Cl, heat and add NH_4OH.
II. Filter, add NH_4OH and pass H_2S gas.
III. Pass H_2S gas into acidified solution of mixture.
Steps will be used in the following order.
(a) I, II and III (b) III, I and II
(c) III, II and I (d) I, III and II

71. A solution when diluted with H_2O and boiled, gives a white precipitate. On addition of excess NH_4Cl/NH_4OH, the volume of precipitate decreases leaving behind a white gelatinous precipitate. Identify the precipitate which dissolves in NH_4OH/NH_4Cl

(a) $Zn(OH)_2$ (b) $Al(OH)_3$
(c) $Mg(OH)_2$ (d) $Ca(OH)_2$

72. Na_2CO_3 cannot be used in place of $(NH_4)_2CO_3$ for the precipitation of V group because

(a) Na^+ interferes in the detection of V group
(b) conc. of CO_3^{2+} is very low
(c) Na will react with acid radicals
(d) Mg will be precipitated

73. A white sodium salt dissolves readily in water to give a solution which is neutral to litmus. When silver nitrate solution is added to the solution, a white precipitate is obtained which does not dissolve in dil. HNO_3. The anion could be

(a) CO_3^{2-} (b) Cl^- (c) SO_4^{2-} (d) S^{2-}

74. Consider the following observation:

$M^{n+} + HCl \longrightarrow$ white precipitate $\xrightarrow{\Delta}$ water soluble

The metal ion M^{n+} will be

(a) Hg^{2+} (b) Ag^+ (c) Pb^{2+} (d) Sn^{2+}

75. Which reagent can be used to identify nickel ion?

(a) Resorcinol (b) Dimethyl glyoxime
(c) Diphenyl benzidine (d) Potassium ferrocyanide

76. Upon treatment with ammoniacal H_2S, the metal ion solutions that precipitates as a sulphide is

(a) Fe (III) (b) Al (III)
(c) Mg (II) (d) Zn (II)

77. Which of the following anion is not tested with layer test?

(a) Bromide (b) Iodide (c) Chloride (d) Nitrite

78. An aqueous solution of a substance gives a white precipitate on treatment with dilute hydrochloric acid, which dissolves on heating. When hydrogen sulphide is passed through the hot acidic solution, a black precipitate is obtained. The substance is a

(a) Hg^{2+} salt (b) Cr^{2+} salt
(c) Ag^+ salt (d) Pb^{2+} salt

79. Dimethyl glyoxime and $NaHSO_3/NH_4CNS$ are used to distinguish and separate Cu^{2+} and Ni^{2+}. These are used in order

(a) HSO_3^-/CNS^- then DMG
(b) DMG then HSO_3^-/CNS^-
(c) at random
(d) given reagent are not suitable

80. The reagent NH_4Cl and NH_4OH will precipitate

(a) Ca^{2+} (b) Al^{3+}
(c) Mg^{2+} (d) Zn^{2+}

81. In the chromyl chloride test, the reagent used is

(a) K_2CrO_4 (b) CrO_3
(c) $K_2Cr_2O_7$ (d) $(NH_4)_2Cr_2O_7$

82. Alums can be represented by general formula $M_2SO_4 \cdot M_2'(SO_4)_3 \cdot 24\,H_2O$ in which

(a) M is bivalent metal and M' is trivalent metal
(b) M is trivalent metal and M' is monovalent metal
(c) M is monovalent metal and M' is trivalent metal
(d) M and M' both are bivalent metals

83. Copper sulphate solution, when added to an excess of ammonium hydroxide, forms a complex compound due to

(a) $[Cu(NH_3)_2]^{2+}$ (b) $[Cu(NH_3)_4]^{2+}$
(c) $[Cu(NH_3)_6]^{2+}$ (d) Cu^{2+}

84. On addition of conc. H_2SO_4 to a chloride salt, colourless fumes are evolved but in case of iodide salt, violet fumes come out. This is because

(a) H_2SO_4 reduces HI to I_2
(b) HI is of violet colour
(c) HI gets oxidised to I_2
(d) HI changes to HIO_3

85. $CuSO_4$ is decolourised on addition of KCN, the product is

(a) $[Cu(CN)_4]^{2-}$ (b) $[Cu(CN)_4]^{3-}$
(c) $Cu(CN)_2$ (d) CuCN

86. A gas X is passed through water to form a saturated solution. The aqueous solution on treatment with silver nitrate gives a white precipitate. The saturated aqueous solution also dissolves magnesium ribbon with evolution of a colourless gas Y. Identify X and Y.

(a) $X = CO_2, Y = Cl_2$ (b) $X = Cl_2, Y = CO_2$
(c) $X = Cl_2, Y = H_2$ (d) $X = H_2, Y = Cl_2$

87. When $BaCl_2$ is added to an aqueous salt solution, a white precipitate is obtained. The anion among CO_3^{2-}, SO_3^{2-} and SO_4^{2-} that was present in the solution can be

(a) CO_3^{2-} but not any of the other two
(b) SO_3^{2-} but not any of the other two
(c) SO_4^{2-} but not any of the other two
(d) All of them

88. When Cl_2 water is added to a salt solution containing chloroform, the chloroform layer turns violet. Salt contains

(a) Cl^- (b) I^-
(c) NO_3^- (d) S^{2-}

89. Unknown solution of salt 'A' $\xrightarrow{K_4[Fe(CN)_6]}$ chocolate ppt. is obtained. Which of the following radicals will be confirmed?

(a) Ni^{2+} (b) Cu^{2+}
(c) $4S_2SO_3^{2-}$ (d) SO_3^{2-}

90. Fe^{2+} ion can be distinguished from Fe^{3+} ion by

(a) NH_4SCN (b) $AgNO_3$
(c) $BaCl_2$ (d) $Al(OH)_3$

91. Sodium nitroprusside when added to an alkaline solution of sulphide ions produce a

(a) red colouration (b) blue colouration
(c) purple colouration (d) brown colouration

92. A suspension containing insoluble substances ZnS, CuS, HgS, Ag_2S, and FeS, is treated with 2N HCl. On filtering, the filtrate contained appreciable amounts of which one of the following groups?

(a) Zinc and mercury (b) Silver and iron
(c) Copper and mercury (d) Zinc, copper and iron

93. What would you observe if you add excess dil. NaOH solution to $ZnCl_2$ solution?

(a) A white ppt.
(b) A white ppt. which later dissolves
(c) A green ppt.
(d) A green ppt. which later dissolves

94. If Fe^{3+} and Cr^{3+} both are present in group III of qualitative analysis, then distinction can be made by

(a) addition of NH_4OH in the presence of NH_4Cl when only $Fe(OH)_3$ is precipitated.
(b) addition of NH_4OH in presence of NH_4Cl when $Cr(OH)_3$ and $Fe(OH)_3$ both are precipitated; on adding Br_2 water and NaOH, $Cr(OH)_3$, dissolves.
(c) precipitate of $Cr(OH)_3$ and $Fe(OH)_3$ as obtained in (b) are treated with conc. HCl when only $Fe(OH)_3$ dissolves
(d) Both (b) and (c)

95. Which of the following groups constitute basic radicals of fourth group?

(a) $Pb^{2+}, Hg^{2+}, Cd^{2+}$
(b) $Zn^{2+}, Mn^{2+}, Ni^{2+}$
(c) $Al^{3+}, Fe^{3+}, Cr^{3+}$
(d) $Ca^{2+}, Sr^{2+}, Ba^{2+}$

96. To get big sized crystals of Mohr's salt, the hot saturated solution is

(a) allowed to cool by keeping the container in ice
(b) cooled by keeping the container in ice cold water
(c) allowed to cool slowly in air
(d) allowed to cool by placing the container over the mouth of a beaker filled with water.

97. Which of the following cation is dissolved when H_2S is passed through it in the presence of dil. HCl?

(a) Cu^{2+} (b) Ni^{2+}
(c) Zn^{2+} (d) Mn^{2+}

98. $MgSO_4$ on reaction with NH_4OH and Na_2HPO_4 forms a white crystalline precipitate. What is its formula?

(a) $Mg(NH_4)PO_4$ (b) $Mg_3(PO_4)_2$
(c) $MgCl_2$, $MgSO_4$ (d) $MgSO_4$

99. Sometimes, yellow turbidity appears on passing H_2S gas even in the absence of group II radicals. This is because of

(a) sometimes group III radicals are precipitated as sulphates
(b) group IV radicals are precipitated as sulphides
(c) the oxidation of H_2S gas by some acid radicals
(d) group III radicals are precipitated as hydroxides.

100. The brown complex obtained in the detection of nitrate radical is formulated as $[Fe(H_2O)_5NO]SO_4$. What is the oxidation number of Fe in this complex?

(a) +1 (b) +2 (c) +3 (d) 0

Assertion-Reason Questions

Direction (Q. Nos. 1-9) *In the following question Assertion (A) followed by Reason (R) is given below. Choose the correct option out of the choices given below.*

(a) Both A and R are true and R is the correct explanation of A.
(b) Both A and R are true and R is not the correct explanation of A.
(c) A is false but R is true.
(d) A is true but R is false.

1 Assertion (A) Dispersion method is used for preparing lyophilic sols.

Reason (R) In this method, the coarse of aggregates break down into particles of colloidal size.

2 Assertion (A) Phenolic compounds give characteristic colour with neutral $FeCl_3$.

Reason (R) It is the property of all the enolic compounds.

3 **Assertion** (A) The compound acetaldehyde give positive iodoform and Tollen's tests.

Reason (R) The compound acetaldehyde contain —CHO group.

4 **Assertion** (A) 2-hydroxyphenyl acetic acid liberates CO_2 with $NaHCO_3$ and do not gives colour with neutral $FeCl_3$.

Reason (R) Liberation of CO_2 with $NaHCO_3$ indicates the presence of a —COOH group.

5 **Assertion** (A) Heat of neutralisation of acetic acid and sodium hydroxide is only 56 kJ.

Reason (R) Heat of neutralisation of a weak acid or weak base is less than 57.3 kJ.

6 **Assertion** (A) If a mixture contains chlorates, chromyl chloride test for chloride anion will not be performed.

Reason (R) Chlorates on reaction with dil. H_2SO_4 form chlorine dioxide which dissolves in H_2SO_4 and form highly explosive orange yellow solution.

7 **Assertion** (A) After adding thiosulphate ions and starch solution to the reaction mixture (iodide ions with hydrogen peroxide), then the iodine react with thiosulphate instantaneously and cannot colour starch blue.

Reason (R) The rate of reaction can be determined by measuring the time taken for appearance of blue colour with sodium thiosulphate solution.

8 **Assertion** (A) In Mohr's salt *vs* $KMnO_4$ titration, the active constituent of Mohr's salt is ferric sulphate which is oxidised by $KMnO_4$.

Reason (R) In this titration, sulphuric acid should be present in excess otherwise a brown precipitate will be formed.

9 **Assertion** (A) In the preparation of *p*-nitro acetanilide, temprature of reaction mixture should be maintained below 35°C.

Reason (R) In the preparation of *p*-nitro acetanilide, fuming HNO_3 in the presence of conc. H_2SO_4, gives nitronium ion (NO_2^+).

Statement Type Questions

Direction (Q. Nos. 1-5) *In the following questions, two statements (I & II) are given. In the light of the given statements, choose the correct option given below.*

(a) Both Statement I and Statement II are false.
(b) Statement I is true but Statement II is false.
(c) Statement I is false but Statement II is true.
(d) Both Statement I and Statement II are true.

1 **Statement I** The identification of Ni^{2+} is carried out by dimethyl glyoxime in the presence of NH_4OH.

Statement II The dimethyl glyoxime is a bidentate neutral ligand.

2 **Statement I** In Lassaigne's test, when both nitrogen and sulphur are present in an organic compound, sodium thiocyanate is formed.

Statement II If both nitrogen and sulphur are present in an organic compound, then the excess of sodium used in sodium fusion will decompose the sodium thiocyanate formed to give NaCN and Na_2S.

3 **Statement I** The Beilstein test for organic compounds is used to detect halogens.

Statement II It gives blue or green colour when heated over Cu wire loop with halogens.

4 **Statement I** Enthalpy of neutralisation of strong acid and strong base is measured using simple calorimeter.

Statement II Known volumes of standard solution of a base and alkali are mixed and change in temperature is recorded.

5 **Statement I** Lyophobic sols can be easily prepared by shaking.

Statement II Sols of silver halides are prepared by mixing dilute solution of silver salts with alkali halides in equivalent amounts.

6 Select the correct statements from the following.

I. Acetanilide prepared by direct acetylation aniline by using the mixture of equal volumes of acetic anhydride and acetic acid.

II. Nitronium ion attacks on acetanilide to form *p*-nitro acetanilide through the cyclopentadienyl anion.

III. *p*-amino azobenzene is an azo dye prepared from diazoamino benzene.

IV. The compounds containing only $-\overset{O}{\overset{\|}{C}}-CH_3$ group gives iodoform test.

V. Diazoaminobenzene is heated aniline and a little amount of HCl at about 40°C gives *p*-amino azobenzene or aniline.

Choose the correct answer from the options given below.

(a) I, III and V (b) II, IV and V
(c) III and IV (d) I and II

7 Select the correct statements from the following.

I. Add 2-3 drops of KI and starch solution in the test tube then a deep blue or violet colour appears which confirms the presence of NO_2^- anion.
II. When filter paper dipped in lead acetate over the mouth of test tube, filter paper turns green due to the formation of PbS which confirms the S^{2-} ion.
III. Take a glass rod dipped in NH_4OH near the mouth of test tube, white dense fumes of NH_4Cl evolved which confirms the Cl^- ion.
IV. If a mixture contains chlorates, chromyl chloride test for chloride anion should not be performed.
V. A paper dipped in starch solution on the mouth of test tube, paper turns blue which confirms the I^- ion.

Choose the correct answer from the options given below:

(a) I and II (b) I, III, IV and V
(c) II, IV and V (d) I, III and V

8 Select the incorrect statements form the following.

I. In oxalic acid *vs* $KMnO_4$ titration, the oxalic acid solution is heated with dilute. H_2SO_4 upto 50-60°C.
II. In oxalic acid *vs* $KMnO_4$ titration, oxalic acid is a reducing agent and $KMnO_4$ is a oxidising agent.
III. Oxalic acid *vs* $KMnO_4$ titration is carried out in the presence of conc. HNO_3.
IV. In oxalic acid *vs* $KMnO_4$ titration, $KMnO_4$ acts as self indicator for end point detection.
V. Oxalic acid *vs* $KMnO_4$ titration is an example of neutralisation reaction.

Choose the correct answer from the options given below.

(a) II, III and IV (b) II and V
(c) I, III and V (d) IV and V

9 Which of the following statement is correct regarding the determination of strength of aqueous NaOH solution? (**Note** Consider that an appropriate indicator is used.)

I. *Aq.* NaOH in a pipette and aqueous oxalic acid in a burette.
II. *Aq.* NaOH in a volumetric flask and concentrated H_2SO_4 in a conical flask.
III. *Aq.* NaOH in a burette and concentrated H_2SO_4 in a conical flask.
IV. *Aq.* NaOH in a burette and aqueous oxalic acid in a conical flask.

Choose the correct answer from the given options below.

(a) I and IV
(b) II and III
(c) Only IV
(d) Only III

10 Which statement is true with respect to nitrate ion test?

I. A dark brown ring is formed at the junction of two liquids.
II. Ring is formed due to nitroferrous sulphate complex.
III. The brown complex is $[Fe(H_2O)_5(NO)]SO_4$.
IV. Heating the nitrate salt with conc. H_2SO_4, light brown fumes are evolved.

Choose the correct answer from the given option below.

(a) I and IV (b) Only III
(c) Only II (d) I, III and IV

Matching Type Questions

1 Match the Column I with Column II.

	Column I (Cation in flame test)	Column II (Flame colour)
A.	Ba^{2+}	1. Crimson red
B.	Ca^{2+}	2. Apple green
C.	Sr^{2+}	3. Golden yellow
D.	Na^+	4. Brick red

Choose the correct answer from the options given below.

(a) A-1, B-2, C-3, D-4 (b) A-2, B-1, C-3, D-4
(c) A-1, B-3, C-4, D-2 (d) A-2, B-4, C-1, D-3

2. Match Column I with Column II.

Column I (Test / Reagents / Observation(s))	Column II (Species detected)
A. Lassaigne's test	1. Carbon
B. Cu(II) oxide	2. Sulphur
C. Silver nitrate	3. N, S, P, and halogen
D. The sodium fusion extract gives black precipitate with acetic acid and lead acetate	4. Halogen specifically

Choose the correct answer from the options given below.

(a) A-3, B-1, C-2, D-4 (b) A-1, B-4, C-3, D-2
(c) A-3, B-1, C-4, D-2 (d) A-1, B-2, C-4, D-3

3 Match the Column I with Column II.

Column I (Test method)		Column II (Reagent)	
A.	Carbylamine test	1.	CH_3COOH and conc. H_2SO_4
B.	Lucas test	2.	$CHCl_3$ and alc. KOH
C.	Ester test	3.	$C_6H_5SO_2Cl$/*Aq*. KOH
D.	Hinsberg's test	4.	Conc. HCl and $ZnCl_2$

Choose the correct answer from the option given below.

(a) A-2, B-4, C-1, D-3 (b) A-3, B-4, C-1, D-2
(c) A-2, B-1, C-4, D-3 (d) A-3, B-1,C-2, D-4

4 Match the Column I with Column II.

Column I (Metal ion)		Column II (Group in qualitative analysis)	
A.	Fe^{3+}	1.	Group-V
B.	Ca^{2+}	2.	Group-IV
C.	Zn^{2+}	3.	Group-II
D.	Cu^{2+}	4.	Group-III

Choose the correct answer from the options given below.

(a) A-3, B-4, C-2, D-1 (b) A-2, B-4, C-1, D-3
(c) A-4, B-3, C-2, D-1 (d) A-4, B-1, C-2, D-3

5 Match Column I with Column II.

Column I (Reagents used)	Column II (Compound with functional group detected)
A. Alkaline solution of copper sulphate and sodium citrate	1. 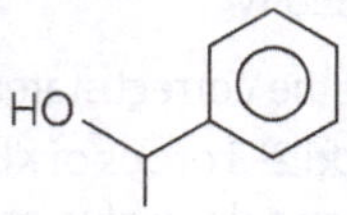
B. Neutral $FeCl_3$, solution	2. 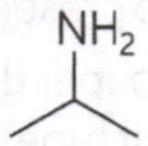
C. Alkaline chloroform solution	3. 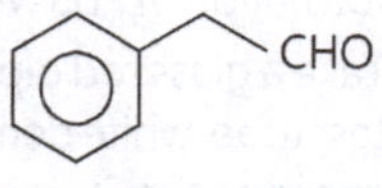
D. Potassium iodide and sodium hypochlorite	4. 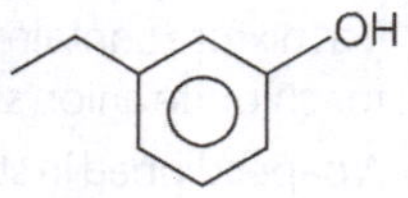

Choose the correct answer from the options given below:

(a) A-3, B-4, C-1, D-2
(b) A-2, B-4, C-3, D-1
(c) A-4, B-1, C-2, D-3
(d) A-3, B-4, C-2, D-1

Numerical Value Questions

1 The mass of NH_3 produced when 131.8 kg of cyclohexanecarbaldehyde undergoes Tollen's test is .... kg. (Nearest integer) Molar mass of C = 12 g/mol, N = 14 g/mol and O = 16 g/mol.

2 20 mL of calcium hydroxide was consumed when it was reacted with 10 mL of unknown solution of H_2SO_4. Also 20 mL standard solution of 0.5 M HCl containing 2 drops of phenolphthalein was titrated with calcium hydroxide, the mixture showed pink colour when burette displayed the value of 35.5 mL whereas the burette showed 25.5 mL initially. The concentration of H_2SO_4 is .... M. (Nearest integer)

3 10.0 mL of 0.05 M $KMnO_4$ solution was consumed in a titration with 10.0 mL of given oxalic acid dihydrate solution. The strength of given oxalic acid solution is .... $\times 10^{-2}$ g/L. (Nearest integer).

4 In the titration of $KMnO_4$ and oxalic acid in acidic medium, the change in oxidation number of carbon at the end point is ....

5 To an aqueous solution containing ions such as Al^{3+}, Zn^{2+}, Ca^{2+}, Fe^{3+}, Ni^{2+}, Ba^{2+} and Cu^{2+} conc. HCl, was added followed by H_2S. The total number of cations precipitated during this reaction is/are

Past Exams' Questions

NEET Archive

1. Given below are certain cations. Using inorganic qualitative analysis, arrange them in increasing group number from 0 to VI. **NEET 2024**

A. Al^{3+} B. Cu^{2+} C. Ba^{2+} D. Co^{2+} E. Mg^{2+}

Choose the correct answer from the options given below.

(a) B, A, D, C, E
(b) B, C, A, D, E
(c) E, C, D, B, A
(d) E, A, B, C, D

2. During the preparation of Mohr's salt solution (Ferrous ammonium sulphate), which of the following acid is added to prevent hydrolysis of Fe^{2+} ion? NEET 2024
(a) Dilute hydrochloric acid (b) Concentrated sulphuric acid
(c) Dilute nitric acid (d) Dilute sulphuric acid

3. Fehling's solution '*A*' is NEET 2024
(a) aqueous copper sulphate
(b) alkaline copper sulphate
(c) alkaline solution of sodium potassium tartrate (Rochelle's salt)
(d) aqueous sodium citrate

JEE Main Archive

4. Match List-I with List-II.

List-I (Test)	List-II (Observation)
A. Br_2 water test	I. Yellow orange or orange red precipitate formed
B. Ceric ammonium nitrate test	II. Reddish orange colour disappears
C. Ferric chloride test	III. Red colour appears
D 2, 4-DNP test	IV. Blue, green, violet or red colour appear

Choose the correct answer from the options given below. JEE Main 2024
(a) A-III, B-IV, C-I, D-II (b) A-I, B-II, C-III, D-IV
(c) A-II, B-III, C-IV, D-I (d) A-IV, B-I, C-II, D-III

5. Lassaigne's test is used for detection of JEE Main 2024
(a) nitrogen and sulphur only
(b) phosphorus and halogens only
(c) nitrogen, sulphur and phosphorus only
(d) nitrogen, sulphur, phosphorus and halogens

6. In the precipitation of the iron group (III) in qualitative analysis, ammonium chloride is added before adding ammonium hydroxide to JEE Main 2024
(a) increase concentration of Cl^- ions
(b) decrease concentration of OH^- ions
(c) increase concentration of NH_4^+ ions
(d) prevent interference by phosphate ions

7. When a solution of mixture having two inorganic salts was treated with freshly prepared ferrous sulphate in acidic medium, a dark brown ring was formed whereas on treatment with neutral $FeCl_3$, it gave deep red colour which disppeared on boiling and a brown red ppt was formed. The mixture contains JEE Main 2023
(a) CH_3COO^- and NO_3^- (b) $C_2O_4^{2-}$ and NO_3^-
(c) SO_3^{2-} and $C_2O_4^{2-}$ (d) SO_3^{2-} and CH_3COO^-

8. Compound that will give positive Lassaigne's test for both nitrogen and halogen is JEE Main 2023
(a) $NH_2OH \cdot HCl$ (b) NH_4Cl
(c) $N_2H_4 \cdot HCl$ (d) $CH_3NH_2 \cdot HCl$

9. Match List-I with List-II.

List-I (Element detected)	List-II (Reagent used/Product formed)
A. Nitrogen	I. $Na_2[Fe(CN)_5NO]$
B. Sulphur	II. $AgNO_3$
C. Phosphorus	III. $Fe_4[Fe(CN)_6]_3$
D. Halogen	IV. $(NH_4)_2MoO_4$

Choose the correct answer from the options given below. JEE Main 2023
(a) A-II, B-IV, C-I, D-III (b) A-III, B-I, C-IV, D-II
(c) A-IV, B-II, C-I, D-III (d) A-II, B-I, C-IV, D-III

10. In base *vs* acid titration, at the end point methyl orange is present as JEE Main 2022
(a) quinonoid form (b) heterocyclic form
(c) phenolic form (d) benzenoid form

11. Fe^{3+} cation gives a prussian blue precipitate on addition of potassium ferrocyanide solution due to the formation of JEE Main 2022
(a) $[Fe(H_2O)_6]_2[Fe(CN)_6]$ (b) $Fe_2[Fe(CN)_6]_2$
(c) $Fe_3[Fe(OH)_2(CN)_4]_2$ (d) $Fe_4[Fe(CN)_6]_3$

12. Given below are two statements.
One is labelled as Assertion (A) and the other is labelled as Reason (R).
Assertion (A) Phenolphthalein is a pH dependent indicator, remains colourless in acidic solution and gives pink colour in basic medium.
Reason (R) Phenolphthalein is a weak acid It doesn't dissociate in basic medium.
In the light of the above statements, choose the most appropriate answer from the options given below. JEE Main 2022
(a) Both A and R are true and R is the correct explanation of A.
(b) Both A and R are true but R is not the correct explanation of A.
(c) A is true but R is false.
(d) A is false but R is true.

13. Which statement is not true with respect to nitrate ion test? JEE Main 2022
(a) A dark brown ring is formed at the junction of two solutions.
(b) Ring is formed due to nitroferrous sulphate complex.

(c) The brown complex is $[Fe(H_2O)_5(NO)]SO_4$.
(d) Heating the nitrate salt with conc. H_2SO_4, light brown fumes are evolved.

14. A compound '*X*' is a weak acid and it exhibits colour change at pH close to the equivalence point during neutralisation of NaOH with CH_3COOH. Compound '*X*' exists in ionised form in basic medium. The compound '*X*' is **JEE Main 2022**
(a) methyl orange (b) methyl red
(c) phenolphthalein (d) eriochrome black T

15. Given below are two statements, one is labelled as Assertion (A) and the other is labelled as Reason (R).
Assertion (A) Permanganate titrations are not performed in presence of hydrochloric acid.
Reason (R) Chlorine is formed as a consequence of oxidation of hydrochloric acid.
In the light of the above statements, choose the correct answer from the options given below. **JEE Main 2022**
(a) Both (A) and (R) are true and (R) is the correct explanation of (A).
(b) Both (A) and (R) are true but (R) is not the correct explanation of (A).
(c) (A) is true but (R) is false.
(d) (A) is false but (R) is true.

16 The dark purple colour of $KMnO_4$ disappears in the titration with oxalic acid in acidic medium. The overall change in the oxidation number of manganese in the reaction is **JEE Main 2022**
(a) 5 (b) 1 (c) 7 (d) 2

17 Reagent 1-napthylamine and sulphanilic acid in acetic acid is used for the detection of **JEE Main 2021**
(a) N_2O (b) NO_2^- (c) NO_3^- (d) NO

18 Cu^{2+} salt reacts with potassium iodide to give **JEE Main 2021**
(a) Cu_2I_2 (b) CuI (c) $Cu(I_3)_2$ (d) Cu_2I_3

19 Which of the following compound is added to the sodium extract before addition of silver nitrate for testing of halogens? **JEE Main 2021**
(a) Hydrochloric acid (b) Sodium hydroxide
(c) Nitric acid (d) Ammonia

20 Which one of the following test used for the identification of functional groups in organic compounds does not use copper reagent? **JEE Main 2021**
(a) Barfoed's test
(b) Seliwanoff's test
(c) Benedict's test
(d) Biuret test for peptide bond

Skill Boosters

1 A white powder, solid '*A*' forms a light green solution with water, which on treatment with potassium hexacyanoferrate (III) gives a blue ppt. On being strongly heated, '*A*' leaves a brown residue and forms a mixture of two gaseous oxides, which turns a dichromate solution green and forms a white precipitate with a $BaCl_2$ solution containing concentrated HCl. *A* is
(a) $CuSO_4$ (b) $Fe_2(SO_4)_3$ (c) $FeSO_4$ (d) $Cr_2(SO_4)_3$

2 Rahul was asssigned a task by his teacher to detect extra elements in some unknown compounds. So, he took sodium to make sodium fusion extract. When he reacted sodium fusion extract with $FeSO_4$ a complex is formed then this complex is reacted with ferric salt and form a magnificant prussian blue colour. The name of the elements detected by this method and the complex by which prussian blue colour formed is
(a) nitrogen, sodium ferrocyanide
(b) sulphur, sodium thionitroprusside
(c) nitrogen, ferric ferrocyanide
(d) chlorine, ferric thiocyanate

3 Abhinav was given 2 mL of solutions *A* and *B* separately. He added aqueous solution of $NaHCO_3$ in both the solutions and then he treated both solutions with neutral ferric chloride solution. Some observations were taken and recorded in the given table.

Solutions	$NaHCO_3$	$FeCl_3$
A	No observation	Violet colour
B	Brisk effervescence	Red colour

The two solutions *A* and *B* are
(a) acetic acid and phenol (b) phenol and acetic acid
(c) formic acid and phenol (d) phenol and oxalic acid

4 In a volumetric redox titration of oxalic acid *vs* $KMnO_4$, dil. sulphuric acid is added to oxalic acid solution to make the solution acidic. The solution is titrated against $KMnO_4$ solution taken in burette till pink colour appears. But it is observed that the reaction is very slow and colour does not appear what change or step is used to make the reaction fast and how this change affect the titration?
(a) Adding more dil. H_2SO_4 to oxalic acid.
(b) Increase the concentration of $KMnO_4$.
(c) Oxalic acid is more in concentration than sulphuric acid and heat it.
(d) Heat the oxalic acid and sulphuric acid solution to 60°-70°C.

5 In a school practical, Ashutosh finds difficulty in identifying the radicals by salts. A observation table is given to him in which experiment and observations are given.

	Experiment	Observations
(a)	Dilute H_2SO_4 is added to hot filtrate and mixture is cooled.	White ppt. is obtained which is soluble in CH_3COONH_4 solution.
(b)	Add KSCN in the third part of blue solution (ppt. of sulphides in test tube and add HNO_3).	Black ppt. is obtained.
(c)	In soluble meta-aluminate add NH_4Cl and boil.	White gelatinous ppt. reappears.

On the basis of the observation table the radicals are
(a) $Cu^{2+}, Pb^{2+}, Al^{3+}$ (b) $Al^{3+}, Pb^{2+}, Ni^{2+}$
(c) $Zn^{2+}, Ni^{2+}, Al^{3+}$ (d) $Pb^{2+}, Cu^{2+}, Al^{3+}$

6 An inorganic compound '*X*' on treatment with concentrated H_2SO_4 produces brown fumes and gives dark brown ring. Compound '*X*' gives precipitate '*Y*' when its solution in dilute HCl is treated with H_2S gas. The ppt. '*Y*' on treatment with concentrated HNO_3 followed by excess of NH_4OH further gives deep blue coloured solution, compound (*X*) is
(a) $Pb(NO_3)_2$ (b) $Pb(NO_2)_2$ (c) $Cu(NO_3)_2$ (d) $Co(NO_3)_2$

7 A solution of *m*-chloroaniline, *m*-chlorophenol and *m*-chlorobenzoic acid in ethyl acetate was extracted initially with a saturated solution of $NaHCO_3$ to give fraction *A*. The left over organic phase was extracted with dilute NaOH solution to give fraction *B*. The final organic layer was labelled as fraction *C*. Fractions *A*, *B* and *C*, contain respectively.
(a) *m*-chlorobenzoic acid, *m*-chloroaniline and *m*-chlorophenol
(b) *m*-chlorobenzoic acid, *m*-chlorophenol and *m*-chloroaniline
(c) *m*-chlorophenol, *m*-chlorobenzoic acid and *m*-chloroaniline
(d) *m*-chloroaniline, *m*-chlorobenzoic acid and *m*-chlorophenol

8 A salt mixture is reacted with dil. HCl to form a white ppt. The precipitate is heated and filtered under hot conditions to give filtrate and residue. When filtrate is cooled it forms white needle like crystals whereas the residue is being reacted with excess of ammonia to give a clear solution. The cations present in the given salt mixture is
(a) Pb^{2+} and Hg^{2+} (b) Pb^{2+} and Hg_2^{2+}
(c) Pb^{2+} and Ag^{+} (d) Pb^{2+}, Hg_2^{2+} and Ag^{+}

Correct Codes

Topical Questions

1. (c)	2. (c)	3. (c)	4. (b)	5. (c)	6. (c)	7. (c)	8. (a)	9. (c)	10. (d)
11. (c)	12. (c)	13. (b)	14. (b)	15. (b)	16. (c)	17. (c)	18. (c)	19. (c)	20. (d)
21. (b)	22. (c)	23. (b)	24. (d)	25. (d)	26. (c)	27. (d)	28. (a)	29. (c)	30. (d)
31. (b)	32. (c)	33. (b)	34. (a)	35. (a)	36. (a)	37. (b)	38. (a)	39. (a)	40. (c)
41. (b)	42. (b)	43. (d)	44. (d)	45. (c)	46. (b)	47. (a)	48. (c)	49. (c)	50. (a)
51. (a)	52. (b)	53. (b)	54. (a)	55. (d)	56. (d)	57. (d)	58. (a)	59. (c)	60. (d)
61. (b)	62. (c)	63. (b)	64. (a)	65. (b)	66. (c)	67. (b)	68. (b)	69. (a)	70. (b)
71. (a)	72. (d)	73. (b)	74. (c)	75. (b)	76. (d)	77. (c)	78. (d)	79. (a)	80. (b)
81. (c)	82. (c)	83. (b)	84. (c)	85. (c)	86. (c)	87. (d)	88. (b)	89. (b)	90. (a)
91. (c)	92. (d)	93. (b)	94. (b)	95. (b)	96. (c)	97. (a)	98. (a)	99. (c)	100. (a)

Assertion-Reason

1. (c) 2. (a) 3. (d) 4. (c) 5. (b) 6. (d) 7. (d) 8. (c) 9. (c)

Statement Type

1. (d) 2. (d) 3. (d) 4. (b) 5. (c) 6. (a) 7. (b) 8. (c) 9. (c) 10. (d)

Matching Type

1. (d) 2. (c) 3. (a) 4. (d) 5. (d)

Numerical Value

1. (60) 2. (1) 3. (1575) 4. (1) 5. (1)

Past Exams'

1. (a)	2. (d)	3. (a)	4. (c)	5. (d)	6. (b)	7. (a)	8. (d)	9. (b)	10. (a)
11. (d)	12. (c)	13. (b)	14. (c)	15. (a)	16. (a)	17. (b)	18. (a)	19. (c)	20. (b)

Skill Boosters

1 (c) 2 (c) 3 (b) 4 (d) 5 (d) 6 (c) 7 (b) 8 (c)

Step by Step

Decoding the Questions

Concept Builders

1. sulphur
2. False
3. Secondary alcohol
4. 2,4-dinitrophenyl hydrazine
5. False
6. Sodium bicarbonate test
7. insoluble
8. True
9. Equivalence point
10. Pink
11. True
12. –57.3
13. Lyophilic
14. False
15. $[FeSO_4 \cdot (NH_4)_2SO_4 \cdot 6H_2O]$
16. endothermic, positive
17. Ba^{2+}
18. Green bead
19. False
20. True
21. chloride, II
22. silver bromide, ammonium hydroxide
23. True
24. dilute HCl
25. Lead chromate ($PbCrO_4$)
26. True
27. III
28. False
29. Na_2HPO_4
30. Sodium metaborate

Topical Solutions

1. (*c*) 2, 4-DNP test is used for the detection of aldehydes.

2. (*c*) The organic compounds containing sulphur when react with sodium metal give Na_2S.

   The Na_2S when react with lead acetate forms black ppt. of PbS.

   $$Na_2S + (CH_3COO)_2Pb \longrightarrow PbS + 2CH_3COONa$$

3. (*c*) Aniline cannot undergo direct nitration.

   Since, HNO_3 is a strong oxidising agent, it oxidises aniline to a black tarry matter.

4. (*b*) Compound '*X*' should be (b).

   Due to presence of $—COCH_3$ group, it gives iodoform test.

   Due to presence of 3° amine group, it does not undergo azo-dye test.

   On the other hand, presence of $PhCOCH_3$ group, it readily undergo 2, 4-DNP test.

5. (*c*)

6. (*c*) The compound which contains —CHO group, gives positive Tollen's test and the compound with $CH_3—\underset{\underset{O}{\|}}{C}—$ group gives positive iodoform test.

   Thus, the compound should be $CH_3—\underset{\underset{H}{|}}{C}{=}O$.

7. (*c*) *m*-cresol is the given organic compound that shows the given solubility profile. *m*-cresol on reaction with 10% NaOH forms 3-methyl sodium phenoxide ion.

8. (*a*) Lucas reagent (concentrated HCl + anhyd. $ZnCl_2$) is used to distinguish between 1°, 2° and 3° alcohols.

9. (*c*) S^{2-} and CN^- anions, if present may interfere by giving white ppt. of AgCN and black ppt. of Ag_2S with $AgNO_3$. Hence, before testing for halogens they are decomposed by concentrated HNO_3.

10. (*d*) Ferric ions generated during the process react with ferrocyanide to form Prussian blue precipitate of ferric ferrocyanide.

    $$6NaCN + FeSO_4 \longrightarrow \underset{\text{Sodium ferrocyanide}}{Na_4[Fe(CN)_6]} + Na_2SO_4$$

    $$Na_4[Fe(CN)_6] + Fe^{3+} \longrightarrow \underset{\text{Ferric ferrocyanide}}{Fe_4[Fe(CN)_6]_3}$$

11. (*c*) The nitration of aniline is difficult to carry out with nitrating mixture since $—NH_2$ group get oxidised which is not required. So, the amino group is first protected by acylation to form acetanilide which is then nitrated to give *p*-nitro acetanilide as a major product.

12. (*c*) Duma's method involved the determination of nitrogen content in the organic compound in the form of nitrogen (N_2).

13. (*b*) $\underset{(A)}{RNH_2} + CHCl_3 + 3KOH \longrightarrow RNC + 3KCl + 3H_2O$

    (where, *R* may be alkyl or aryl group)

    Thus, (*A*) is primary aromatic amine.

14. (*b*)

15. (*b*) Beilstein's test is used for chlorine.

16. (*c*)

17. (*c*)

18. (*c*) Zinc in reaction mixture prevents oxidation of aniline.

19. (*c*) 2° amines, i.e. diethylamine on reaction with nitrous acid give yellow coloured oil liquid of nitrosoamine which is insoluble in alkali.

20. (*d*) Benzoic acid gives buff coloured (pale dull yellow) precipitate while phenol gives green, blue or violet colour with neutral ferric chloride solution.

21. (*b*) Acetate ions gives deep red colour ppt on reaction with neutral $FeCl_3$ solution.

    $$6CH_3COO^- + 3Fe^{3+} + 2H_2O \longrightarrow [Fe_3(OH)_2(CH_3COO)_6]^+ + 2H^+$$

    $$[Fe_3(OH)_2(CH_3COO)_6] + 4H_2O \longrightarrow \underset{\text{(Brown red ppt.)}}{3[Fe(OH)_2(CH_3COO)]} + CH_3COOH + H^+$$

    When phenol reacts with freshly prepared ferric chloride solution and gives violet colour complex.

    $$6C_6H_5OH + FeCl_3 \longrightarrow \underset{\text{Violet colour}}{[Fe(C_6H_5O)_6]^{3-}} + 3HCl + 3H^+$$

22. (*c*) A compounds containing CH_3CHO or $H_3C—\overset{\overset{OH}{|}}{HC}—$ group give positive

iodoform test. The formation of iodoform CHI_3 depends on the presence of $-\overset{O}{\overset{\|}{C}}-CH_3$ group which undergoes iodination to $I_3C-C{=}O$ before producing CH_3I. HCHO does not meet any of this criteria as it does not contain $H_3C-\overset{|}{C}{=}O$ group.

23. (*b*) The compound liberates CO_2 with $NaHCO_3$, so it contains $-COOH$ group and it also gives colour with neutral $FeCl_3$ solution, so it also contains a $-OH$ group directly attached to the benzene ring (i.e. phenol). Hence, the structure of the compound is

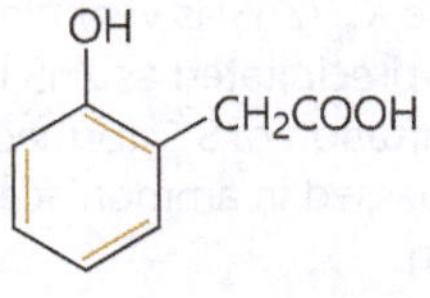

24. (*d*) **25.** (*d*)

26. (*c*) Presence of phenolic group can be confirmed by Liebermann's nitroso test.

27. (*d*) Carbolic acid (phenol) is weaker acid than the other given acids and hence, does not liberate CO_2 on treatment with *aq.* $NaHCO_3$ solution.

28. (*a*)

29. (*c*) Carbylamine test for $-NH_2$ group and Brady's reagent test for the keto group.

30. (*d*)

31. (*b*) Among the given test only Barfoed test cannot used for identifying amino acid, it is used to test the reducing nature of sugar.

32. (*c*)

33. (*b*) The graph that shows the correct change of pH of the titration mixture in the experiment is

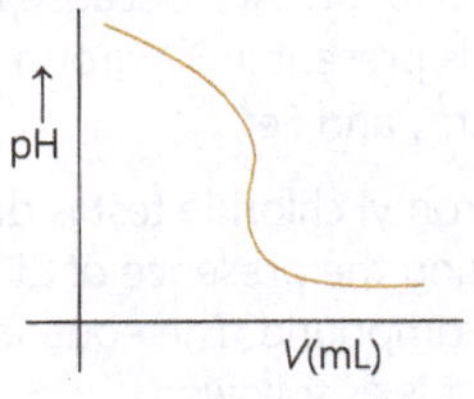

34. (*a*) **35.** (*a*)

36. (*a*) Phenolphthalein is colourless in acid solution (benzenoid form) and pink in alkali (basic) solution (quinonoid form).

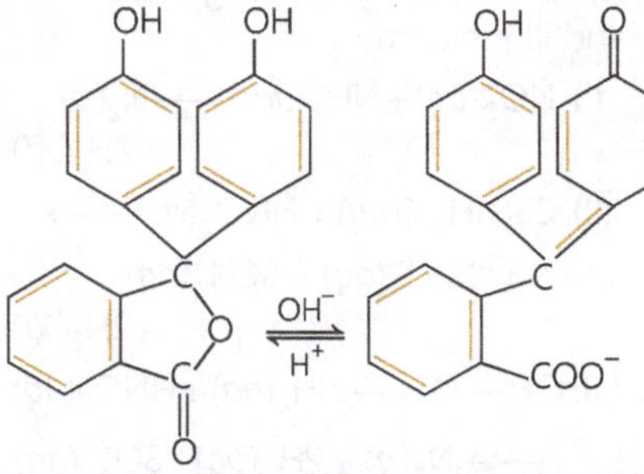

37. (*b*) Strong acid can be used to titrate both strong and weak bases.

38. (*a*)

39. (*a*) For standarising NaOH solution, oxalic acid is used as a primary standard.

40. (*c*) (i) $As_2O_3 + 3H_2S \longrightarrow As_2S_3 + 3H_2O$

(ii) $As_2O_3 + 3H_2O \longrightarrow 2H_3AsO_3$

$2H_3AsO_3 + 3H_2S \longrightarrow As_2S_3 + 6H_2O$

Thus, both reactions take place.

41. (*b*) Statement (b) is incorrect and its correct form is :

In basic or neutral solution, dichromate ions are converted to chromate ions, while in an acidic environment, it reduced to Cr^{3+} ion.

- $Cr_2O_7^{2-} \xrightarrow[\text{Or Neutral}]{OH^-} CrO_4^{2-}$
- $Cr_2O_7^{2-} \xrightarrow{H^+} Cr^{3+}$

42. (*b*) In the titration of oxalic acid *vs* $KMnO_4$, $KMnO_4$ acts as a oxidant as well as a self indicator.

43. (*d*) According to molarity equation

$$n_1 \times M_1 \times V_1 = n_2 \times M_2 \times V_2$$

where, n = change in oxidation number or valency factor $KMnO_4$ reacts with Mohr's salt as

$$MnO_4^- + 8H^+ + 5Fe^{2+} \longrightarrow 5Fe^{3+} + Mn^{2+} + 4H_2O$$

$$n_{KMnO_4} = 5, n_{\text{Mohr's salt}} = 1$$

Hence, $5 \times M_{KMnO_4} \times V_{KMnO_4} = M_{\text{Mohr's salt}} \times V_{\text{Mohr's salt}}$

44. (*d*) The number of moles of Mohr's salt required per mole of dichromate is six.

$$6Fe^{2+} + Cr_2O_7^{2-} + 14H^+ \longrightarrow 6Fe^{3+} + 2Cr^{3+} + 7H_2O$$

45. (*c*) In acid-base titration there is no use of bunsen burner and measuring cylinder.

46. (*b*) In the given experiment following reaction occurs.

$$H_2O_2 + 2I^- + 2H^+ \xrightarrow{\text{Slow}} 2H_2O + I_2$$

Iodine liberated in this reaction, reacts with sodium thiosulphate solution and is reduced to iodide ions.

$$I_2 + \underset{\text{Thiosulphate ion}}{2S_2O_3^{2-}} \xrightarrow{\text{Fast}} \underset{\text{Tetrathionate ion}}{S_4O_6^{2-}} + 2I^-$$

47. (*a*) When 100 mL HCl is added to 35 mL NaOH then 35 mL of HCl is utilised to neutralise NaOH while 65 mL HCl remains as such.

Hence, solution becomes acidic. In acidic solution, the colour of methyl orange is red.

48. (*c*) Equivalent mass of MnO_4^-

$$= \frac{\text{molar mass}}{7-2} = \frac{\text{molar mass}}{5}$$

Equivalent mass of $C_2O_4^{2-}$

$$= \frac{\text{molar mass}}{2(4-3)} = \frac{\text{molar mass}}{2}$$

Milliequivalent of $KMnO_4$

$$= 50 \times 5 \times 0.04 = 10$$

M. eq. of $H_2C_2O_4 = 50 \times 2 \times 0.1 = 10$

49. (*c*) Since, at equivalence point pH is less than 7 it must be the titration curve of strong acid with weak base.

50. (*a*)

51. (*a*) For preparing $Fe(OH)_3$ solution, $FeCl_3$ solution is added dropwise into boiling water.

52. (*b*) Because $KMnO_4$ oxidises HCl into Cl_2 which is also an oxidising agent.

53. (*b*) Let the amount of $K_2Cr_2O_7$ in the mixture be *x* g, then amount of $KMnO_4$ will be $(0.5 - x)$ g.

$$\therefore \left(\frac{x}{49} + \frac{0.5 - x}{31.6}\right) = \frac{100 \times 0.15}{1000}$$

where, 49 is Eq. wt. of $K_2Cr_2O_7$ and 31.6 is Eq. wt. of $KMnO_4$.

On solving we get $x = 0.0732$ g

$$\% \text{ of } K_2Cr_2O_7 = \frac{0.0732 \times 100}{0.5} = 14.64\%$$

54. (*a*) 126 g of oxalic acid = 1 mol of $H_2C_2O_4$

$$2MnO_4^- + 5C_2O_4^{2-} + 16H^+ \longrightarrow 2Mn^{2+} + 10CO_2 + 8H_2O$$

1 mole of oxalate ion require $= 2/5$ mol $KMnO_4$

$$Cr_2O_7^{2-} + 3C_2O_4^{2-} + 14H^+ \longrightarrow 2Cr^{3+} + 6CO_2 + 7H_2O$$

1 mole of oxalate ion require $= 1/3$ mol $K_2Cr_2O_7$.

55. (*d*) 56. (*d*)

57. (*d*) The reaction is proceed as

$$5C_2O_4^{2-} + \underset{\text{Purple}}{2MnO_4^-} + 16H^+ \longrightarrow \underset{\substack{\text{Colourless}\\ \text{(auto-catalyst)}}}{2Mn^{2+}} + 8H_2O + 10CO_2\uparrow$$

58. (*a*) Eq. of $KMnO_4$ used

$$= \frac{50 \times 1}{1000 \times 10} = 0.005$$

$\therefore$ Eq. of Mohr's salt reacted $= 0.005$

$\therefore$ Weight of Mohr's salt needed $= 0.005 \times 392 = 1.96$ g

Thus, percentage purity of Mohr's salt $= \frac{1.96}{3.92} \times 100 = 50\%$

59. (*c*) Strongly acidified solution of barium nitrate gives a white precipitate with sodium sulphate solution.

60. (*d*) The transparent glassy mass consists of boric anhydride and sodium metaborate.

$$Na_2B_4O_7 \cdot 10H_2O \xrightarrow[-10H_2O]{\Delta} Na_2B_4O_7 \xrightarrow{\Delta} \underbrace{\underset{\substack{\text{Sodium}\\ \text{metaborate}}}{2NaBO_2} + \underset{\substack{\text{Boron}\\ \text{oxide}}}{B_2O_3}}_{\text{Transparent bead}}$$

61. (*b*) $Pb[NO_3]_2$ (lead nitrate) is an alkali soluble colourless compound. Hence, formation of lead nitrate complex is not used as a confirmatory test.

62. (*c*) Among the given reagents I, II and III are correct.

(I) $NO_2^-(aq) + NH_4^+(aq) \longrightarrow N_2(g) + 2H_2O(l)$

(II) $CS(NH_2)_2(aq) + HNO_2(aq) \longrightarrow N_2(g) + H^+(aq) + SCN^-(aq) + 2H_2O(l)$

(III) $OH—OS_2—NH_2(aq) + HNO_2(aq) \longrightarrow N_2(g) + 2H^+(aq) + SO_4^{2-}(aq) + H_2O(l)$

63. (*b*) The colourless salt *X* is zinc chloride $ZnCl_2$.

64. (*a*) 65. (*b*) 66. (*c*)

67. (*b*) The reaction is represented as

$$Zn^{2+} + 2NaOH \longrightarrow \underset{\text{White ppt.}}{Zn(OH)_2} + 2Na^+$$

$$Zn(OH)_2 + 2NaOH \longrightarrow \underset{\text{(Soluble)}}{Na_2ZnO_2} + 2H_2O$$

68. (*b*) Metal ions of group IV cations as Co^{2+} and Ni^{2+} are precipitated as black coloured sulphides when H_2S gas is passed through their alkaline salt mixture solutions.

69. (*a*) When chlorine is added, it will displace bromine from bromide and iodine from iodide.

Also, bromine will displace iodine from iodide. The iodine will be present in the organic layer will appear violet.

$$Cl_2 + 2Br^- \longrightarrow 2Cl^- + Br_2$$

$$Cl_2 + 2I^- \longrightarrow 2Cl^- + I_2$$

$$Br_2 + 2I^- \longrightarrow 2Br^- + I_2$$

70. (*b*) As Cu^{2+} belongs to group II so we first pass H_2S into acidified solution of mixture and black ppt. of CuS forms.

Then as Al^{3+} belongs to III group so we filter, boil off H_2S gas and add NH_4Cl, heat and add NH_4OH, white ppt. of $Al(OH)_3$ forms.

After this we filter off ppt. and add NH_4OH and pass H_2S gas, Co^{2+} reacts with H_2S gas and black ppt. of CoS forms.

71. (*a*) The reaction is represented as

$$Zn^{2+} + 2H_2O \xrightarrow{\Delta} \underset{\text{White}}{Zn(OH)_2\downarrow} + 2H^+$$

$$Zn(OH)_2 + 4NH_4OH \xrightarrow{NH_4Cl} \underset{\substack{\text{Complex ion}\\ \text{(soluble)}}}{[Zn(NH_3)_4]^{2+}} + 4H_2O + 2OH^{\ominus}$$

72. (*d*) 73. (*b*) 74. (*c*)

75. (*b*) Dimethyl glyoxime reagent can be used to identify nickel ion.

76. (*d*) Group IV cations like Zn^{2+}, Mn^{2+}, Ni^{2+}, Co^{2+} are precipitated as sulphides . This is because K_{sp}(ZnS) is very high and Zn^{2+} is precipitated as ZnS by high concentration of S^{2-} formed when H_2S is passed in ammoniacal solution.

$$Zn(II) + \underset{\text{(Ammoniacal)}}{H_2S} \longrightarrow \underset{\text{White ppt.}}{ZnS} + 2H$$

77. (*c*) Chloride ion is not tested with layer test as it gives colourless layer hence cannot be identified.

78. (*d*) $PbCl_2$ is soluble in hot water but insoluble in cold water.

$$Pb^{2+} + 2HCl \xrightarrow{\Delta} PbCl_2 \xrightarrow{H_2S} PbS$$

79. (*a*) Dimethyl glyoxime and $NaHSO_3/NH_4CNS$ are used to distinguish and separate Cu^{2+} and Ni^{2+}. These are used in order HSO_3^-/CNS^- then DMG. Ni (II) ions form red ppt. with DMG whereas Cu(II) ions form black ppt. with $NaHSO_3/NH_4CNS$.

80. (*b*) NH_4Cl and NH_4OH precipitates basic radicals of 3rd group in qualitative analysis. Hydroxides of this group have very low value of solubility product. So, this reagent will precipitate Al^{3+} because the radicals present in 3rd group are Al^{3+}, Cr^{3+}, and Fe^{3+}.

81. (*c*) Chromyl chloride test is done for detecting the presence of Cl^- ions of ionic compound. The equation for the test is as follows

$$K_2Cr_2O_7 + 4Cl^- + 6H_2SO_4 \longrightarrow 2CrO_2Cl_2 + 2KHSO_4 + 4HSO_4^- + 3H_2O$$

82. (c)

83. (b) The given reaction is represented as

$$CuSO_4 + \text{excess. } NH_4OH \longrightarrow [Cu(NH_3)_4]SO_4 \text{ or } [Cu(NH_3)_4]^{2+} + 4H_2O$$

84. (c)

85. (c) $CuSO_4$ on addition with KCN. formed $Cu(CN)_2$.

$$CuSO_4 + 2KCN \longrightarrow K_2SO_4 + Cu(CN)_2$$

86. (c) X and Y is Cl_2 and H_2.

The reaction is proceed as

$$\underset{(X)}{Cl_2} + H_2O \longrightarrow HCl + HOCl$$

$$HCl + AgNO_3 \longrightarrow \underset{\text{(White)}}{AgCl} + HNO_3$$

$$2HCl + Mg \longrightarrow MgCl_2 + \underset{(Y)}{H_2(g)}\uparrow$$

87. (d) If CO_3^{2-}, SO_3^{2-} and SO_4^{2-} are present alongwith $BaCl_2$, these can also show white precipitate (as precipitate of all these are also white).

88. (b)

89. (b) The reaction is represented as

$$2Cu^{2+} + K_4[Fe(CN)_6] \longrightarrow \underset{\text{Chocolate ppt.}}{Cu_2[Fe(CN)_6]} + 4K^+$$

90. (a) The chemical compound can be distinguished by NH_4SCN as

$$Fe^{2+} + NH_4SCN \longrightarrow \text{No change in colour}$$

$$Fe^{3+} + NH_4SCN \longrightarrow \text{Red colouration}$$

91. (c) The reaction is proceed as

$$Na_2S + \underset{\text{(Sodium nitroprusside)}}{Na_2[Fe(NO)(CN)_5]} \longrightarrow \underset{\text{Violet coloured Complex}}{Na_3[Fe(ONSNa)(CN)_5]} \text{ or } \underset{\text{Purple colour complex}}{Na_4[Fe(CN)_5NOS]}$$

92. (d) ZnS, CuS and FeS are soluble in (2N) HCl solution. Hence, the filtrate contains zinc, copper and iron. On the other hand, HgS and Ag_2S are insoluble in 2N HCl solution. Hence, Hg and Ag are not present in the filtrate.

93. (b)

$$ZnCl_2 + 2NaOH \longrightarrow \underset{\text{(White ppt.)}}{Zn(OH)_2}\downarrow + 2NaCl$$

$$Zn(OH)_2 + \underset{\text{(Excess)}}{2NaOH} \longrightarrow \underset{\text{(Soluble)}}{Na_2ZnO_2} + 2H_2O$$

Zinc chloride reacts with sodium hydroxide to form white precipitate of zinc hydroxide. It is soluble in excess NaOH to form sodium zincate.

94. (b) If Fe^{3+} and Cr^{3+} both are present then very first solid ammonium chloride and ammonium hydroxide is added slowly till the solution smells of ammonia. Fe^{3+} and Cr^{3+} precipitates in the hydroxide form. For identification, precipitate is treated with NaOH and Br_2 water, yellow colouration confirms Cr^{+3} ion.

$$2NaOH + Br_2 \longrightarrow NaBrO + NaBr + H_2O$$

$$NaBrO \longrightarrow NaBr + [O]$$

$$2Cr(OH)_3 + 4NaOH + 3[O] \longrightarrow 2Na_2CrO_4 + 5H_2O$$

Solution is acidified and treated with lead acetate solution.

$$Na_2CrO_4 + Pb(CH_3COO)_2 \longrightarrow \underset{\text{(Yellow ppt.)}}{PbCrO_4} + 2CH_3COONa$$

95. (b) Zn^{2+}, Mn^{2+} and Ni^{2+} are basic radicals of IV group.

96. (c) In order to get big sized crystals of Mohr's salt the hot saturated solution is allowed to cool slowly in air.

97. (a) Cu^{2+} is a member of group II of basic radicals whereas Ni^{2+}, Zn^{2+} and Mn^{2+} are members of IV group basic radicals.

As only II group members are dissolved in H_2S in presence of dil. HCl, therefore only Cu^{2+} will be dissolved.

98. (a) $MgSO_4$ on reaction with NH_4OH and Na_2HPO_4 forms a white crystalline precipitate, i.e. $Mg(NH_4)PO_4$.

99. (c) The oxidation of H_2S gas by some acid radicals is presented as

$$H_2S \xrightarrow{[O]} H_2O + S\downarrow \text{(colloidal)}$$

100. (a) The oxidation number of Fe in this complex is +1.

Assertion-Reason

1. (c) A is false but R is true.

The correct form of R is :

Dispersion method is used to prepare lyophobic sols.

2. (a) Both A and R are true and R is the correct explanation of A.

3. (d) A is true but R is false.

The correct form of R is

Acetaldehyde contain —CHO group and $CH_3-\overset{O}{\overset{\|}{C}}-$ group that's why it show both positive Tollen's and iodoform tests respectively.

4. (c) A is false but R is true.

The correct form of A is :

2-hydroxyphenyl acetic acid liberates CO_2 with $NaHCO_3$ and also gives colour with neutral $FeCl_3$.

5. (b) Both A and R are true but R is not the correct explanation of A.

The correct explanation of A is :

Heat of neutralisation of acetic acid and sodium hydroxide is less than 57.3 kJ because of the incomplete ionisation of acetic acid.

6. (d) A is true but R is false.

The correct form of R is :

Chlorates on reaction with conc. H_2SO_4 form chlorine dioxide gas which dissolves in H_2SO_4 and form highly explosive orange yellow solution.

7. (d) A is true but R is false.

The correct form of R is :

The rate of reaction can be determine by measuring the time taken for appearance of blue colour with starch solution.

8. (c) A is false but R is true.

The correct form of Assertion is :

In Mohr's salt vs $KMnO_4$ titration, the active constituent of Mohr's salt is ferrous sulphate, which is oxidised to ferric sulphate by $KMnO_4$.

9. (*c*) A is false but R is true.

The correct form of A is :

In the preparation of *p*-nitroacetanilide, the temperature of reaction mixture should be maintained below 10°C.

Statement Type

1. (*d*) Both Statements I and Statement II are true.
2. (*d*) Both Statements I and Statement II are true.
3. (*d*) Both Statements I and Statement II are true.
4. (*b*) Statement I is true but Statement II is false. The correct form of Statement II is :

   Known volumes of standard solution of an acid and alkali are mixed and change in temperature is recorded.
5. (*c*) Statement I is false but Statement II is true. The correct form of Statement I is :

   Lyophobic sols are prepared by two methods namely condensation method and dispersion method.
6. (*a*) Among the given statements, only I, III and V are correct while the other statements II and IV are incorrect.

   Their correct form are

   II. Nitronium ion attacks on acetanilide to form *p*-nitro acetanilide through the sigma complexes.

   IV. The compounds contain $CH_3-\overset{\overset{\large O}{||}}{C}-$ and $CH_3-\underset{}{\overset{\overset{\large OH}{|}}{C}H}-$ group gives iodoform test.
7. (*b*) Among the given statements, Statements I, III, IV and V are correct while the statement II is incorrect.

   The correct form of II is :

   When filter paper dipped in lead acetate over the mouth of test tube, filter paper turns black due to the formation of PbS.
8. (*c*) Among the given statements, Statements I, III and V are incorrect while the statements I and IV are correct.

   The correct form of Statements I, III and V is

   I. In oxalic acid *vs* $KMnO_4$ titration, the oxalic acid solution is heated with dilute H_2SO_4 upto 70-80°C.

   III. Oxalic acid *vs* $KMnO_4$ titration is carried out in the presence of conc. H_2SO_4.

   V. Oxalic acid *vs* $KMnO_4$ titration is an example of redox reaction.
9. (*c*) The strength of NaOH measured by titrating against oxalic by taking NaOH in the burette (volumetric flask) and oxalic acid in the conical flask.
10. (*d*) Ring is formed due to ferrous nitroso sulphate complex.

Matching Type

1. (*d*) The correct match is A-2, B-4, C-1, D-3.
2. (*c*) The correct match is A-3, B-1, C-4, D-2.
3. (*a*) The correct match is A-2, B-4, C-1, D-3.
4. (*d*) The correct match is A-4, B-1, C-2, D-3.
5. (*d*) The correct match is A-3, B-4, C-2, D-1

   A. Alkaline solution of copper sulphate ($CuSO_4$) and sodium citrate is Benedict's solution which is used to test aliphatic aldehydes.

   Hence, it is used to test compound (3) i.e.

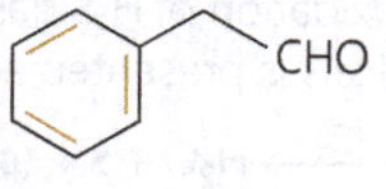

   B. Neutral $FeCl_3$ solution is used to test phenolic compound (4) i.e.,

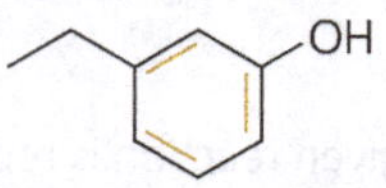

   red, green, purple or blue colouration.

   C. Alkaline chloroform solution is used to detect primary amines (2). i.e.

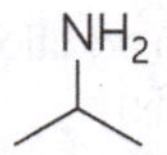

   It is also called isocyanide test.

   D. Potassium iodide (KI) and sodium hypochlorite (NaOCl) gives (I_2 + KOH) which is used to test compounds having

   $CH_3-\overset{\overset{\large O}{||}}{C}-$ or $CH_3-\overset{\overset{\large OH}{|}}{C}H-$

   group. This test is known as iodoform test.

   $$2KI + NaOCl + H_2O \longrightarrow NaCl + I_2 + 2KOH$$

   Hence, compound is (1)

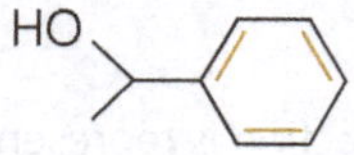

Numerical Value

1. (60)

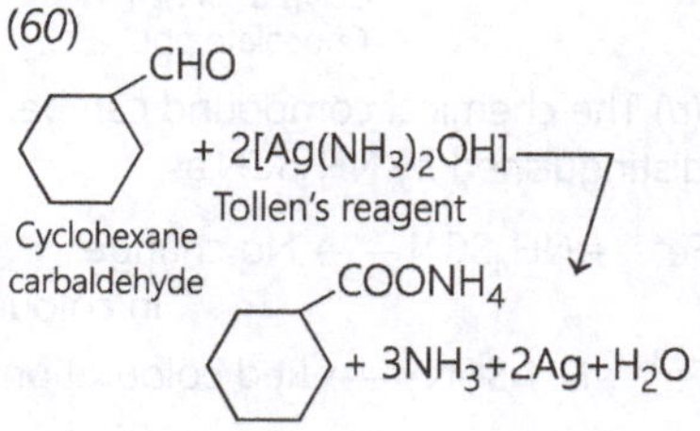

$$w_{NH_3} = \frac{131.8 \times 1000}{112} \times 3 \times 17$$

$$w_{NH_3} = 60 \text{ kg}$$

2. (7) When $Ca(OH)_2$ is titrated against standard solution of 0.5 M HCl, 20 mL volume

$$\therefore \quad n_{\text{Factor}} \times M_1V_1 = n_{\text{factor}} \times M_2V_2$$

$$2 \times M_1 \times 10 \text{ mL} = 1 \times 0.5 \times 20$$

(Since, from 25.5 mL to 35.5 mL, only 10 mL of calcium hydroxide is used)

$$\therefore \quad [M_1 = 0.5 \text{ M}]$$

Now, $Ca(OH)_2$ is titrated with 10 mL of H_2SO_4.

$\therefore \quad 2 \times 0.5 \times 20 = 2 \times M_2 \times 10$

$\therefore \quad [\underset{20\text{ mL}}{M_2} = 1\text{ M}]$

3. (1575) For titration using equation,

$N_1V_1 = N_2V_2$

or $a_1M_1V_1 = a_2M_2V_2$

$a_1 = 5, M_1 = 0.05\text{ M}, V_1 = 10.0\text{ mL},$

$a_2 = 2, M_2 = ?$

$V_2 = 10.0\text{ mL}$

$5 \times 0.05 \times 10 = 2 \times M_2 \times 10$

$M_2 = \frac{0.25}{2} = 0.125\text{ M} = 0.125\text{ mol/L}$

Strength of oxalic acid $= M_2 \times$ Molecular mass

$= 0.125 \times 126$

$= 15.75\text{ g/L or } 1575 \times 10^{-2}\text{ g/L}$

4. (7) $2KMnO_4 + 5H_2C_2O_4 + 3H_2SO_4 \longrightarrow K_2SO_4 + 2MnSO_4 + 10CO_2 + 8H_2O$

Oxdation state of C changes from +3 to +4.

So, at the end point the change in oxidation number of carbon is +1.

5. (1) Only Cu^{2+} get precipitated when HCl followed by H_2S was added. Al^{3+} and Fe^{3+} sulphides hydrolyse in water. Ni^{2+} and Zn^{2+} require basic medium with H_2S to form ppt. Ca^{2+} and Ba^{2+} sulphides are soluble. Hence, we will recieve ppt. of only CuS.

Past Exams'

1. (*a*)

Basic radical	Group number	
(B) Cu^{2+}	II	Group number increases ↓
(A) Al^{3+}	III	
(D) Co^{2+}	IV	
(C) Ba^{2+}	V	
(E) Mg^{2+}	VI	

Hence, the correct order is B, A, D, C, E.

2. (*d*) Dilute H_2SO_4 do not act as oxidising agent which prevent oxidation of Fe^{2+} into Fe^{3+} while concentrated H_2SO_4 will oxidise Fe^{2+} into Fe^{3+}.

3. (*a*) Fehling reagent comprises of two solutions.

Fehling *A* → Aqueous solution of $CuSO_4$.

Fehling *B* → Alkaline sodium potassium tartrate (Rochelle's salt).

4. (*c*) The correct match is

A-II, B-III, C-IV, D-I

- Br_2 water test is a test which is used for unsaturation, in which reddish orange colour of bromine water disappears.
- Alcohol give reddish colour with ceric ammonium nitrate.
- Phenol gives violet colour with natural ferric chloride.
- Aldehyde and ketone give yellow/orange/red colour compounds with 2, 4-DNP, i.e. 2, 4-dinitrophenyl hydrazine.

5. (*d*) Lassaigne's test is used for detection of nitrogen, sulphur, phosphorus and halogens.

6. (*b*) In the precipitation of the iron group (III) in qualitative analysis, NH_4Cl is added before NH_4OH to decrease the concentration of ^-OH ions

$$NH_4OH \rightleftharpoons NH_4^+ + OH^-$$

$$NH_4Cl \longrightarrow NH_4^+ + Cl^-$$

Here, due to presence of common ion, i.e. NH_4^+, the concentration of OH^- decreases in such a way that only group III cation can be precipitated due to their very low K_{sp}.

7. (*a*) According to the question,

$$CH_3COO^- + FeCl_3 \longrightarrow \underset{\text{Blood red colour}}{[Fe_3(OH)_2(CH_3COO)_6]^+}$$

$$\xrightarrow{\Delta} \underset{\text{Red-brown ppt.}}{Fe(OH)_2(CH_3COO)\downarrow}$$

$$2NO_3^- + 4H_2SO_4 + 6Fe^{2+} \longrightarrow 6Fe^{3+} + 2NO\uparrow + 4SO_4^{2-} + 4H_2O$$

$$[Fe(H_2O)_6]^{2+} + NO \longrightarrow \underset{\text{Brown}}{[Fe(H_2O)_5(NO)]^{2+}} + H_2O$$

Thus, the mixture contains CH_3COO^- and NO_3^-.

8. (*d*) Lassaigne's test for both nitrogen and halogen is given by the compound which have C, N as well as halogen atom in the compound. On fusing with Na, $CH_3NH_2 \cdot HCl$ give positive test for both nitrogen and halogen.

$$[CH_3NH_2 \cdot HCl \xrightarrow[\text{Fusion}]{\text{Na}} NaCN + NaCl]$$

NaCN gives positive test for nitrogen.

NaCl gives positive test for halogen (chlorine).

9. (*b*) The correct match is

A-III, B-I, C-IV, D-II.

10. (*a*) In titration, at the end point methyl orange is present as quinonoid form which is red in colour.

11. (*d*) $4Fe^{3+} + 3[Fe(CN)_6]^{4-} \longrightarrow \underset{\text{(Prussian blue in colour)}}{Fe_4[Fe(CN)_6]_3}$

12. (*c*) A is true but R is false.

The correct form of R is :

It dissociates in basic medium and forms conjugate base which is pink in colour.

$$\underset{\text{Colourless}}{HIn} + OH^- \rightleftharpoons \underset{\text{Pink}}{In^-} + H_2O$$

13. (*b*) It ring is formed due to $[Fe(H_2O)_5(NO)]SO_4$ complex ferrous nitrososulphate.

14. (*c*) Phenolphthalein is a weak acid that gives pink colour in basic medium due to formation of ions.

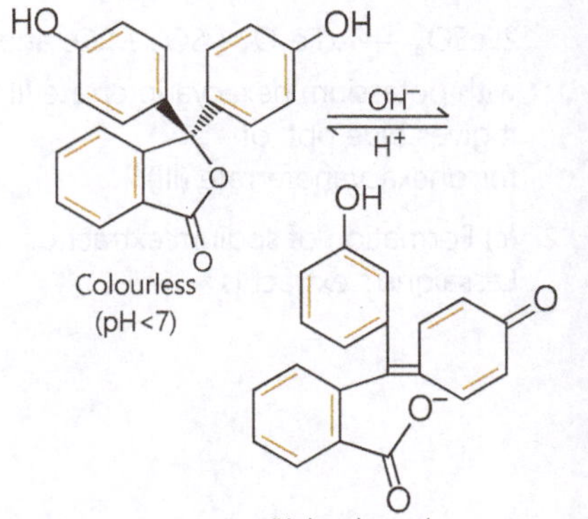

Colourless (pH<7)

Pink coloured (pH > 7)

15. (*a*) Both A and R are true and R is the correct explanation of A.

16. (*a*) $MnO_4^- + 8H^+ + 5e^- \longrightarrow Mn^{2+}$

Oxidation state of Mn changes from +7 to +2.

Therefore, change in oxidation number of manganese is 5.

17. (*b*) 1-naphthyl amine and sulphanilic acid is used for the detection of NO_2^- with the help of acetic acid.

18. (*a*) The reaction is represented as

$$2CuSO_4(aq) + 4KI(aq) \longrightarrow 2K_2SO_4(aq) + Cu_2I_2(s) + I_2$$

Thus, Cu^{2+} salts react with KI and form Cu_2I_2.

19. (*c*) Nitric acid is added to sodium extract before addition of silver nitrate for testing halogens.

Because it decomposes NaCN and Na_2S. So, they do not interfere in the test.

The reaction are as follows

$$NaCN + HNO_3 \longrightarrow NaNO_3 + HCN\uparrow$$

$$\underset{\text{Sodium extract}}{Na_2S} + \underset{\text{Nitric acid}}{2HNO_3} \longrightarrow NaNO_3 + H_2S\uparrow$$

20. (*b*) Seliwanoff's test which is used to distinguish between ketoses and aldoses.

The Seliwanoff's reagent contains resorcinol and HCl.

Skill Boosters

1. (*c*) The compound *A* is $FeSO_4$.

$$2FeSO_4 \xrightarrow{\Delta} Fe_2O_3 + SO_2 + SO_3$$ and with potassium hexacyanoferrate III it gives blue ppt. of ferrohexacyanoferrate (III).

2. (*c*) Formation of sodium extract or Lassaigne's extract is

$$Na + \underbrace{C + N}_{\text{From organic compound}} \xrightarrow{\text{Fusion}} NaCN$$

Unreacted sodium metal reacts with water to form NaOH and H_2.

$$2Na + 2H_2O \longrightarrow 2NaOH + H_2$$

Lassaigne's extract (NaCN and NaOH) react with $FeSO_4$ as follows

$$FeSO_4 + 2NaOH \longrightarrow Fe(OH)_2 + Na_2SO_4$$

$$Fe(OH)_2 + 6NaCN \longrightarrow \underset{\text{Sodium ferrocyanide}}{Na_4[Fe(CN)_6]} + 2NaOH$$

$$4Fe^{3+} + 3Na_4[Fe(CN)_6] \longrightarrow \underset{\text{Ferric ferrocyanide (Prussian blue)}}{Fe_4[Fe(CN)_6]_3} + 12Na^+$$

3. (*b*) (i) Phenol (C_6H_5OH) does not respond to $NaHCO_3$ test and gives violet colour with $FeCl_3$.

(ii) Acetic acid gives brisk effervescence with $NaHCO_3$ and red colour on treating with $FeCl_3$.

4. (*d*) The oxalic acid and sulphuric acid solution is heated to 60°-70° before titrating it with $KMnO_4$ because in cold, reaction is very slow due to slow formation of Mn^{2+}, when the solution is heated liberation of Mn^{2+} speeds up which auto catalyses the reaction.

Mn^{2+} catalysis the redox titration reaction.

5. (*d*) In the basis of observation table, the radicals are basic radicals Pb^{2+}, Cu^{2+} and Al^{3+}.

6. (*c*) On the given observation

$$\underset{\substack{\text{(Anion)}\\(X)}}{NO_3^-} + \underset{\text{(Conc.)}}{H_2SO_4} \longrightarrow \underset{\text{(Brown gas)}}{NO_2\uparrow} + H_2O$$

$$FeSO_4 + \underset{\text{(Conc.)}}{H_2SO_4} + NO_3^- \longrightarrow \underset{\text{(Dark brown ring)}}{[Fe(H_2O_5)(NO)]SO_4}$$

$$Cu^{2+} + \text{Dil. } HCl + H_2S \longrightarrow \underset{\substack{\text{Black ppt}\\(Y)}}{CuS\downarrow}.$$

$$CuS \xrightarrow[\text{HNO}_3]{\text{Conc.}} \underset{(X)}{Cu(NO_3)_2} + NO_2 + S + H_2O$$

$$\xrightarrow[\text{NH}_4\text{OH}]{\text{Excess}} \underset{\text{Deep blue}}{[Cu(NH_3)_4]^{2+}}$$

So, the compound *X* is $Cu(NO_3)_2$.

7. (*b*) Among *m*-chloroaniline, *m*-chlorophenol and *m*-chlorobenzoic acid, only *m*-chlorobenzoic acid will react with $NaHCO_3$.

∴ Fraction of A is *m*-chlorobenzoic acid.

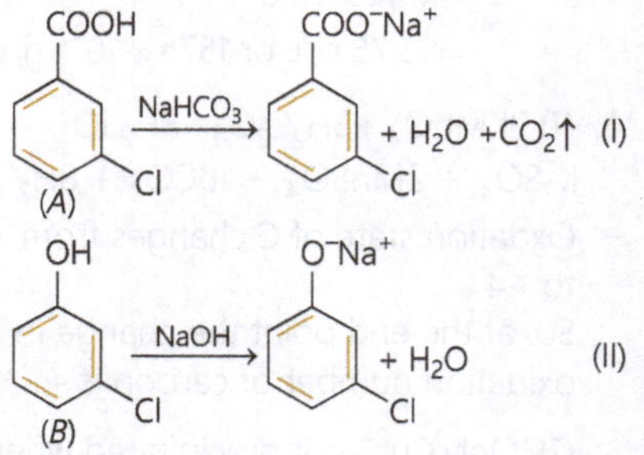

Hence, *A*, *B* and *C* are *m*-chlorobenzoic acid, *m*-chlorophenol and *m*-chloroaniline.

8. (*c*) $\underset{\text{Salt mixture}}{Pb^{2+}, Ag^+} \xrightarrow{\text{Dil. HCl}} \underset{\text{White ppt.}}{AgCl, PbCl_2}$

White ppt.

↓ Heated with distilled water and filter in hot condition.

AgCl (Residue) → Excess NH_3 solution → $[Ag(NH_3)_2]^+$ (Clear solution)

$PbCl_2$ (Filtrate) → Cooled → $PbCl_2$ (White needle like crystals)

The salt mixture contains Pb^{2+} and Ag^+.

Chapter at a Glance
[Chapters 1-12]

Solutions (Chapter at a Glance)

Expressing Concentration of Solutions

Name	Symbol	Formula	Effect of temperature
Mass percentage	%(w/w)	$\frac{\text{Mass of solute}}{\text{Total mass of solution}} \times 100$	No effect
Mass by volume percentage	%(w/V)	$\frac{\text{Mass of solute}}{\text{Total mass of solution in mL}} \times 100$	Changes with change in temperature
Volume percentage	%(V/V)	$\frac{\text{Volume of solute}}{\text{Total volume of solution in mL}} \times 100$	Changes with change in temperature
Strength	g/L (or g/dm^3)	$\frac{\text{Mass of solute in grams}}{\text{Volume of solution in L or dm}^3}$	Changes with change in temperature
Parts per million	ppm	$\frac{\text{No. of parts of solute}}{\text{Total no. of parts of all components of solution}} \times 10^6$	No effect
Mole fraction	χ	$x_A = \frac{n_A}{n_A + n_B}$	No effect
Molarity	M	$\frac{\text{Moles of solute}}{\text{Volume of solution in L or dm}^3}$	Changes with change in temperature
Molality	m	$\frac{\text{Mole of solute}}{\text{Mass of solvent in kg}}$	No effect

Types

I. Based on physical state

- **Solid**
  - Gas – Solid → O_2 in Pd
  - Liquid – Solid → Amalgam of Hg with Na
  - Solid – Solid → Cu dissolved in gold
- **Liquid**
  - Gas – Liquid → O_2 dissolved in water
  - Liquid – Liquid → Ethanol dissolved in water
  - Solid – Liquid → Glucose dissolved in water
- **Gaseous**
  - Gas – Gas → Mixture of O_2 and N_2
  - Liquid – Gas → Chloroform with N_2
  - Solid – Gas → Camphor in N_2

II. Based on concentration

- Dilute solutions
- Concentrated solutions
- Saturated solutions
- Supersaturated solutions

Solid in Liquid

- **Effect of nature of solute and solvent** Like dissolves like, i.e polar in polar and non-polar in non-polar.
- **Effect of temperature** (Follow Le-Chateliers principle)
  Endothermic process ($\Delta H > 0$): Solubility increases with temperature.
  Exothermic process ($\Delta H < 0$) : Solubility decreases with temperature
- **Effect of pressure** It does not have any significant effect on solubility of solids in liquids. It is so because solids and liquids are highly incompressible and practically remain unaffected by changes in pressure

Solubility

It is the maximum amount of solute that can be dissolved in a solvent at a specified temperature.
It depends upon

- Nature of solvent
- Pressure
- Nature of solute
- Temperature

Gas in Liquid

- Solubility increases with decrease in temperature.
- **Effect of pressure**
  Henry law states that the partial pressure of gas in vapour phase is directly proportional to the mole fraction of gas in solution, i.e. $p = K_H x$

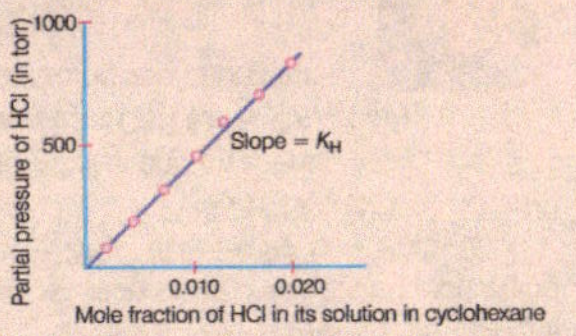

Higher the value of K_H at a particular temperature, the lower is the solubility of the gas in liquid.

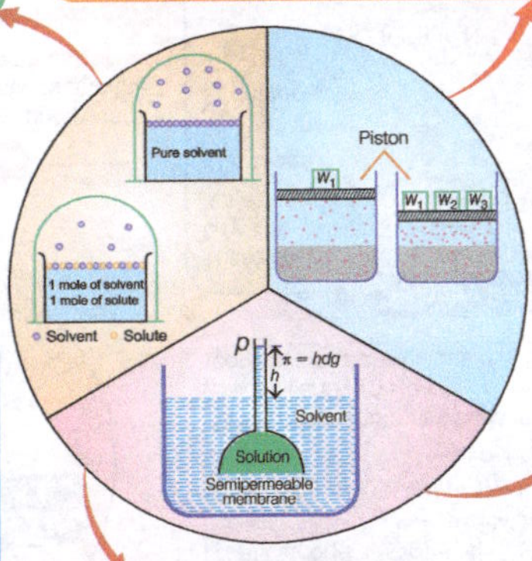

Vapour pressure

The pressure (maximum) exerted by the vapours above the liquid surface in equilibrium with the liquid in a closed system at a given temperature.

$$\text{V.P} \propto \text{Temperature} \propto \frac{1}{\text{Intermolecular forces}} \propto \frac{1}{\text{Boiling point}}$$

Ideal Solutions

A-B interaction are of same magnitude as A-A and B-B interactions, i.e. follow Raoult's law.

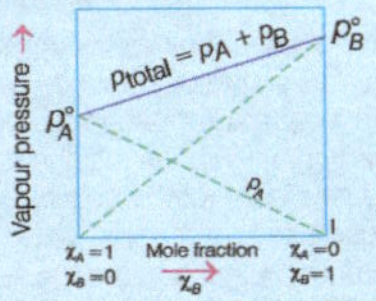

Raoult's Law

This law states that, at a given temperature, for a solution of volatile liquids the partial pressure of each component of the solution is directly proportional to its mole fraction present in solution.

$p_{solution} \propto \chi_{solvent}$

or $p_{solution} = p^\circ_{solvent} \chi_{solvent}$

Raoult's law is a special case of Henry law in which the value of K_H become equal to p_i

Dalton's law

According to Dalton's law of partial pressure, the total pressure (p_{total}) over the solution phase in the container will be the sum of the partial pressure of the components of the solution and is given as:

$p_{total} = p_1 + p_2$

$p_{total} = p_1^\circ \chi_1 + p_2^\circ \chi_2$

Non-Ideal Solutions

A-B interactions are of different magnitude than A-A and B-B interaction, $\Delta V_{mix} \neq 0$ and $\Delta H_{mix} \neq 0$

- **Non-ideal solutions showing +ve deviation:**
  A-B interaction are weaker than A-A and B-B interactins
  $\Delta V_{mix} = +ve$, $\Delta H_{mix} = +ve$ and resulting vapour pressure is higher than that expected. e.g. acetone + benzene
- **Non-ideal solutions showing –ve deviation:**
  A-B interaction are stonger than A-A and B-B interactins
  $\Delta V_{mix} = -ve$, $\Delta H_{mix} = -ve$ and resulting vapour pressure is lower than that expected. e.g. acetone + aniline

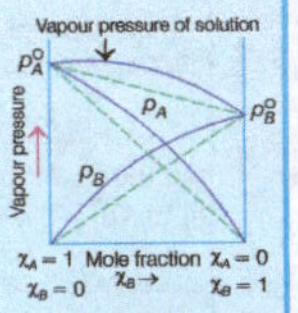

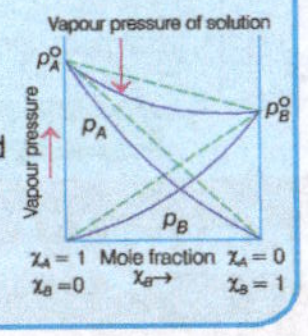

Azeotropes

The mixtures of liquids which boil at constant temperature like a pure liquid and possess same composition of components in liquid as well as vapour phase are called constant boiling mixtures or azeotropic mixtures.

- **Minimum boiling azeotropes**
  They are formed by those liquid pairs which show positive deviations form ideal behaviour. e.g. Ethanol-water mixture.
- **Maximum boiling azeotropes**
  They are formed by those liquid pairs which show negative deviations form ideal behaviour. e.g Nitric acid-water mixture.

Abnormal Molar Mass

When the molecular mass of a substance determined by any of the colligative properties comes out to be different than the expected value. The substance is said to show abnormal molecular mass.

van't Hoff factor (i)

It is defined as the ratio of the experimental value of the colligative property to the calculated value of the colligative property.

$$i = \frac{\text{Normal (calculated) molar mass}}{\text{Obseved/abnormal molar mass}}$$

$$= \frac{\text{Observed colligative property}}{\text{Calculated colligative property}}$$

- In association, observed molar mass has more than that of normal, so i has a value less than one ($i<1$).
- In dissociation, observed molar mass has lesser value than normal, so i is more than one ($i>1$) .
- Modified colligative properties are

$$\frac{p^\circ - p_s}{p^\circ} = i\chi_2, \ \Delta T_b = i K_b m, \ \Delta T_f = i K_f m$$

$$\pi = i\,CRT$$

Colligative Properties

Properties of solutions that are affected by concentration (no. of particles) and not by the properties (size or mass) of solution.

Colligative property $\propto \frac{1}{\text{molar mass}}$

- **Relative Lowering in Vapour Pressure**
  The relative lowering in vapour pressure of an ideal solution containing the non-volatile solute is equal to the mole fraction of the solute at a given temperature.
  It is given by formula $= \frac{p^\circ - p}{p^\circ} = x_2$
  Non - volatile (high B.P.) solute, lowers the V.P. of solvent, by decreasing the rate of evaporation of solvent.

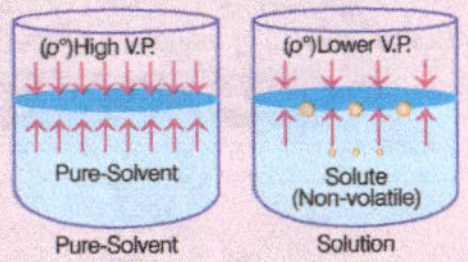

- **Depression in Freezing Point**
  When a non-volatile solute is added to a solvent, the freezing point of the solution is always lower than that of pure solvent as the vapour pressure of the solvent decreases in the presence of non-volatile solute. This difference in freezing point is known as depression of freezing point.

$$\Delta T_f = \frac{K_f \times w_2 \times 1000}{M_2 \times w_1}$$

- **Elevation in Boiling Point**
  When a non - volatile solute is added to a solvent, the boiling point of the solution is always higher than that of pure solvent. e.g. A solution of 1 mole of sucrose in 1000 g of water boils at 373.52 K at 1 atm pressure. This difference in the boiling points of the solution (T_b) and pure solvent (T_b°) is called the elevation of boiling point (ΔT_b) .

$$\Delta T_b = \frac{K_b \times 1000 \times w_2}{M_2 \times w_1}$$

- **Osmosis and Osmotic Pressure**
  Osmosis The phenomenon of the flows of solvent through a semipermeable membrane from pure solvent to the solution is known as osmosis.
  Reverse Osmosis The process of movement of solvent through a semipermeable membrane from the solution to the pure solvent by applying excess pressure on the solution side.
  Osmotic Pressure (π) The osmotic pressure of a solution is the excess pressure that must be applied to a solution to prevent osmosis, i.e. to stop the passage of solvent molecules through a semipermeable membrane into the solution.

$$\pi = CRT = \frac{n}{V}RT$$

Electrochemistry (Chapter at a Glance)

Terms Related with Electrochemical Cell

- **Electrode potential** A potential difference develops between the electrode and the electrolyte due to charge on metal.
- **Standard electrode potential** Electrode potential when concentration of all species in half-cell is unity.
- **Cell potential or EMF of cell** Electromotive force (EMF) is the potential difference, when no current is drawn from the system. It is measured in volts (V).
  $E^\circ_{cell} = E^\circ_{cathode} - E^\circ_{anode}$ or $E^\circ_{right} - E^\circ_{left}$
- **Standard hydrogen electrode** It is a reference electrode against which the electrode potentials of all electrodes are measured.

Nernst Equation

For the reaction, $M^{n+} + ne^- \longrightarrow M$

$E = E^\circ - \frac{RT}{nF} \ln \frac{M}{[M^{n+}]}$ or $E = E^\circ - \frac{RT}{nF} \ln \frac{1}{[M^{n+}]}$

[For pure solids, [M] = 1] or $E = E^\circ - \frac{0.0591}{n} \log \frac{1}{[M^{n+}]}$ at 298 K.

At equilibrium, $E_{cell} = 0$

$E^\circ_{cell} = \frac{0.0591}{n} \log K_c$

For concentration cells, $E^\circ_{cell} = 0$

$E_{cell} = \frac{0.0591}{n} \log \frac{C_2}{C_1}$ where, $C_2 > C_1$

For hydrogen cell, $E = E^\circ - 0.0591 \log [H^+]$

Conductance of Electrolytic Solution

Property	Formula	Units	Definition	Effect of dilution
Conductance (G)	$\frac{1}{R} = \frac{A}{\rho l} = \frac{\kappa A}{l}$	ohm^{-1} = (S)Simens	Reciprocal of resistance	Increases as larger number of ions are produced
Specific conductance (κ)	$\frac{l}{\rho} = G\frac{l}{A}$	$ohm^{-1}\,cm^{-1}$ = Sm^{-1}	Conductance of 1 cm^3 of the conductor	Decreases as number of ions per cm^3 decrease.
Equivalent conductivity (Λ_{eq})	$\kappa \times V = \kappa \frac{1000}{N}$ N = Normality	$\Omega^{-1}\,cm^2\,eq^{-1}$ = $Sm^2\,eq^{-1}$	Conductance of a solution containing 1g equivalent of an electrolyte dissolved in V cm^3 of the solution.	Increases with dilution due to large increase in volume.
Molar conductivity (Λ_m)	$\kappa V = \kappa \times \frac{1000}{M}$	$\Omega^{-1}\,cm^2\,mol^{-1}$ = $Sm^2\,mol^{-1}$	It is conductance of that volume of solution containing one mole of electrolyte.	Increases with dilution due to large increase in volume.

Electrochemical Cells

The most common electrochemical cell is a galvanic cell or a voltaic cell.

- **Galvanic cell** It is an electrochemical cell that converts the chemical energy of a spontaneous redox reaction into electrical energy. Here, the Gibbs energy of the spontaneous redox reaction is converted into electrical work. An example of this type of device is Daniell cell, in which the following reaction occurs:

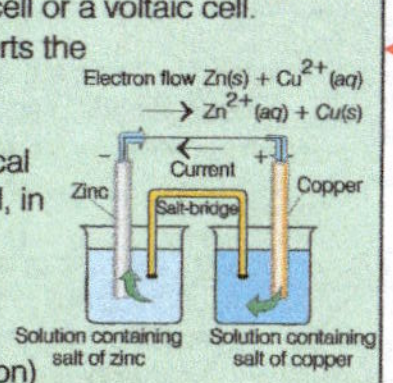

At cathode,

$Zn\,(s) + Cu^{2+}\,(aq) \longrightarrow Zn^{2+}\,(aq) + Cu\,(s)$

$Cu^{2+} + 2e^- \longrightarrow Cu\,(s)$ (reduction half-reaction)

At anode, $Zn\,(s) \longrightarrow Zn^{2+} + 2e^-$ (oxidation half-reaction)

- **Cell representation** Anode | Cathode

$Zn|Zn^{2+}\,||\,Cu^{2+}|Cu$

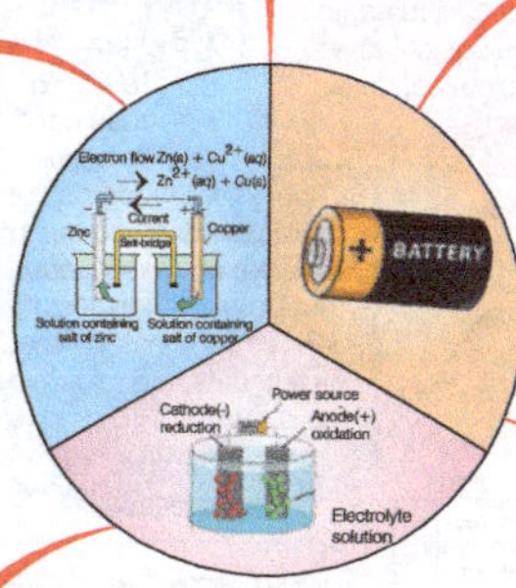

Electrochemical Series

A series of half-cells arranged in increasing order of standard electrode potential.

$\longrightarrow$ Increasing strength of oxidising agent.

$Li^+ < K^+ < Ca^{2+} < Na^+ < Mg^{2+} < Al^{3+} < H_2O < Zn^{2+} < Fe^{2+} < Ni^{2+} < Sn^{2+} < Pb^{2+} < H^+ < Cu^{2+} < Cu^+ < Ag^+ < Hg^{2+} < Br_2 < Cl_2 < O_2 < Au^{3+} < Co^{3+} < F_2$

$\longleftarrow$ Increasing strength of reducing agent.

- Positive E° means the redox couple is a weaker reducing agent than H^+/H_2.
- Negative E° means the redox couple is stronger reducing agent than H^+/H_2.

This series helps in comparing the relative oxidising and reducing power, relative activities of metals and to predict spontanity of the redox reactions.

Faraday's Law of Electrolysis

- **Faraday's first law** it states that the amount of chemical reaction occurring at any electrode by passing current is directly proportional to the quantity of electricity passed through the electrolyte.

$W = Zit$ where, $Z = \frac{\text{Equivalent wt. of element}}{96500}$

- **Faraday's second law** When the same quantity of electricity is passed through different electrolytes the amount of different substances formed are directly proportional to their chemical equivalent weights.

$\frac{w_1}{E_1} = \frac{w_2}{E_2} = \frac{w_3}{E_3}$

Electrolytic Cells and Electrolysis

- **Electrolytic cells** are those cells in which electrical energy is used to carry out non-spontaneous chemical reactions and the reactions takes place in an electrolytic cell is called **electrolysis**.

- Cathode is –ve electrode. - Anode is + ve electrode.

Products of Electrolysis

Electrolyte	Reactions involved		Products	
	At cathode	At anode	Cathode	Anode
Molten NaCl	$Na^+(l) + e^- \longrightarrow Na(s)$	$Cl^-(l) \longrightarrow \frac{1}{2}Cl_2(g) + e^-$	Na (s)	Cl_2 gas
Aq. NaCl	$H_2O(l) + e^- \longrightarrow \frac{1}{2}H_2(g) + OH^-(aq)$	$Cl^-(aq) \longrightarrow \frac{1}{2}Cl_2(g) + e^-$	H_2 gas	Cl_2 gas
Dil. H_2SO_4	$H^+(aq) + e^- \longrightarrow \frac{1}{2}H_2(g)$	$2H_2O(l) \longrightarrow O_2(g) + 4H^+(aq) + 4e^-$	H_2 gas	O_2 gas
Conc. H_2SO_4	$H^+(aq) + e^- \longrightarrow \frac{1}{2}H_2(g)$	$2SO_4^{2-}(aq) \longrightarrow S_2O_8^{2-} + 2e^-$	H_2 gas	$S_2O_8^{2-}$

Corrosion

It is the process of deterioration of a metal from its surface. e.g. Rusting of iron, blackening of Ag, etc.

It is an electrochemical process.

At anode, $Fe\,(s) \longrightarrow Fe^{2+}\,(aq) + 2e^-$

At cathode, $O_2\,(g) + 4H^+\,(aq) + 4e^- \longrightarrow 2H_2O(l)$

$2Fe^{2+}(aq) + 2H_2O(l) + 1/2O_2(g) \longrightarrow Fe_2O_3(s) + 4H^+(aq)$

Prevention The metal surface is coated with paint oil and grease which keeps it out of contact with air, moisture etc.

Kohlrausch's Law

- It is also called **law of independent migration of ions**.
- It states that limiting molar conductivity (Λ°_m) of an electrolyte is the sum of the individual contribution of cation and anion as

$\Lambda^\circ_m(AB_2) = \Lambda^\circ_m(A^{2+}) + 2\Lambda^\circ_m(B^-)$

$\Lambda^\circ_m(NaCl) = \Lambda^\circ_m(Na^+) + \Lambda^\circ_m(Cl^-)$

- The molar conductivity of weak electrolytes at infinite dilution can be calculated using this law.
- It is helpful for the calculation of α and K_a as

$\alpha = \frac{\Lambda_m}{\Lambda^\circ_m}$ and $K_a = \frac{C\alpha^2}{(1-\alpha)}$

Primary Batteries

These are non-rechargeable and cannot be used again.

Dry cell (Leclanche cell) It consists of zinc electrode act as anode and carbon rod act as cathode.

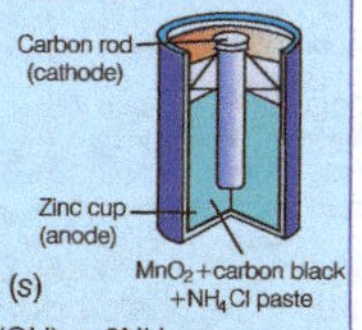

At anode,

$Zn\,(s) \longrightarrow Zn^{2+} + 2e^-$

At cathode,

$MnO_2 + NH_4^+ + e^- \longrightarrow MnO\,(OH) + NH_3$

$Zn(s) + 2NH_4^+\,(aq) + 2MnO_2\,(s) \longrightarrow Zn^{2+}\,(aq) + 2MnO(OH) + 2NH_3$

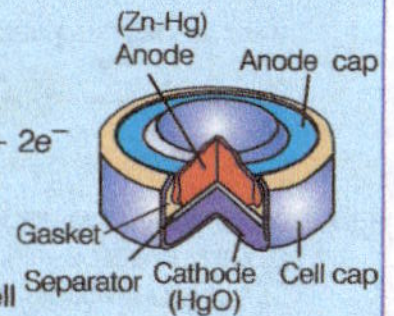

At anode,

$Zn(Hg) + 2OH^- \longrightarrow ZnO(s) + H_2O + 2e^-$

$HgO + H_2O + 2e^- \longrightarrow Hg(l) + 2OH^-$

The overall reaction of the cell is written as

$Zn(Hg) + HgO(s) \longrightarrow ZnO(s) + Hg(l)$

Fuel Cell

- It is a galvanic cell which convert chemical energy of fuel into electrical energy. e.g. $H_2 - O_2$ fuel cell.
- These are more efficient and pollution free.

At anode, $H_2\,(g) + 4OH^-\,(aq) \longrightarrow 4H_2O(l) + 4e^-$

At cathode, $O_2\,(g) + 2H_2O(l) + 4e^- \longrightarrow 4OH^-\,(aq)$

Secondary Batteries

These are rechargeable batteries. During charging, these act as electrolytic cell, e.g. lead storage battery, nickel-cadmium battery.

- **Lead Storage Cell**

Cell reactions during use of battery:

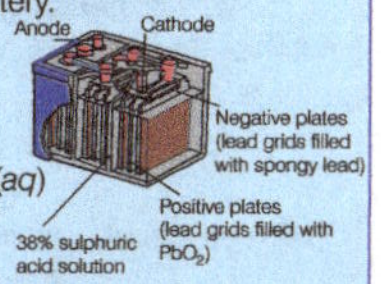

At anode, $Pb\,(s) + SO_4^{2-}\,(aq) \rightarrow PbSO_4\,(s) + 2e^-$

At cathode,

$PbO_2\,(s) + SO_4^{2-}\,(aq) + 4H^+\,(aq) + 2e^- \longrightarrow PbSO_4\,(s) + 2H_2O\,(l)$

Net reaction,

$Pb(s) + PbO_2\,(s) + 2H_2SO_4\,(aq) \longrightarrow 2PbSO_4\,(s) + 2H_2O(l)$

The reverse reaction takes place during recharging

$2PbSO_4\,(s) + 2H_2O\,(l) \longrightarrow Pb\,(s) + PbO_2\,(s) + 2H_2SO_4\,(aq)$

Uses In automobiles and inverters.

- **Nickel Cadmium Cell (or NICAD cell)**

Cell reaction during use of battery:

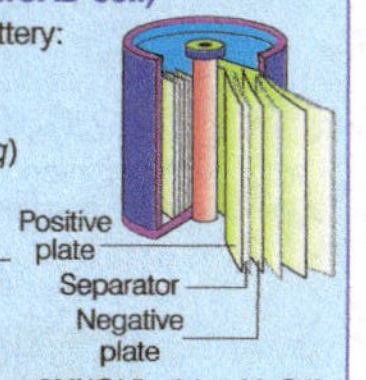

At cathode,

$2Ni(OH)_3\,(s) + 2e^- \rightarrow 2Ni(OH)_2\,(s) + 2OH^-(aq)$

At anode,

$Cd(s) + 2OH^-\,(aq) \rightarrow CdO(s) + H_2O\,(l) + 2e^-$

Net reaction,

$Cd\,(s) + 2Ni(OH)_3\,(s) \longrightarrow CdO(s) + 2Ni(OH)_2\,(s) + H_2O(l)$

The reverse reaction takes place during recharging

$CdO(s) + 2Ni(OH)_2(s) + H_2O(l) \longrightarrow Cd(s) + 2Ni(OH)_3(s)$

Chemical Kinetics (Chapter at a Glance)

Units of Rate Constant

n^{th} order reaction, $\frac{dx}{dt} = k\,(\text{conc.})^n$

$k = \frac{dx}{dt} \times \frac{1}{(\text{conc.})^n} \Rightarrow k = (\text{conc.})^{1-n}\text{time}^{-1}$

- For zero order reaction, (n=0), Unit of k=mol $L^{-1}s^{-1}$
- For 1st order reaction, (n = 1), Unit of k = s^{-1}
- For 2nd order reaction, (n = 2), Unit of k=L $mol^{-1}s^{-1}$

Rate Law Expression and Rate Constant

- The mathematical expression which denotes the rate of a reaction in terms of molar concentrations of reactants. Each term is raised to some power which may or may not be same as the stoichiometric coefficient of the reacting species in a balanced chemical equation.
  For a given reaction, $aA + bB \rightleftharpoons cC + dD$
  Rate $\propto [A]^x[B]^y$; Rate = $k[A]^x[B]^y$
  [x and y may or may not be equal to a and b.]
- **Rate Constant** (k) It is equal to the rate of reaction when concentration of each of the reactant is unity.

Order of a Reaction

- It is the sum of the powers of the concentration terms in the rate law.
  For a given reaction,
  $aA + bB \longrightarrow$ Product Rate $= k[A]^m[B]^n$
  $\therefore$ Order of reaction = $m+n$
- It can be a whole number or a fractional number and can only be determined experimentally.
- It can change with change in conditions such as temperature, pressure etc.
- It is applicable to elementary as well as complex reactions.

Molecularity of a Reaction

- It is defined as the number of molecules of reactant taking part an elementary reaction.
- For a reaction, $aA + bB \longrightarrow$ Product
  Molecularity = $a+b$
- It can only be a whole number.
- It is a theoretical property.
- It is only applicable for elementary reactions.
- It is invariable with change in reaction conditions.
- It has no significance for complex reaction.
  e.g. $2NH_3 \xrightarrow{Pt} N_2 + 3H_2$; Order-0, molecularity-2

Elementary and Complex Reactions

- **Elementary Reactions** Reactions occurring only in one step are called elementary reactions.
  e.g. $N_2(g) + O_2(g) \longrightarrow 2NO(g)$
  $CH_3COOH + C_2H_5OH \longrightarrow CH_3COOC_2H_5 + H_2O$
  Order and molecularities are defined for this step only.
- **Complex Reactions** Reactions involving a sequence of two or more elementary steps are called complex reactions. e.g. $2O_3 \longrightarrow 3O_2$
  Step I $O_3 \rightleftharpoons O_2 + O^\bullet$ (Fast)
  Step II $O^\bullet + O_3 \longrightarrow 2O_2^\bullet$ (Slow)
  Order is defined for the slow step.

Rate of Reaction

- It is the change in concentration of any one of the reactants or products per unit time.
- **Average Rate** It is the rate measured over a long time interval.

$$r_{av} = \frac{-\Delta R}{\Delta t} = \frac{\Delta P}{\Delta t}$$

- **Instantaneous Rate** It is the rate measured over a long time interval. $r_{ins} = \frac{-d[R]}{dt} = \frac{d[P]}{dt}$

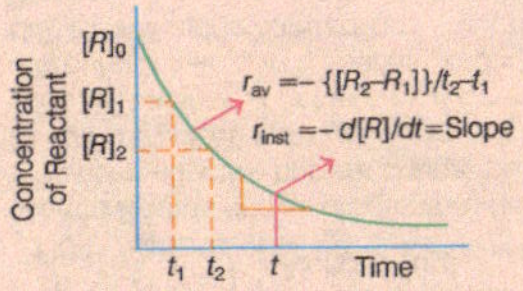

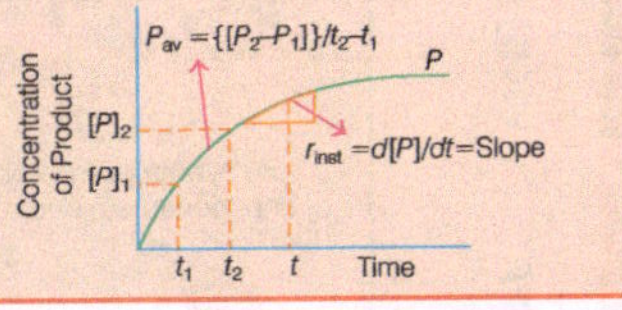

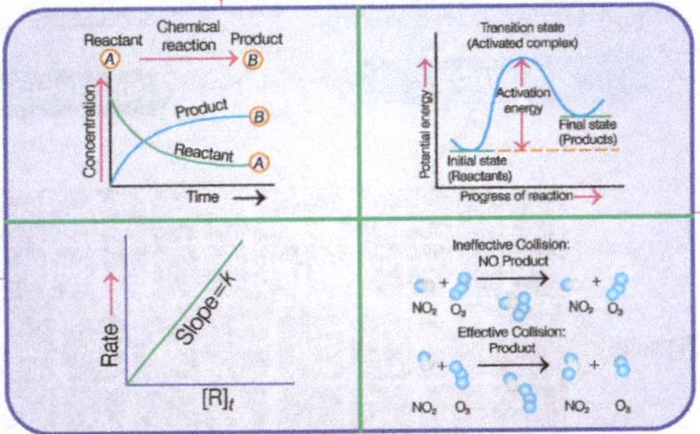

Temperature Dependence of Rate of Reaction

Arrhenius Equation

- Reactant molecules collide with each other.
- These collisions form an intermediate unstable complex.
- Relation between energy required to form this intermediate and rate constant is given as,

$$k = Ae^{-\frac{E_a}{RT}}$$

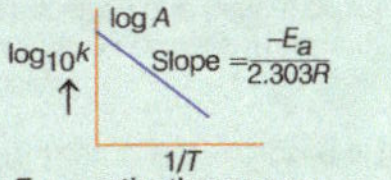

Where, A = pre-exponential factor, E_a = activation energy
R = gas constant, T = temperature (K).

Factor $e^{-E_a/RT}$ in the Arrhenius equation is known as Boltzmann factor.

A plot between $\log k$ and $\frac{1}{T}$ gives a straight line with slope $= \frac{-E_a}{2.303R}$ and intercept $\log A$.

Factors Affecting Rate of Reaction

- **Concentration of Reactants** Increase in concentration increases rate of reaction.
- **Catalyst** It increases the speed of reaction by lowering the energy barrier, i.e. a new path is followed with lower activation energy.
- **Surface Area** Greater the surface area faster is the reaction.
- **Temperature** Generally, the rate of reaction becomes almost double for every 10°C rise in temperature.
- Temperature coefficient $= \frac{k_T+10}{k_T}$
- Rate constant at temperature (T +10°)
- **Physical State of Reactants** Reactions involving gaseous reactants are faster generally.

Half-life Period

- It is the period of time in which the concentration of the reactant is reduced to half of its initial concentration.
  General expression for $t_{1/2}$ different order are as follows
- For zero order reaction, $t_{1/2} = \frac{[A]_0}{2k}$
- For first order reactions, $t_{1/2} = \frac{0.693}{k}$
- For second order reaction, $t_{1/2} = \frac{1}{k[A]_0}$ when $n \geq 2$
- Amount of substance left after n half-lives$= \frac{[A]_0}{2^n}$

Pseudo First Order Reaction

- A reaction which is not truly of first order but under certain conditions becomes a reaction of first order, e.g. hydrolysis of ester.

$$\underset{\text{Ester}}{CH_3COOCH_2CH_3} + \underset{\text{Water}}{H_2O} \xrightleftharpoons{H^+(aq)} \underset{\text{Acid}}{CH_3COOH} + \underset{\text{Alcohol}}{CH_3CH_2OH}$$

Rate=$k[CH_3COOCH_2CH_3]$

- The concentration of water does not get altered much during the course of the reaction. So, the reaction behave as first order reaction. Such reactions are called pseudo first order reaction.

Important Plots

- **Zero Order**

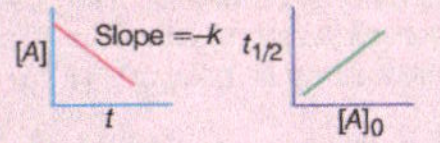

- **First Order**

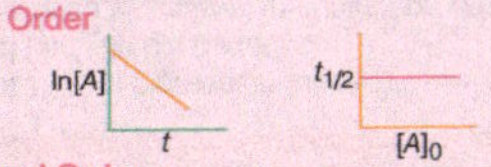

- **Second Order**

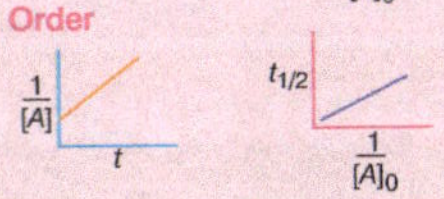

Integrated Rate Equations

- **For Zero Order**
  Rate $=k$, or $k = \frac{1}{t}\{[A]_0 - [A]\}$
  where, k = rate constant, t = time
  $[A]_0$ =initial reactant concentration
  [A] =final reactant concentration at time (t)
- **For First Order**
  Rate $= k \cdot [A]$, $k = \frac{2.303}{t}\log\frac{[A]_0}{[A]}$
- For gas phase reaction,

$$k = \frac{2.303}{t}\log\frac{p_i}{2p_i - p_t}$$

  where, p_i=initial pressure
- **For Second Order**
  (a) When both reactants are equal or with same concentrations.

$$R = k[A]^2 \quad \left(k = \frac{1}{t}\cdot\frac{x}{a\,(a-x)}\right)$$

  (b) When the two reactants have different concentrations.

$$k = \frac{2.303}{t\,(a-b)}\log\left[\frac{b\,(a-x)}{a\,(b-x)}\right]$$

- **For n^{th} order**, $k = \frac{1}{t\,(n-1)}\left[\frac{1}{[A]^{n-1}} - \frac{1}{[A]_0^{n-1}}\right]$
  where, k= rate constant
  $[A]_0$=initial concentration of reactant
  n=order of reaction
  x=concentration of reactant decomposed at time t

Activation Energy

- It is the energy required by the reactant molecules for effective collision to form products.
- Activation energy of a reaction cannot be zero.
  Reaction favours the direction where activation energy is lesser.

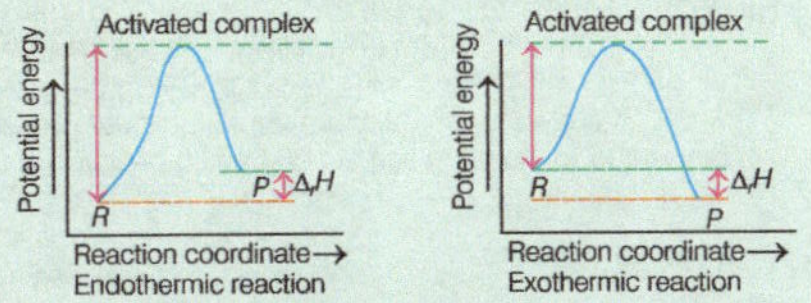

Collision Theory

- Reactant molecules are assumed to be hard spheres.
- Reaction occurs due to collision of reactant molecules.
- Only effective collisions (having threshold energy and proper orientation) give product.
- Threshold energy = Activation energy + Potential energy of reactant.
- **Collision frequency** It is the number of collisions that take place per unit time per unit volume of the reaction mixture.
- Rate = $PZ_{AB}\,e^{-E_a/RT}$
  where, P=probability or steric factor
  Z_{AB} = collision frequency

d & f-Block Elements (Chapter at a Glance)

d-block elements

It consists of four series
(i) 3d series from Sc (21) to Zn (30)
(ii) 4d series from Y (39) to Cd (48)
(iii) 5d series from La (57), Hf (72) to Hg (80)
(iv) 6d series from Ac (89), Rf (104) to Cn (112)

- Electronic configuration $(n-1)\,d^{1-10}\,ns^{1-2}$ [n = 4, 5, 6 and 7].
- Except $_{30}Zn$, $_{48}Cd$, $_{80}Hg$ and $_{112}Cn$, d-block elements are known as transition elements.

Exceptional Configuration

- Due to more stable half-filled configuration Cr from 3d series and Mo from 4d series shows $3d^5\,4s^1$ and $4d^5\,4s^1$ electronic configuration instead of $3d^4\,4s^2$ and $4d^4\,4s^2$ respectively.
- Due to more stable fully-filled configuration of Cu from 3d series and Ag from 4d series shows $3d^{10}\,4s^1$ and $4d^{10}4s^1$ electronic configuration instead of $3d^9\,4s^2$ and $4d^9 4s^2$.

Applications of d-block Elements

- Use of TiO_2 in pigment industry.
- Use of MnO_2 in dry batteries.
- V_2O_5 is used as catalyst in contact process of H_2SO_4.
- $TiCl_4$ with $Al(CH_3)_3$ in used as *Ziegler* catalysts.
- Fe is used as in catalyst in Haber process.
- $PdCl_2$ is used as a catalyst in Wacker process.
- Nickel is used in polymerisation reactions.
- AgBr is used in photographic industry.
- Cu is used in alloy formation like bronze (Cu+Sn) and brass (Cu+Zn).
- Cu, Ag and Au are used for making coins and ornaments.
- Steel, titanium nitride, titanium carbide etc. are used for making artificial joint replacement of bones.
- Tungsten use in making electrical fibres.

Potassium Permanganate ($KMnO_4$)

- **Prepared from the Pyrolusite Ore** (MnO_2)

$2MnO_2 + 4KOH + O_2 \longrightarrow 2K_2MnO_4 + 2H_2O$
$3MnO_4^{2-} + 4H^+ \longrightarrow 2MnO_4^- + MnO_2 + 2H_2O$

- **Commercial method**

$MnO_2 \xrightarrow[\text{Oxidised with air or } KNO_3]{\text{Fused with KOH}} MnO_4^{2-}$ Manganate ion

$MnO_4^{2-} \xrightarrow[\text{in alkaline solution}]{\text{Electrolytic oxidation}} MnO_4^-$ Permanganate ion

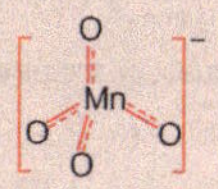

- **Oxidising properties in acidic medium**:

$MnO_4^- + 8H^+ + 5e^- \longrightarrow Mn^{2+} + 4H_2O$
It oxidises I^- to I_2, NO_2^- to NO_3^- Fe^{2+} to Fe^{3+} $C_2O_4^{2-}$ to CO_2.

- **In neutral or faintly alkaline medium**

$MnO_4^- + 2H_2O + 3e \longrightarrow MnO_2 + 4H_2O$
It oxidises $S_2O_3^{2-}$ to SO_4^{2-}, Mn^{2+} to MnO_2, I^- to IO_3^-, etc.

Potassium Dichromate ($K_2Cr_2O_7$)

- **Prepared from Chromite Ore** ($FeCr_2O_4$)

$4FeCr_2O_4 + 8Na_2CO_3 + 7O_2 \longrightarrow 8Na_2CrO_4 + 2Fe_2O_3 + 8CO_2$
$2Na_2CrO_4 + H_2SO_4 \longrightarrow Na_2Cr_2O_7 + Na_2SO_4 + H_2O$
$Na_2Cr_2O_7 + 2KCl \longrightarrow K_2Cr_2O_7 + 2NaCl$

The chromates and dichromates are interconvertible in aqueous solution depending upon pH of the solution.

$2CrO_4^{2-} + 2H^+ \longrightarrow Cr_2O_7^{2-}$ (Orange) $+ H_2O$
$Cr_2O_7^{2-} + 2OH^- \longrightarrow CrO_4^{2-}$ (Yellow) $+ H_2O$

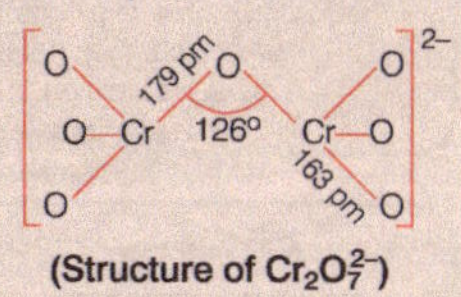

(Structure of $Cr_2O_7^{2-}$)

- **Oxidising Properties**

$Cr_2O_7^{2-} + 14H^+ + 6e^- \longrightarrow 2Cr^{3+} + 7H_2O$
$Fe^{2+} \longrightarrow Fe^{3+} + e^-$; $6I^- \longrightarrow 3I_2 + 6e^-$
$SO_2 + 2H_2O \longrightarrow SO_4^{2-} + 2H^+ + 2e^-$; $C_2O_4^{2-} \longrightarrow 2CO_2 + 2e^-$

The full equation is obtained by adding the half reaction for potassium dichromate to the half reaction for the reducing agent for e.g.
e.g. $Cr_2O_7^{2-} + 14H^+ + 6I^- \longrightarrow 2Cr^{3+} + 7H_2O + 3I_2$

- **Chromyl Chloride Test** $K_2Cr_2O_7 + 4NaCl + 6H_2SO_4 \longrightarrow 2CrO_2Cl_2 + 2KHSO_4 + 3H_2O + 4NaHSO_4$ (CrO_2Cl_2: Chromyl chloride)

Physical Properties of d-block Elements

- Generally, d-block elements are very hard and having low volatility (Zn, Cd and Hg are exceptions).
- Higher **melting and boiling points** due to involvement of d-electrons in metallic bonding.
  - Sc < Ti < V < Cr > Mn < Fe > Co > Ni > Cu > Zn (In period).
  - Zn > Cd > Hg, Cu > Ag ≤ Au [Along group]
- **Atomic Radius** shows progressive decrease along the period, due to increased effective nuclear charge but this decrease in atomic radii become small after midway.
  - Sc > Ti > V > Cr > Mn ≥ Fe ≈ Co ≈ Ni ≤ Cu < Zn
  - Among 3d, 4d and 5d series, order of radii is 3d < 4d ≈ 5d. due to lanthanide contraction.
- **Density** In 3d series, it increases from left to right, Cu being an exception.
- **Ionisation Enthalpy** increases from left to right due to increase in nuclear charge, although the increase is not regular.
- **Oxidation States** shows variable oxidation states due to involvement of ns and $(n-1)d$ electrons in bonding.
  - Highest oxidation states is possible for elements in middle of the series.
  - Stability of higher oxidation states increases down the group with some halides and oxygen.
- **Reactivity and Electrode Potential Values**
  - $E^\circ_{M^{2+}/M}$ increases down the series with exceptions of Mn, Ni and Zn
  - Mn and Zn have stable configuration while Ni has more E° due to high negative ΔH_{hyd}.
  - less negative the E°, better is the oxidising agent.
  - $E^\circ_{M^{3+}/M^{2+}}$: increases down the series with exception of Fe due to stable Fe^{3+} configuration.
- **Magnetic Properties** Magnetic moment increases with the increasing number of unpaired electrons.
- When magnetic field is applied to substances, mainly two types of magnetic behaviour are observed diamagnetism and paramagnetism. Magnetic moment $\mu = \sqrt{n(n+2)}$, n = number of unpaired electrons.
- **Coloured Compounds** Forms coloured compounds due to d-d transition
- **Tendency to form Complexes** Due to small size, high nuclear charge and vacant d orbitals, these elements form complexes.
- **Form Interstitial Compounds** They can easily accommodate the small non-metallic atoms because of spaces between them.
- **Oxides** Oxides in lower oxidation states are basic whereas those with higher are acidic or amphoteric in nature.

Uses of f-block Elements

Lanthanoids

- Form alloys like mischmetal and pyrophoric alloys.
- Used in making magnetic and electronic devices.
- Oxides are used in glass industry and their mixed oxides are used as catalysts in petroleum cracking.
- Recently used in lasers.

Actinoids

- Actinoids are used for the synthesis of transuranic elements.
- Thorium is used in the manufacture of fine rods for atomic reactors.
- ThO_2 is used for making incandescent gas mantles.
- **Uranium** is used in the production of nuclear energy.
- Uranium oxides used in textile and ceramic industry.
- Plutonium is used as a fuel in atomic reactors. and also used in nuclear bombs.

Actinoids

- **Electronic Configuration** [Rn] $5f^{1-14}\,6d^{0-1}\,7s^2$.
- **Ionic size** Gradual decrease along the series due to actinoid contraction.
- Actinoids and many of their compounds are paramagnetic.
- **Oxidation State** The most stable oxidation states is +3. Also, shows different oxidation states like +2, +3, +4, +5, +6 and +7.
- **General Properties**
  - Highly reactive metals.
  - Irregularities in metallic radii.
  - Ionisation enthalpies are lower than that for the lanthanoids.
  - Reacts with boiling water to form oxides and hydrides.
  - Do not react with alkalies.
  - Reacts with HCl easily but only few reacts with nitric acid due to formation of protective oxide layer.

Lanthanoids

- **Electronic Configuration** $4f^{1-14}\,5d^{0-1}\,6s^2$.
- **Atomic and ionic Size** In the lanthanoid series with increasing atomic number, there is a progressive decrease in the size from lanthanum (La) to lutetium (Lu). This contraction in size is known as lanthanoid contraction. In these elements, the added electron enters in the diffused f- orbitals and therefore experiences considerable pull by the nucleus leading to contracts the size of atom. .
- **Oxidation States** Most common + 3, Ce shows +4. Pr, Nd, Tb, and Dy and also show + 4 but only in oxides. Some elements (La, Eu, Yb, Sm) show +2 as well.
- **General Properties**
  - Hardness increases with increasing atomic number.
  - Melting points range between 1000 to 1200 K with exception of Sm (1623 K).
  - Good conductors of heat and electricity.
- Colour they have unpaired electrons in their 4f-orbitals. Thus; ions absorbs visible light by undergoing f-f transition and hence, exhibit colour.
- **Complex Formation** Do not have much tendency to form complexes

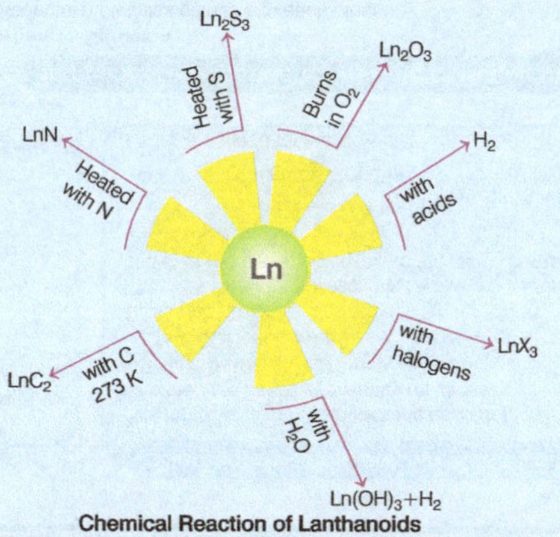

Chemical Reaction of Lanthanoids

Coordination Compounds (Chapter at a Glance)

Werner's theory and Some Terminology

- **Postulates:**
  - Metals show two types of linkages
    (i) Primary valency (ii) Secondary valency
  - Primary valency (Oxidation number) is ionisable, secondary valency (coordination number) is non-ionisable
  - Primary valency is satisfied by negative ions and secondary valency is satisfied by ligands.

Colour	Formula	Solution
Yellow	$[Co(NH_3)_6]^{3+}3Cl^-$	1:3 electrolyte
Purple	$[CoCl(NH_3)_5]^{2+}2Cl^-$	1:2 electrolyte
Green	*trans*- $[CoCl_2(NH_3)_4]^+Cl^-$	1:1 electrolyte
Violet	*cis*- $[CoCl_2(NH_3)_4]^+Cl^-$	1:1 electrolyte

- **Limitations: Could not Explain**
  - Why only certain elements possess complex forming property.
  - Why bonds in coordination compounds have directional nature.
  - Magnetic and optical property in complexes.
- **Ligands** ions or molecules bound to central atom.
  - **Unidentate** Ligand bound to metal ion through a single donor e.g. NH_3, Cl^-, OH^-
  - **Didentate** When ligand can bind through two donor atoms e.g. $C_2O_4^{2-}$ and en $(NH_2CH_2CH_2NH_2)$
  - **Polydentate** When several donor atoms are present in a ligand e.g EDTA.
  - **Ambidentate** When ligand has two donor atoms but either of the two binds to the metal in a complex, e.g. NO_2^- SCN^-.
- **Chelate ligands** When a didentate or polydentate ligand uses it's two or more donor atoms to bind to a single metal atom.
  - Chelate complexes are generally more stable.
- **Homoleptic complexes** Complexes in which a metal is bound to only one kind of donor groups, e.g. $[Co(NH_3)_6]^{3+}$.
- **Heteroleptic complexes** Complexes in which a metal is bound to more than one kind of donor groups, e.g. $[Co(NH_3)_4Cl_2]^+$.

Applications

- Estimation of water hardness using EDTA.
- In extraction of some important metals by complex formation.
- In biological systems e.g chlorophyll, haemoglobin, vitamin B12(cyano cobalamine)
- Used as a catalyst e.g Wilkinson catalyst $[(Ph_3P)_3RhCl]$ in hydrogenation of alkenes.
- In electroplating of articles with gold and silver.
- In use of chelate therapy in medicinal chemistry. e.g. using chelating ligands to remove Cu, Fe, Pb etc. which can be toxic in plant/animal systems.
- EDTA is used in lead poisoning.
- *Cis*-platin *cis*-$[Pt(NH_3)_2Cl_2]$ is used to heat tumors.

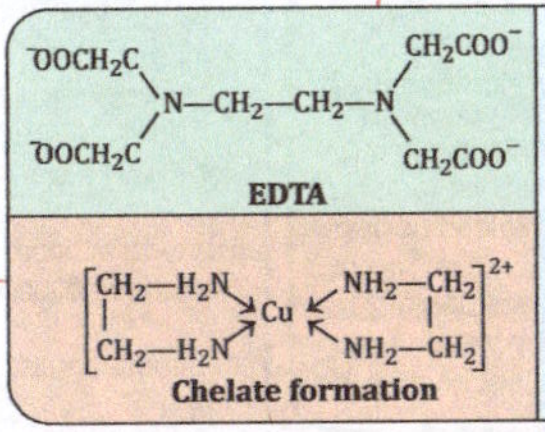

EDTA

Chelate formation

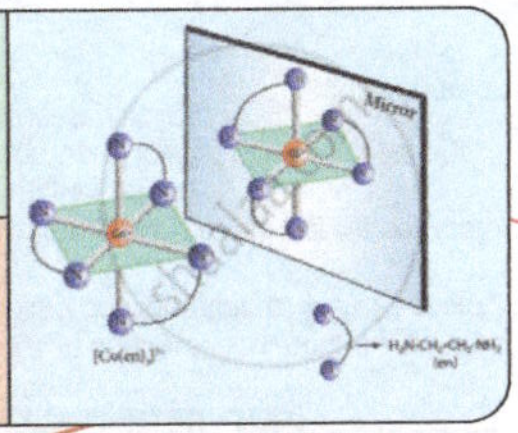

Nomenclature and Isomerism

Nomenclature

For Anionic/Neutral Complexes
- Counter ion name + ligand name with quantity in alphabetical order + metal name + ate + (OS of metal)
- H_2O-aqua, No-nitrosyl, Cl^- - chlorido, CN^- - cyano, etc.

For Cationic Complexes
- Ligand no. + ligand name (alphabetically) + metal name + (OS of metal) + counter ion name (if present).

Isomerism

- **Stereoisomerism**
  - Geometrical—*cis* and *trans* – Optical—*dextro* and *laevo*
- **Structural Isomerism**
  - **Linkage isomerism** shown by complexes having ambidentate ligands. Such as —SCN and —NO_2. e.g. $[Co(NH_3)_5(ONO)]Cl_2$ and $[Co(NH_3)_5(NO_2)]Cl_2$
  - **Coordination isomerism** arises from interchange of ligands between cationic and anionic entities of different metal ions. e.g $[Cr(NH_3)_6]^{3+}[Co(CN)_6]^{3-}$ $[Co(NH_3)_6]^{3+}[Cr(CN)_6]^{3-}$
  - **Ionisation isomerism** occurs when counter ion is itself a potential ligand and displaces ligand in the coordination sphere. e.g. $[Co(NH_3)_5(SO_4)]$ Br and $[Co(NH_3)_5Br]SO_4$
  - **Solvate isomerism** Exchange of solvent molecules inside the sphere with counter ions. If solvent is water, it is called hydrate isomerism. e.g $[Cr(H_2O)_6]Cl_3$ (Violet) and $[Cr(H_2O)_5Cl]Cl_2 \cdot H_2O$ (Grey -green)

- **Geometrical Isomerism**
  - arises in heteroleptic complexes
  - possible in coordination number 4 and 6.

  For coordination number=4;
  - **MA_2B_2 type,**

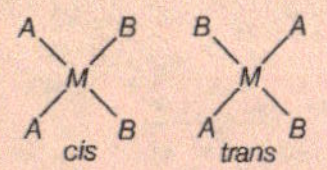

  - **MABXL type**

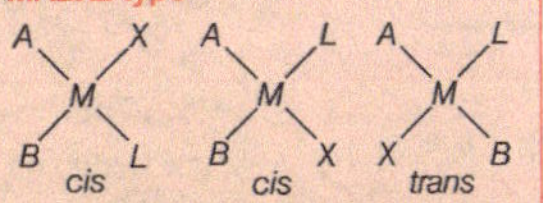

  For coordination number =6:
  - **MA_2B_4 type**

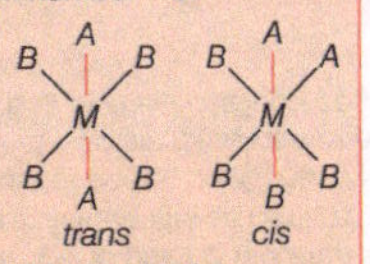

  - other forms will be said to be identical.
  - **MA_2B_2 type** [*B* is didentate ligand]

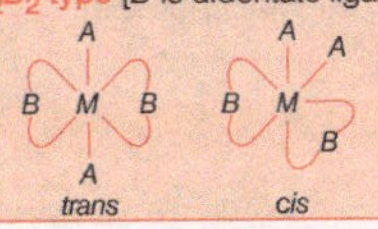

- **Facial isomers**
  - Facial (Fac) if three donor atoms of same ligand occupy adjacent positions at the corners of an octahedral face e.g.

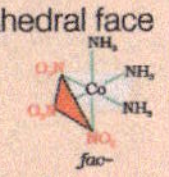

- **Meridional (*Mer*)** When the positions of donor atoms of same ligand are around the meridian of octahedron.

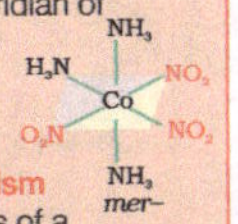

- **Optical isomerism**
  - mirror images of a compound which can not be superimposed on one another.
  - molecules which can not be superimposed are chiral.
  - can either be *dextro* (rotates left to right) or *laevo* (rotates right to left)
  - represented by *d*- and *l* respectively e.g. $[Co(en)_3]^{3+}$

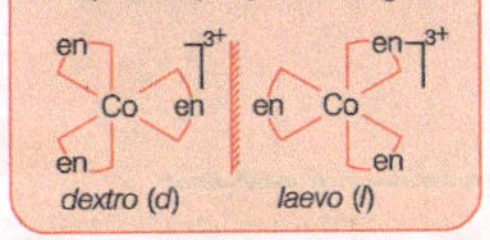

Bonding in Coordination Compounds

- **Valence Bond Theory**
  - Describes the bonding in terms of hybridised orbitals of central metal atom or ion.
  - Central metal atom makes available a number of vacant orbitals equal to its coordination number. The vacant hybrid orbitals form coordinate bond with ligands.

Hybridisation and geometry of complexes

Coord. No.	Type of hybridisation	Geometry of complex	Examples
4	sp^3	Tetrahedral	$[NiCl_4]^{2-}$
4	dsp^2	Square planar	$[Ni(CN)_4]^{2-}$
5	sp^3d	Trigonal bipyramidal	$Fe(CO)_5$
6	sp^3d^2(high spin)	Octahedral	$[CoF_6]^{3-}$
6	d^2sp^3(low spin)	Octahedral	$[Co(NH_3)_6]^{3+}$

- **Magnetic Properties**
  - Complexes can be paramagnetic or diamangetic.
  - Spin-only magnetic moment can be calculated using formula $\mu_s = \sqrt{n(n+2)}$,
- **Limitations**
  - Could not explain colour and spectra of complexes.
  - Does not distinguish between weak and strong ligands.

- **Crystal Field Theory**
  - Consider metal-ligand bonding to be ionic and interactions between metal and ligand to be purely electrostatic.
- **Postulates**
  - Ligands are point charges in case of anions and dipoles in case of neutral molecules.
  - Degeneracy of *d*-orbitals (same energy) is lifted in presence of ligands and splitting occurs.

  CFSE for tetrahedral complexes , $\Delta_t = \frac{4}{9}\Delta_o$

  Δ_o= CFSE of octahedral complexes.

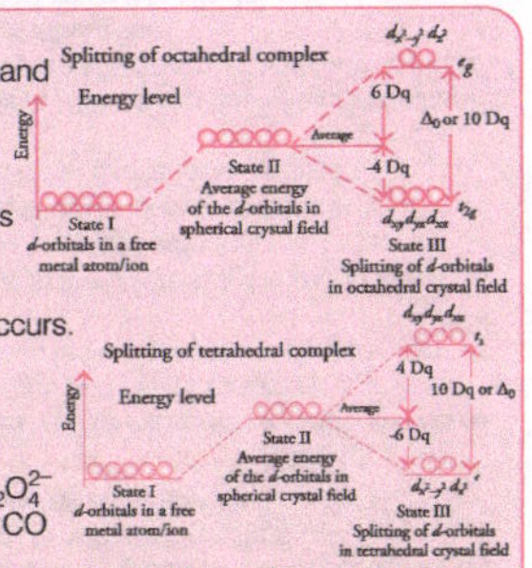

- **Spectrochemical series**

  $I^- < Br^- < SCN^- < Cl^- < S^{2-} < F^- < OH^- < C_2O_4^{2-} < H_2O < NCS^- <$ edta$^{4-} < NH_3 < en < CN^- < CO$
  - For strong field ligands,$\Delta_o > P$, hence pairing occurs and low spin complex forms.
  - For weak field ligands, $P > \Delta_o$, hence no pairing occurs & high spin complex forms.

- **Colour of complexes**
  - Compounds are colourless in absence of ligands.
  - Colour of complexes is due to *d*-*d* transition.
  - With increase in splitting, wavelength of light absorbed is decreased.
- **Limitations of CFT**
  - Could not explain why anionic ligands are weak field ligand while they are stronger point charges
  - Did not take into account the covalent nature of metal-ligand bond.

Jahn-Teller distortion
- If the *d*-orbitals are asymmetrically filled, they will repel some ligand in the complex more than the others. This results in distortion of octahedral complexes.
- Distortion caused by asymmetric filling of t_{2g} is too small to measure.
- Asymmetric filling of e_g orbitals causes a significant distortion.

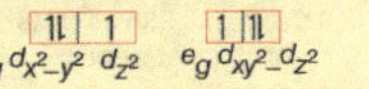

- **Bonding in Metal Carbonyls**
  - *M*–C bond possess both σ and π character.
  - σ- bond forms due to ligand to metal lone pair donation.
  - π-bond forms due to donation of electrons from filled *d*-orbital of metal to π* orbital of CO, known as synergic effect.

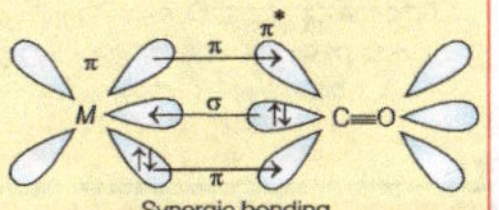

Synergic bonding

Haloarenes & Haloalkanes (Chapter at a Glance)

HALOARENES
HALOALKANES

HALOALKANES

Physical Properties
- Poorly soluble in water.
- Have higher boiling points than those of hydrocarbons of comparable molecular mass.
- BP decrease with increase in branching.
- Density higher than water.
- Dipole moment and solubility decrease with increase in mass.

Preparation
- **Finkelstein reaction**: For converting alkyl chlorides and bromides to iodides.
  $R—X + NaI \rightarrow R—I + NaX$
  (Halogen exchange method → $R—X$)
- **Swart's reaction**: For converting alkyl chlorides and bromides to fluorides.
  $H_3CBr + AgF \rightarrow H_3C—F + AgBr$
- **Free radical halogenation of alkanes**
  $CH_3CH_2CH_2CH_3 \xrightarrow[408^\circ C]{Cl_2, \text{UV-light}} CH_3CH_2CH_2CH_2Cl + CH_3CH_2CH(Cl)CH_3$
- **Addition of HX to alkenes**
  $>C=C< + HX \rightarrow >C(H)—C(X)<$
- **From alcohols**
  - $3ROH + PCl_3 \rightarrow 3R—Cl + H_3PO_3$
  - $ROH + PCl_5 \rightarrow R—Cl + POCl_3 + HCl$
  - $ROH + HCl \xrightarrow{ZnCl_2} R—Cl + H_2O$
  - $ROH \xrightarrow{\text{Red } P/Cl_2} R—Cl$
  - $R—OH + SOCl_2 \rightarrow R—Cl + SO_2\uparrow + HCl$
- **Borodine-Hunsdiecker reaction**
  $RCOO\bar{A}g^{+} + Br_2 \xrightarrow{CCl_4/\text{Reflux}} R—Br + CO_2\uparrow + AgBr$

Reaction with Metals
- $R—X + Mg \xrightarrow{\text{Dry ether}} \underset{\text{Grignard reagent}}{R—MgX}$ (X = Cl, Br, I)
- **Grignard reagent**
  $RMgX + H—G \rightarrow RH + Mg(X)(G)$ $(G = \bar{O}H, R\bar{O}, N\bar{H}_2)$
- **Wurtz reaction**
  $2R—X + 2Na \xrightarrow{\text{Dry ether}} R—R + 2NaX$
- $R—X \xrightarrow{NaCN} R—CN$; $R—X \xrightarrow{AgCN} R—NC$
- $R—X \xrightarrow{R'_2CuLi} R—R'$
- $R—X \xrightarrow{Li} R—Li$

Elimination Reaction
Haloalkanes with β-hydrogen undergo dehydrohalogenation to give an alkene.
- **E1 reaction**
  - 2-step reaction similar to S_N1.
  - Reactivity order of alkyl halides 3° > 2° > 1°.

  e.g. 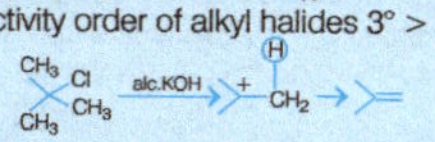
- **E2 reaction**
  - 1 - step reaction similar to S_N2.
  - Proceeds *via* transition state.
  - Favoured by 1° alkyl halides and bulky bases.

  e.g. $CH_3CH_2—Cl \xrightarrow{\text{Alc.KOH}} CH_2=CH_2$

Nucleophilic Substitution of Alkyl halides
$R—X$ with:
- NaOH (KOH) → ROH (Alcohol)
- H_2O → ROH (Alcohol)
- NaOR′ → ROR′ (Ether)
- NaI → R–I (Alkyl Iodide)
- NH_3 → RNH_2 (Primary amine)
- $R'NH_2$ → RNHR′ (Secondary amine)
- R′R″NH → RNR′R″ (Tertiary amine)
- KCN → RCN (Nitrile)
- AgCN → RNC (Isonitrile)
- KNO_2 → R–O–N=O (Alkyl nitrite)
- $AgNO_2$ → $R–NO_2$ (Nitro alkane)
- R′COOAg → R′COOR (Ester)
- $LiAlH_4$ → RH (Hydrocarbon)
- R′–H → RR′ (Alkane)

Nucleophilic Substitution Reactions
Here, X group is replaced by other nucleophiles like $CN^-, NO_2^-, OH^-, NH_2^-$, etc.

S_N1 Reactions
- It is a two step reacton.
- Involves the formation of carbocation intermediate in step - I.
- Involves the inversion of configuration as well as retention, so give racemic mixture if reactant is optically active.
- Rate ∝ [substrate], hence it is a first order reaction.
- Formation of carbocation is the rate determining step.
- Second step is the attack of nucleophile on the intermediate i.e. carbocation.
- Most favourable substrate is a 3° alkyl halide.
- 1° alkyl halide least favourable.
- Solvent conditions of a polar protic solvent favours this type of reaction.

S_N2 Reactions
- It is one step reaction.
- Involves the formation of transition state.
- Favoured by less hindered alkyl halide and non-polar solvent.
- Results in inversion of configuration if reactant is optically active.
- Rate ∝ [substrate] [nucleophile], hence it is a second order reaction.
- Most favoured substrate is a 1° alkyl halide.
- Is favoured in non-polar or polar aprotic solvents like dimethyl sulphide (DMS) and dimethyl sulphoxide (DMSO) etc.
- Less hindered the transition state, faster will be the reaction.

HALOARENES

Physical Properties
- They are heavier than water.
- These are though polar but immiscible with water due to their incapability of forming H–bonds.
- The boiling point of haloarenes are nearly same as that of haloalkanes with same number of carbon atoms.
- Order of boiling point : ArI > ArBr > ArCl > ArF
- B.P of isomers dihalobenzenes → nearly same.
- M. P. of isomers dihalobenzenes → p > o > m

Preparation
- **By electrophilic substitution**
  Toluene + $X_2 \xrightarrow[\text{Dark}]{Fe}$ o-halotoluene + p-halotoluene
- **Sandmeyer reaction**
  Aniline $\xrightarrow[\Delta]{NaNO_2 + HX} Ar—N_2^+X^-$
  $Ar—\overset{+}{N_2}X^- \xrightarrow[X = Cl, Br]{Cu_2X_2/HCl} Ar—X$
  $Ar^-N_2^+X^-$ can be used as a precursor to produce a class of organic compounds.

Reactions with Metals
- With magnesium
  $C_6H_5Br + Mg \xrightarrow[\Delta]{\text{Ether}} C_6H_5MgBr$
- Wurtz-Fittig reactions
  $C_6H_5Br + RX + 2Na \rightarrow C_6H_5R + 2NaX$
- Ullmann reaction
  $2C_6H_5I + 2Cu \xrightarrow[\text{Nitrobenzene}]{100\text{-}350^\circ C} C_6H_5—C_6H_5 + 2CuI$

Electrophillic Substitution Reaction
Aryl halide:
- Halogenation (X_2/halogen carrier)
- Nitration (HNO_3/H_2SO_4)
- Sulphonation (H_2SO_4)
- Friedel-Crafts' alkylation (RX/Lewis acid)
- Friedel-Crafts' acylation (RCOX/Lewis acid)

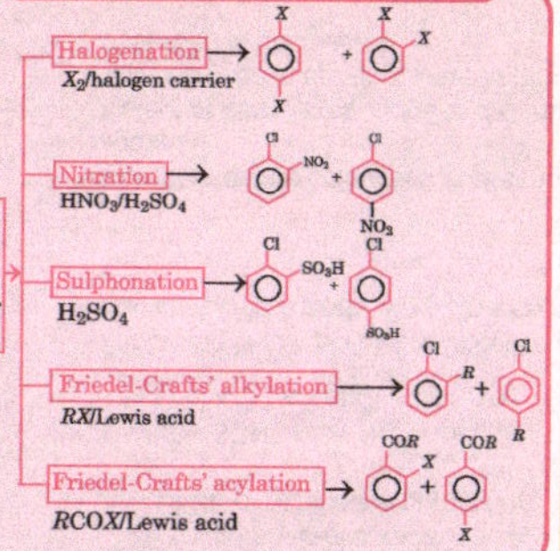

Nucleophilic Substitution Reaction
- Low reactivity due to lesser polar character.
- C—X bond acquires some double bond character and hence stronger.
- Presence of e^- withdrawing groups such as NO_2^-, —CN^- etc. at o- and p- positions w.r.t. halogen → activates the halogen towards nucleophilic substitution.
- Halogen atom is slightly deactivating and o, p-directing (p-product usually predominates).

Some reactions are discussed below

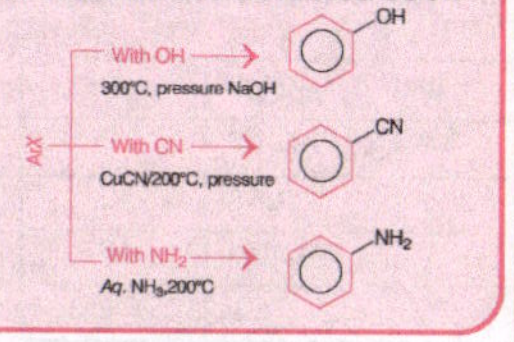

Some Important Examples
Chloretone	$(CH_3)_2C(OH)(CCl_3)$ – Hypnotic
Phosgene	$COCl_2$ – Poisonous gas used in warfare
Chloropicrin	CCl_3NO_2 – Tear gas and insecticide
Iodoform	CHI_3 – Antiseptic
Halothane	FCHClBr – Inhalation anaesthetic
Pyrene	CCl_4 – Fire extinguisher
Freon	CCl_2F_2 – Refrigerant

Polyhalogen Compounds
- **Dichloromethane** (CH_2Cl_2)
  - Used as solvent, propellant and refrigerant.
  - Harms CNS and leads to impaired hearing and vision.
- **Trichloromethane** ($CHCl_3$)
  - Also called chloroform.
  - In air, oxidises to give phosgene ($COCl_2$).
  - Oxidation is checked by using dark coloured bottles and by adding 1% ethanol.
- **Iodoform** (CHI_3)
  - Formed when —CHOH—CH_3 or CH_3CO— group containing compound reacts with alkali and I_2.
  - Used as an antiseptic.
- **Carbon Tetrachloride** (CCl_4)
  - Used as fire extinguisher (under the name pyrene and cleaning fluid.)
  - Leads to liver cancer, ozone depletion, etc.
- **Freons**
  - These are chlorofluoro compounds of methane and ethane.
  - Used as refrigerant and coolant.
  - Leads to ozone layer depletion.
- **DDT**
  - It is p, p-dichlorodiphenyl trichloroethane.
  - Prepared by treating chloral with 2 moles of chlorobenzene.
  - Used as an insecticide.

Reaction of Haloform
$CHCl_3$ with:
- Sunlight, O_2(air) → $COCl_2$ (Phosgene) + HCl (Oxidation)
- Zn/HCl, 2H → CH_2Cl_2 + 3HCl (Reduction)
- Aq. KOH → $HCOO^-K^+ + KCl + H_2O$ (Hydrolysis)
- Ag. powder → $HC\equiv CH$ + AgCl (With Ag)
- $R—NH_2$, KOH → R–NC (Carbylamine reaction)

Stereoisomers
Configurational Isomers
- *cis-trans* Change in configuration around a π-bond.
- *R/S* Given absolute configuration of *R* or *S* according to CIP rule.
- Assign priority to the groups attached. Higher atomic number will get higher priority.
- The H-atom or group of lowest priority is brought vertically in Fischer projection.

R-configuration	S-configuration
Move the arrow in order of decreasing priority. If it rotates clockwise, configuration is *R*.	Move the arrow in order of decreasing priority. If it is anti-clockwise, configuration is *S*.

- **Enantiomers**: Stereoisomers having non-super imposable mirror images are optically active.
- **Diastereomers**: Stereoisomers that are not mirror images of each other.

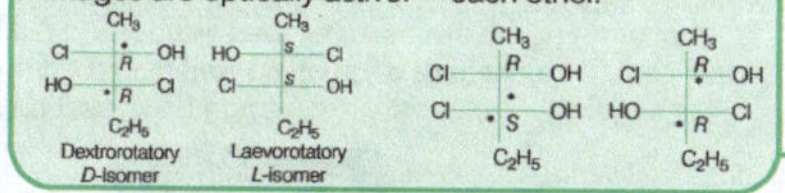

Racemic mixture
If both *d* and *l* enantiomers are present in equal amount (50-50%) then the mixture is optically inactive due to external compensation, the mixture is known as racemic mixture. e.g. Mixture obtained in an S_N1 reaction.

Optical isomers
- Differ in their behaviour towards plane polarised light.
- Must be optically active.
- Dextrorotatory (*D*) if the molecule rotates light towards right or clockwise.
- Laevorotatory (*L*) if the molecule rotates light towards left (anti-clockwise).

Chiral Compounds
- Total number of optical isomers = 2^n (in general)
  n = number of asymmetric carbon atoms
- Total number of optical isomers = $2^{n-1} + 2^{(\frac{n}{2}-1)}$
  n = number of asymmetric carbon atoms (even)
- Total number of optical isomers = 2^{n-1}
  n = number of asymmetric carbon atoms (odd)

Alcohols, Phenols & Ethers (Chapter at a Glance)

Alcohols

Physical Properties

- Lower members are colourless, volatile liquids with a characteristic smell and burning taste.
- Higher members are odourless and tasteless. Alcohol with more than 12 carbon atoms are colourless crystalline solids or liquids.
- Boiling point ∝ number of C-atoms
- Boiling point ∝ (1°>2°>3°)
- Alcohols have higher boiling point than those of hydrocarbons of comparable molecular masses due to H-bonding.
- They are soluble in water due to intermolecular H-bonding
- Solubility ∝ branching

Preparation

Alcohols ←
- (i) $(OAC)_2$ Hg (dil), (ii) $NaBH_4$ ← $CH_3-CH(CH_3)-CH=CH_2$ (Oxymercuration-demercuration)
- (i) B_2H_6, (ii) H_2O_2 ← $CH_3-CH(CH_3)-CH=CH_2$ (Hydroboration oxidation)
- $NaBH_4$ ← RCHO (Reduction of carbonyl compounds)
- NaOH(*aq*)/KOH(*aq*) ← CH_3CH_2Br (Hydrolysis of alkyl halides)
- *R*MgX ← $R_2C=O$ (Reaction with Grignard Reagent)

Classification

- **Monohydric alcohols**
  - 1° alcohols e.g. CH_3CH_2OH(Ethyl alcohol)
  - 2° alcohols e.g. $(CH_3)_2-CH-OH$ (1-methyl ethanol)
  - 3° alcohols e.g. $(CH_3)_3-C-OH$ (tert-butyl alcohol)
- **Dihydric alcohol**
  - A class of alcohol having two hydroxyl groups in each molecule. e.g. CH_2OH-CH_2OH
- **Trihydric alcohol**
  - A class of alcohol having three hydroxyl groups in each molecule e.g. $CH_2OH-CHOH-CH_2OH$
- **Vinylic alcohol** When—OH group is attached to vinylic C atom. e.g. $CH_2=CH-OH$
- **Allylic alcohol**. e.g. $CH_2=CH-CH_2-OH$
- **Benzylic alcohol**, e.g.

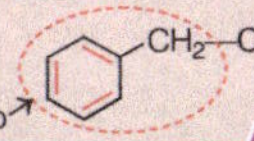

Nomenclature

For naming alcohols, the 'e' of alkane is removed and the ending 'ol' is added.

- Named as alkyl alcohol or alkanols (methanol, ethanol, propanol. etc.)
- For cyclic alcohols, prefix cyclo is used when OH group is present at C–1. e.g. (cyclohexane ring)—OH → cyclohexanol
- For polyhydric alcohols, the number of —OH groups is indicated by adding the multiplicative prefix, di, tri etc.

Distinguishing Test for Alcohols

Alcohol	Dichromate (Oxidation) test	Victor Meyer test	Lucas test
1°	Acid (Orange solution becomes green)	Blood red colour	No turbidity
2°	Ketone (Orange solution becomes green)	Blue colour	Turbidity in 5 minutes
3°	No reaction	Colourless	Turbidity immediately

Chemical properties

- Cleavage of O—H bond (ease of reaction depends on stability of alkoxide ion or phenoxide ion).
  - Alcohols can act as nucleophiles as well as electrophiles
  - Acidity : Phenols > Water > 1° alcohol > 2° alcohol > 3° alcohol
  - *EWG* increases while *EDG* decreases acidity.
- Clevage of C—OH bond (ease of reaction depends on stability of carbocations). Order of reactivity with HX is 3° > 2° > 1°.>CH_3OH

Chemical Reaction

Alcohols →
- Metals: $\xrightarrow{Na} R\bar{O}Na^+ + H_2\uparrow$
- Esterification: $\xrightarrow[RCOX/RCONH_2]{R'COOH/(RCO)_2O/} R'COOR$
- Grignard reagents: $\xrightarrow{R'MgX} R'H + Mg(OR)X$
- Hydrogen halides: $\xrightarrow[HCl]{ZnCl_2} RCl$
- Dehydration: $\xrightarrow[Anhyd.ZnCl_2/Al_2O_3]{H_2SO_4/H_3PO_4/} >C=C< + H_2O$

Alcohols | Phenols | Ethers

Phenols

Preparation

Phenol ←
- NaOH, H^+/H_2O ← C_6H_5Cl Halobenzene (Hydrolysis)
- O_2, H^+/H_2O ← $C_6H_5CH(CH_3)_2$ Isopropyl benzene (Cumene process)
- NaOH, H^+/H_2O ← $C_6H_5SO_3H$ (Sulphonic acid) (Fusion of alkali metal salt)
- NaOH, H_2O ← C_6H_6 Benzene (Hydroxylation of benzene)

Classification

- Monohydric phenols
- Polyhydric alcohols

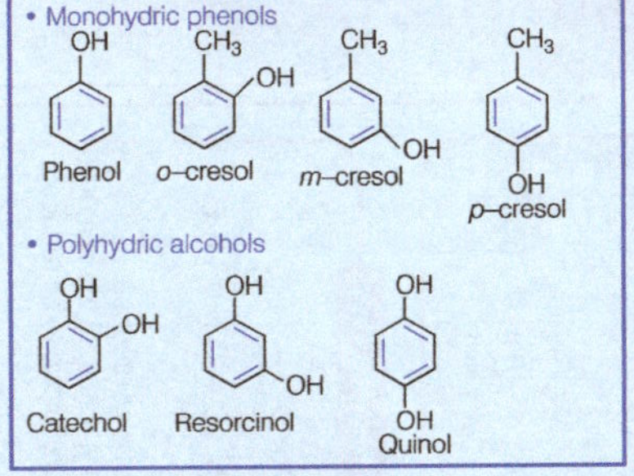

Chemical Properties

PHENOLS →
- Electrophilic substitution reactions
  - Reimer-Tiemann reaction (Alkali + $CHCl_3$) → *o* and *p* -salicylaldehyde
  - Kolbe reaction (CO_2, 140-200°C) → *o* and *p*-salicylate ion
  - Kolbe-Schmidt reaction (CO_2, 5-7 atm pressure, 120-140°C) → *o* and *p*-salicylate ion
- Gattermann synthesis (HCN/HCl, $AlCl_3$, 40°C) → *o* and *p*-salicylaldehyde
- Esterification (with acid or acid derivatives) → Esters
- Lederer-manasse rection (HCHO/acid/base) → Bakelite

Test for Phenol

Test	Observation
$FeCl_3$ test	Violet colour
Br_2-H_2O test	White ppt.
Libermann's nitroso test ($NaNO_2$+ conc H_2SO_4)	Deep green/blue colour which changes into red on dilution.

Physical Properties

- These are colourless liquids or solids with red tint and have carbolic odour.
- Phenols are highly toxic. Due to stronger intermoleculer H-bonding their boiling point are higher than corresponding alcohols.
- They are more miscible with water as compare to alcohols.
- They have high dipole moments and are acidic in nature

Ethers

Structure

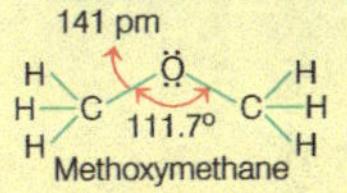

- Bond angle is higher than tetrahedral angle due to high % *s* character in C–O bonds.
- The bulkier *R* group result in the greater forces of repulsion and thus the R_2>O bond angle is 110°.

Classification

- Ethers are compounds having general formula $C_nH_{2n+2}O$.
- A general structure is having two carbon atoms bridged with one O-atom [*R*—O—*R*]
- If both *R* groups are same it is a simple or symmetric ether.
  e.g. CH_3-O-CH_3 or Ph—O—Ph.
- If both *R* groups are different, it is mixed or asymmetrical. e.g. CH_3-O-Ph.

Physical Properties

- C—O bonds are slightly polar due to bent structure.
- B.P. are lower than isomeric alcohols.
- Solubility ∝ 1/Molecular mass (soluble upto three carbon atoms due to H-bonding).
- Ethers upto three carbon atoms are solubles in water due to the formation of intermolecular hydrogen bonds.

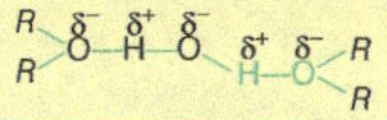

Preparation

1. Williamson's synthesis
   $2ROH \xrightarrow[or\ Al_2O_3,\ 523\ K]{Conc.\ H_2SO_4,\ 413\ K}$ ROR Ether
   $RX + RONa \xrightarrow[-NaX]{\Delta}$ ROR Ether
   It involves S_N2 mechanism of an alkoxide ion on 1° alkyl halide.
2. By reacting alkyl halides with dry silver oxide
   $2RX + Ag_2O \rightarrow ROR + AgX$
3. By dehydration of alcohols
   Dehydration of alcohols for the formation of ethers follows the order. 1°>2°>3°

ETHERS: $CH_3CH_2OH \xrightarrow[413\ K]{H_2SO_4} C_2H_5-O-C_2H_5$ Diethyl ether

Chemical Properties

ETHERS →
- Reactions involving ethereal oxygen
  Action of conc. acids
  $ROR + HCl\ (conc.) \longrightarrow [R_2\overset{+}{O}-H]Cl^-$
- Reactions involving cleavage of carbon-oxygen bond
  (i) With halogen acids,
  $R-OR + HX \xrightarrow{\Delta} R-OH + R-X$
  (ii) With PCl_5
  $ROR + PCl_5 \xrightarrow{\Delta} 2R-Cl$
  (iii) With acid derivatives
  $ROR + (CH_3CO)_2 \xrightarrow[ZnCl_2/\Delta]{Anhy.AlCl_3} 2CH_3COOR$

Aldehydes, Ketones and Carboxylic Acid (Chapter at a glance

Distinction Test

Test	Aldehydes	Ketones
Tollen's test	Silver mirror	No change
Fehling's test (only aliphatic)	Red precipitate	No change
Benedict test (only aliphatic)	Red precipitate	No change
Schiff's test	Pink colour	No change

Physical Properties

- **Physical State** Generally are colourless liquids.
- **Boiling Points** Have higher boiling points than hydrocarbons and ethers of comparable molecular mass due to dipole-dipole interactions.
  - Boiling point of aldehydes and ketones are lower than alcohols of similar molecular masses due to absence of intermolecular hydrogen bonding.
  - Boiling point of ketones are slightly higher than aldehydes due to the presence of two alkyl groups which make carbonyl group more polar.
- Boiling point order : Alcohols > ketones > Aldehydes > Ethers > Hydrocarbons.
- **Solubility decreases with increase in molecular mass.** Lower aldehydes and **ketones are soluble in water.**
  - Aromatic aldehydes and ketones are less soluble than corresponding aliphatic aldehydes and ketones due to large hydrocarlon part in benzene ring.

Structure & Nomenclature

- Organic compounds containing carbon-oxygen double bond, i.e. $>C{=}O$ group are called carbonyl compounds.
- In carbonyl group, π-electron cloud is displaced towards more electronegative oxygen atom.
- The carbon acquires partially positive and oxygen acquires partially negative charge.

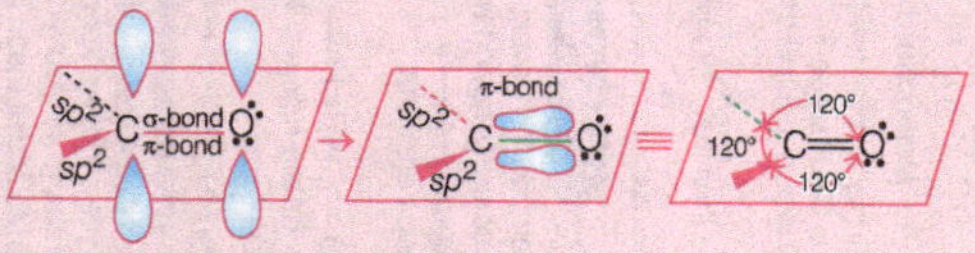

- General formula of aldehyde = C_nH_{2n+1} CHO
- IUPAC name of aldehyde = Alkanal
- General formula of ketones = C_nH_{2n+1} COC_nH_{2n+1}
- IUPAC name of ketones = Alkanone
- The categorisation of aldehydes and ketones is shown below.

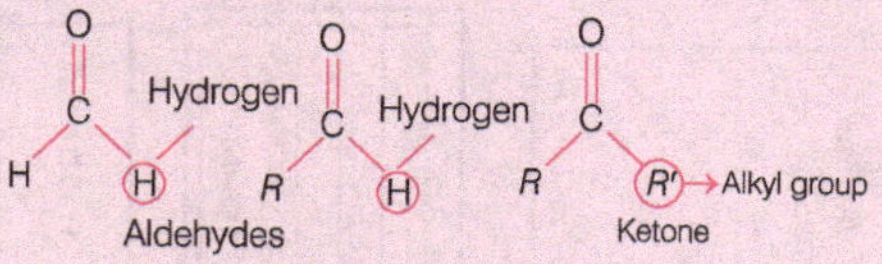

Preparation for Aldehydes & Ketones

- **Hydroboration-oxidation of alkynes**
  $3R—C\equiv CH \xrightarrow[H_2O_2,OH^-]{BH_3,THF} RCH_2—CHO$
- **Hydration of alkynes** $\longrightarrow CH\equiv CH \xrightarrow[H_2SO_4]{1\%\ HgSO_4} CH_3—CHO$
- **Oxidation of alcohols** $\longrightarrow$ 1° alcohol $\xrightarrow{\text{Alkaline } KMnO_4} RCOOH$; 2° alcohol $\longrightarrow R_2CO$
- **Catalytic dehydrogenation of alcohols** $\longrightarrow RCH_2OH \xrightarrow[\Delta]{Cu} RCHO$; $R_2CHOH \xrightarrow[\Delta]{Cu} R_2CO$
- **Ozonolysis of alkenes** $\longrightarrow RCH = CHR' \xrightarrow[Zn/H_2O]{O_3} RCHO + R'CHO$; $R_2C=CR'_2 \xrightarrow[Zn/H_2O]{O_3} R_2CO + R'_2CO$
- **Wacker's process** $\longrightarrow CH_2=CH_2 + \frac{1}{2}O_2 \xrightarrow[H_2O]{PdCl_2\text{-}CuCl_2} CH_3CHO$

Chemical Properties for Aldehydes and Ketones

Nucleophilic Addition Reactions

- **With HCN** $\longrightarrow R—C(=O)—H/R \xrightarrow{HCN}$

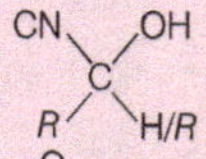

- **With NH_3 and its derivatives** $\longrightarrow R—C(=O)—H/R \xrightarrow{NH_3}$ Schiff's base
- **With RMgX** $\longrightarrow R—C(=O)—H/R \xrightarrow[H_2O]{RMgX}$ Alcohols
- **Addition of alcohols**
  $R—C(=O)—H/R \xrightarrow[\text{HCl gas}]{ROH}$ Hemiacetal or hemiketal $\xrightarrow[-H_2O]{ROH}$ Acetal or ketal.
- **Oxidation** $\longrightarrow RCHO \xrightarrow[\text{Mild}]{[O]} RCOOH$; $R_2CO \xrightarrow[\text{Strong}]{[O]} RCOOH$
- **Reduction** $\longrightarrow R_2CO/RCHO \xrightarrow{NaBH_4/LiAlH_4} R_2CHOH/RCH_2OH$; $R_2CO/RCHO \xrightarrow[NH_2 + NH_2/KOH]{Zn/Hg,\ HCl} RCH_2R/R—CH_3$
- **Haloform reaction** $\longrightarrow RCOCH_3 \xrightarrow[NaOX]{} RCOONa + CHX_3$
  Reaction at α-CH_3 group.
- **Aldol condensation** $\longrightarrow 2RCHO \xrightarrow{NaOH\ (dil.)}$ β-hydroxy aldehyde $\xrightarrow{\Delta}$ α,β -unsaturated aldehyde
  $2R_2CO \xrightarrow{NaOH\ (dil.)}$ β-hydroxy ketone $\xrightarrow{\Delta}$ α,β -unsaturated ketone
- **Cannizzaro Reaction** $\longrightarrow 2RCHO \xrightarrow[\Delta]{Conc.NaOH} RCH_2OH + RCOONa$
  (Aldehyde do not have α-H atom undergo disproportionation on heating with concentrated alkali)

Chemical Properties of Ketones Only

Benzilic acid rearrangement

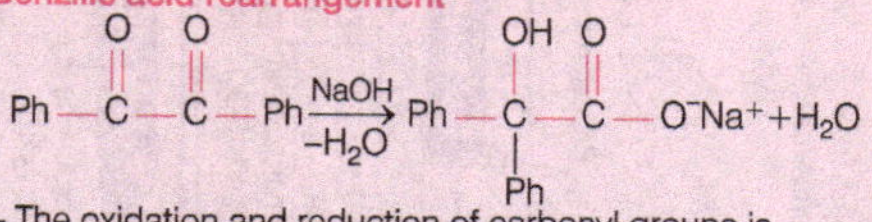

- The oxidation and reduction of carbonyl groups is associated with intermolecular alkyl shift from the carbonyl group to be oxidised to the carbonyl group to be reduced.
- Addition of chloroform

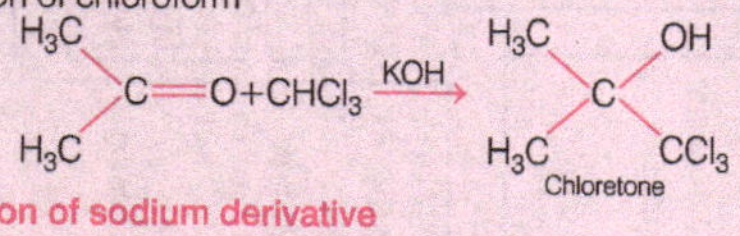

Formation of sodium derivative

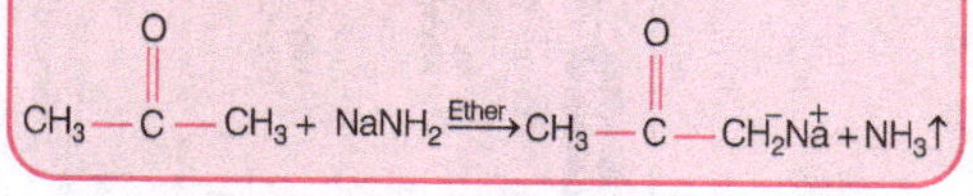

Uses of Aldehydes & Ketones

- Used as solvent in explosive manufacturing.
- Acetone is used in cosmetics and as a nail paint remover.
- Acetophenone is used in flavouring agents.
- HCHO is used in preparing polymeric products.
- Used in drug testing.
- Used in formation of bakelite.
- Cinnamaldehyde is used for treating cold.

Carboxylic Acid

Physical Properties

- Lower acids and derivatives are colourless liquids.
- Exists as dimer in vapour phase.
- Boiling point of carboxylic acids are higher than aldehydes, ketones and alcohols of comparable molecular masses due to intermolecular H-bonding.

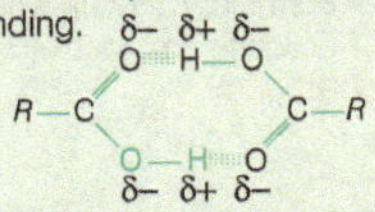

- **Boiling point order** : Carboxylic acids > Alcohols > Aldehydes > Ketones > Hydrocarbons
- Solubility α 1/Number of C atoms α Intermolecular H-bonding

Acidic Strength

- Carboxylic acids are acidic in nature but they are weaker acids than mineral acids.
- They are stronger acids then phenols because the carboxylate ion is more estabilised with resonance as compared to phenoxide ion.
- Electron withdrawing groups increase the acidity of carboxylic acids by stabilising the conjugate base.
- Electron donating groups decrease the acidity by destabilising the conjugate base.
- Dissociate in water to give hydroniumion is acidic due to stable carboxylate ion.

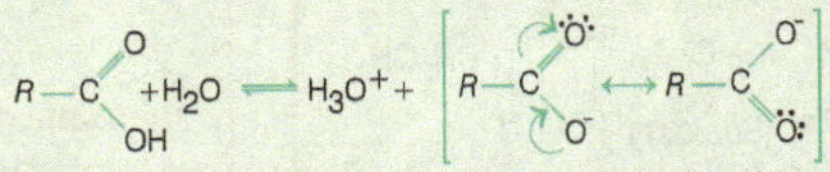

- Hydroxyl group of acids is more acidic than the hydroxyl group of alcohols.
- **Acidity order** Carboxylic Acids > Phenols > Alcohols
- More is the electronegativity of the atom attatced to the carboxyl group, more will be acidity.

Preparation

From Hydrocabons

$$2RCH_3 + 3O_2 \xrightarrow[\text{stearate}]{\text{Manganese}} 2RCOOH + 2H_2O$$

Oxidation of Alcohols

$$2RCH_2OH + 3O_2 \xrightarrow{[O]} RCHO \xrightarrow{[O]} R—COOH$$

Hydrolysis of Esters

$$R—\overset{O}{\overset{||}{C}}—O—R' \xrightarrow{H_2O/H^+} R—\overset{O}{\overset{||}{C}}—OH + R'OH$$

Ozonolysis of alkenes

$$CH_2{=}CH_2 + O_3 \xrightarrow[AgO]{HgO_2} HCOOH + H_2O$$

Formic acid

From Grignard's reagent

$$RMgX + O{=}C{=}O \xrightarrow[\text{ether}]{\text{Dry}} R—\overset{O}{\overset{||}{C}}—OMgX \xrightarrow{H_3O^{\oplus}} R—\overset{O}{\overset{||}{C}}—OH + Mg(OH)X$$

Structure & Nomenclature

Common name Suffix – ic acid at the end
e.g. acetic acid

IUPAC name Suffix – oic acid is added in the name of corrérponding alkane.

Structure:

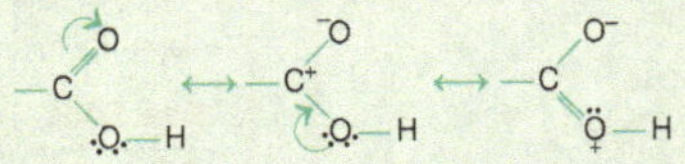

- The bonds to the carboxyl carbon lie in one plane and are separated by about 120°.
- The carboxylic carbon is less electrophilic than carbonyl carbon because of the possible resonance structure.

Uses of Carboxylic Acids

- Used in manufacturing of soaps and detergents.
- In making of drugs e.g. aspirin, vitamin C. etc.
- Used as coagulant in manufacturing of rubber.
- Benzoic acid is used as preservative in food and its salts are used as urinary antiseptic.
- Formic acid is used in leather tanning, textile dyeing and finishing.
- Acetic acid is used in the manufacture of rayon, plastics, rubber.
- It is also used in silk industries.

Chemical Properties

Reactions involving cleavage of C — OH Group

$R—\overset{O}{\overset{||}{C}}—OH$:

- $\xrightarrow[P_2O_5]{+ RCOOH/\Delta}$ $(RCO)_2O$ Anhydride
- $\xrightarrow[-H_2O]{ROH/H^+}$ $RCOOR'$ Ester
- $\xrightarrow[\text{SOCl}_2 \text{ in pyridine}]{PCl_3 \text{ or } PCl_5 \text{ or}}$ $RCOCl$ Acid chloride
- $\xrightarrow[-H_2O_2]{NH_3,\Delta}$ $RCONH_2$ Amide

Reactions involving proton of –OH group

$R—\overset{O}{\overset{||}{C}}—OH$:

- $\xrightarrow{Na}$ $2RCOONa + H_2$
- $\xrightarrow{NaOH}$ $2RCOONa + H_2O$
- $\xrightarrow{Na_2CO_3}$ $2RCOONa + CO_2 + H_2O$
- $\xrightarrow{NaHCO_3}$ $2RCOONa + CO_2 + H_2O$

Reaction involving >C=O Group

$R—\overset{O}{\overset{||}{C}}—OH$:

- (i) LiAlH4/ether or B_2H_6 (ii) H_3O^+(Reduction) $\rightarrow R—CH_2—OH$
- $\xrightarrow[H_2O]{HI, \text{ Red } P}$ $RCH_3 + 2H_2O + 3I_2$
- $\xrightarrow{N_3H, H_2SO_4}$ $RNH_2 + N_2\uparrow + CO_2$

- Benzoic acids are *meta*-directing in nature as they remove electrons through resonance
- The *meta* carbons are more e⁻dense, hence more attractive to an attacking electrophile.

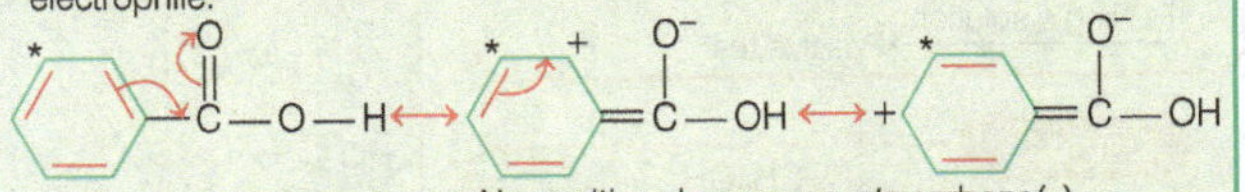

No positive charge on *meta* carbons(*)

- Due to the *meta*-directing nature, benzoic acids do not undergo Friedal craft alkylation or Friedal craft acylation reactions.

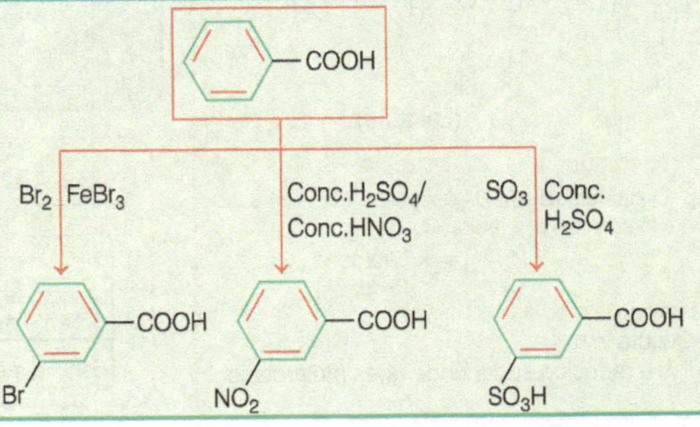

Biomolecules (Chapter at a Glance)

Disaccharides

- Yields two units of monosaccharides on hydrolysis.
- Joined together by glycosidic linkage (—O—).

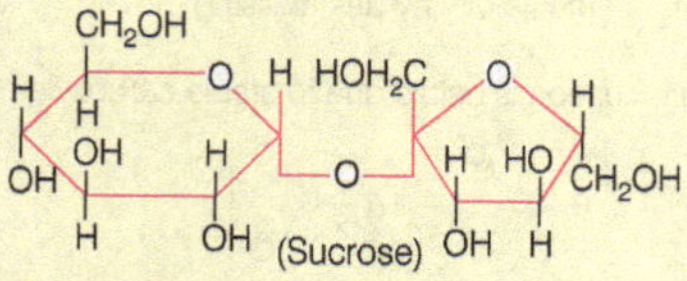

(Sucrose)

• Properties

- It is a non-reducing sugar.
- Is dextrorotatory with $\alpha = +66.5°$
- Mixture of glucose and fructose is laevorotatory.
- α-D-glucose + β-D-fructose $\xrightarrow{-H_2O}$ $(C_{12}H_{22}O_{11})$ Sucrose

• Reactions

Sucrose

- $\xrightarrow{H_2O/H^+}$ α-D- glucose + β-D-fructose is known as inversion of sugar.
- $\xrightarrow{O_2/\Delta}$ $CO_2 + H_2O$
- $\xrightarrow[\Delta]{Burn}$ Caramel

Maltose

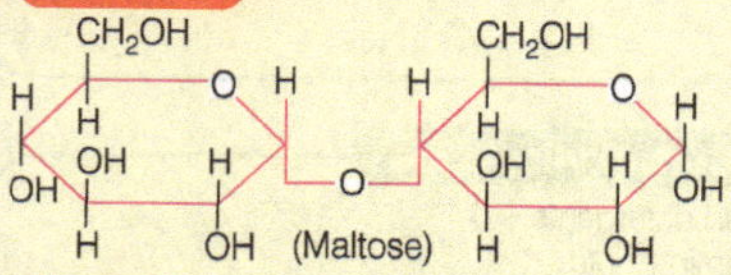

(Maltose)

• Preparation

- Starch $\xrightarrow[Maltase]{H_2O}$ Maltose $(C_{12}H_{22}O_{11})$

• Properties

- It is a dimer of α-D-glucose.
- One glucose unit is non-reducing another is reducing.
- It is a reducing sugar.

• Reactions

Maltose

- $\xrightarrow{H_2O/H^+}$ D-glucose
- $\xrightarrow{\text{Tollen's reagent}}$ Positive test
- $\xrightarrow{\text{Fehling's solution}}$ Positive test

Lactose

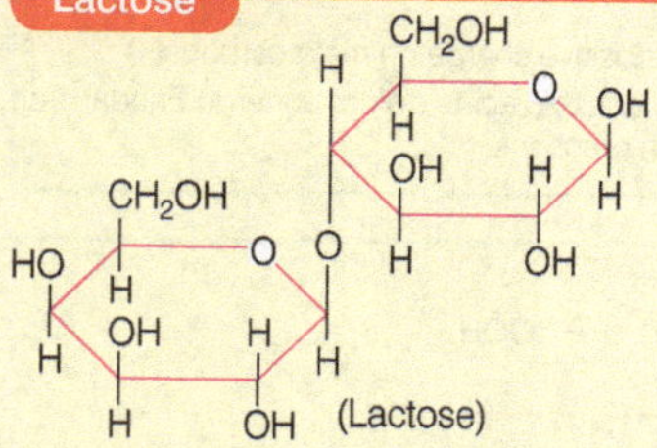

(Lactose)

• Preparation

β-D-galactose + β-D-glucose
(Non-reducing) (Reducing)

⇌ Lactose (Reducing)

• Properties

- Occurs in milk.
- It is a reducing sugar undergoes mutarotation.

• Fructose

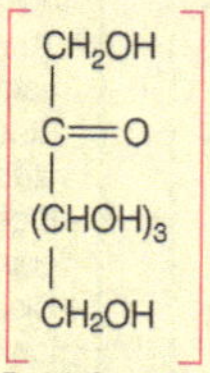

D-(–)-fructose

• Preparation

- Sucrose $\xrightarrow{H_2O/H^+}$ Glucose + Fructose

• Cyclic Structure

- Obtained by addition of —OH at C-5 to —CO group.
- Five membered ring called furanose exists in two forms.

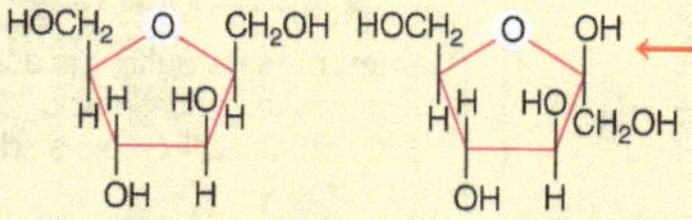

α-D(–)-fructofuranose β-D(–)-fructofuranose

• Reactions

Fructose

- $\xrightarrow{\text{Red P/HI}}$ *n*-hexane
- $\xrightarrow{HCN}$ Fructose cyanohydrin
- $\xrightarrow{NH_2OH}$ Fructose oxime
- $\xrightarrow{\text{Tollen's reagent}}$ Gluconic acid
- $\xrightarrow{Br_2/Water}$ No reaction

Amylopectin

• Properties

- Branched chain polymer of D-glucose.
- Contains D-glucopyranose units coupled together with 1, 6-glycosidic linkage and 1, 4-glycosidic linkage.
- Is insoluble in water.
- Gives maltose on hydrolysis.
- Gives D-(+)-glucose with acids.

Structure

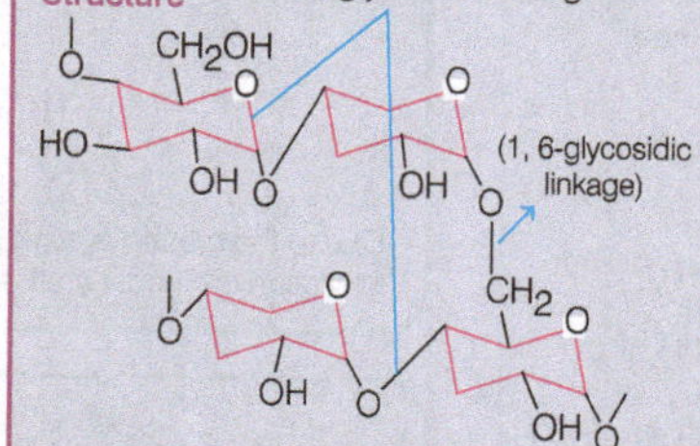

(Amylopectin)

• Reactions

Lactose

- $\xrightarrow{H_2O/H^+}$ or lactose → D-glucose + D-galactose (Equimolar)
- $\xrightarrow{\text{Tollen's reagent}}$ Positive test
- $\xrightarrow{\text{Fehling's solution}}$ Positive test

Monosaccharides

- Smallest unit which can not be hydrolysed.
- Formula: $(CH_2O)_n$ where, $n = 3-7$
- Glucose, fructose etc.

• Glucose

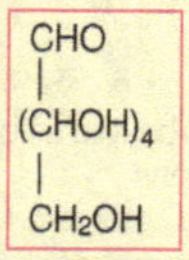

Open chain structure

• Preparation

(i) Sucrose $\xrightarrow{H_2O/H^+}$ Glucose + Fructose

(ii) Starch or cellulose $\xrightarrow{H_2O/H^+}$ Glucose

• Cyclic structure of glucose :

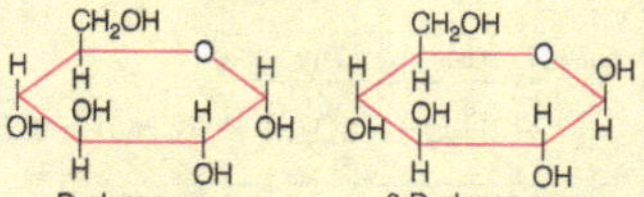

α-D-glucopyranose β-D-glucopyranose

• Reactions

Glucose

- $\xrightarrow{HNO_3}$ Saccharic acid $\xrightarrow{[O]}$ Gluconic acid
- $\xrightarrow{HI/\Delta}$ *n*-hexane
- $\xrightarrow{Br_2/Water}$ Gluconic acid (Test for aldehydic group)
- $\xrightarrow{HCN}$ Cyanohydrin

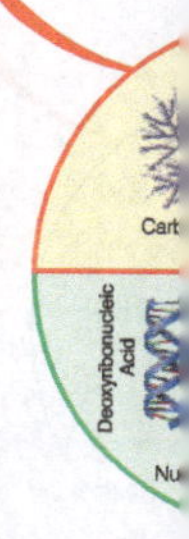

Polysaccharides

- Non-sugars and yields large number of monosaccharides.
- General formula $(C_6H_{10}O_5)_n$.
- e.g. Starch, cellulose, glycogen.

• Amylose

• Properties

- Straight chain polymer of D-glucose.
- Gives blue colour with iodine.
- Contains chained units of α-D-glucopyranose by C_1–C_4 glycosidic linkage. Molecular weight can be between 10000-1000000.

Structure

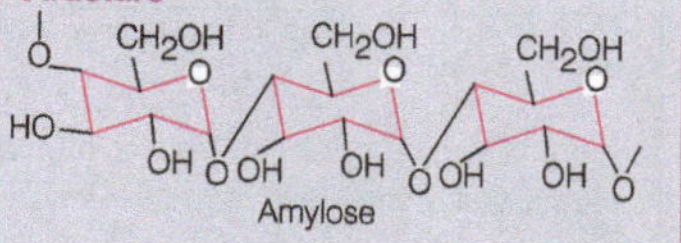

Amylose

Cellulose

• Properties

- Is a colourless solid insoluble in water.
- It is a straight chain polymer.
- Soluble in Schweizer's reagent.
- Is composed of only β-D-glucose units.
- Glycosidic linkage between C_1 and C_4.

Structure

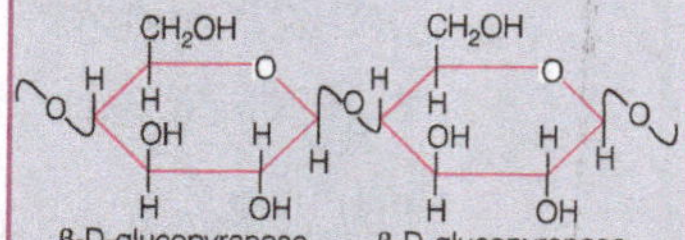

β-D-glucopyranose β-D-glucopyranose

Enzymes

- **Properties**
  - Are biological catalysts that catalyse biochemical reactions.
  - Generally are globular proteins.
  - Increases rate of reactions.
  - Are highly substrate specific.
- **Mechanism**
  - Reduces the activation energy of reaction.
  - Mechanism is known as lock and key model.

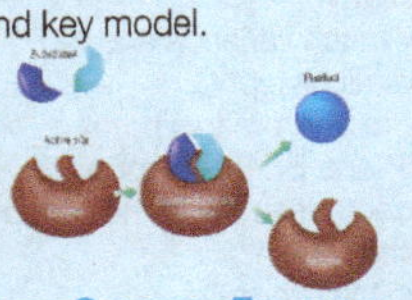

- **Some Common Enzymes**

Enzymes	Reaction catalysed
Amylase	Starch→Glucose
Maltase	Maltose→2-Glucose
Lactase	Lactose→D-Glucose +D-Galactose
Pepsin	Proteins → α-amino acids

Hormones

- Act as intercellular messengers and are governed by endocrine glands.
- **Steroidal Hormones**
  - **(i) Sex Hormones**
    - Includes androgens (testosterone), estrogens (estrone, estradiol) and progesterone.
    - Androgens are generally secreted in testes. Estrogens in ovary and progesterone in corpus luteum.
  - **(ii) Corticoids**
    e.g. Glucocorticoids, found in adrenal cortex.
- **Peptide Hormones**
  - **(i) Insulin** Secreted in pancreas and helpful in blood sugar control.
  - **(ii) Glucagon** Secreted in pancreas and increases blood glucose
  - **(iii) Endorphins** Secreted in pituitary gland and relieves pain
- **Amine Hormones**
  - **(i) Epinerphrine** Secreted in adrenal medulla.
    - Regulates CNS, increases pulse rate.
  - **(ii) Thyroxine** Secreted in thyroid gland and controls metabolism.

Classification

(i) Essential amino acids
- These can not be synthesised in the body.
  e.g. Valine, leucine, isoleucine, arginine etc.

(ii) Non-essential amino acids
- Can be synthesised in the body.
  e.g. Alanine, glutamic acid, aspartic acid, glutamine etc.

- **Properties**
  - Behave like salts rather than simple amines or acids.
  - Exists in Zwitter ion form.
  - Except Gly–, all amino acids are optically active.

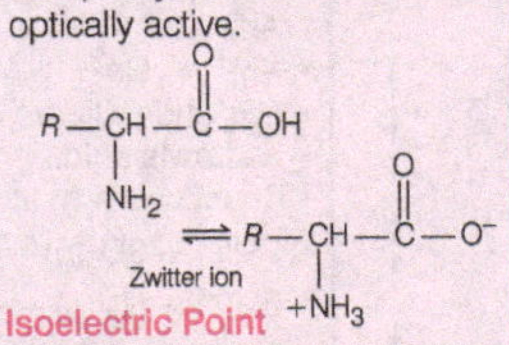

- **Isoelectric Point**
  - pH at which dipolar ion exists as neutral ion.
  - Zwitter ionic forms are amphoteric.

Nucleic Acids

- Are polymers of nucleotides
  Sugar+base+phosphoric acid
- Plays role in transmission of heridity, protein synthesis.
- Are DNA and RNA.
- **Composition**
  - **(i) Pentose Sugar**
    In DNA, β-D-2-deoxyribose.
    In RNA, β-D-ribose.
  - **(ii) Phosphoric acid**
  - **(iii) Nitrogenous Base**
    Adenine (A), guanine (G) and cytosine (C) in both. Thymine (T) in DNA and uracil (U) in RNA.
- **Structures**
  - **(i) Primary** Information regarding sequence of nucleotides in chain.
  - **(ii) Secondary** Two strands of polynucleotides coiled around.
    - Has a double helix form.
    - Contains sugar phosphate units in backbone.
    - Are linked through H-bonds.

Proteins

- These are polymers of α-amino acids linked together with peptide bond.
- This linkage can be dipeptide, tripeptide etc.
  e.g.

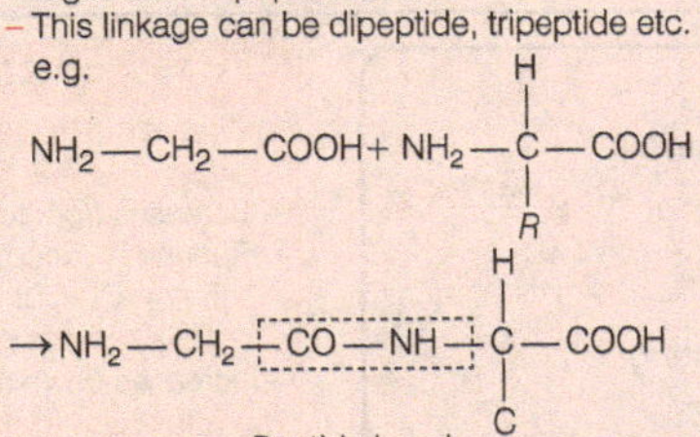

Oligopeptides When 2-10 amino acids are linked together through peptide bond.
Polypeptides When more than 10 amino acids are linked together through peptide bonds.

- **Fibrous Proteins**
  - Have thread like structure and are insoluble in water. e.g. Keratin, myosin.
- **Globular Proteins**
  - Have spherical shapes and are water soluble. e.g. Insulins and albumins.

Amino Acids

- **Introduction**
  - Are organic compounds containing an amino group (—NH_2) and a carboxyl group (—COOH).
  - Can be classified as α, β, or γ...... on basis of relative position of —NH_2 with respect to —COOH.
  - Only α-amino acids are obtained from hydrolysis of proteins.
  - Are building blocks of proteins.

DNA

- **DNA**
  - Has double helix structure.
  - Both strands are complementary to each other.
  - H-bonds are formed between specific pairs.
  - A:::T and C::::G (H-bonds)
- **RNA**
  - It has single strand.
- **Types**
  - *m*-RNA (messenger)
  - *t*-RNA (transfer)
  - *r*-RNA (ribosomal)
- **Functions**
  - **(i) Replication :**
    - Cell divides, DNA molecules replicates and are transferred.
  - **(ii) Protein synthesis**
    - DNA sends message for synthesis of particular protein which is then synthesised by RNA in a cell.

Glycogen

- **Properties**
  - Found in animal cells.
  - Is a reserve of carbohydrates.
  - Gives purple-red colour with iodine.
  - Gives D-(+)-glucose with dilute acid.
  - Structure similar to amylopectin.

Fat Soluble Vitamins

- Soluble in fats and oils and are stored in liver.

Vitamins	Name	Sources	Causes
A	Retinoids	Milk, butter	Night-blindness
D	Ergocalciferol / Cholecalciferol	Milk, fish, liver oil	Rickets
E	Tocopherol	Wheat germ oil, almonds	Muscle weakness
K	Phylloquinone	Leafy veggies	Haemorr -hages

- Vitamin H is neither fat-soluble nor water-soluble.

Tertiary Structure

- **Tertiary Structure**
  - Represents overall folding of secondary structure of proteins.

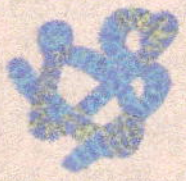

Tertiary structure

- **Quaternary Structure**
  - A3-dimensional fold.

Quaternary structure

Primary Structure

- **Primary Structure**
  - It shows an exact ordering of amino acids.
- **Secondary Structure**
  - **α-helix**
    Twisting of chain due to H- bonds between all NH_2 and COOH groups.
  - **β-pleated Sheet**
    - Polypeptide chains stretched and laid side by side.
    - Held together by intermolecular H-bonds.

Vitamins

- Generally regarded as compounds
- Required in small amounts to perform biological function.
- Are generally necessary for maintenance of optimal growth and health of organism.
- **Water Soluble Vitamins**
  - Soluble in water.
  - Should be supplied regularly and are excreted easily.

Vitamins	Name	Sources	Causes
B_1	Thiamine	Pulses, nuts	Beri-Beri
B_2	Riboflavin	Eggs, Green veggies	Cheilosis
B_6	Pyridoxine	Rice bran, fish	Convulsi-ons
C	Ascorbic acid	Citrus fruits, chillies	Scurvy

Denaturation

- Native shape of protein is destroyed due to heat or coagulation.
- Only 2° and 3° structures are lost. 1° remains intact.
- Biological activity of protein is lost.

p-Block Elements (Chapter at a Glance)

• Anomalous Behaviour of Boron
– Typically semi-metal.
– Cannot extend covalency above four.
– Exhibits allotropy and exists in crystalline and amorphous form.
– Has higher melting and boiling points comparatively.

• Diborane
– Simplest known hydride of boron.
– $4BCl_3 + 3LiAlH_4 \xrightarrow{Ether} 2B_2H_6 + 3LiCl + 3AlCl_3$
– Structure contains two 3 centre-2 electron bridge bonds known as "Banana bonds".

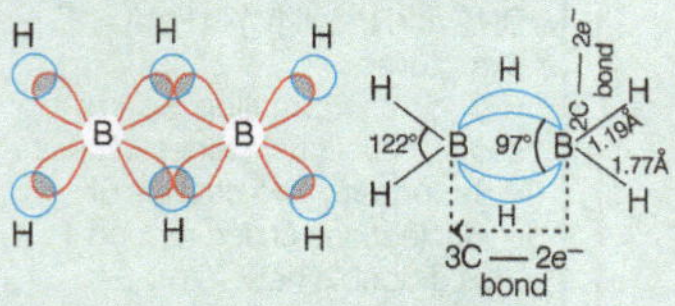

– Is used as a precursor to synthesise other boron compounds borazine.
$3B_2H_6 + 6NH_3 \xrightarrow{\Delta} 2B_3N_3H_6 + 12H_2$

13 Group Elements
[NG] ns^2np^1, NG=Noble Gas

• Physical Properties
(i) Atomic radii B < Ga < Al < In < Tl
(ii) Ionisation enthalpy
– Shows a discontinuity due to poor shielding of *d* and *f*-electrons.
– The order of first ionisation enthalpy is
B > Tl > Ga > Al > In
(iii) Electronegativity B>Tl>In>Ga> Al
(iv) Melting point B > Al > Tl > In > Ga

• Chemical Properties
– Shows +1 and +3 oxidation states.
– Stability of states:
$Al^+ < Ga^+ < In^+ < Tl^+$
$Al^{3+} > Ga^{3+} > In^{3+} > Tl^{3+}$
– BF_3 and BCl_3 are electron deficient and behave as **Lewis acid.**

• Reactions with air
$2M(s) + 3O_2(g) \xrightarrow{\Delta} 2M_2O_3(s)$
$2M(s) + N_2(g) \longrightarrow 2MN(s)$ (*M*=element)

• Compounds with acids and alkalies
$2M(s) + 6HCl(aq) \rightarrow 2M^{3+}(aq) + 6Cl^- + 3H_2(g)\uparrow$
$2M(s) + 2NaOH + 6H_2O(l) \longrightarrow 2Na^+[M(OH)_4]^-(aq) + 3H_2(g)$
[Boron does not react with acids and alkalies.]

• Reaction With halogens
– $2M(s) + 3X_2(g) \longrightarrow 2MX_3(s)$

14 Group Elements
[NG] (ns^2np^2)

• Physical Properties
(i) Covalent radii
– Increases down the group
C < Si < Ge < Sn < Pb
(ii) Ionisation enthalpy
– Decreases down the group but Pb is an exception.
C > Si > Ge > Sn < Pb
(iii) Electronegativity
– Does not show much variation and is almost same for all except C.
(iv) Melting points and boiling point
– Have higher MP and BP than group 13 elements and decreases down the group.
(v) Metallic character
– Increases down the group.

• Chemical Properties
– Common oxidation states are +4 and +2.
– Compounds are generally covalent.
– +4 is more stable for earlier elements (C, Si, Ge).
– +2 is more stable going down the group due to inert pair effect. (Pb^{+2})

p-block ele
ionisation e
and metalli

Group 16 elements [NG] (ns^2np^4)

• Physical Properties
(i) Atomic / Ionic radii
O < S < Se < Te < Po
(ii) Metallic character
O, S, — Non-metal; Se, Te, — Metalloids; Po — Metal
(iii) Melting point and Boiling point
– Both increases down the group.
– Melting point and Boiling point of O are much lesser than S.
(iv) Ionisation enthalpy
– Decreases down the group.
– Lower than those of group-15 elements.
(v) Electronegativity
– O has the highest electronegativity in its groups.
– It decreases down the group.

• Chemical Properties
– Generally – 2 and +2 oxidation state are shown by almost all elements.
– S, Se and Te also exhibit +4 and +6 oxidation state.
– Stability of + 6 state decreases down the group.
– Stability of + 4 state increases down the group.

• Trends in reactivity
(i) With hydrogen
– Acidic nature : $H_2Te > H_2Se > H_2S > H_2O$
– Thermal stability :
$H_2O > H_2S > H_2Se > H_2Te$
– Reducing nature :
$H_2Te > H_2Se > H_2S$
– Melting point and boiling point :
$H_2O > H_2Te > H_2Se > H_2S$
(ii) With halogens
– Stability :
$F^- > Cl^- > Br^- > I^-$
– In case of hexahalides, only fluorides are stable,
$SF_6 > SeF_6 > TeF_6$
– They have octahedral structure.
– SF_6 is exceptionally stable for steric reasons.
– Ease of hydrolysis :
$TeF_6 > SeF_6 > SF_6$
(iii) With oxygens
– Acidic nature decreases down the group for both MO_2 and MO_3 types.
– Reducing property $SO_2 > SeO_2 > TeO_2$

• Allotropes of S.
(i) Rhombic S (α-sulphur)
– Yellow in colour
– Insoluble in water.
– Soluble in CS_2
– Is octahedral in shape.

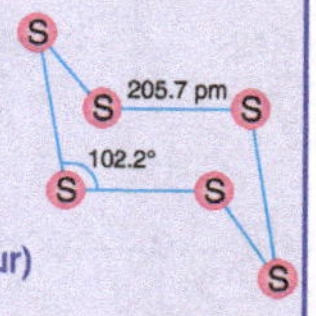

(ii) Monoclinic S (β-sulphur)
– Prepared by melting α-sulphur.
– Soluble in CS_2.
– Is needle shaped crystal.

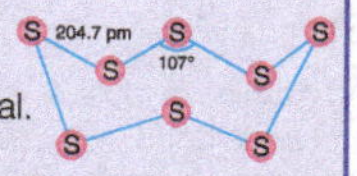

– Both forms have an S_8 ring which has a crown shape.
– In cyclo-S_6, the ring adopts the chair form.

Oxoacids of S
→ H_2SO_3 (Sulphurous acid)
→ H_2SO_4 (Sulphuric acid)
→ $H_2S_2O_7$ (Oleum)
→ $H_2S_2O_8$ (Marshall's acid)

17 Group Elements [NG] (ns^2np^5)

• Physical Properties
(i) Atomic / Ionic radii
– Increases from top to bottom.
– Fluorine is exceptionally small.
F << Cl < Br < I
(ii) Melting point and boiling point
– Increases down the group.
(iii) Ionisation enthalpy
F > Cl > Br > I
– Decreases due to increase in size.
(iv) Enthalpy of dissociation
Cl — Cl > Br — Br > F — F > I — I
(v) Electronegativity
F > Cl > Br > I

• Chemical Properties
– Most **common oxidation** state : – 1.
– **Oxidising power**
F > Cl > Br > I
– Elements exhibit +1, +3, +5 and +7 states as well.
– Fluorine shows unusally high IE, electronegativity due to low F — F (Bond dissociation enthapy).

• Trends in Reactivity
(i) Towards Hydrogen
– F > Cl > Br > I **(Reactivity order)**
– HI > HBr > HCl > HF **(Acidic strength)**
– HI > HBr > HCl > HF **(Reducing character)**
– HF > HI > HBr > HCl **(Boiling point)**
– HF > HCl > HBr > HI **(Thermal stability)**
– HI > HBr > HCl > HF **(Bond length)**
(ii) Towards Oxygen
– Stability of oxides formed by halogens.
I > Cl > Br
– F forms OF_2 and O_2F_2.
– Cl oxides are good oxidising agents.

(iii) Towards Metals
– Ionic character *MF* > *MCl* > *MBr* > *MI*
– Covalent character :
Covalent character ∝ oxidation satate of metal.
(iv) Interhalogen Compounds
– *XX'*, e.g. ICl, ClF.
– XX'_3, e.g. ICl_3, ClF_3.
– XX'_5, e.g. BrF_5
– XX'_7, e.g. IF_7
(v) Psuedohalides
– Univalent negative ions having similar properties to halides ions, e.g. CN^-, SCN^-, OCN^- etc.
(vi) Psuedohalogens
– Dimeric molecules of psuedohalides are psuedohalogens. e.g. $(CN)_2$, $(SCN)_2$ $(OCN)_2$ etc.

Reactions

With oxygen

$M(s) + O_2$ — Limited supply → $MO(g)$; Excess → $MO_2(g)$

Nature of oxides : [GeO-acidic, SnO and PbO (Amphoteric)]

[CO_2, SiO_2 GeO_2 (Acidic), SnO_2 and PbO_2 (Amphoteric)]

With water

- C, Si and Ge are not affected by water.
- Pb is unaffected by water due to protective oxide film formation.
- $Sn + 2H_2O \xrightarrow{\Delta} SnO_2 + 2H_2$ (Steam)

With halogen

- $M + 2X_2 \longrightarrow MX_4$

Order of thermal stability of tetrahalides

$CX_4 > SiX_4 > GeX_4 > SnX_4 > PbX_4$.

- Except CCl_4 other tetrachlorides are easily hydrolysed by water.

• Anomalous behaviour of C:

- Carbon shows −4 to +4 oxidation states.
- Melting point and boiling point of C are very high.
- It can form multiple $p\pi$-$p\pi$ bonds with itself.
- Shows a property called catenation.
- Exists in allotropic forms.

• Allotropes of Carbon

(i) Crystalline allotropes

– Diamond

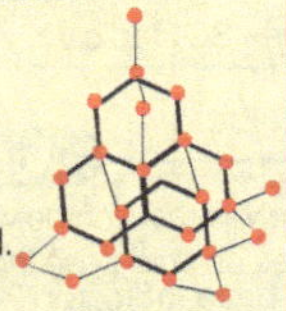

- Rigid 3-D lattice network.
- All carbons are sp^3hybridised.
- Insulator of electricity but a conductor of heat.

• Graphite

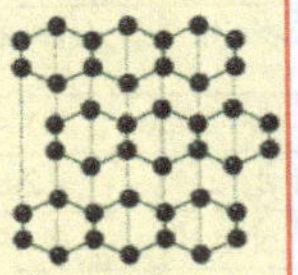

- A layered structure
- Each carbon is sp^2-hybridised.
- Good conductor of electricity.

• Buckminster fullerene

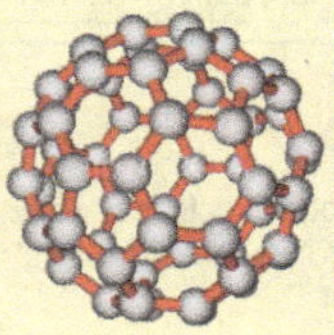

- It is C_{60} molecule.
- Shape like soccer ball.
- Has 20,6-membered and 12, 5-membered rings.
- Each C is sp^2-hybridised.

(ii) Amorphous allotropes

- Carbon black
- Charcoal
- Coke

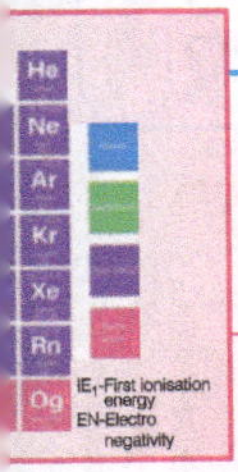

15 Group Elements [NG] (ns^2np^3)

• Physical Properties

N, P, — Non-metals; As, Sb, — Metalloids; Bi, Me — Typical metals

(i) Atomic / Ionic radii

N < P < As < Sb < Bi

(ii) Melting point and boiling point

N < P < As < Sb < Bi (B.P)

N < P < As > Sb > Bi (M.P)

(iii) Metallic character : N < P < As < Sb < Bi

(iv) Ionisation enthalpy : N > P > As > Sb > Bi

(v) Electronegativity : N>P>As>Sb>Bi

• Chemical Properties

- Common oxidation state are − 3, + 3 and + 5.
- +5 state is not stable down the group due to inert pair effect.
- Stability of − 3 O.S decreases down the group due to increase in size.

• Trends in reactivity

(i) Hydrides

Basic character $NH_3 > PH_3 > AsH_3 > SbH_3 \geq BiH_3$

Boiling point $PH_3 < AsH_3 < NH_3 < SbH_3 < BiH_3$

Thermal stability $NH_3 > PH_3 > AsH_3 > SbH_3 > BiH_3$

Solubility in water Soluble – NH_3, PH_3 ;Insoluble AsH_3, BiH_3, SbH_3

(ii) Oxides

- Acidity :

$N_2O_3 > P_4O_6 > As_2O_3 > Sb_2O_3 > Bi_2O_3$

- Acidic strength of oxides of N.

$N_2O < NO$ (Neutral) $< N_2O_3 < N_2O_4 < N_2O_5$ (Acidic)

(iii) Halides

- Stability : $NF_3 > NCl_3 > NBr_3$
- Lewis acid strength :

$PCl_3 > AsCl_3 > SbCl_3$

$PF_3 > PCl_3 > PBr_3 > PI_3$

- Lewis base strength :

$NI_3 > NBr_3 > NCl_3 > NF_3$

• Allotropes of P

(i) White Phosphorus

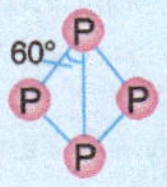

- Catches fire in air

$P_4 + 5O_2 \longrightarrow P_4O_{10}$ White fumes

(ii) Red Phosphorus

- Polymeric chains of P_4.

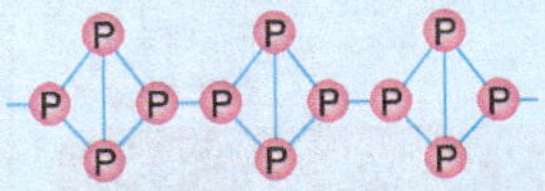

- Gives black phosphorus on heating.

(iii) Black Phosphorus

- Exists as α and β-forms.
- Sublimes in air.

Oxoacids of Phosphorus

- $\overset{+1}{H_3PO_2}$, (Hypophosphorus or phosphinic acid)
- $\overset{+3}{H_3PO_3}$, (*Ortho*-phosphorus acid, phosphonic acid)
- $\overset{+3}{H_4P_2O_5}$, (Pyrophosphorus acid)
- $\overset{+4}{H_4P_2O_6}$, (Hypophosphoric acid)
- $\overset{+5}{H_3PO_4}$, (*Ortho*-phosphoric acid)
- $\overset{+5}{H_4P_2O_7}$, (Pyrophosphoric acid)
- $\overset{+5}{(HPO_3)_n}$, (Poly *Meta*-phosphoric acid)

18 Group Elements [NG] (ns^2np^6)

• Physical Properties

- Are unreactive, chemically, hence termed as noble gases.
- Only exists in monoatomic state.

(i) Ionisation enthalpy

- Have very high IE which decreases down the group

He > Ne > Ar > Kr > Xe

(ii) Atomic radii

- Increases down the group.

He < Ne < Ar < Kr < Xe

- Have abnormally large size due to high inter electronic repulsions.

(iii) Electron gain enthalpy

- Positive due to no vacancy for accepting electrons.

(iv) Melting point and boiling point

- Are low due to weak interatomic dispersive forces. Helium has the lowest boiling point.

He < Ne < Ar < Kr < Xe

(v) Thermal conductivity

He > Ne > Ar > Kr > Xe

• Chemical Properties

- Least reactive due to filled valence shell, high I.E and positive electrons gain enthalpy.
- Only few compounds of Kr are known.

• Trends in reactivity

(i) Xenon-Fluorine Compounds

$Xe \xrightarrow{nF_2}$

- 673 K, 1 bar → XeF_2
- 873 K, 7 bar → XeF_4
- 573K, 60 bar → XeF_6

(n=1,2,3)

(ii) Xenon-Oxygen Compounds

With water

- $XeF_4 \xrightarrow{H_2O} Xe + XeO_3 + HF + O_2$
- $XeF_6 \xrightarrow{H_2O} XeOF_4 + HF$
- $XeF_6 \xrightarrow{H_2O\ (excess)} XeO_2F_2 + HF$

With F donor and acceptors

- $XeF_2 \xrightarrow{PF_5} [XeF]^+[PF_6]^-$
- $XeF_6 \xrightarrow{MF} [XeF_7]^- M^+ [M = Na, K]$
- $XeF_4 \xrightarrow{SbF_5} [XeF_3]^+[SbF_6]^-$

Structure of Compounds of Xenon

- $XeF_2 \rightarrow sp^3d$, Geometry → TBP, Shape → Linear
- $XeF_4 \rightarrow sp^3d^2$, Geometry → Octahedral, Shape → Square planar
- $XeF_6 \rightarrow sp^3d^3$ Geometry → Pentagonal bipyramidal Shape → Distorted octahedral.
- $XeO_3 \rightarrow sp^3$ Geometry → Tetrahedral Shape → Pyramidal
- $XeOF_4 \rightarrow sp^3d^2$ Geometry → Octahedral Shape → Square pyramidal

• Uses

- He used in filling balloons
- Ne used in discharge tubes
- Ar is used mainly to provide inert temperature.

Principle Related to Practical Chemistry (Chapter at a Glance)

Enthalpy of Solution of $CuSO_4$

- The enthalpy of solution of $CuSO_4$ is 16 kcal.
- During electrolysis, when $CuSO_4$ is introduced to water, it dissolves.
- $CuSO_4$ splits into Cu^{2+} and SO_4^{2-} ions.
- Two copper electrodes are immersed in the solution.
- As the result, SO_4^{2-} ions will migrate to the anode and form SO_4 radical.

Preparation of Lyophilic and Lyophobic Sols

- Lyophilic colloids are those in which dispersed phase exhibits a definite affinity for the solvent. They carry little or no charge.
- Lyophobic colloids are those in which the dispersed phase has no attraction for the medium. They carry positive or negative charge.
- Lyophilic colloid is prepared by direct mixing with dispersion medium while lyophobic colloid is not prepared by direct mixing with the medium.

Enthalpy of Neutralisation of Strong Acid and Strong Base

- Enthalpy of neutralisation is the heat evolved when one gram equivalent of the acid is completely neutralised by a base in dilute solution.
- Heat is evolved during neutralisation of an acid with alkali
- It is always constant for a strong acid and strong base as they completely lonise in dilute solution.

Acid-Base Titration

- Involves reaction between an acid and a base.
- Uses an acid-base indicator for making the end point.

Acid-Base Indicator

Indicators	pH range	Colour in acid solution	Colour in alkaline solution
Methyl orange	3.1-4.5	Red	Yellow
Methyl red	4.2-6.3	Red	Yellow
Phenol red	6.4-8.2	Yellow	Red
Phenolphthalein	8.0-9.8	Colourless	Pink

Kinetic Study of Reaction

Iodide Ions With H_2O_2

- H_2O_2 oxidies I^- ions to I_2

$H_2O_2 + 2I^- \xrightarrow[\text{Slow}]{H^+} 2H_2O + I_2$

- I_2 reacts with $Na_2S_2O_3$.

$I_2 + 2S_2O_3^{2-} \xrightarrow{\text{Fast}} S_4O_6^{2-} + 2I^-$

- I_2 + Starch $\longrightarrow$ Blue complex.

Analysis of Basic Radicals

• Group I Cations (Pb^{2+})

- Group reagent : dil HCl

• Tests of Pb^{2+}

- $Pb^{2+} + 2Cl^- \longrightarrow PbCl_2\downarrow$ (Cold O.S) (From HCl) (White ppt.)
- $PbCl_2 + K_2CrO_4 \longrightarrow PbCrO_4\downarrow + 2KCl$ ($PbCl_2$: Soluble in hot water) ($PbCrO_4$: Yellow ppt.)
- $PbCl_2 + H_2SO_4 \longrightarrow PbSO_4\downarrow + 2HCl$ (White ppt.)

Salt Analysis

• Dry Tests

- Physical observation e.g. odour, colour, density.
- Effect of heating, solubility, flame test, charcoal cavity test, borax bead test

• Wet Tests

- For confirmation of analysis of dry tests.
- It is used for analysis of acid and basic radicals.

Titration Curve

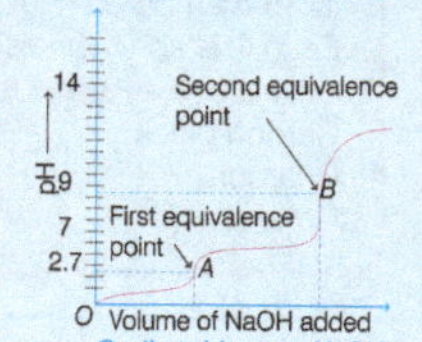

Oxalic acid *versus* NaOH

Titrimetric Exercises

- It is method for quantitative analysis.
- A titrant (known solution) is added to analyte (unknown solution).
- Using $N_1V_1 = N_2V_2$ or $M_1V_1 = M_2V_2$, quantity of analyte is calculated.
- Completion of reaction is marked by end point.
- The end point is detected using indicators.

Group IV Cations Zn^{2+}, Ni^{2+}

Group reagent : H_2S in NH_4OH

- Precipitates as sulphides.

Test for Ni^{2+}

- $3NiS + 6HCl + 2HNO_3 \longrightarrow 3NiCl_2 + 2NO + 3S + H_2O$

$NiCl_2 + 2DMG \longrightarrow$ Dimethyl-glyoximate complex (Cherry red ppt.)

Test for Zn^{2+}

- $ZnS + 2HCl \longrightarrow ZnCl_2 + H_2S$

$ZnCl_2 + 2NaOH \longrightarrow Zn(OH)_2\downarrow$ (White)

- $ZnCl_2 + K_4[Fe(CN)_6] \longrightarrow Zn_2[Fe(CN)_6]\downarrow$ (Blue ppt.)

Group II Cations Cu^{2+}, Pb^{2+}

Group reagent, $\longrightarrow H_2S$ + dil HCl

• Test for Cu^{2+}

- $Cu^{2+} + H_2S \xrightarrow{\text{Dil HCl}} CuS\downarrow$ (Black ppt.)
- $3CuS + 8HNO_3 \longrightarrow 3Cu(NO_3)_2$ (Soluble blue)
- $Cu(NO_3)_2 + 2CH_3COOH \longrightarrow (CH_3COO)_2Cu + 2HNO_3$

$Cu_2[(Fe(CN)_6] \xleftarrow{K_4Fe(CN)_6}$ (Dark brown ppt.)

Group II Anions

- Group reagent: conc. H_2SO_4

• Test for Cl^-

- $HCl + NH_4OH \longrightarrow NH_4Cl\uparrow + H_2O$ (White fumes)

• Chromyl Chloride Test

- $4NaCl + K_2Cr_2O_7 + 3H_2SO_4 \longrightarrow 2CrO_2Cl_2$ (H_2SO_4: Conc.) (CrO_2Cl_2: Chromyl chloride (orange yellow gas))

$+ 2Na_2CrO_4 + K_2SO_4 + 3H_2O$

$CrO_2Cl_2 + 4NaOH \rightarrow Na_2CrO_4 + 2NaCl + 2H_2O$ (Na_2CrO_4: Yellow)

• Test for Br^-

- $NaBr + AgNO_3 \longrightarrow AgBr\downarrow + NaNO_3$ (Pale yellow)

• Test for I^-

- $H_2SO_4 + 2HI \longrightarrow I_2\uparrow + SO_2 + 2H_2O$ (Violet vapours)

• Test for NO_3^-

- $NaNO_3 + H_2SO_4 \longrightarrow NaHSO_4 + HNO_3$ (H_2SO_4: Conc.)
- $4HNO_3 \xrightarrow{\Delta} 4NO_2\uparrow + O_2\uparrow + 2H_2O$ (NO_2: Brown)

• Brown Ring Test

- $[Fe(H_2O)_6]SO_4 \cdot H_2O + NO \rightarrow [Fe(H_2O)_5NO]SO_4 + 2H_2O$ (Brown ring) (Ferrous nitroso sulphate)

Group III Cations Al^{3+}, Fe^{3+}

Group reagent : $NH_4OH + NH_4Cl$

Precipitates as hydroxides.

• Test for Al^{3+}

- $Al(OH)_3 + NaOH \longrightarrow NaAlO_2 + 2H_2O$

$NaAlO_2 + NH_4Cl \xrightarrow[H_2O]{\Delta} Al(OH)_3$ (White gelatinous)

• Test for Fe^{3+}

- $Fe(OH)_3 + 3HCl \longrightarrow FeCl_3 + 3H_2O$

$4FeCl_3 + 3K_4[Fe(CN)_6] \longrightarrow Fe_4[Fe(CN)_6]_3$ (Dark blue colour)

Group V Cations (Ca^{2+}, Ba^{2+})

Group reagent : $(NH_4)_2CO_3 + NH_4OH$

Test for Ba^{2+}

- $BaCO_3 + 2CH_3COOH \xrightarrow{\Delta} CO_2 + H_2O + (CH_3COO)_2Ba$

$2CH_3COOK + BaCrO_4 \xleftarrow{K_2CrO_4}$ ($BaCrO_4$: Yellow ppt.)

Test for Ca^{2+}

- $CaCO_3 + 2CH_3COOH \xrightarrow{\Delta} CO_2 + H_2O + (CH_3COO)_2Ca$

$2CH_3COONH_4 + CaC_2O_4 \xleftarrow{(NH_4)_2C_2O_4}$ (CaC_2O_4: White ppt.)

$\downarrow H^+ / KMnO_4$(Pink)

$10CO_2 + 5CaCl_2 + 2MnCl_2$ (Colourless)

Group III Anion

Test for SO_4^{2-}

- $Na_2SO_4 + BaCl_2 \rightarrow BaSO_4\downarrow 2NaCl.$ ($BaSO_4$: White)
- Lead acetate + $Na_2SO_4 \longrightarrow PbSO_4\downarrow$ (White)

Preparation of Inorganic Salts

Mohr's Salt

- $(NH_4)_2SO_4 + FeSO_4 \cdot 7H_2O \rightarrow FeSO_4(NH_4)_2SO_4 \cdot 6H_2O + H_2O$ (Mohr's salt (Light green))
- Dil. H_2SO_4 is added to prevent hydrolysis of salt.
- To prevent oxidation of Fe^{2+} to Fe^{3+}, water is boiled beforehand.

Group Zero Cations (NH_4^+)

Group reagent : NaOH(dil)

- $NH_4Cl + NaOH \xrightarrow{\Delta} NH_3(g) + NaCl$

NH_3 + NaOH + Nessler reagent $\longrightarrow$ Iodide of million's base (Brown ppt.)

$NH_3 \xrightarrow{HCl} NH_4Cl$ (White fumes)

Potash Alum

Preparation

- $K_2SO_4 + Al_2(SO_4)_3 + 24H_2O \longrightarrow K_2SO_4 \cdot Al_2(SO_4)_3 \cdot 24H_2O$
- H_2SO_4 is added to prevent hydrolysis.

Group VI Cations (Mg^{2+})

Group reagent : $NH_4OH + Na_2HPO_4$

Mg + group reagent $\xrightarrow[-2NaCl]{} Mg(NH_4)PO_4$ (White ppt.)

Detection of Halogen

Lassaigne's extract, acidified with HNO_3 is added with $AgNO_3$ solution. The resultant solution when dissolved in NH_4OH helps in detection of halogen.

$NaX + AgNO_3 \longrightarrow AgX\downarrow + NaNO_3$

$NH_4NO_3 + AgX \longrightarrow [Ag(NH_3)_2 + 2H_2O$

If $X = F^-$, ppt. AgF is white and highly soluble.

If $X = Cl^-$, ppt is soluble.

If $X = Br^-$, ppt AgBr is dull yellow and partially soluble.

If $X = I^-$, ppt AgI is yellow and partially soluble.

Detection of Nitrogen

Lassaigne's extract is boiled with $FeSO_4$. A few drops of $FeCl_3$ followed by acidification with HCl gives bluish green or Prussian blue colour of ferric ferro cyanide.

$2NaCN + FeSO_4 \longrightarrow Na_2SO_4 + Fe(CN)_2 \xrightarrow{NaCN} Na_4[Fe(CN)_6]$

$Na_4[Fe(CN)_6] \xrightarrow{FeCl_3} 12NaCl + Fe_4[(Fe(CN)_6]_3$ (Prussian blue)

Detection of Sulphur

– Presence of sulphur can de detected using following reagents.

– $Na_2S + (CH_3COO)_2Pb \longrightarrow PbS\downarrow + 2CH_3COO^-Na^+$ (Lead acetate; PbS: Black ppt)

– $Na + C + N + S \longrightarrow NaSCN \xrightarrow[With]{FeCl_3} Fe(SCN)_3 + 3NaCl$ (NaSCN: Sodium sulphocyanide; $Fe(SCN)_3$: Ferric sulphocyanide (Blood red))

Detection of Functional Groups

- **Test for Alcoholic (—OH) group**
- **Sodium Test**

– H_2 gas evolves.

– $2ROH + 2Na \longrightarrow 2RO^-Na^+ + H_2$

- **Ceric Ammonium Nitrate Test**

– $ROH + (NH_4)_2Ce(NO_3)_6 \longrightarrow$ Cerium complex $+ 2NH_4NO_3$ (Red colour)

Redox Titration

– Based on reduction-oxidation.
– Titrants used are $K_2Cr_2O_7$.
– Titrant acts as self-indicator. e.g. Oxalic acid versus $KMnO_4$.
– Mn reduces itself from +7 to +2 in acidic medium.
– Colour change from colourless to pink marks the end point.

Test for Phenolic (—OH) Group

- **Litmus Test**

– Converts blue litmus paper to red.
– Phenols are weak acids.
– Do not give effervescence with Na_2CO_3 solution.

- **Ferric Chloride Test**

– Phenol + Ferric chloride (Few drops) $\longrightarrow [Fe(OPh)_6]^{3-}$ (Violet)

- **Liebermann's Nitroso Test**

– Phenol $\xrightarrow{HNO_2}$ p-nitrosophenol $\xrightarrow[H^+]{Phenol}$ Indophenol ion $\xrightarrow{NaOH}$ Indophenol(Blue)

Test for Carbonyl Group

- **Sodium Bisulphite Test**

Both aldehydes and ketones give water soluble crystalline bisulphite products.

$R(R/H)C{=}O + NaHSO_3 \longrightarrow R(R/H)C(OH)(SO_3^-Na^+)$ (Crystalline addition product)

- **2, 4, DNP Hydrazine Test**

Formation of yellow-orange ppt. indicates presence of carbonyl group. $>C{=}O + H_2NHN{-}C_6H_3(NO_2){-}NO_2 \longrightarrow >C{=}N{\cdot}HN{-}C_6H_3(NO_2){-}NO_2 + H_2O$ (2, 4-DNP; Yellow or orange red coloured derivative)

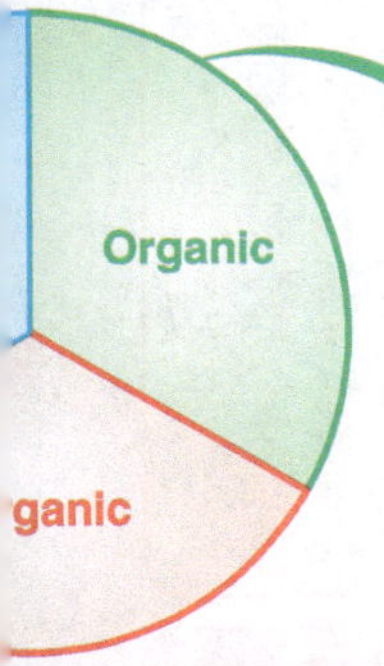

Distinction between Aldehydes and Ketones

- **Tollen's Test**

$RCHO + 2Ag[NH_3]^+_2OH^- \longrightarrow 2Ag\downarrow + RCOO^-NH_4^+$ (Tollen's reagent; Silver mirror)

– Formation of silver mirror confirms the presence of aldehydic group.
– Only aldehydes give this test

- **Fehling Test**

– Fehling solution is made by mixing Fehling A and Fehling B. and is a blue coloured complex of Cu^{2+}.

– $RCHO + 2CuO \longrightarrow RCOOH + Cu_2O\downarrow$ (Red ppt.)

– Only aliphatic aldehydes give this test
– Benzaldehyde is confirmed by malachite green test.
– Reducing sugar show both tests give above.

Distinction between Alcohols

- **Lucas Test**

Lucas reagent : $[ZnCl_2 + HCl]$

Organic compound + Lucas reagent $\longrightarrow$ Solution

– If turbidity appears in solution immediately-3° alcohol.
– If turbidity appears after 4-5 min-2° alcohol.
– If clear solution -1° alcohol.

- **Victor Meyer's Test**

Only 1° and 2° alcohols give this test.

- RCH_2OH (1° alcohol) $\xrightarrow{HI} RCH_2I \xrightarrow{AgNO_2} RCH_2NO_2 \xrightarrow{HONO} R{-}C({=}NOH){-}NO_2$ (Nitrolic acid) $\xrightarrow{NaOH}$ Blood red colour
- R_2CHOH (2° alcohol) $\xrightarrow{HI} R_2CHI \xrightarrow{AgNO_2} R_2CHNO_2 \xrightarrow{HONO} R_2C(NO){-}NO_2$ (Pseudonitrole acid) $\xrightarrow{NaOH}$ Blue colour

Analysis of Acid Radicals

- **Group I Anions**

– Group reagent : dil H_2SO_4

- **Test for CO_3^{2-}**

– $Na_2CO_3 + 2HCl \rightarrow 2NaCl + H_2O + CO_2\uparrow$
– $Ca(OH)_2 + CO_2 \rightarrow CaCO_3\downarrow$

- **Test for NO_3^{2-}**

– $2NaNO_2 + conc.\ H_2SO_4 \rightarrow Na_2SO_4 + 2HNO_2$

$2NO + O_2 \rightarrow 2NO_2\uparrow$ (Brown)

– $2KI + 2NO_2 \rightarrow 2KNO_2 + I_2$

I_2 + Starch $\rightarrow$ Blue colour

- **Test for S^{2-}**

– $Na_2S + H_2SO_4 \longrightarrow H_2S + Na_2SO_4$ (Rotten egg smell)
– $(CH_3COO)_2Pb + H_2S \longrightarrow PbS\downarrow + 2CH_3COOH$ (Black)

Test for —NH_2 Group

- **Azo-dye Test**

– For confirming presence of primary aromatic amines.

– Aniline $\xrightarrow{NaNO_2/HCl}$ Diazonium salt $\xrightarrow{\beta\text{-naphthol}}$ Azo–dye (Orange)

- **Carbylamine Test**

– Formation of a highly toxic isocyanide.
– Only given by primary amines.

$RNH_2 + CHCl_3 + 3KOH \xrightarrow{-3H_2O} R{-}N{\equiv}C + 3KCl$

Test for —COOH Group

- **$NaHCO_3$ Test**

– Gives brisk effervescence

$RCOOH + NaHCO_3 \longrightarrow RCOO^-Na^+ + H_2O + CO_2\uparrow$

- **Ester Test**

– Compounds containing —COOH group gives fruity smelling esters with alcohols.

– $RCOOH + C_2H_5OH \xrightarrow[\Delta]{H^+} RCOOC_2H_5$ (Fruity smell)

Preparation of Organic Compounds

Acetanilide C_6H_5—$NHCOCH_3$

- **Preparation**

– Ph—NH_2 + Acetic anhydride $\longrightarrow$ Acetanilide

- **Properties**

– —$NHCOCH_3$ group is p-directing in nature

Distinguishing 1°, 2° and 3° Amines

- **Nitrous Test**

– 1° amine $\xrightarrow{HNO_2} N_2\uparrow + ROH$
– 2° amine $\xrightarrow{HNO_2} R_2N{=}NO$ (Oily compound)
– 3° amine $\xrightarrow{HNO_2}$ salt formation (Soluble).

- **Hinsberg Test**

– 1° amine $\xrightarrow{\text{Hinsberg reagent}}$ N–alkylbenzene sulphonamide (Soluble in NaOH)
– 2° amine $\xrightarrow{\text{Hinsberg reagent}}$ N,N–dialkylbenzene sulphonamide (Insoluble in NaOH)

p-nitroacetanilide

– p-nitro derivative of acetanilide
– Is used as an intermediate in production of some dyes

$O_2N{-}C_6H_4{-}NHCOCH_3$

– Is prepared by nitration of acetanilide at low temperature

Acetanilide $\xrightarrow[\text{Conc. }HNO_3]{\text{Conc. }H_2SO_4}$ p-nitroacetanilide (major)

Iodoform CHI_3

– Detects carbonyl compounds with α-methyl group.

e.g. —$COCH_3$, —$CH(OH)$—CH_3

– $NaOCl + KI \xrightarrow{Oxidation} KOI + NaCl$

– $CH_3COCH_3 \xrightarrow{KOI} Cl_3COCH_3 \xrightarrow{NaOH} CHI_3$

Aniline Yellow

$C_6H_5{-}N{=}N{-}C_6H_4{-}NH_2$

– Formed by coupling reaction between diazonium chloride and aniline.

– Ph—$NH_2 \xrightarrow{HNO_2}$ Ph—$N{\equiv}N^+Cl^- \xrightarrow{Aniline}$ Aniline yellow

Amines (Chapter at a Glance)

Preparation of Tertiary Amines

- RX(excess) + NH_3 → Mixture of 1°, 2° and 3° amine
- $R—CH_2COR' + NHR''_2 \xrightarrow{Acid} R—C(R)=C—N(R'')_2$
- $RCONR'_2 \xrightarrow{LiAlH_4} RCH_2—N(R')—R'$ (3° amine)

Preparation of Primary Amines

Primary Amines
- $RCN \xrightarrow{LiAlH_4}$ [Reduction]
- $RNO_2 \xrightarrow{Sn/HCl,\ H_2/Pt}$ [Reduction]
- $RCONH_2 \xrightarrow{LiAlH_4}$ [Reduction]
- Phthalimide: (i) KOH (ii) RX (iii) H_2O/OH^- [Gabriel phthalamide reaction]
- $RCOCl \xrightarrow{NaN_3}$ [Curtius method]
- $RCONH_2 \xrightarrow{NaOH,\ Br_2,\ NaOH\ (aq)}$ [Hofmann bromamide degradation reaction]
- $RCONHOH \xrightarrow{HO^-,\ H_2O}$ [Lossen rearrangement]
- $Me_3C—OH \xrightarrow{HCN,\ H_2SO_4}$ [Ritter reaction]
- $R—N{=}C \xrightarrow{H_2O,\ H^+}$ [Hydrolysis]
- $R—C(=O)—OH + N_3H \xrightarrow{Conc.\ H_2SO_4}$ [Schmidt rearrangement]
- $R—C(=O)—H \xrightarrow{(i)\ NH_3,\ (ii)\ H_2/Ni}$ [Reductive amination of carbonyl compounds]

Preparation of Mixture of Amines:

- Hoffman's ammonolysis method
  RI (excess) $\xrightarrow{NH_3/\Delta}$ 1° + 2° + 3° + Quaternary amine
- Reaction of alcohols with ammonia ROH (excess)
  ROH(excess) + $NH_3 \xrightarrow{Al_2O_3}$ 1° + 2° + 3° + Quaternary amine
- Leukart reaction.
  $RCOOMe + HCOONH_4 \xrightarrow{\Delta} RCH(NH_2)Me + H_2O + CO_2\uparrow$

Preparation of Secondary Amines

- Primary amines + RX (excess)
  $\longrightarrow RNH_2 + RX \xrightarrow[\Delta]{NaOH} R_2NH$
- Reduction
  - (i) of isonitriles
    $R—N{\equiv}C \xrightarrow{H_2/Pt} RNHCH_3$
  - (ii) of N-substituted amides
    $RCONHR' \xrightarrow{LiAlH_4} RCH_2—N(H)—R'$
- Reductive amination of carbonyl compounds
  $RCHO \xrightarrow[-H_2O]{R'NH_2} \xrightarrow{H_2/Ni} RCH_2—NH—R'$ (2° amine)

Diazonium Salt

Diazonium Salt
- They have the general formula $RN_2^+X^-$
- They are named by suffix.
- All benzene diazonium salts contain benzene diazonium ion.
  $C_6H_5—\overset{+}{N}{\equiv}N:$
- Primary aromatic amines form arene diazonium salts which are stable for a short time in solution.
- Diazonium salts are strongly electron withdrawing in nature.
- Presence of electron releasing group like $—NR_2$, $—OR$ at *ortho/para* position in the benzene ring stabilises the benzene diazonium ion.

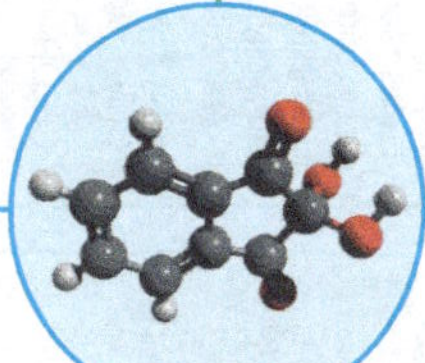

Physical Properties

- These are colourless crystalline solids but acquire colour when exposed to air.
- Due to their ionic nature, they are water soluble.
- Good conductor of electricity in aqueous solutions.
- These decompose easily in the dry state.
- Reacts with water when warmed.

Preparation of Diazonium Salt

Primary aromatic amines react with HNO_2 to form diazonium salts. It is called diazotisation.
- $NaNO_2 + HCl \rightarrow HNO_2 + NaCl$

$C_6H_5—NH_2 + HCl \rightarrow C_6H_5—NH_2\cdot HCl$

$C_6H_5—NH_2\cdot HCl + HNO_2 \rightarrow C_6H_5—N_2^+Cl^- + 2H_2O$

Basicity

- Aliphatic amine > NH_3 > aromatic amine
- 3° > 2° > 1° > NH_3
  [In gas phase or in non aq. solvent]
- 2° > 1° > 3° > NH_3
  [In aq. phase, only — CH_3 subs. amine]
- 2° > 3° > 1° > NH_3
  [In aq. phase, only — C_2H_5 subs. amine]
- In aromatic amines 3° > 2° > 1°.

Chemical Properties

- Coupling Reactions

Benzene diazonium chloride ($ArN_2^+Cl^-$):
- Benzene + NaOH → Diphenyl (Gomberg reaction)
- $—OH$, $—NR_2$, $—NH_2$ → Azo-dye (Coupling reaction)
- HBF_4 → Fluorobenzene (Balz-Schiemann reaction)
- $SnCl_2/HCl$ → Phenyl hydrazine
- Hydrolysis, Δ → Phenol + N_2 + HCl
- $H_3PO_2 + H_2O$ → Benzene + H_3PO_3 + HCl + N_2
- $CuCl + HCl$, $-N_2$ → Chlorobenzene (Sandmeyer reaction)
- Cu/Δ, $-N_2$ → Chlorobenzene (Gattermann reaction)
- $NaNO_2/Cu$ → Nitrobenzene

Importance of Diazonium Salt

- They are useful in the synthesis of a large variety of organic compounds, especially aryl derivatives.
- They find application in the dye and pigment industries and are used to produce dyed fabrics.
- They are used as intermediates for introducing — F, — Br, — Cl, — I, — NO_2, — OH and — CN groups into the aromatic ring.
- Due to their property of breaking down near the ultraviolet light, they are used in document reproduction.

Chemical Properties of Aromatic Amines

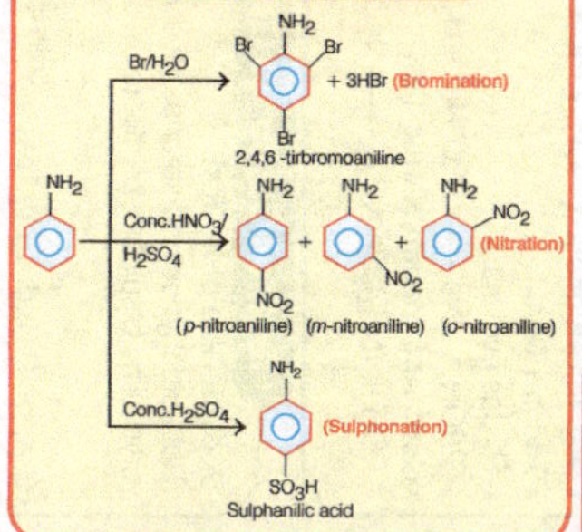

Amines

- They are classified as primary (1°), secondary (2°) and tertiary (3°).
- Quaternary amines exist as salts only and yield amines on hydrolysis.

Degree and Functional Group of Various Amines

Amine	*n*(no. of H-atoms attached to N)	Degree(3-*n*)°	Functional group
$R—N(H)—H$	2	(3-2)° = 1°(primary)	$—NH_2$
R_2NH	1	(3-1)° = 2°(secondary)	$—NH—$
R_3N	0	(3-0)° = 3°(tertiary)	$>N—$

- N-atom possesses four sp^3-hybridised orbitals.
- Due to the presence of unpaired pair of electron, the angle C–N–*E* (where, *E*=C or H) is less then 109.5° i.e. 108°.

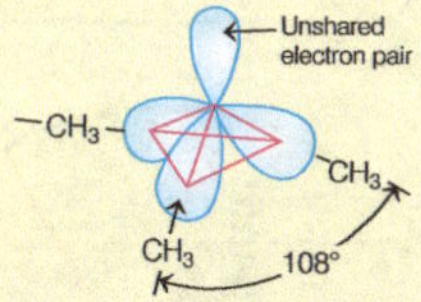

Physical Properties

- Lower amines are gases with ammonical smell.
- They are soluble in water.
- Solublity decreases with increase in alkyl chain.
- Higher boiling points than hydrocarbons of comparable molecular masses due to intermolecular H–bonding.
- Boiling points are lower than those of alcohols and carboxylic acids.
- Order of boiling points of isomeric amines is 1° > 2° > 3°.

Distinguishing Test for Amines

- **Hinsberg Test**
  $C_6H_5SO_2Cl$ + 1° + 2° + 3° amines
  - Clear solution $\xrightarrow{KOH}$ Soluble salt [For 1° amine]
  - PPt. $\xrightarrow{KOH}$ No reaction [For 2° amine]
  - No reaction [For 3° amine]
- **Liebermann's Nitroso Test**
  HONO + 1° + 2° + 3° amines
  - $R—OH + N_2\uparrow + H_2O$ [For 1° amine]
  - $R_2NNO + H_2O$ [For 2° amine]
  - $R_3N^+HNO_2^-$ [Soluble in water] (yellow oil liquid)
- **Carbylamine Test** Given by both aliphatic and aromatic amines but secondary and tertiary amines do not show this reaction.
- **Azo dye Test** Only primary aromatic amines will give orange coloured azo dyes.

Chemical Properties of Aliphatic / Aromatic amines

Amines
- Mineral acids → Salts
- Aqueous solution → Hydroxide
- Acylation $RCOCl$ or $(RCO)_2O$
  - 1° → N-substituted amides
  - 2° → N,N-disubstituted amides
  - 3° → No reaction (as no replaceable H is seen on N of tertiary amine)
- Grignard's reagent → Alkane
- Hofmann elimination → 3° amine + alkene

Further reactions:
- Oxidation with $KMnO_4$
  - 1° → $RCHO$ or $R_2C{=}O$
  - 2° → $R_2N—NR_2$
  - 3° → No effect
- Oxidation with H_2SO_5
  - 1° → Aldoxime or Ketoxime or nitroso alkane
  - 2° → R_2NOH
  - 3° → R_3NO
- With carbonyl compounds
  - 1° → Schiff's base
  - 2° → Enamines
  - 3° → Do not react at all
- With HNO_2
  - 1° → N_2 gas
  - 2° → Yellow oily layer
  - 3° → Water soluble salt
- $CHCl_3$/3KOH → Isocyanides or isonitriles